AUSTRALIAN DICTIONARY

OF BIOGRAPHY

General Editors

BEDE NAIRN

GEOFFREY SERLE

AUSTRALIAN
DICTIONARY
OF BIOGRAPHY

VOLUME 7 : 1891-1939

A-Ch

General Editors
BEDE NAIRN
GEOFFREY SERLE

Section Editors
G. C. BOLTON
K. J. CABLE
R. J. O'NEILL
J. R. POYNTER
HEATHER RADI

MELBOURNE UNIVERSITY PRESS

First published 1979
Printed in Australia by John Sands Pty Ltd,
Artarmon, N.S.W. 2064, for
Melbourne University Press, Carlton, Victoria 3053
U.S.A. and Canada: International Scholarly Book Services, Inc.,
Box 555, Forest Grove, Oregon 97116
United Kingdom, Ireland and Europe: Europa Publications Limited,
18 Bedford Square, London WC1B 3JN

7317

National Library of Australia Cataloguing in Publication data
Australian dictionary of biography. Volume 7.
  1891-1939, A-Ch.
  ISBN 0 522 84185 6

  1. Australia – Biography. 2. Australia – History – 1891-1939.
  I. Nairn, Noel Bede, joint gen. ed.
  II. Serle, Alan Geoffrey, joint gen. ed.
920'.094

PREFACE

This volume of the *Australian Dictionary of Biography*, containing 658 entries by 469 authors, is the first of six for the 1891-1939 section. The two volumes of the 1788-1850 and the four of the 1851-1890 sections have already been published. This chronological division was designed to simplify production, for more than 7000 entries will be included in volumes 1-12. (Volumes 1-2, for 1788-1850, had 1116 entries; volumes 3-6, for 1851-1890, 2053; and 4000 are planned for volumes 7-12). The placing of each individual's name in the appropriate section has been determined by when he/she did his/her most important work (*floruit*). A general index volume will be prepared when the three sections are completed.

The selection of names for inclusion has been the result of much consultation and co-operation. After quotas were estimated, Working Parties in each State and the Armed Services Working Party prepared provisional lists, which were widely circulated and carefully amended. Many of the names were obviously significant and worthy of inclusion as leaders in politics, business, the armed services, the professions, the arts, the labour movement, etc. Many others have been included as representatives of ethnic and social minorities and of a wide range of occupations, or as innovators, notorieties or eccentrics. Many had to be omitted through pressure of space or lack of material, and thereby joined the great mass whose members richly deserve a more honoured place; however, many thousands of these names, and information about them, are accumulating in the Biographical Register at the *Dictionary* headquarters in the Australian National University.

Most authors were nominated by Working Parties. The burden of writing has been shared almost equally by university historians and by a wide variety of specialists in other fields.

The *Australian Dictionary of Biography* is a project based on consultation and co-operation. The Australian National University has borne the cost of the headquarters staff, of much research and of some special contingencies, while other Australian universities have supported the project in various ways. Its policies were originally determined by the National Committee, composed mainly of representatives from the Departments of History in each Australian university. At Canberra the Editorial Board has kept in touch with all these representatives, and with the Working Parties, librarians, archivists and other local experts, as well as overseas correspondents and research assistants in each Australian capital. With such varied support the *Australian Dictionary of Biography* can truly be called a national project.

ACKNOWLEDGMENTS

Special thanks are due to Professor K. S. Inglis for his guidance as chairman of the Editorial Board. Professor J. A. La Nauze has retired; his contribution as chairman is gratefully acknowledged. Those who helped in planning the shape of the work have been mentioned in earlier volumes.

The *Dictionary* is grateful for many privileges extended by the Australian universities, especially the Australian National University.

Within Australia the *Dictionary* is greatly indebted to many librarians and archivists in Canberra and in each State; to the secretaries of many historical and genealogical societies; to the historical research officers of the Australian Post Office; to the Registrars-General of Births, Deaths and Marriages, and of Probates, in the various States, and to Registrars of Supreme and Family Courts, whose generous co-operation has solved many problems; and to the Department of Defence for authenticating many details. Warm thanks for the free gift of their time and talents are due to all contributors and to all members of the National Committee, Editorial Board, and the Working Parties. For particular advice the *Dictionary* owes much to B. G. Andrews, J. J. Auchmuty, M. Austin, P. L. Brown, K. J. Cable, Frank Cusack, B. Gandevia, A. J. and Nancy Gray, N. Gunson, R. F. Holder, J. N. Molony, Heather Radi, F. B. Smith, P. Spearritt, A. K. Stout and G. P. Walsh.

For assistance overseas, thanks are due to Ivan Page, Liaison Officer of the National Library of Australia in London and to his staff; to Alice Gay, Paris, Leonie Glen, London, Deirdre Pescott, Brussels, and Margery Walton, New Zealand; to the archives and/or libraries of the universities of Birmingham, Cambridge, Durham, London and Oxford in England; of Aberdeen, Edinburgh, Glasgow and St Andrews in Scotland; of Florence and Padua in Italy; of Chicago and San Francisco, and of Cornell and Princeton in the United States of America; of Charles University in Prague, Czechoslovakia; Humboldt University, Berlin, and Karl-Marx University, Leipzig, in the German Democratic Republic; the Frederick-Alexander University of Erlangen-Nuremberg, and the University of Marburg, in the Federal Republic of Germany; to University College, Cardiff, Wales; to the Imperial College of Science and Technology and Jews' College, London and the Liverpool School of Medicine, England; to official archives and/or national libraries in U.S.A., Canada, Switzerland, Austria, Norway, Sweden, Wales and New Zealand; to the General Register Office, Edinburgh, and the Public Record Office, London, and County Record Offices; to Bureaux of Vital Statistics in State health departments in New York, Ohio and Utah; the British Embassy, Asuncion, Paraguay; Dictionaries of Canadian and South African Biographies; Army Records Centre, England; public libraries of Boston and Los Angeles; and to other individuals and institutions who have co-operated with the *Dictionary*.

The *Dictionary* deeply regrets the death of such notable contributors as B. W. Champion, A. H. Chisholm, R. Clark, Louise T. Daley, B. T. Dowd, E. W. Dunlop, W. H. Frederick, H. A. K. Hunt, J. S. Legge, G. B. Lincolne, Catherine Mackerras, T. Inglis Moore, S. F. Rowell, J. R. Stevenson, J. H. Thyer, I. A. H. Turner, and W. G. D. Upjohn who, in their several capacities, greatly assisted the work of this and previous volumes.

Grateful acknowledgment is due to the director and staff of Melbourne University Press; to the editorial staff in Canberra: Nan Phillips, Martha Campbell,

ACKNOWLEDGMENTS

Sally O'Neill, James Gibbney, Suzanne Edgar, Chris Cunneen, Frank Brown, Jean Fielding, Merrilyn Lincoln, Ann Smith and Margaret Steven; to Ruth Frappell and Naomi Turner in Sydney; Noeline Hall and Betty Crouchley in Brisbane; Joyce Gibberd and Marlene Cross in Adelaide; Wendy Birman and Margaret Brown in Perth; Beth McLeod, Mary Nicholls and Margaret Glover in Hobart; Mimi Colligan, Ray Duplain, David Dunstan, Jill Eastwood, John Lack, Janet McCalman and Vicky McCalman in Victoria; and to the administrative staff: Dorothy Smith, Norma Gregson, Ivy Meere, Frances Dinnerville and Dorothy McBride.

COMMITTEES

COMMITTEES

AUTHORS

ABBOTT, G. J. :
Burns; Christmas.
ABBOTT, Jacqueline :
Cawood.
ABEYASEKERE, Susan Blackburn :
Blackburn, M.
AHERN, Barbara :
Ahern, T.
AITKIN, Don :
Bruxner.
ALBISTON, Harold E. :
Cameron, S.
ALEXANDER, Fred :
Battye.
ALEXANDER, H. :
Body.
ALLEN, Jim :
Childe.
AMOS, Keith :
Campbell, Eric.
ANDERSON, Hugh :
Beggs; Christie, J.
ANDREWS, B. G. :
Abbott, J.; Adams; Bancks; Bardsley; Broomfield; Chambers.
ANTILL, J. M. :
Barraclough; Bruce, J.
APPLEYARD, R. T. :
Chipper.
ARGENT, A. :
Beardsmore.
ATCHISON, John :
Angus, J.; Brown, T.; Brunskill; Campbell, J. F. & T.
AUSTIN, M. :
Brazenor; Brennan, E.

BADGER, C. R. :
Addis.
BAINTON, Helen :
Bainton, E.
BAIRD, Kathleen :
Baird.
BAKER, D. W. A. :
Archdall.
BALL, G. B. :
Arnold, E.
BANNENBERG, R. J. N. :
Broadbent, J.
BARBALET, Margaret :
Bottrill, D.
BARNES, John :
Baker, C.
BARRETT, John :
Campbell, G.
BATE, Weston :
Brown, F.

BATTYE, O. K. :
Carson, A.
BECKMANN, T. J. :
Brünnich.
BEEVER, E. A. :
Angliss.
BELL, Jacqueline :
Bage; Bourne, E.
BELL, William G. :
Bell, G. J.
BENKO, Nancy :
Barnes, G. A.
BENNETT, Bruce :
Bourke.
BENNETT, J. M. :
Abigail; Blacket, W.; Campbell, J. L.
BENNETT, Scott :
Braddon, E.
BERRY, Dean W. :
Bagot, W.; Brown, M.
BIRMAN, Wendy :
Beadle; Bromham; Burley; Calvert.
BIRTLES, Terry G. :
Birtles.
BLACK, David :
Allen, J.
BLACKBURN, C. R. B. :
Blackburn, C.
BLACKBURN, R. A. :
Blackburn, A.
BLAKE, L. J. :
Asche.
BOLAND, Rodney G. :
Bedford, G.
BOLLEN, J. D. :
Bruntnell.
BOLTON, G. C. :
Anderson, P. C.; Angelo; Barron, H.; Bedford, F.; Bennett, M.; Boyle; Campion, W.
BONNIN, Margriet R. :
Banfield.
BONNIN, Nancy :
Baylebridge.
BOUGHEN, Robert K. :
Brier.
BOYER, Peter :
Broinowski, L.
BRACEGIRDLE, W. S. :
Bracegirdle.
BRADSHAW, F. Maxwell :
Barber, J.
BRETT-CROWTHER, M. R. :
Buddicom.
BRIDGE, Carl :
Butler C.; Cain.
BRIDGLAND, R. J. :
Chapman, R.

BRIER-MILLS, Margery:
Black, W.
BROOMHILL, Ray:
Birrell.
BROWN, George Deas:
Butler, W. F.
BROWN, P. L.:
Austin.
BROWNFOOT, Janice N.:
Bear.
BURFITT, Walter Furneaux:
Burfitt.
BURGIS, Peter:
Bourne, U.
BURNS, R. J.:
Badham.

CABLE, K. J.:
Backhouse; Barff; Batty; Boyce, F. B.
CAIN, Neville:
Benham, F.
CALOV, W. L.:
Armit.
CAMERON, Caroline L.:
Cameron, D. N.
CAMPBELL, Charles:
Benjamin, A.
CAMPBELL, Ruth:
Brennan, A.
CANNON, Michael:
Brodzky.
CARMENT, David:
Chisholm, A.
CARMODY, Freda Vines:
Carter, T.
CARNEGIE, Margaret:
Blackwood; Campbell, J. A.
CARR, Cecil:
Bingle.
CHALMERS, R. O.:
Anderson, C.
CHAMBERS, Don:
Adam, D.
CHAPMAN, G. P. R.:
Ashbolt; Bethune; Booth, N.; Brock.
CHISHOLM, A. H.*:
Barrett, C.; Cayley, N.
CHRISTESEN, C. B.:
Bowen, E.
CLARK, Axel:
Brennan, C.
CLARK, Rex*:
Antill; Bennett, J.; Bidmead; Burley;
Carroll, J.; Cherry, P.
CLARKE, E.:
Barlow, A.
CLELAND, A. B.:
Allard.
CLELAND, Lindsay:
Balsillie.
CLEMENTS, M. A.:
Adamson, L.
*deceased

CLINCH, M. A.:
Cahill, P.
CLOSE, Cecily:
Buchanan, G.
CLYDE, Laurel:
Anderson, E.
COLLIGAN, Mimi:
Amadio; Brahe.
COMRIE-THOMSON, Paul:
Campbell, Elizabeth.
CONDON, Brian:
Adey.
CONDON, Herbert H.:
Atkinson, H.
CONNELL, W. H.:
Aslatt.
COOK, Peter:
Beazley.
COPE, Malcolm:
Brennan, F. T.
CORBETT, Arthur:
Allan, P.; Chinn.
COSTAR, B. J.:
Barnes, G. P.
COULTHARD-CLARK, C. D.:
Airey, H.; Bridges, W.; Cheeseman.
COUNIHAN, Noel:
Cazaly.
CRESCIANI, Gianfranco:
Baccarini.
CRESPIN, Irene:
Chapman, F.
CROSS, Marlene J.:
Brooker.
CROUCHLEY, Betty:
Baynes; Carter, A.
CUNNEEN, Chris:
Abbott, G.; Allen, G.; Anderson, D.;
Ashton, J. and F.; Bjelke-Petersen, H.;
Brown, D; Chelmsford.
CURTHOYS, Ann:
Bennett, Agnes.

DANIELS, J. G.:
Angus, W.
DAVIS, R. P.:
Carruthers, G.
DAWES, J. N. I.:
Bolton.
DE GARIS, B. K.:
Burt.
DENNIS, Alan H.:
Chapple, F.
DERHAM, Frances A. M. L.:
Allen, M.
DE SERVILLE, P. H.:
Baker, Thomas, photographer; Barnett,
H.; Burston; Chomley.
DOUGAN, Alan:
Angus, S.
DOUGLAS, R. A.:
Breinl.
DOWNEY, Michael R.:
Arnold, T.

DRUMMOND, F. H.:
Agar.
DRUMMOND, Neville:
Byatt.
DUCKER, C. H.:
Black, P.
DUNKLEY, Graham:
Cameron, D. J.
DUNLOP, P. R. G.:
Brown, H. Y.
DUNSTAN, David:
Biggs; Brunton; Cabena.
DUNSTON, A. J.:
Butler, T.
DUPLAIN, R. C.:
Bussau; Cameron, James; Chandler, A.
DURIE, E. Beatrix:
Aspinall, J.

EAST, Ronald:
Cattanach; Checchi.
EDDY, J.:
Bergin.
EDGAR, Suzanne:
Ash; Benny; Boehm; Butler, R. L.;
Campbell, A.; Cawthorne.
EDGELOE, V. A.:
Barlow, W.
ELDERSHAW, Shirley M.:
Barclay.
EVANS, Raymond:
Bleakley.

FAIRFAX, Denis:
Carr, W.
FANNING, Pauline:
Binns.
FARMER, M. W.:
Bourne, G.
FARRELL, Frank:
Baddeley; Boote.
FARRER, K. T. H.:
Callister.
FERGUSON, G. A.:
Angus, D.
FIELDER, W. W.:
Andrews, A.
FIELDING, Jean P.:
Borella; Chumleigh.
FINLAY, E. M.:
Adcock
FOLDI, N. S.:
Bugden.
FORD, Edward:
Campbell, A. W.
FORD, Garry R.:
Badger.
FORSTER, Colin:
Bond.
FORSTER, Frank M. C.:
Adam, G.; Allan, R.
FRANKI, G. T.:
Carter, H. J.

FREDERICK, W. H.*:
Brookes, N.
FRENCH, E. L.:
Archer, F.; Buntine.
FRY, Eric:
Barker, T.

GALLON, D. G.:
Carter, H. G.
GARDINER, L. R.:
Carmichael, T.
GARDINER, Lyndsay:
Barrett, E.; Bell, Jane; Carmichael, G.
GARDNER, Susan:
Booth, D.
GEEVES, Philip:
Bennett, A. E.
GIBBERD, Joyce:
Cawthorne; Chapple, P.
GIBBNEY, H. J.:
Ainsworth, G.; Bath; Baynes; Bean, I.;
Bell, F.; Bennett, M; Boyland; Burns;
Chapman, A.
GIBBS, R. M.:
Brookman, G.; Campbell, D.
GIBBS, Ross:
Carlile.
GIBSON, David A.:
Antonieff.
GILES, R. O.:
Brookman, W.
GILL, J. C. H.:
Appel; Blair, J. W.
GILL, Rosemary Howard:
Byrnes.
GILLISON, Joan:
Bon.
GOLDSMITH, D. V.:
Burnage.
GOLDSWORTHY, David:
Burgoyne.
GOLLAN, Robin:
Bowling; Brookfield.
GOODMAN, Rupert:
Barbour.
GORDON, Harry:
Buggy.
GOSS, Noel:
Arnot.
GOW, Neil:
Alderman.
GREEN, O. S.:
Aston.
GREGORY, M. S.:
Burn.
GRIEVE, B. J.:
Blackall.
GRIFFIN, James:
Boismenu.
GUNSON, Neil:
Albiston, W.; Bevan.
GURNER, C. M.:
Butler, A.

*deceased

LAND, William A.:
Barber, G.; Barton, A.
LARGE, Diana:
Benson, L. C.
LAVERTY, John:
Annand.
LAW, Glenda:
Chatfield.
LEA-SCARLETT, E. J.:
Beale.
LE COUTEUR, G. S.:
Aitken.
LEIGHTON, P. F.:
Bradley, J.
LEOPOLD, Elisabeth:
Borthwick; Cann, W.
LE SOUEF, J. C.:
Best, D.
LETHLEAN, Margôt:
Carew-Smyth.
LEVI, J. S.:
Abrahams.
LIEW, K. S.:
Chin Kaw.
LINCOLN, Merrilyn:
Bainton, J.; Bessell-Browne; Bowen, R.
LINCOLNE, G. B.*:
Alcock, A.
LINDSAY, Frances:
Carter, N.
LINGE, G. J. R.:
Butters.
LLOYD, Brian:
Ainsworth, A.
LOGAN, G. N.:
Boyd, W.
LOMAS, L.:
Baker, Thomas, farmer; *Brisbane.*
LONIE, John:
Bagot, E.
LOUGHEED, A. L.:
Campbell, James.
LOUIS, L. J.:
Bailey, H.
LUNDIE, Margaret:
Bailey, M.
LUTTON, Nancy:
Abel.
LYNCH, Lesley G.:
Cazneaux.
LYONS, Mark:
Camfield.

MCCALMAN, *Janet:*
Brenan.
MCCARTHY, John:
Baker, T. C.; Bavin; Bowden; Christie, R.
MCCARTHY, Susan:
Brown, J. T.
MCCONVILLE, Chris:
Bennett, G.
MCCREDIE, H.:
Braddon, H.
*deceased

MCDONALD, D. I.:
Beattie, J. A.
MCDONALD, Lorna L.:
Archer, R. and E.; Blair, J.
MACDOUGALL, R. J.:
Calder, G.
MCEVEY, Allan:
Campbell, A. J.
MCGILL, Maryanne:
Barwell; Bice.
MACGILLIVRAY, Leith G.:
Butler, H.
MCGRATH, Joyce:
Bale.
MCGREGOR, Malcolm:
Brown, H. B.
MCINERNEY, J. M. B.:
Boyd, A. A.
MCINERNEY, Sally:
Chidley.
MCINTYRE, Darryl:
Bennett, A. J.; Braund; Brinsmead.
MCLAREN, Ian F.:
Boreham.
MCLEOD, E. A.:
Allardyce; Bjelke-Petersen, H.
MCLEOD, G. R. C.:
Burke, J.
MCMINN, W. G.:
Cambage.
MCNICOLL, Ronald:
Catani.
MCVILLY, David:
Armstrong, E.
MAHOOD, Marguerite:
Bradley, L.
MANDLE, W. F.:
Baker, R. L.; Bunton.
MANFORD, Toby:
Boan; Briggs.
MARGINSON, Julie:
à Beckett.
MARKS, E. N.:
Bancroft.
MARSHALL, Norma:
Barnes, J.; Best, R.; Blakeley.
MARTIN, A. W.:
Black, R.
MATTHEWS, L. D.:
Cass.
MELLISH, Raoul:
Bustard.
MELLOR, D. P.:
Challinor.
MENDELSSOHN, Joanna:
Bryant.
MILLER, J. S. C.:
Bickersteth.
MILLS, Jenny:
Bunning.
MILLS, Julie:
Bellew.
MILLS, Tony:
Bracy; Carter F. and B.

MINCHAM, Hans:
  Chewings.
MITCHELL, Bruce:
  Alanson; Biddell; Callaghan.
MOLONY, John N.:
  Carr, T.
MORGEN, Margaret:
  Brennan, A.
MORISON, Patricia:
  Carnegie.
MOSSENSON, David:
  Andrews, C.; Chandler, T.
MURPHY, Bernice:
  Auld.
MURPHY, D. J.:
  Bowman, Browne, W.; Carroll, R.; Case.
MURRAY-SMITH, S.:
  Barrett, J. W.; Campbell, F.

NAIRN, Bede:
  Bavister; Beeby; Black, G.; Cann, J.;
  Carmichael, A.
NELSON, H. N.:
  Carpenter.
NICHOLLS, P. L.:
  Ashworth.
NOBBS, Raymond:
  Chapman, E.
NOLAN, Carolyn:
  Beirne.
NOLAN, J. G.:
  Buss.
NORTH, Ian:
  Black, D.

O'CARRIGAN, Catherine:
  Barlow, M.; Bruton.
O'DONNELL, E. J.:
  Bishop.
O'FARRELL, Patrick:
  Barry, J.
O'NEIL, W. M.:
  Anderson, F. & J.
O'NEILL, Sally:
  Arnot; Becke; Card.
ORAM, Nigel:
  Ahuia Ova.
OSBORN, E. F.:
  Albiston, A.
OSBORNE, Graeme:
  Bennett, H.
OSMOND, Warren:
  Atkinson, M.

PALMER, Imelda:
  Benson, L.
PARSONS, George:
  Alston.
PATRICK, Alison:
  Brookes, H.
PAUL, J. B.:
  Allan, J.
PENNY, B. R.:
  Brassey.

PERDRIX, J. L.:
  Baracchi.
PERKS, Murray:
  Charlton, M.
PETTIGREW, C. J.:
  Camfield.
PHILLIPS, Nan:
  Bayldon, F.
PIGGIN, Stuart:
  Abbott, W.
PIKE, A. F.:
  Bailey, A. E.; Carroll, E.; Chauvel, C.
PITCHER, W. B.:
  Bonython, J. Langdon & J. Lavington.
PIXLEY, Norman S.:
  Bell, James.
PLAYFORD, John:
  Baker, R. C.
POYNTER, J. R.:
  Baillieu; Beaurepaire.
PRESTON, James:
  Blanc.
PRUUL, Susan:
  Byrne.
PUREGGER, Marjorie:
  Bulcock.

RADFORD, Joan T.:
  Ampt; Anderson, V.; Avery.
RADI, Heather:
  Ardill; Bowes; Brooks, W.; Bruce, S.;
  Carey.
RADIC, Maureen Thérèse:
  Austral; Castles.
REED, T. T.:
  Bussell.
REEVES, Andrew:
  Andrade; Andrews, J.
REGAN, Kerry:
  Akhurst.
REYNOLDS, John:
  Ashbolt.
RICHARDS, Eric:
  Bruce. T. & W.
RICKARD, John:
  Bayles.
ROBERTSON, Enid:
  Ashby; Black, J.
ROBERTSON, J. R.:
  Angwin.
ROE, J. I.:
  Arundale; Booth, M.
ROE, Michael:
  Alexander, F.; Arthur, R.; Beattie, J. W.;
  Brown, W. J.
ROLLISON, Kay:
  Boyd, J.; Brown, J. D.; Butler, R.
RONALD, Heather B.:
  Chirnside.
ROSENBERG, Louise:
  Boas, A.
ROSENTHAL, Newman:
  Boas, I.

ROUTH, S. J.:
Blacklock.
ROWE, James Brock:
Carlton.
ROWELL, Sydney*:
Bruche.
RUSSELL, E. W.:
Barnett, F.; Broome.
RUSSELL, K. F.:
Allen, H.; Berry, R.
RUTLAND, Suzanne D.:
Benjamin, D.
RUTLEDGE, Martha:
Aronson; Ashton, James, politician;
Bailey, J.; Ball, R.; Barrett, W.; Barton, E.;
Beatty; Boyce, F. S.; Carroll, E.
RYAN, Kevin:
Brennan, F.
RYAN, M. Imelda:
Brennan, M.
RYDON, Joan:
Chanter.

SADLER, P. S.:
Bell, B. C.
SAFFIN, N. W.:
Bromley.
SAUNDERS, Kay:
Buchanan, F.
SCARLETT, Ken:
Ball, P.; Baskerville.
SCOLLAY, Moira:
Anderson, P. M.; Bowling; Brookfield.
SERLE, Geoffrey:
Champion, H. H.
SERLE, R. P.:
Byron.
SHARPE, Margaret:
Ainsworth, A.
SHAW, A. G. L.:
Argyle; Behan.
SHEEHY, Thomas:
Beckett, W.
SHERINGTON, G. E.:
Aspinall, A.; Bee.
SHORTEN, Ann R.:
Bell, B.; Berry, W.
SIERP, Allan:
Ashton, James, artist.
SIMINGTON, Margot Z.:
Cayley, H.
SIMON, Philipp:
Baldwin.
SIMPSON, L. A.:
Bisdee.
SIMPSON, Pat:
Bayley.
SLEE, John:
Canning.
SMART, Judith:
Baines.
SMITH, Ann G.:
Cheel.
*deceased

SMITH, Bernard:
Balfour.
SMITH, R. F. I.:
Butler, R. L.
SOMERVILLE, J. L.:
Benjamin, L.
SOUTHERN, Roger J.:
Calder, W.
SPEARRITT, Peter:
Bradfield.
STANNAGE, Tom:
Bold; Burt.
STAPLES, G. T.:
Burnside.
STARKE, J. G.:
Charteris.
STEWART, Ken:
Bayldon, A.
STEWART, Noël:
Chase.
STIRLING, Alfred:
Bell, A.
STOWELL, Jill:
Cherry, T.
STRACHAN, Robert W.:
Birkbeck.
STRAHAN, Lynne:
Bruce, M.
STUART, Ian:
Champion, H. W.
SULLIVAN, Martin:
Adamson, J.; Airey, P.
SULLIVAN, Rodney:
Casey.
SUMMERS, H. J.:
Browne, R.
SUTTON, R.:
Bartlett; Boswell.
SWAN, R. A.:
Bernacchi, L.; Borchgrevink.
SWEETING, A. J.:
Brand.

TALENT, John A.:
Baragwanath.
TAMBLYN, M.:
Bell, P.
TEALE, Ruth:
Camidge; Campion, F.; Chapman, H.
TEMPLETON, Jacqueline:
Bouton.
THAME, Claudia:
Armstrong, W. G.
THOMAS, David:
Bunny.
THOMPSON, John R.:
Arthur, J.; Broinowski, R.
THOMPSON, Judith:
Boxall.
THOMPSON, Roger C.:
Alcock, R.; Beatham.
THOMSON, Kathleen:
Cameron, A.

A NOTE ON SOME PROCEDURES

Among our authors and readers and, indeed, on the Editorial Board, there is strong disagreement on whether certain facts should normally be included — such as cause of death, burial or cremation details, and value of estate. In this volume our practices have been as follows:

Cause of death: include, except usually in the case of the very old; in practice we include in about two-thirds of the entries.

Burial/cremation: include when details available.

Value of estate: normally include for certain categories such as businessmen, and when the amount is unusually high or low. In recent years, when the practice developed of early distribution of assets in order to avoid estate and probate duties, the sum is not always meaningful; moreover it is not always possible to ascertain the full facts. Hence we have resorted to discretionary use.

Some other procedures require explanation:

Measurements: as the least unsatisfactory solution, we have used imperial system measurements (as historically appropriate), followed by the metric equivalent in brackets. Round metric figures are used when the number is clearly approximate, e.g., 500 miles (800 km).

Religion: stated whenever information is available, but often there is no good evidence of actual practice, e.g., the information is confined to marriage and funeral rites.

[*q.v.*]: the particular volume is given for those included in volumes 1-6, but not for those in this and future volumes. Note that the cross-reference [q.v.] now accompanies the names of all who have separate articles in the *Dictionary*. In volumes 1-6 it was not shown for royal visitors, governors, lieut-governors and those Colonial Office officials who were included.

Small capitals: used for relations and others when they are of substantial importance but not included in their own right.

Five-year rule: a few men and women, whose *floruit* was pre-1940 but who lived to an advanced age, have been excluded on the ground that they died too recently for proper historical consideration. No one is included who died less than five years before date of publication, except some sportsmen whose years of fame were long ago.

xix

CORRIGENDA

Every effort is made to check every detail in every article, but inevitably a work of the size and complexity of the *Dictionary* includes some errors.

Corrigenda have been published regularly with each volume and a list is included with Volume 7, repeating all corrections already made and showing distinctively those made since the publication of Volume 6 (1976).

Only corrections are shown; additional information is not included; nor is any reinterpretation attempted. The only exception to this procedure is when new details become available about parents or births, deaths and marriages.

Documented corrections are welcomed. Additional information, with sources, is also invited and will be placed in the appropriate files for future use.

REFERENCES

The following works of reference have been widely used but have not normally been listed in the sources at the foot of the articles:

D. Blair, *Cyclopaedia of Australasia* (Melbourne, 1881)

D. H. Borchardt, *Checklist of royal commissions, select committees of parliament and boards of inquiry:* part 1 — *Commonwealth of Australia 1900-1950* (Sydney, 1965), 2 — *Tasmania 1856-1959* (1960), 3 — *Victoria 1856-1960* (1970), 4 — *New South Wales 1855-1960* (Melbourne, 1975), 5 — *Queensland 1859-1960* (Melbourne, 1978)

B. Burke, *A genealogical and heraldic history of the colonial gentry*, 1-2 (London, 1891-95)

J. A. Ferguson, *Bibliography of Australia*, 1-7 (Sydney, 1941-69)

J. Fielding and R. O'Neill, *A select bibliography of Australian military history 1891-1939* (Canberra, 1978)

H. M. Green, *A history of Australian literature*, 1-2 (Sydney 1961; 2nd edn, 1971)

J. H. Heaton, *Australian Dictionary of dates and men of the time* (London, 1879)

C. A. Hughes and B. D. Graham, *A handbook of Australian government and politics 1890-1964* (Canberra, 1968);
Voting for the Australian House of Representatives 1901-1964, with corrigenda (Canberra, 1975),
Voting for the Queensland Legislative Assembly 1890-1964 (Canberra, 1974), for *New South Wales . . .* (1975), for *Victoria . . .* (1975), for the *South Australian, Western Australian and Tasmanian Lower Houses . . .* (1976)

F. Johns, *An Australian biographical dictionary* (Melbourne, 1934)

P. Mennell, *The dictionary of Australasian biography* (London, 1892)

E. M. Miller, *Australian literature . . . to 1935*, 1-2 (Melbourne, 1940), extended to 1950 by F. T. Macartney (Sydney, 1956)

Mitchell Library (NSW), *Dictionary catalog of printed books* (Boston, 1968)

W. Moore, *The story of Australian art*, 1-2 (Sydney, 1934)

P. C. Mowle, *A genealogical history of pioneer families in Australia* (Sydney, 1939; 5th edn, Adelaide, 1978)

P. Serle, *Dictionary of Australian biography*, 1-2 (Sydney, 1949)

E. Zalums, *A bibliography of South Australian royal commissions, select committees of parliament, and boards of inquiry, 1857-1970* (Adelaide, 1975)

Australian encyclopaedia, 1-2 (Sydney, 1925); 1-10 (1958)

Dictionary of national biography (London, 1885-1971)

The official history of Australia in the war of 1914-1918, 1-10 (Sydney, 1921-42):
cited under the name of the individual author, together with *first* date of publication of the relevant volume.

also:

British Museum, *General catalogue of printed books*

British Library Bibliographical Services Division, *British national bibliography*

Library of Congress, *National union catalog*

National Library of Australia, *Annual catalogue of Australian publications* (1936-60); *Australian national bibliography* (1961 +)

ABBREVIATIONS USED IN BIBLIOGRAPHIES

A.A.Co.	Australian Agricultural Company	Fr	Father (priest)
AAO	Australian Archives	G, Geog	Geographical
A.B.C.	Australian Broadcasting Commission	GB	Great Britain
		Gen	Genealogical, Genealogists
Ac no	Accession number	gen ed	general editor
ACER	Australian Council for Educational Research	Govt	Government
ACT	Australian Capital Territory	HA	House of Assembly
Adel	Adelaide	HC	House of Commons
Adm	Admiralty, London	Hist	History, Historical
Agr	Agriculture, Agricultural	HL	House of Lords
AIF	Australian Imperial Force	H.M.C.S.	Her Majesty's Colonial Ship
AMA	Australian Medical Association	HO	Home Office, London
		Hob	Hobart
ANU	Australian National University, Canberra	*HRA*	*Historical Records of Australia*
ANU Archives	ANU Archives of Business and Labour	HSSA	Historical Society of South Australia
ANZAAS	Australian and New Zealand Association for the Advancement of Science	*IAN*	*Illustrated Australian News*
		Inst	Institute, Institution
A'sian	Australasian	*ISN*	*Illustrated Sydney News*
Assn	Association		
Aust	Australia, Australian	*J*	*Journal*
AWM	Australian War Memorial, Canberra.	LA	Legislative Assembly
		LaTL	La Trobe Library, Melbourne
		Launc	Launceston
Basser Lib	Adolph Basser Library, Australian Academy of Science, Canberra	LC	Legislative Council
		Lib	Library
		Lond	London
Battye Lib	J. S. Battye Library of West Australian History, Perth	*Mag*	*Magazine*
		Melb	Melbourne
BHP	Broken Hill Proprietary Co. Ltd	MDHC	Melbourne Diocesan Historical Commission (Catholic), Fitzroy
bibliog	bibliography		
biog	biography, biographical	*MJA*	*Medical Journal of Australia*
BM	British Museum, London	ML	Mitchell Library, Sydney
Brisb	Brisbane	MS	manuscript
		mthly	monthly
CAE	College of Advanced Education		
Canb	Canberra	nd	date of publication unknown
cat	catalogue	NL	National Library of Australia, Canberra
Cmd	Command		
CO	Colonial Office, London	no	number
Com	Commission	np	place of publication unknown
CSIRO	Commonwealth Scientific and Industrial Research Organization	NSW	New South Wales
		NSWA	The Archives Authority of New South Wales, Sydney
cttee	committee		
Cwlth	Commonwealth	NT	Northern Territory
		NZ	New Zealand
DNB	*Dictionary of National Biography*	NZNA	New Zealand National Archives
		Oxley Lib	John Oxley Library, Brisbane
ed	editor		
edn	edition	p	page, pages
Edinb	Edinburgh	PAH	*see* RPAH
encl	enclosure	*PD*	*Parliamentary Debates*

ABBREVIATIONS

PMB	Pacific Manuscripts Bureau, Research School of Pacific Studies, ANU	1st S	First Session
		2nd S	Second Session
		2nd s	second series
PNGA	Archives Office of Papua and New Guinea, Port Moresby	SA	South Australia
		SAA	South Australian Archives, Adelaide
PP	*Parliamentary Papers*		
PRGSSA	*Proceedings of the Royal Geographical Society of Australasia (South Australian Branch)*	Sel	Select
		SLSA	State Library of South Australia
priv print	privately printed	SLT	State Library of Tasmania
PRO	Public Record Office	SLV	State Library of Victoria
Procs	*Proceedings*	*SMH*	*Sydney Morning Herald*
pt	part, parts	Soc	Society
PTHRA	*Papers and Proceedings of the Tasmanian Historical Research Association*	supp	supplement
		Syd	Sydney
		TA	Tasmanian State Archives, Hobart
Q	*Quarterly*	Tas	Tasmania
QA	Queensland State Archives, Brisbane	*T&CJ*	*Australian Town and Country Journal*
Qld	Queensland	tr	translated, translation
		Trans	*Transactions*
RAHS	Royal Australian Historical Society (Sydney)	Univ	University
		UPNG	University of Papua New Guinea
rev	revised, revision		
RGS	Royal Geographical Society		
RHSQ	Royal Historical Society of Queensland (Brisbane)	*V&P*	*Votes and Proceedings*
		VHM(J)	*Victorian Historical Magazine (Journal)*
RHSV	Royal Historical Society of Victoria (Melbourne)	v, vol	volume
RMIT	Royal Melbourne Institute of Technology	Vic	Victoria
Roy	Royal	WA	Western Australia
RPAH	Royal Prince Alfred Hospital	Well	Wellington, New Zealand
RWAHS	Royal Western Australian Historical Society (Perth)	wkly	weekly
		WO	War Office, London

A

ABBOTT, GERTRUDE (1846-1934), founder of a hospital for women, was born Mary Jane O'Brien on 11 July 1846 in Sydney, daughter of Thomas O'Brien, schoolmaster, and his wife Rebecca, née Matthews. The family moved in December 1848 to Dry Creek, South Australia, where her father ran a licensed school, then took up farming. In February 1868, taking the name Sister Ignatius of Jesus, she entered the Order of St Joseph of the Sacred Heart, founded at Penola two years earlier by Mary McKillop and Julian Tenison-Woods [qq.v.5,6]. Influenced by Tenison-Woods, she and another nun claimed to witness visions. There was a scandal when the other nun was found to have faked manifestations. Although blameless, Sister Ignatius left the order in July 1872, only four months after she had taken final vows, and returned to Sydney. No longer able to use her religious name, she became known as Mrs Gertrude or 'Mother' Abbott. For the next twenty years she waited in vain for approval to found an order of contemplative nuns. At her establishments in Surry Hills, first in Bourke Street, later in Elizabeth Street, she gathered round her a small community of women who survived chiefly by dressmaking. After Tenison-Woods's death in her care in 1889, she inherited his estate of £609.

In 1893 Mrs Abbott reputedly took in and cared for a pregnant girl brought to her by a policeman. Next year she opened St Margaret's Maternity Home at 561 Elizabeth Street, in the area known as Strawberry Hills. She claimed that the home was 'unsectarian in principle and working', its chief object being 'to provide shelter and care for unmarried girls of the comparatively respectable class'. From March to December 1894 she admitted 9 married and 23 unmarried patients; 3 nurses trained in midwifery that year and 8 were receiving instruction in 1895.

As president of the managing committee, later matron, Mrs Abbott ran the home for the next forty years. She and the women who worked with her were a quasi-religious community and followed an unofficial Rule; she obtained permission for Mass to be celebrated in a chapel at the hospital two or three times a week. In 1904 St Margaret's began to treat diseases of women and opened an out-patients department; doctors also tended cases in near-by homes. In 1910 Mrs Abbott leased, and later bought, from the Sacred Heart nuns a property in Bourke Street near Taylor Square, and the hospital moved there. As it was not recognized officially as a Catholic institution, she raised money for its work and further expansion by a series of large art union lotteries from 1921. That year she received a first government subsidy of £250, and patients' fees outstripped for the first time fees paid by nurses.

In 1926 Sister Magdalen Foley, who had been with her since the earliest days and had been in charge of training nurses, died; from about then Mrs Abbott withdrew from the running of the hospital. She died there on 12 May 1934. That year its annual report recorded 760 patients treated and 619 births registered without any maternal deaths; it was the third largest obstetric hospital in Sydney. After her death, at her wish, it passed to the Sisters of St Joseph, whose order she had left unhappily sixty years before.

G. O'Neill, *Life of Mother Mary of the Cross* (Melb, 1931); T. P. Boland, *Quiet women* (Aust, 1974); J. M. Noone, 'St. Margaret's Hospital . . .', *Aust Hospital*, June 1945; R. J. Murphy, 'Catholic hospitals of Australia', Catholic Medical Guild of St Luke, *Trans*, Sept 1943; *T&CJ*, 8 July 1908; St Margaret's Hospital, Annual reports (ML); Sisters of St Joseph Archives (North Sydney and Goulburn, NSW). CHRIS CUNNEEN

ABBOTT. JOHN HENRY (MACARTNEY) (1874-1953), author, was born on 26 December 1874 at Haydonton, New South Wales, eldest son of (Sir) Joseph Palmer Abbott [q.v.3] and his first wife Matilda Elizabeth, née Macartney. He was educated at The King's School, Parramatta, and attended classes at the University of Sydney before returning to the Hunter valley, where he was working as a jackeroo on a family property when his first contribution to the *Bulletin* was published in 1897.

In January 1900 Abbott left for the South African War as a corporal in the 1st Australian Horse; in May he was commissioned as a second lieutenant in the Royal Field Artillery, but was invalided back to Australia in October. Out of this experience came *Tommy Cornstalk . . .* (London, 1902), one of the earliest examples of Australian war literature. Its success induced Abbott to try his luck as a freelance writer in London. In the several years he remained there he wrote for the *Daily Telegraph*, the *Spectator* and other journals and published four books: *Plain and veldt . . .* (1903), a selection of stories based on his Australian and South

African experiences; two descriptive works, *An outlander in England* (1905) and *The south seas, Melanesia* (1908); and the semi-autobiographical *Letters from Queer Street* ... (1908).

By 1909 Abbott was back in Australia working on a 'shocker' for A. C. Rowlandson [q.v.], proprietor of the New South Wales Bookstall Co.; it was published in 1910 as *The sign of the serpent*. Thereafter he turned primarily to early New South Wales history, churning out over the next forty years hundreds of articles, series and serials, which were published in the *Bulletin*, the *Lone Hand*, *Truth*, the *World's News* and other Sydney journals. His novels such as *The Governor's man* (1919), *Ensign Calder* (1922) and *Sydney Cove* (1923) introduced Governors Bligh, Phillip and Macquarie [qq.v.1,2] as characters, and presented a view of colonial society that reflected his pioneer and Establishment background. Among his other publications were four historical works, including *The story of William Dampier* (1911) and *Ben Hall* (1934), and two based on his schoolboy experiences.

After his works had appeared as serials, Abbott sold the book rights, usually at low cost, to local publishers. Despite the volume of his writing, he was often in financial difficulties; bankrupted in 1923, he was left an annuity of £200 by his uncle W. E. Abbott [q.v.] in 1924 and was awarded a Commonwealth Literary Fund fellowship in 1942. Forced by ill health to stop writing in 1948, he died at Rydalmere Mental Hospital of vascular disease on 12 August 1953. He was buried in the Anglican section of Rookwood cemetery, survived by his wife Katherina, née Wallace, a journalist whom he had married in Sydney on 2 August 1926 according to Roman Catholic rites; as Rena Wallace she had published *A bush girl's songs* (Sydney, 1905). Abbott's use of Macartney as a third name has caused him to be confused with his brother Macartney.

Tall and strong-featured, with 'a face like one of Cromwell's Ironsides', Abbott was 'slovenly colloquial' in speech and had a truculent, contrary side which revealed itself most clearly during his frequent bouts of drinking; a 'throwback to the days of the Rum Corps and Gallows Hill', he is well captured in David Low's [q.v.] *Caricatures* (Sydney, 1915). His historical writing reached a wide audience, but his most significant works are *Tommy Cornstalk* and *Letters from Queer Street*. The first, written 'from the point of view of the Australian ranks', presents a picture of the Australian soldier very much in accord with that eventually established by the Anzac legend. The second is a moving depiction of London poverty.

Aust Defence Dept, *Official records of the Australian military contingents to the war in South Africa*, P. L. Murray ed (Melb, 1912); *The late Alfred Cecil Rowlandson* (Syd, 1922?); N. Lindsay, *Bohemians of the Bulletin* (Syd, 1965); L. Such, 'Three old-timers', *Southerly*, 19 (1958); *Bulletin*, 26 Aug, 23 Sept 1953; J. H. Abbott, *and* Lindsay, *and* Tyrrell papers (ML); Atlee Hunt, *and* Mackaness papers (NL); Bankruptcy papers 23 315/14 (NSWA).   B. G. ANDREWS

ABBOTT, PERCY PHIPPS (1869-1940), solicitor, soldier and politician, was born on 14 May 1869 in Hobart Town, son of John William Abbott, auctioneer, and his wife Mary Ann, née Phipps, and grandson of Edward Abbott [q.v.1]. Educated at The Hutchins School, Hobart, in 1878-87, he was articled to Thomas Edgar Creswell, a Sydney solicitor, in April 1889 and admitted to practice on 2 June 1894. An active member of the Sydney Rowing Club, he played social cricket and was enrolled as a special constable during the 1891 wharflabourers' strike.

Late in 1893 Abbott had bought Norman MacDonald's practice at Glen Innes. On 2 September 1901 at Tamworth he married Elizabeth Matilda, daughter of G. B. Gidley King of Goonoo Goonoo, widow of Colin James Ross and mother of three children; Abbott valued his connexion with old colonial families. He was always an active sportsman: first secretary of the Northern Border Cricket Association, president of the Glen Innes Rifle Club, a keen trout fisherman and breeder of racehorses. He was an alderman on the Glen Innes Municipal Council in 1898-1904 and 1906-14, and in 1910-13 was mayor and president of the hospital board. Backed by the Farmers and Settlers' Association of New South Wales, he was elected as a Liberal to the House of Representatives in 1913 and represented New England until 1919 when he resigned. In the House he was preoccupied with tariffs, decentralization and industrial lawlessness.

Abbott had joined the 4th Infantry Regiment in 1898 as a second lieutenant; he transferred to the 5th Australian Light Horse (New England) in 1903 and in 1905 to the 6th (Hunter River Lancers). He was promoted captain in 1908 and major next year; from 1913 he commanded the 5th Light Horse. Appointed lieut-colonel in the Australian Imperial Force in March 1915, he sailed for Egypt in June in command of the 12th Light Horse, railing in his diary against the wickedness of Germany, but anxious, notwithstanding his rank, to observe the proprieties of Australian egalitarianism. On Gallipoli he was appalled by the ferocity of trench warfare, proud of the Anzacs and scathing about British strategy. He was soon commanding the 10th Light Horse.

Suffering from enteric fever, in October 1915 Abbott was evacuated to England where he commanded Australian staging camps. He often compared the daring and dash of the Australian soldier (however undisciplined) with the slovenly reluctance of his English working-class counterpart, but in 1916 he was disturbed by the number of troops voting against conscription in the referendum. Deeply appreciating the honour of shaking the King's hand four times, he was appointed C.M.G. in June 1917. That year he served with the 63rd Battalion in France, later with the 30th, and was mentioned in dispatches. At the end of 1917 he resumed command of the 12th Light Horse. Recurrence of enteric, the effects of gas and a chronic eye complaint forced his return to Australia in April 1918 and he was released from the A.I.F. in June, although he continued in command of the 12th, now New England Light Horse, until he retired in 1929. In 1919 he was awarded the Colonial Auxiliary Forces Officers' Decoration.

Having re-established his legal practice, in 1919 Abbott organized the Country Party campaign for the State election in New England and accompanied (Sir) Michael Bruxner [q.v.] on his electoral tour. He was president of the Northern New State Movement from 1920. Defeated as a Country Party candidate for the Senate in 1922, he was elected in 1925 but lost his place in 1928. A ready speaker of great charm and humour, Abbott was unpredictable in parliament and sometimes had bitter exchanges with opponents over trivial matters. In 1927-29 he sat on the royal commission on the Constitution, and as a champion of the 'Small Staters' presented several minority reports.

In 1932 Abbott sold his practice to his eldest son Douglas and retired to Tamworth but, soon wearying of idleness, he re-established a practice. He was a member of the Union and Civic clubs in Sydney. In 1939-40 he was commandant of Tamworth civil defence. Survived by his wife, three sons and a daughter, he died in hospital at Tamworth on 9 September 1940 of asthmatic bronchitis and heart failure and was buried in the Church of England cemetery at Glen Innes. His assets were valued for probate at £1662 but his debts amounted to £18 273.

Glen Innes Municipal Council, *The Beardies heritage* (Glen Innes, 1972); *PP* (CA), 1929-31, 2 (16); G. S. Harman, Politics at the electoral level, a study in Armidale and New England, 1899 to 1929 (M.A. thesis, Univ New England, 1965); letters and documents (held by D. W. Abbott & Co., solicitors, Glen Innes); Senator P. P. Abbott papers (held by Univ New England, *and* Dixson Lib, Syd, *and* AAO); P. P. Abbott war diaries (held by D. W. Abbott, Glen Innes).　　　　　TERRY HOGAN

ABBOTT, WILLIAM EDWARD (1844-1924), pastoralist and politician, was born on 1 April 1844 at Muswellbrook, New South Wales, second son of John Kingsmill Abbott (d. 1847), squatter, and his wife Frances Amanda, née Brady. He was educated at The King's School, Parramatta, and briefly at Sydney Grammar School, more because of his mother's belief in the importance of education than her capacity to afford it.

At 16 Abbott took over the family property at Wingen and, by gradually converting leasehold land to freehold, acquired one of the most valuable sheep runs on the upper Hunter. By 1890 he was running almost 21000 sheep and 100 head of Devon cattle on the 30000 acres (12 140 ha) of his Abbotsford estate which incorporated Glengarry and Murrulla stations. In the 1890s he turned from N. P. Bayly's [q.v.3] Havilah merino blood to crossbreds, experimenting first with Lincolns and Romney Marshes from New Zealand, and then Shropshires. Hard working, Abbott was always impatient of any insinuation that the returns enjoyed by pastoralists were excessive.

He experimented with deforestation and rabbit control at Abbotsford and reported his findings to the Royal Society of New South Wales, of which he was a member in 1877-1924. In 1884 he was awarded the society's bronze medal for his paper on 'Water supply in the interior of New South Wales'. In 1890 he included four of his five papers read to the society in *Essays political & scientific*.

Like his brother, Sir Joseph Palmer Abbott [q.v.3], he was an expert on land law and possibly originated the idea of the conditional leasing system in (Sir) Alexander Stuart's [q.v.6] Crown Lands Act of 1884. In 1889 he was elected as a protectionist to the Legislative Assembly for the Upper Hunter and was prominent in carrying the Crown Rents Act of 1890 through the House. However, Abbott was too staunchly individualistic to conform to the policy of Sir George Dibbs [q.v.4]; and after members of his own party accused him of being a 'liar' and a 'cocktail' he spoke rarely in debates. Defeated in the 1891 election, he never again stood for the assembly and was rejected for the 1897 Australasian Federal Convention.

A member of the Pastoralists' Union of New South Wales from its foundation in 1890, Abbott led resistance to the demands of the Amalgamated Shearers' Union of Australasia (later the Australian Workers'

Union). Previously sympathetic to the plight of working men, he was willing to accept the union shearers' agreement for 1891, if allowed to keep existing contracts to shear with non-unionists in 1890. He found W. G. Spence's [q.v.6] refusal to concede this so unreasonable that he resolved to oppose the union with 'every means' in his power; most pastoralists came to the same decision when the A.S.U. called its men out in September. In 1890 Abbott was appointed to the council of the Pastoralists' Union and in 1891, when the A.S.U. decided not to shear at all, he was elected president of the Pastoralists' Federal Council of Australia. His many letters to the press, dwelling on the tyranny and self-interest of union leaders and insisting on 'freedom of contract', were described by labour men as 'vindictive' and 'disgusting'. But he was a fair negotiator: as chairman of the conference with the A.S.U. in August 1891 he refused to 'humiliate the men' by forcing them to accept the pastoralists' definition of freedom of contract, a concession which made a settlement possible.

As president of the Pastoralists' Union in 1894-97 and 1900-10, Abbott was guided by the principles of 'fair dealing and freedom of contract'. From 1902 he was only too pleased to negotiate with the rival Machine Shearers' and Shed Employees' Union, aborting all conferences with the A.W.U. In 1907 he presided over preparation of the pastoralists' case when the A.W.U. took its demands to the Commonwealth Court of Conciliation and Arbitration. The Federal pastoral award allowed some of the union's demands but the president R. E. O'Connor [q.v.] refrained from granting preference to unionists.

Abbott's presidential addresses became increasingly political: by now a convinced free trader, he maintained that meddling legislation by incompetent governments was undermining the pastoral and mining industries on which the growth of the Commonwealth depended. There would be no stock losses even in times of drought, he averred, if sheep could only feed on Hansard. He resigned from the council in 1917 and sold Glengarry about the same time.

In his twenties Abbott was disappointed in love and he never married. Companionable, he was a favourite raconteur and 'beautiful billiards player' in the Australian and Warrigal clubs in Sydney. Abstemious and cultivated, he would drink tea and lace his conversation with quotations from the Bible and Shakespeare. In 1892 he published his *Poems*. Standing 6 ft. 5 ins. (almost 2 m) tall, dressed in coarse tweeds and smoking a capacious pipe, he spoke with slow, deliberate speech and would always end on an upward inflexion of his voice. Abbott died from 'poisoning by arsenic self administered while suffering from acute mental depression following illness' at Murrulla, Wingen, on 14 November 1924 and was buried with Anglican rites beside his mother on a hill overlooking his property. He left most of his estate, valued for probate at almost £81 000, to two Abbott nephews and the income from £2000 to J. H. M. Abbott [q.v.], another nephew.

F. S. Piggin, 'The Graziers' Association: how it began', *Muster*, 7 July 1965, *and* 'New South Wales pastoralists and the strikes of 1890 and 1891', *Hist Studies*, no 56, Apr 1971; *Daily Telegraph* (Syd), 18 Nov 1924; *Pastoral Review*, 16 Dec 1924.

STUART PIGGIN

à BECKETT, ADA MARY (1872-1948), educationist, was born on 18 May 1872 at Norwood, South Australia, elder daughter of Henry John Lambert, Presbyterian minister, and his wife Helen, née Garrett. She was educated at the Advanced School for Girls, Adelaide, and the University of Melbourne (B.Sc., 1895; M.Sc., 1897) where she was awarded the Wyselaskie [q.v.6] scholarship in natural science (biology) and the final honours scholarship in biology. She resided in Trinity College Hostel (Janet Clarke [q.v.3] Hall) for five years and was Annie Grice Scholar in 1892-93. Later she was a founder of the Victorian Women Graduates' Association and chairman of the Janet Clarke Hall Committee in 1923-26 and 1928.

Ada Lambert began teaching science in 1893 at Merton Hall (later Melbourne Church of England Girls' Grammar School). By 1900 she had done some teaching at seven girls' schools in Melbourne and Geelong, and at the Working Men's College. She had also demonstrated in biology at the university but assumed more senior duties in 1898 when Professor (Sir) W. Baldwin Spencer [q.v.] was overseas and in 1899, just before and for some months after the death of Professor Sir Frederick McCoy [q.v.5], she relieved T. S. Hall [q.v.] of his lectures. Her appointment as demonstrator and assistant lecturer in biology during Spencer's central Australian anthropological tour in 1901 was the basis of her claim to be the first woman appointed to lecture at the University of Melbourne.

On 19 February 1903 at Sandringham Presbyterian Church she married Thomas Archibald à Beckett, solicitor, eldest son of Sir Thomas à Beckett [q.v.3]. In 1912, two years after the birth of her third son, she resumed teaching, mainly at Melbourne Church of England Girls' Grammar School; during World War I she also demonstrated in biology at the university. When Scotch

College introduced the subject into its final-year courses in 1921, Ada à Beckett joined the staff full-time, as head of the biology department; she retired in 1937. Remembered as a very competent teacher and a good but not stern disciplinarian, with a 'dignified and commanding personality' and clear, decisive speech, she made significant impact on her pupils, a number of whom entered medicine or allied professions.

Ada à Beckett's extensive involvement with the kindergarten movement and the education of pre-school children began in 1908 when she was elected a foundation vice-president of the Free Kindergarten Union of Victoria; she was president in 1919-39 and a life-president thereafter. She was prominent in establishing the Kindergarten Training College, Kew, in 1916, contributing significantly to the design of courses; she lectured in physiology and hygiene in 1920-23 and was president of the college council in 1926-39. In 1936 she founded the Australian Association for Pre-School Child Development which established the Lady Gowrie [q.v.] model pre-school centres. She was closely involved in creating a community centre on the Housing Commission estate at Fishermen's Bend; the kindergarten established there in 1942 was named after her. Her undoubted abilities as an educator, her 'unique flair for organization', and her position in Melbourne society all contributed to her success. She was appointed C.B.E. in 1935.

Ada à Beckett was active in many women's organizations including the National Council of Women; she was president of the Lyceum Club in 1926-28 and a life member of the Victoria League. She died of cancer at her home in East St Kilda on 20 May 1948 and was cremated at Springvale. Widowed in 1930, she was survived by three sons of whom Edward Lambert was a Test cricketer. A portrait by Charles Wheeler [q.v.] hangs in the Institute of Early Childhood Development, Kew.

Argus, 18 Feb 1927, 20 May 1948; *Age*, 20 May 1948; Registrar's correspondence and related records (Univ Melb Archives).

JULIE MARGINSON

ABEL, CHARLES WILLIAM (1862-1930), missionary, was born on 25 September 1862 in London, son of William Abel, a Congregationalist librarian, and his wife Harriet, née Dobson. A fervent political liberal, Abel migrated when young to New Zealand as a farmworker and lived for a time among the Maoris, winning trust by helping them trade with Europeans. Deciding to become a missionary, he returned to England, entered Cheshunt College and in 1889 applied to the London Missionary Society for appointment to New Guinea. He was ordained in 1890.

Abel began work at Port Moresby on 23 October 1890 and relieved James Chalmers [q.v.3] briefly at Motumotu. In August 1891 he joined F. W. Walker, who had just moved the head station for the east end of New Guinea from Suau to Kwato Island in China Strait. Mainly because of hard physical labour by the two men, Kwato was reasonably habitable by late 1892 and some buildings had been erected. That year he went to Sydney and on 22 November married Elizabeth Beatrice Emma Moxon (1869-1939). At Kwato the Abels and Walker began their teaching programme which, besides elementary subjects and Bible-study, included carpentry for boys, sewing and fine lace work for girls, and sport, especially cricket. Technical education gradually predominated. Walker fell out with the directors of the L.M.S. and resigned in 1896, but the Abels struggled to make Kwato a model station. A feature of the plan was the settlement system whereby native children, segregated as infants from their parents and village life, sold the products of their industry to Samarai. Adult converts also worked at their trades for the mission and became lay evangelists.

Dr R. W. Thompson, foreign secretary of the L.M.S., visited Papua in 1897 and approved this system, but Abel's local colleagues and other missionaries were harder to convince. When he was on furlough in England in 1900, his popular lectures were supplemented by a small pamphlet, *Kwato, New Guinea, 1890-1900*, which gave further details. He was asked to write the L.M.S. children's gift book: *Savage life in New Guinea* was ready by the end of 1901. This was the only substantial book he ever wrote, and critics tend to take statements from it out of context.

Abel's major contributions to Papuan development were yet to come. As Australia prepared to take over the administration, he became more concerned for the future of his people. J. H. Angas [q.v.3] of South Australia donated £1000 for industrial work at Kwato; this allowed Abel to expand with a sawmill. From 1901 he became widely known in New Guinea both for success in teaching good English and for championship of the rights of Papuans in cases against Europeans. His disclosures of the Milne Bay scandals in 1901 made him very unpopular in Samarai but earned him the trust of Papuans. He gained the ear of Alfred Deakin [q.v.], the prime minister, through whom he met Atlee Hunt [q.v.], who encouraged Abel to report on affairs in Papua. When the acting administrator Judge Robinson committed suicide after a royal commission into the Goaribari affray was appointed, a faction supporting European settlement alleged bitterly that Abel had driven Robinson to his death.

During his 1909 furlough he persuaded the directors to let him plant coconuts on land and with money promised to him by friends. This venture, known as Enesi (an acronym of the benefactors' names), was to provide work for Papuans on plantations managed by Abel's converts, and in competition with white traders. He had 500 acres (200 ha) planted within two years but, when other missionaries objected, he agreed to sell the plantations at cost to the L.M.S. if it continued the work. Unfortunately it soon became apparent that the society could not afford to maintain the properties; the deputation sent out to investigate in 1915-16 recommended sale of all but 100 acres (40 ha). Abel would not accept this, and in 1917 travelled to London to confer with the directors. Assisted by influential friends, including three former governors of Papua, he persuaded the society to incorporate the Kwato Extension Association. This enabled him to manage Kwato independently while remaining an honorary missionary; the island was leased to the association for ten years. Some capital was gathered, but the depressed state of the Papuan economy after 1918 demanded another fund-raising tour. In 1921 he and his family went to England, leaving Kwato in the charge of Madge Parkin (1865-1939), his wife's cousin, who had been working there since 1896.

Financially unsuccessful in England, Abel accepted an invitation from the evangelist W. L. Moody to the United States of America. There he found supporters, organized as the New Guinea Evangelization Society, who paid for the education of his four children, who had all decided to become missionaries, and sent him back to Kwato early in 1924 with enough funds to carry on and the promise of a hospital. The next six years saw continual negotiations, often acrimonious, before the L.M.S. agreed to sell Kwato to the Evangelization Society. Abel travelled to America and England in 1929-30 to settle the business, but died after a motor accident in England on 10 April 1930. His ashes were returned to Kwato, where the work was continued by his wife and family.

Abel was a religious fundamentalist and a strong individualist. The Kwato system created an elite through what his critics saw as aggressive recruitment, strict discipline and paternalism. On the credit side it discouraged evangelical gloom and was totally free of racial prejudice. Abel strove to give his people self-respect and to train them in the decision-making which would eventually be required for self-government. He believed that to survive the impact of cultural change Papuans had to acquire European skills. He aimed at the whole life of the Papuan — spiritual, industrial, social, recreational and cultural. They learned their lessons so well that the Kwatos came to consider themselves as a people apart, calling themselves 'insiders' and those not brought up on Kwato 'outsiders'. Neighbouring peoples expressed their admiration for him in religious legends.

R. W. Abel, *Charles W. Abel of Kwato* (New York, 1934); M. K. Abel, *Charles W. Abel, Papuan pioneer* (Lond, 1957); C. Abel, 'The impact of Charles Abel', 2nd Waigani seminar, *History of Melanesia* (Canb & Port Moresby, 1969); P. A. Prendergast, A history of the London Missionary Society in British New Guinea, 1871-1901 (Ph.D. thesis, Univ Hawaii, 1968); A. Holmes, Industrial missions: C. W. Abel and New Guinea education (B.A. Hons thesis, ANU, 1970); A. R. Austin, The history of technical education in Papua 1874-1941 (M.Ed. thesis, UPNG, 1972); D. F. Wetherell, Christian missions in Eastern New Guinea: a study of European, South Sea Island and Papuan influences, 1877-1942 (Ph.D. thesis, ANU, 1974); Abel papers (UPNG Lib); Council for World Missions Archives (SOAS Lib, Lond).

NANCY LUTTON

ABIGAIL, ERNEST ROBERT (1870-1931), solicitor, was born on 21 June 1870 in Sydney, third son of James William Abigail, of Newtown, grocer, and his wife Mary Anne, née Crudgington. After some education at Newtown Public School, Abigail was employed in his father's store. Seeking a better career, and inspired by his elder brother James who became a solicitor in 1890, he passed the matriculation examinations and, as an evening student, attended the University of Sydney (B.A., 1896; LL.B., 1899). He served articles of clerkship to his brother and was admitted as a solicitor on 19 August 1899. On 16 October 1895 at Enmore he had married Mabel Mary Primrose.

Soon setting up in practice independently, he was quickly in command of a large, if sometimes unsavoury, clientele. Mr Justice F. S. Boyce [q.v.] recounted that when 'little Ernie', as he called himself, 'embarked on his profession as a solicitor in the Police and Criminal Courts his success was rapid and complete . . . Some advocates speak over the heads of the jury — little Ernie never did that. His addresses were little more than above ground level — but guileful, shrewd, simple'.

Abigail was involved in 1900 in a preliminary skirmish to the celebrated Coningham [q.v.] divorce case. At first retained by one of the parties, he withdrew after being charged with false swearing concerning the case. Committed for trial at Quarter Sessions, he was acquitted by the jury at the close of the prosecution case without being asked to proceed with his defence. As 'Zero' he wrote *The secret history of the Coningham case* (1901). In 1921 he was again committed for trial. Charged with attempting to suborn a Crown witness, he produced strong testimonials, including those of two District Court judges, that seem to have persuaded the Crown not to proceed.

Despite the tough and tenacious manner in which he practised his profession, Abigail was soft at heart. He was a lover of animals and of flowers; the garden at his Bondi home occupied much of his leisure and won renown for its beauty. Of a charitable disposition, he assisted many of his friends financially; in contrast to his own somewhat deprived upbringing, he indulged his only child, a son, who was indolent and fell into debt.

Abigail amassed a considerable fortune from his practice, property dealings and other investments. In 1929 protracted litigation arose out of a loan he had made on the security of an unregistered mortgage. The allegation that he was carrying on business as a moneylender without statutory licence was rejected by the courts. The Supreme Court, by a single judge, and on appeal, held in favour of Abigail in the contest over the unregistered mortgage; but the High Court reversed those decisions. Abigail instituted an appeal to the Privy Council, but the worry of the case and his disappointment at the behaviour of his son undermined his health.

He succumbed to pneumonia and died on 28 September 1931, survived by his wife and son. He was cremated and his ashes were placed in the family vault at Waverley cemetery. His representatives pursued and won the Privy Council appeal which became a leading decision on aspects of the Torrens [q.v.6] system of registered land titles. His estate was valued for probate at £87 765; in a codicil to his will he disinherited his son, 'so that he does not benefit in my estate to the extent of one shilling'. The will was challenged and its provisions were reviewed after litigation.

T. R. Bavin (ed), *The jubilee book of the law school of the University of Sydney* (Syd, 1940); *Abigail* v. *Lapin, Cwlth Law Reports*, 44 (1930-31), 51 (1934-35); *SMH*, 27 Aug, 29, 30 Sept, 1 Oct 1921, 29, 30 Sept 1931, 3, 12 May 1933; Bankruptcy file 25 812/15 (NSWA).   J. M. BENNETT

ABRAHAMS, JOSEPH (1855-1938), senior rabbi, was born on 1 April 1855 at St Mary Axe, City of London, son of Rev. Barnett Abrahams (1831-1863) and his wife Jane, née Brandon. His father was minister of the Spanish and Portuguese congregation of London and principal of Jews' College, the theological training institution for English Jewry. Joseph received his early education at Jews' College School and went on to the college to begin rabbinical studies and prepare for University of London examinations. He matriculated in January 1873 and received his arts degree in May 1876. He studied at the college until April 1879 when he went to Berlin; there he gained his rabbinical diploma at Dr Hildersheimer's seminary and also attended philosophy classes at the university in 1879-80. He was awarded his Ph.D. at the University of Leipzig in 1881 and his dissertation, *The sources of the Midrash Echah Rabbah*, was published in Berlin in 1883.

That year Abrahams was called to the pulpit of the Melbourne Hebrew congregation. The chief rabbi of the British Empire, Dr Hermann Adler, named him presiding rabbi of the Beth Din (Court of Jewish religious law) for Australia and New Zealand. He was the first Jewish minister to serve in Australia who possessed both a secular university degree and traditional rabbinic ordination. On 16 April 1885 he married Rachel, daughter of Rev. A. B. Davis [q.v.4] of Sydney; they had no children.

Abrahams had an encyclopaedic memory and was an authority on Greek, German, Latin and mathematics. In 1886 he graduated M.A. (*ad eund.*) at the University of Melbourne. He became well known as a competent and scholarly speaker and as the representative of Judaism in the religious life of Melbourne. Unlike his eminent brother Israel (1854-1925), reader in Talmudic and rabbinic literature at the University of Cambridge, who became associated with moves to modernize Jewish practice, Abrahams was resolutely opposed to religious reform. Though he permitted minor changes to the service, such as the introduction of a choir of male and female voices and some English readings, he was staunchly conservative. In 1903 he briefly resigned from his congregational post over a disagreement about the acceptance of converts to Judaism. He was one of the prime founders of the United Jewish Education Board which organized the religious instruction of Jewish children attending state schools and was president in 1896-1901. From about 1899 he was visiting chaplain to metropolitan prisons.

In 1911 Abrahams was summoned to England with the expectation of being offered the post of chief rabbi of the British

Empire. Probably because of the ill health of his wife, he returned to Melbourne without the office. He continued to serve as rabbi until his retirement in 1919, when his congregation began to plan the move from Bourke Street to St Kilda Road.

Abrahams died at St Kilda on 18 August 1938 and was buried in the Fawkner cemetery. His wife had predeceased him in 1931.

Argus, 19 Aug 1938; Melb Hebrew Congregation, Minute-books (Synagogue Archives); documents and letter-book (held by Mr and Mrs Freedman, Ormond, Vic).   J. S. LEVI

A'COURT, ALAN WORSLEY HOLMES; *see* HOLMES A'COURT

ADAM, DAVID STOW (1859-1925), theologian, was born on 9 February 1859 at Langside near Glasgow, Scotland, son of George Adam and his wife Jane, née Constable, schoolteachers. His parents were founders of Langside Academy, where David was educated. He matriculated at the University of Glasgow in 1874 as an arts student (M.A., 1881; B.D., 1884; D.D., 1912), and completed his course with distinction in philosophy, mathematics and Greek. In 1881-85 he studied theology at the Free Church College, Glasgow, topping his exit class. In summer 1884 he read theology at Erlangen University.

The main framework of Adam's thought came from his philosophical education within the Hegelian-inspired tradition of the University of Glasgow. He taught logic and metaphysics at the university in 1881-84 and Hebrew at the Free Church College in 1885-86 when he was also assistant minister at St John's Free Church, Glasgow. Edward Caird described him as 'one of the most distinguished students of his time'.

Late in 1886 Adam was ordained Free Church minister at Banchory-Ternan, Kincardine, in 1890 he went to Kelso, Roxburgh, and in 1895 he became minister of St Andrew's Free Church, Greenock. As devout parish minister of these most fervent and orthodox Free Kirk congregations, he still managed to combine his Hegelian world-view with a staunchly Scottish Evangelical theology. In 1890 he had married Grace, sister of (Professor) W. P. Paterson; they had five sons and a daughter.

In 1907 Adam was appointed to the chair of systematic theology and church history at Ormond College, Melbourne; his references from Principal T. M. Lindsay of Glasgow, Edward Caird and Paterson had crushed those of local candidates. He arrived with his family on 5 February 1908 and was inducted on 11 March. His predecessor, Murdoch Macdonald [q.v.], had been appointed in reaction against the Glaswegian liberalism of Charles Strong [q.v.6]. Adam's portrayal of Hegel as saviour of the faith was hence courageous if theologically vulnerable. His uncompromising public rejection of the theology of Thomas Chalmers, and his assertion that Christian doctrine must adapt itself to modern philosophical truths and to local conditions, at whatever cost to orthodoxy, raised Presbyterian eyebrows.

Adam was a pioneer of Australian ecumenism: he was president of the embryonic Council of Churches in 1910 and the main author of the earliest 'basis of union' for Methodists, Presbyterians and Congregationalists. His breadth contributed much to the success of the infant Melbourne College of Divinity of which he was first registrar, but annoyed the narrowly denominational Professor J. L. Rentoul [q.v.]. However, it did not prevent Adam writing on the superiority of Presbyterianism's conciliar form of church government. From 1916 he was a chaplain with the Australian Imperial Force.

Adam was a keen golfer and interested in fishing and boats. Cycling was a hobby 'from the days when he possessed a penny-farthing machine'. Late in 1924 he began a tour of Chinese, Japanese and Korean mission stations. He intended to visit his missionary daughter and to see Asian Christianity at first hand and so fit it into his picture of God's self-revelation in world history. While in Canton, China, he contracted typhoid fever and pneumonia, and died on 31 January 1925. His amiable nature, mental vigour, adaptability and unselfish commitment were hard to replace. Adam was survived by his wife, four sons (one of whom, (Sir) Alistair, became a judge of the Supreme Court) and a daughter.

Adam's publications included *Cardinal elements of the Christian faith* (London, 1911), *Presbyterianism* (Melbourne [1913]), *Christianity and war* (Melbourne, 1915) and *A handbook of Christian ethics* (Edinburgh, 1925).

Presbyterian Church of Vic, *Procs of the Commission of Assembly*, Nov 1927, and *Procs of the General Assembly*, May 1925; *Presbyterian Messenger* (Vic), Jan-Mar 1908; *Argus*, 3, 9, 13 Feb, 21 Mar 1925; D. Chambers, A history of Ormond College, 1881-1945 (M.A. thesis, Univ Melb, 1966); Book of news-cuttings, Church Union collection, D. S. Adam (ML); information from Sir Alistair Adam, Balwyn, Vic.   DON CHAMBERS

ADAM, GEORGE ROTHWELL WILSON (1853-1924), physician, was born on 22

January 1853 at Leeds, Yorkshire, England, son of George Wilson Adam (d. 1901), Presbyterian minister, and his wife Elizabeth, née Rothwell. The family migrated to New South Wales when he was a child, and in 1861 moved to Victoria where his father served first at Brighton, then at country centres including Koroit, Horsham and finally Urana, New South Wales. In 1867 Rothwell Adam, as he was known in later professional life, entered Scotch College, Melbourne. He matriculated at the University of Melbourne in 1870 but tried farming before determining on a career in medicine. At paternal insistence he went to his father's university, Edinburgh (M.B., Ch.M., 1878). As resident physician in the Edinburgh Royal Maternity Hospital, he was inspired by J. H. Croom (later professor of midwifery, University of Edinburgh); in a similar post at the Glasgow Royal Infirmary he again devoted most of his time to diseases of women.

Returning to Melbourne, Rothwell Adam was registered for practice in Victoria on 7 November 1879 and set up in East Melbourne. Appointed to the honorary staff of the Alfred Hospital in 1881, he resigned in 1888 because of failure to establish there a gynaecological unit. That year he was elected an honorary obstetrician to the (Royal) Women's Hospital, Melbourne, and from 1895 until his retirement in 1913 was gynaecologist there. In 1900 he succeeded W. Balls-Headley [q.v.3] as lecturer in obstetrics and diseases of women at the University of Melbourne. Always interested in teaching, he was a fine lecturer and long endeavoured to improve both the students' and midwives' courses of training. His comprehensive lecture-notes showed careful preparation and logical presentation. In 1884 he received the M.B., Melbourne (ad eund.) and in 1902 was awarded the M.D.

In 1900 a clinical school was established at the Women's Hospital. In the difficult years that followed, the survival of the school and of much else at the hospital depended many times on Rothwell Adam's ethical behaviour, his courtesy, fairness, patience and understanding, and on the great respect he commanded. On his resignation as lecturer in 1913, a warm tribute was paid to his 'personal work and initiative' in building up the system of clinical teaching at the hospital.

His personal and professional distinction is well revealed in three of his papers: the annual lecture arranged by the Melbourne Medical Students' Society (1900), 'Ideals in the pursuit of medicine'; his presidential address to the gynaecology and obstetrics section at the Australasian Medical Congress (1911); and his Listerian Oration pre-

sented to the South Australian branch of the British Medical Association (1922). The last, an account of his part in introducing antisepsis and asepsis into obstetrics in Australia, was a masterly contribution on obstetric teaching. Rothwell Adam was also president of the Medical Society of Victoria and first president of the Melbourne Obstetrical and Gynaecological Society. In nonprofessional life he was a keen golfer and motorist (he had a 1913 Cadillac), took an interest in old Scotch collegian affairs and was a member of the Melbourne Club.

Rothwell Adam died on 26 December 1924 at East Melbourne from rupture of an aneurysm of the abdominal aorta and was buried in Boroondara cemetery. He was survived by his wife Eveline Grace, née Jones (d. 1939), whom he had married on 27 November 1883 at Trinity Church, Melbourne, and by a son and one of their two daughters. He left an estate valued for probate at £21 420.

F. M. C. Forster, *Progress in obstetrics and gynaecology in Australia* (Syd, 1967); *MJA*, 7 Feb 1925; F. M. C. Forster, 'One hundred years of obstetrical and gynaecological teaching in Victoria', *Aust & NZ J of Obstetrics & Gynaecology*, 6 (1966); *Age* and *Argus*, 27 Dec 1924; A. M. Mitchell, The hospital south of the Yarra (Ph.D. thesis, Univ Melb, 1972); Faculty of Medicine minutes, 1913 (Univ Melb Archives).   FRANK M. C. FORSTER

ADAMS, ARTHUR HENRY (1872-1936), journalist and author, was born on 6 June 1872 at Lawrence, New Zealand, son of Charles William Adams (1840-1918), surveyor, crown lands commissioner and astronomer, and his wife Eleanor Sarah, née Gillon. He was educated at Wellington College, and in Dunedin at Otago Boys' High School and the University of Otago (B.A., N.Z., 1894). Against his father's wishes, he abandoned law to become a journalist on the Wellington *Evening Post*, edited by his uncle E. T. Gillon. In 1898 he moved to Sydney, showed his Maori opera, *Tapu*, to J. C. Williamson [q.v.6], and was engaged as literary secretary at £200 a year. A condition was that any dramatic writing he completed should become the property of Williamson, who successfully staged an adaptation of *Tapu*, with music by Alfred Hill [q.v.], throughout Australia in 1904.

In 1900 Adams left to cover the Boxer rebellion in China for the *Sydney Morning Herald* and several New Zealand newspapers. He returned in February 1901 suffering from enteric fever; recovering, he completed a lecture tour of New Zealand and then spent three years as a freelance journalist in England, where he published his first novel, *Tussock land* (London, 1904). By August 1905 he had returned to Wellington and the *Evening Post*; briefly associate editor of the *New Zealand Times*, he joined the Sydney *Bulletin* in October 1906 and replaced A. G. Stephens [q.v.] as editor of its 'Red Page'. In 1909 he succeeded (Sir) Frank Fox [q.v.] as editor of the *Lone Hand*, became editor of the Sydney *Sun* in 1911 and returned several years later to the *Bulletin*.

A widely experienced journalist, Adams was most significant as a literary critic and creative writer. Although inferior to Stephens as a critic, he vigorously championed Australian dramatists, whose works he believed were callously rejected by local theatrical entrepreneurs. His own dramatic efforts began with experiments with Maori music and English romantic history but his forte was urban social comedy, in which he attempted 'to deal dramatically with Australian conditions viewed from an Australian standpoint by the creation of characters essentially Australian. They do not deal with the Bush ... the Australian town-dweller is as typically and as distinctively national as the extinct bushranger'. His most successful play, *Mrs. Pretty and the premier*, was produced by Melbourne Repertory Theatre in 1914 and in London in 1916; with *The wasters*, produced in Adelaide in 1910 and revived in Sydney in 1973, it was included in his *Three plays for the Australian stage* (Sydney, 1914), which show the influence of Ibsen, Shaw, Wilde and Pinero.

Adams's verse ranged from the lyrical elegance and sentimentality of *Maoriland: and other verses* (Sydney, 1899) to the epigrammatic force of *London streets* (London, 1906), a poetic 'guide book' in which his gift for the striking image is displayed. Widely known as a poet before 1914, he announced in the preface to his *Collected verses ...* (Melbourne, 1913) that he was leaving 'the pleasant, twisting by-paths of poetry for the dustier, though more ... direct, highway of prose'. His best novel is *The Australians* (London, 1920), a fascinating glimpse of pre-war Sydney in which he presents, in lucid, simple prose, contemporary views on Englishmen, politicians, art, war and the Australian character. His other novels, sometimes published under the pseudonyms 'James James' and 'Henry James James', include *Galahad Jones* (London, 1910), its protagonist a middle-aged bank clerk with the spirit of knight-errant, and some gay, frivolous and episodic romances. His last, *A man's life* (London, 1929), like his first, is strongly autobiographical and explores themes prevalent in his writing: the tension between romantic idealism and sexual drive; the subjugation of women in marriage and society; the deadening of creativity and idealism by everyday pressures.

'Tall, thin, good-looking in a dark, sallow way', Adams was well known in literary and artistic circles in Sydney. A devoted family man, he had married Lilian Grace Paton at Neutral Bay on 30 September 1908; they settled in one of the first houses on Cremorne Point. Survived by his wife, a son and two daughters, he died of septicaemia and pneumonia in the Royal North Shore Hospital on 4 March 1936, and was cremated with Anglican rites. His estate was sworn for probate at £435.

G. H. Scholefield (ed), *A dictionary of New Zealand biography* (Well, 1940); R. Lindsay, *Model wife* (Syd, 1967); L. Rees, *The making of Australian drama* (Syd, 1973); *Meanjin*, 4 (1945); *Bulletin*, 22 Oct 1908, 1 Oct 1914, 11 Mar 1936, 15 Mar 1950; *Sun* (Syd), 4 Mar 1936; *SMH*, 5, 7 Mar 1936; 9, 27 Aug 1973; *Age*, 23 Feb 1952; Adams scrap-book (ML).

B. G. ANDREWS
ANN-MARI JORDENS

ADAMS, HAMILTON JOHN GOOLD; *see* GOOLD-ADAMS

ADAMSON, JOHN (1857-1922), clergyman and politician, was born on 18 February 1857 at Tudhoe, Durham, England, son of Robert Adamson, shoemaker, and his wife Dorothy, née English. After leaving school at 10 he was apprenticed to his drunken father. Becoming a blacksmith and a total abstainer, he was prominent from 1877 in a local branch of the Amalgamated Society of Railway Employees. A converted Christian before he was 20, Adamson studied for four years at night-school to become a Primitive Methodist lay preacher, then in 1883 married Caroline Jones and migrated to Queensland. They reached Cooktown as bounty passengers in the *Duke of Buckingham* on 21 January 1884. He became Primitive Methodist minister at Stanwell near Rockhampton and served later at Mount Morgan, Georgetown, Maryborough, Ipswich and Boonah.

Adamson was received as a minister of the Presbyterian Church in 1906 but was never posted, probably because he was elected on 18 May 1907 to the Legislative Assembly as Labor member for Maryborough. 'Utterly disgusted with [the] inner workings' of political life, he did not seek re-election in 1909 and subsequently took temporary charges for the Presbyterian Church. In February 1911 he was persuaded to stand again and won Rockhampton at a by-election by sixteen votes.

When Labor won the government

benches in May 1915, Adamson was elected to the cabinet and was appointed secretary for railways. Soon afterwards he became vice-president of the Universal Service League, a vigorous conscriptionist organization which denounced Labor's policy of voluntary military service. Though pressed, he refused to withdraw from the league and was forced to resign from the ministry and the Labor Party on 2 October 1916. The conservative *Brisbane Courier* responded by sponsoring the Adamson Loyalty Testimonial Fund and £309 10s.1d. was subscribed and presented to him in cash and gifts. With understandable optimism he resigned his Rockhampton seat in April 1917, hoping to contest the Senate election for the Nationalists. He was bitterly disappointed when he was omitted from the Nationalist ticket that included H. S. Foll, his former private secretary, and indecisively left his name on the ballot-paper, then belatedly announced his withdrawal. At the State election in March 1918 Adamson unsuccessfully stood as an Independent Democrat against J. A. Fihelly [q.v.], a cabinet minister, Irish Catholic and vehement anti-conscriptionist.

On 13 December 1919, as first-named Nationalist candidate for the Senate, Adamson was elected. In June he had been appointed C.B.E. Neither of these distinctions greatly improved his health: his years in the Senate were punctuated with absences through illness. On 2 May 1922 he was killed by a suburban train at Hendra, Brisbane. Daily newspapers suggested suicide; his chronic ill health and the circumstances surrounding his fall leave some doubt. Survived by his wife, four daughters and two sons, he was given a state funeral and was buried in Toowong cemetery. His estate was valued for probate at £915.

Adamson's death reflected the tragedy of his parliamentary decline from visionary to broken senator. His speeches, homiletic in delivery, were models of careful preparation with arguments supported by contemporary giants such as Sidney and Beatrice Webb and Philip Snowden; they were monuments to his self-education. Genuinely committed to advocating the emancipation of women, Adamson was never confined within the Labor platform. He was parliamentary spokesman for the Central Queensland New State movement, and also bitterly opposed the introduction of Bible teaching in state schools. Yet political life gradually crushed him. Saddened and puzzled by the loss of William Kidston, Peter Airey [qq.v.] and others from the Labor Party, he was further demoralized when, for opposing measures aimed at liberalizing the sale and consumption of alcohol, he was taunted, ridiculed and labelled a wowser – a term he abhorred. He believed that socialism was 'the golden rule applied to every phase of life', but attempts to apply this code led to his political emasculation. His admiration for men such as E. G. Theodore and his friendship with T. J. Ryan [qq.v.] were undermined by his leaving the Labor Party, and his isolation was completed by the temporary rebuff of the Nationalists in 1917. He fell into depths of mental depression and never completely recovered.

E. G. Theodore, *The Labour government of Queensland* (Brisb, 1915); D. J. Murphy, *T. J. Ryan* (Brisb, 1975); D. J. Murphy (ed), *Labor in politics* (Brisb, 1975); *Maryborough Chronicle*, 2 Sept 1909, 3 May 1922; *Brisbane Courier*, 24 Aug, 6 Oct 1916, 3 Feb, 22 Mar, 9 Apr 1917; *Daily Standard*, 2 May 1922.   MARTIN SULLIVAN

ADAMSON, LAWRENCE ARTHUR (1860-1932), headmaster, was born on 20 April 1860 at Douglas, Isle of Man, second son of Lawrence William Adamson, LL.D., grand seneschal of the island and later deputy lieutenant of the County of Northumberland, and his first wife Annie Jane, née Flint. At 10 Adamson was sent to a London preparatory school and in 1874 he entered Rugby School, where he did well in classics and enjoyed all forms of sport. He matriculated in 1879 at Oriel College, Oxford (B.A., Charsley Hall, 1884), and was called to the Bar of the Inner Temple in 1885. After a bout of severe pleurisy he decided to practise law in the warmer climate of New South Wales. Finding the Sydney climate too moist, he moved early in 1886 to Melbourne where he applied to join the Bar and was in due course admitted. Meanwhile he did some private coaching, and also accepted a temporary teaching post at Melbourne Church of England Grammar School; he was awarded his B.A. (*ad eund.*) in May and M.A. in December by the University of Melbourne. In 1887 he became senior resident master at Wesley College and held the post until 1892, teaching English and history and fomenting a new interest in sport.

In 1893 Adamson became resident tutor at Trinity College, University of Melbourne, and for four years lectured there in the evenings and taught at Wesley by day. Late in 1897 the Wesley College Committee informed all members of staff that as a result of its decision to appoint Thomas Palmer [q.v.] as headmaster they were to be dismissed. Adamson, thoroughly disillusioned, moved to University High School, where for four years he was joint headmaster and proprietor with his close friend Otto Krome [q.v.].

In January 1902 the Wesley College Committee set about appointing a new headmaster. In early discussion the name of L. A. Adamson was not mentioned, but when he intimated that he would be willing to accept full financial responsibility for the satisfactory growth of the college, it was decided to appoint him. Adamson took up his position at Wesley in February, and over the next thirty years came to be regarded by many as Australia's most famous headmaster.

Inheritances had left Adamson a wealthy man; while headmaster he made many su' stantial donations to the college. He was often able to return 'home' to England and to indulge in such exciting innovations as motor cars and aeroplanes. In November 1909 he was the first to import an aeroplane into Australia, a Wilbur Wright biplane, although he did not fly it himself. His other interests included dogs, antique furniture, china, bronze, silver, statuary, and green-herb cheese. A devout Anglican, he was a warden at Christ Church, St Kilda, and a deacon of St Paul's Cathedral. He never married.

Adamson always placed great emphasis in the regular school assemblies on good manners, community service, music, sporting achievement, and especially on the maintenance and development of a corporate school spirit. These themes were echoed in the college *Song Book*, which was considerably enlarged during his headmastership; he himself composed many of its words and tunes, including the well-known melody for Newbolt's 'Best School of All'. 'Dicky' Adamson had an unusual gift for talking effectively to individual boys. Two future prime ministers, (Sir) Robert Menzies and Harold Holt, attended the college in his time.

As much as, or more than, his contemporaries, Adamson extolled the effects on character of training and preparation for military service; he was proud of his own family's distinguished military record. He encouraged the college cadet corps, paid frequent tribute to old Wesley collegians who enlisted for active service, insisted on writing the chapter on 'Wesley at War' for the jubilee history of the college (1921), and treasured several volumes of war letters sent to him and other staff members by old boys serving in World War I.

Adamson heavily accentuated the importance of excellence in sport. Sir James Darling in 1969 attributed to Adamson's influence the over-emphasis on competitive sport which he had found in Victorian public schools in 1930. Teams were paraded at school assemblies, and sporting heroes and triumphs were commemorated in school songs; at the same time worthwhile contributions made in other areas could go unrecognized. The first half of Adamson's headmastership was marked by many outstanding team successes, especially in rowing, football and athletics, but at the same time bitter controversies between Wesley and other public schools were highlighted by the press, and Wesley teams and supporters were sometimes accused of poor sportsmanship. Adamson usually defended his boys, emphasizing the dictum that any school must teach its students 'to win decently and lose decently'. He firmly believed that consistently good sporting results helped to increase enrolments: certainly the numbers did increase from 204 in 1902 to 594 in 1920 and fluctuated in the next decade when successes were less frequent.

The strong influence of Adamson's educational ideas and policies on secondary education in Victoria, and the part he played in raising its status, may have been his most lasting achievement. In 1891 he was foundation secretary of the Victorian Institute of Schoolmasters and helped to draft the teachers' registration bill which that body tried to persuade parliament to pass in 1892. In 1898, while at University High School, he initiated and organized a series of teacher-training classes, at that time the only such courses in Victoria. For many years he served on the faculty of arts, council, and schools board of the university. In 1904 Adamson and Krome established the (Incorporated) Association of Secondary Teachers of Victoria and through it Adamson exerted some influence on parliament, which passed the Registration of Teachers and Schools Act in 1905; Frank Tate [q.v.] believed that no one did more to bring about that legislation. By the Act a registration board was established, and Adamson was selected to represent the independent schools. He was keen to initiate a separate system of teacher-training for prospective independent-schoolteachers, and in 1908 the board permitted Wesley College to establish a teacher-training institution which was formally equal in status with the government Training College. From 1911 he was an influential and active member of the recently established Council of Public Education. He was well ahead of his time in his belief that a 'leaving certificate' issued to a student by an approved school should be a sufficient qualification for university entrance. As a member of the university's Board of Public Examinations in 1905-11 and as a leading member of the powerful Schools Board from 1912, he influenced others towards a more liberal view of the role of external examinations in secondary education. In 1903-32 he was secretary and chairman of the Headmasters of the Associated Public Schools.

As president of the Metropolitan Football Association for thirty-seven years, Adamson loudly proclaimed the virtues of amateur sport. For many years he was a delegate to the Victorian Cricket Association, at various times served as its honorary treasurer and president, and in 1906 he became first president of the Australian Board of Control for international cricket; he was president in 1901-05 of the Victorian Amateur Athletic Association. He also served as chairman of the Victorian branch of the Royal Life Saving Society and was president of the Lost Dogs' Home. In 1926 he was appointed C.M.G.

After several years of declining health from diabetes and liver disease, Adamson died of a gastric haemorrhage at Wesley on 14 December 1932, two days before his retirement was to have been announced, and was cremated. His estate, valued for probate at £7073, included bequests to the college and mementos to the staff; H. J. Stewart, his stalwart supporter for thirty years and his personal choice as successor, was executor. A portrait by W. B. McInnes [q.v.] hangs in Adamson Hall at Wesley College.

E. Nye (ed), *The history of Wesley College 1865-1919* (Melb, 1921); F. Meyer, *Adamson of Wesley* (Melb, 1932); *The history of Wesley College 1920-1940*, N. H. MacNeil ed (Melb, 1941); G. Blainey et al, *Wesley College. The first hundred years* (Melb, 1967); J. R. Darling, 'Educational recollections of the thirties', *Melbourne studies in education, 1968-1969*, R. J. W. Selleck ed (Melb, 1969); *A'sian Schoolmaster*, July 1900; *Sketch*, 30 June 1911; *Argus*, 14 Dec 1904; *Age*, 18 Dec 1904, 12 Nov 1912, 31 Oct, 14 Dec 1932; *Punch* (Melb), 8 July 1909, 29 Mar 1917; *Herald* (Melb), 7 July 1910, 26 Apr, 4, 17 May 1911; *Table Talk*, 16 Dec 1926; B. K. Rule, The origins of state secondary education in Victoria (M.A. thesis, Univ Melb, 1961); Council minutes (Inc. Assn of Secondary Teachers of Vic, Melb); Council, Senate, Arts faculty, *and* Schools Board minutes (Univ Melb Archives); Committee *and* Council minutes 1887-1933 *and* Adamson scrap-books 1890-1920 (Wesley College Archives); Education Dept, Special case 1174 (PRO, Vic).

M. A. CLEMENTS

ADCOCK, WILLIAM EDDRUP (1846-1931), journalist and businessman, was born on 31 December 1846 in London, son of George Charles Adcock, cigar manufacturer, and his wife Mary, née Goodwin. George Adcock migrated to Melbourne in 1848 with his wife and infant son and became a bookseller in Bridge Road, Richmond.

William Adcock as a young man had some theatrical experience and dabbled in real estate. He was store-keeping at Gaffney's Creek when on 30 December 1865 with Congregational rites he married Emma Sharples. In 1871 Clarson, Massina [q.v.5] & Co. appointed him editor of the *Richmond Free Press*, but the venture was short-lived. With his wife and three children Adcock sailed in 1872 to Palmerston (Darwin), where next year he opened a general store. He speculated in mining, wrote an article on the Northern Territory for the *Australian Journal* (1873), survived the shipwreck of the vessel in which he was returning to Melbourne for supplies, and was unsuccessful in the first election of councillors for the district of Palmerston in 1874. In 1878 his wife's health failed; Adcock sold out next year for £12 000 and rejoined her in Melbourne.

His successors failed, however, and Adcock took the business over again, in partnership with his brother Herbert Henry, and V. V. Brown. New premises were built at Palmerston and another branch was opened at Derby to serve the goldfields in the Kimberley district of Western Australia. Adcock Bros obtained steamship agencies and built the Victoria Hotel in Palmerston. Adcock himself returned to Melbourne and handled the firm's finances.

In 1885 he went again to the Northern Territory because of financial difficulties resulting from expansion undertaken by his partners without his knowledge. The Town and Country Bank (South Australia) had failed, and its liquidators claimed repayment of overdrafts and loans of £23 000. Adcock formed a new limited liability company, but his offer of settlement was refused, and in February 1888 he and his brother and Brown were declared insolvent. Adcock appealed, thereby initiating proceedings which became unique in Australia's legal history. The adjudication was reversed by the Supreme Court of South Australia, but was reinstated twice before the Full Court confirmed the insolvency in December.

Adcock was advised by his Adelaide solicitors to remain out of the colony to avoid arrest, but guided by his Melbourne lawyer he went to Adelaide and was promptly arrested on 20 December. Except for short periods on bail, he spent the next four years in gaol or in court where, with his counsel (Sir) J. H. Symon [q.v.], he waged a battle with the Insolvency Court, which could hold an insolvent until bail was paid or the case adjudicated. His claim that he could not legally demand the company's books from the Melbourne trustee prevented investigation into the assets of the former Adcock Bros' company, but his defiance of the court delayed his release. He strenuously resisted attempts to prefer the claims of the bank to those of individual creditors, and he bombarded the court, the governor and the Executive Council with affidavits, memorials and appeals for *habeas corpus*. The case became the subject of leading articles in the Melbourne and Adelaide press; Adcock himself published a booklet, *Four years imprisoned and refused a trial* (Melbourne, 1892). In November 1893 he was finally given his discharge, but with his assets liable to seizure if he ever ventured again within the South Australian jurisdiction. Mr Justice Boucaut [q.v.3] was highly critical of his behaviour in court and of his refusal to make full disclosure. The *Register* called him either a 'terribly misunderstood man or a remarkably acute and daring one'.

After his release Adcock engaged in journalism and other business activities in Victoria. In 1900 he went to Coolgardie, Western Australia, to manage mining interests; he also retained a share in the Derby business. Later he helped to establish the mica industry in Victoria.

In 1894-95 Adcock's articles on the gold rush era of Victoria were published anonymously in the *Australian Journal*; a revised version appeared under his name in Melbourne in 1912 as *The gold rushes of the fifties*. About 1910 he succeeded W. E. G. Symons as editor of the *Australian Journal*; he later assisted S. L. Massina until 1926 when he retired.

Adcock died on 18 May 1931 at his home in Kew. He was survived by his second wife Annie Mary Bowcott, née Wheeler, whom he had married in Sydney on 25 April 1898, by five children of his first marriage and by two of his second. He was buried in Burwood cemetery, leaving an estate valued for probate at £1463.

R. G. Campbell, *The first ninety years* (Melb, 1949); E. Hill, *The Territory* (Syd, 1951); D. W. Lockwood, *The front door: Darwin, 1869-1969* (Adel, 1968); *Register* (Adel), 21 Aug 1889-4 Nov 1893; *Table Talk*, 13 Feb 1891, 29 July 1892; *Argus*, 23 May 1931.
                                        E. M. Finlay

ADDIS, WILLIAM (EDWARD) (1844-1917), clergyman, was born on 9 May 1844 in Edinburgh, son of Rev. Thomas Addis — close friend and associate of Thomas Chalmers, founder of the Free Church of Scotland — and his wife Robina Scott, née Thorburn. Educated at Merchiston Castle School, he attended classes at the University of Glasgow in 1859-61 and was awarded the Snell Exhibition in 1862. He matriculated at Balliol College, Oxford, on 12 October 1861, and graduated B.A. with first-class honours in 1866. At Oxford, Addis came under the influence of J. H. Newman and was received into the Roman Catholic Church on 6 October 1866, shortly before his close friend Gerard Manley Hopkins. He joined the Brompton Oratory in October 1868, when he took the name Edward, and was ordained deacon and priest on 20 October 1872. In September 1878 he became priest of a chapel in Lower Sydenham, South London. Elected fellow in mental and moral philosophy in the new Royal University of Ireland in April 1882, he spent six months in Dublin and then returned to Sydenham. In London in 1883, with Thomas Arnold, he published *A Catholic dictionary*.

In 1888 Addis suddenly rejected the Roman faith, married a parishioner Mary Rachel Flood on 5 November and accepted appointment as assistant minister to a former classmate at Glasgow, Rev. Charles Strong [q.v.6] of the Australian Church, Melbourne. He arrived in Victoria with his wife in the *Oroya* on 4 January 1889.

From the first Addis did not enjoy a happy association with the increasingly radical Strong. Their theological, political, economic and social views differed widely. Addis's conservatism attracted the wealthier members of the congregation and, unlike Strong, he was fond of ceremony and liturgical worship. He found his position ambiguous and his relationships to Strong, the congregation and the church's committee of management remained undefined. Misunderstandings between the two men widened the rift and produced factions in the church, particularly over the question of renewal of Addis's two-year appointment. At his request but without consulting Strong, the committee of management met to reappoint Addis. Strong did not pursue his disapproval but objected strongly to the decision being taken without his knowledge. In June 1892 Addis told Strong that he would not seek reappointment and in December announced his plans to leave Victoria in the New Year. He was farewelled by the Australian Church on 20 January 1893 and given a purse of sovereigns. Shortly after, he left with his wife and baby daughter for England where he became minister of the Unitarian High Pavement Chapel, Nottingham.

In Melbourne Addis had contributed to the monthly *Australian Herald* and published *Miracles of the Bible: six lectures delivered in the Australian Church* (1889) and *Lectures on the Trinity and Incarnation* ... (1893). His translation and arrangement of the *Documents of the Hexateuch* was published in 1892.

Addis was appointed professor of Old Testament criticism at the Unitarian training institution, Manchester College, Oxford, in 1899. Still teaching there in 1901 he joined the Church of England and officiated as a priest. In 1910 he resigned from the college and was nominated vicar of All Saints, Knightsbridge, London. Retiring in 1916 to Twickenham, he died in hospital there on 20 February 1917 after being knocked down by a motor van. He was survived by one of his two daughters and a son.

Addis was a fine scholar. The one episode in his life which possibly shows him in an unfavourable light is his brief stay in Melbourne. Yet he commanded the loyalty and affection of many adherents of the Australian Church, while failing to work happily with his chief.

H. Pearson, *Bernard Shaw. His life and personality* (Lond, 1942); C. S. Dessain (ed), *The letters and diaries of J. H. Newman* (Lond, 1961); O. Chadwick, *The Victorian Church*, pt 1 (Lond, 1966); C. R. Badger, *The Reverend Charles Strong* (Melb, 1971).   C. R. BADGER

ADEY, WILLIAM JAMES (1874-1956), educationist, was born on 27 May 1874 near Clare, South Australia, son of Charles George Adey, farmer, and his wife Ann, née Ritchie. He was educated at state primary schools at Redhill and Milbrook, then at Houghton (where he became a pupil-teacher) and Sturt Street, Adelaide. He attended the Grote Street Training College in 1894 and – under special arrangements – the Melbourne Training College in 1907; he passed several subjects part time in 1909-15 at the University of Adelaide, but never graduated. On 17 December 1910 at North Adelaide he married Mabel Edith Dyer (d. 1915) and, on 7 May 1921 at Walkerville, Constance Margaret Weston, a teacher.

Adey was to occupy every rung in the departmental ladder. From 1895 he was a primary teacher at Quorn, Clare, at the inner-city Sturt Street and then the Adelaide Continuation schools. In 1909-19 he was the founding headmaster of Adelaide High School, the Education Department's first such school. He left it to become inspector of high schools in 1919-20. He was superintendent of secondary education for the next nine years and, finally, director of education in 1929-39. He retired at full age, having seen the state schools through the Depression years.

A second choice as director of education, Adey was appointed with an explicit charge to limit himself to carrying out the design of his predecessor W. T. McCoy [q.v.] – and only that. Adey was hard pressed to achieve even that much, but distinguished himself by a notable and sustained defence against unwarranted contractions of popular education. No innovator and no intellectual,

Adey was none the less universally respected for his administrative and teaching ability, and liked for his evident humanity – he was affectionately nicknamed 'Plugger'. He continued to enjoy the esteem of his contemporaries, including even his subordinates, while pursuing policies with whose specifics none of them could have totally agreed.

Adey will be remembered for his part in the 1931 committee of inquiry, appointed to consider cutting the cost of public education. He concurred in the first progress report, which largely enshrined his own policy of saving money by accelerating the consolidation of small primary schools – belt-tightening, without structural change to the system. He dissented from the second progress report, in which his fellow members proposed fees, contractions in post-compulsory schooling, and greater control over entry to high schools, Adey's pride and joy. He opposed the amalgamation of country high schools and insisted that fees be low, with exemptions for those of limited means. When fees were later introduced he minimized the operation of their worst inequalities.

Adey was not an original educational thinker, and his educational writings are not memorable. Following overseas writers, he was somewhat in advance of his local community in seeing the future of secondary education in the single high school, multilateral if highly stratified – a vision not realized for some thirty years. He was very much of his time in stressing education for service, and very much of a type in hoping that education might temper the monotony of work in industry by training the worker to exploit his leisure.

Before and after retirement, he was active in community service: he was a council-member of the University of Adelaide in 1929-50; for many years he presided over the Repatriated Soldiers' Children's Education Board; in 1939 he chaired a government committee inquiring into delinquent and other children in the care of the state, which reported critically and humanely; in 1940-42 he was a member of the Libraries Board of South Australia. He enjoyed cricket, tennis and golf in his spare time. He was appointed C.M.G. in 1935.

Survived by his second wife, and their daughter and two sons, Adey died at his home at Burnside on 23 May 1956, and was buried in the North Road cemetery, Nailsworth.

B. Condon (ed), *Newspaper clippings books . . . Department of Education, 1926-39* (Adel, 1973-76); C. M. Thiele and R. Gibbs, *Grains of mustard seed* (Adel, 1975); *PP* (SA), 1931, 2 (69),

1937, 2 (54), 1939, 2 (44); *Education Gazette* (SA), 15 June 1956; *Observer* (Adel), 17 July 1920; *Advertiser* (Adel), 16, 21 Apr, 28 May, 19 July 1937, 28 May 1956; L. Trethewey, A study of the educational administration of W. J. Adey (Advanced Diploma in Teaching dissertation, Torrens CAE, SA).

BRIAN CONDON

AGAR, WILFRED EADE (1882-1951), zoologist, was born on 27 April 1882 at Wimbledon, England, seventh of nine children of Edward Larpent Agar and his wife Agnes, née Henty. His father was a solicitor and businessman and also the principal founder of the game of hockey in its modern form. He went from a private school to Sedbergh School, Yorkshire, and in 1900 entered King's College, Cambridge, to read zoology. He graduated B.A. in 1903 with a first class in both parts of the Science Tripos (M.A., 1907). At Cambridge he was inspired by William Bateson with an ambition to research in genetics. He tried for a post in the British Museum (Natural History) but then decided that he would prefer an academic position.

In 1904 Agar was appointed demonstrator in zoology at the University of Glasgow, where he found his vocation in teaching and research. His work on the embryology of the lungfish *Lepidosiren* and *Protopterus* led to a fellowship at King's College, Cambridge; this did not entail his leaving Glasgow, for he was obliged only to continue academic and research work. The work on *Lepidosiren* had another important consequence for him. The cells of this fish, being unusually large, offer favourable material for the study of chromosomes and in 1907, aided by grants from the Royal Society and the Balfour Fund at Cambridge, Agar made an expedition to the almost inaccessible Gran Chaco, Paraguay, to collect material for cytological study. His meticulous study of spermatogenesis in *Lepidosiren* provided critical confirmation that the chromosome mechanism could provide a physical basis for Mendel's laws. Another significant contribution to Mendelian theory came from his work on inheritance in parthenogenetic crustacea. He found that apart from rare mutations, the genetic constitution of these crustacea remained unchanged, generation after generation. This work provided the first direct evidence from animals that the segregation of genes is due to the segregation of homologous chromosomes at meiosis.

On the outbreak of World War I Agar, who was a member of the Territorial Reserve of Officers, was posted captain to the 5th (City of Glasgow) Battalion of the Highland Light Infantry which, as part of the 52nd Division, was sent to Gallipoli in June 1915. Agar was adjutant to the divisional base at Alexandria but after a year suffered a severe attack of enteric fever and had to return to England. He remained on home service until he resumed university work early in 1918. During this period he wrote *Cytology* (London, 1920).

In 1908 Agar had married Elizabeth MacDonald in Glasgow; consideration for the future of their young family led him, in 1919, to accept the chair of zoology at the University of Melbourne. In doing so, he feared that he was giving up most of his ambitions; his apprehensions seemed justified when he found that he had to give all the lectures and conduct a large proportion of the laboratory classes without help. However, the appointment of more staff enabled him to resume research; he refused offers of three chairs in British universities and after his retirement in 1948 wrote, 'I believe I have been able to do as much, and as good, work in the University of Melbourne as I should have done in a home university'. His appointment was of special importance to Melbourne. Under his predecessor, Sir Baldwin Spencer [q.v.], teaching had followed almost exclusively the lines of traditional morphology. Agar introduced the newer disciplines of cytology and genetics and these remained his chief teaching interest. His courses were probably the first of their kind in Australian universities. He initiated studies on marsupial chromosomes and his paper on inheritance in cattle seems to have been the earliest in Australia to apply genetical techniques to animal-breeding. In 1921 he was elected to the Royal Society.

From student days, Agar had been interested in the problem of Lamarckian inheritance. Like most biologists he rejected the theory that acquired characters are inherited, but it continued to receive influential support. The most important of Agar's contributions to this controversy was his repetition of an experiment which the psychologist William McDougall claimed had demonstrated the inheritance of the effects of training in rats. It was the most impressive evidence published in support of the Lamarckian theory and none of the many criticisms levelled at it seriously weakened McDougall's claim. However, the results of Agar's properly controlled experiment, continued over twenty years, completely refuted the Lamarckian interpretation of McDougall's experiment.

In his early years in Melbourne, Agar became interested in animal psychology and carried on experiments on the capacity to learn by experience of a range of animals from amoeba to crayfish and snails. These studies over a long period were a source of great pleasure to him. They provided few publications but formed instead a background for his increasing preoccupation with broad biological concepts and the philosophy of science which found expression in *A contribution to the theory of the living organism* (Melbourne, 1943; second edition, 1951). Agar regarded this book as by far his most important contribution to biological theory.

Though retiring by nature, Agar took his full share of administrative work in the university. He was a council-member for many years, twice dean of the faculty of science, and chairman of the professorial board in 1931-34, guiding the deliberations that preceded the appointment of a full-time vice-chancellor. He was a councillor of the Royal Society of Victoria for twenty years and president in 1927-28. His services to science and to the university were recognized by an O.B.E. in 1939 and a C.B.E. in 1948.

Agar's scientific achievements were widely recognized. His scholarship and balanced judgment earned him the respect and trust of his colleagues and students. He wore his distinctions lightly and his kindliness, consideration and unfailing courtesy won wide affection. Beyond his scientific interests, he read widely in philosophy, enjoyed poetry and drama and occasionally did some water-colour sketching.

Agar and his family lived on the university campus until his retirement in 1948 when they moved to Kew. On returning from sabbatical leave in 1926 they had bought a bushland property near Healesville and, a skilful carpenter from boyhood, he built substantial additions to their holiday cottage there. In retirement he continued to research and write but was increasingly troubled by poor health. He had had a coronary thrombosis in 1947 and on 14 July 1951 he died at Kew; survived by his wife, two sons and three daughters, he was cremated.

A portrait by Max Meldrum [q.v.] and a bronze plaque by Andor Meszaros are at the University of Melbourne.

J. G. Kerr, 'Obituary: Prof. W. E. Agar', *Nature*, 168 (1951); 'Annual report to council', Roy Soc Vic, *Procs*, 64 (1952); 'Epitaphs: W. E. Agar . . .', *Melb Graduate*, 3 (1952), no 2; O. W. Tiegs, 'Wilfred Eade Agar', *Obituary Notices of Fellows of the Royal Society*, 8 (1952), no 21; autobiog sketch (held by Dr W. T. Agar, Penshurst, Vic).

F. H. DRUMMOND

AGNEW, ROY (ROBERT) EWING (1891-1944), composer and pianist, was born on 23 August 1891 in Sydney, son of Samuel Agnew, cordial manufacturer, and his wife Maria Jane, née Miller. Educated at Chatswood and Hornsby public schools, he was taught music by Emanuel de Beaupuis, an Italian pianist living in Sydney, then briefly studied composition under Alfred Hill [q.v.] at the New South Wales State Conservatorium of Music. By 1911 Agnew was teaching the piano at Marrickville and beginning to compose 'strikingly original works', abandoning 'the limitations of key and tonal relationship'; in 1913 he published *Australian forest pieces for piano*. His compositions were unknown until Benno Moiseiwitsch played *Deirdre's lament* and the *Dance of the wild men* at a matinée at the Sydney Town Hall in 1920 and helped him to find publishers.

In 1923, through the generosity of friends, Agnew went to London where he studied composition and orchestration with Gerrard Williams. In 1927 his *Fantaisie sonata* was played in London by William Murdoch [q.v.], and published by Augener Ltd of London who later brought out many of his smaller works. The Arthur P. Schmidt Co. of New York issued five of his small pieces in book form, titled *Contrasts* (*c*. 1927). In 1928 he returned to Sydney and in July played at a welcome-home concert at the conservatorium. In August his poem for orchestra and voice, *The breaking of the drought*, was conducted by Hill and encored. At Dorothy Helmrich's farewell concert in July 1929, Agnew played for the first time his *Poem sonata* and next April gave a recital of his works at Burdekin House. On 8 November 1930 at St Mary's Cathedral he married Kathleen Olive, youngest daughter of R. E. O'Connor [q.v.].

In Britain in 1931-34, Agnew performed his works at the Lyceum Club and at George Woodhouse's studio, London, in Glasgow, and for the British Broadcasting Corporation. He returned in December 1934 for an Australian Broadcasting Commission tour and in May 1935 gave two radio recitals of his works. In September he advertised a series of lessons in 'Practical Composition' and in 'General Interpretation and the art of Pedalling' in Melbourne. That year his *Sonata poeme* was published by [G. L.] Allan [q.v.3] & Co. Pty Ltd of Melbourne. In 1936 his *Symphonic poem* for orchestra and voice was performed in Perth with Dorothy Helmrich as soloist. His *Five contrasts*, written originally for the piano, was arranged for string orchestra by his friend John Antill.

From January 1938 Agnew was engaged by the A.B.C. to arrange and compère a weekly session devoted to modern and contemporary composers: it created such interest that it continued for five years. In January he had won the prize for the sesquicentennial celebrations of the Musical Association of New South Wales with his *Sonata ballade* (1939), which he later recorded for the Columbia Phonograph Co. In January 1943 the A.B.C. had records made of Agnew playing some fifty of his own compositions. He had completed in 1940 his last big work *Sonata legend* or *Capricornia*, which was performed at the conservatorium in 1944 by Alexander Sverjensky and published in 1949 as *Capricornia* (*Sonata legend*) by Augener.

Gentle and modest, Agnew was elusive: 'apart from the piano and the home and garden and the flowers he loved so much, life for him was not very real or concrete at all'. He enjoyed walking and surfing. In February 1944 he joined the staff of the conservatorium but he died of septicaemia following tonsillitis on 12 November and was cremated with Presbyterian rites. Childless, he was survived by his wife. His estate was valued for probate at £547.

Agnew had published some ninety piano works as well as many small pieces. His obituarist Neville Cardus claimed that 'his piano music was composed with much warmth of harmony of the romantic flavours current just before [World War I]. He assimilated chordal and development formulae from Scriabin in particular, but he made everything second nature to his essentially lyrical imagination . . . He also had a sure feeling for miniature poems of atmosphere, evocative of sea and dawn and mists'. Roger Covell has found much of Agnew's work repetitive and 'dense and fuzzy', but 'it helped to introduce a note of serious, poetic fancy into Australian music'.

I. Moresby, *Australia makes music* (Melb, 1948); R. Covell, *Australia's music* (Melb, 1967); F. Gordon, 'Roy Agnew: composer', *Lone Hand*, 1 Oct 1920; *Aust Musical News*, 1 Sept 1935; *Sun-News Pictorial*, 22 June 1928; *SMH*, 7, 17 July, 23 Aug 1928, 2 July 1929, 11 Apr 1930, 24 Dec 1934, 20, 25 May 1935, 13 Nov 1944; K. Hince papers (NL).

DOROTHY HELMRICH

AHERN, ELIZABETH (1877-1969), socialist propagandist, usually known as Lizzie, was born on 19 October 1877 at Ballarat, Victoria, daughter of Edmund Ahern, miner, and his wife Eliza, née Kiely, both from Ireland. Lizzie moved to Melbourne as a domestic servant and joined the Abbotsford branch of the Political Labor Council about 1904.

She began her propagandist career with the Social Questions Committee, soon renamed the Victorian Socialist Party, in 1905, advocating unemployment relief. Lizzie was an enthusiastic speaker on street corners and the Yarra Bank and in rural areas. In November 1906 she was arrested and gaoled for ten days for obstruction during the Prahran free-speech fight, after which she visited Broken Hill, New South Wales. Energetic, courageous and determined to the point of stubbornness, she continued her activity in country and suburban areas; a champion of women's rights and a strong internationalist, she became one of the party's most effective propagandists.

Lizzie was a member of the Victorian Socialist Party's executive committee in 1906-08, 1910 and 1917-18; in 1906-07 she was a vice-president. Supporting the party's permeation tactics, she was a delegate to the Political Labor Council's annual conference in 1907 and helped to form the Domestic Workers' Union. She resigned from the P.L.C. late in 1907 in accordance with Socialist Federation of Australia policy.

In October 1908 Lizzie left for Broken Hill. On 10 December, giving her occupation as 'socialist agitator', she married ARTHUR KNIGHT WALLACE (1879-1952) of the Barrier Socialist Propaganda Group in a socialist wedding; Tom Mann [q.v.] was a witness. The couple remained there, with Lizzie an active speaker for the Barrier group, until Wallace was appointed assistant secretary of the V.S.P. in February 1909. The Wallaces supported close relations between the Socialist and Labor parties. Lizzie helped to form the Women's Socialist League in 1909 and Wallace was delegate to the Socialist Federation in 1910. Late that year they moved to Adelaide, where they were active in the Socialist Party of South Australia, and several years later went back to Broken Hill.

In May 1916 they returned to Melbourne, rejoining the V.S.P. and the Labor Party. Both spoke vigorously against war and conscription in 1916 and 1917. In 1916 Lizzie became Caterers' Employees' Union delegate to the Trades Hall Council, secretary of the Women's Anti-Conscription Committee, and delegate to the Labor Women's Central Organizing Committee.

Wallace was the V.S.P.'s financial secretary in 1917-18, publisher-manager of its children's newsletter, *Dawn*, and secretary of the Socialist Co-operative Society during 1919 until his election in November as Labor member for Albert Park in the Legislative Assembly. His parliamentary career was undistinguished; defeated in 1927, he was re-elected in 1929 but, suffering from high blood-pressure, he resigned in 1932 shortly after being appointed to the Geelong Harbor Trust. He was a member of the South Melbourne council in 1929-37 and mayor in 1934. For many years he and his wife ran a small library in Albert Park.

Lizzie remained active with the Labor

Women's Central Organizing Committee until 1934, and was a delegate to the first interstate conference of Labor women in 1929 and secretary to its executive in 1930. She maintained membership of the party's Albert Park branch until her death on 7 April 1969. Buried in Brighton cemetery, she was survived by a daughter; a son had predeceased both parents.

G. Dale, *The industrial history of Broken Hill* (Melb, 1918); *Socialist* (Melb), 3, 10 Nov 1906, 11, 18 Dec 1908, 25 Mar, 14 Oct 1910, 7 Apr, 11 Aug, 22 Sept 1916, 27 Apr 1917; Victorian Socialist Party minutes, 1906-10, 1916-19 (Merrifield collection, LaTL).   GEOFF HEWITT

AHERN, THOMAS (1884-1970), merchant and draper, was born on 23 December 1884 at Ballymacoda, County Cork, Ireland, son of Patrick Ahern and his wife Mary, née McGrath. The family farm could not support six sons: after leaving the village school, Thomas was apprenticed to a Middleton draper and worked for his keep. From 1904 he was employed in Tipperary, Dublin, Kilkenny and Waterford. He applied in 1910 for an assisted passage to Australia in place of a workmate unable to go; using the telephone for the first time, he shouted so loudly that he could almost have been heard in London without it. He sailed early next year and on the advice of a Catholic priest disembarked in Fremantle. Employed by Brennans' drapery at Boulder, he then brought out his fiancée Nora McGrath (1884-1959) and married her in Perth on 19 June 1912. Ahern then moved to Perth as departmental manager for Bon Marché in 1912-18 and manager of Brennans' Perth store in 1918-22.

Advised by Archbishop Clune [q.v.], the family of P. F. Quinlan invited Ahern to manage their drapery and furniture store, Robertson and Moffat's Successors. He insisted on a controlling partnership and opened as Aherns Ltd on 15 May 1922. The firm then had fifty employees and over five hundred in 1970, and never failed to show an annual profit. Ahern gradually bought out the Quinlan shares and became a store patriarch. His kindness to staff helped to solve many family problems and launched many young people; his employees worked hard in return and seldom stood upon the letter of the Shops and Factories Acts.

The business succeeded because of its central position, careful buying and Ahern's strong personality, and expanded into a large departmental store. Some saw Catholic Church influence, though there were many Protestants on the staff, for Ahern was a fervent churchman. An adviser to three

archbishops and many clergy, he was benefactor and friend of many Catholic institutions. In 1927, on the first of several trips to Europe, he was dubbed in Rome a papal knight of St Sylvester.

Late in life Ahern accepted public offices: he was a trustee of Karrakatta cemetery (1938-42), a justice of the peace (1940-70), patron of the Claremont Football Club (1940-69), president of the Retail Traders' Association of Western Australia (1945-47) and president of the Perth Chamber of Commerce (1954-55). He raced three horses, played golf and was a regular swimmer. His birthday parties in a Perth club were famous.

Ahern maintained active control of the firm and in his last years enthusiastically supported proposals by his sons for suburban expansion. He died on 22 May 1970, survived by three sons and two daughters, and was buried at Karrakatta. His portrait by Vernon Jones hangs in the company's boardroom.

West Australian, 23 May 1970; *Record* (Perth), 28 May 1970; family information.
BARBARA AHERN

AH KET, WILLIAM (1876-1936), barrister, was born on 20 June 1876 at Wangaratta, Victoria, only son and fifth child of Ah Ket, storekeeper and grower and buyer of tobacco, and his wife Hing Ung, who were married in Melbourne in 1864. His father had arrived in Victoria in 1855 and after some years on the goldfields established one of the earliest tobacco-farms on the King River. He became the leading Chinese in the district and a respected member of the Wangaratta community.

William was educated at Wangaratta High School and at home by a Chinese tutor. He was one of the few Australian-born Chinese proficient in both Chinese and English, and in his early teens acted as a court interpreter. It was his father's wish that he should qualify for the law in his countrymen's interests. Ah Ket matriculated in 1893 and entered law at the University of Melbourne, completing a single subject before proceeding to his articled clerk's course in 1898. He won the Supreme Court Judges' Prize in 1902, completed his articles with Maddock & Jamieson and was admitted to practice in May 1903. He read with (Sir) Stewart McArthur [q.v.] and signed the Bar roll in June 1904.

In the 1900s Ah Ket was active in the Chinese community's opposition to restrictive and discriminatory legislation, both State and Federal. In 1901 he helped to create a committee to agitate against the proposed immigration restriction bill. He was a member of the Chinese Empire Reform Association of 1904 and of the Anti-Opium League of Victoria, organizations which supported modernization and social reform among Chinese at home and abroad. He was a delegate to the first interstate Chinese convention held at Melbourne in 1905. As adviser and publicist Ah Ket was prominent in opposition to the Bent [q.v.3] government's attempts between 1904 and 1907 to drive the Chinese out of occupations where they competed with Europeans, by requiring licensing of Chinese workers under the Factories and Shops Acts. He defended his people in *A paper on the Chinese and the Factories Acts* (Melbourne, 1906), and was co-founder and president of the Sino-Australian Association, which was the first Australian-Chinese club. In 1912-13 Ah Ket visited China as the delegate of the Victorian Chinese Chamber of Commerce to participate in the election of overseas Chinese to the new parliament of the Republic. He was acting consul-general for China in 1913-14 and in 1917.

Ah Ket built up a healthy practice at the Victorian Bar, specializing in civil law. He was in the front rank of pleaders and became renowned as a fine cross-examiner – quietly spoken, courteous and shrewd – and as an outstanding jury man. He acquired a considerable reputation as a negotiator of settlements. Ah Ket's colleagues remembered him with warmth and affection as an amiable and gregarious man, greatly respected for his ability and integrity. He was an excellent after-dinner speaker, a prominent Freemason and a keen punter and golfer.

On 16 November 1912 he had married Gertrude Victoria Bullock at the Kew Methodist Church. They had two sons – one became a solicitor and the other a medical practitioner – and two daughters. Ah Ket died of arteriosclerosis and renal failure at Malvern on 6 August 1936, and was cremated after an Anglican and Masonic service. His estate was valued for probate at £4342.

J. H. C. Sleeman, *White China* (Syd, 1933?); A. Dean, *A multitude of counsellors* (Melb, 1968); R. G. Menzies, *The measure of the years* (Melb, 1970); *Wangaratta Bi-weekly Dispatch*, 3, 6 June 1896; *Wangaratta Chronicle*, 3, 6 June 1896, 19 Nov 1902, 18 July 1908, 20 Nov 1912, 8 Aug 1936; *Age*, 21 Nov 1902, 7, 8 Aug 1936; *Argus*, 7 Aug 1936; C. F. Yong, The Chinese in New South Wales and Victoria, 1901-1921 (Ph.D. thesis, ANU, 1966).

JOHN LACK

AHUIA OVA (1877?-1951), Papuan court interpreter, was probably born at Hohodae, a Koita section of the village complex of Hanuabada, Port Moresby, Papua. His father lived in the Koita village of Kila Kila and after his death Ahuia lived in Hohodae with his mother's kin. His paternal ancestors came from the Hood Peninsula and his maternal forbears were Nara (Lala) who lived to the north of Galley Reach. He had little claim to the hereditary leadership in Hohodae which C. G. Seligman, the anthropologist, attributed to him.

Ahuia was employed as domestic servant and cook at Government House and by European officials. One of his employers took him on leave for six weeks to Cooktown, Queensland. He later served as a village constable for five years and by 1914 was interpreter at the Central Court, retiring from government service in 1918. He won considerable influence throughout Hanuabada and beyond and became first president of the Hanuabada Council. From 1929, when he was not re-elected as Hohodae councillor, his leadership came under attack. His powerful position to that date was partly gained through the support of Europeans, especially that of Sir Hubert Murray [q.v.], lieut-governor of Papua in 1909-40.

When the Port Moresby villages were evacuated during World War II, Ahuia worked at the Roman Catholic Mission at Yule Island. After the villagers returned in 1945, he met with great hostility in Hohodae and in 1948 returned to his father's village of Kila Kila. He died, lonely and partly blind, on 23 April 1951.

A man of great intelligence, courage and initiative, Ahuia acted at different times as interpreter and informant to the anthropologists Seligman, B. Malinowski and F. E. Williams [q.v.]. The eventual collapse of his tribal leadership was partly due to occasional abuse of power but mainly to his dependence on European support. While his impact on Papuan history was limited, his career, as expressed in his autobiography, reveals the problems faced by an intelligent and literate Papuan in times of rapid social change. He had to try to reconcile the conflict between traditional values and those of the West. He was more than once banned from membership of his local London Missionary Society church because he had married polygamously. In an article published in the *Papua Annual Report* for 1923, he condemned traditional dancing which had come under the disapproval of the church, and he burned his regalia. Later he returned to organizing traditional dances and feasts. He became a Roman Catholic, maintaining that he 'must believe both religions, L.M.S. and Catholic ... It is because I understand that they are working for one god'.

Several times married, he had no children.

C. G. Seligman, *The Melanesians of British New Guinea* (Cambridge, 1910); F. E. Williams, 'The reminiscences of Ahuia Ova', Roy Anthropological Inst, *J*, 69 (1939); C. S. Belshaw, 'The last years of Ahuia Ova', Roy Anthropological Inst, *Man*, 51 (1951), no 230.   NIGEL ORAM

AINSWORTH, ALFRED BOWER (1827-1920), civil engineer and public servant, was born probably in Brussels, only son of Thomas Hargreaves Ainsworth (1795-1841) and his wife Jane, née Bower. His grandfather was a prominent Lancashire cotton industrialist. His father moved to Holland in the 1830s and there established a weaving school and bleachworks important in the history of the modern Dutch textile industry. After schooling in France and Germany, Ainsworth attended the University of Liège, Belgium, in 1845-48, served articles in Brussels and then joined a London firm of consulting engineers.

On 6 November 1851 at Hornsey, Middlesex, he married Elizabeth, daughter of William Sugden; they migrated in the *Caroline Agnes* and arrived in South Australia on 6 May 1852. Ainsworth briefly conducted a grammar school in Adelaide before moving to Victoria where in 1854 he was in Geelong. In November he was appointed a temporary assistant surveyor at a salary of £250. By 1856 his position was confirmed and he carried out extensive survey work in the Western District; in 1860 his salary was £500. His wife accompanied him, bearing children at Lake Terang, Hexham and Warrnambool.

In 1863 the family moved to Melbourne and late in the year Ainsworth went to the new remote goldfield of Wood's Point. At a salary of £70, in January 1864 he became mining surveyor and registrar of the North Jordan subdivision of the Beechworth mining district; he took his family in on horseback two years later. Seven further children were born there. As mining declined after 1864 his area of responsibility was extended. In 1866 he was appointed acting mining surveyor for Jericho and by 1869 covered the divisions of Gaffney's Creek and Big River. He retained all but Jericho till 1879 and from 1873 was also inspector of mines. Alexandra was added to his territory when by 1879 he was forced by financial difficulties to move to that town, and in 1886 he became mining surveyor for Yea. He was surveyor for the Borough of Wood's Point for periods from 1870 to 1891, and shire engineer of Alexandra in 1881 and of Howqua at Jamieson in 1891-98. Ainsworth was an expert horseman, but many of the early reefs in the more rugged areas were accessible only on foot; when roads were built his one concession to age was to drive his one-horse buggy, even in the winter snows of Wood's Point. His endurance became a local legend. From Alexandra he continued his tireless travel to carry out surveys and gather statistics which were published in the quarterly reports of mining surveyors and in the local press. His fine map of Wood's Point (1866) was lithographed, published by the Mining Department and widely circulated.

R. B. Smyth's [q.v.6] *The gold fields and mineral districts of Victoria* (Melbourne, 1869) contained a ten-page contribution by Ainsworth on the discovery of the Wood's Point reefs. When diamond drilling began there in 1886, he fixed the sites for the first bores for the Department of Mines. Although drilling was suspended in 1890, his choices were vindicated by later successes at the Morning Star reefs. His evidence to the royal commission on gold-mining (1891) advocated the latest technical advances and was highly practical. He was well aware of health hazards to miners and recommended dissemination of mining education by lectures at mechanics' institutes in smaller gold towns. In a generation not noted for conservation, he condemned the ruthless cutting of timber for the mines and advocated establishment of reserves and plantations.

Ainsworth was fiercely loyal to the mountain districts and the men with whom he worked. His writings, maps and drawings confirm that he was highly literate; his work has a ring of sincerity and conscientiousness, and in practical mining matters his advice was dependably accurate. Unlike many of his professional contemporaries, he was not listed as shareholder in any mining company.

Ainsworth's excellent eyesight enabled him to use survey instruments into old age. He held most of his mining appointments until he was about 90, and lived at his home, Summerlands, Alexandra, to within six months of his death, aged 92, on 29 May 1920 at Murrumbeena. He was buried at his beloved Alexandra, predeceased by his wife and survived by eight of his fifteen children.

Wood's Point Times, 28 Feb, 16 May, 30 June 1866; *Alexandra Times*, 25 Aug 1868; *Jamieson and Wood's Point Chronicle*, 29 May 1886, 11 June 1887, 22 May 1892; *Alexandra and Yea Standard*, 18 June 1920; *Mansfield Courier*, 26 June 1920; R. B. Smyth papers (LaTL).   BRIAN LLOYD
MARGARET SHARPE

AINSWORTH, GEORGE FREDERICK (1878-1950), public servant and businessman, was born on 20 June 1878 at Lambton,

New South Wales, one of twelve children of John Ainsworth, miner and teacher, and his wife Sarah, née McKean. At 15 he joined the Department of Public Instruction as an assistant teacher but, becoming interested in science, transferred to the Commonwealth service on 31 January 1910 as an assistant in the meteorological branch, Department of Home Affairs. Seconded to (Sir) Douglas Mawson's [q.v.] Australasian Antarctic Expedition, he led the Macquarie Island party from December 1911 to November 1913 and his long report, published in Mawson's *The home of the blizzard* (London, 1915), remains an important source about the island.

On 16 October 1915 Ainsworth was commissioned in the 62nd Infantry Battalion, Australian Military Forces. In November 1916 he appeared in court without recorded rank as complainant in prosecuting the editor of the Brisbane *Daily Standard* for a censorship breach. In July 1917 he was formally appointed special-duty officer in the Counter Espionage Bureau, which had been set up early in 1916 by Major (Sir) George Steward [q.v.], and was made honorary captain on 24 September. Ainsworth was responsible in Brisbane for control of agents investigating the activities of the Lutheran Church, anti-war groups and the Russian Association, besides collection and analysis of information from censored letters and other sources. He was associated with investigations into internment by Sir Samuel Griffith [q.v.]. Demobilized in 1918, he carried out almost the same functions as inspector in charge of Commonwealth Police, Queensland. In later years he spoke of a journey on the trans-Siberian railway but his claim to have been at the Versailles peace conference with W. M. Hughes [q.v.] in 1919 is unproven.

Ainsworth transferred to the Prime Minister's Department on 18 April 1921 as head of a new foreign section, established by Hughes as a counterbalance to the Pacific branch of E. L. Piesse [q.v.], created by Hughes's rival W. A. Watt [q.v.]. Ainsworth went to London in 1923 as foreign-affairs officer with the delegation to the Imperial Economic Conference, and attended the International Labour Organisation meeting at Geneva as sole Australian delegate. Returning to Australia in mid-1924, he was given six months furlough but saw no future in the public service after the fall of his patron and resigned from 31 December — a decision he later regretted.

Until 1929 Ainsworth managed the Melbourne motor-parts firm of Kellow [q.v.]-Falkiner Pty Ltd, then went to New Zealand as general manager for the Chrysler Corporation. He returned to Queensland about 1932 as general manager for the Barnet

Glass [q.v.] Rubber Co. Ltd. Early in 1935 he resigned and in July became State organizer for the United Australia Party.

After racing losses, Ainsworth moved to Sydney about 1937. He owned a delicatessen in Leichhardt, lived in Vaucluse, delivered radio talks on the Antarctic, and was briefly employed again in meteorology during World War II. He died intestate in Royal Prince Alfred Hospital on 11 October 1950 of pyelonephritis and uraemia and was cremated with Congregational rites. He was survived by his wife Mary Catherine Statham, whom he had married in 1917 at Murwillumbah, and by a daughter; a son had predeceased him. His estate was valued for probate at £2450.

A tall, angular man with a commanding manner, Ainsworth's acid judgments of people included a reference to Winston Churchill as 'a bumptious bullfrog'. His dramatic rise and fall in the public service was probably linked to his admiration for Hughes.

Ainsworth's brother William (1875-1945) was a railway worker who became secretary of the New South Wales Locomotive, Engine-drivers, Firemen and Cleaners' Association in 1911-35. He was a Labor member of the Legislative Council in 1925-34 and worked closely with J. B. Chifley.

Queensland and Queenslanders (Brisb, 1936); *Daily Mail* (Brisb), 3 Nov 1916; *Courier Mail*, 9 July 1935; A391, history file, *and* CP772, item 1, *and* A1, 33/1365 (AAO, Canb); information from Dr J. W. Muller, Syd.   H. J. GIBBNEY

AIREY, HENRY PARKE (1842-1911), soldier, was born on 3 August 1842 at Kingthorpe, Yorkshire, England, son of Henry Cookson Airey, Indian Army officer, and his wife Emily, née Parke. Educated at Marlborough College and the East India Co.'s Military College at Addiscombe, he went to India on graduating in 1859, and was commissioned ensign in the 101st Regiment (Royal Bengal Fusiliers) in 1861. He served on the north-west frontier for six years and was promoted lieutenant in 1863.

Airey retired from the army in 1866 and arrived in Sydney in August. By 1868 he had established himself as a sugar-planter at Cleveland, Queensland; in February that year he married Florence Ada McCulloch at St Mark's Anglican Church, Darling Point, New South Wales. He later bought a property at Georges Hall near Liverpool, and when a third battery was added to the colony's permanent artillery he obtained a lieutenancy in 1877.

In 1885 he accompanied the New South Wales contingent to the Sudan and served as aide-de-camp to General Sir Arthur Fremantle, governor of Suakin, during the advance on Tamai. On his return Airey applied for a captaincy with the New South Wales Field Battery, but his commanding officer, Lieut-Colonel W. Spalding, refused to recommend him because he had 'displayed a want of zeal and energy' in carrying out his duties as a field battery officer on active service. A court of inquiry, convened in December 1885, exonerated Airey and he was promoted captain with effect from the previous March.

In 1886 he volunteered to accompany the Burmese Expedition as a special-service officer and was attached to General Sir George White's staff. He was severely wounded, was awarded the Distinguished Service Order for 'coolness under fire and marked gallantry', and was thanked by the Viceroy of India. On returning to Sydney he resumed duty with the colony's field artillery forces. He was promoted major in June 1893, then spent several months training in India; he became lieut-colonel in August 1895, and was appointed honorary aide-de-camp to the governor in November 1896.

In February 1900 Airey left for South Africa in command of the New South Wales Citizens' Bushmen's Contingent which saw action in Rhodesia and the Transvaal. His force was present at the relief of Mafeking and was ambushed by a strong Boer commando near the Magato Pass on 22 July. After eight hours of fighting, reinforcements arrived and the Boers were driven off; at one stage Airey had tried to surrender his whole force to the enemy by insisting that a white flag raised by one isolated party applied to the whole unit. From November he commanded 'B' area of Cape Colony. He returned home in January 1902 with a reputation for being a 'dashing officer' and an 'intrepid and popular leader', and was appointed C.M.G. that year.

Airey retired, albeit reluctantly, on 1 September 1902 with the rank of honorary colonel. Soon afterwards he went to South Africa where he became a stock and grain farmer; after a long illness he died at Panplaats, Transvaal, on 9 October 1911, survived by his wife, two sons and four daughters. Though always a controversial figure, Airey was undoubtedly a gallant and able soldier and, in spite of his domineering personality, was popular with the men he commanded. His interests, in keeping with his restless nature, were riding, hunting and driving. He was a particularly skilled horseman and for several years was master of the Sydney Hunt Club.

C. N. Robinson, *Celebrities of the army* (Lond, 1900); L. Creswicke, *South Africa and the Trans-*vaal war, 6 (Edinb, 1901); J. Stirling, *The colonials in South Africa, 1899-1902* (Edinb, 1907); *V&P* (LA NSW), 1883-84, 6, 335, 338, 417, 1885-86, 1, 207, vol 2, 237, 1887-88, 1, 189, 1894-95, 5, 402, 1896, 1, 324, 1900, 4, 807 and report; *J* (LC NSW), 1885-86, 40, 495-551; C. D. Clark, 'The Aireys', *Sabretache*, Jan 1974; *SMH*, 8 Feb 1900, 16 Oct 1911; *Sydney Mail*, 18 Jan 1902; *The Times*, 16 Oct 1911; *Bulletin*, 19 Oct 1911; E. Barton papers (NL).

C. D. COULTHARD-CLARK

AIREY, PETER (1865-1950), schoolteacher, politician and writer, was born on 9 January 1865 at Dalton-in-Furness, Lancashire, England, son of Peter Airey, labourer, and his wife Mary, née Akrigg. With his brother Samuel and his widowed father, he emigrated to Maryborough, Queensland, in 1875. Three years later he became a pupilteacher at Bundaberg North with the Department of Public Instruction. He was appointed an assistant teacher at Maryborough in 1883, and then to schools at Bundamba, Rockhampton, Mount Morgan, Charters Towers and Hughenden and the Central School for Boys in Brisbane. He led his colleagues in publicly demanding substantial salary increases, and was president and vice-president of the East Moreton Teachers' Association, the largest branch of the Queensland Teachers' Union. On 1 February 1901 he was made head-teacher of Hughenden, allegedly as punishment.

In June 1901 Airey resigned and was elected unopposed for Flinders, becoming the first state-school teacher to represent Labor in the Legislative Assembly. He soon became whip and secretary of the parliamentary Labor Party. In September 1903, when W. H. Browne and William Kidston [qq.v.], Labor's parliamentary leaders, resigned from caucus to enter a 'Lib-Lab' coalition, Airey was elected leader of the Labor Party and president of the central political executive. He held these positions until April 1904 when he filled the cabinet vacancy caused by Browne's death and for a few days replaced him as secretary for mines and public works; he then became home secretary. An erstwhile supporter of the liberalism of Sir Samuel Griffith [q.v.], Airey was always reformist though never avowedly socialist, and found it impossible to support the socialist objective passed by the Labor-in-Politics Convention of May 1905. This resolution led to the split during the next convention in March 1907 when Airey with Kidston and his supporters left the Labor Party. He was defeated in a three-cornered contest for Flinders on 18 May 1907. Because of a premiers' conference and illness, Kidston delayed the naming of his new cabinet and Airey remained home secretary until 3 July 1907 when he was appointed minister without portfolio with a seat in the Legislative Council. After the government fell in November, he won South Brisbane at the elections for the assembly in February 1908 and became treasurer in Kidston's new ministry. When Kidston joined the conservative Robert Philp [q.v.] in a coalition in October, Airey was dropped from the cabinet and withdrew support. Defeated at the election in October 1909 he then went into semi-retirement.

In 1916 he helped form a branch of the Universal Service League, a body advocating compulsory military service. Airey chaired, organized and spoke at meetings in Brisbane and country centres, and as secretary-treasurer of the league worked for W. M. Hughes [q.v.]. On 15 November 1916 at a meeting of interstate conscriptionists he seconded the motion leading to the conference of 9 January 1917, at which he represented Queensland, which founded the Nationalist Party.

A keen student, Airey became a gifted linguist, specializing in German and proficient in French and Latin. He was known as a brilliant speaker and an able administrator whose political success seemed assured; but he preferred writing. Before his election he had established himself as a versifier and essayist. He contributed frequently to the *Bulletin*, his chief publisher, and also wrote under the pseudonyms 'P. Luftig', 'Philander Flam' and 'Furness Born' in the *Queenslander*, *People's Newspaper*, *Boomerang*, *Worker* and, later, *Steele Rudd's Magazine*. The *Bulletin* described his verse in 1904 as 'a task entered upon as doggedly and conscientiously as the correction of school exercises and with as little poetic inspiration', but admitted occasional flights of something better.

After leaving parliament Airey lived partly by writing and partly from investments; indeed, he never took another regular job but lived at Birkdale near Brisbane on a farm bought in 1921 and worked by a son. He sat on the Cleveland (Redland) Shire Council in 1924-27 and in May 1924 became employers' representative on a board investigating the need for a farm workers' award. Six of the nine children born of his marriage to Martha Watts Lintern on 29 December 1897 shared an estate sworn for probate at £19 426 after he died of heart failure on 10 August 1950 at Birkdale.

'I started life as a joyous enthusiast and regenerator', he said of himself, 'but I have come to the conclusion that an essential preliminary to social reform is the extermination of two-thirds of the social reformers'.

D. J. Murphy (ed), *Labor in politics* (Brisb, 1975); *Qld Education J*, Oct 1897, Aug 1898; *Brisbane Courier*, 18, 26 July 1897, 8 Mar 1898, 12 Aug 1899, 25 Mar 1907, 26 Oct 1908, 13, 21, 24 July, 8, 10, 11, 17, 24 Aug 1916; *Worker* (Brisb), 25 May 1907; *Daily Mail* (Brisb), 11 May 1908; *Daily Standard*, 21 July 1916; M. G. Sullivan, Education and the Labor movement in Queensland 1890-1910 (M.A. thesis, Univ Qld, 1971); Register of arrivals, Imm/115 (QA); Register of teachers (male) vol 4 (QA); information from P. L. Airey, Camp Hill, Qld.

MARTIN SULLIVAN

AITKEN, GEORGE LEWIS (1864-1940), pastoralist and woolbroker, was born on 4 February 1864 at Langi Willi, Skipton, Victoria, son of James Aitken and his wife Jane (Jeannie), née Lewis. James Aitken owned Langi Willi with Philip Russell [q.v.6] of Carngham until 1870, when he acquired Banyenong West, Donald. He was also a partner in Dalgety, (J.) Blackwood [qq.v.4,3] & Co., Melbourne; when it was incorporated under the title of Dalgety & Co. Ltd in 1884, he became joint managing director, with A. R. Blackwood [q.v.], and sole managing director from 1889 until his death in 1905.

George was reared a Presbyterian and from 1875 attended Scotch College, Melbourne, later serving on the school's council. In 1882 he joined Dalgety, Blackwood & Co., managing and developing the extensive stock and station business of Dalgety, Melbourne. Shortly after his father's death he was appointed branch sub-manager, in 1910 joint manager, and in 1915 Melbourne manager.

Active in the Melbourne Woolbrokers' Association, he impressed his colleagues with his foresight. He was chairman in 1911-12 and 1917-18, significant years for the wool industry. From 1916 wool disposal was controlled by the Central Wool Committee, and in 1918 contracts were executed to purchase the clip during the war and one year thereafter. The orderly disposal of stocks seriously concerned brokers, who formed the Federated Wool Selling Brokers of Australia. Aitken considered the federation's authority too limited. In July 1919 the National Council of Wool Selling Brokers was constituted and Aitken, its principal architect, was first president, holding office in 1919-24 and 1926-36. He established the council's authority, and emphasized his national approach in discussions with the Central Wool Committee on the powers of the British Australian Wool Realization Association Ltd over disposal of stocks.

Aitken's objective was co-operation between growers, brokers and buyers. He contended that if these interests worked together risks of interference with the industry's organization would be minimized, and he thus consistently opposed schemes to stabilize wool values proposed by growers in 1930 and 1936. In 1932 he established the London committee of the National Council of Wool Selling Brokers to maintain contact with market developments in Europe, and that year he headed a brokers' delegation to a Federal government committee of inquiry into the wool industry.

Aitken's conviction that wool was 'the backbone of Australia's prosperity' motivated his dedicated service to the pastoral industry. Concerned that applied research in the field was inadequate, in 1927 he founded and became chairman of the Australian Pastoral Research Trust, established to promote scientific and economic research into wool production. He stressed the need to reduce costs if competition from artificial fibres was to be effectively countered. Disappointed that the trust failed to attract adequate financial support from woolgrowers, he still persisted with a research programme to demonstrate that costs could be controlled only 'by tackling the task of eliminating stock diseases and thus reducing the cost of handling'.

Aitken was chairman of the Tubbo Estate Co. Pty Ltd, and for many years honorary treasurer of the Australian Sheepbreeders' Association and the Pastoralists' Association of Victoria. As Dalgety's manager he was a member of the local board of the British and Foreign Marine Insurance Co. Ltd, and became its chairman. In the late 1920s he actively supported the Australian Inland Mission in its efforts to establish an aerial medical service based on Cloncurry, Queensland. Donations from the National Council of Wool Selling Brokers assisted the scheme's foundation.

Of powerful physique – in his youth a keen rower and prominent footballer – Aitken had a dominating personality but was regarded as both kindly and just. He was a generous supporter of St George's Presbyterian Church, Windsor, and a member of the Australian and Melbourne clubs. In 1935 he was appointed C.B.E. for his services to research in the pastoral industry. On 28 November 1894 he had married Alice Gorton Burt of Bindi station, Gippsland; when he died of cardiac disease at his home in East St Kilda on 27 February 1940, his wife, his son and two daughters survived him. He left an estate valued for probate at £38 264.

Dalgety's Review (A'sia), 1 Aug 1910; *A'sian Insurance and Banking Record*, July, Oct 1936, Mar 1940; *Argus*, 28 Feb 1940; *Pastoral Review*, 11 Mar 1940; Memorandum of Association 1884 (Dalgety & Co. Ltd Archives, Melb); Presidential addresses 1921-37 (National Council of Wool Selling Brokers of Aust, Syd).

G. S. LE COUTEUR

AKHURST, DAPHNE JESSIE (1903-1933), tennis-player, was born on 22 April 1903 at Ashfield, Sydney, second daughter of Oscar James Akhurst, lithographer, and his wife Jessie Florence, née Smith. She showed promise as a pianist and won prizes at eisteddfods as a child. After schooling at Miss E. Tildesley's [q.v.] Normanhurst until 1920 and at the State Conservatorium of Music (D.S.C.M., 1922), she became a music teacher and performed at concerts and music clubs.

At school Daphne had shown natural ability at tennis. Although self-taught, she won the New South Wales schoolgirls' singles championship in 1917-20. Her first major win in the County of Cumberland ladies' singles in 1923 was the beginning of a long series of victories at State and national levels. In 1925 she defeated her Victorian rival Miss E. F. Boyd in the Australasian championships; women's matches were not usually popular, but her determined play in the final brought cheers which delayed the men's championship event on an adjoining court. She dominated this event for the next five years, winning in 1926, 1928, 1929 and 1930, when she retained permanently the Anthony Wilding Memorial Cup. She won the Australasian ladies' doubles title five times and the mixed doubles four times, partnered in 1928 by the Frenchman Jean Borotra.

Although described as shy and self-effacing, Daphne Akhurst was a keen competitor with a 'temperament that treats tennis as purely a game'. Her consistency in match play was no doubt developed in practice with local players Norman Peach, Jack Crawford and J. O. Anderson at her home club, The Western Suburbs Association, Pratten Park.

In 1925 the New South Wales Lawn Tennis Association had financed the first overseas tour by an Australian women's team. They succeeded against Wales, Scotland, Ireland and Holland but could not match the experience of England and the United States of America. Akhurst, rated as an outsider at the All England Lawn Tennis Club championships at Wimbledon, reached the quarter-finals of the ladies' singles, losing to English player Miss J. Fry 6-2, 4-6, 3-6. *The Times* noted her effort against a hard-hitting opponent by recalling 'those early Australian stonewallers who seemed to have no strokes, but who never got out'. Another

Australian women's team was sent overseas in 1928; this time they won all thirteen matches. At Wimbledon, Akhurst outdid her previous success and reached the singles and doubles semi-finals and, partnered by Crawford, the mixed doubles final. She performed better than any of the Australian men and was ranked by *Ayres' Almanac* third in the world after Helen Wills and Senorita E. dé Alvarez. The *Referee*, more generous, claimed she was the best all-round player in the world.

On 26 February 1930 at St Philip's Church of England, Sydney, Daphne Akhurst married Royston Stuckey Cozens, a tobacco manufacturer, and retired from serious competition soon after winning the Australian ladies' doubles championship in 1931. They had one son. She died on 9 January 1933 of an ectopic pregnancy and, after a service at St Anne's, Strathfield, was cremated.

Her capacity to retrieve and 'ability to run about like a gazelle untiringly' had been responsible for her success and for an Australian-title record that lasted until broken by Nancy Bolton in 1951.

NSW Lawn Tennis Assn, *Tennis Handbook* (Syd, 1933); NSW State Conservatorium, *Prospectus* (Syd, 1963); J. Pollard, *Ampol's Australian sporting records*, 2nd ed (Syd, 1969); *Woman's World*, 1 Mar 1926; *Argus*, 2 Feb 1925; *The Times*, 30 June 1925, 5 July 1928; *Referee* (Syd), 1 Feb 1928; personal information from Mr R. S. Cozens, Bayview, NSW.   KERRY REGAN

ALANSON, ALFRED GODWIN (1863-1943), educationist, journalist and author, was born on 19 November 1863 at Hargraves, New South Wales, son of Richard Chapman and his wife Sarah, née Chapman. His father was born Roger Godwin Alanson at Liverpool, England, and had changed his name to Richard Chapman soon after his marriage in Melbourne in 1858, allegedly in response to an advertisement seeking an heir to money left to relations of his wife. As Chapman he was an untrained teacher in New South Wales country schools in 1861-65 and 1869-83.

Alfred Godwin Chapman was a pupil-teacher at Redfern in 1878-81 and, after six months training, in 1882 became teacher in charge at Frogmore near Young, on £216 a year. In 1884-99 he taught at Woonona, and on 22 December 1885 at Bulli married Sarah Crane, a sewing mistress at the school. A very successful teacher, he was rated in 1895 by the local inspector as the best and most popular in the district. As secretary, manager and player in the district team in 1893-95, he helped to establish country

matches for the Southern Districts (Illawarra) Cricket Association. After his father's death in 1897 his mother arranged next year for all the family to revert to the name Alanson.

After years asking to transfer, in 1900 Alanson opened a new school in the fast-growing Sydney suburb of Kensington. His salary was lower than in 1882 because of depression salary cuts. In 1907 he moved to Randwick Public School where he stayed as it grew to become a superior public school with a boys' intermediate high school and a girls' domestic department. He retired in 1929, having made 'Alanson's School' famous. He was respected and well loved by former pupils who regularly called at his home at Randwick. For years he was a vice-president of the Randwick District Cricket Club and a trustee of Queens Park.

Alanson was active in the New South Wales Public School Teachers' Association, formed in 1899 to represent the industrial and professional interests of state school teachers. He was first elected to its executive in 1904 and was president in 1909-10. A tall well-built man, he had a fine presence and became well known as an orator. He led the association's resistance to the formation in 1911 of a Labor-inspired teachers' union, was elected the teachers' advocate before the 1917 royal commission into the public service, and moved the main resolutions at important meetings in 1918. He ably expressed the resentment of teachers after years of unimproved salaries during wartime inflation, and their determination to become a professional force and a well-organized trade union under the arbitration system. Alanson was also active in the Australian Teachers' Federation formed in 1921, of which he was president in 1923-24, and in the Federated State School Teachers' Association of Australia formed in 1924. He was its general secretary in 1929 when it appeared in the High Court, unsuccessfully seeking registration as a Federal trade union. In 1932 as a political lobbyist he secured rapid amending legislation to enable State superannuation cheques to be honoured during the feud between the Commonwealth and J. T. Lang's [q.v.] governments.

Alanson had considerable experience in writing and journalism. As Chapman he published *Notes on practical lessons in grammar* (1896) and then wrote three adventure books for boys. From May 1908 to August 1914 he contributed an unsigned weekly column on education to the *Sydney Morning Herald*. In 1919-39 he edited *Education*, the monthly journal of the New South Wales Teachers' Federation, and established a nice balance between details of its meetings, membership and campaigns, and articles on teaching techniques, syllabuses, and general cultural and political topics.

Before World War I Alanson's Australian patriotism was overshadowed by his admiration of the British Empire, and he rejected trade unionism and arbitration for teachers and public servants. During the war he launched a campaign for citizenship training to strengthen national life and to teach children that Germany could never be trusted again. In the 1920s he emphasized Australian history and literature, and was prominent in the movement which resulted in the building of Henry Lawson's [q.v.] statue in Sydney. At the same time he preached internationalism and the virtues of the League of Nations. His last book was *Kurnell; the birthplace of Australia* (1933). An Anglican, he maintained a family pew, although he attended church seldom. He loved going to the races, gambling and drinking beer. A persistent but unconfirmed rumour says that he made money from selling the Bulli soil with which the Sydney Cricket Ground pitch was made.

Alanson died on 1 August 1943 at his home at Randwick of coronary occlusion and was buried in Rookwood cemetary. He was survived by his wife and three sons.

B. A. Mitchell, *Teachers, education, and politics* (Brisb, 1975); *Aust J of Education*, 1903-12; *Education* (Syd), 1919-39, 20 Sept 1943; *SMH*, 8 Nov 1928; school files (NSWA).

BRUCE MITCHELL

ALBERT, MICHEL FRANÇOIS (1874-1962), music publisher, was born on 26 March 1874 at Kharkov, Russia, son of JACQUES ALBERT, horologist, and his first wife Sophia (d. 1890), née Greenberg. Jacques had been born on 1 January 1850 at Fribourg, Switzerland, son of Otto Albert, optician, and his wife Rose, née Lachôme. After serving his apprenticeship to a clockmaker in Switzerland, he moved round Europe as a journeyman horologist. In Kharkov from the early 1870s, he later went to Moscow. He arrived in Sydney via Rockhampton, Queensland, with his wife and two children on 10 December 1884.

Jacques Albert set up business as a watch- and clock-mender at Newtown, where the sound of his violin attracted music-lovers to his shop. In 1890 he decided to import violins, moved to premises in King Street, and adopted the boomerang as the firm's trade mark. He also published handbooks on health, diet, cookery and conundrums. On 26 June 1901 at the Baptist Tabernacle he married a widow Annie Maria Hare (d. 1903), née Hay, and that year was naturalized. Albert died of a perforated gastric ulcer on 9 July 1914 in the *Bellita* off Mackay, Queensland, and was buried in Waverley cemetery, Sydney. He was survived by a son and daughter of his first marriage and by his third wife Maria Eliza Blanche (d. 1950), née Allen, whom he had married on 10 February 1904, and by their son (Professor) Adrien Albert.

Frank, as he was widely known, was educated at Newtown Public, Fort Street and Sydney boys' high schools. In 1894 he joined his father in partnership under the style of J. Albert & Son and in 1896 became sole proprietor of what had become a music selling and publishing business. On 25 March at St Andrew's Cathedral he married Minnie Eliza Buttel. He expanded the firm and concluded licensing arrangements with overseas publishers for Australia and New Zealand. In the late 1890s he had taught music and about 1917 set up the Albert College of Music in Boomerang House, King Street. In 1919 he visited Europe and the United States of America. He was naturalized in 1920.

In 1929 Albert became a director of the Australian Broadcasting Co. Ltd, formed by J. Albert & Son with Union Theatres Ltd and Fullers' [qq.v.] Theatres Ltd, which successfully tendered to the Commonwealth government to provide radio programmes and ran the National Broadcasting Service. When their contract expired in 1932, the government set up its own authority, the Australian Broadcasting Commission. In 1933 Albert's Australian Broadcasting Co. acquired the licence for the commercial station 2UW in Sydney and, later, stations in Queensland at Brisbane, Toowoomba, Maryborough and Rockhampton. Albert was a founding director of the Australasian Performing Rights Association and of Waddington's Theatres Ltd, which ran a chain of Sydney suburban cinemas. When J. Albert & Son gave up retailing in 1933 to concentrate solely on music publishing, he formed Albert Investments Pty Ltd which acquired many urban and rural properties.

Albert was a motoring and yachting enthusiast. He was an early member of the Royal Automobile Club of Australia and in 1905 a founder and rear commodore of the Motor Boat Club (Royal Motor Yacht Club) of which he was commodore in 1912-20. In 1909 he bought the New Zealand yacht *Rawhiti* and that season won the Royal Prince Alfred Yacht Club championship. He was elected to the Royal Sydney Yacht Squadron in 1920 and won many races in the next decade with *Rawhiti*; he was also a life-member of the Royal Yacht Club of Victoria. Founding secretary in 1927-35 and president in 1936-37 of the Geographical

Society of New South Wales, he became a fellow of the Royal Geographical Society of London.

Albert was an active Freemason, a director of the Rachel Forster Hospital for Women and Children and a councillor of the Civic Reform Association of Sydney Ltd. In 1940-62 he was a member of the executive committee of the Australian Red Cross Society and from 1943 sat on its divisional finance committee. He gave generously to St Paul's College (University of Sydney), the Royal Australian Naval College and other causes, and endowed St Edmund's Church, Pagewood, in memory of his elder son. Over the years he had donated many small sums to the university and in 1944 gave £10 000 towards establishing a chair of music, which was not filled until 1948.

Survived by his second son (Sir) Alexis, Albert died on 19 January 1962 at his home, Boomerang, Elizabeth Bay, where he had lived since 1902; he was cremated with Anglican rites and his ashes were buried in the family vault at Waverley cemetery.

P. R. Stephensen (ed), *Sydney sails* (Syd, 1962); *SMH*, 27 Jan 1927; information from Sir Alexis Albert, Vaucluse, and Mr P. Geeves, Blakehurst, NSW.

ALBISTON, ARTHUR EDWARD (1866-1961), clergyman, was born on 19 August 1866 at Emerald Hill, Melbourne, son of Joseph Albiston (1829-1919), a Wesleyan Methodist minister, and his wife Elizabeth Barbara, née Rowbotham. His father had arrived from England in 1854; his mother came to Melbourne to be married in 1857 and died in 1875 leaving a family of ten children. Albiston was educated at Wesley College, under the classicist A. S. Way [q.v.6]; in 1883 he was senior prefect and dux of the school, with special prizes in Greek and Latin, mathematics and science. His modest distinction as a long-distance runner and oarsman is consistent with his longevity; he was to play golf when 92 and preach at 94. At the University of Melbourne in 1888 he was awarded the final honours exhibition in natural sciences (B.A.); he became senior resident-master at Wesley.

In 1889 Albiston was received as a candidate for the Wesleyan ministry and was first appointed to Denham Street, Hawthorn. He visited England in 1891, returned to South Melbourne, and was ordained and sent to Mildura in 1893. On 6 April at Essendon he had married Harriette Skinner (1874-1952). His subsequent appointments were to Launceston, Tasmania (1896), Prahran (1899, 1910), Hawthorn (1902, 1917), the Central Mission, Melbourne (1907), and Brunswick and Coburg (1914). Secretary of the Victorian and Tasmanian Annual Conference in 1918 and president in 1919, he was secretary-general of the Australasian Methodist Conference in 1935-37 and president-general in 1938-41.

Albiston was best known for his work as professor of theology at Queen's College, University of Melbourne, in 1920-37. His success was due to a solid background in other disciplines, wide reading and an original, independent mind. Despite the efforts of W. H. Fitchett [q.v.], who urged him to write a book because he had 'the finest mind of us all', he wrote little; only a few special addresses have survived in print. He had extraordinary powers as an orator, using dramatic intensity and vivid gestures. The clarity of his thought was conveyed through a highly sensitive choice of words; he prepared sermon notes carefully but never took them into the pulpit.

Several handwritten volumes of sermon notes indicate the quality and direction of Albiston's thought. He was a liberal Protestant, a humanist and an evangelical. He drew heavily on the Fourth Gospel and Paul with their rejection of the letter and commendation of the spirit. To him, institutions were suspect, as was any belief which was not essential. Called a 'Methodist Quaker' by his friends, he once addressed the Society of Friends on 'The advantage of an unseen Christ'. He considered that Christians were too ready to honour external aspects of faith, and their continuing peril was a reversion to legalism. Yet he valued the Church as the salt of the earth and light of the world, as men raised to their full potential in Christ. By originality and analytic skill he reached further into the New Testament than did many Protestant liberals; like the German founders of this tendency he understood Paul and the evangelical centre of Paul's thought.

Albiston was convinced that the Methodist Church had an essential role. Even his liberal tolerance was openly Wesleyan, as was his careful, simple, scholarly analysis of scripture. To the end, he wrote out the scriptural text of his sermon in Greek or Hebrew. His retiring address as president-general in 1941 was a commendation of Methodist spirituality and classical humanism.

Albiston lived at Auburn in active retirement until his death in hospital at Richmond on 20 June 1961; he was cremated. His three sons and only daughter survived him. Walter Albiston [q.v.] was a nephew.

E. H. O. Nye, 'A prince of preachers', *Heritage* (Vic), 1963, no 14; *Spectator* (Melb), 24 Mar 1920, 28 May 1941, 7, 28 June 1961; Methodist Church

(Vic), *Minutes of the annual conference*, Melb, Oct 1961; MSS (held by Miss M. Albiston, Hawthorn, Vic).   E. F. OSBORN

ALBISTON, WALTER (1889-1965), Congregational minister, was born on 25 July 1889 at Moonee Ponds, Victoria, son of Herbert Rowbotham Albiston, clerk, and his wife Eva Jessie, née McCure. He grew up in Ballarat where his grandfather, Rev. Joseph Albiston, father of A. E. Albiston [q.v.], was minister of Barkly Street Methodist Church. After education to the sixth grade at state schools, he lived for a time on a relation's farm at Beech Forest. Through a school friendship he attended Dawson Street, Ballarat, Congregational Sunday School and Christian Endeavour, passing through a religious crisis in 1906. He moved to Malvern to continue under the tuition of Rev. G. W. Legge, while employed as an enameller of bicycles, and was accepted as a home missionary by the Congregational Union of Victoria in 1908, serving as assistant at Bruthen in Gippsland. In 1909 he entered the Congregational College of Victoria with a reputation as a 'powerful preacher'; he was ordained in 1914. On 26 December that year at Huonville, Tasmania, where he had served as student pastor, he married Gladys Marsh.

Albiston first ministered at Warrnambool, earning a reputation for vigorous support of conscription and Empire loyalty in the controversy with Archbishop Mannix [q.v.]. He became so involved in the campaign that he returned to Ballarat before the Federal election of 1918, founded the Victorian Protestant Federation, of which he remained secretary for forty-six years, and issued a manifesto in opposition to the 'Mannix-Ryan Combination'. With Herbert Brookes [q.v.] he was a founder of the monthly *Vigilant*: through its pages a relentless campaign was waged on such issues as government funding of religious hospitals and schools and alleged Roman Catholic lobbying of government for special consideration. The activities of Mannix, John Wren [q.v.] and others were continuously investigated. In 1920 Albiston opened the federation's office in Collins Street, Melbourne. Having made his home at North Balwyn in 1922, he gathered the East Kew (later North Balwyn) Congregational Church where he was deacon and frequently preacher.

In October 1925 Albiston was elected secretary of the Congregational Union of Victoria and Home Mission superintendent, taking up his duties after a world tour. His appointment coincided with the adoption of a new constitution designed to increase efficiency and to make the Union more influential in the life of its constituent churches. During his thirty-one years in office, Albiston pursued these aims vigorously. A natural administrator, he had a retentive memory and a good business sense. He initiated lay-preacher training and camps at Torquay for young men. A convinced ecumenist, he was a foundation member of the Joint Commission on Church Union and helped to lay the foundations of the Uniting Church in Australia.

Albiston was elected secretary of the Congregational Union of Australia and New Zealand from 1941 until 1954 when he became president. In this capacity he sat on many committees, including the Federal Inter-Church Immigration Committee. He served as president of the Congregational Union of Victoria in 1937-38 and 1957-58. In 1941 he had been appointed part-time chaplain with the Royal Australian Air Force and later visited war zones; before retiring in 1961 he had become principal chaplain for 'other Protestant denominations', with the rank of air commodore.

Regarded as a 'gifted controversialist', Albiston was tireless and vocal in his pursuit of social justice, and earned the respect of political and trade union leaders over social issues. Despite his strong Protestant bias his ecumenical interests broadened in later life to include the Catholics, with whose chaplains he had good *rapport*. A Freemason, he held the position of grand chaplain and was a foundation member of several lodges. A colleague described him as 'an elder statesman, a pillar of the Church, a man to lean on'; though a strict disciplinarian, he was also a man of 'very tender and quick sensibilities'. He was a keen and able sportsman, captain of eleven of the twelve Australian Rules football teams of which he was a member in Tasmania and Victoria, and a cricketer till his early fifties; three of his sons and a grandson were League footballers. An outstanding marksman, he observed the opening days of duck and quail shooting as well as the opening of the trout season. He died of myocardial infarction on 2 January 1965 when fishing on the River Murray near Tocumwal, New South Wales, survived by his wife, two daughters and six sons, of whom one was in the Congregational ministry.

R. Rivett, *Australian citizen; Herbert Brookes* (Melb, 1965); E. M. McQueen, *The story of a church* (Melb, 1966); *Vic Congregational Year Book*, 1914-65; *Congregationalist* (Melb), Feb 1965; *Age*, 4 Jan 1965; *Vigilant*, Jan-Feb 1965; Congregational Union of Vic, Papers (LaTL); family information.   NIEL GUNSON

ALCOCK, ALFRED UPTON (1865-1962), electrical engineer and inventor, was born on 22 September 1865 at Hawthorn, Victoria, eldest son of Henry Upton Alcock and his wife Jane, née Webb, both of whom were Irish-born. At the age of 30 Henry Alcock had migrated to Melbourne in the *Africa*, arriving on 15 April 1853. He briefly tried the goldfields but soon returned to his old trade of cabinet-making. He set up a sawmill and moulding works and began manufacturing billiard tables, trading from 1860 as Alcock & Co.; by 1901 the firm had branches in Perth and Brisbane. Alcock became known as one of the best judges of timber in the colony and developed highly skilled techniques of seasoning wood. His tables won many awards and, although not a billiard player himself, he arranged tours of leading British players to Victoria and received hundreds of testimonials from users all over the world. In 1863 he published in Melbourne his *Epitome of the game of billiards* which reached a fifth edition in 1901 as *The Alcock book of billiards*. Survived by three sons and four daughters, he died on 6 August 1912.

Alfred was educated at Geelong Church of England Grammar School from 1879 and then worked in his father's factory. In his spare time he taught himself applied electricity; at 16 he charged a Leyden jar from a wine bottle spinning in a lathe, and later demonstrated water-boiling and cooking by electricity to his friends. He applied for his first patent in December 1883: for 'improvements in electrical apparatus for registering numbers such as for billiard marking'. Many other applications followed in the next few years; Alcock showed remarkable inventive talent, the technical ability to design and the craftsman's painstaking skill to construct his own prototypes. His work attracted notice and in 1889 he was admitted to membership of the Institution of Electrical Engineers, London.

In the mid-1880s Alcock became interested in electricity-supply to the public. He had constructed a dynamo and in 1888 he and his father established a generating-station in Corr's Lane, Melbourne. The Ganz transformer was introduced to Australia during this year and the system of supply adopted by Alcock was single-phase alternating current. Next year he formed the A. U. Alcock Electric Light and Motive Power Co. and developed a larger station in Burnley Street, Richmond. By 1893 he was supplying 15 000 lights as far away as Footscray. Under the provisions of the Electric Light and Power Act 1896, Alcock's company was granted an Order in Council which gave permission to continue its works in Melbourne, Richmond, Fitzroy, Collingwood, Kew and South Melbourne but not permis-sion to extend further. In 1899 the firm was taken over by the Brush Electrical Engineering Co. of England and a new venture, the Electric Light and Traction Co. was formed, with Alcock a director. This supplied electricity throughout many Melbourne suburbs and later formed the basis of the retail distribution system of the State Electricity Commission.

Alcock's earliest major invention was a device for electrically co-ordinating the range-setter and fire-control for artillery, which was tested successfully at Port Phillip Heads; in 1897 he formed a small company to promote it. Not long after his marriage in August that year to Jessie McFarlane, he went to England where the War Office gave him facilities at Tilbury and Shoeburyness fortresses to develop his device. When after three years the British government refused to commit itself to purchasing the invention, Alcock returned to Melbourne. He received no recompense for his work for the War Office, but there is evidence to show that it pioneered the application of electrically co-ordinated range-setting and fire-control to naval vessels. While in England Alcock had also invented an electrically operated ship's telegraph. A British company became interested in this and invited him to join the firm, but he refused.

In 1910 Alcock moved to Perth to manage the family business there. About that time he began work on a model which some fifty years later was acknowledged by the Westland Aircraft Co. as the basis of the modern hovercraft. The working model of his device, tested successfully before government officials and the press in Perth in 1912 and later in Melbourne and Sydney, consisted of a wooden platform with an electric motor mounted upof it which drove both a compressor and a propeller. From the compressor, air was pumped beneath the platform to provide a cushion of air, while the propeller provided motive power. Alcock called the method of travel 'floating traction' and hoped that his invention might be used in the outback. A provisional patent was taken out in 1914 but financial backing was lacking and the patent was allowed to lapse.

In 1917 Alcock returned to Melbourne with his wife and family and entered into partnership with Herbert del Cott. From 1923 the firm co-operated with the Foundation Co. of London in converting Melbourne's cable trams to electric traction. Alcock was also experimenting with a meat-defrosting process based on an earlier device by which he had seasoned timber for billiard tables by passing an alternating current through it. In 1923 he visited England and demonstrated his defrosting process at Smithfield Market, but despite wide interest it was not developed commercially apart from use by a few passenger liners.

In 1927 Alcock retired to England; the family had always been a close one, and the parents wished to join their son, who was studying at Cambridge, and their two daughters. For the next twenty-three years they lived in or near London but mainly at Surbiton, Surrey. Alcock continued to work on his defrosting process and in the mid-1930s designed a cabinet to disinfect library books, but most of his research was in the field of physics. During World War II he helped to manage a small engineering operation set up by his son-in-law to produce components for the Air Ministry.

After moving to Budleigh Salterton near Exeter, about 1950, Alcock died at Exmouth on 1 February 1962; his wife died a month later.

A. Sutherland et al, *Victoria and its metropolis*, 2 (Melb, 1888); L. H. Hayward, *The history of air cushion vehicles* (Lond, 1963); *Argus*, 4 Oct 1886, 7 Nov 1892, 7 Aug 1912, 21 Jan 1924, 31 May 1941; *Table Talk*, 22 Sept 1893; *IAN*, 1 July 1896; *West Australian*, 3 June 1966; information from Mr Kelvin Alcock, Kelvin Court, Glasgow.

G. B. LINCOLNE*

ALCOCK, RANDAL JAMES (1853-1927), merchant, was born on 20 July 1853 at Collingwood, Victoria, eldest son of Edmund Alcock, a London-born painter and decorator, and his wife Mary Ann, née Ramsey, of Montreal, Canada. His parents were married in New York in 1850 and migrated from London to Victoria in 1851. Leaving school at 13, Alcock joined James Service [q.v.6] & Co., import merchants and shipping agents, as a junior clerk. He showed such rare judgment of men and affairs that Service made him managing partner when he was only 33. His fellow businessmen elected him president of the Melbourne Chamber of Commerce for three consecutive terms in 1895-98. In 1896 the Victorian government appointed him to a board of inquiry into the telephone system and over the years consulted him on economic matters. After Service's death in 1899 Alcock bought his interest in the company and continued under the same name in partnership with James Ormond. They promptly expanded its prospering wholesale grocery and shipping operations by taking over the Robur Tea Co. In 1918 Alcock became sole proprietor. He was also chairman of directors of the Royal Bank of Australia and of the Mercantile Mutual (fire and marine) Insurance Co. Ltd. His motto was 'I must be thorough'.

In 1912 Alcock had made his fourth overseas trip when, representing the Melbourne Chamber of Commerce, he attended imperial and international congresses in London and in Boston, United States of America; he found overseas travel 'a most liberal education'. He was a council-member of Trinity Grammar School and Trinity College, University of Melbourne, and helped to found Swinburne [q.v.] Technical College. For many years Alcock lived at Hawthorn where he was a leading member of St Columb's Anglican Church. He was a lay canon of St Paul's Cathedral, a trustee of the Church, and for many years honorary treasurer of the Victorian Mission to Seamen. A justice of the peace, he was active in the Australian Health Society, the Philharmonic Society and many other charitable and community activities, and was a founder of the Royal Melbourne Golf Club. His 'highly esteemed' luncheon colleagues at Scott's Hotel included G. Swinburne, Sir William McBeath and Sir William McPherson [qq.v.]; there 'public affairs were sifted with close criticism and constructive argument'.

Highly respected as a leader of Melbourne's business community and for his power of decision, persistence and genial temperament, Alcock seemed an obvious candidate for parliament. One journalist wrote in 1912 that 'if only men like R. J. Alcock could be installed in our Parliaments the whole business of politics would very soon undergo a radical change'. He resisted requests to stand for election but, influenced by Service, took a keen interest in politics and actively supported Federation. He was a stalwart of the Liberal and National parties, campaigning at the local level for Federal and State candidates, and in particular for McPherson. His advice and judgment were often sought by political leaders.

On 12 August 1879 at Melbourne, Alcock had married Sarah Louisa Watt. They had no children, but Alcock was an encouraging and understanding uncle and friend to many young people, virtually adopting five and bringing two into his own household. A shortish man, with a rolling gait, he was an inveterate pipe-smoker. He always went to work by public transport, clad in morning dress and top hat; his office was simple and bare. His skill in mental arithmetic was impressive, but he was not a great reader: his spare time was taken up with charities and the Church. He died of cancer at his home, Crossakiel, Hawthorn, on 30 May 1927 and was buried in Boroondara cemetery; a large crowd attended his funeral service at St Paul's Cathedral. His estate was valued for probate at £865 816 and included generous legacies to relations, friends, employees and servants as well as the university, the

Church of England and charities. He also directed that £40 000 be invested as the Randal and Louisa Alcock Fund, from which annual legacies were to be distributed. The fund came into operation on 1 January 1935 after his wife's death the previous August.

Weekly Times (Melb), 11 May 1895; *Traveller* (Syd), 16 May 1896, 22 May 1897, 26 Mar 1904; *Age*, 29 Apr 1898, 31 May 1927; *Aust Storekeepers & Traders J*, 31 Jan 1911; *Punch* (Melb), 4 Apr 1912; *Argus*, 31 May, 2 June 1927.

ROGER C. THOMPSON

ALDERMAN, WALTER WILLIAM (1874-1935), soldier, was born on 17 February 1874 at Hobart Town, son of William Alderman, railway overseer, and his wife Eliza Miller, née Laurence. When he was 6 the family had moved to Melbourne where he was educated privately – probably by his father, an Englishman fluent in seven languages. He became a picture-framer by trade and in 1892 joined a militia unit, the 2nd Victorian Regiment, as a private. In March 1901 he joined the Australian Military Forces and was appointed to the instructional staff. He was a sergeant when he married Rose May Turner at East Melbourne on 16 March 1905. He was commissioned lieutenant in July 1910.

In November 1913 Alderman went to Auckland for exchange duty with the New Zealand Military Forces. His promotion to captain came in July 1914, and when war broke out he joined the New Zealand Expeditionary Force as adjutant of the 1st Auckland Battalion. His unit sailed with the first Australian convoy, and Alderman was wounded at the landing at Gallipoli on 25 April 1915. He rejoined his battalion in August, was promoted major and was in charge of one of the last detachments to leave Anzac Beach on 20 December. For his services in the Gallipoli campaign he was appointed C.M.G. in June 1916.

On the Western Front Alderman, now lieut-colonel, was given command of the newly formed 2nd Auckland Battalion which went into the Armentières sector in mid-May 1916. He remained in command during intensive trench warfare until late June when he was evacuated in ill health. In July he was mentioned in dispatches. He spent a year in England, briefly serving at New Zealand headquarters and then commanding and training the reserve battalions. He returned in August 1917 to the 1st Auckland Battalion and led it throughout the third Ypres offensive, then headed a school for non-commissioned officers. In March 1918 he commanded his battalion in the Somme region, later acted as brigade commander, and took part in the final Allied offensive in the Amiens-Hazebrouck area. That year he was twice mentioned in dispatches and in December was awarded the Distinguished Service Order.

Alderman's service with the New Zealanders ended on 10 February 1919. He was appointed lieut-colonel in the Australian Imperial Force, returned to Australia in June, was discharged in July, and resumed general instructional duties with the Australian Military Forces, quickly regaining his wartime rank. He served in various staff appointments in Hobart, becoming district base commandant in 1923, and was then transferred to Sydney as assistant adjutant and quartermaster general. His final appointment was to Brisbane where he served as general staff officer, 11th Mixed Brigade, from 1928 until his retirement on 17 February 1934 with the rank of honorary colonel.

Survived by his wife, two daughters and a son, Alderman died of cancer at his Auchenflower home on 24 December 1935 and was cremated. A man of considerable personal charm but a strict disciplinarian when it came to training soldiers, he had excelled at instructional work. The historian of the Auckland Regiment commented on his 'genius for organization' and considered him 'unmatched in the N.Z.E.F.' as a training officer.

F. Waite, *The New Zealanders at Gallipoli*, in *Official history of New Zealand's effort in the great war*, 1, 2 (Well, 1921); H. Stewart, *The New Zealand division, 1916-1919* (Well, 1921); S. S. Allen, *2/Auckland, 1918* (Auckland, 1922); O. E. Burton, *The Auckland Regiment* (Well, 1922); *London Gazette*, 3 June, 11 July 1916, 28 May, 27, 31 Dec 1918; *Reveille* (Syd), Dec 1932, Oct 1936; *Mercury*, 3 June 1916; *Brisbane Courier*, and *Telegraph* (Brisb), 26 Dec 1935.

NEIL GOW

ALEXANDER, FREDERICK MATTHIAS (1869-1955), physiotherapist, was born at Table Cape, north-west Tasmania, on 20 January 1869, son of John Alexander, blacksmith, and his wife Betsy, née Brown. John's father Matthias had suffered transportation for joining the 'Captain Swing' riots of 1830. Frederick attended the local school and was tutored out of hours by his perceptive teacher. He first worked as a clerk at the Mount Bischoff mine, Waratah. Already he felt a lifelong urge for somewhat melodramatic theatre; he revelled in Shakespeare and as a hobby recited ballads to the miners. About 1890 he went to Melbourne, took lessons in acting and began to give public readings. He spent the early

1890s in New Zealand, largely in Auckland, but in 1894 returned to Melbourne.

By then Alexander had turned to teaching stage skills, especially breathing and voice production. Further, he already maintained that correct posture was essential to physical, emotional, and spiritual health. Modern civilization, he came to believe, had caused mankind to get head, neck, and trunk awry. The individual made the disastrous mistake of relying on *feel* of muscular comfort; it was necessary to 'inhibit' such response and to impose 'primary control' on the 'psycho-physical unity'. He never quite succeeded in finding the words to express his meaning; touch, charisma, and exhortation were his media.

In 1899-1904 Alexander worked in Sydney where in December 1903 he publicly argued that his breathing method might cure tuberculosis. He received support from the pediatrician C. P. B. Clubbe [q.v.] and the surgeon (and stage enthusiast) W. J. S. McKay and planned to publish a book. Instead, in 1904 he moved to London and wider fame. Here too his first pupils came from the stage, Henry Irving among them. Alexander's scope was widening, however, as became evident in his first major publication, *Man's supreme inheritance* (1910). This attempted to spell out the ideas which underlay 'the Alexander method'. William James, F. W. H. Myers, and I. P. Pavlov were acknowledged; warmest praise went to R. W. Trine, propounder of 'the New Thought'. This suggests the provenance of Alexander's ideas. He had a modest place among those thinkers of the early twentieth century, inspired especially by Nietzsche and Bergson, who strove to achieve a new, creative intensity of human feeling and performance. The quality of Alexander's intellect, while not contemptible, was limited: his forte was actually to imbue many pupil-patients with this intensity.

From 1914 Alexander also taught regularly in the United States of America and his clients included many eminent people: John Dewey, Aldous Huxley, G. B. Shaw, Gerald Heard, Wesley C. Mitchell, William Temple, Stafford Cripps, Major C. H. Douglas. Dewey adapted Alexander's notions into his writings on education while Huxley presented them in various books, notably *Eyeless in Gaza* and *Island.*

Alexander was only a little affected by this acclaim. He continued to write books expounding his views, but always saw his teaching as a profitable business rather than a cult or subject for academic inquiry. He enjoyed good living and was a fanatic gambler on racehorses. Even some admirers have seen him as akin to the confidence man who really did discover how to make gold

bricks. According to E. Maisel, in 1920 Alexander married a widow, 'an Australian actress' Edith Mary Parsons Young, née Page; they had adopted a daughter; the marriage was unhappy well before Mrs Alexander's death in 1938; and he had a housekeeper-mistress and a natural son by her. From the 1890s Alexander had been assisted by a brother Albert Redden, while later another brother Beaumont was close to him professionally and personally.

During World War II Alexander moved with his school to Massachusetts. Although he remained active into old age, his influence receded after the war. He died in London on 10 October 1955 and was cremated. Interest in him revived strongly in the late 1960s, perhaps prompted by the neo-romanticism of those years refurbishing the notion of expanded consciousness. The most dramatic manifestation came from Professor Nikolaas Tinbergen: accepting the 1973 Nobel Prize in Physiology/Medicine, he said that Alexander's 'story of perceptiveness, of intelligence, and of persistence, shown by a man without medical training, is one of the true epics of medical research and practice'. A secondary literature on Alexander has developed steadily.

E. Maisel, *The Alexander technique* (Lond, 1974); M. Roe, 'F. M. Alexander: a prophet from Australia', *JRAHS*, 60 (1974); N. Tinbergen, 'Ethology and stress diseases', *Science*, 185 (1974).

MICHAEL ROE

ALEXANDER, SAMUEL (1859-1938), philosopher, was born on 6 January 1859 in George Street, Sydney, third son of Samuel Alexander, saddler, who had migrated from London in 1845, and his wife Eliza, née Sloman, from Cape Town. His father died a few weeks after Samuel was born, but left his wife fairly well-to-do. The family moved to St Kilda in Melbourne in 1863 or 1864. Alexander was educated at home by governesses and tutors and at private schools before entering Wesley College in 1871. He won the major scholarships at the school and in 1874 all three exhibitions at the matriculation examinations. A contemporary, Dr Felix Meyer [q.v.], remembered him as being tall, unusually handsome, of charming personality, yet reserved and thoughtful. Late in life, Alexander recalled Wesley as being a very good school, especially for its efficiency and many-sidedness, and its headmaster M. H. Irving [q.v.4], who gave him personal tuition, as 'a remarkable man' whose sixth-form lessons were 'always a delight'.

He began an arts course at the University of Melbourne in 1875, and that year won exhibitions in classics and mathematics, in which he seemed equally talented. In 1876 he was awarded honours in nine arts and science subjects and exhibitions in Greek, Latin and English; mathematics and natural philosophy; and natural science. His mother was persuaded to support an attempt to win a scholarship to Oxford or Cambridge, and in May 1877 Alexander sailed for England. He was awarded a scholarship to Balliol College, Oxford, being placed second to J. W. Mackail, and proceeded to an outstanding first class in *literae humaniores* in 1881. In 1882 Lincoln College elected him to a fellowship, the first held by a professing Jew at either Oxford or Cambridge. In 1893 he became professor of philosophy at the University of Manchester where he remained for the rest of his life.

In 1902 Alexander brought his mother, aunt, two brothers and sister from Melbourne to Manchester. He never returned to Australia, but he retained contact with Irving, and with his school and university friends Meyer and Dr J .W. Springthorpe [q.v.], and was a member of the English committees of advice which recommended appointment of W. R. Boyce Gibson [q.v.] and of his son A. Boyce Gibson to the chair of philosophy in the University of Melbourne in 1911 and 1935.

When Alexander was a student, Oxford philosophy was predominantly idealist, and he was under this influence when he won the Green prize essay in moral philosophy, published as *Moral order and progress* in 1889; but he soon moved away to an approach related to biology and psychology. His other early publications included *Locke* (1908), as brilliant and influential as it was short, articles in *Mind*, and presidential addresses to the Aristotelian Society, mainly on theory of knowledge and on values, which he termed 'tertiary qualities'. In 1916-18 he gave the Gifford Lectures in the University of Glasgow, under the title *Space, time and deity*, published 'with some revisions' in 1920. It was, as he said, 'part of the widely-spread movement towards some form of realism in philosophy'. This major work made him for some time the most famous British philosopher of his day. It was remarked that 'no English writer has produced so grand a system of speculative metaphysics in so grand a manner' since Hobbes's *De Corpore* in 1650. It was also the last such work, for the creation of metaphysical systems went out of fashion. Outside the field of philosophy Alexander gave many light-hearted and beautifully written addresses, notably some on literary figures including Dr Johnson, Jane Austen, Molière and Pascal, posthumously collected as *Philosophical and literary pieces*. His later

philosophical work was mainly on aesthetics. John Anderson [q.v.] and his school at the University of Sydney were strongly influenced by Alexander's realism and naturalism.

Alexander was a left-wing liberal in politics and a staunch supporter of feminism; he was an early advocate of Zionism and a friend of Chaim Weizmann, first president of Israel, whom he introduced to Lord Balfour. Alexander's 'magnificent head, his massive forehead, his patrician Roman-Jewish profile, his patriarchal beard', all contributed to his majestic presence. He was handicapped for much of his life, however, by deafness. He became a Manchester institution: 'his benevolent and distinguished figure in his comfortable academic old clothes, perched on the inseparable bicycle . . . became as familiar and as affectionately legendary as that of Kant taking his punctual walk through the streets of Konigsberg'. In 1913 he was elected a fellow of the British Academy, in 1930 he became the first Australian-born appointee to the Order of Merit, and he received many other honours.

Alexander died unmarried on 13 September 1938. His ashes lie in Manchester Southern cemetery in the section reserved for the British Jewish Reform Congregation. His estate of some £16 000 was left mainly to the University of Manchester. A theatre at Monash University, Melbourne, is named after him; a cast of his bust by Epstein stands in its foyer.

J. A. Passmore, *A hundred years of philosophy* (Lond, 1957); G. Blainey et al, *Wesley College. The first hundred years* (Melb, 1967); Prefatory memoir, S. Alexander, *Philosophical and literary pieces*, J. Laird ed (Lond, 1939), and for bibliog; A. B. Gibson, 'Samuel Alexander: an appreciation', *A'sian J of Psychology and Philosophy*, 16 (1938); H. Munz, 'Professor Samuel Alexander', Aust Jewish Hist Soc, *J*, 1 (1941), pt 6; *Manchester Guardian*, 6 Jan 1959.

ALLAN, JOHN (1866-1936), premier, was born on 27 March 1866 at Chintin near Lancefield, Victoria, seventh child of Andrew Allan, farmer, and his wife Jane, née Kirkpatrick, who were married in 1855 at Galston, Ayrshire, Scotland, before migrating to Australia. In 1873 Andrew selected land to the west of what is now Kyabram. From the late 1870s he led one of the strongest of the early farmers' unions. In 1878 fifty-six Goulburn valley settlers marched down Collins Street, Melbourne, demonstrating for a railway; it was granted in 1883 and Andrew Allan drove the last spike at Kyabram in March 1887. During the 1880s he was president of the North Eastern and Goulburn Valley Agricultural and Pastoral

Society, a water commissioner and prominent in establishing the breakaway Rodney Shire. He was also an active Presbyterian layman.

John Allan successfully established a wheat and dairy farm north of Kyabram at Wyuna South. As a young man he was an enthusiastic cricketer, and was active in the local Caledonian and debating societies: he had a striking, resonant voice and a pleasant bass singing tone. On 10 February 1892 he married Annie Stewart, daughter of a Kyabram farmer.

Allan was a Deakin shire-councillor for many years and president in 1914-15. As a commissioner of the Rodney Irrigation Trust he supported local irrigators, and he was a founding director and later chairman of the Kyabram Butter Factory. During World War I he was prominent in forming the Victorian Farmers' Union and in 1917 was its successful candidate for the Legislative Assembly seat of Rodney; he became the acknowledged leader of the five V.F.U. members.

When Allan entered parliament, politics were volatile, but from March 1918 the (Sir Harry) Lawson [q.v.] ministry was to last for five and a half years. The V.F.U. was faction-ridden: it had been formed from three distinct rural movements with differing political orientations, ranging from the conservatism with which Allan was identified to a radical rural populism characteristic of the Mallee settlers. It needed to capture seats from the Labor Party as well as from the Nationalists, and from the outset resisted close identification with conservative interests. In parliament V.F.U. members rarely sat as a bloc; and even when the party's increase to thirteen members in the 1920 election gave it the balance of power, the lack of cohesion persisted.

By August 1923 Lawson was threatened both by the V.F.U. and a Nationalist faction. On 5 September he submitted his resignation to the governor and, when asked to form another government, made places available for five V.F.U. members and for (Sir) Stanley Argyle [q.v.]. John Allan became deputy premier and chose his group's five ministers. He himself became president of the Board of Land and Works, commissioner for crown lands and survey and minister for immigration.

In choosing to join Lawson, Allan and his team placed themselves at odds with powerful forces within their own party organization and also on an equivocal footing with their cabinet colleagues. The ministry was formed on the basis of an electoral pact between Nationalists and the V.F.U. Although Allan kept a copy of the memorandum setting out this agreement, he never made its contents known beyond, presumably, his V.F.U. colleagues in the ministry, for the very good reason that it would have been repudiated. Lawson left Allan in no doubt that the continuance of the composite ministry depended on strict observance of their agreement. Bitter opposition within the V.F.U. to participation in the government came to a head at its party conference of March 1924, and a split was avoided only by the adoption of a compromise agreement that the composite ministry should end with the parliamentary session. Lawson then acted swiftly: he resigned on 14 March and was commissioned to form an all-Nationalist ministry. However, exhausted, he resigned the premiership in April in favour of Sir Alexander Peacock [q.v.] on the understanding that he would become Speaker; the V.F.U. successfully nominated (Sir) John Bowser [q.v.] against him.

The June 1924 election still left the V.F.U. holding the balance of power. On 16 July the Peacock government was defeated on a Labor no-confidence motion carried by V.F.U. support. They kept a Labor ministry led by G. M. Prendergast [q.v.] in office until November, then reached agreement with the Nationalists on the terms for another composite government. When Prendergast was defeated on 12 November, the governor commissioned Allan as premier.

Allan's accession to the premiership after only seven years as a member of the assembly says much for the political skills he developed in that cockpit of uncertain loyalties. That he had ambition is beyond doubt. One of the Nationalists who held office under him believed that the Lawson-Allan ministry had been almost aborted by Allan's ambition to become premier himself and take office without any form of alliance between Nationalists and V.F.U. He certainly negotiated a tough deal with Peacock in November 1924, for his party was given a disproportionate share of the spoils of office. A contemporary profile of Allan attributed to him 'an astuteness in negotiation that his appearance belies . . . A dull-looking, heavy man, with the lumbering walk of a born rustic, he has deceived many into a belief that he is politically negligible'.

During the Allan-Peacock government, which lasted for two and a half years, both parties to the coalition were torn by internal dissension deriving from decisions of earlier ministries. In May 1924 Peacock had introduced a redistribution bill designed to adjust the city-country ratio to 100:44 and to increase the assembly by three city members. It was opposed by some Nationalists as not going far enough, and by some V.F.U. members as giving too much power to the city, and was defeated. The Prendergast ministry had attempted to catch the farmers' vote and drive a wedge between the V.F.U. and the Nationalists, particularly through a proposed compulsory wheat pool. Labor now attempted to revive the scheme and, as in the past, a handful of V.F.U. members led by (Sir) Albert Dunstan [q.v.] voted with Labor against their colleagues. During the 1925 session the Allan-Peacock government had to sacrifice much of its programme through its dedication to redistribution – a scheme which it had to allow to lapse against Labor's blocking tactics. In 1926, however, the electoral boundaries were redrawn, setting a city-country ratio of 100:47. During the 1926 session alone the government survived eleven defeats, and was saved five times by the Speaker's vote. In September Dunstan launched the breakaway Country Progressive Party, and the V.F.U. became known as the Victorian Country Party at this time.

At the election of 9 April 1927 the Labor Party numbers were unaltered while those of the Nationalists and Country Party were reduced; Dunstan's group won four seats. Various proposals for replacing the coalition with an alternative non-Labor administration came to nothing. Eventually Allan resigned on 13 May and on 20 May the Labor leader E. J. Hogan [q.v.] became premier. In addition to his office as premier, Allan had held the water-supply portfolio, and from 24 August 1926 the responsibilities of minister for railways and vice-president of the Board of Land and Works.

Allan did not sit again on the government front bench until May 1932, and then not as premier. The Hogan ministry had been replaced in November 1928 by the Nationalists led by Sir William McPherson [q.v.] who ignored Allan's offer of a coalition. Hogan led Labor back to office in December 1929. The Victorian Country Party and the Country Progressive Party now settled their differences and, after prolonged negotiations, formed the United Country Party under Allan's leadership but with Dunstan as his deputy. Following an election in May 1932 Argyle formed a United Australia Party ministry which included three Country Party members: Allan, Dunstan and G. L. Goudie. Allan was appointed minister for agriculture and vice-president of the Board of Land and Works, retaining these positions until 20 March 1935, when the Country Party withdrew from the government. Having been displaced from the party leadership in 1933, Allan was by then a waning influence in Country Party counsels, so his bitter opposition to his party's withdrawal counted for little. An all-Country Party ministry led by Dunstan and relying on Labor support took office, but

Allan was excluded. He remained on the back-benches until his death from subacute bacterial endocarditis at Wyuna South on 22 February 1936. He was survived by his wife, four sons and two daughters and, after a state funeral, was buried in Kyabram cemetery. His estate was valued for probate at £22 628.

John Allan stood out as the main conservative influence in the Victorian Country Party. In his eyes the Labor Party was suitable only for being kept out of office, unless Nationalist leaders were proving intractable. Then Labor had its uses as a countervailing force to demonstrate the strength the Country Party could wield through holding the balance of power. Tactics of this kind did not make Allan a popular figure in parliamentary circles, yet he had personal qualities which saved him from the obloquy which was to be Dunstan's portion. 'Honest John' was regarded as a hard fighter but a fair opponent, with a genial, imperturbable disposition and great physical vigour; he was scrupulous in matters of personal honour. He gave the impression of homeliness, but had a shrewdness that his appearance and speech belied. His death was the occasion for a most impressive demonstration of affection by the people of his district.

W. H. Bossence, *Kyabram* (Melb, 1963); H. W. Forster, *Waranga 1865-1965* (Melb, 1965); L. G. Houston, *Ministers of water supply in Victoria* (Melb, 1965); B. D. Graham, *The formation of the Australian Country Parties* (Canb, 1966); F. Howard, *Kent Hughes* (Melb, 1972); *Argus*, 22 Feb 1926; *Table Talk*, 1 Apr 1926; *Age*, 24 Feb 1936; *Aust Worker*, 4 Mar 1936; Eggleston papers (NL).

J. B. PAUL

ALLAN, PERCY (1861-1930), civil engineer, was born on 12 July 1861 in Sydney, son of Maxwell Rennie Allan, later undersecretary, Colonial Secretary's Office, New South Wales, and his wife Frances, née Stubbs, and grandson of David Allan [q.v.1]. Educated at Calder House, Sydney, Percy joined the roads branch, Department of Public Works, as a cadet on 8 September 1878. As a member of the Warrigal Football Club, he toured New Zealand in the 1886 Rugby side and later was a referee. He became assistant draftsman in 1882 and chief draftsman on 5 November 1889. His training by pupilage continued under senior engineers within the department in accordance with the conditions prescribed by the Institution of Civil Engineers, London, although some of his contemporaries were pioneers in academic schools of engineering. Appointed assistant engineer for bridges on 1 January 1895, he was promoted a year later to engineer-in-charge of bridge design. The swing bridges carrying city traffic at Pyrmont and Glebe Island are among the structures standing as monuments to his skill.

In 1900-08 Allan assumed increased responsibility for rivers, artesian bores, water-supply and drainage. His work included supervising the construction of Sydney's sewerage system with ocean outfalls. In 1908-11 he was district engineer at Newcastle, responsible for water-supply and drainage and for the harbour in which he constructed the northern breakwater designed by E. M. de Burgh [q.v.]. He personally designed and built additional coal-loading wharves and cranes. In 1911 he was promoted chief engineer for public works, Newcastle, but next year returned to Sydney as assistant to J. Davis [q.v.], director-general of public works. When railway construction was transferred to the railway commissioners and the position of director-general was abolished, Allan, who had been acting since January 1917, was confirmed on 14 July 1918 as chief engineer, national and local government works, at £1250 a year. When he retired in 1927 his department had designed 583 bridges in his time.

In 1908 at Newcastle Allan was a founder and first president of the Northern Engineering Institute of New South Wales. His lecture with lantern slides, 'The construction of the new Pyrmont bridge', was the first of many contributions to its meetings. He was active also from 1900 as a member of the Institution of Civil Engineers, London, to which he presented four papers: 'Port improvements at Newcastle, New South Wales' (delivered personally in London by Davis and awarded a Telford Premium in 1921), 'Georges River bridge', 'The Wagga Wagga timber bridge, N.S.W.' and 'Pyrmont bridge, Sydney, N.S.W.'. The recorded discussions of these papers in London show a lively interest in the achievements of colonial engineers. Allan remained an honorary member of the Northern Engineering Institute and of its successor, the Newcastle division of the Institution of Engineers, Australia. He was a member of the American Society of Civil Engineers and of the Australasian Pioneers' Club.

At the Roman Catholic Church, Hawthorn, Melbourne, on 11 November 1890 Allan had married Alice Mary, daughter of C. M. Trangmar, farmer. He and his wife were keen golfers. He died of angina and cardiac failure at his home at Double Bay on 7 May 1930 and was buried in the cemetery at South Head. He was survived by his wife and two sons who inherited his estate valued for probate in New South Wales and Victoria at £6158.

Northern Engineering Inst of NSW, *Papers*, 1908-12; Inst of Civil Engineers (Lond), *Procs*, 212 (1920-21); Inst of Engineers (Aust), *J*, Nov 1931; staff records (Dept of Public Works, Syd).

ARTHUR CORBETT

ALLAN, ROBERT MARSHALL (1886-1946), physician and professor of obstetrics, was born on 24 February 1886 at South Brisbane, twin son of James Allan, Scottish-born merchant, and his wife Elizabeth Balloch, née Stark. He was educated at the Brisbane Church of England Grammar School and at Scots College, Sydney, from which he matriculated in 1904. He went on to study medicine at the University of Edinburgh (M.B., Ch.B. Hons, 1910). Attracted to obstetrics and gynaecology, he furthered his experience by working as a resident for six months at the Rotunda Hospital, Dublin, obtaining there the diploma of licentiate of midwifery. He then toured the major European teaching centres, becoming proficient in French and German. He was assistant master of the Rotunda Hospital from November 1911 until August 1914 when he enlisted as a temporary lieutenant in the Royal Army Medical Corps. In December the degree of M.D., with honours, was conferred on him *in absentia* by the University of Edinburgh for a thesis on the action of pituitary extract during labour.

Allan had a distinguished war record. He served in France from October 1914 for fourteen months, was mentioned in dispatches, and then was posted to Mesopotamia where he won the Military Cross. As a captain he was invalided to India with dysentery and then to Queensland, arriving there late in 1916. His letters to his father were published anonymously in Brisbane: *Letters from a young Queenslander* (1915) and *Mesopotamia and India* (1916). In 1917 he was medical superintendent of Brisbane General Hospital and in April 1918 enlisted as a captain in the Australian Imperial Force. *En route* to England he served at Sierra Leone and arrived in London in October. After the Armistice, he gained his F.R.C.S. (Edinburgh), returned to Brisbane late in 1919, and practised there as a specialist in obstetrics and gynaecology until 1925. He was appointed honorary obstetrician to the Lady Bowen Hospital and assistant gynaecologist to the Brisbane General Hospital. He was honorary secretary of the Queensland branch of the British Medical Association, and was a vigorous and efficient honorary coadjutor secretary of the Australasian Medical Congress held in Brisbane in 1920. In July 1923 he was promoted major in the Australian Military

Forces. At St Augustine's Church, Hamilton, on 9 November 1920 he had married Maryanne Eleanor Dines Bracker, daughter of a grazier.

In November 1925 Allan took up a two-year post in Melbourne as director of the Obstetrical Research Committee, set up after an inquiry into the conditions of midwifery in Victoria. He investigated maternal mortality and morbidity, the state of obstetrical practice and related research, and reported in November 1926 and April 1928. His practical approach, keen observations and well-founded recommendations won general approval; the report remains a milestone in the history of obstetrics in Australia.

Allan then began private practice in Melbourne. He was appointed to the honorary staff of the (Royal) Women's Hospital, honorary obstetrician to the Melbourne District Nursing Society and examiner for the Midwives' Board. He became a central councillor of the Victorian Bush Nursing Association to which he gave enthusiastic lifelong service. He was elected fellow of the recently founded College of Surgeons of Australasia (later the Royal Australasian College of Surgeons).

As an immediate result of his report a chair of obstetrics was established in the University of Melbourne. Allan was the obvious choice and was appointed in July 1929; he also became State director of obstetrics. In addition, he was to be available for consultation in difficult cases of confinement at both the Women's and Queen Victoria hospitals. Without delay he toured Britain, Europe and North America to assess progress in his speciality. He began work in Melbourne in 1930 and his influence on undergraduate teaching was immediate. He continually revised his lecture notes, and lengthened the time of training in residence at the Women's Hospital. His teaching was noted for conscientious and careful preparation rather than for dramatic presentation, for he eschewed the flamboyant. He appreciated the need for improvement in care of the new-born and supported the appointment in 1929 of Dr (Dame) Kate Campbell as clinical lecturer in infant welfare. He sought also to improve postgraduate training and in 1932 established at Melbourne the first Australian diploma of obstetrics and gynaecology. In 1933 the university conferred on him the degree of M.D. (*ad eund.*). Next year, on another study trip abroad, he was made an honorary fellow of the American College of Surgeons. In clinical work Allan's strength lay in sound opinion in consultation rather then in technical operative skill. He shared the obstetric side of the Women's Hospital work with senior colleagues in private practice; in gynaecology, his teaching was restricted almost entirely to didactic university lectures. Consistently active in university affairs, in 1944 he was appointed dean of the faculty of medicine.

Allan was a foundation fellow and an enthusiastic supporter of the Royal College of Obstetricians and Gynaecologists (London), and became vice-president, an honour not previously conferred on a member residing outside Britain. He was chairman of the college's Australian reference committee in 1941 and his foresight and endeavour were largely responsible for its high standing in Australia; the standard of preparation which he demanded from candidates from Melbourne became traditional. He held many other offices: honorary secretary and president of the Victorian branch of the B.M.A. in 1937; chairman of the Nurses' Board and of the examiners for its midwifery examination; and chairman of the Federal inquiry in 1944 into the medical aspects of the decline in the birth rate, which resulted in a sterility clinic at the Women's Hospital. He gave several valuable formal lectures, of which the most important were the Listerian Oration to the South Australian branch of the B.M.A. (1927), the Anne MacKenzie Oration (1936) and the presidential address to the Victorian branch of the B.M.A. (1938). He was a lifelong supporter of the Presbyterian Church, an omnivorous reader and a passionate follower of Rugby Union football.

Marshall Allan, as he was known, was no seeker after hollow status. Handsome, 'of well-proportioned build and with twinkling eyes', he had great knowledge and, although at times rigid in his opinions on religion, politics and international affairs, was essentially modest, unpretentious and kindly. After a severe coronary occlusion in 1945 he rested and then gradually resumed full duties, but died on 29 July 1946 after a further episode, and was cremated. He was survived by his wife, a son and a daughter; his estate, valued for probate at £18 001, was left to his wife. He is remembered by the Marshall Allan Prize in obstetrics and by the Marshall Allan Library at the Royal Women's Hospital.

C. E. Sayers, *The Women's* (Melb, 1956); G. Blainey, *A centenary history of the University of Melbourne* (Melb, 1957); F. M. C. Forster, *Progress in obstetrics and gynaecology in Australia* (Syd, 1967); 'Our new professors', *Speculum* (Melb), 126 (1930); *MJA*, 7 Sept 1946; C. Macdonald, 'The Fetherstons and their colleagues', *MJA*, 12 Jan 1957; F. M. C. Forster, 'One hundred years of obstetrical and gynaecological teaching in Victoria', *Aust & NZ J of Obstetrics & Gynaecology*, 6

(1966); L. Townsend, 'Robert Marshall Allan – a man of purpose', *MJA*, 9 Nov 1974; *Age*, 30 July 1946.   FRANK M. C. FORSTER

ALLAN, STELLA MAY (1871-1962), journalist, was born on 25 October 1871 at Kaiapoi, South Island, New Zealand, seventh child of Daniel Henderson, clerk, formerly of Wick, Caithness, Scotland, and his wife Alice, née Connolly, of Adare, Ireland. Scholarships took her to Christchurch Girls' High School, and then to Canterbury University College. She graduated B.A. in 1892 with first-class honours in languages and literature, and M.A. in 1893. Among her contemporaries and lifelong friends were (Baron) Ernest Rutherford and (Sir) George Julius [q.v.]. In 1890-91 she was the first woman in New Zealand to begin a law course, later working for a legal firm while completing her degree. The study of law had always been open to women in New Zealand but its practice was still barred to them and Stella encountered opposition to her work in a law office; her case was one which led to amending legislation in 1896 allowing women to practise as barristers or solicitors. However, on gaining her LL.B. in November 1897 she did not apply for admission to the Bar. Instead, she became the Wellington-based correspondent and leader-writer for the *Lyttleton Times*. Her appointment, the first for a woman, was not welcomed by the all-male Press Gallery, and special permission had to be obtained from a subcommittee of the House before her presence was accepted.

In 1900 at Christchurch Stella married Edwin Frank Allan (d. 1922, aged 54), senior leader-writer for the Wellington *Evening Post*. Widely read and a gifted mathematician, Allan was an Englishman, educated at Westminster School and the University of Oxford; he had been with the British Foreign Service in Peking but had retired because of recurrent malaria. He later became noted for his masterly weekly summary of cables during World War I.

In 1903 Stella Allan came to Australia when her husband was invited to join the staff of the Melbourne *Argus* as foreign affairs leader-writer and parliamentary man. In Melbourne the Allans soon joined a large group of stimulating intellectuals. Alfred Deakin [q.v.] and his wife Pattie were close friends and the two women had a mutual interest in social welfare and women's affairs. Stella Allan continued writing for newspapers and joined the Women Writers' Club, succeeding Ada Cambridge [q.v.3] as president. In 1912 she was a foundation member and later president of the Lyceum Club.

In 1907 the *Argus* commissioned her to write a series of articles on the first Australian Women's Work Exhibition held in October. They aroused much interest and next year the *Argus* invited her to join its full-time staff and begin a weekly section on the particular interests of women. She adopted the *nom de plume* 'Vesta' and called the column 'Women to Women'. Her work was unique in an Australian daily paper at that time. Her pages extended to cover every aspect of women's affairs, children's interests and community welfare, and 'Vesta' became a household word for authoritative information and advice on such matters. An excellent needlewoman and first-rate cook herself, she thoroughly tutored her staff in the work and needs of women in both country and city, as well as providing the usual training for cadet journalists. She conducted interviews and also visited the country to see at first hand the results of bushfires, mouse plagues, droughts and floods. In 1910 she was one of three women foundation members of the Australian Journalists' Association.

Described in her early days as tall, with brown curling hair and rosy complexion, wide-open blue eyes and a 'quiet confidence', Stella Allan had a full family and social life, but she found time to become deeply involved in community affairs. She was an original committee-member of the Victorian Association of Crèches and of the Free Kindergarten Union of Victoria, and had much to do with the early days of the Victorian Bush Nursing Association, the Baby Health Centres Association and the Queen Victoria Hospital. She was a member of the National Council of Women, first in New Zealand and then in Melbourne, and of the Country Women's Association from its inception.

A witty, fluent speaker with a pleasant, well-modulated voice and a direct manner, in 1924 she was appointed substitute delegate for Australia to the fifth assembly of the League of Nations at Geneva and was a delegate to the second Pan Pacific Women's Conference in Hawaii in 1930. A meeting held in the Melbourne Town Hall in 1938 by representatives of all the main Victorian women's organizations paid special tribute to her work and influence. She retired next year to England where she continued to write for the *Argus*, contributing articles on the experiences of women and children in wartime. In 1947 she returned to Melbourne where she lived quietly until her death on 1 March 1962. Cremated with Presbyterian rites, she was survived by three of her four daughters.

In New Zealand, her sister Mrs Elizabeth Reid McCombs (1873-1935) became the first woman member of parliament in 1933, while her brother A. G. Henderson was a distinguished journalist.

J. M. Gillison, *A history of the Lyceum Club* (Melb, 1975); A. A. Wheeler, 'Women's clubs', *Centenary gift book*, F. Fraser and N. Palmer eds (Melb, 1934); *Christchurch Star-Sun*, 2 May, 26 Aug, 16 Oct 1958; *Advertiser* (Adel), 3 Mar 1962; family papers (held by author).

PATRICIA KEEP

ALLARD, SIR GEORGE MASON, (1866-1953), chartered accountant, was born on 28 December 1866 at Brixton, London, son of George Allard, provision merchant, and his wife Kezia, née Thatcher. He was educated at United Westminster Grammar School, then joined the London staff of the Australian Joint Stock Bank. He arrived in Sydney in 1888 and remained with the bank until 1895. On 18 March at St John's Church of England, Ashfield, he married a widow Emma Victoria Oliver, née Conves; they visited England that year.

On their return in 1896, Allard began practice as a public accountant and remained independent until 1920. From 1899 he was secretary of the Institute of Bankers of New South Wales and editor of its *Journal* for many years. He was also secretary of the Sydney banks' clearing house. Registrar of the council of the Corporation of Accountants of Australia from 1903, in 1909 he became a councillor (and later vice-president) of the new Australasian Corporation of Public Accountants. From 1914 he lectured on banking practice in the department of economics and commerce at the University of Sydney. During World War I he was honorary treasurer of the Citizens' War Chest Fund for the New South Wales division of the Australian Comforts Fund and chairman of the citizens' committee of the Red Triangle Fund.

In 1917 Allard was appointed royal commissioner to inquire into the working of the public service of New South Wales. In 1918-20 he presented reports to the government on the administration and efficiency of the Public Service Board, the Department of Lands, and the Department of Works including Walsh Island Dockyard, Newcastle; on the State trawling industry and other government industrial undertakings; on the administration of Acts relating to state children; and on retrenchment of officers in the Metropolitan Board of Water Supply and Sewerage.

In 1920 Allard had joined Yarwood Vane & Co. and the firm's name was changed to Yarwood Vane & Co. with G. Mason Allard. In 1923 he and the firm were commissioned by the Commonwealth government to report on expropriated properties and businesses in New Guinea. One of three government-nominated directors of Amalgamated Wireless Australasia Ltd, he was chairman in 1922-31 and with (Sir) Ernest Fisk [q.v.] visited Britain and Canada in connexion with the establishment of the beam wireless service between Great Britain, Canada and Australia. From the 1920s he was for many years chairman of directors of Beard Watson & Co. Ltd and Sargood Gardiner Ltd. He was knighted in 1926, was a councillor of the Sydney Chamber of Commerce, and in 1933-34 was one of a large committee to inquire into the system of examinations and secondary school courses. Following the incorporation by royal charter in 1928 of the Institute of Chartered Accountants in Australia, Allard was a vice-president until 1932, president in 1932-41 and councillor until 1948; he was also chairman of its New South Wales council in 1928-32 and a councillor until 1953. Keenly interested in shaping the affairs of the organizations to which he belonged, he had a profound influence on the accountancy profession and wide impact on the business and banking world. A reticent man, he took care in speaking and writing to ensure that his words carried precise meaning. He had a sense of humour, 'a keen and subtle understanding', and 'a natural courtesy . . . with a capacity for hard work'.

A member of the Union Club from 1917 and of the Royal Australian Historical Society, Allard lived for many years at Wahroonga, and enjoyed golf, boating and motoring. He died on 1 May 1953 and was cremated at Northern Suburbs. Predeceased by his wife in 1952, he was survived by a son and a daughter. His estate was valued for probate at £45 294.

Commerce (Syd), 1 July 1930; *SMH*, 2 May 1953; History of the Institute and earlier accountancy bodies (Institute of Chartered Accountants in Australia, Syd).

A. B. CLELAND

ALLARDYCE, SIR WILLIAM LAMOND (1861-1930), governor, was born on 14 November 1861 at Bombay, India, son of Colonel James Allardyce, military surgeon, and his wife Georgina Dickson, née Abbott. After education at the gymnasium school, Aberdeen, Scotland, and Oxford Military College, England, in 1879 he was appointed clerk and interpreter in the Provincial Department in Fiji and, in 1882, stipendiary magistrate. Rapid promotion to senior posts followed: appointed colonial secretary in July 1902, that year he acted for two months as governor and was appointed C.M.G. A member of the legislative and executive councils, he was an efficient, tough-minded administrator and upholder of the native policy of Sir Arthur Gordon and Sir John Thurston. With 'a profound insight into Fijians' and expert in their language, he edited the first official newspaper in Fijian. Allardyce was governor of the Falkland Islands in 1904-14. He was active in establishing a profitable whaling industry, but was concerned about conserving resources. To reduce isolation, he worked towards the establishment in November 1912 of a radio station. Governor of the Bahamas in 1915-20, he was promoted K.C.M.G. in 1916.

In 1895 at Bacchus Marsh, Victoria, he had married Constance Angel (d. 1919), daughter of Molesworth Greene [q.v.4]. In 1920 he married a widow Elsie Elizabeth Goodfellow, née Stewart. On 16 April Allardyce became governor of Tasmania, at a time when that office was under question. In September a Labor Party motion for its abolition was defeated in the House of Assembly on the Speaker's vote. Next February Allardyce complained to the colonial secretary about the inadequacy of his salary of £2750; in August he was told by the premier W. H. Lee [q.v.] that there was not the 'remotest possibility' of the assembly agreeing to an increase in his salary or allowances. No longer able to afford to hold office, Allardyce decided to take three months leave before retiring, and asked that the governor's remuneration and allowances be the subject of a statement in parliament. On 30 November 1921 that statement was followed by a successful motion in the assembly for the abolition of the office of governor, though a week later the Legislative Council rejected a similar motion.

Praised, even by those opposed to future appointment of State governors, for the expert and whole-hearted way in which they had carried out their duties, the Allardyces left Tasmania on 27 January 1922. He was governor of Newfoundland in 1922-28, and in 1927 was promoted G.C.M.G. He retired in 1928 and during the next year was a director of the Viking Whaling Co. Ltd, an Anglo-Norwegian venture. Survived by his wife and by the two daughters of his first marriage, he died of cancer on 9 June 1930 at Wokingham, Berkshire, England.

V&P (HA Tas), 1920, 54, 1921, 166, (LC Tas), 1921, 59; Great Britain: Dominion Office and Colonial Office List, 1930; Mercury, 21 Jan 1920, 24, 25, 27 Jan 1922, 11 June 1930; Examiner (Launc), 2 Dec 1921, 25, 27 Jan 1922, 11 June 1930; World (Hob), 19-21, 24 Jan 1922; papers (Scott Polar Research Inst, Cambridge Univ, Eng); private papers (held by Mrs A. Jennings, Hob); official records (National Archives of Fiji, Suva); GO 34/2 (TA); Premier's Dept, 1/350/110, 1/365/110, 1/373/110 (TA); information from Hon. Philip A. Snow, Sussex, Eng.   E. A. McLEOD

ALLEN, GEORGE THOMAS (1852-1940), public servant, was born on 23 August 1852 at Geelong, Victoria, son of Thomas Watts Allen, bootmaker, and his wife Esther Elizabeth, née Odell, and elder brother of (Sir) Harry Brookes Allen [q.v.]. Educated at Flinders National School, Geelong, in 1868 he completed first year of an arts-law course at the University of Melbourne. He joined the Victorian Treasury as a clerk in December 1871 and by 1895 had risen to the position of accountant to the Treasury.

In 1901 Sir George Turner [q.v.], establishing the Commonwealth Treasury, chose Allen to be its first secretary; with J. R. Collins [q.v.] as assistant, he formed the department and settled methods of collecting revenue. Allen's permanence during the political instability of the first decade of the Commonwealth was of importance to the financial management of Australia. He had a leading hand in the budget speeches delivered during his term of office, and was 'the buttress and the support, the tutor and the guide' of all the early treasurers. Melbourne Punch in 1909 described him as a modest man and a formalist, 'a model of respectful studied politeness. His figure and his manner are straight and stiff as a ramrod'. He helped to draft the Act establishing the Commonwealth Bank in 1911, and was considered for the post of first governor of the bank, subsequently taken by (Sir) Denison Miller [q.v.]. Allen attended the 1911 Imperial Conference as an adviser to Prime Minister Andrew Fisher [q.v.]. In 1909 he had been appointed commissioner for pensions under the Old Age Pensions Act; next year invalid pensions were added to his duties and in 1912 he was made commissioner under the Maternity Allowance Act.

In 1910 Allen had acquired new duties under the Australian Notes Act, and his signature appeared on the new currency notes. In 1913 the Melbourne Herald commented that, though his methods were unobtrusive and his disposition retiring, 'his power in federal finance was something to be reckoned with'. Awarded the Imperial Service Order in 1903, he was appointed C.M.G. in 1913.

Allen retired on 14 March 1916. His chief interests were music and gardening; for many years he was treasurer of the Church of England home for boys at Canterbury,

Victoria. Leaving an estate sworn for probate at £15 670, he died, unmarried, on 20 April 1940 at his home in Kew, and was buried in the local cemetery.

L. F. Fitzhardinge, *William Morris Hughes, a political biography*, 1 (Syd, 1964); *Punch* (Melb), 16 Sept 1909; *Herald* (Melb), 24 July 1926, 22 Apr 1940; *Age*, 22 Apr 1940.   CHRIS CUNNEEN

ALLEN, SIR HARRY BROOKES (1854-1926), pathologist and medical administrator, was born on 13 June 1854 at Corio Terrace, Geelong, Victoria, second son of Thomas Watts Allen, bootmaker, and his wife Esther Elizabeth, née Odell, and younger brother of G. T. Allen [q.v.]. He was educated at Flinders School, Geelong, and in 1869-70 at Melbourne Church of England Grammar School where he showed unusual brilliance. He had passed the examination for the Civil Service of Victoria when 12. In 1871 he entered the medical course at the University of Melbourne where he topped the class every year and graduated M.B. in 1876 with first-class honours. He was then appointed demonstrator in anatomy, pathologist to the Melbourne Hospital and sub-conservator of the museum of anatomy and pathology, thus settling at once his future career.

In 1878 he obtained his M.D. and next year the recently introduced degree of B.S. He was honorary secretary of the Medical Society of Victoria in 1879-87 and in 1879-83 edited the *Australian Medical Journal*. While Professor G. B. Halford [q.v.4] was in England in 1880, Allen lectured in anatomy, physiology and pathology. Appointed lecturer in anatomy and pathology next year, he prepared with Halford a report on the medical school which recommended a new chair. This was accepted in 1882 when Allen was appointed professor of descriptive and surgical anatomy and pathology, while Halford retained physiology. Allen served as dean of the faculty of medicine in 1886-90 and 1896-1924.

His administrative skills were sought by bodies outside the university, particularly the government. In 1883-84 he was a member of the Central Board of Health and the board of inquiry on tuberculosis in cattle. He was chairman from 1888 of the royal commission on the sanitary state of Melbourne: three reports condemned in the strongest language the scandalous state of Melbourne's sanitary arrangements, and led to the Public Health Act of 1889, the Mansergh [q.v.5] report and the introduction of a water-borne sewage system. In 1888 Allen was also chairman of the intercolonial royal commission into schemes for extermination of rabbits in Australasia. Next year he was general secretary of the Intercolonial Medical Congress. In 1890 he visited Britain and Europe where he studied advances being made in pathology and the relatively new science of bacteriology. He secured recognition of Melbourne medical degrees by the General Council of Medical Education and Registration and was the first Australian graduate to be registered in Britain.

Returning to Melbourne in February 1891, Allen inaugurated the study of bacteriology under Thomas Cherry [q.v.]. He also presented to the Victorian government reports on information he had gained while abroad. The most substantial was on hospital construction and management, while other subjects included the recognition of Melbourne medical degrees, sewerage, the metropolitan water-supply, isolation of infectious diseases and establishment of an institute of preventive medicine.

On the voyage back to Australia Allen had met Ada Rosalie Elizabeth Mason, some eight years his junior, who was travelling with the countess of Jersey as governess to her daughters. On 11 November 1891, with vice-regal blessing, they were married at Sutton Forest, Moss Vale, New South Wales. They had three daughters: Edith Margaret, a journalist, who worked on the *Argus* and *Australasian* but was best known for her cooking notes in the *Herald* under the pseudonym 'Sarah Dunne'; Mary Cecil [q.v.]; and Beatrice (Biddy), a musician.

Allen was elected to the Council of the University of Melbourne in 1898, filling the vacancy left by the death of Sir Anthony Brownless [q.v.3]. By 1906 it was possible to reduce his teaching load: R. J. A. Berry [q.v.] was appointed professor of anatomy and Allen became professor of pathology; the chair of physiology had already been filled by W. A. Osborne [q.v.]. In that year Allen drew up the deed of union between the Medical Society of Victoria and the Victorian branch of the British Medical Association, becoming president of the combined body in 1907. He was active in negotiating for establishment of an Australian Institute of Tropical Medicine which was opened in Townsville in 1909 under Anton Breinl [q.v.]. The eighth session of the Australasian Medical Congress was held in 1908 with Allen as president. For part of 1912 and 1913 he was overseas as a member of the executive committee of the 16th International Medical Congress, London. While in Britain he was admitted to the honorary degree of LL.D., University of Edinburgh.

In 1912-15 Allen was deeply involved in

establishing the Walter and Eliza Hall [qq.v.] Institute. He approached the trustees of the W. and E. Hall Trust Fund with plans for a centre of preventive medicine, but R. G. Casey [q.v.3], one of the trustees, was more interested in general medical research. Negotiations between the trustees, Allen and the Melbourne Hospital were eventually completed by March 1915 when the institute was formed.

In 1914 the medical school celebrated its jubilee and in the New Year honours Allen was knighted. The profession presented him with his portrait by E. Phillips Fox [q.v.]; this was destroyed in the Wilson Hall fire in 1952 but a replica by his daughter Mary Cecil was hung in the pathology department. Late in 1914 he received an honorary LL.D. from the University of Adelaide.

From the early 1900s Allen gradually withdrew from commitments outside the university. By 1923 his health had begun to fail and after a succession of strokes he resigned his chair in 1924 and died on 28 March 1926. He was buried in the Melbourne general cemetery and was survived by his wife and daughters. He left his estate, valued for probate at £5939, to his wife. Lady Allen died in England on 12 December 1933. During World War I she had been very active on Red Cross committees and had organized the Army Nurses' Club. She was a founder of the Victoria League in Melbourne and was interested in the movement to establish a women's college at the university. A devout Anglican, she was president of the Mothers' Union in Melbourne in 1918-33.

Allen was an excellent pathologist and an able teacher who adopted a highly practical approach to the teaching of his subject, essentially based on post-mortem examination and study of the specimens so obtained. In his lifetime he built up a remarkable museum in his department containing some 15 000 specimens, most of which he mounted and described himself. It was, however, his quite outstanding administrative ability which placed him before the medical and lay public and gave him a unique position in medical politics. Aided by a remarkably good memory, he had the facility of being able to digest all the facts about some problem or discussion, read all related references and documents and prepare admirably succinct but complete memoranda.

Because of his ability, faculty left administration of the medical school largely in his hands. Once it was functioning to his liking he did not initiate or encourage changes. He developed the school on the firm basis laid down by Brownless and came to regard it as his personal responsibility. Both men made outstanding contributions to medical education at the university.

Tall and bearded with a commanding, almost imperious presence, Allen appeared aloof, even gruff, to his students. This aloofness masked an inherent shyness, for he had a deep interest in the students and kept notes on their later careers, particularly those who enlisted in World War I. His plans for expansion of the school to cope with the large numbers returning from active service were detailed and comprehensive and were completed and carried out before the close of hostilities. Always precise in his speech, he frowned on unusual idiom and colloquial phrases, for in all he did he strove for perfection. He was not an exciting lecturer, his voice was calm and monotonous and he seldom showed emotion; prepared notes were issued to students and references given for additional reading. His teaching was soundly based and closely related to the specimens in the museum.

To those interested in pathology he could be friendly and helpful and he inspired many whom he trained. He had fixed ideas and was intolerant of rebels. His staff received little encouragement to do research and he did none himself, yet good work was done in his department by devoted colleagues. He could be arbitrary and sometimes harsh to those he disliked, and in committee he was often severe and sometimes dictatorial. He made comparatively few close friends. Apart from his work, which to him was all-absorbing, he was fond of good literature and music, interested in art, a keen philatelist and, perhaps rather surprising to those who did not know him, wrote verse. His poem 'Australia's dead; Alma Mater and the war', first published in *Speculum*, the student magazine, was later included in an anthology of Australian verse. Although no athlete, he was a strong swimmer and enjoyed walking. Another side of his character is seen in his many carefully concealed acts of charity.

Allen wrote few scientific papers, but his notes for students were issued in book form in 1919. The bulk of his writing is seen in his presidential and other addresses and in the voluminous reports and memoranda he prepared for the government and the university.

Univ Melb Medical School Jubilee (Melb, 1914); K. F. Russell, *The Melbourne Medical School 1862-1962* (Melb, 1977); R. Cameron, 'Recollections of Sir Harry Brookes Allen', *The Melbourne School of Pathology* (Melb, 1962); *MJA*, 10 Apr 1926; *Lancet*, 1926, no 1; E. S. J. King, 'The story of the Melbourne School of Pathology', *MJA*, 28 July 1951; 'People we know', *Punch* (Melb), 22 Oct 1908; *Argus*, 29 Mar 1926; Allen papers (Univ Melb, Archives *and* Dept of Medical History).

K. F. RUSSELL

ALLEN, JOSEPH FRANCIS (1869-1933), architect, civil engineer and politician, was born on 6 August 1869 at Mount Perranzabuloe, Cornwall, England, son of William Allen, carpenter, and his wife Salome, née Williams. When 10 he came to Parramatta, New South Wales, with his parents, and in 1884 was articled to the Sydney architect Gordon Mackinnon. He then worked for Rhodes & Co., civil engineers, and from 1894 managed the workshops of Henry Simon & Co., milling engineers. In 1896 he moved to Western Australia where, after working as an assistant engineer on the Fremantle harbour works, he commenced private practice as an architect with Allen & Nicholas in 1898. His works included the East Fremantle Town Hall, Fremantle Trades Hall and Geraldton flour mills, as well as the *Westralian*, the first steel ship built in Western Australia. On 25 September 1900 he married Jean Symington Buntine.

In 1903 Allen won a seat on the East Fremantle Council and held it, but for one year, until his death. He served as mayor in 1909-14 and became property-owners' representative on the East Fremantle Tramways Board and a member of the board of the Fremantle Public Hospital.

After an unsuccessful attempt in 1912, Allen entered State parliament in 1914 as a Liberal member for the West Province of the Legislative Council, defeating W. Somerville [q.v.] by eight votes after a recount. In 1918 he attacked the National Coalition government over an agreement for the right to construct wheat-handling equipment. The validating bill was defeated but Allen was said to have admitted representing his former employer Henry Simon & Co. He became chairman of committees in the council in August 1919 but was defeated in the 1920 election. Henceforth his political influence was to be exclusively outside parliament. He stood unsuccessfully for Fremantle in the assembly in 1921, for the Senate in 1922 and for the West Province of the council in 1923.

Early in 1921 Allen became chairman of the West Australian divisional council of the Australian National Federation. This included three constituent bodies — the Liberal League, the National Federation and the National Labor Party; the first two amalgamated to form the National League with Allen as founding president. He retained the position after the league absorbed other groups in December 1924 to form the United Party.

Allen tried often to conclude election pacts with both State and Federal Country parties. His task was complicated by Country Party disunity and the opposition of some leading Nationalist members who ad-vocated amalgamation or active competition — the policy of 'fuse or fight'. They probably nullified his attempt to negotiate a joint National-Country Party Senate ticket in 1922; his success in so doing in 1925 was due to pressure from Federal leaders and financial backers. In 1926 he was opposed again when he sought a pact for the Legislative Council election. When the party repudiated him publicly, he resigned as president in March with two other senior executive members.

Allen remained prominent in public affairs. In 1928 he became chairman of the Rottnest Island Board of which he was a foundation member in 1917, and in 1931 he was elected mayor of East Fremantle for the second time. He also held office in the Fremantle Municipal Tramways and Electric Lighting Board, Fremantle Chamber of Commerce (president in 1921-25 and 1933), the Royal Institute of Architects and the local Rotary club. Throughout his life in Western Australia he was active in Presbyterian and Masonic affairs. He died suddenly on 23 May 1933: his body was found in the Swan River near his home; the coroner found no suspicious circumstances. Survived by a daughter, he was buried in the Presbyterian section of the Fremantle cemetery.

J. S. Battye (ed), *Cyclopedia of Western Australia*, 1 (Adel, 1913); *West Australian*, 19 May 1914, 10, 12, 23 Mar 1926, 24, 25 May 1933; D. W. Black, The National Party in Western Australia, 1917-1930: its origins and development with an introductory survey of 'Liberal' Party organisation, 1901-1916 (M.A. thesis, Univ WA, 1974).

DAVID BLACK

ALLEN, LESLIE HOLDSWORTH (1879-1964) and SIR CARLETON KEMP (1887-1966), scholars, were sons of Rev. William Allen (1847-1919) and his wife Martha Jane, née Holdsworth, a teacher. William, whose father was a contractor, migrated to Melbourne in 1852, was educated at Scotch College and trained at the Congregational College of Victoria. In 1871-90 he held pastoral appointments at Sandhurst (Bendigo), Maryborough and Carlton, and in 1885-86 was chairman of the Congregational Union and Mission of Victoria. He was joint-editor for a time of the *Victorian Independent*, published *Random rhymes* (Melbourne, 1886), had a prize-winning cantata performed at the Centennial International Exhibition, and wrote a national anthem, 'God save our austral land', later sung in Queensland schools. In 1890 he moved to Petersham, New South Wales, became a prominent evangelical and ecumenical spokesman in Sydney, and was chairman of the New South Wales Congregational Union in 1894-95. He served at Greenwich from 1908 to 1917 when he retired. He was strongly opposed to the theatre, which several of his four sons and two daughters adopted as an engrossing hobby.

Leslie was born on 21 June 1879 at Maryborough, was educated at state schools and Newington College, Sydney, then studied English and classics at the University of Sydney (B.A., 1904; M.A., 1920). He won a travelling scholarship, and at the University of Leipzig completed in 1907 a doctoral dissertation on the personality of Shelley. After his return to Sydney he lectured part time at the university until appointment in 1911 as senior lecturer in classics and English at the Teachers' College.

On 22 December 1915 at Chatswood, Allen married Dora Bavin, a New Zealander. She was tubercular, and this led him to seek a post in the hills: in 1918 he became professor of English at the Royal Military College, Duntroon. His work was undemanding and allowed him to pursue his wide cultural interests. A friend of (Sir) Lionel Lindsay and an early admirer of Roland Wakelin [qq.v.], he collected works by Australian painters. He produced several plays at Duntroon and for the Canberra Society of Arts and Literature. He published a wide range of scholarly articles, translated German plays for Dent's Everyman's Library, and wrote several volumes of poetry and a book of children's verses.

In 1931 Allen accepted the congenial post of sole lecturer in English and classics at the new Canberra University College. Next year his wife died; their only son had died in childhood. He became a member of the Commonwealth Book Censorship Advisory Committee in 1933, and chaired the Literature Censorship Board from 1937 and later its appeals committee. He died at Moruya, New South Wales, on 5 January 1964, survived by his only daughter. The Haydon-Allen building at the Australian National University is in part named after him. He had made a notable contribution to the cultural life of early Canberra.

Carleton, or 'C.K.' as he came to be known, was born on 7 September 1887 at Carlton, Melbourne. He was 3 when the family moved to Sydney, and was educated at Newington College and the University of Sydney (B.A., 1910) where he read classics and won a scholarship to Oxford. At New College he studied jurisprudence under Vinogradoff,

took first-class honours in 1912 and was elected Eldon Law Scholar in 1913.

Allen was a captain in the 13th Battalion, Middlesex Regiment, in World War I, was wounded, and was awarded the Military Cross in 1918. Elected Stowell Civil Law Fellow of University College, Oxford, in 1920, he remained a fellow of the college in one capacity or another for the rest of his life. In 1926 he spent a year as Tagore professor at the University of Calcutta and published his lectures there as *Law in the making* in 1927; it became an established classic and he completed a seventh edition in 1964. In 1929 he was appointed professor of jurisprudence at Oxford, but in 1931 became the second warden of Rhodes House. He filled this office with great distinction and he and his wife Dorothy Frances, née Halford, whom he had married at Oxford in 1922, won the affection and respect of generations of Rhodes scholars.

Allen wrote in a lucid and lively manner and was always interesting; his depth of scholarship could elude the superficial reader. He expressed his individualist philosophy in *Bureaucracy triumphant* (1931); other works included *Law and orders* (1945), *The Queen's peace* (1953), *Law and disorders* (1954) and *Aspects of justice* (1958); he also wrote two novels. On his retirement in 1952 he was knighted; he had been elected to the British Academy and appointed K.C. in 1945.

'C.K.' had been a keen amateur actor and cricketer. He was stalwart in appearance, despite a weak heart, with thick white hair and a neat moustache. He died at Oxford on 11 December 1966 and was survived by his second wife, Hilda Mary Grose, whom he had married in 1962, and by a son and daughter of his first marriage. His portrait by James Gunn is in Rhodes House.

Their elder brother HORACE WILLIAM ('Barney') was born at Maryborough on 31 January 1875, was educated in Melbourne at Scotch and Haileybury colleges and the University of Melbourne, where he took honours in classics with T. G. Tucker [q.v.], and graduated B.A. in 1896 and M.A. in 1898. He tutored in classics from 1897 at Ormond College, University of Melbourne, of which he was vice-master under D. K. Picken [q.v.] from 1915 until his retirement in 1944. Allen was an inspiring and lively teacher; his wit was delightful and never palled. He enlisted in the Australian Imperial Force in 1917, became an honorary captain in the Education Service in 1919, and compiled his university's *Record of active service 1914-18* (1926). He was president of the Classical Association of Victoria for many years and a keen fly-fisher and ice-skater. He died, unmarried, on 13 August 1949 at Frankston.

A. Sutherland et al, *Victoria and its metropolis*, 2 (Melb, 1888); G. E. Hall and A. Cousins (eds), *Book of remembrance 1914-1918* (Syd, 1939); Congregational Union NSW, *Yearbook*, 1919, 1920; *Aust Christian World* (Syd), 4 July 1919; *Congregationalist* (Syd), 1 Aug 1919; *T&CJ*, 27 Oct 1894; *SMH*, 25 June 1919; *Spinner*, 1 Sept 1925; *Age*, 15 Aug 1949; *Canb Times*, 7 Jan 1964; *The Times*, 12 Dec 1966; family papers (held by Miss J. Allen, Griffith, ACT).   K. C. WHEARE

ALLEN, MARY CECIL (1893-1962), artist, writer and lecturer on art, known in the United States of America as Cecil Allen, was born on 2 September 1893 in Melbourne, second daughter of Professor (Sir) Harry Brookes Allen [q.v.] and his wife Ada, née Mason. Mary Cecil and her sisters Edith Margaret and Beatrice (Biddy) were born and brought up on the campus of the University of Melbourne in one of the houses provided for professors; they were educated by governesses, their parents, a fine library and travel. At May Vale's art class for children her work 'surpassed all others'.

In 1910 Mary Cecil qualified for entrance to the faculty of arts at the university, but she preferred the Art School of the National Gallery of Victoria. Her course there, begun in 1910, was interrupted when in 1912-13 she went with her family to England, where she attended the Slade School of Fine Art. Back in Melbourne, this experience and her intellectual gifts made both her and her work conspicuous at the gallery school in 1913-16. A rapid-fire of words expressing ideas and theories in light and lilting cadences attracted a circle each morning until Mary Cecil bade them begone: 'We must work'. She became successful as a painter of portraits and landscape, and especially as a lecturer on art. Study of tonal impressionism with Max Meldrum [q.v.] in 1922 changed her vision and style.

Florence Gillies, an American visitor to Melbourne, was so impressed with Mary Cecil's lectures that she engaged her as a guide to European galleries; they left Australia in January 1926. After eight months, chiefly in Paris, she was invited to lecture in New York and thenceforth made her home in the United States. The Metropolitan Museum, Columbia University and many other institutions appreciated her gifts. 'She was able to increase one's ability to comprehend visually what had previously been puzzling', Marion Scott has commented. 'She did this by using words with great economy, words which were so lucid that they created no barrier between one's eyes and the work of Art'. Mary Cecil had golden hair, intensely blue eyes, and a good figure which she never lost. Not beautiful, she was often described as distinguished, graceful, vital, unforgettable.

In 1930 she arranged the first New York exhibition by Australian artists, at the Roerich Museum, New York City. The exhibition, opened in February 1931, attracted large attendances and much interest. She lectured with it, on tour.

In August 1935 she visited Melbourne until June 1936; the years since Mary Cecil's departure had seen little change in Melbourne's art but much in hers. Her exhibition at Gill's Gallery aroused a storm of protest; only loyal friends bought pictures, later confessing that they would not dare hang them at home. However, she lectured, led discussion groups; in teaching serious full-time studio painting and *plein air* landscapes she gave participants an understanding which acted as a ferment to local slow-moving conservatism. Only in the Bell and Shore [qq.v.] drawing school did she find full appreciation.

Mary Cecil visited Australia again from January to September 1950, when she held an exhibition at Georges Gallery with good sales, and also from November 1959 to April 1960 when only one painting was left unsold after her exhibition at Australian Galleries. All these pictures were conceived and painted in the United States and brought with her. On both visits she lectured to capacity audiences. She also made sketches with elaborate written notes of colour and terrain; subjects included Alice Springs, Coober Pedy opal-mines, sheep-stations, Wilson's Promontory and mountain forests. Translated into pictures they sold well in the United States, but Australia acquired none of them.

From 1950 Mary Cecil lived and worked in the art colony of Provincetown, Massachusetts. In New York she had taught art at a famous private girls' school in 1930-44 and had her own art school in 1941-45. She held shows at the Roerich Museum, Delphic Gallery and American-British Art Centre, New York, and exhibited with group-shows at the Metropolitan and Brooklyn museums and elsewhere. She lectured to many academic institutions, clubs and societies in New York and New England.

Mary Cecil Allen died at Provincetown on 7 April 1962. Neighbours who called to take her to early morning Communion at the Anglican Church found her seated in a chair — dead. Her death was recorded as 'sinus arrest, cause unknown'. Although still an Australian citizen, she was buried at her sisters' request in the Provincetown cemetery in sight of the Pilgrim Monument.

In 1962, the Lyceum Club, Melbourne, held a memorial exhibition. In 1963 a Mary Cecil Allen Memorial Lecture was established by the Art Teachers' Association of Victoria. Her publications include *The mirror of the passing world* (New York, 1928) and *Painters of the modern mind* (New York, 1929).

Woman's World, 1 Feb 1927; *Age*, 14 Apr 1962; MS of book on M. C. Allen by Maie Casey, Frances Derham, et al (held by Mrs F. Derham, Kew, Vic).
FRANCES A. M. L. DERHAM

ALLUM, MAHOMET (1858?-1964), camel-driver, herbalist and philanthropist, was born in Kandahar, Afghanistan. Selling Arab horses and camels to the British Army enabled him to travel through Asia; he probably arrived in Australia between 1884 and 1890. He worked with camels, delivering supplies and provisions to inland townships and stations, and also as a station-hand, butcher, storekeeper, sailor and mine-hand. He was in both Broken Hill and Western Australia for some years and is known to have been in Kalgoorlie in 1903.

In 1928 or 1929 he settled in Adelaide, at a time when dissatisfaction with conventional medical practitioners was enabling herbalists and faith-healers to flourish. Allum lived in Adelaide for most of his remaining life, dispensing herbal mixtures and advice from his house in Sturt Street, asking no payment but accepting donations and giving freely to charities. He claimed that the gift of healing had been handed down in his family for 400 years and referred to himself as 'God's messenger'.

In 1935 he was charged with having posed as a medical practitioner while not registered under the Medical Practitioners Act. He marshalled over forty witnesses to attest that he had never represented himself as a doctor. The crown prosecutor described him as a 'quack', a particularly cunning, very shrewd and deceitful Afghan whose pose of humility and cloak of piety were not congruous with his appearance and his 'vindictive methods' against the medical profession, whose members Allum described as 'devil's agents who have made their money their God'. He was convicted and fined, but the publicity brought more customers. Allum was in court again in 1936 for the alleged publication of scandalous material about a police magistrate, but managed to evade conviction.

His dyed hair, swarthy skin and dark piercing eyes, his showy jewellery, love of publicity, and the devotion of his followers, all made him a controversial and memorable figure. In 1934, when he visited Afghanistan, 10 000 people had petitioned him to remain in Adelaide. His popularity, healing powers and charity were attested to by his patients (and himself) in published testimonials, including many advertisements in the *South Australian Police Journal*, and in a 32-page pamphlet he published.

Allum married in 1940, with Moslem rites, Jean Emsley, a patient; next year, when he was about 83 and his wife 20, a daughter was born. In 1953 the family travelled to Afghanistan, intending to remain. His wife died, and Allum returned in 1954 with his daughter to Adelaide, where he resumed practice as a herbalist.

A devout Moslem, Allum never learned to read or write English but, aided by his wife and friends, he wrote letters to the press and published at least fifteen pamphlets: on Islam, the Koran, illness and his healing powers. He died on 21 March 1964 at his large home at Everard Park; he was commonly stated to have been 108, but the entry on his death certificate was 106. The funeral procession from the mosque to the Centennial Park cemetery was over a mile long. Allum's estate, sworn for probate at £11 218, was nearly all willed to institutions which cared for children.

M. Brunato, *Hanji Mahomet Allum* (Leabrook, SA, 1972); *SA Police J*, 24 Jan, 26 Feb, 23 Mar, 24 June, 22 Aug, 25 Sept, 25 Nov 1935; *News* (Adel), 8, 27 Nov, 3, 5 Dec 1935, 23 Mar 1964, 13 Jan 1965; *Advertiser* (Adel), 9, 29 Nov, 4, 6 Dec 1935, 23 Jan 1936, 6, 13 July 1937, 24 Jan 1953, 15 May, 20, 21 Sept 1954, 8 Oct 1957, 17, 23, 24 Mar 1964, 15 Jan 1965; *Sunday Mail* (Adel), 7, 14 Nov 1964; A.B.C., Personalities remembered (copy, SAA).
VALMAI A. HANKEL

ALSOP, RODNEY HOWARD (1881-1932), architect, was born on 22 December 1881 at Kew, Melbourne, eighth and youngest child of John Alsop, actuary and trustee-manager to the State Savings Bank of Victoria, and his wife Anne, née Howard. He early showed great gifts in both drawing and model-making, skills encouraged by his poor health which kept him in passive convalescence; when he was 15 his realistic panorama of the siege of Delhi was put on public display. While still a pupil at Cumloden, St Kilda, he worked on Saturday mornings for the architects Hyndman and Bates.

After an operation in 1899 to ease his asthma, he went with his family on a tour of Europe which embraced English church and domestic architecture, the Paris Exposition (1900) and Italian art centres. On his return to Melbourne in 1901 he was articled with Hyndman and Bates and in 1906, after admission to the Royal Victorian Institute of Architects, he entered partnership with F. L. Klingender; Alsop was reputedly the designer, and Klingender the practical partner.

In 1921 he joined Kingsley Henderson [q.v.] and Marcus Martin in a practice that created the distinctive Temperance and General Mutual Life offices in several State capitals. Alsop is credited with the notion that these buildings should have a tower of similar character and all be the same colour. From September 1924 until 1931, when he joined A. Bramwell Smith, he practised alone.

In all the partnerships, Alsop is acknowledged as a design architect and a sensitive specialist in domestic work. His crowning achievement was the Winthrop Hall in the Hackett [q.v.] buildings at the University of Western Australia; his designs for them had won first place in the 1926 world-wide competition which he had entered with C. H. Sayce. The commission led to a legal dispute between Sayce and Alsop, from which the former withdrew.

Before World War I Alsop's distinctive house designs were dominated by gables in the English domestic manner, but afterwards he turned towards an arcaded Italian Renaissance mode. Like his friend Professor Leslie Wilkinson [q.v.] he endeavoured to develop an appropriate Australian style by expressing the planning requirements of a building in terms of the architecture of southern Europe. Alsop was also a respected designer of furniture and shared a skill in landscape design with his wife Dorothy Hope, daughter of Sir Nicholas Lockyer [q.v.], whom he had married in June 1912 at Toorak; their only child died in 1915.

Tall and slight, of ready wit and fine features, Alsop was described as 'a true Edwardian gentleman, a man of impeccable manners, and thoroughly good company'. He was admired for his use of simple and unusual materials to create interesting and delightful effects, and his designs often drew together various artists and craftsmen as contributors to the architecture, which to Alsop was always an art. In his mature years, he was a fellow of the Royal Victorian Institute of Architects and a councillor. He was an active member of its board of architectural education and the first director of the University of Melbourne's architectural atelier. On one of his five trips to Europe he represented the institute at the 1925 International Congress of Architects at Budapest. A number of his papers, including one on the importance of travel to the development of an architect, are published in the institute's *Journal*.

Alsop died suddenly of bronchitis and asthma on 26 October 1932; he had just been awarded the 1932 bronze medal by the Royal Institute of British Architects for his Winthrop Hall — a singular honour. Survived by his wife, he was buried in Brighton cemetery.

F. Alexander, *Campus at Crawley* (Melb, 1963); Roy Vic Inst of Architects, *J*, May 1933; *Aust Home Builder*, Nov 1932; *Building and Construction* (Melb), 5 Nov 1932, 23 July 1935; D. H. Alsop, Rodney Howard Alsop, architect (B.Arch. report, Univ Melb, 1970); P. Navaretti, Index of architects and their work: 1900-1940 (B.Arch. report, Univ Melb, 1971).   GEORGE TIBBITS

ALSTON, JAMES (1850-1943), manufacturer, was born on 21 September 1850 at Southwark, London, son of Thomas Alston, plasterer and later a pottery-ware manufacturer, and his wife Kezia, née Edwell. Little is known of his early life, but he arrived in Victoria in 1861 or 1863 and spent some years on the goldfields. In the mid-1860s he was apprenticed to the iron trade in Ballarat, serving four years in general engineering, before establishing himself in 1874 as an agricultural implement-maker and blacksmith at Warrnambool. There, on 25 May he married Mary Sophia Georgina O'Sullivan, daughter of a shopkeeper.

Alston had long had an interest in pumps, but from the early 1870s he began to realize that the windmill offered the real solution to tapping the resources of artesian water. Moreover, if the design could be perfected, windmills could also meet the immense demand for power to drive sawmills, shearing machines and other implements efficiently and economically. Alston began working on improvements to windmills and by 1884 was ready to apply for a patent for his design. His windmills, constantly improved over the next two decades, were of iron (later steel) construction, of a circular form, and with curved sails. In the next two years he applied for patents for an attachment to ploughs, and for an 'improved trough or flume coupling', but his windmills were in such demand that by 1890 he was able to devote himself almost entirely to their manufacture and installation. By then hundreds of them were operating in the Western District of Victoria, and he was well on his way to dominating the market in the other Australian colonies and in South Africa. In 1897 Alston moved to Melbourne to be closer to his sources of raw materials and to save freight costs, recognizing that the capital was now the only real location for an enterprising manufacturer. Close to Queen's Bridge at Moray Street, South Melbourne, Alston built a large, modern factory, equipped with machinery which he had himself invented or adapted. A fair, paternalistic employer, he concentrated on training and keeping a skilled workforce; low labour mobility helped to ensure efficiency, economy and reliability. His management abilities, as well as his entrepreneurial and inventive skills, made him a formidable capitalist.

Alston was a manufacturer; he had few other interests. He perfected a number of inventions which were of great assistance to the rural community, such as the steel water-trough for stock, but took little part in public life. MARY ALSTON (1856-1932), on the other hand, made up for his lack of community involvement. She bore him four sons and three daughters, ran his large house, Majella, in St Kilda Road from the late 1890s, and also involved herself whole-heartedly in an impressive range of charitable activities. Both she and her husband were Catholics, but her 'philanthropy recognised no boundary of creed', and at her death on 13 December 1932 she was president of the Women's Hospital, patroness of the central executive of St Vincent's Hospital, a vice-president of the Victoria League and president of the Loreto Free Kindergarten. Her other concerns included the Queen Victoria and the Alfred hospitals, the Society for the Prevention of Cruelty to Children and the City Newsboys' Society. During World War I she had been a zealous worker for the Red Cross and she was also a member of the Lyceum Club. She was remembered for her unassuming generosity, her old-world dignity of manner and her kindly charm.

Alston died at his home on 27 July 1943, survived by three daughters and three sons; he was buried in the Melbourne general cemetery and left an estate valued for probate at £236 691. He was probably the last of the Victorian manufacturers who in the 1870s and 1880s had made that colony the industrial leader of Australia. The size of the market for certain products seemed to promise a new industrial revolution, a basic change in the Victorian economy. However, while there was manufacturing, there was not industrialization, which was to come much later. Alston's period had been the pre-war years; little is heard of him after 1914. His business was still prosperous, his products still innovative, but the dreams of his generation had faded. Australian manufacturing had become a tariff-protected sector, used by politicians to absorb surplus labour and employing a derivative technology. James Alston and his fellow entrepreneurs had promised much more; the promises now rust on farms all over Australia.

J. Smith (ed), *Cyclopedia of Victoria*, 1 (Melb, 1903); F. Wheelhouse, *Digging stick to rotary hoe* (Melb, 1966); *Scientific Australian*, 20 June 1900; *Age*, 14 Dec 1932, 31 July 1943; *Argus*, 2 Aug 1943.

GEORGE PARSONS

AMADIO, JOHN (BELL) (1884-1964), musician, was born at Christchurch, New Zealand, eighth child of Samuel Biddle Taylor, merchant, and his wife Eliza, née Wilson. Widowed in November 1884, Eliza took the family to Wellington, where in 1890, aged 39, she married a 22-year-old carpenter and flautist Henry Antonio Amadio, whose surname her children assumed. Under his stepfather's guidance John displayed early talent as a flautist; his half-brother Adrian also played the flute while his older brother Henry Henville took up the clarinet, oboe and bassoon.

About 1900 the Amadio family moved to Australia, first to Sydney and then to Melbourne. In 1901 John was engaged as principal flautist with J. C. Williamson's [q.v.6] Italian Opera Company. Next year (Dame) Nellie Melba [q.v.] reputedly offered to take him on tour with her to England but his stepfather decided that he was too young. During Melba's 1911 Australian tour, however, he was principal flute for her opera company. He played in the Marshall Hall [q.v.] orchestra in 1903-12, performed in concerts as soloist or in association with visiting and local artists, and in 1909-20 taught the flute at the University Conservatorium of Music. On 6 January 1915 at Brighton he married the pianist Leonora Soames Roberts.

In July 1918 Amadio toured New Zealand. Next year he decided to further his career abroad, and gave a farewell concert in Melbourne on 28 November. In Europe he accompanied Luisa Tetrazzini on tour and gained international repute as a virtuoso flautist; Sir Henry Wood remarked of his playing with the Hallé Orchestra, 'the finest tone I have ever heard'.

Amadio and his wife had separated in 1919, and in 1925 she divorced him, naming Florence Austral [q.v.] as co-respondent. Amadio and Austral were married soon after, and for the next fifteen years they made concert tours of Europe, America and Australia as associate artists. Their visits to Australia in 1930 and 1934-36 were greeted with enthusiasm by both the press and the critics; his warm playing of Bach and Mozart proved a popular complement to Austral's operatic arias and lieder. In 1934 the couple gave a series of recitals for the Australian Broadcasting Commission; like Austral, Amadio made many recordings, his first in 1920. In 1936 he appeared as associate-artist with the organist (Sir) William McKie.

By 1940 Austral and Amadio had gone their separate ways. During the war years Amadio played with London orchestras, notably the International Ballet, and in concerts for the Armed Forces. In 1947 he returned to Australia, playing for the Melbourne Symphony Orchestra, occasionally as soloist, and was principal flute in the Tasmanian Symphony Orchestra in 1956. From 1959 he lived in Melbourne in semi-retirement, caring for his ailing sister Lenna (Evelyn) Gunderson, of whom he was particularly fond. His main public appearances were at open-air concerts at the Myer [q.v.] Music Bowl, and it was at a rehearsal for one of these that he died of coronary occlusion on 4 April 1964, aged 80. He was survived by two daughters of his first marriage, one of whom was Judy (Lenore), a flautist and music teacher.

Charming yet rather aloof in his personal relations, Amadio kept his warmth for his music. A superb technician, although by strict aesthetic standards something of a showman, his musicality gave him great rapport with singers for whom he played obbligatos: the soprano Glenda Raymond has spoken of him as unequalled as an intuitive accompanist. Other members of the family noted for their musicianship include his nephews Clive and Neville, sons of Henry Henville Amadio.

I. Moresby, *Australia makes music* (Melb, 1948); *Aust Musical News*, 1914-16, Feb 1923, Sept 1936; *Gramophone and Talking Machine News*, Apr 1924; *Listener In*, 28 July 1934; *Argus*, 29 Nov 1919, 15 Sept 1925, 18 July, 3 Aug 1934; A.B.C. Archives (Syd); information from John Amadio's pupils.

MIMI COLLIGAN

AMBROSE, THEODORE (1880-1947), medical practitioner, was born on 9 August 1880 at Mitcham, South Australia, youngest of five children of William Ambrose, schoolmaster, who died two years later, and his wife Helen Harvey, née Finlayson, who died in 1891. He was then reared by his Scots grandparents, whose son John Harvey Finlayson [q.v.4] was editor of the *South Australian Register*.

Ambrose, an Anglican, was educated at Way College and began his medical education in Adelaide, moving to Sydney where he graduated M.B., Ch.M. in 1902. His sister Ethel graduated in medicine from Adelaide in the same year. She became the first woman resident medical officer at Perth Public Hospital and was later a medical missionary. Ambrose held appointments at Sydney Hospital as junior resident medical officer, resident pathologist and bacteriologist (1903) and senior resident, registrar

and assistant superintendent. In 1904 he married Clara Beatrice Young, a nurse born at Canberra. The next year he followed his sister to Western Australia and entered general practice at Mount Magnet. He moved to Perth in 1906 and remained in general practice at Subiaco for nine years, holding honorary positions as visiting medical officer for the Home of Peace for Incurable Cases and the Hospital for Infectious Diseases at Subiaco from 1908. He was appointed to the honorary medical staff at Perth Public Hospital as assistant physician, then physician. Appointed assistant surgeon in 1915, he devoted himself thenceforth to specialist surgery and moved to St George's Terrace. He was senior outdoor surgeon to the hospital in 1917, and later senior consultant. He held similar appointments at the Children's Hospital from 1912. As senior consultant to both major hospitals Ambrose was Perth's leading surgeon for many years, successfully introducing new techniques, particularly in abdominal surgery and radical mastectomy. His operating skill was enhanced by ambidexterity and by extreme deafness which helped his concentration in the theatre but prevented him addressing meetings. Instead he contributed to Australian medical journals.

Ambrose was a foundation fellow of the Royal Australasian College of Surgeons and regularly attended Australasian Medical Congresses until the mid-1930s. He was an enthusiastic member of the Western Australian Turf Club and its honorary surgeon. He owned many racehorses and in 1922 won the West Australian Derby.

Ambrose moved to Mount Lawley in 1937 and suffered a coronary occlusion the next year. In 1940 when he ceased practice the board of the Children's Hospital appointed him honorary consultant for life. Despite ill health Ambrose, as captain in the Australian Army Medical Corps Reserve, sailed that year as ship's surgeon in a convoy carrying explosives to England. He then worked for the Eastern Extension Cable Co. on Fanning Island in mid-Pacific for two years; his wife refused to be evacuated and worked as a teacher and nurse. Ambrose returned to general practice in Western Australia at Brookton, Cue, Meekatharra and Norseman. He became ill at Norseman following a fall and was flown to Perth, where he died three days later on 8 October 1947 of arteriosclerosis and renal failure. He was buried at Karrakatta cemetery. His estate was valued for probate at £2428. One of four daughters and one of three sons graduated in medicine.

L. (Mrs W. H.) Hinton (ed), *Ethel Ambrose* (Lond, 1937?); J. H. Stubbe, *Medical background* (Perth, 1969); A'sian Medical Congress, *Trans*,

1905, 1920, 1927, 1929, 1934; *MJA*, 17 Jan 1948; *West Australian*, 9 Oct 1947; Children's Hospital, Minute-book 1935-46, *and* annual report 1948 (Princess Margaret Hospital, Perth); family information.   PRUE JOSKE

AMPT, GUSTAV ADOLPH (1886-1953), chemical analyst, was born on 19 July 1886 at Hawthorn, Victoria, son of Gustav Adolph Ampt, engineering draftsman, formerly of Germany, and his wife Emilie Clara Adelaide, née Sander. He attended University High School and qualified for matriculation in 1901, entering the University of Melbourne in 1904 to study engineering. The next year he transferred, for health reasons, to the less physically strenuous science course, gaining exhibitions in second-year chemistry and natural philosophy in 1906. He qualified B.Sc. in chemistry in 1907, but the accidental death in January 1908 of his sister Gertrude, a musician, just before his honours examination, left a psychological barrier to his seeking further degrees.

In 1908-10 Ampt held government research scholarships, totalling £250, for analytical work on plant foods and the quartz microbalance. It was carried out in the laboratories of the university and of the Commonwealth Defence Department where he was employed in 1908-18. He visited Britain in 1908 for experience in explosives analysis and later combined his chemical duties with inspection of defence establishments throughout the Australian Commonwealth. At the height of anti-German hysteria in World War I he suffered a completely unfounded attack upon his loyalty, but was appointed by Professor Masson [q.v.] as a part-time demonstrator in the university's chemistry department. There in 1919 he completed work for the Advisory Council of Science and Industry on tin-plate substitutes, for which he was awarded the (F. S.) Grimwade [q.v.4] Prize for applied chemistry.

Ampt became (senior) demonstrator (1921), lecturer (1926) and senior lecturer (1936), instructing later-year classes in practical analytical chemistry and supervising the diploma courses in public health and analytical chemistry. For thirty years his meticulous instruction left an indelible impression upon students: the training they received in skill, accuracy, and integrity in chemical analysis was a hallmark of Melbourne's chemistry graduates. He organized superbly, but initiated few educational changes. Chemical consulting, mainly as a referee when professional analysts differed, occupied some of his time.

During World War II Ampt co-operated in investigations upon tungsten purity, optical glass and chemical warfare. He contributed regularly to analytical studies of rocks, developed numerous methods of chemical analysis and gained international recognition, particularly in his work in association with the Massachusetts Institute of Technology in 1949-50 on methods of rock analysis. Staff and senior students benefited from his kindly and hospitable disposition; he appreciated humour if not directed against himself.

For over twenty years from 1921 Ampt was examiner and syllabus adviser in technical school and public examination chemistry, superintendent of the public examinations in Melbourne in 1933-47, and office-bearer in and frequent scientific contributor to the Melbourne University Chemical Society from 1907, the Society of Chemical Industry of Victoria from 1909 and the Australian Chemical Institute from 1918. He was a keen philatelist.

Illness dogged his later life. He died on 4 May 1953 of hypertensive cerebro-vascular disease, only a year after retirement, survived by his wife Margaret Helen, née Boyne, whom he had married at Camberwell on 16 October 1913, a daughter and two sons. He was cremated with Presbyterian rites, leaving an estate valued for probate at £13 936.

J. Radford, *A history of the chemistry department of the University of Melbourne* (Melb, 1978); *Melb Univ Mag*, 1907, 1920; *Science and Industry*, 1 (1919); Roy Aust Chemical Inst, *Procs*, 20 (1953); *Univ Melb Gazette*, May 1953; Soc of Chemical Industry Vic, Records and minutes 1919, 1947, 1949 (Basser Lib, Canb); Science Faculty minutes 1905, 1908-10, 1939, 1953 (Univ Melb Archives); box 459/15, 1915 (AAO, Brighton, Vic).

JOAN T. RADFORD

ANDERSON, CHARLES (1876-1944), museum director, was born on 5 December 1876 at Moa, Stenness, Orkney Islands, Scotland, third son of John Anderson, crofter, and his wife Margaret, née Smith. From Stenness Public School, a succession of bursaries enabled him to attend Kirkwall Burgh School and the University of Edinburgh (M.A., 1898; B.Sc., 1900; D.Sc., 1908). After every vacation he returned from the Orkneys with a barrel of herrings and sacks of oatmeal and potatoes on which he subsisted. He won six medals in science subjects and excelled in English literature and Latin; on graduating, he took charge of Ben Nevis Observatory.

On 22 July 1901 Anderson was appointed mineralogist at the Australian Museum, Sydney, and on 18 January 1902 at the Roman Catholic Church, Manly, he married

Elsie Helen, daughter of Throsby Robertson, engineer. His doctorate in 1908 was awarded for research into morphological crystallography and the chemistry of minerals in Australia. He determined the elements for a number of local minerals, carried out a comprehensive study of 'Cerussite crystals from Broken Hill, N.S.W., and Muldiva, Queensland', and proved that the axial ratios of azurite from Mineral Hill, New South Wales, differed from those of that mineral from Chessy, France (usually given as standard). He published his findings mainly in the *Records* of the Australian Museum and the *Proceedings* of the Royal Society of New South Wales. In 1916 he produced a valuable *Bibliography of Australian mineralogy*.

Anderson was appointed director of the Australian Museum on 14 February 1921. In 1911 he had visited and reported on important European museums: he now instituted the display of animals in large habitat groups. He immediately started the *Australian Museum Magazine* (later *Australian Natural History*) and was a frequent contributor. He changed his field of research to vertebrate palaeontology on which he published seven papers; his most notable achievement was the reclassification of *Meiolania* (the extinct horned turtle) based on examination of material from Lord Howe Island. In 1938 he wrote a *Guide to the Australian Museum and its contents*.

With an international reputation in two fields, Anderson gave 'abundantly of his rare gifts of scholarship and versatile scientific knowledge' to help others. He was president in 1924 of the local Royal Society, its editorial secretary in 1935-43 and chairman of its geological section in 1935-36. President of the Anthropological (1930-31), Linnean (1932) and Geographical (1941-42) societies of New South Wales, he was also a fellow of the Australian and New Zealand Association for the Advancement of Science, and a corresponding member of the American Museum of Natural History, New York, and of the Zoological Society of London. He lectured in crystallography at the University of Sydney in 1923-24. In December 1940 he retired, but in June 1942 joined the staff of Communications Censorship as his contribution to the war effort.

Anderson subscribed to no religious beliefs. Widely read and a good linguist, he had a whimsical sense of humour, great personal charm and simple tastes: he enjoyed golf, trout-fishing, and singing Scottish songs such as 'Fhairshon swore a feud/Against ta clan MacTavish'. With an abiding love for his native Orkneys, he firmly maintained that Orcadians were of Scandinavian rather than of Scottish ancestry. He used dog German as a lingua franca with his assistant Marcel Aurousseau, who recalled that when measuring crystals on the goniometer, an intricate piece of apparatus, his favourite song was 'There was a wee cooper who lived in Fife,/Nicketty, nacketty, noo, noo, noo'.

Anderson died from coronary occlusion at St Vincent's Hospital on 25 October 1944 and was buried in South Head cemetery. He was survived by his only son, a veterinary surgeon, and by two daughters. His estate was valued for probate at £2750.

Aust Museum Mag, 28 Dec 1940; Aust Museum, *Records*, 21 (1941-47); *Aust J of Science*, Dec 1944; Roy Soc NSW, *Procs*, 79 (1945); W. R. Browne, 'Some builders of geology in New South Wales', Aust Academy of Science, *Records*, 2 (1971), no 1; C. Anderson letters (held by Mr M. Aurousseau, Balgowlah, NSW); printed cat (ML); family information.
    R. O. CHALMERS

ANDERSON, SIR DAVID MURRAY (1874-1936), naval officer and governor, was born on 11 April 1874 at Newton-by-Chester, England, second son of General David Anderson, colonel of the Cheshire Regiment, and his wife Charlotte Christina, née Anderson. Educated at Stubbington, in 1887 he became a cadet at the Royal Naval College, Dartmouth, went to sea two years later and thereafter rose steadily in the service. He commanded the royal yacht *Victoria and Albert* in 1908. That year he married Edith Muriel Teschemaker, a New Zealander.

Promoted captain three years later, Anderson was flag captain in the *Hyacinth* on the Cape Station in 1913-17, and was appointed C.M.G. for services in operations leading to the surrender of Dar-es-Salaam. In 1918-19 he commanded the battleship *Ajax* in the Grand Fleet and in 1921-22 was aide-de-camp to King George V. After a posting in England, as dockyard superintendent at Milford Haven, he was promoted rear admiral in 1922 and next year was made C.B. He was senior naval officer on the Yangtze River, China Station, in 1923-25. Vice admiral from 1927, he commanded the Africa Station for two years. He had qualified as an interpreter of French and spent two years at Geneva as a British naval representative at the League of Nations. In 1930 he was appointed K.C.B. and next year was promoted admiral. He retired at his own request on 1 July 1932.

Sir Murray Anderson was governor of Newfoundland in 1932-35. When, because of financial difficulties, representative government was suspended there, he presided over the Commission of Government, and his personal charm and tact helped to ease a difficult situation. In November 1935 he was appointed governor of New South Wales. *En route* he was taken ill, and spent six weeks in hospital in Perth. He was sworn in at Sydney on 6 August 1936. Because of his recurring illness, Lady Anderson ably undertook many official duties on his behalf. On 29 October he collapsed suddenly and died of a cerebral haemorrhage the next day. After a memorial service in Sydney, his body was shipped to England and buried in Fittleworth cemetery, Sussex. His widow was appointed D.B.E. in 1937.

Great Britain: Dominions Office and Colonial Office List, 1935; *Annual Register*, 1936; *SMH*, 6 Nov 1935, 30 Oct 1936; *The Times*, 30 Oct 1936.

CHRIS CUNNEEN

ANDERSON, ERNEST AUGUSTUS (1859-1945), bishop, was born on 24 March 1859 at Milton Damerel, Devonshire, England, fourth son of Rev. William Dyer Anderson and his wife Mirianne, née Harrison. He was educated at Bedford Grammar School and Queens' College, Cambridge (B.A., 1882; M.A., 1895), where he was an athlete, rower and footballer. He went to North Queensland as a mission preacher in 1882, was made deacon, and on 13 May 1883 ordained priest. On 13 August at Mackay he married Amelia Constance Isabel Ross (d. 1917). He was incumbent of Holy Trinity there in 1884-86, and rector of St Thomas's, Hughenden, in 1886-91; from 1889 he was also an honorary canon of St James' Cathedral, Townsville. In 1891 Bishop Stanton [q.v.], newly translated to Newcastle, New South Wales, appointed him to St Paul's, West Maitland, where he became known as a vigorous Low Church preacher.

In 1894 Anderson succeeded S. Linton [q.v.5] as bishop of the Riverina. He was consecrated at St Paul's Cathedral, London, on 29 June next year, then raised money for his diocese before returning to New South Wales; he was installed in St Paul's Pro-Cathedral at Hay on 11 February 1896.

Anderson had experienced in Queensland similar bush conditions to those he would meet in the Riverina, a see of over 70 000 square miles, with fourteen parishes worked by fifteen clergy. He was faced immediately with the financial collapse of his diocese. Its Episcopal Endowment Fund had been largely depleted through the dishonesty of a solicitor. After two court cases, by 1915 some £11 000 of the original £15 000 had been rescued. Meanwhile Anderson had been paid less than half the annual £800 he had been promised and had spent his personal fortune in maintaining his position as bishop, furnishing Bishop's Lodge, Hay, and educating his children; it was twenty-two years before he was free of debt.

From 1915 motor cars made diocesan travel easier, but Anderson still had to make long annual tours on unmade roads. He had many difficulties with clergy whose churchmanship differed from his, or who had failed in other parishes but were accepted for the Riverina diocese because of the difficulty of recruitment to isolated bush parishes. In 1915 tension reached a peak when E. A. Frost, rector of Broken Hill, was tried at Hay for heresy and breach of ecclesiastical discipline. The panel did not find his High Church views heretical, but he was forced to leave the diocese because of the bishop's hostility. During Anderson's episcopate thirty-two churches and many rectories were built and the number of clergy increased. Diocesan finances after 1920 were stable.

Anderson was an able artist and painted a mural in his pro-cathedral. He had a magnificent china collection and was an authority on roses. On 19 January 1925 at Auckland, New Zealand, he married a widow Margaret Jane Boyd, née Miller-Crook. He resigned his see on 30 June and retired to Auckland where he died on 5 April 1945, and was cremated. He was survived by a son and four daughters; his second son had been killed in action in 1917. His portrait is held by descendants at Hay.

Church of England, *Diocese of Riverina Year Book*, 1896-1924; *T&CJ*, 8 Dec 1894; *Riverine Grazier*, 14 Feb 1896, 7 Nov, 12 Dec 1924, 10 Apr 1945; *Hillston Spectator*, 13 April 1917; Riverina Papers, *and* correspondence (Riverina Diocesan Registry, Narrandera, *and* held by Mrs R. Matthews, Hay).

LAUREL CLYDE

ANDERSON, SIR FRANCIS (1858-1941), philosopher and educationist, was born on 3 September 1858 at Glasgow, Scotland, son of Francis Anderson, manufacturer, and his wife Elizabeth Anna Lockart, née Ellison. Educated at Old Wynd and Oatlands public schools, at 14 he became a pupil-teacher, a tutelage he detested. In 1876 he matriculated at the University of Glasgow (M.A., 1883), where he had a distinguished career; he won the prize for the outstanding graduate of his year, and was awarded the Clark philosophical fellowship which entailed assisting Professor Edward Caird for two years. He taught English literature during the absence of the professor concerned and studied in the theological faculty with the intention of entering the ministry, but was apparently not ordained. Nevertheless, in 1886 he migrated to Melbourne to become an assistant to Rev. C. Strong [q.v.6] in his Australian Church.

Instead of returning to Scotland as he had intended, Anderson in 1888 was appointed a lecturer in logic and mental philosophy at the University of Sydney. Soon he was also giving the evening course in English, for which he was paid extra. In 1890 he became first Challis [q.v.3] professor of logic and mental philosophy, despite strong competition from notable British applicants. Anderson was to write very little on the subject he professed, but was to be remarkable as a teacher and educational reformer. In a pamphlet published in 1903, *On teaching to think*, he set out his aims — to make his students use their brains and to bring out the best in them. In his lecture-room 'questions were asked and discussion encouraged'. Whatever subject he lectured on, 'his exposition was always delightful; his early training in the classics, his beautiful voice, his dramatic sense, all joined to produce a profound effect upon his classes'. 'Hating dogma himself', wrote G. V. Portus [q.v.], 'he would not be dogmatic to others. Fighting bureaucracy outside, he encouraged criticism from his students within'.

Anderson's philosophical position was 'Christian Idealist', predominantly Hegelian, but tempered by the earlier traditional Scottish line of thought which emphasized the self and moral values. His lectures soon settled into a pattern: a first course of logic and psychology, followed by a second and third ringing annual changes on the triad, ancient philosophy, modern philosophy, and social, moral and political philosophy. He covered an enormous range in all three of the advanced courses; in the first two his descriptions stressed the historical and critical approach. In his examination-papers he raised important issues in their historical settings and looked critically at the proposed solutions; despite his Christian Idealism, he seemed to be tolerant of other views. In his third advanced course, he ranged well outside philosophy, as conventionally defined, and concentrated on the relations between philosophy, religion, science and society; he managed to include ethics, education, economics, politics, and sociology in which he was keenly interested. It was perhaps too broad-ranging. His former students testify to his passionate yet critical pursuit of the truth. The more remote observer, viewing what little evidence remains, might see him as no doubt passionate, no doubt stimulating, but nevertheless somewhat restricted by his preconceptions in the pursuit of the truth. In philosophy he seems to have left too much unquestioned. In 1897 he was presi-

dent of the mental science section of the Australasian Association for the Advancement of Science, Brisbane, and in 1907 presided over its social and statistical science section in Adelaide; he read a paper, *Sociology in Australia: a plea for its teaching*, to the Sydney meeting in 1911 and published it next year.

Through his work for the Kindergarten Union of New South Wales, he had met Maybanke Susannah Wolstenholme, née Selfe [q.v. Anderson], who was thirteen years his senior; on 2 March 1899 at Balmain they were married according to Congregational rites. In respect of education in New South Wales, Anderson left little unquestioned and little unanswered; Maybanke encouraged him. In a stirring address on 26 June 1901 to the annual conference of New South Wales Public School Teachers' Association, he smote the public school system hip and thigh. He castigated the pupil-teacher system of training and the role of the teachers' colleges, and alleged that too few future or present teachers attended the university, even part time. He complained about the over-scholastic and rigid curricula of the primary and of the emerging secondary schools and the relative absence of study of the natural, physical and social sciences; he criticized the predominance of 'drill' and 'cramming' in teaching and the absence of 'inquiry'. He deplored the role of the school inspectors who, instead of encouraging innovation, assessed teachers in terms of their conformity to established norms. His audience was enraptured: 'Women were standing on chairs waving their handkerchiefs and parasols, men were stamping and shouting and shaking hands with perfect strangers'. The authorities at first derided his attack, a reaction which led him to write a number of newspaper articles in the *Daily Telegraph* and a pamphlet on *The public school system of New South Wales*. Finally the Knibbs-J. W. Turner [qq.v] royal commission was appointed in 1902 to examine his criticisms. After a study tour overseas, it found largely in support of Anderson and his proposed reforms, many of which were implemented after Peter Board [q.v.] became director of education.

One of Anderson's ambitions was to convert teaching into a profession in the best sense of that term. In 1909 he used the three slogans: 'Train the Teacher, Trust the Teacher and Pay the Teacher'. By this time, with Board's aid, he had broken the back of the old pupil-teacher system, the Teachers' College was established and its first principal Alexander Mackie [q.v.] in 1910 also became professor of education in the university.

Anderson had proposed reforms in the

university such as the broadening of its matriculation requirements to include English, a foreign language, mathematics and a science, and a new chair in economics (attained in 1913) accompanied by chairs of politics and sociology, for he believed that economics should not be taught in purely financial and commercial terms without a political and social context. He also promoted more intensive study of psychology, believing it to be perhaps the one essential component in the education of teachers. He handed over the first course to his assistant H. T. Lovell [q.v.] and encouraged him to develop an advanced psychology course as an alternative to the regular second-year philosophy subject.

A fellow of the senate in 1914-16 and 1919-21, and dean of the faculty of arts in 1914-15 and 1920-21, Anderson promoted adult education through the University Extension Board and, as chairman of the joint committee for tutorial classes from 1916, defended the participation of the Workers' Educational Association of New South Wales. He resigned his chair at the end of 1921 and was made emeritus professor. He declined an offer to have his portrait painted; instead, at his suggestion his work was commemorated by two mural panels by Norman Carter [q.v.] for the philosophy lecture-room. In 1922 he helped to found the Australasian Association of Psychology and Philosophy and that year published for it a monograph, *Liberty, equality and fraternity*; he was first editor of its *Journal* in 1923-26. His 'Notes from the editor's chair', as well as the material he accepted from local and overseas authors, revealed the breadth of his interests. He was president of the local League of Nations Union for many years, although he had doubts about the capacity of the league to enforce peace, and was chairman of the Council of Social Service of New South Wales until 1941.

At the end of 1926 the Andersons visited Britain and Europe; Maybanke died in Paris next year. After his return to Sydney Anderson married Josephine Wight (d. 1953) on 20 January 1928 at St Saviour's Cathedral, Goulburn, and again visited Europe. He was made an honorary LL.D. by the University of Glasgow in 1927 and was knighted in 1936. Anderson died at his home at Woollahra on 24 June 1941, and was cremated with Anglican rites; he was childless. His estate was valued for probate at £1527.

G. V. Portus, *Happy highways* (Melb, 1953), *and* 'Francis Anderson — professor and citizen', *Hermes*, Nov 1921; *Aust J of Science*, 4 (1941-42); H. T. Lovell, 'In memoriam', *A'sian J of Psychology and Philosophy*, 19 (1941); *SMH*, 27 June 1901, 15 Nov 1921.
                                    W. M. O'NEIL

ANDERSON, HENRY CHARLES LENNOX (1853-1924), public servant, was born on 10 May 1853 at sea, son of Robert Anderson, later a police inspector, and his wife Margaret, née Hewson. The family reached Sydney in the *Empire* on 27 July. Educated at Sydney Grammar School and on a scholarship at the University of Sydney (B.A., 1873; M.A., 1878), he won the University Prize in 1872, the Belmore Medal for agricultural chemistry in 1873, and the Hercules Robinson prize for Shakespearian scholarship and literature in 1877. From 1873 he had taught at Sydney Grammar School. On 24 March 1880 at the Macquarie Street Presbyterian Church he married Harriet Lily Lloyd. Two years later Anderson became an examiner in the Department of Public Instruction and helped to reorganize its curricula and examinations; in 1889 he was vice-chairman of the Board of Examiners. A militiaman, he was promoted lieutenant, 1st Regiment, Volunteer Infantry, in 1885 and captain in 1888; he resigned in 1892. With his younger brother (Sir) Robert M. McC. Anderson [q.v.], he was a founding member of the United Service Institution in 1889.

For twenty years Anderson carried out analysis and other work in agricultural chemistry 'as a hobby and recreation' and invested every shilling he had in a farm and orchard at Penrith. On 10 February 1890 he was appointed New South Wales's first director of agriculture; his department was formed haphazardly as a branch of the Department of Mines. He had to contend with catastrophic wheat losses from rust, widespread disease in plants and animals, pests such as rabbits, prickly pear, phylloxera and water hyacinth, and grossly inefficient farming methods. Within four months he edited and largely wrote the first issue of the *Agricultural Gazette of New South Wales*; he soon gathered the nucleus of a departmental scientific staff. In 1891 he established Hawkesbury Agricultural College on 'a sound, scientific and practical foundation' and next year the Wagga Wagga Experiment Farm. He acquired land for other agricultural colleges and farms for demonstration purposes, and made elaborate plans for free distribution of seeds, plants and cuttings and for a travelling demonstration unit to show farmers efficient dairying methods. Plants, trees, shrubs, seeds and insects of all types were to be botanically identified or entomologically classified and catalogued.

In August 1893 Anderson's department was virtually closed down and on 1 September he was appointed principal librarian of the Free Public Library at a reduced salary, a position for which he had 'no desire'. Continuing questions in parliament about his evidence to the royal commission into the civil service on 'political appointments' in the Department of Mines culminated in a select committee and a whispering campaign about his maladministration of the library. Hampered by an inadequate building and an outdated catalogue, he instituted annual stock-taking in 1894 (the first since 1885), helped country students by lending them 'small parcels of reference books', and became internationally known for 101 rules of cataloguing with the use of subject headings. In 1896 he published *Guide to the catalogues of the Reference Library*... (fourth edition, 1902). He also ran classes for his staff, and employed women for the first time. In 1897 he attended the Second International Library Conference in London, and acquired for New South Wales Governor King's [q.v.2] manuscript journal of his voyage to Sydney as a lieutenant in the *Sirius*. From 1901 he was also registrar of copyright and that year introduced the Dewey system of cataloguing.

Anderson believed in 'a National, and not a Municipal, Library' and emphasized the need to have books which 'reflect and give a history of the morals of certain ages'. In 1895 the library's name was changed at his instigation to the Public Library of New South Wales. After an introduction that year by Rose Scott [q.v.] to D. S. Mitchell [q.v.5], Anderson 'assiduously cultivated' him and, with the concurrence of the trustees, ordered books for him and acted out-of-hours as his secretary. In October 1898 Mitchell told him to notify the trustees of his intended bequest of his unrivalled collection. Anderson voluntarily moved out of his house attached to the library to accommodate the 10 000 volumes that Mitchell transferred.

In 1900 a Legislative Assembly select committee on the working of the free public library inquired into Anderson's alleged abuse of postal concessions, the inclusion of some of Judge Wise's [q.v.6] books among 5000 volumes sold to Angus & Robertson [qq.v.], undue preference shown to those booksellers as agents for the library, and the presence of 'decidedly "blue"' books. Its report exonerated Anderson and strongly recommended early selection of a site for and erection of a commodious library. In 1905 when the bequest seemed to be slipping away, the premier (Sir) Joseph Carruthers [q.v.] at last intervened, and work started on the Mitchell wing; Anderson was responsible for its basic design.

In 1905 he became director of the State's new Intelligence Department and from January 1907 government statistician as well. Anderson was then appointed acting under-secretary and director of the new, independent and stronger Department of

Agriculture in January 1908. Friend and colleague of William Farrer, A. J. Perkins [qq.v.] and William Lawrie, he contributed many articles to the *Agricultural Gazette* in 1910-11. At the first Dry Farming Conference in Australia, held in Adelaide in March 1911, he was impressed by the extension of wheat-growing in South Australia, and the advantages of superphosphate and fallowing in winter; New South Wales was still relatively backward in its agriculture.

A fellow of the Senate of the University of Sydney in 1895-1919, Anderson was a trustee of St Andrew's College in 1896-1924 and helped to establish the faculties of agriculture and veterinary science in 1910. He was also joint honorary secretary of the Dreadnought Fund, chairman of the local branch of the New Settlers' League of Australia, a life vice-president of the Highland Society of New South Wales, secretary of the original committee which raised funds for the erection of the Robert Burns statue, an active member of the Farrer memorial committee, and a Shakespearian scholar. Although he had been a brilliant organizer, Anderson reflected on 'the futility of much of his labour' in his reminiscences written soon after his retirement in April 1914. Gordon Richardson described him as 'the ablest man ever to call himself a librarian in this country', gaining an international reputation in 'the classic age of librarians'.

Anderson died of heart failure on 17 March 1924 at Wollstonecraft and was buried in the Presbyterian section of Rookwood cemetery. Predeceased by his only son, he was survived by two daughters. His estate was valued for probate at £13 688.

J. R. Tyrrell, *Old books, old friends, old Sydney* (Syd, 1952); G. D. Richardson, 'The colony's quest for a national library', *JRAHS*, 47 (1961); *V&P* (LA NSW), 1892-93, 1, 586, 1894-95, 3, 55 — evidence, p276, 1895, 1, 142, 219, 1896, 2, 157, 159, 1900, 4, 591-739, Report . . . relating to proposed Mitchell Library, 1905, 4, 1335; *SMH*, 18 Mar 1924; Rose Scott correspondence (ML).   C. J. KING

ANDERSON, JOHN (1893-1962), philosopher, educator and controversialist, was born on 1 November 1893 at Stonehouse, Lanarkshire, Scotland, son of Alexander Anderson, schoolmaster, and his wife, Elizabeth, née Brown. His father reputedly had both socialist and anti-clerical convictions and exerted a great influence on his son. After attending Hamilton Academy, Anderson matriculated at the University of Glasgow. His first concern was with mathematics and physics and he turned primarily to philosophy only late in his undergraduate career. He won prizes in many subjects, including political science, Greek, logic and political economy. In 1917 Anderson graduated Master of Arts with first-class honours in philosophy and in mathematics and natural philosophy. That year he was awarded the Ferguson Scholarship in Philosophy and in 1919 the Shaw Philosophical Fellowship, both in open competition with graduates of all four Scottish universities. As holder of the Shaw Fellowship he was required to deliver four public lectures, which he did in February 1925 on 'The Nature of Mind'. Some of his early published papers were probably based on these lectures.

Immediately upon graduation Anderson began lecturing at the University College of South Wales and Monmouthshire (Cardiff) (1917-19), the University of Glasgow (1919-20) and at the University of Edinburgh (1920-26). He taught over a wide range of philosophy at both elementary and advanced levels: logic, metaphysics, the history of ancient and of modern philosophy, ethics and the philosophy of mind. During this period he was preparing his Shaw lectures, working out his general philosophical position and drafting a textbook on logic which unfortunately was never published. On 30 June 1922 he married Janet Currie Baillie, a fellow-student at both Hamilton Academy and the University of Glasgow; their one son was born in Scotland.

Anderson occupied the Challis chair of philosophy in the University of Sydney from 1927 to 1958. Over the years he was probably the professor most often in the news as a result of controversial utterances not fully comprehended by those who took exception to them. He was probably the most original philosopher ever to have worked in Australia. Others, later, have been equally distinguished or have had greater international recognition. Though Anderson came under many influences, he was not strictly speaking a member of a wider movement. He found building-blocks here and there from which to construct his own philosophical edifice after supplying his own cement and after reshaping the stones. Unfortunately the edifice was never expounded in a comprehensive treatise, but its outlines were clear in his lectures and journal-articles.

He was greatly influenced by Greek philosophy, as interpreted by the Scottish scholar John Burnet, and by Hegel; for all that Anderson came to reject the Absolute Idealism in which he had been trained. Of twentieth-century philosophers, William James, G. E. Moore and Bertrand Russell, the American new 'realists' and, especially, the Australian-born Samuel Alexander [q.v.], laid the foundations of his thinking.

Outside philosophy in the narrower sense, Freud, Marx and the 'political pluralists' of Orage's journal *New Age* all left a permanent mark on him. But Anderson's interpretation of his predecessors and his contemporaries was often highly original, not to say idiosyncratic, and he followed none of them in detail. His general position was pluralistic. Everything, whether it be a physical object, a human mind, or a society is, he argued, a plurality of co-operating and competing activities, each of them in turn a complex plurality. There are no ultimates, whether in the form of total wholes of which everything is a part, elementary units of which it is made up, or a self-subsistent Being on which it depends. It follows that one can never know anything whatsoever through-and-through. In Heraclitus's phrase one has always to 'expect the unexpected'. There is no higher or better way of knowledge than experience, an experience, however, which is not of simple sensations but of complex situations. Even mathematics and logic are corrigible in the light of further experience.

In ethics and aesthetics, Anderson defended the view that our judgments are objective. His aesthetics was closely linked with the formalism of Roger Fry; his ethics had few forerunners. Good, he argued, is a characteristic of certain forms of mental activity, of love, courage, the contemplation and creation of beauty, the spirit of production, the spirit of inquiry. These are not to be thought of as 'ends'; they are acquired, if at all, by 'catching' them from others, rather than by deliberate pursuit. Other ethical notions, such as 'rights', he defined in purely sociological terms.

A central feature of Anderson's teaching was a call for a critical approach to everything. Nothing was to be deemed to be above criticism and nothing was to be allowed to play an obscurantist role in dampening or suppressing criticism. He saw censorship, patriotism, religion and some social conventions such as 'good taste' as having this effect, and consequently he attacked each of them, both within and outside the university. Despite his seriousness in these matters, he had a light-hearted wit or at any rate turn of phrase which endeared him to some but, because it could be so devastating, antagonized others.

Within the university he played three important roles: as a teacher, as a critic and controversialist, and as a conservationist or protagonist of the preservation of an intellectual emphasis and of scholarly standards. The same can be said of his extra-university activities.

Anderson never had much time for Hegelian dialectical materialism turned upside down by Marx as a philosophy, or with Marxist political theory, but he had originally a strong sympathy with some aspects of the Marxist political objectives. So after his arrival in Australia he associated with the communist movement. He wrote for their journals, sometimes under a nom-de-plume, but became disillusioned with the Stalinist party-line; he worked for a time with the Trotsky dissident group but became disenchanted with them also. He could not put up any longer with dialectical materialism or with the servile state which he saw was being imposed by the doctrine of the dictatorship of the proletariat. He was deemed by some to have become after this a conservative in politics. He would be better described as a liberal, pluralist democrat. Liberal he always was, but conservative in the ordinary sense, in politics, ethics, aesthetics, epistemology and metaphysics, he never was. In logic he was conservative but with a liberal touch. When Bertrand Russell and others were reforming traditional logic on one unconventional line, Anderson was reforming it on a much less radical line and he had no sympathy for what they were doing. He was always in one sense conservative in education, adopting what he regarded as a classical position; he insisted that a high intellectual demand be made by any study, that it call for the exercise of criticism and that high standards always be required. In respect of procedures in education, he was conservative; he had no stomach for the new-fangled. He did not endear himself to many of his colleagues when he maintained that courses aimed at professional preparation had no place in a university. The study of the humanities, the sciences (physical and biological) and the social sciences was the prime task. The teaching and learning of professional skills and procedures should in his view be engaged in outside a university.

Through the obvious originality of his philosophical position, aided by his friendliness to and interest in his students but not by any oratorical skills (for he lacked them), Anderson had a tremendous impact on his students. Though he was insistent on high standards, he was not intemperate in blowing on his own shorn lambs. It was not easy to gain a first-class honours from him, but he had a generous judgment of what could be expected from the ordinary run of diligent pass students. There was a continuing central core of adherents, the Andersonians, who adopted his philosophical position in its various aspects with unqualified enthusiasm. They subjected what they encountered in their other courses and in discussion with their fellows to the critical scrutiny which Anderson urged, but it cannot be said that they always subjected his realist empi-

ricism to the same critical scrutiny. When the best of them did adopt this critical attitude to Anderson's own views they became considerable philosophers, legal and other social theorists, literary scholars, historians and so on in their own right. The stamp of Anderson, nevertheless, remained on most of them.

Outside his formal class-room teaching he had a considerable influence on both his own and other students through his activities over many years in the university's Freethought and Literary societies. He helped to found the one and revamp the other. He introduced students to the study of James Joyce in the early 1930s, not an easy task as much of Joyce's work was banned. In the mid-1930s a copy of *Ulysses* circulated among his students, with 'A Book of Common Prayer' in gold letters on its spine.

Anderson was a keen and valuable member of the professorial board and of many of its committees, of the faculty of arts and of other bodies. He had an impeccable knowledge of by-laws, precedents and previous policy decisions. He never wanted anything to be agreed to without rigorous scrutiny, detailed discussion and working over the grounds for and against the matter. He always did his 'homework' with the greatest of care. If on a selection committee considering applicants for a vacancy, whether in anthropology, economics, an ancient or modern language, history, law or psychology, he would not only read with care the referees' reports but he would go on to find out who the referees were, and would read samples of the short-listed candidates' published works. Being by office a member of the board of studies in divinity, he attended its meetings with unfailing regularity and took part in its debates — not because he supported religious studies in the university but because he wanted to do his best to ensure that, granted the university had them, they were conducted in the best possible academic manner.

Anderson opposed many proposals put before the professorial board. He usually lost, but he made their proponents put forward a more reasoned case than they had originally done. As a rule he lost because he could not summon the numbers, but he did not often lose the argument. He moved many motions, and if these were for the adoption of the recommendations of a committee on which he had served they were usually carried. If they were something he had initiated they were almost invariably lost. On one occasion not long before his retirement he moved a motion and argued for it at length, the chairman called for a seconder and someone responded; he called for discussion and after a moment of silence put the motion; there was a murmur of 'ayes' and no 'noes'. Later as the chairman walked out of the meeting he said to him, 'John, I'm pleased that your motion was carried', and he replied, 'But, Bill, the bastards didn't discuss it'.

The foregoing may suggest that Anderson was an austere, somewhat contrary, disembodied intellect. To his students and to some outsiders there was another side to his nature: he was the only arts professor in the university in the 1930s who was not aloof from students; he hob-nobbed with them in the quadrangle, ate lunch with them in the Union; he regularly had afternoon tea with a little coterie outside the university. He had students to his home at Turramurra in the week-end for afternoon tea and tennis; on these occasions his wife Jenny played the friendly but intellectual hostess. Anderson liked to sing Scottish and blues songs in his pleasant light tenor voice: he composed a few blues of his own and set the 'Ballad of joking Jesus' in *Ulysses* to music and added a few stanzas. He liked to jive, to swing or whatever was the appropriate action accompanying the popular musical mode of the day.

Anderson was often a controversial figure outside as well as within the university. In 1931 he gave a lunch-hour talk on patriotism to the Freethought Society. He attacked various patriotic shibboleths as obscurantist and touched on war memorials for good measure. The local press, except for the *Labor Daily* which gave him space for reply, erupted. Many State parliamentarians condemned him and the senate of the university censured him. He was, however, unrepentant and probably enjoyed the situation, as it exposed what he regarded as the forces of obscurantism and invited a wider audience critically to examine what he considered an important issue. In 1943 he addressed the New Education Fellowship in a series entitled 'Religion and Education'. In his contribution Anderson argued that religion and education were antipathetic and that religious influences should be bundled out of education. Again there was an outcry in parliament, with public demands that the senate do something about him. On this occasion, the senate replied by saying that its establishing Act provided that there be no religious tests in the university and refused, perhaps uncomfortably, to do anything. Possibly its failure twelve years earlier to restrain him made its members reluctant to try again. Whatever the reason, it was an important assertion of university autonomy. Shortly after his retirement, another public attack on him was initiated by a fanatical Catholic surgeon and supported by a Protestant judge and an evangelical Anglican archbishop who laid about Anderson and some of his colleagues – who were scarcely Andersonians – for alleged anti-moral teachings. He was disappointed that some of his colleagues denied their involvement in the alleged teaching. The attack on him was unfair, but he used the opportunity to assert the right that nothing – even his own teaching – be treated as sacrosanct.

Survived by his wife and son, Anderson died of cerebro-vascular disease on 6 July 1962, and was cremated. That year a collection of most of his major papers, some forty in number, was published posthumously as *Studies in empirical philosophy*; important papers such as 'Some questions in aesthetics' and 'Religion in education' were omittted. The bibliography of 119 items included many book-reviews, generally much longer than usual, and some but not all of his more ephemeral writing. His portrait by William Dobell is held by the University of Sydney.

J. A. Passmore, 'Introductory essay', J. Anderson, *Studies in empirical philosophy* (Syd, 1962) and 'Philosophy', *The pattern of Australian culture*, A. L. McLeod ed (Ithaca, 1963); J. L. Mackie, 'The philosophy of John Anderson', *A'sian J of Philosophy*, 40 (1962); J. Anderson papers (Univ Syd Archives).   W. M. O'NEIL

ANDERSON, MAYBANKE SUSANNAH (1845-1927), feminist and educationist, was born on 16 February 1845 at Kingston-on-Thames, Surrey, England, daughter of Henry Selfe, plumber, and his wife Elizabeth, née Smith. She arrived in Sydney in January 1855 with her parents and brothers including Norman [q.v.6] and was educated as a teacher, which she later attributed to her mother's 'strong personality'.

On 3 September 1867 at St Philip's Church of England, Sydney, Maybanke married Edmund Kay Wolstenholme, a timber merchant from West Maitland; by 1871 they were living at Balmain and he later became an accountant. Late in the 1870s the Wolstenholmes moved to the outskirts of Marrickville and by 1882 had built a large new home, Maybanke, in spacious grounds. Deserted by her unemployed husband in December 1884, she began to advertise a school next year. Over the next decade she built up a considerable reputation for Maybanke College through its modern teaching methods, the success of its pupils, especially in university examinations, and through her own public activities. In 1892 she divorced Wolstenholme for desertion, under Sir Alfred Stephen's [q.v.6] Divorce Amendment and Extension Act.

In 1891 Maybanke was a foundation

vice-president of the Womanhood Suffrage League of New South Wales and president in 1893-96. From 1892 she was also a member of the Women's Literary Society, a group which had serious intellectual and feminist aspirations, and in 1893 was a founder and secretary-treasurer of the Australasian Home Reading Union which sought to spread systematic reading by establishing small study circles in country areas. Next year she published and edited her own fortnightly paper, *Woman's Voice*: 'democratic but not revolutionary; womanly but not weak; fearless without effrontery; liberal without licence'. Lack of finance as well as the pressure of numerous other activities led her to abandon it eighteen months later after her friend Margaret Windeyer [q.v.] refused to take it over. In 1895 she had helped to set up the first free kindergarten at Woolloomooloo, and continued work with the Kindergarten Union of New South Wales and as secretary of the Playgrounds Association of New South Wales until the 1920s. About 1898 she sold Maybanke College and was for a time registrar at the Teachers' Central Registry in George Street.

On 2 March 1899 Maybanke Wolstenholme married with Congregational rites (Sir) Francis Anderson [q.v.], professor of philosophy at the University of Sydney, and devoted herself increasingly to university activities. A regular speaker and hostess, she was an organizer of the University Women's Society and gave special attention to the Women Evening Students' Association, perhaps because it symbolized the spirit of bold self-help that women needed to grasp the opportunities becoming available to them. Through the National Council of Women of New South Wales, she organized the Citizens' Association which worked to allow women the right to be elected to municipal councils.

For some years after their marriage the Andersons lived at Manly, then acquired a place at Pittwater where Maybanke could farm and garden, knit and sew, as well as write numerous pamphlets and pieces for the press. In 1919 she published *Mother lore*, a handbook on developing the intelligence of babies and the education of young children. A member of the Royal Australian Historical Society, she published the 'Story of Pittwater' in its *Journal and Proceedings* (1920). Later the Andersons moved to Hunters Hill and Maybanke again set about compiling a local history, which she read to the society in 1926. As well, she wrote a chapter on the position of women for M. Atkinson's [q.v.] *Australia: economic and political studies* (Melbourne, 1920).

Towards the end of that year the Ander-

sons set off on a third tour of Europe. Maybanke sent articles about her travels to the *Sydney Morning Herald* until she died on 15 April 1927 at St Germain-en-Laye, Paris. Predeceased by two sons and two daughters, she was survived by two sons of her first marriage to whom she left her estate, valued for probate at £2725. Harry Wolstenholme became a solicitor and an amateur ornithologist of repute.

Hermes (Syd), 1927, no 1; *Hesper*, 1927, Lent; *SMH*, 11 Nov 1892, 16 Oct 1911, 19, 20 Apr 1927; *Woman's Voice*, 1894-96; *Lone Hand*, Feb 1914; *Daily Telegraph* (Syd), 21 Apr 1915, 19 Apr 1927; Windeyer papers, box 19 (ML).

BEVERLEY KINGSTON

ANDERSON, PETER CORSAR (1871-1955), educationist, was born on 16 February 1871 at the manse of Menmuir, Forfarshire, Scotland, son of Rev. Mark Anderson, Presbyterian minister, and his wife Jane, née Corsar. He was educated at Madras College, St Andrew's, from which he won a bursary to the United College in the University of St Andrew's. Here his career was distinguished and versatile. A prizeman in Hebrew and church history, he was also president of the students' representative council, a champion rifle-shot, and a golfer of such prowess that in 1893 he won the amateur championship of Great Britain. After graduating B.A. in 1892 he studied theology at St Mary's College and in 1895 was licensed in divinity by the Church of Scotland, but did not pursue this calling because of a breakdown in health. He took a recuperative journey to visit a brother in Western Australia, but moved on to Victoria, where in 1896-1904 he became an assistant master at Geelong Church of England Grammar School.

In 1904 Anderson was appointed headmaster of Scotch College, Perth. A formidable task confronted him: established in 1897, the school was sited in grossly inadequate temporary premises, and suffered from the ineffectualness of the first headmaster John Sharpe. Some of the college council considered that the venture should be discontinued; others sought a solution in a move to a new site at Swanbourne, seven miles (10 km) west of Perth, where a benefactor offered land. Anderson at once insisted that, unlike his predecessor, he should participate in council meetings, and soon proved himself a vigorous organizer amply capable of ensuring the success of the move.

Anderson was headmaster for forty-one years, retiring in 1945. During this period enrolments rose from 59 to 410; more than 3000 boys passed through Scotch in his time. The first decade of his régime was marked by the provision of science laboratories, a cadet corps, sports grounds and a boatshed. By 1914 Scotch was established as one of the four leading independent boys' schools in Western Australia, and for the next thirty years Anderson was doyen among the Protestant headmasters, setting an educational model whose influence extended well beyond his own college. He was especially insistent on the need to provide an alternative system to the government high schools; it gratified him that many Scotch graduates later became prominent in the business and professional life of the State. He was less memorable as a teacher of English and history than as a masterful administrator, careful in times of financial stringency but insistent on bold planning whenever opportunity permitted. Impressively built and inclined to be set in his opinions, he earned the nickname 'Boss', but was respected for his scrupulous fair-mindedness and capacity for hard work. Legends generated around him, such as the yarn that he once caned the entire school in an attempt to put down smoking. If one or two of his younger masters found him intellectually mediocre, the majority held him in great respect even during his last difficult wartime years. He was appointed C.B.E. in 1947.

On 5 July 1899 at Hawthorn, Victoria, Anderson had married Agnes Henrietta Macartney of Mansfield; they had six sons and seven daughters. Bedridden in his last years with rheumatoid arthritis, he died on 26 August 1955 at his home at Swanbourne, close to Scotch College, and was cremated. His wife and eleven children survived him.

A. A. Phillips, 'Three schoolmasters', *Melbourne studies in education, 1976*, S. Murray-Smith ed (Melb, 1976); *Scotch College Reporter*, 1906-45; *Smith's Weekly*, 25 Sept 1926; *West Australian*, 10 Oct 1945, 27 Aug 1955; M. Uren, Scotch College history (1968, Library, Scotch College, Swanbourne, WA).   G. C. BOLTON

ANDERSON, PHYLLIS MARGERY (1901-1957), pathologist, was born on 13 January 1901 at Petersham, New South Wales, daughter of James Robert Anderson, medical practitioner, and his wife Mary, née Kendall. She was educated at the Methodist Ladies' College, Burwood, and the University of Sydney (M.B., Ch.M., 1925), where she was a director of the Women's Union and a member of its debates committee.

In 1926 Phyllis Anderson became a pathologist at the Royal Alexandra Hospital for Children, and in 1927-40 was senior resident pathologist. She became closely involved with her patients and carried out research into children's diseases such as the gastroenteritis epidemic of 1928-29, von Gierke's glycogen-accumulation disease, and diphtheria, and was a regular contributor to the *Medical Journal of Australia*. By 1941 she was working under the auspices of the university's department of bacteriology, where in 1945 she became a teaching fellow and later a part-time lecturer; although reserved by nature, she was popular with her students. Some of her research at the university was concerned with malaria, tuberculosis, whooping-cough, and the development of techniques for taking swabs and growing cultures. She was partly responsible for the transition of the Rachel Forster Hospital for Women and Children into a teaching hospital.

Throughout her career Phyllis Anderson was also involved in the interests of medical women: in 1928 she was a founder of the Medical Women's Society of New South Wales; in 1935-49 she was an office-bearer and president in 1945-46. In 1938 she became a member of the Royal Australasian College of Physicians and a fellow in 1947. She represented medical women on the standing committee of Convocation of the University of Sydney in 1950-57 and was women's representative on the council of the State branch of the British Medical Association in 1951-54.

A lover of music and ballet, Phyllis Anderson was a member of the overseas advisory committee of the Royal Academy of Dancing. Widely read, she had 'an immense fund of kindness, sympathy and wisdom' as well as 'the habit of accuracy of thought and economy of speech'. A colleague claimed that 'many qualities contributed to the high standard of her work — a first-class intellect, scientific integrity and fierce personal honesty, human understanding, humility and a powerful sense of humour'.

She died of hypertensive cerebro-vascular disease in the Royal Prince Alfred Hospital on 29 November 1957. Unmarried, she had no family in Australia. Her estate was valued for probate at £49 814; she bequeathed £47 000 to the faculty of medicine, University of Sydney, from which the Phyllis Anderson Research Fellowship was established in 1959.

PP (NSW), 1947-48, 1, 208, 1950-52, 1, 731, 1957-58, 1, 566, 1959-60, 1, 899; Royal Alexandra Hospital for Children, *Annual Report*, 1926, 1927, 1940, 1942, 1943; *MJA*, 10 May 1958; *A'sian Annals of Medicine*, Aug 1958; *Syd Univ Gazette*, Oct 1958; *SMH*, 7 Sept 1935, 30 Nov 1957, 9 May 1958.   MOIRA SCOLLAY

ANDERSON, SIR ROBERT MURRAY McCHEYNE (1865-1940), businessman and administrator, was born on 6 August 1865 at The Mint, Sydney, third son of Robert Anderson, sergeant of police and native of Aberdeenshire, Scotland, and his wife Margaret, née Hewson. Educated at Sydney Grammar School, he matriculated in 1882 and joined the Bank of New Zealand. After service in New Zealand, he became manager of the George Street, Sydney, branch. He was commissioned in the 2nd Infantry Regiment in December 1886, promoted lieutenant in 1891 and captain on 27 April 1894; next day he resigned his commission but remained in the reserves. With his brother H. C. L. Anderson [q.v.] he was a founding member of the United Service Institution. On 6 August 1891 he had married Jean Cairns, daughter of Robert Amos of Elizabeth Bay.

In 1897-1900 Anderson was city treasurer and then town clerk of Sydney. Always eager for new challenges he entered commerce and, as a partner in (Sir) Allen Taylor [q.v.] & Co., became prominent in the timber and shipping industries. In 1904 he visited the United States of America, England and South Africa for the firm. His business and administrative acumen soon attracted the attention of the Commonwealth government. In 1911-12 he was a royal commissioner on the sugar industry, and in 1915 advised (Sir) George Pearce [q.v.], minister for defence, on the reorganization of the paymaster's branch, and reported on the business management of the Postmaster-General's Department and of the Department of Home Affairs.

On 8 December 1915 Anderson was commissioned as colonel and appointed deputy quartermaster general of the Australian Imperial Force in Egypt. He was instructed to remedy abuses in the contract and supply system, set up a canteen organization and infuse strict business management into the A.I.F. abroad. In Egypt he closed loopholes for petty corruption in the ordnance and fodder accounting systems, and instituted proper auditing and control of stores. He also did valuable work connected with rest camps in the Middle East and the Anzac Hostel in Cairo. On 1 August 1916 he was appointed commandant of Administrative Headquarters in London. In this capacity he represented the Department of Defence, dealing directly with the War Office, and was Lieut-General Birdwood's [q.v.] link with A.I.F. training depots in England. Aided by an expert staff, within two months Anderson organized a complete financial readjustment with the War Office by setting a fixed rate per soldier, instead of the complicated system of accounting for every item of clothing and equipment. In December he was promoted brigadier general and in January 1917 was appointed C.M.G. and K.C.M.G. in May.

A fiercely Australian patriot, Anderson became involved in a dispute with his superiors over the composition of the Imperial Mounted Division and the question of appointing Australians to high command outside the A.I.F. Though his will did not prevail, more protection of Australian interests was certainly needed at the time and his interference was not without certain good effects. He was impatient with bureaucracy and 'officialese', on one occasion telling the secretary of defence 'There is time to go round with an oil can . . . another to go around with a spanner'. He expressed to Sir John Monash [q.v.] his distrust of permanent soldiers, who would 'close up their ranks very solidly against the outsider, specially if that outsider possesses outstanding abilities'. C. E. W. Bean [q.v.] claimed that Anderson could be aggressive if thwarted and that his 'reign at headquarters was not altogether a happy one, since, though gifted with a keen sense of humour and quick intelligence, he lacked the faculty of retaining the complete confidence of his colleagues'.

In June 1917 Anderson returned to Australia via France and Egypt; he was ill for several months after being shipwrecked on his way home. In 1918 he went to New Zealand where he chaired a royal commission on Defence Department expenditure; later that year he was appointed an adviser to the Commonwealth Treasury.

After the war Anderson advised the New South Wales government on financial and commercial matters, although 'all my sympathies are Federal'. In 1920-22 he was in England on business and promoted Commonwealth migration. From the mid-1920s he was again prominent in the Sydney business community. He was deputy chairman of Mount Kembla Collieries Ltd, chairman of the Australian Mutual Fire Insurance Society Ltd, a director of the Australian Gaslight Co. from 1927 and deputy chairman in 1932-39. His clubs were the Union, Sydney, and the Gresham, London, and he was vice-president of the Highland Society of New South Wales.

About medium height and build, with large luminous eyes, Anderson had an attractive personality. With great drive which owed much to a very able and strong-minded mother, he loved a business or administrative challenge and to use his abilities to the full. He had a shrewd and wide insight into human nature and the affairs of business. As a royal commissioner and investigator he was particularly thorough, yet quick and accurate, and his reports are notable for their acuity and directness. Anderson died of paralysis agitans at his home at Double Bay, Sydney, on 30 December 1940 and was cremated with Presbyterian rites. Three sons and four daughters survived him and inherited his estate, valued for probate at £42 921.

A graduate of the University of Sydney (B.A., 1890), Lady Anderson took an active interest in women's and children's welfare: she was an office-bearer in the Women's Club, represented the National Council of Women at conferences and was a founder and first president of the Rachel Forster Hospital for Women and Children. She died after a long illness in December 1928.

C. E. W. Bean, *The A.I.F. in France*, 3 (Syd, 1929); G. E. Caiden, *Career service* (Melb, 1965); *PP* (Cwlth), 1914-17, 4, 341, 5, 339; Appendix, *J* (HR NZ), 1918, 2, H-19c; *Sydney Mail*, 21 Apr 1894; *Punch* (Melb), 9 Jan 1913; *SMH*, 22 Dec 1928, 1 Jan 1941; Fisher papers (NL); Allen Taylor & Co., Letter-book (ANU Archives); MP133/1, 153/8, 729/4, 324/4, 943/1,2, M62/52 (AAO, Melb).

G. P. WALSH

ANDERSON, VALENTINE GEORGE (1885-1969), chemical analyst, was born on 11 June 1885 at Hotham, Victoria, son of Frederick Anderson, compositor, and his wife Louise Jane, née Heinrichsen. His father died when he was 2 and he was brought up by his mother, whom he supported from the time he could earn a living. He was educated at a state school in Ballarat and at the Ballarat School of Mines where in 1904 he took an assayer's certificate with credit in metallurgy and was appointed assistant demonstrator in chemistry for 1904-05. He then joined the chemistry department of the Working Men's College, Melbourne, as lecturer and demonstrator for two years; he also taught at Wesley College. In 1908-09 he took over D. Avery's [q.v.] advisory role to the Melbourne and Metropolitan Board of Works, and was analyst for the inspector of explosives.

Anderson began practice on his own account in 1910 as associate to Avery, and was his partner from 1915 in the firm known as Avery & Anderson, analysts. In 1913-15 the University of Melbourne granted him government scholarships totalling £250 to undertake research from his own laboratories into nitrogen in rain-water. The work was partly sponsored by the British Association for the Advancement of Science; it was reported to and by them and published, with high praise, in the *Journal of the Royal Meteorological Society* in 1915. From 1916 Anderson advised the Commonwealth on

the availability of potassium from alunite, ash and kelp, on fuel economy, and on setting up the white earthenware pottery industry. In 1920-26 he established himself as a leading consultant in industrial chemistry, an able problem-solver, and an upright honourable man. In 1925-46 he lectured part time in applied chemistry at the University of Melbourne, transmitting his industrial experience to senior students in lectures which were informative but not inspiring.

Known as 'V.G.', Anderson was an associate member (from 1918) and fellow (from 1921) of the Society of Chemical Industry of Victoria and was president in 1922. He was also a member of the Society of Chemical Industry (Great Britain), the Royal Institute of Chemistry, London, the (Royal) Australian Chemical Institute (president, 1947-48), the American Chemical Society and the Royal Society of Victoria (president, 1957-58). He contributed to many journals. He lacked the innovatory spirit of his partner, but was widely consulted on problems requiring persistence and chemical perspicacity. As an analyst, trained in accuracy and reproducibility as well as in research, he contributed immeasurably to the compilation and interpretation of the chemistry of Australia's water supplies. His two papers in the Australian Chemical Institute's *Journal and Proceedings* in 1945 on 'Some effects of atmospheric evaporation and transpiration on the composition of natural waters in Australia' are widely acknowledged by environmental chemists. In World War II he advised the Commonwealth government on water supplies.

There were two sons of Anderson's marriage in 1912 to Ethel Grace, née Butchers (d. 1950). In 1962 he married a widow Matilda Hansford Butchers, née Goyen. He died at Canterbury on 22 August 1969 and was cremated with Presbyterian rites, leaving an estate valued for probate at $57 626.

G. Currie and J. Graham, *The origins of CSIRO* (Melb, 1966); *Science and Industry*, 1 (1919); Roy Soc Vic, *Procs*, 83 (1969); Roy Aust Chemical Inst, *Procs*, 37 (1970); Annual reports 1912-15 (Univ Melb Archives); Advisory Council of Science and Industry, Minutes 1916-19 *and* Cwlth Inst of Science and Industry, Annual reports 1921-22 (CSIRO Archives, Canb). JOAN T. RADFORD

ANDERSON, WILLIAM (1868-1940), theatrical entrepreneur, was born on 14 January 1868 at Sandhurst (Bendigo), Victoria, son of James Anderson, miner, and his wife Jane, née Matthews. He left school at 10 to help support the family, and became a bookseller and a billposter at the Royal Princess Theatre. In 1889 he was Bendigo agent for the MacMahon [q.v.] brothers, theatrical managers on the Victorian provincial circuit, and showed an early entrepreneurial flair by opening a roller-skating rink in Bendigo. By 1893 he was manager for various companies touring Bendigo, Ballarat and Geelong, including that of Charles Holloway, for whom he had become business manager by 1895.

On 30 November 1898 at St Patrick's Cathedral, Melbourne, Anderson married Eugenie Marian Duggan, leading lady in the Holloway company, based at the Theatre Royal, Melbourne. Eugenie, daughter of Dennis Duggan and his wife Mary Ann (Marianne), née Welch, was one of a theatrical family which included her brothers P. J. and Edmund [q.v.] and sister Kathleen. An ardent Shakespearian, she studied under Mrs G. B. W. Lewis (Rose Edouin), and made her first appearance as Juliet at the Theatre Royal in 1890. She was soon in Dan Barry's [q.v.3, J. R. Atkins] company, and joined Holloway in 1895. Not long after their marriage Anderson took over the Holloway company, and Eugenie became leading lady in his 'Famous Dramatic Organisation', formed in 1900.

From now on Anderson had at least two permanent companies, one sharing the Melbourne Theatre Royal and the Sydney Lyceum with his friend and rival in melo-drama, Bland Holt [q.v.4], and another touring Australia and New Zealand. He was now well known as the youngest theatrical manager in Australia. On 1 December 1906 he opened 'Wonderland City', a large fun-fair on the waterfront at Tamarama Bay, south of Bondi in Sydney, which he claimed cost him £20 000 and which was dubbed the Coney Island of Australia. At this time Anderson was very wealthy, maintaining large houses in Melbourne and Sydney and spending and entertaining lavishly. A great lover of sport, he owned racehorses and at the Bendigo Jockey Club's meeting in November 1913 won the President's Plate with his mare The Beggar Maid, named after a favourite role of his wife. Genial in personality, he was very popular with his companies and had the reputation of never sacking a needy employee.

In 1908 Anderson built the large King's Theatre in Melbourne (opened in July), and next year visited England where he engaged Olive Wilton [q.v. Cornell] and Roy Red-grave for his company. In contrast to J. C. Williamson [q.v.6], he made it his policy to foster local talent. He is best remembered for the spectacular Australian melodramas he staged at the Theatre Royal and King's, Melbourne, including *The squatter's*

daughter (1907), a drama based on Ben Hall [q.v.4], and *The man from outback* (1909) by 'Albert Edmunds' (Edmund Duggan and Bert Bailey [q.v.]). These melodramas made a great feature of bush settings and exhibi-tions of country skill such as whip-cracking and wood-chopping; in *The squatter's daughter* several sheep were shorn on stage. In 1910 Anderson presented a film of this play, said to be the longest yet made in Australia and featuring the original cast, at his new open-air Olympia Theatre in Syd-ney. Unlike most managers of his day he was never an actor, but he collaborated in writ-ing two melodramas, produced in 1910, for the King's: *The winning ticket*, a drama of the Melbourne Cup, and *By wireless tele-graphy*, based on the Crippen case, with Temple Harrison and Roy Redgrave as re-spective co-authors.

In 1911 'Wonderland City', whose initial popularity had not been revived even by such stunts as a couple married on ele-phant-back, had to be closed, having vir-tually ruined Anderson financially. Though he retained nominal lesseeship of the King's, Melbourne, until 1915, he handed over the theatre to Bailey and Duggan, who staged their famous dramatization of *On our selec-tion* in 1912. From the end of World War I until the late 1920s he was based at the Prince of Wales Theatre in Adelaide, with his daughter Mary often playing leading roles. In 1929 he staged a season of old-style melodrama at the King's, but it closed earlier than advertised; the lurid sensation-drama on which his reputation had been built had been largely superseded as popular en-tertainment.

In the 1930s Anderson returned to Mel-bourne to live. The last show in which he had an interest was a pantomime, *Sinbad the sailor*, staged by Charles Wenman at the King's in 1939. Eugenie, who had conducted a drama school after her retirement from the stage, died at St Kilda, Melbourne, on 2 November 1936, aged 64. Survived by their daughter, Anderson died of chronic nephri-tis at St Kilda on 16 August 1940; he and his wife were buried in the Melbourne general cemetery.

H. Porter, *Stars of Australian stage and screen* (Adel, 1965); E. Irvin, 'The great Australian play', *Quadrant*, Jan 1976; *Punch* (Melb), 23 Jan 1908; *Herald* (Melb), 10 Feb 1958; *Daily Mirror* (Syd), 15 May 1963; Anderson collection (ML).

                                        MARGARET WILLIAMS

ANDRADE, DAVID ALFRED (1859-1928), and WILLIAM CHARLES (1863-1939), anarchists and booksellers, were born at Collingwood, Victoria, sons of Abraham

Da Costa Andrade, storekeeper, and his wife Maria, née Giles, both from Middlesex, England. David was born on 30 April 1859 and William on 12 October 1863. William had to leave school early, studying at night after working long hours in a drapery shop. Both brothers were active in Joseph Symes's [q.v.6] Australasian Secular Association, but their increasing advocacy of anarchist theory led to tension within that primarily freethought society. In May 1886, they helped to form the Melbourne Anarchists' Club: author of its 'Prospectus', David was elected secretary, and was also chief organizer and theoretician. Via the American periodical, *Liberty*, he developed a commitment to Proudhonist anarchism, a libertarian doctrine of individual emancipation (in his case consciously artisan-orientated) rather than mass revolution.

David set up as a bookseller, stationer, newsagent and printer at North Brunswick and later at his 'Liberty Hall' in Russell Street, Melbourne. An active speaker, he was also founder of the Melbourne Co-operative No. 1, a workshop at Albert Park. He contributed news and theoretical items to overseas anarchist papers, but his more significant works were published locally: *Money: A study of the currency question* (1887); *Our social system* (n.d.); *An anarchist plan of campaign* (1888); and a utopian novel, *The Melbourne riots and how Harry Holdfast and his friends emancipated the workers* (1892).

When the Anarchist Club dissolved in 1888, David sought unsuccessfully to revive the Sunday Free Discussion Society. In the early 1890s he became secretary to the Unemployed Workers' Association in Richmond, concerned to encourage co-operative production and assist in land settlement, themes which had been central to his novel. He turned to the South Sassafras village settlement when, in 1894, business failure reduced him to near destitution, and became a '10-acre selector', storekeeper and mailman. His later years are obscure. He died in hospital at Wendouree on 23 May 1928 and was buried in St Kilda cemetary.

By 1887 Will had moved to Sydney with his wife Emma Louisa, née Wickham, whom he had married at the Richmond registry office on 3 February 1886. He represented the Anarchists' Club at the Australasian Freethought Conference in Sydney, staying there to become a 'dealer in progressive works'. He did not succeed in establishing an anarchists' club and sought to influence the newly formed Australian Socialist League. After some time in Mackay, Queensland, he returned to Melbourne, set up in a grocery business and became interested in acting. In 1898 he started a bookshop at 201 Bourke

Street, moving in the late 1920s to Swanston Street. Andrade stocked mainly theatrical and conjuring books and supplies, but his shop also became a significant propaganda and organizing centre for emergent socialist groups throughout Australasia. His imports of radical literature ordered by left-wing groups were detained several times during World War I, but an intelligence report vouched for his 'good character'. He was an active anti-conscriptionist but later withdrew from political activity, though still radical in outlook. Through Percy Laidler [q.v.], manager of the bookshop until the late 1920s, Andrade's published the first Australian editions in translation of several of Lenin's works.

In 1920 Andrade moved to Sydney, opening a branch in Central Square, later transferring to 173 Pitt Street. His first wife had died in Melbourne in 1894 and on 6 September 1907 at North Sydney he married Hilda Champion Sinclair with Unitarian rites; their only son later managed the Melbourne business. Andrade made three trips to Europe between 1910 and 1935; in 1910 he also visited the United States of America. He was surfing at South Steyne beach on 11 November 1939 when a dumper flung him into shallow water; he died at Manly District Hospital half an hour later, survived by his wife, their son, and two daughters of his first marriage.

S. A. Rosa, *The truth about the unemployed agitation of 1890* (Melb, 1890); H. Coulson, *Story of the Dandenongs* (Melb, 1959); B. Walker, *Solidarity forever* (Melb, 1972); S. Merrifield, 'The Melbourne Anarchist Club 1886-1891', *Bulletin* (Aust Labour Hist, Canb), no 3, Nov 1962, *and* 'The formation of the Melbourne Anarchist Club', *Recorder* (Labour Hist, Melb), no 1, July 1964, *and* 'David Alfred Andrade', *Recorder*, no 5, Mar 1965; *Honesty*, Apr-June, Aug, Oct, Nov 1887, Feb, Apr-June, Aug, Nov 1888; *Tocsin*, 12 May, 1 Dec 1898; M. MacNamara, A view of society: Melbourne anarchists in the 1890s (B.A. Hons thesis, Univ Melb, 1972); W. Andrade papers (ML); information from W. S. Andrade, South Blackburn, Vic.

ANDREW REEVES

ANDREWS, ARTHUR (1848-1925), medical practitioner, historian and numismatist, was born on 4 February 1848 at Brickendon, Hertfordshire, England, son of Samuel Andrews, contractor, and his wife Maria Ann, née Thornton. One of a large family, he studied medicine at St Bartholomew's Hospital London (M.R.C.S., England; L.S.A., London, 1869). While resident physician there, he gained valuable experience in coping with a serious outbreak of smallpox and then practised at Farnham, Surrey. In 1872 he studied surgery, the ear, and skin diseases in Vienna, and travelled in Italy and Switzerland before returning to England to practise briefly at Stowmarket, Suffolk.

Worried about his health, Andrews left for Australia in the *Yorkshire* and arrived in Melbourne on 21 February 1874. Registered in New South Wales on 13 April, he became the partner of R. N. Cobbett at Albury and in June became public vaccinator. On 19 August 1875 he married Edith Emma Cookson (d. 1876), and that year succeeded Cobbett as government medical officer and visiting surgeon to Albury gaol. In the 1880s he was honorary medical officer at Albury Hospital and Benevolent Asylum.

Andrews's practice extended over a wide area of the Riverina and upper Murray. He habitually travelled by buggy-and-pair, carrying a saddle in times of flood, and bred his own horses, chosen for speed and stamina. After a long fight he practically stamped out typhoid fever in the area and following a serious outbreak of smallpox in 1913, when only one case reached Albury, he met every train crossing the border to check passengers suspected of carrying the disease.

Involved in the life of the town, Andrews was deputy sheriff for fifteen years and served on the committee of the reformed Albury and Border Pastoral, Agricultural and Horticultural Society in 1879-1919, being several times president. He was also president of the Mechanics' Institute, the school board and the Parents' and Citizens' Association. He interested himself in the local co-operative butter factory and gas company, and was prominent in reconstituting the Albury District Hospital and Training School for Nurses. A skilful taxidermist, he was largely responsible for numerous specimens of wildlife mounted and exhibited in the town museum. A foundation member of the Albury Club, he was also a Freemason of high standing.

Fascinated by numismatics in general, Andrews collected Australian tokens in particular and contributed articles about them to the *Antiquarian Gazette*. He gave his collection to the Mitchell Library, Sydney, and in 1921, at the request of the trustees, published a handbook, *Australasian tokens and coins*. In 1914-17 he was first president of the Numismatic Society of Victoria and in 1921 became president of the Australian Numismatic Society. Andrews was also a local historian of repute. His publications included *History of Albury* (1912), *First settlement of the upper Murray, 1835-1845, . . .* (1920) and articles in the *Victorian Historical Magazine*. Enjoying carpentry, he made furniture for his house.

After retiring in 1919 Andrews lived at Cremorne, where he died of cerebro-vascular disease on 14 February 1925; he was buried in the Northern Suburbs (Church of England) cemetery. He was survived by his second wife Caroline Mary Lemarchand, whom he had married in Melbourne on 17 April 1879, and by their son and three daughters. His estate was valued for probate at £4959.

Numismatic Soc of Vic, *Record of the foundation of the society* (Melb, 1924); W. A. Bayley, *Border city*, 2nd ed (Albury, 1976); family information.

W. W. FIELDER

ANDREWS, CECIL ROLLO PATON (1870-1951), director of education, was born on 2 February 1870 in London, son of John Marshall Andrews, vicar of St Jude's, Grays Inn Road, and his wife Lucy Ann, née Nash. He was educated at Merchant Taylors' School and St John's College, Oxford, graduating with second-class honours in classics and humanities in 1892 (M.A., 1898). After teaching in 1893-96, he became resident tutor at Battersea Teachers' Training College. He arrived in Western Australia early in 1901, recruited by the inspector general of schools, (Sir) Cyril Jackson [q.v.], to be first principal of the new teachers' training college at Claremont. He came with a promise of succeeding Jackson and did so early in 1903; he was to direct the Education Department for twenty-six years. In 1900 he had married Bertha Arnold Agnew; they had three children.

The movement of population from declining goldfields to the new wheat-belt required provision of several hundred one-teacher schools; this strained the resources of the department. However, Andrews's upgrading of rural education was one of his major contributions: the primitive bush schools of the pre-1914 era were transformed in efficiency by the 1920s. He ensured a concurrent improvement in the size and quality of the teaching service through monitors' classes, Normal schools and, ultimately, development of secondary education.

In 1911 Andrews attended the Imperial Education Conference in London, investigated education in Great Britain, Europe and Canada and was able to incorporate some of the ideas collected into his own system. The institution of state high schools was his most notable achievement. He firmly advised successive ministries that the private secondary schools were inadequate. The announcement that the government would establish a state high school precipitated attacks from the influential *West*

Australian and the headmasters of the private schools; Andrews dominated the ensuing controversy and thereby confirmed the government's wavering convictions. The Perth Modern School opened in 1911; the reputation which it acquired enabled Andrews to extend the system to the eastern goldfields and the main rural centres. Although he failed to secure a second metropolitan high school, he established a number of post-primary central schools. Creation of the Perth Modern School and of the University of Western Australia allowed him to replace the old elementary schools by seven-year primary schools. At the secondary level central schools led to the externally examined junior certificate, and high schools provided two further years for the leaving certificate and matriculation.

Besides the constant problems of a large area and sparse population, Andrews faced other difficulties. Economic recessions, harsh living conditions endured by many rural teachers, and salary cuts enforced by governments in financial difficulties stimulated the West Australian State School Teachers' Union to join other public service unions in the strike of July-August 1920. Peter Board [q.v.] of New South Wales, employed in 1921 as a royal commissioner into the affairs of the Education Department, absolved Andrews from blame for the strike and for alarming increases in expenditure.

During the difficult post-war period Andrews criticized the protracted withholding of teachers' annual salary increments by government and the abolition of the kindergarten classes in schools. Whenever conditions were propitious he introduced wide-ranging changes, including curriculum developments, improvements in teaching methods, the encouragement of Parents' and Citizens' associations from 1918 and medical inspection of pupils. He inaugurated the Correspondence School in 1918 and enlarged the scope of evening or continuation classes.

A foundation member of the senate, Andrews was also pro-chancellor of the university in 1912-29. He saw his university work as an extension of his role in government and eventually sought to perpetuate the appointment of his departmental successors to the pro-chancellorship. His experience helped the university to formulate workable administrative practices and he was a useful link with government, but he was never able to secure grants commensurate with those received by his department.

In 1906-12 Andrews was officer commanding cadets for the Commonwealth Military Forces in Western Australia; he was promoted major in 1906 and lieut-colonel in 1910. An active botanist, he collected specimens, published articles on the native flora and was an enthusiastic gardener. He played tennis and golf and enjoyed rowing and swimming. He was a member of the Anglican synod over a long period.

After retiring in June 1929, Andrews returned to England and lived at Sanderstead, Surrey, until his death on 14 June 1951.

J. S. Battye (ed), *Cyclopedia of Western Australia*, 1 (Adel, 1912); F. Alexander, *Campus at Crawley* (Melb, 1963); D. Mossenson, *State education in Western Australia, 1829-1960* (Perth, 1972); *V&P* (LA WA), 1921-22, 1 (4); *West Australian*, 4, 5 Aug 1908, 29 June 1929.   DAVID MOSSENSON

ANDREWS, ERNEST CLAYTON (1870-1948), geologist, was born on 18 October 1870 at Balmain, Sydney, second child of Fearleigh Leonard Montague, artist, and his wife Alice Maud, née Smith. At 3 he and his sister were unofficially adopted by John Andrews and his wife Mary Ann, née Bennett. He spent his boyhood in the St George district of Sydney, where his dour and puritanical stepfather kept a Wesleyan denominational school in which Andrews at 7 was set to teach younger pupils. The precocious and sensitive boy's upbringing was strict and practical. Largely self-taught, he spent only six months at a public primary school. Enforced reading of the Bible and secret perusal of English and classical authors were early and enduring influences: he learned much of the Bible and T. B. Macaulay's poetry by heart. At 16 he became a pupil-teacher at Hurstville, qualified to enter the Teachers' College, Sydney, and graduated from the University of Sydney (B.A., 1894) with second-class honours in mathematics. He then taught for four years at Bathurst, where he developed an interest in natural history.

At the university he had fallen under the spell of (Sir) Edgeworth David [q.v.] and in 1898 presented his first geological paper, on an area near Bathurst, to the Sydney meeting of the Australasian Association for the Advancement of Science. Chosen by David, he spent June to December in Fiji and Tonga collecting coral reef material and data for Professor Agassiz of the Harvard University Museum of Comparative Zoology. This experience opened up vistas of further geological research. He attended university classes in geology and chemistry and in July 1899 joined the Geological Survey Branch of the New South Wales Department of Mines and Agriculture at a salary of £300. In 1901 with Charles Hedley [q.v.] he examined the

Queensland coast and Barrier Reef; in 1902-03 and again in 1904 he visited New Zealand and attracted overseas interest by indicating the importance of glacial corrasion. He published a somewhat exacting school textbook, *An introduction to the physical geography of New South Wales*, in Sydney in 1905.

In 1908, invited by the eminent geologist G. K. Gilbert, Andrews went to the United States of America, where he examined the Californian Sierras and made the first ascent of Mt Darwin. He also visited Canada, England and Europe and met such other noted geologists and physiographers as A. Penck, T. C. Chamberlain and Professor A. M. Davis of Harvard University. On 30 October 1909 at Mosman, Sydney, Andrews married Florence Anne Winn Byron (d. 1923).

He made detailed examinations of the Forbes-Parkes, Cobar, Canbelego and other mining fields in 1909-12, and wrote three important papers on the theory of erosion, including 'Corrasion by gravity streams', read in draft by Davis. Taught field botany by his friends R. H. Cambage, J. H. Maiden [qq.v.] and Hedley, he published notable papers in 1913-16 on the development and distribution of the orders Myrtaceae and Leguminosae and on the 'Geological history of the Australian flowering plants'. He stressed the geological importance of plant distribution and used his knowledge of flora to map boundaries of rock types in heavily timbered country. In 1914 he made confidential valuations of mines, including Great Cobar and Mt Lyell, for Commonwealth tax purposes; in 1917 with Davis he examined the coral reefs of New Caledonia and the New Hebrides and began work on the Broken Hill lode. On 1 March 1920 he was appointed government geologist of New South Wales at £750 a year. His term of office was marked by revision and extension of certain coalfield surveys, investigations of artesian water resources, and publication of his epic *Broken Hill district* (1922) and *Mineral industry of New South Wales* (1928).

Andrews was also active in the administration of Australian science. He was a councillor of the Royal Society of New South Wales (president 1921), and the Linnean Society of New South Wales (president 1937); honorary general secretary (1922-26), acting president (1928-30) and president (1930-32) of the Australasian Association for the Advancement of Science (A.N.Z.A.A.S.); Australian delegate to the second Empire Mining and Metallurgical Congress (1927); chairman of the Australian branch of the International Oceanographic Committee of the Pacific; president of the Australasian Institute of Mining and Metallurgy (1929); a

foundation and executive committee-member (1922-42) of the Australian National Research Council; and a trustee of the Australian Museum for twenty-four years. He led the Australian delegation to the Pacific Science Congress in 1929, 1933 and 1939.

Desiring to prepare 'some helpful note on the powers that exist in man for his own advancement and happiness' and a concise scientific statement on the origins of mountains, Andrews retired in 1930. His last publications included two small books embodying his personal philosophy, *The increasing purpose* (1939) and *The eternal goodness* (1948) and several papers; an unpublished manuscript 'The plan of the earth' was sent to the Geological Society of America in 1944. He received many honours and distinctions including the David Syme [q.v.6] prize and medal of the University of Melbourne for scientific research (1915); the [W. B.] Clarke [q.v.3] medal of the Royal Society of New South Wales (1928); the Lyell medal of the Geological Society, London (1931), and the Mueller [q.v.5] medal of the Australian and New Zealand Association for the Advancement of Science (1946). Andrews was an honorary member of the Washington Academy of Sciences, honorary fellow of the Royal Society of New Zealand and of the Geological societies of London and America. He was Australian associate-editor of *Economic Geology* and a corresponding member of the American Museum of Natural History. In 1927 he gave the Silliman lectures at Yale University and in 1942 the Clarke Memorial Lecture to the Royal Society of New South Wales.

Andrews had a sound grasp of a wide variety of geological subjects and showed keen powers of observation and marked originality of treatment. He made basic contributions to geomorphology, especially to the Tertiary history of the New England plateau, and may be regarded as the founder in Australia of structural economic geology as applied to ore bodies. He followed in the best traditions of David, Gilbert, Davis and the early explorer-geologists in what he called 'the heroic period' of Australian geology.

Slightly built, with a sensitive and gentle expression, Andrews was beloved for his modesty, self-effacement and guilelessness. He never lost his youthful and schoolmasterly habits: in his papers, often prolix, he used apt classical allusions, once felicitously likening the geologist to 'Antaeus of old, who must draw strength from continual contact with the Earth'; in speech he was wont to be a little didactic. In lectures and talks he made frequent use of simple explanation and homely analogy. His memory, mental energy and powers of concentration were remarkable. He had indifferent health for much of his life and kept to a rigid and frugal diet, yet his physical energy was exceptional; most of his field-work whether in the snow country or the desert was done on foot. Music was one of his great loves.

Andrews died of arteriosclerosis on 1 July 1948 at his residence at Bondi and was cremated with Methodist rites. Childless, he was survived by his second wife Mabel Agnes, née Smith, whom he had married on 16 July 1929. His estate was valued for probate at £3638.

Roy Soc NSW, *Procs*, 83 (1949); Geological Soc of America, *Procs*, Apr 1949; Linnean Soc of NSW, *Procs*, 72 (1952); E. C. Andrews papers (Basser Lib, Canb).   G. P. WALSH

ANDREWS, JOHN ARTHUR (1865-1903), anarchist and journalist, was born on 27 October 1865 at Sandhust (Bendigo), Victoria, son of John Andrews, clerk, and his wife Eliza Mary Ann, née Barnett, both London-born. Andrews entered Scotch College, Melbourne, in October 1879 and matriculated in 1881. He became a clerk in the Department of Mines on 13 February 1882 but was dismissed for insubordination in December 1886. He then earned a living from journalism, contributing paragraphs, verse and articles to Melbourne *Punch*, the Sydney *Bulletin* and the Melbourne *Herald*. In 1888 he edited the *Australian* for the Australian Natives' Association.

From early 1887 Andrews was active in the Melbourne Anarchists' Club as a debater and public speaker. He emerged as a leading theoretician; his idealistic anarcho-communism, derived from Kropotkin, competed with D. Andrade's [q.v.] anarchist-individualism for hegemony within the club. In 1888 he edited the final issues of the club's journal, *Honesty*.

Recurrent ill health and the collapse of the Anarchists' Club led Andrews to abandon Melbourne. In 1890 he was briefly sub-editor and reporter for the *Alexandra and Yea Standard*, which first reported Lieut-Colonel Tom Price's [q.v.] order, during the maritime strike, to 'Fire low, and lay them out' if necessary. He moved to New South Wales where he edited *Anarchy* (1891), published a magazine, *The Revolt*, and regularly expounded the tenets of philosophical anarchism in the Sydney Domain. In 1893-94 he reported for the *Mudgee Guardian*. Returning to Sydney early in 1894 he produced *A Handbook of Anarchy*. Its publication led to his arrest on an arbitrary technical charge and he was sentenced to three months gaol. In December he was arrested again, charged with 'seditious libel' in *The Revolt*, and sen-

tenced to five months gaol.

Imprisonment disillusioned Andrews with New South Wales. He sold his printing machine and returned to Victoria, where he published a pamphlet entitled *Each according to his needs* (Carlton, 1895) and a short-lived magazine, *Reason*, during 1896. He modified his anarchism in these later years. Dissatisfied with decrying abstract concepts of the state, he now differentiated between Victorian emphasis upon personal independence and initiative and the fawning colonialism of the New South Wales government. While anarchism remained his ideal of human organization, in his last years he was credited with giving assistance to aspiring Labor politicians and was highly esteemed in the labour movement.

Andrews was an enthusiastic correspondent for international anarchist journals and in 1897 he was offered a post with the American publication, *Firebrand*. In a vain attempt to raise the fare to the United States, he went to Sydney where he stayed until at least 1899 reporting for the *Australian Workman* and *Australian Worker* and aiding another attempt to establish an anarchist society. Andrews was a fair linguist and claimed a good knowledge of geology and mining, law and public business. He was also a gifted writer of verse of which four volumes were published. Through his friendship with Bernard O'Dowd [q.v.] he was appointed editor of *Tocsin*, but some months later, in August 1902, he entered hospital in Melbourne suffering from tuberculosis. On hearing of his illness the Trades Hall Council passed a resolution of sympathy.

Self-sacrificing to the point of asceticism, Andrews remained an enigma to his many and diverse friends. He ate little, wore the scantiest of clothing and his hair long, and was 'given to the use of Eastern narcotics'. But his intensity of purpose, honesty and gently ironic humour reflected an innate kindness that deeply affected friends who deplored the debilitating effect privation had upon him. He never married. He died in hospital on 26 July 1903 and was buried in Boroondara cemetery.

E. Lane, *Dawn to dusk* (Brisb, 1939); S. Merrifield, 'The Melbourne Anarchist Club 1886-1891', Aust Labour Hist, Canb, *Bulletin*, Nov 1962, *and* 'John Arthur Andrews', Labour Hist, Melb, *Recorder*, May 1965, Oct 1966; *Bulletin*, 7 Jan 1893, 31 Mar 1900, 16 Aug 1902, 28 Mar, 6 Aug 1903; *Aust Star* (Syd), 21 Feb 1895; *Tocsin*, 9 Apr, 28 May, 30 July 1903; *Worker* (Syd), 1 Aug 1903; M. MacNamara, A view of society: Melbourne anarchists in the 1890s (B.A. Hons thesis, Univ Melb, 1972); Dwyer papers (ML); Andrews papers (Merrifield collection, LaTL).

ANDREW REEVES

ANGELO, EDWARD HOUGHTON
(1870-1948), politician, was born on 29 July
1870 at Jhansi (now in Uttar Pradesh), India,
eldest son of Captain Edward Fox Angelo
(1836-1902), who claimed descent from the
ancient Calabrian family of Tremamondo
Malavolti, and his wife Mary, née Col-
quhoun. He served with the 28th and 1st
Regiments in the Crimea and India in
1854-78, retiring as lieut-colonel to become
commandant of the Tasmanian forces in
1880-82. Appointed inspecting field officer in
Western Australia in 1882, he resigned to
become government resident at Roebourne
(1886) and Bunbury (1889) before ending his
career as superintendent of the Aboriginal
prison at Rottnest (1890-97). He left a reputation as a gentlemanly and conscientious
official, but too much given to formality and
fuss.

Edward H. Angelo was educated at The
Hutchins School, Hobart, and High School,
Perth. He joined the Public Works Department in 1884 and became treasury clerk at
Roebourne in 1887. On his father's departure
he joined the local branch of the Union Bank,
was transferred to Perth in 1892 and sent to
open the Carnarvon branch in 1902. In 1907
he resigned to found a stock and station
agency and was joined in 1914 by his brother
Alexander Castell. Edward became chairman of the Gascoyne Race Club, two years
president of the Carnarvon Chamber of
Commerce, three years chairman of the
Gascoyne-Minilya Road Board and mayor of
Carnarvon in 1910-15. After such a record
his election to the Legislative Assembly as
Nationalist member for Gascoyne followed
almost inevitably in 1917.

In politics Angelo was a single-minded
and effective advocate of the development of
the North-West. Never an aspirant to ministerial office, he left the Nationalists with M.
P. Durack [q.v.] to join the Country Party in
1920 because of North-West grievances, but
returned later to his old allegiance. He urged
the expansion of trade with south-east Asia
and pushed the tourist potential of the
North-West (he was a keen fisherman himself), but was less successful in advocating
the Gascoyne district for dairying. His main
triumph was the establishment of the ban-
ana-growing industry through irrigation on
the Gascoyne. Having himself made the first
experiment in local production in 1908, he
pressed various governments until in 1930
F. J. S. Wise was appointed as tropical adviser to the Department of Agriculture and
conducted research which encouraged
further development. Land was thrown open
for settlers, the first commercial crop was
exported in 1932, and the industry is still the
soundest example of tropical agriculture in
the North-West. Ironically it was Wise who

as a Labor candidate defeated Angelo at the
1933 elections; but in 1934 he was returned
to the Legislative Council as Nationalist
member for North Province and sat until
1940. He sometimes emerged from retirement to comment on northern development
and penal reform, and contributed some
vivid and valuable reminiscences of early
days in the North-West to the *West Australian* in 1946.

A justice of the peace from 1903, Angelo
was a local director of the Colonial Mutual
Fire Insurance Co. and chairman of directors of Carnarvon Traders Ltd and Nor'-
West Plantations Ltd. On 22 February 1894
at Scots Church, Fremantle, he had married
Frances Mary Peirl (d. 1944); they had three
daughters. He died at Mount Lawley on 1
October 1948 and was buried in the Anglican
portion of Karrakatta cemetery. His estate
was valued for probate at £4757.

West Australian, 4 May, 8 June, 27 July, 17 Aug,
14 Sept, 5, 19 Oct 1946, 3 Oct 1948; letters and
news-cuttings held by Miss V. A. Angelo, Mount
Lawley, WA.   G. C. Bolton

ANGLISS, Sir WILLIAM CHARLES
(1865-1957), butcher, meat exporter and
pastoralist, was born on 29 January 1865 at
Dudley, Worcestershire, England, eldest
son of William Angliss, tailor, and his wife
Eliza, née Fiddian. He was educated at
Hawkhurst, Kent. Engaged in the butchering trade from his youth, he worked first in
London with an uncle and then, after two
and a half years in New York, migrated to
Queensland, arriving at Rockhampton in
1884. After working for a year in Brisbane
and then in Sydney, he moved to Melbourne
where he opened his own butcher's shop in
North Carlton in 1886. The business prospered: in 1892 he opened larger premises in
Bourke Street in the city and that year began
to export frozen meat. Displaying from the
start immense capacity for work, intense
dislike of waste, attention to detail, flair for
exploiting new products and new markets,
and willingness to gamble, over the next
thirty years he became the dominant figure
in Australia's highly competitive meat export trade.

Angliss first exported frozen meat to the
goldfields of Western Australia, later to the
imperial forces fighting in South Africa and
finally to Britain, using freezing facilities
provided by the Victorian government.
When these proved inadequate he built his
own works at Footscray; opened in 1905,
they were for many decades the largest in
Victoria. By World War I he had begun also
to export meat from New South Wales,

South Australia and New Zealand, and had opened offices in London and Liverpool to handle his rapidly expanding business. To consolidate his activities in New South Wales, he bought meatworks at Forbes in 1914 and at Riverstone near Sydney in 1920. He extended his operations to the Queensland beef export trade, purchasing works at Brisbane in 1924 and, jointly with his New South Wales rival F. J. Walker, at Rockhampton in 1927. To complement his export activities, Angliss also bought or leased numerous pastoral properties in the three eastern States, including some in partnership with Australia's 'cattle king' Sir Sidney Kidman [q.v.]. The last and largest addition to his pastoral empire, in 1929, was a group of cattle stations previously operated by the Queensland government; capable of supporting 80 000 head of cattle, the leasehold alone of these properties cost him £250 000.

Over the years Angliss established several companies to administer his expanding and diversifying interests. The family, which included his brother Albert Henry, always had a majority shareholding and he himself exercised tight personal supervision of their activities. By the early 1930s it was claimed that his was the largest personally controlled meat enterprise in the British Empire. However by then he was approaching 70, had no prospective successor, and the business was ripe for take-over. In 1933 the large British firm of Vesteys, already active in the Australian trade, expressed interest in acquiring his Victorian business, and after keen negotiation finally bought the whole Angliss meat business for £1½ million early in 1934. Angliss retained his pastoral properties and during his subsequent 'retirement' acquired interests in a wide range of business activities. He was chairman for many years of the Eagle Star Insurance Co. Ltd, Benbow Mills Pty Ltd, Clifton Brick & Tile Co. and Premier Printing Co., and director of the Mutual Store, Davies Coop & Co. Ltd, Australian Cement Ltd, Hume Pipe Co. Ltd, Hume Steel Ltd and several other companies. By 1950 he was reputedly the wealthiest man in Australia. In his later years he also financed the establishment of a food-trades school, named after him, and actively supported various charities including the Salvation Army and movements to settle migrant children in Australia. In 1939 he was knighted.

In 1912-52 Angliss was a member of the Legislative Council of Victoria, representing Southern Province, a predominantly mixed-farming electorate to the north of Melbourne. A conscientious, highly respected but not ambitious parliamentarian, he was usually unopposed at elections. His most important political achievement followed his appointment as official business consultant to the Australian delegation at the Ottawa Imperial Conference in 1932. For Australia, one of the most favourable results of this conference was a system of preferential controls which boosted meat exports; it was generally acknowledged that Angliss, with his unrivalled expertise, had played a major role.

Active and retaining a 'freshness of spirit' to the end, Angliss at 92 was still reporting at his desk at 9.30 every morning; he usually sported a flower in his buttonhole and was 'always ready to interrupt his work with a dissertation on the unbounded possibilities of Australia'. In old age he was a keen bowls and deck quoits player and enjoyed a Saturday night game of draughts. He did not smoke and was a temperate drinker.

On 31 March 1919 Angliss had married Jacobena Victoria Alice Grutzner at St Columb's Church, Hawthorn; they had one daughter. He died at his Auburn home, Benbow, on 15 June 1957, and was buried in Box Hill cemetery after a service at St Paul's Cathedral. His wife and granddaughter survived him. The Angliss estate was valued for probate at more than £4 million, of which £1 million was set aside in his will for the creation of a charitable trust.

J. V. Angliss, *Sir William Angliss* (Melb, priv print, 1960); E. A. Beever, A history of the Australian meat export trade, 1865-1939 (Ph.D. thesis, Univ Melb, 1968).   E. A. BEEVER

ANGUS, DAVID MACKENZIE (1855-1901), bookseller, was born on 12 July 1855 at Thurso, Caithness-shire, Scotland, youngest son of David Angus, stonemason, and his wife Elizabeth, née Sutherland. The family moved to Edinburgh in the early 1870s. David was educated there and apprenticed to Maclaughlin & Stewart, booksellers; he then worked as a sales assistant in William Brown's bookshop in Princes Street. Consumptive, he was advised to seek a warmer climate and, after a false start, arrived in the *Austral* on 3 November 1882 in Sydney, where his eldest brother Donald, a carpenter, was already living.

Angus worked in the Sydney branch of George Robertson [q.v.6] & Co. of Melbourne for about eighteen months and met there George Robertson [q.v.], who was no relation to the head of the firm. Hoping to open his own shop with £50 that he had saved, he negotiated with London publishers and his former employers in Edinburgh, who promised support. His first shipment consisted of about ten cases of second-hand books from Young J. Pentland, a fellow-apprentice. Angus rented a small shop at 110 Market Street and sent out a circular dated 10 June 1884, advertising his enterprise and promising special attention to country orders. He soon doubled his shop space, but after about a year his health broke down; he sought the drier air of Mudgee, leaving the shop in charge of an American whose ignorance of bookselling endangered the business. George Robertson, aware of Angus's difficulties, offered to become a partner; in January 1886 for £15, his total capital, he was admitted to a half-share in the business which from that date was styled Angus & Robertson. Donald Angus became the firm's book-keeper.

Angus returned to Sydney early in 1886 and on 27 May at the Pitt Street Presbyterian Church married Jane Lindsay Telfer. He did not share Robertson's interests in publishing Australian books and collecting and selling rare items relating to Australasia and the Pacific; however he developed a profitable trade in medical works, in which the firm long held a leading position, and also concentrated on buying libraries and trading in general second-hand books. In 1890 the firm moved to 89 Castlereagh Street (where it remained until 1971) and a new partnership-agreement for ten years was drawn up with capital of £2331.

'Trim, red-bearded and bright-eyed', Angus was usually gentle and tolerant, but became impatient with customers who haggled. He retired from the firm in ill health in 1899 and next year sold his share in the business to Robertson's new partners, Richard Thomson and Frederick Wymark [q.v.], then returned to Scotland. Survived by his wife and two sons, Angus died of tuberculosis in Edinburgh on 21 February 1901. His estate in New South Wales was valued for probate at £6019.

J. R. Tyrrell, *Old books, old friends, old Sydney* (Syd, 1952); *Daily Telegraph* (Syd), 25 Feb 1901; *SMH*, 26 Feb 1901; Angus & Robertson papers (ML).   G. A. FERGUSON

ANGUS, JAMES (1836-1916), railway contractor, was born on 8 November 1836 at Auchterarder, Perthshire, Scotland, son of James Angus, farmer, and his wife Elizabeth, née Cuthbert. He was educated locally, and became a turner and sawyer; on 29 June 1863 at Blackford he married Charlotte de Vernet Moodie and migrated with her to New Zealand. As a sawmiller at Invercargill, he was well placed to make the classical move into railway contracting and, for example, supplied 50 000 sleepers for the Bluff-Winton-Kingston railway. When the

initial railway boom ended in 1879 Angus moved to Sydney where an association with J. Monie and E. Topham led to the formation of Topham, Angus & Co., a firm which built a duplication of Gjedsted's tramway and the initial tracks for steam-trams in the city and suburbs. After this partnership was dissolved about 1884, Angus & Co. played a major role in railway construction in New South Wales and Victoria, winning in the former colony contracts worth £606 943, including duplication of the Granville-Picton line in 1888-92.

In 1890 Angus bought the Minchinbury estate at Rooty Hill from Charles Mackay, enlarged the vineyard and cellars and, from 1901 with Leo Buring [q.v.3] as manager, began making sparkling wines. Minchinbury champagne won prizes at exhibitions in Australia and London, including gold medals in 1909-12 at the Brewers' exhibitions, London. In November 1913 he sold the estate of phylloxera-resistant vines, the entire stock, good-will and book debts to Penfold [q.v.5] & Co. for about £50 000, then a record in the Australian wine-trade. Angus & Son kept the larger part of the property to run sheep.

Although still resident at Artornish Hall, Rooty Hill, Angus concentrated on interests in the Clyde Engineering Co. Ltd, the Vale of Clwydd Colliery Ltd, the Clyde Brick Co. and the New South Wales Cement, Lime & Coal Co. Ltd. He was also a vice-president of the Royal Agricultural Society of New South Wales, a foundation member of Blacktown Shire Council, a life member of the Nepean Cottage Hospital board, an advocate of the Warragamba dam, a leading elder of the Presbyterian Church and vice-president of Burnside Presbyterian Orphan Homes. Angus was accidentally killed at Rooty Hill railway station on 12 April 1916 by the 'Fish' express; he was survived by his wife, two sons and a daughter. His estate was sworn for probate at £172 862.

Angus's second son JOHN HENRY SMITH was born at Invercargill on 11 August 1875. He accompanied his family to Sydney and was educated at Newington College and at Scots College, where he was the first head-prefect. He gained experience on the New Zealand & Australian Land Co. Ltd's Pareora station at St Andrews, New Zealand, then was taught by his father the 'Angus tradition of home building, temple building, city building and empire building'. He ran the retained part of Minchinbury and acquired Bareenong, near Forbes. After his father's death he became chairman of Clyde Engineering Co. Ltd, the Vale of Clwydd Colliery Ltd, Hydraulic Power, Electric & Hydraulic Lifts Ltd and of several small companies mining coal and lime. A vice-president of the Royal Agricultural Society from 1917, Angus was a member of its wine and finance committees. He was also president of Blacktown Shire Council and of the local agricultural society, and a member of the New South Wales and Tattersalls clubs. John Angus died in St Vincent's Hospital, Sydney, on 11 January 1937 and was buried in the Presbyterian section of St Mary's cemetery. He was survived by a son and a daughter by his wife Fanny Oatley, née Cleeve, whom he had married at Penrith on 29 March 1912. His estate was valued for probate at £106958.

J (LC NSW), 1880-81, 1, 385-86; *Appendix to J* (HR NZ), 1883, 2, 100; *V&P* (LA NSW), 1892-93, 6, 563, 565-68; *Government Gazette* (NZ), 5 Feb 1875, 23 Nov 1876; *Agr Gazette* (NSW), 12 (1901); Roy Agr Soc (NSW), *R.A.S. Annual*, 1906, 1917, 1929; *SMH*, 20, 21 Oct 1909, 12, 13 Nov 1913, 15 Apr 1916, 12 Jan 1937; *Nepean Times*, 15 Apr 1916, 15 Jan 1937; information from Mr J. Angus, Vaucluse, *and* Blacktown Municipal Council, NSW.

JOHN ATCHISON

ANGUS, SAMUEL (1881-1943), theologian, was born on 27 August 1881 at Craigs near Ballymena, County Antrim, Ireland, eldest son of John Cowan Angus, farmer, and his wife Sarah, née Harper. He attended Craigs National School and was privately coached in Latin by his great-uncle William Cowan. He went on to the Collegiate School, Ballymena, then won a scholarship to Queen's (University) College, Galway, affiliated to the Royal University of Ireland (B.A., 1902; M.A., 1903).

Angus decided to study for the ministry of the Presbyterian Church and enrolled for the divinity degree at Princeton Theological Seminary, United States of America, and also at Princeton University (M.A., 1905; Ph.D., 1906). His local minister, Dr G. R. Buick, wrote to his friend Woodrow Wilson, then president of the university, commending his protégé. Angus found Wilson aloof, but recognized a great classicist in A. F. West, head of the postgraduate classical school. He worked on North African Latin Christianity and Greek inscriptions and philosophy. Although he also completed the seminary's course, including honours Hebrew, he refused to devote himself full time to theological studies and forfeited the seminary's degree and a scholarship of $100 a year.

Angus tutored privately in classics at Princeton and lectured at Chautauqua, New York, then worked on Hellenistic Greek and New Testament criticism at Hartford Theological Seminary, Connecticut, and spent a semester at Marburg, Germany. In 1907 he married a widow Katherine Duryea,

daughter of J. E. Walker of New York. It was a most happy marriage although she was for many years an invalid. From 1910 Angus regarded Edinburgh as his headquarters where he found academic community with many distinguished scholars, but from October to January 1912 he attended theological faculty at the Humboldt University of Berlin. He then delivered the Gay lectures at Louisville Presbyterian Theological Seminary in Kentucky. Later in 1912 the United Free Church of Scotland licensed him as a probationer for the ministry and he was appointed chaplain of the Scotch Church in Algiers. He visited classical sites in North Africa and Greece and vividly depicted his experiences there in his short volume of memoirs, *Alms for oblivion* (Sydney, 1943).

In May 1914 the General Assembly of the Presbyterian Church of New South Wales elected Angus by 105 votes to 55 to its chair in New Testament exegesis and theology within the faculty of theology, St Andrew's College, University of Sydney. He was ordained by the Presbytery of Sydney and inducted as professor in March 1915. He settled into a house at Turramurra.

Angus carried on research into the Graeco-Roman mystery-religions and their influence on the development of early Christianity. The result was two notable books, *The mystery-religions and Christianity* (London, 1925) and *The religious quests of the Graeco-Roman world* (London, 1929). He had already in 1914 published *The environment of early Christianity*. He accepted many visiting academic appointments in the United States and received honorary degrees from the Queen's University of Belfast (D.Litt., 1923), the University of Glasgow (D.D., 1924) and the Assembly's College, Belfast (D.D., 1929). He continued to publish scholarly books and articles. At the University of Sydney he was a councillor of St Andrew's College from 1926, curator of the Nicholson [q.v.2] Museum of Antiquities and was prominent in the foundation of the board of studies in divinity in 1936.

Angus found his faculty academically and theologically conservative; it had attracted only one truly professional theological teacher, Andrew Harper [q.v.]. By its standards Angus's theology was radical. He had increasingly reacted against conservative lecturers at Princeton seminary and was deeply impressed by the European 'higher criticism' of his formative years. Following Harnack, he contrasted 'the religion of Jesus' with 'the religion about Jesus', to the latter's detriment; through critical study of the New Testament documents, he believed that the original message and figure of the historical Galilean could be discerned. The historicity of the virgin birth, the physical resurrection of Jesus and the ascension were questioned, as were current interpretations of the atonement. When he made a belated acquaintance with Karl Barth and H. E. Brunner, he scorned them as reactionaries. He was attracted by the Neo-Platonists, especially by Plotinus, and by F. D. E. Schleiermacher's notion of divine immanence, and was convinced of the need for personal religious experience. Angus became the friend and colleague of other liberal Protestant theologians in the 'Heretics' private discussion club which he helped to found in 1916. He co-operated with them formally in the united faculty based at St Andrew's College. As a teacher he influenced and inspired many young men of the post-war generation, but his teaching aroused much opposition and public criticism in his own and other churches.

Angus's orthodoxy was questioned first in the Presbytery of Sydney and later in the 1932 General Assembly of the Church. His colleagues at the Theological Hall mostly rallied to his support. The affair became a *cause célèbre* for the next decade, involving much time in church courts, presbytery, the New South Wales and Australian general assemblies, and the latter's judicial commission. Many pamphlets were written, and attempts made at compromise and reconciliation. Significantly, and partly because of Angus's personal charm and undoubted religious devotion, no formal legal charge of heresy was ever laid. War, especially after 1941, diverted the Church's attention. Angus's wife had died in 1934 and he suffered facial paralysis that impaired his speech. The case concluded in 1942 when the Church's procurator, Bryan Fuller, Q.C., successfully moved in the Australian assembly, that 'all communications dealing in any way whatever with the case of Dr Angus be discharged from the business paper, without prejudice to the rights of any of the parties; and that any of the parties concerned may obtain the restoration of any of the matters to the business paper by motion passed pursuant to notice'. Through all this Angus continued to teach, and at the 1943 New South Wales assembly read a paper on the Christian ministry. He died of cancer in the Scottish Hospital, Paddington, on 17 November, and was cremated; he had no children. His estate was valued for probate at £31 694.

His portrait by Jerrold Nathan is in St Andrew's College, where a memorial lecture hall is named after him.

C. Harper, *The auld sinner* (Syd, 1938); A. Dougan, *A backward glance at the Angus affair* (Syd, 1971); Minutes of NSW General Assembly *and* of Presbyterian Church of Aust, 1932-43 (Presbyterian Lib, Assembly Hall, Syd).

ALAN DOUGAN

ANGUS, WILLIAM (1871-1965), agriculturist, was born on 4 June 1871 at Keithhall, Aberdeenshire, Scotland, son of Alexander Angus, farmer, and his wife Agnes, née Cassie. Angus had a technical education at an Aberdeen teachers' college and in London before going in 1897 to the University of Aberdeen, where he graduated B.Sc. (Agriculture) in 1900. He then taught at Stirling High School and the Knox Institute, Haddington, lectured at the West of Scotland Agricultural College, Glasgow, and the Yorkshire College, Leeds, and became principal of Cheshire County Council Agricultural College at Holmes Chapel.

In December 1904 Angus arrived in South Australia by the *Himalaya* to become professor (later director) of agriculture and secretary to the minister of agriculture. His work took him all over the State and led to the establishment of five government experimental farms. In 1906-07 the departments of fruit, dairying, poultry and veterinary affairs were put under his control. He experimented with wheat, potatoes and manures, lectured to farmers, published numerous articles and taught and examined at Roseworthy Agricultural College. In the department he stressed the need for statistics and the dissemination of information about scientific farming. In 1908 his powers were amended to cover only experimental agriculture. On 25 March 1907 he had married Edith Porter at Gilberton. He had briefly been a second lieutenant in the 16th Australian Light Horse in 1906-07.

In October 1910, following a change of government, a parliamentary select committee on the export depot and agricultural department condemned the government's unprofitable management of egg-marketing. Evidence was heard from two senior officers of Angus's lack of tact and failure to delegate responsibility to heads of sections. He did not appear before the committee, and resigned. Although he was 'a man of strong views', early principals at Roseworthy also sometimes had strained relations with the department.

Angus then spent a year farming with his brother John at Noora, joined the Liberal Union and helped defeat the Labor government at the 1912 elections. He offered himself as an experienced candidate, who had made 'land and its management and productive capabilities his especial study', and became a member of the House of Assembly for Victoria and Albert in 1912-15 and Albert 1915-21. He chaired royal commissions on the Aboriginals (1913 and 1916) and on the wheat scheme and rural industries (1918, 1919 and 1921), and was a member of the 1918 commission on the acquisition and disposal of wheat. He was chairman of committees in 1920 and secretary of the parliamentary Liberal Party.

In 1921 Angus returned to farming, successively at Loxton, Hackham, Gumeracha, and inner-suburban Gilberton where he planted experimental wheat plots. In 1934-44 he taught at Scotch College, Mitcham. Well liked as a teacher, he reorganized the agricultural science course, established a model farm and planted a small orchard. Interviewed by the *Advertiser* in 1960, he claimed he had collaborated in wheat-breeding experiments with W. J. Farrer, F. B. Guthrie and Daniel McAlpine [qq.v.], whom he met at Australasian Association for the Advancement of Science meetings. Angus had chaired the agricultural section of the 1911 congress in Sydney and contributed a paper, 'The relation of science and this section to the further development of Australian agriculture'.

Survived by his wife, daughter and son, he died in a private hospital at College Park on 15 May 1965, and was buried in West Terrace cemetery.

H. T. Burgess (ed), *Cyclopedia of South Australia*, 1 (Adel, 1908); *J of Agr and Industry* (SA), Dec 1904, Jan 1905; *J of Agr* (SA), May, July 1905, Apr 1906, Aug, Sept, Oct, Nov 1910; *Scotch College Mag* (SA), 48 (1965); *Observer* (Adel), 24 Dec 1904, 20 Aug, 8, 15 Oct, 31 Dec 1910, 8 May 1920, 23, 30 Apr 1921; *Register* (Adel), 26, 29 Jan, 14 Feb 1912; information from Mr A. J. Angus, Medindie, SA.

J. G. DANIELS

ANGWIN, WILLIAM CHARLES (1863-1944), carpenter and politician, was born on 8 May 1863 at St Just in Penrith, Cornwall, England, son of Benjamin Angwin, tin-miner, and his wife Mary, née Taylor, who died when William was a baby. His father remarried. Educated at a Methodist school and apprenticed to a carpenter, he left Cornwall in 1882 to work as a builder in Cumberland where he joined social reform movements and worked for the temperance cause. In 1884 he married Sarah Ann, daughter of Jacob Sumpton of Hensingham, Cumberland.

Angwin migrated to Victoria in 1886 and in 1892 moved to Western Australia where he worked for Sandover & Co. in Fremantle until 1904. Active in temperance, unionism and local government he helped form the East Fremantle Municipal Council in 1897, was a member until 1927 and mayor in

1902-04. He also worked on the Fremantle Municipal Tramway and Electric Lighting Board in 1910-26 and the management board of the Fremantle Public Hospital.

Defeated in 1901 for the Legislative Assembly seat of East Fremantle, he won it in June 1904. In August, when H. Daglish [q.v.] became the first Labor premier, he selected Angwin for the seventh and last place in his cabinet, as honorary minister. The ministry fell in August 1905 and was crushed at the October elections. Angwin was narrowly beaten by J. J. Holmes, his opponent of 1901 and 1904, but successfully petitioned and won easily on 13 November 1906 when Holmes withdrew. He held the seat, later called North-East Fremantle, till 1927, concentrating particularly on developmental politics, liquor laws, and health and other social issues.

After Labor's landslide win in October 1911 Angwin, as honorary minister in John Scaddan's [q.v.] cabinet, managed immigration and launched many non-controversial projects. In 1914 his diligence earned him the only vacant portfolio, that of works and industries. He was worried by teething problems of the recently established State enterprises. His most difficult task was to justify the letting of a dubious contract, without tenders, to S. V. Nevanas & Co. Ltd for a State meatworks at Wyndham. When Nevanas abandoned the contract Angwin was prominent in defending the erring ministers, Scaddan and W. D. Johnson [q.v.]. The government almost fell on the issue in November 1915, but survived until the following July.

Angwin joined some colleagues in vigorous advocacy of conscription during the 1916 referendum campaign. When the pressure of events in the eastern States forced the State Labor Party to split in April 1917, he remained with the official rump but continually sought reconciliation. By April 1918 he was third in the party's parliamentary hierarchy and had added wheat legislation to his former interests. After the 1924 election he became deputy premier to P. Collier [q.v.]. As minister for lands, immigration and industries his main concern was with land settlement, particularly the group settlements in the south-west established by Sir James Mitchell's [q.v.] government to develop dairying. He tried to cut expenses, re-negotiated the agreement with the British and Australian governments and set up a royal commission which reported in 1925; but he was as anxious as Mitchell to reduce the State's dependence on imported dairy products and made no big change in the scheme.

Angwin resigned in April 1927 to become agent-general in London for six years. In

1933 he was appointed C.M.G. In 1935 and 1938 he chaired two royal commissions on wheat and in 1936 presided over the Rural Relief Trust. He died at his Fremantle home on 9 June 1944 leaving an estate valued for probate at nearly £16 000. He was survived by a son and a daughter; Benjamin Angwin, M.C., another son, had died in 1919 aged 33.

A moderate, pragmatic man, keen to develop his State's resources and institutions, Angwin opposed entry into the Federation, was critical of the way it harmed his State, and was lukewarm about the Fisher [q.v.] government's attempts to increase Federal powers. In November 1918 he praised the soldiers, men of 'the old bulldog breed', who upheld the honour of Australia and of the British flag. Thomas Bath [q.v.] believed that 'he had ordinary abilities but got places because of his tremendous diligence and application'.

J. S. Battye (ed), *Cyclopedia of Western Australia*, 1 (Adel, 1912); *Morning Herald* (Perth), 29 June 1904; *West Australian*, 29 June, 10, 11 Aug 1904, 13, 14 Nov 1906, 21, 23 Nov 1914, 10 June 1944; J. R. Robertson, The Scaddan government and the conscription crisis 1911-1917 (M.A. thesis, Univ WA, 1958).   J. R. ROBERTSON

ANNAND, FREDERICK WILLIAM GADSBY (1872-1958), businessman, soldier and town clerk, was born on 7 May 1872 at Toowoomba, Queensland, son of James Annand, rural worker, and his wife Harriet, née Gadsby. Educated at Toowoomba High School he worked for the Australian Mutual Provident Society and on Burenda station in the Warrego District before establishing an agency business at Toowoomba in 1895. With George A. Leichney he founded an accounting firm in 1899. Licensed under the Local Auditors' Board, he became auditor for local authorities in the area.

Annand left the partnership in 1905 to manage the Brisbane Permanent Building and Banking Co. Ltd (now the Bank of Queensland). Despite reconstruction in 1898 the management was still defective. His tough, realistic, but judicious control progressively overcame legacies of depression and drought, restored financial soundness, and led to profitable expansion.

Annand joined the Queensland Defence Force and became a lieutenant in the 2nd Battalion, Queensland Mounted Infantry, in Toowoomba in 1897. After transferring to Brisbane he joined the Royal Australian Engineers, was promoted captain to command the 5th Field Company, then major on 6 February 1911, commanding the 3rd Field Company and later the 23rd Engineers (Signal Company). Annand left Australia as major commanding the 7th Field Company, R.A.E., Australian Imperial Force, during 1915; promoted lieut-colonel in March 1916, he organized and commanded the 2nd Australian Pioneer Battalion. He was mentioned in dispatches four times, wounded in November, received the Distinguished Service Order for an action on 29 December and was awarded a Bar for gallantry at Montbrehain on 5 October 1918. After the war he commanded the 15th Battalion in the Citizen Military Force and, after promotion to colonel on 31 March 1926, the 7th Infantry Brigade, Queensland, until 1930; he retired from the army on 19 May 1932.

In 1919 Annand had resumed management of the Brisbane Permanent Building and Banking Co. After two terms as an alderman of the Hamilton Town Council and one as mayor in 1924, he was appointed town clerk of Greater Brisbane next year. When the Metropolitan Water Supply and Sewerage Board was dissolved amid charges of mismanagement and patronage, Annand supervised its absorption by an already efficient city administration. He was accustomed to command, and frustration led him to resign as town clerk in 1931 when the Moore [q.v.] government established a municipal executive committee. Fortunately he was able to resume his position at the Building and Banking Co., from which he resigned on 26 September 1936 to 'take a more active part in public affairs'. He was immediately elected a director of the company and later acquired several other directorates.

Public-spirited and with strong religious convictions, Annand was president of the Young Men's Christian Association in Brisbane, a life member of the United Services Club, president of the Brisbane Rotary Club, and was keen on bowls and yachting. He was a deacon of the City Congregational Church and became deputy grand master of the Masonic Lodge. He died on 22 June 1958 at his Ascot home, survived by his wife Helen Alice, née Robinson, whom he had married on 1 June 1898, and by three sons and two daughters. His estate was valued for probate at £23 857. His son Douglas Shenton (1903-1976) became a distinguished artist.

Annand's brother JAMES DOUGLAS (1875-1952), born at Toowoomba on 21 January 1875, had interests in various Toowoomba retail houses, a grazing property and a real-estate partnership. While in the retail trade he became president of the Toowoomba Traders' Association. He entered the city council in 1921 and served as mayor in 1924-30, 1933-49 and 1952. In 1925-47 he was chairman of the Local Authorities Association of Queensland. He represented Toowoomba in the Legislative

Assembly in 1929-32 and East Toowoomba in 1934-35. He died on 7 August 1952, survived by his wife Isabella Julia, née Walker, whom he had married on 17 March 1904, and by one son and two daughters.

Queensland and Queenslanders (Brisb, 1936); G. Greenwood and J. Laverty, *Brisbane 1859-1959* (Brisb, 1959); R. S. Marriott (ed), *100 years of progress* (Toowoomba, 1960); *Brisbane Courier*, 20 May 1925, 23, 26 June 1958; History, compiled from bank records (Bank of Queensland, Brisb); City Council minutes, 1925, 1928, 1931-32 (Town Hall, Brisb).   JOHN LAVERTY

ANNEAR, HAROLD DESBROWE (1865-1933), architect, was born on 16 August 1865 at Happy Valley, Sandhurst (Bendigo), Victoria, son of James Desbrowe Annear, miner, and his second wife Eliza Ann, née Hawkins. Annear had six much older stepsisters, two sisters and a brother alive when his father died in 1883. He was educated at the Hawthorn Grammar School. In 1883 he was articled to the architect William Salway (d. 1903) who had arrived in Victoria in 1854 and served articles with J. Reed [q.v.6]. Salway had toured Asia, worked in China in 1868-75, and after returning to Melbourne in 1876 had built up an extensive practice.

About 1889 Annear left Salway to set up on his own. His talents were already recognized within the profession: he had received awards for sketches published in building journals and for an illustrated essay on English Gothic architecture. His papers on John Ruskin (1889) and on methods of architectural criticism (1893), delivered before the Victorian Institute of Architects, were later published in Melbourne and show him to be a staunch admirer of Ruskin and the American H. H. Richardson, whom he called 'the greatest modern architectural genius'. They also reveal his deep commitment to the arts and crafts movement and to the concept that architecture is an art, not a profession.

In 1900 Annear became a foundation member and first president of the T-Square Club, which was centred on the Working Men's College and embraced artists, craftsmen and architects. In 1903 he outlined the club's orientation in an address which was later published: 'Now the fellowship of this trinity is considered valuable, in order that the artist might be more architectural, that the architect might be more artistic, and that both might be better craftsmen'. He held doggedly to these views and never joined the professionally oriented Institute of Architects. In practice his opinions were ex-

pressed in designs which were often praised for bringing artist, architect and craftsmen together.

Annear's earliest designs were in an adapted American-Romanesque manner. However, he also worked in a variety of modern styles; his most distinctive early design, possibly influenced by the Viennese Sezession style, was the Springthorpe memorial in the Kew cemetery (1897), described by the *Argus* in 1933 as 'the most beautiful work of its kind in Australia'. In his own words he was a 'developed specialist' — that is 'a man who finds, after diligent study and much experience of architectural history, that the best expression of his work is obtained when he designs in the style with which he is in thorough artistic sympathy'.

In 1902-03 Annear planned three houses for which he is best known: 32, 34 and 38 The Eyrie, Eaglemont. These were free and decorative adaptations of a half-timbered, roughcast, and Marseilles tiles genre called, in Victoria, Queen Anne style. They were planned so that one space could freely flow into another, with built-in cupboards and distinctive, vertically sliding windows. His own house, 32, contained his monogram, derived from Dürer's, in stained glass. He persisted with the half-timbered and roughcast designs into the 1920s but from about 1910 also contrived a related form of expression: a gabled house with half-timbering applied only as an abstracted pattern in the upper parts of gable-ends. In this manner he designed a house for the artist Norman Macgeorge [q.v.] at Alphington (1910) where the garden was laid out by Blamire Young [q.v.]. Another example was a house at 4 Como Avenue, South Yarra (c.1920-25). For his two distinctive designs, Broceliande (also known as Troon) at 224 Orrong Road, Toorak (1918, demolished), and Inglesby at 97 Caroline Street, South Yarra (1919, demolished), Annear has been incorrectly type-cast as a proto-functionalist and a forerunner of the International Style in Melbourne. His writings, the variety of his architectural designs, and his commitment to architecture as an art, all contradict that interpretation. Both Broceliande and Inglesby indicated the influence on him of the West Coast of America and the Spanish Mission Revival, and his continuing desire to create an Australian architecture by adapting that of countries climatically and geographically related to southern Australia.

While much of Annear's work resulted either from commissions by fellow artists or from wealthy clients, he expressed his desire for a universal Australian domestic architecture through a publication, *For every man his home*, edited by him in 1922, which included modest villa designs featuring open-air rooms, American West Coast bungalow forms and rough-cast walls. His other writings include a chapter in *Domestic architecture in Australia*. Although he was chiefly a designer of houses, a major work outside the field of domestic architecture was the reconstruction of Menzies Hotel, while his most novel design was a triumphal arch over Princes Bridge for the visit to Melbourne of the duke and duchess of York in 1901. He also designed the Elwood Beach kiosk (1920, demolished).

After World War I, Annear prepared several fine, simple designs which freely used the classical vocabulary. Notable among these are the graceful Church Street bridge, Richmond (1924), and Cloyne at 609 Toorak Road (1929), which has a jewel-like quality and is unified by the judicious repetition of a Venetian window motif. Such excellent buildings as Cloyne have unjustly been presented as an embarrassment by some of Annear's later admirers, but he believed those who argued for a utilitarian architecture were asking for a non-architecture: they 'did not know definitely what architecture consists of'. In fact he pursued throughout a tempered eclecticism.

For many years Annear was an instructor in architecture and drawing at the Working Men's College. In World War I he was involved in Red Cross work and organized street decorations for button days. He also influenced the selection of the site for the Shrine of Remembrance. He was a foundation member and supporter of the Arts and Crafts Society, an authority on and collector of antique furniture and *objets d'art*, and a skilled designer of furniture. Stout and jaunty, with a round, smooth, rosy face, Annear usually wore a monocle. To Joan Lindsay he was 'what is known as a "character", and [he] gloried in it'. She describes him in middle age as a devotee of good living, who 'loved to play host in his studio cottage in South Yarra where he dispensed hospitality in true eighteenth century style ... He was so witty so indiscreet and so truly loved beautiful things that only the most strait-laced clients objected to his eccentricities and occasional full-blooded lapses into vulgarity ... In all things he was rococo, standing for a touch of fantasy in suburbia'.

On 25 July 1891 at Carlton registry office he had married Florence Susan Chadwick, but by World War I his irascible artistic temperament had led to his wife's estrangement. He had diabetes for some years but died of hypertensive heart disease on 22 June 1933 at St Kilda, and was cremated. He was survived by two sons and by his wife to whom he left his estate valued for probate at £348.

S. U. Smith and B. Stevens (eds), *Domestic architecture in Australia* (Syd, 1919), special no, *Art in Australia*; R. Boyd, *Victorian modern* (Melb, 1947), and *Australia's home* (Melb, 1952); G. Woodful, 'Harold Desbrowe Annear ...', *Architecture in Aust*, Feb 1967; *Aust Builder and Contractors' News*, Jan 1888, June 1894; *Building and Engineering J*, July 1893; *Punch* (Melb), 9 July 1925; *Argus*, 23 June 1933.   GEORGE TIBBITS

ANSTEY, EDWARD ALFRED (1858-1952), builder and politician, was born on 6 July 1858 at Port Elliot, South Australia, third son of Charles John Anstey, carpenter, and his wife Eliza, née Cererher. Educated at Port Elliot Public School he was apprenticed as a joiner to Samuel Trigg. He completed his indentures in the building trade and moved to Adelaide in 1882. On 9 February 1884 he married Mary Ann Glenie; they had two daughters. After five years as a journeyman carpenter he began on his own in 1888 and entered partnership with M. H. Gerard in 1894; they specialized in shop construction and fitting.

Anstey was on the Kensington and Norwood council in 1892-93 and, after moving, was elected to Burnside District Council in 1905. In the 1880s he had been an 'earnest worker for the bettering of the condition of the masses' and prominent in the East Torrens labour committees; he was a foundation member of the United Labor Party of South Australia in 1891. Anstey became president of the State branch in 1914-15 and a member of the Federal executive of the Australian Labor Party. In 1908 he won the State seat of Adelaide in a by-election and held it until 1915 when, after electoral redistribution, he secured North Adelaide. He resigned from the A.L.P. in 1916 over conscription, became a foundation member of the National (Labor) Party, and held North Adelaide as a Nationalist in 1918.

Anstey had been whip in 1915-16 in Crawford Vaughan's [q.v.] ministry. In the Nationalist-Liberal coalition ministry of A. H. Peake [q.v.], he held the agriculture, repatriation and crown lands and immigration portfolios in 1918-20 and chaired the State War Council. In March 1920 Peake's demand for unconditional support from the Nationalists led Anstey to resign from the ministry. While chairman of the Nationalist parliamentary party he helped the Progressive Country Party and representing it in 1921 narrowly lost North Adelaide. An ardent land reformer, he had been a fluent speaker on taxation and political economy.

In 1920 Anstey had been appointed to the council of the South Australian School of Mines and Industries. He became organizer at Minda Home for retarded children; a resourceful fund-raiser, he was secretary in 1927-37 and from 1946 a vice-president. He was honorary treasurer of the Kindergarten Union of South Australia in 1925-27 and was closely involved with literary and dramatic societies.

Anstey was the epitome of early South Australian Labor leaders: a strict teetotaller, leading Freemason and committed Protestant. After retirement he was a keen bowler, but later suffered from partial blindness. He spent his last four years at Geelong, Victoria, where he died on 2 July 1952. Buried there in the Western cemetery, he was survived by his daughter Amy; his estate was sworn for probate at £879. His portrait is in the South Australian Archives.

H. T. Burgess (ed), *Cyclopedia of South Australia*, 2 (Adel, 1909); T. H. Smeaton, *The people in politics* (Adel, 1914); H. G. Viney, *A century of commerce in South Australia* (Adel, 1936); *Adelaide News* and *Advertiser* (Adel), 5 July 1952.

DEAN JAENSCH

ANSTEY, FRANCIS GEORGE (1865-1940), politician, was born on 18 August 1865 in London. His father Samuel, of Devon yeoman stock, had died five months earlier. The boy was cared for on a family farm until his mother Caroline, née Gamble, married John Lank, a stableman. The family travelled through the Midlands and to London in search of work. Frank remembered a kind and warm stepfather, but John's hot temper and trade union beliefs cost him several jobs. Between times, Caroline, a school-teacher, supported the family; it was an unsettled and often a meagre existence. Frank's formal education was a few years at Board school — 'more Bible than grammar, more fear of hell than earthly geography, more crawlsome obedience to one's "betters" than knowledge of how to fight the battle of life'.

Aged 11, Frank stowed away on a full-rigged passenger vessel bound for Australia. He jumped ship in Sydney and signed on as 'bosun's boy' in a ship working the Pacific islands trade. For ten years he knew the brutality of seafaring life, and joined the Seamen's Union in 1883. He sailed to Asia and through the Pacific; what he saw of the coolie and Kanaka trades left him with a hatred of slave labour, a strong belief in White Australia, and a romantic interest in island life. He read widely, kept a common-place-book, and wrote sketches and verse.

Signing off, Anstey carried his swag in search of casual work. While driving a hearse in Sale, Victoria, he met Katherine Mary Bell McColl, daughter of a policeman,

and married her in 1887; two sons were born in 1889 and 1891.

The Ansteys moved to Melbourne where Frank became a cleaner at the Working Men's College. He interested himself in the Knights of Labor, in David Andrade's [q.v.] Anarchists' Club, and in the Social Democratic Federation which supported the Trades Hall Council in 1891 in forming a Progressive Political League. He soon became a leading speaker and writer for the Labor cause. With fellow S.D.F. member Tom Tunnecliffe [q.v.], in 1898 he founded the Victorian Labour Federation, a Rochdale-type co-operative, which prospered briefly. Its rules barred members of parliament as office-bearers; both Tunnecliffe and Anstey entered the Legislative Assembly within five years. Anstey helped found the Tramway Employees' Association and was its president for many years.

He served for eight years from 1902 as member for East Bourke (later Brunswick), his main interest being to attack monopoly in land ownership and banking and to advocate public ownership. John Curtin, a fellow member of the Brunswick Labor Party, became his friend and follower. In 1904, with his parliamentary colleague Charles McGrath [q.v.], Anstey rode a bicycle on the first of several organizing tours through eastern Victoria. Admired for his oratory, he lectured regularly for Tom Mann's [q.v.] Victorian Socialist Party as well as for the Labor Party, and he wrote extensively for *Tocsin* and *Labor Call*, which he edited for some years. Suffering from a debilitating sickness which dogged him throughout life, he took a health trip to England in 1907; his expenses were met from a fund raised by his friends. He sent back perceptive reports of the British and European labour movements.

In 1910 Anstey became member of the House of Representatives for Bourke. His stand on public control of finance made him a strong supporter of the creation of the Commonwealth Bank. The outbreak of World War I caused a breach with his close associate W. M. Hughes [q.v.]. For Anstey, it was 'a war of rival capitalists . . . its inevitable outcome the enslavement of labour'. He conflicted with the Labor government over its budgetary policies and its use of war precautions regulations against opponents of the war. In 1915, he published *The kingdom of Shylock*, the circulation of which was suppressed, in which he argued that 'this war makes the living worker a slave, and fills the treasury of Shylock to overflowing'. (When he revised the book for republication in 1921 as *Money power*, he deleted many of the anti-Semitic references). Having failed to convince caucus, he walked out and offered his resignation to the Victorian Labor executive, which refused to accept it.

Anstey was, with Frank Brennan [q.v.], the first Labor parliamentarian to speak for the Australian Peace Alliance. When the Industrial Workers of the World leader Tom Barker [q.v.] was arrested for publishing an anti-war poster, Anstey sent his support and asked for copies; the police suspected him of conspiratorial activity. Although he was not against conscription for a people's army (a view which caused him some trouble in the labour movement), he campaigned prominently against the referenda of 1916 and 1917. In the 1917 election he condemned Hughes for having betrayed his party and principles to the 'Trusts, Combines and Monopolies, the Profiteers, Exploiters and the great vested interests of capital'.

In March 1918 Anstey sailed on his second trip to England, via the United States of America. In both countries, and in Europe, he met labour and socialist leaders. While he was in England, W. A. Watt [q.v.], the acting prime minister, appointed him a member of an imperial press mission, in which capacity he visited the Western Front and met allied war leaders and publicists. On his return in 1919, he published *Red Europe* which welcomed the 'social revolution' in Russia and forecast the universal advance of the 'drum-beats of the Armies of Revolution'.

In 1922 Anstey became assistant leader of the Labor Party in the House of Representatives. He was appointed next year to the royal commission on navigation, which inquired into the use of non-Australian shipping in the coastal trade, a 'cheap labour' policy which he condemned. He was a trenchant critic of the Bruce-Page [qq.v.] coalition, saying of Bruce that 'he delighted the masses with his unlimited promises, and the wealthy by the fact that he never fulfilled them'. In March 1927 caucus accepted his resignation as assistant leader and commiserated with him on his ill health; he said privately that he had acted out of disgust with the intrigues against his leader Matt Charlton [q.v.], who was soon replaced by James Scullin [q.v.] for whom Anstey had worked in the 1906 election. He took a health trip to the Mandated Territory of New Guinea; on his return, he became a co-director with John Wren [q.v.] and a major shareholder of a New Guinea gold mining company, which failed to prosper.

Labor won a majority in the House of Representatives in October 1929. Caucus elected Anstey to cabinet and Scullin gave him the portfolios of health and repatriation. The Depression overwhelmed everyday administration, and Anstey led a fight within caucus for his financial ideas. He argued for a double dissolution to break the strangle-hold of the Senate. He condemned the bankers and financiers as 'cormorants and vultures . . . whose sole aim is to devour the living standards of the Australian workers'. He urged that the government take direct control of the Commonwealth Bank and expand credit in order to reduce unemployment. In 1930 he published *Facts and theories of finance* to support his case. He moved successfully in caucus for the extension by one year of a maturing public loan but Scullin, then in London, overruled the decision. He had hoped for the support of E. G. Theodore [q.v.] but did not get it, and said the Labor ministers were 'mere Yesmen to the bankers'.

Anstey told caucus that he preferred the Lang [q.v.] Plan to the Scullin government's policies. Caucus dropped him from cabinet; he was, he said, glad to escape with his life. Now 64, he announced that the 1931 election would be his last. For the first time, he just scraped home. He served three last dispirited years and 'selected obscurity and left the limelight and dollars to wiser and more saintly men'.

In retirement, Anstey and his wife lived in Sydney on his scanty savings. In 1938 he met George Nicholas [q.v.] at a favourite place, the race-track. Nicholas thanked him for his help during the war in gaining a permit for the manufacture of aspirin and later sent him a cheque for £500, to which Anstey gave a 'hearty welcome'. After his wife's death, he returned to Melbourne, where he died of cancer on 31 October 1940. As a boy, he had gone with his father to hear the free-thinker Charles Bradlaugh; his will directed that there should be 'no followers or flowers, or praise, prayers or preachers' to mark the cremation. Wren named a colt for his 'great friend' Anstey, and the Victorian government named a railway station in his honour.

Frank Anstey lived his life in the memory of the poverty of his childhood and the harshness and inhumanity of his young manhood. He won his own education and way in the world. Like many self-educated men, he sought a simple explanation of social injustice — in his case, the depredations of private finance capital. His wit, love of words and sense of drama made him one of the greatest and most loved radical orators and writers of his time. He flayed his political foes, but with such style and grace that he made few enemies. He was generous to a fault and had little financial benefit from his long career. A free-thinker and a Freemason, he enjoyed the friendship and patronage of John Wren; but he never betrayed his deeply held beliefs. He was a better publicist than a politician; he ended his days in disillusion and disappointment, believing that his country and his class were as far away as ever from his early dream:

Man rises in his strength and looks around
While in his sight the dawn of reason breaks.

J. T. Lang, *The great bust* (Syd, 1962); J. Robertson, *J. H. Scullin* (Perth, 1974); *Overland*, no 31, 32, 1965, no 33, 1965-66; *Labor Call*, 25 Apr 1907, 7 Nov 1940; *Tocsin*, 15 Dec 1905; Anstey papers (NL).

IAN TURNER*

ANTHON, DANIEL HERBERT (1890-1951), soldier, was born on 9 August 1890 at Petersham, New South Wales, son of Daniel Christopher Anthon, Danish master-mariner, and his wife Eliza Alice, née Brown. After a primary school education he worked as a clerk and in 1912-14 was employed in Port Moresby by Burns Philp [qq.v.] & Co. Ltd, merchants and shipowners.

Anthon enlisted in the Australian Imperial Force on 3 May 1915, was posted to the 20th Battalion and embarked for Egypt seven weeks later. He first saw action at Gallipoli towards the end of August when his battalion relieved the 3rd Light Horse Brigade at The Nek, and then served at Russell's Top until the evacuation. Anthon was promoted corporal on 17 March 1916 and next day left Egypt for the Western Front where he fought in the early stages of the Somme offensive — at Le Bridoux in May and June and at Pozières in July. On 7 August, during the battle for Pozières Heights, he was wounded and did not rejoin his unit until November. Promoted sergeant next month, he was sent to England for officer training and, on being commissioned second lieutenant in June 1917, returned to the front. During the battle of Menin Road he was wounded for the second time but remained on duty and was awarded the Military Cross for 'great initiative in superintending and consolidating after the battalion objective had been gained at Hannebeek Wood'. In October he was promoted lieutenant.

In the early months of 1918 Anthon was involved in patrolling and raids and on 11 March was wounded again; for bravery at Mont St Quentin on 30 August, he was awarded the Distinguished Service Order for capturing a strongly held machine-gun post, raiding a trench and taking fifty-four prisoners. A month later, near Beaurevoir, he ran forward through heavy machine-gun fire and, single-handed, captured an enemy-held farm; this action earned him a Bar to his Military Cross. His final honour was mention in a dispatch by Sir Douglas Haig.

Anthon returned to New South Wales in June 1919 and was discharged from the A.I.F. in October. On 3 May 1922 he married Violet Mary Stacy at Croydon. After farming at Wildes Meadow and Bowral in 1921-28 he was employed by Southern Portland Cement Ltd at Berrima as a foreman and later as a clerk. He was active in local affairs as a justice of the peace, churchwarden and Oddfellow. During World War II he served with the 2nd and 13th Australian garrison battalions and commanded military detention barracks at Holsworthy in 1941 and Orange in 1942-43. While demanding a rigid standard of discipline from the soldiers in his charge he was regarded as a fair man. In 1946 he was awarded the Australian Efficiency Decoration, and was placed on the retired list in June 1948, with the rank of major.

Survived by his wife, two sons and two daughters, Anthon died from heart failure at his Moss Vale home on 4 September 1951, and was buried in the local Anglican cemetery.

C. E. W. Bean, *The story of Anzac*, 2 (Syd, 1924), and *The A.I.F. in France*, 4, 6 (Syd, 1933, 1942); *London Gazette*, 28 Dec 1917, 1 Feb, 8 Mar, 11 July 1919; The war diary of the 20th Battalion (AWM); information from Mr F. S. Anthon, Moss Vale, NSW.

J. B. HOPLEY

ANTILL, JOHN MACQUARIE (1866-1937), soldier, was born on 26 January 1866 at Jarvisfield, Picton, New South Wales, second surviving son of John Macquarie Antill, grazier, and his wife Jessie Hassall, née Campbell. His paternal grandfather was Major Henry Colden Antill [q.v.1], aide-de-camp to Governor Macquarie [q.v.2]. Educated at Sydney Grammar School, he was working as a surveyor when he joined the New South Wales Mounted Rifles in 1889. Commissioned as a captain on 19 January, he raised and commanded the Picton Squadron. Four years later he was sent to India by Major General (Sir) Edward Hutton [q.v.] and attached to the 1st Battalion, Devonshire Regiment, and the 2nd Dragoon Guards for training. On his return in 1894 he was commissioned in the colony's Permanent Military Forces and appointed to the instructional staff.

In November 1899 Antill was promoted major and given command of A Squadron, New South Wales Mounted Rifles. The unit saw active service in South Africa and took part in the relief of Kimberley and operations in the Orange Free State, Transvaal and the Orange River Colony from February to November 1900. A senior officer described him as 'a dashing and capable leader in action, and remarkably cool under fire'. He returned to Australia in January 1901 but in March went back to

South Africa with the 2nd Battalion, New South Wales Mounted Rifles. From April to October he saw action in western and eastern Transvaal, taking part in the capture of Potgieter's convoy on the River Vaal in May and of De La Rey's convoy of wagons, cattle, ammunition and other stores. In eastern Transvaal he was involved in many night marches which resulted in the capture of over 1000 prisoners. For his distinguished services he was appointed C.B. in 1900, twice mentioned in dispatches, awarded the Queen's South Africa Medal with seven clasps, and made a brevet lieut-colonel. After his return home he married Marion Agnes Wills-Allen at St James's Church, Sydney, on 24 October 1901. There were two daughters of the marriage which was dissolved in 1914.

In 1902-04 Antill served on the instructional staff of the Permanent Military Forces in New South Wales and in 1904-06 was aide-de-camp to Governor-General Lord Northcote [q.v.]. Placed on the retired list, he worked at Jarvisfield as a grazier until 1911 when he rejoined the active list as commandant of the Special School of Instructors at Albury. In April 1914 he was promoted lieut-colonel and next October was appointed brigade major with the 3rd Light Horse, which embarked for Egypt on 25 February 1915. The brigade fought at Gallipoli as infantry and Antill took temporary command on 20 September during operations at Russell's Top and Monash Valley. Among the last troops to be evacuated in December, his brigade returned to Egypt and in January 1916 he was promoted substantive colonel and temporary brigadier general. After operations in the Sinai Desert, they were sent to reinforce the Anzac Mounted Division at Romani in August, arrived too late for the fighting there, but joined in pursuit of the Turks.

From 18 September Antill commanded the 2nd Infantry Brigade in operations at Ypres and the battle of the Somme, but sickness forced his evacuation to England in November. Next March he took command of the 16th Infantry Brigade, then forming on Salisbury Plain, but it was soon disbanded. Antill returned to Australia in September 1917 and his appointment with the Australian Imperial Force ended on 12 December. For his war service he was appointed C.M.G. and mentioned in dispatches. Instructional duties followed and in 1918 he became assistant adjutant general in Victoria; later that year he was appointed commandant in South Australia. In 1921-22 he was chief instructor of the Central Training Depot at Liverpool, New South Wales. He retired on 26 January 1924 with the honorary rank of major general.

In retirement, Antill spent several years at Jarvisfield and later lived at Manly and Dee Why. His pastimes were gardening, woodwork, reading and bowls. As a young man he had excelled at boxing and fencing under Larry Foley's [q.v.4] tuition; he retained a keen interest in these sports and in horsemanship. He was also encouraged to write by his 'adopted daughter', Rose Antill de Warren, a journalist, and in 1936 they published *The emancipist*, a three-act drama about the life of William Redfern [q.v.2]. After a three-year illness he died of cancer at Royal Prince Henry Hospital on 1 March 1937, and was cremated.

Tall, spare and wiry, brusque in manner and speech, Antill was recognized throughout his career as a courageous soldier, an able leader, a stern disciplinarian and a shrewd judge of men, with a flair for moulding those under his command to his ideal of what a soldier should be. This ideal was in the traditional British pattern.

Antill's brother Robert Henry (1859-1938), who inherited Jarvisfield, was a prominent pastoralist and a noted breeder of Ayrshire cattle. He was chairman of the Picton Pastures Protection Board in 1901-28 and served as district coroner for forty-two years.

Aust Defence Dept, *Official records of the Australian military contingents to the war in South Africa*, P. L. Murray ed (Melb, 1912); A. C. N. Olden, *Westralian cavalry in the war* (Melb, 1921); C. E. W. Bean, *The story of Anzac*, 1, 2 (Syd, 1921, 1924); T. H. Darley, *With the Ninth Light Horse in the great war* (Adel, 1924); H. S. Gullett, *The A.I.F. in Sinai and Palestine* (Syd, 1923); *V&P* (LA NSW), 1894-95 (5), 402; *Reveille* (Syd), 1 June 1937; *Pastoral Review*, 16 Aug 1938; *Punch* (Melb), 25 Feb 1915; *SMH*, 3 Mar 1937.   REX CLARK*

ANTONIEFF, VALENTIN ANDREEVICH (1877-1962), Russian Orthodox priest, was born on 4 March 1877 in the Ekaterinoslav region of southern Russia (Dnepropetrovsk region, Ukrainian Soviet Republic), son of Andrei Zahar Antonieff, priest, and his wife Alexandra Grigorievna, née Stadnitzky. A brilliant student, Antonieff attended Mariupol Church Seminary and the Ekaterinoslav and Ardon theological seminaries; he graduated from Ardon as dux in 1905. He won a scholarship to the Caucasus Theological Academy, but in 1908 he was obliged to discontinue his studies there.

Antonieff had joined the Imperial Russian army in 1899 and in World War I, as chaplain to the 1st Siberian Infantry Division, was twice wounded and three times decorated, once by the Tsar. On the outbreak of the civil war in 1918, he joined the White Russian army and was appointed dean of Steppe Corps (3rd Division) under General Verzhbitsky. Later, as principal chaplain to the 2nd Siberian army, he had command over 108 priests and 4 deans. He left Russia through Vladivostok in 1922 and, after a year in Shanghai, sailed for Australia in the *St Albans*, landing in Townsville, Queensland, on 23 September 1923. He worked briefly as a labourer on construction of the Cairns-Innisfail railway, then in the mines at Mount Mulligan for three and a half years.

Antonieff had married Maria Mikhailovna Mikhaelsky at Ekaterinoslav in 1907. She and their four children stayed in Russia until he was able to bring them to Australia in December 1924. The family moved in 1927 to Brisbane, and for a time Antonieff served as a stoker on the coastal steamer, *Canberra*.

The 1920s had seen a great influx of Russian immigrants to Queensland, and the work of the Russian Orthodox Church had to be expanded. Father A. Shabasheff had established the Church in 1921 among Brisbane families and, when newcomers settled in the rural areas, particularly in the Callide valley and the Childers district, another priest was clearly needed. Antonieff resumed his ministry, and the successful establishment of the Church outside Brisbane was due largely to his missionary zeal.

When Shabasheff departed for the United States of America in 1929, Antonieff became acting head of the Russian Orthodox Church in Queensland for three years. In 1932 he was confirmed in the appointment of archpriest and incumbent of the Cathedral of St Nicholas in Brisbane. As archpriest he travelled extensively throughout Queensland, visiting Russian communities. A bearded patriarchal figure, he consolidated the rather sparse foundations left for him by his predecessor, and founded Sunday schools and a library. He was naturalized in 1939. Faced with a further post-war increase of Russian migrants, the synod of the Russian Orthodox Church Abroad appointed Antonieff protopresbyter of the Church in Australia on 17 December 1951. This position, equivalent to monsignor in the Roman Catholic Church, gave him the primacy of his Church. He held it until a bishop was appointed from overseas, then ministered in Queensland until ill health forced him to retire from full-time duty in 1961. Survived by five children, he died at his Brisbane home on 26 August 1962 and was buried in Toowong cemetery.

A portrait of Antonieff, painted by A. J. Martin in 1970, is held by the Antonieff family. His private papers, including a number of treatises on aspects of the Russian Orthodox faith, were transferred to the mother church in the United States.

Brisbane Courier, 27 Aug 1962; *Russian Truth* (Melb), 28 Aug 1962; *Unification*, 7 Sept 1962; A659-40/1/289 (AAO).   DAVID A. GIBSON

APPEL, JOHN GEORGE (1859-1929), lawyer, farmer and politician, was born at South Brisbane on 15 March 1859, son of George Appel [q.v.3] and his wife Maria Jane, née Haussmann, the first European female born at the German Mission at Zions Hill (Nundah), Moreton Bay.

After primary education at the Normal School, Adelaide Street, Brisbane, he became at 10 a foundation scholar of the Brisbane Grammar School. From there he went to a private school conducted by Rev. D. A'Court. Passing the preliminary examination for solicitors of the Supreme Court of Queensland, he was articled on 3 June 1875 to G. V. Hellicar of Thompson & Hellicar. Some of his five-year articles were served with Thompson, Foxton & Harvard. He later read in the chambers of K. ff. Swanwick, barrister-at-law. Aged 20, he passed his finals but had to wait until he came of age to be admitted, on 3 August 1880. Meanwhile he had married Ruth, only child of the wealthy James Sutherland of Hill Side, Breakfast Creek, Brisbane, on 18 March 1879.

Appel practised in Brisbane and when James Howard Gill [q.v.4], who married Appel's sister Annie Louise, began practice in Ipswich, the two became partners, with Appel conducting the head office. When Gill became crown solicitor on 7 May 1885, Appel worked alone until 1887 when he went to Townsville on account of ill health. He stayed there until 1889 when he abandoned the law for a farm in upper Nerang Valley. Despite residence in Townsville he was master of the Brisbane-based North Australian Lodge No. 1, United Grand Lodge of Queensland, in 1888-89.

Appel's two homes were Windermere at Hamilton and Sea Glint at Elston (now the heart of Surfers Paradise) near his farming and dairying interests at Glencoe, upper Nerang. He was a member of the Hamilton Shire Council in 1890-1908 and was chairman twice; after Hamilton became a municipality he was twice mayor. In 1902 he also became a member for six years of the Nerang Shire Council. Appel attended many conferences of the Local Authorities Association of Queensland after its foundation in 1896. He was a long-serving president of the Southport Horticultural and Agricultural Association, and a member of the Queensland Fish Board.

Appel stood in 1893 for the electorate of Nundah as an Independent Liberal Democrat but was defeated. Fourteen years later, supporting Robert Philp [q.v.], he failed to win Albert, then based on Southport. He won the seat in February 1908 by a handsome majority and retained it until his death in 1929.

Appel joined William Kidston's [q.v.] ministry on 29 October 1908 as secretary for mines and public works and found his true *métier* as home secretary on 29 June 1909. After the mines portfolio was returned to him on 22 October, he held both portfolios under Kidston and later Digby Denham [q.v.] until 26 February 1915 when, at odds with Denham, he avoided dismissal by a strategic resignation. Although C. A. Bernays [q.v.3, L. A. Bernays] asserts that Appel loved being a minister and regarded the home secretaryship as his own, he was never again in power. Health legislation and codification of the Local Authorities Act and amendments were his most considerable achievements. Because of his long and intimate knowledge of local government he was called the 'Local Authorities Home Secretary'. Appel was early involved in the Farmers' Parliamentary Union (Liberal members representing rural electorates), the forerunner of the Country Party in Queensland. After the 1915 election he led this body in the Legislative Assembly until 1918.

Appel was famous for his tours in the government steamer *Otter*; in 1914 one such trip went as far north as Daru on the coast of south-western Papua. His yacht *Alert* was well known in Moreton Bay, the Southport Broadwater and the Nerang River. He was deeply interested in The Southport School and gave a prize for dux of the school, which was later endowed as a memorial to him and is still given. He was a gifted amateur singer with a wide following. He died on 19 March 1929 at Clayfield from drinking tainted water at Sea Glint some weeks before, survived by his wife, two daughters and a son. Premier McCormack [q.v.] saw him as a broadminded, generous man with a genial temperament. A. E. Moore [q.v.], his party leader, said he was a big-hearted, simple gentleman; honorable, generous and kindly to a fault. Spencer Browne [q.v.] noticed 'the soul of an artist, the heart of a child, and the strength of a Greek wrestler'.

S. Stephensen (ed), *Annals of the Brisbane Grammar School 1869-1922* (Brisb, 1923); C. A. Bernays, *Queensland — our seventh political decade, 1920-1930* (Syd, 1931); D. J. Murphy (ed), *Labor in politics* (Brisb, 1975); *Brisbane Courier*, 30 Oct 1908, 24 Feb 1915, 20 Mar 1929; *Daily Mail*, 24-27 Feb 1915; ED/3/64-113, 1870-78 (QA).

J. C. H. GILL

APPLEFORD, ALICE ROSS; *see* ROSS-KING

APPLETON, WILLIAM THOMAS (1859-1930), businessman, was born on 2 May 1859 at Leeds, Yorkshire, England, son of Thomas Appleton, bookbinder, and his wife Mary, née Burnley. His mother's brother William had established a profitable import-export agency in the Port Phillip District; the Appleton family visited him in Melbourne in late 1859 just before his death, but soon went back to England. William Thomas was educated at Wharfdale College, Yorkshire, before returning to Victoria with his parents in 1869 to settle in Geelong. He completed his education at Melbourne Church of England Grammar School in 1872-73. As a youth he was a keen horseman and interested in many sports.

In the late 1870s Appleton joined his brother (Colonel) George Burnley (1850-1945) in his Geelong woolbroking and stock and station agency. On 27 April 1882 he married Elizabeth Jane, daughter of John Traill, a founder and then chairman of Huddart [q.v.4], Parker & Co. Pty Ltd whose Geelong office Appleton joined about 1884. Manager there early in 1887 and later of the Melbourne office, he was appointed to the board in 1894 and became managing director in 1898. In 1910-30 he was also chairman of the company, which in the 1890s had consolidated its position in the Australian coastal trade, extended its operations to New Zealand and secured a majority interest in the Hebburn and Metropolitan collieries at Maitland and on the South Coast, New South Wales.

Appleton was an able and energetic organizer in the field of industrial relations. His thorough understanding of shipping management and his mastery of detailed administration assisted him as architect and advocate of the Australasian Steamship Owners' Federation, which grew into a very powerful organization; he was its founding chairman in 1899-1903, and in 1908, 1911-16, 1920-21 and 1925-30. First appointed as a shipowner representative on the Melbourne Harbor Trust in November 1906, Appleton was chairman from April 1911 until the trust was reconstituted in February 1913, and was thereafter a senior commissioner. Throughout, he was a staunch advocate of harbour improvements and strongly supported the trust's long-term plan for new dock construction. Appleton Dock on the north side of the River Yarra was named after him.

For twenty-five years Appleton was an active council-member of the Melbourne

Chamber of Commerce, of which he was president in 1914-16. He was also president of the Associated Chambers of Commerce of Australia in 1915-16 and had been president of the Geelong branch and a representative at congresses in London. He was chairman of several shipping and colliery companies, a director of Amalgamated Wireless Australasia Ltd, and had been a trustee of the Geelong Savings Bank and a founding director of the Western and Wimmera Districts of Victoria Freezing Co. Ltd. In 1910 he intended to stand at the Kooyong Federal by-election but at the last moment withdrew in favour of the Liberal Party's nominee, Sir Robert Best [q.v.]. During World War I Appleton held a number of temporary official posts. He also attended the inaugural National Laboratory Conference in early 1916 and took part in later negotiations which eventually led to the formation of the Council for Scientific and Industrial Research.

Appleton died of cancer on 16 February 1930 at his home in Malvern, and was cremated with Presbyterian rites. He was survived by his wife, two daughters and three of his five sons of whom the eldest had been killed at Pozières in 1916. His estate was valued for probate at £131 323. One of the most influential men in the Australasian shipping world, Appleton was respected by both shipowners and maritime unions for his strength of leadership and fairness of judgment.

Huddart Parker Ltd, *Huddart Parker Limited 1876-1926* (Syd, 1926); B. Hoare, *Jubilee history of the Melbourne Harbor Trust* (Melb, 1927); Melbourne Harbor Trust, *Port of Melbourne official handbook* (Melb, 1933); G. Currie and J. Graham, *The origins of CSIRO* (Melb, 1966); *Southern Sphere*, March 1911; *Punch* (Melb), 1 Feb 1912; *Age*, 17 Feb 1930; Huddart, Parker & Co. Ltd records (Univ Melb Archives); family papers (held by Mrs J. M. McMillan, Richmond, Vic.).

G. R. HENNING

ARCHDALL, MERVYN (1846-1917), clergyman, was born on 24 June 1846 near Clonmel, Ireland, son of Rev. William Rowley Archdall and his wife Catherine, née Archdall. His father was a Church of Ireland priest until sectarian violence drove him to England. Educated at Durham School and Corpus Christi, Cambridge (B.A., 1870; M.A., 1883), Archdall was ordained deacon in 1869 and priest next year. In 1869-73 he was curate of St George's, Kendal, Westmorland, and then became district secretary of the London Society for Promoting Christianity among the Jews. This enlivened his interest in the Old Testament which he

reverenced as mankind's real history – God's progressive revelation culminating in the incarnation. Archdall later founded a Sydney branch of the London Society and his condemnation of pogroms won him the affection of Australian Jewry. In 1882 Bishop Barker [q.v.3] invited him to St Mary's, Balmain. He first married on 14 September in Stettin, Germany, Martha Caroline Christine Karow, daughter of a Lutheran pastor. They reached Sydney in the *Potosi* on 27 November.

Archdall soon became the polemical leader of the already predominant Evangelicals in the Sydney diocese, for he never let his 'doctrines sag or melt together like lollies in a bag'. Although fair, courteous and disliking controversy, he so propounded his principles that some claimed he provoked prejudice and strife. In many published addresses and theological pamphlets he criticized Darwinism, rejected much higher criticism and denounced Higinbotham's [q.v.4] 'Christless Christianity'. *Lithurgical right and national wrong . . .* (London, 1900) was 'distinguished . . . by profound learning and accurate scholarship'. In 1898 he helped to found the Protestant Church of England Union and was a leader of the Australian Protestant Defence Association.

Rome's iniquities appalled Archdall. Roman Catholics were Christians in spite, not because, of their Church; he learnedly demonstrated many pagan survivals in Roman liturgy and government. Heathenism, he wrote, 'has its fulfilment in the Papacy'. He deplored Anglican latitudinarianism and was shocked when bishops tried to remove certain Old Testament passages from the Prayer Book to relieve the Church from defending their historical accuracy. Ritualism was worse; 'First, it comes purring gently and with feline step, and only asks for "toleration". But once tolerated it soon threatens . . . until it can safely show and use its claws'. Scripture, not tradition, was his touchstone. Both episcopacy and government by presbyters were scriptual; the former was not essential for valid orders. Surplice, academic gown and tippet alone were legal vestments.

Archdall argued learnedly and read Scripture and the fathers in the original languages. When studying French, Dutch or German theologians he could become oblivious of time and forget to go to bed. He prized patience, careful investigation and weighing of evidence. He loved words and used philology to elucidate Scripture. His faith, while a living experience, rested on wide historical knowledge, especially of the apostolic, sub-apostolic and Reformation eras.

Archdall laboured earnestly in his parish

but scorned a popular style. His carefully prepared sermons were beyond many hearers. One reported he was kept awake by Archdall's enthusiasm as though he were listening to a song in some foreign language. He judged hymns by their doctrine and forbade Newman's 'Lead kindly light' for it omits God's name. He condemned abbreviating Christian names as demeaning baptism and disdained increasing his congregation by 'Pleasant Sunday Afternoons'. He taught theology at home to many young clergymen. Donald Baker, later bishop of Bendigo, won his wife Rosa from Archdall's home.

Archdall persuaded his diocese to accept deaconesses for teaching and pastoral work; in 1891 he founded Bethany for their training and long supported it with a quarter of his income. In 1902 he became a canon of St Andrew's Cathedral and in 1908 incumbent of St Stephen's, Penrith. He retired to Drummoyne in 1913 where he died of cardiac disease on 22 November 1917; he was buried in the Field of Mars cemetery. His wife, daughter and two sons survived him. His estate was valued for probate at £1005.

Archdall's eldest child Mervyn (1884-1957), medical practitioner and journalist, was a captain with the Australian Army Medical Corps in 1917-18 in France and Belgium. In 1930-57 he edited with great distinction the *Medical Journal of Australia*. He insisted on high scientific standards, on publishing results of Australian medical research in Australia and on preserving the purity of the English language, of which he thought Fowler but an indifferent guarantee. His brother, Henry Kingsley (1886-1976), was an eminent Anglican clergyman, headmaster and academic in Australia, New Zealand and England. In 1922 he published in Sydney *Mervyn Archdall*, a memorial of his father.

Australian Christian World (Syd), 30 Nov 1917; *Aust Church Record*, 7 Dec 1917; *MJA*, 14, 21 Sept, 14 Dec 1957; *Punch* (Melb), 13 Dec 1917; *The Times*, 3 Mar 1976; S. N. Hogg, Balmain past and present (ML).   D. W. A. BAKER

ARCHER, FRANCIS HENRY JOSEPH (1886-1958), schoolmaster, was born on 18 March 1886 at Ballarat, Victoria, eldest of four children of Henry Archer, hairdresser, formerly of London, and his wife Emma Olivia Josephine, née Whitten, whose parents were Irish immigrants. He went to Urquhart Street State School and in 1900 won a scholarship to Grenville College, whose headmaster, A. A. Buley, insisted he take eight subjects at matriculation and physics at the Ballarat School of Mines. He was dux

in 1902, did a third matriculation year and then in 1904 began teaching at Ballarat Church of England Grammar School. Obliged to support himself at the University of Melbourne, he became a resident master at Caulfield Grammar School in 1907, and attended evening lectures (B.A., 1911; M.A. and Dip.Ed., 1913). Archer considered a post in 1912 at the Royal Australian Naval College, studied in 1914 for M.A. honours in the university's French department, which held him to be of professorial calibre, and completed the second part of the Australian College of Theology's licentiate in theology. He chose a teaching career for its pastoral opportunities. In 1913 he was recommended for an exchange teaching post in England under a scheme of the League of Empire, but the outbreak of war prevented him taking it up. On 6 January 1915 he married Lillie Verran Morcom, an accomplished Ballarat pianist.

Highly regarded as teacher, churchman and sportsman (he played for Ballarat against the South African cricketers in 1911), Archer was appointed in 1917 headmaster of Trinity Grammar School, Sydney, founded four years earlier and controlled by the parish of Holy Trinity, Dulwich Hill. An Evangelical, he fitted easily into the archdiocese, which supported his efforts to make Trinity a modern public school, and he coped patiently with the difficulties of parochial control. By 1921 the enrolment had risen from 121 pupils to 186. Fearing a possible collapse of the school as a result of the measles and influenza epidemics of 1918-19 he moved the boarders to Austinmer near Wollongong, organizing studies at home for day-boys.

In 1923 Archer returned to Melbourne to Caulfield Grammar School as headmaster, at the invitation of its owner-principal W. M. Buntine [q.v.]. On Buntine's retirement in 1932 when control passed to a council, Archer was appointed headmaster. Aiming to give 'opportunity to the individual pupil to reveal the possibilities dormant in him' he diversified the curriculum, extended extracurricular activities, and gave pupils a share in managing the school. Distrustful of urban values and impressed by the successful experiment at Austinmer, he was at no pains to build a 'great brick fortress' at Caulfield. Instead, he established at Yarra Junction the first rural education centre for an Australian suburban school. The enrolment increased from 525 in 1932 to 852 in 1954, when he resigned. His savings were depleted by inflation, and for two years until his retirement in 1957 he took a part-time post at Brighton Grammar School. He had made his only visit to Britain and Europe in 1951.

Archer had deep religious convictions and

broad human sympathies. Religious affiliations or ethnic origins had no place in his judgment of staff or pupils, and he regarded as unscriptural and insulting the doctrine that non-episcopal ordinations were invalid. He chaired a committee of the Victorian Council for Christian Education in Schools appointed to construct a syllabus for secondary schools, and contributed to the first of its series of booklets, *Sizing things up* (Melbourne, 1944), edited by R. Mathias. He was a councillor of Ridley College in 1934-56, a warden of the vestry of St Mary's, Caulfield, active in the Church of England Men's Society, and chairman of the Caulfield branch of the Missionary Service League. In 1938 he was appointed to the board for electing the archbishop of Melbourne, and in 1943 became a lay canon of St Paul's Cathedral.

Archer died on 20 February 1958 of coronary vascular disease and was survived by his wife and three sons. A portrait by Margery Withers is at Trinity Grammar School and one by Rollo Thompson is at Caulfield Grammar School. Memorial windows are in the chapel of Trinity Grammar and in St Mary's Church.

C. E. Latham and A. Nichols, *Trinity Grammar School* (Summer Hill, 1974); Trinity Grammar School, *Triangle*, Dec 1975; Advisory Council minutes 1913-24 (Trinity Grammar School, Summer Hill); F. H. J. Archer papers and news-cuttings (held by Mr F. K. Archer, Elwood, Vic); information on F. H. J. Archer (Caulfield Grammar School, Vic).

E. L. FRENCH

ARCHER, ROBERT STUBBS (1858-1926), pastoralist and company director, born on 21 May 1858 at Croydon, Surrey, England, and EDWARD WALKER (1871-1940), pastoralist, businessman and politician, born on 12 December 1871 at Croydon, were sons of David Archer [q.v.1] and his wife Susan, née Stubbs. They were educated at Whitgift Grammar School, and Edward also attended King's College School, London.

Robert worked first for his father's firm of commission merchants in London, but in 1880 arrived at Gracemere near Rockhampton, Queensland, with his brother John, as book-keeper. Within a year he succeeded his uncle Thomas [q.v.1] as manager of Archer & Co. He continued to improve the Shorthorn and Hereford studs, established in 1856 and 1862 respectively, by importing high quality bulls. He was recognized as an authority on cattle-breeding from 1891 when he was awarded second prize by the National Agricultural and Industrial Association of Queensland for his treatise on aspects of managing the two breeds. He was also respected as a cattle-judge at Brisbane and Sydney shows.

Archer pioneered cattle-dipping in central Queensland and in 1898 the Queensland government appointed him to the Tick Commission to study methods of combating the scourge. In 1890 he introduced a share dairy-farming system with 600 cows bred from the Gracemere Ayrshire stud which supplied Rockhampton and Mount Morgan with milk, cheese and butter. He also experimented with pasture-improvement, irrigation and ensilage, long before such practices were common; his 1882 silo was said to be the first in Queensland. When the dairying project was abandoned in 1914 he established a Red Poll stud. He improved his firm's herd by crossing Red Polls with Shorthorns, and his bulls raised the standards of northern Australian herds generally; he himself believed this to be his most valuable contribution to the cattle industry.

Archer was a director of Mount Morgan Gold Mining Co. Ltd (1896-1926), chairman of directors (1904-11), and managing director and acting general manager (1912). In Rockhampton he was president of the Agricultural Society (1895-1903, 1905-26), a trustee of the Grammar School (1899-1907), and chairman of the Harbour Board (1907-09, 1910-13, 1915-24). In the controversy between Port Alma and Broadmount, he favoured Port Alma because it required no dredging.

A deeply compassionate man who seldom rejected a plea for help, Robert Archer was generous to local charities, and during World War I was prominent in forming the Stockowners' Red Cross Fund and the Returned Men's Cattle Committee. In 1889 he had married Alice Manon, daughter of Ernest Marwedel and his wife Marie, née Geh, of Toowoomba. Their two sons and daughter were all associated with the pastoral industry. He died of cardiac failure at Rockhampton on 29 December 1926 and, as he had requested, was carried to the family burial ground in a farm wagon 'symbolical of the conveyance used by the Archers' when they settled at Gracemere. His estate was valued for probate at £12 621.

After completing his education Edward worked with the British India Steam Navigation Co. of London in 1891-94, and then migrated to Canada to learn prairie farming. In 1897 he arrived at Gracemere as book-keeper and became a partner in R. S. & J. Archer. From 1900 he was manager of Targinnie station and of the small goldmine within its boundaries in which he had invested. He was chairman of the Port Curtis Co-operative Dairy Co. in 1904-07 and he also served several terms on the Calliope and Fitzroy shire councils.

Edward represented Capricornia in 1906-10 in the Commonwealth parliament, sitting with the Free Trade party. He then set up a stock and station agency in Brisbane and also managed the Auto Screw Dropper Co. In March 1914 he won Normanby in the Legislative Assembly of Queensland. His outgoing and attractive personality and his education and varied experience were eminently suited to parliament but he was again defeated in May 1915 because of the rising strength of the Labor Party in central Queensland.

Archer then managed Coolibah station briefly before moving to Fifteen Mile cattle station, which he managed until his retirement to near-by Rockhampton in 1931. He served there as an executive member of the United Graziers' Association of Queensland, and was president of the agricultural society in 1927-40, and chairman of the Harbour Board in 1933-39. In Sydney on 18 May 1901 he had married Ada Jessie Rhoades by whom he had two daughters and a son. He died in Rockhampton of renal disease on 1 July 1940, leaving an estate valued for probate at £4507. Like his brother Robert, he was buried with Anglican rites in the Gracemere private burial ground, not far from the homestead built by their uncles in 1858.

National Agr and Industrial Assn of Qld, *Journal*, 1891; A. Archer, 'Fitzroy Waters – from sheep to cattle and coal', *JRHSQ*, 9 (1971-72); *Graziers' Review*, 11 Jan 1927; *Pastoral Review*, 15 Jan 1927, 16 July 1940; Archer papers *and* R. S. Archer letter-books, 1899-1926 (ML); information from Mrs J. Archer, Gracemere, Mr A. Archer, Clayfield, and Mrs C. Murray, Yeronga, Qld.

LORNA L. MCDONALD

ARCHIBALD, JOHN (1845-1907), businessman and politician, was born on 15 December 1845 at Penston, Haddington, Scotland, son of Robert Archibald, coal-mine manager, and his wife Janet, née Henderson. Educated at a local Free Church school, he became a teacher with the London Council of Education for four years, then migrated to Queensland in 1863. He worked for Cribb [q.v.3] & Foote of Ipswich until 1870, then became manager at Harrisville for J. & G. Harris [q.v.4]. Transferred by the firm to Ipswich about 1874, he resigned in 1878 and on 21 July became clerk of petty sessions at Charters Towers. Promoted in July 1884 to police magistrate and warden at Ravenswood, he was transferred to Warwick in June 1887 and resigned from the government service on 19 April 1888.

Archibald joined W. H. Barnes [q.v.] in operating flour-mills on the Darling Downs and was taken into partnership; he spent five years as financial director of the firm, then sold his interests in Barnes, Archibald & Co. He formed a partnership with Samuel Crowther and in December 1895 they floated the Dominion Milling Co. Ltd. A successful businessman, Archibald joined the boards of Carricks Ltd, Queensland Trustees Ltd and the Daily Mail Newspaper Co. In 1896 he stood for Warwick in the Legislative Assembly but, having complied with a party request to withdraw in favour of T. J. Byrnes [q.v.], was called to the Legislative Council next year by the premier Sir Hugh Nelson [q.v.]. There he opposed Federation, but showed a keen interest in mining legislation and restriction of Asian immigration. His private interests lay in the Methodist Church, Freemasonry and local government; he was mayor of Warwick in 1890 and 1897. He settled at New Farm in Brisbane about 1900 and died there on 20 May 1907 of valvular disease of the heart. His estate, valued for probate at £34 642, was left mainly to his widow Frances Amelia, née Herbert, whom he had married at Harrisville on 19 January 1872. He was survived by three sons and four daughters.

Archibald's eldest son ROBERT JOHN (1874-1939) was born on 16 June 1874 at Ipswich and began his education at Charters Towers and Ravenswood. He won a scholarship to Brisbane Grammar School for 1887-89, and in 1890 became a clerk in Barnes, Archibald & Co. By 1896 he was manager in Toowoomba for the Dominion Milling Co. Ltd. When the firm became associated with the Brisbane Milling Co. in May, he was appointed Brisbane manager, and in 1902 general manager of the joint enterprise. The 1915 royal commission on the supply and distribution of wheat and flour revealed that the Archibald interests, through their branches at Brisbane, Toowoomba, Roma, Pittsworth and Maryborough, controlled two-thirds of the mills in Queensland. He became chairman of the combine in 1924 when it was joined by White Rose Flour Ltd of Sydney.

Archibald was also chairman of the Queensland Trustee Co., Finney Isles & Co. and Carricks Ltd. He held directorates in Foggitt Jones, United Provisions, Luya Julius, Solomon Islands Rubber, Manara Plantations and the Daily Mail Newspaper Co., and was on the local board of the Australian Mutual Provident Society. In 1923 he stood unsuccessfully for Ithaca in the Legislative Assembly.

Like his father Archibald was a fervent Methodist, serving as organist and choirmaster of the West End church for thirty years and on the Church's Epworth House

Trust. Unlike his father, he had sporting interests in golf, bowls and motoring, and was president of the Austral Choir. He died at Brisbane on 1 August 1939. His estate, sworn for probate at £88 614, was left mainly to his wife Lilian Amy, née Merry, whom he had married at Brisbane on 9 April 1902, and to their three children.

V&P (LA Qld), 1885, 3, 36, 1900, 2, 378, 3, 163; Brisbane Courier, 21, 23, 25 May 1907; Toowoomba Chronicle, 22 May 1907; Courier Mail, 2 Aug 1939; company registers, book 8 (QA).

ARCHIBALD, WILLIAM OLIVER (1850-1926), politician, was born on 3 June 1850 at St Pancras, London, son of Thomas Archibald, a cabinetmaker from Edinburgh, and his wife Margaret, née Blackwood. William was orphaned at 10 and after basic education at national schools in London was apprenticed to the Protestant piano-building trade. A staunch supporter of W. E. Gladstone, he studied radical theorists and read T. B. Macaulay's essays so often that he knew them almost by heart. At 16 he joined the London Debating Society and quickly became a confident speaker. He belonged to the St Pancras Workingmen's Club, the Workingmen's Club and Institute Union, and the Reform League.

In 1879, being unemployed, Archibald migrated to New Zealand but moved on to New South Wales and Victoria before arriving about 1882 in South Australia, where he worked in the country and on the Port Adelaide wharves. He was a government employee in the Islington railway workshops in the late 1880s, and on 14 May 1887 in Adelaide married Rose Owens.

Archibald was a member of the executive council of the Railway Service Mutual Association, chairman of the Port Adelaide Working Men's Association in 1895 and a member of and prominent lecturer at Adelaide's Democratic Club. A foundation member of the United Labor Party in South Australia, he was its choice to represent Port Adelaide for the House of Assembly in 1893 and topped the poll. He retained this seat at the five succeeding general elections but retired from State parliament before the 1910 election. A hard-working member who always thoroughly mastered his subject, Archibald sat on six commissions and select committees and successfully piloted several bills through the House. Most notable were an Act of 1898 allowing for the establishment of free libraries in corporate towns, the Moneylenders' Act of 1903, an amended workmen's compensation Act of 1904, which it is said he also drafted, and an Act of 1907 to amend the law regarding distress for

rent. He had been president of the State branch of the Labor Party in 1901-02 and as chairman of its parliamentary party in 1905-08 was influential in the Tom Price-A. H. Peake [qq.v.] government of 1905-09. He led attempts to maintain the coalition after Price's death.

As Labor's candidate for the Federal seat of Hindmarsh in 1910, Archibald was elected unopposed; he proved to be a useful backbencher. Next year he joined a party of parliamentarians who visited England for the coronation of George V. He held his seat in the 1913 and 1914 elections and on 17 September 1914 became minister for home affairs in Andrew Fisher's [q.v.] government. When Fisher resigned in October 1915, caucus did not elect Archibald to the W. M. Hughes [q.v.] ministry. Next year he resigned from the party over conscription and followed Hughes into the National Labor Party. Minister for trade and customs from 14 November to 17 February 1917, he was then dropped from the Nationalist ministry. Returned at the 1917 election, he lost his seat in 1919. Archibald had been an impressive minister: rugged and strong with burly physique, bow legs and a bullet-like head, he was vehement, logical and analytical in approach. Although his aspirates were 'always in confusion' and one observer claimed 'he slaughters the English language with pitiless ferocity every time he talks', T. H. Smeaton [q.v.] summarized his faithful contribution to the labour movement as 'based upon a sound judgement' and 'fairness to political opponents'. Others admired his reasonable radicalism and commented that he was 'one of the best-read men in the Federal parliament ... whose speeches were invariably listened to with interest and respect'.

After the death of his first wife Archibald married a widow Elizabeth Pollard at Port Adelaide on 20 January 1903. In 1919 she died and he married for the third time, on 20 December next year, Marie Schmett, a divorcee. He was briefly a bookseller and lived at Semaphore, but later moved into the People's Palace, a Salvation Army home in Pirie Street, where he died intestate on 28 June 1926 leaving assets valued at £399. Survived by his wife and a daughter and son of his first marriage, he was buried in West Terrace cemetery.

H. T. Burgess (ed), Cyclopedia of South Australia, 2 (Adel, 1909); T. H. Smeaton, The people in politics (Adel, 1914); B. Dickey, 'South Australia', Labor in politics, D. J. Murphy ed (Brisb, 1975); PD (SA), 1896, 1898, 1903, 1904; Observer (Adel), 17 June 1893, 6 May 1899, 3 July 1926; Aust Worker, 28 Jan 1905, 30 June 1926; Punch (Melb), 8 Dec 1910, 18 Feb 1915; Advertiser (Adel), 29 June 1926.

DEAN JAENSCH

ARDILL, GEORGE EDWARD (1857-1945), evangelist and social worker, was born on 17 December 1857 at Parramatta, New South Wales, second son of Joshua Ardill, plasterer, and his wife Anna Maria, née Johnson. The family were Baptists. After elementary education at Parramatta, he took an office job and then in 1883 briefly set up in Pitt Street, Sydney, as a stationer and printer. While still in his 20s he devoted himself to full-time charity organization. Already attracted to the gospel temperance movement, he started the Blue Ribbon Gospel Army, a temperance organization which long remained under his personal direction. He joined the Local Option League on its formation in 1883, and later the New South Wales Alliance, serving it for some thirty years as councillor, honorary treasurer, and secretary in 1900-03.

In taking the gospel to the godless at late-night street meetings, Ardill discovered destitute and homeless women. With characteristic practicality, he set about providing shelter and in 1890 formed the Sydney Rescue Work Society to help finance his work; it became a major charitable organization, attracting support from (Sir) Samuel McCaughey and Ebenezer Vickery [qq.v.5,6]. In 1884 an All Night Refuge and the Home of Hope for Friendless and Fallen Women were opened, the latter a lying-in hospital to which later he attached a commercial laundry where the women were gainfully employed and given 'training'. In another home, the Crusade to Women operated to reclaim the penitent, especially those saved from drink. He ran two other homes for discharged prisoners in 1884-91.

So that the mothers from the Home of Hope could take work where a child was not acceptable, Ardill soon was involved in providing for the unwanted children. In 1886 he founded the Society for Providing Homes for Neglected Children, which opened Our Babies' Home that year, Our Children's Home at Liverpool in 1887 and, in 1890, Our Boys' Farm Home at Camden where older boys were to be trained on near-by farms. In the 1890s Ardill was organizing crêches in the city. By then he was reputedly a director of twelve societies: his work was becoming less directed to rescuing the fallen than to providing for the needy.

On 8 September 1885 at the Baptist Church, Bathurst Street, Ardill had married Louisa (1853-1920), daughter of Thomas Wales. She had had experience as an evangelist in England and, after her arrival in Sydney in 1883, in the Blue Ribbon Gospel Army and the Woman's Christian Temperance Union. She served on the executive of the latter, superintended its franchise department in 1901-02, and represented it on the New South Wales Alliance for many years. Louisa also shared her husband's work, taking prayer-meetings, acting as supervisor from time to time in one or other of the homes and, notably, as matron-superintendent of the Home of Hope hospital, which provided under her direction and instruction a training centre for midwifery: in 1900 seventy-six trainees passed the external examinations, their fees amounting to about a tenth of the hospital's income. As it came to be used more by private patients in separate rooms, it was renamed South Sydney Women's Hospital. Extensions were made in 1904 and 1911, and surgical and gynaecological departments added. Louisa died in 1920 after a long illness but the hospital continued until World War II without government subsidy.

Ardill was less successful in extending his other institutions, despite persistent effort and ingenuity in fund-raising, such as publicity in his quarterly magazine, *Rescue*. By adopting the cottage home as his model, he had considerable staff expenses and substantial mortgages to pay off. Repeatedly in financial difficulties and occasionally vilified in the press for failing to publish accounts, he juggled the funds, paying current expenses from building appeals and foregoing some of the modest allowance due to him as director of the Rescue Work Society. Although he had successfully sued the *Australian Workman* for libel in 1891, he was severely reprimanded by the 1898-99 royal commission on public charities for sometimes failing to pay employees and also for his leniency in not forcing his unfortunate women out to work and allowing some to be admitted for a second illegitimate child. Prepared in principle to agree with the commissioners, he was kinder in practice: government subsidies (received since 1893) ceased. Although he remained executive director of the children's and the babies' homes until 1945 the numbers in his care gradually declined.

Interested as an evangelist in the Aboriginals, Ardill joined the New South Wales Aborigines Protection Association, which financially supported D. Matthews's [q.v.5] mission. Secretary from 1886, he was involved in the removal of the Maloga settlement. Ardill joined the Aborigines Protection Board in 1897, representing the association. A regular visitor to its stations, he became the board's most active member, a vice-president by 1909 and its effective policy-maker. Convinced of the need for positive policies to change the situation of Aboriginals, Ardill set about making them 'useful members of the State' by taking the children away from the Aboriginal community, putting them to work in private homes or on station properties, and placing others, too young for work, in his homes. The 1909 Act conferring the requisite authority on the board to place or 'apprentice' neglected children was largely due to his efforts, as was the reorganization of the board's work. In 1915, again on his recommendation, amendments to the Act strengthened the board's hand, but were condemned as 'reintroduction of slavery', and by the secretary of the Australian Aborigines Mission as attacking Aboriginal family life. Whether on account of these objections or on other grounds, Ardill had over-reached himself. He had pestered the government for more money and over the appointment of inspectors, and in 1916 was forced off the board.

Ardill was an expert lobbyist. He was a founding member of the Social Purity Society in 1886 and later secretary of its vigilance committee on public morals, and a founder and in 1890 secretary of the New South Wales Society for the Prevention of Cruelty to Children. He successfully campaigned for an affiliation Act establishing a woman's right to support from the putative father of her child before its birth, and for a children's court, but failed to get the age of consent raised from fourteen to seventeen. He was convinced that where women were destitute and without recourse to support, infanticide occurred.

The Ardills were ecumenical ahead of their times: both were prepared to conduct services or speak in other churches. A member of the Evangelical Council of New South Wales, Ardill helped to organize some of the special missions which in the early years of the century drew attendances of 50 000 to 100 000, and was joint secretary for the J. Wilbur Chapman and Charles Alexander mission of 1908. He later served as local secretary for the Australasian Chapman-Alexander Bible Institute. In his latter years the United Preachers' Association of New South Wales was especially dear to him.

Awarded an M.B.E. in 1934 for commnity service, Ardill died on 11 May 1945 at Stanmore and was buried in Waverley cemetery with Anglican rites. His estate was valued for probate at £13 356. Survived by a son and daughter, he was predeceased by his second wife Kelsie Hannah, née Starr, whom he had married on 5 October 1921; before and after marriage she helped to run the mission's office. Probably the friend giving the funeral oration came closest to the essential Ardill: 'He loved to plan and scheme and contrive in the interests of causes dear to his heart'.

His daughter KATIE LOUISA (1886-1955) was born on 3 August 1886 at Knox Street. Familiar with her mother's hospital from early childhood, she was educated at Wellesley College and the University of Sydney (M.B., Ch.M., 1913), then did a year's residency at Royal Prince Alfred Hospital before being appointed honorary anaesthetist and out-patients' medical officer at South Sydney Women's Hospital. On the outbreak of World War I she sought in vain to enlist, proceeded to England and, under direction of the British Red Cross Society, went to a Belgian hospital, and afterwards with the British Army to Napbury, the Dover military hospital, and the Citadel hospital, Cairo. In 1920 Katie resumed her hospital appointment, which continued until 1950, and set up a practice in gynaecology in Macquarie Street, providing a regular free clinic for servicemen's wives and children. On 1 June 1921 in St Andrew's Cathedral she married Charles Christie Brice, a law student and later an accountant.

Katie Brice had lectured for the St John Ambulance Association in 1913. She joined the St John Ambulance Brigade in 1920, was later on the association's executive committee from 1938, was deputy chairman in 1947-48 and was the first woman in New South Wales to serve as its chairman, in 1950-55. She had been awarded an O.B.E. in 1941. Admitted to the Order of St John of Jerusalem as a serving sister in 1938, she was created dame of grace of the order in 1952. Both the Red Cross and the St John Ambulance felt her presence: with a stentorian, brash and husky voice, 'smoking perennially', she handled meetings with authority and was willing to debate any question with fire and gesticulation. In Britain in 1952 she studied methods of treatment for atomic blast. Survived by her husband, she died in St Luke's Hospital on 3 January 1955 and was cremated after a service at St Andrew's Church of England, Roseville. Her estate was valued for probate at £25 506.

Ardill's son GEORGE EDWARD (1889-1964) was born on 18 October 1889 at Darlinghurst and was educated at Stanmore Public School and Newington College. After farming near Coraki, in 1916 he bought a dairying property near Gunning, where he established himself in 1921 as an auctioneer and agent, and later as a garage proprietor. Active in producer organizations and community affairs, he was branch secretary of the Primary Producers' Union and the Graziers' Association of New South Wales, and secretary of the Gunning Pastoral, Agricultural and Industrial Society. He helped to found a dramatic and literary society and was a noted performer; he was also a Methodist lay preacher and a Freemason. He served on Gunning Shire Council in 1920-34 and 1938-41 and was president in 1923 and 1927-28.

Ardill won the Yass seat in the Legislative Assembly for the Nationalists in 1930, holding it until 1941. As a parliamentarian his performance was sound, and in 1937 he was rewarded by appointment as government whip. He spoke sparingly but effectively, addressing himself to local issues and the great concerns of the time — the terrible unemployment, the distressing position of the indebted farmers, and the fear of extremism. He was prominent in the Sound Finance League of Australia. Yet the cause which he rose to defend with greatest vigour was that of the Aborigines Protection Board, which he joined in 1936, giving strong support to the amending Act that year which again extended its control over the Aboriginals. Although sincerely concerned for their improvement, he was heavily paternalist and believed they were 'especially feckless'. He regarded the board's eminent vice-president A. P. Elkin as a 'foolish critic'. Appointed to the reconstituted Aborigines Welfare Board in 1940, he continued to serve on it to 1945, without noticeable influence on policy.

In later life Ardill was able to indulge his hobbies — poultry and pigeons; he founded and was president of the All Leghorn Club, and was also president of the Pigeon Fanciers' Society of New South Wales. In 1945 he became executive director of the Society for Providing Homes for Neglected Children, taking charge of the remaining two homes until he died of emphysema and coronary occlusion on 13 July 1964 at Concord; he was cremated with Baptist rites. He was survived by his wife Emma Booth, née Olive, whom he had married on 7 June 1911 at Bungawalbyn, and by a son and four daughters. His estate was valued for probate at £16 584.

Cyclopedia of N.S.W. (Syd, 1907); *V&P* (LA NSW), 1899, 2nd S, 1, 191–274; *Rescue* (Syd), 1894–1914; *Poultry*, 14 Aug 1964; *SMH*, 23 Feb, 1 May, 4 Sept 1884, 11 June, 4 Nov 1885, 8 Oct 1886, 14 Apr 1890, 2 July 1892, 17 July 1920, 30 Sept 1932, 12 May 1945, 5 May 1955; *Smith's Weekly*, 4 Feb 1950; *Goulburn Evening Post*, 30 July 1964; D. P. Dwyer, The New South Wales Aborigines Protection Board 1909–1923 (B.A. Hons thesis, Univ Syd, 1973); D. Matthews papers (ML); Aborigines Protection Board, Minute-books, *and* Attorney-General, Special bundles 7779 (NSWA); news-clippings (held by Mr G. E. Ardill, Goulburn, NSW).   HEATHER RADI

⚬

ARGYLE, SIR STANLEY SEYMOUR (1867-1940), premier and medical practitioner, was born on 4 December 1867 at Kyneton, Victoria, son of Edward Argyle and his wife Mary, née Clark. His mother was born in Sydney; his father had migrated from Derbyshire thirty years before and, following (Sir) Thomas Mitchell's [q.v.2] explorations, had been a successful pioneer squatter in north-eastern Victoria before moving first to Sandhurst (Bendigo), and then to Kyneton.

Educated at Hawthorn Grammar School and under Dr G. H. Crowther [q.v.] at Brighton Grammar School, Argyle entered the University of Melbourne in 1886 to study medicine. In his last year, 1890, as a senior student at Trinity College, he was involved in the famous protest against the alleged maladministration of the warden Dr Leeper [q.v.]. He was expelled for 'contumacy' after chairing a student meeting and, with two others who were expelled and thirty-four who left in sympathy, quitted the college in a long procession of hansom cabs. It may be doubted if the *Age* was justified in claiming that the affair was a manifestation of 'the spirit of insubordination' then being exhibited in the great maritime and shearers' strikes; Argyle did not remain a rebel and showed little sympathy with police protesters against alleged injustice thirty years later.

After graduating (M.B., 1890; Ch.B., 1891), Argyle went to England, and in 1892 obtained the conjoint M.R.C.S., L.R.C.P. diploma before studying bacteriology at King's College, London, but financial difficulties arising from the bank smash compelled him to return home after two years, when he set up as a general practitioner in Kew. There he soon showed his interest in the supply of pure milk, and in 1898 founded the Willsmere Certificated Milk Co., of which he was a director until 1920. On 24 January 1895 at Holy Trinity Church, Kew, he had married Violet Ellen Jessie Lewis. Three years later he was elected to the local council, and served as mayor for two terms in 1903-05; in that office he began the agitation for the removal of the Kew Lunatic Asylum. In 1908, soon after he had begun to specialize in X-ray work, he was appointed 'medical electrician and skiagraphist' (called 'radiologist' in 1920) at the Alfred Hospital; in the next six years he succeeded in obtaining assistance from the government in buying radium, and from the Walter and Eliza Hall [qq.v.] Trust for building an electrical pavilion; in 1924 he obtained funds for additions to it when he became director of radiology.

During World War I Argyle served as skiagraphist in the 1st Australian General Hospital in Cairo, where, like many others, he fell foul of (Sir) James Barrett [q.v.]; he took a radiology unit to Lemnos in 1915 and later, as consultant radiologist to the Australian Imperial Force, served in France and England before returning home in April

1917 with the rank of lieut-colonel. A Collins Street specialist of some standing, he was elected to the council of the Victorian Branch of the British Medical Association in 1918, and was its vice-president in 1923 and 1924 and president in 1925. By then he had entered the Legislative Assembly, winning Toorak in 1920 as an independent Nationalist against Barrett, the endorsed party candidate. He criticized secretive party selections and, while opposing government interference with private enterprise, strongly supported policies of development, irrigation, assistance to primary producers, a good milk-supply, voluntary charitable support for hospitals, compulsory health insurance, and scripture-reading in state schools. As a back-bencher and busy doctor he was not an unduly active member, but he urged greater expenditure on the university and on public health, and strongly supported both the government's hospital and charities bill, reiterating his objections to its interference in the internal management of hospitals, and the metropolitan milk bill, which was intended to improve the quality of Melbourne's milk. After the latter was held up in the Legislative Council in 1921, he was nominated to a committee to consider amendments, and visited New Zealand to report on milk-supply there; an amended measure was enacted in 1922.

Like other 'metropolitan liberals', of whom he was the most important, Argyle was not entirely happy with the existing Lawson [q.v.] ministry. His group contributed to the pressure which compelled its reconstruction on 7 Sepember 1923 (and soon afterwards the resignation of the economically minded treasurer Sir William McPherson [q.v.]); he then took office as chief secretary and minister of health, posts which he held under Lawson and his successor, Sir Alexander Peacock [q.v.], until 18 July 1924.

Faced almost at once with a police strike in November 1923, Argyle was adamant in refusing to re-employ those whom he described as 'mutineers' who, he insisted, had broken their oath. Although he immediately carried the Police Pensions Act, which met one of the most important grievances of the strikers, he refused to order a full inquiry into the condition of the force; however, the short-lived Prendergast [q.v.] government did so, and after Argyle had returned to office he hoped that his selection of Brigadier General Blamey as chief commissioner in 1925 would lead to reforms.

Argyle was chief secretary and minister of health again under John Allan [q.v.] from 18 November 1924 to 20 May 1927, and under McPherson from 22 November 1928 to 12 December 1929, a year when he felt compelled to give up his Alfred Hospital appointment, though he continued as consulting radiologist there. He introduced a mental deficiency bill in 1926, but it failed to pass owing to lack of time, and he never brought it up again (though he was to welcome its reappearance in 1939). He was more successful in carrying a redistribution of seats bill (which had failed in 1924) that, while correcting many anomalies, set the 'normal' number of voters in country electorates at about one half that of city ones; as minister, he accepted compulsory voting and the abolition of plural enrolments which he had previously opposed. Argyle supported borrowing for development and for creating 'outer ports' away from Melbourne. In the public health field, he did not move the Kew Asylum, but he invited Dr M. McEachern from the United States of America to report on hospital problems generally, and warmly supported his advocacy of establishing paying wards in public hospitals. In 1927, with Professor Berry [q.v.], he visited the United States to investigate medical training establishments there, and to enlist the aid of the Rockefeller Foundation for financing medical research. He strongly recommended establishing a teaching hospital adjacent to and allied with the university.

In opposition in 1927-28, Argyle opposed the financial agreement as giving too much power to the Commonwealth, and an unemployment insurance scheme as likely to lead to socialism; when back in office next year under McPherson, he was able to reserve the site near the university for the Melbourne Hospital. The government was defeated at the election at the end of 1929. Argyle was knighted on 1 January 1930, and later that year he was chosen to lead his party and the Opposition. He steadily refused to criticize the Labor government for past extravagance, for which he argued all sections of the community were 'equally blameworthy', living 'in a fool's paradise', but he strongly and consistently urged it to economize in expenditure, to reduce wages and rates of taxation while widening the field of taxpayers, and to insist that the unemployed should work in return for their sustenance payments. This policy he implemented immediately he returned to office in May 1932, after the disintegration and electoral defeat of the Hogan [q.v.] government.

Now premier, treasurer, and minister for health, Argyle appointed a non-political committee to approve relief works, and by paying rates which were 'under award' though higher than those for sustenance without work, he was able, without increasing total expenditure, to raise the number employed on them. Other emergency measures he adopted were to charge fees at the State high schools, and to adjust the payments due to the State from those who had borrowed money under the various closer settlement schemes; to assist private enterprise, his government forbade the 'socialist' practice of the State Electricity Commission selling electrical appliances. At the election in 1935, Argyle's United Australia Party lost several seats to the Country Party and, although the two parties had faced the electorate as allies, the latter decided to leave his ministry when he refused to give them more portfolios; faced with combined Labor-Country Party opposition, the government was defeated in the Legislative Assembly, and on 2 April he became leader of the Opposition again. Powerless in the assembly, his effective work was over, though he remained leader of his party.

Argyle suffered in later years from chronic bronchitis and emphysema of which he died at Toorak on 23 November 1940. Cremated after a state funeral, he was survived by his wife, two sons and two daughters. His estate, valued for probate at £9090, included a citrus orchard at Lake Kangaroo near Bael Bael. A bust by Paul Montford is in Parliament House, Melbourne.

A competent administrator and a man of the utmost integrity, Argyle had given unstinting service to the State and to his profession, but his contributions were perhaps limited by a lack of imagination and by the outlook possessed by most men of his position in the first half of the century, despite his anxiety to improve particular aspects of the community's life that came specifically under his notice.

J. A. Grant (ed), *Perspective of a century . . . Trinity College* (Melb, 1972); J. Hetherington, *Blamey, controversial soldier* (Canb, 1973); *PD* (Vic), 1921-40; *Age* and *Argus*, Sept-Oct 1920, Sept 1923, 25 Nov 1940; A. M. Mitchell, The hospital south of the Yarra (Ph.D. thesis, Univ Melb, 1972).

A. G. L. SHAW

ARMFIELD, LILLIAN MAY (1884-1971), policewoman, was born on 3 December 1884 at Mittagong, New South Wales, daughter of George Armfield, labourer, and his wife Elizabeth, née Wright. Educated locally, she wrote a clear hand, could spell and cope with arithmetical problems. About 1907 she became a nurse at the Hospital for the Insane, Callan Park, Sydney, where she looked after female inmates. She left in 1915, favourably recommended by the medical superintendent for her competence and kindness to patients, to apply for a newly established post in the police force. When recruited as probationary special constable on 1 July 1915, she was 5 ft. 7¾ ins. (1.72 m) tall, weighed 12 st. 10 lbs. (80.74 kg), and had light brown eyes, brown hair and a fair complexion. She was described by her interviewing-officer as 'very intelligent, tactful, shrewd, capable . . . Character undoubtedly good and a very suitable candidate'. Lillian Armfield was paid 7s. 6d. a day, no uniforms were provided and no overtime or expenses were allowed. After a years probation she was enrolled as a special constable and was obliged to sign an agreement with James Mitchell, inspector-general of police, binding her to the same discipline as her male colleagues, but she was deprived of any right to compensation for injuries received in carrying out her duties and had to renounce all superannuation rights.

The experiment of Lillian Armfield's appointment was watched with interest overseas, for she was one of the first plain-clothes female detectives, exercising the same powers of arrest as male colleagues and working side by side with them. Although her work primarily concerned women and girls, it often led her into cases involving murder, rape, theft, drug-running, the white slave traffic – indeed the whole catalogue of crime. Often it led her into danger as when she disguised herself to gain admittance to suspected houses and, having done so, remained inside to open the door to the raiding police. Although brave she was also sensible and recognized that discretion could be the better part, as when she picked up her skirts and ran for her life from 'Botany Mary' (a cocaine-runner caught in the act), who came after her with a red hot flat-iron. Lillian Armfield was much concerned with the social aspects of her work. Much of it was preventative, such as tracing runaway girls and inducing them to return to their homes before they came to serious harm, or warning young women of the dangers of a bullet-wound or razor-slash through associating with known criminals.

Although the value of her work was officially recognized, promotion was slow. By 1 November 1923 Lillian Armfield had become a special sergeant, 3rd class, and by 1 January 1943 had risen to 1st class. In 1947 she was awarded the King's Police and Fire Service Medal for outstanding service and, after her retirement on 2 December 1949, aged 65, the Imperial Service Medal. She was presented with an illuminated address and £200 by the lord mayor of Sydney; the Police Department allowed her £455 6s. 5d. in lieu of extended leave of absence, but she received no superannuation. In 1965 she was granted a special allowance of £3 10s. a week by the government of New South Wales, and relinquished her 10s. a week old-age pension. During her latter years she lived at the Methodist Hostel, Leichhardt; she died on 26 August 1971 at Lewisham Hospital, and was cremated with Church of England rites.

V. Kelly, *Rugged angel* (Syd, 1961); *SMH*, 23 Dec 1949, 16 July 1965, 27 Aug 1971; *Daily Mirror* (Syd), 17 May 1950; L. M. Armfield file (Public Relations, Police Dept, Syd).   HAZEL KING

ARMIT, HENRY WILLIAM (1870-1930), medical journalist, was born on 9 July 1870 at Islington, London, son of William Armit, later secretary to the Hudson's Bay Co., and his wife Sara, née Lipman. Educated at Cheltenham College, he went to the RheinischeFriedrich-Wilhelms-Universität, Bonn, Germany, to study physics and chemistry. His early training may have encouraged his passion for accuracy in observation and expression and perfection in grammatical construction. He returned to England in 1887 and studied medicine at St Bartholomew's Hospital, London (M.R.C.S., England; L.R.C.P., London, 1894). After hospital experience in the north of England and London, on 14 October 1896 at Bad Godesberg, Germany, he married Maria Josephine Gertrude, daughter of Dr E. Pohl.

After general practice at Torquay, travel in Germany, and work as a locum tenens, he settled at Wembley, London, in 1900. He engaged in research into immunity and other subjects at the Lister Institute of Preventive Medicine under (Sir) Charles Martin [q.v.]. From 1902 Armit published in English and German learned journals. In 1901 he had joined the external staff of the *British Medical Journal* and translated articles from German periodicals. He organized the British section at the International Hygiene Exhibition in Dresden, 1911, and lectured daily in German to visitors.

In 1913 Armit was appointed by the Australasian Medical Publishing Co. Ltd as editor of a proposed new national journal, and arrived with his wife and daughter in Sydney on 4 June 1914. The first issue of the *Medical Journal of Australia* appeared on 4 July. He volunteered when war was declared, but was put on the reserve list. He contended with rising costs of paper and printing and shortage of advertising revenue, by setting up a type-setting machine in the B.M.A. Building in Elizabeth Street; he soon acquired a first-hand knowledge of printing techniques. In the early 1920s Armit advised the company to expand its printing activities and in 1925 'The Printing

House' at Glebe was functioning. He set high scientific and journalistic standards and, by courage, tenacity and hard work, built up a flourishing journal with an international reputation. As editor, he was a prolific writer.

Armit was a member of the Royal Society of New South Wales from 1915, and an honorary member of the Australian Veterinary Association whose journal he helped to found. He was also a vice-president of the local branch of the League of Nations Union, associate editor for Australia of the *Journal of Industrial Hygiene*, and chairman of the typography committee of the Standards Association of Australia.

Although not a big man physically, Armit had an imposing presence and courtly manner, with a deep booming voice and hearty laugh. Generous to his staff and solicitous for their welfare, he earned their respect for his knowledge of typography and his understanding of their professional problems. He died suddenly of tonsillitis and septicaemia at his home at Woolwich near Hunters Hill on 12 March 1930 and was buried in the Anglican section of Northern Suburbs cemetery. He was survived by his wife and daughter, whom he left in straitened circumstances.

MJA, Mar, Apr 1930; Aust Veterinary Assn, *Handbook*, May 1970.   W. L. CALOV

ARMSTRONG, EDMUND LA TOUCHE (1864-1946), librarian, was born on 12 August 1864 at Herne Hill, Geelong, Victoria, fourth son of John Simpson Armstrong (d. 1884), barrister, crown prosecutor and acting judge of the County Court, and his wife Alice, née O'Dell. His parents had migrated to Victoria from Ireland in 1858. Sixth of ten children, Edmund was educated at Scotch College, Melbourne, and studied part time at the University of Melbourne (LL.B., 1893; M.A., 1899).

Armstrong joined the Public Library of Victoria in December 1881 as a junior assistant at a salary of £50. By 1891 he was listed as assistant at £300 and by 1895 was principal assistant in the reference library. On 29 August 1896, after the premature death of M. F. Dowden, he was appointed librarian and secretary to the trustees of the Public Library, Museums, and National Gallery of Victoria. According to his memoirs he then decided not to practise at the Bar but to assist the trustees 'to carry on the work of the institution'. On his retirement on 30 April 1925 it was recorded that he had served conscientiously and diligently and had 'proved himself not only a learned and accomplished librarian, but also a most capable administrator'.

Armstrong opposed separation of the four sister institutions. He looked back to Sir Redmond Barry's [q.v.3] concept and to the British Museum's model of a display of knowledge, creation and achievement all in the one institution: he was a curator of knowledge rather than a disseminator of information. His name will always be associated with the octagonal, domed reading-room, suggested by him in 1905 and opened on 14 November 1913. Although he intended it to incorporate the best features of the British Museum and Library of Congress reading-rooms, it was criticized from the outset as being inefficient with regard to space, lighting, heating and comfort.

Much, however, was achieved while Armstrong was chief librarian: grants from the government and gifts from the Felton [q.v.4] Bequest enabled the library to grow in size and prestige. The Dewey decimal system of classification was introduced in the lending library in 1899 and in the reference library in 1910-15, the travelling libraries were revived and expanded in the 1900s and the country lending service began in 1920. He was secretary of the Library Association of Australasia in 1896-1902 and editor of the *Library Record of Australasia* in 1901-02. He was also the author and co-author of two carefully compiled histories of the library, museums and gallery covering the period 1856-1931.

Armstrong did not marry and gave much of his life to his work. In recreation, he was a member of the Wallaby (walking) Club (and by 1946 its oldest member), the Yorick and the Metropolitan Golf clubs and the Royal Empire Society. He was respected widely although his natural reserve and caution made him seem remote from his staff. His tall figure and regular features gave him a dignified appearance which matched his courteous demeanour and tactful and conservative attitudes. He died of coronary vascular disease at his home at East Malvern on 15 October 1946 and was privately cremated at Springvale. A portrait by Bernard Hall [q.v.] is in the State Library of Victoria.

Armstrong's eldest brother THOMAS HENRY was born on 2 April 1857 in Dublin and was educated at Geelong Church of England Grammar School, Geelong College, and Trinity College, University of Melbourne (B.A., 1880; M.A., 1883). Ordained deacon by Bishop Moorhouse [q.v.5] in December 1880 and priest a year later, he was successively curate of Christ Church, St Kilda (1881-83) and Christ Church, Hawthorn (1883), first vicar of St Columb's, Hawthorn (1883-94), and archdeacon of Gippsland (1894-1902). He was rural dean of Sale (1896-99), and a canon of St Paul's Cathedral and examining chaplain to the bishop of Melbourne (1899-1902). On 24 February 1902 he was consecrated first bishop of Wangaratta, retiring on 31 March 1927. In his term the bishop's lodge was built, St Columb's Hall for the education of clergy established and a cathedral partially completed. In 1903 he was awarded an honorary D.D. by the University of Trinity College, Toronto, Canada.

After his retirement Armstrong was acting incumbent of St John's, Toorak, and was president of the Melbourne College of Divinity in 1930. Low Church in outlook, he was described as energetic, cheerful and sympathetic. He was handsome and tall, with a strong physique and a red beard. On 19 May 1892 he had married Marion Ruth, daughter of Henry Henty [q.v.4]. He died of coronary thrombosis on 23 March 1930, survived by a son and a daughter. After a service at St Paul's Cathedral he was buried in Boroondara cemetery.

'The State Library building', *La Trobe Lib J*, Oct 1970; *Church of England Messenger* (Vic), 4 Apr 1930, 1 Feb 1935; *Argus*, 27 Mar 1925, 24, 26 Mar 1930, 15 Feb 1935, 17 Oct 1946; *Wangaratta Chronicle*, 2 Apr 1930; E. La T. Armstrong, Fifty years of the P.L.V.: some recollections and some notes (LaTL); E. M. Miller, Some Public Library memories 1900-1913, *and* L. Scott, Mainly from memory 1908-1926 (LaTL); Public Library, Museums and National Gallery of Victoria, Minutes 26 Mar 1925 (SLV); news-cuttings on loan from J. H. B. Armstrong (LaTL).   DAVID McVILLY

ARMSTRONG, WARWICK WINDRIDGE (1879-1947), cricketer, was born on 22 May 1879 at Kyneton, Victoria, son of John Andrewartha Armstrong, clerk and later solicitor, and his wife Amelia Mary, née Flynn, both of whom were Tasmanian-born. He was educated at Cumloden College, St Kilda, and University College, Armadale, made a name for himself in schoolboy cricket and quickly graduated to the South Melbourne and Melbourne clubs. He also played football for South Melbourne.

Statistics reveal the measure of Armstrong as a cricketer. He represented Victoria in 1899-1922, scoring 6615 runs at an average of 51.7 and taking 244 wickets at 22.68 runs each; he was captain for many years. Between 1901 and 1921 he played in 42 Tests against England, a record bettered to that time only by S. E. Gregory [q.v.4]. He made 2172 runs averaging 35.03, and took 74 wickets at 30.92. On his retirement he was one of four Australian batsmen who had scored more than 2000 runs against England. On each of his four English tours he made more than 1000 runs; on three tours he took more than 100 wickets.

Wisden, referring to the 1902 series, claimed that few players had rendered better service on a first tour. Armstrong was in his prime from 1905 to 1909. In 1905 in England he made 2002 runs and took 130 wickets. In the Test at Lord's he captured 6 wickets for 35 runs in the second innings on a good wicket. He played little Test cricket in his thirties, mainly because of World War I. Yet in his early forties he enjoyed a glorious 'Indian summer'. In 1920-21, aged 41, he became the only Test captain to win all five matches in a series, and scored three centuries, including his highest Test innings of 158. Later in 1921 he won the first three Tests in England (the last two were drawn), headed the bowling averages for the tour, and hit three centuries in four matches, including 303 against Somerset.

As captain, Armstrong was immensely knowledgeable and a stern disciplinarian; he seemed to have no nerves and was at his best on big occasions. Though he had few stylish pretensions, his ability to 'murder' any type of bowler made him an invaluable middle-order batsman. As a bowler he specialized in 'straight' leg-breaks, but his impeccable length and uncanny field-placement earned vital wickets. He was one of the greatest all-rounders the game has known.

Physically, Armstrong was an impressive man, sometimes known as 'the Big Ship'. To get fit on the way to England in 1921 he shovelled coal in the stokehold for two hours daily, but his weight on arrival was 22 stone (139.71 kg). He towered over an opposing captain when they tossed the coin; the bat seemed like a teaspoon or a toothpick in his hands; but he was nimble enough between wickets and in slips.

Neville Cardus described Armstrong as 'Australian cricket incarnate'. He was one of the 'characters' of Test cricket, an Australian version of W. G. Grace: abrasive, cantankerous, with strong likes and dislikes and cast-iron convictions. In 1912 he was one of the six who defied the new board of control, on the issue of the players' right to appoint their own manager, and stood down for the Test series. Early in 1921, when disciplined by the Victorian selectors, indignation meetings in the city culminated in a rally of some 8000 outside the members' entrance to the Melbourne Cricket Ground while the match against the Englishmen was in progress. Later that year at Manchester he told England's captain, the Hon. Lionel (Lord) Tennyson, that he was breaking the rules in declaring an innings closed; sat on the pitch, while the crowd heckled him, when the umpires upheld his point; then unwittingly broke the rules himself by bowling two overs in succession. At best he maintained an armed truce with the game's administrators.

Armstrong retired in 1921 from the secretarial staff of the Melbourne Cricket Club to represent a firm importing Scotch whisky. Next year, in London, his *Art of cricket* was published. He played his last game for Melbourne in 1927 and occasionally reported on cricket for the newspapers. About 1934 he moved to Sydney and became general manager in Australasia for James Buchanan & Co. Ltd, whisky distillers. On 16 July 1913 he had married Aileen Veronica O'Donnell, daughter of a Gundagai grazier; she predeceased him. He died of pulmonary embolism complicating venous thrombosis at his Darling Point home on 13 July 1947, and was buried in the Catholic section of South Head cemetery. Nearly all his estate, valued for probate at £105 813, was left to his only son. The museum at the Melbourne Cricket Club holds his tent-like shirt, capacious trousers and enormous boots.

K. Dunstan, *The paddock that grew* (Melb, 1962); R. Grace, *Warwick Armstrong* (Camberwell, 1975); *Age* and *Argus*, 15 July 1947; *Herald* (Melb), 29 Oct 1955.   S. M. INGHAM

ARMSTRONG, WILLIAM GEORGE (1859-1941), physician, was born on 29 May 1859 at Leigh, Essex, England, eldest son of Lieutenant Richard Ramsay Armstrong, R.N., [q.v.3] and his wife Eliza Susannah, née Malet, of Jersey, Channel Islands. He was educated at King's School, Canterbury, and about 1873 went to New Zealand with his mother. In 1878 the family settled at Hunters Hill, New South Wales, and he attended Sydney Grammar School. He worked on the *Singleton Argus* in 1878 and next year was a sub-editor on the *Sydney Mail*. While attending the University of Sydney (B.A., 1884; M.B., Ch.M., 1888), he taught at his old school.

After a nine-year engagement, on 9 February 1888 Armstrong married Elizabeth Jane, daughter of Rev. C. F. Garnsey [q.v.4], at Christ Church St Laurence, Sydney. He practised medicine at Merriwa, Emmaville and Bowral before going to England in 1894; next year at the University of Cambridge he gained the necessary qualifications for a diploma in public health (conferred retrospectively in 1912) and became a fellow of the (Royal) Sanitary Institute, London. As part of his studies he visited the famous 'consultations de nourrissons' conducted by Pierre Budin at the Charité hospital, Paris, and was deeply impressed by this scheme to advise mothers on the feeding and care of infants.

On his return to Sydney, Armstrong was appointed medical officer of health for the Metropolitan Combined Sanitary Districts of Sydney in March 1898 and became city health officer in 1900. Four years later he launched the infant welfare movement, three years before his more famous colleague Truby King in New Zealand. In 1905, as president of the public health section of the Australasian Medical Congress in Adelaide, he published an important article, 'Some lessons from statistics of infant mortality in Sydney', in its *Transactions*. He believed that approximately half of the 106 infant deaths (in their first year) per 1000 live births in 1901-05, had occurred because of mismanagement of feeding, and that mothers should be educated in the care and breast-feeding of babies rather than in the overseas trend of providing impoverished mothers with ready-made artificial baby-food.

Armstrong engaged a qualified health visitor to advise mothers of all new-born infants in the city of Sydney. In 1912, when two additional staff were employed to cover the inner suburbs, 4686 visits were made. Armstrong's team referred those needing regular supervision to the Alice Rawson School for Mothers at Darlinghurst, founded in 1908 as a subsidized voluntary agency. In 1914 both operations were combined under the Baby Clinic Board, of which Armstrong was president. The movement expanded rapidly, despite administrative problems, and by 1918 there were twenty-eight clinics in New South Wales. After 1919 the board worked closely with the new Royal Society for the Welfare of Mothers and Babies. In the *Medical Journal of Australia*, 28 October 1939, he claimed that the sharp decrease in infant mortality was partly due to his advisory and supervisory programme.

In 1913 Armstrong had transferred to the restructured Department of Public Health as senior medical officer of health and deputy-director-general. In 1904-20 he lectured at the university. Over the years he sat on several government administrative boards. He was esteemed for his work during major epidemics of bubonic plague, smallpox and pneumonic influenza on which he reported extensively in the *Proceedings* of the Royal Society of Medicine, London, and in the *Medical Journal of Australia*. Influenced by the ideals of J. Ashburton Thompson [q.v.], he advocated disease-prevention through environmental control, sanitary improvement and public education. After acting for a year, from 1 July 1922 Armstrong became director-general of public health and president of the Board of Health until he retired on 28 May 1924; he stayed on the board until 1941. He was

medical superintendent of Anthony Hordern [q.v.4] & Sons Ltd until 1935.

With a trace of his father's restlessness, Armstrong frequently moved house. As a young man he enjoyed billiards, tennis, swimming, cycling and photography; later he owned a small yacht and gardened. He took his family to almost every Gilbert and Sullivan opera professionally staged in Sydney. In 1925 he visited Jersey to see his sister Amy, who had married her cousin Reginald Malet de Carteret, seigneur of St Ouens Manor. Armstrong died at Vaucluse on 27 December 1941 and was cremated with Anglican rites. He was survived by his wife, a daughter and a son John Malet, who had a distinguished career in the Royal Australian Navy.

PP (NSW), 1914-15, 4, 169, 1923, 2, 1205; *MJA*, 28 Feb 1942; C. Thame, Health and the state (Ph.D. thesis, ANU, 1974); information from Mrs M. E. Arundel, Greenwich, NSW.   CLAUDIA THAME

ARNOLD, ELLEN (1858-1931), missionary, was born on 5 July 1858 at Aston, Warwickshire, England, daughter of Alfred Arnold, commercial traveller, and his wife Ellen Jane, née Seager. The family migrated to Adelaide in 1879 and joined the Flinders Street Baptist Church where Ellen was influenced by Rev. Silas Mead [q.v.5]. She became a teacher and after brief medical training, left in October 1882 for Furreedpore, India, backed by the South Australian Baptist Missionary Society. Practical and ascetic, she expected 'hard work, discouragements, fever, ague, cholera, disagreeableness, privations'. In fact she was invalided back to Australia to convalesce in 1884 when she toured most of the colonies and New Zealand.

This 'crusade of Ellen Arnold' fixed East Bengal as the mission field for Australasian Baptists. She enlisted four women who returned to Bengal with her in 1885; the group was known as 'the five barley loaves'. A 'fine, impulsive, carry-all-before-you sort of woman' who travelled widely by boat and pony, Arnold helped initiate medical and educational work at Furreedpore. A building project she supervised ran the mission into debt so, to save the expense of her support, she transferred in 1886 to the New South Wales Baptist Missionary Society and pioneered its work in Comilla. With some difficulty she secured land and began building a mission house in 1889. In 1892 she went to Pabna, where most of the rest of her life was spent preaching and establishing schools and dispensaries, mainly in the villages of Bera and Ataikola. In 1905 she reminisced: 'At one time they hooted me out of the village [Ataikola]; now they growl when I go away, and rush for me when I come! What has done it? My poor blundering attempts at medical work . . .'.

Ellen Arnold's strong will sometimes made co-operation with her colleagues difficult, especially in 1913 when she was almost forced to retire. But the Bengalis, in whose language she was fluent, loved her and she was a driving force in the establishment of the East Bengal Baptist Union. She urged intercolonial co-operation long before the federation of Australian Baptist mission work occurred in 1913. In 1919 she was awarded, but declined to accept, the Kaisar-I-Hind medal for public service in India. She served seven terms in Bengal, spending all but one (England, 1909) of her furloughs in Australia rallying support for missionary work.

In March 1930 on the eve of her expected retirement, the East Bengal Baptist Union took over her work, but after a few months in Australia Arnold returned to India against the wishes of the home board and her colleagues. Settled at Ataikola, she became a voluntary worker until she died there on 9 July 1931 after refusing surgery for a malignant growth. Donations financed the building of the Ellen Arnold Memorial Dispensary at Ataikola. The Bangladesh Baptist Union observes the anniversary of her death as 'Ellen Arnold Day'.

D. F. Mitchell, *Ellen Arnold* (Adel, 1932); *Truth and Progress*, Nov, Dec 1892; *Our Indian Field*, Aug 1931; Furreedpore Mission Cttee, Minute-books (Burleigh College, Adel); Log-books of Comilla *and* of Pabna Zenana work (Aust Baptist Missionary Soc Archives, Melb).   G. B. BALL

ARNOLD, RICHARD ALDOUS (1849-1923), public servant, was born on 9 February 1849 at Stradbrook, Paterson River, New South Wales, eldest son of William Munnings Arnold [q.v.3], and his wife Ellen Augusta, née Smith. After private tuition he was educated at Rugby School, England, then spent a year in Germany and returned to Sydney late in 1866. On 3 January 1867 he joined the public service and in May became a clerk in the roads branch of the Department of Public Works at £200 a year. In October 1868 he was temporarily transferred to the Legislative Assembly staff and became permanent next January. Advancement was rapid while his father was Speaker: after two promotions he became clerk of select committees in February 1873, then clerk of records in May, and his salary rose to £400. He was joined on the staff by two brothers.

An enthusiastic sportsman, Arnold helped to organize Rugby football in the colony. He founded in 1870 and captained the Wallaroo Club and from 1874 was an office-bearer of the Southern Union (later New South Wales Rugby Football Union). In 1868 he had joined the Volunteer Artillery as a gunner; in 1871-78 he was second lieutenant attached to No.4 Battery and indulged his interest in rifle-shooting. He was a founder in 1872 and later secretary of the Sydney Amateur Athletic Association.

On 21 April 1881 at the parish church, Lower Sydenham, Kent, England, Arnold married Annie Emma, daughter of William Kent, late manager of Jondaryan station, Queensland. In 1888 he was promoted assistant clerk of the Legislative Assembly at £750 and in February 1904 he was appointed clerk. He soon made the sensible innovation of combining certain common papers of the Legislative Assembly and Legislative Council into joint volumes, but most of his years as clerk were quiet. The framework established during the great reforms to Standing Orders in 1885-95 endured for forty years; Arnold's task was consolidation as the State parliament adjusted to the Federal system. Although he was somewhat overshadowed by J. J. Calvert [q.v.3], the long-serving clerk of the parliaments, relations with his staff and the Speakers he served were usually harmonious. In 1910 he edited Speaker W. McCourt's [q.v.] decisions and in 1910-11 managed smoothly the election and tenure of J. H. Cann [q.v.], the first Labor Speaker.

However in 1911-13 Arnold had considerable differences with H. Willis [q.v.], whose passionate but misguided notions of a Speaker's position and administrative powers led to clashes; he privately complained that 'at no time' did Willis ask him 'for advice, assistance, or opinion' about staff arrangements but rather 'put me on my trial'. Arnold took nine months leave on full pay in 1911 but disagreements continued throughout Willis's term.

Arnold retired in April 1916 and lived at North Sydney until about 1921. He died of chronic nephritis at Bowral on 23 May 1923 and was buried in the Church of England cemetery. He was survived by two sons and three daughters who inherited his estate, valued for probate at £8138.

G. N. Hawker, *The parliament of New South Wales, 1856-1956* (Syd, 1971); R. A. Arnold diary (Parliamentary Lib, Syd); E. S. Marks sporting collection (ML).   G. N. HAWKER

ARNOLD, THOMAS FRANCIS (1897-1960), soldier and farmer, was born on 5 May 1897 at Watraba, South Australia, son of

William Berry Arnold, sheep-farmer, and his wife Alice Lydia, née Paine. He spent his childhood on St Francis Island, Nuyts Archipelago, which his father had leased for grazing, and was educated privately before attending Norwood State School, Adelaide. When he was 16 his mother died and he returned home and worked on the island until the outbreak of World War I.

Arnold enlisted in the Australian Imperial Force on 7 September 1915; he embarked for France next February with reinforcements for the 10th Battalion and joined his unit at Pozières late in July. On 31 October 1916 he was transferred to the 48th Battalion and went into the front line, first at Flers and later at Gueudecourt. He soon showed aptitude for scout work and, during a patrol action before the first battle of Bullecourt, narrowly escaped death when he broke through the enemy wire and surprised a German sentry-post. At Bullecourt on 11 April 1917 he excelled in patrolling and was awarded the Military Medal. Promoted lance corporal, then corporal in May, he won his second award, the Distinguished Conduct Medal, for 'conspicuous gallantry and devotion to duty' at Messines on 11 June. This time he went out with a bombing patrol and captured two enemy strong points containing field guns; on the same day he took a prisoner and gained useful information. Arnold was promoted lieutenant in October and after fighting at Passchendaele took part in the defence of Amiens. For bravery near Albert early in April 1918 he won the Military Cross: despite heavy machine-gun fire he maintained communication between the companies of the 48th Battalion and contact with its headquarters. He later served as an intelligence officer during the attack on Monument Wood and remained with his unit in the Villers-Bretonneux sector until July. He went into the line for the last time at Flechin in September and was mentioned in dispatches.

Arnold returned to South Australia in May 1919 and resumed sheep-farming in partnership with his father. On 17 June 1922, at the Congregational Stow Memorial Church, Adelaide, he married Edith May Daniel, a second cousin whom he had met in England during the war. They lived on St Francis Island until 1927 and, when the water suddenly dried up, sold their stock and moved to the Monto district, Queensland. There Arnold selected and cleared 650 acres (263 ha) of brigalow and softwood scrub and within four years had established a successful dairy farm; he later bought a beef-cattle property in the same area and remained there until 1959. Survived by his wife, a son and a daughter, he died of progressive muscular atrophy on 14 November

1960 at Yeppoon, and was cremated at Rockhampton.

A tall, well-built man with a pleasant disposition, Arnold was a popular and prominent figure in the Monto community. He belonged to various ex-servicemen's clubs, was a foundation member of the Monto Masonic Lodge, and during World War II commanded and trained the local home guard detachment; he also served as an intelligence officer for part of the war. While at Monto he gained something of a reputation as a water-diviner; another of his hobbies was deep-sea fishing.

C.E.W. Bean, *The A.I.F. in France*, 4, 5 (Syd, 1933, 1937); *London Gazette*, 6 July, 24 Aug 1917, 16 Sept, 31 Dec 1918; *Advertiser* (Adel), 6 Sept 1917; *Morning Bulletin*, 16 Nov 1960; *Monto Herald*, 17 Nov 1960; 48th Battalion, AIF, war diary (AWM); information from Mrs E. M. Arnold, Sandgate, Qld.   MICHAEL R. DOWNEY

ARNOT, ARTHUR JAMES (1865-1946), electrical engineer, was born on 26 August 1865 at Hamilton, Scotland, son of William Arnot, commercial agent, and his wife Elizabeth Helen, née Macdonald. After a grammar school education, he attended the West of Scotland Technical College, Glasgow, and then entered the London workshop of an Anglo-American electrical engineering company, while studying part time. In 1885 he was appointed assistant engineer of the Grosvenor Gallery power station where he worked with S. Z. de Ferranti, pioneer of the transmission of electrical power at high voltage.

In 1889 Arnot arrived in Melbourne under a two-year contract to erect a large alternating-current plant for the Union Electric Co. In March 1891 he was appointed first electrical engineer for the city council; in August he married Cornelia Ann (d. 1947), daughter of Councillor C. J. Ham [q.v.4]. Arnot installed a comprehensive system of street lighting for Melbourne city in 1891-92; designed and managed in 1894-1901 the council's Spencer Street power station; helped to draft the Victorian Electric Light and Power Act of 1896; and extended the council's supply to private lighting in 1895 and to traction in 1899. He was described in 1896 as a man of 'considerable enterprise ... versatile, determined, hard-working'. In 1892 and 1899 he studied developments in electrical engineering in Britain, Europe and the United States of America.

Arnot was elected a member of the Institution of Electrical Engineers, London, in 1899 but let his membership lapse in 1906; he held office in the Victorian branch of the institution and later became a member and president of the Electrical Association of New South Wales. He was examiner in electrical technology for technical schools in Victoria, and in 1897-1901 was a councillor of the Working Men's College.

In September 1901 Arnot resigned from the Melbourne City Council to become Australasian manager of the British company, Babcock & Wilcox Ltd; he visited the head office in London before taking up his post in Sydney in June 1902. In the next few years the firm supplied plant for Sydney's tramways and electric light, for the electric tramway systems of Christchurch and Auckland, New Zealand, and for power generation on the Western Australian goldfields. From a head office staff of four in 1901, under Arnot's managership the firm grew to an organization in 1929 which included large boiler-making works, and branch offices in Newcastle and all mainland State capitals.

On the outbreak of war in 1914 Arnot had volunteered for service abroad but was detained in Australia. He had been a lieutenant in the Submarine Company, Victorian Engineers, from 1894, transferring to the reserve of officers in 1900; he resigned his commission in 1912. In July 1915 he was recommissioned into the Australian Engineers, Australian Military Forces; next month he was promoted captain and in October 1916 major. From June 1918 to April 1919 he was director of works in the Department of the Chief of Ordnance. He transferred to the reserve again in 1920 and retired in 1925 with the rank of major.

From 1910 Arnot had also taken an active interest in farming. He had bought a property at Batlow in southern New South Wales for his two sons, planting 100 acres (40 ha) of it in apple and pear trees. When the sons turned to sheep-farming about 1924 he took over the running of the orchard from them. He was a keen fisherman and after the war was a member of the Union and the Royal Sydney Golf clubs.

In 1928 Arnot became a key witness in a scandal which involved allegations of corrupt dealings between the former Sydney Municipal Council and the firm of Babcock & Wilcox, over the letting of a contract in May 1926 to instal plant at the Bunnerong power station. During a royal commission of inquiry set up in June 1928 Arnot, who had negotiated the deal on behalf of his firm, alleged that S. J. Maling, a former alderman, had demanded £10000 to secure the contract. In his report, Mr Justice Harvey [q.v.] censured Arnot but decided that pressure for the bribe had come from Maling, who was later sentenced to six months imprisonment;

Babcock & Wilcox were ordered to pay a substantial fine.

Arnot retired from the firm in September 1929, making his home at Batlow where he was active in local organization of the fruit industry. About 1940 he moved to Camden and later to Castle Hill, where he died on 15 October 1946. He was survived by his second wife Dora Christine, née Shewan, whom he had married in Los Angeles in 1927, by their two children (the younger aged 6) and by four children of the first marriage. He was cremated with Presbyterian rites.

J. Smith (ed), *Cyclopedia of Victoria*, 1 (Melb, 1903); *Cyclopedia of N.S.W.* (Syd, 1907); J. T. Lang, *I remember* (Syd, 1956); Batlow Hist Soc, *Batlow*, E. Herring ed (Syd, 1975); *Scientific Australian*, 20 June 1896; *Table Talk*, 7 July 1893; *SMH*, 18 May, 6, 23 June 1928; *Argus*, 25 July, 1 Aug, 11 Dec 1928, 2 Mar 1929; information from Babcock & Wilcox Ltd, Lond and Aust.   NOEL GOSS
                                        SALLY O'NEILL

ARONSON, ZARA (1864-1944), journalist and charity worker, was born on 4 September 1864 in Sydney, daughter of Moritz Baar, merchant of Hanover and London, and his wife Zillah, née Valentine. Taken to Europe at 3, she was educated at Bradford Girls' Grammar School, Yorkshire, England, and at Weisbaden, Germany. She returned to Sydney in 1879 and attended Mrs Morell's school. At the Great Synagogue on 25 October 1882 she married a 32-year-old merchant Frederick Aronson (d. 1928). They lived at Woollahra near her father, who now imported Indian and Chinese wares.

Known as Mrs Fred. Aronson, she became active in local charities and was a member of the committees of the Sydney Industrial Blind Institution and the Thirlmere and the Queen Victoria homes for consumptives. In the 1890s she turned to feminist activities and was an original member of the Women's Literary Society. A founder of the National Council of Women in 1896, she was its corresponding secretary in 1900-01 and honorary secretary in 1906-08. Encouraged to write by Lucy, wife of Henry Gullett [q.v.], she contributed to the *Australian Town and Country Journal* and the *Illustrated London News*. In 1897-1901 as 'Thalia', she edited the women's pages in the *Sydney Mail*, and published *XX*th *century cooking and home decoration* (1900), which included some of her own recipes (not all kosher) and ideas for economic decorating.

By 1899 her husband had set up Frederick Aronson & Co., wholesale jewellers and importers. In 1901 she accompanied him when he took charge of the Melbourne branch of the firm. Back in Sydney, she edited the *Home Queen* in 1903-04 and wrote much of it herself, including the theatrical and fashion columns; the literary page was written by the wife of B. R. Wise [q.v.]. She told Miles Franklin [q.v.] that 'Country people are without a country womans paper of their own & this fact makes me almost sure of its ultimate success. I am not a bit afraid of the work you consider may be laborious — work never hurts me it is the worry that wears'. In the following years she edited the fashion pages in the *Town and Country Journal* and the *Sunday Times* (Sydney), and was Sydney correspondent of the Brisbane *Telegraph*. About 1912 Aronson set up a branch of his jewellery business in Perth and Zara joined the staff of the *Western Mail*. Described as a 'most capable journalist', she wrote directly on to her typewriter.

In Sydney again in 1914 she was an original member of the executive committee of the New South Wales division of the British Red Cross Society, and organized and ran the depot which distributed over a million books and magazines during World War I. She also raised some £500 for the Junior Red Cross by the proceeds of her *Excel cookery book*. In February 1925 she resigned from the Red Cross executive committee in protest against the society's funds being expended on other than ex-servicemen. During the visit of the United States Navy to Sydney in August she organized canteens for the sailors.

By 1918 Zara Aronson had started the Mary Elizabeth Tea Rooms in King Street which she ran until the 1930s; a by-product was her *Mary Elizabeth cook book*. In September 1925 she became foundation secretary of the Socety of Women Writers of New South Wales and in 1930 its president; she was also a founder of the local branch of John O'London's Literary Circle. In 1930-37 as Zara Baar Aronson she contributed irregularly to the *Sydney Morning Herald*. Plump and handsome, she was a bright conversationalist and loved reading and house decoration. She was awarded the O.B.E. in 1936. Survived by a son and a daughter, she died at her house at Darling Point on 1 July 1944 and was buried in the Jewish section of Rookwood cemetery.

Table Talk, 5 Sept 1901; *SMH*, 20 Oct 1919, 3 Feb 1925, 23 June 1936, 3 July 1944; *Woman's World*, 1 Oct, 1 Nov 1927; *Hebrew Standard of A'sia*, 6 July 1944; Miles Franklin papers (ML).

MARTHA RUTLEDGE

ARTEM; *see* SERGEEV

ARTHUR, JOHN ANDREW (1875-1914), lawyer and politician, was born on 15 August 1875 at Castlemaine, Victoria, son of John Andrew Arthur, goldminer, and his wife Sarah Ann, née Elsbury. Despite frequent moves with his family around Victorian mining towns, he showed considerable promise as a scholar. He was awarded a state scholarship which took him to Grenville College, Ballarat, for three years. He went on to the University of Melbourne where he first read arts (B.A., 1895). Achieving brilliant results each year, including the award of the Wyselaskie [q.v.6] Scholarship in political economy and the Exhibition in Roman law, he completed his Master of Arts (1897), his Bachelor of Laws (1898) and his Master of Laws (1901). At university he showed a deep interest in social questions; he stood out as a serious, natural scholar. Warmly regarded by his teachers, particularly Rev. E. H. Sugden [q.v.], master of Queen's College, Arthur became a tutor at Queen's in logic and philosophy, political economy and history, and law, prior to his admission to the Victorian Bar in 1901. On 1 January 1903 at Maldon, he married Lillie Ada Dabb.

Arthur's entry into professional practice just preceded the establishment of the Federal courts: the High Court of Australia and the Commonwealth Court of Conciliation and Arbitration. He quickly earned a reputation as a skilful constitutional and industrial lawyer, particularly in cases before the Arbitration Court, and he was soon acknowledged as one of the leading authorities on trade unionism. In 1907 he represented the Agricultural Implement Makers' Union in the case that led to the Harvester judgment and the evolution of the basic wage concept. It is not surprising that this branch of legal practice should have led him to a career in Federal politics. As a member of the Australian Labor Party, he stood for Bendigo in 1913 and narrowly defeated Sir John Quick [q.v.], its incumbent since Federation. Arthur entered the legislature as one of the most widely admired and promising politicians the young Commonwealth had seen. His speech on the 'test' bill on preference to unionists was the best in that important debate. At the same time, he continued his career as an industrial advocate, travelling frequently between parliament in Melbourne and courts in Sydney.

Following the double dissolution in 1914, Arthur easily held Bendigo. But the combination of heavy professional responsibilities as counsel for the Australian Tramways Employees' Association in a case before the High Court and the demands of the election campaign seriously strained his health. He knew his kidney complaint would be fatal, but was determined 'to die in harness'. An enforced rest following the election, which had brought his party into government, was broken by his attendance at the caucus of 17 September that elected him to the new cabinet. He was sworn in later that day as minister for external affairs before returning to his sick-bed. In the following weeks his health worsened; he lapsed into a coma and died on 9 December 1914, aged 39, at his home in The Avenue, Parkville; he was survived by his wife, two daughters and two sons.

Allowing for exaggerated estimates of a man's worth which follow an untimely death, there seems to have been every indication that Arthur was destined for an outstanding career. He was regarded as one of Labor's most brilliant recruits, and there were suggestions, even before his entry into Federal politics, that he would eventually be appointed to the High Court. His death was widely mourned and glowing tributes to his 'lovable personality' and 'fertile mind' were paid by members on both sides of the House before the state funeral and his burial in Coburg cemetery.

Punch (Melb), Nov 1912; *Age*, and *Argus*, 10 Dec 1914; *Aust Worker*, 17 Dec 1914; Atlee Hunt papers (NL).   JOHN R. THOMPSON

ARTHUR, RICHARD (1865-1932), social reformer and medical practitioner, was born on 25 October 1865 at Aldershot, England, son of Rev. David Arthur, Church of Scotland chaplain to the army, and his wife Isabella, née Simpson. He was educated at Dover College, then at the universities of St Andrews (M.A., 1885) and Edinburgh (M.B., Ch.M., 1888; M.D., 1891). He practised in Edinburgh's slums, but soon fell ill from typhoid fever. He visited Australia and worked with J. B. Nash at Wallsend, New South Wales. On 19 March 1890 at Coolangatta he married Jessie Sinclair, daughter of David Bruce, a Presbyterian minister.

The couple travelled to Europe; in 1890-91 Arthur studied hypnotism in France and wrote a thesis on its therapeutic uses for his Edinburgh doctorate. He returned to medical missionary work, now in London, but again his health suffered and late in 1891 the Arthurs went to Sydney. He made his home at Mosman, where he practised, and made a comfortable living, his main interests being the eye, ear-nose-and-throat, and dental work. He moved his practice to Macquarie Street about 1900 and served as an honorary to the Royal North Shore Hospital and Sydney Hospital. Hypnosis retained his sympathy, and he used it in nervous and other cases. He was a director of Royal Prince Alfred Hospital in 1917-20 and 1927-31 and of Sydney Hospital in 1924-32.

Always busy in public affairs, in 1892-93 Arthur worked towards creating a political faction devoted to temperance and other moral reforms. At the 1894 election his energies shifted to the Free Trade and Land Reform Association, on the radical fringe of support for (Sir) George Reid [q.v.]. Arthur concentrated on preaching moral purity in the next years, and he was also fairly active against the South African War. In 1904 he was elected to the Legislative Assembly for Middle Harbour, as a Liberal and Reform candidate with temperance and Protestant backing. He stayed in parliament as a non-Labor member throughout his life, representing North Shore in 1920-27 and Mosman in 1927-32. Most of his ideas and causes persisted over the years, but their emphasis fluctuated. He worked through parliament, pressure groups, and the written word. His prose was clear and sharp, but his personal impact was nondescript or even comical.

Early in the century Arthur was a prime advocate of Australia's need for defence against Japan. In mid-1907 he urged the Commonwealth government to invite the American fleet to Australia, and ever claimed that he originated this idea. Apart from building armed forces, he argued, Australia should sacrifice luxury in order to subsidize migration and closer settlement. From 1905 he was founding president of the Immigration League of Australasia; some notoriety attached to his encouraging southern Europeans to settle tropical Australia.

Arthur fully supported World War 1, but modified his martial enthusiasm. Instead he concentrated on the welfare of returned servicemen, especially by seeking to provide them with good, cheap homes. During the war, he also gave much care to the problems of venereal disease and chaired a select committee on its prevalence in 1915-16; the pertinent New South Wales Act of 1918, providing for notification and treatment, was largely his work.

From 1916 Arthur became well known as Australia's pioneer advocate of child endowment. His particular stresses were that endowment should be given for all children without a means test, and from taxation on luxury and profit. He became very aware in the 1920s of the extent and effects of poverty in Sydney, while remaining sympathetic to rural needs and helping to inspire the Country Women's Association of Australia (1922). He preached simplicity in all things, especially diet, praising milk and fruit as elixirs of life. As chairman of the royal commission on lunacy law and administration in 1923, Arthur (a long-time eugenicist) urged special training and institutions for defectives. He was much readier than most public figures to discuss sexual matters and birth control.

Earlier in the decade Arthur was at odds with National Party leadership, but in 1927 he became minister for public health under (Sir) Thomas Bavin [q.v.]. The oncoming depression restricted his plans, but the Health Department gave increased attention to venereal disease, tuberculosis, and maternal and baby welfare. New legislation created the Hospitals Commission, the Milk Board, and the Board of Optometrical Registration. The first two Acts did not altogether represent his own views, however, and he failed to carry a dearly cherished mental defectives bill. Ill health weakened his ministerial performance.

In opposition from November 1930, Arthur concentrated on helping the unemployed. Land settlement still seemed to him the country's prime need. The response to his death from cancer on 21 May 1932 showed that 'the Little Doctor' was held in real, if somewhat patronizing, affection. He was cremated with Anglican rites, and was survived by his wife, son and two daughters. His estate was valued for probate at £9711.

P. H. Douglas, *Wages and the family* (Chicago, 1925); *MJA*, 16 July 1932; R. Arthur papers (ML).

MICHAEL ROE

ARUNDALE, GEORGE SYDNEY (1878-1945), theosophist, was born on 1 December 1878 at Wonersh, Surrey, England, son of Rev. John Kay, preacher, and his wife Mary Ann Elizabeth, née Arundale. His mother died in childbirth and his father went to Australia. Adopted by his aunt Miss Francesca Arundale, a wealthy theosophist, George took his mother's maiden name. Educated at school at Wiesbaden, Germany, and Linton House, London, Arundale graduated from St John's College, Cambridge (B.A., 1898; LL.B., 1899; M.A., 1902), thus completing a gentleman's education.

Arundale joined the Theosophical Society in 1895, and in 1902, after experiencing 'soul-awakening' on hearing Annie Besant, dedicated himself to her service. He went to India in 1903 to teach history at her Central Hindu College, Benares, and became headmaster in 1907 and principal in 1909-13. In 1910-15 — when his life was dominated by her adopted son Krishnamurti, identified by theosophists as 'Vehicle of the World Teacher' or 'Messiah' — Arundale was

mostly in Europe. He instituted the preparatory Order of the Star in the East in 1911, editing its journal *Herald of the Star* until 1913.

During World War I Arundale assisted the British Red Cross Society in London, and was briefly general secretary of the Theosophical Society of England and Wales. In 1916 he returned to India to support Mrs Besant's Home Rule for India League, and was interned in 1917. They also founded the Indian Boy Scouts' Association and the short-lived theosophical National University, Madras, which conferred Arundale's honorary D. Litt. in 1924, a title that he used thereafter.

In April 1920 Arundale married 16-year-old Shrimati Rukmini Devi, daughter of Pandit Nilakanta Sastri; she later founded the Kalâkshetra Classical Dance Company after seeing Pavlova dance in Sydney. He also joined the Liberal Catholic Church, claiming to be clairvoyant, and from 1925 was its regional bishop of India. Late that year he openly doubted Krishnamurti's 'possession', and in the ensuing crisis he and his wife were brought to Sydney, then a major theosophical centre, by C. W. Leadbeater [q.v.]. The society's compound, The Manor, Mosman, was his headquarters until mid-1931.

Arundale dominated the Theosophical Society in Australasia as its general secretary (1926-28), chairman of the theosophical broadcasting station 2GB, editor of the *Australian Theosophist*, and co-editor of the *Australian Star News*. He joined local groups like the Good Film League and League of Nations Union, edited an Australia-India League *Bulletin* and, deploying theosophical resources, enunciated a patriotic political platform through the monthly *Advance Australia* (1926-29), and the Fidelity News Service. To promote comradeship, patriotism and imperial unity, on Armistice Day 1929 he co-founded the Who's for Australia? League, instantly attracting 4000 members according to its newspaper. An able preacher and experienced publicist, Arundale simultaneously formulated political responses and supported advanced causes, from a theosophical base.

Although perhaps marking time personally, Arundale's commanding presence gave leadership during Australian theosophy's most vital but perturbing period. In the early 1930s he returned to Madras and, while maintaining Australian connexions, wrote, lectured and travelled as world president of the Theosophical Society from 1934. He died childless on 12 August 1945 at Adyar, Madras; his funeral pyre at the Garden of Remembrance near Adyar Beach was lit by his wife.

M. Lutyens, *Krishnamurti* (Lond, 1975); Theosophical Soc, Aust Section, *Advance Australia*, 1926-29; *Aust Theosophist*, 1926-31; *Theosophist*, 67 (1945); *The Times*, 13, 16 Aug 1945.

J. I. ROE

ASCHE, THOMAS STANGE(R) HEISS OSCAR (1871-1936), actor-manager, was born on 24 January 1871 at Geelong, Victoria, son of Thomas Asche, land agent and hotelier, and his second wife Harriet Emma (Lily), née Trear. Oscar's father THOMAS was born in August 1826 at Christiania (Oslo), Norway, graduated in law from the University of Christiania in 1851, and arrived at Melbourne in the *Gibson Craig* on 27 August 1854. Golden-bearded and prodigiously strong, he worked as a goldfields trooper and miner, then as a Ballarat storekeeper; a reef, lead and gully were named after him. On 17 August 1855 at his home at Golden Point he married Jane Wier, by whom he had one surviving son. By August 1860 he had settled as innkeeper at Camperdown; in October he was naturalized. His wife died and on 13 September 1866 at Christ Church, Geelong, he married Harriet Emma, whose father Colonel William Trear owned Mack's Hotel. From 1866 as an all-powerful speculator Asche sometimes managed to arrange and almost to preside over the sale of crown lands, wanted by squatters, at auctions where his men dominated the bidding.

In Geelong he became a town councillor in 1870 and acquired Mack's Hotel on 24 March 1871. In November 1876 he moved to the Union Club Hotel, Melbourne, and some ten years later to the Royal Hotel in George Street, Sydney. After heavy financial losses in 1893 he had to sell the Royal but from 1896 ran the Imperial Hotel, Wynyard Square. He died there of chronic kidney disease on 2 November 1898 survived by his wife, one son of his first marriage and two sons and three daughters of the second.

Oscar was educated at Laurel Lodge, Dandenong, and from 1884 at Melbourne Church of England Grammar School, where his academic progress was aided by a flair for memorizing. He left school at 16 with a deep interest in theatre from his acquaintance with actors who frequented the Royal Hotel; but he was also keen to go on the land. He claimed to have visited China and Fiji, was briefly apprenticed to an architect, learned to box from Larry Foley [q.v.4], and spent a few months 'humping his bluey' through southern New South Wales, accompanied by two dogs and a pocket edition of Shakespeare's plays. In 1890 he decided finally to make his career in the theatre; his father paid his fare to Norway to study under actor-manager Bjørn Bjørnson at Christiania, where he met Ibsen. On advice he went to London where he studied speech with Walter Lacy and Henry Neville and watched the acting of Ellen Terry, Henry Irving and others. In March 1893 he had his first London part in *Man and woman* at the Opéra Comique Theatre, but that year his father had to stop his £10 weekly allowance. Living precariously at times, Oscar found work with (Sir) F. R. Benson's touring Shakespearian company. In June 1899 at Hindley, Lancashire, he married Lily Brayton who had joined the company in 1896.

In 1901 Lily was engaged by Herbert Beerbohm Tree in London. Asche also joined Tree but was released to play Freddy Maldonado in Pinero's *Iris*, his first prominent part in London. He also played opposite Ellen Terry in *Much ado about nothing*, and appeared in many Shakespearian plays. In 1904 Asche and Lily Brayton formed a company (with Oscar as actor-manager) to play at the Adelphi Theatre. *The taming of the shrew* became a very successful item in their repertoire. They then leased His Majesty's Theatre, opening in 1907 with *Attila*. This soon made way for Asche's entrancing production of *As you like it*; he expounded his unorthodox interpretations of Shakespeare in an arrangement of this play published in 1907.

In 1909 Asche took the full company for a triumphal eighteen-months tour of Australia. He opened to packed houses at the Theatre Royal with *The taming of the shrew*, then presented *Othello*, *As you like it*, *The merchant of Venice*, and in the new year, *Count Hannibal* and *The virgin goddess*. He played two seasons in Sydney and three in Melbourne.

Back in London in 1911, Asche began a two-year season of *Kismet*, a lavish Arabian nights fantasy with Oscar as the beggar Hajj and using original lighting techniques. He took *Kismet* to Australia and New Zealand from early 1912 until August next year. In Brisbane he met Rider Haggard and discussed with him the stage adaptation of his novel, *A child of the storm*. This was presented as *Mameena* in London in October 1914, but was not a financial success; Asche yearned for another *Kismet*. He found the answer in *Chu Chin Chow*, for which he wrote 'book' and lyrics in two weeks. Opening on 31 August 1916, the show broke all records with a five-year season; as author Asche received £200 000 and as actor-producer £500 weekly. In 1917 he produced *The maid of the mountains*; he also wrote another successful musical, *Cairo*, which opened in 1921.

In July 1922, under contract to J. C. Williamson [q.v.6] Ltd, Asche left England for a third tour of Australasia. His wife refused to join him. He included *Chu Chin Chow* and *Cairo* as well as Shakespeare in his popular repertoire. Despite quarrelling with Williamson's over production and finance, he managed to recapture some of the pleasures of his earlier visits by staging lavish picnics, attending race meetings and making a camping tour of the coast between Sydney and Melbourne in his chauffeur-driven Rolls-Royce. After further disagreement, his contract was abruptly terminated in June 1924; he left Melbourne soon after.

In England Asche encountered more trouble. Greyhound-racing, which he had taken up during his 1909 Australian tour, cost him £45 000; he owed over £40 000 in taxes and his £100 000 Sugley Farm in Gloucestershire had to be sold when he became bankrupt. His wife helped him by backing his new but unsuccessful musical, *The good old days of England*. He wrote his memoirs, *Oscar Asche: his life. By himself* (London, 1929) and two novels (1930). In 1932 he directed his wife in her last stage appearance. Ill and impoverished, he rejoined her at Marlow, Buckinghamshire. He died at near-by Bisham of coronary thrombosis on 23 March 1936, and was buried in the riverside cemetery there. They had no children.

A powerfully built, virile figure 'glowing with health' in his early years, Asche became grossly fat in old age. He was a keen sportsman and had been a good cricketer, a wicket-keeper by preference. A man of great gusto, most impressive as an actor, an innovator and perfectionist as a producer, an extravagant generous incurable optimist, Asche was a splendid showman.

Oscar Asche . . . by himself (Lond, 1929); H. Pearson, *The last actor-managers* (Lond, 1950); W. R. Brownhill, *The history of Geelong and Corio Bay* (Melb, 1955); M. L. Kiddle, *Men of yesterday* (Melb, 1961); H. Porter, *Stars of Australian stage and screen* (Adel, 1965); P. Hartnoll (ed), *The concise Oxford companion to the theatre* (Oxford, 1972); *Lone Hand*, 1 Apr 1909; *Home*, Dec 1922; *Argus*, 10, 14, 16 June, 4, 9 July, 15 Nov 1924; *Sunday Herald*, 19 Oct 1952; *Daily Mirror* (Syd), 30 June 1973; Asche family papers (held by Mr Justice A. Asche, South Yarra); information from P. L. Brown, Newtown, Vic.

L. J. BLAKE

ASH, GEORGE (1859-1897), journalist, lawyer and politician, was born on 19 September 1859 in Southwark, London, son of James Ash, journeyman baker, and his wife Eliza Ann, née Goodfellow. In his teens Ash ran away to sea but was brought back and put to work in a warehouse. In 1877 he went to South Africa, where he joined the staff of the *Kaffrarian Watchman* in King William's Town and enlisted as a volunteer in order to report the Kaffir war.

In 1879 Ash migrated to South Australia and worked on the Mount Gambier *Border Watch* and the *Narracoorte Herald*. He bought the latter in December 1880 with J. B. Mather. Within three years they had paid off their loan and established a reputation for integrity and fearlessness. The editorial tone was strongly anti-squatter; some felt Ash 'looked upon himself as a heaven-born reformer sent down to set us all straight'. In 1885 he married Nellie Malcolm; they had five children. In 1886 he was elected to the Narracoorte District Council.

On 9 April 1889 Ash wrote an article attacking a local landowner. Libel was alleged and the case attracted much debate over freedom of the press. Ash ably conducted his own defence but, having alleged perjury, was not allowed to bring evidence in support. The plaintiff eventually won on a legal technicality, but public sympathy lay with Ash. Despite the success of a sustaining fund, he was forced to sell the paper and by August was bankrupt.

Contesting the district of Albert at the April 1890 election, Ash supported free trade, increased land tax, women's suffrage, payment of members and Federation, and continued his popular crusade against dummying; he became the youngest member of the House of Assembly. A commentator described him as full of brain, backbone and tongue, eccentric, 'a smart man — but not a discreet one'. Encouraged by (Sir) Samuel Way, (Sir) J. H. Symon and C. C. Kingston [qq.v.], Ash consolidated his hard-won legal experience by matriculating in 1891 and studying law; he worked for Kingston as an articled clerk.

Phenomenally industrious, Ash would leave parliament at midnight, walk home to Woodville and, after brief rest, begin his office work and studies. He won the Stow Prize in 1892 and 1893 and topped his final year of law. In December 1894 he was admitted to the Bar, and became Kingston's partner, although they were not aligned politically. Ash headed the poll again in Albert at the 1893 and 1896 elections when he was associated with the conservative National Defence League. He had sat on the 1892 shops and factories commission. A teetotaller and non-smoker, he was a diligent official visitor to Adelaide's two lunatic asylums. His agitation for separation of retarded children from adult lunatics resulted in 1894 in government consent to subsidize the building of Minda Home. Ash wrote articles in the *Advertiser* seeking subscriptions and was honorary secretary of the founding committee.

Late in 1896 his doctor warned that he was overworking dangerously. Ash soon contracted typhoid fever, but still was selected as a delegate to the 1897 National Australasian Federal Convention. He did not attend, having died on 23 February 1897, aged 37. 'The good always die young' he had once joked. Ash was buried in West Terrace cemetery; his estate was sworn for probate at £1200.

Some had deplored Ash's apparent veering from a liberal to a conservative stance; his friends described it as consistent independence. Kingston admitted that Ash's dogged individualism and conscientious pontification over trivial details would have prevented his joining a government, but believed that he had become 'a potent voice in the parliament'.

Minda Home, *Fifty years of sympathetic care and practical service* (Adel, 1948); *SA Institutes J,* June 1931; *Register* (Adel), 17 July-6 Aug 1889, 17, 19, 21, 25 Mar, 4, 7, 11 Apr 1890; *Observer* (Adel), 9 Aug, 13 Dec 1890, 27 May 1893, 27 Feb 1897; *Advertiser* (Adel) and *Border Watch,* 24 Feb 1897; J. H. Symon papers, 1736/1/825 (NL); Register no 301, 1894 (Supreme Court, SA).

SUZANNE EDGAR

ASHBOLT, SIR ALFRED HENRY (1870-1930), businessman, was born on 6 March 1870 at Christchurch, New Zealand, son of Alfred Ashbolt, printer and manager of the *New Zealand Times,* and his wife Mary, née Nuthal. Educated at schools in Christchurch and Wellington, he was articled at 15 to T. Kennedy Macdonald, a businessman and politician. He passed accountancy examinations and at 19 became junior book-keeper with the *New Zealand Times* at £3 a week.

In 1891 Ashbolt went to Tasmania to join the merchants A. G. Webster [q.v.6] & Son of Hobart, as junior book-keeper, and rose to chief clerk at 26. He also managed the Sun Fire Insurance office and the Peninsular & Oriental Steam Navigation Co. agencies. In 1898 his application to become town clerk of Hobart failed. Leaving Webster in 1901, he became junior partner in the firm of Tasmania's leading industrialist (Sir) Henry Jones [q.v.], then beginning expansion as fruit processors, timber-millers, ship-owners and shipping agents. Ashbolt was involved in the growth of the Hobart branch of the company, which became Henry Jones (Co-operative) Ltd, and in its spread to all mainland States, and to New Zealand, South Africa and England. Other undertakings in which he had interests included Charles Davis Ltd, ironmongers, and Foreman Foundry and Enamelling Co. Ltd; he was also involved in two unsuccessful attempts to extract zinc from Tasmanian ores by the new electrolytic process. His most successful venture was the Tongkah Harbour Tin Dredging Co. (Thailand), which in 1919 paid dividends of £517 500. He was also a leading member of a construction syndicate which carried out projects in Tasmania, Victoria and other States.

In 1906 Ashbolt attended a conference which advised the Commonwealth on regulations under the Commerce (Trade Descriptions) Act of 1905. He was an active member, sometime president, of the Hobart Chamber of Commerce which he represented at the 1913 world conference in London. *En route* he had visited Germany and seen the early Zeppelins, which stimulated an abiding interest in airship travel. A member of the first State War Council and the Munitions Committee during World War I, he also worked for voluntary organizations including the Red Cross Society. He was consul for Russia in Tasmania until he resigned on the outbreak of the revolution. For some years he was Tasmanian commercial representative of the British Board of Trade.

Ashbolt was appointed agent-general for Tasmania in London in 1919. With characteristic thoroughness he sought for investors in the State's industries; his canvassing ranged from British machine tools to the marketing of imperial and colonial timbers. As a result of his efforts, several British firms established branch factories in Tasmania. An enthusiast for Empire development and imperial protection, he was vice-president of the British Empire Producers' Association, executive committee-man for the Australian pavilion at the British Empire Exhibition, Wembley, and a strong proponent of development of an Empire airship (Dirigible) service. With government consent he was advisory director to the Leverhulme group while in England. He also secured for the Royal Society of Tasmania the letters (1837-43) of Lady Franklin [q.v.1] to her sister.

Returning via North America to Hobart in September 1924, Ashbolt rejoined A. G. Webster & Son and became managing director. Next year he was knighted. In the United States he had investigated the introduction to Australia of the manufacture of celotex from sugar-cane refuse. He explored other new fields for his company, including the supply and servicing of labour-saving farm machinery and the buying and international marketing of the rare mineral, osmiridium, being mined at Adamsfield. He encouraged the pioneer growing and processing of flax and other exotic crops, but these enterprises were hampered by severe commercial recession.

He also backed Tasmanian Paper Pty Ltd at Kermandie which perfected a technique for making paper pulp from the groundwood of the *Eucalyptus regnans*, a successful process subsequently taken over by the Australian Newsprint Mills at Boyer.

Ashbolt was an Anglican and a prominent Freemason — sometime superintendent of the Tasmanian District Grand Royal Arch Chapter of Scotland. He was a member of the Tasmanian (Hobart), Windham and Ranelagh (London) and the Australasian Pioneers (Sydney) clubs. A leading lawn tennis player and sculler, he had helped found the Sandy Bay Rowing Club and became president of the Royal Hobart Golf Club. He had been married twice: in 1904 to Alice Mabel Frederica Howe (d. 1918 without issue), and in 1919 to Muriel Wayne Walker. From 1915 he lived at Lenna, formerly the home of Alexander McGregor [q.v.5]. After Jones's death in 1926 Ashbolt was undisputed leader of the commercial community in southern Tasmania. In failing health from about 1928, he died of cerebral haemorrhage on 24 January 1930, survived by his wife and their two children; he was buried in Cornelian Bay cemetery. His estate was sworn for probate at £47 225.

R. A. A. Sherrin and J. H. Wallace, *Early history of New Zealand*, T. W. Leys ed (Auckland, 1890); *The Times*, 12 Aug 1920, 13, 29 July, 2, 17, 26 Nov 1921, 9 Feb, 14 Sept, 23 Oct, 16 Dec 1923, 3 July 1924, 1 Jan 1925, 25 Jan 1930; *Mercury*, 20 Apr 1928, 25 Jan 1930; family papers (held by Mr A. Ashbolt, Sandy Bay, Tas).

G. P. R. CHAPMAN
JOHN REYNOLDS

ASHBY, EDWIN (1861-1941), estate agent and naturalist, was born of Quaker stock on 2 November 1861 at Pleystowe Capel, Surrey, England, son of James Ashby, tea merchant, and his wife Eliza, née Sterry. A delicate child, he had little formal education but was encouraged in his natural history interests by his parents, both critical field naturalists. He worked for his father, then visited Australia for his health in 1884-87 and migrated to Adelaide in 1888 with his elder sister. On 6 May 1890 he married Esther Maria Coleman; they had two sons and two daughters.

There were three main facets to Ashby's life: his work as a land and estate agent, his passionate interest in natural history, and his involvement with the Society of Friends. Having failed at wattle-bark-growing in the South-East, about 1890 he joined a cousin's firm of land and estate agents and financiers; later, as Saunders & Ashby, they owned much of Eden Hills, which they largely developed. In 1902 the Ashbys moved to Blackwood in the Adelaide hills and established the property, Wittunga, in virgin bushland. He retired in 1914 but continued an independent business from his home. In 1918 he visited North America.

Ashby was an avid collector of birds, butterflies and other insects, shells (particularly chitons) and plants. A critical observer, with infectious enthusiasm, he wanted to share each new discovery. He published over eighty papers in ornithology alone, and named or discovered several new birds. But his most outstanding contributions were on chitons, recent and fossil, on which he was a world authority, discovering over twenty new taxa. His collection, presented to the South Australian Museum in 1932, was considered the best of its kind.

Wittunga began as a formal English gentleman's garden, but as Ashby became increasingly fascinated by Australian native flora, he specialized in its cultivation, collecting numerous plants from the bush throughout Australia. He experimented with methods of cultivation and evolved the 'Ashby system' of watering, giving plants a soaking every three to four weeks instead of the usual light surface watering. Speaking and writing often, he introduced many Australians to their unique flora. A 1934 bushfire burnt part of Wittunga garden, gutted the house and destroyed many of his records and collections. Fortunately many bird-skins and chitons were in the Museum, but material burnt included some 'type' specimens. At 73 he could not rebuild these, but instead enlarged his horticultural interests by establishing an Australian native-plant nursery; over 300 tried and proven species were offered cheaply. An enlightened conservationist, he worked to preserve wildlife reserves such as Flinders Chase, and was a prime mover in securing Chauncy's Line Reserve.

For many years Ashby was one of the Quakers' most widely known members, speaking at public meetings and on the radio, and writing to the press on such issues as peace and temperance. His life exemplified his belief: 'Six working days are a better index of what we are than one Sunday'.

A member of many learned and scientific organizations, Ashby was elected a fellow of the Linnaean Society of London and a corresponding fellow of the American Ornithologists' Union. He was a councilmember of the Royal Society of South Australia in 1900-19, and president of the Royal Australasian Ornithologists' Union in 1926. He died at Wittunga on 8 January 1941, and was interred in the Friends' Burial Ground, West Terrace, Adelaide. His daughter Alison is a distinguished collector and painter of

Australian flora. His garden has been preserved by the gift of his son Keith and his family, who in 1965 donated 35 acres (14 ha) to the Board of Governors of the Botanic Garden, Adelaide.

Blackwood Mag (SA), 1 (1914); *Aust Zoologist*, 4 (1925-27), pp 340-42; *Emu*, 40 (1941); Malacological Soc Lond, *Procs*, 25 (1942); Roy Soc SA, *Trans*, 65 (1941); Roy Zoological Soc NSW, *Procs*, Aug 1941; *Observer* (Adel), 20 Mar 1926; *Express and J*, 18 May 1935; Esther Ashby, Diaries and farm journals (held by Mr Eric Ashby, Mt Alma, Inman Valley, SA); minute-books and documents (Religious Soc of Friends SA, Regional Meeting, North Adel, *and* SAA). ENID ROBERTSON

ASHCROFT, EDGAR ARTHUR (1864-1938), electrical engineer and metallurgist, was born on 5 September 1864 at Sunderland, County Durham, England, son of George Ashcroft, civil engineer, and his wife Sophia, née Davey. He trained as a mechanical and electrical engineer for five years, before accepting appointment at Broken Hill, New South Wales, with the Broken Hill Proprietary Co. Ltd to direct the installation of its electric light plant. He worked as an electrician for the company, and as a metallurgist experimented in the treatment of silver-lead sulphide ores; he was assisted by Dr Carl Schnabel of Clausthal, Germany, in the preparation of his report in 1891. In 1893 with John Howell he invented a steam generator using hot slag. In 1894 he patented a complex electrolytic process for recovering zinc from refractory sulphide ores. Late that year he left B.H.P. and, with the financial support of other mining company promoters, the process was tested successfully on a small scale at Broken Hill and in England, and approved by Schnabel. The Sulphide Corporation (Ashcroft Process) Ltd was floated in London next year with a capital of £1 100 000, and it bought Ashcroft's process and the Broken Hill Central Mine. In 1895-97, when he was a councillor of the Australasian Institute of Mining Engineers, he took out further patents in Australia and the United States of America.

At Cockle Creek, near Newcastle, New South Wales, the world's first electrolytic zinc works was erected in 1897 at a cost of £250 000, to the inventor's specifications and under his control. Although his theory was sound, both the plant and process had to be modified, and Ashcroft lacked managerial experience. In less than a year the works had almost been dismantled; he had overestimated profits and under-estimated costs, and later claimed that low grade ores had been responsible for commercial failure.

The Sulphide Corporation dissociated itself from Ashcroft and his process, and succeeded as an orthodox mining smelting company. The *Australian Mining Standard's* accusation that he made 'a very large amount of money in selling what he knew was worthless to his company' was never substantiated.

A member of the Institution of Mining and Metallurgy, London, from 1895, Ashcroft returned to England, and in June 1898 his paper to the institution on 'The treatment of Broken Hill Sulphide ores by wet extraction process, and the electrolytic deposition of zinc' aroused considerable controversy. He joined James Swinburne and continued to work in his London laboratory on a wet electrolysis system for separating chlorides and related problems. He published in such journals as the *Transactions* of the Electrochemical Society, New York. In the early 1920s he described himself as a research chemist and in 1933 his paper on 'Chlorine smelting with chloride electrolysis' was read to the Institution of Mining and Metallurgy.

Ashcroft retired to Ancrum House, Roxburghshire, Scotland, and died on 24 August 1938 at Polton, Midlothian; he was survived by his wife Irene, née Dulier.

Described by (Sir) Richard Threlfall [q.v.] as having 'that peculiar combination of imaginative faculty with sound horse sense which, more than anything else differentiates the born inventor', Ashcroft was fascinated with developments in an area of rapidly changing technology. His complicated process consisting of twenty operations failed commercially, but not before the original 'Sulphide Corporation advanced the electrolytic process further than any other individual or company in the world'.

G. Blainey, *The rise of Broken Hill* (Melb, 1968); Inst of Mining and Metallurgy (Lond), *Trans*, 6 (1897-98), 48 (1938-39); *Aust Mining Standard*, 29 Apr 1893, 27 Jan 1897, 22 Oct 1898; J. W. Turner, The development of coal mining and manufacturing in Newcastle 1800-1900 (Ph.D. thesis, Univ Newcastle, 1977); Gibbs, Bright & Co. papers (Guildhall Lib, Lond). J. W. TURNER

ASHTON, JAMES (1859-1935), artist, was born on 4 April 1859 on the Isle of Man, England. He grew up in the city of York where he was apprenticed to a pharmacist and attended the school of art before gaining a scholarship to the National Art Training School (Royal College of Art) at South Kensington, London. At 17 he returned to York, taught art and worked as a gilder and carver. On 27 December 1880 he married Mary Elizabeth Rawlings Turnbull.

Ashton arrived in Adelaide on 11 January

1884 and decided to become a professional painter. He spent twelve months looking for work before a job teaching art at Prince Alfred College enabled him to bring out his wife and son. He established the Norwood Art School in 1886 in two cramped rooms of the Norwood Town Hall where he taught sketching, china-painting and painting in oil and water-colours. In 1895 he returned to England where he paid £240 for three months lessons from Henry Moore, R.A., an eminent marine painter at York. He gained a diploma and on 28 June was elected a member of the (Royal) Society of Arts, London.

Ashton was affiliated with the Royal Drawing Society and, after his return to Adelaide via Europe and Egypt, instituted its examinations and much-prized certificates at Ashton's Academy of Arts, which he opened in Victoria Square in 1896. It later moved to Flinders Street, then Grenfell Street. Through the highly regarded academy, 'Jimmy' influenced many painters who later became well known: his son (Sir) John William, Gustav Barnes, Hans Heysen [qq.v.] and Ivor Hele. Ashton insisted on basic proficiency in drawing: on the wall of his studio hung a plaque inscribed 'He that attempts to run before he can walk must surely stumble and fall'.

His association with Prince Alfred College lasted nearly forty years; he was a jovial popular teacher who allowed the boys to develop their own interests but encouraged them to copy early masters. In 1925 he presented the school with a valuable art collection and he bequeathed his library to it.

Ashton had presided in 1896 over the Adelaide Easel Club, a group of rebels dissatisfied with Adelaide's art Establishment. In 1912-14 he was a member of the Commonwealth Art Advisory Board. A trustee and honorary fellow of the (Royal) South Australian Society of Arts, he was its president in 1914-17 and vice-president in 1931; in 1926 and 1929 he won the society's seascape prize. He encouraged six South Australian country towns to begin art collections and his own paintings were bought by galleries in Broken Hill, Bendigo, Perth and Colombo. He was a justice of the peace and a Freemason.

In 1927 Ashton, a rubicund tubby figure with silver hair and waxed moustache, who usually wore a flower in his lapel, retired to live in a terrace by the sea at Brighton. Here, between nine trips to Ceylon (Sri Lanka) and despite painful arthritis, he continued painting his favourite subject, the sea. He was an effective draftsman and a loving, careful observer of nature, though by later standards rather sentimental. His best seascape, 'The Moon Enchanted Sea', is in the National Gallery of South Australia. In 1934 his oil portrait, now held by the family, was painted by Leslie Wilkie [q.v.]. On 2 August 1935 Ashton died of intestinal obstruction due to hernia in Wakefield Street Private Hospital, Adelaide, and was buried in St Jude's Anglican cemetery, Brighton. He was survived by his wife (d. 1945), daughter and son; his estate was sworn for probate at £889.

M. A. Overbury and H. E. Fuller, *A history of the S.A. Society of Arts, Inc. 1856-1931*, W. Sowden ed (Adel, 1933); N. Benko, *Art and artists of South Australia* (Adel, 1969); Roy Soc of Arts, *J*, 43 (1895); A. Ashton, 'James Ashton, South Australia's veteran painter and teacher . . .', *Art in Aust*, Nov 1935; *Observer* (Adel), 21 July 1894, 8 Aug 1896, 13 June 1925; *Advertiser* (Adel), 11 Apr 1896, 3, 6 Aug 1935; *Mail* (Adel), 9 Aug 1913; A.B.C., 'Personalities remembered', no 37 (SAA).

ALLAN SIERP

ASHTON, JAMES (1864-1939), newspaperman, politician and businessman, was born on 8 May 1864 at Ashby near Geelong, Victoria, fifth child of James Ashton, coffee-roaster and later a sharebroker, and his first wife Mary Ann Kinsman, née Brittan. About 1871 the family moved to Sandhurst (Bendigo) where James was educated at the Sandhurst Grammar School until he was 10, when he started work in a printing office and was paid 2s. 6d. for a 54-hour week. At 13 he went with his family to Echuca, and worked on two local newspapers before moving to New South Wales where he became a compositor on the *Hay Standard* at £2 5s. a week. Two years later he joined Cramsie, Bowden & Co., station suppliers, and as relaxation ran in amateur athletics; in 1884-88 he worked in their Melbourne office and was active in 'a big church debating society'.

In 1888 Ashton returned to Hay and for £1000 bought a half-share in the *Riverine Grazier*. He sold out in 1892 and bought the *Narrandera Argus*. As a free trader and supporter of (Sir) George Reid [q.v.], in 1894 he was elected to the Legislative Assembly for Hay, which he represented until 1898. He had campaigned vigorously in his newspaper against 'landlordism' and advocated a perpetual leasing system and a tax on land based on its unimproved value. An able debater, he refused office under Reid. On 6 March 1899 at Sutton Forest he married Helen Willis, granddaughter of J. S. Willis [q.v.6] and a relation of E. W. Knox [q.v.].

In 1897 Ashton had strongly opposed equal representation of the States in a powerful Senate. He proposed that no alterations to the Constitution be made without the consent of every State, proportional representation for electing the Senate and a national referendum to break deadlocks. Realizing that his constituents thought differently on Federation, in 1898 he won Goulburn, which he represented until August 1907. In 1901 he was defeated narrowly for Riverina in the House of Representative elections, in part because of his 'expressed sympathies with the Boers' in the South African War.

In 1904-07 Ashton was secretary for lands under (Sir) Joseph Carruthers [q.v.]. He was harassed throughout his term by the allegations of bribery and improper conduct against W. P. Crick [q.v.], his predecessor, which culminated in a royal commission into the administration of his department and in criminal charges being laid against Crick. In 1906 he introduced a bill, which lapsed, to transfer the routine administration of the Department of Lands to three commissioners, because he believed that a man with political duties and 'tempestuous disputes to attend to' had no time to attend to necessary detail. That year he reduced the number of staff in an effort to improve efficiency. Long an advocate of closer settlement on scientific lines, he ably administered land resumptions made under the Closer Settlement Acts. Sickened by politics, he did not stand for election in 1907 and was nominated to the Legislative Council on 24 September. When the ministry was reformed by (Sir) Charles Gregory Wade [q.v.] in October he was minister without portfolio until he resigned on 25 June 1909, having been briefly acting premier.

As 'a protective measure' Ashton qualified for the Bar but was not admitted. In 1910 with Sir Samuel McCaughey [q.v.5] he became a shareholder in and director of the Coreena Pastoral Co., which owned Coreena sheep-station near Barcaldine and cattle-stations elsewhere in Queensland. It was an investment which 'put me on Easy Street', and made possible everything that happened afterwards'. He became attorney and adviser to McCaughey and to the New Zealand & Australian Land Co. Ltd of Edinburgh, and later was chief executor of McCaughey's will.

During World War I, as an executive of the Australian Red Cross Society, Ashton became closely associated with its president Lady Helen Munro Ferguson [q.v.]; later he often consulted her about McCaughey's bequest of £500 000 to benefit the dependants of ex-servicemen. In 1919 Ashton's wife was appointed O.B.E. for her work for the Red Cross. In 1920-24 he was a senator of the University of Sydney and in 1920-21 chairman of the Commonwealth board of inquiry into Federal and State taxation. He

contributed articles to the *Sydney Morning Herald* on closer settlement, the Northern Territory and current political issues in the 1920s and 1930s.

Assiduous in attendance at the Legislative Council, Ashton organized opposition to J. T. Lang's [q.v.] attempts to abolish the Upper House in 1926 and attempted radical legislation such as the mortgages bill of 1932. He did not stand for election to the reconstructed council in 1934. A Labor member paid tribute to his 'wonderful knowledge and an extraordinary gift of self-expression ... he was relentless in his criticism, but ... was always fair and logical'.

After World War I Ashton was chairman of the Mutual Life & Citizens Assurance Co. Ltd in 1927-39, and of the Commercial Banking Co. of Sydney in 1933-38, was sometime chairman of the Union Trustee Co. of Australia Ltd and a director of Anthony Hordern [q.v.4] & Sons Ltd. By 1933 he had acquired properties in New South Wales for each of his four sons, James, Robert, Geoffrey and Philip, who formed a famous international polo team from 1927. Ashton, who had twice been to the United States of America, visited England in 1930 when his sons went there to play. He was also 'an enthusiastic cricket fan'.

Survived by his wife (d. 24 October) and sons, he died of cancer on 6 August 1939 at his waterfront home, Tueila, Double Bay, where he had lived since 1903, and was cremated with Anglican rites. His estate was valued for administration at £23 279.

PP (NSW), 1906, 2, 73-4, and evidence; Farmers and Settlers' Assn (NSW), *Reports*, 1905-06; *Aust Mag* (Syd), 1 Aug 1910; *Pastoral Review*, 16 Sept 1939; *SMH*, 30 Dec 1924, 3 Feb 1925, 13, 14 Feb, 7 July 1930, 1 June 1932, 26 Apr, 22 Sept 1933, 7 Aug 1939; *Goulburn Evening Penny Post*, 12 July 1933; *Country Life and Stock and Station J*, 11 Aug 1933; information from G. G. Ashton, Markdale, Binda, NSW.

MARTHA RUTLEDGE

ASHTON, JAMES (1861-1918) and FREDERICK (1866-1941), circus proprietors, were sons of JAMES HENRY ASHTON and his second wife Elizabeth, née Critchley. Their father, whose real name may have been Wild, was reputedly a clog-dancer and circus performer from Colchester, Essex, England, who had arrived in Australia in the 1840s. After success as a 'bold and fearless' equestrian at Radford's Amphitheatre, Hobart Town, in 1848-49 and at Port Phillip, he performed at John Malcolm's Amphitheatre, Sydney, in September 1851 and later at J. S. Noble's Olympic Circus. His first wife Mary died aged 19 at Maitland in 1852, and next year at Hanging Rock, near Tamworth, he married Elizabeth Critchley. By May 1854 he had formed Ashton's Royal Olympic Circus and for the next thirty-five years he toured eastern Australia with his variously grandly titled circus. He was in South Australia in 1865, but his name became a household word especially in the country areas of New South Wales and in Queensland as far north as Rockhampton. He acquired a reputation for developing Australian talent: the Wirth family [q.v.] joined his troupe for a time, and he often featured Aboriginal performers such as the acrobatic rider Mungo Mungo.

James junior was born at Ipswich, Queensland, in 1861 and Frederick at Boorowa, New South Wales, on 28 September 1866. They and their brothers and sisters were soon being featured as clowns, riders, musicians, tumblers and high-wire performers in what was, during the mid-1870s, one of Australia's largest travelling circuses, with a splendid brass band, about 40 horses, 12 vehicles and a tent said to be capable of seating 800 people. Advertisements in 1875 featured 'Master James Ashton . . . the most sensational gymnast of the present day, actually standing on his head upon the flying steed', and 'ballet-dancing on the tight-rope'. In 1884 at Armidale, New South Wales, James married Elizabeth Ryan, and at Walgett in 1887 Frederick married her sister Ellen.

After their father died at Gladstone, Queensland, on 17 January 1889, James carried on the circus, sometimes in partnership with Frederick. While other circuses dominated in Sydney in the 1890s Ashtons' continued to tour the bush towns of New South Wales and Queensland. In 1904-05 James was engaged with the Fitzgerald Brothers' Circus, and with it toured New Zealand. By December 1905 he had re-formed his own troupe and in 1906-07 was in partnership with Walter St Leon. In 1909 James combined with one Stillman in a circus and buck-jumping show, and in 1913 his troupe featured the 'Flying Colleanos', of whom Con was later to be a tight-rope performer of international fame. While travelling with Sole's circus James, aged 57, drowned in the Macquarie River at Dubbo, New South Wales, on 9 May 1918 and was buried in the Roman Catholic cemetery. He was survived by his wife and nine children, of whom most became circus and vaudeville performers.

After World War I Frederick, known as 'Flash Fred', a fine circus bandsman, small, dark and an immaculate dresser, was sole proprietor, and continued to entertain in the outback. He died on 17 February 1941 at Randwick, survived by his wife and ten children; he was buried in the Catholic section of Rookwood cemetery. His descendants still carry on the family circus.

N. Fernandez, *Circus saga – Ashtons* (Syd, 1971); *Cornwall Chronicle*, 20 Jan 1849, 26 Jan 1850; *SMH*, 1, 3 Sept 1851, 23 July 1855; *ISN*, 6 May 1854, 30 June 1855; *Advertiser* (Adel), 28 Mar 1865; *T&CJ*, 2, 16 Jan, 29 May 1875; *Bulletin*, 9 Feb 1889, 16, 30 May 1918; *People* (Syd), 22 Apr 1953; information from Mr & Mrs D. Ashton and family, of the circus, and Mr M. St Leon, Wahroonga, NSW.

CHRIS CUNNEEN

ASHTON, SIR JOHN WILLIAM (1881-1963), artist, was born on 20 September 1881 at Clifton, York, England, son of James Ashton [q.v.], artist, and his wife Mary Elizabeth Rawlings, née Turnbull. He migrated to Adelaide with his parents and was educated at Prince Alfred College in 1889-97, then did odd jobs in his father's studio and studied drawing part time. He met Hans Heysen [q.v.], who became a lifelong friend. In 1900 Will left for England to work under the seascapist Julian Olsson at St Ives, Cornwall. He spent the winter of 1902-03 at the Académie Julian, Paris, with E. Phillips Fox, David Davies [qq.v.] and Heysen.

In 1904 Ashton had work accepted by the Royal Academy of Arts, London, and the Salon des Artists Français, Paris, but next year he returned to Adelaide. The sale of 'Boulevard Montparnasse, Paris' for 150 guineas to the National Gallery of South Australia enabled him to marry May Millman (d. 1958), one of his students, on 31 January 1906 at Christ Church, North Adelaide. After holding successful exhibitions in Sydney, Melbourne, Perth and Adelaide, in 1908 he won the Wynne prize for landscape. In 1912-14 he painted in Britain, Europe and Egypt. Back in Australia for a year, he felt his prospects were better overseas, and took his family to London in 1915. Prevented by an arthritic condition from joining the Australian Imperial Force, he became a voluntary driver. He advised the South Australian gallery and private collectors, and supported his family by examining for the Royal Drawing Society of which he was a member.

Ashton returned to Sydney in 1917 and next year was commissioned by the Commonwealth government to depict the La Pérouse [q.v.2] monument at Botany Bay as a gift to France. He made frequent overseas trips, sometimes with such artists as Lionel Lindsay and Charles Bryant [qq.v.]; he returned again and again to Paris. He won the Wynne prize in 1930 and in 1939. Will Ashton had worked mainly in oils from about 1910. He was fascinated by the effects of changing light on white, such as snow, cloud and foam, and his most characteristic works are impressionist seascapes and landscapes. He used a free and vigorous treatment in impasto, while not departing from design and good draftsmanship. Lindsay wrote that Ashton had caught the changing Paris landscape 'with such a fine truth and vision, that you will go far in Europe today to find so able a painter'.

In 1937, hoping that he 'could be of value to the artists here', Ashton became director of the Art Gallery of New South Wales, and almost immediately had to organize the sesquicentennial exhibition of Australian art. Aware of the gallery's inadequacies, he managed to improve the lighting, but other plans were postponed because of World War II. In 1941 he accompanied an Australian exhibition to the United States of America and inspected galleries there and in Canada. In 1944-47 he was director of David Jones' [q.v.2] Art Gallery. A member of the Commonwealth Art Advisory Board from 1918, Ashton was chairman in 1953-62. He was a member of the Royal Institute of Oil Painters, London, a vice-president of the Australian Painter-Etchers' Society, and a member of the Society of Artists, Sydney, being awarded its medal in 1944. He was appointed O.B.E. in 1941 and knighted in 1960.

Ashton died of cancer at his home at Mosman on 1 September 1963 and was cremated with Anglican rites. He was survived by three sons of his first marriage and by his second wife Winfreda Isabel Hoggard, née Luxmoore, a widow whom he had married on 6 February 1961. His estate was valued for probate at £25 195. William Dargie's portrait of Ashton was bought by the Commonwealth government.

The life and work of artist Sir William Ashton (Syd, 1961); *Art in Aust*, June 1929; *B.P. Magazine*, June 1937; R. H. Croll papers (LaTL).

KATHERINE HARPER

ASHTON, JULIAN HOWARD (1877-1964), journalist, critic and artist, was born on 9 August 1877 at Islington, London, eldest child of Julian Rossi Ashton [q.v.] and his first wife Eliza Ann, née Pugh. He reached Melbourne with his parents in April 1878. In 1883 the family moved to Sydney where Ashton attended Bondi Public School and Sydney Boys' High School. He was 'brought up in a Bohemian home': his interests were musical, artistic and literary. In 1896-1903 he attended his father's art school where he met Mary Ethel Roberts, whom he married on 27 January 1908.

Ashton's first short story was published in 1904 by the *Bulletin*, for which he continued to write under the pen name 'Hassan'. He also did line portraits for the Sydney *Daily Telegraph*, wrote for British magazines such as the *Pall Mall Gazette* and *Chambers's Journal*, and occasionally sold paintings at Society of Artists exhibitions. In 1906 he joined the *Sydney Morning Herald* as a junior shipping reporter, and in 1908 moved to Melbourne and the *Argus* as a general reporter and, from about 1910, music critic. In June 1916 he returned to Sydney and joined the *Sun*; by 1922 he was writing seven leaders a week as well as literary, music and art reviews. In 1924 he became editor and in 1926, as associate editor, resumed criticism and leader-writing, covering everything from sport to politics. He also wrote 'Nature notes' for the *Sunday Sun and Guardian* and contributed frequently to *Art in Australia*. An avowed conservative and anti-communist, Ashton strongly criticized J. T. Lang [q.v.] and joined the New Guard. An aggressive opponent of modernism, which he regarded as 'artistic Bolshevism', he dismissed the 1919 Wakelin and de Maistre [qq.v.] exhibition of experiments in Post-Impressionism as 'elaborate and pretentious bosh'.

Ashton would have been a full-time artist but for the need to support his family; his earlier works in pastel and oil were fresh and poetic interpretations of sea and countryside, but a stilted realism characterized his later work. In 1938 he won the Sydney sesquicentenary prize for landscape. A member of the Society of Artists, he resigned in 1934 over the election of Wakelin; in 1939 he joined the more conservative Royal Art Society of New South Wales and was its president in 1942-45. Although he strongly disagreed with the award of the 1943 Archibald [q.v.3] Prize to William Dobell, he kept out of the ensuing court case because he believed 'no court of law could bring down judgement on a matter of artistic opinion'.

Ashton entertained many visiting musicians at his Mosman home and about 1930 suggested the formation of the first Sydney String Quartet. He was also a keen entomologist and gave his collection of cicadas to the Australian Museum. His wife died in December 1945, and in March 1946 he resigned from the *Sun* to devote himself to painting and reading. He died on 30 April 1964, and was cremated with Anglican rites; his ashes were placed in a rock near his home. He was survived by a daughter and three sons of whom Cedric Howard is a noted cellist, and Julian Richard an artist and teacher. His estate was valued for probate at £33 019.

Ashton is represented in the New South Wales and Victorian State galleries. His portrait by Paul Delprat is held by the family.

SMH, 1 May 1964; Howard Ashton, Flee from the Press, *and* family papers (held by Mrs M. R. Delprat, Mosman, and Mr J. Richard Ashton, Curl Curl, NSW).   KATHERINE HARPER

ASHTON, JULIAN ROSSI (1851-1942), art teacher and artist, was born on 27 January 1851 at Addlestone, Surrey, England, elder son of a wealthy American, Thomas Briggs Ashton, and his Florentine wife Henrietta, daughter of Count Rossi. Soon after his birth the family moved to Gulval, Cornwall, where his father, an amateur painter, encouraged the artistic leanings of Julian and his brother George. About 1862 the Ashtons moved to Totnes on the River Dart, where Julian attended the local grammar school, but his father died and the family, now in financial straits, went to London. Julian had art lessons from an old friend of his father whose teaching he described as 'the most helpful I ever had'. At 15 he took a job in the civil engineering branch of the Great Eastern Railway and attended the West London School of Art at night; after three years he joined a firm of ironmongers as a draftsman, but soon left to become a successful illustrator for such journals as *Chatterbox* and *Cassell's Magazine*. In 1873 he spent a few months at the new Académie Julian in Paris; he returned to illustration in London and had work accepted by the Royal Academy of Arts. On 1 August 1876 at Hackney he married Eliza Ann Pugh (d. 1900).

Ashton, with his wife and son, reached Melbourne in the *Cuzco* on 18 June 1878, to work on David Syme's [q.v.6] *Illustrated Australian News*. His decision to migrate was seemingly dictated by a lifelong asthmatic condition. In 1881 he joined the Melbourne-based *Australasian Sketcher* and in 1883 moved to Sydney to work on the *Picturesque atlas of Australasia*: until 1886 he travelled extensively throughout Australia drawing points of interest; he also drew for the *Bulletin*.

In 1886 Ashton began to teach privately. In 1892-95 he conducted classes at the Art Society of New South Wales of which he had been president in 1887-92. Artistic professionalism was a vexed question and in 1895 Ashton joined a new professional body, the Society of Artists, Sydney. Sacked from his teaching position, he established his own school in King Street, moved it to the Queen Victoria Markets in 1906 and renamed it the Sydney Art School. In George Street from 1935 it became the Julian Ashton School and always enjoyed a considerable reputation:

among his students were G. W. Lambert, E. Gruner, J. J. Hilder, Thea Proctor, S. Ure Smith [qq.v], William Dobell, Jean Bellette and D. Dundas.

His wife Eliza had literary and musical interests and was a social writer for the *Daily Telegraph* in the 1890s. She was a foundation member and councillor of the Womanhood Suffrage League of New South Wales, which she later embarrassed by her outspoken criticism of marriage, and was on the committee of the Women's Literary Society.

In 1889-99 Ashton was a trustee of the National Art Gallery of New South Wales and was responsible for its enlightened patronage of local artists. He bought the first Streeton [q.v.] for the gallery, 'Still Glides the Stream and Shall Forever Glide', in 1890 for £70. Questions were asked in parliament about the number of his own paintings bought by the trustees; he had played no part in their selection. He organized the 1898 exhibition of Australian art in London at the Grafton Gallery, and used his influence with Sir Henry Parkes [q.v.5], B. R. Wise and benefactor Howard Hinton [qq.v.] among others, to promote the work of Hilder, Norman Lindsay [q.v.] and the Australian Impressionists.

In 1897-98 Ashton was president of the Society of Artists which in 1903 amalgamated with the Art Society of New South Wales to become the Royal Art Society of New South Wales. In 1907 he led a successful move to re-establish the Society of Artists, and was president until 1921 and vice-president until 1940, when he returned to the Royal Art Society. Because of Ashton's domination, the society became strongly identified with his art school.

In 1892 Ashton had been commissioned by George Adams [q.v.3] to decorate the 'Marble Bar' at his well-known hotel. He was behind the establishment in 1911 of the Fine Arts Society's gallery and shop in Bligh Street, the first to deal solely in Australian art. He also lectured and wrote frequently, especially for *Art in Australia*.

Ashton was a well-established artist in both oils and water-colour. He claimed his 'Evening, Merri Creek' (1882) was the first *plein air* painting done in Australia. His early landscapes had a distinctly Australian feeling of light and space. He was also known for his romantic figure-paintings, many done at beaches near his home at Bondi. He painted the portraits of, among others, Parkes and Archbishop Kelly [q.v.]. About 1914 his sight began to deteriorate, first with colour blindness (said to be yellow and blue) and later with a condition that severely limited his peripheral vision; this, in addition to his asthma, forced him to reduce his activities, although he remained vocal on art matters, particularly modernism, which he condemned for bad draftsmanship and poor craftsmanship. Awarded the Society of Artists' medal for distinguished services to Australian art in 1924, he was appointed C.B.E. in 1930, and won the Sydney sesqui-centenary prize for a water-colour in 1938. He published his reminiscences, *Now came still evening on*, in 1941.

Strong, white-haired and ruddy-faced, Ashton had a military-type moustache. He bathed in the sea all the year round, cultivated his vegetable patch and, 'as a bit of a fancier', tended his poultry. Lionel Lindsay [q.v.] found him 'a generous friend, a fine enemy'. An inspired teacher although less gifted as a painter, he dominated artistic circles in Sydney for over fifty years. 'No other man did so much towards making the place of art in the community better understood and appreciated'. In *Home* (March 1924) Arthur Jose [q.v.] named him as one of 'the seven greatest living Australians'.

Ashton died on 27 April 1942 at Bondi and was cremated with Anglican rites. He was survived by two of his four sons and a daughter of his first marriage, and by his second wife Constance Irene, née Morley, whom he had married on 8 September 1902. His estate was valued for probate at £4343. His portrait by George Lambert is in the Art Gallery of New South Wales.

His brother GEORGE ROSSI (b. 1857) studied at the South Kensingto, School of Art and became a black-and-white illustrator for the London *Graphic*. In 1877-78 he represented the *Illustrated London News* at the Kaffir war and next year joined Julian on the *Illustrated Australian News* in Melbourne; together they covered the capture of the Kelly [q.v.5] gang at Glenrowan. He was among the first sketch-artists of the *Bulletin*, drew also for the *Australasian Sketcher*, the *Illustrated Sydney News* and the *Picturesque atlas of Australasia*, and was art editor and artist for *Victoria and its metropolis*. In 1886-88 he was a member of the Art Society of New South Wales and the Australian Artists' Association (Victoria). In 1893 he returned to England where he continued to illustrate for various papers and toured music-halls with a lightning-sketch routine. He published *Australasian sketches* (London, 1895). He had married Blanche Brooke, daughter of George Coppin [q.v.3], and settled on the River Dart with his wife and two sons.

The Julian Ashton book (Syd, 1920); K. Campbell, Julian Rossi Ashton . . . as art politician (B.A. Hons thesis, Univ Adel, 1974); D. Thomas, Julian Rossi Ashton . . . a bibliography (ML); H. Heysen letters (NL); H. Ashton, Autobiography, Flee from the Press, *and* family papers (held by Mrs M. R. Delprat, Mosman, and Mr J. Richard Ashton, Curl Curl, NSW.
                                    KATHERINE HARPER

ASHWORTH, THOMAS RAMSDEN (1864-1935), publicist, was born on 5 December 1864 at Richmond, Victoria, son of Thomas Ramsden Ashworth and his wife Mary Jane, née Leeson. His father, educated at Eton and Jesus College, Cambridge, had migrated to Australia, married in 1862 and in 1869 graduated M.B. at the University of Melbourne. Dr Ashworth later practised at Bombala, New South Wales; on his death there in 1876 his wife returned to Melbourne with the five children.

At 13 Thomas ran away to sea. Four years later he was in Melbourne working as a carpenter and builder, and studying architecture. He practised as an architect for many years, was elected a fellow of the Royal Victorian Institute of Architects in 1916, and in the early 1920s was associated with H. D. Annear [q.v.] in designing the Church Street Bridge, Richmond. He had also set up as an estate agent in 1893, buying land at Middle Park and building a series of houses in a street named after him; he later built a block of nine flats in St Kilda Road.

Ashworth was a founder of several companies including the Union Can Co. and was for many years a director of Bussell, Robson Pty Ltd, clothiers. In 1910-17 he was chairman of the canister-makers' section of the Chamber of Manufactures. He was president in 1920-34 of the Victorian Employers' Federation and also held office in its Australian council. In 1927 he founded the Employers' Federation Insurance Co. Ltd and chaired its board of directors.

In 1897 Ashworth had failed to win the Legislative Assembly seat of Albert Park. He was president of the Victorian division of the Free Trade and Liberal Association in 1898-1902 and as its candidate stood unsuccessfully against (Sir) Isaac Isaacs [q.v.] for the Federal seat of Indi in 1901. Next year he stood as a ministerial candidate against Isaacs's brother in the State seat of Ovens. Campaigning on a platform of retrenchment, especially in relation to the public service, he won comfortably. In the Legislative Assembly he remained consistent to the principles which he had put forward in a book, written with his brother, entitled *Proportional representation applied to party government . . .* (Melbourne, 1900). In 1904 he was defeated for Hampden.

Ashworth's brief parliamentary career left a deep impression on him. Although he took pride in the fact that after 1920 the Employers' Federation had no formal ties with political parties, he was an active commentator on public affairs. As a publicist he demonstrated lucidity and wide reading – he owned a substantial reference library – and his abilities were recognized by his colleagues: he was a member of many delegations and committees. In 1919-22 he severely criticized W. M. Hughes [q.v.], and did not spare his successor S. M. (Viscount) Bruce [q.v.] for lavish spending and reckless borrowing.

In 1927-29 Ashworth was a member of the royal commission on the Constitution and with two Labor politicians wrote a minority report advocating greater Commonwealth powers. Greatly impressed by the views of R. Windeyer [q.v.] on this subject, Ashworth campaigned for him when he stood as an independent in the Federal seat of Warringah in 1929. This action displeased some of his Employers' Federation colleagues, who considered he had become cranky and tried to force his resignation as president.

As the Depression deepened, the constitutional question became less important for Ashworth although the fundamental issue remained: 'the awards of industrial tribunals tended to obviate the necessity for honest and efficient labour'. Under his leadership the Federation mobilized public opinion against the Scullin [q.v.] ministry and Ashworth undoubtedly contributed to the anti-Labor atmosphere before the 1931 Federal election by his criticism of party politics, of timorous politicians and of the high wage-levels forced on industry by arbitration. The change of government did not alter the substance of his comments.

In the last years of his life Ashworth lived at Frankston where he had built a model poultry-breeding farm. In 1888 at St Silas' Church, South Melbourne, he had married Emily Ashweek, who died in 1922. Six years later he married Marguerita Adele Young at St James' Old Cathedral; both marriages were childless. Survived by his wife, he died of arteriosclerotic heart disease in hospital at Fitzroy on 23 August 1935 and was buried in the Melbourne general cemetery. He left an estate valued for probate at £27 087 and in his will requested that the University of Melbourne set up in his name a chair or lectureship or a biennial prize in sociology. His portrait by Streeton [q.v.] is held by the Victorian Employers' Federation.

Liberty and Progress, Feb, Oct 1920, Jan, Oct 1921; *Employers' Mthly Review*, Sept 1929; *Industry and Trade*, Oct, Dec 1929; *Wangaratta Chronicle*, 16, 20 Mar 1901, 16 Mar 1904; *Ovens and Murray Advertiser*, 25, 27 Sept, 4 Oct 1902; *Camperdown Chronicle*, 2 June 1904; *Argus*, 5, 27-29 Oct 1926, 6 Apr, 12 Aug, 17 Nov 1927, 12 Sept, 11 Oct, 21 Dec 1928, 24 Sept 1929, 24, 25 Sept 1930, 18, 22, 30 Sept 1931, 22 Apr, 17 June, 4 Oct, 24 Nov 1933, 24 Aug 1935; *Labor Daily*, 9 Oct 1929; *Age*, 24 Aug 1935; Council and executive minute-books 1919-35 (Vic Employers' Federation, Melb); family information.   P. L. NICHOLLS

ASLATT, HAROLD FRANCIS (1885-1958), soldier and bushworker, was born on 16 November 1885 at Stoneham, Hampshire, England, son of Francis Aslatt, brick manufacturer, and his wife Emily Laura, née Babot. When 23 he migrated alone to Australia and before World War I worked as a teamster and station-hand in the Griffith district of New South Wales.

Aslatt enlisted in the Australian Imperial Force on 16 November 1914 and embarked for Egypt next February with reinforcements for the 13th Battalion. He first saw action on 26 April 1915 when his unit landed at Gaba Tepe and took over the defence of Monash Valley. The 13th Battalion historian was later to name Aslatt as among the unit's 'most distinguished in those early days'. Promoted lance corporal on 4 November and corporal on 3 December, he remained at Anzac until the evacuation and then returned to Egypt; on 10 March 1916 he was transferred to the newly formed 45th Battalion. For the next two months he was involved in training and defensive activities in the Canal zone; he also began a course of instruction in the operation of the new Stokes gun and on 16 July, shortly after his arrival in France, was transferred to the 4th Light Trench Mortar Battery. Though they lacked experience and full training, the artillerymen of the 4th Australian Division went straight into the battle of Fromelles as reinforcements; they then withdrew for further training. In August they supported the 4th Canadian Division at Ypres and rejoined their own division there in September.

In 1917 Aslatt served with the 4th Divisional Artillery at Bullecourt in April, at Messines in May and June, and at Passchendaele in September; he was promoted sergeant on 23 June. Early in 1918 his battery was in action at Villers-Bretonneux and he was awarded the Military Medal for 'conspicuous gallantry and valuable service in command of a mortar near Albert on 5 April'. The citation noted that, although exposed to heavy machine-gun and mortar fire, he 'carried out his work as if on parade at a practice shoot'. Next June he received the Meritorious Service Medal for 'continuous good and gallant service in the field'. In the second half of 1918 he took part in the counter-offensive near Amiens and, for 'conspicuous devotion to duty' at Bellenglise in mid-September, was awarded the Distinguished Conduct Medal; 'his cheerful and energetic manner set an example which had good effects on all around him'.

After the Armistice, Aslatt undertook a five-month course in marine engineering in England and was demobilized on his return to Australia in March 1920. For the next nineteen years he worked as a prospector and bushworker in New South Wales. When World War II broke out he joined the 11th Garrison Battalion in Sydney and served for five years. He was discharged in June 1944 and returned to bush work. In 1957 he settled at Maiden Gully near Bendigo, Victoria, and died there, unmarried, on 15 October 1958 of coronary vascular disease. He was buried in Bendigo cemetery.

C. E. W. Bean, *The story of Anzac*, 1, 2 (Syd, 1921, 1924); T. A. White, *The fighting Thirteenth* (Syd, 1924); C. E. W. Bean, *The A. I. F. in France*, 3-6 (Syd, 1929, 1933, 1937, 1942); J. E. Lee, *A brief history of the 45th Battalion, A. I. F. 1916-19* (Syd, 1962); *London Gazette*, 17 June, 16 July 1918, 8 Mar 1919.   W. H. CONNELL

ASPINALL, ARTHUR ASHWORTH (1846-1929), clergyman and school principal, was born on 23 June 1846 at Southeram, Yorkshire, England, son of John Aspinall, an Australian-born innkeeper, and his wife Sarah, née Ingham. He came to Sydney as a child and was educated at Rev. Miles Moss's private school and later under Dr Boag and Rev. B. Quaife [q.v.2], close associates of Rev. J. D. Lang [q.v.2] for whom Aspinall retained a lifelong admiration. In 1867 he attended Sydney Mechanics' School of Arts and entered the University of Sydney (B.A., 1889; M.A., 1912) in 1870 but withdrew that year after contracting scarlet fever. During his convalescence, he completed a course in divinity at Camden College. Although his education had been Congregationalist, he was ordained as a Presbyterian minister in 1873.

Aspinall's first thirteen years in the ministry were spent at Forbes where he sought to emulate the ideals of Lang by organizing church administration, building churches there and at Condobolin, and writing about the local scene. He was an active Freemason. On 22 November 1877 at Wandoo Wandong, near Obley, he married Helen Strahorn, daughter of a pastoralist. In 1887 he returned to Sydney and next year assumed charge of St Luke's Church, Redfern. He completed his university degree and in 1891 was moderator of the General Assembly of the Presbyterian Church of New South Wales.

In 1892 Aspinall, backed financially by his wife's family, supported plans to establish a Presbyterian boys' secondary school in Sydney. Despite opposition within the as-

sembly, he helped Rev. Archibald Gilchrist and Rev. W. Dill Macky [q.v.] to draw up a constitution for the school and leased the New Brighton Hotel at Lady Robinson's Beach, Rockdale. In 1893, after Gilchrist had refused, Aspinall was appointed first principal of Scots College, assuming full financial responsibility for and control over its affairs.

Aspinall wanted to develop a college primarily for boarders, based on the ideals of Thomas Arnold. He stressed religious and moral principles, gentlemanly conduct and intellectual ability rather than success in examinations. Despite the depression, the school opened with thirty-five boys and the number soon rose to one hundred. Many early pupils were sons of his old parishioners and most continued to be of Scottish descent. In 1895 he leased St Killians from the (Daniel) Cooper [q.v.1] estate and the school moved to Bellevue Hill where it could develop splendid playing-fields: sport was an important part of the curriculum. Scottish traditions were emphasized by establishment of the kilted cadet corps in 1899 and a pipe-band in 1900. Bearded and thickset, with bristling whiskers, Aspinall won the respect of the boys, despite his short temper and severe discipline that included corporal punishment and ridicule. In 1901 he bought the lease of St Killians and after long negotiations sold it to the Presbyterian Church in 1906 for £7000; he was guaranteed a further six years as principal.

In 1901-05 Aspinall was a founding committee-man of the Australian Historical Society and president in 1904. A fine Elizabethan scholar, he increasingly 'withdrew from his school world' to immerse himself in scholarship, and in 1912 was awarded a master's degree for his thesis on 'the metaphysical significance of the Renaissance'. In his final years as principal he became increasingly 'apoplectic', enrolment dwindled, the buildings fell into disrepair and unrest culminated in a brief strike by the boys.

In 1913 Aspinall retired and visited Britain where his wife died in 1915. He lived at Turramurra, consoled by his books and garden, until he died on 9 June 1929; he was cremated. His only daughter Jessie [q.v.] and four sons all became medical practitioners; his youngest son was killed in action in Belgium in 1917.

M. Munro, *In old Aspinall's day* (Syd, 1961), and for bibliog; *JRAHS*, 48 (1963), p 311; *Scotsman*, June 1914, June 1918, Dec 1967; *SMH*, 30 Jan 1893, 18 Dec 1896; Carruthers papers (ML); memoirs of Dr A. Gilchrist (ML); J. D. Lang papers and letters (ML); S. D. Stevenson family papers (ML); M. R. L. Bee at Scots (Scots College Archives).

G. E. SHERINGTON

ASPINALL, JESSIE STRAHORN (1880-1953), medical practitioner, was born on 10 December 1880 at Forbes, New South Wales, only daughter of Rev. Arthur Ashworth Aspinall [q.v.] and his wife Helen, née Strahorn. After the family moved to Sydney in 1887, she was educated at the Presbyterian Ladies' College, Croydon, Rivière College, and Miss Gurney's Kambala where she excelled at history; she then studied medicine at the University of Sydney (M.B., Ch.M., 1906).

Her appointment in 1906 as the first female junior medical resident officer at Royal Prince Alfred Hospital caused a furore when its Conjoint Board refused confirmation. Her father took immediate action: in a long letter to the *Sydney Morning Herald* on 9 February he drew attention to the injustice of the board's action. There were editorials in the leading newspapers in the eastern States, with a flood of letters to the editors and protest meetings by women's groups. One commentator concluded that 'Miss Aspinall will pass into history as a noble martyr, while the men who threw her out will be bracketed with Bloody Jeffreys, Torquemada and Judas Iscariot'. The board of directors on 2 March resolved that female residents would 'be exempted from attendance on certain cases', and the Conjoint Board resolved that 'Dr Aspinall be appointed for this year, but that her appointment is not to be taken as a precedent'. Her male colleagues in residence presented her with a gold watch in sympathy.

In June 1907 Jessie Aspinall was appointed junior house-surgeon at the General Hospital, Hobart, and in 1908 was resident medical officer at the Women's Hospital, Crown Street, Sydney. She then set up practice at Lyon's Terrace and for a time was school doctor for Scots College. In 1911 she moved to Wyoming, Macquarie Street. On 22 June 1915 at St Killian's Church, Potts Point, she was married by her father to Ambrose William Freeman [q.v.], a mining engineer living at Taiping, Perak, in the Federated Malay States. In 1916-22 she bore four children and accompanied her husband for two sojourns in Malaya before the family settled in her father's house, St Killians, Potts Point, where she continued to live after her husband's death in 1930.

Jessie Freeman was for many years a member of the Sydney executive of the Victoria League, the National Council of Women and the appeals committee of the Young Women's Christian Association. During World War II she was vice-president of the Darlinghurst branch of the Australian Red Cross Society. In 1941 she gave Berida, her house at Bowral and three acres of land, to the Red Cross; it was used as a convales-cent home for ex-servicemen. She had been made a life-governor of the Women's Hospital in 1908.

Jessie Freeman was a devout Presbyterian, had great determination, a fearlessness that 'evoked general admiration', notable professional skill and 'undoubted charm'. She became a legend in the medical world at a time when female practitioners were uncommon. She died of arteriosclerosis at Haberfield on 25 August 1953, and was cremated. Survived by two sons and two daughters, she was followed in medicine by her youngest daughter Jessie (Chantek) Freeman. Her estate was valued for probate at £100 164.

M. Munro, *In old Aspinall's day* (Syd, 1961); The Women's Hospital (Syd), *Annual Reports*, 1907, 1908; *Red Cross News*, June 1941; *MJA*, 5 Dec 1953; M. Little, 'Some pioneer medical women . . .', Syd Univ Post-graduate Cttee in Medicine, *Bulletin*, 14 (1958-59); W. A. Freeman, 'An Australian's impressions of Malaya', *Home*, 1 Mar 1921.

E. BEATRIX DURIE

ASTON, MATILDA ANN (1873-1947), blind writer and teacher, was born on 11 December 1873 at Carisbrook, Victoria, youngest of the eight children of Edward Aston, bootmaker, and his wife Ann, née Howell. Her parents had migrated from Gloucestershire to Kapunda, South Australia, in 1855 and two years later moved to Carisbrook.

Tilly, as she was commonly known, had defective eyesight from birth. Happily her parents took every opportunity to draw her attention to the beauty of nature, so endowing her with a fortune of vivid memories which later inspired and illuminated her homely verse, her pleasant and musical poems, and her remarkably authentic prose sketches. At a private school she learned to read from large-type books and to write and to memorize poetry, but just before her seventh birthday she became totally blind. In 1881 her father died and her mother extended her work as district nurse to support the family. Six months later Tilly was rescued from boredom by Thomas James, an itinerant blind missionary who introduced her to the Braille method of reading. The choir of the Victorian Asylum and School for the Blind, St Kilda, then visited Carisbrook, and at the urging of its leader, Rev. W. Moss [q.v.5], Tilly enrolled as a boarder at the school on 29 June 1882. At 16 she matriculated and began an arts course at the University of Melbourne, but lack of Braille textbooks and nervous prostration forced her to abandon it in her second year. While convalescent and trying to earn a living as a music-teacher, Tilly realized the plight of the blind for whom there was no succour. Her own struggle for independence had gained her many friends; aided by them and the Australian Natives' Association, she established in 1894 the Victorian Association of Braille Writers (later the Victorian Braille Library). Next, with a few friends, she founded and became first secretary of the Association for the Advancement of the Blind; she was president in 1947.

In 1913 Tilly Aston applied for the Education Department post of head of the School for the Blind. After teacher-training she took up the appointment but was never fully accepted by some of the staff and officials of the Royal Victorian Institute for the Blind who did not approve of a blind teacher. At the same time she was required to sever her connexion with the blind societies she had helped to found. Thus, although she enjoyed teaching, her years at the school were not happy. When in 1925 she had to retire, in ill health after a slight stroke and a fall, the management of the school tardily recognized her services by appointing her a life-governor. The Education Department arranged to pay her a weekly allowance of £2 in lieu of superannuation.

Tilly Aston's writing career had been interrupted by her years at the school. In 1901 she had published her first book, *Maiden verses*. In 1904 she won the Prahran City Council's competition for an original story. *The Woolinappers or, some tales from the by-ways of Methodism* was published in 1905 and from September 1908 'The straight goer' was serialized in the *Spectator*. Her later books, which she drafted in Braille and then typed, included *Singable songs* (1924) and *Songs of light* (1935); 'Gold from old diggings' was serialized in the *Bendigo Advertiser* from August 1937 and *Old timers* was published in 1938. She believed *The inner garden* (1940) contained her best work. Her sense of humour and courage are shown in her *Memoirs of Tilly Aston* (1946), written while a member of the Bread and Cheese Club. All her books were published in Melbourne. For twelve years she edited and largely wrote *A book of opals*, a magazine issued in Braille for use in Chinese missionary schools. She was awarded a Commonwealth grant in 1935 and twice received the King's Medal for distinguished citizen service. She was also a keen exponent of Esperanto and corresponded with fellow linguists all over the world.

On leaving school Tilly had lived with a brother and their mother in Melbourne until about 1913 when her brother married and her mother died. She then moved to her own house in Windsor where a devoted housekeeper-companion cared for her. She died there of cancer on 1 November 1947 and was buried in St Kilda cemetery; her estate was valued for probate at £1149. A year later the Midlands Historical Society and Carisbrook school children erected a cairn to the memory of this indomitable woman.

B. Bilton, 'They also taught', *Educational Mag* (Vic), Mar 1971; *New Idea*, Sept 1909; G. A. Hunter, 'Tilly Aston', *All About Books*, Aug 1936; *Focus (Melb), May 1947; Age*, 3 Nov 1947; J. Burke, 'Beacon for the blind', *Parade*, Dec 1973; *Weekly Times* (Melb), 15 Oct 1904; Assn for the Blind, *and* Braille Talking Book Lib, *and* Roy Vic Inst for the Blind, Records (Melb); C. H. Souter papers, 1481 (SAA); P. Whelan papers MS 534, 2449 (NL); printed cat (ML).　　　　　　　O. S. GREEN

ATKINSON, EVELYN JOHN RUPERT (1881-1961), poet, was born on 2 February 1881 at Sandhurst (Bendigo), Victoria, son of Dr Harry Leigh Atkinson (1832-1915) and his third wife Eva, née Moulden. Paternal ancestors included many medical practitioners and Anglican clergy. Harry Atkinson was educated at Beverly Grammar School, Yorkshire, England, entered the Leeds Free Hospital in 1849 and graduated L.S.A. (London) and M.R.C.S. (England) in 1858. After experience in Yorkshire, London and Paris hospitals, he migrated to Victoria in 1859 as surgeon to the *Suffolk*. Next year he was appointed to the Bendigo Hospital and in 1862 began private practice, which he continued with distinction until his death. Dr Atkinson was a masterly businessman who was a director of many important Bendigo mining companies and a shrewd investor in land. He became one of the largest landowners in Victoria; his pastoral properties included at various times Terrick West, Ravenswood, Auchmore, Barwonleigh and Yarrabrob. He married five times and at his death on 14 July 1915 his estate was valued for probate at £209 586.

Rupert was educated at St Andrew's College, Bendigo, before being sent to England with his elder brother Evelyn Leigh to attend Rugby School and later Dover College. Evelyn Leigh went on to the University of Oxford but about 1900 Rupert returned to Australia to work on his father's properties. He became manager of Ravenswood, but by June 1909 styled himself as a 'journalist living in Sydney' when, in Melbourne with Free Christian rites, he married Marie Domec-Carrè; they settled at Bendigo. After his father's death Rupert inherited much property and decided to study medicine. He matriculated at the University of Melbourne, but three and a half years later abandoned the course to devote himself to literature. For the next four decades, almost uniquely in Australian letters, Atkinson was to lead the life of a leisured gentleman, poet and playwright.

Always prolific, he published six volumes of poetry between 1906 and 1921. *A flagon of song* (Melbourne, 1920) is his own selection of his better work; the title indicates affinity with his friend Hugh McCrae [q.v.]. For the most part it is introspective but forceful philosophical verse, though he sometimes wrote lyrics and long narratives. Before 1920 he became interested in combining film with stage-drama and wrote *Key to the adaptation of the best of Shakespeare's plays to the stage-cinema-interaction process for the production of drama* (New York, 1920). Between 1919 and 1928 he published several plays, including two involving 'cinematic back-projection'. Most of them were studies in abnormal psychology; some had energy and exuberance; none are known to have been publicly performed. In his plays and poetry both, Atkinson's language rarely matched the quality of his concepts.

He travelled widely in the 1920s and was associated with E. A. Vidler [q.v.] in the Australian Institute of the Arts and Literature, launched in August 1921. Vidler published most of Atkinson's plays. According to Jack Lindsay, Atkinson was 'a talented writer of verse and of plays in which he tried to define his own tormented split-up being, his sense of living several lives at the same moment ... a restless disappointed man, printing his own work hastily and unable to settle to anything definite — poetry or whisky or travel, an intellectual or a playboy role'. He confessed himself to be a decadent, but was also generous with his wealth, subsidizing his friends' publications and, as Philip Lindsay [q.v.] warmly recalled, seeing them through impoverished patches. Widely regarded as an important poet between the wars, Atkinson dropped from literary view in the later part of his life.

He died at East Melbourne on 6 February 1961, predeceased by his wife in 1954, survived by two sons and two daughters and leaving a considerable estate. In his will he requested that he be cremated without Christian rites. At his dying wish *We gods in masquerade* (Brisbane, 1964), verse written in old age, was published posthumously.

P. Lindsay, *I'd live the same life over* (Lond, 1941); G. L. C. Rees, *Towards an Australian drama* (Syd, 1953); J. Lindsay, *Fanfrolico and after* (Lond, 1962); R. D. FitzGerald (ed), *The letters of Hugh McCrae* (Syd, 1970); *Spinner*, Jan 1925; *Pastoral Review*, 16 Sept 1915; *Bendigo Advertiser* and *Bendigo Independent*, 15 July 1915; E. J. R. Atkinson, letters (NL) *and* letters received (ML); information from Dr L. Atkinson, East Brisb, Qld.

ATKINSON, HENRY BRUNE (1874-1960), clergyman and orchidologist, was born on 17 March 1874 at Gordon, Tasmania, son of Rev. Henry Dresser Atkinson and his wife Sarah Ann, née Ward. Descended from English clergymen, his father had known Truganini [q.v.6] who, legend suggests, nursed Henry Bruné. They lived in various rural and coastal parishes where his father encouraged an interest in natural history, particularly orchids. He was educated at Stanley State School, the Church Grammar School, Launceston, and the University of Tasmania (B.A., 1899).

Atkinson was ordained deacon at Holy Trinity Church, Launceston, on 24 March 1901 and priest at St David's Cathedral, Hobart, on 17 September 1902. In 1904 he went as vicar to Ringarooma and Derby, where he met Helen Bertha Knight of Christchurch, New Zealand, a great-niece of Jane Austen; they were married there on 21 June 1905. In 1906-10 he was curate to his father at Evandale. He completed the building of St Peter's Church at the Nile; he took up motor-cycle racing, moved to Forth and Leven parish in 1910 as rector before going in 1911 to Devonport. Here he developed into an excellent preacher, enjoyed cricket, golf and rifle-shooting and became a Freemason. From 1914 he was an elected member of the diocesan council; he was also a representative in the general synod of the dioceses of Australia and Tasmania.

In 1916 Atkinson became rector of Holy Trinity Church, Hobart, where he attracted large congregations, established branch churches and extended buildings. Next year he took part in a national mission of repentance and hope to Grafton and Brisbane dioceses. In Hobart he irritated sections of the public and clergy by his vigorous preaching against poverty and the city's slums, but in 1920 he was chosen to accompany Bishop R. S. Hay [q.v.] to the Lambeth Conference in England. While he was away his parish was administered by Rev. H. M. R. Rupp [q.v.] who revived Atkinson's interest in orchids. On his return he began to collect and classify the Tasmanian varieties, eventually recording twenty-four previously unknown species. *Caladenia atkinsonii* Rod. was named after him. In 1919-25 he was vice-warden of the university senate and in 1923 was elected to the Royal Society of Tasmania.

In 1924 Atkinson became archdeacon of Darwin, and in 1928 of Launceston and Darwin centred on Hagley, where he added a graceful spire to the Gothic church of St Mary. He was now responsible for all Tasmania north of Conara, the west coast and Flinders and King islands. In 1942-44 he administered the Tasmanian diocese during the absence of the bishop and after his death. He was revered for his work on the boards of Anglican schools in Launceston.

Atkinson retired to Launceston in 1949 to his garden, shells, music and books, but he continued preaching until the last week of his life. Survived by his daughter, he died at Riverside, Launceston, on 16 June 1960, two months after his wife; his ashes were placed in the chancel of Holy Trinity Church, Launceston.

Church of England Year-book, Diocese of Tasmania, 1906, 1955; *Church News* (Hob), Mar 1914, Nov 1928; *Tas Mail*, 16 Aug 1920; *Mercury*, 25 Sept 1942, 17 May 1944; *Examiner* (Launceston), 17 June 1960; Diocese of Tasmania, Clerical Registers, 5/223-224, 229, 684, 760, 6/216, 500 (Church House, Hob); family papers held by Miss S. Atkinson, Launceston, Tas.

HERBERT H. CONDON

ATKINSON, MEREDITH (1883-1929), educationist and publicist, was born on 3 January 1883 at Hartlepool, County Durham, England, third son of Meredith Atkinson, blacksmith, and his wife Margaret, née Thompson. He was educated until 18 at the Hartlepool Grammar and Technical School. In 1902-04 he held a King's scholarship at St John's College, Battersea, part of the London Day Training College, then went to Keble College, Oxford (B.A., 1908), where he also gained diplomas in education (1909) and in economics and political science (1911). On 20 December 1910 at the Parish Church, Hartlepool, he married Margaret Freeland (d. 1924). In 1911-14 he was an extension lecturer for the University of Durham. During these years he became a disciple of Albert Mansbridge, the originator of the Workers' Educational Association in England.

In March 1914 Atkinson arrived in Sydney with his family to take up his appointment as organizer of tutorial classes at the university, on the recommendation of Mansbridge; from 1916 he was also lecturer in economic history. In 1915-18 he was president of the Workers' Educational Association of New South Wales, worked closely with David Stewart [q.v.], and regarded himself as a missionary for the movement throughout Australia and New Zealand.

Atkinson's efforts to bridge the gap between the university and the worker were seriously undermined by his passionate campaign for conscription as secretary of the Universal Service League in 1915-16. In December 1916 the central council of the W.E.A. formally dissociated itself from his views. His advocacy had also embarrassed his university colleagues; moreover they accused him of empire-building and shoddy administration, and resented his overt pressure for promotion to professorial rank. His administrative and personal ambition led to conflict with the University Extension Board and the new joint committee for tutorial classes. However, Atkinson attracted attention as a lecturer, orator and polemicist on a wide range of subjects. He organized a conference on trade unionism, and edited its findings as *Trade unionism in Australia* (1915).

Atkinson was increasingly criticized by his former conscriptionist colleague (Sir) Mungo MacCallum [q.v.]. Tired and petulant, he resented opposition and, through his friendship with (Sir) W. Harrison Moore [q.v.], in 1917 was appointed director of tutorial classes with professorial status at the University of Melbourne. Again his attempts to absorb the extension board clashed with both academic and trade union prejudice. Again he was seen as a blatant careerist, this time for his advocacy of sociology as a valid discipline. His most important work, *The new social order: a study in post-war reconstruction* (Sydney) was published in 1919. He also edited *Australia: economic and political studies* (1920); similar collections of essays by specialists in related subjects became the most common genre for sociological writing about Australia.

After World War I Atkinson became a pacifist and internationalist. In 1921 he took leave 'for private purposes', went to England, and resigned from the university and the W.E.A. on 1 January 1922. In February he visited the Soviet Union as an honorary famine commissioner. Later that year, with financial backing from Herbert Brookes [q.v.], he acquired a controlling interest in *Stead's Review* and returned to Melbourne as editor. As a businessman Atkinson was incompetent, and the journal's circulation and finances quickly ran down. Before leaving for England he had floated a company styled Quick Gears Pty Ltd, which failed; he and his co-directors were sued in the Supreme Court for fraudulent misrepresentation, but were acquitted in 1924. He ventured into private publishing as Meredith Atkinson Press; *Stead's Review* collapsed in 1926 and he went to London.

Atkinson became literary secretary for the New Health Society and was lecturer on economics for the University of Cambridge's board of extra-mural studies. He contributed to the revived *Stead's Review*, the *Nineteenth Century and After* and other journals. Never robust and always inclined to overwork, he died in London on 13 May 1929 of aortic valve disease. He was survived by his second wife Isobel Marion, grand-daughter of Professor Charles Badham [q.v.3], whom he had married in Melbourne on 21 March 1925, and by two sons and a daughter of his first marriage.

A man of great charm and stormy temperament and intellect, Atkinson played an important role in the early establishment of the W.E.A. in Australia and in the advocacy of sociology as a recognized discipline in universities. He remained an outsider in academic circles.

H. Heaton, 'Personalities 1913-1922', *Highway*, 1 Oct 1923; F. Alexander, 'Sydney University and the W.E.A. 1913-1919', *Aust Q*, Dec 1955; *Punch* (Melb), 16 May 1918; *Table Talk*, 22 Nov 1923; *The Times*, 15 May 1929; A. Wesson, formal adult education in Victoria 1890-1950 (M.Ed. thesis, Univ Melb, 1971); T. Rowse, Australian Liberals' theories of consensus and national character (M.A. thesis, Flinders Univ, 1976); F. W. Eggleston, *Confidential notes: journalists and press barons* (Menzies Lib, ANU); correspondence file, 1917 (Univ Melb Archives). WARREN OSMOND

ATTIWILL; *see* RICHARDSON, ETHEL TRACY

AULD, JAMES MUIR (1879-1942), artist, was born on 19 June 1879 at Ashfield, New South Wales, third son of Rev. John Auld, Presbyterian minister, and his wife Georgina, née Muir. He was educated at Ashfield Public School and at Sydney Grammar School. While employed as a clerk by the Ashfield Borough Council he enrolled in night classes in drawing at Ashfield Technical School and spent much of his spare time drawing and sketching the foreshores of Sydney Harbour. He resigned in 1907 to become a professional artist, and studied with J. S. Watkins; later he joined Julian Ashton's [q.v.] Sydney Art School.

About 1906 J. Muir Auld (as he signed his works) began to show oils at the annual Royal Art Society of New South Wales exhibitions, but he first became known in Sydney as a black and white artist, contributing regularly to the *Sydney Mail* and the *Bulletin*. In 1909 he visited England to study the work of English painters, particularly Constable and Wilson Steer, and precariously supported himself by pen-and-ink drawings for magazines such as *London Opinion*.

About 1911 Auld returned to Australia and in 1918 settled at Dee Why near fellow artists Roland Wakelin and Lawson Balfour [qq.v.] in an environment suited to Post-Impressionist *plein air* painting. On 1 July 1914 Auld had married with Presbyterian rites a divorcee Maggie Kate Kane, née Bell.

That year he completed his earliest securely-dated oil, a portrait of 'Thelma', his step-daughter. Besides landscapes, he painted some subject pictures and portraits: 'The Broken Vase' and a portrait of the poet Roderic Quinn [q.v.] were bought early by the National Art Gallery of New South Wales.

Auld exhibited frequently with the Society of Artists, Sydney, of which he was a member. In the 1920s he joined the well-known commercial art firm, Smith & Julius, and illustrated several books. In 1931 he moved to Thirlmere, south-west of Sydney, where he spent the rest of his life alone — eschewing even a radio in his small cottage. Here, however, according to Wakelin, he painted the best of his landscapes, achieving 'a deeper penetration into the mysteries of light and shade'. He was awarded the 1935 Wynne Prize for 'Winter Morning', a study of trees and sky which had 'a stimulating sense of wind, and flying cloud' and showed the artist's partial adoption of the palette knife. Auld had three one-man exhibitions at the Macquarie Galleries, Sydney, in 1928, 1936 and 1938, and had also exhibited in London and Paris. He was a foundation member of the Australian Academy of Art in 1938.

Auld died of tuberculosis on 8 June 1942 in Camden District Hospital. His estate was valued for administration at £52. In December the National Art Gallery of New South Wales held a memorial exhibition. Self-portraits are in the Mitchell Library, Sydney, and the Art Gallery of New South Wales; he is also represented in public collections in Adelaide, Brisbane, Melbourne, Armidale and Manly.

Art Gallery (NSW), *Loan memorial exhibition of pictures by J. Muir Auld* (Syd, 1942), and *A catalogue of Australian oil paintings . . . 1875-1952* (Syd, 1953); *Society of Artists book* (Syd, 1942); *Art in Aust*, 3 (1917). BERNICE MURPHY

AUSTIN, SIDNEY (1846-1906), AUSTIN ALBERT (1855-1925), EDWIN HENRY (1860-1909), and EDWARD ARTHUR (1875-1940), were respectively nephew and son-in-law, second son, fourth son, and grandson and great-nephew, of Thomas Austin [q.v.1] of Barwon Park, Winchelsea, Victoria. All had a pastoral setting and became minor politicians.

Sidney, seventh and youngest son of John Austin, Thomas's eldest brother, and his wife Eleanor, née Collins, was born at Baltonsborough, Somerset, England, on 16 May 1846. Early in 1864 he followed his brothers Josiah, Benjamin and Albert [q.v.3] to Victoria. Trained by the first and third, he became a station-owner in 1870 and from 1874, as part-lessee, managed in succession Avalon for his uncle James Austin [q.v.1] and Barwon Park for Thomas Austin's estate. In 1881 his name enlarged the title of the Geelong woolbrokers Dennys, Lascelles [qq.v.4,5] & Co. In 1888 he extended his rural interests into New South Wales, through his partnership with his first cousin Frank Mack in Narromine station near Dubbo. His surviving Narromine letter-book (500 pages), although clearly only a fraction of his correspondence, displays his capacity, vision, literacy and professional business standards.

Centred upon Geelong, he combined the functions of pastoral expert and progressive citizen. In 1886 he became a council-member of Geelong Church of England Grammar School; in 1888, a Geelong town councillor and also member for South-Western Province in the Legislative Council. He was mayor in 1896-98 and held his parliamentary seat until 1904 when ill health caused his retirement. After renting Lunan, the mansion of J. F. Strachan [q.v.2], in 1892 he bought a verandahed brick and stone bungalow at Newtown, added a floor and called the result Larneuk. His wife Harriet Mary, Thomas Austin's second daughter, whom he had married in 1871, died there in 1901. He died there also, on 8 May 1906, of chronic nephritis. As chairman of the inaugural council of Geelong Church of England Girls' Grammar School, he had just clinched its foundation and chosen its first headmistress, Elsie F. Morres [q.v.]. In 1922 the school expanded from The Hermitage into Larneuk, and renamed it Austin House. It was demolished when in 1973 the school forsook Newtown for Highton.

Austin Albert and Edwin Henry, whose mother Elizabeth Phillips Harding had married their father Thomas in Melbourne in 1845, were both born at Barwon Park: Austin on 23 November 1855 and Edwin on 23 August 1860. From April 1864 until 1873, when he left as an unofficial prefect and captain of field games, Austin attended Geelong Grammar School. Edwin joined him there in July 1872 from Ballarat College, going on to Scotch College, Melbourne, in 1878. Austin and Edwin both became active landholders and local legislators. Austin was member of the Legislative Assembly for Grenville in 1902-04 and of the Legislative Council for South-Western Province in 1913-25. Edwin was M.L.A. for Ripon and Hampden from 1892 until 1900 as a conservative. In 1906-09 he was M.L.C. for Nelson Province.

Physically short but quick and tough, Austin captained the Geelong Football Club's victorious teams of 1879 and 1881 and then concentrated upon productive activities which stretched from Commeralghip station, Rokewood, as far as the Balmoral, Heywood and Stawell districts, but were centred upon Narmbool and Larundel stations in the timbered hills near Elaine. There he and his wife Winifred, daughter of John Cameron of Morgiana station, near Hamilton, brought up two sons and three daughters as a well-knit family in comparatively primitive country. He was pragmatic, direct and neatly humorous. 'The happiest people', he would tell his family, 'are those who get things gradually. Failure is not a crime, but low aim is'. When a daughter at school in Melbourne wrote for leave to learn fencing, he assented — and added wryly that it might be useful on the property. Austin died at Geelong of cerebro-vascular disease on 29 July 1925 leaving an estate valued for probate at £60405.

On 10 June 1884 Edwin married Jessie Isabella, daughter of Thomas Shaw, government surveyor and grazier near Ararat. He leased Gorrinn station in that district for some six years from 1883, bought St Enochs, near Beaufort in 1888, but about ten years later sold it and settled on Colvinsby at Dobie. He died of nephritis at Stawell on 30 November 1909, survived by his wife, two daughters, and a son Rex who succumbed to meningitis in 1914.

Edwin and Austin were well informed sheepmen. Edwin established a stud merino flock near Ararat. In 1895 he was president of the Australian Sheepbreeders' Association and at various times served as head of both the Ararat and Beaufort agricultural societies. He was also a Ripon shire councillor in 1888-97 and president there in his turn. Austin's civic emulation was expressed through his youngest brother Herbert Arthur, his partner and afterwards his neighbour, a Buninyong shire councillor for thirty-five years and mayor of Geelong in 1909.

Edward Arthur was Sidney's fourth son. He and his elder twin Arthur Edward were born at Avalon station, near Geelong, on 3 July 1875. Both, like their younger brother Alfred Victor, became staff-members of Dennys, Lascelles, Austin & Co.; but Victor died in 1903 and Arthur in 1910. By 1911 the other brothers, Sidney Augustus Napier and Thomas Phillips, were managing the family's stations in New South Wales (Wambianna and Cobborah, which they bought individually in 1926), and Edward was his firm's secretary. In 1916, however, he resigned to become secretary and bursar of Geelong Grammar School. He had taken his father's place on the school council in December 1906, and became its honorary secretary in 1907.

In 1895 Edward ('Ned') had been school captain and a matriculated athlete. Knee injury failed to impair his interest in balanced development. He contributed business skill and painstaking wisdom; robust, uncensorious sympathy; a knack with the ugly duckling. He gained satisfying momentum through perception of the divine in common experience. The single-seater Swift in which he began his years of daily motoring between Corio and Geelong, where, being single, he lived with his married sister, presaged his ultimate renunciation of salary. Helped by his sister, he had until 1914 continued the tented holiday camps at Lorne which Arthur and he had arranged as leaders of a young men's Anglican group. He became a diocesan councillor, but was a lay reader at Fyansford for thirty-four years, and was president of the Fyansford cricket club until it was dispersed by World War I. He understood small boys and straightforward men, and delighted to be host to congenial company; but at times he became too serious for half-baked youth. Yet critics of his occasional resonant school-chapel sermons seldom if ever doubted Ned's integrity, or accused him of unjustified interference. His unobtrusive but positive Christian faith was influenced by his conception of J. B. Wilson and J. L. Cuthbertson [qq.v.6,3]. His *Light blue days* (Melbourne, 1927), a book of seventy-eight poems, deficient in execution but sincere in feeling, defined his motives and loyalties. He held several public offices, and in 1932 won the Legislative Assembly seat of Geelong as a last-minute candidate for the United Australia Party. But politics dismayed him. In 1935 he lost to his Labor opponent without regret.

Ned Austin was middling tall and solidly built, with warm brown eyes, a firm handshake, square features, and a ruddy, weather-beaten look. His bushwhacking elder brothers used to banter him, but with ingenuous gumption he replied in kind. Thomas's ornithological Cobborah collection, now in the National Museum, Melbourne, suggests a common interest. Others were also shared.

Trusted friend and adviser of successive headmasters, still actively employed, Edward died suddenly of hypertension and cerebro-vascular disease at his home, Claremont, Geelong, on 1 May 1940. He left an estate valued for probate at £28 372, with generous bequests to the Church of England and to Geelong Grammar School. Cuthbertson's 'In Memoriam S.A.' could have been written for both father and son:

Ashes to ashes, dust to dust —
Yet his clear spirit lives,

And from the kingdom of the good and just
A benediction gives.

Geelong Grammar School, *History and register* ... (Geelong, 1907); A. Henderson (ed), *Early pioneer families of Victoria and Riverina* (Melb, 1936), and *Australian families*, 1 (Melb, 1941); Mrs A. S. Gray, *Austin family tree* (priv print, 1948); I. Southall, *The story of The Hermitage* (Melb, 1956); Mrs R. A. Austin, 'The Austin family in Australia', *VHM*, 36 (1965); Geelong Grammar School, *Annual*, 1875-76, and *Quarterly*, July 1906, Oct 1911, and *Corian*, 1914-May 1940; S. Austin letter-book (held by Geelong Hist Soc); rate-books (Geelong *and* Newtown City councils); records (Geelong Grammar School); family information.

P. L. BROWN

AUSTRAL, FLORENCE MARY (1894-1968), singer, was born on 16 April 1894 at Richmond, Victoria, only daughter of William Wilson, a Swedish carpenter formerly known as Wilhelm Lindholm, and his wife Helena Mary, née Harris, a dressmaker. Her father died in 1895 and her mother set up in business; in 1903 she married 28-year-old Syrian book-keeper John Fawaz, a staunch Methodist. The singer was known as Florence Fawaz until 1921 when she adopted the professional name of Florence Austral.

Austral received no early vocal training but in 1913 went to Ballarat to sing in the renowned South Street competitions. She won first prize in the mezzo-soprano section and second prize in two others. At the suggestion of adjudicator Fritz Hart [q.v.], she took lessons with Madame Elise Wiedermann [q.v. Pinschof] who was then at the Conservatorium of Music, Albert Street, Melbourne. In 1917 she won an entrance exhibition to the University Conservatorium where Wiedermann was then teaching. At 25, with first-class honours in second-year diploma and first-year bachelor of music, she decided to make singing her career. After a farewell concert on 22 September 1919, when critics praised her voice for its 'remarkable size and great beauty', she left to study Italian opera in New York. She appeared at festivals in Boston and Chicago, afterwards auditioning at the Metropolitan Opera House, New York. A contract was offered but arguments arose over a proposed début in Chicago. Homesick and disillusioned by what she regarded as corrupt practices at the Metropolitan Opera, she decided to return to Australia. However, she broke her journey in London and remained there.

Florence Austral first appeared in London at a Sunday concert at the Albert Hall early in 1921. She successfully auditioned for Covent Garden but it was not until 16 May 1922 that she made her début there under the auspices of the British National Opera Company. At short notice, without stage or orchestral rehearsal for the part, she replaced Elsa Stralia [q.v.] as Brünnhilde in Wagner's *Die Walküre*. She was an instant and lasting success. Thereafter it was recognized that Austral was an operatic phenomenon, a tireless worker of easy temperament with a voice unequalled in quality and power, particularly suited to the Wagnerian roles in which she was to excel.

She continued with the British National Opera Company at Covent Garden until the end of the famous International Season of 1924. Her many engagements at this time included contracts with (Sir) Landon Ronald and the Royal Albert Hall Orchestra, Sir Henry Wood's Queen's Hall Orchestra, and the Hallé Orchestra in Manchester. On 20 January 1923 she appeared for the only time with Melba [q.v.] in an evening of operatic excerpts. In the 1920s she began recording on acoustic discs and made the earliest of her many electrical recordings; her Wagnerian discs established her reputation.

Austral had known John Amadio [q.v.] from student days in Melbourne. Her marriage to him at Hampstead, London, on 15 December 1925, two months after his divorce, caused a rift with her parents which their visit to London failed to mend: she was not permitted to see her mother again.

With Amadio, Austral returned to Australia in 1930, giving her first concert in Sydney on 24 May and in Melbourne on 21 June. Critics exclaimed over her 'perfectly wonderful voice, amazing skill ... lively intelligence ... glowing intensity, all informed by unerring judgment'. Back in Europe in November, she contracted to sing at the Berlin State Opera. During a performance of *Die Walküre* she found herself unable to stand without help, the first public evidence of her long battle with multiple sclerosis. She later attributed her 'wooden acting' to its early effects.

Austral had made the first of six successful tours of North America in 1925. With Amadio, these tours were resumed in 1931-32 and 1932-33. Her English recital tours also continued but she did not appear at Covent Garden again until 1933. She toured Holland in 1931 and 1933-34.

In April 1934 Austral and Amadio returned to Australia for a season of concerts in capital cities and large country towns. The critics noted her vitality and the 'infectious air of personal enjoyment' in her performance. In September Sir Benjamin Fuller [q.v.] engaged her for his season of 'Grand Opera', and Australians saw her in her famous operatic roles for the first time. When the season ended early in April 1935, Austral and Amadio continued to tour Australia, making several successful broadcast recitals as well, but by the end of 1936 Austral had returned to London. During World War II she appeared for occasional benefit concerts, but her career was at an end.

In late July 1946 she returned alone to Melbourne and in 1954 took up an appointment to teach at the newly formed Newcastle branch of the New South Wales State Conservatorium of Music. She retired in ill health at the end of 1959. When she later became paralysed, the Florence Austral Association paid for her care. She died of cerebro-vascular disease in a church home for the aged at Mayfield, Newcastle, on 15 May 1968, and was cremated with Methodist rites.

B. and F. Mackenzie, *Singers of Australia* (Melb, 1967); *Musical Courier* (New York), 23 Dec 1926; *Opera*, Mar 1955, July 1968; *Music and Dance*, 1960, Oct 1962, Sept 1963; *Record Collector*, 14 (1962); *Musical Times*, Jan 1963; *Argus*, 23 Sept 1919, 15 Sept 1925, 12 May, 23 June 1930, 2 Apr, 11, 18 June 1934, 8 June 1939; *Herald* (Melb), 8 June 1962, 16 May 1968; *Age*, 15, 22 Aug, 2 Oct 1962; *SMH*, 26 Mar 1965.

MAUREEN THÉRÈSE RADIC

AVERY, DAVID (1871-1956), chemical consultant, was born on 22 February 1871 at Bungaree, Victoria, eldest son of David Avery and his wife Elizabeth, née Kiel, pioneering farmers. He was educated at Mount Pleasant State School, the Ballarat School of Mines and Grenville College; he qualified for matriculation in 1887 and in 1889 entered the University of Melbourne where he was a resident at Queen's College. Wyselaskie [q.v.6] scholar in natural science in 1890, he specialized in chemistry and technical chemistry, taking the honours examination for B.Sc. in March 1892 and winning the Kernot [q.v.5] Research Scholarship for Chemistry. His research under Professor Masson [q.v.] was mainly on the chemistry of hyponitrites; he graduated M.Sc., the second on the university's roll, in March 1894. He tutored at Queen's, Ormond and Trinity colleges and contributed actively to the University Science Club and to college sport.

In 1897, after two years of study towards a medical degree, Avery married Gertrude Elizabeth Hall (M.A., 1897), a specialist in modern languages and stepsister of the scientist T. S. Hall [q.v.]. That year Avery began his career in industrial chemistry, managing a cyanide process for extracting gold from low-grade ores for a mining company at Mount Egerton. He returned to Melbourne as head of the chemistry department at the Working Men's College in 1899-1911. He later entered private practice and in 1915, with V. G. Anderson [q.v.] as partner, established the firm known as Avery & Anderson. Among organizations consulting Avery were the Melbourne and Metropolitan Board of Works, Amalgamated Zinc (de Bavay's [q.v.]) Ltd and the Electrolytic Zinc Co. of Australasia Ltd. He advised Amalgamated Zinc on aspects of flotation processes for the separation and extraction of zinc and lead from the tailings of mines at Broken Hill; after 1916 he was also consultant to Electrolytic Zinc on electrolytic extraction of lead, zinc and aluminium, being joint-holder of several patents. He served from 1916 on the executive and special chemicals committees of the newly formed Commonwealth Advisory Council of Science and Industry and in 1919 (when he suffered a severe attack of encephalitis) was appointed for two years to the executive of the Institute of Science and Industry.

In 1923 Avery persuaded Amalgamated Zinc to consider the manufacture of pulp and paper from Australian hardwoods by extending the successful laboratory investigations sponsored by the Institute of Science and Industry. He and L. R. S. Benjamin [q.v.] visited England and Holland in 1924; they met with little success in persuading British papermakers to undertake commercial tests on Australian eucalypts by sulphite-pulp processes, but trials in Holland produced paper, though of poor quality. Avery, now a director of Amalgamated Zinc, took an option on forest land in the Huon Valley, Tasmania, in 1926 and there Amalgamated Zinc, through its subsidiary, Tasmanian Paper Pty Ltd, financed a pilot pulp and paper mill at Kermandie. Benjamin joined Avery in 1927 and two and a half years later, after overcoming numerous technical difficulties, they produced newsprint from *Eucalyptus regnans*. The crash of the New York Stock Exchange ended plans for commercial expansion.

Avery gave valuable service to education. In Britain and Europe in 1908-09 he studied developments in technical education. He was a matriculation examiner in chemistry for the University of Melbourne and an external examiner for higher degrees. A vice-president of the Working Men's College, he also sat on the councils of technical schools. In 1922 he chaired an apprenticeship conference convened by the Victorian minister of labour, and in 1931 served on a board of inquiry into the administration of the Victorian Education Department.

Avery was a foundation member and office-bearer of the Society of Chemical Industry of Victoria (founded 1901), the Melbourne University Chemical Society (1904) and the Australian Chemical Institute (1918), and a member of the Australasian Institute of Mining and Metallurgy in 1920-29. He urged the Society of Chemical Industry of Victoria to sponsor and finance research at technical colleges. He was an executive member of the Victorian business and excursion subcommittees organizing the 1914 meeting of the British Association for the Advancement of Science. In 1924 he was elected president of the Rotary Club of Melbourne.

Avery was a man of principle, kindly, trusted and well liked. His general philosophy and religious faith are revealed in his twenty-five pages of verse, *The quest of man* (Melbourne, 1938). From 1933 he virtually retired to his property, Greenacres, at Harkaway, Berwick, where he died on 27 October 1956; he was cremated with Methodist rites. He was survived by his only daughter, who practised medicine. His estate was valued for probate at £30 283.

L. J. Blake (ed), *Vision and realisation*, 1 (Melb, 1973); L. R. East, *The Kiel family and related Scottish pioneers* (Nunawading, 1974); *Alma Mater* (Univ Melb), 1 (1896), 3 (1898), 5 (1900); L. R. Benjamin, 'The challenge of the eucalypts', *Appita*, 13 (1959); *Science and Industry*, June 1920; J. A. Rawson, A history of the Australian paper making industry, 1818-1951 (M.A. thesis, Univ Melb, 1953); Council minutes, 1901, 1903, 1905, 1910, 1913 (Soc of Chemical Industry of Vic).

JOAN T. RADFORD

B

BACCARINI, ANTONIO (1887-1971), merchant, was born on 7 July 1887 at Avellino, Italy, son of Pasquale Baccarini (d. 1919), and his wife Maria Italia, née Vason. In 1900 Antonio moved to Florence when his father was appointed professor of botany at the Instituto di Studi Superiori (University of Florence); he qualified as a chemist in 1913 and as a doctor in science in 1915.

From 1913 Baccarini served in the Italian army; discharged early in 1915, he was almost immediately recalled for service in World War I and was soon promoted captain. Late that year he was posted to London and bought supplies for the Italian army commissariat. On 28 November 1917 at St Peter's Italian Church, Holborn, he married Ruth King. In February 1918 he was recalled to the front and acted as liaison officer between the British and Italian commands; in August 1919 he was awarded the British Military Cross and later was appointed a cavaliere of the Crown of Italy.

Baccarini and his wife visited Australia in 1922, arriving in Sydney on 12 September in the *Moreton Bay*. Liking it, they decided to settle. He soon became prominent in business circles and was a founder that year of the Italian Chamber of Commerce in Australia. In 1923 he bought an interest in an import and export firm, W. Plant & Co. Ltd, and often wrote for the Sydney newspaper *Italo-Australian*, explaining the nature and the policies of Mussolini. In 1925 he was a founder of the local Dante Alighieri Art and Literary Society and was its president in 1927-35. He was a member of the Royal Society of New South Wales from 1923.

Baccarini visited England and Italy in 1927-28, and upon his return to Sydney lectured in Italian for the University Extension Board. In 1931 he was naturalized; describing himself as an agent, he lived at Woollahra until 1953. In the 1930s he wrote articles and lectured on his native country's culture, language and literature and was responsible also for the production of some modern plays. In 1938-40 he conducted special language courses for teachers for the Department of Education. In 1936 Baccarini's pamphlet, *What for?*, supporting Fascist aggression against Ethiopia, had attracted the attention of the Australian government for its objectionable comments on the British Empire. He was interned from June 1940 until March 1944.

After World War II, as a lecturer, Baccarini continued to be involved in the affairs of the Italian community in Sydney and con-tributed to several ethnic newspapers. In 1948 he again attracted the attention of the government with a speech praising Mussolini and Fascism at a reception for the Italian Opera Company. He divorced his wife in 1951 and married Phyllis Hope Raymond, a schoolteacher, on 6 March 1954. He died on 6 February 1971 in Balmain Hospital and was buried in the Northern Suburbs Catholic cemetery, survived by a son of his first marriage and by his second wife.

Italian Bulletin of Aust, 17 June 1927; *Sunday Telegraph* (Syd), 5 Dec 1948; *Daily Telegraph* (Syd), 9 Dec 1948; G. Cresciani, Fascism, anti-Fascism and Italians in Australia, 1922-1945 (M.A. Hons thesis, Univ Syd, 1978).

GIANFRANCO CRESCIANI

BACKHOUSE, BENJAMIN (1829-1904), architect, and ALFRED PAXTON (1851-1939), judge, were father and son. Benjamin was born at Ipswich, Suffolk, England, son of Benjamin Backhouse, stonemason and builder, and his wife Elizabeth Prentice, née Fuller. He worked with his father and as a builder on his own account. On 20 August 1849 he married Lydia Warne Johnson, by whom he had seventeen children. Financial losses induced him to migrate to Victoria in 1852. He practised as a builder and then as an architect at Geelong and, with a partner, at Ballarat. After an unprofitable return to London in 1860, he went to Brisbane where he prospered as an architect and became an alderman. In 1868 he removed to Sydney.

Backhouse soon developed a large architectural practice with branches at Newcastle and Bathurst. He was secretary of the Institute of Architects of New South Wales in 1871-73 and, on a visit to England in 1886, was made an associate of the Royal Institute of British Architects. Wider interests began to engage his attention. He joined the City of Sydney Improvement Board in 1879 and was its chairman in 1880-92. He helped found the Sanitary Reform League in 1880, investigated sanitation whenever he could and worked tirelessly for a better urban sewerage system; he joined the Metropolitan Board of Water Supply and Sewerage in 1895.

Backhouse was an earnest social reformer, strongly influenced by his reading of Carlyle, Ruskin and William Morris. In the depression he was chairman of the Pitt Town Co-operative Settlement and an exponent of slum clearance. Appointed to the Legislative Council in 1895, he was sympathetic to Labor's programme while taking an independent radical line. He died, aged 75, on 29 July 1904, survived by his second wife Emma Sanday, née Byrnes, a divorcee whom he had married on 16 December 1903, and by seven sons and four daughters. Although a Swedenborgian in early life, he was buried in the Anglican section of Rookwood cemetery. His estate was sworn for probate at £9638.

Backhouse's second son Alfred Paxton was born at Ipswich, Suffolk, England, on 25 May 1851, the year of the Great Exhibition; he received his second Christian name in honour of its architect. He lived with his family in England, Victoria and in Queensland where he attended Ipswich Grammar School. Entering the University of Sydney, he graduated with honours in 1872 (M.A., 1875). After teaching at Sydney Grammar School, he was admitted to the Bar on 16 December 1876.

Backhouse's legal career prospered. He became a crown prosecutor in 1878, an acting District Court judge in 1884 and a permanent member of the bench that year. He acted on occasions as a Supreme Court judge, notably when he presided at the trial of the Broken Hill strike leaders in 1892. Commercial and maritime matters were his principal interests. His over-leniency in criminal cases, notably in the T. E. Rofe conspiracy trial in 1895, led to strong criticism and may have cost him a permanent place on the Supreme Court. He retired in 1921, but remained active in public life.

Backhouse's interests were as varied and as vigorously pursued as those of his father. At different times, he was president of the New South Wales Rowing Association, the United Charities Fund, the Navy League and the Benevolent Society of New South Wales. A keen student of history, he was a long-term councillor of the Royal Australian Historical Society; he was also a member of the Sydney Philharmonic Society.

Backhouse served on the Senate of the University of Sydney in 1887-1939. When the 1912 amending legislation created new conditions for the appointment of senators, his lifetime tenure was specifically confirmed. He was acting chancellor in 1892-94, 1896-99 and 1911-14, and a fellow of St Paul's College until 1928 when he resigned on a matter of domestic policy. An original member of the Sydney University Union, he helped to reconstitute it as a large-scale club in 1913 and was its lifelong supporter. Interested in music and drama, and in all kinds of organized sport, he fostered these outside and inside the university. For over half a century Backhouse and the University of Sydney were virtually synonymous.

On 4 February 1879 he had married Kate Marion, daughter of Robert Hills; they had no children. He died at his home at Elizabeth Bay on 1 August 1939 and his estate was sworn for probate at £31 397. Although Backhouse had been brought up as a Swedenborgian, he had become a member of the Church of England and, after a service at St John's Church, Darlinghurst, was buried in Rookwood cemetery. His portrait by John Longstaff [q.v.] is held by the university.

Sydney Univ Union, *The Union book of 1902* (Syd, 1902); J. M. Freeland, *The making of a profession* (Syd, 1971); H. T. E. Holt, *A court rises* (Syd, 1976); *Union Recorder*, 10 Aug 1939; *SMH*, 30 July 1904; *Bulletin*, 6 Oct 1904; B. Backhouse papers (ML); A. P. Backhouse papers *and* University minutes 1887-1939 (Univ Syd Archives).

K. J. CABLE

BADDELEY, JOHN MARCUS (1881-1953), trade unionist and Labor politician, was born on 20 November 1881 at Burslem, Staffordshire, England, son of George Billinge Baddeley, innkeeper, and his wife Mary Elizabeth, née Bailey. He was brought to Australia as a small child by his parents who settled at Newcastle, where his father found work as a coalminer. He left Merewether Public School at 11 to work at odd jobs round the Glebe colliery near Merewether and at 16 followed his father to the coal-face. On 22 February 1902 he married Harriet, daughter of John Churchill, a local miner.

In 1908 Baddeley moved to Cessnock, working at the Neath then at the Aberdare Extended collieries. He was soon well known as a cricketer and first-grade footballer and local trade union and civic leader. He became secretary of the Aberdare Extended miners' lodge and then northern district president of the Colliery Employees' Federation in 1914-22. In 1914 he also served on the Cessnock Shire Council, and was first vice-chairman of the Cessnock District Hospital Board and a member of the board of Cessnock Co-operative Store. In 1915 he became first president of the Australasian Coal and Shale Employees' Federation (the Miners' Federation) which had finally succeeded in linking Australian coalminers into a single union. In 1920 he was appointed by the Commonwealth government to the Coal Industry Special Tribunal.

As a militant socialist trade union leader, Baddeley worked closely with A. C. Willis [q.v.] and other left-wing unionists to strengthen and revitalize the labour movement by amalgamation and closer organization. Difficult conditions in the coal-mining industry ensured that the Miners' Federation remained at the centre of radical trade unionism throughout World War I and into the 1920s. At the All-Australian Trade Union Congress in Melbourne in 1921, Baddeley successfully moved the report on industrial organization which sought to create 'one big union' of the working class. Though this rigid and doctrinaire scheme proved impractical, the 'one big union' movement did help to prepare the ground for the founding of the Australasian Council of Trade Unions in 1927. In 1919 Baddeley had supported moves to form the breakaway Industrial Socialist Labor Party but, along with many other supporters of this party, he rejoined the Australian Labor Party when it adopted the socialist objective put forward by trade unionists in 1921.

Baddeley was elected to the Legislative Assembly in 1922 as a member for Newcastle and in 1925-49 represented Cessnock. He served as secretary for mines and minister for labour and industry in J. T. Lang's [q.v.] Labor government in 1925-27. With Willis, he drafted a series of Acts implementing diverse union policies, including measures designed specifically to benefit coalminers. In 1926-27 he toured Britain, Europe and the United States of America to study mining methods. He regained his former portfolios in the Lang ministry of 1930-32, and in 1931 introduced a bill to nationalize the coal industry; it lapsed with the dismissal of Lang in 1932 and large-scale reorganization of the coal industry was delayed until the 1940s. As deputy leader of the party he supported Lang in the faction struggles which racked the New South Wales Labor Party in the 1930s. Nevertheless he finally abandoned 'the Big Fella' under pressure from unionists, and supported moves which led to Lang's replacement as leader by (Sir) William McKell in 1939.

With the return of a Labor government under McKell in 1941 Baddeley became deputy premier, colonial secretary and secretary for mines; in 1944-47 he was also minister for national emergency services. He continued in the same portfolios in James McGirr's ministry in 1947-49 and in 1948-49 was also minister for labour and industry and social welfare. He was second only to McKell in adapting State government policies to the national war effort and guiding New South Wales through the social and economic dislocation accompanying the return to peace. Baddeley was acting premier from August to December 1948 when he suffered a heart attack in Parliament House. He resigned on 8 September 1949 to become director of State coal-mines and chairman of the State Mines Control Authority until 1953. A keen gardener and student of natu-

ral history, he was the moving force behind the Fauna Protection Act of 1948. He died of cerebro-vascular disease at St Luke's Hospital, Darlinghurst, on 1 July 1953 and was cremated with Anglican rites. He was survived by his wife, two sons and three daughters; his estate was valued for probate at £4869.

Throughout his career Baddeley excelled mainly as an administrator, combining formidable organizing ability with sincere concern for the welfare of the working class. As a socialist propagandist he lacked the theoretical competence of Willis; as a politician he was overshadowed by leaders of the stature of Lang, McKell and McGirr. Despite his socialist principles he won repute as a conservative on many social and moral questions, especially while colonial secretary in the 1940s. He was also strongly criticized for obstructing the introduction of mechanized and labour-saving techniques in the mining industry. Yet he had few peers as an arbitrator in major industrial disputes, as a co-ordinator of labour and management throughout the difficult years of World War II, and as a faithful representative of the miners who elected him to parliament.

J. T. Lang, I remember (Syd, 1956); R. Gollan, The coalminers of New South Wales (Melb, 1963); I. Turner, Industrial labour and politics (Canb, 1965); E. Ross, A history of the Miners' Federation of Australia (Syd, 1970); H. Radi and P. Spearritt (eds), Jack Lang (Syd, 1977); Newcastle Morning Herald, 18 Feb, 6, 8, Apr 1922, 7 Sept 1949, 2 July 1953; SMH, 16 May 1945, 11 Sept 1949, 2 July 1953; Sun (Syd), 3 July 1953; I. E. Young, The impact of J. T. Lang on the N.S.W. Labor Party, 1929-1943 (M.A. thesis, Univ NSW, 1963).

FRANK FARRELL

BADGER, JOSEPH STILLMAN (1851-1934), electrical engineer and administrator, was born on 28 November 1851 at De Ruyter, New York, United States of America, son of Joseph A. Badger and his wife Almyra, née Coon. He is said to have been educated at Whitewater, Wisconsin, and in Illinois at Woodstock and Hedding College, Abingdon.

Badger began work in the 'telephone business' in 1882, joined the Edison Company's railroad department in 1890 and in 1894 was transferred to the factory at Schenectady, New York. He came to Queensland during May 1896 on behalf of the General Electric Co. to electrify the Brisbane Tramway Co.'s system. He joined the latter, became its chief electrical engineer in 1897 and by 1899 was general manager. As managing director from about 1914, he visited the United States frequently, including 1914, 1919 and 1922.

Able, courageous and ruthless, Badger would stretch the law to its uttermost limits when the interests of his firm were at stake. When the new electric cars were delayed he converted worn-out horse-cars; in the first seven years he added over thirty-three miles (53 km) of suburban track to the system. He refused to accept trade unionism, decreed that union badges could not be worn on duty, and suspended the many employees who refused to submit. Over-confident leaders of the militant Australian Labour Federation saw an issue of principle and called a general strike which paralysed Brisbane from 18 January to 5 February 1912, then collapsed. None of the tramway strikers was ever re-employed by the company.

In 1917 the Ryan [q.v.] Labor government launched a bill to buy out the tramway company when its concession expired. Clauses in the bill forbidding payment for lines laid without authority and a concurrent attempt to force fare-reductions brought threats of a boycott on Queensland by English financiers. A select committee reported on both bills in July 1919. Both government and company appointed valuation boards in 1920, and the issues of payment for goodwill, lines illegally laid, and non-tramway business undertakings such as power-supply almost reached the Privy Council. Badger retired in February 1922 to a 'fruit ranch' in California and on 1 January 1923 the tramways were handed to a trust. Badger, who had gained a local and international reputation as a standard-bearer of capitalism, died at Monrovia, California, on 22 November 1934 and was buried in Live Oak mausoleum.

A pious Presbyterian and political Republican, described as 'humorless and self-conscious' and arrogant and philanthropic, Badger is said to have used the Bible he kept prominently on his desk as his business guide. He believed in staff welfare, engaged nurses for sick employees and their families, and sometimes paid personally for extended hospitalization. His accomplished photography records much of Brisbane tramway history. He was an early motorist and a member of the Royal Automobile Club of Queensland and of other professional, cultural and social bodies. He supported the Queensland University Extension Committee and much of his book-collection is now in the university's library.

Badger had married Carrie Mabel Hewitt in Elgin, Illinois, in 1882; she died in Brisbane on 7 July 1909, leaving two sons. On 24 June 1914 in the United States he married Marion Stirling of Toowoomba; they had no children.

H. S. M. Woodrow, *The Queensland government and the Brisbane tramways* (Lond, 1918); G. R. Steer, 'Brisbane tramways: their history and development', *JRHSQ*, 3 (1937-47), no 3; *Brisbane Courier*, May-June 1896, 15 Jan-29 Feb 1912, 30 Nov 1917, 22 Aug 1922; *Age*, Jan-Feb 1912; *Telegraph* (Brisb), 22 Nov, 4, 30 Dec 1917, 24 Mar 1918; *Daily Standard*, 1 Dec 1917; *The Times*, 8 Jan 1918; *Daily Mail* (Brisb), 20 Aug 1922; G. Strachan, The Brisbane general strike of 1912 (B. A. Hons thesis, Univ Qld, 1972); CRS/203, 205 (QA).

GARRY R. FORD

BADHAM, EDITH ANNESLEY (1853-1920), headmistress, was born on 6 December 1853 at Louth, Lincolnshire, England, eldest daughter of Rev. Charles Badham [q.v.3] and his first wife Julia Matilda, née Smith (d. 1856). She was educated at Dinant, France, and by her father, who was headmaster of the Birmingham and Edgbaston Proprietary School from 1854. He recognized her gift for languages and took a great interest in her upbringing. In 1867 she arrived in Sydney with her father, who had been appointed professor of classics at the university, her stepmother and nine brothers and sisters. Women were not admitted to the university, but Edith studied, with Badham, all the subjects in the arts course and became so proficient that she assisted in his work and corrected public examination papers. In 1883-84 she kept house for her brother at Tenterfield. From 1884 she taught privately.

A devout Anglican, Miss Badham was a member of the provisional committee formed to establish a high school for girls under the auspices of the Church. She was keenly aware of the depressed economic conditions: her offer to act as principal for six months at a nominal salary was accepted. The school was formally opened on 17 July 1895 in a terrace-house in Victoria Street, Darlinghurst, in the presence of six bishops among other dignitaries, and with only one pupil. Six months later it was named the Sydney Church of England Grammar School for Girls, and grew so rapidly that in 1896 it moved to larger premises at Potts Point.

Edith Badham shared many of her father's forthright views on the purpose and nature of education. She believed that it should develop intellectual discipline and strong moral character, and that this could best be achieved by study of classical languages. At the first annual prize-giving, she declared that Latin was being studied by even the 'smallest children in the school', which made the teaching of English grammar unnecessary; she assured parents that it was possible for a girl to learn Greek and Latin without at all desiring to step out of 'her proper and subordinate place in the scheme of Creation'. No radical feminist, she shared the Victorian middle-class traditions in which she had been reared. In *Cosmos Magazine*, April 1895, she roundly condemned Australian literature on the grounds that it was insufficiently developed and unworthy of usurping the place of European classical literature. Although the *Bulletin* claimed that the school taught nothing but 'boating, Shakespeare and the Bible', the curriculum included English language and literature, French, mathematics, modern and ancient history, geography, and botany and geology for older girls, as well as a wide range of extra subjects such as music and art. Miss Badham herself taught Latin, Greek and French and formed La Réunion Française, attended by outsiders as well as pupils. She regularly took girls rowing on Saturday mornings.

Under Miss Badham the S.C.E.G.G.S. continued to grow: a kindergarten was opened in 1900 and next year the school moved to larger premises at Barham, Forbes Street. She became principal when branch schools were opened at Bowral in 1906 and North Sydney in 1911. She had always detested cramming for examinations and opposed the introduction of the intermediate and leaving certificate examinations. However the school was registered with the Department of Public Instruction in 1914. After several visits, she published *A trip to Java* (1909) and *Java revisited and Malaya* (1912).

Edith Badham was described as 'tiny and neat in person — her pretty light hair, now brownish fair. It was crinkled and vital; so much so that one expected sparks. Her skin finely etched; still like a rose-petal; her spotless clothes stiffly starched. She walked briskly with a quick, triumphant little patter of feet ... and she stood rigidly upright before her class vibrating — one might say — scintillating — with life — her steel grey eyes still very humorously bright'. Miss Badham died of pneumonia at Mosman on 17 May 1920, and was buried in St Thomas's Church of England cemetery, North Sydney. She left her estate, valued for probate at £1260, to her sister Julia Jackson. In 1926 the school chapel, that Edith Badham had always wished for, was dedicated to her memory.

S.C.E.G.G.S. Council, *Sydney Church of England Girls' Grammar School, 1895-1955*, W. Sharland ed (Syd, 1958); *Syd Diocesan Mag*, 1 June 1920, Oct, Nov 1930; S.C.E.G.G.S., *Lux*, June 1945, jubilee no; *N.Z.L. Q Mag*, June 1923; *SMH*, 18, 19 May 1920.   R. J. BURNS

BAGE, ANNA FREDERIKA (1883-1970),

university teacher, was born on 11 April 1883 at St Kilda, Victoria, daughter of Edward Bage, wholesale chemist, and his wife Mary Charlotte, née Lange. When her father, a junior partner in Felton, Grimwade [qq.v.4] & Co., died in July 1891 his widow took the three children to England where she enrolled them in the Oxford High School for girls. Returning to Melbourne in 1894, Freda went to Fairlight School. Inspired by her father's amateur scientific interests, she entered Janet Clarke [q.v.3] Hall, University of Melbourne, in 1901, and after failing first year graduated B.Sc. in 1905 and M.Sc. with second-class honours in 1907. She then worked as a junior demonstrator in biology, sharing the MacBain [q.v.5] Research Scholarship in 1907 and winning a Victorian government research scholarship in 1908. Next year she read two papers to the Royal Society of Victoria, then went to England on a King's College, London, research scholarship; her work under A. Dendy [q.v.] in 1910-11 led to a fellowship of the Linnean Society. Returning to the University of Melbourne as senior demonstrator, she was appointed lecturer in charge of biology at the University of Queensland in 1913, and became first principal of The Women's College within that university on 8 February 1914.

Miss Bage travelled widely in Queensland on official visits to encourage women to attend the university and to gain rural support for her college. From 1914 she drove and serviced a car, and competed in hill-climbs and reliability trials despite assertions that she was unladylike. As a biologist interested in fauna and flora she became president of the Field Naturalists' Club in 1915 and was a foundation member of the Barrier Reef committee. She was a member of the university senate in 1923-50.

Freda Bage's extra-mural interests were wide. In World War I she was a member of the Queensland recruiting committee and in both wars was president of university women's war work groups. Later she was honorary treasurer and vice-president of the State branch of the Australian League of Nations Union and in 1926 and 1938 she was sent to Geneva as a substitute delegate to the League of Nations Assembly. She was an original member of the National Art Galleries' Association, the Twelfth Night Theatre and the Brisbane Repertory Society. A hockey enthusiast, she managed the first hockey team in Australia to travel interstate, from Melbourne to Adelaide in 1908, and was president of the Queensland Women's Hockey Association in 1925-31.

Miss Bage was always interested in women's organizations and activities, being honorary secretary of the National Council of Women, Queensland, for some years and president of the Women's Club in 1916, and the Lyceum Club, Brisbane, in 1922-23. In particular the organization of university women concerned her and she took the lead in forming the Queensland Women Graduates' Association (later the Queensland Association of University Women). She was president of the Australian Federation of University Women in 1928-29, and represented it at several overseas conferences of the International Federation of University Women; as a tribute to her work the A.F.U.W. established a Freda Bage scholarship. Appointed O.B.E. in 1941, she retired in 1946 and the university conferred an honorary doctorate of laws on 26 April 1951. She died of cerebral arteriosclerosis in Brisbane on 23 October 1970, and was cremated with Anglican rites. Her estate was sworn for probate at $59 566: beside numerous personal legacies, it provided scholarships in Melbourne as memorials to her brother and funds for Melbourne and Queensland universities and their women's colleges.

A forerunner of women in public life in Queensland, Freda Bage was an unpretentious person despite her strong personality. Her portrait by William Dargie hangs in The Women's College, University of Queensland.

Her brother Edward Frederic Robert, born on 17 April 1888, graduated in civil engineering at the University of Melbourne in 1910, worked in the Queensland Railways, then joined the regular army. He served with distinction on the Mawson [q.v.] Antarctic expedition in 1910-13, joined the Australian Imperial Force in 1914 and as a captain, second-in-command of the 3rd Field Company of Engineers, was killed in action at Gallipoli in May 1915. His mother founded a commemorative engineering scholarship at the University of Melbourne in 1917.

A sister Ethel Mary (1884-1943), M. A., achieved some notice in 1926 by accepting management of a garage in Kew, Victoria, to honour the memory of a friend, Alice Anderson, who had founded it.

Her uncle Charles, born on 7 October 1859 at Colac, Victoria, graduated in medicine from the University of Melbourne in 1881, practised in South Yarra till 1923 and, having been Alfred Felton's personal physician, served as a trustee of the Felton Bequest from 1904 and as chairman from 1910. He died on 7 December 1930.

A biographical register of Queensland women (Brisb, 1939); J. R. Poynter, *Russell Grimwade* (Melb, 1967); H. F. L. Brotherton, *A college is built* (Brisb, 1973); *Woman's World*, 1 Dec 1927; *Argus*, 8 Dec 1930, 23 Aug 1943; *SMH*, 18 Aug 1938; records (Janet Clarke Hall *and* Univ Melb Ar-

chives); information from Miss G. Hughes, Miss H. Marks and Dr L. Perrett, The Women's College, Univ Qld.   JACQUELINE BELL

BAGOT, EDWARD DANIEL ALEXANDER (1893-1968), businessman and political organizer, was born on 25 December 1893 at Henley Beach, South Australia, son of Edward Arthur Bagot, who had been an Anglican clergyman, and his wife Harriet Lilian, née Massy-Dawson. He spent his childhood in Western Australia and in England where he was educated at private schools at Framlingham and Lowestoft, Suffolk. At 15 he was trained at Ilford in wireless telegraphy; this led to a job with Marconi's Wireless Telegraph Co. In 1912 he was second operator on the *Olympic* when it assisted the stricken *Titanic*.

Bagot returned to South Australia before World War I and in 1915 joined the Postmaster-General's Department in Adelaide as an engineer operator. On 20 September 1916 he married Christobel Ballantyne Bollen at West Adelaide. Next day he embarked for service with the Australian Imperial Force as a lieutenant, 1st Australian Wireless Signal Squadron. He served in Mesopotamia, was twice mentioned in dispatches and promoted captain in 1918, and wrote the squadron's history. In 1919 he returned to Australia, depressed about his prospects as a civilian. He soon returned to Mesopotamia where he organized a trading company and was a director of the *Times of Mesopotamia*. His wife joined him, and their only son was born in 1922 at Basra where Bagot was secretary of the British and Arab chambers of commerce. In 1924 he became managing director of the Eastern Transport Co., which pioneered the Beirut-Bagdad-Teheran cross-desert motor-mail service.

In 1925 Bagot returned home and established an Adelaide-Darwin motor-transport service which eventually failed. In 1928 he began working in insurance and, while president of Adelaide's Constitutional Club, in October 1930 he and others founded the Citizens' League of South Australia, a militant, rightist, political organization. As its full-time secretary until 1936, Bagot was able but rambunctious, at times overbearing, and politically naive in his public and private statements. He led local protests against the appointment of Sir Isaac Isaacs [q.v.] as governor-general. He participated in the anti-Labor Emergency Committee of South Australia, established by leading members of the Liberal Federation to contest the 1931 Federal elections but which was largely motivated by fear of Bagot's league; with Labor defeated and economic recovery at hand, the league's influence faded. Bagot had been a typical example of the many former A.I.F. officers who were prominent in sporadic conservative political organizations during the Depression.

At the 1934 Federal elections Alec Bagot stood unsuccessfully for Adelaide as an independent but held the Southern seat in the South Australian Legislative Council in 1938-41. In 1944 at Broken Hill he joined the Government Insurance Office of New South Wales, did well and moved to Sydney. He edited the institution's journal, *Security*, from 1946 and in 1951 was promoted to production supervisor. He retired in 1963 and two years later published a well-researched biography, *Coppin the great, father of the Australian theatre*.

Bagot suffered from chronic lymphatic leukaemia for four years before he died on 12 June 1968 in Sydney; his body was returned to Adelaide for burial with Anglican rites. His wife survived him; their son had been killed in action in 1943.

NSW Government Insurance Office, *Security*, 10 (1957), no 1; *Observer* (Adel), 22 May 1926; *Advertiser* (Adel), 13 June 1968; A. Bagot, Roaming around (SLSA).   JOHN LONIE

BAGOT, WALTER HERVEY (1880-1963), architect, was born on 17 March 1880 at North Adelaide, son of John Bagot, pastoralist, and his wife Lucy Josephine, née Ayers. His grandfathers Charles Hervey Bagot and Sir Henry Ayers [qq.v.1] had been pioneer settlers in South Australia. He was educated at the Collegiate School of St Peter and apprenticed to the architect E. J. Woods for four years. In 1902 Bagot went to England where he studied architecture at King's College, University of London, won the silver medal of the Worshipful Company of Carpenters and in 1904 gained associateship of the Royal Institute of British Architects. In 1905 he returned to Adelaide and formed the firm of Woods & Bagot (later Woods, Bagot, Laybourne-Smith & Irwin). He also lectured in architectural history at the South Australian School of Mines and Industries for five years. On 18 November 1908 at St Peter's Cathedral he married Josephine Margaret Barritt.

Bagot's architectural preference was for classical and traditional designs: he saw 'the striving for novelty as one of the great dangers of modernism' and came to hate 'the glasshouses of the modern architect'. He was architect for St Peter's Cathedral in 1907-45 and for the Roman Catholic archdiocese in 1905-26; for the latter he designed the chapel of the Convent of Mercy and additions to St Francis Xavier's Cathedral. As architect to the University of Adelaide in 1910-45 he designed the Bonython [q.v.] Hall, completed in 1936, and the Georgian style Barr-Smith [q.v.6, R. B. Smith] Library and associated structures. As the university grew he battled for congruity in its buildings.

In 1924 the Adelaide City Council had appointed him a referee under the Building Act, 1923. Bagot believed that the simplicity of Italian domestic architecture and of English Georgian offered the best models for South Australia's Mediterranean climate. He considered that buildings needed 'the caressing of trees to temper their hardness': the Italianate garden of his summer home in the hills was planted with exotic conifers and he was a governor of the Botanic Garden and a commissioner of the National Park, Belair. A supporter of plans to beautify Adelaide's park lands, he was a sponsor of the National Trust of South Australia.

Bagot was a passionate traveller in Europe and Italy and lectured on Italian painting at the National Gallery of South Australia. In 1962 he was made a knight of the Order of Merit of the Italian Republic for his work with the Australian-Italian Association. He was president of the South Australian Institute of Architects in 1917-19, and he was made a life fellow of the Royal Australian Institute of Architects on his retirement in 1960.

Bagot was said to have had a facility for developing excellent relations with workmen engaged on his projects. In 1948-50 he was president of the Adelaide Club, of whose founders he wrote a history (1957), and he belonged to the Pioneers' Association of South Australia. His wife described him as moving 'perfectly among the great ones'; the Bagots were concerned to show that in Adelaide 'some of us knew the way to do things as well as any citizen of the world'. Predeceased by his wife and survived by two daughters and a son, he died at North Adelaide on 27 July 1963. His estate was sworn for probate at £212 837. A portrait by Ivor Hele is held by the family.

J. M. Bagot, *Reveries in retrospect* (Adel, 1946); *Architecture in Aust*, Dec 1963; *Advertiser* (Adel), 9 July 1960, 30 July 1963; records of principal architectural works executed by E. J. Woods and W. H. Bagot 1886-1944 (SAA); family information from Mrs M. J. Chatterton, Lyndoch, and Miss M. E. Bagot, Gilberton, SA.   DEAN W. BERRY

BAILEY, ALBERT EDWARD (1868-1953), actor and theatrical manager, was born on 11 June 1868 at Auckland, New Zealand, second son of Christopher Bailey, farmer, and his wife Harriette Adelaide, née

Colgan [q.v. McCathie]. About 1879 his mother remarried, moved to Sydney and founded a large drapery store. Educated at the Cleveland Street Public School, Bert then worked as a telegram-boy and at a skating-rink, before entering vaudeville as a tambourine player and singer. In 1889 he joined a touring theatrical company led by Edmund Duggan [q.v.] and played leading roles in numerous melodramas, pantomimes and even grand opera throughout Australia. In 1900 he joined William Anderson's [q.v.] company in Sydney as a comedian. On 11 February 1902 at the Anglican Church of St Matthias, Paddington, he married an actress in the company, Ivy Isobel Gorrick.

With Duggan, Bailey wrote an Australian outback melodrama, *The squatter's daughter*, first produced by Anderson in 1907. It was highly successful commercially and became a regular stage favourite. In 1910 Bailey supervised the production of a film version with himself playing a comic 'new chum' and Duggan the bushranger Ben Hall [q.v.4]. Their partnership continued for many years and, sometimes using the combined pseudonym 'Albert Edmunds', they wrote many plays including *The man from outback* (1909) and *The native born*. In 1912 they presented their most popular success, *On our selection*, based loosely on the stories of 'Steele Rudd' [q.v. A. H. Davis]. Bailey starred as Dad Rudd, the irascible and stubborn old farmer, with the Shakespearian actor Fred MacDonald as his slow-witted son Dave; both actors remained closely identified with the roles for the rest of their lives. *On our selection* was performed repeatedly on the Australian stage until the early 1930s. In 1920 Bailey took the play to London but it failed after one month, although the critics praised his performance.

In 1912 Bailey had formed a long-lasting business association with Julius Grant and leased Anderson's King's Theatre, Melbourne. As Bailey & Grant they became one of the strongest theatrical entrepreneurial teams in Australia and produced many Australian plays. In 1921 he scored a success in *Jefferson wins through* at the King's Theatre, and next year for E. J. and Dan Carroll [q.v.], produced *The sentimental bloke*, adapted for the stage from C. J. Dennis's [q.v.] poem; he later took the part of Ginger Mick. A commercially disastrous season of Shakespeare followed in Sydney.

In 1932 Bailey emerged from one of his several retirements to co-direct with K. G. Hall and star in a film version of *On our selection* for the new Cinesound studio in Sydney. The film was a record box-office hit and three 'spin-offs' followed, all starring Bailey and MacDonald as Dad and Dave: *Grandad Rudd* (1935), *Dad and Dave come to town* (1938) and *Dad Rudd, M.P.* (1940). Bailey finally retired in 1940. In his leisure he enjoyed boating and bowls and was a member of the Savage Club, Melbourne, and Tattersall's and Rose Bay Bowling clubs, Sydney. Predeceased by his wife in 1932 and survived by his only daughter, he died on 30 March 1953 at his home at Darlinghurst, and was cremated with Anglican rites. His estate, valued for probate at £32 527, included shares in McCathie's Pty Ltd.

Physically robust, a teetotaller and a vigorous raconteur, Bert Bailey had a commanding presence on and off the stage. Dedicated to the encouragement of Australian theatre, he was always scrupulously honest and trustworthy. Critics often attacked his plays as crude farce or sentimental melodrama but, especially in his role as Dad Rudd, he enjoyed constant mass endorsement for his work.

H. Porter, *Stars of Australian stage and screen* (Adel, 1965); E. Reade, *The Australian screen* (Melb, 1975); K. G. Hall, *Directed by Ken G. Hall* (Melb, 1977); G. Hervey, 'Success and its makers', *Lone Hand*, 1 June 1914; *Theatre* (Syd & Melb), 1 July 1919; *Bulletin*, 25 Jan 1912; *T&CJ*, 17, 24 Apr 1912; *Punch* (Melb), 12 June 1913, 6 Mar 1919; *Australasian*, 24 Sept 1921, 6 Dec 1922; *Herald* (Melb), 23 Aug 1923; *Sunday Herald*, 5 Apr 1953; *Daily Mirror*, 15 Oct 1956; A. F. Pike, The history of an Australian film production company: Cinesound, 1932-1970 (M.A. thesis, ANU, 1972); information from Miss Doreen Bailey, Darlinghurst, NSW.

A. F. PIKE

BAILEY, ARTHUR RUDOLPH (1863-1938), pharmacist, was born on 21 August 1863 at Ballarat West, Victoria, son of Christopher Bailey, Irish-born merchant, and his wife Ellen, née Jones. He was educated at Ballarat College and became a commercial photographer in Ballarat, in Melbourne (where he was associated with J. W. Lindt [q.v. 5]) and at Charters Towers, Queensland. He was a medal-winner at the Colonial and Indian Exhibition, London, in 1886. He entered the Victorian College of Pharmacy in 1890 and was registered as a pharmacist on 10 October 1894. He then opened a business in Glenferrie Road, Malvern, where he worked throughout his life. On 4 February 1895 at Christ Church, Hawthorn, he married Margaret McNeil Tough.

Bailey was a council-member of the Pharmaceutical Society of Victoria in 1901-37 and president in 1903-06, 1912-15 and 1924-25. For over thirty years he represented his profession on the Food Standards Committee appointed under the provisions of the Health Act and was a driving force behind the Pure Foods Act. Elected to the Pharmacy Board of Victoria in 1912, he remained a lifelong member, was president in 1919-23, 1929-30 and 1935-36, and represented it at every interstate conference in that period. From 1909 he was a prominent leader of the Australian Pharmaceutical Conference of which he was president in 1913-23, and through it was one of the leading workers in producing the first Australian Pharmaceutical Formulary. In 1915 with Dr Sidney Plowman he compiled a *Digest of the new and more important features of the British pharmacopaeia—1914*, published by the Victorian government. From 1920 he was a director of the *Australasian Journal of Pharmacy* and became chairman of its publishing company.

Bailey gained early debating experience in the Australian Natives' Association and was president of the Malvern branch in 1903-04. He was also a conscientious magistrate on the Malvern bench, a prominent Freemason and a Rotarian. Described as hefty yet dapper, with a waxed and pointed moustache, usually with a flower in his buttonhole, he was a popular leader of his profession.

Bailey died at Malvern on 25 April 1938, survived by his wife, a daughter and three sons who became pharmacists. He was buried in Brighton cemetery and left an estate valued for probate at £24 922.

A'sian J of Pharmacy, 30 May 1938; records (Pharmacy Board of Vic, Parkville); family information.

BAILEY, HENRY STEPHEN (1876-1962), politician, was born on 9 September 1876 at Ballarat East, Victoria, youngest child of Thomas William Bailey, Kentish-born stoker, and his wife Margaret, née Kemple, of County Galway, Ireland. After education at a state school and St Patrick's College, Bailey became a clerk with a legal firm in Ballarat. Membership of the local debating society developed skills and brought him into contact with future Labor leaders, including J. H. Scullin [q.v.]. Soon after his marriage on 11 February 1902 at St Patrick's Cathedral, Ballarat, to Blanche Mary Nicholson (d. 1914), he went to the South African War as a lieutenant in the 4th Battalion, Australian Commonwealth Horse, returning later that year.

Bailey then settled at Port Fairy as a solicitor's clerk and set about establishing a solid political base. He was secretary of the town's racing club (racing was a lifelong interest) and in 1906-15 borough councillor, serving as mayor in 1912-13. Meanwhile, his activities in the Political Labor Council culminated in endorsement for the Legislative Assembly seat of Port Fairy. At the 1914 election he narrowly defeated the sitting Liberal, J. F. Duffus, despite the latter's appeal to the substantial Roman Catholic community on the education issue, while Bailey (though himself a Catholic) stood by Labor's opposition to grants to denominational schools.

In parliament Bailey was an informed speaker with an unadorned style free from personal invective. He was an enthusiastic champion of issues such as rail services and freights, land (especially soldier) settlement, and the need to develop industries and port facilities in his electorate. An effective local member, he held Port Fairy with ease until the seat was eliminated by the 1926 redistribution; next year he won adjacent Warrnambool for Labor for the first time. His success in country electorates secured for him considerable standing in his party; he became known as a spokesman for the moderate and rural elements of Labor policy, and as one who had stood loyally to principle in the conscription crisis. Thus in the Labor ministries of G. M Prendergast [q.v.] in 1924 and of E. J. Hogan [q.v.] in 1927-28 and 1929-32, Bailey became president of the Board of Land and Works, commissioner of crown lands and survey and minister of water supply.

The second Hogan minority Labor government was to be overwhelmed by the Depression crisis. Bailey was not in sympathy with the radical demands pressed by militant industrial labour, and supported the Premiers' Plan in defiance of a party ultimatum in early 1932 threatening expulsion. At the election following the government's defeat in April, his loyalty to his lifelong associate Hogan, who continued to support the plan, and his attacks on the central executive of the party cost him his endorsement; he stood as Premiers' Plan Labor candidate, only to be defeated by J. V. Fairbairn [q.v.] of the United Australia Party. After Labor's débâcle, the central executive expelled the intransigent supporters of the plan, including Bailey on 17 June. He was the only dissident to respond to a summons to defend his case, and again the only one to apply (unsuccessfully) to rejoin the party at its annual conference in January 1933.

In November Bailey contested a by-election for Warrnambool as an independent, but lost on preferences. The politician, without a seat or a party, then joined the Country Party, but failed to win Wannon at the 1934 Federal election. However, at the State election next year he won for the United Country Party his old seat of Warrnambool. His history and interests and his moderate political views made for an easy transfer to the Country Party, which under (Sir) Albert Dunstan [q.v.] stood for rural rehabilitation and promised relief for workers. Bailey's qualifications ensured him a place in Dunstan's government, formed with Labor support in April 1935; he became minister without portfolio (2 April 1935-22 June 1936), minister of labour (22 June-28 July 1936), chief secretary (22 June 1936-14 September 1943) and attorney-general (26 April 1938-14 September 1943).

The Dunstan government did not leave a remarkable legislative record though Bailey, carrying heavy responsibilities, was an active minister: the Companies Act of 1938 was regarded as his major achievement. The ministry was caught up in some scandals, but while there were allegations of improper practices relating to the licensing laws, racing, and the attempt to introduce night trotting, none against Bailey himself were sustained.

The defeat of the Dunstan government ended Bailey's career as a minister. He held his seat for a further seven years but in May 1950 was defeated, partly because he had long since left the district. He had for many years lived in Alma Road, St Kilda, on a property which he had divided into self-contained flats. He died there on 26 July 1962 and was buried in the Catholic section of St Kilda cemetery. Bailey was survived by his second wife Elizabeth, née Gibson, whom he had married at East Melbourne on 23 August 1928, by their two sons and a daughter, and by two sons of his first marriage. His estate was valued for probate at £33 608.

L. J. Louis, *Trade unions and the Depression* (Canb, 1968); *PD* (Vic), 1914-50; *Port Fairy Gazette*, 1905-26; *Labor Call*, 11 Sept 1924, 2, 9 Feb 1933; *Age*, 18 Sept 1943, 27 July 1962; family information from Mr P. Bailey, Bentleigh, Vic.   L. J. LOUIS

BAILEY, JOHN (1871-1947), trade union leader and politician, was born on 14 June 1871 at Manus Creek, New South Wales, second son of native-born parents, Thomas Henry Bailey, labourer, and his wife Rosanna, née Reilly or Colman. He left school at an early age to help his father, then worked as a shearer. On 20 November 1891 he married Esther Elphick at Tumut, where he lived until 1917.

'A bare-knuckles fighter', Bailey 'literally fought his way upwards' in shearing sheds. Determined to improve country working conditions, in 1901 he joined the Political Labor League and became an organizer for the Australian Workers' Union. 'Quick of temper and rough of tongue', he 'aimed to be the ruthless party boss', according to J. T. Lang [q.v.], one of his opponents. He was president of the A.W.U. central branch in 1915-33 and New South Wales vice-president of the general executive in 1914-23 and 1927-33. A member of the central executive of the State branch of the Australian Labor Party in 1916-18, he had helped to organize opposition to conscription, and the unions' take-over of the party and changes of the rules. He shunned newspaper publicity, rarely made long speeches and preferred to operate behind the scenes. In 1917 he had been defeated for the Federal seat of Eden-Monaro, but next year won a by-election for Monaro in the State Legislative Assembly; he represented Goulburn in 1920-25.

From 1916 Bailey and the A.W.U. had played a powerful role in the State executive, surviving a challenge from 'One Big Union' enthusiasts in 1919. Frustrated in his ambition for cabinet office, he supported J. J. G. McGirr [q.v.] and indulged in faction fights, plotting in 1920-22 against successive Labor premiers John Storey and James Dooley [qq.v.]; Bailey's allegations involved Dooley and T. D. Mutch [q.v.] in a royal commission on charges of bribery. For much of the 1920s, with the A.W.U., he was embroiled in a bitter struggle with A. C. Willis [q.v.] and the Coal and Shale Employees' Federation to dominate the State Labor party machine. In 1922 he stirred the sectarian issue which contributed to the defeat of Labor at the general election, and, to win Catholic support, had J. H. Catts [q.v.] expelled from the party by using faked delegates' badges.

At the 1923 State A.L.P. conference, Bailey was accused of complicity in the use of sliding-panel ballot-boxes. A committee chaired by Willis found him guilty. Allegations were also made about the 'crook' delegates' badges and 'his diabolical plotting to ruin his adversaries'. He was expelled from the party, as 'a menace not only to the Labor Movement, but also to the body politic'. Supported by H. E. Boote [q.v.], he was exonerated by the A.W.U.'s own inquiry, but next year E. G. Theodore [q.v.] investigated the ballot-box scandal for the party's federal executive and found the charges against Bailey proven, thereby earning his enmity. In 1925 P. C. Evans won £50 damages from Bailey who alleged that he had been financed by the Nationalist Party in the 1920 election for Goulburn.

Unable to contest Goulburn in 1925 as a Labor candidate, Bailey fought a rearguard action with the backing of the *Australian Worker*. He flirted with the Communists in 1924 but, after the 'Red Rules' were carried at the 1927 party conference, he railed against foreign plots and any connexion with Moscow. He denied responsibility for implicating Theodore and P. E. Coleman [q.v.] in charges respecting the sale of Federal seats. In December 1929 Bailey, after 'a spectacular libel suit', won £4500 damages from Willis and others for their report which had led to his expulsion from the party in 1923.

In the 1930s he was strongly anti-Lang and, as vice-president of the New South Wales federal branch of the Labor Party in 1931-34, found himself working with Theodore; in 1931 he was defeated for the Senate. Early in 1933 he and his lieutenants were out-manoeuvred and defeated in the A.W.U. State elections; but he made a surprise comeback as State president in 1938, only to have the ballot voided by the union's federal executive. He had spent part of the intervening years gold-prospecting. From 1930 he was honorary chairman of the Central Australia Gold Exploration Co. which financed an expedition to find L. H. B. Lasseter's [q.v.] lost reef. In 1931-32 he was a director of the *World*.

Survived by his wife, two sons and two daughters, Bailey died after falling off a ladder at Stanmore, Sydney, on 26 October 1947 and was cremated. His estate was valued for probate at £4822. In his lifetime he contributed substantially towards the improvement of conditions of rural workers. To the *Sydney Morning Herald* Jack Bailey was a legendary figure—'a sort of emperor in the world of rural labour, and the most theatrical figure in his union's history'.

I. L. Idriess, *Lasseter's last ride* (Syd, 1931); J. T. Lang, *I remember* (Syd, 1956); L. F. Crisp, *Ben Chifley* (Melb, 1961); I. Young, *Theodore* (Syd, 1971); *Aust Worker*, 14 Nov 1918, 26 Sept, 3, 10 Oct, 21 Nov 1923; *Smith's Weekly* (Syd), 8 Mar 1919; *SMH*, 11, 13, 16 Aug, 17, 19, 21 Nov 1923, 22 Apr, 24, 25 Nov 1924, 16 Jan, 19, 20 June 1925, 4, 8 Aug 1928, 27, 29, 30 Nov, 3-6 Dec 1929, 4 Mar, 9 Dec 1931, 7 Mar 1933, 18, 19 Jan 1938, 27 Oct 1947; I. E. Young, Conflict within the New South Wales Labor Party 1919-1932 (M.A. thesis, Univ Syd, 1961); F. Farrell, International socialism and Australian labour (Ph.D thesis, ANU, 1975); Bailey papers (ML).   MARTHA RUTLEDGE

BAILEY, JOHN FREDERICK (1866-1938), horticulturist, was born on 5 August 1866 at Brisbane, son of Frederick Manson Bailey [q.v.3], botanist, and his wife Anna Maria, née Waite. Educated at the Normal School, Brisbane, and at Divinity Hall, the Presbyterian training college, in 1889 he became assistant to his father in the botanical branch of Queensland's Department of Agriculture. They travelled widely throughout the colony to collect, describe and evaluate its flora, and published their discoveries: John's appeared in the *Queens-*

land Agricultural Journal. He published articles on economic botany (1897) and on the plants of the rabbit-infested country, Bulloo River (1898); but his most notable work at this time was his 'Report on the timber trees of the Herberton district, North Queensland' (1899) which discussed the utility of trees on the Atherton Tableland. In 1901 he was a member of an expedition to the Gulf of Carpentaria with Dr W. E. Roth [q.v.], the northern protector of Aboriginals.

In 1905 Bailey became director of the Botanic Gardens, Brisbane, and developed his interests in horticulture and economic botany, writing articles for popular publications and continuing his work on tropical timbers. He was active in the Royal Society of Queensland as secretary in 1893-1905 and president in 1909, and he was also secretary for ten years of the Horticultural Society. He lectured effectively on botany at the Queensland Agricultural College and on his father's death in 1915, while remaining director of the gardens, also became government botanist.

Two years later Bailey was offered the directorship of the Botanic Garden, Adelaide. One reason he accepted was that South Australia was prepared to fund its gardens more generously than Queensland. In 1917-32 he ensured that the Botanic Garden was confirmed in the floricultural emphasis which had developed since the death of M. R. Schomburgk [q.v.6]. Bailey changed the garden's landscape, introducing 'windowing' effects, and popularized its displays of bedding flowers, particularly dahlias. A modest, unassuming director, his policy was to 'follow nature just as closely as ever' he could. By 1925 he was said to have effected 'striking' aesthetic improvements. He visited country towns to advise on the planting of parks and the eastern States to confer with other directors. He was president of the Dahlia Society of South Australia, vice-president of the State branch of the Wattle Day League and an office-bearer in the Field Naturalists' Section of the Royal Society of South Australia.

Upon retiring in 1932 Bailey returned to Brisbane, where he died of coronary vascular disease on 19 May 1938. He had married Agnes Sophia Rayer in Brisbane on 21 December 1893. They had a daughter and two sons: Frederick Manson was commissioner for forests in New South Wales in 1970-71 and John Rayer became curator of the Botanic Gardens, Brisbane.

Adelaide Botanic Garden, *Centenary volume 1855-1955* (Adel, 1955); *V&P* (LA Qld), 1906, 2, 146, (SA), 1918, 3 (89); R. H. Pulleine, 'The botanical colonisation of the Adelaide plains', *PRGSSA*, 35 (1935); C. T. White, 'The Bailey family and its place in the botanical history of Australia', *JRHSQ*, 3 (1936-47); *Observer* (Adel), 30 June 1923, 18 Apr 1925; Aust botanists biog files (Basser Lib, Canb).   PETER VALLEE

BAILEY, MARGARET ANN MONT-GOMERY (1879-1955), headmistress, was born on 9 June 1879 at Toowoomba, Queensland, eldest child of John Bailey, farmer, and his wife Jane, née McCurdy. Educated at the Newnham School for Girls, Toowoomba, she won an exhibition to the University of Sydney (B.A., 1900), then taught at Rockhampton Girls' Grammar School in 1900-03 and 1908-11 and at Girton College, Toowoomba, in 1903-07. In 1912-14 she studied abroad. Unable to make herself – an honours graduate in French – understood in Paris, Margaret Bailey became interested in modern methods of language teaching; she gained the International Phonetic Association (University College, London) diplomas in English, French and German, as well as the diploma of education from the University of London, while studying at the London Day Training College. She also studied German at the famous 'Institut Tilly' in Berlin, run by William Tilly, an Australian.

In 1914 Margaret Bailey joined the staff of Ascham School, Darling Point, Sydney, and in September with Kathleen Gilman Jones [q.v.], another staff-member, bought the school from the retiring headmaster H. J. Carter [q.v.]. In 1916 Miss Bailey became principal and sole proprietor of Ascham, and committed the girls to a khaki uniform by buying material from army disposals. Interested in overseas educational developments and able to enlist the enthusiastic co-operation of her staff, in 1922 she introduced a modified version of the 'Dalton plan' into the senior school, after learning about it from a staff-member Eva Fry, who had been sent a copy of a letter and an article describing the scheme in the *Times Literary Supplement* (20, 27 May 1920). This plan, evolved by Helen Parkhurst, an American admirer of Maria Montessori, took its name from the high school at Dalton, Massachusetts, where it was applied in 1920. At Ascham there were from two to four lessons a week in each subject and assignment-work was done in free periods or at home. Although pupils were encouraged to work ahead if they wished, the week's work in all subjects was generally expected to be completed within the week. The plan, with some modifications, has been carried on by her successors; the self-directed method of study and individual assistance available in free periods has benefited both the quicker and slower learners.

A gifted and enterprising teacher, Margaret Bailey taught classics to senior classes and was an early exponent of the direct method of teaching French. Known to her pupils as 'Mab', she treated each girl as an individual. In 1937 she incorporated the school as a non-profit-making company with a council of governors. A life-governor herself, she resigned as principal in 1946. The school had become one of the best known in Australia and the 74 pupils of 1914 had increased to almost 400. An excellent businesswoman, she had financed by her own efforts the purchase in 1930 of The Knoll (now called Macintosh House after her colleague and dearest friend), as well as the construction of three new buildings. Sir Edward Knox's [q.v.5] house, Fiona, was bought in 1948. No financial appeals were ever made to parents.

Margaret Bailey was active in the Headmistresses' Association of Australia and the New Education Fellowship. She was also vice-president and president of the Sydney University Women Graduates' Association, an executive member of the Australian Federation of University Women and a councillor of the rival Kambala Church of England School for Girls. A practising Presbyterian, she showed her eagerness for exact knowledge and openness to new ideas in her keen interest in critical work on biblical texts and the controversial reinterpretations of Dr Samuel Angus [q.v.]. She died peacefully in her sleep on 5 June 1955 at Roseville and was cremated. She left her estate, valued for probate at £26629, to her sister and eldest niece. Her portrait by H. F. Abbott is at Ascham.

M. Flower (ed), *The story of Ascham School* (Syd, 1952); M. D. Roberts, *50 years of the Dalton plan* (Syd, 1972); Ascham School, N. Weekes papers (ML *and* Rare Books Div, Fisher Lib, Univ Syd); information from Mrs A. Weekes.
                              MARGARET LUNDIE

BAILLIE; *see* LAMINGTON

BAILLIEU, WILLIAM LAWRENCE (1859-1936), financier and politician, was born on 29 April 1859 at Queenscliff, Victoria, second son of JAMES GEORGE BAILLIEU and his wife Emma Lawrence, née Pow. James was born at Haverfordwest, Pembrokeshire, England, on 13 March 1832. He was the third son among fifteen children of Lambert Francis Baillieu (1802-1861), dancing-master and musician, and grandson of Etienne Lambert Baillieu(x), who had come to Britain about 1790 from Liège, where the family had been embroiderers and mercers. At 17 James went to sea. In January 1853, while anchored in quarantine inside Port Phillip Heads in the *Priscilla*, he decided to escape the attentions of a drunken master by swimming to land, not to the nearest beach but to Queenscliff, two miles across a wild water-way. After a short time in hiding James gained employment as a boatman in the health service. He attended the arrival of the *Australia*, loaded with female government immigrants, and on 3 November married one of them, Emma Pow, a 'strong healthy and most lovely girl', baptized at Marksbury, Somerset, on 25 November 1838. The young couple lived first in a tent and then in a cottage on the beach at Queenscliff, where ten sons and four daughters were born to them.

James spent thirty years in the government service — as a boatman for health and customs, and after 1881 as a lighthouse-keeper at Point Lonsdale — but he also involved himself in the growth of Queenscliff to a fashionable watering-place. In 1881 he erected a large hotel, grand enough to attract the governor of Victoria for holidays. The thirteen Baillieu children who survived infancy attended the Queenscliff Common School — where they came under the influence of Robert Jordan, a notable teacher — and were active in local sporting events, especially boating and horse-racing, two family passions. James retired from the lighthouse service to share the management of the hotel with his third son George. Both were prominent in local affairs, each serving as mayor. James was described as 'very independent and honest in his opinions', though 'not what is known as a sharp businessman'. Nevertheless the family achieved some wealth as well as local notability, though only George was to remain at Queenscliff; the rest of the family moved to Melbourne in 1885. When James died at Camberwell on 10 December 1897, his sons buried him at Queenscliff, at his own request without benefit of undertaker or hearse; they themselves prepared him for burial, and bore him to his grave on a wagonette. Emma survived him, remaining a dominant figure in the family until her death in 1908.

It became a tradition among the Baillieus to regard loyalty to the family as the highest duty of all, and a family company formed later was named simply 'Mutual Trust'. William Lawrence became the pivot around whom the family fortunes, and much else in Australia, turned. The eldest son, James Lambert (1855-1890), worked briefly with him; the next three were little involved in William's affairs, but the five youngest all played significant roles in business. EDWARD LLOYD (1867-1939), known as 'Prince', became a sharebroker, pastoralist and racehorse owner. Arthur Sydney (1872-1943) made his career in the family estate agency, and as a company director. Richard Percy Clive (1874-1941), known as 'Joe', was a foundation partner with Prince in the family sharebroking firm. Norman Horace (1878-1955) and Maurice Howard Lawrence (1883-1961), known as 'Jac', were both sharebrokers and company directors. Two of the Baillieu daughters married close business associates of William. The network of business relationships which developed around the Baillieus had little formal structure, and friends and rivals alike referred to it as a 'group' rather than an empire.

At 14 'Willie' Baillieu left school for a job in the Queenscliff branch of Henry 'Money' Miller's [q.v.5] Bank of Victoria. 6 ft. 4 ins. (193 cm) in height and a notable athlete, he loved boating which won him an influential friend in 1878 when he joined the crew of the yacht sailed by the wealthy Edward Latham [q.v.5], founder of the Carlton brewery. An extraordinarily close friendship developed; 'deep affection, perhaps unusual between men, bound us together intimately', Baillieu later wrote. He fell in love with Latham's only daughter Bertha Martha (1865-1925), an attachment he announced to the Queenscliff population by naming his own small boat after her.

In 1882 William transferred to the bank's branch in the mining town of Maryborough. There he met the mayor Alfred Outtrim [q.v.] and B. J. Fink [q.v.4], a powerful promoter of Victoria's boom, whose brilliant younger brother Theodore [q.v.] was to become a friend and an abiding — and liberal — influence. Baillieu also became friendly with Donald Munro, son of James [q.v.5]. In 1885 he left the bank and moved to Melbourne where he joined Donald Munro in an estate agency, with financial support from James Munro's Federal Bank and a personal guarantee from Latham.

As an auctioneer the 26-year-old Baillieu was a resounding success. With the land boom at its height there was no lack of agents trying to sell their fellow citizens real estate, at the same time lending them the money to buy it. He was described as 'the greatest auctioneer of all'; he had imagination as a promoter, a compelling presence on the stand, and a speed in disposing of business which left onlookers gasping. In 1887 Munro & Baillieu surpassed all others in the volume of business done, selling land worth more than £3 million. At 28 Baillieu became a noted figure in the Melbourne business world, which knew him henceforth as 'W.L.'. On 7 December at St Jude's Church of England, Carlton, he married Bertha

Latham, and went to live with her parents in their mansion at Kew. Bertha's mother died in 1894, and next year Latham married William's sister Emma Elizabeth, who thus became her brother's mother-in-law.

The young auctioneers inevitably became involved in land speculation themselves, in a business community deeply enmeshed in an intricate game in which Victorians borrowed money from London to lend to each other, unhindered by banking laws protecting society against its own financial recklessness. Munro & Baillieu encountered liquidity problems as early as 1889, and met them, in the fashionable way, by accelerating both borrowing and lending. The collapse, when it came in 1891-92, was perhaps the most complete of all recorded bank crashes. The Victorian government passed legislation under which formal bankruptcy could be avoided if creditors agreed to compound the debts of firms or individuals, with the approval of the court. Munro & Baillieu had no hope of surviving the collapse of several land companies with which they were involved, especially while James Munro's Federal Bank lurched towards disaster. In July 1892 Theodore Fink, as Baillieu's solicitor, applied to the court for permission to call a meeting of creditors, a less happy task than his role as master of ceremonies at W.L.'s wedding. On 26 July, at separate gatherings, creditors of the partnership and of Baillieu himself agreed to accept 6d. in the pound. More remarkable than W.L.'s involvement in the land boom was his exceptionally expert recovery from the depression, though the later success of the Baillieus made it inevitable that this early discomfiture would echo in public memory.

The partnership with Munro was dissolved in 1892, and his first step in restoring his fortunes was to establish W. L. Baillieu & Co. as a new estate agency, in which he was soon joined by his younger brother Arthur. At about the same time Prince Baillieu formed, with Clive, the sharebroking firm of E. L. & C. Baillieu. The brothers worked closely together, dealing in land and shares and, increasingly, in mining property. Mining was to fascinate W.L. all his life: his first involvement seems to have been in organizing the exploitation of the black coal-seam at Outtrim, Gippsland, in 1890, while thirty years later he was grub-staking osmium prospectors in Tasmania. The Baillieus became deeply involved in the Indian summer of Victorian gold-mining, with the deep-lead Duke United at Maryborough their first major success. Even more spectacular was the Jubilee quartz-mine at Scarsdale, bought in 1889; its success was

largely due to technical innovation, which W.L. was already adept at organizing though he himself had no technical training.

He had an increasing number of local associates in mining and other ventures, but the chief source of capital had still to be sought in England. E. L. & C. Baillieu had built up a considerable arbitrage business with London brokers, and in 1897 W.L. set sail for Britain to broaden this connexion. London had reason to look askance at young colonials 'with a bit of quartz in one hand and a magnifying glass in the other', and W.L.'s success in gaining acceptance in useful circles in the City illustrates his persuasive personality. A friend described him at this time as 'one of the wicked bears who are always ranging around the world with a view of getting as much out of it as possible', and there must have seemed a strong predatory element in W.L.'s unceasing search for profitable fields. A longer perspective suggests that behind his obvious delight in managing and making money – he is said to have become very rich by the turn of the century – he had also a more elevated instinct for national development, which he identified, habitually but not exclusively, with mining and related industries.

In August 1901 W.L. was elected to the Victorian Legislative Council as member for the Northern Province. Sitting as a non-party member he supported liberal policies of economic development and moderate social reform, including old-age pensions, increases in teachers' salaries and factory legislation (showing special concern for procedures to avoid and settle strikes). He supported the White Australia policy, but defended Chinese against discrimination. Years later the Labor member George Prendergast [q.v.] observed that 'he was generally considered a somewhat liberal-minded man in view of his great wealth at that period'. When John Murray [q.v.] became premier in 1909, Baillieu accepted office as minister of public health and commissioner of public works and was government leader in the council. In 1912, when Murray was succeeded by W. A. Watt [q.v.], W.L. relinquished his portfolios, but continued as honorary minister and government leader in the council. He was content with a political power that was unobtrusive but real, and much greater than his formal positions implied.

In 1902 Prince temporarily withdrew from E. L. & C. Baillieu to spend a highly profitable decade as a member of the London Stock Exchange. In 1904 W.L. handed over management of the estate agency to Arthur, as his own interests became more diverse; henceforth he described his profession simply as 'investor'. Theodore Fink had invited him to be a director of the *Herald* in 1893 and he joined Fink on the board of Wunderlich [q.v.] Ltd in 1908. In 1904 he had joined three other boards: the Dunlop Pneumatic Tyre Co. of Australasia Ltd; the Mount Morgan Gold Mining Co. Ltd; and the Carlton Brewery Ltd (in response to a solemn petition from its directors, prompted by respect for his abilities as well as for his wife's substantial shareholding). In the same year Montague Cohen [q.v.] introduced him to A. J. F. de Bavay [q.v.], the Belgian chemist of the Foster brewery, who was devising a flotation process for extracting metals from the mountains of tailings around the Broken Hill silver-lead mines. W.L. was impressed, and with Prince and Cohen formed de Bavay's Treatment Co. Ltd (re-formed in 1909 as Amalgamated Zinc (de Bavay's) Ltd) to exploit the process.

Despite his preoccupation with Victorian gold-mining, W.L. had long had interests in mining ventures in Tasmania and New South Wales, and in 1906 he was to join the board of the important Hampden-Cloncurry copper-mine in Queensland. His involvement with Broken Hill had a different order of significance; he committed himself to the future of the great lode with a boldness of vision for his own and the national future. His principal associates included the Australian-born London sharebrokers Lionel Robinson and William Clark; Lionel's younger brother W. S. Robinson [q.v.]; Francis Govett, another London stockbroker, with extensive interests in Western Australia; John L. Wharton, H. J. Daly and the American mining engineer and future president, known locally as 'Hail Columbia' Hoover [q.v.]. In 1905-06 the group brought together a number of related interests in Broken Hill. W.L. joined the board of the reconstructed North Broken Hill Mining Co. (after 1912 North Broken Hill Ltd), of which he was to be chairman in 1926-31. With Robinson Clark & Co. he raised capital to develop the mine, only to find that its future lay in the despised Victoria Cross lease, which Prince and W.L. had bought as a speculative bargain in 1902 and sold to Norths in 1904. Norths provided de Bavay with a site for a flotation plant, and dumps of tailings. In 1906 W.L. joined Clark, Hoover and Govett in forming the Zinc Corporation to exploit another flotation process; the corporation eventually became a great mine-owner as well as a processor when it acquired the Broken Hill South Blocks in 1911. In 1912 a new company, Minerals Separation and de Bavay's Processes Australia Pty Ltd, was formed with W.L. as chairman, to develop flotation processes for other minerals. W. S. Robinson later wrote

that 'no metallurgical development of the last fifty years ... added so much to the wealth of the world as the flotation process ... The part our group played was mostly due to W. L. Baillieu, whose belief in the success of flotation never wavered'. At the time when Broken Hill Proprietary was deciding that its future lay in iron and steel and away from Broken Hill, these loosely-related Anglo-Australian groups entrenched themselves at the northern and southern ends of the lode; they drew the old Broken Hill South Silver Mining Co. into their orbit as well as North Broken Hill Ltd and with new processes and new ore discoveries proved that there was more wealth in the famous Hill than had yet been removed from it.

Among W.L.'s other interests at this time was the Melbourne Electricity Co., whose advisory board he joined in 1908. Anxious to develop electricity generation from brown coal deposits in the La Trobe valley, he formed first a syndicate and later the Great Morwell Coal Mining Co. By 1914 a plan had been drawn up, with the involvement of Siemens of Berlin, to establish a Lurgi plant in the valley, the gas to be piped to Melbourne for electricity generation. When, in 1918, the State Electricity Commission was eventually established, Baillieu spoke proudly in the Legislative Council of his long 'obsession' with the prospect of massive electrification from brown coal, and claimed that the terms under which private enterprise had been willing to launch it 'would have been highly satisfactory to the State, and absolutely fair'. The public debate had convinced him, reluctantly, 'that the country would not permit the great undertaking to be taken up by private enterprise'.

In 1910 W.L. built his group a home in Collins Street. A massive building, it housed the offices of some fifty companies of vastly varying significance, all provided with common services by Secretariat Pty Ltd, founded by W.L.'s brother-in-law Edward Shackell. Collins House became, for sixty years, the symbol of Australian capitalism to its socialist critics; its rivals called it 'Glenrowan House' and alleged that its motto was 'when on thin ice skate fast'. The very scale of the Baillieu success aroused envy and animus, just as the qualities which brought that success inspired admiration in associates. The young W. S. Robinson, brought up with prejudices against land-boomers and Baillieu in particular, came to regard him as 'the greatest of all men who set out to develop Australia': Robinson admired his boldness of conception, and what W. M. Hughes [q.v.] described as 'his dauntless courage and tenacity of purpose'. W.L. himself once complained to fellow directors that 'the trouble with you fellows is that you're more concerned with not being wrong than with being right'. Although his formal education was not extensive, he had great natural skill with figures, and an earthy directness of speech and writing. A shrewd judge of men, he sought technical advice wisely and used it well, negotiated with subtlety and force and chose excellent managers whom he supported loyally. He also had the rare quality of valuing diversity of view; 'in every good zoo', he remarked, 'you've got to have one of every kind of animal'. If there remained an enigmatic quality in his personality, it lay less in any ethical ambiguity – despite the murmurings of business rivals less clever than he – than in his reticence concerning his deepest motives, his preference for informal rather than formal authority, and his disdain for public honours; he twice rebuffed offers of a knighthood.

His private life was simple, though he lived well. Heathfield, his home in Camberwell, was large and comfortable, and Sefton, which he built at Mount Macedon early in the century, included a golf course among its amenities. W.L.'s four sons and four daughters were born between 1889 and 1904; CLIVE LATHAM (BARON BAILLIEU) (1889-1967), the eldest, left Melbourne Church of England Grammar School in 1908 for Trinity College in the University of Melbourne, proceeding to Magdalen College, Oxford, in 1911 to read law. He rowed for Oxford in 1913, was called to the Bar of the Inner Temple in 1914, and married William Clark's daughter Ruby in 1915. W.L. was an attentive father. His social life was restricted to his family and a few close friends, such as the architect W. R. Butler, the artist (Sir) Arthur Streeton, and in later years (Sir) Keith Murdoch [qq.v.]. In middle age he developed a strong interest in country life, and acquired a number of properties, mainly in Queensland and Victoria. Two of his sons, Harry Latham and Tom Latham, made their careers as pastoralists; the youngest, James Latham, trained for the law.

When war broke out in 1914 Baillieu expressed surprise and apprehension, predicting economic dislocation and serious unemployment: 'My thoughts fly particularly to the working classes, who will be most seriously affected by hostilities', he told the Legislative Council. Australian base-metal mining was heavily dependent on German contracts; Baillieu took part in the rapid negotiation of a government guarantee for copper producers, which protected Mount Morgan and Hampden-Cloncurry, and in August he called a conference of Broken Hill companies and unions at Collins House which produced a plan for half-time working to prevent extensive lay-offs on the Hill. Before the war Broken Hill had also relied on German and other foreign smelters for processing half its lead output and almost all its zinc. The brash beginnings of Hughes's campaign against German dominance in the metals trade annoyed Baillieu, but when the minister recruited W. S. Robinson as architect of a new Imperial structure for the industry W.L. became a crucial, if wary, supporter. Robinson had persuaded W.L. that the war would be a long one, and revived the proposal that the Collins House group should acquire B.H.P.'s large smelter at Port Pirie. The Broken Hill Associated Smelters Pty Ltd was formed to take over the works in May 1915; W.L. was chairman in 1915-33, and under Robinson and Colin Fraser [q.v.] the works were rejuvenated and production greatly increased. At about the same time W.L. was involved in arranging for Mount Morgan, with Hampden-Cloncurry, to replace German interests as shareholders in Electrolytic Refining and Smelting Co., which operated a copper refinery at Port Kembla. Production was increased, and a fabricating plant was established by a new company, Metal Manufactures Ltd, incorporated in 1916 with W.L. on the board.

Australian capacity to smelt zinc remained extremely limited. Baillieu had inspected processes in Germany in 1911, but it was not until 1915 that the Collins House group explored the possibility of establishing electrolytic smelting of zinc in Australia, collecting information and experts in the United States of America; W.L., knowing that only Tasmania had electricity resources capable of supporting zinc smelting, negotiated with its government and chose a site at Risdon. In 1916 the Electrolytic Zinc Co. of Australia Ltd was formed; technical problems in the pilot plant caused almost everyone but W.L. to panic, but skill and luck averted disaster. The attempt to raise £1 million in 1920, the largest float of its kind in Australia to that time, seemed likely to fail disastrously until he pledged the entire resources of Mutual Trust – in effect the Baillieu family fortunes – in support of the expansion of the plant. This act, which sufficed to save the company, was described by Robinson as 'one of the boldest actions in Melbourne's financial history'. It was too bold for two of the Baillieu brothers; convinced that 'William was off his head' they vainly sought ways of dissuading without confronting him.

W.L.'s wartime activities were not restricted to the mining industry. In August 1914 he attended the prime minister's conference on economic policies for war, and he remained 'much within the vortex of things'. His work as chairman of the Victorian State Munitions Committee in 1915-18 was highly praised by the minister for defence, and in 1918 he joined Treasurer Watt's Commonwealth Finance Council to plan post-war reconstruction. In 1915 he also contributed to policy-making in the marketing of primary production, when he urged compulsory government purchase and resale of the wheat crop. His proposal is said to have influenced the establishment of the compulsory pool scheme, under the Australian Wheat Board, in 1916. He advocated the pool as an exception to his general rule that 'the less the government interferes with trade the better it is for the community and for itself'; indeed he argued later for a merely voluntary pool, though by that time his opposition was mainly to the strident demands of the nascent Country Party, which he saw as the harbinger of 'socialism'.

The emergence of militant country organizations was but one symptom of the increasing bitterness which developed in the later years of the war. As early as 1916 W.L.'s moderate interventionism had been attacked, in his own electorate, as too liberal. He reacted to the new militancy of the Left with an outspoken championing of free enterprise, supported Hughes in the conscription debate, and contemptuously rebutted an attack mounted on him in Federal parliament in August 1917 by Frank Anstey [q.v.], who revived the allegation of German associations. When the Victorian government fell, there were rumours that W.L. would seek the premiership, but instead he resigned his offices in November 1917; he later accepted the unofficial leadership of the Legislative Council. Early in 1922 he retired from the council; in a farewell statement to his constituents he attacked both the Country Party's sectionalism and Labor's socialism, expressing the fear that the two might combine.

Although Baillieu did not escape the prevalent hardening of general political attitudes, he retained much of his liberal pragmatism on specific issues. In labour relations he remained flexible and innovative, though sometimes abrasive in particular negotiations. He fully supported (Sir) Gerald Mussen's [q.v.] introduction at Port Pirie of staff amenities and safety standards unprecedented in the area: Mussen had been sent early in 1919 to Broken Hill to improve workers' conditions but he had been forced to withdraw when the 'Big Strike' of 1919-20 erupted. W.L. did not visit Broken Hill during the strike, though he chaired a committee of company representatives in Melbourne; his role at an important meeting of management and unions which was ul-

timately called at Collins House is said to have been liberal and constructive. E. J. Holloway later praised his attitude in labour matters, and gave him the main credit for accepting proposals for the famous 'lead bonus'. W.L. also gave thought to international aspects of the labour question: in 1919 the Australian government sent to Hughes at the Versailles Conference his proposal 'for a democratic programme to secure better conditions for working men'.

During the war W.L. had expressed concern for the future of Australian servicemen. With his brothers he donated £25 000 – the largest single gift – to the Australian Soldiers' Repatriation Fund in 1918, and after the war they purchased a mansion in Brighton to become, as Anzac House, a repatriation hostel for disabled veterans. The brothers also set up the Baillieu Educational Trust for the benefit of the children of dead or wounded soldiers. Three of W.L.'s sons had served with distinction in France and Britain: Clive returned with the rank of lieut-colonel, after serving in the Australian Flying Corps and then the Royal Air Force (1918-19); he was appointed O.B.E. and was mentioned in dispatches. Harry served in the British Army, winning the Military Cross for gallantry on the Western Front; Tom joined the Australian Flying Corps and was awarded the Distinguished Flying Cross. By this time their mother's health was failing; Bertha Baillieu died in 1925, and her unmarried daughter Vere took her place as housekeeper at Heathfield and Sefton, homes which remained the centre of W.L.'s existence.

W.L.'s life in his sixties was, however, scarcely autumnal. As W. S. Robinson later recalled, 'the chief never really grew old'. He joined new boards – for example Yarra Falls Ltd in 1924, and Austral Silk and Cotton in 1927. Ever on the watch for new ventures, he explored the potential value of copper and oil in New Guinea and irrigation in Western Australia, and would have pursued the development of the vast ore body discovered at Mount Isa in 1923 had early reports not discouraged him. Under his chairmanship Amalgamated Zinc began in 1924 to investigate the possibility of establishing a paper industry in Tasmania, and in 1927 the Collins House group joined in forming Tasmanian Paper, forerunner of a company which established production in 1936. W.L. was said to be especially sympathetic to this venture because it satisfied three criteria he now applied to new investments: the product was equally important in war or peace; the raw material was available in Australia and war would not cut off supplies; and the product was not subject to substitution. The lessons of 1914 had been well learned, and another lesson also: the emergence of political extremism persuaded him that mere mining leases were a form of property too subject to the whims of unpredictable governments, while processing and manufacturing had greater security if soundly based.

The manipulation of money itself never ceased to fascinate him, and he enjoyed his almost legendary status as 'Australia's Money King'. Prime Minister (Viscount) Bruce [q.v.] recalled his embarrassment when a Baillieu syndicate under-bid the Australian government's regular London agent in tendering for a Commonwealth Loan. For reasons of continuity Bruce felt obliged to accept the higher London bid; he explained his motive to W.L. and was surprised and impressed when he made neither public nor private protest.

By the 1920s the international strength of the Collins House group was well established. W. S. Robinson's London office as 'controller' for the group gained an impetus of its own; W.L. supported Robinson in the decision to join in the British Metals Corporation rather than set up a separate marketing organization for the Broken Hill group. In 1926 it was decided that W.L.'s son Clive, who had gone to the Melbourne Bar after the war, should join the burgeoning London operation; he was well established there by 1929 when his father and Robinson were jointly awarded the gold medal of the Institute of Mining and Metallurgy 'in recognition of their services in the mineral development of the Empire'.

The Depression, rather than development, was to dominate W.L.'s last years. The slump in metal prices in 1926 presaged wider disasters. The Hampden-Cloncurry copper-mine closed, all W.L.'s financial adroitness was required to save the Port Kembla refinery, and Broken Hill itself was hard pressed to avoid drastic retrenchments. Now much quoted in the press, he looked to increased population and American investment as the country's chief remedies, but the Wall Street slump brought new dimensions of difficulty. In 1930 W.L. pleaded for major efforts to rationalize industry, and to break down 'the wall of suspicion' dividing employer and employee. He rejected orthodox remedies for the Depression: 'such deflation would bankrupt half the businesses in Australia, and who would employ all the staffs and employees?'. (He was himself secretly subsidizing the employment of professional men in state investigatory projects.) He was more sympathetic to the Premiers' Plan than most businessmen, and was wrestling with 'a scheme to lower capital values by an agreed writing down which would reduce the interest bill', when his health suddenly collapsed

in 1932. Symptoms of physical restlessness, loss of memory, uncharacteristic indecision, and irrational fears – including a belief that he was insolvent – beset him. Unable to work, he retired from most of his offices; Clive and Vere took him to Britain, where he died of pneumonia on 6 February 1936, and was buried at Windlesham, Surrey. To the surprise of many, but not of those who knew his skill in avoiding unnecessary financial commitments, his estate was valued at under £60 000.

Prince Baillieu lived on until 14 July 1939. He had worked closely with W.L., but to the public he was best known as a racing man; a member of the Victoria Racing Club Committee from 1895, and honorary treasurer from 1918 until his death, he owned in whole or part many famous horses, including the 1924 Melbourne Cup winner Backwood (in which W.L. had a share) and the legendary Ajax, which in 1937-40 won 36 out of 46 races, including 18 in succession. He once remarked that he had kept his business records exactly to the farthing, but had no idea of the extent of his racing investments. He had a substantial property, Elleston, in New South Wales. Like other Baillieus, he was an active Freemason. On his death-bed he told his nephew that 'everything the Baillieu family has they owe to your Uncle Willie'; and one-fifth of his estate of almost £500 000 was left to the University of Melbourne Library 'in memory of William Lawrence Baillieu'.

The most prominent Baillieu of the next generation was W.L.'s eldest son Clive. His career was international, with its focus in London rather than Melbourne, but he always regarded himself as an Australian who happened to live and work much of the time in Britain. Circumstances delayed the launching of his business career until his mid-thirties, but its progress then was meteoric. After a period working with Robinson in the London office, he joined the board of the Zinc Corporation and immersed himself in mining matters. In 1936 he and Robinson established the New Broken Hill Consolidated mine to the south of the Zinc Corporation leases, and saw it become 'the heart of the field'. The Zinc Corporation, drifting apart from the original Collins House group, merged with the Imperial Smelting Corporation Ltd to become the Consolidated Zinc Corporation in 1949; after a further merger, Baillieu became in 1962-65 deputy chairman of Rio Tinto Zinc Corporation Ltd, a giant company with interests in America, Europe and Australia. These, and related interests, made him a force in the world mining industry.

Baillieu was also involved in insurance, in banking (on the boards of the English,

Scottish and Australian Bank from 1929 and the Midland Bank from 1944), and in the New Zealand Loan and Mercantile Agency Ltd from 1924, becoming joint president in 1962-65 after the formation of Dalgety & New Zealand Loan Ltd. The company he always regarded as chief among his loyalties, however, was Dunlop Rubber Co. Ltd whose board he joined in 1929; he became deputy chairman in 1945, chairman in 1949 and president in 1957, and saw it develop into a highly diversified industrial giant. His involvement with the international rubber industry brought him close links with the United States, and a concern for the stability of rubber supplies which became important in the period of emergency in post-war Malaya.

Clive shared his father's pragmatic liberalism. In 1928 he was approached to stand for the House of Commons as a Liberal, but decided against a political career. His involvement in public affairs was, however, continuous. In 1929-39 he sat as the United Kingdom representative in Australia on the Imperial Communications Advisory Committee, and in 1930-47 was an Australian representative on the Imperial Economic Committee. As Europe darkened into war, he was, with Bruce, one of the principal interpreters of Australian opinion to Britain, and vice versa. He was appointed C.M.G. in 1929 and K.B.E. in 1938.

When war broke out Baillieu was asked to go to the United States, where he played a very effective part organizing supplies of raw materials. A skilled, patient negotiator, who listened with courtesy and could sum up discussion with a persuasively phrased proposal, he proved as effective in Allied councils as he was in boardrooms, and he had an almost unrivalled knowledge of world trade in raw materials.

Returning to Britain, Baillieu was asked by the government to act as chairman of the Fairey Aviation Co., then in difficulties. In 1944 he became deputy chairman of the Federation of British Industry; as its chairman in 1945-47, and as a member of the National Industrial Council in 1945-53, he was deeply involved in efforts to revitalize British industry after the war. Twenty years earlier, he and his father had tried to persuade Australians to seek capital from America and not to rely, through mistaken loyalties, on London alone; in 1948 in Melbourne he argued that Britain's greatness was not over, and that Australia should participate in her recovery. That year he led a trade mission to Argentina; in 1950 he made a world tour of Dunlop plants, pausing in Melbourne to warn of the dangers of communist insurgency in south-east Asia. In 1953 he was created Baron Baillieu, of Sefton

in Australia and Parkwood in Surrey, the first Australian hereditary peer with sons to succeed him.

Lord Baillieu gave time to causes, as well as to companies and governments. He was deeply interested in the English Speaking Union, spanning as it did his own allegiances to Britain, Australia and the United States, and was its chairman from 1951. He was a member of the General Advisory Council of the British Broadcasting Corporation in 1947-52, and after 1958 a governor of the National Institute of Economic and Social Research. Always concerned to improve the quality of management, he chaired the Committee on Industrial Management which produced the 'Baillieu Report', was a member of the first council of the British Institute of Management, and later its first president.

Late in life he showed particular concern for the preservation of business archives and, especially, for the collection being gathered by the University of Melbourne. He died suddenly in Melbourne on 19 June 1967, predeceased by his wife in 1962; his will provided for the transfer of his own rich collection of papers to a suitable repository in Australia, and also revealed the usual strong sense of family identity in expressing the hope that a suitable biography of W. L. Baillieu would be written.

His eldest son William Latham (b. 1915) succeeded to the title. He was killed in an accident in 1973 and the title passed to his son James William (b. 1950). The first Lord Baillieu was also survived by two other sons and a daughter.

G. Blainey, *The rush that never ended* (Melb, 1963); M. Cannon, *The land boomers* (Melb, 1966); W. S. Robinson, *If I remember rightly*, G. Blainey ed (Melb, 1967); *Argus*, 7, 8 Feb 1936; *Age*, 15, 17 July 1939; 19 June 1967; *Herald* (Melb), 19 June 1967; papers of Sir Colin Fraser, of W. S. Robinson and of Broken Hill companies (Univ Melb Archives); papers of 1st Lord Baillieu, including J. H. Reynolds, Memoir of W. L. Baillieu (held by Lord Baillieu's trustees); family and business papers (held by Mr Darren Baillieu, Toorak, and Mr Everard Baillieu, Melbourne).   J. R. POYNTER

BAINES, SARAH JANE (1866-1951), feminist, was born on 30 November 1866 in Birmingham, England, daughter of James Edward Hunt, gunmaker, and his wife Sarah Ann, née Hunt. At 11 Jennie was sent to work in Joseph Chamberlain's ordnance factory. Three years later she joined her parents in Salvation Army work, speaking from the platform and playing the cornet; on reaching the rank of lieutenant she was appointed evangelist to an independent working man's mission in Bolton where she also acted as police court missionary to women arrested. She later joined the temperance movement and the Independent Labour Party. On 26 September 1888 at Bolton she had married a bootmaker, George Baines; between 1890 and 1899 she bore five children.

About 1905 Jennie Baines joined the Women's Social and Political Union, the women's suffrage organization formed by the Pankhursts in 1903. In April 1908 she was made a full-time organizer in the Midlands and north of England on a wage of £2 a week. Travelling from her base at Stockport, she planned demonstrations, set up new branches and addressed meetings. One of the first to advocate militant methods, she was imprisoned some fifteen times for her part in protests and was the first suffragette to be tried by jury; in prison, she went on hunger-strikes five times but was never force-fed because her health was too frail. Soon after her release from gaol in 1913 she was smuggled into Wales with her husband, two sons and surviving daughter; as the 'Evans' family, in December they arrived in Melbourne, which had been chosen as refuge because it was the headquarters of the Women's Political Association which had links with the Women's Social and Political Union.

Jennie Baines settled with her family in Fitzroy and began working for the Women's Political Association in January 1914, supporting Vida Goldstein's [q.v.] candidacy for the Federal seat of Kooyong. To some extent she was overshadowed by the arrival in Melbourne of the more flamboyant Adela Pankhurst [q.v.]. Both joined the Women's Peace Army in July 1915 (Jennie was elected an officer in February 1917); both helped to organize a women's employment bureau that year, and they campaigned tirelessly against the war and conscription in 1916-17. Both joined the Victorian Socialist Party of which Jennie was made an executive officer in September 1917. Unlike Adela, Jennie retained her connexion with both the Peace Army and the Women's Political Association until they disbanded in 1919.

Jennie Baines's primary concern was the welfare of women. For a month from 23 August 1917 she and Adela Pankhurst led marches organized by the militant Women's Peace League to protest to the Federal government against profiteering and the prohibitive cost of living. On 30 August she, Adela Pankhurst and another were arrested; on 4 September she was sentenced to nine-months gaol but was released pending appeal, and in October the conviction was quashed on a legal technicality. In December 1918 she was fined for displaying the red flag on the Yarra Bank. She was finally tried and gaoled for six months on 18 March 1919 for refusing to pay the fine or to sign a bond not to fly the red flag again. Resorting to her old tactic of the hunger-strike, for four days she went without food and drink before being released after a special Saturday meeting of Federal cabinet; she was reputedly Australia's first prisoner on a hunger-strike. Her defiant action won her acclaim from the Left, and eulogies and verses in her honour appeared in the *Socialist* and the *Woman Voter*. From the country, where she had temporarily retired to recover, she wrote: 'I will not, nor will I allow the workers if I can prevent it, to be cowed and driven by the miserable curs and creatures of political superstition and treachery, supported by their equally depraved hirelings and tools, who will commit any atrocity against the intelligence and physique of humanity in the name of "law and order" and for pay and position'.

Jennie Baines continued to work both in the Socialist and Labor parties. In 1928 she was appointed a special magistrate in the Children's Court at Port Melbourne, where the family had moved in 1926. Her activities after World War II were curtailed by encroaching blindness; she died at Port Melbourne on 20 February 1951 and was cremated, survived by her husband and three children. Although she lost her early Christian conviction, the evangelical imperative always coloured her commitment to the cause of women and socialism; her work also demonstrated the close links between women's radical political organizations in Britain and the Dominions.

C. Pankhurst, *Unshackled*, F. W. Pethick-Lawrence ed (Lond, 1959); E. S. Pankhurst, *The suffragette movement* (Lond, 1931; New York, 1971); *Woman Voter*, 3 Feb 1914, 18 Sept 1917, 13 Apr, 6 June 1918, 10 Apr 1919; *Socialist* (Melb), 14, 28 Sept 1917, 28 Mar, 11, 25 Apr, 2 May, 25 July 1919; *Age*, 31 Aug, 5, 21, 25 Sept, 3 Oct 1917; *Herald* (Melb), 18, 20, 21 Mar 1919; *Pix*, 13 Mar 1943; Baines papers (Fryer Lib, Univ Qld); information from Miss M. Stevenson, Red Hill, Qld, *and* Mrs E. Baines, Beaumaris, Vic.   JUDITH SMART

BAINTON, EDGAR LESLIE (1880-1956), musician, was born on 14 February 1880 at Hackney, London, son of Rev. George Bainton, Congregational minister, and his wife Mary, née Cave. He was educated at King Henry VIII School at Coventry, where his musical gifts became apparent. At 9 he played in his first concert and in 1896 won an open scholarship to the Royal College of Music, London, where his teachers included (Sir) Charles Stanford and

Franklin Taylor; he was awarded the Tagore medal.

In 1901 Bainton was appointed professor of pianoforte and composition at the Conservatoire of Music, Newcastle upon Tyne, and became principal in 1912. At the parish church at Long Benton, Northumberland, on 31 July 1905 he had married his student Ethel Frances Eales. Active in the city's musical life, he was conductor of the Newcastle Philharmonic Orchestra in 1911-34. Visiting Germany for the Bayreuth music festival in 1914, he was caught by the outbreak of war and interned in Ruhleben camp with other musicians. He organized a madrigal society known as 'Bainton's Magpies', conducted an orchestra, played piano concertos, lectured on musical and literary subjects, and composed vigorously. In 1918 he was invalided to The Hague before resuming his position at Newcastle.

'An accomplished but minor figure in the gentler English traditions of the earlier twentieth century music', Bainton was a prolific composer of choral, symphonic and chamber works. He was often inspired to set poetry to music 'with a masterly instinct for imagery'; close friends included the poets Gordon Bottomley and Wilfrid Gibson. As an examiner for the Associated Board of the Royal Schools of Music, he made several tours of Australia, Canada and India.

In 1934 Bainton was appointed director of the New South Wales State Conservatorium of Music, and that year was awarded an honorary doctorate of music by the University of Durham and elected a fellow of the Royal College of Music. He arrived in Sydney with his wife in the *Cormorin* on 31 May. Steeped in the English musical traditions of orchestral, operatic, chamber music and general scholastic training, Bainton was filled with enthusiasm for the task ahead. Within a few months he conducted the first concerts of the future Sydney Symphony Orchestra and had founded the conservatorium's opera school, which in August 1935 performed Gluck's *Orpheus and Eurydice* on a stage so defective that it was described by one critic as 'equivalent to putting on Wagner's *Parsifal* in an ordinary theatre'. Thereafter the school staged two operas a year.

Bainton revived chamber music concerts and concert tours to country centres, started classes for military bands, built up the string quartet and choir, increased the number of orchestral concerts, and as conducter introduced many unfamiliar works to Sydney audiences. He firmly believed in broadcasting as a means of musical education and encouraged the music club movement; he often adjudicated at the City of Sydney Eisteddfod. Between teaching, conducting,

playing, examining and lecturing, he still found time to compose. He attracted good teachers and raised the standards for the conservatorium diploma; due to his influence music became a full subject at intermediate and leaving certificate examinations. A Bach scholar, he conducted the *Mass in B minor* in 1936; from 1939 the Easter performance of the *St Matthew Passion* under his direction became an annual event. His wife and daughter Helen were also active musicians.

In 1942 Bainton conducted his *Symphony in D minor* in Sydney and Melbourne and in 1944, at the conservatorium, the first performance of his opera, *The pearl tree*. The libretto based on a Hindu legend was written by R. C. Trevelyan, and the sets were designed and painted by Bainton's daughter Guendolen and her artist husband Harold Abbott. The score was praised by Neville Cardus, who found the performance 'one of the richest and most potential seeds ever sown for the future of music in this country'. At his farewell concert at the conservatorium in 1946 Bainton conducted the first performance of his *An English idyll*.

When he reached retiring age the number of students at the conservatorium had increased from 750 in 1934 to over 2000. In 1947 he toured Canada and Ceylon and next year New Zealand. He loved walking, and in 1935 had climbed the Milford Track in New Zealand. After the death of his wife in 1954, Bainton completed his *Symphony in C minor*. He was drowned after suffering a coronary occlusion while swimming at Lady Martin's Beach, Point Piper, on 8 December 1956, and was cremated with Anglican rites after a service at St Andrew's Cathedral. Belonging 'to a golden age of English culture . . . that recognized the connection between a musical education and an education in letters', he had enriched the musical life of Sydney at a time when it was suffering from starvation.

H. P. Greene, *Charles Villiers Stanford* (Lond, 1935); H. J. Wood, *My life of music* (Lond, 1938); E. Blom (ed), *Grove's dictionary of music and musicians*, 5th ed (Lond, 1954); G. Bottomley and Paul Nash, *Poet & painter*, C. C. Abbott and A. Bertram eds (Lond, 1955); R. H. Bainton, *Pilgrim parson* (New York, 1958); H. Bainton, *Remembered on waking* (Syd, 1960); D. E. Tunley, 'Thoughts on the music of Edgar Bainton', *Westerly*, June 1963; E. L. Bainton diaries (ML) *and* papers and press-cuttings (Conservatorium of Music, Syd).

HELEN BAINTON

BAINTON, JOHN RICHARD (1867-1924), electrical engineer, was born on 10 September 1867 at Geneva, Switzerland, son of Richard Bainton, British master mariner, and his wife Anna Marie, née Dénériaz. Brought up in Kent, he received little formal education and at 13 left home to work for a shipbuilding company in London. He was later apprenticed to the Gulcher Electric Light & Power Co. of Battersea and, on qualifying as an electrical engineer, worked at Earle's Shipyards, Hull.

Bainton came to Australia in 1889 as the agent for Woodhouse & Rawson, a London engineering firm. Seven years later, having decided to settle, he became managing engineer for Edge & Edge, a Sydney firm of electrical contractors. Always keenly interested in innovative engineering, he visited the United States of America in 1898 to study the Bell automatic telephone system and was partly responsible for its later introduction into Australia in the early 1900s. In 1900, while still employed by Edge & Edge, Bainton converted to electric power T. Sawell's [q.v.6] steam tramway linking Brighton-le-Sands and Rockdale: this was Sydney's pioneer electric tramway. That year he became president of the Electrical Association of New South Wales and served for two successive terms.

In 1903 Bainton secured the Australian agency for Dick, Kerr & Co. of London and within a year had fulfilled its contract to supply the generating plant for Sydney's original electric lighting scheme. In the same year he also set up in business with James Nicholson, managing director of Sydney's Waygood Elevator Co. They established the Standard Electric Elevator Co. and over the next few years introduced the electric lift into Australia; their firm became known as Standard Waygood early in 1909.

On 23 April 1910, on one of his frequent trips to England, Bainton married Mabel Beatrice Maria Vernon at St Mary's Anglican Church, Shortlands, Kent. They lived at Point Piper until 1922 when, for the sake of Bainton's health, they moved to the Blue Mountains. By the end of World War I the Bainton-Nicholson firm, then called the English Electric Co. of Australia, was among the largest engineering concerns in the country. One of Bainton's last projects was preparing an unsuccessful tender for the Sydney Harbour Bridge in 1924.

Bainton was tall and slightly built with pleasant features; his appearance and quiet personal charm belied the sterner qualities of relentless drive, determination, and astuteness in negotiation that made him so successful in business. He was a member of the Institution of Electrical Engineers, London, and of the American Institute of Electrical Engineers. He was a keen motorist and his De Dion-Bouton was among the first private cars in Sydney; in 1897 he had introduced the motor cycle to Melbourne, alarming pedestrians and horses alike as he rode along St Kilda Esplanade. He also took an active interest in photography and wireless technology; he rose to the rank of captain in the Corps of Australian Engineers. He was a Freemason from 1894.

A long-term sufferer from asthma, Bainton died suddenly of cardio-respiratory disease at his Wentworth Falls home on 13 June 1924 and was buried in the local Anglican cemetery. He was survived by his wife, a son and a daughter. The J. R. Bainton Prize, which he endowed, is awarded annually by the Institution of Engineers, Australia.

English Electric Co. of Aust, *Tender ... for Sydney Harbour Bridge* (Syd, 1924); Electrical Assn of NSW, *Procs*, 1906-14; Inst of Engineers (Aust), *Trans*, 5 (1924), and *Q Bulletin*, July 1924; *Cwlth Engineer*, 1 July 1924; *Argus*, 31 May 1897; *SMH*, 14, 16 June 1924; family papers and information supplied by Mr J. V. Bainton, Darling Point, and Mrs M. Lamrock, Wahroonga, NSW.

MERRILYN LINCOLN

BAIRD, ADAM (1873-1954), engineer and businessman, was born on 19 May 1873 at Ballarat, Victoria, son of William Baird, accountant, and his wife Janet, née Paton, both of whom were from Ayrshire, Scotland. He won scholarships to Grenville College, Ballarat, and in 1890 to Ormond College, University of Melbourne. He graduated with honours in 1896 in civil engineering, then went to Western Australia, surveying and erecting mining machinery at Coolgardie, Kalgoorlie and Menzies.

In 1896 Baird's brother William founded a hardware business in Coolgardie and it was soon extended to Kalgoorlie and Boulder. In 1899 Adam followed other brothers and sisters into the firm, which opened a shop and a rural mail-order house in Perth in 1903; from about 1910 it was housed in Baird's Arcade, designed by Adam. Retail interests were diversified and their catalogue became widely known as the 'Farmer's Bible'. After incorporation as a limited company in August 1917, Bairds moved its headquarters to Murray Street in 1919. On 6 February 1906 at Ballarat Adam had married Eliza Armstrong, daughter of a solicitor H. W. Morrow.

During World War I Baird represented the Chamber of Commerce on the State Munitions Supply Committee in 1915 and became secretary of its engineering sub-committee. He was honorary secretary of the War Munitions Supply Co. of Western Australia in 1915-16, then volunteered for munitions work in England and was away till 1919.

Although Baird controlled the accounts of the family company, his main concerns were service to customers and staff welfare. He drafted a profit-sharing agreement in 1919; it was not then implemented, but the firm introduced a subsidized mutual-aid plan and a health insurance scheme for staff long before these became common practice. During the Depression Baird worked to avoid staff retrenchment, and saved many farmers from ruin by extending credit, accepting payment in kind and helping with marketing. He followed similar policies in World War II, during which he deferred his retirement. He remained chairman of directors after the death in 1947 of his brother William, who had throughout been managing director, but passed much responsibility to his only son Hugh. Survived by his wife, son and two daughters, Baird died on 9 February 1954 at his Peppermint Grove home. Hugh Baird died in 1965 and in 1969 the Myer Emporium bought out the firm.

Baird had been a founding director in 1919 of Plaimar Ltd which produced extracts, essences and perfumes from Western Australian native plants. He was also a director of its subsidiary, Industrial Extracts Ltd, which developed a process for producing tannin from wandoo trees. He was an early member of the faculty of engineering at the University of Western Australia, served on the councils of Scotch College and the Presbyterian Ladies' College and gave generously to both, and was treasurer of his local Presbyterian church. Sir Walter Murdoch [q.v.], with whom he had shared a college study, thought him 'one of the best men I have ever known, and the most modest'.

Bairds Limited: a short history of the company, A. McCracken ed (Perth, 1972); *West Australian*, 7, 21 Aug, 4, 6 Oct 1915, 13 July 1916; Business, family and personal papers (held by author); family information.   KATHLEEN BAIRD

BAIRD, JOHN LAWRENCE; *see* STONEHAVEN

BAKER, CATHERINE (1861-1953), teacher, was born on 23 April 1861 at Cappoquin, County Waterford, Ireland, youngest daughter of Francis Wilson Baker, heraldic painter, and his wife Catherine, née Sheffield. She was brought to Victoria as a child and was educated at North Williamstown State School. In 1881 she entered the state teaching service, and in 1886 was appointed to take temporary charge of a one-teacher school at Wanalta Creek near Rushworth. During the ten months she spent teaching there and at near-by Bur-ramboot East, she became friendly with members of the Furphy family, including Joseph [q.v.] who came on a visit from Shepparton. Impressed by 'the only girl in the Eastern Hemisphere who knew who Belisarious was', Furphy, nearly twenty years her senior, was glad to have her as a friend. They corresponded, and met when Furphy visited Melbourne. From 1887 to 1898 Kate Baker taught at her old school at North Williamstown as a junior assistant, and thereafter had various appointments as an infant-teacher until she retired in 1913. Although afflicted with increasing deafness, she had been a capable teacher: the rest of her long life was devoted to the memory of Furphy, whose death in 1912 affected her deeply.

Kate Baker's belief in his ability had helped to sustain Furphy during the long labour of writing *Such is life*, eventually published in 1903. The novel had made little impact on the public, and at the time of his death he was little known: Kate resolved to gain proper recognition for him. As she said in 1936: 'That was my life-work; its fulfilment my reward. I desire no other'.

Dependent upon her small pension, she lived frugally. In 1916 she edited and published at her own expense *The poems of Joseph Furphy*; in 1917 she purchased from the *Bulletin* the 825 unbound copies of *Such is life* remaining from the original edition of 2000, and reissued them with a preface by Vance Palmer [q.v.]. Her rescue of *Rigby's romance* from the files of the Broken Hill *Barrier Truth* led to its publication in an abridged form in 1921. She addressed literary societies, wrote newspaper articles, and sent copies of Furphy's published work to libraries throughout the world. In 1937 her efforts to publicize him and other local writers were acknowledged officially by award of the O.B.E. More important to her, perhaps, was the award of the S. H. Prior [q.v.] Memorial Prize in 1939 for an essay, 'Who Was Joseph Furphy?', by Miles Franklin [q.v.] who had incorporated Kate's written recollections. It was expanded into *Joseph Furphy; the legend of a man and his book* and published in 1944, the same year in which a new and unabridged edition of *Such is life* finally appeared.

Though her 'life-work' was done, Kate's enthusiasm was undiminished. Unworried by total deafness, she continued to support Melbourne literary societies until extreme old age. She died at Camberwell on 7 October 1953 and was cremated with Methodist rites. Though of gentle disposition, Kate could be very stubborn and determined, especially where her affections were concerned. She was not remarkable for any intellectual gifts, and her championship of *Such is life* owed more to devotion to its author than to her critical perception. It is for her work as 'Furphy's gallant standard-bearer' that she is, and deserves to be, remembered.

Education Dept (Vic), *Vision and realisation,* L. J. Blake ed (Melb, 1973); Kate Baker Collection (NL); V. and N. Palmer papers (NL).

JOHN BARNES

BAKER, HENRY HERBERT (1867-1940), optician, was born on 6 October 1867 at Yeovil, Somerset, England, son of William Baker, bank clerk, and his wife Mary Ann, née Watson. He became a clerk in his grandfather's firm, W. Watson & Sons. Partly because of incipient phthisis, he came to Melbourne to represent his firm at the Centennial International Exhibition in 1888. Arriving in May, he found prospects so promising that he arranged to open a branch of the business and for his brother Frank to join him. They carried a range of cameras, microscopes, telescopes and surveying instruments, mainly of Watson manufacture. On 16 April 1891 at Carlton he married Clara Ingham with Congregational rites.

Baker had wide interests. He took the English course in optics and sight-testing and about 1900 obtained the diploma of the Spectacle Makers' Company. He lectured widely on optical matters, astronomy and X-rays, discovered in 1895. Early in 1896 coils and vacuum tubes were obtained to supply those interested in making trials; the firm, under Baker, played an important role in making available the benefits of X-rays and in 1921 a factory for manufacturing electro-medical equipment was established. An 'enthusiastic student of science', Baker was a member of various astronomical, microscopical and photographic societies. He was founder and in 1911-14 first president of the Victorian Optical Association. He studied defects in the refraction of the eye and the firm's rooms were equipped with the most modern instruments for testing eyesight and correcting disorders.

Henry and Frank Baker had acquired the Australian business in 1903, when their uncle T. P. Watson died. The firm was registered as a proprietary company in 1916 and as a public company in 1919 with Henry as managing drector; the name W. Watson & Sons Ltd was retained in honour of his grandfather. Sydney henceforth became the headquarters of a business covering the chief cities of Australia and New Zealand; the company built and moved into the substantial Watson House in Bligh Street in 1928. After relinquishing the post of managing director, Henry remained as chairman

until 1940. He regarded his staff as a kind of 'family' and was closely concerned with their welfare.

Baker was a member of the Royal Society of New South Wales from 1919 and, later, of the local Microscopical Society. An outstanding member of the British Astronomical Association from 1932, he served as honorary librarian, secretary in 1936-39 and president of the New South Wales branch in 1939-40. He was a member of the Congregational Church, Killara, and active in such organizations as the Rotary Club of Sydney, the Killara Community Service Club, and the Millions Club of New South Wales, which supported immigration.

Baker became somewhat deaf and founded Deaf Aids Ltd as a subsidiary of W. Watson & Sons. Although he experimented with hearing aids, he did not use one and his deafness gave some impression of aloofness. He died of coronary occlusion after a surgical operation on 13 August 1940 in St Luke's Hospital, Darlinghurst, and was cremated. He was survived by his only son Arnold, who became a director of W. Watson & Sons.

J. Smith (ed), *Cyclopedia of Victoria,* 2 (Melb, 1904); W. Watson & Sons Ltd, *A brief history* (Syd, 1928), and *X-rays* (Syd, 1938), and *Salute to the X-ray pioneers of Australia* (Syd, 1946); *Scientific Aust,* 20 Sept 1905; Roy Soc NSW, *Procs,* 75 (1940); British Astronomical Assn, *J,* 51 (1941); records (Watson Victor, Syd); information from Mrs Alison Leslie, Canterbury, Vic.   HARLEY WOOD

BAKER, REGINALD LESLIE (SNOWY) (1884-1953), sportsman and showman, was born on 8 February 1884 at Surry Hills, Sydney, son of George Baker, an Irish-born Sydney Municipal Council clerk, and his wife Elizabeth Jane, née Robertson. Very blond, he was called 'Snowy' from childhood; he was educated at Crown Street Public School and, reputedly, learned horsemanship at dawn work-outs on Randwick Racecourse. In 1897-99 he won a series of swimming championships for his school, swam and played water polo for the East Sydney Swimming Club, and in 1901 finished second to R. Cavill [q.v. F. Cavill] in the State half-mile championship. He did not, as was later claimed, study engineering at the University of Sydney or win several 'blues'; he may have worked for the Colonial Sugar Refining Co. as an engineering draftsman. He played Rugby Union for Eastern Suburbs and represented New South Wales at half-back against both Queensland and the touring Great Britain side in 1904. A 'rare tackler . . . and as hard a player for his weight as has been seen in the game', he played for Australia in the first Test. As an oarsman, he rowed for the Mercantile Rowing Club in championship maiden and junior fours and eights in 1905-06; he was also a capable cricketer.

Baker served as a trooper with the New South Wales Lancers from about 1902, gaining the rank of sergeant and excelling in a variety of military sports: over the years he won many prizes in such activities as fencing (with the sword and bayonet), wrestling on horseback and tent-pegging. A fair shot, he was 'a decidedly handy man in the event of a foe descending on our peaceful shores'. In 1902 he took up boxing; for many years he weighed 11 st. 7 lb. (73 kg). In 1905 he became New South Wales amateur middleweight champion and next year retained his title, won the same belt in Victoria, and became the heavyweight champion of both States.

In December 1906, farewelled by 1000 people in Sydney including a boatload of twenty young ladies who pursued him to the Heads, Baker left for England to compete in the Amateur Boxing Association's championships, but contracted enteric fever and pneumonia. However, he boxed in the 1908 Olympic tournament held in London in October, three months after the games proper. As a middleweight he won three fights in the one day, two of them by knockouts, to reach the final which he lost narrowly on points to J. W. H. T. Douglas. He visited Scotland, Ireland, Scandinavia and Europe and performed at both exhibition and competition level, mainly in aquatic sports. He was welcomed as a distinguished athlete at gentlemen's sporting clubs wherever he went.

Returning to a considerable welcome in Sydney in December 1908, Baker began to capitalize on his athletic and boxing fame and opened a physical culture establishment, with mail-order courses, in Castlereagh Street. On 31 March 1909 at St Mark's Anglican Church, Darling Point, he married 37-year-old Ethel Rose Mackay, daughter of a squatter and widow of Augustus Daniel Kearney, a Victorian physician and notable tennis player. A journalist of skill, Baker contributed to the Sydney *Evening News* in 1908-10, published a book, *General physical culture* (Melbourne, 1910), and in 1912 began *Snowy Baker's Magazine*, a penny monthly that attained a circulation of over 3000 in its two years of existence.

Meanwhile he had become involved in H. D. McIntosh's [q.v.] Stadiums boxing organization, mainly as a referee; at times controversial, Baker wore green trousers and a felt hat, later evening dress. In December 1912 he arranged the purchase of the Rushcutters Bay Stadium for £30 000

and soon, with John Wren [q.v.], had Baker's Stadiums in Melbourne, Adelaide and Brisbane, and was following McIntosh's policy of bringing international boxers to Australia. In July 1914 the stadium staged its first Les Darcy [q.v.] fight and Baker soon controlled the Maitland boxer's engagements. He was annoyed when Darcy left Australia secretly in October 1916, and had to face accusations thereafter that he had been largely responsible for the boycotting and even the death of Darcy in the United States of America in May 1917. Baker always denied the charges and seems conclusively to have disproved them face-to-face with a Maitland committee of inquiry in October.

He tried three times to enlist in the Australian Imperial Force, but was prevented by a spinal injury; instead he devoted himself to fund-raising concerts. Boxing declined in popularity and he put on shows and filmnights at the stadium. Baker moved into the film business in 1918, and played a secret agent in *The enemy within* and a stationhand in *The lure of the bush*. In 1919 he was co-producer with E. J. Carroll [q.v.] and starred as a boxing parson in *The man from Kangaroo*, as a bushranger in *The shadow of Lightning Ridge*, and as a jackeroo in *The jackeroo of Coolabong* (1920). All his roles featured his horsemanship, with his famous grey, Boomerang.

In August 1920 Baker left for the United States of America to further his film career, but although he did appear in some movies, succeeded rather as a coach and instructor in athletic feats and as a businessman. In 1933 he became a director and major operating partner of the Riviera Country Club, near Santa Monica, California, and spent an active life largely as a riding instructor to Hollywood stars and as a polo player. In the early 1930s he had contributed a column to the Sydney *Referee*. He re-visited Australia briefly in 1925, 1932 and 1952.

Survived by his wife and a step-daughter, Baker died of cerebro-vascular disease on 2 December 1953 at Los Angeles, and was cremated. His estate in New South Wales was valued for probate at £39 111. His stature as an athlete depends largely upon the enormous range rather than the outstanding excellence of his activities; it was as an entrepreneur-showman, publicist and businessman that he seems in retrospect to have been most important.

His brother WILLIAM HAROLD (1887-1962), was born on 29 September 1887 in Sydney. He was a notable swimmer, winning three New South Wales championships in 1906 and captaining the Australian water polo team. He played Rugby football for Australia three times against New Zealand and won boxing and wrestling championships.

With Snowy he worked for Stadiums Ltd and refereed many of Darcy's most important fights, including the one against Fritz Holland on 12 September 1914 when he disqualified Darcy for a foul. He was described as a 'man with a marble mouth and a jaw of steel. A man of ice with frozen eyes and a frozen voice'. Captain of Maroubra Surf Club in 1900-10, on 28 January 1910 he took part in a famous surf rescue of over 100 people at Cronulla Beach and was awarded the Albert Medal for bravery; a public subscription for him raised £1000 in its first week. He died on 17 October 1962 at Woollahra, survived by a daughter and by his wife Nellie Innes Sara, née Crawshaw, whom he had married on 12 June 1912.

His brothers Frank, who joined the film industry in Los Angeles in the 1920s, and Ernest were water polo players; Frederick was an amateur welterweight champion of Australia, and refereed for Stadiums Ltd.

R. Swanwick, *Les Darcy, Australia's golden boy of boxing* (Syd, 1965); E. Reade, *Australian silent films* (Melb, 1970); *People* (Syd), 27 Sept 1950; *Parade*, Oct 1959; *Referee*, 1908, Dec 1912-Dec 1913, 31 Oct 1917, 13 Apr 1932; *Punch* (Melb), 19 June 1913; *SMH*, 4 Dec 1953.   W. F. MANDLE

BAKER, SIR RICHARD CHAFFEY (1841-1911), barrister, pastoralist and politician, was born at North Adelaide on 22 June 1841, eldest son of John Baker [q.v.3] and his wife Isabella, née Allan. He was educated at Eton and Trinity College, Cambridge (B.A., 1864; M.A., 1871), where he was a keen oarsman. Called to the Bar at Lincoln's Inn in June 1864, he returned home in the same year and set up in practice with Charles Fenn. In 1873 he entered into partnership with Dr William Barlow [q.v.].

In April 1868 Baker became the first South Australian-born member of the colonial legislature, being elected at the head of the poll for Barossa in the House of Assembly. His father was a prominent member of the Legislative Council and in May 1870 the unusual spectacle was witnessed of father and son on the same day successfully moving no confidence motions in Strangways's [q.v.6] land-reforming ministry. Baker then became attorney-general in J. Hart's [q.v.4] ministry of 1870-71, and the first locally born minister of the Crown. He resigned from cabinet to manage his ailing father's affairs, and did not stand at the 1871 general election, although he had again been returned at the head of the poll for Barossa in the previous year. His father's extensive pastoral and other interests occupied Baker for two years, and afterwards he visited England and the Continent, representing South Australia at the Vienna International Exhibition in 1873. Upon his return early in 1875, he was offered and declined a place in the A. Blyth [q.v.3] ministry. At the general election that year he failed to regain his former seat, the only defeat he suffered during his political career.

In 1877 he became the first native-born member to be elected to the Legislative Council; the whole colony then voted as one constituency and Baker came third in the poll. In 1885 he won the Southern seat which he represented without interruption until the formation of the Australian Commonwealth. Baker had been minister of justice and education in Colton's [q.v.3] ministry in 1884-85. In 1885-86 he visited England to negotiate a postal union between Great Britain and the Australian colonies. In recognition of the success of this important mission he was appointed C.M.G. in 1886. During the visit he also acted as commissioner for South Australia at the Colonial and Indian Exhibition.

A tenacious and courageous fighter for his beliefs and a staunch guardian of the rights of the Upper House, Baker was for many years its most influential member. Aware that his conservatism did not meet with the approval of the majority of the population of the colony, he resolved to delay what he considered to be hastily conceived or unworkable legislation. He did not, however, adopt an unrealistic, reactionary stance: although strongly opposed in 1887 to the payment of members of parliament, he saw that it was inevitable and contented himself with deferring the introduction of the measure for three years.

The success of candidates nominated by the United Labor Party at two by-elections for the Legislative Council in May 1891 prompted Baker to form the National Defence League, a body of pastoralists, business and professional men which stood for 'the preservation of law, order and property' and was opposed to 'all undue class influence in Parliament', particularly with regard to progressive land taxes and statutory arbitration machinery. Members of both Houses endorsed by the league led the attack on C. C. Kingston's [q.v.] radical liberal ministry of 1893-99, and a number of important bills were rejected or severely amended in the Upper House where Baker succeeded Sir Henry Ayers [q.v.3] as president in December 1893. He immediately resigned from the National Defence League, of which he had been founding president, on the ground that the occupant of such a position should sever all connexions with a political party. He was appointed K.C.M.G. in 1895.

The most colourful event in Baker's political career had occurred in December 1892. It arose through Kingston making some reflections on Baker in reference to the collection of funds in 1889 for the building of the Trades Hall in Adelaide, whereupon Baker denounced his opponent as a coward, a bully and a disgrace to the legal profession. Kingston retaliated by claiming that Baker was 'false as a friend, treacherous as a colleague, mendacious as a man, and utterly untrustworthy in every relationship of public life'. Characteristically, Kingston did not stop at that and procured a pair of matched pistols, one of which he sent to Baker accompanied by a communication appointing the time for a duel in Victoria Square on 23 December. Baker informed the police, who arrested Kingston with a loaded revolver at the designated venue; he was bound over to keep the peace for twelve months. After the incident, Baker snubbed Kingston on all but official occasions.

Baker deserves to be better remembered as one of the founding fathers of Federation. He was a member of the Federal conventions of 1891 and 1897-98. The deliberations of the former were given direction and precision by his publication, *A manual of reference to authorities for the use of the members of the National Australasian Convention* ... (Adelaide, 1891). In Deakin's [q.v.] opinion he 'was at this time in advance of all his [South Australian] colleagues in federal knowledge and in the federal spirit'. Baker subsequently wrote a number of pamphlets on Federation. At the 1897-98 convention, he played a part in the unsuccessful attempt to prevent Kingston's election as president but managed to keep him off the important drafting committee. Baker was elected to the arduous position of chairman of committees; his knowledge of parliamentary procedure, together with his tact and firmness, made him an ideal choice.

His major contributions to the debates were his arguments in favour of a powerful Senate, which were constantly used by delegates from the smaller colonies, and his suggested abandonment of the British model of cabinet government. At the 1891 convention he had moved that the Senate be given equal power with the House of Representatives over all legislation, but the motion was lost 16-22, and instead the celebrated 'compromise', which provided that the Senate could not initiate or amend money bills, was agreed upon. Although Baker at the time found few supporters for his views on the incompatibility of Westminster-style responsible government and a federal system in which the States were to enjoy in the Senate co-equal power with the House of Representatives, the importance of this question was revived in the light of

political developments in 1975. Baker was adamantly opposed to the principle that the Federal ministry should be responsible only to the House of Representatives and he suggested the adoption of a modified version of the Swiss form of executive, with an equal number of ministers elected by (and responsible to) both houses of parliament. Despite his failure to convince a majority of the delegates, Baker did not retreat into embittered isolation; his major objective was to bring about a federated Australia.

He resigned the presidency of the Legislative Council in 1901 to stand successfully for the Senate in the first Commonwealth parliament. He was elected first president of the Senate, and, consistent with his previous views, he refused to take sides in the debates between free traders and protectionists. He was widely respected for his fairness, decision and ability. He wanted the Senate to be able to hold its own against the House of Representatives, believing that this was the only way in which the small States' rights could be preserved. In 1903 he represented the Commonwealth at the Delhi Durbar when King Edward VII was proclaimed emperor of India. In 1904 he was re-elected president of the Senate, but retired from political life in 1906 because of ill health. Despite Baker's strenuous attempt to maintain the Senate's position of equality with the Lower House, its importance was already subsiding.

So much of Baker's time was devoted to politics that his work at the Bar was necessarily restricted, and his appointment as a Q.C. in July 1900 did not gain unanimous approval from the legal profession. Through his father's estate, and as chairman of the Queensland Investment and Land Mortgage Co., he had extensive connexions with the pastoral industry, and was also a director of Elder Smith [qq.v.4,6] & Co. Ltd, the colony's largest woolbrokers. He was involved in the development of mining in South Australia, particularly copper in northern Yorke Peninsula; in 1890 he had been elected to the board of the Wallaroo and Moonta Mining and Smelting Co. He also held interests in various Broken Hill mining companies. For thirteen years, at different periods, he was chairman of the Adelaide Club; he presented it with the chair which he had used as president of the Senate. As chairman of the South Australian Jockey Club in 1888-1909, Baker played a leading part in regulating horse-racing and it was mainly through his efforts that parliament legalized the use of the totalizator machine on race-courses. He was also president of the Royal Agricultural Society, a member of the board of the Botanic Garden, a trustee of the Savings Bank, and a staunch Anglican.

Baker died of diabetes and chronic nephritis at his country estate, Morialta, Norton Summit, on 18 March 1911, and was buried in North Road cemetery. Predeceased by his wife Katherine Edith, née Colley, whom he had married at Glenelg on 23 December 1865, he was survived by a daughter and two sons. His estate was valued for probate at £64 000. Portraits in oils hang in the Adelaide Club, Parliament House, Adelaide, and Parliament House, Canberra.

T. A. Coghlan, *Labour and industry in Australia*, 4 (Lond, 1918); G. C. Morphett (ed), *The Bakers of Morialta* (Adel, 1946); *Observer* (Adel), 31 Dec 1892; *Advertiser* (Adel), and *Register* (Adel), 20 Mar 1911; records, PRG 38 (SAA); note-books (held by Lady Hawker, Bungaree, Clare, SA).

JOHN PLAYFORD

BAKER, RICHARD THOMAS (1854-1941), botanist and museum curator, was born on 1 December 1854 at Woolwich, Kent, England, son of Richard Thomas Baker, a blacksmith at the naval dockyard, and his wife Sarah, née Colkett. He was educated at Woolwich National School and Peterborough Training Institution and gained science and art certificates from South Kensington Museum. He was engaged by the School Board for London as a senior assistant-master in 1875 but resigned in July 1879 to travel to Australia, arriving in September.

Baker became science and art master and senior house-master in June 1880 at Newington College, Sydney, where he remained for eight years before resigning to visit Europe and the United States of America. On 15 January 1888 he was appointed assistant curator to J. H. Maiden [q.v.], curator of the Technological Museum, Sydney, and published his first scientific paper (with Maiden) in 1891. In charge of the museum from 1896, he was appointed curator on 5 September 1898, and economic botanist in 1901; he also had charge of branch museums at Goulburn, Bathurst, Newcastle, Albury and West Maitland. On 3 December 1890 at the Wesleyan Church, Ashfield, he had married a widow Ann Hebblewhite, née Dawson.

Although Bosisto [q.v.3] and Mueller [q.v.5] had recently pioneered the eucalyptus oil industry, phytochemistry as a science was virtually unknown. Into this potentially fertile field Baker plunged with enthusiasm, supported by his colleague H. G. Smith [q.v.]. Generally their work was oriented towards the commercial applications of the various natural products of the flora—such as essential oils, gums and resins; but Baker was an originator and mere compilations of data held little interest for him. From the date of his first major work with Smith, *Research on the eucalypts, especially in regard to their essential oils* (Sydney, 1902), his theories were challenged by many Australian botanists, although his work was often praised overseas.

The corner-stone of Baker's work on the eucalypts, which he elaborated in the second edition of his book in 1920, was his assertion that each species of *Eucalyptus* was characterized by an oil of comparative chemical constancy, that there was a relationship between the leaf venation and the composition of the oil, and that chemical characteristics should be accorded equal value with morphological characters in the establishment of species. The last statement particularly aroused the ire of more orthodox botanists. Although more efficient methods of investigation have led to a substantial modification of Baker's theories, he and Smith were pioneers of modern chemotaxonomy as a recognized discipline, and their work enabled the eucalyptus oil industry to be established on a firm commercial basis.

Baker was reserved and reticent in family matters but, 'energetic, fiery and domineering', he enjoyed the controversy his theories provoked, even though this led to confrontations with such botanists as Maiden who, ironically, had introduced him to the disputed subject. He wrote to a colleague that 'opposition [to his work] was so great that individuals and deputations waited on me and asked me to give it up or I would wreck my scientific future'. His daughter recalls that at this time he often quoted Carlyle; 'The degree of vision that dwells in a man is a correct measure of the man'. In 1918 he told the governor-general Sir Ronald Munro Ferguson [q.v.]: 'I didn't mind the opposition for I love a fight . . . I append a copy of one of the letters,—its a gem! I get an immense amount of fun out of it'.

Baker published over 120 scientific papers dealing with *Melaleuca, Leptospermum, Prostanthera, Angophora* and other essential-oil-bearing genera. In 1908 he issued a small book, *Building and ornamental stones of New South Wales* (which he greatly expanded in 1915). It was followed in 1910 by *Research on the pines of Australia* (with Smith), *Cabinet timbers of Australia* (1913), and *The Australian flora in applied arts* (1915) in which he warmly advocated the waratah as Australia's national flower and its use as a motif. He regarded *Hardwoods of Australia and their economics* (1919) as his major work and dedicated it to Munro Ferguson. After his retirement from the museum in June 1922, Baker and Smith collaborated in producing *Woodfibres of some*

Australian timbers ... (1924). All these books were not only scientifically and practically important, but are a lasting tribute to the quality of Australian book production at the time. A talented artist, he illustrated several of his own books as well as numerous scientific papers.

In addition to his scientific research work, Baker built up and redisplayed the museum collections and aimed at making up-to-date information on technology available to the commercial world; he was especially proud of his applied-art collections. In 1913-24 he lectured in forestry at the University of Sydney. Baker was a member of the Linnean Society of New South Wales from 1888 and a councillor in 1897-1922, also a member of the local Royal Society from 1894. Awarded the Mueller Medal by the Australasian Association for the Advancement of Science in 1921, and the Royal Society's [W. B.] Clarke [q.v.3] Medal in 1922, he was a corresponding fellow of the Linnean Society of London, an honorary member of the Pharmaceutical societies of Great Britain and New South Wales and of the Philadelphia College of Pharmacy (and Science), Pennsylvania.

In his long retirement Baker retained his 'characteristic keenness and enthusiasm' by corresponding with a wide circle of friends in Australasia and overseas. He collected both old and modern china and in 1938 joined the Royal Australian Historical Society. He died at Cheltenham on 14 July 1941 and was buried with Anglican rites in the Methodist section of Rookwood cemetery. Predeceased by his wife, he was survived by a married daughter. His estate was valued for probate at £7820.

Roy Soc NSW, *A century of scientific progress* (Syd, 1968); *A'sian J of Pharmacy*, 22 (1941); *Aust J of Science*, 4 (1941); Linnean Soc NSW, *Procs*, 67 (1942); Roy Soc NSW, *Procs*, 76 (1942); Novar papers (NL); family papers and letters (Museum of Applied Arts and Sciences, Syd).   J. L. WILLIS

BAKER, THOMAS (1840-1923), farmer, was born in Ireland, eldest son of Edmond Baker and his wife Bridget, née Macnamara, farmers near Ennis, County Clare. Prompted by the potato famine, in 1851 the family took an assisted passage in the *Lady Elgin* to South Australia; on learning of the discovery of gold, they disembarked in March 1852 at Melbourne where employment was immediately offered by J. G. Ware of Camperdown. In October 1854 Edmond died after a fall from a horse. In 1857 his elder boys took employment with a government surveyor who appointed young Thomas foreman of a surveying party. He had had little schooling, and now read J. S. Mill, the speeches of Bright and Gladstone, and any books procurable. Biddy Baker taught her family to follow the Catholic faith, to avoid gambling, racing and bad language, and to practise thrift. After leasing a farm from J. and P. Manifold [q.v.2], the family selected land at Glenormiston under the 1865 Land Act, and prospered. In 1882, soon after his marriage on 15 February to Rosanna Despard, daughter of the Mortlake shire president, Thomas left the family partnership and leased land on the shores of Lake Colac.

At home among Colac's lakes and soft green hills, Baker saw the agricultural potential of the fertile soil on the pastoral runs. In 1885 he bought land on Cororooke, one of the four estates of Robertson Bros [q.v.6, W. Robertson] and, by inducing an onion-grower from the Bellarine Peninsula to sow a trial crop, proved that Colac land was as productive as the best in the colony. In 1887 he formed a syndicate to subdivide Dr D. E. Stodart's Corunnun estate on Lake Corangamite near Colac. From December 1888 Corunnun was offered for sale and lease in small lots, until the primitive sheep-walk employing four hands became a prolific onion and potato-growing area supporting 4000 tenants and workmen. Usually attired in gentleman's top hat and tails, the tall and strongly built Baker, with full grey beard cut short, became a familiar sight as he cut the huge paddocks into small holdings. The response from the Warrnambool district was remarkable; men from Killarney, Crossley and Koroit, most of them Irish Catholics, 'good fellows and good farmers', set the cultural and social pattern of the district. In 1892 Baker canvassed to form the Colac Dairying Co., which gave another thrust to local development.

From his Corunnun homestead Baker now worked to improve community life. For twenty-eight years he was a zealous councillor of Colac Shire and president in 1895-96. In 1894 he defeated the entrenched squatter, C. L. Forrest, for the Legislative Assembly seat of Polwarth; closer settlement, decentralization, and their handmaiden, transport, were his chief interests. Partly due to the over-enthusiastic support of his co-Religionists, his parliamentary life lasted only one term, to September 1897. Between 1890 and 1920 he supported the local farmers' association, the People's Party and the Victorian Farmers' Union. His logical presentation of the case for railways connecting surrounding districts with Colac had notable results between 1889 and 1922. Although in time he became better known as a stock, land and general commission agent based in Colac than as a farmer, he never deserted the cause of the onion and potato men. Always aware that growing root crops was one of the few ways for a working man to become a landowner, he originated export schemes and promoted plans for co-operative marketing; in 1910 Cororooke was the largest onion-growing centre in Australia. Shrewd and strong-willed, though speaking quietly and courteously with a marked brogue, he guided many rowdy meetings of angry onion-growers towards constructive action.

The respected patriarch of an industry, Baker died on 29 December 1923 at Coragulac House, aged 83, and was buried in the Camperdown cemetery. He was predeceased by his wife and was survived by five sons and two daughters; he left an estate valued for probate at £27 365.

J. Smith (ed), *Cyclopedia of Victoria*, 2 (Melb, 1904); *Table Talk*, 26 July 1895; *Colac Herald*, 29 Jan 1917, 31 Dec 1923; *Colac Reformer*, 6 Dec 1919; *Farmers Advocate*, 22 July 1920; *Argus*, 31 Dec 1923; M. G. Finlayson, Victorian politics 1889-94 (M.A. thesis, Univ Melb, 1964); Mackinnon papers (LaTL).   L. LOMAS

BAKER, THOMAS (1854-1928), photographic scientist and philanthropist, was born on 23 June 1854 at Montacute, Somerset, England, son of Charles Baker, blacksmith, and his wife Ann, née Beaton. The family migrated to Adelaide in 1865, where Charles began business as blacksmith, wheelwright and coachbuilder. Thomas joined his father but left to become a pharmaceutical chemist at Maryborough, Queensland, in 1876. There, on 26 January 1877 at St Paul's Church of England, he married ALICE (1855-1935), daughter of William Edward Shaw, postmaster at Raymond Terrace, New South Wales, and his wife Emma, née Coombe.

By 1881 the Bakers had moved to Melbourne where Thomas matriculated in six subjects and began medicine at the university in 1882, only to discontinue it the next year. He started experimenting with the production of photographic dry plates and by 1884 had sufficiently mastered the technique to begin business, with an office in the city and a laboratory at Abbotsford. Tradition has it that Baker, his wife and her sister Eleanor (1857-1948) used to work by night developing photographs and spend the day taking orders.

In 1887 Baker went into partnership with J. J. Rouse as importers and producers of photographic material. Rouse, a forceful extrovert, attended to sales while Baker, quiet and earnest, directed production and worked in the laboratory. Branches were opened in other colonies in 1890-92 and Rouse took charge of the Sydney office.

Baker & Rouse grew to be the largest suppliers of photographic material in Australia at a time when, with the development of the Eastman camera, there was a boom in amateur photography. In 1908 the firm amalgamated with the London Kodak company to form Kodak (Australasia) with Baker and Rouse as joint managing directors. A larger factory was built and production of new material, including rollfilm, began; in 1924 the firm manufactured the first X-ray film in Australia. Baker's commercial interests were not limited to photography; during World War I he had been associated with munitions production and he spent much money in search of oil in Australia and New Zealand.

In appearance Baker must have seemed the quintessence of the successful Edwardian businessman, wearing a silver imperial and motoring up to town from his seaside estate in a Rolls-Royce. He remained an approachable man, however, and was distinguished from fellow industrialists by his interest in scientific research and philanthropy. In both he was supported by his wife. Childless, they helped their relations generously and provided their employees with a company doctor. Often their donations were anonymous but they were known to have supported, among other charities, the Red Cross, the Big Brotherhood, Toc H and the Limbless Soldiers. At the end of his life Baker was president of the Melbourne Rotary Club.

Their greatest benefaction was to the Alfred Hospital. In 1913 Baker gave money for cancer research, and later took his friend Dr J. F. Mackeddie to England where they investigated a new cure for tuberculosis. Financed by Baker, Mackeddie set up a biochemistry department at the Alfred in 1922. When the new building was opened in 1926 the Bakers announced that they would maintain the laboratory for the next five years, enabling research to be carried out; their first grant, paid characteristically in a lump sum, was £20 500. The laboratory was named after the Bakers and Eleanor Shaw. In 1927 Baker decided to increase his support, but died suddenly at Mornington on 4 December 1928. His wife and Eleanor Shaw, with J. J. Rouse and his family, continued to help the Baker Institute during the Depression. Under the wills of Thomas and Alice Baker and Eleanor Shaw a trust was set up to underwrite the research work of the institute, which by 1974 had received nearly $4 million, as well as to aid other charities.

Besides her support for the Women's Hospital and the Talbot Colony, Alice Baker was prominent in the National Council of Women and represented Australia at the Toronto meeting of the International

Council of Women. Baker received no public honours; Alice Baker was appointed C.B.E. in 1933. She died on 20 March 1935 at South Yarra.

J. Cato, *The story of the camera in Australia* (Melb, 1955); *A'sian Photo-Review*, 15 Dec 1928; *Argus*, 23 Jan 1926, 6 Dec 1928, 22 Mar 1935; T. E. Lowe, The Thomas Baker, Alice Baker and Eleanor Shaw Medical Research Institute ... 1926-1975 (copy at Baker Institute).

P. H. DE SERVILLE

BAKER, THOMAS CHARLES RICHMOND (1897-1918), soldier and airman, was born on 2 May 1897 at Smithfield, South Australia, eldest son of Richmond Baker, schoolmaster and farmer, and his wife Annie Martha, née Gardner, and nephew of Thomas Baker [q.v.] photographic scientist. He was educated from 1911 at the Collegiate School of St Peter, Adelaide, where he won the Farrell Scholarship, rowed, played tennis and football and was a member of the cadet corps. On leaving school in 1914 he became a clerk in the Adelaide branch of the Bank of New South Wales.

Enlisting on 29 July 1915, Baker embarked in November for the Middle East as a reinforcement gunner for the 6th Field Artillery Brigade; his battery, the 16th, moved on from Egypt to France, arriving in time to take part in the first battle of the Somme. As a gunner he showed considerable courage. He won his first Military Medal on 15 December 1916 in an action near Gueudecourt: as part of an observation team sent forward to record the fall of shot and to secure the range for a bombardment, he repeatedly repaired broken telephone lines while under heavy fire. Shortly after this episode he was awarded a Bar to his Military Medal when, at great personal risk, he put out a fire in a gun-pit containing ammunition.

Though he had proved himself a competent gunner, Baker centred his hopes on joining the Australian Flying Corps. As a boy his chief hobby had been making model aeroplanes and in France aerial combat captured his imagination. In August 1917 he remarked that he was 'almost green with envy' on seeing Allied aviators in action. When an opportunity arose in September he transferred to the A.F.C. as an air mechanic, but he was selected for flying and sent to England to No. 5 Training Squadron; he made his first solo flight in March 1918. On 15 June he graduated as a Camel pilot and next day, with a total of 57 hours 40 minutes flying time, joined No. 4 Fighter Squadron as a second lieutenant. Baker's operational career extended from 23 June, when he first

crossed the lines, to his death in a fierce battle against odds over Ath on 4 November. During this period he destroyed eight enemy aircraft and was credited with having forced down four more. Several of these victories were against the highly effective Fokker biplane fighter; often he closed to ten or twenty feet before destroying them. He had been promoted lieutenant on 27 June. Award of the Distinguished Flying Cross and promotion to captain were both posthumous; his D.F.C. citation referred to 'exceptional initiative and dash'.

Baker had a forceful yet pleasant personality, was a fine pilot and became a steady, respected flight-leader. He often quoted Shakespeare in his letters. He was buried in the communal cemetery, Escanaffles, Belgium, and a stained-glass window is dedicated to his memory at St John's Church of England, Halifax Street, Adelaide.

E. J. Richards, *Australian airmen: History of the 4th Squadron, A.F.C.* (Melb, 1918); *Bank of New South Wales roll of honour* (Syd, 1921); F. M. Cutlack, *The Australian Flying Corps ... 1914-1918* (Syd, 1936); *London Gazette*, 19 Feb, 21 Aug 1917, 8 Feb 1919; *Mail* (Adel), 15 Nov 1919; No. 4 Squadron, Letters, log books and war diary (AWM); family papers (held by W. A. J. Baker, West Beach, SA).

JOHN McCARTHY

BALDWIN, JOSEPH MASON (1878-1945), astronomer, was born on 9 September 1878 at Carlton, Victoria, third son of Joseph Baldwin (d. 1887) and his wife Emma Maria, née Graham. His father, Yorkshire-born, had migrated to Victoria in 1870 and in 1885 became senior inspector of schools. His maternal grandfather Andrew Graham (1815-1908) was a distinguished British astronomer who took great interest in his grandson's development and training.

Baldwin was educated at South Melbourne College and University High School, matriculating in 1897, and for six months worked at the Melbourne Observatory where the director P. Baracchi [q.v.] became his tutor. He was then a scholar for four years at Queen's College, University of Melbourne, and a fellow for another year. Specializing in physics and mathematics, he graduated B.A. (1900), B.Sc. (1901), M.A. (1902) and D.Sc. (1913). He tutored at Trinity College and taught at Wesley College. After a period of lecturing at the Ballarat School of Mines he returned to the university where he conducted research for eighteen months with Professor (Sir) Thomas Lyle [q.v.]. In 1906 he was awarded an 1851 Exhibition scholarship which enabled him to continue his research in astrophysics abroad. He spent six months at the Royal Observatory at the Cape of Good Hope and then visited the Potsdam, Paris, and English and American observatories. At Cambridge, England, on 8 March 1907 he married Jessie Redmond of St Kilda, Victoria.

While overseas Baldwin accepted Baracchi's invitation to become his chief assistant from June 1908; he took up duties on his return to Melbourne in November. After Baracchi's retirement in 1915 Baldwin became acting director, and in 1920 government astronomer. The observatory's main activity at the time was observation of the Melbourne zone for the International Astrographic Catalogue; its reduction was achieved under Baldwin's direction. The first three volumes were presented between 1926 and 1929 but, although Baldwin had prepared the remaining material for printing, subsequent volumes were published posthumously. His other activities included establishment of the Geophysical Observatory at Toolangi in 1919, study of the earth's magnetic elements, and work for recording exact time for the time-signal service; variable star-work was also undertaken, the results of which were published in America. He led a party to Goondiwindi, Queensland, for the observation of the total solar eclipse in 1922. In 1943 the Victorian government decided to close the observatory. Baldwin continued briefly as officer-in-charge of the time service for the Commonwealth Solar Observatory, Mount Stromlo, before retiring in March 1944.

Baldwin was a council-member of the Royal Society of Victoria in 1920-45 and president in 1925-26, publishing several papers in the society's *Proceedings*. In 1930-31 he was president of Section A, Australian and New Zealand Association for the Advancement of Science; he was a fellow of the Institute of Physics and of the Royal Astronomical Society, London, publishing in the latter's monthly notices. He kept up his connexion with the university as a non-teaching member of the faculty of science from 1916, as a member of the standing committee of convocation from its establishment in 1923, and as president of the University Association in 1930-31.

Baldwin was remembered as large, loosely built, kindly and courteously soft-spoken, a competent worker, deeply immersed in his studies and always helpful to his staff, but perhaps not sufficiently tough and practically versed in the art of dealing with politicians. His first wife had died in 1935; on 6 January 1938 in Sydney he married Florette Jessie Bostock. He died of pneumonia on 6 July 1945 while on holiday at Southport, Queensland, survived by his second wife and by two sons and a daughter of the first marriage. He was cremated at Brisbane.

Melb Observatory, *Astrographic Catalogue*, 1926-63; *Aust J of Science*, Dec 1945; Roy Soc Vic, *Procs*, 58 (1946); *Punch* (Melb), 26 June 1913, 19 May 1921; family papers (held by Mrs Jessie Harley, Clayton, Vic).   PHILIPP SIMON

BALE, ALICE MARIAN ELLEN (1875-1955), artist, was born on 11 November 1875 at Richmond, Victoria, only child of William Mountier Bale (1851-1940), naturalist and inspector of customs, and his wife Marian, née Adams (d. 1915). A specialist in hydroids, W. M. Bale was a foundation member of the Field Naturalists' Club (1880), secretary of the Microscopical Society of Victoria (1882) and member of the Royal Society of Victoria. He published several papers on Victorian hydroids and on his death left many of his specimens and books to the National Museum and the National Herbarium, Melbourne.

Alice Bale spent her earliest years at the home of her paternal grandparents in Richmond, and attended the Erin Street State School. By 1886 her parents had made their home at 83 Walpole Street, Kew, where Alice lived for the rest of her life. In 1885-92 she attended the Methodist Ladies' College and distinguished herself in music and literature. She had early decided to be an artist and took private lessons from May Vale and a few from Hugh Ramsay [q.v.]. She was elected to membership of the Victorian Artists' Society in 1894; her first picture hung was at its exhibition in October 1896.

Alice Bale was enrolled at the Gallery School in 1895, where in the course of her studies she won nine major prizes and in 1902 was a strong contender for the travelling scholarship; she attended for two more years but did not compete for prizes. She became noted for her paintings of flowers; Bernard Hall [q.v.] held her work in high regard and a print of her 'Scabiosa' (purchased 1922) was for years one of the few available coloured reproductions of pictures in the National Gallery of Victoria. Her landscapes and interiors were mostly painted at Castlemaine, where she had a house and studio, and at Kew; she never left Victoria. Miss Bale became a consistent and respected exhibitor with the Women's Art Club (later the Melbourne Society of Women Painters), and she edited the journal of the Victorian Artists' Society from 5 March 1918 until its last issue in February 1919. She rarely missed a council meeting of 'the Vics'' during her two terms in office in 1914 and in the stormy years between October 1916 and November 1918 when Max Meldrum [q.v.] was president. It was then that a group of supporters present in Meldrum's studio decided to form the Twenty Melbourne Painters; Alice Bale was the first and lifelong secretary. Explaining the origin and aims of the society, she wrote in 1920: 'we desire nothing but sincerity and a humble study of nature, from which alone all art, whether decorative or realistic, draws any enduring life'.

From 1923 her membership of the Australian Art Association (disbanded in 1933) enabled her to exhibit annually with major artists from all States. Two of her paintings were in the 1923 exhibition of Australian art in London. In 1933 her group portrait, 'Mr. and Mrs. Carl Hampel', was hung at the Royal Academy and her 'Portrait of a lady' was exhibited at the Salon of 1939 in Paris. She also exhibited with The Half Dozen Group of Artists in Brisbane in 1943-48 and in 1946 painted a commissioned portrait of Major General Vasey for the Australian War Memorial.

Articulate and formidable in controversy, Miss Bale wrote many letters to newspapers on issues ranging from the appointment of a new director of the National Gallery of Victoria to the preservation of trees and modernism in art. Adrian Lawlor [q.v.], although opposed to her traditionalism, admired her 'sense, character and intelligence'; she reminded him of Dame Ethel Smyth.

On 14 February 1955 Alice Bale died in the Royal Melbourne Hospital after an operation for cancer; she was buried in the Church of England section of Boroondara cemetery. From her estate, valued for probate at £46 353, a perpetual scholarship bearing her name was established. Her portrait by William Rowell [q.v.] is in the Castlemaine Art Gallery where there are seven of her paintings; others are at Walpole Street and in public collections in Melbourne, Sydney, Adelaide, Brisbane, Ballarat and Mildura.

L. B. Cox, *The National Gallery of Victoria, 1861 to 1968* (Melb, 1970); *V.A.S.*, 23 Apr 1920; *Art in Aust,* Mar 1924, Dec 1926; *Age*, 3 Aug 1929; J. McGrath, The Australian Art Association, 1912-1933 . . . (B. Soc. Sci. special study, RMIT, 1974); Vic Artists' Soc, Minute-books (LaTL); Art cats and news-cuttings (SLV); Public Lib . . . of Vic records (PRO, Vic); family papers (held by Perpetual Trustees Aust Ltd, Melb).   JOYCE MCGRATH

BALFOUR, JAMES LAWSON (1870-1966), artist, was born on 17 August 1870 at Fitzroy, Melbourne, son of James Balfour, artist, and his wife Elizabeth, née Hart. His father came from Scotland where the family returned in 1872. Lawson grew up in an artistic and musical environment: his father and uncle had their own studios and his ancestors had made 'damask designs for the linen trade'. He spent two years at Herkomer School at Bushey, Hertfordshire, England, and exhibited with the Royal Society of British Artists and the New Watercolour Society in 1892-93. He continued his training in Paris, spending one year with F. Cormon, and three at the Académie Julian under W. Bouguereau, Benjamin Constant and Jules LeFebvre.

Balfour began his professional career in Ireland as a painter of horses, dogs and babies. He was living in Bangor, County Down, when he exhibited 'Sunday Morning' at the Royal Academy of Arts in 1899. In 1900 he went to New Zealand and at Christchurch on 29 April 1904 married Eva Hulston. He moved to Sydney in 1912 and became a noted portrait painter. He was commissioned to paint prominent citizens such as Governor Sir Dudley de Chair, Sir Normand Maclaurin and Sir Charles Mackellar [qq.v.], A. B. Weigall [q.v.6], and fellow artists Charles Bryant and W. Lister Lister [qq.v.], his lifelong friend. He gave private lessons for many years and in 1922-24 directed the Balfour Art School, assisted by Reginald Payten.

Contemporaries found Balfour quiet and retiring. He was one of the first to discover the possibilities of the Dee Why area as a sketching ground, and settled there. His competent formal portraits tended towards a conventional tonal rendering but were distinguished by their sophisticated technique and knowledge of oil as a medium. His artist friends were more informally posed, with staccato dashes of colour to enliven the surface. His imaginative figure drawings revealed the high proficiency of his French academic training. In 1919-31 Balfour was an exhibiting councillor of the Royal Art Society of New South Wales; he had become a fellow in 1922 when the society was reconstituted. In 1932 he was elected to the committee of the Manly Art Gallery and Historical Collection and was a vice-patron in 1955-66.

Predeceased by his wife, Balfour died on 9 February 1966 at Woy Woy, and was cremated with Anglican rites. His estate was valued for probate at £1401. Balfour's work is represented in the art galleries of New South Wales, South Australia, Queensland, and Belfast, Northern Ireland, the Robert McDougall Art Gallery, Christchurch, New Zealand, and the Manly Art Gallery. His portrait of Sir Joseph Banks [q.v.1] is in the Commonwealth collection.

Art in Aust, May 1923, Dec 1926; De Berg interview with Lawson Balfour, Dec 1961 (Tape recording NL).   JOCELYN HACKFORTH-JONES
BERNARD SMITH

BALL, GEORGE (1892-1916), soldier, was born in 1892 at St Petersburg (Leningrad), Russia; he was a natural-born British subject. Nothing is known of his early life. In August 1911 he migrated alone to Australia, arriving in Melbourne on the German ship *Seydlitz*, and from 1912 until the outbreak of World War I worked as a vigneron's clerk at Rutherglen, Victoria.

One of the district's first volunteers, he enlisted as a private in the Australian Imperial Force on 18 August 1914 and was posted to the 7th Battalion. His unit embarked at Melbourne in mid-October and on arriving in Egypt went into training at Mena. Ball first saw action on 25 April 1915 at Gaba Tepe where he was wounded during the landing; he rejoined his battalion on 26 May and in its next major engagement, the battle for Lone Pine, won the Distinguished Conduct Medal for 'conspicuous gallantry'. On 6 August, after all the officers and non-commissioned officers in his party had been killed or wounded, he 'took command ... in an isolated post, and held the enemy in check until reorganization had been effected'. Six days later he was promoted temporary corporal and, apart from a rest period spent with his battalion at Mudros, remained at Gallipoli until the evacuation on 20 December 1915. Ball was confirmed as corporal on 4 December and was mentioned in a dispatch by General Sir Ian Hamilton.

Following a period of outpost duty in the Canal Zone the 7th Battalion sailed for France on 26 March 1916. On 3 May they went into a relatively quiet sector of the line near Fleurbaix and then moved to Ploegsteert. In July and August the battalion took part in the battles for Pozières, suffering heavy casualties. The Ypres sector, their next post, was calm by comparison, and on the night of 30 September they raided enemy trenches near Hollebeke. Ball, a temporary sergeant since February, led one section of the raiding party along the German defences, 'himself killing five or six of the enemy and displaying great courage and initiative'. For his role in this and similar encounters he was awarded a Bar to his D.C.M. Five weeks later, on 5 November, he was killed by a shell near Gueudecourt on the Somme battlefield.

A tall man, 'all muscle and bone', Ball was described by the 7th Battalion historian as one of the unit's 'most fearless and resolute' soldiers. Always called 'the Russian', in spite of his excellent command of English, he was as formidable an adversary in the boxing stadium at Mena Camp as in the trenches. Away from the battlefield he took great delight in entertaining with his mandolin, which was frequently raffled to pay his debts from crown and anchor and later bought back when winnings permitted. Ball has no known grave but his name is commemorated on the Villers-Bretonneux Memorial, France.

C. E. W. Bean, *The story of Anzac*, 1, 2 (Syd, 1921, 1924), and *The A.I.F. in France*, 3 (Syd, 1929); A. Dean and E. W. Gutteridge, *The Seventh Battalion, A.I.F.* (Melb, 1933); *Norddeutscher Lloyds Shipping Lists*, 21 Aug 1911; *London Gazette*, 11, 28 Jan, 14 Nov 1916; *Rutherglen Sun*, 21 Aug 1914; Seventh Battalion war diary (AWM).
WILLIAM JAMIESON

BALL, PERCIVAL (1845-1900), sculptor, was born on 17 February 1845 at Westminster, London, son of Edward Henry Ball, carver, and his wife Louisa, née Percival. Showing early artistic talent, he studied at the Royal Academy of Arts schools, London, winning several gold medals and prizes. Between 1865 and 1882 he exhibited twenty-four works at Royal Academy exhibitions. About 1870 he went to Paris and then to Munich and Rome, where he lived for some eight years; his work in marble received high praise.

Troubled by asthma and bronchitis, in 1884 Ball sought the milder climate of Australia; heavy drinking was probably another reason for his voluntary exile from Europe. After six months in Sydney he settled in Melbourne and established a studio in Collins Street East; by 1888 he had moved to 9 Collins Street.

In 1886-87 Ball completed James Gilbert's statue of Sir Redmond Barry [q.v.3] and the memorial was placed outside the Public Library, Melbourne. Another work commissioned in 1886 was a marble bust of Bishop Moorhouse [q.v.5], now at the La Trobe Library. In 1889 he completed a statue of Scottish hero Sir William Wallace for the Ballarat Botanical Gardens. He executed a number of portrait busts, including one of the bookseller and publisher George Robertson [q.v.6]. He produced a small model in 1890 for the proposed memorial to Francis Ormond [q.v.5]; the full-scale figure was completed in 1892 and cast in bronze in Melbourne. This work was more realistic than most of Ball's sculpture: a contemporary wrote that he 'has managed to produce a most faithful likeness of features and expression of his subject, and he has also succeeded in catching Mr. Ormond's attitude and bearing in ordinary conversation'. It was not until June 1897 that the statue was erected and unveiled outside the Working Men's College, at a cost of some £1200.

Ball also received commissions from the other colonies. The relief panel, 'Phryne before Praxiteles', on the outside wall of the Art Gallery of New South Wales, was commissioned by the trustees in 1898. It was completed by 1900 and Ball was sent to London to superintend the casting in bronze. Local critics suggested that Australian craftsmen could cope with the casting, or that skilled craftsmen should be brought to Australia. Unfortunately Ball died in London of heart failure due to asthma and bronchitis on 4 April 1900 before his work was completed. He was unmarried. By 1903 the relief was cast and erected; skilfully designed, it is a typical Victorian academic work, which hints at the sensuous behind the cover of an acceptable classical myth.

Ball had exhibited with the Society of Artists in Sydney and in 1886 was a member of the Australian Artists' Association and the Victorian Artists' Society. Examples of his work are in the National Portrait Gallery, London; Peel Park, Salford, England; the Art Gallery of New South Wales; and the La Trobe Library, Melbourne.

E. Benezit, *Dictionnaire critique et documentaire des peintres, sculpteurs . . .*, 1 (Paris, 1911); *Table Talk*, 31 Aug 1888, 1 Aug 1890; *IAN*, 1 Mar 1892; *Argus*, 8 June 1897; *A'sian Art Review*, 1 Jan 1900.
                                                    KEN SCARLETT

BALL, RICHARD THOMAS (1857-1937), engineer and politician, was born on 14 September 1857 at Surry Hills, Sydney, eldest son of George Ball, farmer, and his wife Ann, née Hooper. His parents had reached Sydney on 23 August from Devonshire, England, as bounty migrants in the *Zemindar*. After his father's death his mother married Jabez Francis and moved to Rooty Hill. Richard was educated at the Eastern Creek Public School, then was employed by Chapman & Co., engineers, and the Atlas Foundry & Engineering Works. He was working as a blacksmith at Brisbane Street, Sydney, when he married Esther Arnold, a dressmaker, on 6 May 1880 with Baptist rites.

In 1881 Ball bought Burn & Son's foundry at Goulburn and had various partners until 1885 when he established R. T. Ball & Co. From 1888 he carried out government railway contracts 'as a commercial speculation' on borrowed capital, and in 1890 set up a branch called the Rolling Stock Works. In 1894 his estate was sequestrated with debts of over £6000 and the works forcibly sold at a loss; he received his certificate of discharge

in 1895. An alderman on the Goulburn Municipal Council in 1887-94, he had been mayor in 1890 and 1891.

In 1895 Ball went to Albury to help construct the local waterworks. He was elected to the Legislative Assembly for Albury as a free trader in July 1895 but was narrowly defeated in 1898 after opposing equal representation of the States in the Senate and the lack of machinery to break deadlocks. He petitioned in vain against the return of his opponent as 'guilty of undue influence and intimidation'. He was now practising as a mechanical engineer in Sydney. About 1911 he moved to Petersham and at Goulburn re-established R. T. Ball & Co., later managed by his son.

Defeated for Albury in 1901, he represented Corowa in 1904-20 and 1927-37 and Murray in 1920-27. A member of the Farmers and Settlers' Association, Ball was one of a group of members who tried to form a country party in 1914-15. In 1916-20 he was secretary for public works and minister for railways in W. A. Holman's [q.v.] National ministry. Minister for agriculture from April to June 1922 in Sir George Fuller's [q.v.] coalition government, he was then again secretary for public works and minister for railways and State industrial enterprises from June 1922 until June 1925. Administrative ability and business and engineering knowledge contributed to Ball's success as secretary for works. In 1918 he established the ship-building industry at the Government Dockyard at Walsh Island, Newcastle. He carried legislation to construct 526 miles (846 km) of new branch railways and to build bridges, water-supply, sewerage and harbour works, and conducted government industrial enterprises in a business-like manner. In 1922 he skilfully piloted through parliament an Act to ratify the border railway and bridges agreement with Victoria which helped to develop the Riverina; and after fifty years of controversy, as a non-party measure, carried the Sydney Harbour Bridge Act authorizing work to start.

Ball urged the union of all anti-socialist parties in the early 1920s and, as a good local member, supported the Riverina New State Movement. However in April 1932 he left the United Australia Party and joined the United Country Party. He was a trustee of the National Park in 1933-37 and an associate member of the Institution of Engineers, Australia, which he had helped to found. He enjoyed playing bowls and billiards. Ball died on 30 October 1937 at Marrickville, and was cremated after a state funeral at the Central Baptist Church. He was survived by two sons and two daughters of his first marriage, and by his second wife Lillie May

Hume, née Gettens, a divorcee whom he had married on 26 January 1926 at the Baptist Church, Stanmore. His estate was valued for administration at £5211.

E. W. Hine, *A parliamentary veteran* (Corowa, 1937); R. T. Wyatt, *The history of Goulburn*, 2nd ed (Syd, 1972); *Aust National Review*, 20 Feb 1924; *SMH*, 6 Apr 1932, 15 Sept, 1 Nov 1937; Bankruptcy file 8562/5 (NSWA).   MARTHA RUTLEDGE

BALSILLIE, JOHN GRAEME (1885-1924), engineer and inventor, was born in Brisbane on 11 September 1885, second son of James Pearson Balsillie, wholesale warehouseman, and his wife Eliza, née Johnston, both of whom were Scottish-born. Brought up by an uncle after his father's death in 1889, he was educated at the Brisbane Boys' Central School and Brisbane Grammar School. In December 1901 he became a clerk in a warehouse, attending the Technical College part time until, in 1903, he went to England to study electrical engineering. He worked in the Armstrong-Whitworth workshops and was coached by a cousin who was a school principal. In May 1904 he invented a magnetic detector and in August joined a company erecting wireless telegraph stations in England and then in Russia. After working in Germany, Siberia and China for about five years, he formed in England the British Radiotelegraph Co. which marketed the 'Balsillie System' of wireless telegraphy, judged in 1911 to be an infringement of the Marconi patent.

Balsillie had been elected associate member of the Institution of Electrical Engineers in 1910. Next year he met Prime Minister Andrew Fisher [q.v.] in London and on 31 July was appointed engineer for radiotelegraphy, within the Australian Postmaster-General's Department, to establish a coastal maritime communication service. By late 1915 there were twenty stations around Australia, using a new system which survived an action for infringement of patent brought by the Marconi Co. in 1912 and settled to the government's advantage in 1915. That year an inquiry into another patent dispute lapsed before evidence was taken. In September wireless telegraphy was transferred to the Department of the Navy and Balsillie resigned in December, though with a retaining fee as consulting engineer for six months.

He had become interested in rainfall stimulation and by April 1915 had designed an apparatus, the 'Balsillie Rain Stimulation and Procuration Plant', which was purchased by the Department of Home Affairs; he operated it in arid country at Bookooloo,

on the transcontinental railway, from May 1916 and later at Wynbring and Tarcoola. Patents were subsequently granted. Plants also established at Hopetoun and Boonoke survived temporary closure in 1919. The Commonwealth meteorologist disputed the experimental stations' claimed increase in rainfall; a report by Balsillie was tabled in parliament, but operations ceased in January 1921 after press and parliamentary criticism. In September his work, which had cost over £6000, was referred to the Institute of Science and Industry. In 1919 and 1920 he had obtained patents for improvements in light projection and reflectors with application to vehicle headlights. Commercial manufacture of his 'Flatlight' reflectors took him to the United States of America.

Fair, with a high forehead, Balsillie smoked a pipe, wore pince-nez, and though usually immaculately dressed could 'jump into overalls and do the dirtiest work'. He was described as a 'scholarly man and a brilliant conversationalist of courtly manners'. Unmarried, he died of nephritis in Cincinatti on 10 July 1924 and was cremated.

R. Curnow, 'The origins of Australian broadcasting, 1900-1923', I. Bedford and R. Curnow, *Initiative and organization* (Melb, 1963); *SMH*, 29 Dec 1915; *Punch* (Melb), 13 July 1916; *Bulletin*, 9 Dec 1959; J. G. Balsillie papers (NL); Attorney-General's Dept, Correspondence files CRS A432 (AAO, Canb); PMG, Correspondence files MP 341/1 (AAO, Melb).   LINDSAY CLELAND

BAMFORD, FREDERICK WILLIAM (1849-1934), politician, was born at Dubbo, New South Wales, on 11 February 1849, son of Frederick Bamford, builder, and his wife Mary Anne, née McKay. He was educated at Toowoomba, Queensland, where his family lived from 1854. Apprenticed to a carpenter at 14, he probably worked round Toowoomba for nearly twenty years; he was married there on 7 September 1871 to Mary Ann Miller.

Bamford and a partner began cabinet-making at Mackay in July 1882; they quarrelled and dissolved the partnership in December and Bamford was declared insolvent in April 1884. He was employed in September 1885 as inspector of railway bridges around Cairns and was discharged from bankruptcy in November. In 1892 he transferred to Bowen and early in 1894 became licensee of the Sportsman's Arms. He joined a Democratic Association in December 1895, was its candidate for Bowen in the general election next April, but was narrowly defeated. He moved to the Railway Hotel, became local secretary of the Licensed Victuallers' Association, joined the

Chamber of Commerce and was elected to the municipal council in 1897; next year he was mayor of Bowen. After failing in a second parliamentary candidature in March 1899, he resigned from the municipal council in July and worked on a Townsville newspaper. In 1901 he became the official Australian Labor Party candidate for the Federal seat of Herbert. Campaigning against Kanaka labour on the northern sugar-fields, he won the seat narrowly.

Bamford was soon known in parliament as a competent speaker, an advocate of White Australia and a keen and consistent supporter of subsidies and protection for the sugar industry. He was a member of the royal commissions on old-age pensions (1906), the Tasmanian customs leakage (1911), chairman of the commissions on the pearling industry (1913) and the New Hebrides mail services (1915), temporary chairman of committees in the House of Representatives in 1911-22, and a member of the standing committee on public works in 1920. In 1902-16 Bamford was vice-president of the Waterside Workers' Federation, and established a friendship with W. M. Hughes [q.v.], who was president over the same period.

Bamford had always shown his concern for Australian defence, which to him was founded on unquestioned loyalty to Great Britain and, after 1914, on vigorous prosecution of the war in Europe. He urged conscription for overseas service as early as July 1915, being the first member of the House of Representatives openly to do so. He was expelled from the A.L.P. on 30 October 1916, joined Hughes in the walk-out from caucus on 14 November and became minister for home and territories in the National Labor government of 1916-17. He was connected with no important legislation, however, and his brief spell in the ministry was more a recognition of his personal ties with Hughes, outspoken support of conscription and general popularity than of noteworthy ability. His widely appreciated affability, together with respect for his age and parliamentary service, brought him appointment as chairman of committees and deputy Speaker from 1923 until his retirement from parliament in 1925. Although not very active in the position, he was reasonably efficient and impartial.

Bamford's career was remarkable mainly for his continued electoral success as a Nationalist after 1916 in an electorate normally safe for Labor. This was chiefly a consequence of his widespread personal popularity, as well as his earnest support of the sugar-farmers' cause. He thus exemplified a political tradition of North Queensland where personality is often a particularly important ingredient of electoral success.

After his retirement, Bamford spent nine years in comfortable obscurity in Sydney, where he died on 10 September 1934. He was cremated with Anglican rites, and was survived by three sons and two daughters. 'Everyone likes Fred', the Brisbane *Worker* had declared in 1914, and this judgment was shared by colleagues and constituents.

P. Weller (ed), *Caucus minutes, 1901-1949* (Melb, 1975); *V&P* (LA Qld), 1887, 3, 1250-51; H. McQueen, 'Who were the Conscriptionists?', *Labor Hist*, no 16, May 1969; *Worker* (Brisb), 26 Feb 1910, 6 Aug 1914; *Punch* (Melb), 21 Dec 1916; *SMH*, 12 Sept 1934; D. W. Hunt, Federal politics in the Herbert electorate, 1915-1925 (B.A. Hons thesis, James Cook Univ, 1974); Waterside Workers' Federation of Aust, Federal Council minutes, 4 Feb 1902, 15 Aug, 19 Sept 1916 (ANU Archives); Qld Labor Party, Central Political Executive minutes, 30 Oct 1916 (Labor House, Brisb).

D. W. HUNT

BANCKS, JAMES CHARLES (1889-1952), cartoonist, was born at Enmore, Sydney, on 10 May 1889, son of John Spencer Bancks, an Irish railway-porter, and his wife Margaret, née Beston. Brought up at Hornsby in a family he remembered as a 'living comic strip', Bancks left school at 14, worked as a wool clerk, office-boy and lift-driver, and practised drawing in his spare time. In 1911 his first cartoons were published in the *Comic Australian* and, from 20 August 1914, in the *Bulletin*. After the *Bulletin* guaranteed him £8 a week for his drawings, he became a full-time artist and took lessons from Julian Ashton and Dattilo Rubbo [qq.v.]. He worked mainly as caricaturist and cartoonist; his work showed the influence of L. Hopkins, P. May [qq.v.4,5] and A. Vincent [q.v.], although he most admired Will Dyson [q.v.] among Australian artists.

In November 1921 Bancks began drawing 'Us Fellers', a colour comic-strip for the Sunday issue of the Sydney *Sun*. One of the minor characters in the first issue was Ginger Smith, a small red-headed boy in a black waistcoat. By the time he became Ginger Meggs in April 1922 he had a muff-wearing girl-friend, Minnie Peters, a rival for her affections in Eddie Coogan, and had gathered about him a gang of mates, including Benny and Ocker. For the next thirty years, weekly in the *Sunday Sun* and also from 1924 in the *Sunbeams book, adventures of Ginger Meggs*, he experienced under Bancks the joys and tribulations of urban life: the joys of cricket and football, wangling ice-creams out of Italian shop-keepers, and toughening up curly-headed 'sooks' named Cuthbert and Clarence: the tribulations of brushes with the law over broken windows, with the bully Tiger Kelly against whom the only defence was a rotten tomato or a catapult, with his largely unsympathetic parents and with schoolteachers. These basic ingredients of the strip were established in its first year, but Bancks developed an increasing strength of line and use of planned areas of black; linguistically there was a gradual 'improvement' of Ginger's language. Throughout his adventures Ginger remained sturdily optimistic, self-confident, cunning and quick-thinking; part larrikin, part battler, part philosopher and part humourist, he became Australia's most famous boy. His 25th birthday was celebrated in the wards of children's hospitals in several States.

In the late 1920s Bancks penetrated the overseas syndication market; by the time 'Us Fellers' changed its *Sunday Sun* title to 'Ginger Meggs' in November 1939, the strip had reached audiences in England and the United States of America as well as throughout Australia, and had been translated into French and Spanish for readers of *La Presse* in Montreal and *El Muno* in Buenos Aires. On visits overseas Bancks met fellow cartoonists, including Walt Disney; in 1948 Ginger appeared on American television. Plans to introduce the strip into Europe were largely thwarted by the outbreak of World War II, but it reached the Pacific via *Guinea Gold*, issued by the Australian Army.

In 1923-26 Bancks lived in Melbourne: from 1922 'Us Fellers' had also appeared in the *Sun-News Pictorial*, for which he drew 'Mr. Melbourne day by day' and 'The Blimps'. Based thereafter in Sydney, he married Jessie Nita (d. 1936), daughter of E. J. Tait [q.v.], on 15 October 1931 at Darling Point. She was well known as a stage and dress designer, and collaborated with Bancks on the dialogue and costumes for the musical comedy *Blue Mountain melody*, staged by J. C. Williamson's [q.v.6] in 1934 with Madge Elliott and Cyril Ritchard as the leads. Bancks also wrote for newspapers, was prominent in club life and racing circles, and much in demand as an after-dinner speaker. The highest-paid Australian cartoonist of his day, he was gentle, generous, an indefatigable charity-worker and warm in his encouragement of Australian artists; in 1946 he funded a £1000 travelling scholarship for a black-and-white artist under 25. In 1949 Bancks signed a new ten-year contract with Associated Newspapers Ltd, but repudiated it in 1951 when the company failed to fulfil its obligation to publish 'Ginger Meggs' on the front page of the *Sunday Sun*'s comic supplement. Bancks won the ensuing court cases and moved to the rival *Sunday Telegraph*; Ginger helped to increase its circulation.

Bancks died suddenly of coronary vascular disease at Point Piper on 1 July 1952 and was cremated with Anglican rites. He was survived by his second wife Patricia, née Quinan, whom he had married at Yuma, Arizona, United States, in 1938, and by a daughter. In 1978 'Ginger Meggs' left the *Sunday Telegraph* for the *Sun-Herald*.

Whether Bancks influenced or merely reflected the mores of Australian society can only be conjectured; but it is at least possible that the popularity of Ginger Meggs entrenched nicknames like 'Ginger' and 'Ocker' within Australian English, and consolidated schoolboy attitudes towards the gang, the 'opposite sex', and such figures of authority as parents, policemen and schoolteachers.

A. Ashton, *Sydney savages 1934-55* (Syd, 1955); V. Lindesay, *The inked-in image* (Melb, 1970); J. Horgan (ed), *The golden years of Ginger Meggs* (Lond, Adel, 1978); *Salt*, 8 Oct 1945; *Current Affairs Bulletin*, 23 Dec 1963; *Comic Australian*, 28 Oct 1911; *Bulletin*, 20 Aug 1914, 16, 30 May 1918, 29 Jan 1920, 2 July 1924, 9 July 1952; *Sunday Sun*, 1921-51; *Sun-News Pictorial*, 11 Sept 1922, 6 Jan, 10 Feb 1923; *SMH*, 16 Oct 1931, 18 Aug 1934, 23 Mar, 4 Sept 1936, 27 May 1939, 21 May 1944, 23 Nov 1946, 1 July 1947, 8 Mar, 4, 5 Apr, 1, 3, 12 May 1951, 2 July 1952, 21 July 1968; *Pix*, 9 Mar 1940; *Daily Telegraph* (Syd), 2 July 1952; *Sunday Telegraph* (Syd), 6 July 1952; Bancks entry (ML picture cat); information from Mrs P. R. Bancks, Woollahra, NSW, *and* V. Lindesay, Ripponlea, Vic.

B. G. ANDREWS

BANCROFT, THOMAS LANE (1860-1933), medical naturalist, was born on 2 January 1860 at Lenton, Nottinghamshire, England, son of Dr Joseph Bancroft [q.v.3] and his wife Anne, née Oldfield. The family arrived in Brisbane in October 1864. From the Normal School and the Brisbane Grammar School, Bancroft entered Edinburgh University in 1878, graduated M.B., Ch.M. in 1883 with the bronze medal for botany, and then spent a year at the Manchester Infirmary where he became an expert photographer. As a boy, he had assisted in his father's experiments and his own interests lay in scientific inquiry, but his ambition to hold a full-time research appointment was never fulfilled.

Bancroft spent 1885-86 working in the hospital at Geraldton (Innisfail), Queensland, where in the rain forest he found new poisonous plants. He began pharmacological studies and in 1886-94 tasted over one thousand plants, tested more than 150 extracts and published ten papers. After a year at Christchurch Hospital, New Zealand, he practised from 1889 to 1894 in Ann Street, Brisbane, with his father and his cousin Peter Bancroft. In 1892 he investigated 'Birdsville disease' in horses and 'zamia poisoning' in cattle for the Queensland government, and in 1893 published the first Australian record of bacteria in the root-nodules of legumes.

Bancroft inherited his father's experimental farm and pemmican factory at Deception Bay, moved there in 1894, and next year on 10 July married Cecilia Mary (1868-1961), daughter of Archdeacon Thomas Jones of Brisbane. Of their two children, Mabel Josephine (1896-1971) became a noted parasitologist. At Deception Bay he did his best work: he discovered that female mosquitoes, thought to be short lived and dependent on blood meals, would survive for weeks on banana. In 1899, using *Culex fatigans* mosquitoes which he had reared and fed on a patient with filariasis, he defined and illustrated each stage of the larval worm over a developmental period of about sixteen days. In 1904, working with the related heart-worm of the dog, he proved that the infective larvae break out from the tip of the mosquito's proboscis, thus completing research begun by Patrick Manson in 1878.

Moving to Brisbane in 1904, Bancroft served as quarantine officer for the port of Brisbane, and held temporary appointments with the State Health Department in 1905-06 to investigate dengue fever, beriberi and suspected cases of plague. Dengue was thought to be transmitted by *Culex fatigans*; he correctly suspected but failed to prove that the day-biting *Aedes aegypti* was the carrier. In 1908 he published a review of Queensland mosquitoes.

Bancroft became government medical officer that year at Stannary Hills, a mining settlement west of Cairns, then in 1910 at Eidsvold on the Burnett River. Here he investigated the Queensland lung-fish *Neoceratodus forsteri*, which he believed nearly extinct. He set up a rearing-tank to provide embryological and other material for research workers, discovered that the hatchlings briefly became amphibious, and thus succeeded in fostering them through the difficult early stages; his proposal for a hatchery and laboratory on Stradbroke Island elicited meagre support. Appointed medical officer at Palm Island in 1930 – a frustrating experience – in 1932 he retired to Wallaville on the Burnett River, where he died of cerebral haemorrhage on 12 November 1933. He was buried in Toowong cemetery, Brisbane.

Bancroft undertook many other investigations ranging from blood parasites of birds to Aboriginal food-plants and hybridization of cotton. From 1884 to 1932 he collected plants for the Queensland Herbarium and animals for the Queensland Museum, and freely provided material for fellow scientists which led to recognition of many new species in such diverse groups as freshwater algae, eucalypts, mosquitoes, fruit-flies, spiders, fish and snakes, many of which were named after him. He was elected a corresponding member of the Zoological Society of London in 1923.

Shy, kindly and generous, Bancroft shunned publicity. He was uncompromising on matters of principle and could not be persuaded to modify opinions based on his own observations. This sometimes led him into public debate that embarrassed the departments he worked for. In the absence of suitable employment, his potential as a research scientist was unfulfilled. Absorbed in natural history, however, he made indirect contributions to knowledge over an even wider field than his personal research on which he published eighty-four papers.

I. M. Mackerras and E. N. Marks, 'The Bancrofts: a century of scientific endeavour', Roy Soc Qld, *Procs*, 84 (1972), and for bibliog.

E. N. MARKS

BANFIELD, EDMUND JAMES (1852-1923), author and naturalist, was born on 4 September 1852 at Toxteth Park, Liverpool, England, son of Jabez Walter Banfield (1820-1899), printer, and his wife Sarah Ann, née Smith. Jabez had served his apprenticeship with a Liverpool printer, but migrated to Victoria in 1852 and followed the gold rushes. On 20 November 1854 his family sailed in the *Indian Queen* to join him. A founding partner in the *Maryborough and Dunolly Advertiser*, Jabez moved to Ararat in 1857 and started the *Ararat Advertiser*; it was owned by the family until the 1960s. He became a leading local citizen: treasurer to the borough council and the hospital board of management for some thirty-five years, magistrate, churchwarden and lay preacher, secretary to the cemetery trustees, and popular public reciter and reader of Dickens [q.v.4], Shakespeare and other classic authors.

Educated at an Ararat church-school, Edmund became a reporter and printer's assistant for his father, relaxing on weekend natural history trips in the Grampians. In the 1870s he worked on the Melbourne *Age* and the Sydney *Daily Telegraph*, and in 1882 became reporter and sub-editor with the *Townsville Daily Bulletin* in Queensland. In 1884, probably with the backing of Burns Philp [qq.v.] & Co., he travelled to England; while there an eye injured in childhood was removed, and he met Bertha Golding, who migrated to Townsville to marry him on 3 August 1886 at St James' Anglican Church. He had published *The Torres Straits route from Queensland to England* in Townsville in 1885.

Banfield reported Robert Philp on his first election campaign in 1886, and in 1890 organized fund-raising functions for the North Queensland separation movement. Although he took professional responsibilities seriously, he felt that he lacked 'those qualities which make for dutiful citizenship' and was enraged by political, professional and personal wrongs, real and imagined. He camped with friends on Dunk Island near Tully and in September 1896 applied for a thirty-year lease of part of the island. Diagnosed as tubercular and in nervous collapse, he resigned from the North Queensland Newspaper Co. and, partly blind, with a palsied hand and a deaf wife, settled on Dunk Island from 28 September 1897.

Banfield's health rapidly improved and on 4 January 1900 he selected 320 acres (129 ha); in 1913 a further 40 acres were added in his wife's name. Though he relieved for the *Townsville Bulletin* in 1901 and visited New South Wales and Victoria in 1911, his life henceforth was spent almost entirely on Dunk. He grew maize, vegetables, coffee and fruit, and kept farm animals, but was unable to live on the proceeds. An apiary was destroyed by birds which he refused to kill because he considered the island a sanctuary and hoped it would become a national park. His income to maintain himself, his wife, and Irish servant and occasional Aboriginal helpers never exceeded £100 a year; the community lived on seafood, goat meat, poultry, fruit, vegetables, milk and eggs, with occasional provisions from the weekly steamer. An 'erratic diary' of nature observations became the basis of articles and books which were studded with quotations from copious reading. He corresponded with naturalists throughout the world, and a species of rat discovered by him on the island was originally named *Uromys banfieldi*. His articles, sometimes under the pen-names 'Rob Krusoe' and 'Beachcomber', appeared in the *Lone Hand*, North Queensland newspapers, and the *Queensland Geographical Journal*. He wrote by hand until he obtained a typewriter late in life.

Banfield was commissioned by the government to write *Within the Barrier* (Townsville, 1907), a tourist guide to the coastal areas of North Queensland. His most famous work, *The confessions of a beachcomber* (London, 1908), later translated widely, was dedicated to Philp on whose recommendation he had become a justice of the peace in 1899. *Confessions* was followed

by *My tropic isle* (London, 1911), much of which had appeared originally in the *North Queensland Register* as 'Rural homilies', and by *Tropic days* (London, 1918). Surprised at the interest of the world in his 'prosaic' life, he described himself as a 'sedate and determined man' who resented gratuitous violations of his privacy; at least one enthusiastic reader arrived unannounced hoping to share his idyllic existence. *Last leaves from Dunk Island* (Sydney, 1925), published posthumously, was a collection of sketches compiled by A. H. Chisholm largely from *Townsville Daily Bulletin* articles.

On 2 June 1923 Banfield died of peritonitis; his wife was alone for three days before her signals were noticed by a passing steamer. He was buried on the island by the ship's crew; subsequently, a cairn was erected over his and his wife's graves. His estate, sworn for probate at £1916, was composed chiefly of shares in Townsville newspapers. Although his clichéd style and archaic usages have dated his books, Banfield was an enthusiastic promoter of Australia and a passionate spokesman for the preservation of North Queensland in its natural state. His island, however, became a tourist resort.

H. C. Perry, *Memoirs of the Hon. Sir Robert Philp . . . 1851-1922* (Brisb, 1923); A. H. Chisholm, *Birds and green places* (Lond, 1929); J. W. Frings, *My island of dreams* (Lond, 1936); C. L. Barrett, *Koonwarra* (Lond, 1939); G. C. Bolton, *A thousand miles away* (Brisb, 1963); L. L. Banfield, *Green pastures and gold* (Canterbury, 1974), and *Colonists of the early fifties: J. W. & S. A. Banfield* (priv print, nd); Joseph Jones, *Radical cousins* (Brisb, 1976); C. L. Barrett, ' "The Beachcomber" and his tropic isle', *Aust Museum Mag*, Oct 1923; A. H. Chisholm, Introduction to *Last leaves from Dunk Island* (Syd, 1925), and to *The confessions of a beachcomber* (Syd, 1933, 1968); J. Barrymore, 'The Beachcomber', *Townsville Daily Bulletin*, June 1923; information from Miss L. L. Banfield, Ararat, Vic.

MARGRIET R. BONNIN

BARACCHI, PIETRO PAOLO GIOVANNI ERNESTO (1851-1926), astronomer, was born on 25 February 1851 at Florence, Italy, son of Giovanni Battista Baracchi, a Tuscan Army officer of independent means, and his wife Anna, née Paoletti. He was educated by private tutor and later at a school in Florence where he studied mathematics and astronomy. After taking a degree in civil engineering, probably in Florence, he served briefly in the Italian Army as an engineer.

Early in 1876 Baracchi and his friends C. Catani and E. Checchi [qq.v.] sailed from Hamburg in the *Fritz Reuter* for New Zealand, but found little opportunity to practise their professions. They moved on to

Australia, reaching Melbourne in September. Within a few weeks the three friends had gained appointments in the Victorian Public Service. Baracchi began work as an assistant at the Melbourne Observatory on 1 November but by March 1877 had joined Catani and Checchi in the Department of Lands and Survey as a draftsman; in July 1880 he passed his land surveyor's examination with credit. In October 1882 he was transferred back to the observatory when R. L. J. Ellery [q.v.4], the government astronomer, selected him to go to Port Darwin to take part in a project to determine Australian longitudes. After successfully completing his task, Baracchi returned to Melbourne in April 1883 and in August became third assistant, in charge of the Great Melbourne Telescope, undertaking a review of the southern nebulae. On 30 June 1886 at St Mary's Catholic Church, St Kilda, he married the wealthy Catherine (Kate) Petty.

In 1892 Baracchi was promoted to first assistant and when Ellery retired on 30 June 1895 he became acting government astronomer. His position was not confirmed however until 27 December 1900, nor was a chief assistant appointed to replace him until 1907 when J. M. Baldwin [q.v.] joined the staff. Until then, Baracchi wrote, 'we were left, a band of four, to carry out the meridian and astrophotographic work'. Moreover, from 1895 there were no funds for publishing the observatory's records.

Baracchi was best known to the general public as official weather-forecaster for the colony, a role that he did not like. To him, 'popular meteorology' was 'of little practical value except as an amusement, and of doubtful credit to science'. In 1902 he supported the opinion that meteorological work carried out by astronomical observatories should be placed under Commonwealth control, and that the observatories, relieved of these duties, should remain independent State institutions. In 1906 the Meteorology Act gave control of weather services to the Commonwealth and by the end of 1907 the Melbourne Observatory was freed of its meteorological function—and never regained its former status.

In February 1910 the Commonwealth government invited Baracchi and a party of four to the Yass-Canberra area to select a suitable site for an astronomical observatory. With a 9-inch (23 cm) refractor, donated by J. Oddie [q.v.5], Baracchi established a small observatory on Mount Stromlo in May 1911. He and Baldwin alternately spent one week in six testing the site until May 1913; a month later Baracchi reported that it 'fulfilled the most essential requirements for any class of delicate astronomical work'. He led expeditions to ob-

serve solar eclipses to Bruny Island, Tasmania, in 1910 and to the Tongan archipelago in 1911. In 1914 he wrote a chapter, 'Astronomy and geodesy in Australia' for the *Federal Handbook* of the British Association for the Advancement of Science.

He was elected a fellow of the Royal Astronomical Society in 1884, and in 1897 the Italian monarch conferred upon him the Order of Knight Commander of the Crown of Italy; Baracchi was thereafter often referred to as Commendatore. He had been naturalized on 10 June 1895. A member of the Royal Society of Victoria from 1887, he was president in 1908-09 and a trustee in 1914-22. He was a man of 'particularly likable disposition, with a genius for making friends'. Ellery had written in 1895 that 'Baracchi's attainments in all branches of science involved in Observatory work are of the highest order'. His concentration on scientific rather than managerial and political matters, however, did little to help the Melbourne Observatory keep pace with overseas institutions.

Baracchi's wife died in 1908. In 1915 he retired and in 1922 visited Europe for two years; after his return he lived at the Melbourne Club. He died of cancer on 23 July 1926 and was buried in Melbourne cemetery, leaving his estate, valued for probate at £32 679, to his only son Guido (1887-1975), a foundation member of the Communist Party of Australia.

J. Smith (ed), *Cyclopedia of Victoria*, 1 (Melb, 1903); Board of Visitors to the Observatory, Reports, *V&P* (LA Vic), 1883, 4 (51), 1884, 4 (86), *PP*, 1903 (2nd S), 2 (28), 1907, 2 (7), 1911, 2 (3); *Australasian*, 17 July 1897, 21 Aug 1915; *Table Talk*, 27 Feb 1902; *Punch* (Melb), 21 Feb 1907, 8 Apr 1909.   J. L. PERDRIX

BARAGWANATH, WILLIAM (1878-1966), surveyor, geologist and public servant, was born on 1 August 1878 at Durham Lead near Ballarat, Victoria, son of William Baragwanath, Cornish-born surveyor, and his wife Margaret Hunter, née Herberton, of Glasgow. He was educated at state schools at Durham Lead and Garibaldi, and later at the Victoria College and the Ballarat School of Mines. In 1894-97 he was articled to Robert Allan, land and mining surveyor, whom he assisted with topographic and underground surveys at Maldon, Daylesford and Ballarat. He joined the Department of Mines in 1897, and studied part time to pass the land surveyor's and mining surveyor's examinations in 1902-03; he received the certificate of geologist of the Ballarat School of Mines in 1911.

In 1897 Baragwanath was assistant surveyor and draftsman in the department's survey of the Walhalla goldfield, and was in charge from 1898 until 1900. Successive geologic, topographic and mine surveys of the Castlemaine-Chewton, Aberfeldy, Berringa and Ballarat goldfields earned him an enviable reputation for precision, perseverance and attention to detail, qualities he was to require of his juniors. Late in 1916 he began investigating the La Trobe Valley brown-coal region, selecting bore sites, carrying out topographic surveys and assisting in management of the coal-winning operations; he accumulated much of the data used later by the State Electricity Commission to establish the Yallourn open-cut mine and power-house. In 1922 he was appointed director of geological survey, in 1924 chief mining surveyor, and in 1932 secretary for mines; in 1934 he had to give up the last because of the depression-induced expansion of the mining industry, especially gold. He retired in 1943, but was retained as a consultant to the Department of Mines until 1950. He was a member of the State committee for the Council for Scientific and Industrial Research in 1920-50, president of the Royal Society of Victoria in 1944-45, and a councillor of the Ballarat School of Mines in 1916-50; he was made a fellow of the Victorian Institution of Surveyors in 1958, and was appointed O.B.E. in 1952.

Baragwanath developed an unrivalled and encyclopaedic knowledge of the mining geology of Victoria. His memory for mine, bore and old assay data, the modifications of mine names (even of obscure 'scratchings'), and the chronology of discoveries, incidents and personalities became legendary; it was primarily for this reason 'Mr Barry' was retained as departmental consultant. His advice was highly valued by the mining industry because his opinions were invariably judicious and his optimism guarded. It was his pleasure to provide anyone with detailed information on geology and mining in Victoria, for geology and mining were his life; his favourite hobby was building model ships.

Baragwanath had argued from analogy with oil-bearing sequences elsewhere in the world that the Tertiary rocks of east Gippsland could be petroliferous. In 1922 the Department of Mines tested his theory by drilling a line of bores west of the Gippsland lakes; it was an unsuccessful experiment, but he lived to see his theory vindicated when off-shore drilling of the same sequence from 1964 led to the discovery of the Bass Strait oil and gas reservoirs. His major publications consist of four memoirs and eight bulletins of the Geological Survey of Victoria and about seventy shorter papers covering a wide spectrum of economic geology. His memoir on the Aberfeldy district attracted international attention because of his discovery of what were then the most ancient land plants, named *Baragwanathia* in his honour; unfortunately publication was delayed for over fifteen years until 1925.

Baragwanath died on 20 September 1966 at Prahran, and was cremated. He was predeceased by his wife Clara Ethel, née Jones, whom he had married at the Presbyterian Church, Flemington, on 9 May 1900, and was survived by two sons and six of his seven daughters. His estate was valued for probate at $99 024.

G. Blainey, *The rush that never ended* (Melb, 1963); *Aust Surveyor*, 4 (1932), 21 (1967); *Mining and Geological J*, 6 (1970); Dept of Mines Archives (Melb).

JOHN A. TALENT

BARBER, GEORGE WALTER (1868-1951), medical practitioner and administrator, was born on 20 November 1868 at Prestwich, Lancashire, England, son of Charles Worthington Barber, merchant, and his wife Isabella, née Loughborough. Educated at Whitgift Grammar School, London, he later became a cadet on the *Conway*, the merchant navy training-ship at Birkenhead, and in 1884 joined the *Star of Russia* as an apprentice crewman. Within a year he had to leave the sea because of defective eyesight; he then studied medicine at the University of London (M.R.C.S., England, L.R.C.P., London, 1891) and after holding appointments at the Bedford County and Lewes hospitals, became a ship's surgeon with the Peninsular and Oriental Steam Navigation Co.

About 1895 Barber migrated to Western Australia and began private practice at Kalgoorlie; he married Janet Watson Salmond at Christ Church, Springwood, New South Wales, on 8 August 1896. He was appointed district medical officer for Kalgoorlie in October 1907 and remained in the goldfields area until 1911. Commissioned lieutenant, West Australian (Volunteer) Medical Staff, in September 1900, he later enlisted in the Australian Army Medical Corps and was promoted captain in 1905. He was assigned to the 1st Battalion Goldfields Infantry Regiment three years later and served with this unit until 1911 when he moved to Perth to take up an appointment as Commonwealth medical officer at Kalamunda. There, he kept up his links with the militia and was promoted major in the A.A.M.C. on 2 July 1912.

When war broke out in August 1914 Barber was mobilized as senior medical officer to the Fremantle Garrison. In October he was appointed major in the Australian Imperial Force and sailed for Egypt on 14 December as registrar and second-in-command of the 2nd Australian Stationary Hospital. After the landing at Gallipoli his hospital was based on the *Gloucester Castle* and the *Franconia*, dealing with casualties from the Peninsula. Barber became its commanding officer on 20 November, was promoted lieut-colonel on 1 January 1916 and temporary colonel next month, and was made assistant director of medical services for the 4th Australian Division which left for France in June. He was mentioned in dispatches in July and served at Pozières and Mouquet Farm in August and September. While stationed in the Somme region he increased the effectiveness of field medical units by moving regimental aid-posts closer to the lines, increasing the number of stretcher-bearers and instituting new hygiene and sanitation regulations. His standing orders later became the basis of those for the Australian Corps. He was awarded the Distinguished Service Order in January 1917 and was confirmed as colonel next month.

Throughout 1917 Barber remained with the 4th Division, serving at Bullecourt, Messines and Passchendaele, and was mentioned in dispatches three times. On 8 April 1918 he was made deputy director of medical services for the Australian Corps. His skill as an organizer and administrator was most fully appreciated in mid-1918 when trench warfare gave way to mobile warfare; adapting quickly, he reorganized his field medical units so successfully that the evacuation of the wounded and the provision of medical supplies continued smoothly. His arrangements for the battles of the Hindenburg Line, Polygon Wood and Messines are regarded as models of careful organization and efficiency. In 1918 he was twice mentioned in dispatches and on 1 January 1919 was awarded the Croix de Guerre; he was appointed C.B. in June.

Barber returned to Australia in October 1919 and was made principal medical officer for the 5th Military District (Perth) on 1 January 1920. Although he was discharged from the A.I.F. a month later, he retained this position until 1 August 1921, when he became deputy director of medical services for the district. He was president that year of the Western Australian branch of the British Medical Association. In May 1925 he was appointed, with the rank of colonel and temporary major general, to the Permanent Military Forces as director general of medical services at Australian army headquarters, Melbourne. He was confirmed major general on 9 March 1927 and was also made director general of medical services for the Royal Australian Air Force and the Department of Civil Aviation. He held these offices until his retirement from the army on 20 August 1934. The last seventeen years of his life were spent in a quiet semi-rural practice at Kalamunda.

Survived by his wife, a son and three daughters, Barber died at Perth on 24 July 1951, and was cremated. A portrait by George Bell [q.v.] hangs in the Australian War Memorial, Canberra.

C. E. W. Bean, *The story of Anzac* (Syd, 1921), and *The A.I.F. in France* (Syd, 1929, 1937); A. G. Butler (ed), *Official history of the Australian Medical Services . . . 1914- 18*, 1, 2 (Melb, 1930, Canb, 1940); *Government Gazette* (WA), 27 Aug 1909, 11 Aug 1911; *London Gazette*, 11 July 1916, 1, 2 Jan, 1 June, 28 Dec 1917, 1 Jan, 28 May, 31 Dec 1918, 7 Jan, 3 June, 11 July 1919; *Aust Army Orders*, 23 Oct 1920; *MJA*, 25 Aug 1951; *Listening Post*, Aug 1951; *Herald* (Melb), 21 July 1934.

WILLIAM A. LAND

BARBER, JOHN ANDREW (1873-1958), Presbyterian minister, was born on 4 March 1873 at Ellerslie, Victoria, eighth child of Alexander Barber, farmer, and his wife Sarah, née Esler, both from County Antrim, Ireland. Barber was educated at a state school and at Scotch College, Melbourne. An undergraduate from 1892 at Ormond College, University of Melbourne, he studied arts (B.A., 1898) and theology. After assisting at Scots Church, Melbourne, he was ordained and inducted as minister at Beaufort on 5 June 1900. On 31 October that year at Elsternwick, he married Maggie Rorke, daughter of a Presbyterian clergyman.

In 1904 Barber was called to the important congregation of Hamilton where, due to his efforts, a new church was built in 1907. In November 1909 John Flynn [q.v.] joined him briefly as an assistant to the shearers' mission Barber had founded. The two shared an interest in the inland and Barber helped Flynn to write his *Bushman's companion* (Melbourne, 1910).

In 1915 Barber was transferred to Woollahra, New South Wales, and thence to West Hawthorn, Victoria, in 1918. When Flynn, now with the Australian Inland Mission, began his campaign for a wireless service and flying doctor scheme, Barber as convener of the Presbyterian Church's Inland Mission Council of Victoria took up the cause. Energetic and practical, he organized the funds required to launch the scheme successfully. In 1927 he accepted the post of patrol organizer for the mission and in June left Melbourne with Dr George Simpson on a motor tour of central and northern Australia, inspecting hospitals and arranging for the establishment of an aerial ambulance at Cloncurry. On his return to Melbourne an aerial medical advisory committee was formed, with Barber as chairman. He made similar patrols each year until 1933 when, desiring semi-retirement, he accepted a call to Gisborne. Besides overseeing the work of the travelling padres, Barber had also acted as superintendent of the mission while Flynn was overseas in 1929-30.

In July 1935 Barber's organizing skills were enlisted again when he was appointed administrator for the General Assembly of the Presbyterian Church. He sought complete retirement in 1939 but in 1941 accepted a call to Richmond where he remained until 1947. After some casual ministerial work, he took charge of the Moreland congregation in 1951 and became chaplain at Pentridge gaol, work which he greatly enjoyed.

Barber had a flair for setting people at ease and enthusing them with any task he had on hand; he was a splendid public speaker and raconteur. Of large physique, in his youth he had been an outstanding sportsman; he was a keen huntsman and a good shot. He bred Irish setters and on country rounds of the parish was usually accompanied by gun and dog. He always wore clerical garb, however, even in the outback. He combined a deep religious faith and a theology that verged on the fundamentalist with a tolerance and broadmindedness that made him a popular figure throughout the inland. Barber had much to do with the promotion of the Flynn legend, and had himself suggested the title for Ion Idriess's book published in 1932. But while Flynn was the visionary, Barber's business acumen and common sense were vital to the implementation of the flying doctor service.

Barber died at East Melbourne on 7 January 1958, and was cremated. He was survived by his wife and two sons, of whom the elder (Sir) Edward Hamilton Esler became a judge of the Victorian Supreme Court.

I. L. Idriess, *Flynn of the inland* (Syd, 1932); G. Simpson, *Australian Inland Mission personalities* (Gisborne, 1958); W. S. McPheat, *John Flynn, apostle to the inland* (Lond, 1963); *Argus*, 10 Sept 1926, 18 May, 3 June, 17 Aug 1927, 3 July 1935; family information.   F. MAXWELL BRADSHAW

BARBOUR, GEORGE PITTY (1867-1951), headmaster, was born on 27 January 1867 at Williamstown, Victoria, son of Robert Barbour [q.v.3] and his wife Catherine, née Pitty. Educated at Sydney Grammar School in 1878-81 and in classics at the University of Sydney (B.A. 1887; M.A.,

1889), he won the (Sir Daniel) Cooper [q.v.3] scholarship in classical studies and was a founder of the magazine *Hermes*.

Barbour taught at Sydney High School for a year, founding its magazine the *Record*, then joined Sydney Grammar School in 1889-1910 as classics and sports master. As a pupil at Sydney Grammar he had been in its 1883 cricket team, said to be the best ever. He played club cricket with Burwood which he represented on the State association from 1902. In 1907-09 he was a member of the Australian Cricket Board of Control and was chairman in 1908-09. He also represented New South Wales at Rugby Union in 1888 and tennis in 1891.

Barbour became headmaster of Toowoomba Grammar School in 1910 and over twenty-five years built it into one of the best public schools in Queensland, especially by broadening the curriculum. He was a liberal voice for broadmindedness and tolerance against bias and bigotry. In the Arnold tradition, he emphasized hard work and disciplined study. He developed boardinghouses, the prefect system, the cadet corps and sport and continued himself to play competitive sport in Toowoomba for many years. After retirement in 1935, he settled at Roseville in New South Wales; he died on 7 September 1951 and was cremated. He was survived by his widow Isabella Fredericka, daughter of Rev. Frederick Hibberd, whom he had married in the Baptist church at Ashfield on 3 April 1890, and by four sons and four daughters.

His son ERIC PITTY (1891-1934) was born on 27 January 1891 in Sydney. Dux of Sydney Grammar School, he too distinguished himself at cricket while young; his aggregate of 2146 runs in 1908-09 was a school record. Entering the University of Sydney's medical school he played for New South Wales in 1910-14 and was selected for South Africa in 1914 but the tour was cancelled. He graduated M.B. in 1915, enlisted in the Australian Imperial Force and sailed for Egypt in October and after service in Egypt, England and France was demobilized in 1919 as medical officer of the 2nd Divisional Train. He represented the A.I.F. against England at cricket. On return Barbour practised medicine at Dorrigo in 1919-23, Stockton in 1923-29 and at Kensington until his death on 7 December 1934. He wrote on cricket for the *Sydney Morning Herald* and the *Sydney Mail*, and published two textbooks, *The making of a cricketer* and *Cricket coaching*, and *Anti bodyline* in collaboration with Alan Kippax [q.v.]. He married Jessie Nicholson and was survived by two sons and two daughters.

Another son Robert Roy Pitty (b. 1899) was Queensland Rhodes Scholar in 1920, master of St Andrew's College, Adelaide, in 1928-36, warden of Melbourne University Union in 1940-54 and senior lecturer in classics 1954-67. His son Peter was director-general of the Australian Security Intelligence Organisation in 1970-75.

R. Goodman, *Toowoomba Grammar School 1875-1975* (Toowoomba, 1976); Toowoomba Grammar School, *School Mag and Old Boys Register*, Nov 1934; *Sydneian*, Dec 1954; Archives (Toowoomba Grammar School); EDU/BC 359-362 (QA); family papers (held by R. R. P. Barbour, Berwick, Vic, Miss K. Meyer, Willoughby, NSW).

RUPERT GOODMAN

BARCLAY, DAVID (1846-1929), banker and company director, was born on 18 April 1846 in Hobart Town, youngest son of David Barclay, watchmaker and silversmith, and his wife Margaret, née Strachan. He was educated at The Hutchins School and at the High School, Hobart, and received his Associate of Arts (second class) in 1863 with prizes in pure mathematics and natural philosophy. After working for a year as a junior clerk in the Survey Department and Commissioner of Crown Lands Office, in 1866 he joined the Commercial Bank founded by John Dunn [q.v.1].

On 9 September 1873 at Hobart he married Grace Agnes Salier; they had seven daughters and two sons. By 1884, when Barclay joined the Tasmanian Club, he had become manager of the bank, whose name was now changed to the Commercial Bank of Tasmania Ltd. In 1904, on the death of his brother Charles [q.v.3], David succeeded him as managing director and carried on the tradition of sound administration until the take-over by the English, Scottish and Australian Bank Ltd in 1921. He negotiated this sale, realizing that the rate of progress had outgrown the resources of his shareholders; he continued as an advisory director to the E.S. & A. until his death.

Barclay was known for his sound knowledge of finance, reliable judgment and business tact: while he was in charge the bank's business more than doubled. Urbane in manner, with a neat beard and billowing moustache, he was a shrewd judge of character, always willing to support the man rather than the professed security. He helped many who subsequently made great contributions to the State's economic growth. He saw himself as not merely a financial agent but a banker whose institution had a part to play in community and national development.

When he had completed fifty years service in 1916, Barclay was presented with an illuminated address and a purse of sovereigns by representatives of the prominent citizenry of Hobart, and with an address by his devoted bank staff. He had been a justice of the peace from 1895 and was a director of many companies including mining groups, the Union Steam Ship Co. of New Zealand Ltd, Davies Brothers Ltd and the Perpetual Trustees, Executors, and Agency Co. of Tasmania Ltd. He died in Hobart on 20 June 1929, survived by his wife and all his children except a son who was killed in World War I. Barclay's estate, sworn for probate at £36 124, included generous provision for numerous Hobart charities.

Cyclopedia of Tasmania, 1 (Hob, 1900); *Hobart Town Gazette*, 2 Oct 1863; *Tas Mail*, 3 Feb 1916; *Weekly Courier* (Launc), 7 Apr 1921; *Mercury*, 21 June 1929; LSD 72/2 (TA).

SHIRLEY M. ELDERSHAW

BARDOLPH, DOUGLAS HENRY (1893-1951) and KENNETH EDWARD JOSEPH (1895-1964), newspaper publishers and politicians, were born at Manly, New South Wales, on 18 February 1893 and 11 August 1895, the third and fourth sons of Henry Bardolph, labourer and later a building contractor, and his wife Mary, née Taggart. They were educated in Victoria, where Kenneth studied architecture at the Working Men's College in 1911-12 and served his apprenticeship under William Pitt [q.v.]. From 1914 he was employed by the Commonwealth government for two and a half years, working on the plans for the Federal capital under W. B. Griffin [q.v.]. At the end of World War I the family moved to Adelaide and became involved in newspaper publishing and politics; Kenneth also practised as an architect.

Douglas became prominent as publisher and editor of the *Unley News* (1918-23) and of the *South Australian Worker* from 1924. He entered politics, joined the Australian Labor Party, was an Adelaide city councillor in 1927-29, and was State president of the Clerks' Union in 1929-30. He became involved in a bitter pre-selection battle in 1929 against S. R. Whitford [q.v.] for nomination for a Legislative Council by-election; a special A.L.P. council-meeting declared null and void the ballot which Bardolph had won, and both brothers were expelled from the party for canvassing for votes. Each was a supporter of J. T. Lang [q.v.], and they had close links with the party in New South Wales. They printed in Adelaide *Labor Weekly*, the official organ of the New South Wales Labor Council; in this connexion Kenneth later successfully sued the New South Wales government for breach of a contract entered into with the prior Lang government. They organized visits to South Australia by Lang and his supporters, and Kenneth worked in New South Wales for a period, assisting Lang and campaigning for E. J. Ward in his initial election for the Federal seat of East Sydney.

In 1931 when the South Australian branch of the A.L.P. expelled most of its parliamentary members, including the L. L. Hill [q.v.] ministry, for accepting the Premiers'‹ Plan, Douglas officially launched the Lang Labor Party in that State. Despite a strong tendency towards fragmentation, and notwithstanding frequent defections to the A.L.P., the new party's representatives, including Douglas, won all three seats in the electorate of Adelaide in the 1933 State election; objection to Bardolph's victory was taken unsuccessfully to the court of disputed returns. Douglas had dominated the local Lang party, 'suffered no superior and brooked no equal'; opponents claimed it was essentially his personal political machine. When the A.L.P., the Parliamentary (Hill) Labor and Lang Labor parties amalgamated in 1934, both the Bardolphs were formally reinstated, but in August 1935 Douglas was again declared outside the party for non-payment of the levy on parliamentarians. He held his seat as an Independent Labor member in 1938 and 1941, continued his attempts 'to clean up the dirty stable of the A.L.P.', and had an enviable reputation as an eloquent and hard-working parliamentarian. He lost in 1944 to the endorsed A.L.P. candidate and unsuccessfully sought re-election in 1947 and 1950. A bachelor, he died of cancer on 2 February 1951 at Croydon; his estate was sworn for probate at £2437.

Kenneth was president of the United Trades and Labor Council of South Australia in 1929-30, a member of the interstate executive of the Australian Council of Trade Unions, and vice-president of the South Australian Lang Labor Party in 1932-33. He remained within the A.L.P. after reinstatement in 1934. He was an unsuccessful candidate for the Federal seat of Adelaide in 1934 and in 1937, but was elected to the Legislative Council in 1941 where he served for twenty-three years and became deputy leader of his party. Bardolph was elected a fellow of the Royal Australian Institute of Architects in 1951. Chairman of the State Manpower Advisory Committee in World War II, he was again president of the Trades and Labor Council in 1941-43, was State president of the A.L.P. in 1944-46 and in 1950-51, and was several times a delegate to federal conference. On 29 March 1927 he had married Mary Josephine Dineen; she and their six children survived him when he died in Adelaide on 9 November 1964. Both brothers were Catholics.

D. Hopgood, 'Lang Labor in South Australia', R. Cooksey (ed), 'The great Depression in Australia', *Labour Hist*, 1970, no 17; R. Pettman, 'Factionalism in the South Australian A.L.P., 1930-1933', *Labour Hist*, May 1975, no 28; *Advertiser* (Adel), 8 Nov 1932, 3 Feb 1951, 10 Nov 1964.

DAVID ST LEGER KELLY

BARDSLEY, WARREN (1882-1954), cricketer, was born at Warren, New South Wales, on 6 December 1882, son of William Bardsley, teacher, and his wife Rachel Hannah, née Readford. At the Forest Lodge Superior Public School at Glebe, where his father taught for over forty years from 1883, he developed the dedication to practice that characterized his career; his schoolmates included 'Tibby' Cotter [q.v.], the fast bowler. At 17 Bardsley played for Glebe in the Sydney first-grade competition, made his State début in 1903-04, and won selection in the Australian team to visit England in 1909.

On tour Bardsley became established as an opening batsman, topped his side's averages and aggregates with 2180 runs at 46, and was named as one of *Wisden's* cricketers of the year. Making 136 and 130 in the Oval Test, he became the first player to score a century in each innings of a Test match, sharing with Syd Gregory [q.v.4, D. W. Gregory] an opening partnership of 180 that stood as an Australian Test record for over fifty years. Bardsley made further tours of England in 1912, 1921 and 1926. On the first he again headed the averages and aggregates with 2441 runs at 51; on the second his consistency helped lay the solid foundation on which the successes of W. W. Armstrong's [q.v.] side were built; on the third he carried his bat for 193 in the Lord's Test and captained Australia at Headingley and Old Trafford. He retired from representative cricket at the end of the 1926-27 Australian season, having amassed 17 031 runs in first-class matches at an average of just under 50; against England he had scored 1334 at 33 and in all Tests 2469 at 40. Until 1933 he continued playing grade cricket with Western Suburbs, the club he had joined in 1919; his aggregate of 12 110 runs at 50 is a record for the Sydney first-grade competition.

A serious man, a non-smoker, teetotaller and vegetarian, Bardsley was of medium height, solidly built and round-faced. He had an upright stance at the wicket, was strong on the cut and the drive, and adept at working the ball off his legs. His orthodox batting lacked the flair of Clem Hill [q.v.], the left-hander with whom he is most often compared, but English observers in particular paid tribute to his 'classical' style. His achievements, at a time of rapid advancement in bowling techniques, depended on the soundness of his play, to which were added unquenchable keenness and thorough preparation; on the 1909 tour he was invariably first at the ground, 'casing the joint for stealing runs'. Bardsley had most success in England; the habit acquired in childhood of early morning practice on damp wickets is usually advanced as the reason. He seldom bowled, but was a fine fieldsman in the deep.

Bardsley served briefly as a New South Wales and Australian selector, and in 1936 shared a testimonial with Jack Gregory [q.v.], which yielded £1500. In 1899-1920 he had worked as a clerk in the accounts branch of the Department of the Attorney-General and Justice and from about 1920 was an agent for English firms. He died suddenly of coronary vascular disease at Clovelly on 20 January 1954 and was cremated with Presbyterian rites. He was survived by his wife Gertrude Muriel, née Cope, whom he had married at Strathfield on 15 September 1945.

E. H. D. Sewell, *Triangular cricket* (Lond, 1912); J. B. Selby (ed), *50 years of cricket ... Western Suburbs District Cricket Club* (Syd, 1946); J. Fingleton, *Masters of cricket from Trumper to May* (Lond, 1958); B. Frindall, *The Kaye book of cricket records* (Lond, 1968); R. Robinson, *On top down under* (Syd, 1975); *V&P* (LA NSW), 1883-84, 7, 912; *Wisden Cricketers' Almanack*, 1909-10, 1913, 1922, 1927, 1938, 1955.　　　B. G. ANDREWS

BARFF, HENRY EBENEZER (1857-1925), university administrator, was born on 9 July 1857 at Tahaa Island, Society Islands, youngest son of Rev. John Barff of the London Missionary Society, and his wife Amelia, née Banes. The family came to Sydney in 1865; at Camden College, where he was educated, he met Congregational families who were influential in academic circles and he was to retain and extend those contacts. In 1873 he went to the University of Sydney (B.A., 1876; M.A., 1882), where he won the (Solomon) Levey and the (Thomas) Barker [qq.v.2,1] scholarships and graduated with the University Prize (Medal) in mathematics. Barff then became master of studies and in 1879 an assistant examiner and acting lecturer in mathematics. Next year, as acting registrar, he found his true niche in the administration; he was confirmed as registrar in 1882. He was also titular librarian in 1893-1914.

On 6 September 1899 at Holy Trinity Church Barff married Jane Foss, daughter of H. C. Russell [q.v.6]; she had graduated in classics in 1886 (M.A., 1889) and had been tutor to women students. Jane Barff was active in women's education, in charitable and church activities, and as president of the University Women's Settlement in 1915-24. Barff compiled *A short historical account of the University of Sydney ...* (1902) to commemorate its golden jubilee. In 1913 he helped to reconstitute the Sydney University Union, of which he had been a founding member in 1874. Next year he contributed a descriptive article on the university to the *Handbook* of the British Association for the Advancement of Science for its Sydney session in 1914.

For over forty years Barff was the chief administrator, responsible to the senate for all its aspects, save those within the province of the professors. In recognition of growing executive complexity in 1914 he added the office of warden to that of registrar, acquiring a general co-ordinating authority. In fact he had been steadily increasing the range of his responsibilities. In 1880 there were one teaching faculty, four professors and a handful of students; by 1924, when Barff retired, there were ten faculties, and over 3000 undergraduates. The university had survived an economic depression and World War I, quadrupled its buildings, helped to bring about a transformation in secondary education and emerged as a major tertiary institution. Throughout, Barff retained close personal contact with staff and students and kept firm control of the entire administrative process. His complete dedication to the university made him a popular figure, while an impressive dignity of bearing earned him, in his later years, an awesome respect. When he left office it was found necessary to create the position of vice-chancellor. He was appointed C.M.G. in 1923 and served briefly on the senate in 1924-25.

Barff had been a member of the Royal Society of New South Wales from 1896; he enjoyed playing golf and was a member of the Royal Sydney Golf and University clubs. In 1922 he visited the United States of America and, next year, South Africa. Survived by his wife and daughter, he died of cerebro-vascular disease on 2 May 1925 and was buried in the Anglican section of Waverley cemetery. His portrait by John Longstaff [q.v.] is owned by the University of Sydney.

Sydney Univ Union, *The Union book of 1902* (Syd, 1902); J. A. Garrett and L. W. Farr, *Camden College, a centenary history* (Syd, 1964); Roy Soc NSW, *Procs*, 59 (1925); *Union Recorder*, 7 May, 18 June 1925; *ISN*, 21 June 1890; *Daily Telegraph* (Syd), 14 Apr 1915; *SMH*, 4 May 1925; Senate minutes (Univ Syd Archives).　　K. J. CABLE

BARKER, STEPHEN (1846-1924), trade unionist and politician, was born in Sussex, England, son of Stephen Barker, farmer, and his wife Hannah, née Nagle. Little is known of his early years: by the 1860s he was living in Melbourne. A presser by trade, he claimed to have been employed as a lad in Victoria's first clothing factory; he knew what it meant to work from 6 a.m. to 6 p.m. and was to give vehement evidence in 1893 to the Factories Act Inquiry Board against 'sweating'. After employment in some of the largest clothing manufacturing houses, including Sargood, Son & Co. and Solcberg & Son, he worked in the retail and wholesale trade in Launceston, Tasmania, and in New Zealand at Wellington and Auckland. He was back in Melbourne by April 1874 when he married Jane Laughton, a servant, at St John's Church of England, La Trobe Street. He then worked for Godfrey Barthold and for Beath, Schiess & Co. until ill health forced him to leave. In the 1890s he operated a small business in North Melbourne as a tailor and dyer.

About 1875 Barker helped to found the Pressers' Society, but he was not a member until 1890; in 1894 he played a major part in its revitalization. He was president of the union in 1894-96 and 1900-01, secretary in 1899, and its delegate to the Trades Hall Council from 1892 to 1902 when the pressers, under his guidance, joined with the cutters and trimmers to form the Victorian Clothing Operatives' Union.

Barker was president of the T.H.C. in 1897-98, a member of the Eight-Hours Committee in 1896-98 and full-time secretary of the council in 1901-10, succeeding J. G. Barrett [q.v.]. As president and then treasurer of the T.H.C. Organizing Committee in 1900-02, he helped to set up wages boards for some sixty unions; he represented the clothing trade on its board from 1897 until 1907, when he lost the confidence of the union over his recommendations for a reduction in piece-work rates. Although he was exonerated by a T.H.C. committee and lauded as an 'honourable conscientious and hard-working colleague', he henceforth took his seat on the council as a delegate for the Musicians' Union, of which he was an honorary member.

The *Bulletin* remarked that Barker must have looked ironically on the eight-hours monument opposite the Trades Hall, for 'he worked about 96 hours a week'. His strength was as an organizer: the T.H.C. was administered with system and method and nursed to growing authority, as the movement took advantage of the slow return to prosperity after the long depression years. Barker helped to untangle many industrial conflicts: he abhorred strikes except as a last resort and won a reputation as a man of moral courage, fair, and trustworthy. As a public speaker, however, he was frequently militant, described as 'torrential' and 'unreportable'. He was said to have been the principal mover in the formation of the Political Labor Council in 1902, and was its secretary next year.

In 1899 Barker was defeated in the North Melbourne Council election, and made an unsuccessful bid against W. A. Watt [q.v.] for the Legislative Assembly seat of North Melbourne. He was a local councillor from 1901 and mayor from September to October 1905 when North Melbourne was formally annexed to the city of Melbourne; he received public congratulations for his part in the amalgamation. In December he stood unsuccessfully in the Melbourne City Council elections. After Federation Barker ran for the Senate in 1901, 1903 and 1906 before succeeding as one of Labor's victors in 1910; he was defeated in 1919, but returned in a famous victory over G. Swinburne [q.v.] in 1922.

Rotund and ruddy-faced, Barker wore a trim beard and moustache. A justice of the peace, he was prominent in the temperance movement and supported women's franchise; from December 1907 he was a council-member of the Working Men's College. A staunch anti-conscriptionist, he was a member of the parliamentary delegation to the Western Front. Long a resident of North Melbourne, Barker made his home in St Kilda about 1911. Aged 79, he died of cancer on 21 June 1924 in a private hospital at Toorak, and was buried in Brighton cemetery. He was predeceased by his wife and survived by three sons and two of his four daughters. His estate was sworn for probate at £2327; he had given books from his extensive library to the St Kilda branch of the Labor Party, of which he was president when he died.

PP (LA Vic), 1895-96, 3 (44), 1902-03, 2 (31); *Table Talk*, 29 Mar 1906; *Punch* (Melb), 21 July 1910; *Argus*, 23 June 1924; *Bulletin*, and *Labor Call*, 26 June 1924; Clothing & Allied Trades Union of Aust, Federal office records (ANU Archives).

BARKER, TOM (1887-1970), was born on 3 June 1887 at Crossthwaite, Westmorland, England, eldest child of Thomas Grainger Barker, farm labourer, and his wife Sarah, née Trotter. As a boy he worked on farms, ran away to Liverpool, then enlisted in the army, under age. Discharged as medically unfit after three years service, he migrated to New Zealand in 1909. In Auckland he was a tram conductor, active trade unionist and secretary of the New Zealand Socialist

Party, working with future leaders of the Labour Party, such as H. E. Holland [q.v.], M. J. Savage, Peter Fraser and Robert Semple. Attracted by industrial unionism he became an organizer for the Industrial Workers of the World. In Wellington during the violent strikes of 1913 he was arrested, charged with sedition and released on a bond.

Early in 1914 Barker arrived in Sydney where he was soon editing the I.W.W. paper, *Direct Action*. After August 1914 the I.W.W. was the most determined and vociferous opponent of the 'capitalist war'. Barker, who had escaped gaol on a technicality in 1915, was sentenced to twelve months imprisonment after his arrest in March 1916, but released in August after an aggressive campaign to free him. Meanwhile the deep and bitter divisions over conscription were coming to dominate Australian life. The I.W.W., glorying in its stance of vanguard opponent to conscription, attracted militant and radical support; Prime Minister W. M. Hughes [q.v.] branded it as a set of vicious traitors. Barker, still at liberty after the arrest and imprisonment of twelve members on charges of treason, personified the I.W.W. propaganda which continued defiantly after the organization was declared unlawful in December 1916. His most famous anti-conscription poster, the subject of a serious charge, read: 'TO ARMS!! Capitalists, Parsons, Politicians, Landlords, Newspaper Editors, and Other Stay-at-Home Patriots. Your Country Needs You in the Trenches! Workers, Follow Your Masters!' He and the remaining members were arrested next year at the time of the general strike in New South Wales and before the second conscription referendum in December. Barker was held in gaol until deported to Chile in 1918.

In South America he organized seamen; in Moscow he was enthused by Lenin to work for the Kuzbas project of industrialization in Siberia and recruited technicians for it in the United States of America for five years to 1926. Later he worked for the Soviet petroleum export organization, visiting Australia briefly in 1930-31, and settled in London. As a member of the Labour Party, councillor and in 1959 mayor of St Pancras Borough, he was energetic in political, welfare and cultural fields until his death on 2 April 1970. He was survived by his wife Bertha, a Polish-born ballet-dancer.

Barker roamed the world as a worker and organizer, basing himself on the simple tenets of class struggle and socialism. In Australia, a time of crisis thrust him into prominence. Elsewhere he served the cause at hand selflessly. He was a slightly built man, lively in speech and manner, fighting his battles with laughter.

L. C. Jauncey, *The story of conscription in Australia* (Lond, 1935); E. C. Fry (ed), *Tom Barker and the I.W.W.* (Canb, 1965); I. Turner, *Sydney's burning* (Melb, 1967); *Labour Hist,* May 1970, no 18.

ERIC FRY

BARLOW, ANDREW HENRY (1836-1915), bank officer and politician, was born in August 1836 at Wanstead, Essex, England, son of John Henry Barlow, merchant, and his wife Eliza Ann, née Burnstead. He arrived with his father in Sydney in 1848 and on 11 July 1851 joined the Bank of Australasia. In December 1855 he became sub-accountant in the Sydney branch and between that year and 1884 he served in Melbourne, Newcastle, Auckland, Tamworth, Brisbane and Ipswich, Queensland, where he became manager in 1878. In January 1885 he was retired on a pension because of a chronic liver condition. He was elected to the Legislative Assembly for Ipswich on 5 May 1888. A logical rather than a fluent speaker, Barlow opposed Chinese immigration and supported the eight-hour bill, but favoured plural voting because he believed that unrestrained democracy fostered despotism.

As secretary for public lands and agriculture in the Nelson [q.v.] ministry between 1893 and 1896, Barlow introduced the relatively unsuccessful Communities Land Settlement Act of 1893 which provided for co-operative land settlement. The Crown Lands and the Agricultural Lands Purchase Acts of 1894, which encouraged 'grazing homesteads' and enabled the Land Board to purchase land for selection as agricultural farms, were more successful. When his health failed in 1896, he resigned his portfolio on 6 March at his wife's request, but was persuaded to represent the government in the Legislative Council. He continued as minister without portfolio in three ministries until he resigned on 11 September 1899 when (Sir) James Dickson [q.v.], as premier, supported Federation, which Barlow strongly opposed. He was severely criticized in parliament in 1897 for his role in the Queensland National Bank scandal. In 1893 Nelson and Barlow had declared the bank sound, but by 1896 it had a huge deficit and further investigations revealed gross mismanagement amounting almost to corruption.

Barlow was out of office in 1899-1903 because he disapproved of Robert Philp [q.v.], but from September 1903 to November 1907 he was secretary for public instruction; after a second Philp ministry he held the post again from February 1908 to June 1909. Assisted by J. D. Story [q.v.] as under-secretary, he made plans for state high schools and departmental control of technical colleges ('the poor man's university') which were implemented by his successors. In 1910 he was appointed to the first Senate of the University of Queensland. In 1909-15 Barlow was again minister without portfolio and leader of the government in the Legislative Council. Now trusted adviser-in-chief to the various premiers rather than a popular politician, he was referred to as 'the continuous minister'; he often substituted for other ministers and was several times acting premier.

Tall, with a pronounced shoulder hump, Barlow was tactful, shrewd and witty, but sometimes unpleasantly obsequious. Throughout his parliamentary career, he adhered sincerely to his basic liberal principles even though his cabinet affiliations frequently changed. He maintained a paternalistic attitude to 'the poor man' but was bitterly hostile to socialism and the Labor Party.

Barlow suffered a cerebral haemorrhage and ten days later died on 29 March 1915 at his Toowong home; after a state funeral he was buried at Toowong cemetery with Anglican rites. His estate was valued for probate at £7271. In 1873 he had married Eleanor Marion Outridge; they had one son.

C. A. Bernays, *Queensland politics during sixty years* (Brisb, 1919); *Echo* (Brisb), 12 Dec 1896; *Queenslander*, 9 Sept 1893; *Daily Standard*, 29 Mar 1915; *Brisbane Courier*, 30, 31 Mar 1915; D. P. Crook, Queensland politics, 1900-1915 (B.A. thesis, Univ Qld, 1957); I. Tyrrell, The reform of state education in Queensland 1913-1939 (B.A. thesis, Univ Qld, 1968); T. O'Sullivan, Reminiscences of the Queensland parliament, 1903-15 (Oxley Lib, Brisb); ANZ Bank Archives (Melb).

E. CLARKE

BARLOW, CHRISTOPHER GEORGE (1858-1915), Anglican bishop, was born in 1858 in Dublin and educated at Brecknock College, Wales. He entered his stepfather's manufacturing firm in London, but resigned his partnership to become secretary to his lifelong friend George Henry Stanton [q.v.6], appointed bishop of North Queensland. Made a deacon on 18 December 1881, Barlow served his curacy at Mackay under Albert Maclaren; after ordination on 24 September 1882, he became rector of St Paul's Church, Charters Towers, for three years. Barlow's sympathy, insight and humour endeared him to his people. He was a man's man with a powerful and attractive personality. In 1885 he was transferred to St James' Pro-Cathedral, Townsville, where his unobtrusive nature, organizing abilities and spiritual qualities were valued by clergy and laity. With Stanton, he worked to collect funds for the cathedral which he himself was to consecrate as one of his first episcopal acts.

On Stanton's translation to Newcastle, Barlow was elected to succeed him, becoming the first man ordained in Australia to be elected bishop by an Australian synod. As he had no university degree the appointment was challenged, but he was immediately granted a Lambeth D.D. by the archbishop of Canterbury. After consecration in Sydney on 25 July 1891, he left for England to recruit priests. He was enthroned in Townsville on 10 April 1892 and for the next ten years travelled constantly throughout the diocese. Financially tried by droughts, cyclones and depression, Barlow still successfully reorganized diocesan and parish incomes and widened the Church's activities. He encouraged mission work among the Aboriginals at Yarrabah, among the Pacific islands sugar-workers at Mackay and on the Herbert River, and among the Chinese in Townsville, Cairns and Charters Towers. Realising that his diocese was too large for one bishop, he gathered funds for the new diocese of Carpentaria which was created on 28 November 1900. It was once regarded as his greatest achievement, but the wisdom of its creation came to be questioned.

In his churchmanship, there was a gradual change from his original Evangelicalism towards a more moderate liberalism with its emphasis on spirituality in worship and the personal faith of the clergy. In an address to the New South Wales Provincial Synod in 1907, he deplored party bigotry within the Church and pleaded for more tolerance and humanity towards differing points of view. The strain of a tropical climate, long visitation tours and frequent attacks of endemic diseases weakened his health, and in 1902 he accepted an invitation to the diocese of Goulburn, New South Wales.

Barlow was enthroned in St Saviour's Cathedral on 23 April. He found an under-manned diocese still bedevilled by the acrimonious Rossi [q.v.6] dispute and financially crippled by a long drought. To strengthen the links of the bishop with the scattered parishes, he divided the diocese into four archdeaconries on the lines of the plan initiated by Bishop Mesac Thomas [q.v.6]; he founded the *Southern Churchman* (1902), and by reorganizing the Church Society increased support from £600 to nearly £3000 a year. This financial stability enabled him to subsidize the poorer districts, establish a clergy superannuation fund and provide for clerical training. In 1907 all diocesan accounts were amalgamated and this facilitated the general management of financial affairs. The establishment of a full-time diocesan registry, the collation of a record of diocesan land, and the building of many churches and rectories indicate the strength of his administrative policy. Other visionary projects, such as the Bishopthorpe High School for Girls' at Goulburn and a theological college, both set up in 1906, failed through lack of funds.

Barlow was a warm, humane man of simple faith, a courteous peacemaker but authoritative when necessary. Signing himself 'your affectionate bishop', he befriended his clergy and shared their personal problems. On his return from England in 1908 he bought, and became probably the first Australian bishop to drive, a motor car. To remedy the loneliness and intellectual frustration of the country clergy, he often lived for months in one centre. He also instituted 'quiet days' and conferences of clergy during synod meetings. He was a lonely man, and the burden of responsibility for matters like the complicated legal aftermath of the Rossi dispute oppressed him. He sometimes lacked wisdom and foresight, but his love of people overcame much that was less attractive.

Barlow's health deteriorated and he had to take several periods of leave. After his house, Bishopthorpe, was burned down in 1914, he resigned on 31 March 1915 and died, unmarried, at Cooma rectory on 30 August of uraemia; he was buried in Goulburn cemetery. His estate was sworn for probate at £2861; the major bequest was £1000 to the diocese of Goulburn for clerical training. The high altar in St Saviour's Cathedral is a memorial to him.

The diocese of Carpentaria (Thursday Island, 1913, 1927, copy Fryer Lib, Univ Qld); J. O. Feetham and W. V. Rymer (eds), *The North Queensland jubilee book 1878-1928* (Townsville, 1929); R. T. Wyatt, *The history of the diocese of Goulburn* (Syd, 1937); E. C. Rowland, *The tropics for Christ* (Townsville, 1960); *Southern Churchman* (Goulburn), 15 Sept, 15 Oct 1915; *Aust Church Q,* 29 June 1936; K. Rayner, Attitude and influence of the Churches in Queensland on matters of social and political importance 1859-1914 (B.A. Hons thesis, Univ Qld, 1951), *and* The history of the Church of England in Queensland (Ph.D. thesis, Univ Qld, 1962); C. G. Barlow, Letter-book 1907-10 (St Mark's Inst of Theology, Canb).

            JOHN CHARLES VOCKLER
               BARBARA THORN

BARLOW, MARY KATE (1865-1934), charity worker and women's leader, was born in County Limerick, Ireland, daughter of John McDonagh and his wife Helena, née O'Gorman. She was educated at the Convent of the Faithful Companions, Laurel Hill, Limerick. In 1884 she came to Australia to visit her aunt Bedelia, wife of William Hughes. On 29 April 1887 at St Mary's Cathedral, Sydney, she married John Bede Barlow, architect; they lived at Airmount, Waverley, now the Christian Brothers' College.

Mary Barlow became active in fund-raising for institutions designed by her husband such as the Sacred Heart Hospice for the Dying, Lewisham Hospital, and St Vincent's Hospital Nurses' Home. In 1911 she joined the new Catholic Women's Association of New South Wales and, after the resignation of Lady Strickland in 1914, she was president until 1934. She dominated her committee and instituted Our Lady's Charity Guild, supervised the opening of a library, visited hospitals and prisons, and raised funds by organizing lectures, social evenings, and concerts directed by William Caspers, organist at St Mary's Cathedral. By 1917 she had planned the Hostel for Business Girls which was soon extended to accommodate thirty-two.

Mary Barlow served on the committees of the National Council of Women, the Victoria League, the Travellers' Aid Society, the Society of Women Writers, the Good Film League, the Prisoners' Aid Association, and the Women's Loyalty League. For the Sydney Industrial Blind Institution, she founded the Sacred Heart Braille Writers' Association to translate Catholic literature. During the Eucharistic Congress of 1928, she presided over the first Catholic women's conference, attended by some 500 delegates who set up the Australian Council of Catholic Women. For her work she was created dame of the Holy Sepulchre; in 1916 she had been awarded the Cross of Leo. In 1930-34 she was first editor of the *Catholic Women's Review*.

Known to her friends as 'Queenie', Mary Barlow was a gifted speaker with a keen sense of humour and was proud of her Irish heritage. She was beloved for her charm and ready sympathy. A connoisseur and keen collector of fine china and etchings, she was also knowledgeable about jewels and literature, especially poetry. Survived by two daughters, she died of suppurative arthritis of the hip in St Vincent's Hospital on 27 May 1934, aged 69, and was buried in South Head cemetery after a requiem mass at St Mary's Cathedral conducted by Archbishop Kelly [q.v.]. Her husband had predeceased her in 1924 and their only son had been killed in action at Gallipoli.

Catholic Women's Review, 19 June 1934; *Catholic Press,* 31 May 1934; *Freeman's J* (Syd), 31 May 1934; Catholic Women's Assn of NSW, Minute-book (Syd Diocesan Archives, St Mary's Cathedral); records (Catholic Women's League, Syd);

family papers (held by Mr L. A. Barlow, Artarmon, NSW).
CATHERINE O'CARRIGAN

BARLOW, WILLIAM (1834-1915), barrister and university administrator, was born on 19 February 1834 in Dublin, second son of Peter Barlow, barrister. In 1851 he entered Trinity College, Dublin (B.A., 1855; LL.D., 1884), where he won a gold medal for oratory in the College Historical Society. In 1858 he was called to the Irish Bar and in 1870 he married Emma Sarah Ardill.

The Barlows arrived in South Australia on 25 June in the *Carnaquheen*. He was immediately admitted to the South Australian Bar and practised alone until 1873 when he formed a partnership with (Sir) Richard Chaffey Baker [q.v.], which lasted until his retirement in 1909. On 18 December 1874 Barlow had been appointed part-time registrar of the new University of Adelaide. He was involved with its decision to fight for the controversial right to award science degrees and to confer degrees on women; they were admitted to lectures in 1876 and in 1881 the university enrolled them for degrees.

In 1882 Barlow relinquished the duties of registrar, librarian and clerk of the senate and was elected to the university council. Dean of the faculty of law in 1883, its inaugural year, and in 1890-91, he was chairman of the finance committee in 1897-1905. He was chairman of the board of musical studies in 1901-04 and again in 1906, and vice-chancellor of the university from 1896 until his death. Barlow was popular with graduates and students, some of whom he assisted unostentatiously when they needed money.

He was a warden, trustee and synodsman for Christ Church, North Adelaide, for over thirty years, and church advocate, a member of the standing committee and chancellor of the diocese of Adelaide for thirteen years. He was a Mason, having joined in Dublin the Venerable Lodge of St John and the Military Lodge, of which he became worshipful master. In Adelaide he helped found the Mostyn and St Alban's lodges, and in 1907 became past deputy grand master of the Grand Lodge of South Australia. In 1914 he was appointed C.M.G.

Although a retiring man, Barlow was widely respected and was said to have a genial disposition. Tall and spare, he presented on ceremonial occasions at the university a sharp physical contrast to the chancellor, Sir Samuel Way [q.v.]. His major publication was the authoritative 483-page *Local Courts Act, rules and forms, and Special Magistrates Confirmation Act . . .* (Adelaide, 1890), which cited more than 1200 cases.

Barlow regularly attended evening concerts at the Elder [q.v.4] Conservatorium of Music. He had been a member of the Adelaide Club since 1875. The Barlows were childless and, after his wife's death in 1912, he looked forward to his own demise as a release. Aged 81, he died at his home in North Adelaide on 19 April 1915, and was buried in North Road cemetery, Collinswood. His estate, sworn for probate at £22 818, went to cousins and professional associates.

William Barlow: in memoriam (Adel, priv print, 1915); E. J. R. Morgan, *The Adelaide Club 1863-1963* (Adel, 1963); W. G. K. Duncan and R. A. Leonard, *The University of Adelaide, 1874-1974* (Adel, 1973); *Advertiser* (Adel), and *Register* (Adel), 20 Apr 1915; records (Supreme Court, SA, *and* Univ Adel).   V. A. EDGELOE

BARNES, GEORGE POWELL (1856-1949), and **WALTER HENRY** (1858-1933), businessmen and politicians, were born in Castlemaine, Victoria, sons of Hiram Barnes and his wife Catherine, née Dawes; George was born on 20 September 1856 and Walter on 7 September 1858. Their father was a senior driver for Cobb [q.v.3] & Co. and in 1865 took sixteen coaches from Bathurst to Brisbane; in 1868 he inaugurated the Brisbane-Gympie-Maryborough run. Both boys were educated at the Ipswich and Brisbane Normal schools; Walter completed his education with Rev. C. Ogg at the Presbyterian College, Brisbane.

George worked in T. F. Merry's Toowoomba store in 1868 and later held similar jobs at Gympie, Brisbane and Warwick. After opening his own store at Warwick in 1874, he married Merry's daughter Mary Cecilia in 1879; they had eight children. In 1880 he laid the foundation of his business success by joining Walter and Merry in a produce firm, Barnes & Co. Ltd.

Walter worked first for Cobb & Co., then with Uhl's saddlery in Brisbane. He left the Postal Department in 1884 to work for Barnes & Co., managed the company's Roma Street store in Brisbane and then became managing director. On 5 June 1888 he married Katherine Edmonds; they had one son. Barnes won the Legislative Assembly seat of Bulimba as a ministerialist in 1901 and held it until 1915. He regained the seat in 1918 and held it until 1923 when he successfully transferred to the near-by seat of Wynnum and held it until his death. He was secretary for public lands in the Philp [q.v.] government of 1907-08 and, although he was initially left out of W. Kidston's [q.v.] first ministry, in June 1909 he was appointed secretary for public instruction and in October was also given responsibility for public works. When D. F. Denham [q.v.] succeeded Kidston in February 1911, Barnes became treasurer and secretary for public works. He held these offices until the government's defeat in 1915.

As secretary for public instruction, Barnes managed the bill to establish the University of Queensland in 1909, although Kidston was its chief architect. His most controversial action as a minister was his passing in 1912 of the Industrial Peace Act in the wake of the general strike. Despite his assurance that its 'liberal provisions' would render all future strike action unnecessary, the Opposition leader David Bowman [q.v.] described it as 'the worst, the most tyrannical, and most coercive Bill that has ever existed in any part of Australia'. The labour movement regarded him henceforth as a class-biased reactionary.

While he never attained goverment leadership, Walter Barnes was the subject of an unorthodox method of selecting an acting premier. In 1914 Denham decided to visit England. Normal practice required that he should nominate a deputy to preside in his absence. There was such keen competition for the position between Barnes and (Sir) James Blair [q.v.] that Denham, reluctant to exercize his right of appointment lest it cause further discord in the ministry, organized a ballot of government members. The fact that Barnes won the election handsomely suggests that had he and the government not been defeated in 1915, he might well have eventually become premier.

After his defeat Barnes concentrated on business but maintained a close interest in public affairs. At the height of the conscription controversy in 1916, he wrote to the *Brisbane Courier* accusing two State ministers of making disloyal speeches. When he returned to parliament in 1918, the Labor Party was firmly entrenched in government; in January 1920, he was elected deputy to E. H. Macartney [q.v.], leader of the Opposition. In 1924 the previously faction-ridden non-Labor parties united to form the Country Progressive National Party which, under the leadership of A. E. Moore [q.v.], ended Labor domination of Queensland politics by its victory at the 1929 general election. Because the new party lacked ministerial experience, Moore overlooked Barnes's advanced age and made him treasurer. Known for his financial and economic caution, orthodoxy and conservatism, Barnes considered the Depression was caused by waste and government extravagance; only by reducing public expenditure and the costs of production, he argued, could Queensland be led out of its economic difficulties. He was an implacable opponent of the 'pump-priming' policies of Federal Treasurer Theodore [q.v.] and was a vigorous advocate of the Premiers' Plan. When the Moore government was defeated in 1932, Barnes held his seat with a reduced majority. The difficult years of office had seriously affected his health, however, and he died in Brisbane on 19 February 1933. Buried in South Brisbane cemetery with Methodist rites, he left an estate valued for probate at £6862.

George Barnes was politically less conspicuous but commercially more prominent than his younger brother. He entered parliament in 1908 as the farmers' representative for Warwick, having failed to take the seat in 1906 and 1907. Subsequently he joined successively the Liberal, Nationalist, United, and Country Progressive National parties, but held Warwick until his retirement in 1935. His parliamentary duties as a back-bencher were light, and he expanded Barnes & Co. into one of the major produce firms in south Queensland and diversified into flour-mills and dairy-farming. He was preoccupied all his public life with closer settlement and railway expansion. He died at Brisbane on 9 December 1949, leaving an estate valued for probate at £6384, and was buried in Warwick cemetery with Methodist rites.

George Barnes was a long-serving member of the Warwick Shire Council, while his brother was a Coorparoo shire councillor for twenty-five years and was five times elected chairman. Both were devout Methodists. George was a total abstainer and a temperance leader, while Walter was president of the Brisbane City Mission and of the Young Men's Christian Association; his close involvement with the Church earned him the sobriquet 'Bishop Barnes'. George was also involved with a plethora of community and industry groups in Warwick, including the Chamber of Commerce, the Co-operative Dairying Co., the School of Arts and the Technical College.

C. A. Bernays, *Queensland politics during sixty years* (Brisb, 1919); K. A. Austin, *The lights of Cobb and Co.* (Adel, 1967); *Brisbane Courier*, 19 Apr 1907; *Queenslander*, 23 May 1929, 23 Feb 1933.

B. J. COSTAR

BARNES, GUSTAVE ADRIAN (1877-1921), artist, was born on 9 May 1877 at Islington, Middlesex, England, eldest son of John William Barnes, plasterer, and his wife Ann Eliza, nèe May. The family migrated to Adelaide when Gustave was young and by 1889 his father had formed the firm, Barnes & Neate, builders, plasterers and modellers.

Gustave entered the business, also studied the violin, and joined a group of young artists painting in the Adelaide hills. His friend Hans Heysen [q.v.] described him as 'always an enthusiast . . . out at sunrise and you couldn't get him back till dark'. From 1896 he attended classes at James Ashton's [q.v.] Academy of Arts.

In 1900 Barnes went to Britain, played violin in Sir Edward Elgar's second orchestra, and attended night classes at the Royal College of Art, South Kensington. He was also employed at the Royal Doulton pottery works, designing, modelling and painting. Later, scholarships enabled him to study full time at the college and in 1908 he exhibited a water-colour, 'Suffolk Marshes', at the Royal Academy of Arts. He probably worked for a time in Scotland: he married Annie May, a factory worker, at Kirkcaldy on 4 June 1909 and Heysen spent a summer with him in Fifeshire.

After the death of his father in 1912 Barnes returned to Adelaide to run the family business. In England he had collected old prints, engravings and etchings; his expertise led to an appointment in 1915 to the Public Library, Museum and Art Gallery of South Australia, as artist and art supervisor. He was to sort and arrange the print collection for exhibition, help select works for the gallery, and supervise modelling. A sensitive man and a vegetarian, Barnes was conspicuously unassertive, but in his gallery lectures on the development of local art he emerged as 'a cultured and convincing speaker'.

During World War I Barnes's large-scale model of Gallipoli Peninsula was displayed in the public library. A larger relief map went to the Department of Defence's war museum. A bronze bust of Frederic Chapple [q.v.] was commissioned from Barnes by Prince Alfred College old boys and presented to the school in 1918. That year he was promoted curator of the gallery and regularly exhibited rural landscapes with the South Australian Society of Arts. The gallery bought 'Monarch of the Glen', 'Morning in the Hills' and 'Mount Barker from Crafers'. He also played violin in Hermann Heinicke's [q.v.] ensemble.

After a complicated respiratory illness lasting two months, Barnes died on 14 March 1921, survived by his wife and two daughters. He was buried in Payneham cemetery and his estate was sworn for probate at £1886. He had just been appointed to a position in the National Gallery of Victoria. Sir William Sowden [q.v.], lamenting his death, praised his modesty and cultural versatility. In April, to assist his family, an exhibition of his work was held by the Society of Arts. He had been an artist of considerable promise, who had worked as designer, modeller, etcher, and especially landscape-painter in oils and water-colours.

C. Holme (ed), *Art of the British Empire overseas* (Lond, 1917); N. Benko, *Art and artists of South Australia* (Adel, 1969); J. Johnson and A. Greutzner (eds), *Dictionary of British artists 1880-1940* (np, 1976); *PP* (SA), 1915 (13), 1918 (13), 1919 (13); *Advertiser* (Adel), 15 Mar, 15 Apr 1921; *Register* (Adel), 15, 30 Mar, 5 Apr 1921; *Observer* (Adel), 1 Sept 1928; Museum, Public Library and Art Gallery of SA records (SLSA); information from the Misses Barnes, Mitcham, SA.

NANCY BENKO

BARNES, JOHN (1868-1938), trade union official and politician, was born on 17 July 1868 at Hamilton, South Australia, son of John Thomas Barnes, a drover who had emigrated from Somerset, England, and his wife Mary, née Comerford, from County Clare, Ireland. He was educated at the local state school but went to work as soon as possible, for when he was 6 his father had died. He had numerous jobs: tar-boy, rouseabout, picker-up, shedhand, shearer, timber-getter and handyman. At 17 he became an itinerant worker, carrying in his swag works by Adam Smith, Henry George [q.v.4] Robert Blatchford and Henry Lawson [q.v.]. In his own words, 'You could hardly get a job, let alone one that was well paid'.

In 1886 Barnes moved to Broken Hill, where he met E. Grayndler [q.v.]. Next year he joined the Shearers' Union (later the Australian Workers' Union) and almost fifty years later could still display his first membership ticket. While at Broken Hill he became the A.W.U. agent, and was subsequently its first organizer in South Australia. In 1908 he succeeded Grayndler as secretary of the Victoria-Riverina branch at Ballarat, and remained in this post until 1913 when he was elected to the Senate.

Barnes was on the parliamentary executive of the Labor Party in 1914-16, and in 1916-17 was a member of the Commonwealth Prices Regulation Board. He retained his connexions with Ballarat, where he was known as a forceful anti-conscription speaker. Defeated in 1919, he returned to the A.W.U. until 1922, when he was re-elected to the Senate. In 1923-25 he was again one of Labor's parliamentary executive. He was a member of the Victorian executive of the party for sixteen years, having been president in 1918.

Barnes was president of the A.W.U. from 1924 until his death; the union's support gave him formidable strength within the Labor Party. In the Scullin [q.v.] government he was assistant minister for works in

1929-31, and vice-president of the Executive Council in 1931-32; his policies were moderate, and he faithfully supported the prime minister. He was party leader in the Senate from 1932 until defeated in the 1935 election. He was re-elected in 1937 but, after a long illness, died of cancer in the Mercy Hospital, East Melbourne, on 31 January 1938. In 1898 at Kapunda, South Australia, he had married Ellen Charlotte Camba Abbott; she and their son and five daughters survived him. After a state funeral conducted by Canon Crotty of Christ Church, St Kilda, Barnes's funeral procession passed through the city, paused outside the Trades Hall, and continued to the Melbourne general cemetery. His estate was valued for probate at £1018.

Natural shrewdness and physical and mental vigour compensated for Barnes's lack of formal education. He was not an initiator of policy, but was a skilled politician and unfailingly supported his party and union. The *Australian Worker* commented at his death: 'In days when Labor has so often been betrayed by self-seekers and lovers of loot, it is good to be able to say of a representative of the workers that he was incorruptibly faithful from the beginning to the end of a long and strenuous career'. He was a forceful debater, but his charm, good nature and freedom from malice ensured his popularity.

Barnes appears to have embodied the characteristics of the legendary and archetypal bush worker. Sir George Pearce [q.v.] described him as 'a breezy, unconventional character . . . with a whiff of the shearing-shed about him'; he was also a notorious practical joker. In his days at Ballarat, he, J. McKissock and J. McNeill [q.v.] were known as the 'Three Musketeers of the Trades Hall'. They made a pact that when one of them died, the survivors would plant a Cootamundra wattle on the grave, and the union would do the same for the last of the trio. In July 1938 McNeill planted a wattle by Barnes's grave, where another memorial was erected by the A.W.U. in 1943.

G. F. Pearce, *Carpenter to Cabinet* (Lond, 1951); *Labor Call*, 18 July 1912, 3 July 1930, 3 Feb 1938, 18 Feb 1943; *Aust Worker*, 21 Feb 1934, 2 Feb 1938; *Argus* and *Ballarat Mail*, 1 Feb 1938; J. Barnes material (held by Mr. A. Williams, Ballarat).

NORMA MARSHALL

BARNETT, FREDERICK OSWALD (1883-1972), social reformer, was born on 28 September 1883 at Brunswick, Victoria, twin son of Charles Barnett and his wife Elizabeth, née George, both from Cornwall, England. Charles Barnett, a quarryman, was thrown out of work in the early 1890s after the building boom collapsed. Oswald attended the Albert Street, Brunswick, State School where, after entering the Victorian Education Department in 1898, he became monitor and then pupil-teacher. Although praised by the district inspector and promoted, he resigned in 1902 to become a clerk in the office of the master in equity and lunacy. By 1920 he had qualified as a public accountant and he left the civil service to set up his own practice, later known as F. Oswald Barnett & Co. In 1929 he was elected a fellow of the Institute of Chartered Accountants in Australia, of which he became a Victorian councillor. On 6 January 1909 at the Brunswick Methodist Church he had married Elizabeth Mary Hyett: they had four daughters and a son.

Barnett was an active Methodist. In 1923 a visit to an inner-city slum shocked him deeply and, concerned for the welfare of the children in particular, he enlisted the aid of young Methodists in a campaign which led to the establishment of the Methodist Babies' Home in South Yarra in 1929. At the same time he was studying part time at the University of Melbourne (B. Comm., 1928); his master's thesis of 1931, based on the result of 150 questionnaires, was published in 1933 as *The unsuspected slums*.

Barnett set up a study-group of forty people drawn from various community organizations, who met weekly in his office to discuss problems of housing reform. His group soon widened its activities to form the nucleus of the slum-abolition movement of the early 1930s. In his public campaign Barnett used a combination of scientifically gathered data and sometimes emotional presentation; he urged his audiences to write to the premier (Sir) Albert Dunstan [q.v.], who finally agreed to inspect the slums for himself. In 1936 the premier appointed a Housing Investigation and Slum Abolition Board, of which Barnett was a member: it recommended establishment of a housing scheme run by a commission of experts, a policy which his group had long advocated. When the Housing Commission of Victoria was set up in 1938 Barnett became vice-chairman until 1948, when he declined reappointment.

Barnett frequently contributed to public discussion of housing, poverty and related issues through newspaper articles, public addresses and pamphlets, which included, with W. O. Burt, *Housing the Australian nation* (1942) and, with Burt and F. Heath, *We must go on: a study in planned reconstruction and housing* (1944). In 1941-49 he was a director of the City Mutual Life Assurance Society Ltd and chairman from 1946 of its Victorian board, but he was asked to resign when it was known that he was auditor to Australia-Soviet House, Melbourne. In 1952 his was virtually a lone voice attacking proposals for multi-storey flats as public housing, in an address from his familiar platform, the Pleasant Sunday Afternoon at Wesley Church. For a generation he served the Victoria-Tasmania Methodist Conference as a leader of influential Bible classes, as a lay preacher of distinction, and as a member of many welfare committees. He published several collections of verse and a booklet on the divinity of Christ.

In 1962 Barnett formally retired from his accountancy firm. His first wife had died in 1956; in 1959 he married a widow Florence Emily Fowles, née Orr. He died at Box Hill on 3 May 1972 and was cremated. His wife, and the children of his first marriage survived him; his estate was valued for probate at $37 401.

Barnett was a humanitarian, idealist and enthusiast, and an astute organizer and polemicist who influenced the lives of many people; his Methodism had a practical stamp.

C. A. Grant, *500 Victorians* (Melb, 1934); J. S. Gawler, *A roof over my head* (Syd, 1963); E. W. Russell, *The slum abolition movement in Victoria, 1933-37* (Melb, 1972), and for biblog; *New Spectator*, 24 May 1972; *Argus*, 23 Feb, 2, 8 July, 26 Aug, 11 Oct 1935, 28 Dec 1943, 10 Jan, 10 Mar 1944, 22 Nov 1945, 26, 27 June 1946; *Herald* (Melb), 10 Feb 1948, 25, 26 Aug 1952, 20 May 1972; *Age*, 11 Feb 1948, 14 Jan, 25 July 1952; *Sun-News Pictorial*, 10, 11, 26 Feb 1948, 25 Aug 1952.   E. W. RUSSELL

BARNETT, HENRY WALTER (1862-1934), photographer, was born on 25 January 1862 at St Kilda, Victoria, son of Lewis Barnett, merchant, and his wife Alice, née Jacobs, both London-born Jews. Barnett began as a studio assistant to Robert Stewart of Bourke Street about 1875. A fellow-assistant was Tom Roberts [q.v.] who remained a close friend until late in life; Barnett claimed to have arranged the first sale of a Roberts painting in 1881. At 21 Barnett set up a studio in Hobart but sold out to his partner in 1884, and travelled via the United States of America to London, where he joined the society photographers W. & D. Downey.

Returning to Australia, Walter Barnett opened the Falk Studios in Sydney in 1885. He soon became one of the leading portrait photographers in the country, distinguished for his ability to bring out bone-structure and texture of the skin. Among professionals he was noted for his thorough methods and for his flair in conducting business. He made more studies of his sitters than was usual; a perfectionist, he employed highly skilled craftsmen and ran his studio stylishly and without attention to cost, asking previously unheard-of fees. Apart from his plutocratic clientele, his most notable sitters were visiting actors and actresses, especially those brought out by his friend J. C. Williamson [q.v.6]; Bernhardt sat for him during her tour of the colonies. On 18 July 1889 in Sydney he married 20-year-old Hilda (Ella) Frances Clement Forbes; the couple became known for their lavish entertaining although reputedly Barnett never smoked and rarely drank.

While returning from a visit to London in 1896, Barnett met Maurice Sestier, an employee of the Lumière brothers, who was stranded in Bombay. Barnett recognized the potential of motion film and brought Sestier to Sydney. In November 1896 Barnett took Sestier with him to film scenes of the Melbourne Cup. These, with scenes of Sydney Harbour which Sestier had developed in Barnett's studio dark-room in September and October, are among the first moving film to be shot in Australia: they were given their première in Sydney in December. Although his connexion with the cinema did not last long, Barnett's place in the history of Australian cinematography is assured.

About 1898 Barnett left for London where he soon established himself as a leading photographer, with a studio at Hyde Park Corner and later in Knightsbridge. His sitters included the royal family and many prominent in English society. The portraits, printed on specially prepared paper from platinotype and placed on flexible vellum mounts, resembled, in the opinion of an English obituarist, fine mezzotint engravings. The negatives, on glass and varnished, were still in perfect condition forty years later and formed a library of photographs illustrating the development of style and technique, taken by 'one of the fathers of professional photographic portraiture'. Barnett was prominent in the Royal Photographic Society of Great Britain and a foundation member of the Professional Photographers' Association. From all accounts he was a man of vigorous personality and cosmopolitan taste, somewhat aloof in manner and dedicated to his work.

In 1920 Barnett sold his business and retired to the south of France. He had always preferred the company of artists (Streeton [q.v.] considered Barnett had a 'good, strong appreciation for the beautiful') and now devoted his attention to the collection and sale of contemporary French art. In early 1927 he brought an exhibition of Provençal paintings to Melbourne, but an offer to arrange an exhibition of Impressionists and Post-Impressionists was rejected by the trustees of the National Gallery. In 1933 in

Paris Barnett published a pamphlet critical of the trustees of the Felton [q.v.4] Bequest, urging them to buy works of the contemporary French school rather than pay inflated prices for works by old masters. A plan to write an account of artistic life in Australia in the 1880s, using his correspondence with Roberts, was announced in 1933, but he died on 16 January 1934 at Nice, survived by his wife, whose portrait by Longstaff [q.v.] is now in the Art Gallery of South Australia. Barnett's death attracted little notice in his own country, though Jack Cato was later to claim that his work represented the culmination of nineteenth-century photography in Australia.

R. H. Croll, *Tom Roberts, father of Australian landscape painting* (Melb, 1935); *Smike to Bulldog – letters from Sir Arthur Streeton to Tom Roberts*, R. H. Croll ed (Syd, 1946); J. Cato, *I can take it* (Melb, 1947), and *The story of the camera in Australia* (Melb, 1955); M. Wasson, *The beginnings of Australian cinema* (Melb, 1964); E. Reade, *Australian silent films* (Melb, 1970); *British J of Photography*, 26 Jan 1934.   P. H. DE SERVILLE

BARNETT, PERCY NEVILLE (1881-1953), author and book-plate authority, was born on 13 September 1881 at Christchurch, New Zealand, son of Neville [q.v.3] Barnett and his wife Mary Constance Isabel, née Rahn. His father had migrated to New Zealand in 1875 and became organist at St John's Church, Christchurch, and later at St Matthew's, Auckland. The family moved to Sydney in 1887 when Barnett, an Anglican, was appointed organist at St Mary's Cathedral. He taught music and became a critic for the *Sydney Morning Herald*.

Percy Neville (known as Neville) was educated at Fort Street High School. In 1898 he entered the Bank of New South Wales, working in several branches until compelled by ill health to retire to Sydney from the Cooma office in 1918. On 3 June that year at St Michael's Church of England, Wollongong, Barnett married Gabrielle Joyce Havelock Vidal. Earlier, when a knee injury prevented him playing sport, he had taken up book collecting and the study of book-plates, and had developed a taste for fine editions. His enforced retirement enabled him to make an intensive study of his hobbies.

Barnett's publications were often issued in small *de luxe* and standard editions with genuine colour-prints pasted in by hand. They included *The bookplate in Australia . . .* (1930), *Pictorial book-plates* (1931), the first general book on the subject issued in Australia, and *Armorial book-plates . . .* (1932). He spent ten years collecting the 102 different plates that he tipped-in to each of the 275 copies of *Woodcut book-plates* (1934): it had a foreword by Lionel Lindsay [q.v.] and represented the work of eighty artists in twenty countries. His major work, *Australian book-plates . . .* (1950), involved nine years research and the personal tipping-in of 30 000 examples, some of which he hand-coloured. He also issued elaborate souvenir brochures relating to his more important works.

In the 1930s Barnett became interested in Japanese wood-block colour-prints; he imported 40 000 prints and specially designed endpapers from Japan for a series of charming books including *Japanese colour-prints* (1936), *Colour prints of Hiroshige* (1937), *Hiroshige* (1938), *Figure prints of Japan* (1948) and *Japanese art* (1953). Unable to replenish his stock during World War II, he had to restrict *Glimpses at Ukiyo-ye* (1940) and *Nishiki-ye: brocade prints of Japan* (1941) to eleven and fifteen copies.

Barnett not only wrote the text; he also designed and published each work, and signed and numbered each copy of limited editions. A perfectionist at a time when the second-rate satisfied many people, Barnett chose the best materials available: he procured type-fonts from Germany, used hand-made paper, and imported vellum from England, board from Scotland, silk from China and brocade from Japan. His books were printed in Sydney at the Beacon Press, whose proprietor H. P. Mortlock was a dedicated craftsman.

After an improvement in health, Barnett returned to the bank in 1933 as librarian at the head office, a post he retained for the rest of his life. He reorganized and widened the scope of the library, but his return to work gave him less time for his hobbies. Apologizing to a friend in 1939 for not having replied to a query, he wrote: 'these books are my excuse – a whole-time job with only one's leisure time to do them in'.

In 1951 his friends honoured him with a striking book-plate which had been designed by Gayfield Shaw. They also printed a booklet, *P. Neville Barnett and his books*, containing tributes from admirers in Australia and abroad. Barnett's scarce and valuable publications have been keenly sought by collectors. They became highly regarded in the United States of America and elsewhere: Queen Mary, in particular, valued his productions. He received awards of merit in international competitions for book-plate designs and won world-wide repute as an authority. Honorary secretary of the Australian Ex Libris Society, in 1930 he edited its *Journal*, and was also vice-president of the New Zealand Ex Libris Society and of the Book-plate Association

International, Los Angeles. In 1931-37 he was general secretary of the Australian Painter-Etchers' Society.

Barnett was a man of short stature, friendly and unassuming, and a Christian Scientist. Survived by his wife, son and daughter, he died at Mosman on 5 June 1953, and was cremated. His estate was valued for probate at £4911.

A century of journalism. The Sydney Morning Herald (Syd, 1931); H. B. Muir, *A checklist of ex libris literature published in Australia* (Adel, 1942); A. Milgrom et al, *P. Neville Barnett and his books* (Syd, 1951); W. A. Orchard, *Music in Australia* (Melb, 1952); G. Farmer, *Private presses and Australia* (Melb, 1972); *Etruscan*, Sept 1953; *NZ Free Lance*, 8 Apr 1948; *Sunday Herald*, 7 June 1953; *SMH*, 20 June 1953; staff records (Bank of NSW Archives, Syd).   J. P. HOLROYD

BARR SMITH, SIR TOM ELDER; *see* SMITH, SIR TOM ELDER BARR

BARRACLOUGH, SIR SAMUEL HENRY EGERTON (1871-1958), mechanical engineer, was born on 25 October 1871 in Sydney, eldest son of William Henry Barraclough, clerk, and his wife Hannah Arabella, née Egerton. He was educated at Sydney Boys' High School and the University of Sydney (B.E., 1892). Awarded an 1851 Exhibition travelling scholarship, he attended Sibley College of Engineering, Cornell University, United States of America (M.M.E., 1894), and while there was an editor of the *Sibley Journal of Engineering*. After travelling in North America, he returned to Sydney in 1895 and became lecturer-in-charge of the department of (applied) physics at the Sydney Technical College and taught physics at Sydney High. He thoroughly reorganized his department and introduced a more modern syllabus, and also helped to edit the *Australian Technical Journal*. In 1897 he was appointed assistant lecturer in mechanical engineering under Professor W. H. Warren [q.v.6] in the Peter Nicol Russell [q.v.6] school of engineering at the university; he also lectured in military engineering in its department of military science.

Barraclough published numerous articles, often connected with steam engines and boilers, in the engineering journals and the *Journal and Proceedings* of the Royal Society of New South Wales; his *Abridged mathematical tables ...* (1907) was republished several times. In 1901-02 he was founding president of the Sydney University Engineering Society. Lawrence Hargrave [q.v.] consulted him in 1908 about a suitable engine for his planned 'lightest and most compact' flying machine. Despite being granted the right of private practice in 1904 and promotion to assistant professor in 1908, he applied unsuccessfully in 1909 for the chair of engineering at the University of Melbourne. He was president of the Engineering Association of New South Wales in 1914-15.

In October 1899 Barraclough had been commissioned in the Corps of Australian Engineers; in 1908 he transferred as captain to the Australian Intelligence Corps. Promoted major in 1914, he served with Intelligence as senior assistant censor until the end of 1915 when he visited India, Egypt, France and Great Britain on behalf of the Commonwealth government. In his report he advised that 'the best way of helping the British munitions effort and the future inauguration of the Australian arsenal would be to send to Great Britain ... as many Australian workers as possible'. At the end of 1916 he returned to London as honorary lieut-colonel in charge of the Australian munitions workers in England and France. By 1918 some 5000 skilled men had reached England and he had built up a staff of about 150 to look after the men's welfare and discipline. At the end of the war Churchill praised 'the great success of a unique scheme'. Barraclough was appointed C.B.E. (military division) in 1919 and next year was promoted K.B.E.; he was also awarded the Volunteer Officers' Decoration. He remained in England until 1920 when the last of the men and their dependants were repatriated.

Barraclough had been appointed professor of mechanical engineering in the University of Sydney in 1915. He was dean of the faculty of engineering in 1924-33 and 1936-41, and a fellow of the senate in 1925-33 and 1938-56. An interesting teacher and good administrator, he had a profound influence on the advancement of engineering education. He had an infectious enthusiasm for research and worked hard to foster travelling scholarships. Dignified and immaculately dressed, he was careful of speech, cheerful and kindly. For twenty years he was chairman of the Australian Student Christian Movement.

Sir Henry served his profession outside the university as a fellow of the Society of Engineers, a member of the institutions of Civil and Mechanical Engineers, and a foundation member of the Newcomen Society, all of London. He was a councillor of the Royal Society of New South Wales, and president of its engineering section, and president of section H of the Australian and New Zealand Association for the Advancement of Science in 1937. As a councillor and president in 1935 of the Institution of Engineers, Australia, he helped to obtain the grant of its royal charter in 1938 and next year was awarded its Peter Nicol Russell Memorial Medal. He also served on the Australian National Research Council, the council of the Standards Association of Australia and on various local advisory committees. He was a member of the Australian Club, Sydney, the Royal Sydney Golf Club, the Athenaeum Club, London, and Phyllis Court, Henley-on-Thames, England.

Barraclough died at Sydney Hospital on 30 August 1958 and was cremated with Congregational rites. He was survived by his wife Mona Edith, née Rossiter, whom he had married at Bishopscourt, Melbourne, on 22 August 1927, witnessed by (Viscount) Bruce [q.v.] and his wife.

Inst of Engineers (Aust), *J*, 30 (1958); *SMH*, 1 Sept 1958; Barraclough papers (Univ Syd Archives).   J. M. ANTILL

BARRETT, CHARLES LESLIE (1879-1959), naturalist and journalist, was born on 26 June 1879 at Hawthorn, Victoria, third son of Thomas Barrett, Tasmanian-born builder, and his wife Rebecca, née Chipperfield, of Essex, England. At an early age he became interested in natural history and with two friends E. B. Nicholls and C. P. Kinane spent week-ends at an engaging spot east of Melbourne; as a result he wrote in the *New Idea* a series of pleasant articles entitled 'Our bush hut on Olinda'. These became the subject of his first book, *From range to sea: a bird lover's ways* (1907), a sensitive group of essays that led to many other writings on natural history.

Meanwhile in 1906 Barrett had joined the staff of the Melbourne *Herald* and for the next thirty-three years informed the public on natural history matters through feature articles, answers to correspondents, and books such as the Sun nature and travel books, edited by him and published under the auspices of the Herald and Weekly Times Ltd.

Barrett had no formal scientific training but was an associate and friend of specialists in the Field Naturalists' Club of Victoria (from 1899), the Entomological Society of Victoria and the Royal Australasian Ornithologists' Union, of which he was a foundation member in 1901 and assistant editor of its publication, *Emu*, in 1910-16. He was prominent in the formation of the Bird Observers' Club in 1905 and was a fellow of the Royal Zoological Society of London and a corresponding member of the Zoological Society of New York. In 1925-40 he edited the *Victorian Naturalist*.

In Adelaide on 12 June 1911 Barrett married Florence Ellen Williams, a trained nurse. In June 1916 he enlisted in the Australian Imperial Force and joined the Camel Brigade Field Ambulance which left for Egypt in May 1917. He edited an issue of the Field Ambulance's journal, *Cacolet*, and in April-December 1918 the monthly *Kia-ora Coo-ee*. A visit to the Nile valley left him with a lifelong interest in Egypt.

After World War I Barrett travelled widely throughout Australia: by 1935 he had visited the Great Barrier Reef, explored the Nullarbor Plain area, and crossed central and northern Australia with his wife as companion and 'assistant naturalist'. He published numerous works of travel and natural history, some aimed specifically at youthful readers. In 1920-27 he also edited the boys' paper *Pals*. During World War II he visited troops in northern Australia and New Guinea, lecturing on practical bush lore. When his son Donald settled in New Guinea after the war Barrett paid him several extended visits. In 1953 he was awarded the Australian Natural History Medallion.

Barrett was of stocky build, remembered as a courteous man who always went out of his way to be friendly and co-operative; an inveterate pipe-smoker who 'enjoyed spinning a good yarn'; he spoke in a soft, rather high pitched and emphatic voice. He died of cancer in Melbourne on 16 January 1959 and was cremated, survived by his son and daughter. His collection of New Guinea and Pacific books from his fine reference library was left to his son, who later presented them to the Administrative College of Papua and New Guinea, Port Moresby.

S. C. Yocklunn (ed), *The Charles Barrett collection of New Guineana: an author checklist*, 2nd ed (Port Moresby, 1969); F. S. Colliver, 'Charles Leslie Barrett ...', *Vic Naturalist*, 76 (1959-60); *Emu*, 59 (1959); information from Mr R. T. M. Pescott and Dr J. H. Willis, Melb.

         A. H. CHISHOLM*

BARRETT, EDITH HELEN (1872-1939), medical practitioner, was born on 29 October 1872 at Emerald Hill, Victoria, eighth child of Dr James Barrett and his wife Catherine, née Edkins. Educated at South Melbourne College, in 1888 she matriculated in eight subjects but did not sign the matriculation roll until 1897 when she began a medical course at the University of Melbourne; she graduated M.B. in 1901 and M.D. in 1907. Four of her brothers, including (Sir) James [q.v.], were also doctors. Edith was resident medical officer at the Melbourne Hospital in 1901 and three years later joined the honorary medical staff of the

Queen Victoria Hospital, from which she retired in 1934.

Edith Barrett was in general practice first in South Melbourne and then in Collins Street. Her practice was never extensive and she made only a bare livelihood from it. Her interests and energies were devoted rather to a number of voluntary organizations, particularly those concerned with improving medical and social conditions for poorer women and children. She was a foundation member of the National Council of Women in Victoria in 1902, and in 1911-15 and 1921-26 was its honorary secretary. Her constructive approach to social problems is evident in the council's work, particularly in the founding of the Bush Nursing Association of Victoria in 1910; Edith was a member of its first central council as a representative of the Victorian Women's Medical Association.

In November 1914, when her brother James sailed with the Australian Imperial Force for Egypt, Edith replaced him as honorary secretary to both the Bush Nursing Association and the Australian branch of the British Red Cross Society. She held the position at the B.N.A. till 1920 when he again took over and she became honorary assistant secretary until 1935. The association's headquarters was at 105 Collins Street where both Edith and James practised; it is likely that the routine administration and correspondence fell to the honorary assistant.

A full-time paid secretary was employed at the Australian Red Cross from 1915, and James did not resume the honorary position on his return; Edith held it till 1928. Her main Red Cross activities, however, were with the Victorian division, of which she was a foundation committee-member, remaining on both council and committee until 1936-37. During the war she had been active on numerous divisional committees; for this work she received both the O.B.E. and the C.B.E. in 1918.

Edith had been an enthusiastic motorist from pre-war days, even doing her own car-repairs. She enjoyed gardening, and recommended fruit-growing and bee-keeping as combining the 'utilitarian with the health giving'. In 1912 she was a foundation member of the Lyceum Club and a trustee until 1926. She died on 1 February 1939 of a heart condition at a nursing home in Malvern, and was buried in Brighton cemetery. She had been an indefatigable worker for humanitarian causes, intelligent and sensitive, oblivious of her own material advancement or comfort. She was always overshadowed by her brother, especially at the B.N.A. The mental collapse which darkened the last years of her life caused her to be forgotten even before she died. Of the associations which she had served, only the National Council of Women noted her death.

E. Scott, *Australia during the war* (Syd, 1936); *Lone Hand*, 1 Sept 1914; *Argus*, 3 Feb 1939; Bush Nursing Assn of Vic, Annual reports 1911-39, *and* central council minutes 1914-37 (Melb); British Red Cross Soc, Aust Branch, Annual reports 1914-39, *and* Vic Division annual reports 1914-39 (Melb); National Council of Women (Vic), Executive *and* Council minutes 1902-39 (Melb); family information.   LYNDSAY GARDINER

BARRETT, SIR JAMES WILLIAM (1862-1945), ophthalmologist and publicist, was born on 27 February 1862 at Emerald Hill (South Melbourne), eldest child of James Barrett, physician, formerly of Oxfordshire, England, and his wife Catherine Oliver, née Edkins; she died when young James was 12.

Barrett was educated at a private elementary school, Melbourne Church of England Grammar School and Carlton College, where he was dux. In 1876 he matriculated and entered the University of Melbourne (M.B., 1881; Ch. B., 1882); he was the first secretary of the Medical Students' Society in 1880. He worked for two years as a resident medical officer at the Melbourne Hospital where he became a strong advocate of antisepsis and gathered powerful statistical evidence against the old ways; in 1883 he published his first paper, *Typhoid fever in Victoria*. In October he went to London (M.R.C.S., 1884; F.R.C.S., 1887); his professor at King's College, G. F. Yeo, remarked on his earnestness, quickness, assiduity, urbanity, and courtesy. He taught at King's College, Moorfields Ophthalmic Hospital and elsewhere, gaining his main source of income from coaching in physiology for F.R.C.S. examinations, and visited Austria and Germany, where he met Robert Koch. He developed a lifelong affection for German language, literature and music, together with an attachment to the scientific rationality and agnosticism of T. H. Huxley [q.v.1]. He researched into the anatomy of the mammalian eye, published seventeen papers, and decided to spend his life in London on investigative work, but in 1886 he was called back to Australia for family reasons.

In Melbourne Barrett took up private practice and in 1887 became part-time demonstrator in physiology and histology at the university under his revered mentor, Professor G. B. Halford [q.v.4]. That year he passed M.D. and in 1888 Ch.M. He continued research into the eyes of animals and began a long association with the Victorian Eye and Ear Hospital. On 31 October 1888 at

South Yarra he married Marian, née Rennick (d. 1939), the 27-year-old widow of F. J. Pirani; Charles Strong [q.v.6] of the Australian Church officiated.

In 1897 Barrett took up a lectureship in the physiology of the special senses which he was to carry on for forty years, earning a reputation as a 'lucid, simple and informed' teacher. In 1901 he was elected to the university council. An exponent of 'national efficiency', he urged closer attention to vocational training. He recommended the university's affiliation with the teachers' and veterinary colleges, and its involvement in agricultural and commercial education: he reiterated his views in 1902 to the royal commission on the university. He could claim some credit for the introduction of 'professional' courses including mining engineering (1901), education (1902), dentistry (1906), and agriculture (1911). Barrett also took a close interest in medical education. He fought for a revision of the curriculum which was adopted in 1911, and in 1913 advocated clinical chairs. He was joint secretary of the committee appointed that year to inquire into the university's administration, and saw its thorough-going survey translated into legislative action in the Act of 1923.

In 1912 Barrett visited the United States of America and was deeply impressed with the universities' 'energy, drive, liberal support and receptivity to new ideas', particularly that of Wisconsin. In London he helped to set up the Universities Bureau of the British Empire, and organized a parliamentary delegation to Australia which he and (Sir) George Fairbairn [q.v.] funded.

By 1914 Barrett had an assured professional and public reputation (C.M.G., 1911), a family, and a fine house and property, Palmyra, with a 338-foot (103 m) frontage on Lansell Road, Toorak, where wallabies grazed to the delight of passing schoolboys. On the outbreak of World War I he became honorary secretary of the Australian Red Cross and in October he joined the Australian Imperial Force with the rank of major (serving without pay until the following May, when he was promoted lieut-colonel). In December he sailed in the *Kyarra*, arriving in Egypt on 13 January 1915. He was posted to the 1st Australian General Hospital at Heliopolis as registrar and oculist and was also consultant to the British forces in Egypt; he nurtured a close connexion with the director of medical services, Major General Sir R. W. Ford. He was also executive officer of the Australian Red Cross Society in the region. In June he was appointed by Ford, quite irregularly, as 'Assistant Director of Medical Services, Australian Forces', thus securing authority

which went far beyond the 1st A.G.H.

Barrett's shambling figure, often with gaiters on the wrong legs or spurs upside down, was militarily grotesque, but he was enabled to carry out his varied duties by 'immense energy and astonishing indefatigability, great organising and administrative ability, and intellectual capacity, and social flair'. Yet in doing so he made bitter enemies. By 5 April Lieut-Colonel J. W. Springthorpe [q.v.], a student contemporary, was writing in his diary that Barrett was 'playing himself in everywhere with the bigwigs', while sections of a virulent diary written by Major (Sir) Stanley Argyle [q.v.], referring to Barrett as the 'octopus of Heliopolis', were circulated in Melbourne drawing-rooms.

Barrett, however, was more the victim of an inexperienced administration than of his own personal characteristics. By July the 1st A.G.H. had become 'administratively unmanageable' and in August, as a result of a War Office inquiry into its affairs, its commanding officer and Matron Jane Bell [q.v.] were recalled to Australia. Barrett was relieved of all military duties but was permitted to retain his Red Cross work. However, Springthorpe had circulated in Australia a lengthy and substantially inaccurate charge against his administration in this field. Early in September Barrett was asked to resign by the council of the Australian Red Cross. He did so and immediately asked for an inquiry, which exonerated him, as did a further inquiry into the affairs of the 1st A.G.H. that was set up at his request. Shortly after, Barrett was ordered home.

With his military career in the Australian forces clearly at an end, Barrett brought off a remarkable defensive *coup* by arranging to be invalided to London on two months sick leave. There he quickly made as many influential friends as possible. In January 1916 he was ordered home again, but his busy involvement in military, political and diplomatic intrigue resulted in the Australian government assenting to his transfer to the British Army. He resigned from the A.I.F. in February 1916, and returned to Egypt in the Royal Army Medical Corps in the same rank as before. In 1916-17 he served as consulting aurist to the Egypt Expeditionary Force, and in 1917 as president of the invaliding and classification boards for most of Egypt. Although the attacks on him and the death of his son Keith in France in 1917 had brought him to a low ebb, he became active in the British Red Cross and the Young Men's Christian Association in the area, and wrote, with P. E. Deane [q.v.], *The Australian Army Medical Corps in Egypt* (1918). He also published in London his collected articles in two volumes, *The twin ideals: an educated commonwealth* (1918), *A vision of the possible: what the R.A.M.C. might become* (1919), and *The war work of the Y.M.C.A. in Egypt* (1919). He ended the war with a K.B.E., a C.B. and an Egyptian order — honours which may have softened his relentless determination to have legal vengeance on Springthorpe, Argyle, and the Melbourne *Age* and *Herald*.

In 1919 Barrett returned to Australia and decided to enter politics. He organized a branch of the National Party in Toorak, with himself as chairman and his daughter as secretary, and won pre-selection there for the 1920 Legislative Assembly election. But his enemies persuaded Argyle to stand as an independent Nationalist, and he easily defeated Barrett.

Barrett now busied himself with professional and public affairs, apparently developing a cynical attitude to politics. His major interest was the University of Melbourne, of which he became vice-chancellor in 1931, deputy chancellor in 1934 and chancellor in 1935-39, while continuing to sit on almost innumerable university committees. He retired from teaching in 1937. While bitterly unpopular with the professors, whom he regarded as employees to be kept in their place, on council he reigned supreme. He was imperturbable in debate, having 'a supreme forensic gift: his capacity to put his point in a few sentences was remarkable'. So too was his capacity to prepare his cases, the usual reason why 'Barrett got his way again'. In the absence of a salaried vice-chancellor until 1934, he was an extremely important administrator; nevertheless he supported the appointment of (Sir) Raymond Priestley [q.v.], who soon found his position intolerable. In 1937 a major confrontation, in which council had to support the vice-chancellor, marked the end of Barrett's most active participation in university affairs.

He was never popular in the medical profession, being regarded as a leading physician but a somewhat heroic surgeon. Yet it was a mark of Barrett's commanding presence that his profession paid him his greatest honour when, in 1935 at the annual meeting of the British Medical Association, held in Australia, he was elected as the new president; he gave an incisive presidential address on hospital problems. When the Ophthalmological Society of Australia was established in 1939 he, as a matter of course, became its first president.

From the 1890s Barrett had maintained a voluminous writing to the press, especially the *Argus*, while his list of public and charitable commitments was formidable. Even at 75, he was active on twenty-eight committees, being president of twelve, vice-president of two, chairman of seven and honorary secretary of three. He promoted the Workers' Educational Association, inviting Albert Mansbridge to Australia in 1913, paying the fares himself. He was chairman of the National Parks Committee, and president of the Town Planning and Playgrounds associations and the Japan Society. Other public questions of interest to him were decimalization, proportional representation, Empire affairs, venereal disease, neglected children, technical education, immigration, the League of Nations, preventive medicine, pure milk, baby clinics and a world calendar. By general agreement his most important work was the foundation in 1910 of the Bush Nursing Association movement, aided by his sister Edith [q.v.], which had a remarkable effect on rural health. By 1945 there were sixty-seven bush nursing hospitals and fifteen nursing centres in Victoria, all owing their existence to his initiative — his 'greatest and his noblest memorial'.

In music Barrett made another major contribution. An able pianist, in 1902-13 he took over the business management of G. W. L. Marshall Hall's [q.v.] orchestral concerts. After the war he helped to form the University Conservatorium Symphony Orchestra and from 1923 worked closely with the young violinist-conductor (Sir) Bernard Heinze to develop support for serious music; in 1932 they had the satisfaction of seeing the university orchestra merge into the Melbourne Symphony Orchestra. Heinze believes Barrett's influence was critical in building the standard of classical music in Melbourne to a point where it caught the public taste, and indeed sees his hand in the subsequent development of the Australian Broadcasting Commission's presentation of symphonic music. Barrett married Heinze's sister Monica Ernestine, aged 51, in St John's Catholic Church, Heidelberg, on 4 December 1940.

Barrett was a practical visionary, a rare combination. Lord Horder in 1935 said of him that he seemed 'to have been a pioneer in all the things that one could think of by which the human race might be bettered and improved'. Despite his almost complete lack of humour, especially about himself, he recognized that he possessed an 'unconquerable propensity for having a finger in every pie'. He was dogmatic and ruthless but was guided by the vision of civic virtue. Only some of his childhood friends ever called Barrett 'Jim'. He was a 'remorselessly purposeful' golfer. One of the paradoxes about him is that, despite his prowess and immense talents, despite his achievements, he was not only an unpopular man but also a widely ridiculed one. No doubt his physical ungainliness had something to do with satirical attacks on him and perhaps too a reputation for busybodiness and over-reaching himself. But Barrett was neither a dilettante nor ineffective; he was an extraordinarily capable operator on many fronts, and his very competence aroused jealousy. He concentrated on power and influential connexions rather than on public relations and popularity; he said of Melbourne doctors of his generation that they had 'never been accustomed ... to brook control of any description'. He did not bear grudges, and was generous and kind to many; he lived unostentatiously, gave generously to very many causes and did not seek wealth. But he could be mean, especially to those near him, and his treatment of his associate, Dr Ethel Parnell, has occasioned criticism. None the less, if not a great man, he had elements of greatness.

Barrett, who had long had bronchitis, and a complete heart block for two and a half years, died at his home at Toorak on 6 April 1945 of cerebral haemorrhage, and was buried in Melbourne general cemetary. He was survived by his second wife and by three daughters and a son of his first marriage. His estate was valued for probate at £58 437.

A. G. Butler (ed), *Official history of the Australian Army Medical Services... 1914-18*, 1 (Melb, 1930); *Lancet*, 14 Apr 1945; *MJA*, 14 July 1945; *British J of Ophthalmology*, 29 (1945); Ophthalmological Soc of Aust, *Trans*, 5 (1945); Soc for the Preservation of the Fauna of the Empire, *J*, Dec 1945; *The Times*, 7 Apr 1945; J. W. Barrett papers (AWM, and Univ Melb Archives); Springthorpe papers (LaTL); family information; interviews.

S. MURRAY-SMITH

BARRETT, JOHN GEORGE (1858-1928), tinsmith and politician, was born on 17 December 1858 at Carlton, Melbourne, fourth child of George Barrett, carpenter, and his wife Jane, née Elliott, both London-born. His father had been active in early agitation for reform of working conditions and was for seven years secretary of the North Melbourne branch of the Victorian Industrial and Protection League; John remembered being taken as a child of 8 to a (Sir Graham) Berry [q.v.3] rally at the Princess Theatre.

Barrett attended St Mary's Anglican School at Hotham from 1863 to 1870, when he was apprenticed to a firm of tinsmiths. At school he was 'diligent and industrious', carrying into later years a taste for study and general reading, especially in the fields of history, political economy and trade union literature; no athlete, he would watch an occasional cricket or football match.

In 1883 with F. H. Bromley [q.v.] and a former schoolfellow David Wyllie, Barrett founded the Tinsmiths' Society, and won reforms in hours and wages. Barrett succeeded Bromley as secretary of the society, which both men represented on the Trades Hall Council. Later he held office as T.H.C. secretary in 1893-1901, having been twice president and a leading member of its executive and of its parliamentary committee, which worked for the election of union candidates to the Victorian parliament. After the maritime strike of 1890 he was a council delegate to a conference which considered establishing a court of conciliation and arbitration, and was one of a sub-committee of four set up to draft a scheme for legislative action. He served as a council-member of the Working Men's College in 1888-95, and in 1899 he was appointed a member of the royal commission on technical education.

In 1892 Barrett contested the Legislative Assembly electorate of Carlton South. He won the seat in a by-election in March 1895, but lost it in 1897 by a narrow margin. He was described as a thoughtful man, of medium height, slender with a rather delicate appearance and a 'quiet grave, pale face'. Later a commentator recalled his cherub-like expression as he 'talked Labour Socialism in a Sunday School voice'. Among the political principles to which Barrett was pledged were an unimproved land tax, reform of the Legislative Council, protection to native industry, female suffrage, prohibition of Chinese and coolie labour, and Federation. His two-hour speech criticizing the weak points of the first Federation bill led to many requests for him to speak on the subject in country centres. In 1897 he served on a royal commission on law reform.

In 1901 Barrett was elected as one of Victoria's six senators to the first Federal parliament. He left the Labor Party before the 1903 election, when he was defeated as an Independent. He then directed his energies to temperance work, becoming secretary of the Victorian Alliance in 1904 and superintendent of the department of law and vigilance for the Victorian Prohibition League. In 1907 and 1917 he made two further attempts to re-enter State politics.

Barrett died on 19 May 1928 in a Melbourne hospital of pulmonary embolism after an operation for gastric ulcer, and was buried in Fawkner cemetery. On 29 April 1882, the day before her death, he had married Mary Henderson Duncan, a victim of Bright's disease. Three years later, at the High Church Presbyterian Manse, Geelong, he married her sister Anne Isabel Claudina Duncan, who predeceased him; he was survived by their five daughters and a son.

A'sian Hardware, 1 July 1902; *Table Talk*, 29 Mar 1895, 25 Apr, 9 May 1901; *Leader* (Melb), 23 Mar 1901; *Punch* (Melb), 19 July 1906; *Argus*, 21 May 1928; C. J. Kellaway, The Melbourne Trades Hall Council: its origins and political significance, 1855-1889 (Ph.D. thesis, La Trobe Univ, 1973); H. B. Higgins papers (NL); Eight-Hours Anniversary Cttee, Minutes 1877-93 (ML); minutes, 1877-93 (Trades Hall Council, Melb).

CARLOTTA KELLAWAY

BARRETT, WALTER FRANKLYN (1873-1964), film cameraman and director, was born at Loughborough, Leicestershire, England, son of William Brown, hatter, and his wife Matilda, née Hopwell. Brought up by an aunt, he played the violin in the Theatre of Varieties, Bath, for 30s. a week and devoted his spare time to photography. About 1895 he probably joined his father and brother John Henry in Wellington, New Zealand, working as a clerk for his father.

While touring with theatre orchestras from about 1900 he experimented with moving pictures: early films included a 'fake' boxing match with 'Dummy Mace' (1901), the royal tour of the duke and duchess of Cornwall and York, and a science fiction movie, *A message from Mars*, from the play (1903). In 1901 he had sent some photographs to London and in December won the Thornton Pickford prize of £15. Barrett sold his scenic films to the Charles Urban Trading Co. Ltd, visited England and worked for eight months with that firm. Back in Australia in 1904, he was the first person to film the Melbourne Cup from start to finish, and then shot more scenic films for the New Zealand and New South Wales railways. Although he signed the register as Brown, he was already known as Barrett when, as a widower, he married Mabel Muriel Pile in Perth on 10 December 1906.

Barrett joined the Melbourne office of Pathé Frères in 1908 and filmed *The sea coasts of New Zealand* and in 1909-10 *South Sea Island films*. He often showed great physical courage to get rare pictures: he crossed Cook Strait on a special platform built over the side of the ship to film the famous pilot dolphin 'Pelorous Jack', and hired a small launch to photograph the erupting volcano on Savaii Island.

West's Pictures took over Pathé in 1911, and Barrett remained as cameraman, supervising production; he also made several feature films. In 1913 West's merged with Australasian Films Ltd, and he joined the Fraser Film Release & Photographic Co. as film maker and buyer, and next year visited New York. His reputation as a director grew: in 1918 he photographed *The lure of the bush* for E. J. Carroll [q.v.], featuring the exploits of 'Snowy' (R. L.) Baker [q.v.], and in 1919 directed *Struck oil* starring Maggie Moore [q.v.5]. Although the plot of *The breaking of the drought* (1920) was old-fashioned, Barrett's realistic photography of the drought scenes was praised by the critics and led indirectly to the tightening of Commonwealth censorship laws. In 1920 he formed his own film company with Barry Kenwood, a solicitor, and in 1921-22 made three features, *A girl of the bush*, which 'had a distinctive spirit of "documentary realism" ', *Know thy child* and *A rough passage*. They all revealed 'his sensitive eye as a photographer of Australian landscapes'.

In mid-1922 Barrett's company failed, partly because of Australasian Films' monopoly over cinemas. In 1925 he became manager of the Capitol Theatre, Sydney. He joined Hoyts' Theatres Ltd in 1927 and managed its cinemas at Neutral Bay, Mosman, Arncliffe, Clovelly and Woollahra. Predeceased by his wife, he died at Randwick on 16 July 1964, aged 91, and was cremated after an Anglican service. He was survived by a married daughter Harrie Marrett, known on the stage as Miss Todd Barrett.

Roy Com on the moving picture industry in Aust, Report, *PP* (Cwlth), 1926-28, 4, 1371; *Theatre Mag* (Syd), 1 Jan 1917; *Picture Show*, 1 Aug 1920, trade supp; *Everyone's*, 11 Dec 1920; *A'sian Picture Mag*, 1 June 1921; *Showman*, Aug, Sept, Oct 1950; *Cinema Papers*, Apr 1974; *SMH*, 17 July 1964; information from Mr Ross Cooper, Melb, Mr A. Pike, Canb, and Mr C. Sowry, Wellington, NZ.

MARTHA RUTLEDGE

BARRON, ELLEN; *see* CHATFIELD

BARRON, SIR HARRY (1847-1921), soldier and governor, was born on 11 August 1847, son of Charles Barron of Denmark Hill, Surrey, England, and his wife Elizabeth, née Pigeon. Educated privately and at the Royal Military Academy, Woolwich, he was commissioned lieutenant in the Royal Artillery in 1867 and enjoyed the steady promotion of a successful peace-time professional officer: from captain in 1879 to major general in 1904. He was chief instructor in 1897 at the School of Gunnery, Shoeburyness, then commander of the Royal Artillery in the Thames district (1900-04) and in Malta (1904-08), being appointed C.V.O. in 1907 and K.C.M.G. on his retirement.

Barron became governor of Tasmania from September 1909 to March 1913, then governor of Western Australia until February 1917. Completely inexperienced in politics, he met more than his fair share of minor constitutional crises, but handled them safely. In October 1909, just after his arrival in Hobart, Sir Neil Lewis's [q.v.] government was beaten through the defection of some of its members; Barron summoned the leader of the Opposition, John Earle [q.v.], to form Tasmania's first Labor government, but on his immediate defeat refused him a dissolution and commissioned Lewis to form another and more durable ministry. His judgment was more generally approved in this case than in December 1912, when he granted a dissolution at the request of the Liberal premier A. E. Solomon [q.v.], who had lost a vote of confidence. The Labor *Daily Post*, then agitating for abolition of the office of governor, described him as 'a conservative partisan'.

In Western Australia Barron refused the Labor premier John Scaddan [q.v.] a dissolution in July 1916 when he was defeated in the Legislative Assembly by a combination of Liberal and Country party members, and commissioned the Liberal leader F. Wilson [q.v.] to form a ministry. In February 1917, because the Labor Party broke pairs with the Country Party, the Wilson government was four times defeated in the House. When Wilson sought a dissolution he too was refused, Barron stating that it was important to avoid the turmoil and expense of a general election at a time when legislation was needed to look after returned servicemen, and when an election was in any case due within eight months. Instead, Barron summoned the Country Party leader F. E. S. Willmott [q.v.], and won from him an undertaking to restrain hostilities against the Wilson ministry for the remainder of the session. These manoeuvres were followed by a Labor motion of no confidence in the Wilson government which led to the most tumultuous scenes ever experienced in the State legislature; by that time, however, Barron was no longer in Government House, and only one or two Labor back-benchers ventured even a hint of criticism of his actions.

Barron retired to Weybridge, Surrey. He was made colonel commandant of the Royal Artillery in 1920, and died on 27 March 1921. He had married in 1877 Clara Emily, daughter of Major General T. Conyngham Kelly, C.B.; they had one daughter.

A. B. Keith, *Responsible government in the Dominions*, 1, 2nd ed (Oxford, 1928); *Mercury*, 28 Dec 1912; *West Australian*, 13 Mar 1913, 3-8, 26, 27 Feb 1917.
            G. C. BOLTON

BARRON, JOHANNA (1865-1948), Brigidine nun known as Mother Paul, was born at Knockeen, County Waterford,

Ireland, daughter of Thomas Barron and his wife Mary, née Power. She was educated at Butlerstown National School and at the Brigidine Convent, Abbeyleix, where she became a postulant in 1882 and in 1885 a professed Sister of the Brigidine Order.

In 1888 Mother Paul was one of five Brigidine Sisters, three from Abbeyleix and two from Goresbridge, who were selected from volunteers to found a convent at Ararat, Victoria. They arrived there on 16 November and in 1889 opened St Mary's Primary School, with an attendance of sixty children, and a select school with, initially, seven pupils. These Sisters had been brought to Ararat by Bishop James Moore [q.v.5] of Ballarat, but there were already three Brigidine communities in the colony in the diocese of Bishop Crane [q.v.3] of Sandhurst: at Echuca and Beechworth (both founded in 1886) and at Wangaratta (1887). Bishop Moore maintained that the churches could achieve little without Catholic schools and Catholic education. Although the Sisters likewise rejected the secular spirit of the day and emphasized the religious aspect of their teaching, their educational aims were not narrowly sectarian. Their reputation as teachers was high, and the curriculum offered by the select school in 1889 was both liberal and comprehensive.

The Ararat foundation flourished. It is not primarily as an educator, however, that Mother Paul is remembered, but as an administrator, unifying the Victorian foundations which had inherited the Irish tradition of autonomy. In 1889 all the Irish and Australian houses amalgamated and New South Wales and Victoria became one Province, which in 1896 was divided in two. In this time of reorganization and rapid expansion – the original Australian foundations were themselves forming new communities – the role of mother provincial was critical. In Victoria Mother Paul held this position from 1908 for the unusually long period of twelve years. From 1920 to 1932 she was superior at the Albert Park and Ararat convents, before serving a further six years as mother provincial. In 1938-44 she was again superior at Albert Park, where she died on 15 October 1948, aged 82.

In her work of amalgamation Mother Paul was assisted by her personal links with the Sisters from the Irish founding houses, her devotion to the traditional Rule of the Order, in itself a unifying force and a force for equality within the Order, and her command of canon law. Conservative rather than flexible, she united a keen intelligence with a strong but kindly personality; her administrative skill was undoubted.

M. Gibbons, *Glimpses of Catholic Ireland in the*

eighteenth century (Dublin, 1932); *Ararat Advertiser*, 16 Nov 1888, Jan 1889; *Advocate* (Melb), 9 Mar 1889, 21, 28 Oct 1948; *Tribune* (Melb), 6 Dec 1934; Mother Paul Barron, An account of the establishment of the Novitiate, *and* Annals of Albert Park, Ararat, Echuca and Mentone Brigidine convents (Malvern Convent, Vic).

WILMA HANNAH

BARRY, JOHN (1875-1938), Catholic bishop, was born on 18 June 1875 near Freemount, County Cork, Ireland, eldest son of 10 children of Simon Barry, farmer, and his wife Mary. His parents were intensely religious: a brother became president of an American seminary and two sisters were nuns. Educated at the parish school and at St Colman's College, Freemount, he studied for the priesthood at St Patrick's College, Maynooth, where he was ordained on 18 June 1899.

Barry left for Australia that year, arriving in Melbourne on 8 November. After serving as curate at Dandenong and St Kilda East, he was parish priest at Mansfield in 1907-12; he travelled overseas in 1910. In 1912 he took over the new parish of Balaclava and in March 1917 was appointed by Archbishop Carr [q.v.] administrator of St Patrick's Cathedral and chancellor of the archdiocese of Melbourne. On Carr's death two months later, he was confirmed in his offices by Archbishop Mannix [q.v.], and was prominent in administering the building funds of Newman College, University of Melbourne, and of Corpus Christi College, Werribee. In 1920, during Mannix's absence overseas, Barry was in charge of the archdiocese. He won repute as a hard-working and efficient organizer, a man of active holiness and a genial and considerate host. From the same Irish diocese as Mannix, he had his trust and friendship.

On 5 March 1924 Barry was appointed bishop of Goulburn and was consecrated there on 29 June by the apostolic delegate, Dr B. Cattaneo. In his diocese, which included Canberra, he became known as a 'building bishop' despite the onset of the Depression. He renovated Saints Peter and Paul's Cathedral, Goulburn, made large extensions to the Hospital of St John of God, extended the orphanages and founded a technical school and a diocesan library. He also began to develop Catholic institutions in Canberra with moves in 1927 towards the erection of a church, school and convent and plans for a cathedral worthy of the nation's capital. A strong advocate of systematic visitations, he travelled incessantly within his diocese. He became known throughout Australia for his vigorous sponsorship of the Holy Name Society, which he saw as the main area of activity for Catholic Action.

Possessing restless energy, 'a flair for diplomacy and a never-failing sense of humour', Barry was popular both with his own flock and other denominations. He became ill in February 1938 while attending the Regional Missionary and Eucharistic Congress at Newcastle, and died of coronary occlusion in Lewisham Hospital, Sydney, on 22 March. After a well-attended funeral at which Mannix read the oration, he was buried in the Catholic cemetery at Kenmore, Goulburn. His estate was valued for probate at £1912.

W. F. Whyte, *Monsignor P. M. Haydon* (Syd, 1952); R. T. Wyatt, *The history of Goulburn*, 2nd ed (Syd, 1972); A. J. McGilvray, *The hallowed high adventure* (Syd, 1973); *Our Cathedral Times*, 10 Apr 1938; *Footprints*, July 1971; *Catholic Press*, 6 Mar 1924, 24, 31 Mar 1938; *Goulburn Evening Penny Post*, 23, 25 May 1938; Syd Archdiocesan Archives (St Mary's Cathedral).

PATRICK O'FARRELL

BARRY, JOHN ARTHUR (1850-1911), author and journalist, was born at Torquay, Devon, England. Orphaned young, he persuaded his guardian to apprentice him at 13 to the Orient Steam Navigation Co. He served his time under sail and eventually received his first mate's ticket. In the 1860s he was apparently on the Australia run, and in 1870 followed the gold rush to the Palmer diggings in North Queensland. In the next few years he seems to have engaged in droving, digging, boundary riding and other outback occupations. He returned to the sea about 1877, this time to the coastal trade of eastern Australia, and in steam as well as sail. In 1879 he went back to the land, accepting a position as overseer and station-manager, probably near Scone, New South Wales.

Barry seems to have remained there until 1893, when he returned to England for a holiday. One of the results of his trip was the publication of his first book, *Steve Brown's bunyip, and other stories* (London, 1893), a collection of pieces which had earlier appeared in English and Australian journals and newspapers. Rudyard Kipling, who had some slight acquaintance with Barry, contributed introductory verses. Having little taste for London life and less for the English winter, Barry returned to Sydney in about six months. After another period of station life, he joined the staff of the *Evening News* in 1896, and retained a close connexion with it and to a lesser extent with the *Australian Town and Country Journal* until 1911. He enjoyed yachting and playing chess with his friends. Unmarried, he died of chronic myocarditis at his home at North Sydney on 23 September 1911, aged 61. He was buried in the Anglican section of the Gore Hill cemetery and left an estate valued for probate at £1521 to his friends.

Barry was a prolific if superficial writer. Some of his newspaper series such as 'The city of Sydney' and 'The fleets of the golden fleece' have historical interest. His fiction, both novels and short stories, is in part at least autobiographical, and has two principal subjects: the sea and the Australian outback. His chief works include *Luck of the native-born* (London, 1898), *A son of the sea* (London, 1899), *Red lion and blue star, with other stories* (London, 1902), and *South sea shipmates* (Sydney, 1913) with an unsigned biographical preface. These books are boyishly exciting romances and sometimes explicitly directed towards a juvenile audience. Yet his contemporaries saw him as lacking 'a genius for advertisement' rather than ability; according to the *Bulletin*, 5 October 1911, 'Faithfulness and honesty were the keynotes of all he wrote, and he shrank from anything that looked like literary log-rolling. He was a man who was entirely lovable – one of those gentle souls who did not know how enemies were made'.

SMH, 25 Sept 1911; *Bulletin*, 28 Sept 1911.

H. P. HESELTINE

BARTLETT, CHARLES HENRY FALKNER HOPE (1853-1916), soldier, was born on 1 August 1853 at Maitland, New South Wales, son of Falkner Hope Bartlett, pastoralist, and his wife Hephzibah Elizabeth, née Hallett. He was educated by private tutors and trained as a solicitor but did not practise. In 1872 he joined the East Maitland Company of the Northern Battalion, New South Wales Volunteer Force, and was commissioned captain in March 1875. When the Force was reorganized three years later, he reverted to the rank of lieutenant, but was again made captain in October 1880. He resigned from the volunteer infantry on 21 November 1883 and next day joined the New South Wales Permanent Military Forces; immediately commissioned captain, he was appointed adjutant of the 1st Australian Infantry Regiment.

In 1885 Bartlett went to the Sudan as adjutant of the New South Wales infantry contingent. He took part in the advance on Tamai, the only notable skirmish of the campaign, was mentioned in dispatches, and was awarded the Egypt Medal and clasp and the Khedive Star, the standard campaign decorations. On returning home he resumed duty with the 1st Regiment. In 1887 he went to England on leave and, while there, obtained permission to undergo military instruction. He was attached to the 1st Manchester Regiment at Aldershot in July, and next month attended a course at the School of Musketry, Hythe; he later completed another course there, qualifying as an instructor in the operation of Nordenfelt and Gardner machine-guns. He was promoted major that year and on 20 December 1888 married Ada Louisa Gale at St Thomas's Anglican Church, Willoughby, New South Wales.

In 1893-95 Bartlett served as deputy assistant adjutant general at New South Wales headquarters; he became adjutant of the 3rd Australian Regiment in 1895, was promoted brevet lieut-colonel in 1899, and was appointed to the administrative and instructional staff of the 3rd and 4th Regiments in 1902, then to the instructional staff at State headquarters, Commonwealth Military Forces, in 1904. Two years later he became assistant adjutant general and chief staff officer there. His last appointment, on 23 December 1909, was as aide-de-camp to the governor-general, the earl of Dudley [q.v.]; he retired, with step in rank to colonel, on 1st April 1912. He was a foundation member and councillor of the United Service Institution of New South Wales.

Bartlett died of pneumonia on 17 June 1916 at Woollahra, survived by his wife and two sons and predeceased by his only daughter. After a service at St Matthias Anglican Church, Paddington, he was buried in South Head cemetery with full military honours.

A man of exceptional tact and loyalty, with a firm grasp of administrative and tactical procedures, Bartlett was a staff officer of outstanding merit. As director of many training and promotion courses he made a significant contribution to the training of volunteers.

F. Hutchinson and F. Myers, *The Australian contingent* (Syd, 1885); T. Archer, *The war in Egypt and the Soudan*, 4 (Lond, 1887); *The First Australian Infantry Regiment, Militia (NSW)* . . . *1854-1904* (Syd, nd); R. Clark, *New South Wales Soudan contingent* (Canb, 1972); B. W. Champion (ed), *Hunter Valley register, 1843-84*, 1 (Newcastle, 1973); *Government Gazette* (NSW), 20 Sept 1848, 29 Mar 1899; *London Gazette*, 25 Aug 1885; *SMH*, 21 June 1916; Bartlett papers (AWM); information from Mr H. R. H. Bartlett, Merimbula, NSW.

R. SUTTON

BARTON, ALAN SINCLAIR DARVALL (1886-1950), medical practitioner, was born on 12 March 1886 at Bathurst, New South Wales, son of Robert Darvall Barton, grazier and author of *Reminiscences of an Australian pioneer* (Sydney, 1917), and his wife Fanny Blanche, a daughter of John Smith [q.v.6], sheep-breeder; he was a first cousin of A. B. Paterson [q.v.]. Educated at All Saints' College, Bathurst, and the University of Sydney (M.B., Ch.B., 1909; Ch.M., 1910), he became resident medical officer and registrar at Sydney Hospital in 1910-11. Two years later he began private practice at Coonabarabran.

When World War I broke out Barton enlisted in the Australian Imperial Force and was commissioned captain, Australian Army Medical Corps, on 14 November 1914; he was posted to the 2nd Australian General Hospital and sailed for Egypt. After serving with the 1st Australian Division at Mena Camp, he joined No.1 Australian Casualty Clearing Station at Anzac Beach in September 1915. Plans for the Allied withdrawal from Gallipoli assumed that the badly wounded would be left behind and taken out later under the Red Cross flag; Barton's offer to stay with them was accepted. As it turned out, all the wounded were evacuated on 20 December and he commanded one of the last medical parties to leave the beach. He rejoined his clearing station at Serapeum, Egypt, and accompanied it to France in April 1916. It was soon to deal with the heavy casualties from the battle of Fromelles.

In France Barton quickly gained a reputation as a skilful and dedicated surgeon and spent most of his time in casualty clearing stations close to the front lines. The demands made on surgical teams were extreme; they often worked shifts of sixteen to twenty-four hours in the operating theatres, and at the same time were required to keep pace with new developments in the treatment of wounds. In August Barton was attached to a British station near Amiens where many gas and gangrene victims were treated. Promoted major on 14 November, he was transferred next month to No.2 Australian Casualty Clearing Station at Armentières; he was still there in June 1917 when casualties poured in from the battle of Messines. In that month the station admitted over 7000 casualties, evacuated almost as many again, and performed over 1000 operations. Barton was mentioned in dispatches in June and December and was awarded the Distinguished Service Order on 1 January 1918. He remained at Armentières until March and was then posted to the 2nd Australian General Hospital at Boulogne. His final service was with a British clearing station near Péronne during the final attacks on the Hindenburg Line; on 28 December he was again mentioned in dispatches.

In February 1919 Barton married Dorothy Ellena Duffy at St Philip's Anglican Church, Sydney. His A.I.F. service ended in March, and in August he published a paper on his work in Allied casualty clearing stations; this drew attention to new techniques for the closure of wounds and to the use of gas and oxygen as anaesthetics. Late that year he settled at Singleton and over the next twenty-six years built up an extensive private practice. He became a fellow of the Royal Australasian College of Surgeons in 1928. In 1946 he retired to Gosford and, survived by his wife, a son and three daughters, died of coronary occlusion on 18 May 1950.

A. G. Butler, *Official history of the Australian Army Medical Services. . . 1914-18*, 1-2 (Melb, 1930, Canb, 1940); W. A. Steel and J. M. Antill, *The history of All Saints' College, Bathurst, 1873-1963* (Syd, 1964); *London Gazette*, 1 June, 24 Dec 1917, 1 Jan, 28 Dec 1918; *MJA*, 23 Aug 1919; Barton papers (AWM).   WILLIAM A. LAND

BARTON, SIR EDMUND (1849-1920), federationist, first prime minister and judge, was born on 18 January 1849 at Glebe, Sydney, third son and youngest child of William Barton and his wife Mary Louisa, née Whydah; his eldest brother was G. B. Barton [q.v.3]. William had arrived in Sydney from London in 1824 as accountant to the Australian Agricultural Co. After a quarrel with Sir William Parry [q.v.2], he had resigned in 1832 and his subsequent career as a financial agent and sharebroker was chequered. With nine children to be provided for, his wife, who was exceptionally well educated, ran a girls' school in the 1860s. Edmund, known as Toby to his schoolmates, was educated at Fort Street Model School for two years and in 1859-64 at Sydney Grammar School, where he began a lifelong friendship with R. E. O'Connor [q.v.], and was school captain in 1863 and 1864.

In 1865 Barton matriculated at the University of Sydney. Next year he won a prize for classics and the £50 (William) Lithgow [q.v.2] scholarship. In 1867 he studied under Professor Charles Badham [q.v.3], who gave him a lasting love of Greek and Latin, and won the (Sir Daniel) Cooper [q.v.3] scholarship. He graduated B.A. in 1868 and M.A. (by examination) in 1870. He learned to debate at the Sydney Mechanics' School of Arts. From May 1868 he had worked for a solicitor H. B. Bradley [q.v.3] and from June 1870 with a barrister G. C. Davies. On 21 December 1871 he was admitted to the Bar. Although slow to get briefs, in May 1872 he was junior counsel for the defence of the notorious murderer Alfred Lester.

As a boy Toby had loved fishing and cricket; a fair batsman, but an atrocious fieldsman, he played for the university in 1870 and 1871. Later he organized several intercolonial matches and umpired in some major games including New South Wales v. Lord Harris's English XI which was interrupted by a riot. In 1870, when visiting Newcastle with a team, he confided to his diary that 'Jeannie Ross is beautiful, and sings like a bird, and is a dear'; they became engaged in 1872. He warned her: 'You do not know the depths of my poverty and the slenderness of my chances'. In 1875 he accompanied Sir Alfred Stephen [q.v.6] on circuit to Grafton as his associate; later that year he was briefly an acting crown prosecutor, and again in 1878, but failed in other efforts to get a government appointment. On 28 December 1877 at the Watt Street Presbyterian manse, Newcastle, he married Jane (Jean) Mason Ross, daughter of an English engineer and hotelkeeper.

In 1876 and 1877 Barton was defeated for the University of Sydney seat in the Legislative Assembly, but won it in 1879. Although he generally opposed the Parkes-Robertson [qq.v.5,6] coalition ministry, strongly supported its 1880 Education Act. In November he was elected unopposed for Wellington, and won East Sydney in 1882, thinking it 'almost unnecessary' to say that he was a free trader.

On 3 January 1883 Barton became Speaker. In a turbulent parliament, he displayed a sound knowledge of constitutional law and T. E. May's *British parliamentary practices*. The youngest Speaker yet, he revelled in the clubbable atmosphere of parliament and earned the *Bulletin*'s nickname, 'Toby Tosspot', but was able to give clear decisions at 5 a.m. after disorderly sittings. He displayed quickness of perception, tact, courtesy and firmness. Next year he was forced to introduce new standing orders to control such rowdy and abusive members as D. Buchanan, J. McElhone [qq.v.3,5] and A. G. Taylor [q.v.6], who was twice suspended from parliament by a vote of the House; the second time Barton had to order his removal by the serjeant-at-arms. Taylor claimed his suspension was illegal and won £1000 damages against him; the decision was upheld by the Privy Council.

In September 1885 Barton told L. J. Brient [q.v.], editor of the *Daily Telegraph*, of his 'determination not to be permanently "shelved"' after the defeat of Sir Alexander Stuart's [q.v.6] ministry. Despite Governor Loftus's [q.v.5] opinion that Barton was the probable leader of an emerging strong third party, Brient's intrigues to bring about a coalition ministry between him and (Sir) George Dibbs [q.v.4] came to nothing. Barton refused the attorney-generalship under Dibbs and was again elected Speaker.

Bradley urged him to give more attention to his professional career: 'there will be directly no man at the General Bar but Salomons [q.v.6] to compete with you!' Whatever hard work and 'late hours and late habits' the Speakership involved, it was compensated for by a salary of £1200. In the years 1883-86 his earnings at the Bar had been £720, £630, £1114 and £901.

On 31 January 1887 Barton resigned as Speaker, and on 2 February was nominated to the Upper House. He rejected Parkes's offer of the vice-presidency of the Executive Council and leadership of the government in the Legislative Council. On 25 May he regretfully refused office as attorney-general, because he could not bring himself 'to concur in the financial projects of the Government'. However in January-March 1889 he held that portfolio in the Dibbs Protectionist ministry and, as *ex officio* leader of the Bar, he took silk on 8 March. In October he chaired the first National Protection Conference held in New South Wales but declined leadership of the Protectionist Party.

From the early 1880s Barton spent many convivial hours at the Athenaeum Club, where 'wit sparkled while the wine flowed freely', with fellow members such as J. F. Archibald and W. B. Dalley [qq.v.3,4], Julian Ashton, Louis Becke, Thomas Butler, and (Sir) James Fairfax [qq.v.]. Here in the mid-1880s he discussed a Federal legislative body with A. Inglis Clark [q.v.3]. Handsome, with 'finely chiselled features', curling black hair starting to grey and 'beautiful black eyes that glowed with enthusiasm', Barton grew portly with age and good living, but still enjoyed fishing. Part of his charm was his generosity, even temper and ability to keep silent; his conversation rarely lacked 'humour or wit'. An omnivorous reader, he loved the theatre – especially Shakespeare and the opera – and appreciated music and art. He was a fellow of the university senate in 1880-89 and 1892-1920, and a trustee of the Public Library of New South Wales.

Ardently believing in Australia's destiny as a nation, Barton congratulated Parkes in October 1889 on his Tenterfield address, and at a crowded meeting in the Sydney Town Hall in November, supported Federation. Familiar with Clark's draft constitution, sent to him on 12 February 1891, he criticized Parkes's proposed resolutions for the National Australasian Convention: he thought it 'of the highest importance that just proposals' should be formulated at once on the New South Wales fear of 'surrenders' on the seat of government and possible 'dismemberment' against its consent.

As a delegate to the convention in Sydney in March, Barton impressed Alfred Deakin and (Sir) John Downer [qq.v.] with his address on the Federal resolutions. He urged that the 'territorial rights' of the colonies should remain intact and, on the divisive question of protection, took it 'as a matter of course' that soon after Federation 'trade and intercourse ... shall be absolutely free'. Believing that the Lower House should rest 'upon universal suffrage', he advocated that the second chamber should also be representative and argued that the power of such a senate to amend money bills would cause less friction than an outright veto. He begged the convention and colonial parliaments to 'secure the abolition of the jurisdiction of the Privy Council'. When Clark succumbed to influenza, Barton became a member of the drafting committee, and 'strenuously and industriously' devoted himself to its work, winning the praise of its chairman Sir Samuel Griffith [q.v.].

He soon had to uphold the draft constitution bill against (Sir) George Reid [q.v.], who maintained that certain clauses were unfair to New South Wales. On 12 June 1891 Barton resigned from the Upper House and in the general election contested East Sydney with Reid. He astounded political circles when he announced that 'So long as Protection meant a Ministry of enemies to Federation, they would get no vote from him'. He bitterly attacked Reid and asserted that on Federation 'Mr. Dibbs is a daily conundrum. What can we do but give him up?' Praised by the *Sydney Morning Herald* for his stand on principle, he topped the poll.

In the new parliament Barton voted in all major divisions with Parkes, who remained in office with Labor Party support. In August, again refusing office, he explained that he did not see its acceptance 'as a public duty' at that time. The government fell in October, and Parkes persuaded him to take over leadership of the Federal movement in New South Wales.

On 23 October Barton became attorney-general, with the right of private practice, in Dibbs's new Protectionist ministry, which was lukewarm towards Federation. Assailed on all sides, he defended himself: 'if the question of Federation is to be satisfactorily handled ... its conduct should be in the hands of a Minister, and that Minister, an ardent Federationist'. He had extracted a promise from Dibbs of ministerial support for the Federal resolutions, to be introduced early in the next session. However, his acceptance of a protective tariff to remedy the large treasury deficit roused a storm of criticism and charges that he was putting 'provincial protection first, and Federation in the dim future'. Many free traders in his electorate felt betrayed.

Barton worked hard and late to introduce order and punctuality into his department.

Also acting premier while Dibbs was in England from April to September 1892, he had to contend with the Broken Hill miners' strike. He refused to send military forces to keep order as he wanted to 'avoid undue causes of irritation', but did dispatch fifty policemen. When the leaders were charged with conspiracy in September, he instructed the crown prosecutor to conduct all cases 'with absolute fairness', but accepted advice to transfer the trial to Deniliquin, as no Broken Hill jury was likely to convict, thus provoking the antagonism of Labor members and the *Australian Worker*. Preoccupied with the strike, hindered by indifferent colleagues, and encumbered with a complex electoral bill, Barton was unable to introduce the Federal resolutions until 22 November: he finally carried them on 11 January 1893. Frustrated in his attempts to get the draft constitution bill considered in committee, he was caught up in the depression and bank crisis in May and had to pilot the bank issue and current account depositors bills through the assembly.

In December 1892 Barton had visited Corowa and Albury and, with local co-operation, had set up branches of the Australasian Federation League. In July 1893 the Central Federation League was formed in Sydney; blaming Barton for failing to get the draft bill considered in parliament, Parkes disapproved of him seeking support from the people. Throughout the winter Barton was attacked in the press by Parkes and B. R. Wise [q.v.]. Exhausted, he visited Canada from July to September.

In October the resolutions were finally considered in committee, but the adjournment was carried. They had not been restored to the order-paper by December when Barton and O'Connor, minister of justice, were challenged in the House for holding briefs against the Crown in *Proudfoot* v. *the Railway Commissioners*. He immediately returned his brief and Governor Duff [q.v.] reported that 'the matter would have ended there', but Barton defended the right of cabinet ministers 'in their professional practice, to appear against a government department' in the courts. The adjournment was carried against them and Barton immediately resigned.

An able attorney-general, he had gained valuable administrative and ministerial experience, but his reputation as a Federation leader had suffered and both free traders and Labor members now distrusted him. In the general election of July 1894 he was defeated for Randwick. When Reid precipitated another election a year later Barton told Parkes that 'a return to active politics would be just now disastrous to the interests of my family';

throughout the 1890s his finances were precarious. However, reconciled with Parkes, he campaigned for him.

Barton devoted the next three years to tireless work for Federation. He left the organization of the leagues, springing up all over the colony, to non-political enthusiasts – but was always willing to give advice – while he 'stumped the country', addressing some 300 meetings. He was helped by a band of 'young disciples' such as Atlee Hunt, (Sir) Robert Garran and (Sir) Thomas Bavin [qq.v.]; Garran recorded that at Ashfield Barton triumphantly asserted that 'For the first time in history, we have a nation for a continent and a continent for a nation'. He kept in close touch with prominent federationists in other colonies and by March 1897 he had become 'the acknowledged leader of the federal movement in all Australia': his prestige had been vastly increased by 'his years of patient advocacy'. He was elected to the Australasian Federal Convention, first of forty-nine candidates.

On 22 March the convention met in Adelaide. Barton was elected leader and, later, chairman of the drafting and constitutional committees. Night after night Barton drove the drafting committee to exhaustion but it produced a constitution by mid-April. He was alert, patient, willing to explain, to intervene and to make notes of amendments for drafting. He was rarely provoked, except by (Sir) Isaac Isaacs [q.v.], whom he rebuked as 'a pedant'; he unwisely neglected some of his suggestions.

Before Reid left to attend Queen Victoria's Diamond Jubilee, he recommended Barton's appointment to the Legislative Council to take charge of the draft bill. Barton demurred as 'he had been sitting for months as arbitrator' in *McSharry* v. *the Railway Commissioners*, and could not withdraw from the case because of the 'enormous hardship' to both parties. However, Reid considered his continuance as sole arbitrator 'perfectly consistent', and he was appointed to the council on 8 May. This freed J. H. Want [q.v.], Reid's attorney-general, to attack the draft bill in a council already intransigently opposed to Federation. So many damaging amendments were carried that on 26 August Barton refused to have anything more to do with the mutilated bill and claimed 'you might as well say you would improve a horse by cutting his legs off!'

When the adjourned convention met in Sydney in September to consider the 286 amendments proposed by the colonial legislatures, Barton kept the delegates to their task. The convention reconvened in Melbourne on 20 January 1898. The summer was hot and by March the members were irritable and weary of inconclusive debates on finance, rivers and railway freights. Barton kept on until the drafting committee was satisfied, but blunders crept in: he defended the wording that trade and commerce should be 'absolutely free'. J. A. La Nauze has paid tribute to Barton's achievement. 'There were men in the Convention more eminent and more industrious in their common professions; more learned in constitutional law; equally devoted in the preceding decade to the profitless cause of federation; more prominent and experienced in politics. Yet he led them all, with an authority never questioned, and sustained by the visible and irrefutable example of plain hard work and conscientious devotion to a task'.

The convention finally rose on 17 March and Barton returned home to campaign for the referendum to approve the draft constitution bill. Strong opposition from leading businessmen and the *Daily Telegraph* was reinforced when Reid adopted an equivocal attitude. In June the referendum failed by 8504 votes to reach the required minimum of 80 000. Barton, who had been warned by Governor Hampden [q.v.], realized that concessions would have to be made if New South Wales were to accept the constitution.

On 22 July 1898 Barton resigned from the council to stand against Reid in the general election. He advocated three modifications to the bill: the Federal capital to be in New South Wales, cancellation of the (Sir Edward) Braddon [q.v.] clause on finance, and removal of the three-fifths majority at a joint sitting to resolve a deadlock. No match for Reid's wit, he was narrowly defeated in 'a historic political duel'. In September he won a by-election for the Hastings and Macleay assembly seat after a bitter campaign against Sydney Smith [q.v.], who was assisted by J. H. Young [q.v.6].

Back in the assembly Barton was immediately elected leader of the Opposition and soon had to face fierce criticism for his association with the McSharry case, which had lasted for more than two years. At the head of a motley group of Federalists who were also protectionist and of protectionists who were anti-Federation and anti-Reid, Barton, somewhat inconsistently with his reputation as 'Australia's noblest son', now pursued tactics of harassment against Reid and turned a blind eye to the obstructive antics of his dubious supporter W. P. Crick [q.v.], thereby endangering the new Federal resolutions. After Reid had won important concessions at a premiers' meeting in January 1899 and carried the Enabling Act for a second referendum in April, he and Barton campaigned together. Leaving the main railway-lines, Barton drove through the bush in a buggy, speaking at towns, villages and homesteads, often driving through the night. On 29 June 1899 the draft constitution bill was approved by 107 420 votes to 82 741.

In August it seemed likely that Reid would be defeated in the House; Barton resigned as leader of the Opposition as, unacceptable to the Labor Party, he could not form a government. He refused the attorney-generalship when, after complex manoeuvring, (Sir) William Lyne [q.v.], a strong opponent of Federation, became premier. He resigned from parliament on 7 February 1900.

In March Barton, accompanied by his wife, arrived in London as leader of the Australian delegation invited by Joseph Chamberlain to explain the constitution to the Imperial government. Instructed to press for its passage without amendment through the British parliament, he soon found that Chamberlain, backed by influential pressure from Australia, was adamant on restoring the right of appeal to the Privy Council. Barton and the other delegates wasted no opportunity to publicize their cause; they accepted numerous invitations to speak, and stressed that the bill had been approved by the Australian people. Chamberlain offered a compromise whereby the settlement of constitutional issues would be left to the High Court, while the right of appeal to the Privy Council was restored for other cases. The earl of Jersey [q.v.] told Barton that the concession 'could only have been obtained by tact, firmness & the confidence you inspired'.

Barton was elected an honorary member of twelve famous clubs in London and awarded an honorary LL.D. by the University of Cambridge. Back in Australia by September, he corresponded with the Colonial Office about the details of the inauguration of the Commonwealth of Australia. It was widely believed that he would be first prime minister, although Sir Frederick Darley [q.v.4] complained to Sir Samuel Way [q.v.]: 'Barton is bad enough, though I suppose he is certain to be C.[hief] J.[ustice]; but he is not so bad as either Kingston or Symon [qq.v.]. Barton does not command respect here. He is undoubtedly an able man, and might have been a distinguished man at the Bar, but he is too lazy to work, and has therefore but little experience. He is unfortunately in very impoverished circumstances ... a sum of money has been collected . . . for the benefit of his wife and his children's education'.

However, Barton thought it 'his duty to remain in politics for a time', and it came as a shock, both in England and Australia, when on 19 December 1900 the earl of Hopetoun [q.v.], the governor-general, asked Lyne to form the first Commonwealth min-

istry. Barton refused to serve as attorney-general and, after frantic use of the telegraph by Deakin, Lyne failed to form a ministry; Barton was commissioned to do so and on Christmas Day named his cabinet, which included his friends Deakin and O'Connor, Kingston, and the three premiers (Earl) Forrest, Sir George Turner [qq.v.] and Lyne. Barton himself was prime minister and took the portfolio of external affairs: it was fitting that Australia's first prime minister was native-born.

The proclamation of the Commonwealth on 1 January 1901 was followed by banqueting and great celebrations, but before the royal tour of the duke and duchess of York could begin, Barton had the elections to win to become prime minister in his own right. He opened his campaign at West Maitland on 17 January with a statesmanlike speech: he favoured moderate protection to raise sufficient money for the States and the Commonwealth and would resort to direct taxation if extra funds were needed in an emergency. He infuriated many Queenslanders by declaring for 'a white Australia', but this was an electoral masterstroke in the other States, both unifying and liberal; he favoured old-age pensions and conceded female suffrage to his more radical colleagues. On 24 January he was appointed a privy councillor.

Barton was elected unopposed for Hunter, and all his ministers were returned. In the House of Representatives he had to depend on the Labor members for a majority; in the Senate he was in a minority. Parliament was opened in Melbourne on 9 May by the duke of York. The first session was largely taken up with procedural matters; however Barton carried the Immigration Restriction Act, and the Pacific Island Labourers Act which provided for the repatriation of Kanakas. The early introduction of this legislation pleased Labor, was cheap to implement (unlike old-age pensions) and tested the fledgling Commonwealth's power against the Colonial Office, which insisted on the substitution of a European for an English language dictation test. Barton acted swiftly to conciliate the Japanese acting consul-general H. Eitaki, who claimed a conflict between the Act and the Queensland protocol to the Anglo-Japanese Treaty. In 1905 Barton was granted permission to retain the insignia of the Japanese Order of the Rising Sun (first class). In December 1901 he had acceded to an official British request to send a Commonwealth contingent to the South African War.

It took all Barton's tact and courtesy to manage his team of leaders, whom he did not try to discipline. Moreover, to the despair of his private secretaries Hunt, then Bavin, he gave too much time to 'importunate callers', forgot engagements, had no love for administration, and had never enjoyed political intrigues or manoeuvring. His hold on parliament was precarious, and he 'had somehow to contrive a different majority for almost each piece of legislation'. He took a keen interest in setting up the Commonwealth Public Service and securing for it 'only the most competent of officers'. Despite a warm association with Hopetoun, he delayed in putting to parliament the question of an £8000 allowance for the governor-general, and permitted the bill to be amended out of recognition. Hopetoun resigned, but Barton had already left for England to attend the delayed coronation of Edward VII and the Colonial Conference of 1902. Already a convert to the Admiralty's policy of fleet concentration, he negotiated a new naval agreement: mainly actuated by considerations of expense and practicability, he believed an Australian navy was for the future and pledged £200 000 to maintain the British squadron based on Sydney. The new agreement provided for more modern ships and for the local training of Australian seamen as part of the Royal Naval Reserve.

Having refused a knighthood in 1887, 1891 and 1899, Barton now accepted the G.C.M.G. He also received the freedom of the City of Edinburgh, an honorary D.C.L. from the University of Oxford and was made an honorary bencher of Gray's Inn. On his way home he visited the Pope and accepted from him a medallion; for this he was scurrilously attacked by Rev. W. Dill Macky [q.v.], who organized a petition signed by 30 000 Protestants.

As minister of external affairs Barton was primarily concerned with immigration, but he took a deep interest in questions connected with the Pacific. Although early in 1901 he had asserted that Australia could have 'no foreign policy of its own' and implied that the Empire should speak as one, he equally believed that the British government should adopt the Australian point of view on the Pacific Islands. With 'a greater sensitivity for imperial diplomacy in the midst of the Boer War' than other ministers such as Deakin, he tried to damp down public agitation for an aggressive policy while, from as early as February 1901, he pressed the Colonial Office to appoint an international tribunal to settle land disputes with the French in the New Hebrides. In August he sent Wilson Le Couteur there, as Australia's first spy. As the Colonial Office did nothing, and he received no promise of action at the Colonial Conference, his attitude hardened. In 1903 he refused the British suggestions of a joint protectorate or partition, and urged the Colonial Office to acquire

the New Hebrides either by purchase or treaty. He offered to pay £250 000 for their acquisition and all costs of administration. After he left office he recommended to Hunt that if the Colonial Office continued to do nothing, the government should publish the correspondence.

In January 1903 Barton clashed with the governor-general Lord Tennyson [q.v.] over the role of his official secretary (Sir) George Steward [q.v.] in confidential communications with the Colonial Office, and reminded the governor-general 'that it was his duty to accept the advice of his Ministers'. Although parliament was proving difficult to manage, Barton was able to carry the Naval Agreement Act after a prolonged struggle in committee. In July Kingston resigned over differences in cabinet about the conciliation and arbitration bill. On 23 September 1903 Barton resigned and a few days later became senior puisne judge of the new High Court of Australia. Way told Darley: 'Barton seems to me to have a judicial mind, though he certainly has not powers of lucid expression . . . [he] did not want to leave politics, but his friends wanted him to go to the Bench to provide for his family. His party was getting dissatisfied with his leadership'.

Hunt, while noting his chief's 'brilliancy of perception', had complained of the difficulty of getting work done and of his 'want of personal energy, his disregard of time, both his own and other people's, his habit of taking so much to drink that he becomes slow of comprehension and expression'. He had always worked with 'amazing concentration and speed' but irregularly, and often late at night. Bavin later wrote of Barton as prime minister: 'He was impatient of questions of detail. Though he was always genial, he was too easy going to bother about humouring weaknesses or vanity of other members. He had little or no interest in the game of politics for its own sake. But it would be quite wrong to suppose that this means his term of office was a failure . . . He not only played the chief part in planning the machine and inducing the people to accept it, but he took the leading part in bringing it into action'.

Barton proved an unexpectedly good and 'scrupulously impartial' judge; possessing 'one of the keenest and quickest of intellects', he readily grasped the essential issues and arguments in a case and discussed them in court with perception and courtesy in his 'rich and beautifully modulated voice'. The width of his reading in British and American appeal cases was displayed in his sound constitutional opinions. He also proved a careful expositor of the many branches of private law needed for non-constitutional cases, which made up most of the court's appellate jurisdiction. At first he and O'Connor relied heavily on Griffith's greater learning and experience; Barton frequently concurred or adopted joint opinions, 'often pocketing his own reasons for the judgment', but from 1906 he increasingly wrote separate opinions and developed a characteristic style, on occasions strongly dissenting from his colleagues. In 1911 he was acting chief justice.

With Griffith and O'Connor, Barton shared a 'balancing' view of the Federal system on most constitutional questions and endeavoured to preserve autonomy for the States. They devised the doctrine of 'implied immunity of instrumentalities', which prevented the States from taxing Commonwealth officers, and also prevented the Commonwealth from arbitrating industrial disputes in the States' railways. They also developed the doctrine of 'implied prohibitions' and narrowly interpreted Federal powers in commercial and industrial matters, but in the steel rails and wire-netting cases in 1908 they held that the Commonwealth's fiscal powers included competence to tax goods imported by State governments. Barton fully agreed that the Commonwealth's defence power included extensive control of the civilian economy in World War I. He particularly desired to keep Commonwealth industrial arbitration power within narrow bounds, and began the *laissez-faire* interpretation of the guarantee of freedom of interstate trade which later prevailed in the court. Chief Justice (Sir) Adrian Knox [q.v.] claimed that Barton's 'mastery of constitutional law and principles was unsurpassed, and to this he added a thorough knowledge of the principles of common law'.

The High Court sat in all the State capitals – Barton often stayed or dined with old friends and colleagues and now had time to go to the races. He continued to enjoy 'the warm pleasures of life' and in the summer law vacations took his family to Tasmania. An affectionate husband and father, Barton had a special affinity with his eldest daughter Jean, who in 1909 married (Sir) David Maughan [q.v.]; Hunt frequently recorded how much he 'loved children'. In 1915 Sir Edmund visited England with his wife and daughter: his son Wilfred, who had been the first New South Wales Rhodes Scholar, was serving with the British Army in France. On 10 June Barton was sworn into the Privy Council by the King and sat on its Judicial Committee in several cases. In 1919 he was disappointed at not succeeding Griffith as chief justice.

Barton died suddenly of heart failure at Medlow Bath in the Blue Mountains on 7 January 1920, and after a state funeral service at St Andrew's Cathedral, was buried in the Church of England section of South Head cemetery; he had been a Freemason. He was survived by his wife, four sons and two daughters, and his estate was valued for probate at £6565. His portrait by Norman Carter [q.v.] hangs in Parliament House, Canberra, and one by John Longstaff [q.v.] is in the High Court, Sydney.

The adulation of his supporters gave Barton much to live up to: as a politician he had lacked astuteness and, probably, ambition, and as a barrister neglected his profession for politics. Yet for twelve years he gave all his energy to the cause of Federation and in 1897-98 rose to the heights of oratory, dedicated leadership and sustained hard work. As prime minister he played an important part in setting up the Commonwealth administrative machine and in making Federation a practical reality. As a High Court judge he was distinguished and alert to ensure that the Constitution should function smoothly. For a 'lazy' man, his achievements were great. Moreover he lived life to the full and always enjoyed the company of his fellow men. Knox claimed that it was 'given to few men to inspire as he did, a feeling of affection in those with whom he came into contact in every phase of life. This rare gift, springing from a nature richly endowed with the Divine gift of sympathy, conferred upon him a distinction all his own'.

J. Reynolds, *Edmund Barton* (Syd, 1948); J. A. La Nauze, *The Hopetoun blunder* (Melb, 1957); R. R. Garran, *Prosper the Commonwealth* (Syd, 1958); A. Deakin, *The federal story*, J. A. La Nauze ed (Melb, 1963); J. A. La Nauze, *The making of the Australian constitution* (Melb, 1972); M. Rutledge, *Edmund Barton* (Melb, 1974); R. Norris, *The emergent Commonwealth* (Melb, 1975); N. Meaney, *A history of Australian defence and foreign policy, 1901-23*, 1 (Syd, 1976); *PD* (NSW), 1893, 1572, 1897, 3459, 1898, 1062, 1121; *Cwlth Law Reports*, 27 (1919-20); *Daily Telegraph* (Syd), 18 Sept 1897; *SMH*, 9 May 1927; C. Cunneen, The role of governor-general in Australia 1901-1927 (Ph.D. thesis, ANU, 1973); E. Barton papers (NL), *and* correspondence, and collection of news-cuttings, 1900-20 and vol 203 (ML); Bavin papers, Deakin papers, Groom papers, Atlee Hunt papers and Novar papers (NL); Parkes correspondence (ML); External Affairs, Correspondence 1901-03, A6, A8, *and* New Hebrides correspondence, A35, A1108 vols 2, 3, 10,11, 14 (AAO, Canb); Sir Samuel Way, PRG 30/4 p74, 30/5/7 p168 (SAA); printed cat (ML); information from Professor G. Sawer, Canb.

MARTHA RUTLEDGE

BARWELL, SIR HENRY NEWMAN (1877-1959), lawyer and premier, was born on 26 February 1877 in Adelaide, son of Henry Charles Barwell, clerk and produce merchant, and his wife Clara, née Brooke. Educated at Whinham College and the Collegiate School of St Peter, he graduated from the University of Adelaide (LL.B., 1899) and was admitted to the Bar that year. He practised at Clare for nine months, then went to Port Pirie. As partner in a successful practice, Barwell & Hague, he was solicitor to the local corporation and successful counsel for the defence in seven murder trials. He was prominent in the Port Pirie School of Mines, the Mechanics' Institute, and the local branch of the Liberal Union of South Australia. On 19 August 1902 he married Anne Gilbert Webb at Clare.

In 1915 Barwell entered the House of Assembly for the district of Stanley and moved to Adelaide. He was a clear and logical debater: the confident, arrogant tone of his maiden speech was characteristic of his style – 'I am here and I have come to stay'. He defended the restricted franchise for the Legislative Council by arguing that Labor should not 'secure absolute political control over the capital that employs labor, and over the superior intellect that governs that labor'. Caustic about 'the pettifogging parochialism' of parliamentarians, he was proud to be labelled a Tory and a conservative. From the start he vehemently expressed his own views, irrespective of party policy, and gained many enemies both within and outside his party. This outspokenness on delicate issues finally overshadowed his substantial contribution to the administration of the State.

When the Labor government resigned in 1917 following the split over conscription, Barwell became attorney-general and minister of industry in A. H. Peake's [q.v.] Liberal Union government. He lost this portfolio a month later when a Liberal-National coalition government was formed. Following the 1918 elections, he again became attorney-general, and minister of industry in charge of town planning, for which he established a new department headed by Charles Reade [q.v.]; he published two papers on soldiers' settlements and town planning in 1918 and 1919. A 1919 Act provided for the establishment of a garden suburb at Mitcham, but the far-reaching Town Planning and Development Act, 1920, which Barwell introduced and strongly supported, was shorn of its effectiveness in the Legislative Council.

In March 1920 the coalition was dissolved after years of friction between the two parties. Thus, when Peake died and Barwell became premier a few weeks later, his government consisted solely of Liberals, although it depended for support on Nationalists. Some felt he had 'effected a Cromwellian usurpation' and the Opposition claimed he had found difficulty in gathering a ministry. But Barwell, who had already demonstrated his talent for efficient management, promoted several rivals to powerless positions and took firm command of his cabinet. His policy was enunciated in 1922 when he said: 'we want sound and safe administration . . . The less legislation the better'. Major changes included the appointment in 1921 of a royal commission on the public service which aimed to effect improvements in method and economies in administration. Barwell thought the service 'overmanned and inefficient'. He tackled in a far-sighted way the rehabilitation, through a £5 million programme, of the State's notoriously uneconomic railways, personally recruiting a brilliant American expert, W. A. Webb [q.v.], as director. New passenger-cars became known as 'Barwell Bulls'.

He also attempted to abolish the State arbitration system by the industrial disputes bill, 1922. Together with his avowed intention of reducing wages, it was seen as a direct attack on labour, and earned him much hostility in the community and in parliament, where the Nationalists voted with Labor to defeat the bill.

During the 1922 parliamentary recess Barwell visited England and was appointed K.C.M.G. While there he launched a short-lived 'Barwell Boys' immigration scheme, through which youths were brought to South Australia and indentured to farmers; the aim was to replace the 6000 South Australians killed in World War I. However, this was overshadowed by the controversy, aroused on the eve of his departure from London by his public statement that the Northern Territory should be developed by coloured labour. In spite of the storm of protest, he repeated his views in a letter to *The Times*. Although he emphasized that he was speaking as a private citizen, this seriously embarrassed the Liberal Union, caused a no confidence motion at the opening of the 1922 session of parliament, and became a factor in the Liberals' 1924 electoral defeat. Hostility from the temperance lobby and unease about award of railway contracts to American firms were also relevant. He remained parliamentary leader, but was encouraged by friends to enter Federal politics. When Senator J. V. O'Loghlin [q.v.] died in 1925 the Liberals used their numbers to elect Barwell to replace him, although this was a departure from precedent as O'Loghlin had been a Labor man – the Labor leaders strongly protested. Barwell's intransigence continued to alienate Federal colleagues; he was an uncompromising defender of the rights of small States, and his relations with Prime Minister

(Viscount) Bruce [q.v.] were not happy.

In 1928 Barwell resigned to become South Australia's agent-general in London. A fervent imperialist, he made many speeches on 'reciprocal trade and reciprocal preference'. He was a director of a trust company there after his term expired in 1933. Back in South Australia in 1940, after an unsuccessful attempt to win pre-selection for Stanley, he retired from politics. By this time he was very deaf and could not return to the Bar. He was an active synodsman in the Anglican Church, and until his death filled positions on various State boards, most notably that of the South Australian Housing Trust, of which he was deputy chairman in 1945-59. For many years he had had symptoms of arteriosclerosis and he died of cerebro-vascular disease at his Unley Park home on 30 September 1959, survived by his wife, three daughters and a son; he was cremated. His estate was sworn for probate at £1811.

R. I. Jennings, *W. A. Webb, South Australian Railways commissioner, 1922-1930* (Adel, 1973); *PD* (SA), 1915, 1299, 2333, 1922, 62, 350; *Observer* (Adel), 10 June 1922, 26 Dec 1925; *Advertiser* (Adel), and *The Times*, 1 Oct 1959; records (Supreme Court, SA).   MARYANNE MCGILL

BASEDOW, HERBERT (1881-1933), anthropologist, geologist, explorer and medical practitioner, was born on 27 October 1881 at Kent Town, Adelaide, youngest son of Martin Peter Friedrich Basedow [q.v.], newspaper proprietor, and his second wife Anna Clara Helena, née Muecke. Educated at the Higher Public School, Hanover, Germany, and Prince Alfred College in Adelaide, he attended the University of Adelaide in 1898-1902 (B.Sc., 1910) and the South Australian School of Mines and Industries.

In 1903 Basedow was a member of the South Australian Government North-West Prospecting Expedition, led by L. A. Wells [q.v.]; he studied natural history and geology, and compiled a detailed journal on the Aboriginals, collecting a vocabulary of about 1500 words of the Aluridja (Western Desert) and Aranda languages. Next year he published anthropological notes on the journey and in 1915 his full journal appeared, containing outstanding photographs of tribal Aboriginals.

From 1905 Basedow assisted H. Y. L. Brown [q.v.], the government geologist, and was able to further his study of Aboriginals. His 1907 account of the western coastal tribes of the Northern Territory is especially valuable for its data on the Larakiya of the Darwin area. In 1906 he had begun to study the Aboriginal art and rock carvings in

the Adnjamatana tribal area (Flinders Range) which he described in a paper read in Berlin next year.

Basedow studied medicine and anthropology at Breslau University in 1907-09 (Ph.D., 1908), at Heidelberg in 1909 and at Göttingen in 1909-10 (M.D., Ch.D.). At Breslau he worked with the famous anthropologist Hermann Klaatsch. Basedow carried out anatomical and pathological research on the collections of Australian skeletal materials in the Hunterian Museum of the Royal College of Surgeons, London. While abroad he looked into the making of brown coal briquettes for the South Australian government; on his return to Adelaide late in 1910 he was employed as assistant government geologist and government medical officer for remote districts.

He resigned in May 1911 to take up the position, newly created by the Federal government, of chief protector and chief medical inspector of Aboriginals at Darwin. Basedow approached this work with enthusiasm and energy, but he was over-idealistic and became rapidly disillusioned and dissatisfied. To the dismay of his loyal staff, he resigned in August, after only forty-five days in the Northern Territory. He claimed the Aborigines Act, 1911, was unworkable, yet before taking up the post he had ignored requests to discuss possible amendments with the minister. He was averse to being supervised by the Territory's acting administrator who had found him 'tactless and unpractical', lacking 'balance of mind' and entertaining 'unwarrantedly large ideas of his position'.

Basedow entered private medical and geological practice in Adelaide and continued to publish on anthropology in learned journals. He was one of the few men of his time actively interested in recording traditional Aboriginal life. In 1914 he and Rev. H. Howard [q.v.] failed to persuade the respective governments to declare 60 000 square miles (155 000 km²) in the Tompkinson, Mann and Musgrave ranges an Aboriginal reserve. As leader of a search for munition minerals in the northern Kimberleys of Western Australia in 1916, he found time to gather valuable ethnological data on this area, published in an article in 1918.

On 4 June 1919 Basedow married Olive Nell Noyes in Adelaide; they had no children. In August they made a medical tour of the north-east of the State, and next year made a longer medical relief expedition, funded by the South Australian and Commonwealth governments, to tend, examine and report on the prevalence of disease among Central Australian Aboriginals; his wife acted as nurse. They visited Hermannsburg mission station where he thought the work of Rev. Karl Strehlow [q.v.] the best of its kind in many similar centres he had seen. Basedow examined 600 Aboriginals and returned to press again for a hinterland reservation, because of the danger of complete extermination of some tribes. He reported humanely and expertly to the Commonwealth on the urgency of the Aboriginals' medical plight, and suggested appointment of a medical officer at Alice Springs. The Commonwealth government respected his views, but, remembering its previous contract, looked on Basedow sceptically.

From this time he employed two Aboriginal girls in his home at Kent Town, and became a vigorous controversialist in the local press on behalf of Aboriginals. In the early 1920s he led a search for the remains of Ludwig Leichhardt [q.v.2], and visited Java. In 1925 Basedow published *The Australian Aboriginal*, a positive contribution at a time when little detailed material was available to the public. Basedow was not a socio-cultural anthropologist and was not in a position to provide a systematic analysis of Aboriginal life. However, the book encapsulated his experience with the race over twenty years.

In 1926 Basedow led the First Mackay [q.v.] Exploration Expedition on a geographical and scientific investigation of the south-west of the Northern Territory; it included a wireless-outfit and photographic and recording apparatus. He collected Aboriginal songs and other material in the Petermann Ranges where his language skill proved essential to the expedition's success. To spell the camels, he and Donald Mackay walked almost two-fifths of the 1300 miles (2092 km) covered. They established good relations with local Aboriginals, fixed the correct position of Ernest Giles's [q.v.4] landfalls, and explored unknown country north of his route. In 1928 Basedow made 'his most important piece of zoological and anthropological research' when he led the Second Mackay Exploration Expedition towards the Gulf of Carpentaria and into the heart of Arnhem Land.

In 1927 he had been successful in his second attempt to represent Barossa in the House of Assembly for the Country Party; defeated in 1930, he was re-elected as an Independent in 1933. His chief purpose was to assist the Aboriginals. One newspaper said that he had been elected because of his 'belovedness': others saw his failure to shine in parliament as due to an 'inability to work with others'. Easily riled, he was impatient of those who did not share his vision.

An early conservationist, Basedow wanted sanctuaries and national parks to preserve rare inland flora and fauna. Many insects and plants and a mollusc he discovered were named after him. Chairman of several central Australian mining companies, he promoted the search for oil and in the 1920s was president of the Australian Petroleum Association in Melbourne – he also partnered his brother as a vigneron. Sometime chairman of the Aborigines' Protection League, he was a member of the Royal Geographical Society of Australasia, and an honorary corresponding member of the Royal Anthropological Institute of Great Britain and Ireland, publishing in its journal. He was also a fellow of the Geological societies of London and Berlin and belonged to other learned societies in Germany.

An unusually tall, sinewy man with great broad shoulders, Basedow was to be seen in Adelaide in summer striding along in his grey silk sun-helmet, noticeable for his height and the remoteness of his gaze. Survived by his wife, he died suddenly of peripheral venous thrombosis on 4 June 1933 at Kent Town, and was buried in North Road cemetery. His obituary in *Nature* claimed that, 'since the death of Sir Baldwin Spencer [q.v.] Dr Basedow had been generally recognized as the first authority on the aborigines of Australia'. In 1934 the Australian government bought part of his rare ethnological collection, which is in the Australian Institute of Anatomy, Canberra.

In 1935 his *Knights of the boomerang* was published. In it Basedow had wished 'to appear as one of the Aborigines', whom he described as 'simple but unapproachable, humble but dignified, barbarous but kind-hearted, and ungrateful but generous'. He castigated Australians for their 'racial homicide', and their failure to 'protect or give the vote to Aborigines'. It was frequently said of him, after his early death, that he would have achieved greater eminence if he had not spread his remarkable talents so widely.

Roy Soc SA, *Trans*, 28 (1904), 29 (1905), 31 (1907); Roy Anthropological Inst, *Man*, 13 (1913), and *J*, 44 (1914); *PRGSSA*, 15 (1915), 17 (1918), 29 (1927-28); *Geog J*, 74 (1929), no 5; *Nature*, 17 June 1933; *Argus*, 15 Sept 1911; *Mail* (Adel), 20 Dec 1919, 18 Sept 1926; *Observer* (Adel), 15, 20 May 1926, 28 July 1928; *Queenslander*, 12 Apr 1928; *Chronicle* (Adel), 8 June 1933; *Bunyip* (Gawler), 9 June 1933; *Country News* (Adel), 10 June 1933; PRG 324, *and* biog notes and records under Basedow (SAA); H. Basedow, A1 12/2149, A3 NT 22/2805, 14/7104 (AAO, Canb); ML printed cat under Basedow   IAN HARMSTORF

BASEDOW, MARTIN PETER FRIEDRICH (1829-1902), teacher, newspaper proprietor and politician, was born on 25 September 1829 at Dreckharburg near

Hamburg, Hanover, son of Christian Friedrich Basedow, teacher, and his wife Helena Catherine. He was educated by his father and at the gymnasium at Winsen, then taught in the Vierlande region near Hamburg. Hoping to earn a better salary as a teacher, he arrived in South Australia in the *Pauline* on 1 April 1848 but could get work only as a station-hand in the Murray River district. On 5 August 1850 he was naturalized.

That year Basedow opened a Lutheran school at Tanunda and in 1852 received a licence and a grant, in the form of a salary of £100, from the Central Board of Education. His school, of about eighty pupils, was praised by an inspector for its orderliness and the range of its science teaching. It was recognized as the best German school in the colony and when he resigned in 1864 the board commended him for his services. In 1856 his parents and his seven brothers and sisters had arrived in the colony.

In 1863 Basedow had established the *Tanunda Deutsche Zeitung;* he had for several years been part-owner and accountant of the previous paper, *Süd-Australische Zeitung.* From 1865 he was a justice of the peace and in 1864-76 was chairman of the Tanunda District Council. On 8 February 1868 he married Anna Clara Helena Schrader, a widow (d. 1921); his first wife Johanna Maria Kiesewetter, whom he had married at Tanunda in 1852, had died in 1867. Basedow gave evidence to the 1868 select committee on the Education Act, expressing progressive ideas which he was to pursue both in his journalistic and parliamentary career: that education should be free, compulsory, broad, humane and moral.

In 1870, in a bid to widen its appeal, Basedow changed his paper's name to the *Australische Deutsche Zeitung* and in 1874 moved to Adelaide. Here, he and his father-in-law and partner Carl Muecke [q.v.5] amalgamated the journal with the now Adelaide-based *Süd-Australische Zeitung* to form in January 1875 the *Australische Zeitung*, the sole South Australian German-language newspaper.

In 1876-90, as well as editing his newspaper, Basedow represented Barossa in the House of Assembly. He was not an exciting speaker: as (Sir) J. W. Downer [q.v.] put it, he 'had not aspired to brilliancy', but 'his light shone steadily'. Basedow's views, however, particularly on education, were respected, and for three months in 1881 he was minister for education. He sought improvements in the status and conditions of teachers and opposed payment by results, which he believed led to rote learning and was contrary to the idea that education should fit a child to live a full life; in his opinion the low

quality of teachers was caused by the pupil-teacher system. Basedow maintained that unless the state produced intelligent, upright children it jeopardized its existence. He attacked the prevailing idea that educating workers' children wasted public money. In 1879 he had moved an amendment to a bill which later resulted in the formation of Roseworthy Agricultural College, which his paper had long advocated. 'A true representative of enlightened liberalism', he was the only parliamentary member appointed to the 1881 commission on the working of the Education Acts and was also on the 1887 board of inquiry into technical education.

In 1890 Basedow visited Europe and next year represented South Australia at the Universal Postal Congress in Vienna. He returned in 1893 and in 1894-1900 represented the North Eastern District in the Legislative Council. He tried to interest the House in German legislation on sickness, accident, invalidity and old-age insurance; his lectures, *Workers' insurance in Germany* (Adelaide, 1899), were published to spread these ideas.

Although Basedow allegedly decided not to stand again for election in 1900 because of the unpopularity of his pro-Boer sympathies, he had successfully bridged the gulf between Englishman and German. For while a Lutheran, a strong believer in German culture and a president and trustee of the Deutsche Club, he also held several directorships in public and private institutions in Adelaide. Survived by his wife and eleven children, he died with aortic valve disease on 12 March 1902 and was buried in the North Road cemetery. His estate was sworn for probate at £14 000.

PP(SA), 1861 (131), 1862 (30), 1868-69 (56), 1881 (122); *PD (SA)*, 1877-79, 1894; R. B. Walker, 'German-language press and people in South Australia, 1848-1900', *JRAHS*, 58 (1972); *Pictorial Aust*, Sept 1894; *Register* (Adel), 1 Apr 1848, 19 July 1877, 31 Mar 1890; *Advertiser* (Adel), 14 Mar 1902; *Observer* (Adel), 15 Mar 1902, 25 June 1921; *Australische Zeitung*, 19 Mar 1902; *Bulletin*, 5 Apr 1902; Central Board of Education, Minutes 12 May 1852 (SAA); private papers (Mr B. Basedow, Linden Park, SA).

IAN HARMSTORF

BASKERVILLE, MARGARET FRANCIS ELLEN (1861-1930), sculptor, was born on 14 September 1861 at North Melbourne, eldest child of Edgar Arthur Baskerville, ironmonger, and his wife Sarah Francis, née Moseley. John Baskerville, the printer, was an ancestor.

Margaret spent her youth in Ballarat, where she attended Miss Quinlan's School for Ladies. Later the family returned to Melbourne where her father set up as a tobacconist in Bourke Street. She studied at the National Gallery school in 1880 and 1882-85 under O. R. Campbell and G. F. Folingsby [qq.v.3,4], and attended Saturday afternoon life classes conducted by C. D. Richardson [q.v.]. In 1886 she was licensed to teach with the Victorian Education Department, for which she worked for sixteen years.

Margaret Baskerville soon determined to become a sculptor. However she continued to produce water-colours and oil paintings; in 1899 her 'Study of Wallflowers' won a diploma at the Greater Britain Exhibition and was shown in Paris in 1900. By 1902 she was a full-time sculptor, running private afternoon classes at her studio behind the Assembly Hall in Collins Street. Her works at this time included 'Gathering Flowers', 'Nature's Mirror', 'Fern Gatherer' and 'The Book of Fate'. By 1904 she had saved enough to go to London where she studied at the Royal College of Art under Professor Lanteri and had instruction in marble carving from Galmuzzi. Her work won the praise of Auguste Rodin who visited the college twice while she was a student there. From London she visited Paris, Rome, Florence and Switzerland. After her return to Australia in 1906 she assisted Richardson in their Collins Street studio; on 23 December 1914 they were married at St John's Church of England, East Malvern. She was then 53 and Richardson 61.

In 1907 Margaret Baskerville had won six prizes for sculpture at the Women's Work Exhibition held in Melbourne. Her first commission, for which she was paid £1000, was the Sir Thomas Bent [q.v.3] memorial, Brighton. Begun in 1911 and unveiled on 20 October 1913, the over-life-sized statue is of bronze on a pedestal of granite and is probably her best-known work. Other commissions followed. The James Cuming [q.v.] memorial (1915-16), for which she did her own marble carving, was placed at Footscray. In 1916 she produced a circular marble plaque in memory of Ernest Wood for St Paul's Cathedral, Melbourne, and in 1922 as a war memorial for Alexandra, Victoria, a bronze figure of a soldier leaning on his rifle; the pose is conventional and the style simple realism. In a subsequent memorial for Maryborough, unveiled on 24 October 1926, she depicted in bronze a soldier on the battlefield. Her Edith Cavell memorial, St Kilda Road, Melbourne, was unveiled on 11 November 1926. She also produced three life-sized figures of Daphne, Echo and Persephone for the remodelled restaurant in the Hotel Australia, Collins Street; these figures were presumably demolished with

the hotel in 1938. With her husband she worked on two bas-reliefs for the foyer of the Capitol Theatre, opened in 1922.

Margaret Baskerville produced a number of portrait heads and busts, particularly of children. She showed her work regularly throughout her life and exhibited for the last time in 1929. A foundation member of and office-bearer in the Yarra Sculptors' Society (1898-1909), she was also a member of the Victorian Sketching Club, the Women's Art Club, the council of the Australian Institute of the Arts and Literature, and the Austral Salon; as a member of the Victorian Artists' Society she vigorously defended her husband in controversies while he was president. She predeceased him on 6 July 1930 at Brighton, and was cremated. The Brighton City Council has a number of her works.

E. A. Vidler, *Margaret Baskerville, sculptor* (Melb, 1929); W. Moore, 'Sculpture and architecture', *Architecture* (Syd), Apr 1925; *New Idea*, 1 Dec 1902, 6 Oct 1905; *Woman's World*, 1 May 1922; *Argus*, 28 Oct 1913; *Maryborough and Dunolly Advertiser*, 26 Oct 1926; National Gallery school records (SLV); information from Dr M. Rose, Melb.

KEN SCARLETT

BASSETT, SAMUEL SYMONS (1840-1912), vigneron, storekeeper and pastoralist, was born on 26 March 1840 at St Enoder, Cornwall, England, son of William Bassett, landowner, and his wife Phillippa, née Batten (or Letcher). Migrating to New South Wales in 1856, he gained colonial experience on the Hunter River with his uncle John Christian, went to the Maranoa District in Queensland in 1858, and became overseer of Euthulla station.

Grapes had already been grown on the adjacent Mount Abundance station and, perhaps because of his Hunter Valley experience, Bassett planted vines on the banks of Bungil Creek just north of the developing town of Roma. Using local cuttings and some from Toowoomba, he established a vineyard on freehold land purchased in June 1866. Despite his limited knowledge of either vine-growing or wine-making, he gradually expanded his Romavilla vineyard and orchard to 60 acres (24 ha) and was soon selling wine locally. Although he tried unsuccessfully to sell Romavilla in 1879, he persisted with development and by 1889 had the largest vineyard of seven in the Roma area, yielding 200 gallons of wine to the acre (2250 litres to the hectare). By 1884 he had a cellar and a wine-making plant.

Bassett began business as a storekeeper and wine merchant in Roma in partnership with A. J. Skinner from 1874 and was on his own in 1880-92. He also held interests in the pastoral runs Mount Maria (1875-88), Brigham (1876-88), Tarawinnabah (1876-88), Winneba (1877-88), Red Cap (1878-88), Bassett (1882-88) and Protection (1885-88), all in the Warrego District and in partnership with Skinner and Robert Douglas. After considerable losses Bassett and Skinner withdrew.

Returning to wine, Bassett began marketing operations which eventually covered eastern Australia. He also sold grapes to colonial and overseas markets, packing them in sawdust for safe transit. His wines won prizes at the Brisbane Exhibition in 1902 and at interstate and overseas shows. In 1903 the Romavilla marketing list included port, muscat, amontillado, burgundy, madeira, chablis, hock, claret, sherry, champagne and sauterne. Irrigation was introduced before 1900.

Despite poor health in the latter half of his life, Bassett was an enterprising, energetic, tough businessman, respected as a benevolent taskmaster by his family. He died of pulmonary tuberculosis on Christmas Day 1912, survived by his wife Isabella, née Cameron, whom he had married at Roma on 27 July 1871, and by six sons and three daughters of their fourteen children. His estate was valued for probate at £823.

Romavilla had involved a heavy contribution from the family. Bassett's sons, Lionel, Samuel and Kenneth, travelled for the firm and Samuel, before leaving the business for the pastoral industry, was manager of the vineyard. His twin WILLIAM AUGUSTUS (1887-1973) took increasing responsibility for the wine-making operations. Born at Roma on 27 April 1887 and educated there and at The Armidale School, New South Wales, William was sent to Sydney by his father to learn the wine-making art from Leo Buring [q.v.3, T. G. H. Buring]. Returning to Roma he joined the family business, working in the winery. When his father died William took over the total management of Romavilla. He continued the family's success in retail-marketing of wine and exhibiting at various shows.

Like his father, Bassett was interested in grazing, holding at various times Crochdantigh near Muckadilla, Karoola Park and Ventura Downs in the Surat district, and Mooga Hills near Roma. On 8 June 1911 at Roma he married Ruby Maiden who predeceased him in 1971. Actively managing Romavilla into his old age, he died after a short period of illness on 4 December 1973, aged 86. The business was then sold. He had been a respected member of the business community and a strong supporter of local interests. He was survived by one daughter and three sons and left a gross estate of $85 113 to his family.

Queensland and Queenslanders (Brisb, 1936); R. B. Taylor, *Roma and district, 1846-1885*, 2nd ed (Roma, 1959); Viticulture and wine-making in the southern districts, *V&P* (LA Qld), 1889, 4, 25; *Western Star*, 28 Dec 1912, 7 Dec 1973; H. Spencer, 'The Bassett family', Roma pioneer families (Oxley Lib, Brisb); Ecclesiastical file 13/102, SCT/P848 (QA); LAN/N6, N63, AB12 (QA); information from S. S. Bassett jnr, Bundilla, Roma, and Mrs D. R. Lalor, Orange Hill, Roma.

PAUL D. WILSON

BATCHELOR, EGERTON LEE (1865-1911), politician, was born on 10 April 1865 in Adelaide, son of Capel Baines and Elizabeth Batchelor. His father, a photographer, died when Batchelor was very young and his mother was left to raise three sons. He was educated at the North Adelaide Model School and when 12 became a pupil-teacher there. He also taught at an early age in a secondary school at the North Adelaide Church of Christ. Although he showed promise as a teacher, Batchelor's fascination with mechanics led him at 17 to become an apprentice engine-fitter in the government engineering plant at Islington. After eleven years at this trade, during which he worked in country towns and was promoted to foreman, he resigned to take up politics. On 10 January 1890 he had married Rosina Mooney in the Christian Chapel in Adelaide and they lived in the city.

Batchelor was a central figure in the South Australian labour movement as early as his twenties. He joined the Amalgamated Society of Engineers (Adelaide) in 1882, was elected to executive office almost immediately and was president four times in 1889-98: he was also a member and president of the Railway Service Mutual Association. First elected as a delegate to the Trades and Labor Council in 1889, he was its treasurer in 1892 and secretary next year. With this record of service to the movement, it is not surprising that he was one of the leading foundation members and a driving force in the formation of the United Labor Party in 1891: he was elected secretary for four years from 1892 and president of the party in 1898. An automatic choice by the U.L.P. for its first electoral contests in South Australia, he was pre-selected to contest the House of Assembly election on 15 April 1893 for West Adelaide. He won a notable victory: a confirmation that the Labor Party had 'arrived' in the colony, and an indication of personal support for Batchelor. He topped the poll, defeating a sitting minister and relegating C. C. Kingston [q.v.], arguably the colony's strongest politician, to second place. He supported opening up land under a leasing system; factory, steam-boilers and workmen's lien legislation; a state bank; and women's suffrage. He retained first position at the elections of 1896 and 1899.

Batchelor was on the front bench in parliament from the start. A prominent party spokesman in all major debates, he was secretary of the Parliamentary Labor Party in 1893-97 and leader, after the death of J. A. McPherson [q.v.], from 1897 until 1899. Following the fall of the Kingston ministry in December 1899 and the brief interregnum of V. L. Solomon [q.v.], Batchelor was invited to join (Sir) Frederick Holder's [q.v.] goverment. Although the Labor Party pledge of 1899 refused the right of members to join a non-Labor administration, caucus released Batchelor from this constraint: Holder's was essentially the old Kingston ministry with which Labor had associated closely. Batchelor resigned from caucus and from the leadership and became the first Labor member in Australia to join a non-Labor ministry, with the party's unanimous approval. He remained in the Holder administration as minister of education and of agriculture until he resigned from State parliament in 1901. His main achievement while minister was the organization of a scheme to enable pupil-teachers to receive two years university education as part of their training.

Batchelor was elected to the House of Representatives in 1901, and was the only South Australian Labor member in that House in the first parliament. When the State was divided into districts for the 1903 election, Batchelor left to a colleague J. Hutchinson [q.v.] what would have been his 'natural' (and safe Labor) district of Hindmarsh, and defeated the sitting member Solomon in Boothby. He retained this seat in the 1906 and 1910 elections, at least partly as a result of a strong personal vote, for, following his death, Boothby was won easily by a Liberal. Batchelor was never defeated in an election throughout his parliamentary career.

In 1901 he had acted briefly in June as party leader and had been one of the committee which framed the constitution and rules of the Federal parliamentary party. As the only Labor member with considerable cabinet experience, he and J. C. Watson and W. M. Hughes [qq.v.] chose the first Labor ministry in 1904; he then believed that 'responsibility will do great good not only to the Labor members but to the working class generally throughout Australia'. He took the portfolio of home affairs, and in the Fisher [q.v.] ministries of 1908-09 and 1910-13 was minister for external affairs until his death. When Watson retired as leader in 1907, Batchelor was one of four nominated by caucus to succeed him, but he

withdrew from the contest. He was a consistent supporter of alliance with the Liberals until the 1908 change of policy. A member of the Australian delegation to the 1911 Imperial Conference in London, he was principal spokesman on trade and foreign policy: *The Times* praised his 'sound commonsense and cool judgment'. In 1911 Batchelor took over responsibility for the Northern Territory. Believing that 'the treatment of the natives formed the blackest page' in Australia's history, he quickly moved to establish reserves, to aid 'preservation of the native tribes' and to 'ameliorate the present conditions'. He appointed the enlightened anthropologist Herbert Basedow [q.v.] as protector, and two medical assistants.

A 'vigorous, wiry-looking abstemious man', Batchelor was, however, never robust. On 8 October 1911, when climbing Mount Donna Buang near Warburton, Victoria, with fellow members of the Wallaby Club, he collapsed from a heart attack and died immediately. After a memorial service in Melbourne, his body was returned to Adelaide for burial in West Terrace cemetery. He was survived by his wife and six children, and his estate was valued for probate at £3200. A locality near Darwin was later named after him.

Throughout his career Batchelor was a leader of the moderate wing of the Labor Party and a driving force for reforms. A committed Christian, an active member of the Churches of Christ, he was determined to provide greater opportunities for working people. He was versatile in both his profession and in his recreations; he retained his interest in education and literary affairs, and was a constant speaker at meetings in South Australia and interstate. Both his colleagues and his political opponents praised his diligence, honesty and sincerity. 'Batch', as his friends called him, was respected for his 'energy, organising talent and general ability', and as a speaker who was 'clear and forcible, marshalling facts with great care and precision' in perfect English: no orator, he was a good debater, and always calm and good-tempered when others were excited.

After his death the *Bulletin* remarked: 'It is questionable if any man in the Australian Parliament was more popular or more deserving of popularity, and in point of intellect he ranked either first or a good second among the members of the Fisher ministry'. Batchelor had a 'philosophic mind, seeking to weigh fairly the arguments on both sides to elicit the truth'. His popularity was partly due to his dislike of doctrinaire stances. In *The Labor Party and its progress* (1895) he wrote that while solidarity was important, 'the United Labor Party does not by any means include the whole of the party of progress': that 'no party is run exactly on the lines I think best ... [but] by joining that party whose aims and policy are nearest my own, I can ensure the success of some of those things I want to see brought about ... and use my voice and vote to convert the other members of the party to my way of thinking'. This approach evoked such descriptions of him as 'a man of much natural ability who possesses the entire confidence of his fellow workers' and whose 'unassuming manner masked a fund of quiet wisdom'.

J. J. Pascoe (ed), *History of Adelaide and vicinity* (Adel, 1901); H. T. Burgess (ed), *Cyclopedia of South Australia*, 2 (Adel, 1909); T. H. Smeaton, *The people in politics* (Adel, 1914); S. O'Flaherty, *A synopsis of the formation ... of the Australian Labor Party, South Australian Branch* (Adel, 1956); *PP* (SA), 1900, 3 (44); *Pictorial Aust*, June-July 1893; *Review of Reviews* (A'sian ed), 20 May 1904; *Observer* (Adel), 14 Apr 1894, 16 July 1898, 14 Oct 1911; *Punch* (Melb), 11 Aug 1904; *The Times*, 3 Mar, 1 June, 9 Oct 1911; *Advertiser* (Adel), 9-11 Oct 1911; *Age*, 9 Oct 1911; *Bulletin*, 12 Oct 1911.

DEAN JAENSCH

BATES, DAISY MAY (1863-1951), welfare worker among Aboriginals and anthropologist, was born on 16 October 1863 in Tipperary, Ireland, daughter of James Edward O'Dwyer, gentleman, and his wife Marguarette, née Hunt. Her mother died in Daisy's infancy and she had an unstable childhood. On the death of her maternal grandmother she was put, aged about 8, in the care of Sir Francis Outram's family in London.

Suspected of having contracted pulmonary tuberculosis, she migrated to Australia in 1884 and lived briefly at Townsville, Queensland, as a guest of Bishop G. H. Stanton [q.v.]. Late that year she was employed as a governess at Berry, New South Wales. On 17 February 1885 at Nowra she married Jack Bates, a cattleman; they had a son Arnold in 1886. She showed only a distant attachment to husband and son, leaving both in Australia when she returned to England in 1894 for what turned out to be a stay of five years. In London she worked on the *Review of Reviews*, learning the craft of journalism which was to become a crucial source of income when she lived with the Aboriginals.

Daisy Bates returned to Australia in 1899. Interested in an allegation in *The Times* about atrocities against Aboriginals in north-west Australia, she went to the Trappist mission at Beagle Bay, north of Broome. Here she had her first long contact with Aboriginals while working at this decaying settlement and its market gardens.

The north-west also saw the start of her inquiries among the local Aboriginals when in 1901 she temporarily rejoined her husband on the cattle-station at Roebuck Plains, where tribes from the Broome district were camped. Her curiosity about the camp's disputes and scandals led her to investigate their roots in kinship. She started to collect vocabularies and saw sacred and secret ritual life. These eccentric interests further estranged her from her husband, and she finally left him after a harrowing ride overlanding cattle from Broome to Perth in 1902.

Daisy Bates had already shown such anthropological promise that in 1904 she was appointed by the Western Australian government to research the tribes of the State. Next year this task was temporarily narrowed to a study of the Bibbulmun tribe of the Maamba reserve in the south-west, where she conducted her first concentrated period of field-work. She recorded wide-ranging data on language, myth, religion and kinship.

In an important 1905 paper on marriage laws she showed the equivalences of the four-section system for northern tribes and those to the south. By 1910 she had completed a substantial manuscript on the Aboriginals. Its publication was fatally delayed by the arrival from Britain of an expedition, led by A. R. Radcliffe-Brown [q.v.], to study the social anthropology of Aboriginals of the north-west. Because of her experience Daisy Bates was appointed a member of this expedition but she turned herself to welfare, moved by the miseries of the sick and elderly Aboriginals enforcedly exiled on the islands of Bernier (the males) and Dorré (the females). Her anthropological knowledge showed her that to physical distress were added the mental agonies of unnatural juxtapositions of tribe and kin. She claimed that it was there that the Aboriginals gave to her the affectionate name 'Kabbarli', meaning grandmotherly person.

In 1912 she established the first of the harsh, isolated camps for which she became renowned. She camped at Eucla amongst the remnants of the Mirning tribe on the southern fringe of the Nullarbor Plain. She was invited to attend meetings in eastern capitals in 1914 of the anthropological section of the British Association for the Advancement of Science. To attend, she arranged a crossing of 250 miles (400 km) over the southern Nullarbor Plain in a small cart pulled by camels.

She returned in 1915 to the Mirning's area, but this time to the eastern margin near Yalata. In 1918, during a brief stay in

Adelaide, she failed to extract from the South Australian government a protectorship and money for medical work. Nevertheless, she set off for a stay of sixteen years at Ooldea, a permanent water-hole on the trans-Australian railway around which Aboriginals had gathered. Here the travelling public could see her remarkable welfare work. In 1920 she was appointed a justice of the peace. Three visits by royalty brought her fame and she was appointed C.B.E. in 1934.

At Ooldea in 1930 Daisy Bates had been befriended by the writer Ernestine Hill [q.v.], who aided her return to Adelaide in 1935 and the writing of her autobiography, 'My natives and I', serialized in several newspapers. Those episodes dealing with the latter part of her life were edited into *The passing of the Aborigines* (London, 1938). To prepare her papers for the national collection the Australian government had, in 1936, given her a stipend. The sum was insufficient for normal living so she chose to do the work in a tent at Pyap on the River Murray. This episode successfully ended in 1940 with the transfer of ninety-nine boxes of papers to the Commonwealth National Library.

Still with some government stipend, she was living in 1941 in the railway siding of Wynbring, east of Ooldea. Her letters show that old age and failing health were at last making such an austere life untenable. By 1945 she was back in Adelaide, where a secretary who worked with her briefly found her 'an imperialist, an awful snob . . . a grand old lady'. She died in an old people's home at Prospect on 18 April 1951, leaving an estate valued for probate at £66.

Though applauded for the self-sacrifice of her welfare work, Daisy Bates had no illusion about her own motives, which she privately identified with those that had previously impelled her to enjoy such sports as hockey, tennis and fox-hunting.

She wrote some 270 newspaper articles about Aboriginal life, valuably sensitive accounts of cultures customarily presented in the press as unintelligibly bizarre. However, her repeated, emphatic assertions concerning Aboriginal cannibalism aroused much controversy. She strongly opposed miscegenation; her belief that Aboriginal full-bloods would become extinct unless segregated from Europeans was proved wrong by the population statistics of the years following the *Passing*. Nevertheless her widely read defeatist views helped prod governments into action in medicine and child care.

Radcliffe-Brown had likened her mind to a well-stocked but very untidy sewing-basket. Her anthropology found little favour with anthropologists and her papers lay dormant for three decades, though latterly they have received some scholarly attention. The usefulness of the collection as a resource of anthropological information lies in the strong empirical thread in her research, coupled with a precocious manifestation of the anthropological method of living with one's subject. She had been careful 'never to intrude my own intelligence upon' the Aboriginals. Her place in Australian folklore has been formalized by the opera, *The young Kabbarli*, written by Lady Casey to music by Margaret Sutherland. Her achievements remain the subject of sustained controversy.

E. L. G. Watson, *But to what purpose* (Lond, 1946); J. Greenway, *Bibliography of the Australian Aborigines . . .* (Syd, 1963); E. Salter, *Daisy Bates* (Syd, 1971); R. V. S. Wright (ed), *Archaeology of the Gallus site, Koonalda cave* (Canb, 1971); E. Hill, *Kabbarli* (Syd, 1973); R. Needham, *Remarks and inventions* (Lond, 1974); *Vic Geog J*, 23-24 (1905-06), p36; A'sian Assn Advancement of Science, *Report of Meeting*, 14 (1914); Roy Anthropological Inst, *Man*, June 1975; *Australasian*, 14 May, 6, 27 Aug 1921; *The Times*, 20 Apr 1951; *SMH*, 29 Aug 1959; *Sydney Mail*, 16 Sept 1972; *Sunday Telegraph* (Syd), 22 Oct 1972; P. Biskup, Native administration and welfare in Western Australia, 1897-1954 (M.A. thesis, Univ WA, 1965); Daisy Bates papers (NL).

R. V. S. WRIGHT

BATH, THOMAS HENRY (1875-1956), miner, politician, farmer and co-operator, was born on 21 February 1875 at Hill End, New South Wales, son of Thomas Henry Richard Bath, itinerant miner, and his wife Sarah Ann, née Barrow. With only a primary schooling he began work as a miner and sailed for the West Australian goldfields in 1896. Used to the traditional solidarity of mining camps, he slipped easily into the cosmopolitan world of goldfields unionism and, after briefly returning to New South Wales, joined the Amalgamated Workers' Association on its foundation in 1897. Induced to become secretary of a local chapter of the American Knights of Labor, he represented it at the Coolgardie Trade Union Conference of 1899 and in September 1900 became first editor of the *Westralian Worker*. Though not a trained journalist, he was intelligently self-educated and had a flair for polemical writing. The paper was an immediate success but did not improve when Bath gave way in July 1901 to the professional Wallace Nelson. He invested later in a disastrous paper called *Democrat*, run by Nelson.

As secretary of the Kalgoorlie and Boulder Trades and Labor Council Bath was involved in faction-fighting between miners' unions, and his membership of socialist ginger groups provided some of the impetus for the election of six Labor members to the Legislative Assembly in April 1901. When John Reside, member for Hannans, died in December Bath won the selection ballot and the election. Though his fluency and orderly mind were ideal parliamentary qualities, Henry Daglish [q.v.] did not include him in the first Labor ministry of August 1904 and he became chairman of committees. However, Daglish chose him for lands and education when the ministry was reconstructed in June 1905. When the government fell in August and the party crashed at the October election, Bath's reputation for rigid probity won him leadership of the dispirited rump.

A government land-settlement scheme gave Bath a 160-acre (65 ha) wheat farm north of Tammin, expanded subsequently to 733 acres (297 ha). He held his Kalgoorlie suburban seat until 1911. In 1907-10 he shared with Julian Stuart [q.v.] the editorial chair of the *Westralian Worker* but was so weary by 1909 that he planned to abandon politics. He was persuaded to remain in parliament but gave up the leadership and his editorial work. John Scaddan [q.v.], whose self-education he had supervised, succeeded him as leader and became premier in October 1911. Bath administered lands and agriculture until November 1914 when he resigned the portfolios and his Avon constituency to devote his life to farming. An original university endowment trustee of 1903, he helped to establish the University of Western Australia as a royal commissioner in 1910 and as a senator in 1912-19. He was also a committee-member of the Public Library and Museum of Western Australia.

Bath had long preferred co-operation to socialism as a social panacea and from 1922 was a leader in the farmers' co-operative movement represented by Westralian Farmers Ltd. He was a trustee of the wheat pool from 1925 and in May 1927 attended an International Wheat Pool conference at Kansas City. He wrote regularly on the economics of wheat in *Wesfarmers Gazette* which he edited for a time, and in the *Primary Producer*; his pamphlets on similar topics warned against the coming depression. For several years he was unpaid secretary of the Co-operative Federation of Australia. From the mid-1930s he was an active exponent of the bulk handling of wheat; in 1943-48 he was vice-chairman, then chairman of Co-operative Bulk Handling Ltd which disposed of the whole State crop. In 1948 he was appointed C.B.E.

Bath died of coronary occlusion at his Mount Lawley home on 6 November 1956, and was cremated. His wife Elizabeth Maria Jane, née Fensome, whom he had married at Kalgoorlie on 27 July 1904, predeceased him by many years; he was survived by one son and two daughters. His estate, valued for probate at £6714, was left to his children excepting two bequests to sisters and eight to charities.

Slim, dark, dapper and quiet, Bath returned in old age to the Methodist faith of his youth but though serious, he was never solemn. To his children, he was sometimes witty and was 'soppy about Shakespeare'. His passion was expressed as a foundation member of the Shakespeare Club in 1930 and as president in 1940-45 of the Perth Repertory Society and as a vice-patron in 1946-55. In both the main phases of his career he was the rock on which others depended. The Labor Party used him until he was worn out. The wheat pool relied on him to persuade farmers of the need for price reductions. An obituarist said of him, 'It was his voice and his pen that gave [the co-operative movement] purpose, that informed its spirit and defined its direction'. The remark was equally true of his work for the labour movement.

Truthful Thomas, *Through the spy-glass* (Perth, 1905); J. S. Battye (ed), *Cyclopedia of Western Australia*, 2 (Adel, 1913); J. Sandford, *Walter Harper and the farmers* (Perth, 1955); F. Alexander, *Campus at Crawley* (Melb, 1963); H. J. Gibbney, 'Western Australia', *Labor in politics*, D. J. Murphy ed (Brisb, 1975); Trades Union and Labor Conferences (WA), *Reports*, 1899-1910; Aust Labor Federation (WA) Conferences, *Reports*, 1910-15; *Wesfarmers News*, 15 Feb 1962; H. J. Gibbney, Working class organization in West Australia from 1880 to 1902 (B.A. Hons thesis, Univ WA, 1949); J. R. Robertson, The Scaddan government and the conscription crisis 1911-17 (M.A. thesis, Univ WA, 1958); Parliamentary Labor Party (WA), Minutes (Battye Lib, Perth).

H. J. GIBBNEY

BATTY, FRANCIS DE WITT (1879-1961), Anglican bishop, was born on 10 January 1879 at Waltham Green, London, youngest son of Rev. William Edmund Batty and his wife Frances Beatrice, née Jebb. Named after his mother's ancestor, the Dutch patriot Jan de Witt, he was usually known by his second name. Waltham was a poor parish and in 1892 his father accepted the living of Finchley in a residential district of London. The change of surroundings and his education at St Paul's School in 1890-97 helped to give him that ease of movement amid the governing classes which was to be one of his chief characteristics. He entered Balliol College, Oxford, graduating with a second-class in *Litterae Humaniores* in 1902 (M.A., 1905).

Balliol exercised a decisive influence on Batty who responded with a lifelong affection for the college. He was a wide and intelligent reader all through his life; he was not a professional scholar but Oxford gave him a sound understanding of philosophy, classical literature and some history. More important, he made friends with men who were to be future leaders in church and state, became aware of Britain's imperial obligations and opportunities, and acquired that sense of high moral responsibility combined with an aloofness of manner and a rueful acknowledgment of the weaknesses of lesser mortals which he always retained.

Family influence and the impression made by a junior undergraduate, William Temple, later archbishop of Canterbury, were important in Batty's decision to enter the Church. He declined an offer to read theology at Balliol and in 1902 entered Wells Theological College. Here he obtained an insight into the corporate spiritual life, was grounded in liberal religious learning and came to disdain those Church 'parties' whose contests were then particularly virulent. On 4 October 1903 he was made deacon and became an assistant curate at Hornsey, a London suburb. His vicar, St Clair Donaldson [q.v.], gave Batty thorough tuition in his craft. When Donaldson was appointed bishop of Brisbane in 1904, Batty went as his domestic chaplain and secretary. Priested by the Bishop of London on 29 May he reached Brisbane on 19 December.

Batty lived at the official residence with the bachelor archbishop and was soon asked to assist in much of the administration of the diocese. He also helped at the cathedral, took religious instruction classes and in 1909-16 edited the *Brisbane Church Chronicle* and lectured at St Francis's (Theological) College. Significantly, he accompanied Donaldson, and sometimes represented him, at meetings with governors, politicians and ecclesiastics. He acquired a wide knowledge of the workings of church and state, an easy familiarity, which he treasured, with important people, and a somewhat Olympian attitude, enhanced by his quizzical sense of humour, to local problems and personalities. He probably learned little about 'grass-roots' conditions — his attitude to local radicalism and later to the conscription referenda made this evident.

Although he could never wholly identify himself with Queensland, Batty's sense of commitment became deeper. He was made sub-dean and canon residentiary of St John's Cathedral in 1916, and as such took over the whole responsibility for the running of the cathedral and was closely involved in the St Martin's War Memorial Hospital Appeal. He spoke frequently in the diocesan synod and represented his diocese in the wider councils of the Church. While lamenting what seemed to be a decline in standards, he worked vigorously for the Australian College of Theology, becoming a fellow in 1924. He published pamphlets on Church reunion and the ministry of healing. When Donaldson was translated to Salisbury in 1921, Batty, though severely tempted, chose not to follow him home. His relations with the new archbishop, Gerald Sharp [q.v.], were generally good. With Rev. C. T. Dimont, he publicly stated his debt to his mentor in *St. Clair Donaldson* . . . (London, 1939). Meanwhile, his links with Queensland became stronger. On 7 January 1925 he married Elizabeth Meredith Davis (1893-1972), matron of St Martin's Hospital. That year he became dean of Brisbane and in 1930 succeeded his friendly rival H. F. Le Fanu [q.v.] as coadjutor bishop. He retained his deanship and acted as administrator of the diocese in Sharp's absence.

Batty was elected bishop of Newcastle, New South Wales, and enthroned on 3 March 1931. He thought it 'the most enviable diocese in Australia': compact in area but varied in composition, with a strong intellectual tradition, a good supply of clergy and a large endowment in a pastoral property. He had family ties with the district and had long venerated the founder-bishop William Tyrrell [q.v.6]. He rejected the chance of becoming bishop of Adelaide in 1941.

In depression-ridden Newcastle, Batty encouraged the registrar and diocesan trustees to reduce reliance on the endowment and to provide for greater financial responsibility by the parishes. While this policy freed funds for special projects and promoted parochial self-reliance, it bore hardly on the weaker areas. He was less successful in coping directly with the problems of people in mining parishes — he lacked the common touch of his predecessor G. M. Long [q.v.] but was made acutely aware of the challenge to the Church posed by current social issues.

Batty found at St John's College, Morpeth, a group of scholars, including E. H. Burgmann, Roy Lee and A. P. Elkin, who, in a series of publications, were trying to relate Christianity to modern developments in sociology, politics and international affairs. His meeting with Temple during a visit to Britain in 1933 stimulated his own thinking on these lines. In 1955 the college came under the sole control of Newcastle and he hoped that a connexion would be set up with the new university college. Under him Newcastle became a focal point for earnest thinking about contemporary issues in a Christian context. During World War II the Christian Social Order Movement received strong support and Batty himself, stimulated by a Roman Catholic journalist and under the enthusiastic patronage of the governor, Lord Wakehurst, initiated 'Religion and Life Week'. Batty became a radio broadcaster of distinction, although he failed to secure a licence for a Church radio station at Newcastle. At the 1948 Lambeth Conference, he played a considerable part in social justice discussions and was not committed to a distinct secular position. His (Bishop) Moorhouse [q.v.5] lectures in 1939 had made it clear that he held to traditional propositions; they were published as *Human nature* (Sydney, 1941). He criticized the conservative stance in theology and politics but he was also a strong critic of some Labor government policies of the 1940s.

Batty was associated with Donaldson in early discussions for reform of the 'legal nexus' between Australian dioceses and the Church of England and emerged as a proponent of the draft constitution first tabled in 1926. Although consistently English in his loyalties, he actively opposed those who feared the jurisdictional independence of an Australian Anglican tribunal. He always disliked extremes of churchmanship and the ecclesiastical quarrels motivated by them. In the later 1940s he supported strongly, though with some compunction, Bishop Wylde of Bathurst in the 'Red Book' case, fearing a revival of divisions over ritual. By 1945 Batty had emerged as the 'minister in charge of the Bill' (as he termed himself). Despite patient negotiation he had to confess by 1950 that the prospect of agreement seemed remote, but enough consensus was reached in 1955 for legislative action to begin. He was widely regarded as one of the principal architects of the constitution which was received in 1961. He also favoured an ecumenical approach and was a persistent exponent of discussions about Christian reunion. From 1937 he belonged to a group of Anglican and Protestant churchmen who studied possible bases of agreement, although he remained reluctant to proceed too rapidly.

In the 1950s Batty remained active, travelling overseas, and promoting new lines of Christian thought. It is probable that his diocese, faced with post-war problems of expansion and finance, would have benefited more by his direct attention, but he became increasingly content to leave these affairs to his subordinates. He did not resign until 1958, when he was in his eightieth year, and then presided over the synod which elected his successor. Batty lived in quite active retirement at Double Bay, Sydney. Survived by his wife, he died on 3 April 1961 and was buried in Morpeth cemetery, next to W. Tyrrell, whom he had commemorated in a short play, and whose centenary of appointment he had celebrated with much ceremony in 1947.

A. P. Elkin, *The diocese of Newcastle* (Syd, 1955); Church of England (Brisb), *Reports of the Procs of Synod*, 1904-30, and General Synod, *Procs*, 1905-60; 'Synod reports', Church of England, *Diocese of Newcastle Year Book*, 1930-58; F. de W. Batty, Memoirs (Diocesan Registry, Newcastle); Batty papers (St James's Church, Syd, *and* held by Mr M. R. Hardwick, 180 Phillip St, Syd); Elgin papers (held by earl of Elgin, Dunfermline, Fife, Scotland); Verney papers (held by Sir Ralph Verney, Middle Claydon, Buckinghamshire, Eng); Wakehurst papers (ML); Wylde-Batty correspondence (Diocesan Registry, Bathurst, NSW).

K. J. CABLE

BATTYE, JAMES SYKES (1871-1954), librarian, was born at Geelong, Victoria, on 20 November 1871, son of Daniel Battye, wool-weaver, and his wife Maria, née Quamby, both of whom were from Yorkshire, England. After winning a Victorian state schools exhibition in 1884, he went to Geelong College, then to the University of Melbourne (B.A., 1891; LL.B., 1893). He was an assistant at the Public Library of Victoria in 1889-94, then became chief librarian of the Victoria Public Library in Perth. Battye was soon a significant, if junior, member of the group of Western Australian public officials who worked under the leadership of Premier Sir John (Earl) Forrest and his associates Bishop C. O. L. Riley and the publicist (Sir) J. Winthrop Hackett [qq.v.].

From 1912 until his death Battye was general secretary of the amalgamated library, museum and art gallery; Hackett and Riley were the first two presidents of the trustees. Battye had personally selected the basic book-stock of the library and later readers were often impressed by the range and depth of early accessions. By 1903 he had raised the number of books to 50 000, which grew to 100 000 by 1911. Yet by 1945 there were still only 175 000 volumes, while the parliamentary grant, which in 1905 had been £4000 for the library alone, was a mere £8500 for the three combined institutions. Though some progress was made after World War II with new trustees and some able professional staff, it is doubtful whether more than 10 000 books were added to the library in Battye's last ten years of office. Although the library was castigated in both the Munn- (E.R.) Pitt [q.v.] report of 1935 and the McColvin report of 1947, it must be admitted that Battye's professional work probably suffered after 1929 from discouragement when his finances, still recovering from wartime economies, were further crippled by the Depression.

The record of the library's development as a repository of West Australian history was broadly similar. In twenty-five years of keen personal and professional interest in the history of the State, Battye acquired official records of the Colonial Secretary's Department in 1903 and of the Treasury in 1918. Concern about the destruction of valuable records led to the establishment in 1923 of a Public Records Committee chaired by him. Revived in 1929 as the State Archives Board, it survived until 1943 but its activities were more sporadic than effective. Meanwhile his work in compiling the *Cyclopedia of Western Australia* (Adelaide, 1912-13) and the *History of the north west of Australia* (Perth, 1915), and in writing his *Western Australia: a history* ... (Oxford, 1924), brought some valuable private papers into the library. This last book remained the standard work in his lifetime, won him a University of Melbourne D.Litt., and enhanced his local reputation as a scholar. Battye helped to establish the Western Australian Historical Society in 1926 and chaired the State executive of the Centenary Celebrations Committee. He backed the successful effort by his trustees in 1945 to secure government finance for a State Archives within the library and supported the first archivist Miss M. F. F. Lukis, but she had little more material to work on initially than the library had held in the 1920s.

Battye's physical height, commanding presence, unfailing self-confidence, impressive knowledge of relevant facts and his increasing skill in manipulating both large audiences and committees were valuable assets in public life. He was secretary of the Wesley Church Trust for most of his life, occupied official circuit and mission positions, and was a member of the Wesley College board. He was president of the Children's Hospital board in 1911-13, chairman of the board of governors of the High (Hale) School in 1911-23, and honorary secretary of the Victoria Institute for the Blind.

As secretary to Hackett's royal commission of 1909-11, Battye won and held a seat on the first university senate. While Hackett remained chancellor, Battye continued to act as though he were little more than his secretary. Subsequently, he became increasingly active as warden of convocation in 1920 and 1922-23, chairman of the finance committee, and pro-chancellor in 1931-36; he then succeeded Sir Walter James [q.v.] as chancellor until 1943. When the university had neither a full-time vice-chancellor nor a registrar, Battye undertook much detailed work and some important decisions fell to him. Long after the need had passed, he sought unsuccessfully as chancellor to re-

capture such responsibilities; a competent chairman of the senate, Battye no doubt influenced some members but had little effect on major policy decisions. He rarely revealed constructive imagination and, despite a certain skill and finesse in negotiation, was no match for the subtler academic minds. Partly because of his relatively low public service standing, his achievements as ambassador for the university were limited.

Battye was initiated into the Masonic craft in 1898. Having resigned his initial lodge membership in 1903, he was nominated by Hackett and Riley next year as an affiliate member of another lodge. Thereafter, his rise was meteoric. He prided himself that before holding grand lodge offices as president of its board of general purposes, deputy grand master and finally grand master from 1936, he had 'never held any office in a subordinate lodge other than that of Worshipful Master'. He laid the foundation stone for a new Central Masonic Temple during the grand lodge's jubilee celebrations of 1950 while in his fifteenth term as grand master. That year he was appointed C.B.E.

University and Masonic responsibilities, with crippling arthritis, diabetes and consequential failing eyesight, hampered his work as a librarian. There was increasing criticism of the backwardness of the State's public library services and of Battye's failure to give effective leadership. In 1950 he was still sufficiently active and influential to secure the withdrawal of a bill which would have placed the library under the control of a new board. By 1953, the trustees informed the premier that Battye was 'no longer in a fit condition to carry out the duties of his office'. Since he claimed life tenure, an abortive attempt was made to devise terms of retirement that would suit all parties. The State cabinet had just agreed on a revised version when he died on 15 July 1954. He was survived by his wife Sarah Elizabeth May, née Jenkins, whom he had married in Melbourne on 15 May 1895, and by five of their seven children.

Battye's portrait, in chancellor's robes, hangs in the senate room of the University of Western Australia, and another, in grand master's regalia, is in the Freemasons' Hall, Terrace Road, Perth. His most fitting memorial is the J. S. Battye Library of West Australian History, established as an adjunct to the new State Reference Library in 1956.

N. R. Collins and H. C. Forster, *Golden jubilee history ... Grand Lodge of Western Australia ... Masons* (Perth, 1950); F. Alexander, *Campus at Crawley* (Melb, 1963); P. Biskup, 'The Public Library of Western Australia, 1886-1955', *Aust Lib J*, Jan 1960; Public Lib, Museum and Art Gallery,

FRED ALEXANDER

BAVIN, SIR THOMAS RAINSFORD (1874-1941), lawyer and politician, was born on 5 May 1874 at Kaiapoi near Christchurch, New Zealand, son of Rev. Rainsford Bavin, a Methodist minister from Lincolnshire, England, and his New Zealand-born wife Emma, née Buddle. He was educated at Auckland Grammar School and, after his father's call to Sydney in 1889, at Newington College. He taught at his old school and as an evening student attended the University of Sydney where he was editor of *Hermes*, became a lifelong friend of (Sir) John Peden [q.v.], and graduated B.A. in 1894 with first-class honours in logic and mental philosophy. He won the (Sir George) Wigram Allen [q.v.3] Scholarship and graduated LL.B. in 1897 with first-class honours and the University Medal.

Bavin was admitted to the Bar on 28 May 1897 and shared chambers with B. R. Wise [q.v.]. Here he met (Sir) Edmund Barton [q.v.], who inspired him with the cause of Federation; he campaigned vigorously for the Constitution bill at the 1898 referendum and that year unsuccessfully contested Canterbury for Barton's National Federal Party. He taught briefly at the law school and in 1900 was acting professor of law at the University of Tasmania.

Next year Bavin became private secretary to Barton, and wrote many of his speeches. When Barton was appointed to the High Court in 1903, Bavin became his associate, while remaining private secretary to the new prime minister Alfred Deakin [q.v.]. He was encouraged by both men, who became lifelong friends, and learned some of his political philosophy from them. On 6 February 1901 at St Andrew's Church of England, Summer Hill, he had married Edyth Ellen, daughter of F. E. Winchcombe [q.v.]; neither she nor her father approved of politics as a career for Bavin.

In 1904 he returned to Sydney to practise as a barrister in University Chambers. At first briefs were scarce and he supplemented his income by coaching: one of his students was W. M. Hughes [q.v.]. He also wrote newspaper articles and in 1907, while Deakin was in England, took over his 'Australian Correspondent' column in the London *Morning Post*; on Deakin's return they shared it until 1911. Briefed by trade unions and the government, in 1908 Bavin was junior counsel for the defendant in the important constitutional case over steel rails, *The Attorney General of New South Wales* v.

The Collector of Customs for New South Wales. From 1911 he chaired the royal commission on food supplies and fish; he resigned in 1913 but Premier J. S. T. McGowen [q.v.] dissolved the unwieldly commission and appointed Bavin alone to inquire into food supplies and prices. Shocked by the great difference in prices received by producers and those paid by customers, he went to sea with the trawlers and followed the catch through every agency until it reached the consumer. He checked each item of food in like manner and roundly condemned the whole system of marketing through middlemen. His most important proposal was to set up a kind of anti-monopoly bureau with powers to investigate prices and to recommend prosecution of trusts and combines.

Bavin lived at Chatswood; in 1911-14 he was an alderman on the Willoughby Municipal Council and became widely known on the North Shore. He had not abandoned his political ambitions and told Deakin that 'I can't rid myself of my desire to go into federal politics . . . I should much rather be in politics with a small practice, than out of politics, with a big one'. Perhaps partly because of his sympathy with much of Labor's social welfare programme, he lost Liberal pre-selection for East Sydney and Cook in 1910 and North Sydney in 1911. A strong believer in Imperial federation, next year he became a foundation member of the New South Wales group of Round Table and helped to prepare articles for its quarterly review.

Bavin had been a member of the Australian National Defence League in 1906-09. During World War I he advocated compulsory military service for those without domestic responsibilities, and with J. D. Fitzgerald [q.v.] became joint secretary of the Universal Service League in 1915. In 1916 he won Progressive pre-selection for Albury, but the elections were deferred. In 1917 he narrowly won the Legislative Assembly seat of Gordon as a Nationalist, on a platform which included proportional representation, continuation of six-o'clock closing, and reforms in the production, handling, marketing and distribution of food and combines. Rejected as medically unfit for active service, from 20 December 1917 he served with the Royal Australian Naval Brigade as a lieut-commander on part-time intelligence work inquiring into reports of enemy action at sea.

In parliament Bavin became strongly critical of W. A. Holman's [q.v.] National government and in 1919 called for the resignation of the minister of agriculture W. C. Grahame [q.v.]. Disenchanted with the Nationalists' lack of a constructive policy and their aura of corruption, at a party meeting in January 1920 he unsuccessfully moved no confidence in Holman as leader and resigned from the party. He rejoined G. S. Beeby's [q.v.] Progressives, won Ryde in the 1920 elections and became their deputy leader in October. On 20 December 1921 he was attorney-general for seven hours in (Sir) George Fuller's [q.v.] short-lived ministry; he held the same portfolio in Fuller's second ministry in 1922-25. Responsible for the government's controversial industrial legislation, such as the restoration of the 48-hour week, he was frustrated in his attempts to simplify the arbitration system. He was narrowly elected leader of the Nationalists in 1925.

As leader of the Opposition Bavin underestimated J. T. Lang [q.v.], but with the help of the Legislative Council had some success in modifying some of his social legislation. In 1926 Bavin was strongly criticized by his party for opposing the Bruce-Page [qq.v.] referendum seeking additional powers over industrial matters for the Commonwealth; his allies in the 'No' campaign included the Australian Workers' Union, J. S. Garden, Sir Arthur Robinson [qq.v.], Lang and (Sir) Robert Menzies. Moreover, his support of adult franchise at local government elections was not popular with the Nationalists.

In 1927 the National and Country parties agreed not to oppose each other at the election and Bavin committed himself not to repeal Labor social welfare legislation, although he later did so. He formed a coalition ministry with E. A. Buttenshaw [q.v.], in which he was premier and colonial treasurer. Ironically, one of his most far-reaching acts was to sign the Commonwealth-States financial agreement setting up the Loan Council. Long a believer in graduated income tax, he enraged his own supporters with his Income Tax (Management) Act of 1928, in which the incomes of husband and wife were added together, and taxes were increased on higher incomes. He carried the Constitution (Legislative Council) Amendment Act, 1929, making abolition of the council impossible without a referendum. Largely successful in taking direct religious faction-fighting out of politics, he spoke at the opening of the 1928 Eucharistic Congress at St Mary's Cathedral. Some of his young ministers such as (Sir) Bertram Stevens, D. H. Drummond and (Sir) Michael Bruxner [qq.v.] had solid achievements, but the coalition was uneasy and Bavin was troubled by persistent ill health.

While he was in England from April to August 1929, trying to negotiate a new loan, Buttenshaw removed rural workers from the basic wage award. Bavin had mishandled the timber strike and was confronted with trouble on the coalfields: he presented a plan to reduce the price of coal, which included a 1s. wage-cut. When the miners rejected it, the Northern Collieries' Association began a lock-out on 2 March. The Federal attorney-general ordered the prosecution of John Brown [q.v.] and a joint Commonwealth-State royal commission on the industry was set up. By October coal was allegedly running short in Sydney and Bavin decided the government would lease the Rothbury mine. 'Free labour' was recruited in Sydney and the colliery was picketed: in an ensuing skirmish a miner was shot dead by police, who had been attacked with stones. Bavin was uncompromising in his stand that the men must accept a wage reduction; he was believed by many to have promoted the owners' interests. The pits remained closed until May 1930.

In the face of depression in 1930 Bavin reduced the salaries of public servants and politicians, restored the 48-hour week, employed men on public works projects at under-award wages and imposed an income tax levy of 3d. in the £ for unemployment relief. In August at the Premiers' Conference he adhered to the 'Melbourne agreement' to balance budgets.

In the election campaign in October Bavin could only prophesy gloom and stress the need for self-sacrifice: Lang won a landslide victory. He remained leader of the Nationalists despite silent disapproval from prominent members of the National Association. He regarded the All for Australia League as a threat to democracy and, despite the support of Nationalist branches for the league's proposed fusion with the National Party, Bavin continued to distrust its motives. Faced with a challenge by Stevens, he resigned as leader in March 1932; the United Australia Party was formed without further opposition.

Bavin was appointed K.C.M.G. in 1933 and that year a volume of extracts from his speeches was published. He resigned from parliament on October 1935 on being appointed a Supreme Court justice. Plagued by continued ill health, he sat mainly in chambers and in causes, and was 'characterized by the same high standards as had distinguished his political career'. Outside politics, he had long found mental refreshment trout-fishing in the Snowy River, near Khancoban, with close friends such as (Sir) John Latham and A. J. Arnot [qq.v.]. He was founding president of the League of Nations Union in 1920 and president of the Sydney University Law Society in 1907 and 1922-41. He belonged to the Royal Sydney Golf Club and the Australian and University clubs and helped to organize the Rotary movement. A man of wide culture, and considerable learning in literature and art, he shared a love of music with his wife and was a founder of the Sydney Repertory Theatre Society. He was also a committee-man of the Bush Book Club of New South Wales. In 1934-41 he was president of the Australian Institute of International Affairs and chaired the 1938 British Commonwealth Relations Conference at Lapstone in the Blue Mountains. In 1940 he edited *The jubilee book of the law school of the University of Sydney 1910-1940*. Invited to give the Macrossan [q.v.5] lectures at the University of Queensland in 1940, he became ill, and they were read for him and published as *Sir Henry Parkes, his life and work* (1941).

Survived by his wife, son and three daughters, Bavin died of cancer on 31 August 1941 at his home in Bellevue Hill, and was cremated after a state funeral service at St Andrew's Cathedral. He had abandoned Methodism when a student and, a confirmed Anglican, had worshipped at St Mark's Church, Darling Point. His estate was valued for probate at £519. His portrait by Jerrold Nathan is held by the Sydney University Law School.

Bavin regarded life as 'a high adventure', and some of his actions appeared quixotic. He was, in fact, a decided mixture: a political liberal, yet in later life a social conservative; imbued with a Deakinite vision of social justice, he opposed Lang's social welfare programme; he defended parliamentary democracy, yet the union movement in New South Wales came with some justification to see him as an enemy. Reserved and aloof, Bavin lacked magnetism as a leader, although he was greatly admired for his courage both as a politician and in refusing to be defeated by his lingering illness. With his medium height, medium build and regular features, he was the despair of political cartoonists.

I. N. Steinberg, *Australia – the unpromised land* (Lond, 1948); Univ Syd Union, *Union Recorder*, 11 Sept 1941; *Aust Law J*, 19 Sept 1941; *Aust Q*, Sept 1941; M. Savage, 'A high adventure', *Aust Q*, Dec 1941; *Round Table*, 31 (1941-42); *Otago Daily Times*, 6 Sept 1941; Bavin papers (NL); Carruthers papers (ML); Deakin papers (NL); Latham papers (NL).   JOHN McCARTHY

BAVISTER, THOMAS (1850-1923), trade unionist and politician, was born at Sheffield, Yorkshire, England, son of Joseph Bavister, platelayer, and his wife Kesiah, née Langley. On the death of his father next year the family moved to Bedfordshire where he was educated at a local school. At 14 he was a messenger boy, later becoming an apprentice bricklayer. In 1871 he returned to Sheffield and joined the United Operative Bricklayers' Trade Society of Great Britain and Ireland. He was soon prominent in the society and for six years was secretary of the local branch; he became a member of the central executive and in 1877-82 was assistant secretary of the general council. He represented the union at the 1875 Trades Union Congress in Glasgow and joined in the demonstration supporting Samuel Plimsoll in London. He had married Harriet Green with Wesleyan Methodist rites at Luton, Bedfordshire, on 3 September 1873. In 1883 they migrated to Sydney.

Bavister worked at his trade and joined the United Operative Bricklayers' Society of New South Wales. He became active in it and was pleased to find that it had the 'closed shop' and working hours of forty-six per week in summer and forty-seven in winter – he had sought similar conditions in England as his political awareness had been stirred by 'Lib-Labism'. He became his union's delegate on the Trades and Labor Council at a time, 1889-90, when it was preparing to found a political party. He also won repute as a temperance worker and supporter of thrift through friendly societies; he was one of the significant minority of tradesmen who purchased homes in the suburbs; he lived at Ashfield, a long walk from the station.

Bavister was an ideal candidate in his constituency of Canterbury for the Labor Electoral League at its first parliamentary attempt in 1891. The electorate was large, sparsely settled on its perimeter, with many middle-class and some working-class voters nearer the city, and was a free-trade stronghold; Labor won two of its four seats. In parliament he signed the initial caucus pledge and, when the party split in December, he was among the seventeen 'solids'– all free traders except J. S. T. McGowen [q.v.]. He became the parliamentary party secretary, but in 1892 he was reported to the central executive for voting contrary to the platform; he was one of eight members at the unity conference in November 1893, but he refused to sign the new caucus pledge. Early in 1894 he sought J. H. Carruthers' [q.v.] political help assuring him that 'I am not one of the fanatical violent section of Trades Unionists'. Although he won as an independent Labor candidate that year he was a free trader when he retained the seat in 1895. B. R. Wise [q.v.] beat him by five votes in 1898.

Bavister was secretary of the Building Trades Council in 1895-99, and an active delegate of the Sydney Labor Council in 1900-08. He was employed by the Department of Public Works and by 1910 was foreman of works at Long Bay gaol. Aged 72, he died on 2 January 1923 at Kogarah and was buried in the Methodist section of Rookwood cemetery, survived by a son.

B. Nairn, *Civilising capitalism* (Canb, 1973); *V&P* (LA NSW), 1891-92, 5, 774; *Daily Telegraph* (Syd), 2 July 1891, 2 Aug 1894; *SMH*, 4, 5 Jan 1923; *Bulletin*, 11 Jan 1923; Carruthers papers (ML); Sydney Labor Council minutes, 1900-08 (ML).

BEDE NAIRN

BAYLDON, ARTHUR ALBERT DAW-SON (1865-1958), poet, was born on 20 March 1865 at Leeds, Yorkshire, England, son of Charles Henry Bayldon, solicitor, and Matilda Maria, née Dawson. As a student at Leeds Grammar School, he won prizes for swimming, and developed an appreciation of poetry through the scholar J. R. Tutin. His parents having died while he was young, he travelled widely in Europe and, he claimed, in the United States of America and India. In his early twenties he published two volumes of verse which, in their conventional evocation of delight and despair, display a bookish regard for nineteenth-century English poets and an attraction towards Victorian Romantic diction.

Bayldon arrived in Brisbane in 1889, practised freelance journalism, and lost his possessions and money in a flood. In the 1890s he became a prominent *Bulletin* poet and 'Red Page' critic who embodied many of that paper's characteristics and myths. Independent, egalitarian, egotistic, ostentatious and convivial, he confessed, however, to 'desolate brooding', restlessness and a stoicism relieved by religious faith. His occupations between 1890 and 1930 included those of swagman, rouseabout, phrenologist, full-time motto-writer, lighter-owner, salesman of his own books, insurance agent, picture dealer, clothier's agent, teacher of English composition, literary lecturer, editor of and canvasser for a comic monthly, tea-merchant, private secretary, and advertisement-writer. In cities and towns in Queensland and New South Wales, he recited his verse and, like the poet R. H. Horne [q.v.4], performed 'fancy swimming strokes' for a fee.

Bayldon's poetry was dominated in these years by melancholy realism in depicting the swagman's life, drought, sordid aspects of cities, and the bush as 'hell'. But he wrote in a happier and occasionally more 'majestic' tone on themes of liberty, egalitarianism, his personal philosophy, and his experience of a more Arcadian Australian landscape. His frequently derivative and tritely aphoristic style is interesting as the product of an educated Englishman's adaptation to a nationalistic Australian environment. Bayldon was modest about his poetry, but sensitive about the 'little encouragement . . . shown to an Author in Australia'. Less distinguished than his contemporaries Brunton Stephens [q.v.6], A. G. Stephens and Christopher Brennan [qq.v.], like them he extended the scope of the *Bulletin*'s literary criticism beyond national subject-matter; he wrote brightly and frankly on Byron, Tennyson, Longfellow and Browning as well as on local authors.

Bayldon was in Brisbane in 1897, and published his *Poems* there that year; in 1900 he moved to Orange, New South Wales, where he married Maude Bernard Leighton on 16 June 1902; they had no children. A collection of short stories, *The tragedy behind the curtain*, was published in Sydney in 1910, but a novel and various other works remained unpublished. His verse included *Collected poems* (Sydney, 1932) and four other volumes.

During and after World War I Bayldon turned more to patriotic, democratic and optimistic themes. He had settled in Sydney in the 1920s or earlier. In 1930 he suffered 'another breakdown', which he attributed to overwork as a canvasser; though he kept his job he was granted a Commonwealth literary pension of £52 a year. When he died at the Home of the Little Sisters of the Poor, Randwick, on 26 September 1958, he had outlived his wife and all the *Bulletin* poets of the 1890s except Will Ogilvie and his friend Dame Mary Gilmore [qq.v.]. He was buried in the Roman Catholic section of Botany cemetary.

H. A. Kellow, *Queensland poets* (Lond, 1930); *Aust Worker*, 23 June 1910; *SMH*, 4 Oct 1958; news-cuttings (ML); A. G. Stephens letters (Fryer Lib, Univ Qld); information from Mrs A. Flood, Hazelbrook, NSW.

KEN STEWART

BAYLDON, FRANCIS JOSEPH (1872-1948), master mariner and nautical instructor, was born on 23 April 1872 at Partney near Spilsby, Lincolnshire, England, second son of Rev. Joe Wood Bayldon and his wife Jessie Caroline, née Nicholls. He was educated at King Edward VI Grammar School, Spilsby. In 1887 he was apprenticed to Devitt & Moore, shipowners, and became a cadet officer in their passenger clippers, *Rodney, Harbinger* and *Illawarra*, sailing to Australia via Cape of Good Hope and returning round Cape Horn. Successful in examinations for first mate in 1894 and for extra-master in 1896, he transferred to steamers later that year.

In 1897-1901 Bayldon was with the Canadian-Australian line, plying between

Vancouver and Sydney, as an officer on the *Aorangi* and the *Warrimoo*. He was on the Burns, Philp [qq.v.] & Co. Ltd's *Moresby* in 1901-02, and was chief officer and master for the Pacific Islands line for the next eight years. In March 1905 he searched for and found the disabled and drifting *Pilbarra* near New Caledonia.

Bayldon had been commissioned in the Royal Naval Reserve in 1898 and was promoted lieutenant in 1907 in recognition of his work in hydrography: while sailing the south-west Pacific, he had co-operated in Royal Navy surveys, correcting somewhat sketchy charts and adding new detail, including the Bayldon Shoals, near Tulagi, Solomon Islands, named officially in 1912 by the Admiralty. His observations of the zodiacal light were published by the British Astronomical Association in its journals in 1898-1900, and by the Lick Observatory, United States of America, in 1900. His treatise *On the handling of steamships during hurricanes on the east coast of Queensland* (Sydney, 1913) was highly commended by master mariners.

On 2 July 1898 in Sydney, with Catholic rites, Bayldon married Stella Clare, daughter of shipowner Captain William Summerbelle. He retired from the merchant service in 1910, highly qualified in all branches of seamanship, a marine surveyor and a compass adjuster. On 3 May he opened the Sydney Nautical Academy (later the Sydney Nautical School), 'catering for all types of nautical certificates and later on for Civil Aviation licences as well'; he had some 3000 successful students. He sold the school to Captain W. D. Heighway in 1947, and it later formed the basis of navigation studies at Sydney Technical College.

Ardently interested in maritime history and exploration, Bayldon was a fellow of the Royal Australian Historical Society and contributed articles to its journal, including one in 1925 on the journeys of Torres [q.v.2] from the New Hebrides to the Moluccas. In 1929 the Hakluyt Society severely criticized it in their volume, *New lights on the discovery of Australia* (series 2, number 64). Bayldon, who had first-hand detailed knowledge of Torres Strait and near-by areas, was incensed and took every opportunity to counteract what he considered were 'most misleading deductions'.

Bayldon was a fellow of the Royal Geographical Society of London and a foundation councillor of the Geographical Society of New South Wales; he was also president of the local League of Ancient Mariners and vice-president of the Shiplovers' Society. A member of Australia's 150th Anniversary Celebrations Council, he was responsible for the rigging and outfitting of the scale model

of H.M.S. *Supply* of 1788. He was appointed M.B.E. in 1938.

Bayldon was a member of the parish council of St Mark's Anglican Church, Darling Point. He died at his home at Edgecliff on 21 July 1948 and his ashes were scattered over the Bayldon Shoals. He was survived by his son Dr Francis Wood Bayldon. His extensive nautical collection is now at the Mitchell Library.

'The doyen of Australian seafarers', Bayldon was a quiet, gentle man with a 'wealth of experience and ability, and well respected', 'remarkable in that day and trade for his erudition and gentility'. His brother officers knew him as 'Gentle Annie', but 'he was not a prude, for he drank, smoked and swore'. He was, in part, the model for Captain Dobbin in Kenneth Slessor's poem of that name.

Aust Geographer, 3 (1929), no 6; *Pan-Pacific Who's Who*, 1940-41; *Navy* (Syd), Dec 1948; *SMH*, 4 July 1931, 5 Dec 1964; Mackaness papers (NL); G. A. Wood papers (Univ Syd Archives); family and other information.   NAN PHILLIPS

BAYLEBRIDGE, WILLIAM (1883-1942), writer, was born on 12 December 1883 at East Brisbane, son of George Henry Blocksidge, estate agent, and his wife Kate, née Bell. Christened Charles William Blocksidge, he adopted the name Baylebridge without legal change soon after 1925. He was educated at Woolloongabba State School, at Brisbane Grammar School, and by a private tutor David Owen, a classical scholar who became a close friend and a major influence. He chose a writer's career, which divided him bitterly from his father, a rigid Methodist who was absorbed in local business and politics.

In 1908 Blocksidge went to England with his friend Robert Graham Brown. He was financed at first by his maternal grandmother and by his mother's half-sister Celia Grace Levin (or Leven), but later lived as a poor scholar in cheap rooms, probably by pseudonymous hack-writing. He toured the Continent with his aunt and sister, and published eight books of verse and two of prose in England, beginning with *Songs o' the south*; most were private printings. He was influenced at this time by the writings of Friedrich Nietzsche, either directly or diluted by various English interpreters, and developed a mystic nationalistic scheme of metaphysical philosophy akin to that later espoused in Nazi Germany: he presented it publicly in *National notes* (1913). This burden proved too much for his poetic talent, and his pleasure in archaic constructions often resulted in obscure versification.

Early in World War I Blocksidge tried to enlist from London in the Australian forces, but was told that he could do so only in Australia or, possibly, in Egypt. Spencer Browne [q.v.] later reported helping him out of trouble with the British military authorities in Cairo when he arrived there mysteriously with no satisfactory explanation for his presence. He claimed subsequently to have done special literary work for the British Secret Service. He returned to Queensland in 1919 and, after living briefly on a family farm at Mount Gravatt, writing occasionally for Brisbane papers, he settled in Sydney. He made a living by using a private income for operations on the Stock Exchange. When the marriage between his sister Muriel and his friend Brown collapsed in 1923, he helped her set up house at Manly, living himself in a room in Macquarie Street in the city. His mother and sisters later settled in a house which he bought for them at Wahroonga.

Baylebridge wrote continually, revised constantly and published versions of earlier work under new titles so frequently that his output is a bibliographer's nightmare. The Mitchell Library contains twenty-one books produced during his life, many of which are clearly revisions. In 1922 he published *An Anzac muster*, a complex epic of Anzac in 'Miltonic prose'. Unable to find a publisher to match his own standards of book production, he continued to publish privately and established the Tallabila Press in 1934; thenceforth he appeared under that imprint.

Baylebridge died, unmarried, in Sydney on 7 May 1942, shortly after a heart attack brought on by fighting a bushfire which threatened his country cottage at Blackheath. His estate, valued for probate at £18158, was left to his mother and sister, with a large provision for an annual poetry prize in memory of 'my benefactress Grace Leven' and for the publication of his own work. The will was contested by relations, but upheld in 1947.

Tall, fair, handsome and athletic, Baylebridge was said to be a good conversationalist and raconteur who sang well and could play the violin, cello, fife and banjo. Nevertheless he had few friends, guarded his privacy rigorously, shunned literary society, resolutely refused nearly all invitations for publication in anthologies, and was regarded by many as a mysterious recluse.

No two critics agree on his work. Frederick T. Macartney accused him of habitual larceny and applied to him W. S. Gilbert's verse, 'If this young man expresses himself in terms too deep for me,/Why, what a very singularly deep young man this deep young man must be!' T. Inglis Moore saw him as the only Australian poet with a philosophy.

H. M. Green placed him with the intellectuals alongside C. J. Brennan [q.v.], devoted fourteen pages to his work, admitted all the faults pointed out by other critics, and asked whether he was 'a minor talent enlarged by an immense determination and enormous pains or a major talent handicapped by an effort overstrained, a taste insufficiently cultivated and an element of the counterfeit'. Judith Wright, in more sympathetic vein, admired Baylebridge's sincere attempts 'to relate humanity to some wider and greater unity' and 'to find some basis for a new faith for mankind'. 'It is ironical', she wrote, 'that a man dedicated to the forwarding of life's creative impulse should find himself in the position of Canute bidding the waves to stand still'. No one understood his dilemma more clearly than Baylebridge himself:

> All that I am to Earth belongs:
> This Heaven does me violent wrongs ...
> True Earth am I, of Earth I'm knit –
> O, let me be at peace with it!

H. A. Kellow, *Queensland poets* (Lond, 1930); T. I. Moore, *Six Australian poets* (Melb, 1942); C. H. Hadgraft, *Queensland and its writers* (Brisb, 1959); N. Macainsh, *Nietzsche in Australia* (Munich, 1976); *Southerly*, 16 (1955), 35 (1975); *Aust Literary Studies*, 7 (1975-76), no 2; *Quadrant*, Mar-Apr 1975; *Westerly*, Mar 1975; *SMH*, 19 Jan 1935, 17 Oct 1936, 4 May 1940, 16 May 1942, 22 May 1943; *Bulletin*, 10 Aug 1938; W. Baylebridge MSS (ML); H. M. Green MSS (NL and Mrs D. Green, Canb); V. and N. Palmer papers (NL); P. R. Stephensen correspondence (ML); family and personal information.   NANCY BONNIN

BAYLES, NORMAN (1865-1946), politician and solicitor, was born on 1 February 1865 at Prahran, Victoria, sixth child of William Bayles [q.v.3], merchant, and his wife Isobel, née Buist. The family lived in Toorak. Norman was educated at Toorak and Scotch colleges and in 1883 attended classes at the University of Melbourne. Later he practised as a solicitor and became a member of the firm of Bayles, Hamilton & Wilks. On 18 February 1897 at Campbell Town, Tasmania, he married Marion Elizabeth Clarke, who died in 1915 leaving no issue. On 11 September 1917 he married a widow, Roma Mary Hill Neill, née James; they had one son.

When young, Bayles achieved renown as a tennis player, and was three times joint holder of the Victorian doubles championship; (Sir) Norman [q.v.] and (Dame) Mabel Brookes were his friends. He had gained political experience campaigning for D. Gillies [q.v.4] and (Sir) George Fairbairn [q.v.] before he won the Legislative Assembly by-election in 1906 for the highly prized Toorak constituency. He retained something of a dashing image, though Melbourne *Punch* thought that 'his mannerism had always suggested the aesthetic — the drawing room as against the football field'. In his maiden speech he declared his intention of playing the game, and jovially warned other members that 'if they hit hard they must not expect him not to do the same, because he had a rather good left, and a good counter, too'.

Bayles, as befitting the representative of Toorak, soon established a reputation as one of the most conservative members. He opposed the land tax and resisted Sir Thomas Bent's [q.v.3] closer settlement legislation. Never afraid to pursue an independent line, he helped to expel Bent from office in 1909; during World War I he was a member of the so-called 'Economy Party', which was critical of Sir Alexander Peacock's [q.v.] government. On moral issues he was responsive to the women's vote and always received a good deal of female support; he favoured legislation to suppress the gaming business of John Wren [q.v.], and voted for the continuation of six-o'clock closing after the war. However, fourteen years of politics were enough for him and he retired in 1920.

Bayles was long a member of the Council of Scotch College; he also served on the committee of the Melbourne Cricket Club and was a trustee of the Melbourne Cricket Ground. He was a member and for many years treasurer of Toorak Presbyterian Church and also took an active interest in the Alfred Hospital. He listed motoring as a hobby and his bright yellow motor car was said to have been a Collins Street West landmark. In the 1920s and 1930s he was a constant traveller abroad, claiming to have covered 300 000 miles (480 000 km) in a decade; the excuse he gave was the educating of his son at Winchester College. Bayles died at his home in Toorak on 25 September 1946, predeceased by his wife, and was buried in St Kilda cemetery. His estate was valued for probate at 82 640.

E. H. Sugden and F. W. Eggleston, *George Swinburne* (Syd, 1931); M. Brookes, *Crowded galleries* (Melb, 1956); *PD* (Vic), 1906, 2116; *Australasian*, 20 Feb 1897; *Punch* (Melb), 23 Oct 1917; *Age*, and *Argus*, 26 Sept 1946; K. Rollison, Groups and attitudes in the Victorian Legislative Assembly, 1900-1909 (Ph.D. thesis, La Trobe Univ, 1972).   JOHN RICKARD

BAYLEY, ARTHUR WELLESLEY (1865-1896), discoverer of the Coolgardie goldfield, was born on 28 March 1865 at Newbridge, Victoria, son of John Bayley, butcher, and his wife Rosanna, née Williams. Educated in 1875-82 at the Rupanyup State School, he went to North Queensland at 16 and prospected at Charters Towers, Hughenden, Normanton and the Palmer. He worked with his brother Tom in 1882-85 and first met his later partner William Ford (1852-1932) at Croydon. When the gold ran out there Bayley returned to Victoria, then decided to try Western Australia. Arriving in Perth in 1887, he walked to Southern Cross and worked as a miner to raise money. A trial of the tinfield at Greenbushes left him broke. He moved to the Ashburton goldfield in the North-West, walking the 280 miles (450 km) from the coast and arriving almost destitute early in 1890; a few weeks later he struck a rich patch.

He returned to Perth and set out by land again for the north with a mate called Taylor. On the Murchison goldfield they divided £3000 for three months work and Bayley was able to return to Victoria for a holiday. He went back to Perth, met Ford and planned a joint expedition. At Mount Kenneth, 250 miles (400 km) to the northeast, poison-bush killed their horses and they had to walk to Newcastle (Toodyay) for replacements. They moved out again for the Gnarlbine Rocks along (C. C.) Hunt's [q.v.4] track, and eventually reached a native well called Coolgardie and began prospecting. Ford made the first discovery at Fly Flat late in August 1892. Soon after, a party of Irishmen appeared, but the value of the find was successfully concealed from them. Bayley went into Southern Cross for supplies early in September and was followed on his return by a party of new-chums led by Tom Talbot. When Bayley delivered 554 ounces (15·7 kg) at Southern Cross on 17 September, he accused Talbot's party of attempting to jump the claim. Talbot and his friends, on the other hand, maintained firmly for many years that Bayley and Ford had cheated them. Bayley, they said, had diverted their attention while Ford had moved his claim pegs to embrace the most valuable ground which they had first found and worked. Bayley, however, reported the find to warden J. M. Finnerty [q.v.] at Southern Cross and was granted the reward claim. He thereby legally revealed the discovery and gained the distinction of being the first to mine gold at Coolgardie.

In March 1893 Ford and Bayley sold out to Sylvester Browne, brother of T. A. Browne [q.v.3], and Gordon Lyon for £6000 and a sixth interest in the mine. On 24 May at Albany, Bayley married Catherine, daughter of A. A. Fagan, a bricklayer. He returned to Victoria in 1894, apparently without his wife, and bought a farm near

Avenel which his brother Tom managed. Arthur Bayley's unostentatious generosity, always accompanied by a wish for luck, made him many friends in the district. When he died at Avenel of hepatitis and haematemesis on 29 October 1896, his estate, sworn for probate at £28 831, was left mainly to his brother. His wife, who was not mentioned in the will, was living on an annuity in Western Australia early in the twentieth century.

J. Smith (ed), *Cyclopedia of Victoria*, 3 (Melb, 1905); J. Reside, *Golden days* (Perth, 1929); M. Uren, *Glint of gold* (Melb, 1948); *Aust Mining Standard*, 18 Nov 1893; *Seymour Telegraph*, 3 Nov 1896; *Kalgoorlie Miner*, 14 Oct 1948; *People* (Syd), 13 Mar 1963.   PAT SIMPSON

BAYNES, HARRY (1858-1920), GEORGE (1862-1907) and ERNEST (1864-1930), butchers and meat exporters, were sons of William Henry Baynes (1833-1898), butcher, and his wife Sarah, née Robinson. Harry was born on 16 December 1858 at Hawthorn, Victoria. His father moved to Brisbane in 1859, joined Isaac and Hugh Moore on Barambah station in the Burnett district and on Condamine Plains on the Darling Downs, established a butchering business in South Brisbane, and represented the Burnett in the Legislative Assembly in 1878-83. Harry was educated at Brisbane and Sydney Grammar schools, then worked on Condamine Plains and Barambah. In 1881 he joined his father and uncles in Brisbane in the Graziers' Butchering Co. and the Graziers' Meat Export Co., established in 1880. On 12 June 1883 in the Baptist Church, South Brisbane, he married Annie Brookes; they had five children.

The companies were sold in 1885 to a new partnership of the three Baynes sons and George Hooper, who was replaced in 1888 by John V. Francis. The firm undertook meat preserving in leased premises at Queensport, and had nearly thirty suburban shops as well as a plant at Belmont for fellmongering, wool-scouring and soap-making; it also operated a factory at South Brisbane to supply cooperage, saddlery and vehicles. The business seemed prosperous, but the four inexperienced partners were soon in trouble from incompetent accounting and excessive personal drawings. In 1894 they registered the Graziers' Butchering and Meat Export Co. Ltd with power to take over the assets of the two older companies, which in 1897 they allowed to become insolvent. The Baynes brothers were bankrupt for a time but were discharged in March 1898 and immediately registered a new firm, Baynes Bros. George left the firm in 1899 and Ernest in 1912. With a new partner John

Stitt, Harry, who was primarily a cattleman, again reorganized the firm in 1918 as Baynes Ltd.

Harry served for many years on the Woolloongabba Divisional Board and Stephens and Belmont shire councils. On 27 August 1920 he died of a heart attack and was buried in the Congregational section of South Brisbane cemetery. His estate, valued for probate at £39 107, was left to trustees charged to carry on the business for his family; managed by Stitt and two of Baynes's sons, the firm closed down in 1937.

George was born on 3 April 1862 in South Brisbane and was educated at Toowoomba Grammar School. He specialized in sheep and managed the Belmont plant until his retirement after suffering a stroke in 1899. He had married Agnes Petrie at Brisbane on 22 September 1886, and after her death married Florence Emma Eyres at Ballarat, Victoria, on 3 July 1895; they had four children. He lived at Narrabeen, New South Wales, from 1899 and died there on 20 September 1907. He was buried with Church of England rites in Waverley cemetery and his estate was sworn for probate at £3968.

Ernest was born on 1 February 1864 at South Brisbane. He began his education privately under W. A. J. Boyd [q.v.], then attended Horton College in Tasmania and Toowoomba Grammar School from 1878. After several years as a jackeroo and drover, he went to Western Australia, spent some years on the Kimberley goldfield, made a friend of M. P. Durack [q.v.], and was employed by Sir Thomas McIlwraith [q.v.5] to seek potential sugar-lands in the west. On his return he joined the family firm as superintendent of the retail outlets, and married Annie Celia Jones at St Andrew's Anglican Church, South Brisbane, on 5 April 1889. He retired in 1912, was widowed in 1929 and died on 22 September 1930 of cerebro-vascular disease at St Martin's Hospital. He was buried in South Brisbane cemetery, survived by two daughters; he left an estate valued for probate at £11 796.

Enthusiastic sportsmen, the Baynes brothers shared special interests in water sports and the turf. George and Ernest were prominent at school in football and cricket; both later held debentures in the South Brisbane Cricket Ground. Harry and George raced *Koala* in the Royal Queensland Yacht Squadron; Harry was vice-president of the Queensland Rowing Association in 1900 while Ernest, an active oarsman in the 1880s, became president in 1902. All three were on the committee of the Queensland Turf Club, Ernest in 1894-95, George in 1893-95 and Harry in 1895-1919; Harry was a steward, Ernest a judge and George an owner.

In his retirement Ernest devoted most of

his time to the breeding and judging of quality stock. A council-member of the National Association from 1892, he was its chairman in 1920-23 and president in 1924-30. Until 1920 he was ringmaster of the association's annual Brisbane exhibition; a grandstand at its grounds was named for him in 1923. He had a national reputation as a judge of horses and in 1911 selected Akbar, a Durbar charger, for the prince of Wales; he was a member of the Southern District Stallion Board, and frequently adjudicated horse-classes at shows in Melbourne, Sydney and Adelaide. His own horses included the champion buggy-horse, Comet, and the high-jumper, Spondulix.

W. F. Morrison, *The Aldine history of Queensland*, 2 (Syd, 1888); W. B. Carmichael and H. C. Perry, *Athletic Queensland* (Brisb, 1900); S. Stephenson, *Annals of the Brisbane Grammar School, 1869-1922* (Brisb, 1923); M. Durack, *Kings in grass castles* (Lond, 1959); Roy National Agr and Industrial Assn of Qld, *Report of Council*, 1920, and *Review*, 1931; P. Fynes-Clinton, 'The beef industry in Queensland', *JRHSQ*, 6 (1959-62) no 4; Commercial Publishing Co. of Sydney, Ltd, *Annual Review of Qld*, 1 (1902) no 1; *Pastoral Review*, Oct 1907, Sept 1920, Oct 1930; *Telegraph* (Brisb), 28, 31 Aug 1920; *Graziers' Review*, Oct 1930; company file no 231, book 7 (QA); liquidation files 1639/1897 (Supreme Court, Brisb); information from Mr H. Baynes, Hamilton, Qld, *and* Toowoomba Grammar School.   BETTY CROUCHLEY
                                    H. J. GIBBNEY

BAYNTON, BARBARA JANE (JANET AINSLEIGH) (1857-1929), writer, was born on 4 June 1857 at Scone, New South Wales, youngest daughter of John Lawrence, carpenter, and his wife Elizabeth, née Ewart, who had arrived in Sydney from Londonderry, Ireland, as bounty immigrants in the *Royal Consort* on 9 November 1840. However Barbara later alleged that her father was Captain Robert Lawrence Kilpatrick of the Bengal Light Cavalry. By 1866 the Lawrences had moved to Murrurundi. Educated at home, Barbara enjoyed the works of Dickens [q.v.4] and the Russian novelists; she became a governess with the Fraters at Merrylong Park, south of Quirindi. On 24 June 1880 at Tamworth Presbyterian Church she married Alexander Frater junior, a selector. Next year they moved to the Coonamble district, where she bore two sons and a daughter.

In 1887 Frater ran off with Sarah Glover, a servant in his household; Barbara took her children to Sydney, instituted divorce proceedings and was granted a decree absolute on 4 March 1890. Next day at St Philip's Church of England, claiming to be a widow, she married a 70-year-old widower

Thomas Baynton, who was a retired surgeon with literary and academic friends who visited his home at Woollahra. Financially secure, Barbara began to add to her husband's collection of Georgian silver and antiques. Robust and vigorous, overflowing with vitality, she also began to write short stories, verse and articles for the *Bulletin*. Her first story, 'The tramp', was published in December 1896. A. G. Stephens [q.v.] became a close friend.

After failing to find a publisher in Sydney for her collection of six short stories, in 1902 Barbara Baynton visited London where, with the help of Edward Garnett, the critic, *Bush studies* was published that year by Duckworth & Co. She did not romanticize bush life and showed a savage revulsion against its loneliness and harshness. 'A dreamer', 'The chosen vessel', 'Scrammy' and 'Squeaker's mate' are chilling tales of terror and nightmare, built up detail by detail rather than by atmosphere and the supernatural. Stephens reviewed *Bush studies* in the *Bulletin*, 14 February 1903: 'So precise, so complete, with such insight into detail and such force of statement, it ranks with the masterpieces of realism in any language'. To Vance Palmer [q.v.], 'Bush church' and 'Billy Skywonkie' had 'a robust masculine humour'. Writing powerfully, with economy of style, Baynton used certain symbolic and recurrent themes, notably the strong maternal instinct, the loyalty of the dog, the isolation of the bush and a bitter insistence on man's brutality to woman, which gave unity to the stories and lifted them above the plane of simple realism.

In 1903 Barbara Baynton returned to Sydney where her husband died on 10 June 1904, leaving her his whole estate, valued for probate at £3871. She began investing on the Stock Exchange, particularly in the Law Book Co. of Australasia Ltd of which she later became chairman of directors. An astute businesswoman, she also bought and sold antiques and started her fine collection of black opals from Lightning Ridge. She contributed occasional forceful articles to the *Sydney Morning Herald* on the 'Indignity of domestic service' and other women's issues. She spent the next years between Australia and London, where she lived 'in a succession of increasingly fine houses', surrounded by Cinese lacquer, Chippendale furniture, ornate porcelain and silver. Something of a celebrity in literary circles, she entertained lavishly and knew many famous people. She found time to write her only novel, *Human toll* (London, 1907) which, despite its melodrama and 'unsure management of structure', included in A. A. Phillips's opinion 'some of her most characteristic writing . . . and maturer insights into human behaviour'. During World War I she opened her house in Connaught Square to British and Australian soldiers, and in 1917 published *Cobbers*, a reissue of *Bush studies* with two new stories, including 'Trooper Jim Tasman'.

On 11 February 1921 Barbara Baynton married Rowland George Alanson-Winn, fifth baron Headley, president of the Society of Engineers and of the Muslim Society in England, and a sportsman. Next year he became bankrupt. Outraged when he refused the throne of Albania, she returned to Melbourne in a huff. She built a house at Toorak, near her daughter Penelope who had married (Sir) Henry Gullett [q.v.] in 1912, and furnished it with Queen Anne and Georgian pieces. Bored with it, she sold its contents with such success that she returned to England and brought back another shipload of antiques. Dark, with heavily lidded, watchful eyes, she loved jewellery, especially opals and pearls, and beautiful clothes. With considerable charm, 'a devastating wit', a caustic tongue and a domineering personality, she had the ability to amuse and impress people. W. M. Hughes [q.v.] found her 'a remarkable woman'.

Lady Headley died of cerebral thrombosis at her home at Toorak on 28 May 1929 and was cremated. Her estate was sworn for probate at £160 621. She was survived by her first and third husbands and by two sons and a daughter of her first marriage; a son by her second husband had died in infancy. Robert Guy Frater, her second son, inherited her adventurous spirit: he went to the South African War at 15, raised soldiers for a Chinese warlord, served in the Archduke Ferdinand's bodyguard at Sarajevo and, with his brother, fought with the British Army in World War I. Her portrait by John Longstaff [q.v.] is held by the Frater family.

S. Krimmer, 'New light on Barbara Baynton', *Aust Literary Studies*, Oct 1976, and for bibliog; Supreme Court, W. J. Windeyer divorce notebooks, 1889 (NSWA); information from Mrs R. Baxter, Syd.

BEADLE, JANE (1868-1942), Labor leader, feminist and social worker, usually known as Jean, was born on 1 January 1868 at Clunes, Victoria, daughter of George Darlington Miller, miner, and his wife Jane, née Spencer. She left school early to keep house for her widowed father, then endured a term of sweated labour in the Melbourne clothing trade, which left an indelible impression and inspired many of her future activities. On 19 May 1888 at Carlton she married the militant ironmoulder Henry

Beadle. Within six weeks he was in a six-months strike and was subsequently boycotted by employers. Settled at Footscray, Jean supported her husband and helped to organize a Victorian woman's relief committee for the Broken Hill strikers of 1892 and a union of female factory workers. An associate of Dr William Maloney [q.v.], she joined the Women's Suffrage Alliance and, from 1898, was prominent in the Women's Political and Social Crusade.

In 1901 the family moved to Western Australia, where Jean organized a Labor women's organization at Fremantle in 1905 and profited from the advice of Tom Mann [q.v.], Keir Hardie and Ramsay MacDonald and his wife. When the Beadles moved to the goldfields in 1906, she formed the Eastern Goldfields Women's Labor League, representing it at the Trade Union Conference of 1907. On leaving Kalgoorlie in 1914 she donated her presentation purse of sovereigns to striking woodcutters. Joint delegate with Mrs J. B. Holman from the Labor Women's Club to the first Labor Women's Conference at Perth in October 1912, Jean Beadle was elected inaugural president. Her first motion was to request the State government, in order to increase employment, to establish a clothing factory to manufacture uniforms needed by civil servants. She retained the chair for thirty years; during her term important issues included peace, disarmament, women's status, health, education, maternity allowances, pensions and child endowment. Although a committed anti-conscriptionist, she was, nevertheless, a reconciling mother-figure to the labour movement in the split in 1916-17. As vice-president of the Labor Women's Central Executive at its creation in 1927, she was soon appointed to the State Executive of the Labor Party and was a candidate for Senate pre-selection in 1931.

Associated with the Children's Court since 1915, Jean Beadle was appointed a special magistrate in 1919 and next year was among the first women to take the oath for the Perth magisterial district. She was a foundation member of the Women Justices' Association, in which she frequently held office, and took the lead in forming a similar association in Victoria. For many years she was an official visitor to the women's section of Fremantle Prison. In the 1920s she was vice-president of the Workers' Education Association. During the Depression, she served as treasurer to the West Perth Relief Committee and was adviser to young people seeking work near her West Perth home.

Jean Beadle was co-opted to the executive of the Women's Service Guild about 1912. At its instigation in 1915, she presided over a successful protest meeting against the government's plan to extend Perth Hospital instead of building a separate maternity hospital; she later became a member of the King Edward Memorial Hospital Advisory Board and was secretary from 1921.

A small woman, always neat and immaculately dressed, Jean was a fluent and convincing speaker, highly regarded by her many friends. Survived by two sons and a daughter, she died on 22 May 1942 at her West Perth home, and was buried in the Methodist section of Karrakatta cemetery. Her death was commemorated by a special message in the *Westralian Worker* by Prime Minister John Curtin, who quoted Alexander Pope:

Here rests a woman, good without pretence,
Bless'd with plain reason, and with sober
    sense . . .
So unaffected, so composed in mind;
So firm, yet soft; so strong, yet so refined.

B. M. Rischbieth, *March of Australian women* (Perth, 1964); *Westralian Worker*, 25 Oct, 1 Nov 1912, 27 Oct, 3 Nov 1933, 29 May 1942; *Dawn* (Perth), 15 June 1926, 17 June 1942; *Daily News* (Perth), 2 July 1928, 17 June 1942; J. Beadle, King Edward Memorial Hospital (1936, Battye Lib, Perth); Aust Labor Party (WA), State Executive file 1688A/340, 454 *and* Premier's Dept (WA), file 279/20 (Battye Lib, Perth).   WENDY BIRMAN
EVELYN WOOD

BEAL, GEORGE LANSLEY (1869-1952), public servant, was born on 20 September 1869 in Brisbane, son of James Charles Beal, government printer, and his wife Mary Elizabeth, née Callaghan. Educated in Brisbane and at Newington College, Sydney, he joined the Queensland Public Service in January 1887 in the Government Printing Office and was appointed clerk there from January 1891.

Beal transferred to the Auditor-General's Office in 1897, becoming an inspector by 1899, examiner of accounts by 1902, and treasury inspector by 1905. In 1907 he joined the Treasury as accountant and registrar of Government Savings Bank inscribed stock. In 1915 he was promoted to chief clerk and accountant of the Treasury, and was then under-secretary from 1 January 1917 to 1 September 1926 when he was appointed auditor-general. He was also a member of the Brisbane Tramways Trust from November 1922 until December 1925 and chairman from 14 February 1925, and first chairman of the State Stores Board in 1923-24. From 1912 he had been a fellow of the Federal Institute of Accountants.

Early in 1917 Beal, as under-secretary of the Treasury, was involved in legal proceedings resulting from the T. J. Ryan [q.v.] government's attempt to regulate the wartime meat industry: separate writs for damages were issued against E. G. Theodore [q.v.] and Beal, as agents of the government, following the detention of Mooraberrie station cattle. The consolidated case, which was eventually resolved in the High Court, favoured the plaintiff.

Beal's first report as auditor-general, for 1925-26, ignited a political controversy for Premier W. McCormack [q.v.] over the state purchase some years earlier of the Chillagoe smelters and silver-lead mines at Mungana, North Queensland. The smelters had been running at a loss and Beal had been consulted in 1924 about writing off the accumulated deficit. In his official capacity he reported the continuing losses, questioned the assessment of ore values and cited examples of irregular accounting methods adopted by the smelters' manager. A. E. Moore [q.v.], the Opposition leader, called for a royal commission which McCormack refused; instead, he empowered Beal to make a special investigation of the Chillagoe enterprise. His report, which appeared in August 1927 but not before McCormack had closed the smelters and accepted the manager's resignation, confirmed gross mismanagement of public funds, over-valuation of assets and questionable payments to preferred individuals. On the basis of his disclosures, Moore promised a royal commission if elected in May 1929, and next year redeemed his pledge by appointing J. L. Campbell [q.v.] to investigate what came to be known as the Mungana affair. Campbell found numerous irregularities in the acquisition and operation of the smelters and mines, some of which involved Theodore and McCormack; unsuccessful civil proceedings were instituted against them in 1931. Campbell also criticized 'the tacit connivance or, at least, the accommodating silence of the auditor-general' in the mismanagement of the enterprise. In a special report to parliament in September 1930, Beal made it clear that the reference was to his predecessor, and recapitulated his detailed adverse reports of 1926-28, rebutting any charge against his own integrity.

During his term of office, the auditor-general's responsibilities increased considerably with the growth in complexity of government and his added authority over local government accounts. Beal was a capable and conscientious public servant who remained a perfectionist throughout his career. Awarded the Imperial Service Order in 1929, he retired on 19 September 1939, after serving a record term. On 12 December 1893 in Brisbane, with Free Methodist rites, he had married Clementine Helen Godfrey;

they had no children. He died at Wynnum on 14 October 1952 and was cremated; his estate was valued for probate at £8126.

C. A. Bernays, *Queensland – our seventh political decade, 1920-1930* (Syd, 1931); C. Lack, *Three decades of Queensland political history, 1929-1960* (Brisb, 1962); *PD* (Qld), 1926, 597-604, 1315-42, 1936, 1737-40; *Courier Mail*, 19 Sept 1939; Roy Com on Mungana & Chillagoe mines, ROY/15-16, Ecc. file 1952/1755 (QA).   PAUL D. WILSON

BEALE, OCTAVIUS CHARLES (1850-1930), piano manufacturer, was born on 23 February 1850 at Mountmellick, Queen's County (Leix), Ireland, son of Joseph Beale, woollen manufacturer, and his wife Margaret, née Davis. In December 1854 he and his mother joined his father and brothers in Van Diemen's Land. In Hobart Town Mrs Beale founded a small school, one of several which amalgamated into The Friends' School. Brought up as a Quaker, Beale was sent back to Ireland in 1859 to be educated for six years at Newton School, Waterford. At 16 he entered a Melbourne hardware firm, Brooks, Robinson & Co., and at 23 set up a branch in New Zealand; he returned to Melbourne and became a partner two years later. On 9 October 1875 at the Congregational Church, Woollahra, Sydney, he married Elizabeth Baily, who bore him thirteen children. She died in 1901 and Beale married her sister Katherine on 4 March 1903.

After a brief association with Hugo Wertheim in Melbourne as sewing-machine importers, he moved to Sydney about 1884 and established Beale & Co., Ltd, piano and sewing-machine importers; he was managing director until 1930. In 1893 at Annandale he established a large piano factory. Beale & Co. made all their own components and introduced a revolutionary improvement, the all-iron tuning system, patented in 1902. He also made sewing-machines. With J. C. Watson [q.v.] he had been joint honorary treasurer of the Pitt Town Co-operative Settlement in 1894, and as a large employer of labour, maintained 'a friendly association' with trade unions.

In 1903 Beale was a member of the New South Wales royal commission on the decline of the birth-rate and on the mortality of infants. Believing that the inquiry had failed to stem the social change that disturbed him, he continued to pester the Commonwealth government about 'secret drugs' and abortifacients, the use of which was 'ruining the moral fibre of the nation'. Authorized by the prime minister Alfred Deakin [q.v.], in 1905-06 he collected information in the United States of America, Britain and Europe and on his return was appointed to act at his own expense as a royal commissioner into secret drugs, cures and foods. In 1908 Beale presented his report, which was chiefly distinguished by its moralistic tone and reliance on opinions rather than evidence, and had to be purged of some of its wilder claims before publication. He was criticized by some members of parliament, and legislation had to be enacted to give him the protection of retrospective privilege. His racialist and strongly pro-natalist population theories were aired again in his *Racial decay: a compilation of evidence from world sources* (Sydney, 1910), which merited its later description as 'quite the oddest book ever published in a field where there are many competitors'.

Beale was founding president of the Federated Chambers of Manufactures of Australia, and president later of the New South Wales Chamber of Manufactures and of the Chambers of Commerce of the Commonwealth of Australia. As State president of the National Protection League, he kept Deakin, an old ally, informed on political matters in Sydney and complained of Sir William Lyne [q.v.] losing himself 'in the torrent of his own invective'. As early as 1905 he was discussing a possible *rapprochement* with the free traders; and, an advocate of 'Empire preference', he lunched with Joseph Chamberlain in London in 1906. He encouraged the 'fusion' of the non-Labor parties, and was present at Deakin's meeting with (Sir) Joseph Cook [q.v.] on 24 May 1909.

A good linguist, Beale had revisited Europe and England in 1908 for the Franco-British Exhibition, of which he was a commissioner. He had three sons on active service and was often in London with his family in World War I. He became a fellow of the Royal Historical Society and of the Royal Society of Arts; as a liveryman of the Company of Musicians he was admitted freeman of the City of London in 1918. Back in Sydney, Beale was a trustee of the Australian Museum and of the New South Wales Savings Bank. At his home, Llanarth, Burwood, he grew rare plants in his garden, particularly orchids; he was knowledgeable about botany and Australian timbers. Fascinated by the ritual and history of Freemasonry, he became an Anglican and joined the Christian Masonic orders. He combined the refinement of a classical education with the forcefulness of a successful man of affairs. While his letters suggest a quiet confidence, his family remembered him as a stern paterfamilias in the Victorian manner.

Beale was killed in a motor accident at Stroud, New South Wales, on 16 December 1930 and was buried in St Thomas's Church of England cemetery, Enfield. He was sur-

vived by six sons and four daughters of his
first marriage and by his second wife.

Aust Museum Mag, 16 Jan 1931; *Lone Hand*, 1
Nov 1907, 1 July 1911; *SMH*, 17, 31 Dec 1930; O. C.
Beale, Correspondence MS2281, 2822 (NL); Deakin
papers (NL); family papers (ML); Report on secret
drugs, CRS A2 9/3562 (AAO, Canb).

NEVILLE HICKS
E. J. LEA-SCARLETT

BEAN, CHARLES EDWIN WOODROW
(1879-1968), historian and journalist, was
born on 18 November 1879 at Bathurst, New
South Wales, eldest of three sons of Edwin
Bean [q.v.3] and his wife Lucy Madeline, née
Butler, of Hobart Town. The Beans were an
Imperial family. Edwin was born in Bombay,
son of a surgeon-major in the army of the
East India Co. and Charles was named after
Henry Woodrow, who had worked in India
under Macaulay. They were also a family
for whom Thomas Arnold's innovations in
schooling were important. Woodrow was
the original at Arnold's Rugby of a character
in *Tom Brown's schooldays* who protects a
smaller boy against bullying. Edwin Bean
was among the first pupils in 1862 at Clifton
College, one of the new boarding-schools
founded to diffuse Arnoldian education.
When Charles was born his father had been
in Australia six years and was headmaster of
All Saints' College, Bathurst. Charles entered its preparatory school in 1886. In 1889
his father was forced by ill health to resign
and took the family to England.

For two years the Beans spent summer in
Oxford and winter in Brussels, where
Charles learned French and drawing. In
1891 his father became headmaster of
Brentwood School in Essex, which his own
father had attended. Charles was a pupil
there in 1891-94 and then entered Clifton.

He was a schoolboy in love with England
and Empire. In its thirty years Clifton had
become rich in Imperial tradition. Such old
boys as Douglas Haig and William Birdwood
[q.v.] were serving in the Bengal Lancers
and the Egyptian Army; and while Bean was
at school another old boy, Henry Newbolt,
published the verses in which the cry 'Play
up! play up! and play the game!', learned on
the school cricket field, saves the day on the
field of battle. Bean acquired at Clifton, he
recalled, 'a real interest in literature, & in the
classics', and played much cricket. He was
known at first as 'The Rum'Un' for his
Australian accent; in his last year he was
made head of his house.

In 1898 Bean won a scholarship to Hertford College, Oxford (B.A., 1902; B.C.L.,
1904; M.A., 1905), where he read classics
(preferring history to philosophy) and simplified his prose style, having 'determined never, if possible, to write a sentence
which could not be understood by, say, a
housemaid of average intelligence'. He
graduated with second-class honours and,
like his father before him, missed a place in
the Indian Civil Service; had he got a first or
a place in India (he reflected later), he might
never have returned to Australia. He studied
law, still living on his scholarship, and in
1903 was called to the Bar of the Inner
Temple. He taught briefly at Brentwood,
travelled to Teneriffe as a tutor, and sailed
for Sydney in 1904. He was admitted to the
New South Wales Bar that year.

While waiting for clients he was an assistant master at Sydney Grammar School,
and wrote some articles for the *Evening
News*, edited by A. B. Paterson [q.v.]. As
associate to Sir William Owen [q.v.] and two
colleagues he saw much of New South Wales
on circuit in 1905-07. He wrote a book, illustrated by his own drawings, about Australia as seen by a returned native. 'The
impressions of a new chum' could not find a
publisher, but the *Sydney Morning Herald*
printed eight articles out of it from 1 June
to 20 July 1907, under the general title
'Australia', by 'C.W.'. He saw Australians
as the best of Britons, and celebrated the
bushman rather as Kipling sang of other
outriders of Empire.

Bean resolved to live by writing rather
than teaching or the law, and on Paterson's
advice went to the *Sydney Morning Herald*,
which took him on as a junior reporter in
January 1908 after he had spent eight hours
a day for four months learning shorthand. In
August he was assigned as special correspondent in H.M.S. *Powerful*, flagship of the
Royal Navy squadron on the Australian
Station, to report the visit of sixteen
American warships – the Great White Fleet.
Bean wrote a book based on his reports, with
photographs, drawings and a water-colour
frontispiece by the author, and had it published at his own expense. *With the flagship
in the south* (London, 1909) was among other
things a plea for an Australian navy.

In 1909 Bean was sent to the far west of the
State to do a series of articles on the wool
industry. He was unenthusiastic, he admitted later. 'And then it flashed upon him that
the most important product of the wool industry was men; it was responsible for
creating some of the outstanding national
types'. He savoured the difference between
Englishmen and Australians, and between
rural and urban types in Australia. He liked
the tough, resourceful boys of the outback.
The articles were published as *On the wool
track* (London, 1910). The assignment produced another series of articles, based on a
journey down the Darling in a small

steamer, for the *Sydney Mail*. These too became a book, whose title referred jocularly to a great Imperial preoccupation of the day: *The dreadnought of the Darling* (London, 1911). Bean was to cherish a passage which began with an account of comradeship in the back country and ended with a prophecy that if ever England were in trouble, she would discover 'in the younger land, existing in quite unsuspected quarters, a thousand times deeper and more effective than the more showy protestations which sometimes appropriate the title of "imperialism", the quality of sticking . . . to an old mate'.

Bean had started at the *Sydney Morning Herald* on £4 a week. By 1909 he was earning £9; two other papers made him offers, which he declined. He took to writing leading articles, and paragraphs for the *Mail*, as well as carrying a heavy load of reporting, and nearly collapsed from over-work.

In 1910-12 Bean represented the *Herald* in London, living with his parents. He reported the building of the battle-cruiser *Australia* and the light cruisers *Melbourne* and *Sydney*. His book *Flagships three* (London, 1913) incorporated these reports and much of his first book, *With the flagship*. Early in 1913 he returned to Sydney as a leader-writer. He disliked the job, and managed to get several assignments out in the country. From late June 1914 he was writing a daily commentary on the European crisis.

In September the Imperial government invited each dominion to attach an official correspondent to its forces. (Sir) George Pearce [q.v.], minister for defence, invited the Australian Journalists' Association to nominate a man, and in a ballot of members Bean won narrowly from (Sir) Keith Murdoch [q.v.] of the Melbourne *Herald*. Pearce expressed to Bean the hope that he would later write the history of Australia's part in the war.

He travelled to Egypt with the first contingent of the Australian Imperial Force, as a civilian who was regarded as a captain for such purposes as precedence in the mess. He wrote a booklet, *What to know in Egypt . . . a guide for Australasian soldiers* (Cairo, 1915). An early dispatch, explaining why 'a handful of rowdies' were being sent home, aroused resentment. A savage set of verses accused him of 'wowseristic whining' and declared that he could not be an Australian. Early in April he left Egypt with the main body of the A.I.F. which joined the Mediterranean Expeditionary Force.

Bean went ashore at Anzac Cove on Gallipoli about 10 a.m. on 25 April 1915, some five and a half hours after the first landing. Two weeks later he accompanied two Australian brigades in a costly and unsuccessful attack at Cape Helles. For the help he gave to wounded men under fire on the night of 8 May he was recommended for the Military Cross; as a civilian he was not eligible, but was mentioned in dispatches. His bravery became a legend, and erased whatever hostility remained from his dispatch about the first of the returned soldiers. Australians at home read a detailed account of the landing, in the papers of 8 May. It was not by Bean, whose first dispatch was held up by the British authorities in Alexandria until 13 May, but by the English correspondent Ellis Ashmead-Bartlett. Both accounts were much reprinted. Bean's was the more precise, for he had seen more. The English reporter betrayed surprise that untrained colonials had done so well; Bean was seeing what he hoped confidently to see: the Australian soldiers, as he described them, were displaying qualities he had observed out in the country.

He was the only correspondent to stay on Gallipoli from April to December. On 6 August he was hit by a bullet in the right leg. Determined not to be taken off to a hospital ship, he hobbled to his dugout and lay there until 24 August, having the wound dressed each day, until he was well enough to get out and watch the fighting. At the evacuation he carried off writing and drawing by soldiers which he edited as *The Anzac book* (London, 1916). Bean contributed photographs, drawings, and two pieces of verse: 'Abdul', in which the Turkish enemy is honoured for having 'played the gentleman', and 'Non nobis', an affirmation that although we cannot understand why the dead have died and we live, there must be some beneficent purpose which all the destruction of war is serving. In 1946 these verses, set to music by Dr A. E. Floyd [q.v.], were included in the Australian supplement of the Church of England's *The book of common praise*.

In 1916-18 Bean was in France to observe every engagement of the A.I.F. Some dispatches were published as *Letters from France* (London, 1917). The historian's task grew larger in his mind. At first he thought of one volume, but in France he conceived a grander work which would be literally a monument to the men of the A.I.F. − 'the only memorial which could be worthy of them', he decided, 'was the bare and uncoloured story of their part in the war'.

Late in 1918 Bean took leave in the south of France and wrote *In your hands, Australians* (London, 1918), an Australian version of the world-wide hope that the survivors of war would perform peaceful deeds which justified the years of death. The last and longest chapter was about education. Early in 1919 he went back to Turkey on a journey described in a book eventually published as *Gallipoli mission* (Canberra, 1948). He studied the field of battle as the Turks had seen it and reported to the Commonwealth government on how the Australian graves should be disposed and maintained. In May he returned to Australia, writing on the way home his recommendations for the official history and for a national war memorial which 'for all time' would 'hold the sacred memories of the A.I.F.' The government accepted his proposals. Late in 1919 the historian, his staff and their crates of records moved into the homestead of Tuggeranong near Canberra, to create *The official history of Australia in the war of 1914-1918*.

On 24 January 1921 at St Andrew's Cathedral, Sydney, he married Ethel Clara Young, a nursing sister at the Queanbeyan hospital whom he first met when she visited Tuggeranong to play tennis. The ceremony was conducted by the dean, A. E. Talbot [q.v.], who had been a chaplain on Gallipoli.

The first two volumes of the history, *The story of Anzac*, appeared in 1921 and 1924. Bean had been suffering pain for several years from a kidney ailment, and in 1924 he went with his wife to England for treatment; a kidney was removed. Doctors advised a warmer climate; so the Beans left Tuggeranong for Sydney, where they lived at Lindfield in a house named Clifton, and the staff and records moved to Victoria Barracks.

Bean himself wrote six volumes about the infantry divisions: the two on Gallipoli, and four on France. He edited eight more, and he and a colleague annotated the volume of photographs. The last volume appeared in 1942. The series contained nearly four million words. In Australian historical writing nothing had ever been done on such a scale; and there had been no military history anywhere quite like Bean's.

'Its theme', he wrote, 'may be stated as the answer to a question: How did this nation, bred in complete peace, largely undisciplined except for a strongly British tradition and the self-discipline necessary for men who grapple with nature ... react to what still has to be recognized as the supreme test for fitness to exist?' His answer, in plain prose dense with personal detail, had been foreshadowed in a passage of *In your hands, Australians*: 'the big thing in the war for Australia was the discovery of the character of Australian men. It was character which rushed the hills at Gallipoli and held on there'.

Bean brought a democratic and colonial scepticism to bear on the assumption that the dispatches of high commanders were the best source of information about what actually happened when men went into battle.

His own diaries (226 note-books) were full of the evidence about 'what actual experiences, at the point where men lay out behind hedges or on the fringe of woods, caused those on one side to creep, walk, or run forward, and the others to go back'.

Bean's approach differed from that of the British war historians, whose work was official not only in sponsorship but in texture: history written by generals, not by an honorary captain. The British volumes had no biographical footnotes of the sort that were essential to Bean's method because he wanted to show that the participants were 'a fair cross-section of our people ... that the company commander was a young lawyer and his second in command and most trusted mate a young engine driver and so on'.

The *Official history* was published by Angus & Robertson [qq.v.], Sydney, and paid for by the Defence Department. The government accepted Bean's request that it be uncensored, though he had to yield when the Australian Commonwealth Naval Board insisted on removing critical passages from A. W. Jose's [q.v.] *The Royal Australian Navy*. Each volume had to go to the minister for defence before printing, but only once (outside the naval volume) was a passage questioned, and 'the matter was easily settled'. By 1942, 150 000 copies had been sold—an average of some 10 000 a volume. Bean's one-volume abridgement of the series followed, as *Anzac to Amiens* (Canberra, 1946).

The story of Anzac ended with a declaration that 'it was on the 25th of April, 1915, that the consciousness of Australian nationhood was born'. That view of the nation was embodied not only in Bean's writings but in the Australian War Memorial, which rose in Canberra as a storehouse for the records of war, a popular museum for its relics, and a temple to honour its victims. Bean saw it opened in 1941, was made chairman of its board in 1952, and lived to see it become the most popular tourist resort in the national capital, visited by more people than ever opened a page of the war histories on sale in the foyer.

His attitude to warfare changed. Before 1914 he had regarded war as an evil but awesome thing, not to be welcomed, but not to be flinched from. Looking back later, he saw that when politicians and the press asked a young man whether he was prepared to die for his country, that 'splendid question' helped to blind civilized nations to the folly of warfare. Bean became an active member of the League of Nations Union, believing in the league as guardian of peace. Horror of war led him to support Chamberlain's conciliation of Hitler. He went on hoping that Hitler would keep his pledges—would play the game—until the German invasion of Czechoslovakia; and on 21 March 1939 a letter from Bean appeared in the *Sydney Morning Herald* under the heading 'Recantation'.

In Sydney he founded the Parks and Playgrounds Movement of New South Wales, which tried to make the city a little more like the country, and was involved in the Town Planning Association. These activities gave him his first experience of local politics, and led him to dismay at corruption. The Depression shook him: his own salary, fixed by contract, was unaffected by the reduction imposed on public servants, including his associates on the *History*; but he insisted that his pay be cut too. Until he saw the mass unemployment of the 1930s he was a virtual stranger to the socialist tradition. Now he became interested in planning to reduce inequalities, and grew curious about the Soviet Union.

In the new war Bean did several jobs. He wrote a pamphlet, *The old A.I.F. and the new* (Sydney, 1940), and was employed in 1940 by the Department of Information to provide liaison between the chiefs of staff and the press. He became chairman in 1942 of the new Commonwealth Archives Committee, and did more than anyone else to create the Commonwealth Archives. In 1943 he published *War aims of a plain Australian*, deploring the failure of his people to enact the ideals for which World War I had been fought. As in his tract of 1918 his answer was 'Educate, and educate!'.

In 1947-58 Bean was chairman of the promotion appeals board of the Australian Broadcasting Commission. He and his wife visited England in 1951. They returned on a migrant ship on which he was employed as a migration officer. He wrote a commissioned history of the 'independent and corporate' schools of Australia, using as title words from a poem by Newbolt about Clifton chapel: *Here, my son* (Sydney, 1950). Earlier works found new readers when *On the wool track* (1945, 1963, 1967) and *The dreadnought of the Darling* (1956) were republished.

In his last book, *Two men I knew. William Bridges and Brudenell White, founders of the A.I.F.* (Sydney, 1957), Bean told the story, related also in volume VI of the *Official history*, of his own 'high-intentioned but ill-judged intervention' on behalf of White and against Sir John Monash [qq.v.] when a successor to Birdwood as commander of the Australian Corps was being chosen in 1918.

The sense of values established in boyhood remained steady; the opinions derived from it went on changing. Before 1914 Bean had employed serenely the notion of an English race, and briskly defended White Australia. By 1949 he was arguing for ad-

mission of immigrants from Asia rather than perpetuation of 'a quite senseless colour line'.

More than once Bean declined a knighthood. He accepted a D.Litt. in 1931 from the University of Melbourne and an honorary LL.D. in 1959 from the Australian National University, an institution which he had been one of the first to foresee. In 1930 he was given the Chesney Gold Medal of the Royal United Service Institution.

In 1956 he and his wife moved from Lindfield to Collaroy, to another house named Clifton. Early in 1964, aged 84, Bean was admitted to the Concord Repatriation General Hospital, and died there on 30 August 1968. He was cremated after a memorial service in St Andrew's Cathedral. He had not been a regular churchgoer, believing (he said in 1948) that 'the question whether God existed or not could make no difference to conduct'. The congregation sang his verses of 1915, 'Non nobis', and heard Angus McLachlan speak of the 'devotion, amounting almost to worship' that he won from friends.

An author at Gallipoli described him as 'Captain Carrot' because of his hair colour, a man 'with the face of a student . . . He was rather tall and rather thin, with a peaky face and glasses'. He had a light voice, and an accent close to standard English but retaining the Australian 'a'.

The Australian War Memorial has his portrait by George Lambert [q.v.] and a bust by John Dowie.

K. S. Inglis, *C. E. W. Bean, Australian historian* (Brisb, 1970); A. W. Bazley, 'C. E. W. Bean', *Hist Studies*, no 53, Oct 1969; B. N. Primrose, Australian naval policy 1919 to 1942. A case study in Empire relations (Ph.D. thesis, ANU, 1974); C. E. W. Bean, Account for Effie—a memoir (1924, AWM).   K. S. INGLIS

BEAN, ISABELLE (1862-1939), nurse, theosophist and feminist, was born in 1862 at Salisbury, Wiltshire, England, daughter of William John Gater, ironmonger, and his wife Elizabeth, née Knight, daughter of an Anglican clergyman. Reared in an atmosphere of religious liberalism, she trained as a nurse for nine months at Salisbury Infirmary in the early 1880s until illness led her to migrate to Australia. On 5 February 1886 in a registry office at Redfern, Sydney, she married Erik Gustaf Edelfelt, son of an aristocratic Swedish Army captain. Edelfelt, who had had some scientific training, had gone to New Guinea in 1884 as a collector of natural history specimens, and returned there in 1886 as an agent for Burns Philp [qq.v.] Ltd at Motu Motu near Port Moresby.

Armed with her own revolver, Isabelle sometimes accompanied him on his frequent journeys and was described in an official report as 'an enterprizing and courageous lady'. In 1888 Edelfelt was employed as government agent at Samarai, where a relatively comfortable residency enabled her to entertain all kinds of visitors.

Sir William MacGregor [q.v.5] did not re-employ Edelfelt and, soon afterwards, the couple left New Guinea to settle in Rockhampton, Queensland, where he practised as a dentist. While he went to Sweden in 1894 Isabelle undertook further training as a nurse at the Women's Hospital in Melbourne. On his return he practised for a time in Brisbane until driven by tuberculosis to the drier climate of Freestone Creek on the Darling Downs, where he died on 1 February 1895.

Isabelle then became a sought-after obstetric nurse. Partly inspired by Edelfelt's psychic interests, she joined the infant Theosophical Society and met William George John, a Brisbane insurance accountant. When he moved to Sydney in 1901 to become general secretary of the Australian Theosophical Society, she married him on 23 November in a private home at Ashfield, with Presbyterian rites. As virtual assistant general secretary of the society, Mrs John ran classes in theosophical theory and practice and spoke regularly at Sunday meetings in the Sydney Domain. She still found time for social work round the city wine-bars and for house-to-house canvassing on issues such as raising the age of consent. Her robust common sense and gift for practical exposition were valuable assets to any cause. In 1908 she toured the Commonwealth with Mrs Annie Besant, as secretary and general factotum, during a national lecture tour.

John died in 1917 and on 2 March 1922 Isabelle was married to his successor Dr John Willoughby Butler Bean in the Liberal Catholic Church of St Alban, Regent Street, Sydney, by C. W. Leadbeater [q.v.]; C. E. W. Bean [q.v.], the bridegroom's brother, was witness. Isabelle continued her work for the society as secretary to special ventures like the Order of the Round Table and Krishnamurti's Order of the Star of the East.

When Bean resigned from the society in 1924, they spent six months in Tasmania; then after several locums he set up a practice in Roseville, New South Wales. In 1927-32 he was a medical officer in the Queensland Department of Public Instruction, then practised privately in Queen Street, Brisbane. Mrs Bean continued her public life as a vice-president for many years of the Women's Non-Party Association, a body devoted to developing social welfare

through political pressure, and as a delegate for the theosophical Order of Service to the National Council of Women. She died of hypertensive cerebro-vascular disease at her South Brisbane home on 14 May 1939, and was cremated with the rites of the Theosophical Society.

Although she claimed to have seen visions, Mrs Bean was essentially a practical person. Her favourite aphorism was: 'If each one would sweep his own doorstep, then the village would soon be clean'.

J. W. Lindt, *Picturesque New Guinea* (Lond, 1887); A. Wichmann, *Nova Guinea*, 2 (Leiden, 1910) pt 2; A. R. Nethercot, *The last four lives of Annie Besant* (Chicago, 1963); *British New Guinea Annual Reports*, 1887; *Theosophy in Aust*, Aug, Sept 1939; *Telegraph* (Brisb), 16 May 1939; J. P. Thompson letter-book (Oxley Lib, Brisb).

H. J. GIBBNEY

BEAR (BEAR-CRAWFORD), ANNETTE ELLEN (1853-1899), feminist, was born in East Melbourne, eldest daughter of John Pinney Bear and his wife Annette Eliza, née Williams. Bear had come to Victoria from Devon, England, in 1841 and joined his father in a prosperous stock and station agency, which he sold about 1857 before going back to England. The family returned to Victoria in 1860 and Bear established the Tabilk (Chateau Tahbilk) vineyard on the Goulburn River. He was a member of the Legislative Council for Southern Province from 1863 until 1878 when he retired, settling in England for ten years. He died at Tabilk vineyard on 27 October 1889.

Annette Bear had three brothers and five sisters. Their father believed in giving his daughters 'every educational advantage' and Annette was taught by governesses in Australia and England before attending Cheltenham Ladies' College, Gloucestershire. After some time in France and Germany she trained in social work in England, gaining experience of work in city slums and in London's New Hospital. She met leaders of the women's movement and became well known as an active member of the National Vigilance Association.

In April 1890 Annette rejoined her mother in Victoria. She became a leading force in the growing women's movement which was then most concerned with gaining the franchise. Annette Bear believed that 'the vote would be the most effective instrument for improving conditions of life'. She used her fine organizing abilities to strengthen and eventually unite the existing suffrage societies. With the support of the Woman's Christian Temperance Union, she formed the Victorian Women's Suffrage League.

Then, on her initiative, the United Council for Women's Suffrage was founded in 1894, with representatives from organizations interested in the cause; she was first president and later honorary secretary. The council lobbied politicians and municipal councillors and organized a monster petition in favour of women's suffrage, but failed to persuade members of the Legislative Council to allow the passage of a franchise bill.

Annette Bear also helped to educate women for public work. An accomplished and logical speaker, she trained other women in the art; Vida Goldstein [q.v.], who accompanied her to meetings, was shown how to handle hecklers and answer questions. Annette constantly addressed W.C.T.U. and suffrage meetings and also encouraged women to gain election to school boards of advice. She helped to obtain amendments to legislation affecting women, including the raising of the age of consent to sixteen, and the appointment of women as factory inspectors and to the Benevolent Asylum Committee. She also saw the need for police matrons and women to administer the Infant Life Protection Act (1890), and was one of the first members of the Society for Prevention of Cruelty to Children and of the Victorian Vigilance Society. She was undoubtedly a stimulus and inspiration to Victorian feminists of the time. Perhaps her most enduring achievement was the foundation in Melbourne of the Queen Victoria Hospital for Women, which grew out of her concern for the welfare of unmarried mothers and their children; she organized the successful Queen's Willing Shilling fund in 1897 to launch the scheme but did not live to see the hospital opened.

In 1894, aged 41, Annette had married William Crawford, a solicitor nine years her junior, and was thereafter known as Mrs Bear-Crawford. Her marriage brought her happiness but did little to change the even flow of her life. Beatrice Webb described her as a 'gentle-tempered intelligent woman who keeps me company in the dowdiness of her dress'. Domestic, affectionate and well-read, she had a 'lovable, sunny nature', but as an ardent feminist she believed strongly in women's equality with men; the *Age* reported in an editorial of 22 September 1897 that she had 'uttered the rather astounding dictum that most things worth having were originally produced by women. Man, she said, is destructive, while woman is constructive'.

In November 1898, after a farewell evening at the Prahran Town Hall, she left for England to attend the Women's International Conference. Her husband joined her in London only three weeks before she died of pneumonia, on 7 June 1899, aged 46. On 4 July a memorial service was held in St Paul's Cathedral, Melbourne; in 1902 a statue was unveiled in London to her memory and, in tribute to her work in England and Australia, her English friends placed a bronze plaque on the wall of Christ Church, South Yarra.

Women's Political Assn, *Life and work of Miss Vida Goldstein* (Melb, 1912); *Queen's Willing Shilling testimonial* (Social Science pamphlets, vol 42, SLV); B. Webb, *The Webbs' Australian diary, 1898*, A. G. Austin ed (Melb, 1965); Mrs. F. Anderson, 'Women in Australia', M. Atkinson (ed), *Australia: economic and political studies* (Melb, 1920); A. Henry, 'Marching towards citizenship', F. Fraser and N. Palmer (eds), *Centenary gift book* (Melb, 1934); *Aust Herald* (Melb), Sept 1899; *Aust Woman's Sphere*, 1 Sept 1900, 10 Mar, 10 June 1902, Jan 1905; *Age*, 22 Sept 1897; *Table Talk*, 19 June 1902; J. A. Hone, The movement for the higher education of women in Victoria in the later nineteenth century (M.A. thesis, Monash Univ, 1965); J. N. Brownfoot, Women's organisations... in Victoria c.1890 to c.1908 (B.A. Hons thesis, Monash Univ, 1968); Julia Rapke, Vida Goldstein (NL); Alice Henry papers *and* Rischbieth collection (NL).

JANICE N. BROWNFOOT

BEARDSMORE, ROBERT HENRY (1873-1959), soldier and public servant, was born on 12 August 1873 at Marrickville, New South Wales, son of William Beardsmore, carpenter, and his wife Sarah Ann, née Grimes, both of whom were born in England. Educated at Sydney High School and the University of Sydney (B.A., 1895), he became a clerk in the public service in July 1890 and worked in the Department of the Postmaster-General in 1890-97, the office of the Public Service Board in 1897-99 and the Chief Secretary's Department in 1899-1914. He was secretary of the Aborigines Protection Board in 1904-14. On 5 February 1901 had married Ethel Mary Clack at St Adrian's Anglican Church, Summer Hill.

Beardsmore joined the militia in 1895 and was commissioned second lieutenant in the 2nd Infantry Regiment, New South Wales Military Forces; he was promoted captain in 1905 and major in 1914, two years after he had been transferred to the 24th Infantry Regiment. On the outbreak of World War I, Beardsmore volunteered for service with the Australian Naval and Military Expeditionary Force which captured and occupied German New Guinea. He then enlisted in the Australian Imperial Force on 5 August 1915 as a major in the 30th Battalion, and reached Egypt in December. In June 1916 his battalion embarked for the Western Front and on 19-20 July had a bloody baptism in the battle of Fromelles. Beardsmore, who was awarded the Distinguished Service Order for conspicuous gallantry, was wounded early, but continued to lead his company for ten hours before having his wounds dressed; the citation praised his 'great coolness and courage'. He was promoted lieut-colonel on 28 July and appointed to command the 32nd Battalion. In January 1917 he was mentioned in dispatches; next April he was transferred to the general list on account of his health, and was placed in charge of the 5th Australian Division base depot at Etaples. He later became a staff officer for demobilization at Australian depots in the United Kingdom.

Beardsmore was discharged from the A.I.F. on 13 February 1920 and resumed employment with the New South Wales Public Service as an accountant in the Department of Lands. In December 1929 he organized the police camp at the Rothbury colliery near Maitland when, in an attempt to reopen the mine, the State government gave armed police protection to non-unionists and a violent clash followed. In his capacity of chief accountant to the department, in 1932 Beardsmore was to precipitate the final chain of events which led to the dismissal of the premier J. T. Lang [q.v.]. On 10 May the government issued a circular instructing its officers to pay into the State Treasury all revenue collected in New South Wales; this contravened an earlier Commonwealth proclamation which directed that any revenue due to the Federal government should be paid into the Commonwealth Bank. Beardsmore was the only departmental executive who refused to comply with the State order. His action forced a crisis: Governor Sir Philip Game [q.v.] ruled the circular was illegal and on 13 May dismissed the Lang government. Beardsmore had been sent on indefinite leave and later resigned from the service. He became treasurer of the Australian Jockey Club in 1935-49 and was also a member of the State Superannuation Board; from 1947 he was a director of B. J. Heath Pty Ltd, crockery merchants. He had been appointed M.B.E. in 1938.

An extrovert by nature, Beardsmore was a keen sportsman whose favourite recreations were horse-racing, golf, poker and rifle-shooting; in 1919 he had captained the Australian rifle team at Bisley and he was the first president of the Metropolitan District Rifle Association of New South Wales. Survived by a son and a daughter, he died at Burwood on 25 December 1959, and was cremated.

S. S. Mackenzie, *The Australians at Rabaul...* (Syd, 1927); C. E. W. Bean, *The A.I.F. in France*, 3, 4 (Syd, 1929, 1933); B. Foott, *Dismissal of a premier* (Syd, 1938); H. Sloan, *The purple and gold... the 30th Battalion, A.I.F.* (Syd, 1938); *London Gazette*, 26 Sept 1916, 2 Jan 1917; *Daily Telegraph* (Syd), 12-14 May 1932; *SMH*, 14 May 1932.

A. ARGENT

BEATHAM, ROBERT MATTHEW (1894-1918), soldier, was born on 16 June 1894 at Glassonby, Cumberland, England, son of John Beatham, papermaker's foreman, and his wife Elizabeth, née Allison. While still in his teens he migrated alone to Australia and was working at Geelong, Victoria, as a labourer when he enlisted in the Australian Imperial Force on 8 January 1915.

Beatham embarked for Egypt in April and was returned to Australia on medical grounds in July. He re-embarked in September with reinforcements for the 8th Battalion and six months later moved on to France where he was twice wounded in action — at Pozières in August 1916 and Passchendaele in October 1917. When the great Allied offensive was launched on 8 August 1918, his unit was among those ordered to advance from Harbonnières and capture the high ground of Lihons north of Rosières. On approaching this German strong point on 9 August the 8th Battalion, its supporting tanks knocked out by heavy artillery fire, was halted by a line of machine-guns. Private Beatham's company worked its way forward to enfilade the enemy position and, assisted by Lance Corporal W. G. Nottingham, he rushed forward and bombed the crews of four guns, killing ten men and capturing ten others. This action enabled the battalion to renew its advance. Later the same day when nearing its objective on the southern slope of Lihons it was again halted by German reinforcements. Beatham, though wounded, rushed another machine-gun and bombed and silenced it, but was riddled with bullets. He was buried at Heath cemetery, Harbonnières. His award of the Victoria Cross was posthumous. The citation praised his 'most conspicuous bravery and self-sacrifice' which had 'inspired all ranks in a wonderful manner'.

K. R. Cramp, *Australian winners of the Victoria Cross... 1914-1919* (Syd, 1919); C. E. W. Bean, *The A.I.F. in France*, 1916-18 (Syd, 1929, 1933, 1937, 1942); L. Wigmore (ed), *They dared mightily* (Canb, 1963); *London Gazette*, 14 Dec 1918.

ROGER C. THOMPSON

BEATTIE, JOHN WATT (1859-1930), photographer and antiquarian, was born on

15 August 1859 at Aberdeen, Scotland, son of John Beattie, master house-painter and photographer, and his wife Esther Imlay, née Gillivray. After a grammar-school education he migrated with his parents and brother in 1878, and struggled to clear a farm in the Derwent Valley, Tasmania. He soon turned to his life's work. From 1879 he made many photographic expeditions into the bush, becoming a full-time professional in 1882 in partnership with Anson Bros whom he bought out in 1891. Gifted with both physical zeal and craftsman skills, he probably did more than anyone to shape the accepted visual image of Tasmania. An admirer of W. C. Piguenit [q.v.5], Beattie stressed the same wildly romantic aspects of the island's beauty. His work included framed prints, postcards, lantern-slides and albums, and was the basis for a popular and pleasing set of Tasmanian pictorial stamps (in print 1899-1912).

In the 1890s Beattie broadened his entrepreneurial work. His museum of art and artefacts became one of Hobart's sights and showed his enthusiasm for local history. Convictism at Port Arthur and the Aboriginals were conspicuous among his interests, but he gathered and dealt in all kinds of material (including gossip). He was appointed the colony's official photographer in 1896, and thereafter worked hard in support of tourism. His own illustrated lectures had much success, and he prepared sets of slides (with solid, informed commentary) for wider distribution. Tasmania's promise of health and minerals ranked high in this propaganda.

Making a business of Tasmaniana never corrupted Beattie. While sometimes over-imaginative in historical reconstructions with pen and camera, he had a scholarly sense. His accounts of Port Arthur, for example, steered between sensation and sentimentality, and he confronted the horror of European-Tasmanian relations. 'For about 30 years this ancient people held their ground bravely against the invaders of their beautiful domain', he wrote of the Aboriginals. While supporting and investing in the development of minerals, Beattie also urged conservation of fauna and flora. Among his attachments were the Minerva Club, wherein Hobart's liberal intellectuals gathered around Andrew Inglis Clark [q.v.3], and he joined Bishop H. H. Montgomery and Professor W. J. Brown [qq.v.] in establishing the historical and geographical section of the Royal Society of Tasmania in 1899. The society had elected Beattie to a fellowship in 1890, and he gave the key-note historical address at the Tasmanian centenary celebrations of 1904 (published as *Glimpses of the lives and times of the early Tasmanian governors*).

An opportunity for exotic photography came in late 1906 when Beattie toured the Western Pacific, including Norfolk Island. In 1912 Roald Amundsen entrusted him with developing plates taken on the first trek to the South Pole. Thereafter, highlights came fewer, and family portraits thicker, although Beattie retained his various interests. In 1927 the Launceston Corporation paid £4500 for much of his collection, which remains in the Queen Victoria Museum; after his death, further items (many slides, and objects relating to Port Arthur and the Pacific) went to the Tasmanian Museum, Hobart. The business he established survived in 1978, still selling his work.

A fine-looking man, Beattie was likeable if volatile. Jack Cato, a kinsman and pupil, declared him not only 'the finest landscape photographer of his age' but also 'by far the best known man in the island, and the most popular'. Montgomery was more subtle, although hardly less admiring: 'All you say of your struggles and hopes reminds me of the old Beattie! Your life consists of much keener joys than most people enjoy – and you must put up with gloom too' (1907). Beattie's long commitment to theosophy, dating from the foundation of a lodge in Hobart in the early 1890s, may be explained by his romanticism, but was later tempered by membership of the Methodist Church.

He died suddenly of heart disease in Hobart on 24 June 1930, survived by his wife Emily Cox, née Cato, member of a long-settled Tasmanian family, whom he had married in 1886, and by their two daughters. His estate was valued for probate at £871.

J. Cato, *I can take it* (Melb, 1947), and *The story of the camera in Australia* (Melb, 1955); Beattie papers in the Allport and Crowther collections (SLT); Beattie and Hurst papers in the Roy Soc (Tas) collection (Univ Tas).   MICHAEL ROE

BEATTIE, JOSEPH ALOYSIUS (1848-1920), medical practitioner, was born on 14 April 1848 at Athlone, Ireland, son of Robert Ettingsall Beattie, civil engineer, and his wife Margaret, née Mangan. Educated at Trinity College, Dublin, he won the gold medal of the Pathological Society and was admitted as licentiate, Royal College of Surgeons in Ireland (1877) and King and Queen's College of Physicians in Ireland (1878). He was briefly clinical assistant and demonstrator of anatomy at Steevens Hospital, Dublin.

Beattie arrived in Sydney on 21 October 1878 as surgeon superintendent in the migrant ship *La Hogue*, and for a time lived with F. N. Manning [q.v.5] before being appointed assistant medical officer, Hospital for the Insane, Parramatta. In 1881 he became resident medical officer at the Quarantine Station, Sydney, and on 24 November 1882 resident medical superintendent at the Coast Hospital and Sanatorium, Little Bay.

Next year Beattie was asked to initiate a new migration service in association with the Orient Steam Navigation Co. On his first visit to the Plymouth Immigration Depot he reported favourably upon conditions and the work of the immigration officer T. H. Phillips. On 12 December 1883 he left Plymouth in the *Abergeldie* on the inaugural voyage of the new steamship migration service. Over the next three years he made five trips, having the direct medical care of 3127 migrants.

On 1 October 1886 Beattie was appointed surgeon superintendent at the Liverpool Asylum for infirm and destitute men, which was little more than a hospital for the chronically ill and destitute; he was given the right of private practice. Under his direction it became the principal hospital for the treatment of males suffering from pulmonary tuberculosis until the State sanatorium at Waterfall was established in 1909. In addition, a number of cancer patients and others with 'every disease under heaven' were treated in spartan accommodation.

In September 1891 Beattie was granted six months leave and travelled extensively abroad. In 1901 he represented the New South Wales government in London at the British Congress on Tuberculosis; his short report was criticized for being perfunctory and vague. As part of a campaign from 1903 to have consumptive and cancer patients moved elsewhere, his administration of the asylum came under criticism because of its primitive conditions and unhygienic system of waste disposal. That year he was appointed to the Medical Board of New South Wales. Beattie went overseas again in 1910 to study recent developments in the treatment of cancer; his interest in this disease had been quickened by the claims of local quacks, whose patients often ended their days under his care.

His long association with the poor convinced Beattie that old-age pensions were not in the best interests of recipients who would be imposed upon and neglected by relations. Nevertheless he was regarded by his many patients as 'the friend of the aged poor'. He was a remarkable organizer, despite paying 'little attention to detail'. Gifted with literary ability and a ready wit, he had few equals as a companion, while 'the brilliancy of his conversation was a by-word'. He remained at Liverpool Asylum until 13 April 1916 when he retired after suffering a stroke

some months previously.

Beattie, a bachelor, died on 27 November 1920, and was buried in the Catholic cemetery, Liverpool. His estate was valued for probate at £24 281; he left the residue to Catholic charitable institutions in Dublin.

Blue Book, *V&P* (LA NSW), 1883-84, 7, 55-56, 1887, 5, 36, 1890, 3, 995 (pp 33, 39); *PD* (NSW), 1903, 2nd S, 1950; *Government Gazette* (NSW), 5 Sept 1879, 8 Aug 1884, 13 Nov 1903, 11 Feb, 14 Apr 1916; *MJA*, 18 Dec 1920; *SMH*, 4, 6, 7 Feb 1884; *Truth* (Syd), 28 May 1899; *Cumberland Argus*, 19 Dec 1903; *Daily Telegraph* (Syd), 30 May 1914, 5 May 1916; *Freeman's J* (Syd), 2 Dec 1920; Col Sec, Grants to officers, migrant ships 1884, *and* Reports by immigration agents 1874-84 (NSWA).

D. I. McDonald

BEATTY, RAYMOND WESLEY (1903-1973), bass-baritone and teacher of singing, was born on 22 June 1903 at Narrandera, New South Wales, son of James McIntyre Beatty, schoolteacher, and his wife Marie, née Weissel. He was educated at East Maitland High School and the State Conservatorium of Music, where he studied singing under Roland Foster [q.v.] and in 1923 won the Dame Clara Butt scholarship, followed by two others. In November 1926 he gave the first of many recitals with his fellow-student Heather Jean Kinnaird, contralto, whom he married at St Stephen's Presbyterian Church on 21 August 1935. In 1928 he won the Welsh delegation's vocal championship for New South Wales.

Beatty had a 'robust bass-baritone voice', appeared in conservatorium opera productions, and was successful in oratorio and concert performances with the Royal Philharmonic Society of Sydney and the Welsh Choral Society. In November 1930 he had an enthusiastic reception at his farewell concert before leaving for Britain next February. He achieved some success in England, singing at orchestral concerts in Bournemouth, Bristol and Northampton; he also sang for the British Broadcasting Corporation and in 1932 gave a recital at the Wigmore Hall, London. Next year he broadcast in the United States of America. On his return in September 1933 the *Sydney Morning Herald* music critic wrote that, although Beatty's voice retained 'its intrinsic force and quality', he had become overenthusiastic 'on the subject of diction' and 'the flow of the music was chopped into a disturbing staccato'.

On his honeymoon in New Zealand in 1935, Beatty worked for its Broadcasting Service. Both he and his wife were in demand as soloists and used air travel to keep appointments as far apart as Townsville, Queensland, and Sydney on successive nights. In the 1936 Australian Broadcasting Commission grand opera season of seven months, Beatty, with Florence Austral [q.v.], sang title roles in *Don Pasquale* and *The Marriage of Figaro*, and Dr Bartolo in *The Barber of Seville*. He toured Australia as a soloist with (Sir) Malcolm Sargent in 1936, 1938 and 1939. He went to New Zealand for the A.B.C. in 1940, achieving an 'outstanding success' at the centenary celebrations — especially as a soloist in *Elijah*, and as Mephistopheles in a stage production of Gounod's *Dr Faustus*. He also appeared with Sir Thomas Beecham later that year in Australia. Credited by Foster with over 200 performances in the *Messiah*, he sang annually in the *St Matthew Passion*.

On 30 June 1941 Beatty enlisted, saw active service in the Australian hospital ship *Manunda* and was in Darwin during the bombing; he was discharged on 4 April 1945. He had taught privately since 1934; in 1946-73 he taught singing and voice production at the Conservatorium of Music. He sang in 1947 in A.B.C. concert versions of *The Barber of Seville* and *Peter Grimes*.

Beatty lived at Lindfield and enjoyed swimming and tennis for relaxation. Survived by his wife and two sons, he died of cerebro-vascular disease in Royal North Shore Hospital on 5 December 1973 and was cremated with Methodist rites. He had a wide repertoire: as well as arias and oratorio from Mozart, Handel, Brahms, Verdi and Schumann, he was interested in folk-songs, and often included the works of modern British composers.

R. Foster, *Come listen to my song* (Syd, 1949); *SMH*, 16 Nov 1926, 3 Dec 1928, 12 Nov 1929, 8, 17 Nov 1930, 9 May, 21 Nov 1931, 23 Jan, 11 Jun 1932, 1 Nov 1933, 29 Oct 1935, 29 Aug 1936, 20 Nov 1937; *Argus*, 26 Feb 1936.   MARTHA RUTLEDGE

BEAUCHAMP, seventh EARL (1872-1938), governor and politician, was born on 20 February 1872 in London, and baptized William, elder son of Frederick Lygon, 6th Earl Beauchamp and his first wife, Lady Mary, daughter of the 5th Earl Stanhope. Educated at Eton College and Christ Church, Oxford, he succeeded his father in 1891, inheriting 5000 acres (2023 ha) in Worcestershire. He was a devout High Churchman and was associated with the Christian Social Union and the Christ Church mission in London's East End.

Although he had been mayor of Worcester at 23 and a member of the London School Board for two years, Colonial Secretary Joseph Chamberlain's offer of the governor-ship of New South Wales surprised no one more than Beauchamp. He had not contributed to party funds or sought preferment. In London politics he was aligned with the Progressives not the conservative Moderate Party. He 'scarcely knew where was the colony & certainly nothing about it . . . The offer was very nearly forthwith refused, so ridiculous did it appear to me'.

Beauchamp's arrival in May 1899 was unforgettably preceded by publication of a message in verse, adapted from Kipling: 'Greeting! your birthstain have you turned to good'. Other gaffes and misunderstandings followed. At Cobar, in September 1899, he offended French colonists by condemning the Dreyfus trial and expressing pride in being an Englishman not a Frenchman. Cartoonists made predictable Beecham's Pills jokes. And his attendance at the dedication of the Roman Catholic St Mary's Cathedral antagonized the Evangelical Council and others dismayed by his High Church beliefs.

Unperturbed by *Bulletin* verbal and pictorial caricature, Beauchamp enjoyed the company of local writers and artists, befriending in particular Victor Daley and Henry Lawson [qq.v.]. The latter — who went to England at Beauchamp's expense — spoke of the governor as being 'a fine, intelligent cultured gentleman' who 'understood and loved the bush people of Australia'. He assiduously visited country districts, and was praised for the innovative invitation of a group of suburban mayors to lunch.

Like other late nineteenth-century governors, Beauchamp was neither powerful nor purely ornamental. He exercised limited prerogatives and influence in an increasingly radical and nationalist environment. His own behaviour — such as punctiliously climbing into carriages ahead of his lady companions — stimulated further criticism from those ill-disposed to colonial symbols.

After he had left Australia, Beauchamp admitted that the governor's duties 'do not take much time — sport cannot absorb one's whole attention & other interests are necessary'. Tracing missing children and spouses, selecting a doctor for Fiji, arranging London University external examinations, were routine gubernatorial activities. He could also oversee contract negotiations for the Pacific Cable, display admirable equanimity during the outbreak of bubonic plague of March-October 1900, and discreetly stimulate commercial and political resistance to the proposed extension of the contract time for sea mail deliveries. He was closely involved in arranging the participation of New South Wales contingents in the

South African War and in China following the Boxer uprising.

Although disappointed with colonial politicians and bureaucracy, Beauchamp admired the absence of bribery in New South Wales government. Sustained by sage counsel from Chief Justice Sir Frederick Darley [q.v.4], Beauchamp's constitutional conduct was exemplary. He was not bamboozled by (Sir) George Reid [q.v.] — in 1899 the governor earned Chamberlain's commendation by refusing a prorogation, and later a dissolution, knowing that (Sir) William Lyne [q.v.] could form a government with Labor support.

After Federation the governor's status and salary were reduced. The inexperienced Beauchamp was an impediment to Lyne's campaign to have the governor-general appointed as governor of New South Wales as well. Ostensibly to leave Government House free as a temporary residence for the first governor-general, Beauchamp went on leave on half-pay in October 1900 and did not return. His commission as governor 'in and over the State of New South Wales and its Dependencies in the Commonwealth of Australia' was proclaimed on 1 January 1901 though he was not present.

On 26 July 1902 Beauchamp married Lady Lettice Mary Elizabeth Grosvenor, daughter of Earl Grosvenor, eldest son of the 1st duke of Westminster. He joined the Liberal Party and was lord president of the council and first commissioner of works in the Asquith government from 1910 to 1915. A resolute free trader, he played a conciliatory, but ineffectual, role during the Liberal strife of 1916 to 1923, and was Liberal leader in the House of Lords from 1924 to 1931.

Threatened with divorce and criminal proceedings that would reveal his homosexuality, Beauchamp resigned all of his appointments except the lord wardenship of the Cinque Ports, and went into exile in 1931. He lived in Germany, Italy, and France, and made several world tours, visiting Australia in 1932, 1934 and 1938. He died of cancer in the Hotel Waldorf-Astoria, New York, on 14 November 1938, leaving £140 993; his title and estate passed to his eldest son.

G. N. Hawker, *The parliament of New South Wales, 1856-1965* (Syd, 1971); M. Mahood, *The loaded line* (Melb, 1973); R. Gillespie, *Viceregal quarters* (Lond, 1975); *PD* (NSW), 1899-1900; Beauchamp papers (family possession and ML); Governor's papers 4/1401 (NSWA); CO papers (microfilm, ML and NL).

CAMERON HAZLEHURST

BEAUREPAIRE, SIR FRANCIS JOSEPH EDMUND (1891-1956), sportsman, businessman and civic leader, was born on 13 May 1891 in Melbourne, eldest son of Francis Edmund de Beaurepaire, sailor, tram-conductor, trader, and (later) hotel proprietor, and his wife Mary Edith, née Inman. At Albert Park State School, and later at Wesley College, he showed skill in several sports and an unusual talent for swimming.

Beaurepaire was dark-haired and stocky, with exceptionally powerful shoulders. The swimming style he developed, a modification of the popular trudgen stroke, proved effective over both short and long distances; at that time the crawl was thought too exhausting for anything but sprints. He won his first Victorian titles in 1906 at the age of 14, and in 1908 won three titles in the national championships at Perth. That year he made his first trip overseas, to represent Australia at the Olympic Games in London. The tour began badly — he collapsed after six miles (9.65 km) of a fifteen-mile (24.13 km) race in the Thames — but he won the English half-mile and mile championships. At the Olympics Beaurepaire took second place in the 400 metres and third in the 1500 metres, and was fourth in a 100 metres semi-final. He also won races in France, Germany and Belgium before returning home.

1910 was Beaurepaire's greatest year in competitive swimming. With twelve Australian championships to his credit he was sent on a European tour, in the course of which he set world records for 300 yards and for 200, 300 and 500 metres, and won seven English titles — from 100 yards to the mile — six of them in record time. He was undefeated in forty-one championships and first-class races, and the Helms Athletic Foundation of America awarded him its trophy for the best athlete of the year.

In 1911, when Beaurepaire became a swimming instructor with the Victorian Education Department, he was declared a professional and debarred from amateur competition. He indulged an interest in motor cycling with an attempt on the 24-hour endurance record, riding a Triumph around Albert Park Lake.

With the outbreak of war Beaurepaire enlisted in the Australian Imperial Force and was posted as a second lieutenant, but became medically unfit after a serious appendicitis attack. In 1916 he went overseas as a Young Men's Christian Association commissioner, serving with the 1st and 3rd Divisions in England and France, and gaining warm commendation from Sir John Monash [q.v.] for his work. He was invalided out in 1918, after an attack of trench fever. In July 1915 he had married Myra Gertrude, daughter of newspaper proprietor N. B. McKay, and niece of H. V. McKay [q.v.], at the Presbyterian Church, Albert Park. A son and a daughter were born of the marriage.

After the war Beaurepaire did not return to his position as an instructor, and worked for a time as an insurance salesman. Eligible once again to compete as an amateur, he made a remarkable comeback. At the Antwerp Olympic Games of 1920 (where his sister Lily was also a representative) he was unplaced in the 400 metres final, but came third in the 1500 metres and was one of the team which came second in the 800 metres relay race. In 1921, while living in Sydney, he won five titles in the Australian championships, helping to win the Kieran [q.v.] Shield for New South Wales as he had earlier won it for Victoria. In 1924, in Paris, he competed in the Olympic Games for the last time, taking third place in the 1500 metres final and second place yet again in the 800 metres relay race. It is remarkable that in so brilliant a career, having held fifteen world records, Beaurepaire never won first place in an Olympic final.

A man of much mental as well as physical energy, Beaurepaire found a suitable sphere of business enterprise when, with a Canadian acquaintance, he formed the Advanx Tyre Repair Co. in Sydney in 1920. In 1922 he decided to return to Melbourne, and founded the Beaurepaire Tyre Service there, with his brother-in-law Oscar McKay as partner. The business prospered, thanks largely to Beaurepaire's skill in choosing staff with the necessary technical abilities, and his persuasive qualities as salesman and promoter. In 1933 the Olympic Tyre and Rubber Co. Pty Ltd was formed, becoming a public company in 1936; by 1952 its paid-up capital was £3 500 000. Production of electric cables was begun in 1940, with profitable war-time government contracts, and Olympic Cables Ltd was formed as a separate company. In 1953 Olympic Consolidated Industries was formed as a holding company for all Beaurepaire enterprises.

In 1928 he won a by-election for Gipps Ward and became a Melbourne city councillor. In 1940-42 Beaurepaire was lord mayor, and was especially active in raising wartime patriotic and charitable funds. He was knighted in 1942, and in the same year was elected to the Legislative Council, where he sat until 1952. He was an unsuccessful United Australia Party candidate for the Senate in 1943. His political views were generally conservative, but he was more interested in fostering particular projects than in ideological positions.

Beaurepaire was very active in support of the *Herald* Learn-to-Swim campaign, which he helped to found in 1929 and which he served as president for twenty-four years. He fostered the installation of municipal swimming pools, and also financed a dressing-room complex at Albert Park. Among many acts of philanthropy, the largest was the gift of £200 000 to the University of Melbourne for a sports centre.

Sir Frank Beaurepaire was one of the chief sponsors of the proposal to hold the Olympic Games in Melbourne in 1956. He attended meetings of the International Olympic Committee in London and Helsinki, and of the International Olympic Conference in Rome, and was for a time chairman of the Victorian Olympic Council and of the Olympic Games Organizing Committee. There was dissension in the organization; Beaurepaire lost an election for the chairmanship of the council and resigned from the committee, ostensibly for health reasons. His sudden death at Melbourne from aortic stenosis on 29 May 1956 was, however, quite unexpected; he was cremated with Presbyterian rites. His estate was valued for probate at £938 610. The Beaurepaire Centre at the University of Melbourne, opened after his death, was completed in time for use as a training site during the Melbourne Olympics, and is a fitting memorial to Beaurepaire's rare combination of sporting and business ability.

G. Lomas, *The will to win* (Melb, 1960); *People* (Syd), 21 Sept 1951; *Age* and *SMH*, 30 May 1956.

J. R. POYNTER

BEAZLEY, WILLIAM DAVID (1854-1912), politician, was born on 7 October 1854 in London, son of William Beazley, carpenter, and his wife Elizabeth Ann, née Parker. He arrived in Melbourne with his parents early in 1855. At 14 he became an apprentice saddler and harnessmaker and remained in that trade until he entered business as an estate agent in Collingwood in 1886. For some years he was in partnership with C. W. S. Aumont; he retired about 1898 but allowed his name to remain in the firm.

In August 1887 Beazley was elected to the Collingwood Council, serving as mayor in 1894-95, 1899-1900 and 1900-01. His association with the district remained intense throughout his life. He was active in several local businesses, principally the Denton Hat Mills and in co-operative building societies; in community affairs, particularly those concerned with friendly societies and technical education; and in local swimming and cricket clubs. However, Beazley was best known for his interest in football, being conspicuous among the founders of Collingwood Football Club in 1892; he was president in 1892-1911. He expected that the club would help subdue larrikinism and promote integration and a sense of responsibility, with the extra advantage that it 'would confer a great boon on Collingwood, as the matches would be sure to draw immense crowds, and be the cause of much money being spent in the district'.

Beazley became one of the members for Collingwood in the Legislative Assembly on 28 March 1889. He held the seat until 1904, when he won the new contiguous seat of Abbotsford. From the beginning he was regarded as a radical or 'advanced liberal', and he was quick to declare an association with the Melbourne Trades Hall Council and the proto-Labor members of the late 1880s. He stood for Labor at the election of 1892 and was successful, though the party was not; in the next decade he was loosely associated with it, but in 1900 stood as a Liberal, and it was only from 1902 when it finally established its identity that Beazley was committed to Labor.

He was an ardent protectionist. Interested in finance, he was for some years member and later chairman of the Committee of Public Accounts and was a member of the royal commissions into state banking (1894-95) and old-age pensions (1897-98). He was chairman of committees in 1897-1903. As deputy Speaker in 1902-03 and then Speaker until 1904, Beazley was noted for his impartiality and for the 'promptness and equity' of his decisions. In parliament he was respected for his gentle expression of convictions, and in his electorate for his local involvements and his assiduous attention to all matters affecting Collingwood.

Beazley never married. He was devoted to his mother who was a well-known worker for the poor of the district until her death, aged 90, on 26 October 1911 at their home in Bath Street, Collingwood. Beazley died of pneumonia on 28 June 1912 and was buried in Melbourne general cemetery, leaving an estate, valued for probate at £11 221, which was bequeathed to the Working Men's College, the Collingwood Technical School and the Old Colonists' Homes.

D. W. Rawson, 'Victoria', *The emergence of the Australian party system*, P. Loveday et al eds (Syd, 1977); *PD* (Vic), 1912, 20-22; *Leader* (Melb), 27 Apr 1889; *Argus*, 27 Oct 1911, 29 June 1912.

PETER COOK

BECKE, GEORGE LEWIS (LOUIS) (1855-1913), author, was born on 18 June 1855 at Port Macquarie, New South Wales, son of Frederick Becke, clerk of petty sessions, and his wife Caroline Matilda, née Beilby, both English-born. Becke received little formal education before 1867 when the family moved to Sydney and he attended Fort Street Model School. Two years later, with his brother Vernon, he took passage to San Francisco and was away for nineteen months. At 16 he stowed away to Samoa, taking a job in Apia as a book-keeper. He was 18 when he met the notorious Captain 'Bully' Hayes [q.v.4] who was to become a central character in his later writings. Early in 1874 Hayes signed Becke on as supercargo on the *Leonora* which, some ten weeks later, sank off Kusaie, stranding the survivors there. When a British warship arrived in pursuit of Hayes six months later, Becke was arrested for piracy and taken to Brisbane. Acquitted, he joined the Palmer River gold rush, worked at Ravenswood station (1877), and as a bank clerk in Townsville (1878-79).

By April 1880 Becke was in the Ellice Islands, employed as a trader. Next February he opened his own store at Nukufetau and there married Nelea Tikena. Later that year he lost everything in a shipwreck and for the next few years worked in New Britain and at Majuro in the Marshall Islands.

Late in 1885 Becke returned to New South Wales and on 10 February 1886 at Port Macquarie, he married Elizabeth (Bessie) Mary Stuart, née Maunsell (d. 1932). He worked in Sydney as a contract draftsman for the Lands Department until they went to Townsville, Queensland, in 1888. He was assistant secretary to the New South Wales branch of the Royal Geographical Society of Australasia for a few months in 1890 before accepting a post in the islands again. He returned to Sydney from Noumea in January 1892.

Unable to find regular work, Becke turned to writing. His friend Ernest Favenc [q.v.4] persuaded him to put his South Sea yarns on paper and introduced him to J. F. Archibald [q.v.3]. His first signed story, "Tis in the blood', appeared in the *Bulletin* on 6 May 1893. *By reef and palm*, a collection of short stories, was published in London in 1894 and reprinted three times that year. Further collections of stories followed in 1896 and 1897. Becke went on to write thirty-four books, including six novels in collaboration with W. J. Jeffery [q.v.] and seven on his own account. Bertram Stevens [q.v.] called him 'a born story-teller', an impressionist-realist yet without imagination and little conscious art. Becke later paid tribute to Archibald for teaching him 'the secrets of condensation and simplicity of language'.

He sold all his books outright and success brought him no wealth; in April 1894 he was declared bankruptm In 1896 he separated from his wife (who tried to divorce him in 1903 and 1910) and left for England, accompanied by his daughter Nora (b. 1888) and by Fanny Sabina Long (1871-1959). In

London Becke was received as a celebrity. He and Sabina lived at Eastbourne, where their two daughters were born, and later in Ireland and northern France; he visited Jamaica in 1902. He raised finance in 1908 to back an expedition to the Pacific to record folk-lore. On 22 July, before leaving for Suva via New Zealand, he and Sabina went through a form of marriage at St Pancras Register Office.

By 1909 Becke had returned to Sydney. He still wrote for the *Bulletin* but creditors hounded him, he was drinking heavily, and he spent the last two years of his life ill and alone. He died of cancer on 18 February 1913 in his room at the York Hotel, King Street; friends in the *Bulletin* office arranged his burial in Waverley cemetery. He was predeceased by two sons and survived by three daughters.

R. S. Browne, *A journalist's memories* (Brisb, 1927); A. G. Day, *Louis Becke* (New York, 1966); *Government Gazette* (Qld), 28 August 1875; H. E. Maude, 'Louis Becke . . .', *Pacific Islands Mthly*, Oct 1956, *and* 'Louis Becke: the traders' historian', *J of Pacific Hist*, 2 (1967); *Australasian*, 28 Nov, 12 Dec 1903; *Bulletin*, 20, 27 Feb 1913, 15 June, 7 Sept 1955; application for appointment to the Ellice Islands (copy held by Mr H. E. Maude, Canb); A. G. Stephens papers, uncat MSS 248 (ML).

SALLY O'NEILL

BECKETT, CLARICE MARJORI-BANKS (1887-1935), painter, was born on 21 March 1887 at Casterton, Victoria, daughter of Joseph Clifden Beckett, bank manager, and his wife Elizabeth Kate, née Brown. Her grandfather was John Brown, a Scottish master builder who had designed and built Como House and its gardens in Melbourne.

Clarice was a boarder at Queen's College, Ballarat, until 1903, before spending a year at Melbourne Church of England Girls' Grammar School. She showed artistic ability, and after leaving school took private lessons in charcoal drawing at Ballarat. As a genteel young lady she had her 'coming out' there and spent her spare time sketching, reading, listening to music and writing verse. In 1914-16 she took lessons in drawing from Frederick McCubbin [q.v.] at the Melbourne Gallery School but then chose to study under Max Meldrum [q.v.]. Constantly encouraging, though often fiercely critical, Meldrum regarded Clarice as a very gifted artist; in later years he confided to one of her contemporaries his belief that he had helped to break the shell around her abnormally shy personality.

In 1918 Joseph Beckett retired and settled in the Melbourne bayside suburb of Beaumaris. Here Clarice spent the rest of her life as an artist. She took subject-matter from what would seem commonplace to others, such as a strip of wet tar-sealed road, bordered with telegraph poles. Her preferences were for the diffuse light of early morning; delicately restrained sunsets; dusk; misty days with a glimpse of a tram or T-model Ford; lights glowing in the fog. Whilst her contemporaries were revelling in the effects of broad sunlight, she was seeking to reinterpret her own restricted environment in subtle relationships of shape, colour and composition. She painted swiftly and compulsively, never reworking and seldom signing her canvasses. The brushwork was flat, the paint thinned and smoothed into the canvas. Her output was prolific: many boards were painted on both sides, sometimes with another canvas stuck on top of the first or second painting. She exhibited usually with Meldrum's other students; very few of her paintings were sold in her lifetime. She regarded herself as a realist and remained loyal to Meldrum's teachings, though not his literal practice; for years she would take her works for his appraisal, and most of her canvasses bear his assessment, A, B or C, on the back.

When in the late 1920s Clarice became more enmeshed in household duties and the nursing of frail parents, her painting time became limited, but she still managed to wander the cliffs of Beaumaris with her home-made cart filled with painting equipment. She quietly enjoyed summer camps at San Remo with a small gathering of Justus Jorgensen's students. In these last years her work flourished and developed; she used colour to reinforce form and there was a daring release of design. In 1934 her mother died: on 7 July next year Clarice, exhausted, died of pneumonia in a hospital at Sandringham. She was buried in the Cheltenham cemetery.

A memorial exhibition, assembled by her sister and father, was held at the Athenaeum Gallery in May 1936. In 1971 a major exhibition of her paintings was mounted at the Rosalind Humphries Galleries in Melbourne; a group of these was purchased for the National Gallery, Canberra.

Homage to Clarice Beckett 30th Oct-20th Nov 1971 (exhibition cat, Rosalind Humphries Galleries, Melb); *Herald* (Melb), 4 May 1936; *Sun-News Pictorial*, and *Argus*, 5 May 1936; *Australasian*, 23 May 1936; *Age*, 1 June 1957; *SMH*, 26 Jan 1975.

ROSALIND HOLLINRAKE

BECKETT, WILLIAM JAMES (1870-1965), politician, was born on 10 June 1870 at Prahran, Victoria, son of Samuel Beckett, Irish-born cab proprietor, and his wife

Margaret, née Cameron, of Glasgow, Scotland. He was educated at state and private schools. On 22 February 1893 at St Matthew's Church of England, Prahran, he married Alice Maud Street. About then he set up business with his brother Henry as Beckett Bros, furniture brokers of Fitzroy, advertising as buyers and sellers of 'billiard tables, pianos, organs, and all descriptions of good household furniture purchased for prompt cash, from 1s to £1,000'. Beckett established a house at Footscray and later moved to Fitzroy; from about 1930 he lived at St Kilda. By then he had retired from the furniture business which was still run as Beckett Bros.

He had grown up to appreciate quality horse-stock, and had early developed an interest in racing and trotting activities which brought him into contact with John Wren [q.v.]. This association influenced his embarkation upon a lifelong career of racing and politics. He became an owner-breeder of horses: in the late 1890s he owned a livery stable off Bourke Street, Melbourne, which he later transferred to a site near the business at Fitzroy. In the early 1900s he raced the champion trotter Lightfoot. Beckett held office in the Victorian Trotting Association (formed in 1908) and was its chairman for thirty years after 1919 when it had become known as the Victorian Trotting and Racing Association and had acquired Wren's trotting and racing interests. Beckett was also president of the Ascot Racing Club for many years. In 1948 the association became the Melbourne Racing Club and he was its chairman in 1949-50. He also served for nineteen years as a trustee of the Victoria Amateur Turf Club, which controlled the Caulfield Racecourse Reserve.

In 1914 Beckett entered both local and State politics as a Labor candidate. In August he won a seat on the Fitzroy City Council, serving until August 1932 with terms as mayor in 1921 and 1925. In September 1914 he entered the Legislative Council as member for Melbourne North Province, holding the seat until his defeat in June 1931; in 1934 he won Melbourne East (later Melbourne) Province, retiring in April 1952. He held the portfolios of mines and of forests, and was also vice-president of the Board of Land and Works in the Prendergast [q.v.] government of July-November 1924. He was minister of forests and of public health and vice-president of the Board of Land and Works in the two E. J. Hogan [q.v.] ministries in 1927-28 and 1929-31. From 1940 he was Labor Party leader in the Legislative Council and from 1943 unofficial leader of the House.

Beckett was a Freemason. A member of the St Kilda Foreshore Committee, to the age of 90-odd he swam daily at the beach. He was appointed C.B.E. in January 1953. He had suffered from cancer of the lip for thirty years before his death of bronchopneumonia on 7 May 1965 at St Kilda. He was survived by his son and daughter and was buried in St Kilda cemetery. His estate was valued for probate at £31 979.

PD (Vic), 1931, 618, 1952, 750; *Weekly Times* (Melb), 6 Sept 1903; *Labor Call*, 19 July 1920; *Age*, and *Sun-News Pictorial*, 8 May 1965; minute-books and reports (Fitzroy Municipal Council); MS collection (LaTL).
THOMAS SHEEHY

BEDFORD, SIR FREDERICK GEORGE DENHAM (1838-1913), governor, was born in England on 24 December 1838, son of Vice Admiral Edward James Bedford. Entering the Royal Navy in July 1852, he served in the Crimean War, was promoted lieutenant in 1859, commander in 1871 and captain in 1876. In 1877 he commanded the *Shah* in action against a Peruvian ship and consolidated his reputation in 1884-85 by organizing the Nile flotilla in the relief of Khartoum. He married Ethel Turner at Ipswich, Surrey, on 28 October 1880, was appointed C.B. in 1886 and in 1888-91 was an aide-de-camp to the Queen. He was a lord commissioner of the Admiralty in 1889-92 and 1895-99. His work as commander of the Cape Station in 1892-95 won him a K.C.B. He was promoted vice admiral in 1897.

Bedford became governor of Western Australia in 1903 at a time when several naval officers were being appointed to govern Australian States. He arrived with his wife in Perth on 24 March and soon became popular. The main political events of his term of office were the brief reign of the State's first Labor government under Henry Daglish [q.v.] in 1904-05, and a minor constitutional crisis in September 1907: (Sir) Newton Moore [q.v.] resigned the premiership after the rejection by the Legislative Council of land tax legislation, but was soon persuaded to resume office and to resubmit his proposals in a modified form.

Bedford and his wife travelled widely in Western Australia and his name is perpetuated in two small townships, Bedford, and Bedfordale, and in a number of geographical features. He was fond of children and took a special interest in the State Schools Amateur Athletic Association. His brisk and distinct manner of speech and sometimes unorthodox sense of humour gave added emphasis to his regular fervent expositions of the doctrine of Empire.

Bedford declined the invitation of the government to extend his term, pleading the needs of his family. Parliament farewelled him with a dinner at which he confessed to having been terrified of making a fool of himself as a governor. He left Perth by train on 14 April 1909, boarded the *Charon* at Geraldton and returned to England via Singapore. After living in retirement at Weybridge, Surrey, he died at Walton on 30 January 1913.

J. S. Battye (ed), *Cyclopedia of Western Australia*, 1 (Adel, 1912); *Who Was Who* (Lond), 1897-1915; *The Times*, 1 Feb 1913.

G. C. BOLTON

BEDFORD, GEORGE RANDOLPH (1868-1941), journalist, mining speculator and politician, was born on 27 June 1868 at Camperdown, Sydney, sixth surviving child of Alfred Bedford, miniaturist, and his wife Elizabeth, née Wilcox. His father had migrated to Sydney from Yorkshire about 1859 and, to feed his family, had been forced into house-painting. Educated at Newtown Public School, Randolph at 14 found work as an office-boy with a firm of Sydney solicitors. Two years and several jobs later, he humped his swag across the western plains of New South Wales, earning 6d. a rabbit-skull and carrying copies of Carlyle's *French Revolution*, Shakespeare and the Bible. He spent a year in Hay as a clerk, then in Wagga Wagga joined Edmund Duggan's [q.v.] struggling repertory company and enjoyed 'the merriest and most irresponsible time I ever knew'.

At Albury Bedford read the *Bulletin* for the first time and 'thereby entered a new world'. Diverse jobs included four months as a clerk on a Murray River paddle-steamer. After working on a newspaper at Bourke, he was writing for the *Broken Hill Argus* by 1888 and was captured by the excitement of the mining-boom. He modelled his style on the *Bulletin*'s and began to contribute. He worked briefly on the Adelaide *Advertiser*, then moved to Melbourne where he was employed by the *Age* for about two years. At Fitzroy on 14 February 1889, with the rites of the Free Church of England, he married Mary Henrietta Arrowsmith (d. 1953), a vivacious strong-willed actress. In 1892 he briefly owned the *Toora and Welshpool Pioneer*, a small Gippsland newspaper.

Bedford survived the depression as a freelance journalist and in 1896 in Melbourne he launched his mining and literary journal, the *Clarion*; it was illustrated and part-edited by (Sir) Lionel Lindsay [q.v.] who became Bedford's lifelong friend. A militant Australian nationalist, he advocated republicanism, 'White Australia', vigilance against the Japanese, a parochial form of socialism, and a military alliance with the

United States of America. The journal was supported with advertising from Lionel Robinson and later by the colonial governments in special numbers. The *Clarion*'s notable contributors included A. G. Stephens, Louis Esson, Ambrose and Will Dyson, and Norman and Percy Lindsay [qq.v.]. With the Lindsays and Dysons, Bedford was a founder of the Bohemian Ishmael Club.

Having launched the *Clarion*, Bedford visited the mines at Zeehan and Mount Lyell, Tasmania, and spent a year or more following gold in Western Australia where, through his habit of 'grub-staking' prospectors, he promoted at considerable reward the deep alluvial goldfield at White Feather (Kanowna); he was then at Chillagoe and Mount Garnet in North Queensland off and on for a year. Between visits to mining fields, he was defeated as a Liberal for the Victorian Legislative Assembly seats of Eastern Suburbs in 1897 and Bourke West in 1900. He did not join the Labor Party until after Federation, but he always sympathized with Labor, partly because it was the 'only Australian party'.

In 1901-04 Bedford took his wife and family to England and thence to Italy. His first novel, *True eyes and the whirlwind*, was published in London in 1903, and another, *The snare of strength*, appeared in 1905; both were largely autobiographical. His *Bulletin* travel-notes were later published as *Explorations in civilization* (1914). After returning to Australia, Bedford visited New Guinea in July 1905 and severely criticized the delays in dealing with applications for land; after the findings of the 1906-07 royal commission on Papua, he took up 10 000 acres (4000 ha) at Milne Bay in 1908, but did not develop it. Meanwhile in 1906 he had been involved in mining syndicates on the Seymour and Leichhardt rivers, and near Cloncurry, in North Queensland. Later that year, after failing to get Protectionist endorsement, he unsuccessfully contested Cook for Labor in the House of Representatives elections.

An incurable optimist, 'Randolph the Reckless' dreamt up a 'fourteen-million acre' cattle scheme in the Northern Territory but, as he himself said, 'no man could have had better chances or messed them up more by attempting out of mere exuberance of strength to do too much'. He got into financial difficulties: the *Clarion* failed in 1909 and in 1914 he had trouble paying the fees due on his remaining Northern Territory grazing licences. Meanwhile, between visits to New Guinea and the Solomon Islands, China, Japan, Europe and the United States of America, he wrote his play, *White Australia, or the empty north*, staged in Melbourne in 1909; he contributed articles in

1910-12 to the *Lone Hand* on mining, shipping and the potentialities of the Mount Kosciusko area, and also wrote short stories for the *Bulletin* and another novel.

By 1912 Bedford and his wife had separated, and about 1915 he settled in Brisbane with Ada Billings, who bore him a daughter. In 1915-16, in the columns of the Brisbane *Worker*, he bitterly opposed conscription. He wrote two more novels and in 1918-22 he spasmodically produced the trade journal, *Australasian Timberman and Ironmaster*.

A friend of E. G. Theodore [q.v.], in 1917 Bedford had been nominated to the Queensland Legislative Council, pledged to its abolition. Next year he resigned to contest the Legislative Assembly seat of Carnarvon, lost, and was reappointed to the council, which was abolished in 1922. He won a by-election for Warrego, the Australian Workers' Union stronghold, in 1923 and held it until 1941; he resigned it in 1937 to contest unsuccessfully the Federal seat of Maranoa, but re-won Warrego. A formidable debater and master of caustic repartee, he was impatient with parliamentary formalities and rebellious against party discipline, so was never elected to cabinet. In 1921 he visited the United States on a publicity campaign for the Queensland government.

Politics did not prevent Bedford speculating in mining; he lost heavily in tin-mining in the Federated Malay States and searching for oil near Roma, Queensland. In 1924, with John Wren [q.v.], he floated the Mount Isa Proprietary Silver-Lead No Liability Co.; its profitable sale for £125 000 was attacked in the Queensland parliament in 1929. In 1931 he was one of the first at the Cracow goldfield; as a director of the Golden Mile Cracow (No Liability) Co., he unsuccessfully sued the Brisbane *Telegraph* for £20 000 damages for publishing a letter criticizing the administration of the company, and on appeal was awarded negligible damages. In 1935 he was saddened by the death of his daughter Vera, a noted opera-singer and composer.

Resonant if sometimes rough in voice, Bedford broadcast intermittently in the 1930s, and in 1939-41 made three series of talks for the Australian Broadcasting Commission. A prolific author, he also penned verse, sometimes reputedly published under the pseudonym 'Martin Luther', and words for patriotic songs. He wrote at a furious pace, mostly without pause or reflection, and usually refused to revise his work; he excelled as a descriptive writer and was never dull. One of his short stories, 'Fourteen fathoms by Quetta Rock', was republished in standard anthologies. His writings reflect his adventurous spirit, romantic idealism and passionate love of Australia. With

piercing blue eyes, hawk-nose and blond moustache, Bedford 'seldom removed his great slouch hat' because of his bald head. Warm-hearted and generous to a fault, he had an enormous sense of humour and was reputed to be able to out-drink any man in Queensland. To Vance Palmer [q.v.] 'there was no finer raconteur', but on occasions he could be coarse and devastatingly rude.

Bedford died on 7 July 1941 of coronary thrombosis in the Lister (later the Holy Spirit) Hospital, Brisbane, which he had planned, built and owned. He was survived by his wife, three sons and two daughters, and by Ada Bedford and their daughter. His estate was insolvent, with its largest debt of nearly £2000 owing to John Wren. Bedford's autobiography, *Naught to thirty-three*, was published posthumously in 1944.

G. Blainey, *Mines in the spinifex* (Syd, 1960); C. Lack (ed), *Three decades of Queensland political history, 1929-1960* (Brisb, 1962); N. Lindsay, *Bohemians of the Bulletin* (Syd, 1965); L. A. Lindsay, *Comedy of life* (Syd, 1967); R. Lindsay, *Model wife* (Syd, 1967); *Overland*, no 26, 1963; *Bulletin*, 12 Feb 1894, 4 Jan 1912; *Australasian*, 30 Oct 1920; *SMH*, 4 June 1924, 26 Oct 1929, 18 Nov 1933, 9 Feb, 28 July 1934, 6 Feb, 30, 31 May 1935; Bedford papers (Oxley Lib, Brisb); Deakin papers (NL); A1 and A3 series lists (AAO, Canb).

RODNEY G. BOLAND

BEDFORD, ROBERT; *see* BUDDICOM

BEE, JAMES (1864-1941), headmaster, was born on 23 December 1864 at Oamaru, New Zealand, son of James Bee, clerk, and his wife Marion Dickson, née Guthrie, both Scottish-born. He was educated at Oamaru Grammar School where he became a pupil-teacher in 1878. In 1884 he won an exhibition and attended the University of Otago (B.A., N.Z., 1887; M.A., 1888) and Dunedin Training College where he gained a teacher's certificate in 1887. A good athlete, he played Rugby for a New Zealand team against New South Wales in 1884 and 1886. On 8 January 1890 at Hoopers Inlet near Dunedin, he married Wilhelmina Young, who was to provide strong encouragement throughout his career. He was senior mathematics master at Wellington College for eighteen years and continued his studies at Victoria University College (B.Sc., N.Z., 1902; M.Sc., 1905).

In January 1907 Bee was appointed headmaster of the Presbyterian Ladies' College, Melbourne. An innovator, he soon introduced physics and chemistry into the curriculum and had a properly equipped laboratory built; this led to a generation of medical and scientific women. As the enrolment grew, he added commercial and domestic science courses and encouraged sport. A musician as well as a fine sportsman, Bee proved himself a 'first-rate teacher and born educator, as interested in the welfare of the least as of the most gifted girls and vividly aware that book-learning is only a part of what there is to be learnt at school'. An elder of the Cairns Memorial Presbyterian Church, he was a councillor of the Association of Secondary Teachers of Victoria and a member of the Schools Board of the University of Melbourne.

In July 1913 Bee was appointed principal of Scots College, Sydney, in succession to Rev. A. A. Aspinall [q.v.]. Enrolment had fallen very low, while the reorganization of New South Wales education in 1910-12 presented the prospective challenge of an expanding state high school system. He was supported by Rev. R. G. MacIntyre [q.v.], chairman of the college council, who foresaw the possibilities arising from the development of Sydney's eastern suburbs. Under their guidance a new class-room block was built, boarding accommodation increased and land bought for playing fields. The college benefited from the growing demand for secondary education and the increased support for such schools during and after World War I. Enrolment grew from 54 pupils in 1914 to 305 in 1924.

Bee espoused an educational philosophy based on the English public school tradition adapted to the Australian environment. He encouraged the teaching of science and mathematics and emphasized character-building through team sport (he acted as his own sportsmaster), development of school spirit and loyalty to the Empire. He was a firm disciplinarian and, while generally popular, somewhat distant in his relations with staff and pupils. After MacIntyre retired in 1920, Bee lost his close relationship with Scots College Council. The school continued to expand in the 1920s but he resented council intrusion into college affairs; with the onset of the Depression his last years as principal were rather difficult, but in 1932 he was president of the Headmasters' Association of Great Public Schools of New South Wales. He had been an elder of the Woollahra Presbyterian Church from 1921.

Bee retired in 1934 and died of coronary occlusion at his home at Rose Bay on 30 October 1941; he was cremated. He was survived by his wife, one of their twin sons and three daughters; the other son had been killed in action in World War I. His estate was valued for probate at £2558. As a young man he had worn a magnificent flamboyant moustache, 'a strangely dashing ornament for the face of a serious, gentle and rather shy man'.

J. C. Beaglehole, *Victoria University College* (Well, 1949); M. O. Reid, *The ladies came to stay* (Melb, 1960); K. Fitzpatrick, *PLC Melbourne* (Melb, 1975); *Scotsman*, June 1914, Feb 1924, Feb 1929, Nov 1934; 'The Scot we know', *Scottish A'sian*, Sept 1919; *Wellingtonian*, Dec 1941; C. Turney, 'The advent and adaptation of the Arnold Public School tradition in New South Wales', *Aust J of Education*, 10 (1966), 11 (1967); M. R. L. Bee at Scots (Scots College Archives, Syd); family information.   G. E. SHERINGTON

BEEBY, SIR GEORGE STEPHENSON (1869-1942), politician, judge and playwright, was born on 23 May 1869 at Alexandria, Sydney, second son of English-born Edward Augustus Beeby, book-keeper, and his wife Isabel, née Thompson. Educated at Crown Street Public School, on 3 July 1884 he became a pupil-teacher at Macdonaldtown (Erskineville) Public School under Peter Board [q.v.], but because of defective eyesight he soon left and drifted into several jobs – in a bulk iron store, as a debt-collector, as a book-keeper and stenographer in the law firm of Creagh & Williams, and as an accountant. In 1890 he attended Henry George's [q.v.4] meetings and became a single taxer; next year he was secretary of the first Labor Electoral League formed at Newtown and helped in the return of two local Labor candidates at the general election. In 1892 he became editor and manager of the *Bowral Free Press* and on 9 March married Helena Maria West at Camperdown Church of Christ.

Unemployed by December, Beeby returned to Sydney; early in 1893 he went to Hillgrove and organized Labor in the New England district. He had become one of the chief propagandists of the new Labor Party, stressing the need for parliamentary solidarity. In August he represented the Hillgrove league at a meeting in Sydney, and argued for a conference 'representative of all Labor leagues, trade unions and democratic political organizations'; but the radical groups were excluded from the resulting Labor unity conference held in November. By then he had left the single taxers – who labelled him 'bumptious Beeby' while he referred to their 'idiotic effusions' – and had joined the Australian Socialist League. He gave significant support to J. C. Watson [q.v.], who led the campaign for Labor solidarity based on a party pledge and the sovereignty of annual conferences. Beeby became his deputy, ably defending the executive, mainly against George Black [q.v.]. He ran for Labor at

Armidale in the 1894 elections and, as editor-proprietor, began the *New England Democrat* with £50 capital and one compositor. He fought a long and active campaign, consolidating his knowledge of rural problems, but lost narrowly. Joined by W. A. Holman [q.v.], he moved his newspaper to Hillgrove, but it soon failed and they returned to Sydney broke. Next year with Watson, Holman and others he was charged with conspiring to defraud in connexion with the short-lived Labor paper, the *Daily Post*, but he was cleared.

Beeby survived the mid-1890s depression by intermittent clerical work and freelancing. His difficulties increased with the birth of three children. He obtained work at 35s. a week with the legal firm of Lawrence & Rich and studied law. In 1901 he was with M. J. Brown and on 16 November was admitted as a solicitor, afterwards founding the firm of Beeby & Moffatt, which specialized in industrial matters. He had remained active in the Labor Party and in 1904 ran for Leichhardt, but lost. In 1907 he failed at a by-election in Blayney, a country seat, but won it at the August general election. He soon ranked third behind J. S. T. McGowen [q.v.] and Holman as a leading Labor parliamentarian. His industrial expertise helped him, with Holman, to obtain an amendment to (Sir) Charles Wade's [q.v.] 1908 Industrial Disputes Act to make the trade or industrial union an effective unit in the arbitration system. He was admitted to the Bar in 1911.

Beeby had developed as a vigorous speaker, not brilliant but effective and well prepared. Of medium height, he wore trim spectacles and waxed and curled his spruce moustache. He was almost painfully aloof, upright and formal; he preferred to be addressed as 'Beeby', and in 1911 was still writing to his old comrade as 'Dear Watson'. But a subtle sense of humour had gradually modified his youthful earnestness as his reading extended to Oscar Wilde and G. B. Shaw. He was a great theatre-goer and a bad chess-player.

Beeby became minister of public instruction and for labour and industry in the first Labor government in 1910. He at once co-operated with Board in having regulations approved under which public high schools were to be established and conducted; he also encouraged Board in his plans for continuation schools. On 11 September 1911 he was transferred from public instruction to the lands portfolio: the objective of his Land Act next year was to assist settlers with little capital to make a living. But most of his time and energy were devoted to new labour legislation, resulting in the Industrial Arbitration Act, 1912. On balance the Act stressed the need for social harmony rather than the interests of employees; it set up a new system of conciliation; it removed imprisonment as a penalty, but tightened up the collection of fines, and involved unions in the conduct of their members, with a maximum penalty of £1000. It purported to 'repress' rather than 'prohibit' lock-outs and strikes, but prosecutions against strikers continued to increase. Beeby's adherence to Labor was seen to be sapped at the very time he was chafing at the party's direction to its members to support the transfer of certain State powers, including labour, to the Commonwealth.

Beeby was disillusioned with the form political parties had taken; and argued that the Labor Party had developed a conservatism of its own. He wanted more freedom of choice for voters and more independence for candidates. He was not a States righter but sought a complete review of the Federal Constitution to vest 'in the central Parliament . . . all functions, with power to allocate duties to State Legislatures'. His persistent radicalism showed in the demand 'either for the abolition of the Senate or equality of franchise in [its] election'. On 9 December 1912 he resigned from parliament and the Labor Party. Rumours that Holman and others would join him in a 'Centre Party' were not substantiated. He regained his seat on 23 January 1913 after a bitter campaign. At Armidale in March he proposed the formation of a 'National Progressive Party', and in July began negotiations with the Farmers and Settlers' Association. At the general election in December he ran thirteen candidates, but all lost — including himself at Waverley, to the Labor man. He renewed his discussions with the F.A.S.A. in July 1915 and the Progressive Party was founded with Beeby as leader; it proposed preferential voting, extension of Federal powers and the formation of new States. In February 1916 a pact was reached with the Liberal Party to combine against the Labor Party.

The conscription crisis of that year split the labour movement and in November Holman reformed his government as a National ministry. Although Beeby had grown apart from the premier, he joined the new cabinet as minister of labour and industry with a seat in the Legislative Council; at the 1917 general election he won Wagga Wagga in the assembly. He soon examined the need for a review of industrial law; he denounced 'the revolutionary doctrines preached by some militant union leaders' and reaffirmed his belief in arbitration. Next year he amended the Industrial Arbitration Act declaring certain strikes illegal and setting up a Board of Trade with power to declare a living wage; overall, according to H. V.

Evatt, the Act 'would make any *effective* strike punishable'. While piloting the arbitration amendment bill through the assembly in February, Beeby threatened to resign over the terms of the government contract with H. Teasdale Smith [q.v.] & Co., but Holman placated him.

Beeby's leadership of the Progressive Party was questioned in October prior to his trip to the United States of America and Britain in December: the F.A.S.A. wanted to make it more of a country party and his urban style now grated with farmers. He returned on 9 July 1919 and soon resigned his portfolio. The *Sydney Morning Herald* said he had resigned three times from two cabinets; but his political base seemed insecure, and he had long been disgruntled with Holman; specifically he objected to four administrative acts of the government, especially to a contract negotiated by W. C. Grahame [q.v.], minister for agriculture, for the sale of wheat without public tenders.

In August Beeby strongly supported J. Storey [q.v.], leader of the Labor Party, in a demand for a second inquiry, and widened the attack on Holman to include alleged dubious dealings with H. D. McIntosh [q.v.]. A further royal commission was inconclusive, but Beeby's charges and his campaign embarrassed the government in the March 1920 elections. Labor won, Holman lost his seat and Beeby was returned for Murray, but W. E. Wearne [q.v.] defeated him for the leadership of the Progressives in April. On 9 August Premier Storey announced Beeby's appointment as a judge of the Industrial Court of Arbitration and president of the Board of Trade, which the government intended to administer new legislation on profiteering and price control. In September he was appointed a royal commissioner to inquire into the effects of a proposed decrease from 48 to 44 hours per week in the iron and building trades; his report supported the reduction.

In 1912 *Melbourne Punch* had predicted that 'a judgeship is [Beeby's] real objective'. He also aspired to be a playwright and over the years had recorded details of his wide experiences, which he now began to put into dramatic form. In 1923 he published *Concerning ordinary people*, containing four long and two short plays, ranging from tragedy to farce. They all feature dialogue rather than action, argument rather than plot; but they engage attention with their warm, human understanding. Beeby's characters tend to be garrulous silhouettes, but their humanity glows through his respect for them. His debt to Shaw is clear, especially in 'Potter and clay', 'a comedietta in two episodes'. His intimacy with the law and industrial relations enabled him to present a compelling

court-room scene in 'Point o'view', and authentic portrayals of men on strike. In a speech from the stage on 11 July 1925 he explained that the play's central idea was to stress the need for tolerance and mutual respect in the settlement of strikes. He supported 'little theatres' and sought municipal and state aid for them. He was a founder of the Players' Club, which produced several of his works, including *Merely Margaret* on 10 September 1927.

Beeby kept his sense of humour apart from his public life. But it emerged clearly in his comedies and farces: in 'The banner'—in which the author draws on his country newspaper experiences—Golly, a remittance man, reveals that 'Boondi has five hotels, three general stores, two blacksmiths, three churches, a dancing academy, a philharmonic society, a Band of Hope, and five poker schools. What more can civilization offer?' This play is the basis of 'The lost Plantagenet' (Golly), serialized in the *Australasian* early in 1928. *In quest of Pan* (1924), a vacation fantasy, convincingly satirized in verse certain contributors to *Vision* and *Poetry in Australia*, and uncovered a bawdy streak in Beeby:

> Above the waist
> Let them be chaste
> Most ornately descriptive.
> But lower down,
> To save a frown
> Use phrases more elusive.

He also wrote several short stories and a light novel, *A loaded legacy* (1930).

In 1920-22 Beeby complemented on the bench much of the industrial legislation of the Storey-Dooley [q.v.] Labor governments. On 1 January 1921 he became the judge of the Profiteering Prevention Court, and next month he sat as a Special Court in connexion with the Eight Hours (Amendment) Act 1920. His decisions lent support for a general 44-hour week and helped to stabilize prices. But, with the (Sir George) Fuller [q.v.] government in 1922-25, he reverted to routine Industrial Court work. In 1926 the J. T. Lang [q.v.] Labor ministry reformed the arbitration system, abolishing the Board of Trade and establishing an Industrial Commission to replace the court: A. B. Piddington [q.v.] was made industrial commissioner and Beeby took over District Court and sessions work. The same year the Commonwealth Court of Conciliation and Arbitration was reconstituted with full judicial powers and he was appointed to it on 2 August. By December he had clashed with the Waterside Workers' Federation, and in March 1927 he suspended the hearing of a case involving it. In November, concerned about attacks on the 44-hour week, he sought advice from H. B. Higgins [q.v.]

about the 'serious danger of the [Commonwealth] court being used to defeat State Labor legislation'; he asked 'Can the C'wealth without power to directly legislate on hours of employment give to [its court] power to legislate on such a question?'

In July 1928 Beeby broke his leg in a Melbourne street and did not return to the bench until December 1929. By then the effects of the Depression were being felt and in the coalminers' case next February he asked, 'Will not the whole of Australian profits, prices, values, and probably wages have to come down to a lower plane?' Again his notion of social harmony jarred with the labour movement. In September 1931 the Scullin [q.v.] Federal government appointed him as a royal commissioner to inquire into the prosecution of J. Johnson in 1928; he reported that no miscarriage of justice had occurred. He visited England in 1936 on six months leave. On his return his popularity with trade unionists continued to decline and, as president of a coal-mining conference, he was criticized by R. James, M.H.R., in 1938. But he was made chief judge of the Commonwealth Arbitration Court in March next year, and in June was appointed K.B.E. Seriously ill, he retired in 1941. On 18 July 1942 he died at Killara, Sydney, of cerebrovascular disease and was cremated with Anglican rites; his wife, a son and three daughters survived him.

Unlike Holman and W. M. Hughes [q.v.] before their defections, Beeby had not achieved the highest parliamentary office through the Labor Party, though he knew in 1912 when he seceded that the premiership was within his grasp. By then he understood the peculiar outlook and needs of country people and realized that a significant number of them, however progressive, could not identify with city people, especially trade unionists: concurrently, he had come to see that 'All civilized countries are searching for a way' to foster agreement between labour and capital. He remained a radical, but he saw the Labor Party as constricting and conservative, with an alien and nihilistic element adhering to it in 1916. He proved a notable judge, often in conflict with militant unions, but ensuring the growth of the whole arbitration system on a socially harmonious base. At the same time he emerged as a successful author and playwright, demanding attention for the authenticity of his characters and situations.

His daughter DORIS ISABEL (1894-1948) was born on 30 July 1894 at Stanmore. She was educated at Sydney Church of England Grammar School for Girls and at the University of Sydney as an unmatriculated arts student. In September 1920 she became her father's associate and moved with him to the Commonwealth Arbitration Court in 1926. In 1931 she was the secretary of his Johnson royal commission.

Doris Beeby went to London in March 1939 and joined the Spanish Relief Movement, which helped refugees from the civil war. She joined the Communist Party of Great Britain, and on her return to Sydney next year joined the Australian Communist Party. In 1942-45 she was an organizer for the Sheetmetal Workers' Union and sought higher wages for women through the Women's Employment Board. For the *Tribune* and the *Australian Women's Digest* she wrote about women's wage-gains and their growing role in trade unions during World War II. After a long illness she died of cancer at Castlecrag on 17 October 1948 and was cremated.

H. V. Evatt, *Australian labour leader* (Syd, 1942); U. Ellis, *The Country Party* (Melb, 1958); B. Nairn, *Civilising capitalism* (Canb, 1973); G. S. Harman, 'G. S. Beeby and the first Labor electoral battle in Armidale', *Labour History Bulletin* (Canb), 1 (1962), no 3; A. Landa, 'The State industrial system', *NSW Industrial Gazette*, 109 (1962), no 3, supp; 'George S. Beeby and the new party', *Lone Hand*, 1 Apr 1913; *T&CJ*, 16 Jan 1907; *Punch* (Melb), 19 Dec 1912, 6 Sept 1917; *SMH*, 24 Jan 1913, 20 July 1942; *Table Talk*, 26 Jan 1928; *Smith's Weekly* (Syd), 10 Aug 1940; Kate Baker papers (NL); G. S. Beeby letters (LaTL); H. E. Boote papers (NL); Carruthers correspondence (ML); J. C. Watson papers (NL).   BEDE NAIRN

BEGGS, THEODORE (1859-1940), ROBERT GOTTLIEB (1861-1939) and HUGH NORMAN (1863-1943), pastoralists and sheep-breeders, were sons of Francis Beggs and his wife Maria Lucinda, née White. Born at Malahide, Ireland, in 1812, Francis Beggs entered Trinity College, Dublin, in 1828 and later farmed his father's Malahide estate. Soon after his marriage in July 1849 he migrated to Port Phillip with his wife, brother George and sister Sophia, arriving in Geelong next March. He purchased the rights to Gnarkeet, near Lismore, and lived there until 1859 when he became partner to George in Mount Cole, or Eurambeen, near Beaufort; as G. and F. Beggs they built up a fine merino stud flock.

Theodore, seventh child of Francis, was born at Geelong on 17 August 1859. He was educated by a tutor, and on his father's death in 1880 became manager and a trustee of the Eurambeen estate. Three years later he and his brothers Robert and Hugh joined in a pastoral partnership that leased and purchased several large properties in the district. When the partnership was dissolved by mutual consent in 1913, Theodore became sole owner of Eurambeen.

For some thirty years Beggs was a councillor of Ripon Shire and was twice president. From 1910 until his retirement in 1928 he was member for Nelson Province in the Legislative Council. He voted there to keep large properties intact and led local opposition to the acquisition of Trawalla estate for soldier settlement in 1919, causing his critics to allege that he thought 'more of a bit of dirt than he thinks of a man'. He was a director of the Ballarat Trustees, Executors & Agency Co. Ltd, a member of the Australian Sheepbreeders' Association, Victorian delegate to the Pastoralists' Federal Council in 1915 and was widely known as a judge of merino sheep. He was a member of the Melbourne, Australian and Ballarat clubs. In 1906 Theodore was described as 'a thoughtful man, not easy to best in argument, and though most amiable in disposition, a "sticker" in conference'. On 3 December 1918 he married Agnes Jane Walpole. He died on 2 April 1940 at Eurambeen and was buried there in the family cemetery, survived by his wife and their four daughters.

Robert Gottlieb was born at Eurambeen on 21 September 1861 and was also educated privately. He worked on the property until 1882 when he became a partner with his brother Francis (1850-1921). In December 1882 he married Maria, daughter of A. B. Balcombe [q.v.3], who died next year giving birth to a son. He then joined Theodore and Hugh, managing their joint property, Hopkins Hill, at Chatsworth, until 1913 when he took it over himself together with part of Nareeb Nareeb, at Glenthompson, which the partners had bought in 1909. In 1920 he bought some of Mawallok, near Beaufort, which he renamed Buln Gherin. Apart from sheep-breeding his great interest was the growing of trees, especially native species which he raised from seed. Like his brother Hugh, he was a councillor for the Leigh and Mount Rouse shires. In September 1905 he had married Amy, daughter of Colonel P. R. Ricardo [q.v.]. She became State president for three years of the Country Women's Association and, survived her husband, together with their three sons and two daughters and his son by his first marriage, when he died on 12 July 1939. His estate was sworn for probate at £30 377.

Hugh Norman was born at Eurambeen on 6 June 1863. He was educated at Wesley College, Melbourne, and spent three years in a bank before joining Theodore and Robert on the land. He managed their property, Swanwater, near St Arnaud, until 1909 and then Nareeb Nareeb until 1913, when he purchased 12 800 acres (4856 ha) of that property, including the homestead. He was for many years an executive member, and later trustee, of the Graziers' Association of Victoria, and was president of the Australian Sheepbreeders' Association. Hugh, like his brothers, was a practical and efficient sheepman; he too publicly expressed alarm in 1919 at what he termed the 'indiscriminate resumption of land' for closer settlement. In 1897 he had married Mary Catherine Reeves, daughter of Henry Sandford Palmer, former high sheriff for County Tipperary, Ireland: they had four sons and a daughter. He died at Hamilton on 29 November 1943, survived by his wife and a son and a daughter. Both he and Robert were buried at Eurambeen. His estate was sworn for probate at £96 577.

A. Henderson (ed), *Early pioneer families of Victoria and Riverina* (Melb, 1936); H. Anderson, *The flowers of the field* (Melb, 1969); *Pastoral Review*, July 1906, Mar 1915, Sept 1929, Aug 1939, Apr 1940, Dec 1943; *Argus*, 3 Apr 1940; Trawalla Soldier Settlement papers (held by Shire of Ripon, Beaufort); station records (held by Mrs T. Beggs, Eurambeen, Beaufort, Vic).   HUGH ANDERSON

BEHAN, SIR JOHN CLIFFORD VALENTINE (1881-1957), educationist, was born on 8 May 1881 at Footscray, Victoria, ninth child of William Behan, clerk, storekeeper and son of a schoolteacher, and his wife Phoebe Hannah, née Gundry. He was educated at Caulfield Grammar School, where he was dux in 1895, and at University High School in 1896. Winning a scholarship to the University of Melbourne, he enrolled in Trinity College. By 1904 he had won Wyselaskie [q.v.6] and Hastie scholarships, and had graduated B.A., with first-class honours in logic and philosophy and in history and political economy; and also gained an LL.B. with first-class honours, winning the Supreme Court Prize. Later that year he was chosen to be Victoria's first Rhodes Scholar; his selection aroused considerable criticism, since to many his qualifications seemed too exclusively intellectual.

At Oxford he read law at Hertford College. In 1906 he took first-class honours in both his B.A. in jurisprudence and his B.C.L. — uniquely in the same year — and won both the Vinerian and Eldon law scholarships; he also gained first-class honours at the Middle Temple in his Bar finals, with more prizes which brought the total value of his awards to £3000. In 1907 he returned to Victoria to marry, on 30 July at Brighton, Violet Greta Caldwell. He was appointed lecturer in law at University College, Oxford, where two years later he won the Stowell Civil Law Fellowship; in 1914 he was appointed dean. In 1915-17 he served in the ministries of munitions, food, and national service, before returning to Melbourne to succeed Dr A.

Leeper [q.v.] as warden of Trinity College.

Behan's ambition was to realize the aim stated by the college founders that Trinity should be an incorporated body, governed on the Oxford model by a provost and fellows, instead of by an external council. He perceived that, to achieve this, the college finances must be put in order and endowments for scholarships and stipends procured. Taking over in April 1918, he found the buildings dilapidated and the college in debt; he told the council that £20 000 would have to be raised at once and £100 000 within ten years. His strenuous efforts raised £60 000 by the end of 1919 and a further £30 000 by 1925, but later he was handicapped by a quarrel with an important council-member F. P. Brett, who was anxious to reduce Anglican (as opposed to Protestant) and episcopal influence in college affairs, and who finally, in 1931, secured a further gift (of £20 000) conditional on the council removing the rights of all the bishops in Victoria to be *ex officio* members. Behan agreed that such a demand was inadmissable, but the issue had raised such clerical anxieties as to increase opposition to his own proposals for incorporation and internal government. To his intense disappointment, in December 1933 the council adjourned their consideration of this matter *sine die*.

The immediate cause of this vote was the open outbreak of a long-simmering dispute between Behan and the college students. On taking office, the warden had faced a body of servicemen, with whom his legal training, Oxford experience, high academic standards and reserved personality made him somewhat unfitted to deal, and he was further handicapped by a tradition of hostility to 'the Warden'. Although in the mid-1920s his difficulties seemed to be waning, trouble increased after 1930 when the students' club consistently opposed all disciplinary measures; then, although Behan had preserved the college buttery in order to encourage 'civilised drinking', in opposition to considerable prohibitionist sentiment, various incidents in 1933 induced him to close it, whereupon the club resolved to 'adopt a policy directed to procuring the removal of the Warden'. Although the council naturally supported dissolution of the club and refusal to allow members of its committee to return to college, the bishops, in deciding to vote to postpone incorporation, minuted that 'in view of recent events, we cannot agree to allow the College to commence a new epoch under the Wardenship of Dr. Behan'.

Despite these set-backs, Behan then commenced a much easier second half of his wardenship. Earlier in 1933 the council had approved the appointment of a dean, and the tutorial staff was strengthened. Removed from day to day contact with the students, Behan was able to assume the more benign image which soon earned him respect and affection. Tall and spare, always immaculately dressed, he introduced many of his students to the elegance and richness of their mother tongue, to good music (especially Beethoven) in days when this was rare, and set before them a formidable example of good manners, self-discipline and singleness of purpose. A magnificent stone building was opened and named after him; it was to be the first instalment of a master-plan adopted in 1920, but this proved too ambitious and had to be abandoned.

In February 1946 Behan made another attempt to achieve internal self-government, but failed again; however, when he resigned in June, he left a college immeasurably strengthened. He had, almost unaided, raised £140 000 in endowments. He had put its trusts in order, and procured the first Victorian Act (since often copied) allowing the pooling of trust funds for investments. He had arranged with the Royal Australian Air Force for the part-occupation of the university colleges in 1942-45, which relieved their wartime financial problems, and in 1943-44 he conducted, as in 1919, a successful appeal for funds for post-war renovations. He had made Trinity the nearest in Australia to the ideal of an Oxford or Cambridge college; and more than any other individual, he succeeded in preserving for this type of institution an important place in university development.

His achievements had been at the cost of his scholastic work, though he published in 1924 *The use of land as affected by covenants* . . . (London), which earned him the Melbourne degree of LL.D.; in 1921-52 he was secretary to the Rhodes Trust in Australia, and succeeded in improving the work of its selection committees. He retired to Olinda where he was an active churchwarden and completed a substantial manuscript on the early history of the college. In 1949 he was knighted. He died without issue on 30 September 1957 at Olinda.

J. Grant, *Perspective of a century* (Melb, 1972); *The Times*, 8 Oct 1957; Archives of Rhodes Trust in Aust (Univ Melb); Trinity College Archives (Melb).

A. G. L. SHAW

BEIRNE, THOMAS CHARLES (1860-1949), retailer, was born on 9 July 1860 at Ballymacurly, Roscommon, Ireland, son of John Beirne, farmer, and his wife Catherine, née Callaghan. After scanty education at a near-by Franciscan monastery, then at a National school where he excelled at mathematics, he was apprenticed to his cousin Dominick Owens, a draper in Strokestown; in 1880 he went to Gallagher Bros of Ballina. In March 1881 he joined M. D. Piggott of Tuam, County Galway, who befriended him and persuaded him to migrate to Australia rather than to the United States of America. Beirne sailed for Melbourne on the *Lusitania*, arriving in February 1884; 'There was no-one to welcome me' he recorded; 'I was a complete stranger in a strange land'. He was quickly employed by Eyre & Sheppard of Carlton, then by Foy [q.v.4] & (William) Gibson [q.v.].

Piggott, who had also migrated, invited Beirne to partnership in Brisbane, and in February 1886 Piggott & Beirne opened a drapery store in Stanley Street, South Brisbane, then a smart shopping area. Beirne married Ann Kavanagh on 11 April 1887 in St Stephen's Cathedral. Of their ten children, only five daughters survived infancy.

After a disastrous fire in the store in January 1889 and dissolution of the partnership in August 1891, Beirne opened a new store in the then unfashionable Fortitude Valley; he was fortunate, for the great flood of 1893 destroyed South Brisbane as a retail centre. Meanwhile he instituted mail-order arrangements. In 1894 a Scot, James McWhirter, became his manager for one year, then partner for three, eventually opening a rival store across the street. Beirne later reflected that the ensuing competition made the Valley the principal shopping area in Brisbane. He opened a branch at Ipswich in 1892 with his brother Michael as manager, and another at Mackay in 1902.

Beirne avoided possible financial damage from the bank crashes of the 1890s by instituting a direct buying scheme with London in 1896; at home he operated through many small accounts in various towns. In 1898 he became an active member of the Brisbane Traders' Association and was president in 1901. He was trusted by the infant Labor Party; in 1898 he moved the vote of confidence in Frank McDonnell [q.v.], whom he had known in Ireland, and W. G. Higgs [q.v.] as candidates for Fortitude Valley. While visiting Britain in 1905 he was requested by cable to become a member of the Legislative Council; he was appointed on 27 July by the (Sir) Arthur Morgan [q.v.] ministry, and remained a member until the abolition of the council in 1922. He always insisted strongly on his freedom from party ties.

Beirne was universally regarded as a good employer and made several attempts to introduce profit-sharing and staff shareholding schemes, but he was bitterly disap-

pointed at the lack of interest and the petty bickering over status. As a successful businessman with an extensive portfolio of shares, he was a welcome addition to many company boards; the first and most controversial was the Brisbane Tramway Co. which he joined about the time of the 1912 general strike. His public appeal for moderation, in a letter to the *Brisbane Courier*, fell on deaf ears and cooled his relations with the labour movement, but he stayed on the board until the company was bought out by the government. Beirne was also interested in his membership of the Queensland board of the Australian Mutual Provident Society; he was a director in 1916-36, deputy chairman for three years and chairman for seven, and was invited to remain a member for two years after the statutory age for retirement. He was also on the board of the Queensland Trustees, the Atlas Assurance Co. and the British Australian Cotton Association.

Beirne was elected to the Council of the University of Queensland in 1927 and was warden of the university from 1928 until his resignation in 1941. He enjoyed these associations and in 1935, the university's silver jubilee year, he was persuaded to donate £20 000 to establish the T. C. Beirne School of Law rather than bequeath the £10 000 which he had originally intended.

A devout Roman Catholic, he was a close friend and confidant of Archbishop James Duhig [q.v.]. In July 1929 he was awarded a papal knighthood of the Order of St Gregory by Pius XI in recognition of his work for the Church, particularly towards the building of the new Holy Name Cathedral. Throughout his life Beirne helped the Pius XII Regional Seminary, Banyo, and the Mater Misericordiae Hospital, and was also a foundation benefactor of Duchesne College at the university. Accused by an Orange newspaper of sectarianism in 1917, he won £5000 in defamation proceedings. In evidence, he announced that he and his family had voted for conscription.

Beirne's pastimes were mainly connected with his family life and his home, Glengariff, at Hendra, with its beautiful grounds, tennis and croquet courts. He was fond of picnics and Sunday tennis and croquet. At his death Glengariff was given to the Church as a home for the newly appointed coadjutor archbishop.

Beirne retained an active interest in the store until shortly before his death on 21 April 1949. He was buried in Nudgee cemetery. His estate was sworn for probate at £1 251 574 in Queensland and £19 225 in New South Wales, with other assets recorded in Victoria, South Australia, Western Australia and Canada; he was one of the few millionaires in Australia. His estate was left to his family, apart from minor bequests to Catholic educational institutions and some charities.

Newspaper Cartoonists' Assn of Qld, *Queenslanders as we see 'em* (Brisb, 1916); E. Macrossan, *The life story of Thomas Charles Beirne* (Brisb, 1947); Commercial Publishing Co. of Sydney, Ltd, *Annual Review of Queensland*, 1 (1902), no 1; *Brisbane Courier*, 31 May-2 June 1917; *Catholic Advocate*, 30 May, 11 July 1929; *Courier Mail*, 23 Apr 1935, 21 Aug 1947, 22, 23 Apr 1949; *Truth* (Brisb), 24 Apr 1949; *Catholic Leader*, 28 Apr 1949; C. Douglas, And long go it was (Oxley Lib, Brisb); Supreme Court (Qld), file W9/44/49 (QA).

CAROLYN NOLAN

BEJAH, DERVISH (1862?-1957), cameldriver, was born in Baluchistan, India (now Pakistan), son of Dervish Bejah. He served in the Indian Army at Kandahar and Karachi under Lord Roberts and eventually attained the rank of sergeant. Bejah arrived by sailing-ship at Fremantle, Western Australia, about 1890.

In 1896 Lawrence Wells [q.v.], of the South Australian Survey Department, was appointed to lead the Calvert [q.v.] Scientific Exploring Expedition through the central deserts of Western Australia from Mullewa to Derby. Perhaps aware of prejudice against 'Afghans', Wells tried to engage a white camel-man. Fortunately, he failed. In May he left Adelaide by sea, with Bejah as the 'Afghan' in charge of camels. Wells's journal records his growing reliance upon Bejah in a cumulation of hardship and danger. The expedition of seven men and twenty camels formed a depot eighteen days east-north-east of Lake Way. From there Wells set out on a 'flying trip' with Bejah, G. L. Jones and seven camels. Twelve days later he named Bejah Hill. It was Bejah who discovered and tried to destroy poison bush; who was ever ready to gather 'hundredweights' of herbage for camels tethered in poison country; who shepherded them on scanty feed till midnight, tethered them and refused breakfast because his charges had none; who ran to spelled camels 'talking to and playing with them in a most excited manner'.

When the expedition continued northward, with Charles Wells and Jones on a separate line to the west, Lawrence Wells depended heavily on Bejah. They rode or walked together, scouting for water in terrible country, suffering together, almost perishing, rescuing each other. Wells recorded how, riding by night on dying camels, he entrusted the lead to Bejah, with instructions to steer by a star, while he himself slept in his saddle.

Their close attachment, sketched in Douglas Stewart's poem 'Afghan', continued. They found the bodies of Charles Wells and Jones on 27 May 1897. The journal shows Bejah as a skilful and devoted camel-man, a bushman equal to all emergencies, and a man of loyalty, courage, enterprise and endurance. The expedition ended in June. Bejah was later given a reception at Government House, Adelaide, and was presented with the expedition's compass, inscribed for him.

He then settled at Hergott Springs (Marree), where in 1902 he bought three sections of land. On 15 December 1909 he married a widow, Amelia Jane Shaw; they had one son, Abdul Jubbar (Jack). On the outskirts of the town the 'Afghans' had a big camp, with thousands of camels and a corrugated iron mosque. Bejah's camels and their loads of wool and stores were well known throughout the far north of South Australia until he retired in the 1930s to grow date palms. In 1939 C. T. Madigan [q.v.] invited him to lead the camels on his journey through the Simpson Desert; he sent his son instead. A devout Moslem, Bejah attributed his long good health to his faith. The Shell Company film, *Back of beyond* (1954), shows him at prayer. A very tall man, in old age he had a splendid full white beard and wore a gold skull-cap beneath a grey silk turban. Predeceased by his wife, Bejah died in the Port Augusta Hospital on 6 May 1957 and was buried in the local cemetery. Obituaries appeared in *The Times* and Australian newspapers.

Journal of the Calvert scientific exploring expedition, 1896-7 (Perth, 1902); C. T. Madigan, *Crossing the dead heart* (Melb, 1946); G. Farwell, *Land of mirage* (Adel, 1960); *PP* (WA), 1901-02, 3 (46); *Mail* (Adel), 28 Mar 1953; *Advertiser* (Adel), 7 May 1957.

VALMAI A. HANKEL

BELL, ALEXANDER FOULIS (1876-1940), businessman, was born on 1 March 1876 at Paisley, Scotland, youngest child of John Bell and his second wife Euphemia, née Foulis. Aged 10 when he migrated to Queensland with his parents, he remained unmistakably Scottish throughout his life. His father set up in Brisbane as a warehouseman and manufacturers' agent, establishing the family home at Hazlewood, South Brisbane, in whose grounds he could indulge an inherited taste for ornithology.

After education at Brisbane Grammar School, Bell joined the local office of Robert Harper [q.v.] & Co., wholesale grocers, becoming manager in 1906. On 26 December 1911 he married Grace Stewart of

Ipswich. Commissioned a lieutenant in the Queensland Rifles in 1903 and promoted to captain in 1911, Bell was prevented by poor eyesight from active service in World War I; as honorary major with the 8th Infantry (Oxley Battalion) he held a senior administrative post at Enoggera Camp in 1916-17.

In 1917 Bell was transferred to Melbourne to manage the firm's head office in Flinders Lane; two years later he became managing director with (Sir) Robert Gibson [q.v.] as chairman. Bell was a member of the Commonwealth Dried Fruits Control Board from its inception in 1925 until September 1939 and was acting chairman for a time in 1930; his assistance was invaluable in creating orderly overseas market procedures for the industry. Bell was also a member of the honorary committee which organized Australian trade publicity in Great Britain. His close friend and business associate S. M. (Viscount) Bruce [q.v.] sent him to the International Economic Conference at Geneva in 1927; in January that year he had been appointed C.M.G. He was a director and vice-chairman of the Union Trustee Co., a director of the Victorian Board of the Australian Mutual Provident Society, and of the National Bank of Australasia from 1932 until February 1934 when he resigned to join the board of the Commonwealth Bank.

Though a member of the Melbourne and Australian clubs and of the Union Club (Sydney), Bell was an essentially private man, completely unostentatious and shunning publicity: he often remarked that 'the only newspaper columns one's name should appear in are the financial columns'. Kindly, with a pawky Glaswegian wit, he was always helpful to those genuinely seeking advice, especially younger people, but did not suffer fools gladly. He loved skilled horsemanship and good paintings, notably those of Frederick McCubbin [q.v.]. His many friends rightly regarded him as an apostle of financial soundness. He believed in paying cash for everything, thus getting the best prices, and in return he expected cash. There was never a penny owing on his balance sheets.

On 5 September 1939 Bell was appointed chairman of the Central Wool Committee, which carried out the wartime disposal of the Australian woolclip under the terms of contract between the Commonwealth government and Great Britain. His 'unremitting personal attention' to the committee's many problems led to severe .overstrain; he died on 14 August 1940 of cerebro-vascular disease and was cremated. He was survived by his wife and his only daughter, whose career as a medical practitioner had given him great satisfaction. His estate was sworn for probate at £41 720.

A'sian Insurance and Banking Record, 21 Aug 1940; Pastoral Review, Sept 1940; Argus, 1 Jan 1927, 2 Feb 1934, 15 Aug 1940; Courier-Mail, 2 Feb 1934; Age, 15 Aug 1940; information from Aust Dried Fruits Control Board (Melb).

ALFRED STIRLING

BELL, BARBARA (1870-1957), Catholic educationist, was born on 26 July 1870 in Dublin, third child of Hamilton Bell, well-known teacher and a member of the Irish National Council of Education, and his wife Bridget, née Funcheon. After education by the Dominican nuns in Dublin and, later, in Belgium, she taught in Holland with the Ursuline nuns. In June 1895 at Cambridge, England, she passed the examination in theory, history and practice of education conducted by the Teachers' Training Syndicate. Shortly afterwards she was offered a position in Egypt; but then Mother Gonzaga Barry [q.v.3] of Loreto Abbey, Ballarat, Victoria, invited her to assist in the training of teachers for the Institute of the Blessed Virgin Mary. Barbara telegraphed her father for advice. His reply was: 'Australia, unquestionably'.

She sailed in November 1895, intending to stay two years. Initially she worked with the Loreto Sisters at Ballarat, and later at Loreto convents elsewhere. In 1899 Bishop Delaney [q.v.] of Hobart invited her to Tasmania; there she worked in the convent schools of the Sisters of Mercy, lecturing, demonstrating teaching methods and advising on school organization. In 1901-04, at the invitation of Archbishop Carr [q.v.] of Melbourne, she provided courses of training for the Sisters of Mercy, the Presentation Sisters and the Faithful Companions of Jesus at several Victorian convents. In December 1905 she accepted an appointment as mistress of studies and method at the new Central Catholic Training College. Under the guidance of the principal Mother Hilda Benson [q.v.] and Barbara Bell, who held her post until 1909, courses were established for a diploma in education and to prepare student-teachers for the registration qualifications of the Council of Public Instruction. Barbara was a member of the board of examiners of the Teachers' Registration Committee, set up under the 1905 Act. She also travelled to New Zealand where she conducted training courses at several convents and visited other teachers' colleges.

It is not known where Barbara Bell lived between 1910 and 1913 and what formal work, if any, she undertook. For a while she cared for her blind brother; early in 1913 after his death, she joined the Religious of the Sacred Heart in Sydney. Later that year she visited her family in Ireland, continuing her noviceship at Roehampton, England. In 1916 she taught in New Zealand at Timaru, where she also lectured on teaching methods for the nuns. Later, at Elizabeth Bay, Sydney, she was in charge of the teacher-training of young nuns. Subsequently, she returned to Timaru, moving in 1935 to Wellington, and in 1947 to Auckland. She died at Remuera on 18 September 1957.

Barbara Bell's life-work in the training of Catholic women teachers was of particular significance. She introduced contemporary developments in the theory and practice of education in her courses, encouraged teachers to keep abreast of new developments, and urged critical adaptation of those ideas which seemed helpful and educative. She insisted upon thorough preparation of lessons and the maintenance of weekly records of work. Firm but always just as a teacher, she was noted for her ability to use varied methods, and to interest children in drama, poetry, music and art.

Her sister Mary Bridget (1874-1946), known as Molly, came to Australia about 1897 at the invitation of Bishop Gallagher of Goulburn, to conduct teacher-training courses at convents in Albury, Wagga, Goulburn, Yass and elsewhere. In February 1903 she joined the Institute of the Blessed Virgin Mary at Loreto Abbey, Ballarat. After her religious profession in June 1905, Mother M. Baptista continued to work in Loreto schools, at first in Victoria and later in Western Australia. Gentle, firm and thorough, she was considered a fine teacher, who took particular interest in younger children. After her retirement she taught music until prevented by ill health. She died in Perth on 3 October 1946.

R. Fogarty, *Catholic education in Australia 1806-1950*, 2 (Melb, 1959); K. D. Kane, *Adventure in faith* (Melb, 1974); *Cambridge Univ Reporter*, 1893-94, 1895-96; *Advocate* (Melb), 23 Dec 1905, 9 Feb 1907; Lettres Annuelles de la Société du Sacré Coeur de Jésus, 3, 11 (1957-59, Religious of the Sacred Heart, Braybrook, Vic); Central Catholic Training College, Papers and correspondence 1906-24 (MDHC Archives, Fitzroy); Institute of the Blessed Virgin Mary Archives (Loreto Abbey, Ballarat).   ANN R. SHORTEN

BELL, BERTRAM CHARLES (1893-1941), airman, grazier and farmer, was born on 5 April 1893 at Coochin Coochin station, Boonah, Queensland, son of James Thomas Marsh Bell [q.v.], pastoralist, and his wife Gertrude Augusta, a daughter of James Norton [q.v.5]. He was educated at Toowoomba Grammar School and later joined his brothers in managing the family properties, Coochin Coochin and Camboon.

When World War I broke out Bell was visiting England and was asked by the Queensland agent-general to take the first 'Queensland' motor ambulance to France. Arriving at Boulogne in September 1914, he served for six months as an ambulance driver with the Red Cross and the Australian Voluntary Hospital, and then took private flying lessons in England. On 2 May 1915 he was commissioned as a probationary flight sub-lieutenant in the Royal Naval Air Service and was posted to No.1 Squadron, R.N.A.S., at Dunkirk in July. He remained there for eighteen months, carrying out reconnaissance and bomb-dropping missions, correcting naval gun fire and, finally, serving as a fighter-pilot flying Nieuport Scouts. Promoted flight lieutenant in April 1916, he was awarded the Distinguished Service Cross for 'conspicuous skill and gallantry' as a pilot of reconnaissance, photographic and fighter aircraft. In February 1917 he transferred to No.3 Squadron, R.N.A.S., then supporting the Royal Flying Corps at Amiens; in two months service he shot down at least six enemy aircraft. Promoted to flight commander in March, he later received the Distinguished Service Order in the field for 'conspicuous bravery and skill in attacking hostile aircraft' during fourteen combat missions; he was also mentioned in dispatches during this period.

From April 1917 until the end of the war Bell commanded No.10 Squadron, R.N.A.S. Flying Sopwith triplanes and later Sopwith B.R. Camels, it served with the Royal Flying Corps at Droglandt, west of Ypres, from May to October 1917, and remained on the Western Front until the Armistice; by then its pilots had accounted for 321 enemy aircraft. The squadron's final task had been to assist the Belgian Army during the Flanders operation. Bell was later awarded the Belgian Croix de Guerre avec Palme. No.10 was redesignated No.210 Squadron on the formation of the Royal Air Force in April 1918, and Bell held the rank of major from that date. He left the R.A.F. in March 1919 after refusing the offer of a permanent commission, and returned home to manage Coochin Coochin.

On 24 April 1926 Bell married Adeline Grace Barnes at St Mark's Anglican Church, Warwick. They made their home at Aroo, a farm on the Coochin estate, which they converted into one of the most modern in Australia, winning several awards for fodder conservation and farm design. The onset of World War II disturbed Bell; he tried to enlist but was told that his contribution to the war effort should be as a farmer. Early in June 1941 he suffered a breakdown and, survived by his wife, a son and a daughter, died at Brisbane on 15 June.

His brother Victor Douglas Bell, O.B.E., was also a distinguished airman. A major in the R.A.F. during World War I, he commanded No.80 Squadron in 1918-19.

H. A. Jones and W. A. Raleigh, *The war in the air* (Oxford, 1922-37); *London Gazette*, 21 Apr, 12 May 1917; *Reveille* (Syd), 1 May 1935; N.S. Pixley, 'The Bells and Coochin Coochin', *JRHSQ*, 8 (1965-69); P. S. Sadler, 'Bertram Charles Bell: a biographical sketch', *Sabretache*, Apr 1977; *Pastoral Review*, 16 July 1941; B. C. Bell papers, including a draft history of 210 Squadron (held by Miss Pamela Bell, Aroo, Boonah, Qld).   P. S. SADLER

BELL, FREDERICK WILLIAM (1875-1954), soldier and colonial administrator, was born on 3 April 1875 in Perth, son of Henry Thomas Bell, clerk, and his wife Alice Agnes, née Watson. Educated at A. D. Letch's preparatory school and at the government school, Perth, he joined the Western Australian Public Service in November 1894 as a cadet in the Department of Customs where he later became a cashier.

On the outbreak of the South African War in October 1899 Bell enlisted as a private in the 1st West Australian (Mounted Infantry) Contingent. He first saw action at Slingersfontein, and later took part in the relief of Johannesburg and of Pretoria and the battles of Diamond Hill and Wittebergen; on 19 July 1900, in a sharp engagement at Palmeitfontein, he was seriously wounded and was invalided to England. He returned to Perth in February 1901, was commissioned lieutenant in the 6th Contingent on 8 March, and re-embarked for South Africa. On 16 May at Brakpan, Transvaal, while his unit was retreating under heavy fire, he went back for a dismounted man and took him up on his horse. The animal fell under the extra weight and Bell, after insisting that his companion take the horse, covered his retreat; for this action he received the Victoria Cross — the first awarded to a Western Australian.

After his discharge in May 1902, Bell joined the Australian section of the coronation escort for King Edward VII. He then settled in Perth but returned to England, joined the colonial service in 1905 and was appointed to British Somaliland as an assistant district officer in April. Made an assistant political officer later that year he held the post until 1910. While in Somaliland he took up big-game hunting and in 1909 narrowly escaped death when he was badly mauled by a lion. He was assistant resident in Nigeria in 1910-12 and from then until the outbreak of World War I was an assistant

district commissioner in Kenya. In 1914 Bell, who had been commissioned in the 4th Reserve Regiment of Cavalry in August 1907, served in France with the Royal Irish Dragoon Guards. He was mentioned in dispatches and promoted captain in October 1915. On his return to England he was made commandant of a rest camp and promoted major; later, in the rank of lieut-colonel, he commanded an embarkation camp at Plymouth. Two of his three brothers were killed in action with the Australian Imperial Force.

After the war Bell returned to the colonial service as a district commissioner in Kenya. In May 1922 in London he married a divorcee Mabel Mackenzie Valentini, née Skinner, and in 1925 went into retirement in England. His wife died in 1944 and on 20 February 1945 he married a widow Brenda Margaret Cracklow, née Illingworth. He revisited Western Australia in 1947. His wife survived him when he died at Bristol on 28 April 1954.

Aust Defence Dept, *Official records of the Australian military contingents to the war in South Africa*, P. L. Murray ed (Melb, 1912); L. Wigmore (ed), *They dared mightily* (Canb, 1963); *PD* (HC GB), 1925, 2506; *Duckboard*, Mar 1968; *The Times*, 23 Apr 1925, 1 May 1954; *West Australian*, 1 May 1947, 30 Apr 1954.   H. J. GIBBNEY

BELL, GEORGE FREDERICK HENRY (1878-1966), artist and teacher, was born on 1 December 1878 at Kew, Victoria, son of George Bell, public servant, and his wife Clara, née Barlow. He was educated at Kew High School and was expected by his father to take law at the University of Melbourne: the prospect held little interest for him. He enrolled instead at the National Gallery school where he studied in 1895-1903 under Bernard Hall, Frederick McCubbin and George Coates [qq.v.]. He also studied violin with Alberto Zelman senior [q.v.6] and junior [q.v.] and played in the Hawthorn Orchestra and in string groups.

In 1903 Bell went to Europe with Hugh Ramsay [q.v.] and in 1904-06 studied in Paris under Jean Paul Laurens and later in London and at St Ives with Philip Connard. He joined the Chelsea Arts Club and in 1908 became a foundation member of the Modern Society of Portrait Painters. Bell visited Italy several times, and exhibited portraits and landscapes in a tonal realist manner in France, Germany, the United States of America and England, eventually being hung in the Royal Academy. During World War I he was a schoolteacher, then worked in munitions. From October 1918 to the end of 1919 he was an official war artist to the 4th Division of the

Australian Imperial Force; he returned to Australia in 1920 to complete his major war painting, 'Dawn at Hamel 4th July 1918' (War Memorial, Canberra).

Bell started teaching in Melbourne and began his long term as critic for the *Sun-News Pictorial* in 1923-50. He continued to paint in a tonal academic realist style, but became increasingly uneasy about his approach to art. Throughout the 1920s he played the viola in the University Conservatorium Orchestra. On 21 February 1922 at the Congregational Church, Elsternwick, he had married Edith Lucy Antoinette Hobbs.

In February 1932 Bell and Arnold Shore [q.v.] opened an art school in Melbourne. Later that year Bell formed the Contemporary Group of Melbourne. He suddenly left the school for Europe for sixteen months in 1934-35 in order to question his basic approach. He studied drawing with Iain McNab, involving himself in the New English Art Club and in the writings and theories of Clive Bell and Roger Fry, which became the foundation of his own painting and teaching. His basic philosophy is summed up in his catalogue appreciation of the Hugh Ramsay Retrospective (National Gallery of Victoria, March 1943): 'had he [Ramsay] lived he would have seen the modern artists experimenting with the same spatial relationships but using colour . . . as part of the form construction'.

Shore withdrew from partnership a year after Bell's return. In 1937 (Sir) Robert Menzies, while attempting to establish an equivalent to the Royal Academy, threw artists into public controversy. Bell emerged as a leading opponent of the Australian Academy of Art and as a spokesman for 'modern art', and pursued a prolonged public argument with Menzies. In July 1938 he took the lead with a leaflet, *To art lovers*, in forming the Contemporary Art Society of which he became founding president. It was a heterogeneous grouping, however, which included many *avant-garde* painters, especially social realists, as well as the Post-Impressionists whom Bell led. In 1940, distressed by the activities of laymen and communists, he himself seceded with about eighty followers and founded the Melbourne Contemporary Artists.

Bell introduced into Melbourne the teaching of French Post-Impressionism – but it was Cézanne via the New English Art Club, Iain McNab and Clive Bell. George Bell became a strong influence on many artists, such as Peter Purves-Smith [q.v.], Russell Drysdale, Sali Herman and Constance Stokes, and fast became Australia's most influential teacher. He was a close friend of Rupert Bunny and Daryl Lindsay [qq.v.] and during the 1940s was a strong advocate of Drysdale, Danila Vassilieff and Ian Fairweather but denigrated, both publicly and privately, the less formal artists Arthur Boyd, Sidney Nolan, John Perceval and Albert Tucker.

Bell painted regularly throughout his long career. He destroyed many of his early works and this, coupled with his penchant for reworking his old canvases, will tend to diminish his stature as an artist. He is represented in most public galleries by portraits, still lifes and early interiors. He was a prolific figure-draftsman in his later years.

Bell was tall and well built with a craggy face and a shambling gait. He built and sailed small craft for most of his life. In old age he suffered from a heart condition, but continued to teach and paint; a retrospective exhibition was held at the Leveson Street Gallery in 1965 and he was appointed O.B.E. next year. Survived by his wife and daughter, he died at his home at Toorak on 22 October 1966, and was cremated. His estate was valued for probate at $194 175.

Bernard Smith, *Australian painting 1788-1960* (Melb, 1962); J. Hetherington, *Australian painters* (Melb, 1963); *Age*, 5 Nov 1966; G. Bell, When everybody was poor (LaTL).   FRED WILLIAMS

BELL, SIR GEORGE JOHN (1872-1944), soldier, grazier and politician, was born on 29 November 1872 at Sale, Victoria, eldest son of George Bell, farmer, and his wife Catherine, née Hussey. His mother died when he was 5 and his father, left with five young children, soon remarried. Bell received his education at local state schools in Moe, Tanjil and Sale and later helped on his father's farm. In 1892 he joined the Victorian Mounted Rifles, and was one of the Victorian Contingent to Queen Victoria's Diamond Jubilee celebrations in London.

On the outbreak of the South African War in 1899 Bell enlisted as a private in the 1st Victorian Mounted Infantry Company, which joined the Australian Regiment at Cape Town in November. The regiment undertook reconnaissance missions into the Orange Free State and frequently skirmished with the Boers. Bell took part in its two most notable engagements – at Bastard's Nek and Pink Hill – and served with the unit until its disbandment in April 1900. The Victorian Mounted Infantry was then attached to the 4th Mounted Corps of the Imperial Army and fought at the siege of Mafeking, the relief of Johannesburg and the battle of Diamond Hill. By December Bell was back in Australia, but when the British called for reinforcements in February 1901 he re-enlisted as a lieutenant in the 5th Victorian (Mounted Rifles) Contingent. He served in operations in the Transvaal, Orange River Colony and Cape Colony and on 4 January 1902 was severely wounded at Bakkop. He was awarded the Distinguished Service Order and was mentioned in dispatches.

After the war Bell settled in north-western Tasmania and in 1904 took up selections of land at Henrietta and Parrawe. Within three years he had cleared the dense myrtle forests and established two cattle-grazing properties and, though his home and stock were destroyed by bushfire in 1907, his holdings were prospering by 1914. On 25 August he enlisted in the Australian Imperial Force as a second lieutenant in the 3rd Light Horse Regiment and sailed for Egypt in October. He was promoted lieutenant in February 1915 and from May to November served at Gallipoli where his regiment had been sent to fight as infantry. He then served in the Suez Canal zone, was promoted captain on 8 February 1916 and major on 15 April, and took command of the regiment's 'A' squadron. He participated in the early stages of the Sinai campaign, fighting in the decisive battle of Romani on 4 August and in the abortive advances on Katia and Bir el Abd. Attached to the 4th Camel Battalion, Imperial Camel Corps, in October, he saw action during the occupation of El Arish and, after months of patrol work in the western desert, rejoined the light horse at Bir el Abd in March 1917. Promoted lieut-colonel on 14 June, he was given command of the 3rd Light Horse Regiment and soon emerged as 'one of the most aggressive and astute leaders produced by the light horse'. He demanded from his men the same rigid standard of discipline which he imposed upon himself, but they respected him for his fairness, his coolness under fire and his almost uncanny knowledge of what the enemy was going to do next. Under his leadership they played a spirited role in the battle of Beersheba, participated in the capture of the Jordan Valley and on 10 February 1918 took Jericho without opposition. Bell's chief contribution to the main Palestine offensive was made during the advance on Amman when he led his horsemen in an attack on Es Salt. Surprised by the swiftness of their approach, the Turks withdrew without fighting, thereby surrendering a vital stronghold. The later, successful evacuation of British troops from Es Salt was largely due to Bell's initiative and tactical astuteness. He was mentioned in dispatches by General Allenby and next April was appointed C.M.G. Throughout the final stages of the war he remained in the Amman area. Two of his brothers, Gunners Frederick (killed in

action) and Alexander, served with the Australian artillery at Gallipoli, and another, Trooper Arthur, with the 3rd Light Horse Regiment in Palestine.

Bell was demobilized in September 1919 and resumed work on his Tasmanian pastoral properties. On 5 November he married Ellen Rothwell at Yolla. In the Federal elections that year, as the National Party candidate for Darwin, he won by 1000 votes and, except for one term in 1922-25, held the seat until 1943. In parliament he constantly drew attention to inadequacies in national defence policy and was labelled a militarist because of his outspoken advocacy of universal military training and his stand against disarmament. In 1925 he was awarded the Volunteer Officers' Decoration and in 1927 was appointed aide-de-camp to the governor-general; in March of that year he relinquished command of the 26th Light Horse Regiment, a post which he had held since 1920. Bell suffered a personal tragedy in October 1927 when his brother William Robert, a district officer in the British Solomon Islands Protectorate, was assassinated.

Bell was elected chairman of committees in the House of Representatives in 1932 and in 1934-40 was Speaker. At the time of his death Prime Minister Curtin was to praise his wide knowledge of standing orders and the dignity and poise with which he had carried out his office. His rulings were sometimes disputed and his authority was often put to severe test but, as (Sir) Robert Menzies said of him, he always gave his judgments 'with conspicuous fairness'. During his final term in parliament (1940-43), he served on a parliamentary committee inquiring into the operations of the Apple and Pear Marketing Board; in 1941 he was appointed K.C.M.G. Bell was troubled by poor health and in 1943 retired from politics. Survived by his wife, three sons and two daughters, he died of coronary vascular disease on 5 March 1944 and was buried in Burnie Anglican cemetery after a state funeral.

Tall, well-built and striking in appearance, Bell was a man of courage and determination and throughout his life showed exceptional gifts of leadership. In the official war history he was described as 'a sound soldier of wide vision'; as a politician he was recognized as 'a man of irreproachable character, upright and fearless in every respect'. His portrait by Max Meldrum [q.v.] hangs in King's Hall, Parliament House.

Aust Defence Dept, *Official records of the Australian military contingents to the war in South Africa*, P. L. Murray ed (Melb, 1912); H. S. Gullett, *The A.I.F. in Sinai and Palestine* (Syd, 1923); F. M. Blackwell, *The story of the 3rd Australian Light Horse Regiment* (Adel, 1950); *Examiner* (Launc), 6

Mar 1944; *Mercury*, 6-8 Mar 1944; W. G. Bell, The military and political life of Colonel George Bell (NL).   WILLIAM G. BELL

BELL, JAMES THOMAS MARSH (1839-1903), pastoralist, son of James Thomas Bell and his wife Elizabeth, née North, was born on 25 December 1839 at Belmont, a farm near Richmond, New South Wales, inherited by his father from Ensign Archibald Bell [q.v.1]. Educated at The King's School and Sydney Grammar School, he left prematurely when Belmont was sold after the insolvency and death of his father. He worked as a station manager for his uncle George Henry Cox [q.v.3], then bought a share in Therilby East on the Namoi River with John Hobart Cox.

After selling out profitably, Bell leased Tingan and later Glengabba, near Goondiwindi, Queensland. In 1874 he became managing partner with the wealthy Englishman Vincent Colville Hyde in Camboon, a 700-square-mile (1813 km²) leasehold with 22 000 head of cattle. On 24 July 1875 in Sydney he married Gertrude Augusta (1855-1946), daughter of James Norton [q.v.5]. They had eight children, two of whom, Bertram Charles [q.v.] and Victor Douglas, had distinguished records in the Royal Air Force in World War I. Gertrude travelled widely, kept a journal throughout her life and published two novels, *Under the Brigalows* (Melbourne, 1921), set on an Australian cattle-station, and *Sarabande* (London, 1915), set in Egypt.

For the sake of his wife's health, in 1883 Bell bought, with Hyde, the 22 000-acre (8900 ha) freehold property, Coochin Coochin, near Boonah in Queensland coastal country, as a fattening station for their other holdings. They had been the first to introduce Hereford cattle to the Dawson valley and sold much of Coochin to finance a Hereford stud on the residue in 1895. The homestead became noted for hospitality: many distinguished guests stayed there including Edward, prince of Wales, whose autograph is still on the wallpaper in one room. Hyde broke the partnership early in 1900 and moved to Armidale, New South Wales, where he died next year. The Camboon herd of 20 000 in 1897 was reduced to 800 by the drought of 1902. Bell began to restock but suffered a stroke in Toowoomba. He recovered briefly but died at Coochin Coochin on 5 May 1903, and was buried in the Church of England section of Toowong cemetery, Brisbane. His estate was valued for probate in Queensland at £63 327 and in New South Wales at £3915.

His second son ERNEST THOMAS (1880-1930) was born on 31 March 1880 at Camboon. Educated at Toowomba and Ipswich grammar schools, he became manager of Combargno station, near Roma, in 1900 but, after his father's death, joined his brother Francis in managing Camboon and Coochin Coochin. On 17 August 1910 in Brisbane he married Pauline Eva, daughter of Dr W. F. Taylor, M.L.C., and built Aroo homestead on part of Coochin Coochin.

Bell acquired Planet Downs in 1913 and was elected on 24 April to represent Fassifern in the Legislative Assembly as a Liberal. He consistently won absolute majorities, was unopposed in 1929 and died as member for the district. His maiden speech showed him to be a firm and intelligent defender of rural interests; subsequently, he spoke rarely but usually to the point. He was elected as a Nationalist in 1918, a member of the Country and Northern Country Party in 1920, a United candidate in 1923 and a Progressive Country Nationalist in 1927 and 1929; he was a consistent opponent of unionism and of the Labor Party.

The years immediately following World War I were critical for the meat industry, as South American producers began to dominate traditional European markets. More concerned with the affairs of his industry than with political preferment, Bell travelled overseas in 1920 and before his return in March 1921 visited meat-producing establishments in Argentina, Paraguay and Uruguay, and cattle markets in Denver and Chicago. In 1922-25 he was chairman of the Cattle Council formed by the United Graziers' Association of Queensland, and in October 1922 he attended a conference in Melbourne called by the Federal government to establish the Australian Meat Board, on which he became Queensland representative.

Bell attended another Melbourne conference in March 1923, at which combined graziers' organizations created the Australian Meat Council. He was its salaried chairman in 1925-26, but the council failed to satisfy the industry and was disbanded in 1927. He was chairman also of the Queensland Meat Advisory Committee from 1925, and president of the Queensland Stockowners' Association. In 1926-30 Bell was a council-member of the United Graziers' Association and represented it on the Queensland committee of the Australian Overseas Transport Association. He was also a member of the Queensland Board of Advice of the National Bank of Australia in 1928-30, president of the Fassifern Agricultural and Pastoral Association, and a Goolman shire-councillor; fifteen years a council-member of the Royal National Association of Queensland, he was a vice-president in 1922-23 and 1930.

Bell died of renal failure at his home at Ascot on 2 May 1930, survived by his wife, a son and three daughters, and was buried in Toowong cemetery. His estate was sworn for probate at £45 976.

M. J. Fox (ed), *The history of Queensland,* 1 (Brisb, 1919); P. Cox and W. Stacey, *The Australian homestead* (Melb, 1972); N. S. Pixley, 'The Bells and "Coochin Coochin" ', *JRHSQ,* 8 (1965-69), no 4; *Pastoral Review,* 16 June 1930; *Queenslander,* 8 May 1930, 28 July 1932; *Courier Mail,* 11 Aug 1946; Gertrude Bell, Journals and news-cuttings (held by Miss E. Bell, Coochin Coochin, Mount Alford, Qld).   NORMAN S. PIXLEY

BELL, JANE (1873-1959), hospital matron, was born on 16 March 1873 at Middlebie, Dumfriesshire, Scotland, daughter of William Bell, farmer, and his wife Helen, née Johnston. Jane was educated at a small school near Dumfries. When both parents and four of the children died of tuberculosis, Jane and her surviving brother and two sisters were helped by their local Presbyterian congregation to migrate to Sydney, arriving in 1886.

In December 1894 Jane began training as a nurse at the Royal Prince Alfred Hospital, completing her certificate in May 1898. She held various staff appointments until April 1903 when she became matron first at Bundaberg Hospital, Queensland, following her sister Euphemia who had trained at Sydney Hospital, and then in September 1904 at the Brisbane General Hospital. She resigned on 31 July 1906 to go to London where she trained in midwifery at Queen Charlotte's Hospital. In 1907 she was appointed senior assistant superintendent of nurses at Edinburgh Royal Infirmary. She returned to Australia, and in 1910-34 was lady superintendent of the Melbourne Hospital, bringing to the position, besides her sound training and considerable experience, qualities of leadership, determination and vision.

Despite those attributes Miss Bell had a brief, unhappy period overseas with the Australian Army Nursing Service. Appointed lady superintendent of the Third Military District in June 1913, on the outbreak of war she recruited the Victorian section of the nursing staff of the 1st Australian General Hospital; she was principal matron aboard the hospital ship *Kyarra* which left for Egypt in December 1914. At the time the position, status, authority and working conditions of army nurses were undefined. Promoted to matron inspectress in June next year, Miss Bell waged an in-cessant battle with the Army Medical Service, seeking to clarify the position and responsibilities of the nursing service and to place its control and discipline in the hands of its own members. When her staffing recommendations were rejected in July 1915 she asked to be transferred or returned to Australia. In August both Matron Bell and her commanding officer were recalled; she reached Australia in September unaware that an inquiry had been held in the meantime into the administration of the A.G.H. Although she had been unable to defend herself, her stand was vindicated by the court and the way paved for the reorganization in 1916 of the Australian Army medical and nursing services.

On the termination of her A.I.F. appointment in October 1915 Miss Bell was reinstated at Melbourne Hospital. She made many innovations including: replacement of male orderlies by sisters in the operating theatres; the appointment of tutor-sisters to instruct trainees and of a house-sister to supervise the nurses' quarters; and the introduction of a six-week preliminary course. She also persuaded the hospital's committee of management to pay trainee-nurses. Her introduction of a four instead of a three-year course did not survive the passing of the Nurses' Registration Act (1923), for which she had campaigned, but the new rank of staff-nurse, before promotion to sister, filled the hiatus. As working hours were reduced and the staff-patient ratio improved, nurses in the hospital increased from 100 in 1910 to 200 in 1934.

Jane Bell was a foundation member, in 1899, of the Australasian Trained Nurses' Association and in 1910 became a member of the Royal Victorian Trained Nurses' Association (later the Royal Victorian College of Nursing), of which she was president in 1931-34 and 1938-46. She was a member of the Nurses' Board in 1924-50. Qualifications, salaries and working conditions for the profession were her constant concern, and in later years she took part in the development of postgraduate training. She was appointed O.B.E. in 1944. She died at the Royal Melbourne Hospital on 6 August 1959, aged 86, and was cremated after a Presbyterian service.

A. G. Butler (ed), *Official history of the Australian Army Medical Services . . . 1914-18,* 1, 2 (Melb, 1930, Canb, 1940); K. S. Inglis, *Hospital and community* (Melb, 1958); *Una,* May-Aug, Oct 1934, Oct 1959; M. E. Webster, 'The history of trained nursing in Victoria', *VHM,* 19 (1941-42), no 4; *Age,* 7, 8 Aug 1959; S. G. Kenny, The Australian Army Nursing Service during the Great War (B. A. Hons thesis, Univ Melb, 1975); information from Mrs Helen Cattermull, Bundaberg, Qld.   LYNDSAY GARDINER

BELL, JOSHUA THOMAS (1863-1911), barrister and politician, was born on 13 March 1863 at Ipswich, Queensland, eldest son of Sir Joshua Peter Bell [q.v.3] and his wife Margaret Miller, née Dorsey. He was educated privately and at Ipswich and Brisbane Grammar schools; in 1881-85 he attended Trinity Hall, Cambridge, where as president of the Union he debated with such luminaries as Austen Chamberlain. He was called to the Bar at the Inner Temple and in 1888 was a marshal on the Northern Assizes circuit.

Returning in 1889 Bell became a director of the Darling Downs and Western Lands Company whose head-station Jimbour was the family seat. He was Sir Samuel Griffith's [q.v.] private secretary in 1890-92 and then, when the company collapsed, became member for Dalby in the Legislative Assembly in 1893-1911. In 1901 (Sir) Littleton Groom [q.v.] beat him for the Federal seat of Darling Downs.

After membership of the royal commission on land settlement in 1897, Bell became chairman of committees in 1902 and subsequently secretary for public lands in the Morgan and two Kidston [qq.v.] ministries between 1903 and 1908. Home secretary for eight months during 1908-09, he was elected Speaker in 1909, a post which he held with distinction until his death.

'Joey' Bell's appearance, attitudes and 'somewhat pompous' bearing, inherited from his father, were apparently contradicted by his liberal views. Fashionably dressed, he was something of an aloof *poseur* with a superior air which, although it concealed shyness and insecurity, irritated Labor and conservative opponents alike. 'Smitth' of the *Worker* not altogether unfairly parodied Bell's manner in 1901:

> But I'd like to – haw – to dwah
> Your attention, Sir, to – haw –
> To the way our time is wasted;
> Sir, its weally quite a cwime;
> While the Labah membahs theh,
> talk of "Strikes" I do declah
> that this horwid pwickly peah keeps on
> gwoing all the time.

Nevertheless, he was able enough to represent the government in important Land Court cases and was a parliamentarian with an astonishing fluency, an unerring instinct for the correct word, and a mastery of polished, if stylized rhetoric, seldom found among Australian politicians.

Bell's contemporaries considered that his tenure of the Lands Department, during which he encouraged closer settlement, improved public amenities and acquired private estates for small farming, was his main contribution to Queensland's history. His pioneering National Forests Act – perhaps his most important single legacy – and his alleviation of technical difficulties hampering farmers were impressive. His conciliatory role, when the rise of Labor had confused liberals and conservatives, is even more important.

Bell was a skilful electioneer. Hard pressed by Labor in 1893, 1896 and 1902 (when a family scandal temporarily lost him the Roman Catholic vote), his 'pocket-borough' was saved by his local appeal as a superb horseman and native pastoralist, and by provision of three branch railways for the Dalby area and assiduous favours for other constituents. A liberal without a coherent policy, he helped organize the Darling Downs members, then slowly stepped towards more radical attitudes. His liberalism was partly fuelled by his financial collapse: the Bells became virtual grace and favour residents at Jimbour, and he was dependent on his ministerial salary and his wife's income; he then sold Jimbour to the State for agricultural settlement. He could neither bring himself to join organized labour nor stomach the political and social stonewalling of the conservative establishment.

A keen rower and rifle-shot and patron of the arts (he secured the first grant in Queensland for a cultural society), Bell represented an increasingly anachronistic social group – the 'independent Australian Briton'. He combined in his person the manners and education of an English gentleman and the earthy political skills of the native-born, but his failure to attain the heights of brilliant contemporaries like Deakin [q.v.] and to really enjoy the rough-and-tumble of State politics suggested more an Indian summer than a springtime harvest.

On 25 July 1903 Bell had married Catherine Jane, widow of Sydney Jones, a Rockhampton solicitor, and daughter of John Ferguson [q.v.]; they had one son and one daughter. Between July 1910 and his death from septicaemia with peritonitis at Graceville, Brisbane, on 10 March 1911, Bell suffered agony from surgical treatment. A member of the Brisbane Synod of the Church of England, he was accorded a state funeral and buried in Toowong cemetery, high on the hill next to his father. His estate was sworn for probate at £4567.

C. A. Bernays, *Queensland politics during sixty years* (Brisb, 1919); C. P. Trevelyan, *Letters from North America and the Pacific, 1898* (Lond, 1969); D. J. Murphy et al (eds), *Prelude to power* (Brisb, 1970); *Worker* (Brisb), 21 Aug 1901; *Brisbane Courier,* 1 Apr 1907, 11 Mar 1911; *Daily Mail* (Brisb) and *Darling Downs Gazette,* 11 Mar 1911; *Truth* (Brisb), 12 Mar 1911; *Queenslander,* 18 Mar 1911.   D. B. WATERSON

BELL, PETER ALBANY (1871-1957), caterer and philanthropist, was born on 20 April 1871, near Clare, South Australia, son of Peter Bell, farmer, and his wife Jane, née Craig. He had little formal education before moving with his widowed mother to Western Australia in 1887. For six years he was in turn a draper's delivery boy, an inland stockman and a shop assistant; then in 1894 he opened a small shop in Hay Street, Perth, making and selling confectionery and lemon squash. In the next decade he opened more shops and a confectionery factory, and in 1898 studied the soda-fountain trade in the United States of America. On his return he introduced new products and methods, such as pure fruit juices and sundaes, but after Federation the competition of confectionery from the eastern States led him to begin manufacturing cakes and pastry. His shops were transformed into tea-rooms. Albany Bell Ltd, formed in October 1911, ultimately controlled eleven city tea-rooms and three in Kalgoorlie and Boulder. He employed about four hundred workers in the shops and in an attractive model factory at Mount Lawley. All received two weeks annual leave on full pay before awards required it; his goldfields workers also received holiday rail-fares to the coast.

For nearly thirty years Albany Bell's tea-rooms were famous, but in 1925, as chairman of the Master Caterers' Association, he was involved in a disorderly strike lasting over four weeks for a union shop led by the militant Hotel and Restaurant Employees' Union. Wide public criticism of police inaction led to a censure motion against the government. An appeal by Albany Bell Ltd for deregistration of the union failed, but compulsory unionism clauses in the final agreement were modified. Discouraged by the strike, rising costs and fiercer competition, he sold his interest in the business in 1928.

Bell was an early convert to the Churches of Christ and his creed and a social conscience turned him to philanthropy. An enthusiastic member of the Young Men's Christian Association, he volunteered to work for it overseas in 1916, sailed in October in the *Afric* and served in both England and France. He returned home in February 1919 and was discharged in March. He had been commissioned as a justice of the peace in 1909 and had served on the Children's Court; on a business trip to the United States in 1915, he had studied progressive treatment of juvenile delinquents. After retiring from business in 1928, he bought 3750 acres (1518 ha) at Roelands near Bunbury which became the Chandler Home for Unemployed Boys and, later, the Roelands Aboriginal Mission. The annual harvest of a citrus orchard on his own property at Roelands was left in trust for missions and orphanages; it produced an average crop of over 2000 cases in 1965-75. He made many other charitable donations.

Bell died on 14 September 1957, survived by his wife Edith Agnes, née Clark, whom he had married on 11 March 1896 in Adelaide, and by eight of their nine children; he was buried in Karrakatta cemetery. Albany Bell is significant as a manufacturer in the early years of the century when Western Australia lagged behind the other States in developing urban industries.

A. B. Maston (ed), *The jubilee pictorial history of Churches of Christ* . . . (Melb, 1903); J. S. Battye (ed), *Cyclopedia of Western Australia*, 1 (Adel, 1912); *Western Australian Industrial Gazette*, 26 Aug 1925; *Westralian Worker*, 15, 22 May, 6 June 1925; *West Australian*, 20, 23 May 1925, 10 Mar 1956; P. A. Bell, interviewed by R. Wright (tapes 73, 74, Battye Lib, Perth); family information.

M. TAMBLYN

BELLEW, HAROLD KYRLE MONEY (1850-1911), actor, was born on 28 March 1850 at Prescot, Lancashire, England, son of Rev. John Chippendall Montesquieu Bellew, Anglican clergyman, and his wife Eva Maria, née Money. His father was later converted to Catholicism and became a popular preacher. Kyrle was educated at the Royal Grammar School, Lancaster, then was apprenticed in the training ship *Conway*. He joined the merchant navy and about 1869 reached Victoria, where he worked as a labourer, goldminer, station-hand and signwriter.

In Melbourne in 1871 Bellew was engaged by George Coppin [q.v.3] to read W. H. Russell's letters to *The Times* as a lecture accompanying a panorama of the Franco-Prussian War. He became known as a journalist by his court reports in rhyme and graphic sketches for the Melbourne *Herald* and *Daily Telegraph*. On 27 October 1873 at St Patrick's Cathedral he married Parisian-born actress Eugénie Marie Séraphie Le Grand, who bore him a son. Next year he acted at the Solferino diggings in New South Wales. Although advised to shun the stage by a committee of pressmen, including Charles Bright, Marcus Clarke and F. W. Haddon [qq.v.3,3,4], he returned to England in 1875, without Eugénie, and succeeded as an actor. He was associated with the Bancrofts and (Sir) Henry Irving, and in 1885-87 was with Wallack's Theatre in New York, playing romantic comedy roles.

Bellew returned to London and in 1887 formed a touring company, with the American actress Mrs Cora Brown-Potter. They visited Australia in 1890 and opened at the Princess Theatre, Melbourne, on 1 March in *Camille*. The press savagely criticized the couple and their engagement was reduced to six weeks. The Sydney newspapers were more encouraging and their season there was extended. After seeing Bellew's performance in *David Garrick*, Bright admitted that he 'could act, in spite of the opinion to the contrary of his earliest critics'. They gave dramatic recitals at Newcastle, Maitland, Ballarat and Adelaide before leaving in December for England via the Far East and India. The company toured South Africa, the United States of America and England and visited Australia again in 1896, opening in Sydney in V. Sardou's *La Tosca*. He adapted several works for the stage including *Charlotte Corday*, which was seen by Australian audiences. His partnership with Mrs Brown-Potter ended in 1898.

In 1900 Bellew returned to Australia to speculate in gold-mining leases on the Palmer diggings in North Queensland for several overseas syndicates, and he applied to the State government for permission to complete the railway-line from Cooktown to his leases. However his enterprises were never floated. Apart from brief appearances in London he spent his last years in America, where he rejoined Wallack's Theatre.

Bellew died of pneumonia on 2 November 1911 at Salt Lake City, Utah, and was buried with Catholic rites in New York, survived by his son. With a classical Greek profile, windswept hair and romantic good looks, he had popular appeal: 'his manner was ingratiating, his voice penetrating and pleasant, his style forcible and picturesque'.

J. L. Wallack, *Memories of fifty years* (New York, 1889); M. Bancroft, *The Bancrofts: recollections of sixty years* (New York, 1909); P. McGuire et al, *The Australian theatre* (Melb, 1948); A. Bagot, *Coppin the great* (Melb, 1965); *V&P* (LA Qld), 1900, 3, 873, 1901, 4, 323; *PP* (Qld), 1902, 1st S, 3, 340; *Argus*, 22 Feb 1890, 5 Dec 1911; *Sydney Mail*, 15 Aug, 12 Sept 1896; *New York Times*, 3, 5 Nov 1911; *Bulletin*, 11 Mar 1882, 8, 15 Mar, 17 May, 6 Dec 1890, 15 Nov 1902, 18 Jan 1912; 'Mummer memoirs', newscuttings, Vol 23, p85 (ML).   JULIE MILLS

BELT, FRANCIS WALTER (1862-1938), naval commander and lawyer, was born on 30 April 1862 at Adelaide, fourth son of William Charles Belt, barrister, and his wife Penelope Avice Anne, née Woolrych. His English-born parents had migrated to South Australia in 1851. Belt was educated at the Collegiate School of St Peter and, after matriculating in 1878, commenced articles of clerkship with his father's firm; he was ad-

mitted as a barrister and solicitor in October 1884.

From 1884 Belt frequently travelled in Europe, Asia and America and, like his father, became a skilful big-game hunter. On returning from overseas in 1894, he accompanied the W. A. Horn [q.v.] scientific expedition to Central Australia and according to Horn, his brother-in-law, made a useful contribution as a collector and taxidermist. Charles Winnecke, the second-in-command, named Mounts Francis, Edward and William in the MacDonnell Ranges after Belt and his brothers. He resumed legal practice and on his father's death in February 1899 took over the firm in partnership with his brother William. Later that year he went hunting big-game in South Africa and had no sooner returned home when the South African War broke out. Enlisting as a trooper in the 2nd South Australian (Mounted Rifles) contingent, he sailed in January 1900 and saw action at the relief of Prieska, the advances on Johannesburg and Pretoria, and the battle of Diamond Hill; he later served in the Transvaal until March 1901.

In 1908 William Belt died and the firm passed to Francis, who remained in practice until shortly before World War I. On 22 December 1914 he joined the Royal Naval Volunteer Service in England as a lieutenant, next July became a lieut-commander in the Royal Naval Division, and until late 1917 served with various naval armoured-car squadrons in Belgium, Russia, Romania and Galicia. In this period he led an expedition into Persia 'in trying circumstances with conspicuous success'; he was later second-in-command of a squadron throughout the Dobrodja and Romanian operations. During this campaign he was wounded and on 11 November 1917, then an acting commander, was awarded the Distinguished Service Order; he was also awarded the Russian orders of St Anne and St Stanislaus. In 1918 he was sent to the United States of America for special naval service.

After the war Belt visited Adelaide, wound up his practice and returned to England. On 3 July 1915 he had married Violet Mary Selina Lucas-Shadwell at St George's Church, Hanover Square, London; they settled at Mill Court, near Alton in Hampshire. There Belt lived the leisurely life of a country gentleman, spending winters at his villa at Toulon, France. A contemporary described him as 'charming, accomplished, cultured and elegant'; his interests ranged from big-game hunting, carriage-driving and horse-breeding to collecting embroideries and fine china. His wife died in 1927 and three years later he married her friend Marie-Thérèse Bricard. She survived him when he died at Montreux, Switzerland, on 21 August 1938. His estate was sworn for probate at £56 029 in England and £98 723 in South Australia.

C. Winnecke, *Journal of the Horn Scientific Exploring Expedition, 1894* (Adel,1897); Aust Defence Dept, *Official records of the Australian military contingent to the war in South Africa*, P. L. Murray ed (Melb, 1912); J. M. Brown, *'The Almonds' of Walkerville* (Adel, 1970); *London Gazette*, 30 Nov 1917; *Reveille*, 1 Dec 1938; *Observer* (Adel), 27 Sept 1851, 18 Feb 1899, 12 Mar 1927; Collegiate School of St Peter, Records (Adel).

ROBERT HYSLOP

BENHAM, ELLEN IDA (1871-1917), educationist, was born on 12 March 1871 at Allen's Creek, Kapunda, South Australia, third of eleven children of William Hoare Benham, solicitor, and his wife Aimie, née Huggins. She went from Kapunda Model School to the Advanced School for Girls, Adelaide, where she was influenced by the headmistress Madeline Rees George [q.v.]. She studied at the University of Adelaide from 1889 (B.Sc., 1892). After becoming headmistress of Christ Church day school, Kapunda, for two years, she studied in Europe in 1895. She returned to teach science at Dryburgh House School, Adelaide, in 1896-1900, and later at Tormore House School under Caroline Jacob [q.v.] and concurrently at the Advanced School.

Ellen, like most of her brothers and sisters, followed her father's botanical interests. In 1901 the ailing professor of natural science engaged her to give his botany lectures; on his death that year the University of Adelaide confirmed the appointment, thus making her its first female academic. She reorganized the botany curriculum, extending the study of native flora and including field visits. An authority on the identification of plants, in 1906 she was appointed to classify a major collection presented to the university herbarium by the South Australian government.

To extend her knowledge of higher education, Ellen Benham went to England in 1908, teaching at Winchester High School and gaining the Oxford Diploma of Education in an unusually short time. She resumed teaching at Tormore and the university in 1909 and helped found the lively Women Students' Club in which she held office; in 1914 she was a foundation member of the Women Graduates' Club. Owing to illness she reduced her schoolteaching in 1910 and resigned from Tormore at the end of 1911, teaching part time at Akaroa School in 1912. Her university teaching ended that year with the foundation of a chair of botany.

In December 1912 Ellen Benham purchased Walford School, Malvern, South Australia. Her educational aims were based on the pursuit of excellence applied with a judicious combination of idealism and common sense. She had large, well-ventilated class-rooms, gave open-air lessons, and refused to accept 'entertainments or visiting' as an excuse for omission of homework. She consulted parents in order to establish 'the right adjustment of work to the physical and mental powers of the children', and believed that the student's abilities could be extended by the formation of habits of self-reliance, accuracy and thoroughness. She sought to develop each girl's capacity 'to become a useful and effective woman in whatever position she may have to fill'. At Walford she taught botany and physiology, raised academic standards, chose well-qualified staff and offered a balanced curriculum including callisthenics and sport. Influenced by Tormore and by English practices, she introduced hockey and tennis matches, sports days, informal cricket and the prefect system. She appointed an Anglican chaplain, emphasized *esprit de corps* and gave the school a motto: *Virtute et veritate*.

Miss Benham died of hepatic abscess in Adelaide on 27 April 1917 and was buried in Kapunda cemetery. The Benham Wing, incorporating science and class-room facilities, perpetuates her name at Walford Church of England Girls' Grammar School.

H. Jones and N. Morrison, *Walford, a history of a school* (Adel, 1969); R. R. Chivers, *The Benham family in Australia* (Black Forest, SA, 1970); *Tormorean*, 1900-12; *Kapunda Herald*, 14 May 1917; Education Cttee, Minutes 1901-12, *and* Registry files for E. Benham 1901-12 (Univ Adel).

HELEN JONES

BENHAM, FREDERIC CHARLES COURTENAY (1900-1962), economist, was born on 6 March 1900 at Bristol, Gloucestershire, England, son of Charles Courtenay Benham, leather merchant, and his wife Kathleen Grace, née Taylor. He was educated at Katharine Lady Berkeley's Grammar School, then at the London School of Economics and Political Science (B.Sc.(Econ.), 1922; Ph.D., 1928). A student of the redoubtable Edwin Cannan, he graduated with first-class honours and became a research fellow.

In 1923 Benham was appointed lecturer in economics at the University of Sydney under R. C. Mills [q.v.], with whom he published *Lectures on the principles of money, banking, and foreign exchange*... (1925). His non-monetary works were more numerous and significant in the policy milieu of the 1920s. Their focus was Australian, their conceptual frame Cannanian, their theorizing simple but consistent and directed always at the world of affairs. The substance of articles which first appeared in the *Economic Record* in 1926-27 and in such collections as *London essays in economics* (London, 1927) and *The peopling of Australia* (Melbourne, 1928), re-emerged in *The prosperity of Australia: an economic analysis* (London, 1928), for which he was awarded his doctorate.

Using *per capita* real income as the ultimate 'test' of economic success, Benham asked how efficiently the Australian population had exploited its resources. He found its stewardship wanting: because only an unfettered price mechanism would allocate resources ideally over space and time, the tariff and other market interventions had blunted Australia's *per capita* performance and population potential. Securely astride the free-market paradigm, he jousted vigorously with the Tariff Board and those of his colleagues who reasoned, somewhat elliptically, that the tariff-wage system had, up to a point, served the national population ambition.

Benham's place in Australian political economy is assured by three related factors: he added to the short list of pioneer national-income estimates a calculation, the conceptual basis of which first approximated modern ideas; at a time when economics, led by men of little formal background, was establishing itself as an independent discipline in Australian universities, he introduced some rigour into those debates which were helping a fledgling profession towards a sense of identity; and, asserting that 'general principles' would satisfy where his statistical demonstrations might not, he essayed the first comprehensive free-market overview of Australian economic practice in this century.

Benham left Sydney in 1929 to become a Rockefeller research fellow. In 1931-42 he taught at the London School of Economics and became a *rapporteur* to Chatham House on international economic problems. He was economic adviser to the comptroller for development and welfare in the West Indies in 1942-45, and to the commissioner-general for the United Kingdom in south-east Asia in 1947-55. In 1945-47 he had been professor of commerce at the University of London and from 1955 was a research professor at the Royal Institute of International Affairs. He published in the fields of monetary policy, economic welfare, taxation and the problems of underdeveloped countries. A gift for simple exposition was displayed in his enduring *Economics: a general textbook for students* (London, 1938).

'A delightful raconteur' and 'convivial companion', Benham was a fine bridge-player and as 'Fourchette' had written on the game in the *Sydney Morning Herald*. He was appointed C.B.E. in 1945 and C.M.G. in 1950. He died of rheumatic heart disease on 7 January 1962 at St Mary's Hospital, London, survived by his wife Suzanne Henriette, née Paitre, of Paris, whom he had married in London on 10 December 1932, and by a daughter.

N. G. Butlin, *Australian domestic product, investment and foreign borrowing* ... (Cambridge, 1962); C. D. W. Goodwin, *Economic enquiry in Australia* (Durham, N.C., 1966); S. J. Butlin, 'Frederic Benham ...', *Economic Record*, Sept 1962; N. Cain, 'The economists and Australian population strategy in the twenties', *Aust J of Politics and Hist*, Dec 1974; *The Times*, 9 Jan 1962.

NEVILLE CAIN

BENJAMIN, ARTHUR LESLIE (1893-1960), pianist, composer, conductor and teacher, was born on 18 September 1893 in Sydney, son of Abraham Benjamin, commission agent, and his wife Amelia, née Menser. His parents moved to Brisbane in 1896 and he was educated at Bowen House School and Brisbane Grammar School. His family provided a strong informal musical background and, aged 6, he made his first public appearance as a pianist. At 9 he began formal training and in 1907 accompanied his parents on a tour of Europe where he developed the musical discrimination that had been lacking. He finished his schooling in Brisbane, and in 1911 went to London and attended the Royal College of Music for three years as a pupil in composition of Sir Charles Villiers Stanford.

Following the outbreak of World War I, he enlisted in the British Army. He attended the Army Officers' Training Corps and on 29 April 1915 received a temporary commission as second lieutenant with the 32nd Battalion of the Royal Fusiliers, which served in France. On 4 November 1917 he was attached to the Royal Flying Corps as a gunner. Shot down over Germany on 31 July 1918, he was repatriated on 29 November.

In 1919 at the invitation of H. Verbrugghen [q.v.], Benjamin returned to Australia to become professor of piano at the New South Wales State Conservatorium of Music, Sydney. He went back to England in 1921 to advance his career as a pianist and composer, and, as an adjudicator and examiner for the Associated Board of the Royal Schools of Music, toured Australia, Canada and the West Indies.

Benjamin's first published work was a string quartet which received a Carnegie award in 1924, and by 1926 his published music revealed his developing techniques. In 1925 he made his first public appearance as a professional soloist and that year joined the faculty of the Royal College of Music. Among his pianoforte pupils were Benjamin Britten and Peggy Glanville-Hicks. In 1929 he again visited Australia, combining the role of examiner for the board with a series of successful recitals. Back in England he continued his concert career but soon concentrated on composition. His first opera, *The devil take her*, a witty one-act farce, was performed under the direction of Sir Thomas Beecham in 1931. His publications in this period included another opera, a violin concerto and orchestral, solo and vocal works; he was also a prolific composer of good film-music.

At the end of 1938 Benjamin resigned as a professor at the Royal College of Music and settled at Vancouver, Canada, where he was engaged in 1941 to conduct the new Canadian Broadcasting Corporation Symphony Orchestra. In 1944-45 he also worked as a lecturer at Reed College, Portland, Oregon, United States of America. Benjamin's publishers asked him to return to England in 1946 and enabled him to devote his time to composition. He made a successful tour for the Australian Broadcasting Commission in 1950, playing a specially written piano concerto.

At the Festival of Britain in 1951 Benjamin's ballet, *Orlando's silver wedding*, was produced, and his opera, *A tale of two cities* – a romantic melodrama based on Dickens [q.v.4] – won first prize; it was televised in 1953 and successfully produced at Sadler's Wells Theatre in 1957.

Witty and urbane, Benjamin enjoyed London life and theatre. He was a member of the Savile Club and lived at Hampstead. After a serious illness in 1957, he continued to conduct but, in 1960, recurrent illness forced him to interrupt a world tour and return to England. He was admitted to Middlesex Hospital, London, where he died of cancer on 10 April 1960; he was privately cremated.

Benjamin's composition was stylistically eclectic. At heart he was a romantic, who continued to be influenced by Stanford. His music was distinguished by wit and skilful technique with a sure touch for parody and satire; he was also successful with compositions written in a richer emotional and contemplative style, but had difficulty in convincingly overcoming the challenge of reflecting the deeper issues of World War II – as evidenced in his Symphony No.1 written in 1944-45.

D. Ewen (ed), *Composers since 1900* (New York,

1969); J. Murdoch, *Australia's contemporary composers* (Melb, 1972); F. W. Sternfeld (ed), *Music in the modern age* (Lond, 1973); *Tempo* (Syd), Aug 1950; *SMH*, 29 Apr, 14, 21 Sept 1929, 2, 6, Sept 1950, 11 Apr 1960; *The Times*, 10 Apr 1960.

CHARLES CAMPBELL

BENJAMIN, DAVID SAMUEL (1869-1943), merchant and charity worker, was born on 10 April 1869 in Brisbane, eldest son of Maurice David Benjamin, merchant, and his wife Fanny, née Davis. He trained as an architect and practised briefly before moving to New South Wales about 1889. After varied experiences, he was a storekeeper at Junee when he married Ina Muriel Younie Russell on 11 October 1899 in Sydney. In 1903 he became manager of the well-established retail business of Sweet Brothers, drapers, of Newtown and North Sydney. Next year he acquired an interest in the business and in 1906 became managing director.

In 1907 Benjamin was elected a member of the Master Retailers' Association (Retail Traders' Association of New South Wales, 1921) and served on its council in 1907-36. As president in 1918-20 he helped to increase the membership and prestige of the association, and in 1919 founded the *M.R.A. Journal* in which he maintained a keen interest.

Benjamin worked for various philanthropic institutions in the city of Sydney. As a director of the Royal Prince Alfred Hospital in 1919-43 he contributed to the financial and administrative work of the hospital in many ways: he was honorary treasurer in 1924-25 and a member of the house committee; he instituted and organized an appeal for electric lighting in the hospital and was active in its Jubilee Fund campaign of 1923. Benjamin contributed liberally to other public appeals. From 1924 he served on the University Cancer Research Committee which by 1927 had raised over £120 000 for the University of Sydney. In 1919 he was vice-chairman of the influenza administration committee which controlled ambulances during the epidemic. In February 1920 he was appointed chairman of the New South Wales Ambulance Transport Service Board. He became a member of the executive of the St John Ambulance Association and in 1933 was admitted as an associate serving brother to the Order of St John of Jerusalem in recognition of his services.

Benjamin was also a trustee of the National Park, a councillor of the Employers' Federation of New South Wales, and a member of the State executive committee for the Commonwealth Peace Celebrations

(1919). Prominent in the Jewish community, he served on the boards of the Great Synagogue (1921-23) and of the Sir Moses Montefiore Jewish Home (1917-21), and in 1923 was joint treasurer of the New South Wales Jewish War Memorial building fund. A chronic asthmatic, he died of heart failure on 1 December 1943 in Royal Prince Alfred Hospital, and was cremated. He was survived by his wife, who inherited his estate valued for probate at £18 694, and by one of their two sons.

Hebrew Standard of A'sia, 4 July 1919, 27 Aug 1936, 9 Dec 1943; Master Retailers Assn, *J*, July, Sept 1919, July 1920, July 1936, Dec 1943; RPAH Annual reports 1919, 1924-25, 1944 (ML); Annual reports, 1921-23 (Great Synagogue office, Sydney).   SUZANNE D. RUTLAND

BENJAMIN, LOUIS REGINALD SAMUEL (1892-1970), chemist and technologist, was born on 30 April 1892 at Ayr, Queensland, son of Benjamin (Harry) Benjamin, licensed victualler, and his wife Caroline, née Barnett. Educated at Scotch College, Claremont, Western Australia, and the School of Mines, Kalgoorlie, he worked for a time on the eastern goldfields as a metallurgist. On 6 December 1917 he married Florence May McManaway at Sandstone.

Benjamin was introduced to the field of wood-pulping in 1918 by I. H. Boas [q.v.] at the Technical School, Perth; they examined the novel possibility of making paper from eucalypt wood when it was only thought possible to use conifers. He was employed by the newly formed Institute of Science and Industry and the Council for Scientific and Industrial Research until 1928, in charge of eucalypt wood-pulp and cellulose research in Perth and Melbourne. In 1924 he and David Avery [q.v.] attempted unsuccessfully to make newsprint from eucalypts in a paper-mill in Holland. By 1927 Benjamin and his colleagues had examined the soda, sulphite and mechanical processes of pulping eucalypt woods. He had shown in a small trial at Fyansford mill that the soda process was suitable for making printing papers, a result availed of by other hands to establish, in 1938, the Burnie mill of Associated Pulp and Paper Mills Ltd. The sulphite and mechanical processes were then examined in an experimental pulp and paper-mill operated by Tasmanian Paper Pty Ltd at Kermandie in 1928-30, with Benjamin as technical superintendent. Mechanical pulping was proven valuable for newsprint manufacture, but then the Depression halted progress.

Benjamin was superintendent of research and technical control for Australian Paper Manufacturers Ltd, Melbourne, from 1930 to 1932 when he joined (Sir) Keith Murdoch's [q.v.] Derwent Valley Paper Co. Pty Ltd in Hobart. He remained for twenty-four years with this firm, which in 1938 formed Australian Newsprint Mills Pty Ltd, being partnered in this by most of the leading Australian newspapers. In 1934 at Ocean Falls, British Columbia, Benjamin and staff had carried out a large mill-scale test, using 1000 tons (1016 tonnes) of Tasmanian eucalypt, in which the problem of using this wood for making newsprint was largely solved. This assurance led to the erection of A.N.M.'s mill at Boyer near New Norfolk in 1938, with Benjamin as general superintendent. In 1941, the first to do so in the world, they produced newsprint from hardwood, and within a few months were manufacturing at the rate of about 20 000 tons (20 320 tonnes) a year. This was valuable to Australia during World War II; at its close the firm bought bigger machinery and almost doubled output.

In 1956 when Benjamin retired and was appointed C.B.E., it was said that he 'had had the satisfaction, rare to a scientist, of managing the industry he had created in the laboratory'. He continued to act for overseas firms, to work as a consultant to existing mills, and to advise the Tasmanian government on the promotion of aluminium at Bell Bay. He received a concession in 1957 over forests in the south-east and interested capital in establishing a pulp-mill at Kermandie. Before his death he was investigating the economics of wood-chip export to Japan from Weipa, North Queensland. A fellow of the Royal Australian Chemical Institute, he was vice-chairman of the Australian Aluminium Production Commission in 1945-60 and president of the Australian Pulp and Paper Industry Technical Association in 1950. Much of his outlook is summed up in his article, 'The challenge of the Eucalypts', *Appita*, November 1959. Benjamin's success in life was largely due to his possession of the common touch, whether with bushman or premier, and his passion for technical exploitation of a natural resource, be it an ore body or a forest. He died in Hobart on 14 March 1970, survived by his wife and two daughters. His estate was sworn for probate at $121 417.

Jobson's Investment Digest Year Book, 1956; *Newspaper News*, 2 July 1956; *Appita*, 23 (1970), no 6; *SMH*, 12 May 1941, supp; CSIRO records (Canb).
                                    J. L. SOMERVILLE

BENJAMIN, SOPHIA (1882-1962), pioneer of kindergarten work and of parent and sex education, was born on 24 December

1882 in Adelaide, daughter of Phillip Benjamin, journalist and later company secretary, and his wife Minnie, née Cohen, who were orthodox Jews. About 1888 the family moved to Sydney. Educated by governesses until 10, she went for three years to Darlinghurst Superior School, after which she shared governesses and tutors with cousins. Her intelligent and cultured father, for whom she had great respect and affection, contributed breadth and richness to her education: she read widely in history, the arts and philosophy. After gaining the Kindergarten College's diploma in 1905, she took charge of several kindergartens, then lectured to nurses at the Norland Nursing College until she joined the staff of her old college in 1912 as a lecturer in psychology and education; she later became vice-principal. Known as Zoe, she was diminutive in stature, radiated vitality and confidence, and always commanded attention. Her clear logical lectures were punctuated with searching questions. While nervous or reluctant students might quail before her, she encouraged those struggling to think for themselves. At a time when sex education was minimal, students always found her a sympathetic counsellor.

Zoe was continually pioneering new ventures. As a student she could not reconcile the constant direction of children in kindergartens with Friedrich Froebel's concept of creativity, so she won permission to introduce a daily free-play period, a practice which soon spread. In 1910-11 she launched and edited the *Australian Kindergarten Magazine*. Fired with enthusiasm by the Women's Institutes in Britain, in 1924 she established the Free Kindergarten Mothers' Union to enrich the lives of mothers of inner-city children. As president, she organized an annual handiwork exhibition for ten years and later a dramatic society, helping her raw recruits to reach remarkable levels of skill. In 1930 she established a holiday home for children from congested areas.

In 1916 Zoe Benjamin, after presenting a paper on sex training for young children, had been invited by the department of tutorial classes, University of Sydney, to begin child study tuition for parents. Her dynamic, family-centred approach to issues of child development and management was very popular and her classes flourished. In 1937 she resigned as vice-principal of the Sydney Kindergarten and Preparatory Teachers' College to concentrate on parent work; she also gave private consultations at her Hunters Hill home. Colleagues and parents urged her to write, and her pamphlet, *Education for parenthood* (Melbourne, 1944), was described by Professor Tasman Lovell [q.v.] as 'almost perfect in both form and matter', the reader being 'borne along by an unfailing clarity of exposition'. Radio talks for the Australian Broadcasting Commission's 'Kindergarten of the air' were published as *Talks to parents* (London, 1947). Her other publications included *The schoolchild and his parents* (Sydney, 1950). When the New Education Fellowship established a parent-education committee in 1950, she became chief lecturer.

Zoe Benjamin's lively interest in and enjoyment of all types of people made her very perceptive of human situations. The diversity of her interests, ranging from theatre and philosophy to gardening and dressmaking, enabled her to meet people at the point of their own enthusiasms, while her imaginative application of psychological and educational principles equipped her to give sound and practical advice. Long troubled by poor sight, she was blind when she died of cerebro-vascular disease at Hunters Hill on 13 April 1962; she was cremated with Anglican rites. Her estate was valued for probate at £9693. The Zoe Benjamin Memorial Fund was established and in 1963 presented to the Trustees of the Public Library of New South Wales; the Trustees used part of it for an initial purchase of books and have continued to administer the fund.

H. Dumolo, 'Zoe Benjamin', *Syd Kindergarten ... Teachers' College Mag*, Dec 1937; *Ivrian J*, Oct 1938; D. Mohr, '... A woman of infinite interests', *Aust Highway*, Feb 1953; *SMH*, 14 Apr 1962; Z. Benjamin letters (Sydney Kindergarten Teachers' College Archives, and ML); information from Miss M. Ford, Lane Cove, and Mrs C. McNamara, Gordon, NSW.   MARGARET HINSBY

BENNETT, AGNES ELIZABETH LLOYD (1872-1960), medical practitioner, was born on 24 June 1872 at Neutral Bay, Sydney, sixth child of W. C. Bennett [q.v.3], and his first wife Agnes Amelia, née Hays. Educated in England at Cheltenham Ladies' College and Dulwich Girls' High School until her mother's death in 1881, she attended Abbotsleigh girls' school in Sydney from July 1885, then the Girls' High School, Sydney, in 1888-89. She won a scholarship in 1890 and studied science at the University of Sydney (B.Sc., 1894); she was secretary of and a night-school teacher for the Women's Association (later University Women's Settlement).

Finding that female scientists were unwanted, Agnes Bennett worked as a teacher and governess, then left Australia in 1895 to study at the College of Medicine for Women, University of Edinburgh (M.B., Ch.M., 1899). She returned to Sydney in 1901 and set up in private practice in Darlinghurst Road. She soon became a committee-member of the (Church of England) District Nursing Association and gave free medical assistance. Prejudice against female doctors forced her to relinquish her practice, and accept a position on 1 December 1904 as junior medical officer at the Hospital for the Insane, Callan Park. Dissatisfied, in July 1905 she took over the practice of a woman doctor in Wellington, New Zealand, and this time prospered. An outstanding practitioner, she was chief medical officer in 1908-36 at St Helen's maternity hospital, and honorary physician to the children's ward of Wellington Hospital from 1910. In 1911 she completed her M.D. at Edinburgh. She was a consistent defender of women's right to higher education; in 1909 and 1914 she publicly opposed Drs Batchelor and Truby King, who saw higher education as detrimental to women's maternal functions and hence to the human race.

In 1915 Agnes Bennett became the first female commissioned officer in the British Army, when as a captain she worked as a medical officer in war hospitals in Cairo. In 1916-17 she was in charge of a unit of the Scottish Women's Hospitals on the Serbian front. She became the first president of the Wellington branch of the International Federation of University Women in 1923, and represented New Zealand at its world conference at Cracow, Poland, in 1936. She had visited Australia often since 1905, and in 1938-39 was medical officer at the hospital, staffed by flying doctors, at Burketown, North Queensland. She returned to Wellington and in 1939 helped to form the Women's War Service Auxiliary. Between 1940 and 1942 she worked in English hospitals and, on returning to New Zealand, lectured to the women's services on venereal disease and birth control.

Dr Bennett was appointed O.B.E. in 1948; she died in Wellington on 27 November 1960 and was cremated with Presbyterian rites. She had contributed largely to the improvement of maternal and infant medical care in New Zealand, and through example, argument and organization did much to advance women's status. In 1955 and 1956 she had given £10 000 for aeronautical research to the University of Sydney, which inherited the residue of her estate, valued for probate in New South Wales at £26 490.

Her portrait by Charles Hopkinson is held by the Wellington branch of the New Zealand Federation of University Women.

C. and C. Bennett, *Doctor Agnes Bennett* (Lond, 1960), and for bibliog; *SMH*, 26 Dec 1917, 20 May 1939, 12 Dec 1954, 10 Apr 1956, 7 Aug, 2 Dec 1960; W. C. Bennett papers (ML).   ANN CURTHOYS

BENNETT, ALFRED EDWARD (1889-1963), broadcasting executive, was born on 26 September 1889 at Balwyn, Victoria, son of George Jesse Bennett, schoolmaster, and his second wife Harriet Ann, née Bentley. He was educated at Balwyn State School and at Hawthorn College and had become secretary of the Freezing Co. Ltd at Murtoa, when he married Ruby Adelaide Frauenfelder at St James's Old Cathedral, Melbourne, on 11 June 1912. Next year he moved to Shepparton as secretary of the Goulburn Valley Industries Co. Ltd, and about 1919 he went to Western Australia to manage a meatworks at Carnarvon.

In 1922 Bennett began business in Sydney as a public accountant. In 1926 he was appointed manager of the Theosophical Society in Australia's commercial radio station 2GB, which began broadcasting on 23 August. A Theosophist himself from 1920, he reassured doubters that 'we have no axe to grind . . . we have no right to use wireless unless we utilize it for the Nation's uplift and progress'. Although a tiro in show business, he shrewdly assessed public taste, enlisted popular talent from other stations and gave unknown performers a chance. Among those he promoted were Eric, brother of Hollywood actor Ronald Colman, 'Uncle' George Saunders, 'Bimbo' Arthur Hahn, Jack Davey and Charles Cousens.

On Armistice Day 1929, with G. S. Arundale [q.v.] Bennett founded the Who's for Australia? League and became its first president until 1931 when his elder brother Brigadier General H. Gordon Bennett, president of the Chamber of Manufactures of New South Wales, took over. A. E. Bennett placed his faith in 'the discovery of a "strong man"' to lead Australia, and openly admired Mussolini. In March 1931 he became a vice-president of the All for Australia League and later that year, as a United Australia Party candidate, was defeated for the House of Representatives seat of Lang.

Bennett visited the United States of America in 1933-34 and in 1935. He obtained exclusive Australian rights to World Broadcasting Wide Range recordings, introduced radio transcriptions, and helped to found an Australian industry to produce radio programmes locally; he also set up American Radio Transcription Agencies (later Artransa). In 1934-36, as president of the Australian Federation of Commercial Broadcasting Stations, he strongly urged them to defend themselves from government encroachment; he demanded equal status with the Australian Broadcasting Commission, which, he argued, should 'cultivate a civic consciousness – a national sentiment – inculcate a high appreciation of music in Australian homes'. He was also a director of radio stations 3AW Melbourne and 5DN Adelaide.

In 1935 Bennett, feeling threatened by differences among local Theosophists, was appointed managing director of the Theosophical Broadcasting Station Ltd for seven years 'with extraordinarily full powers'. When next year 2GB combined with 2UE, he became managing director of the Broadcasting Service Association Ltd formed to run the two stations and soon sold his shares in the company. Asked to resign in 1937, next year he successfully sued the association for the agreed compensation, and in 1947, with (Sir) Garfield Barwick as counsel, he won a High Court appeal against the commissioner of taxation, maintaining that the compensation was a capital payment.

After Bennett retired he devoted himself to welfare work among children and old men, and became general secretary of the Australian Child Welfare Association. Survived by his wife, son and daughter, he died of coronary vascular disease at the wheel of his car outside his home at Vaucluse on 17 April 1963, and was cremated. His estate was valued for probate at £21 085.

I. K. Mackay, *Broadcasting in Australia* (Melb, 1957); B. Muirden, *The puzzled patriots* (Melb, 1968); R. R. Walker, *The magic spark* (Melb, 1973); K. Amos, *The New Guard Movement 1931-1935* (Melb, 1976); *Radio Trade Manual . . . of Australia*, 1934; J. McCarthy, '"All for Australia": some right wing responses to the depression . . . 1929-1932', *JRAHS*, 57 (1971); *Wireless Weekly*, 3 Sept 1926; *SMH*, 22 Sept 1937, 10 Nov 1938, 24 July, 13 Aug 1947; Rischbieth collection (NL); information from Mr R. E. Bennett, Surfers Paradise, Qld.

PHILIP GEEVES

BENNETT, ALFRED JOSHUA (1865-1946), soldier, educationist and administrator, was born on 10 January 1865 at Dry Valley Farm, Wagga Wagga, New South Wales, son of Barnett Basil Bennett, farmer, and his Irish-born wife Bridget Elizabeth Maria, née Russell. Educated at Wagga Wagga State School and Fort Street Training College, Sydney, he became a teacher with the Department of Public Instruction.

In 1885 Bennett enlisted in the Sudan Contingent as a corporal and saw action in the advance on Tamai. On his return he took up a teaching post at Wagga Wagga and on 10 April 1886 joined the local company of the New South Wales volunteer infantry as a second lieutenant. He was promoted lieutenant in December 1894 (he was then teaching at Windsor) and captain in March 1898. When the South African War broke out in October 1899 Bennett enlisted as a captain in the 1st New South Wales Mounted Rifles and was given command of 'D' Squadron. He was in action from February 1900 to March 1901, was severely wounded at Driefontein on 10 March 1900 and for 'courage and resource' at Bothaville on 5-6 November was awarded the Distinguished Service Order. His unit returned to Australia in April 1901 but Bennett, promoted major on 30 March, was transferred to the 3rd New South Wales Mounted Rifles Regiment and remained until May 1902. He commanded an independent mobile column under General Rimington, was mentioned in dispatches, and later attended the coronation of King Edward VII.

In 1902 Bennett resumed his career in the Department of Public Instruction and was a head teacher in 1914. On 13 August he was commissioned by Colonel H. N. MacLaurin [q.v.] to form the 3rd Battalion, Australian Imperial Force, which he expected to lead, but was appointed second-in-command to his close friend Lieut-Colonel R. H. Owen [q.v.], a regular soldier. The unit reached Egypt in December and went into training at Mena Camp where Bennett, who dealt severely with shirkers and malingerers, was soon nicknamed 'Defaulter's Waterloo'. A week after the landing at Gallipoli on 25 April 1915 he was promoted lieut-colonel and given command of the 4th Battalion. He led this unit during the Turkish attack on 15 May and soon afterwards became commander of the 1st Battalion. He served with distinction in the fierce battles for Lone Pine in August, when he was second-in-command to Brigadier General (Sir) Nevill M. Smyth [q.v.]. Wounded in action, he was evacuated with paratyphoid on 2 September and invalided to Australia; he received the Volunteer Officers' Decoration and was later appointed C.M.G. for his services at Lone Pine. From October 1916 to April 1917 he was in charge of troops on the transport *Ulysses*, then resumed active service in 1918, commanding the 20th Battalion in France from February to June. Invalided from the line, he was appointed commandant of the Australian reinforcements camp at Charleroi, Belgium.

Demobilized in October 1919, Bennett returned to the Department of Public Instruction and became supervisor of evening continuation colleges. On 18 November 1920 he married Catherine Josephine Lawler at St James Catholic Church, Glebe. He remained with the department until 1929 when he was headmaster of Waverley Public School. He was then appointed administrator and chief magistrate of Norfolk Island for a three-year term, after which he went into retirement. He had retired from the Australian Military Forces in 1925 with the rank of colonel; during World War II he served as a manpower officer. Survived by his wife, he died of cancer on 1 August 1946 at Randwick and was buried in South Head cemetery.

Aust Defence Dept, *Official records of the Australian military contingents to the war in South Africa*, P. L. Murray ed (Melb, 1912); C. E. W. Bean, *The story of Anzac* (Syd, 1921, 1924), and *The A.I.F. in France, 1918* (Syd, 1942); E. Wren, *Randwick to Hargicourt . . . 3rd Battalion, A.I.F.* (Syd, 1935); *V&P* (LA NSW), 1887-88, 7, 804, 1889, 3, Blue Book p 41; *PP* (NSW), 1912, 3, 123; *London Gazette*, 19 Apr 1901, 29 July 1902; *Reveille*, 1 July 1937, 1 Sept 1946; *SMH*, 20 June 1932; records (AWM).
DARRYL McINTYRE

BENNETT, GEORGE HENRY (1850-1908), brewer and radical politician, was born in Buckie, Banffshire, Scotland, son of George Bennett, schoolmaster, and his wife Margaret, née Young. He arrived in Victoria with his mother in March 1855, joining his father who later became town clerk of Collingwood. After education at St Patrick's College, he began work with a carrying firm which he managed when only 19. After managing the Victoria Sugar Co. he joined Timothy Lane who had operated a porter-brewing business, known as the Excelsior Brewery, in Collingwood and Richmond from about 1877. When larger firms captured much of the market the partners turned to manufacturing aerated waters and cordials at Richmond. From August 1883 Bennett carried on the business alone. By 1902 his well-equipped factory included stables for fifty-six horses.

Bennett lived at Richmond and was an enthusiastic promoter of local cricket, football and athletics clubs. Long-connected with friendly societies, he held high office in the United Ancient Order of Druids. In 1880 he became the youngest councillor in the colony when he was elected to the Richmond town council; as mayor in 1886-87, he helped to restore faith in an administration maligned because of financial mismanagement. In May 1889 he was elected with W. A. Trenwith [q.v.] to the double-member seat of Richmond in the Legislative Assembly, and was undefeated in the next seven elections. A liberal and protectionist, he joined the radical wing in opposition to the Deakin [q.v.]-Gillies [q.v.4] government. He opposed its handling of the maritime strike and constantly supported measures favouring the working class.

Bennett was president of the Licensed Victuallers' Association for some years, and continually stressed the need for lower duties on liquor and extended trading hours. His support for measures such as the eight-hour day sprang as much from an under-standing of the benefits to employers as from sympathy for the lot of the worker. He chastised fellow employers for antagonism towards trade unions, claiming that 'the employers had obtained all they wanted without coercion'.

Bennett found it increasingly difficult to reconcile his position as a successful industrialist with duties to a working-class electorate. A stubborn opponent of female suffrage, he reneged when confronted by local support for the issue. In 1903 he risked his majority by crossing the floor to vote for the railways employés strike bill: while still professing sympathy for the workers, he maintained that 'if the House allows them to do as they like they will defy the country'. He never held ministerial office but acted as Speaker and chairman of committees.

Bennett held emphatic views yet his integrity and humaneness were unquestioned. His political vision was uncomplicated; his radicalism owed little to ideology and his success was due to a whole-hearted involvement in the local community. However, his paternalism and faith in the common interests of labour and capital grew increasingly irrelevant.

Bennett had married Jessie Mill of Collingwood on 25 September 1879 at St Ignatius' Church, Richmond. He was an active Catholic. On 8 September 1908, aged 58, he died of pneumonia at his home and was buried in Boroondara cemetery, survived by his wife and two of their three daughters. His estate was valued for probate at £17 573. His bust stands outside the Richmond Town Hall, and bears the inscription:

Formed on the good old plan,
A true and brave and downright honest man.

A tear for pity and a hand open as day for melting charity.

J. Smith (ed), *Cyclopedia of Victoria*, 1-2 (Melb, 1903, 1904); *PD* (Vic), 1903, 198; *Aust Brewers' J*, 20 Feb 1898, 20 Feb 1907, 21 May 1910; S. M. Ingham, 'Political parties in the Victorian Legislative Assembly, 1880-1900', *Hist Studies*, no 15, Nov 1950; *Richmond Australian*, 7 Aug, 25 Sept 1880, 6, 20 Aug 1887, Sept-Oct 1908; *Leader* (Melb), 18 May 1889, 28 Feb 1903; *Age*, and *Argus*, 9 Sept 1908; M. G. Finlayson, Victorian politics 1889-94 (M.A. thesis, Univ Melb, 1964).
CHRIS McCONVILLE

BENNETT, HENRY GILBERT (1877-1959), radical, better known as Harry Scott Bennett, was born on 1 June 1877 at Chilwell, Geelong, Victoria, only child of James William Bennett, Bristol-born carpenter, and his wife Charlotte Mary, née Phipps, a schoolteacher. The family moved to Melbourne, where Bennett absorbed rationalism and republicanism from Joseph Symes [q.v.6] and Charles Rose. There also he developed his early socialism, as a foundation member of the Victorian Socialist League in 1897, in H. H. Champion's [q.v.] Social Democratic Party from 1902, and in Tom Mann's [q.v.] Victorian Socialist Party from 1906. After leaving his employment as a draper's assistant for full-time public speaking, he won the Ballarat West seat in the Legislative Assembly for the Political Labor Council in 1904. He worked hard for his constituents, taking a lively interest in education, unemployment and civil liberties and, after his marriage with Unitarian rites to Caroline (Carrie) Thomas on 1 March 1905, seemed securely launched on a parliamentary career. But his eagerness for social change had bred impatience and a conviction that workers needed to be better educated to make the best use of parliament. He resigned his seat in 1907 and returned to full-time educational work. Generous, eloquent, with a gentle humour and a fine, cultivated voice, energetic, a prodigious reader with a photographic memory, he became one of Australasia's finest public speakers.

In 1907 Scott Bennett went to Sydney and worked in H. E. Hollands's [q.v.] International Socialist Club. He travelled widely and was a delegate to the Socialist Federation of Australasia. Late in 1909 he made the first of many trips to New Zealand, working there for the Federation of Labor and the Social Democratic Party and in industrial actions such as the 1912 Waihi strike. In 1913 in New Zealand Bennett was devastated by the death of his young wife, leaving him with two small daughters and a son. Soon afterwards he settled there temporarily as national organizer for the Social Democratic Party. In 1915, still restless over the loss of his wife, he went to the United States of America where he conducted a series of highly successful lecture tours for both the American Socialist Lecture Bureau and the National Rationalist Association. Returning to Australia in 1917 he threw himself whole-heartedly into the anti-conscription cause. He rejoined the Victorian Socialist Party as its principal lecturer and debater, undertook strenuous interstate propaganda tours, pamphleteered, ran speaking and social science classes, wrote for *Ross's monthly of protest, personality and progress*, and was a foundation member of the Y Club. Bennett sought to unify the Socialist movement and equip it with a more effective strategy, but in the turbulent years after World War I both seemed distant. In 1920 he resigned his position with the Socialist Party to return to independent educational work, though his continuing ties were illustrated by his marriage in Sydney in November 1922

to an active party-member, Eliza Jane Joynson, 29-year-old daughter of a shearer.

Increasingly Scott Bennett felt that people had to acquire rational thought processes before they could grasp the importance of Marxist economics. He lectured more frequently under rationalist auspices, ranging over politics, economics, science and astronomy, and was among the pioneers in Australasia of public discussion of social issues such as the nature of marriage, birth control, sexual mores and practices, venereal disease, and mental health. Between 1922 and 1940 he made several successful lecturing tours for the New Zealand Rationalist Society, some of which were sponsored by anti-prohibition interests. He also tutored for seven years in public speaking for the University of Melbourne Extension Board, lectured for the Social Science Forum, promoted Esperanto, worked in the Movement Against War and Fascism and was active in defence of civil liberties – for example in the Book Censorship Abolition League and in the Egon Kisch case. In 1936 he settled in Sydney as lecturer and secretary for the New South Wales Rationalist Association. He lectured in public speaking until 1951 for the Workers' Educational Association and became a familiar figure in the Domain and at Ingersoll Hall, then Sydney's rationalist headquarters. He brought to Sydney rationalism tolerance, an active interest in a variety of progressive movements, and an insistence that rationalists should understand society's underlying economic relationships. This tolerance and his personal integrity ensured that he emerged untarnished from the internal crises that occasionally troubled the movement.

Scott Bennett gave his last public address in March 1959. He had suffered for many years from emphysema and chronic bronchitis and died on 24 May of coronary occlusion at Waverley War Memorial Hospital; his ashes were scattered in Northern Suburbs cemetery. He was survived by his wife and by three children of his first marriage. His only estate consisted of a fine library, now held by the Australian National University, and the enlightenment he gave during his life to thousands of his fellows.

B. Walker, 'Harry Scott Bennett: an appreciation', *Labour Hist*, May 1969, no 16; H. Scott Bennett collection (ANU Archives); papers held by Mrs Dolly Scott Bennett, Chippendale, NSW, *and* by author.   GRAEME OSBORNE

BENNETT, JAMES MALLETT (1894-1922), airman and mechanic, was born on 14 January 1894 at St Kilda, Victoria, son of

James Thomas Bennett, tick-maker, and his wife Henrietta Augusta, née McKendrick. After schooling he trained as a motor mechanic. In 1912 he joined the militia and served for three years with the 49th Battalion.

Bennett enlisted in the Australian Imperial Force on 14 July 1915 and, on the formation of the Australian Flying Corps early next year, was posted to 'C' Flight, No. 1 Squadron, as a mechanic. On arrival in Egypt in mid-April, the squadron's mechanics were split up into several parties and assigned to British units for training. Bennett joined No. 14 Squadron, Royal Flying Corps, and trained as a fitter and turner. After returning to his own unit he was promoted corporal on 24 August; later that year he began duty with No. 67 Squadron, R.F.C., an all-Australian squadron serving with the British Expeditionary Force in Egypt. Except for a brief period spent at its base at Abbassia, he remained with No. 67 Squadron throughout the Sinai and Palestine campaigns. Promoted sergeant in March 1918, he was mentioned in dispatches soon afterwards and was later awarded the Meritorious Service Medal for his distinguished service as an air mechanic.

After the Armistice Bennett and Sergeant W. H. Shiers [q.v.] were invited to act as air mechanics for Captain Ross Smith [q.v.], then attempting the first Cairo-Calcutta flight in a Handley-Page aircraft. Both mechanics received the Air Force Medal for outstanding work under hazardous conditions during the flight. The same crew then carried out a survey by ship of the proposed Calcutta-Koepang (Timor) air route. On 7 July 1919 Bennett was attached to a Royal Air Force unit on the north-west frontier in India; here he superintended the rigging of Bristol fighters for use in reconnaissance and offensive missions during the short but fierce Afghan campaign.

In 1919 the Australian government offered a prize of £10 000 to the first aviator to fly from England to Australia within thirty days. Ross Smith and his brother Keith [q.v.] entered the race with Bennett and Shiers as their mechanics and were the first to reach Darwin. Their success aroused world-wide interest and acclaim. On 22 December the Smith brothers were knighted; Bennett and Shiers received Bars to their Air Force Medals. Popular opinion favoured greater recognition for the mechanics, especially after Ross Smith stated publicly that the success of the flight was mainly due to their skill and zeal. On 19 March 1920 the minister for defence announced that Bennett had been promoted senior warrant officer, class 1; six months later he was granted the honorary rank of lieutenant in the A.I.F. reserve of officers.

Early in 1922 the Smith brothers decided to attempt a round-the-world flight; Bennett and Shiers were again chosen as mechanics. The crew planned to take off from England on 25 April, but on 13 April Ross Smith and Bennett were killed during a test flight at Weybridge, when their Vickers Viking Amphibian crashed. The pioneer aviators were mourned as national heroes and their bodies were brought back to Australia. Bennett was buried in St Kilda cemetery on 19 June 1922 after a lying-in-state at Queen's Hall, Parliament House. An obelisk in his honour was unveiled at St Kilda on 26 April 1927.

Ross Smith, *14,000 miles through the air* (Lond, 1922); F. M. Cutlack, *The Australian Flying Corps ... 1914-18* (Syd, 1923); N. Eustis, *The greatest air race* (Adel, 1969); *London Gazette*, 14 June 1918, 3 June, 26 Dec 1919; *Sea, Land, and Air*, Dec 1919, 1 May, 1 July 1922; *Australasian*, 4 Feb, 15 Apr 1922; *SMH*, 14 Apr 1922; *Argus*, 19 Apr, 16-19 June 1922; *Sun-News Pictorial*, 26 Apr 1927.   REX CLARK*

BENNETT, MARY MONTGOMERIE (1881-1961), teacher and advocate of Aboriginal rights, was born on 8 July 1881 at Pimlico, London, daughter of Robert Christison [q.v.3] and his wife Mary, née Godsall. Because their mother detested life on Lammermoor station in North Queensland, the children were educated mainly by governesses in Sydney, Brisbane, and in Tasmania, Australian country towns and England, but Mary learned nevertheless to share her father's strong affection for the Aboriginals on his run. Artistically gifted, she was a student at the Royal Academy of Arts in 1903-08; she accompanied Christison back to Australia for the sale of Lammermoor, and settled with her parents at Barwell Park in Lincolnshire. On 18 August 1914 she married the 58-year-old Peninsular & Orient captain Charles Douglas Bennett before he left for war service in the Royal Naval Reserve. When he retired from the sea in 1921, they settled in London, where she took an active role in the British Empire League.

In 1927 she published *Christison of Lammermoor*, a biography of her father reflecting his vigorous hostility to trade unionism and his deep sympathy for and insight into Aboriginal society. After her husband died in November, she distributed family papers and mementoes to various institutions and, in October 1930, arrived in Perth to devote the rest of her life to the welfare of Aboriginals.

After short periods with the United Aborigines Mission at Gnowangerup in the south-west and at the Forrest River Mission, she settled late in 1932 at the Mount Margaret Mission near Laverton, managed by Pastor R. M. Schenk who shared her distrust of anthropologists and pastoralists. There she devoted herself principally to unorthodox but highly successful primary teaching of Aboriginal children and the promotion of handicrafts among Aboriginal women. Her teaching was supplemented by tireless agitation for Aboriginal rights, which made her anathema to State officials and politicians. She corresponded widely, persuaded the Women's Service Guild and the Country Women's Association to take up her cause, and was able to use London friends to spread her views outside Australia. After wide British press coverage in June 1933 of her charges of maltreatment, made to the British Commonwealth League, the Western Australian government appointed H. D. Moseley as royal commissioner to inquire into Aboriginal problems. His 1934 report rejected most of her allegations but conceded the need for reforms.

Undeterred by this failure and by frequent illness, Mrs Bennett continued agitation, particularly on behalf of Aboriginal women. She co-operated gladly with small activist groups and in 1938 participated in the Aboriginal day of mourning at the Sydney sesqui-centennial celebrations. About 1940 she returned to England in order to remedy her educational deficiencies. She matriculated at the University of London in 1944 but did not take a degree and returned to Australia about 1950. Soon after, she retired to Kalgoorlie and died there on 6 October 1961; she was buried in the Kalgoorlie cemetery with the rites of the Churches of Christ.

Mary Bennett wrote *The Australian Aboriginal as a human being* (London, 1930) and substantial pamphlets on Aboriginal affairs between 1935 and 1957. She urged Aboriginal bodies to adopt an International Labor Office convention asserting the right of native peoples to independence. Although fluent in French and German, she made no attempt to learn any Aboriginal language and taught only in English. Tall, gaunt, elegant and austere-looking, she cared little for clothes and often dressed in black. She always seemed well off and donated a Christison Memorial Hospital to the Mount Margaret Mission, but her estate in England amounted only to £163.

P. Biskup, *Not slaves, not citizens* (Brisb, 1973); J. Horner, 'Blacks and whites together', *Politics* (Syd), 11 (1976), no 1; CSO 166/32 (Battye Lib, Perth); information from Mrs R. M. Schenk, Esperance, WA.　　　　　　G. C. BOLTON
　　　　　　　　　　　　　　H. J. GIBBNEY

BENNY, SUSAN GRACE (1872-1944), local government councillor and housewife, was born on 4 October 1872 in the Crown Inn, Adelaide, daughter of Peter Anderson, a farmer at Morphett Vale, and his wife Agnes Ellen, née Harriot. The Andersons later owned Springfield, a sheep-station on Yorke Peninsula; Grace, whose mother died when she was nine, grew up there. Later she went to a small boarding-school for girls at McLaren Vale, then returned home and taught her younger sisters. On 16 July 1896 at Springfield, she married her cousin Benjamin, a solicitor (LL.B., 1891) and son of George Benny, Free Presbyterian minister and teacher, and his wife Susanna, née Anderson.

The Bennys established a home, Stoneywood, in suburban Seacliff and raised three daughters and two sons. Grace maintained an interest in poetry and literature; she and her husband built up a valuable library of over 2000 volumes. Active in community life, during World War I she was honorary secretary of the Seacliff Cheer-up Society, and also prominent in the local spinning club, progress association and croquet club. Interested in politics, in 1918 she was president of the women's branch of the South Australian Liberal Union, where she had ensured that equality of divorce for women was placed on the party's platform; in 1918 this became law. Her husband had been mayor of Brighton City Council in 1903-05 and on 22 December 1919 Grace herself became the first female member of a local government council in Australia. Believing that there was work in this area which only a woman was likely to initiate, she represented the newly created Seacliff ward. She kept her seat through two elections, and stood unsuccessfully for mayor in 1922. In 1921 she had been made a justice of the peace. In 1919-26 her husband, a Nationalist, was a Federal senator and member of the 1923 royal commission on national insurance and of the joint committee on public accounts in 1923-25. He resigned from parliament on 27 January 1926 due to ill health and in June was convicted of embezzlement and sentenced to three years hard labour. He was also declared insolvent.

Grace Benny now had to rely on money she had inherited to support her children. Unusually resourceful for a woman of her period who had never worked for a living, she moved into her husband's office in King William Street and opened the Elite Employment Agency. This she ran throughout the Depression, to the mutual satisfaction of both employers and the unemployed, for many of whom she provided a meal and a bed. All her children had a private school education.

Benjamin Benny returned to work as a salesman for Beck's bookshop, but was never really successful. He died on 10 February 1935. Grace, no longer working, in Melbourne on 23 February 1940 married Cecil Ralph Bannister, a tramway worker and clerk twenty years her junior. They lived in Adelaide. Grace died at North Adelaide on 5 November 1944, survived by her second husband; she was buried in the Scots cemetery, Morphett Vale, leaving an estate sworn for probate at £1420. Small and fine-boned, she had been a cheerful, energetic and courageous woman. The Brighton Council named a crescent and a building, which is a centre for women's charity groups, after her. But for her husband's disastrous collapse, she might have achieved more in politics.

H. T. Burgess (ed), *Cyclopedia of South Australia*, 1 (Adel, 1908); H.A.F. Taylor (ed), *History of Brighton, South Australia* (Brighton, 1958); A. V. Smith, *Women in Australian parliaments and local governments, past and present* (Canb, 1975); *Observer* (Adel), 20 Dec 1919, 19 June 1926, 22 Jan 1927; *Advertiser* (Adel), 12 Feb 1935, 7 Nov 1944; minute-books, 22 Dec 1919-18 Dec 1922 (Brighton City Council, SA); GRG 66/5/26, file no 7629 (SAA).   SUZANNE EDGAR

BENSON, LOUISA (1845-1920), religious Sister and educationist, known as Mother Mary Hilda, was born on 12 May 1845 at York, England, daughter of Christopher Benson and his wife Mary, née Stein. Louisa Benson was a convert to Catholicism. In 1865 she graduated with distinction from Notre Dame Training College, Liverpool, and then taught for a time at Hurst Green. She entered the Institute of the Blessed Virgin Mary (Loreto) at Rathfarnham, Dublin, on 10 January 1868. Her first appointment after profession on 10 May 1871 was as principal of Loreto National School, Dalkey, Dublin. She clashed immediately with an inspector, refusing to oblige Irish children to read the strongly nationalist English texts; later she watched with satisfaction as the children danced around a bonfire of the offending books.

In 1876 Mother Hilda arrived in Australia to join the Irish Loreto Sisters who had made their Australian foundation at Ballarat in the previous year, under Mother Mary Gonzaga Barry [q.v.3]. She was appointed principal of St Joseph's primary school, Dawson Street, Ballarat, in March 1877. Thereafter, she was invariably entrusted with the task of opening or staffing new parish schools including those at Redan (1882), Portland (1885) and South Melbourne (1891), and she also took charge of an existing school at Randwick, New South Wales (1896). Clearly she was considered a very able teacher and administrator. St Joseph's, Ballarat, planned along the lines of the Notre Dame practising schools, became a model for parochial schools throughout Australia.

Mother Hilda was also deeply interested in the training of teachers. In 1877 at St Joseph's she introduced a five-year programme for pupil-teachers. Then followed, in 1884, the erection of the Dawson Street Training College which she and Mother Gonzaga planned jointly to meet the needs of diocesan schools. It was one of the earliest Catholic training colleges in Australia and remarkable for its five-year course of study. As foundation-principal, Mother Hilda again drew on her recollections of Notre Dame.

After the Registration of Teachers and Schools Act of 1905, the Victorian bishops sought a principal for the proposed Central Catholic Training College at Albert Park. Evidence suggests that they originally thought of making a secular appointment, probably Miss Barbara Bell [q.v.]; only when Mother Gonzaga rejected this proposal was Mother Hilda named principal and Miss Bell mistress of method. When the college opened on 1 May 1906, Mother Hilda's main responsibility was the moral and social welfare of students, their intellectual training being the special concern of Miss Bell. Within a few years, however, Mother Hilda's influence seems to have permeated all aspects of college life. Former students long recalled her precise, lively mind.

In 1913 she returned to Ballarat, where she spent her last years, seriously afflicted by arthritis. She died at Loreto Abbey, Mary's Mount, on 2 August 1920, and was buried in the new cemetery, Ballarat.

B. Hoare, *The Institute of the Blessed Virgin Mary* (Melb, 1925); M. Oliver, *Love is a light burden* (Lond, 1950); *Age*, 6 Aug 1906; M. Gonzaga Barry letters (Loreto Abbey, Ballarat); M. H. Benson letters (MDHC Archives, Fitzroy); Central Catholic Training College, Register of students 1906-19, *and* prospectus, 1911 (MDHC Archives, Fitzroy); information from Mother Borgia Tipping, Mandeville Hall, Toorak, and Mother Mildred Dew, Loreto Abbey, Ballarat, Vic.

                                         IMELDA PALMER

BENSON, LUCY CHARLOTTE (1860-1943), musician and theatrical entrepreneur, was born on 1 March 1860 in Hobart Town, eldest of ten children of Thomas Westbrook, auctioneer, and his wife Fanny, née Lempriere, a talented singer, and was related to Lempriere Pringle [q.v.]. Lucy was educated privately; she studied singing with del Sarte and Madame Emery Gould, and piano with Herr Guenett of Melbourne and later with Fraulein Mayer and F. A. G. Packer [q.v.5]. When 10 Lucy was playing as organist in three churches each Sunday; later she was organist at four Hobart churches of various denominations.

She had 'a sweet voice that lingered in the memory', sang in many concerts, managed, directed and conducted light operas, and was perhaps the first female conductor of opera in the Australian theatre. She produced most of Gilbert and Sullivan, and had been the female lead in *H.M.S. Pinafore* in 1879. In opera Lucy had met William Benson, whom she married on 2 June 1881 at Bellerive; they had six children.

Her musical career continued unabated: in 1901 she sang before the duke and duchess of York and two years later her choir won the eisteddfod at Bathurst, New South Wales. Returning through Sydney they gave a concert and the *Daily Telegraph* praised their 'high discipline, admirable finish and effective . . . control'. In 1905 Lucy took an enlarged choir, including eight of her family, to South Street, Ballarat, where they won the championship of the Commonwealth. On their return they received a civic welcome in the streets of Hobart from the city band and the inhabitants.

At this stage Lucy Benson, by her musical activities, had raised £1600 for charity. Not surprisingly she was lauded in verse in the press as able to 'undermine a mountain', 'bound to boss the play', and referred to as 'The Great Commanding Spirit of the South' who could 'organize high Heaven'. For half a century there were few musical occasions in Tasmania, religious or secular, in which she had no hand, either as manager, conductor, soloist, director, accompanist or costume designer. Sometimes she combined all these functions. Her teaching, which was based on a thorough grounding in enunciation and the art of breathing, was another important aspect of her career. Percy Grainger [q.v.] praised her pupils and Amy Sherwin [q.v.6], the 'Tasmanian Nightingale', considered her 'one of the best teachers of voice production' in the colonies. Lucy Benson's accompaniments were described as 'magnetic' by one commentator.

In 1913 she moved, and worked in northern Tasmania, but she returned to Hobart in 1928 and took part in broadcasting. For relaxation she specialized in violet-breeding and the raising of prize poultry. She was still organist at St Mark's, Bellerive, when 83. Predeceased by her husband, Lucy Benson died on 14 October 1943 at Sandy Bay and was buried in Cornelian Bay cemetery. One of her sons, Charles, had a successful musical career in London.

Cyclopedia of Tasmania, 1 (Hob, 1900); W. A. Orchard, *Music in Australia* (Melb, 1952); *Examiner* (Launc), and *Mercury*, 15 Oct 1943; *Saturday Evening Mercury*, 19 Jan 1974; family papers and scrap-books (held by Mr D. Taylor, Lindisfarne, Tas).   DIANA LARGE

BENSTEAD, THOMAS ARTHUR (1896-1971), motor cyclist, was born on 21 May 1896 at Leichhardt, Sydney, twin son of Gregory Blades Benstead, butcher, and his wife Edith Grace, née Jones. In 1916 he joined the Newtown Bicycle Club and competed against well-known riders. Employed by Turner Bros, cycle agents, in George Street, about 1917 Benstead was lent a motor bike and came second in an acceleration test. He borrowed a Turner Jap machine from his employers and won a 33-mile (53 km) road race at Goulburn, on a circuit which was severely rain-affected. The first motor cycle he owned was a second-hand 1917 Harley-Davidson, on which he won many hill climbs and acceleration tests. In the early 1920s he joined Bennett & Wood Ltd who sponsored him on Harley-Davidsons.

In that decade Tommy Benstead won more motor cycle races than any other rider in Australia. He competed throughout New South Wales, and in Queensland, Victoria and South Australia, conquering all kinds of tracks: long and short, road, dirt, cinder, concrete, grass and board. On 21 January 1923 he rode from Melbourne to Sydney in 14 hours 43 minutes, lowering the record by 1 hour 36 minutes. At Deagon Racecourse, Queensland, in August 1924 he set three solo and three side-car records, including the Five Mile Solo in which he showed his great skill in cornering. At Brisbane in 1928 he won golden and silver helmets and a silver sash. Next year he won the 'Fast and Furious' shield for which he had dead-heated the previous year. He collected many solo and side-car championships, setting Australian and world records; his trophies included golden and silver stars, gauntlets and helmets. He also took part in petrol-consumption tests and reliability trials. His riding was cool and well calculated, his judgment of just when to use the tactic which would enable him to go to the front and win was admirable. He handled the heavy motor cycles with superlative ease in exceptional conditions. A member of the Motor Cycle Club of New South Wales, Benstead was among the first to insist that protective fences should be erected to safeguard spectators.

On 10 August 1929 at the Baptist Church, Dulwich Hill, he married Jessie McGavin, a tailoress from Edinburgh; they lived at Lakemba and he apparently gave up racing. He continued to work as a salesman, and enjoyed playing tennis. Survived by his wife, two sons and a daughter, Benstead died of coronary vascular disease on 25 January 1971 in the Canterbury Hospital and was cremated with Anglican rites. His estate was valued for probate at $14 192.

Auto-cyclist, 1920-24; *Daily Mirror,* 8 Aug 1959; news-cuttings (held by author). RAY WHITE

BERGIN, MICHAEL (1879-1917), Jesuit priest and military chaplain, was born in August 1879 at Fancroft, Tipperary, Ireland, son of Michael Bergin, mill-owner, and his wife Mary, née Hill. Educated at the local convent school and the Jesuit College at Mungret, Limerick, he entered the Jesuit noviceship at Tullabeg in September 1897. Two years later he was sent to the Syrian mission where English-speakers were needed; he felt the break from home and country very keenly but became absorbed in his missionary work and the exotic customs of the local peoples. After learning Arabic and French he studied philosophy at Ghazir, and in October 1904 began teaching at the Jesuit College in Beirut.

In 1907 Bergin was sent to Hastings, England, to complete his theology studies and was ordained priest on 24 August 1910. After a short time at home he returned to Hastings for further study and then gave missions and retreats in the south of England. He returned to the Middle East in January 1914 and was in charge of Catholic schools near Damascus until the outbreak of World War I; along with other foreigners in Syria, he was then imprisoned and later expelled by the Turkish government. By the time he reached the French Jesuit College in Cairo in January 1915 the first Australian troops had arrived in Egypt, and Bergin offered to assist the Catholic military chaplains. Though still a civilian, he was dressed by the men in the uniform of a private in the Australian Imperial Force and when the 5th Light Horse Brigade left for Gallipoli he went with it. Sharing the hardships of the troops, he acted as priest and stretcher-bearer until his official appointment as chaplain came through on 13 May 1915. He remained at Anzac until September when he was evacuated to the United Kingdom with enteric fever.

Bergin's arrival home in khaki, complete with emu feather in his slouch-hat, caused a sensation among his family and friends. Though tired and weak after his illness, he was anxious to get back to his troops for Christmas. He returned to Lemnos but was pronounced unfit and confined to serving in hospitals and hospital-ships. Evacuated to Alexandria in January 1916, he worked in camps and hospitals in Egypt and in April joined the 51st Battalion, A.I.F., at Tel-el-Kebir. He accompanied it to France and served as a chaplain in all its actions in 1916-17; these included the battles of Pozières and Mouquet Farm, the advance on the Hindenburg Line and the battle of Messines. He was killed at Passchendaele on 11 October 1917 when a heavy shell burst near the aid-post where he was working. He was buried in the village churchyard at Renninghelst, Belgium.

Bergin was awarded the Military Cross posthumously. The citation praised his unostentatious but magnificent zeal and courage. Though he had never seen Australia he was deeply admired by thousands of Australian soldiers, one of whom referred to him as 'a man made great through the complete subordination of self'.

L. C. Wilson and H. Wetherell, *History of the Fifth Light Horse Regiment* (Syd, 1926); Sister S., *A son of St. Patrick* (Dublin, 1932); *51st Battalion Newsletter* (Perth), July 1962; F. Gorman, 'Father Michael Bergin, S. J.', *Jesuit Life,* July 1976.

J. EDDY

BERNACCHI, ANGELO GUILIO DIEGO (1853-1925), entrepreneur, was born on 1 July 1853 at Lozza, Como, Italy, son of Luigi Bernacchi, landowner and lawyer, and his wife Teresa, née Cortellezzi. Educated at a technical school at Varese and for four years at Barmen, Prussia, on 20 September 1876 he married Barbe Straetmans in Brussels. They settled in England where Bernacchi represented the silk-spinning firms, Societa per la Filatura dei Cascami de Seta of Milan and Arles Dufour & Co. of Basle and Lyons. He and his wife and three small children arrived in Melbourne on 13 January 1884 in the *Orient,* and went on to Tasmania next day.

Bernacchi wished to introduce sericulture to the colony and chose Maria Island, which enchanted him. In April the family moved to the former convict settlement of Darlington at the north of the island. Although many colonists were suspicious of the charming, persuasive Italian, the Maria Island Leasing Act was passed on 24 November 1884 granting Bernacchi a lease from 1 January 1885 for ten years at one shilling a year. The conditions included outlaying £10 000 and establishing sericulture and viticulture within twelve months. At the end of the first five years, if the lessee had expended £5000 he would be entitled to select 500 acres (202 ha) on the island as freehold at £1 per acre. If either industry were established by 1895, Bernacchi would be entitled to a forty-year lease at £300 per annum. He soon spent £1000 on improvements to Darlington, planting orchards and 50 000 vines from the de Castella [q.v.3] vineyards in Victoria.

In 1886 Bernacchi was naturalized and invited parliamentarians to inspect the island. They were welcomed with fireworks, brilliant Chinese and Venetian lanterns, and champagne banquets. The first grapes were picked in May. (Sir) Matthew Davies [q.v.4] visited the island and was so impressed that he became Bernacchi's partner. The Maria Island Co. was floated in 1887 with a capital of £250 000 and Bernacchi as resident managing director. The company planned to establish a township and its intended interests included sericulture, wine-making, fruit-growing, farming, cement, limestone and marble, fisheries, and sheep and cattle fattening. Darlington, re-named San Diego, by 1888 was a boom town of about 250 people of a dozen nationalities. Buildings had been repaired and others erected, including a hotel and coffee palace. The island was dubbed 'the Ceylon of Australasia, and a Tasmanian Eden'. In 1888 Bernacchi was appointed a justice of the peace; next year he was to represent Tasmania at the Paris Exhibition but did not attend; and in 1889-92 he was a municipal councillor at Spring Bay, where the family now lived at Louisville.

In 1892 the Maria Island Co. was voluntarily liquidated and Bernacchi went to England where he floated the Land Development and Cement Co. of Tasmania Ltd to produce cement on the island. But a financial crisis, the depression, over-optimism and grandiose ideas contributed to his failure. San Diego again became a ghost-town, its name reverting to Darlington. The Bernacchis and their daughters returned to England about 1897, their son Roderick remaining in Melbourne in charge of his business and his father's interests.

In 1918 Bernacchi returned to Australia as a director of National Portland Cement Ltd, which had an authorized capital of £600 000. (Sir) Robert Knox [q.v.], a director, went to Denmark to buy the best equipment available and supervise its shipping to the island. Production began shortly before Bernacchi became ill and left the island; he died in Melbourne of cerebro-vascular disease on 12 March 1925. Predeceased by his wife, he was buried in Brighton cemetery, survived by three daughters and two of his three sons. His estate was sworn for probate at £481.

The company ceased business in 1930. Prosperous when he had arrived in the colony, Bernacchi had the temperament of a gambler and lived on his wits promoting companies, but he never enjoyed much prosperity. From the 1890s onwards he was stout, with a moustache. He spoke several languages, and was popular, charming and a benevolent employer. The most colourful story about him alleges that he tied bunches of grapes on the vines to impress visiting dignitaries. He built up the island's reputation in Australia and overseas, and frequent newspaper coverage in the 1880s and 1890s used terms such as 'King Diego' and 'His Most Amiable Majesty'. His eldest son, Louis Charles [q.v.], became a distinguished Antarctic scientist.

'Dio' (C. Morton), *Maria Island* (Hob, 1888); M. Weidenhofer, *Maria Island* (Melb, 1977); *PP* (Tas), 1884 (40), 1886 (17, 103, 134, 172); *Age*, 14, 15 Jan 1884, 18 Oct 1886; *Mercury*, 28 Jan, 12 Mar 1884, 25 Apr, 5 May, 13 Oct 1888; *Tas Mail*, 23 Aug 1884, 8 May 1886; *Examiner* (Launc), 18 Jan 1896; family information.   MARGARET WEIDENHOFER

BERNACCHI, LOUIS CHARLES (1876-1942), scientist and Antarctic explorer, was born on 8 November 1876 in Belgium, eldest child of Angelo Guilio Diego Bernacchi [q.v.] and his wife Barbe, née Straetmans. Louis arrived in Tasmania with his parents in 1884 and they settled on Maria Island off the east coast. On 27 February 1886 the family was naturalized.

Bernacchi was educated privately and at The Hutchins School, Hobart (1889-91). From about 1895 he visited the Melbourne Observatory to gain experience in practical astronomy and terrestrial magnetism, and from March 1897 spent a year there training in sextant work and in the use of magnetic instruments. He was influenced by the work of the various Australian Antarctic committees, and showed his interest in both commercial and scientific aspects of Antarctic work through letters to the Tasmanian and Victorian press in 1896-97. In particular, C. E. Borchgrevink's [q.v.] account of his work on the whaler *Antarctic* during 1895 aroused Bernacchi's enthusiasm, and when Borchgrevink organized his *Southern Cross* expedition (1898-1900), he travelled to London to join it as physicist and astronomer; he became the first Australian to work and winter in Antarctica.

Bernacchi wrote a vivid account of the expedition, *To the south polar regions* (London, 1901). The Royal Geographical Society (London) made him a fellow in 1900 and awarded him the Peek Grant. Later he was recruited as physicist for Captain R. F. Scott's British National Antarctic Expedition (1901-04); he was regarded as a tireless and energetic observer and a 'cheerful and loyal friend' to all the party. His scientific writings and Scott's published views testify to the value of his work, and he was awarded the Royal Geographical Society and the King's Antarctic medals as well as the French Cross of the Légion d'honneur (1906). After his return he travelled in Africa and on 10 February 1906 at Preston parish church, Sussex, England, married Winifred Edith Harris; Scott was his best man. Later that year he explored the upper Amazon Basin, Peru. Scott tried to recruit him for his ill-fated second Antarctic expedition (1910-13) but family responsibilities deterred him. He then made a foray into British politics — in 1910 failing twice as a Liberal candidate — invested in rubber plantations in Malaya, Java and Borneo, and maintained a lively interest in the Antarctic.

In World War I Bernacchi was first a lieut-commander in the Royal Naval (Volunteer) Reserve, then worked on the Naval Staff of the Admiralty (anti-submarine division), and later with the United States Navy. In 1919 he was awarded the O.B.E. (military) and the United States Navy Cross. After the war he returned to his rubber interests in south-east Asia. He remained active in scientific organizations such as the Royal Geographical Society, of which he was a council-member in 1928-32, the British Science Guild and the British Association for the Advancement of Science. Plans in 1925 for an expedition of his own to the Antarctic were dropped because of the costs involved. In 1930 he organized the British Polar Exhibition; he published several books on Antarctic matters, including *A very gallant gentleman* (London, 1933), a biography of Captain L. E. G. Oates; and helped to organize the Second International Polar Year (1931-32).

On the outbreak of World War II Bernacchi, with his former rank, returned to the R.N.V.R. to work on the organization of 'Q' ships. But his health was failing and on 24 April 1942 he died at his London home, survived by his wife and their two sons and two daughters.

PP (Vic), 1898, 3 (47); *Geog J*, 99 (1942); R. A. Swan, 'Louis Charles Bernacchi', *VHM*, 33 (1962-63); *The Times*, 25 Apr 1942.

R. A. SWAN

BERRY, RICHARD JAMES ARTHUR (1867-1962), anatomist, neurologist and anthropologist, was born on 30 May 1867 at Upholland, Lancashire, England, son of James Berry, coal merchant, and his wife Jane, née Barlow. His father died before he was born. Supported by his grandfather, he received his early education at Southport,

first at a dame's school and then in 1877 at a private school for boys. Having passed the University of Cambridge local examination at honours standard, he was apprenticed to a firm of shipbrokers in Liverpool. After several years he decided that he wanted to do a medical course at the University of Edinburgh and, having received permission to break his contract, matriculated there in May 1886. In 1891 he graduated M.B., Ch.M., and became house-surgeon to Thomas Annandale, Regius professor of clinical surgery at the Royal Infirmary. In the same year he was president of the Royal Medical Society of Edinburgh, a student group. His prize-winning thesis for his M.D. in 1894 was on the vermiform appendix.

In 1895 Berry became a fellow of the Royal College of Surgeons of Edinburgh and next year was appointed lecturer in anatomy at the school of medicine of the Royal Colleges, where he soon showed his outstanding ability. In 1897 he was elected a fellow of the Royal Society of Edinburgh. He was by now a widely recognized teacher with well-established classes. For relaxation he took to mountaineering, conquering most of the Scottish peaks; he also toured much of Scotland and northern England by bicycle. On 7 August 1900 he married Beatrice Catherine, daughter of Sir Samuel Brighouse, who was also a cyclist and mountain-climber. Berry made several cycling tours of France and Germany with her, for they were both keenly interested in art; moreover he was anxious to improve his German.

In December 1905 Berry was appointed to the chair of anatomy at the University of Melbourne. His typescript autobiography, 'Chance and circumstance', contains an amusing account of his arrival in February 1906, and of the run-down condition of his department: (Sir) Harry Allen [q.v.], who had been professor of both anatomy and pathology, did not like teaching the former and was much more interested in the latter. Berry found little in the way of museum specimens, teaching models, microscopes or other facilities, although he had a keen but small staff — nor did he think much of the university. His students found themselves facing a short, wiry figure with upstanding hair, a grating voice, a forceful personality and a profound knowledge of anatomy which he proceeded to instil with great vigour and stern discipline, stressing the practical aspect. He revolutionized the teaching of anatomy in Melbourne.

Before Berry left Edinburgh he had published a book on surface anatomy and another work, in three volumes, on regional anatomy. The latter formed the basis for his locally published *Practical anatomy* (1914), which remained the text for Melbourne students for some twenty-five years. He received the Melbourne M.D. (*ad eund.*) in 1906. Once he had reorganized his department he became very interested in the Australian and Tasmanian Aboriginals and the metrical and non-metrical features of their skulls. Another of his principal scientific interests was mental deficiency, particularly in children; this resulted in his appointment as consulting psychiatrist to the Melbourne and Children's hospitals and later, when he left Australia, was to become his main subject of research.

Berry designed a new building for the department of anatomy, opened in 1923 and known as 'Berry's Folly', because of its size, but in fact it was a clear example of his far-sightedness for it accommodated without modification the very large classes which followed World War II. In 1925-29 he was dean of the faculty and a member of the university council, and during this time he pressed for expansion of the medical school. In particular, he strongly advocated the move of the Melbourne Hospital to Parkville so that it could be alongside the medical school, for which he planned a building in the south-west corner of the campus across the road from the hospital site. In 1914 he had suggested moving the school to the hospital, but this plan was shelved with the outbreak of World War I.

Berry regarded the close association of hospital and medical school as a vital necessity. However, he ran against considerable opposition, notably from Sir James Barrett [q.v.] and others, and his vigorous criticism of those who did not have his depth of vision and ideals lost him many friends. He was impatient, intolerant and often sarcastic with many of his colleagues. In contrast, to his students he was both sympathetic and compassionate.

In 1927 Berry was invited by the Rockefeller Foundation of New York to tour medical schools and hospitals in North America; he was accompanied by (Sir) Stanley Argyle [q.v.]. Their report firmly favoured rebuilding the Melbourne Hospital on the Parkville site. Berry's plans for location of the medical school were in fact ultimately carried out, just as he had envisaged, but long after he had left Melbourne.

In 1929 Berry unexpectedly resigned from the university to accept the position of director of medical services at the Stoke Park Colony at Stapleton, Bristol, England, and chairman of the Burden Mental Research Trust. There he carried out extensive research into mental deficiency until his retirement in 1940. While in England he served on the council of the British Medical Association, representing the Queensland and

New South Wales branches.

Berry's published work may be divided into two categories: an early part devoted to topographical anatomy and physical anthropology and, later, the brain, both normal and mentally defective. His work on physical anthropology was published in the *Transactions of the Royal Society of Victoria* in two large volumes: on the Tasmanian crania (1909) and on the Australian crania (1914). In 1911 he published *A clinical atlas of sectional and topographical anatomy*, which remains an outstanding authority. *Brain and mind* appeared in New York in 1928, followed next year by his excellent report on mental deficiency in Victoria. The result of his work at Stoke Park Colony was published in London in 1938 in his *Cerebral atlas* of normal and defective brains. Berry also showed talent as a broadcaster: his shrewd and lively radio talks given in Melbourne after his American tour were published at Bristol in 1930.

When Berry left the university, the council had not conferred on him the title of professor emeritus, as was usual. In 1959 Sir William Upjohn, the chancellor, persuaded council that this should be done. Now quite blind, but retaining his impish sense of humour, Berry thanked council for 'this almost post-humous honour'. He died on 30 September 1962 at Clifton, Bristol. His wife had died in 1949; they had one son and two daughters of whom Beatrice married (Professor) I. R. Maxwell of Melbourne.

Berry made a notable contribution to medicine in Victoria. His teaching produced a generation who left their mark on Australian surgery, the foundation of their knowledge being gained in his dissecting-room and museum. Berry was a stimulating and far-sighted administrator, overshadowed in his earlier years in Melbourne by Sir Harry Allen who, however, agreed with many of his plans; it is regrettable that these were frustrated by lack of support from his colleagues. His portrait by Justus Jorgensen hangs in the department of anatomy, University of Melbourne.

K. F. Russell, *The Melbourne Medical School 1862-1962* (Melb, 1977); *British Medical J*, 6 Oct 1962; *Lancet*, 13 Oct 1962; *MJA*, 23 Mar 1963.

K. F. RUSSELL

BERRY, WILLIAM (1857-1928), marine engineer, was born on 2 August 1857 at York, England, son of William Berry, engine-fitter, and his wife Isabella, née Carr. After completing his schooling, he was apprenticed in the locomotive workshops of the North Eastern Railway Co. in 1871. Illness in 1879 led him to migrate to South

Australia next year in the *Aconcagua*. Before leaving he had married Hannah Crawford at York on 9 August.

Berry joined the Adelaide Steamship Co. Ltd, completed his qualifying sea service, and by 1885 had passed his examinations for the South Australian Marine Board's certificate of competency as a first-class engineer; he rose to be a chief engineer with the company. After nearly a decade at sea he was appointed to H.M.C.S. *Protector*. He had joined the newly established Australasian Institute of Marine Engineers in 1881 and was elected honorary secretary of its Adelaide district on 2 July 1883. He resigned on 31 December 1887, partly because of his frequent absence at sea, but was re-elected on 8 April 1889. At the end of 1891 he was dismissed from the *Protector* for objecting to the manning policy for H.M.C.S. *Musgrave*, which had been permitted to sail with a stoker as second engineer. The institute demanded a governmental inquiry into his dismissal; this was refused, but Berry was informed that he might apply for re-engagement in 1892, which he declined to do.

Instead he established himself as a storekeeper and provision merchant at Exeter and became part-time secretary of the Adelaide district of the institute. When it bought its Port Adelaide Chambers in 1912, Berry became full-time paid secretary, and sold his business. He remained in the post until ill health forced his retirement in 1926. He exemplified the pragmatic virtues of the colonial marine engineers who established the profession's traditions in Australia. They characteristically held that, while no quarter was to be given in meeting any challenge to their professional status, the withdrawal of their services was to be considered the ultimate sanction; this principle was applied by Berry and his intercolonial colleagues in the engineers' disputes of 1893 and 1897. As the institute's representative, he was in 1893-1926 a respected warden of the South Australian Marine Board, the governing body for the administration of merchant shipping in South Australia. From 1892 he had prepared students for their certificate of competency examinations.

Berry had been a member of the board of management of the Retail Grocers' Association of South Australia and an advocate for the formation of the Wholesale Co-operative Grocery Co. Ltd of South Australia. Prominent in the Semaphore Methodist Church and a well-known local preacher, he supported the Seamen's Mission Hall and Sailors' Rest at Nile Street, Port Adelaide, for over forty years. He was also president of the Young Men's Guild, Semaphore, and a Freemason. He died of cerebral haemorrhage on 25 October 1928 at his home in Semaphore and was survived by a daughter.

H. T. Burgess (ed), *Cyclopedia of South Australia*, 1 (Adel, 1908); *Sawtell's Nautical Almanac*, 1885-86; Aust Inst of Marine and Power Engineers, *Forty-eighth Annual Report, 1929*; *Advertiser* (Adel), 26, 27 Oct 1928; *Port Adelaide News*, and *Register* (Adel), 26 Oct 1928; Aust Inst of Marine and Power Engineers (Adel District), Minutes 1881-1913 (Branch Archives, Inst Chambers, Port Adel); Aust Inst of Marine Engineers, News-cuttings 1891-1930 (Vic Branch Archives, South Melb).

ANN R. SHORTEN

BERTIE, CHARLES HENRY (1875-1952), librarian and historian, was born at Lionsville, Clarence River, New South Wales, on 18 July 1875, son of Robert Alexander Bertie, goldminer, and his wife Elizabeth, née Smith. At an early age he went with his family to Sydney. He attended evening lectures at the University of Sydney as an unmatriculated student and trained as a metallurgical chemist at Sydney Technical College. He was a vice-chairman of the Sydney Technical College Association and contributed to the *Australian Technical Journal*. About 1899 he joined the Sydney Municipal Council as a junior under the city surveyor and rose to be chief clerk.

From about 1904 Bertie's interests took an increasingly literary bent and he contributed articles on literature to Sydney newspapers. In 1909 he was appointed first librarian of the new Sydney Municipal Library, constructed out of the moribund lending branch of the Public Library of New South Wales. He supported the children's library movement and in 1918 established within the Municipal Library the first public lending library for children in Australia. He visited the United States of America and recorded his impressions in a *Report on the public libraries of the United States* (1923). Bertie modestly assessed his formidable problems and his achievements in an address delivered in 1928 to the Australian Library Conference on 'Organization of a lending library', later published in its *Proceedings*.

Long before retirement for health reasons in 1939, Bertie had become a notable collector of Australiana, as the catalogue of his collections in the Mitchell Library shows. A member of the (Royal) Australian Historical Society from 1909, he was a member of council in 1912-52, president in 1914, honorary secretary in 1921 and honorary research secretary from 1933. He worked in the 1940s with J. A. Ferguson, the noted bibliographer, to reorganize the society's library. Elected an 'original fellow' in 1916, Bertie contributed extensively to its *Journal*

and Proceedings and other periodicals, and
was well known as a lecturer on early Sydney. After a visit to England in 1913 he
worked to have historic sites identified and
marked. His many publications included
*The early history of the Sydney Municipal
Council . . .* (1911), *Story of old George Street*
(1920) and *Old colonial by-ways* (1928). In
1912 he had been appointed editor of a
proposed historical and biographical record
of Australia, an enterprise never completed,
but which became the starting point of the
first edition of *The Australian encyclopaedia*
(1925-26). On seeing the manuscript of
Ralph Rashleigh, the now-famous story of
convict life, Bertie arranged its first publication as *Adventures of Ralph Rashleigh, a
penal exile in Australia 1825-1844* (London,
1929).

Bertie died of cerebral haemorrhage on 19
July 1952 at Cremorne and was cremated. He
was survived by his wife Nellie, née Hutchinson, whom he had married at Toxteth
Church, Glebe Point, on 27 September 1905,
and by a daughter and two sons. His estate
was valued for probate at £3650. He
belonged to the Sydney group of zealots who
gave initial impetus to the systematic study
of Australian history and the collection of
Australiana.

C. H. Bertie memorial journal, *JRAHS*, 38
(1952), pt 5.   JOHN M. WARD

BESSELL-BROWNE, ALFRED JOSEPH
(1877-1947), soldier and businessman, was
born on 3 September 1877 at Auckland, New
Zealand, son of William Henry Brown
(Bessell-Browne), insurance inspector, and
his wife Harriott Maria Searle, née Linton.
The family migrated to New South Wales in
the mid-1880s and Alfred became a pupil at
Camden Grammar School. They later
moved to Western Australia and, after attending Perth High School, Alfred joined the
Patents' Office as a clerk in 1896. That year
he enlisted in the Perth Artillery Volunteers
and by 1899 was a sergeant.

When the South African War broke out,
Bessell-Browne enlisted in the 1st Western
Australian (Mounted Infantry) Contingent
as a private. His unit reached Cape Town in
November 1899, served with the Kimberley
Relief Force and in operations in the
Transvaal, Orange Free State and Cape
Colony. Having been promoted through all
the ranks Bessell-Browne was commis-
sioned lieutenant on 22 April 1900. He re-
turned home with the contingent in March
1901 but immediately re-enlisted in the 5th
Western Australian Contingent, serving as
adjutant, then second-in-command. He was

promoted captain in June, was mentioned in
dispatches in July and received the Distinguished Service Order. On returning to
Perth in April 1902 he resumed his public
service career and on 12 May next year
married Muriel Maud Manning at St
George's Cathedral. He rejoined the Australian Field Artillery as lieutenant, was
promoted captain in 1908, and in 1909 attended a course in military science at the
University of Sydney. That year he resigned
from the public service and went into business as a wholesale merchant.

Bessell-Browne was major commanding
the 37th Battery, A.F.A., when World War I
began. Appointed major in the Australian
Imperial Force on 18 August 1914, he was
given command of the 8th Battery, and left
for Egypt in November. His unit was at
Gallipoli during the landing but, because of
the difficulty of positioning field-guns in the
rugged terrain, its artillery was not brought
ashore until 4 May 1915; 400 infantrymen
hauled two guns on drag-ropes up precipi-
tous slopes to the crest of Plateau 400. Until
August Bessell-Browne commanded this
battery, which bombarded Turkish lines at
Lone Pine; from then until the evacuation he
commanded the 2nd and 3rd A.F.A. brigades
in turn. His final task on Gallipoli was to
destroy guns which could not be taken out.
That year he had been appointed C.M.G. and
mentioned in dispatches.

In March 1916 Bessell-Browne, a lieut-
colonel since 1 January, left for the Western
Front. His 2nd A.F.A. Brigade was posted to
the Somme and in July provided part of the
covering barrage for the attack on Pozières
– one of the earliest creeping barrages. In
September he was made temporary commander of the 1st Divisional Artillery which
served at Flers in the winter of 1916-17.
Promoted colonel and temporary brigadier
general in January 1917, he was in charge of
the 5th Divisional Artillery until the end of
the war and in this period emerged as an
outstanding commander, constantly showing his capacity for solving difficult problems of technique and command. At Polygon
Wood he sent three batteries to cover the
Australians' exposed right flank: this was
probably the first time that defence of a flank
by artillery had been attempted in a
trench-warfare attack. With the transition
to mobile warfare after Villers-Bretonneux
in 1918, he quickly adapted tactics to give
close support to the advancing infantry
during the attacks on the support systems of
the Hindenburg Line and the final penetration at Bellicourt. Here, in its finest performance during the war, the 5th's artillery put
down a creeping barrage at an angle of
ninety degrees from the line of sight to cover
an attack at Le Catelet. In October Bessell-

Browne supported the 30th American Division in the Selle River sector and received the American Distinguished Service Medal. He was appointed C.B. for his services in France and Flanders and was mentioned in dispatches nine times.

Demobilized in July 1919, he resumed work as a merchant. By 1921 he had established an indent agents' firm, Bessell-Browne Ltd, in Perth, and remained its managing director until his death. He served with the Australian Military Forces as a colonel until World War II, when he commanded the Western Australian Volunteer Defence Corps, and retired as brigadier general in 1942. Survived by his wife, three daughters and four of their five sons, he died of cancer on 3 August 1947 and was cremated with full military honours.

Aust Defence Dept, *Official records of the Australian military contingents to the war in South Africa*, P. L. Murray ed (Melb, 1912); C. E. W. Bean, *The story of Anzac* (Syd, 1921, 1924), and *The A.I.F. in France* (Syd, 1929, 1933, 1937); *Statistical Register* (WA), 1897; *West Australian*, 4-6 Aug 1947; Bessell-Browne file (AWM).

MERRILYN LINCOLN

BEST, DUDLEY ROBERT WILLIAM (1844-1928), naturalist, was born on 1 March 1844 at Needham Market, Suffolk, England, son of Alban Thomas Best, pharmacist, and his wife Frances Ann Hunsley, née Thomas. He arrived with his parents in Victoria in the *Sibella* in February 1850. After education at the Model School in Spring Street he joined the firm of Joske Bros, general importers and wine and spirit merchants. In 1886 the firm became known as Joske, Best & Co., with a trade in colonial and imported wines, spirits and ales. Best retired as senior partner in 1916, but for many years continued to visit the city two or three times a week. He was an active Freemason. In his last years he turned his attention to the growing of native plants in the garden of his home at East Kew.

From the age of 12 Best had collected insects, especially beetles, and his hobby continued through adulthood. His main interest was in the study of the *Coleoptera*, in particular the *Longicornia*. He made friends with others interested in natural history, and in the late 1870s a group of enthusiasts, including Best, Charles French [q.v.] and D. Kershaw, decided to form a natural history society. At a preliminary meeting on 6 May 1880, Best was appointed honorary secretary and on 12 May the decision was taken to form the Field Naturalists' Club of Victoria. He continued as honorary secretary for four years until pressure of business forced him

to relinquish the post. For the next twelve years he remained on the committee, serving at one time as treasurer and vice-president (1891-93), but refusing the office of president. In February 1923 he was made an honorary life member.

A tall, bearded bachelor, Best attended several camp-outs and sometimes joined others on collecting trips but, being a reserved man, he mostly preferred to work alone. He obtained many specimens by breeding the beetle larvae in special cages at home. Three species were named after him, including *Morphnos bestii* (*Carabidae*) from the Grampians; these formed part of his collection which he bequeathed to the National Museum of Victoria. Best also contributed papers to the *Southern Science Record* and the *Victorian Naturalist*, some dealing with *Coleoptera* and others describing excursions to various parts of Victoria. Several of these papers were written in collaboration with his lifelong friend Charles French.

Best collapsed and died in his garden on 10 June 1928 and was buried in the Melbourne general cemetery. He left an estate valued for probate at £45 998.

A. Sutherland et al, *Victoria and its metropolis*, 2 (Melb, 1888); *Vic Naturalist*, 45 (1928-29); *Age*, 12 June 1928.

J. C. LE SOUEF

BEST, SIR ROBERT WALLACE (1856-1946), politician and solicitor, was born on 18 June 1856 at Collingwood, Victoria, son of Robert Best, farmer, later customs officer, and his wife Jane, née Wallace, both born in Ireland. Educated at Templeton's school, Fitzroy, at 13 he became a clerk in a Chancery Lane printing office. Joining the firm of W. T. Trollope, equity solicitor, he took articles, matriculated in 1875, studied law at the University of Melbourne and was admitted as a solicitor in 1881. That year, at St Philip's Anglican Church, Collingwood, he married Jane Caroline, daughter of G. D. Langridge [q.v.5].

An alderman on Fitzroy City Council in 1883-89 and 1890-97, Best was mayor in 1888-89 at a time of public building activity by the council, and laid the foundation stone of the Fitzroy Public Library, a fine example of the wealth and exuberance of 'marvellous Melbourne'. He was elected member for Fitzroy in the Legislative Assembly in April 1889, as one of a fine crop of young native-born radicals; he was an admirer of George Higinbotham [q.v.4]. In 1892 he declined a seat in cabinet without portfolio after the reconstruction of the Shiels [q.v.] ministry.

He was chairman of the royal commission on constitutional reform in 1894.

Best reached the apex of his career in colonial politics in 1894-99 when, as president of the Board of Land and Works, commissioner of crown lands and survey and also for trade and customs in the G. Turner [q.v.] government, he was responsible for introducing several important measures, including the tariff reform of 1896, one of the foremost issues in Victorian politics. He was twice acting premier and represented Victoria at the 1897 Premiers' Conference. He gained a great reputation from the 'Best Land Act' of 1898, an important measure which introduced a new principle of classification of land, designed to promote closer settlement and effectively recasting all Victorian land laws. In 1899 he visited New Zealand with W. A. Trenwith [q.v.], investigating labour questions. Sidney and Beatrice Webb described him as 'a young man of the clerk type; red-haired and excitable, habitually overworking himself'.

An ardent advocate of Federation, Best resigned from the assembly in 1901 and was elected to the Senate as a protectionist, becoming chairman of committees in 1901-03. He visited England in 1905 in connexion with a Privy Council appeal. Vice-president of the Executive Council and leader of the Senate from February 1907 until November 1908, he was responsible for introducing tariff and excise bills. He was appointed K.C.M.G. in 1908. He negotiated on behalf of Alfred Deakin [q.v.] to form the 'Fusion' ministry of 1909-10 in which he was minister for trade and customs. Best was not a colourful figure, but he was a conscientious minister and could be relied upon to speak moderately and sensibly in parliament; according to Melbourne *Punch*, he spoke with 'an overwhelming love of adjectives and heavy sentences'. His pleasant manner, grasp of detail and forcefulness as a debater were useful in the Senate where his party was heavily outnumbered, and evident in his piloting of the Deakin-Lyne [q.v.] tariff. He remained interested in Fitzroy and during the years of the Deakin ministries was an assiduous speaker to Liberal groups.

The Labor landslide victory of 1910 meant Best's defeat in the Senate; his request for a recount was refused. Fortunately, William Knox [q.v.], M.H.R. for Kooyong, resigned soon after and Best was returned at the by-election. Always a favourite with the formidable Australian Women's National League, he was frequently a speaker at their meetings during campaigns. This appears to have stood him in good stead in Kooyong, where he achieved solid majorities; the *Fitzroy City Press* commented that he 'did well to pin faith to the feminine fair'.

Best was member for Kooyong until 1922, as a Liberal until 1917 and as a Nationalist thereafter. In 1916 he had supported the introduction of conscription by proclamation. By 1922 dissatisfaction was growing with the W. M. Hughes [q.v.] ministry, and (Sir) John Latham [q.v.] stood against Best as a Liberal, anti-Hughes candidate, supported by the *Argus*. The result of the contest was in doubt for several days: Best did not have an absolute majority; Labor had directed its preferences to Latham and this decided the contest in his favour. Best did not attend the declaration of the poll and abandoned politics.

Throughout his political career, he had maintained his legal practice, having entered into partnership with Theodore Fink [q.v.] in 1886; the firm became Fink, Best & P. D. Phillips in 1889 and Fink, Best & Miller in 1917. He was a devout and prominent Anglican layman in St Mark's parish, Fitzroy. Said to have been a singer, elocutionist and an athlete in his youth, he was sometime president of the Fitzroy Football Club, the Victorian Cricket Association, the League of Victorian Wheelmen and the Victorian Football Association; he built much of his political popularity on his sporting links.

Best's first wife had died in 1901. Next year he married Maude Evelyn Crocker-Smith at Christ Church, St Kilda. Survived by two sons and two daughters of his first marriage and four daughters of his second, he died on 27 March 1946 at Hawthorn after a short illness and was cremated. A year before, he had fallen down some stairs and had never fully recovered although he continued to attend his office. An oil portrait of him is at Fitzroy Town Hall.

J. Smith (ed), *Cyclopedia of Victoria*, 1 (Melb, 1903); B. Webb, *The Webbs' Australian diary, 1898*, A. G. Austin ed (Melb, 1965); *Aust Mag*, 1 Mar 1909; *Argus*, 20 Oct 1890, 28 Mar 1946; *Punch* (Melb), 10 Jan 1907, 19 Nov 1908; *Fitzroy City Press*, 26 Aug 1910; *Age*, 28 Mar 1946.

NORMA MARSHALL

BETHUNE, FRANK POGSON (1877-1942), soldier and clergyman, and JOHN WALTER (1882-1960), clergyman and headmaster, were first cousins and close, lifelong friends. Frank was born on 8 April 1877, second son of Walter Ross Munro Bethune, stock-owner, and his wife Louisa Gellibrand, née Pogson. John was born on 5 November 1882, only son of Walter Ross Munro's brother, John Charles Bethune, lawyer and sheep-farmer, and his wife Annie Emily, sister of Louisa Pogson. They lived on the family estate, Dunrobin, near Hamilton, Tasmania, established by their grandfather W. A. Bethune [q.v.1]; both boys were born there. John's mother died when he was a child, his father moved away and he was raised by his uncle and aunt.

The cousins were educated at The Hutchins School, Hobart, and John also attended the Launceston Church Grammar School. Frank spent some years farming but both completed their education at Selwyn College, University of Cambridge, England, where they read theology and were active in sport. John (B.A., 1904; M.A., 1908) topped his final year with first-class honours and won a university prize; Frank, who won a half-blue for boxing, was rusticated for a term for burning college fences on 'Mafeking night', but also graduated with first-class honours (B.A., 1905; M.A., 1908).

In Tasmania John was ordained in 1905 and was curate of St David's Anglican Cathedral, Hobart, for two years. He was rector of St Paul's Church, Launceston, and chaplain to the Launceston General Hospital in 1908-15. Frank married Laura Eileen Nicholas on 3 January 1907 at Ouse. He was ordained in 1908, and was curate at St John the Baptist Anglican Church, Hobart, and later at Sheffield and Ranelagh parishes.

In World War I John served as chaplain to the army training camp at Claremont. Frank became a fighting padre, enlisting as a private in 1915; he was commissioned as second lieutenant in the 12th Battalion in December. On 2 April 1916 he conducted a service on the troopship *Transylvania* on the way to France, preaching a memorable sermon which was widely reported in the Australian press. 'We are not heroes', he said 'and we do not want to be called heroes . . . We are on that great enterprise, with no thought of gain or conquest, but to help right a great wrong . . .' He rose to the rank of captain, was awarded the Military Cross for bravery in action in 1917, and was wounded twice and gassed. In March 1918 Bethune, then commanding No. 1 section, 3rd Machine Gun Company, was ordered to defend an exposed position at Passchendaele. His group of seven men became isolated, but held the position for eighteen days. Bethune issued the following orders, later described by *The Times* as 'inspiring and famous':

1. This position will be held and the section will remain here until relieved.

2. The enemy cannot be allowed to interfere with this programme.

3. If the section cannot remain here alive, it will remain here dead, but in any case it will remain here.

4. Should any man, through shell shock or other cause, attempt to surrender, he will remain here dead.

5. Should all guns be blown out, the section will use Mills grenades, and other novelties.

6. Finally, the position, as stated, will be held.

They survived until relieved. The orders passed into military history, were circulated throughout the allied armies in France and embodied in British Army Orders until 1940. Twenty-two years later, after the fall of Dunkirk, they were reproduced as posters under the caption 'The spirit which won the last war' and displayed throughout England.

Frank never entirely recovered from his wartime injuries and privations. He returned to Tasmania in 1919 and moved with his family to Dunrobin where he farmed till 1936, assisting occasionally in the Hamilton parish. He died of cerebro-vascular disease in Hobart on 4 December 1942. He was survived by his wife, two daughters and two sons; the elder Walter Angus became a Tasmanian premier. Despite stern qualities, Bethune had been popular with his men and his parishioners. His whimsy was exemplified when, pinned down in a shell-hole by enemy gunfire, he passed the time calculating the cost to Germany of keeping him there.

After the Armistice in 1918, John Bethune accepted appointment as headmaster of the Launceston Church Grammar School, a position he held until 1928. 'Responsible for a new era' at the school, he initiated and supervised its move in 1924 from Elizabeth Street to Mowbray Heights, and was the driving force in raising funds for rebuilding. He reorganized it on the lines of a modern public school: during his period numbers doubled. In 1927 he was appointed C.B.E. for his services to education, and next year he retired. After a period as rector of Wynyard, he was chaplain to the Hobart gaol and active in charity work. A bachelor, he died on 2 October 1960, at Hobart. Like his cousin, he had placed significant emphasis on the values of Empire and the English public school.

B. W. Rait, *The official history of The Hutchins School* (Hob, 1935), and *The story of the Launceston Church Grammar School* (Launc, 1946); C. E. W. Bean, *The A.I.F. in France*, 1917, 1918 (Syd, 1933, 1937); *Reveille*, May 1941; G. H. Stephens, 'Three schools and the Great War', *PTHRA*, 24 (1976), no 3; *Tas Mail*, 19 Jan 1907; *Mercury*, 24 June, 12 Aug 1916, 23, 26 Feb, 27 Apr 1917, 13 June 1919, 19 Apr 1923, 3 June 1927, 5 Dec 1942, 3, 5 Oct 1960; *Examiner* (Launc), 27 Apr 1917, 19 Apr 1923, 3 June 1927; *Daily Post* (Hob), 12 May 1917; *The Times*, 24 Dec 1942; *A'sian Post*, 23 Feb 1956; Bethune family papers (held by Mr V. A. Bethune, Dunrobin, Ouse, Mrs C. F. F. Chapman, Ouse, and Mrs N. A. Thompson, South Hobart).

G. P. R. CHAPMAN

BETTS, SELWYN FREDERIC (1879-1938), judge, was born on 6 February 1879 at Goulburn, New South Wales, second son of Augustine Matthew Betts, solicitor, and his wife Elizabeth Anne, née Thompson, and grandson of Rev. Samuel Marsden [q.v.2]. Selwyn spent his boyhood with his brother Ernest and two sisters at their parents' home, Euthella, Goulburn, and was educated there at King's College. As a boy he lost the sight of an eye through a catapult accident. He served his articles of clerkship with Sydney solicitors Pigott [q.v.] and Stinson. On the motion of R. M. Sly [q.v.] he was admitted to the Bar on 7 May 1903 and from Wigram Chambers built up an extensive practice in both civil and criminal jurisdictions, especially on the southern circuit.

On 13 January 1913 he married Nelle Marion Rodd, an artist and illustrator, who died on 10 October 1915. In London in 1919 he found that she had illustrated an edition of *Grimm's fairy tales*, when he bought a copy for their only child Peter Selwyn.

Betts was commissioned as a second lieutenant in the 3rd Australian Light Horse Regiment in March 1905 and was promoted lieutenant in 1908. He transferred to the 11th Light Horse in 1912 and, retained in Australia as an instructor on the outbreak of World War I, was promoted captain in 1916. Permitted to join the Australian Imperial Force in June 1918, he went overseas as an honorary captain with reinforcements for the 33rd Battalion but arrived after the Armistice. Discharged from the A.I.F. in 1920, Betts retained his connexion with the army, being promoted major in 1922 and lieut-colonel in 1926 when he became divisional legal officer. He was awarded the Volunteer Officers' Decoration in 1925. That year he was a founding committee-man of the Legacy Club of Sydney.

Betts returned to the New South Wales Bar and practised from University Chambers. With Frank Louat he published *The practice of the Supreme Court of New South Wales at common law . . .* (1928), a standard work. On 7 June 1937 he was appointed a District Court judge and chairman of Quarter Sessions for the metropolitan district. In 1935 he had been deputy chairman of the Workers' Compensation Commission of New South Wales for a month and for three months from 1 September 1938 he was also appointed to the Industrial Commission of New South Wales.

Good-natured and popular, Betts was a member of the Australasian Pioneers and Imperial Service clubs and of the Royal Sydney Yacht Squadron. He spent most of his leisure sailing his yacht *Whimbrel* or fishing at Shellharbour. Shortly after trying to prevent a woman falling on to a railway line, he died of cerebral haemorrhage at his home at Mosman on 14 October 1938 and was buried in the Church of England section of Gore Hill cemetery. He left his estate, valued for probate at £14 696, to his son.

In his short tenure of judicial office Betts showed patience, placidity and care, but expressed difficulty in sentencing youthful offenders who were not hardened to crime, and professional men of previous good character.

R. T. Wyatt, *The history of Goulburn* (Goulburn, 1941); *Government Gazette* (NSW), 29 Aug 1935, 11 June 1937, 12 Aug 1938; *Aust Law J*, 18 Nov 1938; *SMH*, 17 Feb, 15 Oct 1938.   H. T. E. HOLT

BEVAN, LLEWELYN DAVID (1842-1918), Congregational minister, was born on 11 September 1842 at Llanelly, Carmarthen, Wales, son of Hopkin Bevan, actuary, and his wife Eliza, née Davies, a Congregational minister's daughter, and was related to prominent Dissenting preachers on both sides of his family. Raised in a cultured home atmosphere, Bevan attended University College School, London, boarding in a pious household where he matched his wits and physical strength with young ministers. He abandoned his plans for a legal career when he was converted by the preaching of Henry Grattan Guinness. A 'fine big boy, with dark flowing locks', he entered New College, then under Dr Robert Halley, father of his friend J. J. Halley [q.v.4], as a lay student in 1858. As an exhibitioner and prizeman he completed his B. A. in 1862 and LL.B. with honours in 1865 at the University of London, spending his last year at University College.

After ordination in 1865, Bevan assisted Dr Thomas Binney [q.v.3] at the King's Weigh House Chapel and in 1869-75 he was minister of Tottenham Court Chapel. He was early influenced by the Christian Socialist movement, and his popular London ministry was characterized by his concern for education and the welfare of the-workers. He won the Marylebone seat on the London School Board on the minority 'free, compulsory and secular' platform in 1873, and in 1866-76 was active as a councillor of the Working Men's College founded in 1854 by F. D. Maurice, whose Bible class Bevan also took over. He preached at social crusades and revival meetings as well as lecturing in English at New College. By 1874, when he ministered for two months at the Central Church, Brooklyn, New York, Bevan had acquired an international reputation. He received calls from leading churches including Collins Street Independent Church,

Melbourne, and finally accepted the ministry of the Brick Presbyterian Church in New York in 1876, becoming moderator of the New York Presbytery in 1880. In 1882, honoured with a Princeton doctorate, he removed to London as minister of the newly formed Highbury Quadrant (Congregational) Church. Such was his interest in social questions and his popularity that he was urged to stand for parliament, with the choice of three Liberal seats in Wales and one in North London, but in 1886, partly for the health of his family and in response to a fourth call, he accepted the ministry of Collins Street Independent Church. With his wife Louisa Jane, née Willett, whom he had married at Southampton on 2 April 1870, and his family, he reached Melbourne in the *Valetta* on 6 November 1886.

For twenty-three years Bevan was a leader of Protestant intellectual life in Melbourne. Although he became less insistent on some of his Gladstonian Liberal beliefs such as Irish Home Rule and free trade, he remained an ardent advocate of educational and social reform. In 1888-89 (also in 1898-99 and 1909-10) he was chairman of the Congregational Union of Victoria and made numerous visits overseas in the interests of wider Congregationalism, serving as a vice-president of its international councils at London in 1891 and Boston in 1899. He was chairman of the jury of education at the Melbourne Centennial International Exhibition of 1888, for which he was honoured by the French government, and in 1891 he served on a parliamentary committee to study the educational systems of France, Germany and the United States. In 1889, during the London dockers' strike, he addressed the public meeting organized in Melbourne by the Congregational Union and the Trades Hall Council to raise funds for strikers' families and, in 1892, with Rev. A. Gosman [q.v.4] he was an advocate of labour colonies. An ardent believer in Australian Federation, based on an imperial federation ideal, he lectured tirelessly, one of his hymns on the subject being published in the Congregational hymnal. In the Federal election of 1901 he resisted pressure to stand against J. C. Manifold [q.v.] for Corangamite. He opposed the White Australia policy, but believed Australia had a right to its own Monroe doctrine in the Western Pacific.

In 1909 Bevan decided to lighten his ministerial load. From 1888 he had lectured in church history at the Congregational College of Victoria and in February 1910 he became principal of Parkin (Congregational) College, Adelaide, holding this position until he died there on 19 July 1918. For twenty-five years he had suffered from diabetes and ultimately from peripheral vascular disease. His successor, E. S. Kiek [q.v.], thought him neither a profound nor exact scholar, but a man of wide culture. The Bevan lectures were given at Parkin in his memory in 1927-56.

Bevan was regarded as a great preacher with a mellifluous voice and 'the fiery eloquence of John Bright' whom he physically resembled. Randolph Bedford [q.v.] described him as 'a pink, portly bishoplike man, his plump and innocent face framed in hair, white and fine as cotton wool'. Conscious of his middle-class station, he retained enough Maurice-type social conscience to insist on equal opportunities in education, especially for women, and to deplore exploitation of the workers such as sweating and organized gambling. His forte, however, was cultural. He delighted in musical evenings and eisteddfods and in creating a salon atmosphere at home and church gatherings, bringing together, for instance, Archbishop Carr, Rabbi Joseph Abrahams [qq.v.], and 'the third wise man', a notorious ragged scholar of the Melbourne streets. Bevan was a bibliophile, collector of antique ceramics, and recognized student of Ibsen. He was also a gifted raconteur, able to draw on personal recollections of the distinguished people he had known in Europe and America, including Gladstone, Mill, Emerson, Holmes and Longfellow. Holding a 'liberal Evangelical' theology and blessed with a sense of humour, he eschewed fundamentalism but joined in evangelistic crusades such as the American-inspired Simultaneous Mission of 1902. Many of his sermons and addresses were published.

His wife LOUISA JANE BEVAN (1844-1933), was born on 11 April 1844 at Norwich, England, elder daughter of John Willett, physician, and his wife Mary Ann, née Oxley. She learned French, German and Italian while sewing for the village poor at Market Lavington, Wiltshire. On her father's death the family moved to Southampton where Louisa became a member of the Above Bar Chapel and taught a young women's Bible class until her marriage. In New York in 1879 she suffered a spinal injury in a fall from a hammock and could never afterwards sit in an ordinary chair.

Louisa Bevan shared her husband's intellectual and musical interests, wrote and illustrated poems and hymns which were occasionally published, and at 60 learned Greek and Sanskrit in order to assist him. She was active in the National Council of Women and in October 1890 organized a women's philanthropic and cultural circle known as Daughters of the Court (afterwards Friends in Council). In 1920 she compiled and edited *The life and reminis-*

cences of Llewelyn David Bevan (Melbourne). She died at the family home, Pen Bryn, at Upper Beaconsfield, Victoria, on 12 September 1933. There were seven children and an adopted daughter. The four sons earned the reputation of 'the brainy, brawny Bevans' at Melbourne Church of England Grammar School, and at Melbourne and British universities: Hopkin Llewelyn Willett (1871-1933) was a mission teacher in Shanghai, then a Congregational minister in South Australia, and married Beatrice, poet and critic, a member of Louisa Bevan's circle and daughter of W. M. K. Vale [q.v.6]; David John Davies (1873-1954) became first judge of the Supreme Court of the Northern Territory; Louis Rhys Oxley (1874-1946) was a professor of law in China; Penry Vaughan (1875-1913) was a professor of physical sciences at Royal Holloway College, University of London. Of the daughters, Sibyl became a medical officer in the New South Wales Public Service.

Portraits in oils by George Webb of Llewelyn and Louisa Bevan are held by the family. A caricature likeness by 'B.A.L.' in the series 'Representative men' was published in the *Leader* in 1901. The Bevan collection of Australian books was purchased by Newman College, University of Melbourne.

J. Currie jnr, *Notes on travel* (Edinb, 1890); J. E. Ritchie, *An Australian ramble* (Lond, 1890); R. Bedford, *Naught to thirty-three* (Syd, 1944); E. S. Kiek, *Our first hundred years* (Adel, 1950); *Vic Congregational Year Book*, 1886-1919; *Congregationalist* (Melb), 1 Aug 1918; *Leader* (Melb), 4 Sept 1886, 24 Aug 1901; *Bulletin*, 6 Sept 1890; *Weekly Times* (Melb), 6 Apr 1895; *Punch* (Melb), 22 Aug 1907; *Advertiser* (Adel), and *Register* (Adel), 20 July 1918; *Argus*, 22 July 1918, 13 Sept 1933; family records (held by Mr M. L. W. Bevan, Stirling, SA, and Mrs C. Western, Canterbury, Vic).

NIEL GUNSON

BEW, GEORGE KWOK; *see* KWOK BEW

BICE, SIR JOHN GEORGE (1853-1923), blacksmith and politician, was born on 25 June 1853 at Callington, Cornwall, England, son of Samuel Sandoe Bice, mine agent, and his wife Elizabeth, née Rowe. He attended a local school and migrated to South Australia with his parents in the *Eastern Empire*, arriving on 20 June 1864. They settled at Moonta where, aged 11, he began working in the copper-mines for the Moonta Mining Co. He soon became a blacksmith's apprentice, and the company's superintendent described him when he left

after eleven years as, 'a competent smith, a careful and intelligent workman'.

On 30 December 1875 at Moonta Bice married Elizabeth Jane Trewenack. Next year he moved to Wilmington in the newly opened up north, to manage a blacksmithing firm for his father-in-law. Two years later he transferred to Port Augusta and in 1881 opened his own agricultural machinery business. A student at night classes, he joined the local literary and debating society and helped found the Masonic Lodge. A member of the town council for eight years, from 1887 he was on the board of advice for the Port Augusta school district, a justice of the peace and a member of the northern district's licensing bench. In 1888-89 he was mayor of the town which he later described as 'the Liverpool of South Australia'.

In 1894-1923 Bice represented the Northern District in the Legislative Council. His early policy was liberal and included support for income taxation, female suffrage and nationalizing water-systems. In parliament his upright character, alertness in debate, and the fact that he could be relied on not to waste time or words, were appreciated. Minister for the Northern Territory and water-supply in 1908-09, he was chief secretary in four later non-Labor governments and several times acting premier. Sir Henry Barwell [q.v.], with whom he served in 1920-23, considered Bice would have been premier if he had been in the Lower House. He was proud of his role in the 1897 lands commission which was partly responsible for the 1899 Pastoral Lands Act; and he chaired an interstate royal commission on border railways in 1911-12.

Big, burly and bearded, Bice was 'a politician of the old school', full of 'strong common sense and rugged honesty'. In 1905 he had been elected by the Institutes Association to a committee to guard their interests in parliament. He assisted in the establishment of several country hospitals and in improvements to facilities and working conditions at the Adelaide Hospital and the Magill Homes. He had been on the board of governors of the Botanic Garden from 1896 and on the council of the School of Mines and Industries from 1898. At home he cultivated a private library; he also enjoyed fishing.

In 1923 when Bice was appointed K.C.M.G. he was enthusiastically arranging Commonwealth participation in the 1924 British Empire Exhibition in England at which he was to represent Australia; but he died of pneumonia on 9 November that year. He was accorded a state funeral and was buried in West Terrace cemetery. Thousands of citizens mourned this 'most able and lovable statesman' who had served parliament continuously for twenty-nine years.

Bice's wife had predeceased him and he was survived by two daughters, and by a son John Leonard Sandoe Bice, who followed his father into the Legislative Council in 1941. His estate was sworn for probate at £2560.

H. T. Burgess (ed), *Cyclopedia of South Australia*, 1 (Adel, 1908); S. H. Roberts, *History of Australian land settlement, 1788-1920* (Melb, 1924); D. W. Meinig, *On the margins of the good earth* (Chicago, 1962); *SA Institutes J*, 24 Sept 1905; *Pictorial Aust*, 1894; *Observer* (Adel), 20 July 1895, 9 June, 17 Nov 1923; *Sydney Mail*, 5 July 1913; *Register* (Adel), 10 Nov 1923; *Bulletin*, 15 Nov 1923; J. G. Bice, A398 A3, 522 (SAA).

MARYANNE MCGILL

BICKERSTETH, KENNETH JULIAN FAITHFULL (1885-1962), headmaster, was born on 5 July 1885 at Ripon, Yorkshire, England, son of Rev. Dr Samuel Bickersteth and his wife Ella Chlora Faithfull, née Monier-Williams. He was educated at Rugby School and Christ Church, Oxford (B.A., 1907; M.A., 1912). After visiting India, he attended Wells Theological College, was ordained in 1910, and accepted a curacy at Rugby Parish Church.

In 1912 Julian Bickersteth went as chaplain to Melbourne Church of England Grammar School. Late in 1915 he returned to England and became senior chaplain in the 56th (London) Division in France and Flanders. His commanding officer admired 'his devotion to the welfare of all ranks': always 'moving about among the troops and sharing both their pleasures and their hardships', Bickersteth was awarded the Military Cross in 1918 and was twice mentioned in dispatches.

In 1919 he was appointed headmaster of the Anglican Collegiate School of St Peter, Adelaide. An English advisory committee had recommended him for his impeccable clerical background, public school education, colonial experience, war service, earnest Christianity and 'social qualifications . . . beyond dispute'. The Rugby headmaster noted his 'transparent sincerity', 'abundant energy', 'strength of will and character'. These qualities were in demand before Bickersteth arrived in Adelaide in 1920, by men there who desired his aid in setting up an Anglican residential college, based on English models, at the university. He joined the university council in 1921 and soon persuaded the Anglican synod to form a committee to plan for a college. When it lapsed, he formed another committee of ex-members of such colleges, which enlisted the support of leading citizens and raised funds: St Mark's College opened in 1925 and

Bickersteth was elected to its council, next year becoming a foundation fellow.

At St Peter's he built up pupil numbers, especially boarders, and improved academic standards. By 1930 this was reflected in excellent public examination results. Bickersteth also introduced the English house-system and compulsory games. A man who never cultivated privacy, he exercised a strong spiritual influence, centred round the chapel, and guided many boys to ordination. Bickersteth was undoubtedly a controversial figure; his definite and uncompromising churchmanship led to some difficulties with the council, particularly on the question of confession, but his headmastership was a landmark in the school's history. He organized the first of the headmasters' conferences for the independent schools in Australia. In 1926 and 1931 Bickersteth visited England, and in 1933 returned there as head of Felsted School, Essex, applying the same gift for living 'at a tremendous pace' and enthusing others. He brought stimulating lecturers and preachers to the school and was popular as a speaker himself.

In 1943 Bickersteth became archdeacon of Maidstone and a residentiary canon of Canterbury Cathedral. He welcomed Commonwealth visitors there and went to South Australia in 1948 seeking funds for the cathedral's post-war restoration. From 1953 he was a chaplain to the Queen and retired in 1958. Two years later he visited Adelaide again where he stayed with Bishop T. T. Reed, an old pupil and friend. At this time he was made one of the first three honorary fellows of the newly founded Australian College of Education. Bickersteth, a bachelor, died at Canterbury on 16 October 1962 while preparing a sermon.

'The history of the college and college register 1925-1935', *St Mark's College Record*, 1936, special supp; St Mark's College, *Lion*, 1962-63; *St Peter's College Mag*, Dec 1962; *Register* (Adel), 6 June 1919; *Advertiser* (Adel), 16 Apr 1960, 19 Oct 1962; *The Times*, 17, 22, 31 Oct 1962; The Collegiate School of St Peter 1847-1947 (SAA); biog file (SAA).

J. S. C. MILLER

BIDDELL, WALTER (VIVIAN HARCOURT) (1859-1933), manufacturer and a founder of the surf life-saving movement, was born on 6 May 1859 at Croydon, Surrey, England, son of Walter Biddell, master confectioner, and his wife Eliza Jane, née Sheppy. He migrated to Sydney about 1877 and became a mercantile agent. On 23 December 1891 at St Stephen's Presbyterian Church, he married Emily Lavinia Harper (d. 1898), who bore him two children; in 1894 they were living at Grafton. About 1896 he returned to Sydney, settled at Waverley, and in 1899 began to manufacture Dr Lee's baking-powder. On 11 October he married Mabel Annie Buttsworth, whom he divorced in 1923.

In 1904, after a nervous breakdown, Biddell tried many cures, but did not recover until he began to sunbathe and to surf daily at Bronte. In the controversy after a man had almost drowned there in February 1907 because the normal life-line with a buoy was fixed too far away, he urged that regular bathers should practise with the line: in April the Bronte Surf Life Brigade was formed, which he claimed was the first club to institute regular drill, discipline and practice, and to turn out trained life-savers. He also organized the purchase of its first surf-boat in 1907, and the two-man look-out mast and shark bell on the beach. When the surfing season opened in October, Biddell protested against the strict dress and beach regulations proposed by the Waverley, Randwick and Manly municipal councils. He believed in the beneficial effects of sun and surf, provided sunbathing was segregated. He particularly criticized Waverley council's neglect of female surfers, and contributed £60 to erect a ladies' dressing shelter at Bronte. In February 1908 he was defeated for the council on a reform ticket. He was president of the Bronte Surf Bathing Association and later acting president of the Surf Saving and Open-Sea Life Association of New South Wales.

A life governor of the Royal Life Saving Society from 1909, Biddell concentrated on training boys and young men in its techniques. He built a gymnasium in his backyard for the Bronte juniors. In the summer of 1909-10 he visited Honolulu and, amid much publicity, conducted demonstrations of release, rescue and resuscitation methods previously thought to be suitable only for calm water. Biddell urged the superiority of his invention, a torpedo-shaped lifebuoy, over the usual belt, line and reel; it was adjudged by a 1912 parliamentary committee to be better in certain surf conditions, but it was a handicap in rough seas. He also invented a heavy cork surf-belt and a three-man surf-boat based on two torpedo-like tubes.

Biddell's baking-powder enterprise ended in 1915. In the early 1920s he had a manufactory at Randwick, and in his retirement lived at Hurlstone Park. Survived by his son, he died in hospital on 23 April 1933 and was buried in the Anglican section of Rookwood cemetery.

Surf-bathing cttee, Report and evidence, *PP* (NSW), 1911-12, 4, 445; *SMH*, 26 Apr 1933; W. V. H. Biddell, Collection of material on Bronte Surf Life Saving Club, etc (ML).   BRUCE MITCHELL

BIDMEAD, MARTHA SARAH (1862-1940), nurse, was born on 5 December 1862 at Guernsey, Channel Islands, daughter of Thomas Benjamin Bidmead, tobacconist, and his wife Anne, née Mason. In 1885, after both parents had died, she migrated to South Australia with her four sisters, arriving on 30 April in the *John Elder*. Having decided on a nursing career, she began training at Adelaide Children's Hospital in July 1886 and was a charge nurse there in 1887-89. For the next eight years she engaged in private nursing, then in 1898 was appointed staff nurse at Burra Burra District Hospital.

In 1899, when the South Australian government decided to send a detachment of nurses to the South African War, Sister Bidmead volunteered and was placed in charge of six nurses who sailed on 21 February 1900. The government paid their fares and guaranteed them a salary of 15s. a week. They were attached to the 2nd General Hospital at Winburg near Cape Town until June, and then transferred to the 10th General Hospital at Bloemfontein where the New South Wales Ambulance Corps was based. The nurses spent most of their time in tented medical wards tending cases of enteric fever and dysentery — diseases which accounted for a high proportion of casualties.

Sister Bidmead wrote regularly to members of the Nurses' Fund Committee describing her experiences; her letters, published in the Adelaide *Observer*, gave a vivid account of conditions in the improvised hospitals and of the struggle against epidemics of contagious diseases. In March 1901 she became ill and after a fortnights leave was assigned to light duties at the 5th Stationary Hospital, Bloemfontein. She later took charge of the 10th General Hospital and on 4 September was mentioned in dispatches. Late in 1901 she went to England in charge of the wounded on a hospital ship. On 10 December she was awarded the Royal Red Cross, the first South Australian to receive this decoration. She also received the Queen's and King's South African Service medals and in June 1902 was presented with the Devoted Service Cross, a decoration awarded by the South Australian Nurses' Association.

After the war Sister Bidmead engaged in private nursing until 1912 when she was appointed superintendent of the District Trained Nursing Society of South Australia, which provided home-nursing care for the poor. Much of the society's success was due to her administrative ability; she remained in charge until her retirement in 1926. She had been secretary of the South Australian branch council of the Australian Trained Nurses' Association in 1920-26.

Short in stature, with a bustling nature, Martha Bidmead was a born leader with an arresting personality, a positive character and a deep rich voice. In retirement she found time for her favourite hobbies: playing bridge and tending the garden at Guernsey Cottage, the home she shared with her sisters at Payneham. She died there of a chronic neurological disorder on 23 July 1940 and was cremated after a service at St Aidan's Anglican Church, Payneham.

Aust Defence Dept, *Official records of the Australian military contingents to the war in South Africa*, P. L. Murray ed (Melb, 1912); SA Trained Nurses' Centenary Cttee, *Nursing in South Australia . . . 1837-1937*, 2nd ed (Adel, 1939); *Advertiser* (Adel), 1 May 1885; *Register* (Adel), 23 Apr, 17 Dec 1900; *Observer* (Adel), 2, 9 June 1900, 19 Jan, 30 Mar, 8 June 1901, 3 May, 7 June, 19 July 1902; District Trained Nurses Soc, 32nd annual report, 1926 (Roy District Nursing Soc, Adel).

REX CLARK*

BIGGS, LEONARD VIVIAN (1873-1944), journalist, was born on 29 March 1873 at Hackney, Middlesex, England, son of James Biggs, a cashier for the Great Eastern Railway, and his wife Mary Ann, née Wrensted. Educated at Enfield Grammar School he became a junior clerk with the Great Eastern. From 1893 he spent two years on the staff of the weekly *Middlesex Gazette*. In 1895-98 he worked in London for the Central News Agency and for the *African Critic*, a financial paper; in 1896, with W. F. Purvis, he published a book on South Africa.

Energetic and intelligent, Biggs took a keen interest in the politics of social reform. He was an active debater and a member of many men's societies. In the 1890s his attention was drawn to the newly formed London County Council and the influence of Fabian socialism in that body; in 1898 he stood for the council as a Progressive candidate. An Anglican, he was particularly influenced by the Christian Socialism of Henry Scott Holland.

After a brief sojourn in South Africa, Biggs arrived in Melbourne in October 1898 and at once began contributing to the *Age*; in April next year he joined the reporting staff. As Federal roundsman in the first decade of the Commonwealth he formed close relationships with Andrew Fisher, (Sir) Isaac Isaacs and, particularly, Alfred Deakin [qq.v.]. As chief of the reporting staff in 1914-20 Biggs supported the recently formed Australian Journalists' Association. He retained English contacts as Melbourne correspondent for the London *Daily Chronicle* in 1898-1918, the *Manchester Guardian*

in 1905-18 and the *New Statesman* in 1913-17.

Biggs had become interested in the Greater Melbourne movement in 1898, a plan for municipal amalgamation modelled on the London County Council. He threw his energy and experience into the debate, and in speeches, pamphlets and articles argued that the proposed body should be democratically based and an instrument of redistributive social reform. However, opponents of the proposal held their ground and the issue remained unresolved in his lifetime. He served a term as member of the Hawthorn City Council in 1911-13.

Biggs was equally active within the Church of England. As a member of synod in 1907 he successfully moved for the establishment of the Social Questions Committee, a body concerned with the social responsibility of Christian citizenship. The committee published various pamphlets, including one by Biggs on the housing problem (1913). He also helped to form the Church of England Men's Society in 1911 and later became its chairman. A member of the council of the diocese and the chapter of St Paul's Cathedral until 1927, he was a lay canon in 1917-27.

In 1920 Biggs left the *Age* and joined the National Union to take charge of political propaganda for the ruling Federal National Party. He fell out with the Nationalists and in 1926 returned to the *Age* as a leader-writer. After the sudden death in December of G. F. H. Schuler [q.v.], he was appointed editor by (Sir) Geoffrey Syme [q.v.] and retained the position until his retirement in 1939. While real power in the *Age* remained in the hands of Syme, Biggs enjoyed his public position, and his energetic and mannered style was a contrast to that of his dour employer.

Biggs's editorship maintained the traditions of the *Age*. As a journal of opinion it campaigned on various public issues with considerable energy and prejudice. Metropolitan authorities such as the Board of Works, together with the State Electricity Commission and the Victorian Railways, were always in its sights. The policy was born of old grudges but also reflected Biggs's concern with a Greater Melbourne Council, which the paper supported. Certainly he professed high ideals concerning the practice of journalism and saw his role as falling within the canons of English liberalism. His 1938 A. N. Smith Memorial Lecture remains an eloquent statement of his beliefs. As editor he expanded the literary section and wrote under the pen names of 'Audax' and 'Ludgate'.

Biggs was appointed in 1943 to membership of a three-man royal commission concerned with the reform of the Metropolitan

Board of Works by the Victorian government. He signed the majority report which recommended a directly elected body with wider powers: the board would be made in effect a Greater Melbourne Council.

Biggs died suddenly of coronary thrombosis at his home at Hawthorn on 20 January 1944 and was buried in Box Hill cemetery. He was survived by his wife Marion, née Row, whom he had married at Canterbury on 2 April 1902, and by three daughters and a son. His portrait by Percy White hangs in the Chapter House of St Paul's Cathedral.

H. W. Malloch, *Fellows all* (Melb, 1943); *PP* (Vic), 1943, 1, 781; *VHM*, 20 (1943-44), no 3; *Church of England Messenger* (Vic), 18 Feb 1944; *Herald* (Melb), 1 Jan 1927; *Newspaper News*, 1 Mar 1933; *Age*, 31 Jan 1944; D. Dunstan, Greater Melbourne 1898-1915: a political controversy (B.A. Hons thesis, Monash Univ, 1974).   DAVID DUNSTAN

BIGNOLD, HUGH BARON (1870-1930), barrister, was born on 22 June 1870 at Calcutta, India, third son of Thomas Frank Bignold, judge, and his wife Sophia Mary, née Howe. Educated at Stafford Grammar School and Buxton College, Derbyshire, England, he completed his studies at Hanover, Germany. On 7 June 1886 in the *Flora* the family arrived in Hobart; next year his father died and Hugh joined the Union Bank of Australia. In 1889 as 'Baroni' he published *Adrian North*, a book of short stories and verse. He matriculated at the University of London in 1892 and two years later moved to the bank's Sydney office. A part-time student-at-law from 1895, he was admitted to the New South Wales Bar in December 1899. On 30 January that year he had married Nellie Elena Gertrude Norton Raines at St James's Anglican Church, Sydney. Next year he resigned from the bank.

According to the *Bulletin*, though he was equipped to have made a success at the Bar, 'a certain nervousness and diffidence handicapped him and his literary tastes interfered with his profession'. Bignold's career consisted largely of writing and editing legal works, mainly commentaries on statutes. His first annotated edition of a New South Wales statute, the *Wills, Probate and Administration Act*, with W. A. Walker (1898), was followed by a series of such works, including one on the Police Offences and Vagrancy Acts (1905 and successive editions). *Bignold's banking manual . . .* (1909) was another work. He was editor of the *Magistrate* in 1905-14 and compiled indexes for New South Wales and Commonwealth statutes. He contributed articles on imperial defence to the *United Service Magazine* and other journals in the early

1900s. He wrote a deal of published and unpublished verse and short stories, and *Likewise* (1919), a collection of epigrams, and frequently contributed to the press on political and economic subjects.

In 1895-1911 Bignold conducted the chess column in the *Sydney Morning Herald*. A prominent player in both Hobart and Sydney, he edited the *Australian Chess Annual* (1896), was vice-president, sometime president of the New South Wales Chess Association, and played against Victoria nine times in 1906-22. He published *Auction simplified* in 1922, and in 1927 was president of the Sydney Auction Bridge Association. From 1924 he was a councillor of the Millions Club of New South Wales.

Bignold died of coronary vascular disease on 24 January 1930 and was cremated. He was survived by his wife, daughter and son Esme, a barrister who was a prominent crown law officer, and later a Supreme Court judge in the Territory of Papua and New Guinea.

Sweet and Maxwell, *A legal bibliography . . .*, 6, 2nd ed (Lond, 1958); *A 'sian Chess Review*, 20 Feb 1930; *SMH*, 25 Jan 1930; *Bulletin*, 19 Feb 1930; CSD 30/19/2088 (TA).

BILLSON, ALFRED ARTHUR (1858-1930), brewer and politician, was born on 11 January 1858 at Wooragee, Victoria, eighth child of GEORGE BILLSON (1817-1886), brewer and politician, and his wife Isabella, née Blades. George was born in Lincolnshire, England, son of Joseph Billson and his wife Elizabeth, née Antill. He grew up in Leicester and as a young man travelled widely. In May 1842 he reached New Zealand where in November he married Isabella; a year later he sailed to South America, then returned to England for three years. Early in 1848 he arrived in Adelaide, and next year joined the Californian gold rushes. Attracted back in 1852 by the Victorian gold rushes, Billson ran a store at Sandhurst (Bendigo) for two years; then in 1856, after another two years in England, he settled north of Beechworth at Wooragee, where he purchased 140 acres (57 ha) and built a two-storey hotel. In 1864-67 he was a publican in the Wood's Point district before finally settling in Beechworth, where he purchased the Ovens Brewery. He erected a larger brewery and aerated waters and cordial manufactory in 1872 and, with his eldest son George Henry, made it a flourishing concern.

Billson was elected to the Beechworth Borough Council in 1868 and was mayor in 1869-71. In May 1877 he won Ovens in the

Legislative Assembly; professedly an independent, he supported the Liberal government of (Sir) Graham Berry [q.v.3] during the 1878 budget crisis and attempted Legislative Council reform. Billson was defeated in July 1880 but regained his seat for the coalition years of 1883-86. He was a sensible, practical politician who supported manufacturing development and assiduously protected his district's interests. Aged 69, he died of heart failure on 9 February 1886 at Beechworth, survived by three sons and two daughters.

Alfred Arthur was educated at the Beechworth Grammar School and Scotch College, Melbourne. On 28 June 1881 at St Paul's Church, Melbourne, he married Laura Annie Fielder. He took over his father's brewery in 1882, steadily improved it under the name of A. A. Billson & Co., and also traded as a wine and spirits merchant. The brewery's speciality, Anglo-Australian Ale, sold well both in Victoria and New South Wales. The soft-drinks and cordial factory also prospered, and a branch was opened at Tallangatta. Billson adapted to the growing temperance movement by launching teetotaller drinks such as Social Ginger Cup. The brewery traded as the Anglo-Australian Brewing Co. Pty Ltd in about 1904-12, then, after amalgamation with an Albury firm, as Border United Co-operative Breweries Ltd; in 1914 it was sold to Murray Breweries Pty Ltd.

Billson took an indefatigable interest in town affairs and foresaw tourism as a means of stemming Beechworth's decline. At various times he was president of the local progress association, hospital board, Liedertafel, choral society, and sporting clubs. An ardent patriot and Federalist, he chaired the Beechworth branch of the Australian Natives' Association in 1898-1900. He was a Beechworth United Shire councillor for twenty-four years and served four terms as president.

After several attempts to enter the Legislative Assembly, Billson won Bogong at a by-election in June 1901. A sturdy, jovial figure with handlebar moustache, he proudly occupied the seat formerly held by (Sir) Isaac Isaacs [q.v.]. To his dismay, he lost Bogong in 1902 but gained the new seat of Ovens two years later and held it for twenty-three years. He was a conscientious back-bencher, with special interests in mining, municipal and liquor-trade legislation. In the Liberal governments of J. Murray and W. A. Watt [qq.v.] he was minister of railways in 1909-12 and in February-December 1913, when he also held mines and forests, and was minister of public instruction and vice-president of the Board of Land and Works from 1909 to February 1913.

As minister Billson supported the enlightened policies of the director of education, Frank Tate [q.v.]. He introduced bills to improve the salaries and promotional opportunities of teachers and steered through the important Education Law Further Amendment Act of 1910 which provided the basis for state high school development and the expansion of technical education. He became increasingly concerned about the population drift from country to city and in 1916-18 was a member of a select committee on the subject. He was an unflagging advocate of tourist development and supported the construction of the Mount Buffalo road and the formation of a tourists' resorts committee in 1922.

In articles published in 1918 and 1919 Melbourne *Punch* accused Billson of belonging to a country faction corner group which embarrassed the government by 'political submarining'; he angrily denied the charge of disloyalty to the National Party government. He was chairman of committees in 1921-26 before retiring from parliament in 1927 because of ill health.

Billson lived in Melbourne from 1916, making his home at Wooragee, Toorak. He died there of coronary vascular disease on 31 October 1930, survived by his wife, three sons and two daughters, and leaving an estate valued for probate at £6047.

L. J. Blake (ed), *Vision and realization* (Melb, 1973); *Aust Brewers' J*, 21 May 1900; *Ovens and Murray Advertiser*, 10 Feb 1877, 5 Mar 1878, 17 Feb 1883, 13 Feb 1886, 16 June 1900, 24, 31 Jan 1903; *Table Talk*, 11 July 1901; *Punch* (Melb), 10 Aug 1911, 1 Aug 1918, 14 Aug 1919; *Age*, and *Argus*, 1 Nov 1930; *Bulletin*, 5 Nov 1930.

CAROLE WOODS

BILLSON, JOHN WILLIAM (1862-1924), trade unionist and politician, was born on 10 January 1862 at Leicester, England, son of William Daniel Billson, shoemaker, and his wife Betsy, née Sharp. His background is obscure but reputedly by the age of 16 he had joined the National Operatives' Union; he was a laster by trade when on 14 October 1882 at the parish church of St Mary, Leicester, he married Sarah Jane Sarson Coverley. In 1886 they migrated to Australia.

One of Billson's first acts on arrival in Melbourne was to enrol in the Victorian Operative Bootmakers' Union. By September 1890 he was elected to its executive committee and as a delegate to the Trades Hall Council; in September 1893 he became both trustee and president, holding office during the bootmakers' strike from September 1894 to January 1895. He left his work to organize the stoppage and was boycotted by employers when he tried to return to his trade, but he refused the union's offer of compensation. He apparently went to Sydney to seek work, but was recalled in March to become general secretary of the union, a position he held for the next six years. In April 1902 Billson chaired the Interstate Boot Trade Conference held in Melbourne, and in 1903 was a delegate to meetings held to discuss a federation of the boot-trade unions. He was also on the Eight Hours' Committee in 1895-1900 and was a delegate to the United Labor Party Conference in July 1896. In February 1897 he was elected to the boot-trade wages board and was involved in establishing boards for other occupations. In June 1900 he was vice-president and in 1901-02 president of the T.H.C.; he was also president of the council's organizing committee in 1901.

In August 1898 Billson had been elected to the Richmond City Council where he worked unsuccessfully for women's representation. After failing in a bid for the Legislative Assembly seat of West Richmond and Jolimont in 1897, he stood for Fitzroy in 1900, winning a seat with (Sir) Robert Best [q.v.]. He moved to the electorate, which he represented for the rest of his life.

Billson spent his political career fighting to improve the conditions of employees and to relieve the plight of the unemployed. He was minister for railways and vice-president of the board of land and works in the Elmslie [q.v.] ministry of December 1913, and during World War I became deputy leader of the Labor Party. He was a hard-working member of the Parliamentary Voluntary Recruiting Campaign Committee in 1915, but he was fervently opposed to conscription: his comments during the referendum campaigns brought him before a police magistrate in Prahran and called forth a tirade of abuse from W. M. Hughes [q.v.]. He was a member of the Standing Committee on Railways in 1907-13 and 1914-24 and became chairman in May-December 1924. He had been a delegate to the federal Labor conferences of 1905 and 1915.

Billson was regarded by many as one of the foremost debaters in the House, who 'put his arguments with force and lucidity, and obviously from the depths of conviction'. Sir Frederic Eggleston [q.v.] remembered him as a modest, unassuming and 'very abstemious' man. He was a member of the Australian Natives' Association and took a close interest in the Fitzroy cricket and football clubs. Illness prevented his inclusion in the Prendergast [q.v.] Labor ministry of 1924, and he died on 23 December. Survived by his wife and two married daughters and predeceased by a son, he was buried in Box Hill cemetery. His estate was sworn for probate at £5841.

PD (Vic), 1925, 1, 27; *Tocsin*, 1 Sept, 13 Nov, 15 Dec 1898, 20 Apr 1899; *Fitzroy City Press*, 16 Nov 1900, 28 Feb 1902; *Argus*, 12 Oct 1916, 5 Feb, 4, 14 Dec 1917, 24 Dec 1924; *Bulletin*, 1 Jan 1925; *Labor Call*, 8 Jan 1925; F. W. Eggleston, Confidential notes: the Victorian parliament as I knew it (Menzies Lib, ANU); Aust Boot Trade Employees Federation, Vic Branch records, T5 series 1, 2 (ANU Archives).   R. KISS

BINGLE, WALTER DAVID (1861-1928), public servant, was born on 12 April 1861 at Newcastle, New South Wales, second son of John Rayden Bingle, and his wife Frances Elizabeth, née Corlette. His paternal grandfather had migrated from Britain and worked as a surveyor of the east coast of Australia. Educated at Newcastle Grammar School, Bingle then spent ten years in his father's shipping agency and commission merchant's firm, Bingle & Co., in Pitt Street, Sydney. Towards the end of this period he served as vice-consul for the Netherlands and Italy. In 1885 he joined the New South Wales Public Service as a temporary clerk. He married Emily Pinhey at Ashfield on 19 October 1887; they had a son and three daughters.

On 1 July that year Bingle had received a permanent appointment in the Department of Lands. He became private secretary to several lands ministers, including J. N. Brunker, H. Copeland [qq.v.3] and (Sir) Joseph Carruthers, and to the premier (Sir) William Lyne [qq.v.]. Bingle was closely involved in pre-Federation conferences and when in 1901 Lyne took home affairs in the first Commonwealth ministry, Bingle transferred to Melbourne with him and was soon promoted to chief clerk. From 1903 he was also marshal of the High Court of Australia and in 1905-06 temporarily assumed the additional duties of chief electoral officer.

In 1898 Bingle had been secretary to the imperial commission which developed a constitution for Norfolk Island, and in 1913 he went to Honolulu as a representative of the Commonwealth to meet the Empire Parliamentary Association delegation to Australia. He was acting head of the Department of Home Affairs in 1907-09 and 1914-16, and became secretary and permanent head of the Department of Works and Railways from 1917, until his retirement in 1926; in 1925 he was also commissioner for war service homes. In 1923 he had been awarded the Imperial Service Order.

Wilfred Blacket [q.v.], the sole member of

the 1916-17 royal commission on the Federal capital's administration, had adversely criticized the former minister and the officers of the Department of Home Affairs for hindering W. Burley Griffin [q.v.] in carrying out the planning of Canberra. It was alleged that Bingle had been obstructive in delaying communication of vital information to Griffin. Blacket concluded in his report that officers, and particularly the minister W. O. Archibald [q.v.], were hostile to Griffin and his design and preferred an alternative departmental plan for the city. Blacket also blamed wasteful expenditure at Canberra on lack of forethought and organization in the department. Bingle had been less directly involved than some of his colleagues. He expressed his views privately to a friend ten years later: 'The more I reflect on the strictures of the Blacket Commission report the more I realise how untrue were the findings as far as my motives were concerned. I honestly tried to do my best to advance Canberra, and to this day think that it would have been better to have had a committee of experts report on the Griffin plan (particularly engineers) and have it adopted by Parliament before proceeding'.

C. S. Daley [q.v.] described Bingle as 'reflective in temperament and easily moved', but 'dignified, of ... kindly disposition, and [with] a good sense of humour when relaxed'. Bingle saw the great danger in Canberra as 'the likelihood of official life creeping in the social life'. 'The highest officially are not always the most desirable socially', he commented in 1927. He died of arteriosclerosis at Brighton, Victoria, on 7 August 1928, survived by his wife and two daughters, and was buried in Brighton cemetery.

PP (Cwlth), 1914-17, 2, 1067, 1917, 2, 1; C. S. Daley, 'Much ado about nothing', Canb & District Hist Soc, *Papers*, 1960; *Herald* (Melb), 23 Jan 1926; Groom papers (NL); Dept of Home Affairs, Papers (AAO, Canb); Dept of Works and Railways, Papers and printed schedules (AAO, Canb).

CECIL CARR

BINNS, KENNETH (1882-1969), librarian, was born on 28 November at Dunfermline, Fifeshire, Scotland, third son of Rev. Fred Binns, Congregational minister, and his wife Henrietta, née Johnstone. The family migrated to Australia in 1890 and he was educated at Cleveland Street Public School and Sydney Grammar School. In 1900 he joined the staff of the Fisher [q.v.4] Library at the University of Sydney and attended night classes in the faculty of arts as a non-matriculated student. On 14 September 1909 Binns married Amy Jane Higgins (d. 1968) at Redfern. Two years later he became a cataloguer in the Commonwealth Parliamentary Library, Melbourne, and in 1919 took over its Australian section. An outstanding early accession was James Cook's [q.v.1] *Endeavour* journal, in the purchase of which in 1923 Binns played a significant part.

His foresight in promoting the erection of a building in Canberra for the growing national collections was nullified by government demands for increased office space. In 1926-27, as assistant librarian, Binns arranged the transport to Canberra of the parliamentary library's 68 000 volumes. From 1 January 1928, on Arthur Wadsworth's [q.v.] retirement, he was parliamentary librarian, but in difficult circumstances: the library was remote from sources of supply and from professional contacts, and accommodation problems continued. He did much to promote the intellectual life of the new capital, especially the Canberra Society of Arts and Literature and the University Association of Canberra; after the university college was established he served on its council. He was an active Congregationalist.

In 1934 Binns became the first Australian librarian to be awarded a Carnegie travelling fellowship; two years later the Carnegie Corporation of New York gave a grant to the library to support a free service for Commonwealth external territories. During World War II he extended facilities to military camps and established liaison offices in Melbourne and London; and in 1943 the Commonwealth National Library accepted temporary responsibility for the custody of archives other than those of armed service departments. The library's training school and film section were established during Binns's administration and he inaugurated some principal bibliographical activities, as well as encouraging research inquiries. He was unusual for his time in seeking university graduates of a high standard for his staff. He had been a leading foundation member of the Australian Institute of Librarians and was its president in 1940-44. He retired in 1947.

In 1930-39 Binns had been the Australian representative for the International Institute for Intellectual Co-operation, and after the war he was a member of the national committee for the United Nations Educational, Scientific and Cultural Organization. He was a member of the Commonwealth Literary Fund's advisory board in 1939-53 and of the Commonwealth Literature Censorship Board for twenty years before becoming its chairman in 1957-64. He was responsible for some of its more enlightened policies, but he did not retire until he was 81 and he and the board drew criticism for the banning of such books as V. Nabokov's *Lolita*. He had also been on the Australian National Film Board for three years from 1945. In 1964 he was appointed C.B.E.

Binns was a cautious, practical man whose period of office had spanned the difficult, restrictive years of the Depression and World War II. Nevertheless the library had emerged as a national institution, and many of its successful developments originated during his administration. He died in Canberra on 27 July 1969 and was cremated, survived by two daughters and by a son Kenneth Johnstone, who was under-treasurer of Tasmania in 1952-76.

Aust Lib J, June 1965; *SMH*, 31 May 1960, 4, 6 July 1964; Groom papers (NL); Parliamentary Library *and* NL Archives (Canb); information from Miss J. Binns, Canb.   PAULINE FANNING

BIRD, FREDERIC DOUGAN (1858-1929), surgeon, was born on 27 May 1858 at Richmond, Surrey, England, son of Samuel Dougan Bird [q.v.3] and his first wife Catherine Emma, née Tate. He arrived in Victoria with his parents in February 1862. Educated at Scotch College, he studied medicine at the University of Melbourne (M.B., 1882; Ch.B., 1884; Ch.M., 1886), with experience at the hospitals of King's and University colleges, London (M.R.C.S., England, 1883). Bird was a founder of the Melbourne Medical Students' Society and the University Rifle Club and was a first-class oarsman and billiards player. Talented, witty and charming, he was tall and striking in appearance with a 'very fine physical presence'. In November 1881, while still a student, he married Lucy Clare Hopkins of Murdeduke, Winchelsea.

In 1884 Bird was appointed a part-time demonstrator of anatomy at the University of Melbourne. In 1887 he became honorary surgeon to out-patients at the Melbourne Hospital and in 1891 to in-patients, a position he held for twenty-three years. He was appointed lecturer and examiner in surgery at the university in 1895. Students found him urbane and helpful, a brilliant lecturer, an excellent clinical teacher and a careful examiner who preferred to teach from his own experience rather than from lessons 'perpetuated in textbooks'. He established a large surgical practice; his private hospital in Spring Street was one of the first to have, besides a well-equipped operating theatre, a pathology laboratory and an X-ray room. He was a highly efficient artist in his technique though neither adventurous nor innovative; he gained a reputation in the surgical treatment of hydatids, following his father's

interest in the disease. His eminence in his profession was due to his personality, his social connexions, his undoubted technical ability and his conscientious care of his patients. He served for many years as surgeon to the Metropolitan Fire Brigade and later as consultant to the Queen Victoria Hospital.

Bird was president of the surgery section at the Australasian Medical Congress held in Adelaide in 1904. He was sometime president of the Medical Society of Victoria, although he preferred not to become involved in council and committee meetings: he doubted the wisdom of any rigid organization of the profession. While in London in 1913 as vice-president of the surgery section of the International Congress of Medicine, he was awarded an honorary fellowship of the Royal College of Surgeons of England.

Bird volunteered for service with the Australian Imperial Force in 1914 and, bearing the cost of his own team of nurses and equipment, he accompanied the first contingent to Egypt. He soon transferred to the Royal Army Medical Corps and in February 1915 was appointed consulting surgeon to the British forces in Egypt with the rank of lieut-colonel. He served at Gallipoli and in Macedonia; after appointment to the Mediterranean Expeditionary Force, he was posted to Southern Command, England. He was three times mentioned in dispatches and for his part in the Gallipoli campaign was appointed C.B.

In May 1918, while still abroad, Bird relinquished his active position at the Melbourne Hospital. After his return he was first president of the Surgical Association of Melbourne in 1920 but resigned in November from the university and in 1923 retired from his practice. From 1880 he was a member of the Melbourne Club and was president in 1926. Widely read, he was interested in art and architecture and was a keen Dante scholar. He enjoyed bush-walking, especially in the Victorian mountains, and was an enthusiastic botanist. His publications in medical journals were not numerous, but were characterized by 'high seriousness and thoughtfulness' and an original writing style.

In his last years Bird was crippled by gout; he died of coronary thrombosis at his home in Toorak on 29 May 1929, survived by his wife, a son and a daughter, and was buried in Boroondara cemetery, Kew. He left an estate valued for probate at £45 761.

MJA, 20 Aug 1921, 6 July 1929; *Argus*, 30 May 1929; Novar papers (NL).   W. D. UPJOHN*

BIRDWOOD, WILLIAM RIDDELL (1865-1951), 1st BARON BIRDWOOD OF ANZAC

AND TOTNES, field marshal, was born on 13 September 1865 at Kirkee, India, second son of Herbert Mills Birdwood, under-secretary to the government of Bombay, and Edith Marion, daughter of Surgeon Major E. G. H. Impey of the Bombay Horse Artillery. Birdwood was educated at Clifton College, Bristol, and the Royal Military College, Sandhurst, England, from which he was commissioned early owing to the Russian war scare of 1885. He was posted to the 12th Lancers in India, transferring in 1887 to the 11th Bengal Lancers. In 1894 he married Jeannette Hope Gonville, daughter of the fourth Baron Bromhead of Lincoln.

By 1914 Birdwood was an experienced and successful officer. He had served in numerous North-West Frontier campaigns and in the South African War, and had held an important frontier command. He had been on Lord Kitchener's staff in South Africa and India, and later recognized Kitchener as 'the greatest influence on my life'. Awarded the D.S.O. and C.I.E. in 1908, he became major general in 1911 and was appointed C.B. He became secretary to the Army Department, government of India, and member of the Viceroy's Legislative Council in 1912, and was already regarded by some as a future commander-in-chief. However, the outbreak of war in Europe turned his career in a wholly unexpected direction.

In November 1914 Kitchener, as minister for war, gave Birdwood command of the forces raised by Australia and New Zealand for service in Europe. He reached Egypt, where they were assembling, on 21 December accompanied by a small, carefully chosen staff. From the beginning, Lieut-General Birdwood struck the note which was to characterize his command throughout the war; he left his staff to get on with their work and went among his troops.

Kitchener at first gave Birdwood command of the troops who were to land on the Gallipoli Peninsula in support of the fleet trying to force the passage of the Dardanelles. Birdwood's report, made after reconnoitring the Straits and discussions with the Royal Navy, convinced Kitchener that a greater military effort was needed; he allotted more troops and appointed General Sir Ian Hamilton to command. Hamilton, disregarding Birdwood's plans, ordered him to land north of Gaba Tepe on the Aegean side of the peninsula, simultaneously with other landings around Helles and on the Asian shore. He was to press inland and cut off the Turks in the southern part of the peninsula. Birdwood insisted on a silent attack before dawn to ensure surprise.

The covering force went ashore on 25 April, a mile north of the designated beach. The consequent confusion was aggravated by the abrupt and lofty ridges, narrow gullies, dense scrub and increasing Turkish resistance. By dark the force was disorganized, the men almost exhausted and their objectives still in enemy hands. The divisional commanders W. T. Bridges [q.v.] and A. J. Godley impressed on Birdwood their doubts about withstanding a counter-attack and urged him to make arrangements with the navy for re-embarkation. This he refused to do but agreed to place their views before Hamilton. The latter's firm refusal to withdraw and his injunction to 'dig, dig, dig until you are safe' ended the first crisis of the campaign.

The impression that Birdwood had made on the Anzacs in Egypt deepened during the seven months on the peninsula when the attackers became a besieged garrison. Daily the short, lean figure of their commander was seen in the front trenches, chatting with the soldiers, noting with professional eye what the amateurs had overlooked and giving orders for its amendment, sharing the risks but never the water that was offered because he knew that every drop had been carried up from the beach. He neither smoked nor drank any form of alcohol but refreshed himself by swimming daily off Anzac—the name he gave the landing place—in spite of enemy fire. 'Birdie's' serene courage won the admiration of all. His concern for the soldiers and his fighting spirit became important factors in Anzac morale. Robert Rhodes James states that his popularity 'was something of a newspaper myth' and quotes an unnamed Australian observer: 'He bored the men and they bored him'. C. E. W. Bean [q.v.], who saw Birdwood at close quarters throughout the war, does not confirm this view; nor does Birdwood's enthusiastic reception by Australians in London on Anzac Day 1916, nor his triumphal progress around Australia and New Zealand in 1920. Whatever the extent of his popularity, there is no doubt of the respect in which he was held for his courage and his example. In Hamilton's memorable phrase, he was 'the soul of Anzac'.

After Bridges died on 18 May 1915 Birdwood temporarily took command of the Australian Imperial Force, but was not formally appointed until 14 September 1916. He had suggested the move and, while admitting his ambition, it must be conceded that, from the standpoint of fairness and military efficiency, this decision was crucial to the future of the A.I.F. which in 1915 had expanded to two divisions and included troops under New Zealand command. Birdwood brought an Australian expert in personnel matters to his headquarters and in September chose Colonel (Sir) Brudenell White [q.v.] from 1st Division Headquarters as chief of staff. Thus began a military partnership which contributed markedly to the development of the A.I.F.

Birdwood's attacks in May and August were costly and mostly unsuccessful — hardly surprising, given the nature of the ground, the lack of depth in the Anzac position and the commanding heights occupied by the Turks. He had held this position against all Turkish efforts. When the question of evacuation was debated in November, Birdwood was the only senior officer opposed to it but it fell to him to command the brilliant operations whereby Suvla, Anzac and Helles were evacuated without loss in December and January. After expanding the A.I.F. to four divisions in Egypt, he sailed for France in command of the 1st Anzac Corps in March 1916.

In France, Birdwood's influence on the A.I.F. was no less important than in Egypt. Successfully resisting General Headquarters' attempt to take charge of Australian administration, he built up the A.I.F. base and training establishments in England and united the five Australian divisions in the Australian Corps. He insisted on retaining command of the A.I.F. in Egypt, but failed either to go himself or to send White to visit the Light Horse and other units.

Birdwood's policy was to appoint Australians to commands and staffs, but pressure from home forced him to accelerate the process. By 31 May 1918, when he handed over the corps to Lieut-General Sir John Monash [q.v.], whom he had recommended as his successor, only one British officer remained in a senior command. Birdwood, who had been promoted general in 1917, went to command the Fifth Army much against his own wishes; he took White as chief of staff and to advise in Australian matters, as he still retained command of the A.I.F. Although most Australian generals supported this arrangement, there was strong opposition from Bean and (Sir) Keith Murdoch [q.v.], the journalist and confidant of W. M. Hughes [q.v.]; they argued that Monash should command the A.I.F. and White the corps as, in their view, Birdwood could not command a British army and efficiently administer the A.I.F. In August Hughes offered Birdwood the administrative command full time and he accepted, while obtaining Hughes's agreement to his remaining with his army until 30 November.

Birdwood was appointed K.C.M.G. (1914), K.C.S.I. (1915), K.C.B. (1917), G.C.M.G. (1919), and was created a baronet and granted £10 000 (1919). He was mentioned in dispatches frequently and awarded many foreign decorations. In the Australian Military Forces he was made a general (1920), field marshal (1925), and honorary colonel of the 3rd Infantry Battalion and the 16th Light Horse; he also received further British honours.

Birdwood toured Australia and New Zealand in 1920 after which he returned to the Indian Army, becoming commander-in-chief in 1925. He retired in 1930. An ambition of which he made no secret was thwarted when Sir Isaac Isaacs [q.v.] was made governor-general of Australia that year. King George V had wished to appoint Birdwood but Prime Minister Scullin [q.v.] insisted on an Australian. However, his election to the mastership of Peterhouse, Cambridge, England, in 1931 was an enjoyable coda to a long and distinguished career. In 1938 he was created Baron Birdwood of Anzac and Totnes.

Birdwood's success as a commander lay in the field of leadership rather than in tactics or organization. Nevertheless he was careful to choose able subordinates and the quality of his staffs was high. His choice of White, widely regarded as the outstanding Australian officer, strengthened his position in dealing with the Australians as well as with higher authority. If he lacked the tactical flair and imagination of General Allenby, he was a very competent professional who set and obtained high standards. In view of the reputation of the Australian Corps when he left it in May 1918, he must be accorded his share of the credit for creating so illustrious a force. Throughout the war he kept up a valuable correspondence not only with the governor-general, the prime minister and the minister for defence but also with bereaved or anxious families in Australia. He also wrote to officers who had been decorated or promoted. When Field Marshal Haig told White that he should command the corps, White's reply was significant: 'God forbid! General Birdwood has a position among Australians which is far too valuable to lose'.

Survived by a son and two daughters, Birdwood died at Hampton Court Palace, Middlesex, on 17 May 1951 and was buried in Twickenham cemetery with full military honours. His autobiography, *Khaki and gown*, had been published in 1941 and a short book of reminiscences, *In my time*, in 1946. Portraits are in the Australian War Memorial and the Royal Military College, Canberra, as well as the National Gallery of Victoria. A town in South Australia bears his name. His elder daughter married Colin Craig, a Western Australian grazier.

C. E. W. Bean, *The story of Anzac* (Syd, 1921, 1924), and *The A.I.F. in France* (Syd, 1929, 1933, 1937, 1942); C. F. Aspinall-Oglander, *Military operations: Gallipoli*, 1-2 (Lond, 1929, 1932); R. R. James, *Gallipoli* (Syd, 1965); E. Bush, *Gallipoli* (Lond, 1975); *Who was who 1951-1960* (Lond);

Birdwood *and* Pearce papers (AWM); Chauvel papers (held by Lady Chauvel, Melb); Novar papers (NL); news-cuttings 1914-51 (AWM).

A. J. HILL

BIRKBECK, GILBERT SAMUEL COLIN LATONA (1876-1947), soldier and public servant, was born on 15 March 1876 at Brisbane, son of Robert Epiphany Birkbeck, grazier, and his wife Francesca Julia Louisa Latona, née Clement; both parents were born in Mexico. After education at state schools, he joined the Queensland Department of Agriculture and Stock on 1 June 1900 and was meat inspector at Normanton in 1901-05 and Mackay in 1905-14. On 17 February 1909 he married a widow Anna Jacinta Mary Elizabeth Thomas, née Antoney, at Holy Trinity Anglican Church, Mackay; they had one son and two daughters.

In April 1908 Birkbeck was commissioned second lieutenant in the 15th Australian Light Horse Regiment, Queensland Mounted Infantry. He was promoted lieutenant in March 1911 and served with this unit (renamed the 27th L.H.R., Australian Military Forces, in 1912) until World War I. On 20 August 1914 he enlisted in the Australian Imperial Force as a lieutenant in 'C' Squadron, 2nd Light Horse Regiment, and was promoted captain on 18 October, two days before embarking for Egypt. After training, his unit was sent to Gallipoli to fight as infantry; it took over the defence of Quinn's Post on 12 May 1915 and three days later Birkbeck was wounded while leading an abortive raid. Wounded again in a Turkish attack at Pope's Hill on 30 June, he was evacuated, and rejoined his unit for the Sinai campaign. He was promoted major on 1 August 1916 and in the battle of Romani commanded 'A' Squadron.

On 15 November Birkbeck's regiment joined Major General Sir Philip Chetwode's Desert Column which attacked the Turks at Magdhaba on 22 December. Swooping on a vital Turkish redoubt from the rear, Birkbeck's troops cut off the only line of retreat. For his 'initiative and excellent leadership' he was awarded the Distinguished Service Order. He commanded 'A' Squadron at Rafa and at the second battle of Gaza and was mentioned in dispatches on 6 July 1917. Later that year he was liaison officer between the Desert Mounted Corps and the 20th Army Corps, then served as second-in-command of his regiment at the battle of Beersheba. He was temporary commander from December 1917 to February 1918 and from May to August, and served in the Jordan Valley until the Turkish

surrender on 31 October.

Birkbeck returned to Australia on 30 April 1919 and was demobilized in June. He resumed work with the Department of Agriculture and was stock inspector at Mackay in 1919-21, Gympie in 1921-34 and Toowoomba in 1934-41. He served as a captain in 'B' Squadron, 27th Light Horse Regiment, A.M.F., and was promoted major in April 1920. Transferred to the 5th L.H.R. in 1921, he commanded it from 1924, when he was awarded the Volunteer Officers' Decoration. Lieut-colonel in 1927, he commanded the 47th Battalion from 1928 to 15 March 1933 when he was placed on the retired list with the honorary rank of colonel.

Birkbeck retired from the public service in 1942 and lived in Toowoomba until he died there of coronary thrombosis on 15 December 1947. He was cremated in Brisbane.

H. S. Gullett, *The A.I.F. in Sinai and Palestine* (Syd, 1923); G. H. Bourne, *Nulli secundus: the history of the 2nd Light Horse Regiment, A.I.F.* (Tamworth, 1926); Blue Books, *PP* (Qld), 1903, 1908, 1909, 1912; *Government Gazette* (Qld), 2 Dec 1933, 10 Feb 1934, Oct 1941; *Courier Mail*, and *Toowoomba Chronicle*, 16 Dec 1947.

ROBERT W. STRACHAN

BIRKS, FREDERICK (1894-1917), soldier, was born on 16 August 1894 at Buckley, Flintshire, North Wales, son of Samuel Birks, groom, and his wife Mary, née Williams. His father died in a coal-mining accident when he was 8. Educated at the local St Matthew's Anglican parish school he later worked as a labourer and steel-rollerman in the near-by town of Shotton.

In 1913 Birks migrated to Australia and worked as a labourer in Tasmania, South Australia and Victoria. Enlisting in the Australian Imperial Force on 18 August 1914, he was posted to the 2nd Field Ambulance, Australian Army Medical Corps, and sailed for Egypt in October. His unit went into action at Gallipoli on 25 April 1915, providing medical support for the 2nd Infantry Brigade. On 26 June, while serving as a stretcher-bearer, Birks was wounded by shrapnel; he resumed duty soon afterwards and remained at Anzac until 9 September. He served in Egypt until March 1916 when the 2nd Field Ambulance left for the Western Front, was promoted lance corporal on 21 April and served throughout the first battle of the Somme as a stretcher-bearer. At Pozières in July, for 'constant good services', he was awarded the Military Medal in the field by General Birdwood [q.v.].

Promoted corporal on 10 August 1916, Birks was selected for officer-training and was commissioned second lieutenant in the

6th Battalion on 4 May 1917; his first major engagement as an infantryman was the third battle of Ypres. On 20 September, while his battalion was advancing on Glencorse Wood, Birks and a corporal rushed a pillbox which was holding up the advance. The corporal was wounded but Birks went on by himself, killed those manning the pillbox and captured a machine-gun. Shortly afterwards he raised a small party and attacked another strong point, capturing sixteen men and killing or wounding nine others. In the consolidation that followed, he reorganized groups from other units which were in disarray. Next day, during an artillery bombardment, he was killed while trying to rescue some of his men who had been buried by a shell. For his 'conspicuous bravery' he was awarded the Victoria Cross posthumously.

Birks was buried in Zillebeke cemetery, Belgium. In 1921 a memorial was erected in his honour in St Matthew's schoolyard, Buckley. His portrait by F. Hornsby hangs in the Australian War Memorial, Canberra.

C. E. W. Bean, *The A.I.F. in France*, 1916, 1917 (Syd, 1929, 1933); A. G. Butler (ed), *Official history of the Australian Army Medical Services ... 1914-18*, 1, 2 (Melb, 1930, Canb, 1940); *London Gazette*, 16 Nov 1917, 8 Nov 1917; *Buckley Parish Mag* (Wales), Nov 1917; *Sydney Mail*, 9 Jan 1918; R. E. Goode and G. F. Green, 2nd Australian Field Ambulance: a short history, 1914-16 (AWM); information from F. H. Birks, Edinburgh, Scotland.

L. WARD

BIRRELL, FREDERICK WILLIAM (1869-1939), typographer and politician, was born on 27 August 1869 at North Adelaide, son of Andrew Birrell, labourer, and his wife Eliza, née Banks. Eliza was deserted by her husband soon after Frederick and his twin brother were born but she and her children were helped by the Thomas family; (Sir) Robert Kyffin Thomas [q.v.6] was general manager of the *South Australian Register*. Frederick joined the paper's printing section and in 1892 became a member of the Typographical Society of South Australia (the Printing Industry Employees' Union). In 1909 he 'realised one of the ambitions of his life' by becoming its president, a position he held for four years; he remained a member for over forty years. In 1911-21 he was its representative on the Printing Wages Board (the Printing Trades Board), and in 1911-26 its delegate to the United Trades and Labor Council and the council and annual conference of the United Labor Party. After several years with the *Register*, Birrell had joined the Labor Party newspaper, the *Daily Herald*, as a linotype operator, and was later

a journalist for it and a member of its board of management. On 15 October 1903 at College Park he had married Ellen Thomas, a machinist.

In 1915 Birrell stood unsuccessfully as a Labor candidate for the safe Liberal seat of Wooroora in the House of Assembly, but polled well. President of the T.L.C. in 1918-20 he believed strikes and lock-outs were 'barbarous', as they often inflicted 'suffering upon the innocent' and that 'anarchy and red revolution have no place in Australian sentiment'. Speaking at his installation as president in 1920 he said: 'It, therefore, behoves us all to tend our energies in the direction of perfecting our arbitration and conciliation machinery'. Birrell was secretary of the State branch of the Labor Party in 1919-20 and president in 1923-24. In 1921 he had entered the House of Assembly, for North Adelaide, and became a quiet, hard-working member. He was not regarded as a gifted orator, spoke infrequently, and was generally seen as a moderate, although in his maiden speech he strongly defended the party's socialization plank. Birrell maintained firm personal support in his electorate and was comfortably returned at the 1924 election. In 1926 the Labor premier John Gunn [q.v.] resigned and in the ensuing reshuffle Birrell became Speaker for seven months.

Because of illness he was unable to take part in the 1927 election campaign, but nevertheless retained his seat. He remained in parliament until 1933 but took little part in debates. In August 1931 the South Australian Labor Party had split over the L. L. Hill [q.v.] government's support for the Premiers' Plan, and twenty-two parliamentarians were expelled from the party. Although Birrell was identified with the Hill group, illness prevented his becoming publicly involved in the controversy. He did not stand in the 1933 election and retired from public life.

Birrell died of cerebro-vascular disease at his home in North Adelaide on 20 January 1939 and was survived by his wife; they had no children.

Daily Herald (Adel), *Labor's thirty years record in South Australia* (Adel, 1923); *A'sian Typographical J*, Aug 1909, Aug, Nov 1911, Oct 1913; *SMH*, 10 Feb 1920; *Observer* (Adel), 31 July 1920, 15 Sept 1923, 18 Sept 1926; *Advertiser* (Adel), 21 Jan 1939; R. Pettman, Factionalism in the A.L.P.: a South Australian case study, 1930-33 (B.A. Hons thesis, Univ Adel, 1967); S. R. Whitford, An autobiography (SAA).   RAY BROOMHILL

BIRTLES, FRANCIS EDWIN (1881-1941), overlander, was born on 7 November

1881 at Fitzroy, Victoria, son of David Birtles, a bootmaker from Macclesfield, England, and his wife Sarah Jane, née Bartlett. He was educated at South Wandin State School, and at 15 joined the merchant navy as an apprentice. In 1899 he jumped ship at Cape Town, South Africa, and tried to enlist with Australian militia, but was attached to the Field Intelligence Department as part of a troop of irregular mounted infantry until May 1902. He returned briefly to Australia, then joined the constabulary in the Transvaal as a mounted police officer. His experiences there equipped him with bushcraft skills in a semi-arid environment and he undertook several cycling and photographic excursions; his police service ended when he contracted blackwater fever.

Birtles disembarked at Fremantle, Western Australia, and on 26 December 1905 left to cycle to Melbourne, an achievement which attracted widespread attention. After brief employment as a lithographic artist, in 1907-08 he cycled to Sydney and then, via Brisbane, Normanton, Darwin, Alice Springs and Adelaide back to Sydney, where he was thereafter based. In 1909 he published the story of his feat, *Lonely lands,* which he illustrated with his own photographs. That year he set a new cycling record for the Fremantle to Sydney continental crossing, then in 1910-11 rode around Australia. In 1911 he was accompanied from Sydney to Darwin by R. Primmer, cameraman for the Gaumont Co.: *Across Australia* was released next year. Birtles had continued on to Broome and Perth, then lowered his record by riding from Fremantle to Sydney in thirty-one days. By 1912 he had cycled around Australia twice and had crossed the continent seven times.

Birtles next turned to the motor car and in 1912 completed the first west-to-east crossing of the continent with Syd Ferguson and a terrier, Rex, in a single-cylinder Brush car. In 1914 with Frank Hurley [q.v.] as cameraman he made *Into Australia's unknown* (1915); next year he retraced their route and was responsible for the film *Across Australia in the track of Burke and Wills* [qq.v.3, 6]; in 1919 he made *Through Australian wilds,* following by car the track of Sir Ross Smith [q.v.]. On his many other trips, with companions such as his brother Clive, he shot much film footage.

On 27 November 1920 at St Paul's Cathedral, Melbourne, he married Frances Knight; they soon separated and she divorced him in 1922. In 1921 he and his companion Roy Fry had been extensively injured when his car caught fire near Elsey station while he was employed by the Prime Minister's Department on a survey mission for the proposed north-south railway to

Alice Springs; he later finished the survey by air. In 1926 he set motoring records from Melbourne to Darwin and Darwin to Sydney (seven days) in a Bean car named 'The Sundowner'. By mid-1927 he had completed more than seventy transcontinental crossings. Impecunious, he depended on manufacturers to sponsor his expeditions and wrote about many of his journeys for newspapers and periodicals.

In July 1928 Birtles became the first person to drive from London to Melbourne, a nine-month part-solo journey completed in 'The Sundowner' which he donated in 1929 to a proposed national museum in Canberra. With M. H. Ellis he undertook an unsuccessful search for L. H. B. Lasseter [q.v.]. In the Depression he spent several years gold-prospecting in arid areas and discovered a payable gold-mine in 1934. On 11 February 1935 at St Mary's Cathedral, Sydney, he married Nea McCutcheon. That year he published *Battle fronts of outback* (Sydney).

Survived by his second wife, Birtles died at Croydon of coronary vascular disease on 1 July 1941 and was buried in the Anglican section of Waverley cemetery.

M. H. Ellis, *The long lead* (Lond, 1927); T. R. Nicholson, *The trailblazers* (Lond, 1958), and *Five roads to danger* (Lond, 1960); I. Bertrand, 'Francis Birtles — cyclist, explorer, Kodaker', *Cinema Papers,* Jan 1974; information from Mrs J. S. Birtles, Nambour, Qld.   TERRY G. BIRTLES

BISDEE, JOHN HUTTON (1869-1930), soldier and pastoralist, was born on 28 September 1869 at Hutton Park, Melton Mowbray, Tasmania, eighth child of John Bisdee, pastoralist, and his wife Ellen Jane, née Butler. His grandfather, John Bisdee [q.v.1], had arrived in the colony in 1821. He was educated at The Hutchins School, Hobart, and then worked on his father's property until April 1900 when he enlisted for service in the South African War as a trooper in the 1st Tasmanian Imperial Bushmens' Contingent.

Bisdee sailed on 26 April and served in operations in Cape Colony, the Transvaal and the Orange River Colony. On 1 September, near Warmbad, Transvaal, he was with a scouting party ambushed by Boers in a rocky defile; six of its eight men were wounded, including an officer whose horse broke away and bolted. Bisdee dismounted, put the wounded man on his own horse and ran alongside, then mounted behind him and withdrew under heavy fire. For this action he received the Victoria Cross — the first awarded to a Tasmanian. Wounded during the ambush, he was invalided home but, on

298

recovering, went back to South Africa as a lieutenant in No. 1 Company, 2nd Tasmanian Imperial Bushmens' Contingent, and served from March 1901 until the end of the war.

After his return to Tasmania Bisdee resumed farming at Hutton Park. On 11 April 1904, at St John's Anglican Church, Hobart, he married Georgiana Theodosia, daughter of Bishop M. B. Hale [q.v.4]. Two years later he joined the 12th Australian Light Horse Regiment, Tasmanian Mounted Infantry, as a temporary lieutenant and was promoted lieutenant in 1908 and captain in 1910; in that year he attended a course of instruction in India. In August 1913 he became commanding officer of his regiment, now the 26th Light Horse.

Bisdee joined the Australian Imperial Force as a captain in the 12th Light Horse on 26 July 1915. Accompanied by his wife, who was to do valuable work in the A.I.F. canteens, he sailed for Egypt in November. He served in operations against the Senussi at Mersa Matruh until a leg wound precluded him from active service; he was seconded as assistant provost marshal, first to A.I.F. Headquarters, Egypt, in March 1916, then two months later to the Anzac Mounted Division. Bisdee was promoted major in September, returned to regimental duty in December and served with the Light Horse throughout 1917. In January 1918 he became assistant provost marshal (Egypt section) of the Anzac Provost Corps; in June he was confirmed as lieut-colonel. He was mentioned in dispatches and appointed O.B.E. in June 1919.

Bisdee was discharged from the A.I.F. in May 1920. A major in the Australian Military Forces from 1915, he was placed on the reserve in 1921 and on the retired list, with the honorary rank of lieut-colonel, in 1929. He had continued to farm at Ashburton, Bridgewater, in Tasmania, the property he had acquired in 1915. While travelling in France in 1926 his wife died. He returned to Tasmania and lived at Tranquility, Melton Mowbray, where he died of chronic nephritis on 14 January 1930; he and his sister (who died next day) were buried in St James's churchyard, Jericho, in the same grave. The Bisdee Memorial Cadet Efficiency Prize, awarded annually at St Virgil's College, Hobart, is named after him.

Aust Defence Dept, *Official records of the Australian military contingents to the war in South Africa*, P. L. Murray ed (Melb, 1912); L. Wigmore (ed), *They dared mightily* (Canb, 1963); *Reveille* (Syd), 31 Jan 1930; *Sydney Mail*, 24 Nov 1900; *Mercury*, 15-17 Jan, 6-7 Feb 1930; *SMH*, 15 Jan 1930; Bisdee papers (Tas Museum and Art Gallery, Hob); I. McAuley, The Bisdees of Hutton Park (TA).   L. A. SIMPSON

BISHOP, CHARLES GEORGE (1895-1931), soldier, labourer and council inspector, was born on 12 September 1895 at Urana, New South Wales, son of Charles George Bishop, labourer, and his wife Violet Jane, née Stripling. He attended Lavington Public School but had no further education after his mother died when he was 11. Before World War I he worked as a labourer, and served for two years with a militia unit, the 44th (Riverina) Infantry Regiment.

Bishop enlisted in the Australian Imperial Force on 3 August 1915 and two months later sailed for Egypt with reinforcements for the 18th Battalion. By May 1916 his unit was in France at Armentières where he distinguished himself in patrolling. On 4 August he was so severely wounded at Pozières Heights that he was unable to return to duty until late December. His battalion remained on the Western Front throughout 1917, fighting at Lagnicourt, Bullecourt, Messines and Passchendaele. Bishop was promoted lance corporal in May, corporal in September and sergeant in October.

In April 1918 he was awarded the Military Medal for leading an attack on an enemy patrol of thirty men at Pont Rouge, Belgium. During a patrol action on 8 March, German scouts had been seen entering a trench; Sergeant Bishop and three men, with covering fire from their mates, assaulted the enemy from a flank and routed them. In September he received the Distinguished Conduct Medal for 'conspicuous gallantry and devotion to duty' on 15 April 1918, while in charge of a mopping up party at Cemetery Copse in the Villers-Bretonneux sector. He had to contend with an unexpectedly large number of Germans, but accomplished his task by bringing in neighbouring troops to assist in a prolonged action. His last encounter with the enemy was at Morlancourt on 19 May 1918. Although wounded in the face during the preliminary bombardment, he took charge of a party and reached the objective, rescued a wounded officer and took his place, until he too was wounded and evacuated. For this action, he was awarded a Bar to his Military Medal.

Bishop's various wounds were severe: he was invalided back to Australia on 20 October. The Armistice was signed while he was at sea and he returned to Albury as a local hero. After discharge from the A.I.F. he resumed his former occupation of labourer and worked on the construction of the Hume Weir until 1924 when he was appointed health and nuisance inspector with Hume Shire Council. In 1922 he had married May Elizabeth Knobel at Thurgoona; they had two children. Bishop was a tall well-built man, popular in the district. He marched on

Anzac Day, but did not dwell on his wartime experiences. He died at Albury on 17 September 1931 of septic pharyngitis and cellulitis after only two days illness, and was buried in the Catholic cemetery. His early death was hastened by the effects of his wounds.

C. E. W. Bean, *The A.I.F. in France*, 1916-1918 (Syd, 1929, 1937, 1942); *London Gazette*, 23 Apr, 3 Sept, 4 Oct 1918; *Reveille* (Syd), 30 Sept 1931; *Sun* (Syd), 20 Oct 1931; 18th Battalion war diary (AWM); records (AWM); information from Mrs M. E. Bishop, Albury, NSW.   E. J. O'DONNELL

BJELKE-PETERSEN, HANS CHRISTIAN (1872-1964), physical culture teacher, was born on 14 April 1872 in Copenhagen, Denmark, son of Georg Peter Bjelke-Petersen, gardener, later master-builder, and his wife Caroline Vilhelmine, née Hansen. His sister was Marie Caroline Bjelke-Petersen [q.v.]. At first educated by his father at home, acquiring a thorough grounding in gymnastics, swimming and the Bible, he later attended schools at Dresden, Germany, and at Copenhagen, graduating from Copenhagen Teachers' College in 1890. The family then went to London and in October 1891 arrived in Tasmania in the *Doric*.

Bjelke-Petersen opened a physical education institute in Hobart in 1892. In 1893 he began training boys in drill and gymnastics twice a week at Friends' High School, and later also taught geography and science there. During the same period he taught gymnastics and German at The Hutchins School and gymnastics at Queen's College. In 1894 he was naturalized. The Education Department employed him in 1902-06 to train teachers in a project of physical culture 'carefully based on physiological principles', which he had devised to replace military-style drills as a compulsory subject in the state schools. His scheme, for both boys and girls, stressed the importance of breathing exercises, deportment drills, physical culture games, and rest between exercises; he argued that 'National Physical Culture would give to the coming generation increased ability to do work with body and brain, and therefore greater prosperity, better health, and . . . greater happiness'. He was on the board of the Young Men's Christian Association in Hobart.

In 1906 Bjelke-Petersen moved to Sydney where, with his brother Harald, he established a physical training institute, and began working in private schools. In 1909 he set up in Melbourne as well. Despite opposition on the grounds that he was not native-born, in 1911-14 he was director of a Commonwealth scheme of physical training

under the Department of Defence and was accredited honorary lieut-colonel. His task was to organize a system for Australian school children and to arrange the training of expert instructors for cadet forces and schoolteachers. He still carried on his private practice. In 1913 he visited England. Terminating his services in 1914, the department praised his work as having 'a lasting and beneficial effect on the manhood of Australia'. In 1918-20 he was inspector of physical training and in 1920-22 honorary consultant for the military forces.

After World War I Bjelke-Petersen's business expanded. The prince of Wales used his facilities in 1920. He sold his Melbourne business to Percy Pearce in 1923. That year he claimed that he gave instruction to more than 5000 pupils in 95 private schools in Sydney; his private and evening-class roll was said to number 1300 per week. In 1924 he rebuilt premises at 68 Elizabeth Street; besides squash and basketball courts, his establishment also included departments for remedial exercises, orthopaedic massage and electrical treatment. Doctors referred numerous patients to him.

Bjelke-Petersen was 'of medium build, slim, but quite heavily muscled, with fair hair, blue eyes and a bright, eager intelligent face'. He retired in 1927 but remained a senior director of the Bjelke-Petersen Institute. In May 1933 at St Paul's Anglican Church, Glenorchy, Tasmania, he married Dorothy Gertrude Leonie Henri. In retirement, feeling the urgent need to stimulate the spiritual side of Australian life, he worked for the Pocket Testament League and for various Christian youth movements. He died at Eaglehawk Neck, Tasmania, on 23 May 1964. A nephew Johannes became premier of Queensland in 1968. His physical culture institute in Sydney still operates.

PP (Tas), 1901 (66); The Friends' School, *School Echoes*, Feb 1893, May 1894; *People* (Syd), 18 May 1955; *SMH*, 27 June 1911; ED 13/102/343 and ED 9/10/287 (TA); official correspondence held by Mrs L. Bjelke-Petersen, Newstead, Tas; information from Sir William Crowther, Hobart, *and* Det Danske Selskab, Denmark.

CHRIS CUNNEEN
E. A. MCLEOD

BJELKE-PETERSEN, MARIE CAROLINE (1874-1969), novelist, was born on 23 December 1874 at Jagtvejen near Copenhagen, only daughter of Georg Peter Bjelke-Petersen, gardener and later master builder, and his wife Caroline Vilhelmine, née Hansen. Marie attended schools in Denmark, Germany and London. When very young she was taken on long walks by her father, who had spartan ideals and instructed his children in subjects ranging from the Bible to Greek mythology and gymnastics. The family migrated to Tasmania in the *Doric*, arriving in Hobart on 13 October 1891, and settled at New Town. Next year Marie's brother Hans [q.v.] established the Bjelke-Petersen Physical Culture School in Hobart; Marie joined as instructor in charge of the women's section and also taught the subject in schools. In 1906 she registered with the Australasian Massage Association and next year with the Teachers and Schools Registration Board, Tasmania. Illness forced her to abandon this career and she then began to write seriously. She was naturalized in 1915.

Her first published stories had appeared in Sydney papers about 1906 under a pseudonym, as her father would have objected. Her first books, published in Hobart, were three romantic religious sketches. *The mysterious stranger* (1913), called a classic by *The Times*, was translated into Arabic and reissued by the Religious Tract Society, London, in 1934. She was encouraged to write novels by William Henry (Will) Dawson, and her first, *The captive singer* (London, 1917), sold over 100 000 copies and 40 000 in Danish. The story was set in the Marakoopa Caves, Tasmania, and inspired by a guide who sang there. She was 42 at the time but her father, on being informed, 'wasn't too pleased': he had hoped that she would become an artist – she did continue to paint oils for many years. Eight more novels, published in London, followed until 1937.

In 1921 the *Triad* (Sydney) commented that she 'was honoured most outside [Australia] . . . Her people are real . . . and their inconsistencies are credible. She is not afraid of passion, though her theme and treatment are entirely . . . respectable'. However, the *Bulletin* gave her 'some nasty whippings . . . they loved making fun of my lovemaking!', she recalled. The *Australasian* reviewed *Dusk* in 1921 and suggested that Bjelke-Petersen should 'be persuaded to exercise a little restraint over both her imagination and her vocabulary'. Her 'flamboyant exuberance' and the 'reckless profusion of her descriptions' were deplored. Her metaphorical depiction of Tasmania's west coast as a 'virile, ferocious beauty' of 'lawless loveliness' who 'flung derisive laughter from unscalable peaks', 'danced in mad glee on dizzy heights' 'and looked unshaken into brain-reeling deeps!' drew particular disfavour. But her style remained florid.

Never an armchair novelist, Bjelke-Petersen's excellent physique and passion for accuracy enabled her, notebook in hand, to go on foot, horseback, dray or bullock-wagon into remote areas. At Queenstown in the 1920s she was the first woman to go underground with working miners; she mixed easily with them and with those on the Savage River osmium fields. The latter was the setting of *Jewelled nights* (1924) which used the vernacular she had noted; it was filmed by Louise Lovely Productions in 1925.

Marie Bjelke-Petersen enjoyed country painting-trips with her close friend Sylvia Mills. She frequently wintered in Brisbane, Sydney or Melbourne, taking a flat where she would hold religious meetings, to which she attracted fans and friends, including a large following of young women, in the manner of many female romantic novelists of her day. She was referred to as Australia's Marie Corelli, for her novels always contained an evangelical theme: in *The captive singer* the hero and heroine marry and sing *Nearer my God to thee*. She felt the modern world lacked sentiment, particularly in 'our spiritual life towards God', but she believed in the advances women had 'made in education and in many other things in recent years'.

As a young woman she was fair, lithe and mannish in dress; later the expensive smart clothes she chose enhanced a graceful femininity. She made early radio broadcasts and in 1935 received a King's Jubilee Medal for literature. She encouraged younger writers, and her experience and practical suggestions were useful in establishing the Tasmanian Fellowship of Australian Writers. Although steeped in mythology Bjelke-Petersen was a sincere Christian who never overlooked the poor and needy. Her fondness for whimsy expressed itself through notes to fairies in letter-boxes in her garden. She continued reading and gardening in her nineties and set some of her verses to music; a selection was recorded in 1969. She died at Lindisfarne, Hobart, on 11 October 1969, leaving an estate sworn for probate at $40 474.

J. Lyng, *The Scandinavians in Australia . . .* (Melb, 1939); *Triad* (Syd), Sept 1921; *New Idea*, 2 Dec 1932; *Woman's Budget*, 5 Apr 1933; *Australasian*, 31 Dec 1921; *New York Times*, 16 Apr 1922; *SMH*, 10 Aug 1934; *Sydney Mail*, 25 Dec 1935; *Mercury*, 14 Oct 1969; C. A. Anderson, 'The fate of an emigrant 20,000 kilometers away from Denmark', Danish radio script 1 Nov 1957, tr by Elin P. Johnston, 1975 (copy held by author); family information from Mrs Neta Stiller, Vine Veil, Guluguba, Qld.

MARGARET WEIDENHOFER

BLACK, DOROTHEA FOSTER (1891-1951), artist, was born on 23 December 1891 at Burnside, Adelaide, daughter of Alfred Barham Black, engineer and architect, and his wife Jessie Howard, née Clark, amateur artist. She was educated at Mrs Fanny Hübbe's private school at Kensington. About 1909 she went to the South Australian School of Arts and Crafts and painted landscapes in water-colours in the manner of its principal, H. P. Gill [q.v.]. In 1911-12 she visited Britain and Europe with her parents. Dorrit went to Julian Ashton's [q.v.] Sydney Art School in 1915; there she adopted oils as her main medium, and soon showed the influences of Ashton and Elioth Gruner [q.v.].

In mid-1927 Dorrit Black went to London and spent three months at the Grosvenor School of Modern Art, where she was attracted by Claude Flight's promotion of colour linocut printing as an original art form. Next year she studied at André Lhôte's academy in Paris and at his summer school, and worked briefly with Albert Gleizes in 1929. Now a disciple of Cubism, she returned to Sydney late that year, held the first of her six one-woman shows in 1930, and exhibited with the Group of Seven, which included Roy de Maistre, Roland Wakelin [qq.v.] and her close associate Grace Crowley. In 1931-33 she conducted the Modern Art Centre, Margaret Street; she produced most of her linocuts in the 1930s.

Dorrit Black travelled overseas with her ailing mother in 1934-35 and then settled in Adelaide. In the late 1930s she worked mainly in water-colours until her studio-house at Magill was completed, when she reverted to oils; she mostly painted landscapes of the Adelaide hills and the south coast. She supplemented a small private income by part-time teaching and occasional sales; and from about 1940 taught landscape painting at the School of Arts and Crafts. That year the National Gallery of South Australia bought her picture 'Mirmande' (1928). Becoming deeply involved in the local art world, she was on the committee of the Royal South Australian Society of Arts in 1938; became vice-chairman of the South Australian branch of the breakaway Contemporary Art Society of Australia in 1942; and in 1944 founded Group 9, where co-exhibitors included H. Trenerry [q.v.].

In 1938, 1945 and 1949 Dorrit Black held one-woman exhibitions at the local Society of Arts and continued to exhibit in Sydney and Melbourne. In the 1940s she wrote private poetry about her unmarried status and religious doubts. She abandoned Christian Science, while a long-standing interest in socialism sharpened; she became an active member of the Australian Labor Party, often writing to the *Advertiser* on politics and art.

Plump, dignified, black-haired and well-groomed, she was regarded as a mother-figure by younger artists. Dorrit Black died in the Royal Adelaide Hospital on 13 September 1951, after a car accident, and was cremated with Unitarian rites. A memorial exhibition was held at the Society of Arts in 1952, but her outstanding role as a pioneer and proselytizer of modernism in Australia was then largely overlooked. A touring retrospective exhibition was organized by the Art Gallery of South Australia in 1975.

I. North, *Dorrit Black* (Adel, 1975); R. Biven, *Some forgotten, some remembered* (Adel, 1976); *Advertiser* (Adel), 14 Sept 1951; information from Mrs Helen Finlayson, Burnside, SA.

IAN NORTH

BLACK, GEORGE MURE (1854-1936), politician and journalist, was born on 15 February 1854 at St James's Square, Edinburgh, son of George Stevenson Black, messenger-at-arms, and his wife Isabella, née Mure. Educated at Thorburn's School, Leith, he matriculated in the faculty of arts, University of Edinburgh, in 1871; two years later he transferred to medicine but left in 1877 without graduating. According to his own account, he 'mixed with the fast set in my youth at home' and migrated to Australia to work as a station book-keeper for 'a wealthy cousin' in Gippsland, Victoria; on the voyage, probably in 1877, he took up with Mrs Georgina Duggan, née Johnson (1850-1924), fought with her husband and was placed in irons; in the colony the liaison led to his early dismissal. About 1878 he moved with her to New South Wales and filled a wide variety of occupations, including billiard-marker and country journalist; in 1889 he settled down in Sydney as sub-editor of the *Bulletin*. By 1891 he had fathered twelve children (five of whom had died) by Mrs Duggan, and was a well-known Domain speaker, School of Arts debater and member of the Socialist and Republican leagues.

In May 1891 Black joined the initial Labor Electoral League formed in West Sydney, which returned four members to parliament. Selected as one of the Labor candidates in June, he campaigned strongly at the general election, stressing the independence of the new party. Labor won all the seats in West Sydney, and thirty-one elsewhere in a House of 141. Black at once set his sights on party leadership, and at the first caucus in July had the original pledge adopted. He followed it up with a cogent parliamentary speech stating Labor's policy of 'support in return for concessions'.

Black's private life hampered him politically. He broke violently with Mrs Duggan and formed an attachment with Mrs

Rosielinn (Rosalind) Clarkson, née Singleton (b. 1866). Anxious to have her company at the 1891 Melbourne Cup, he described her as his wife and got a free railway pass for her. In December W. P. Crick [q.v.] obtained a select committee to investigate the incident; it reported in March 1892 that while Black had acted improperly, he had believed that he had conformed with customary parliamentary practice. No action was taken, but Crick and John Norton [q.v.] pilloried 'Baldy Black' in *Truth*. He replied in kind in the *Australian Workman* — which he edited in 1891-92 — and lectured on 'The polecat element in politics'. In June he sued Norton for £5000 and was awarded one farthing. At St Paul's Anglican Church, Hornsby, on 21 June 1894, he married Mrs Clarkson, nine days after her divorce.

Black's literary and oratorical talents kept him active and influential in the Labor Party. As the party's annual conference and central executive tightened discipline over the parliamentarians in 1891-94 he emphasized their independence and their problems: 'do not trammel them with impracticable regulations', he advised in 1893. Single-member seats applied at the 1894 general election and Black won as a 'non-solidarity' against the endorsed Labor candidate in Sydney-Gipps, the Millers Point area of West Sydney; but when that year's conference reworded the pledge he rejoined the party and retained his seat at the 1895 election. He supplemented A. Griffith's [q.v.] efforts in presenting a theoretical case for Labor and in giving the party a comprehensive appeal: W. Astley [q.v.3] had written to him in 1891 that 'The thoughtful, cultured advocate of labour interests . . . is wanted in the House, even more than the labourer himself'. Black was a skilful pamphleteer and his *Labor in politics* (1893) revealed the portentous 'educational effect' of the parliamentary party, and he pointed out that the Labor members had ensured in the third session that 'The House . . . never was counted out. An entirely new experience for the Parliament'.

Labor selected its ten best candidates, Black among them, to run for the Federal Convention in 1897. None was elected. His discerning analysis of the reasons for the defeat helped to set the stage next year for the withdrawal from the party of members of the Socialist League. He was lukewarm to Federation, and in April 1898 wrote forcibly against the Constitution bill in the *Australian Worker*. But his self-esteem, never exiguous, had outstripped his political stature and at the election that year he told his electorate that he would not beg for votes. He lost his seat. Next year he failed at a by-election for Northumberland and in St

George at the 1907 election.

Black's marriage proved sustaining and he settled down as a successful, though somewhat humourless, journalist. The first editor of the *Barrier Truth* in 1898, he edited the *Australian Worker* in 1900-04, and the *Bathurst National Advocate* in 1908. In 1901 he published *In defence of Robert Burns*, and later consolidated much of his occasional writing and became the party's first historian with his valuable, if self-centred, *History of the N.S.W. Labor Party* (1910) — in 1926-29 he extended and enhanced it in the 7-part *A history of the N.S.W. political Labor Party*. When his wife died, childless, in 1917 his grief was expressed sensitively in *To perpetuate the memory of Rosalind Singleton Black. . .* (1918). He plunged into poetry with *An Anzac Areopagus and other verses* (1923).

Black was elected to the Labor Party's executive in 1901, 1903, 1911 and 1915-16. He returned to parliament as member for the Namoi in 1910, and won again in 1913. He had to mark time until 1915 to join the cabinet: minister for agriculture from 23 February to 15 March, from then he was colonial secretary and, concurrently, minister for public health from 27 April to 15 November 1916. Touches of the ridiculous marked his ministerial career; once, having stumbled over some women in a tram, he announced that he would make leg-crossing illegal on public transport. Like many other early members of the Labor Party, Black's radicalism had strong nationalist and imperialist overtones. He favoured conscription for World War I and when the party split on the issue he was expelled. He was disappointed when W. A. Holman [q.v.] did not include him in the new National ministry in November 1916, and he lost his seat at the 1917 general election; he was appointed to the Upper House that year and was granted retention of the title 'Honourable' for life. In 1918 he became a member of the Federal Film Censorship Board.

In the 1920s Black continued his newspaper writings, being much concerned with the growth of Communism, especially in China, and with reminiscenses of Scotland. On 11 April 1928 at Randwick he married Priscilla Verne Kelly, née Jones. He was granted £52 from the Commonwealth Literary Fund in 1930. Survived by his wife, a son and three daughters he died in the State Hospital, Lidcombe, on 18 July 1936. After a Presbyterian service he was buried in Waverley cemetery. His assets were valued for probate at £627, his liabilities were £802.

C. Pearl, *Wild men of Sydney* (Lond, 1958); B. Nairn, *Civilising capitalism* (Canb, 1973); *V&P* (LA NSW), 1891-92, 5, 751, 1894-95, 1, 969; *Aust Workman*, 19 Dec 1891; *Daily Telegraph* (Melb), 21 Dec 1891, (Syd), 17 Mar 1897; *Aust Worker*, 16, 23,

30 Apr 1898; *Punch* (Melb), 4 Nov 1915; *SMH*, 20 July 1936; George Black papers (ML).

                                    BEDE NAIRN

BLACK, JOHN McCONNELL (1855-1951), botanist, was born on 28 April 1855 at Wigtown, Scotland, third of four children of George Couper Black, procurator fiscal and banker, and his wife, Ellen, née Barham. He was educated at Wigtown Grammar School, the Edinburgh Academy, the College School, Taunton, training ground of many natural scientists, and the commercial Handels-Lehranstalt, Dresden, Germany. He worked in the British Linen Co. Bank in Edinburgh and the Oriental Bank, London, before migrating in 1877 to South Australia with his widowed mother, sister and brother. Another sister Helen, a brilliant scholar, remained in England, married Richard D'Oyly Carte, of Gilbert and Sullivan fame, and successfully managed the opera company's affairs.

Black was unable to find work in a bank in Adelaide and in 1878 tried wheat-farming in salt-bush country at Baroota, where his interest in arid-zone flora and Aboriginal languages was aroused. The farming was uneconomic and in 1883 he returned to the city where he joined the staff of the *South Australian Register*. He later became a senior reporter and respected editorialist on the *Advertiser*, also working as a Hansard reporter on a sessional basis until he was 74. He was a capable linguist and frequently used Arabic, French, German, Italian, Russian and Spanish (as well as shorthand) in his notebooks and diaries. He published three papers in 1915-20 on Australian Aboriginal vocabularies, recording them in *The International Phonetic Alphabet*.

A legacy received on his mother's death enabled Black to retire from journalism in 1903 and to tour South America and Europe. On his return he concentrated on botany. Impressed that the alien weeds, grasses and garden escapes common near Australian towns had rarely been recorded, in 1909 he published *The naturalised flora of South Australia,* well illustrated with his own line-drawings. In 1914 he was bequeathed a further legacy by his sister Helen and began working on indigenous flora. Although self-trained, he was clearly the best systematic botanist in the State for almost fifty years. *The flora of South Australia* was published in four parts in 1922-29, admirably illustrated with Black's habit and dissection drawings and including 2430 species, both indigenous and naturalized. It was indispensable both to local professional and lay botanists and to those concerned with the vegetation of the arid regions of contiguous States. In 1930, as secretary to the Australian and New Zealand Association for the Advancement of Science's committee on botanical nomenclature, Black actively participated in the International Botanical Congress at Cambridge, England.

The need for a revised edition of his book became acute in 1939: at 84 he undertook this exacting task. While slower in pace he was still efficient and worked steadily for twelve years, publishing part 1 in 1943 and part 2 in 1948; part 3 was nearing completion at his death.

Black's concept of species has proved sound, his approach to nomenclatural problems cautious and responsible. He was keenly observant and after a critical appraisal did not hesitate to make decisions in taxonomically difficult genera such as *Eucalyptus, Acacia* and *Stipa.* He was a gifted amateur with strong intellectual discipline; a modest man and a meticulous worker, he was patient with young inquirers seeking his opinion on difficult specimens. He worked largely with his own herbarium (bequeathed to the University of Adelaide), the specimens in which, though often meagre in size, were richly annotated with commentaries, descriptions and sketches; surprisingly few of South Australian species were not represented in it.

Black received many distinctions: honorary lecturer in systematic botany at the University of Adelaide (1927); associate *honoris causa* of the Linnean Society, London (1930); the Sir Joseph Verco [q.v.] Medal of the Royal Society of South Australia (1930); the Mueller [q.v.5] Memorial Medal from A.N.Z.A.A.S. (1932); M.B.E. (1942); the Natural History Medallion from the Field Naturalists' Club of Victoria (1944); and the (W. B.) Clarke [q.v.3] Memorial Medal from the Royal Society of New South Wales (1946).

At Wellington on 11 September 1879 Black had married Alice Denford, who shared his interest in cycling and botany; they had a daughter and three sons. He died at his home, 82 Brougham Place, North Adelaide, on 2 December 1951, and was buried in Magill cemetery. A sketch-portrait by his eldest granddaughter Shirley Clissold was used on the dust-jacket of *Memoirs of John McConnell Black* (Adelaide, 1971) and is held by her.

J. B. Cleland and C. M. Eardley, 'Preface', J. M. Black, *Flora of South Australia,* pt 3, 2nd edn (Adel, 1952); E. C. Black et al (eds), *Memoirs of John McConnell Black* (Adel, 1971); *PP* (SA), 1888, 2 (28); ANZAAS, *Report of Meeting,* 21 (1932); *A'sian Herbarium News,* 1952, no 10; *Vic Naturalist,* 68 (1951-52); Roy Soc SA, *Trans,* 76 (1953), and for publications; *Taxon,* 1 (1952); family papers (held by Miss M. W. Andrew, Adel). ENID ROBERTSON

BLACK, PERCY CHARLES HERBERT

(1877-1917), soldier and goldminer, was born on 12 December 1877 at Beremboke, Victoria, eleventh child of William John Black, farmer, and his wife Ann, née Longmore; both parents were natives of Antrim, Ireland. He was educated at Beremboke State School and became a carpenter before going prospecting on the Western Australian goldfields. In 1901-13 he worked claims at Black Range and Sandstone and was mining at Mount Jackson when World War I broke out.

Black enlisted as a private in the 16th Battalion, Australian Imperial Force, on 13 September 1914 and sailed for Egypt in December. He first saw action at the Gallipoli landing on 25 April 1915 when his unit took over the Pope's Hill zone. Within a week Lance Corporal Black, who headed one of the machine-gun crews, had been highly commended by his commanding officer. Though wounded in the hand and the ear he refused to leave his post until his weapon had been smashed by Turkish bullets. On 2 May he mounted a machine-gun beyond Gully Ridge; his only companion was shot dead but Black, surrounded by Turks and without any assistance, fired into the enemy lines until his ammunition was exhausted. For this action he received the Distinguished Conduct Medal and five days later was commissioned second lieutenant in the field. He was mentioned in dispatches on 5 August, promoted temporary captain four days later, and remained at Gallipoli until the evacuation. C. E. W. Bean [q.v.] later described Black and his No. 2 gunner H. W. Murray [q.v.] as 'men of no ordinary determination' and their 'magnificent' machine-gun section as 'possibly the finest unit that ever existed in the A.I.F.'.

Black was promoted major on 27 April 1916. His unit was posted to the Western Front in June and suffered severe casualties in the battle of Pozières. On 28 August it returned to the front line and two days later Black's 'B' Company was detailed to capture Mouquet Farm. In the attack Black immobilized a machine-gun, killing the gunner, before being wounded in the neck and evacuated. He was later awarded the Distinguished Service Order and the French Croix de Guerre for gallantry at Pozières and Mouquet Farm; he was also mentioned in dispatches twice. His next engagement was the first battle of Bullecourt on 11 April 1917. Tanks, sent in to clear a passage through the wire, failed to reach their objective and the infantry found themselves facing intense machine-gun fire along an unbroken entanglement. Black, commanding the battalion's right flank, led his men through a 'hurricane fusillade', captured the first

trenches and pressed on towards the support-line, but was then shot through the head; he was one of 640 casualties in the 16th Battalion that day. His comrade Harry Murray made an impassioned search for his body; however, he has no known grave and his name is commemorated on the Villers-Bretonneux Memorial, France. The action in which he died is depicted in a diorama in the Australian War Memorial; a near-by painting by Charles Wheeler [q.v.] is entitled 'Death of Major Black'.

Of splendid physique, quiet and unassuming in manner, Black was 'a born leader of men and a natural soldier' and his courage was a byword. Bean once described him as 'the greatest fighting soldier in the A.I.F.'.

C. E. W. Bean, *The story of Anzac* (Syd, 1921, 1924), and *The A.I.F. in France,* 1916-18 (Syd, 1929, 1933, 1937, 1942); C. Longmore, *The old Sixteenth* (Perth, 1929); *London Gazette,* 1 June, 5 Aug 1915, 11 July, 14 Nov, 8 Dec 1916, 2 Jan 1917; *Reveille* (Syd), Dec 1929, Jan 1930, Apr 1933, Oct 1936.

C. H. DUCKER

BLACK, REGINALD JAMES (1845-1928), banker, stockbroker and politician,

was born on 19 March 1845 in Sydney, son of John Henry Black, general manager of the Bank of New South Wales, and his wife Louisa, née Skinner. Educated at Sydney Grammar School, he joined the bank in 1863, serving at Penrith, Bathurst, Goulburn and Glen Innes. He was assistant inspector at head office in 1875-80, then manager at Bathurst until 1882 when he resigned to join the Sydney firm of Jones & Black, stockbrokers and financial agents. He had become a justice of the peace in 1873.

On 26 February 1883 at Guntawang, Mudgee, Black married Eleanor, granddaughter of Richard Rouse [q.v.2] and sister of Richard Rouse junior [q.v.6]. He represented Mudgee in the Legislative Assembly in 1887-91. A free trader, a supporter of Sir Henry Parkes [q.v.5] and a man of few words, he was likely, when he did speak, to apologize for taking the House's time. During the bank crisis of 1893 Sir George Dibbs [q.v.4] reputedly consulted Black and on his written advice introduced the bank issue bill, to make bank-notes legal tender with government guarantee. Other accounts credit Dr H. N. MacLaurin [q.v.] or Dibbs himself with authorship of the idea. On 25 April Black wrote to the *Daily Telegraph* advocating a measure such as was in fact framed, and in 1920 he made no demur when S. H. Smith [q.v.], addressing the Royal

Australian Historical Society in honour of Black's election as president, credited him with being the major influence on Dibbs. The implication is that he was consulted although it cannot be doubted that the measure itself was collectively designed. In 1894 Governor Duff [q.v.] refused Dibbs's recommendation to appoint Black (and six others) to the Legislative Council; however he served there as a taciturn member in 1900-28.

President of the Australian Economic Association in 1896 and 1897, Black contributed articles to its journal, the *Australian Economist,* including 'The banking crisis and its lessons' (1893) and 'The finances of Federation' (1895). He strongly believed that banking problems would best be solved by Federation and uniform laws. From the 1890s he also strongly criticized 'wretched' land legislation and published an address, *Our land laws,* in 1905.

Black was a director of both the Australian Mutual Provident Society and the Bank of New South Wales from 1898 to 1928; he took particular interest in the bank's staff matters and canteen. He was also a founder and from 1920 chairman of the Perpetual Trustee Co., and a director of the Commercial Union Assurance Co. Ltd, the Indemnity Mutual Marine Assurance Co., Goldsbrough Mort [qq.v.4,5] & Co. Ltd, the New South Wales Mortgage Land & Agency Co., Harrison, Jones & Devlin Ltd, the North Shore Gas Co. Ltd, the Sydney Exchange Co. and of the Daily Telegraph Newspaper Co. Ltd.

Black was a director of Sydney Hospital in 1899-1928, and joined the boards of the Royal Alexandra Hospital for Children and the Royal North Shore Hospital. He was a trustee of Sydney Grammar School and president of its Old Boys' Union in 1920, and a councillor of Sydney Church of England Grammar School (Shore). In 1921-26 he was president of the Million Farms Campaign Association. A keen cricketer in his younger days, he kept wickets for the Albert Cricket Club and was later president of the I Zingari, Australia, and Gordon District clubs. He was a member of the Union Club and president of the Australasian Pioneers' Club in 1915-28.

On 30 June 1928 Black died at his home at Wollstonecraft and was buried in the Anglican section of Waverley cemetery. He left an estate valued for probate at £50 524 and was survived by his wife, a son and three daughters; his second son Reginald, M.C., was killed in action in Palestine in 1917.

R. F. Holder, *Bank of New South Wales: a history* (Syd, 1970); *PD* (NSW), 1893; 'The romance of a pioneer family', *JRAHS,* 6 (1920); C. B. Mackerras, 'Sir Norman MacLaurin 1835-1914', *JRAHS,* 54 (1968); *SMH,* 24 Apr 1893, 25 Feb, 6 Mar 1920, 2 July, 3 Aug 1928; *Daily Telegraph* (Syd), 25 Apr 1893; *Bulletin,* 9 May 1903; Board minutes 1863-65 and staff records 1868-82 (Bank of NSW Archives, Syd).

A. W. MARTIN

BLACK, WILLIAM ROBERT (1859-1930), mine-owner and philanthropist, was born on 3 March 1859 at Kildress, County Tyrone, Northern Ireland, son of Robert Black, farmer, and his wife Margaret, née McNeece. He arrived in Queensland on 17 May 1880 in the *Silver Light,* worked around Maryborough as a farm-labourer, timber-cutter and fencer, then moved to Brisbane and delivered coal with a hand-cart for a merchant named Lindsay. By 1885 he was in business for himself, delivering coal with a horse and dray. He extended his interests to coal-transport on the Brisbane and Bremer rivers, and soon controlled a fleet of six launches and twenty lighters.

Continuing good fortune and increasing wealth enabled Black to buy 700 acres (283 ha) of coal-deposits at Bundamba near Ipswich. There he established the Blackheath Colliery and with electric haulage and advanced machinery was soon able to cut 600 tons (tonnes) a day – a State record. When he later bought the Caledonian Colliery at Walloon, he raised its output to 300 tons (tonnes) daily. His purchase of the Abermain Colliery at North Ipswich cost him an additional £8000 for a railway-siding and £40 000 for a new shaft and machinery.

Black retired from business in 1920. For some years he had been busily dispersing his fortune. Small, dark, reserved and a devout Presbyterian anxious to maintain the link between religion and education, he gave mainly to church institutions. He saw his wealth as a trust and believed that 'much had been given that by him much might be done'; all gifts were carefully considered and were usually conditional on others agreeing to make donations. In 1917 he helped to establish Fairholme, the Presbyterian girls' school at Toowoomba, and in 1919 Scots College for boys at Warwick. From 1918 he served on the councils of both the Brisbane Boys' College and Somerville House for girls, a united educational venture by the Presbyterian and Methodist churches. He also assisted in founding Emmanuel College, University of Queensland. Black's donations to the Presbyterian Church in 1919-20 enabled it to employ both a director and a kindergarten and primary supervisor of Sunday schools. Further gifts led to establishment of the Blackheath Home for Children at Oxley in 1923, a children's home at Chelmer in 1927 and old people's homes in both suburbs in 1929. Many other smaller donations to individual congregations enabled the Presbyterian Church in Queensland to expand.

Black died of coronary thrombosis on 2 October 1930 at St Martin's Hospital, Brisbane. He had never married and, after various bequests to relations in the Channel Islands, the residue of an estate valued for probate at nearly £180 000 was left in trust for the Presbyterian Church in Queensland. His black-marble tombstone, erected by the Church in Toowong cemetery, bears only the red hand of Ulster, a cross and two inscriptions: 'Not slothful in business, fervent in spirit, serving the Lord' and 'The righteous showeth mercy and giveth'.

R. Bardon, *Centenary history of the Presbyterian Church of Queensland 1849-1949* (Brisb, 1949); R. Goodman, *Secondary education in Queensland, 1860-1960* (Canb, 1968); Presbyterian Church in Qld, Historical records (Church Archives, Brisb).

MARGERY BRIER-MILLS

BLACKALL, WILLIAM EDWARD (1876-1941), medical practitioner and botanist, was born on 8 July 1876 at Folkestone, Kent, England, son of Walter Blackall, photographer, and his wife Sarah Jane, née Gilbert. As a child he developed a keen interest in wildflowers. Educated at the High School, Oxford, he matriculated on 23 May 1896 as a non-collegiate student of the university and graduated B.A. in 1900 (M.A., 1904). He went on to study medicine (L.R.C.P., London, M.R.C.S., England, 1903; B.M., B.Ch., Oxford, 1904). He developed an interest in mental illness and when the post of medical officer at the Fremantle Asylum was offered him, he accepted, partly for professional reasons and partly from curiosity about Western Australian flora. On 24 May 1904 he married Ethel Gray Eldrid at Oxford and they sailed at once for Perth.

After six years work at the asylum, Blackall entered general practice at Cottesloe and became known as an outstandingly capable physician, surgeon and obstetrician. He was later surgeon to the orthopaedic ward of the Lady Lawley Cottage by the Sea and consultant to the Mosman Park school for deaf children. He served as a volunteer gunner in the Australian Field Artillery for two years, then joined the Australian Imperial Force as honorary captain on 28 June 1916. He embarked on 29 June 1917, served in France with the 1st Australian General Hospital and the 1st Australian Field Ambulance, was declared medically unfit in October 1918 and returned to Australia in December as medical officer of the troopship *Nestor*. Discharged on 15 February 1919, he remained on the Australian Army Medical

Corps reserve as assistant director of hygiene for base headquarters of the 5th Military District until he retired as major in July 1936.

Blackall resumed practice in Cottesloe in 1919 and despite the demands of his professional work found time to take an increasing interest in the native flora. During the early 1920s he met another keen botanist, C. A. Gardner, who later became government botanist. The two men made collecting trips together and collaborated in identifying plants. In 1935 Blackall and his wife went to England where he spent some time at the Kew Herbarium and presented specimens to it. On his return, with two partners in his practice, he devoted more time to botany. Besides identifying wildflowers he developed his talent for drawing and painting them. In 1918, while on active service in France and resting behind the lines before the battle of Mount Kemmell, he had made a delightful watercolour study of a *Primula elatior* plant that he found beside him in a field.

Convinced of the need for a simple illustrated key to the flora of Western Australia, he began work in the 1930s. His wife collaborated, but by 1941 even she believed that it was becoming a tyranny of labour. Blackall knew, however, that he was gravely ill; before completing the task, he died of cancer on 7 October. His wife, a daughter and a son survived him. Gardner honoured him in 1942 by naming a new genus *Blackallia* after him; a new species of *Verticordia* (*V. etheliana*) was named after his wife. A later botanical accolade came in 1974 when R. Carolin created the new genus *Nigromnia* (a play on the name Blackall). The Blackall Prize in the University of Western Australia is awarded annually to the most promising student of botany.

His manuscript, presented to the University of Western Australia in 1948, was completed by B. J. Grieve and published in four parts as *How to know Western Australian wildflowers. A key to the flora of the temperate regions* (1954-75). A reviewer concluded that the work might well be one of the most important botanical manuscripts ever published in Australia. It is Blackall's monument.

MJA, 14 July 1917, 14 Dec 1918; C. A. Gardner, 'Contributiones florae Australiae occidentalis XI', Roy Soc WA, *J*, 27 (1940-41); B. J. Grieve, 'Botany in Western Australia: a survey of progress: 1900-1971', Roy Soc WA, *J*, 58 (1975); *West Australian*, 8 Oct 1941.

B. J. GRIEVE

BLACKBURN, ARTHUR SEAFORTH (1892-1960), soldier and lawyer, was born on

25 November 1892 at Woodville, South Australia, youngest child of Rev. Thomas Blackburn and his second wife Margaret Harriette Stewart, née Browne. He was educated at Pulteney Grammar School, the Collegiate School of St Peter and the University of Adelaide (LL.B., 1913). He had been articled to C. B. Hardy and was admitted as a legal practitioner in 1913.

Although not a sturdy youth, Blackburn enlisted as a private in the 10th Battalion, Australian Imperial Force, in October next year, and landed at Gallipoli on 25 April 1915. C. E. W. Bean [q.v.] concluded that he and another private that day reached a point further inland than any other Australian soldier achieved in the campaign. Blackburn himself was modest and retiring on the matter in later years. He was commissioned second lieutenant in August, and served throughout the Gallipoli campaign and in France in 1916. On 23 July, at Pozières, he commanded a party of fifty men which, in the face of fierce opposition, destroyed an enemy strong point and captured nearly 400 yards (366 m) of trench, Blackburn personally leading four successive bombing parties, many members of which were killed. For this exploit he was awarded the Victoria Cross 'for most conspicuous bravery'. In September he was evacuated sick and was later invested by King George V at Buckingham Palace.

Invalided to Adelaide, on 22 March 1917 Blackburn married Rose Ada Kelly in his old college chapel, and was shortly afterwards discharged on medical grounds. He returned to legal practice and took an active part in the pro-conscription campaigns. In 1918-21 he was Nationalist member for Sturt in the House of Assembly. His speeches usually related to serving and returned soldiers; an exception was a resolution, passed on his motion, in favour of a system of profit-sharing for employees in industry. He continued his practice, but found parliamentary duties a heavy burden and did not seek re-election in 1921. He was a founding member of the Returned Sailors', Soldiers' and Airmen's Imperial League in South Australia and president of the State branch in 1917-21. In 1933-47 he was city coroner, in which office he encountered and ignored criticism for refusing to offer public explanation for any decision not to hold an inquest.

In 1939, having served as a militia officer for fifteen years, Blackburn was promoted lieut-colonel and took command of a motorized cavalry regiment. In 1940 he ceased legal practice and was appointed to command the 2nd/3rd Australian Machine-Gun Battalion, A.I.F., which fought under his command in Syria in 1941.

Blackburn, as the senior Allied officer present, accepted the surrender of Damascus on 21 June, and after the campaign was a member of the Allied Control Commission for Syria. In February 1942 a small Australian force including his battalion was hastily landed in Java; he was promoted temporary brigadier and appointed to command 'Black Force', with orders to assist the Dutch against the rapid Japanese advance. After three weeks vigorous but fruitless resistance, and in spite of Blackburn's reluctance, the Allied forces surrendered: he was a prisoner until September 1945 when he was liberated in Mukden, Manchuria, weakened but not broken in health. In 1946 he was appointed C.B.E. (Military) for distinguished service in Java.

In 1947-55 Blackburn served as a conciliation commissioner in the Commonwealth Court of Conciliation and Arbitration. In 1955 he became a member of the Australian National Airlines Commission and a company director. He had again been State president of the R.S.L. in 1946-49, and was chairman of trustees of the Services Canteen Trust Fund from 1947 to his death; for these and other community services he was appointed C.M.G. in 1955. Next year he attended the gathering of V.C. winners in London. He died suddenly at Crafers of ruptured aneurism of the common iliac artery on 24 November 1960, survived by his wife, two sons and two daughters, and was buried with full military honours in West Terrace cemetery.

C. B. L. Lock, *Fighting 10th . . . A.I.F., 1914-19* (Adel, 1936); L. Wigmore (ed), *They dared mightily* (Canb, 1963); *Rising Sun* (Adel), Jan 1942; *Reveille* (Syd), 1 Apr 1934; Personalities remembered, radio script D5390 (misc) no 43 (SAA).

R. A. BLACKBURN

BLACKBURN, SIR CHARLES BICKERTON (1874-1972), physician and university chancellor, was born on 22 April 1874 at Greenhithe, Kent, England, second son of Rev. Thomas Blackburn (d. 1912), and his first wife Jessie Ann, née Wood. Originally from Liverpool, his father was a noted lepidopterist and throughout his life made major contributions to the collection of the British Museum. In 1876 he took his family to Honolulu, where he was senior Anglican priest, and in 1881 moved to Port Lincoln, South Australia. Charles's mother died in 1885 and his father remarried – one of his half-brothers was A. S. Blackburn [q.v.].

Educated at home, Charles was reading Virgil in the original at 7. In 1886 he went to the Collegiate School of St Peter, Adelaide, with several scholarships, then won another to the University of Adelaide (B.A., 1893), and in 1892 was awarded the John Howard Clark [q.v.3] Scholarship in English literature. He went on to study medicine while working three nights a week as librarian at the Woodville Institute for £25 a year. When the medical school was closed in 1896 he moved to the University of Sydney (M.B., Ch.M., 1899; M.D., 1903); he topped each year of his course and gained his doctorate for a thesis on cystic disease of the liver and kidneys.

Blackburn began his long association with the Royal Prince Alfred Hospital in 1899 as junior resident medical officer. He became senior resident next year and was medical superintendent in 1901-03. From 1903 when he set up in private practice at College Street, he was connected with the hospital as an honorary: assistant physician in 1903-11, physician in 1911-34 and as a consultant until 1972. As chancellor of the university, he was a member of its board from 1942 to 1964. He was also an honorary physician at the Royal Hospital for Women, Paddington, honorary pathologist at the Royal Alexandra Hospital for Children (and a member of its board), and honorary consultant at Prince Henry Hospital. Later he moved his practice to Macquarie Street. On 3 August 1910 he married Vera Louise Le Patourel (1881-1936).

Lecturer in clinical medicine at the University of Sydney from 1913, Blackburn was at first dissuaded from enlisting by Professor (Sir) Anderson Stuart [q.v.] and taught medicine in 1916. However in August he embarked for Egypt with the rank of lieut-colonel in the Australian Army Medical Corps, and served in the 14th Australian General Hospital in Cairo. Twice mentioned in dispatches, he was appointed O.B.E. in January 1919 and returned to Australia later that year. He remained on the reserve and in 1924 chaired the Commonwealth royal commission on the assessment of war service disabilities. In World War II he served as lieut-colonel at the 113th Australian General Hospital, Concord.

A councillor of the New South Wales branch of the British (Australian) Medical Association in 1911-57, Blackburn was chairman of its ethics committee in 1921-72. As president in 1920-21 he supported the move to deport Dr M. M. Herz [q.v.]. Although neither rigid nor self-righteous, he never compromised on ethical matters. He published some twenty-five articles in scientific journals and gave the 1923 Lister Oration in Adelaide. In 1928 he represented the university at the celebrations of the Royal College of Physicians in London and at the Dublin Congress of the Royal Institute of Public Health (London).

In 1930-31 Blackburn was a founding councillor of the Association of Physicians of Australasia; its secretary in 1932, he was president in 1933-35 and in 1934 delivered the (Joseph) Bancroft [q.v.3] Memorial Lecture and the Sir Richard Stawell [q.v.] Oration in Melbourne. Again president in 1937-38, he helped to found the Royal Australasian College of Physicians and was an original fellow and its first president. He was largely responsible for getting government and private donations to set up Sydney headquarters in its historic building in Macquarie Street. In his valedictory address he established and clearly defined the president's role as spokesman for the council and not for himself. He remained active in the college and attended scientific meetings until late in life. Knighted in 1936, he became an honorary F.R.C.P., Edinburgh, in 1938, and F.R.C.P., London, next year.

Blackburn devoted himself unstintingly to the University of Sydney. He was elected to its senate in 1919, lectured part time until 1934 and was dean of medicine in 1932-35. He became deputy chancellor in 1939 and chancellor in 1941. His term covered the period of the university's greatest expansion and he faced many problems: student numbers increased dramatically after World War II, academic staff were poorly paid, and the university was chronically short of funds until the report of the Murray Commission was acted upon in 1959. Meticulous in attendance at senate meetings, he missed only two (when overseas) in twenty-three years, and was a superb chairman. Scrupulously fair, he had an unusual ability to see, and express to others, the difference between personal opinions and principles, while 'his methods of ending futile meetings have become legendary, especially when executed with such exquisite courtesy'; he spoke little but resolved deadlocks in a few words. Through the senate, he indirectly had considerable influence on developments.

When the occasion demanded, Blackburn spoke publicly and forcibly on important issues: he spoke out for the university in 1946 over the State government's non-renewal of a temporary annual government grant, and defended the university's appointment of Dr R. Makinson whose political views were attacked by the press. He encouraged and successfully raised funds for the university's postgraduate medical committee, but suggested the government should financially assist students to take an arts degree before doing medicine or law. A witty after-dinner speaker, he gave innumerable addresses, and also attended, enjoyed and responded to toasts at functions of almost every university society and club, maintaining that 'if your cigar goes out . . . you have spoken too long'. He was a founder of the University Club and a member of the Union Club from 1903.

After twenty-three years, when aged 90, Blackburn retired as chancellor on 12 November 1964; he had conferred 31194 out of the 48853 degrees awarded by the university. He retired from practice next year. The senate appointed him chancellor emeritus and his work was commemorated by the Chancellor's Garden. He had been appointed K.C.M.G. in 1960 and had received honorary doctorates of science from the universities of New South Wales, Tasmania and Queensland, of literature from New England and Sydney, and laws from Melbourne and Western Australia.

Outside the university and his profession Blackburn served on the council of the Australian Red Cross Society and was made an honorary life member in 1960. He took great pride in his vegetable and flower growing, and was a keen beach and trout fisherman. Above all he enjoyed his week-end rounds of golf at Royal Sydney until his nineties and still liked to win: 'his putting remained deadly'. The friend of politicians, academics, diplomats, golfers and patients, in 1965 he was likened to 'Peter Pan' by Sir Robert Menzies.

Blackburn died suddenly, aged 98, at his Bellevue Hill home on 20 July 1972 and was cremated with Anglican rites. He was survived by one of his two sons, Charles Ruthven Bickerton, professor of medicine at the University of Sydney, and by a daughter Vera, who married Philip, son of Sir Philip Game [q.v.]. His estate was valued for probate at $300 158.

His portraits by Joshua Smith and William Dargie are owned by the University of Sydney and another by F. W. Leist [q.v.] is held by the Royal Australasian College of Physicians.

MJA, 21 Feb, 28 Mar 1931, 27 Feb 1937, 12 Nov, 10, 31 Dec 1938, 13 Oct 1964, 21 July 1973; *SMH,* 19 June 1920, 27 Aug 1941, 2 Mar 1943, 27, 30 May 1946, 2 Dec 1950, 7 June 1952, 13 June 1956, 29 Mar, 22 Nov 1960, 10 Apr 1963, 26 Apr, 25 Oct 1964; Royal A'sian College of Physicians Archives (Syd); Univ Syd Archives; family papers (held by author).   C. R. B. BLACKBURN

BLACKBURN, MAURICE McCRAE (1880-1944), lawyer and politician, was born on 19 November 1880 at Inglewood, Victoria, son of Maurice Blackburn, bank manager, and his wife Thomasann Cole, née McCrae. He was a grandson of James Blackburn [q.v.1] and Captain Alexander

McCrae. After his father died in 1887, his mother took her two sons and two daughters to Melbourne, where she worked as a music teacher.

Blackburn was educated at Toorak Preparatory Grammar School and from 1893 at Melbourne Church of England Grammar School. He matriculated in 1896 and, since money was not available for further education, became an office-boy in a legal firm. From 1902 he studied at the University of Melbourne (B.A., 1906; LL.B., 1909) while working as a teacher and librarian. In 1910 he was admitted to the Bar and in 1914 assisted in the consolidation of the statute law of Victoria. In 1922 he founded the firm of Maurice Blackburn & Co., which mainly dealt with trade union law. However, he also appeared in civil and police-court cases, especially those involving civil liberties. On 10 December 1914 he and Doris Amelia Hordern were married by Frederick Sinclaire [q.v.].

Blackburn became interested in politics when he was involved in the anti-sweating campaign and the Gas Consumers' League. He joined the Labor Party about 1908 and was active in the Victorian Socialist Party from 1911, editing its newspaper, the *Socialist,* in 1911-13. An omnivorous reader in politics, history, economics and the literatures of several languages, he was especially influenced by the English liberal and socialist traditions and by guild socialism. One of his guiding beliefs was the complementarity of industrial and political action. Through his generously proffered legal advice, Blackburn proved himself invaluable to the unions and the Labor Party. He was frequently consulted on drafting resolutions and bills, and much of his work is unacknowledged.

In July 1914 Blackburn was elected as Labor member for Essendon in the Legislative Assembly. However, his strong stand against the war cost him the seat in 1917. Despite strong pacifist sympathies he supported the concept of a citizen army, based on compulsory military training for national defence. He consistently opposed conscription for overseas service on the grounds that it could lead to imperialist aggression. Early in World War I his revulsion against the diminution of civil liberties and what he regarded as the useless slaughter in Europe turned him against the patriotic fervour of the times. In a meeting of the two Victorian Houses of Parliament in June 1915, he declared he would not help the recruiting campaign in his constituency. From 1916 he was in the forefront of Labor anti-war activities in Melbourne, addressing anti-conscription rallies and working within the party to force Labor politicians to oppose conscription.

In the pacifist, international socialist atmosphere of the labour movement in the immediate post-war years, Blackburn was at the height of his popularity. He was elected vice-president of the Victorian central executive in 1918 and president in 1919, was editor of *Labor Call* in 1918-20, and frequently tutored for the Victorian Labor College. At interstate Labor conferences he moved and seconded resolutions on peace and conscription, and was prominent in the debate on the socialization objective. At the Brisbane conference in 1921, he achieved a modification of the collective ownership aim when he carried the declaration that the party did 'not seek to abolish private ownership even of any instruments of production where such instruments [were] utilized by their owners in a socially useful manner and without exploitation'. This so-called Blackburn Interpretation was restated in 1948. However, even in the 1920s he was at odds with the party on two issues which proved crucial in his career. When its mood was increasingly anti-militarist and isolationist, he persisted in defending a citizen army and stressed international socialist issues, such as opposition to Mussolini.

Blackburn also had problems in winning pre-selection for parliament. The most dramatic incident occurred at Fitzroy in 1925, when John Wren's [q.v.] group tried to rig the pre-selection ballot; a less-publicized attempt occurred in 1934. Blackburn alienated people by his stubborn independence. Being a strict (though tolerant) teetotaller, he campaigned in parliament for shorter drinking hours and for local option. He was known to be sympathetic towards Communism because in 1924 he opposed the Labor Party's decision to exclude Communists from membership. He was also considered by many to be an atheist or at least anti-Catholic. Raised in the Church of England, he had soon moved beyond the bounds of sectarian Christianity and was for many years a member of the Free Religious Fellowship, a group which held political and literary discussions as well as informal religious services conducted by Sinclaire.

As member for Fitzroy in the assembly from 1925, Blackburn succeeded in carrying his Women's Qualification Act (1926), which aimed at removing discriminations against women in public affairs and professions. In 1927 he was elected to the new seat of Clifton Hill. At the onset of the Depression, he actively opposed the E. J. Hogan [q.v.] Labor government's retrenchment measures, fought to obtain improvements in unemployment relief and attacked the Premiers' Plan as inequitable and ineffectual. He was

president of the Melbourne section of the International Class War Prisoners' Aid, set up to assist the movement of protest by the unemployed. However, he was still highly respected and popular in parliament and was elected Speaker of the assembly in 1933 when Labor was not in office.

Next year Blackburn moved into Federal politics, winning Bourke which he held until 1943. His years in Canberra were dominated by his preoccupation with international Fascism and by clashes with the Victorian executive of the A.L.P., which was more concerned about Communism. During 1935 he became active in the Victorian council of the Movement Against War and Fascism, which many of his fellow members of the Victorian executive regarded as a Communist front. He was also involved in moves to prevent the deportation of the noted Czech anti-Fascist Egon Kisch. The break between Blackburn and the executive was triggered by the Abyssinian crisis. On this issue he was also at variance with the Federal Labor Party; in parliament in October 1935 he voted in favour of sanctions against Italy, thus defying his leader John Curtin. Although the Victorian executive had ruled that Labor members were not permitted to associate with the council, Blackburn continued his activities and was expelled in December. After some wrangling with the executive over terms, he was finally persuaded to leave the council and was re-admitted to the A.L.P. at Easter 1937.

In 1936 Blackburn participated in the campaign against Fascism in Spain, fearing that another world war was imminent. From 1938 he was active in the Australian Council for Civil Liberties, becoming its president in 1940 in close association with Brian Fitzpatrick, its secretary; he often brought before parliament issues referred to him by this council. After the outbreak of war, Blackburn led the Labor opposition to (Sir) Robert Menzies' first national security bill, on the grounds that it needlessly eroded civil liberties and evaded parliamentary control. At first the A.L.P. was in general sympathy with Blackburn's actions, but as the war became more serious most Labor members, apart from a few like Frank Brennan [q.v.] and E. J. Ward, drew away from him, often leaving him as the sole watch-dog for his major concerns: civil liberties and opposition to conscription for overseas service.

However, Blackburn's second break with the party occurred not on these issues but on one related to his earlier expulsion. As a long-time sympathizer with the Soviet Union as a 'great experiment in government', he became active in the Australia-Soviet Friendship League, although he was never a member. The strongly anti-Communist

Victorian central executive excluded Blackburn from the party in October 1941 when he refused to observe its rule that A.L.P. members could not participate in league activities. Ironically, Russia soon became a respected ally, causing the executive to reverse its ruling. But Blackburn did not again apply for readmission to the party: after the Curtin government took office in October 1941 and after Pearl Harbor, he sensed that the tide was turning in favour of conscription for overseas service. From December 1942 he presided over the No Conscription Campaign in Victoria, and was the only member of parliament to vote against the defence bill which introduced limited overseas conscription in February 1943. In August he was defeated in the general election by the official Labor candidate.

At a large meeting of prominent citizens held in his honour in October, a Maurice Blackburn Testimonial Fund was established. On 31 March 1944 he died in Melbourne of cerebral tumour and was buried in Box Hill cemetery, survived by his wife, two sons and a daughter, and by his mother. His estate, which included a fine library, was sworn for probate at £2552.

Unambitious for high office, Blackburn had acted as a conscience of the labour movement. He had always been an admirer of George Higinbotham [q.v.4]; morals and principles dominated both men's political behaviour. He was consistent in the defence of underprivileged groups and of civil liberties, and in his internationalist Socialism. His publications included several pamphlets on the conscription issue. His articles and speeches were models of unimpassioned, reasoned prose; his obvious sincerity and his 'magnificent, rich voice' were impressive, although some complained that he was too calm and thoughtful and that his speeches were like lectures. From 1924 he had been a trustee of the Public Library, Museums, and National Gallery of Victoria. In his personal relationships Blackburn was noted for his simple tastes, his tolerance and his sense of fun. Sir Frederic Eggleston [q.v.] described him as 'the most honest man I have ever met, and chivalrous to a degree'. Large, cheerful, upright, he was regarded most affectionately by almost everyone who knew him.

DORIS BLACKBURN (1889-1970) was born on 18 September 1889 at Auburn, daughter of Lebbeus Hordern and his wife Louisa Dewson, née Smith. Before her marriage she was campaign secretary to Vida Goldstein [q.v.]. A woman of 'great conscience and personal integrity', she supported the Woman's Christian Temperance Union, was president of the Women's International League for Peace and Freedom, and resigned from the A.L.P. in 1938 to remain a member of the International Peace Congress. She was a founder of the Aborigine Advancement League and of the Federal Council for Advancement of Aborigines and Torres Strait Islanders. Other interests included the Save the Children Fund and education, especially pre-school.

In 1946-49 she held her husband's former seat of Bourke as an Independent Labor member. She died in Melbourne on 12 December 1970 and was buried in Box Hill cemetery.

P. Hasluck, *The government and the people, 1939-1941* (Canb, 1952); W. J. Hudson (ed), *Towards a foreign policy, 1914-1941* (Melb, 1967); S. Blackburn, *Maurice Blackburn and the Australian Labor Party, 1934-1943* (Melb, 1969), and for bibliog; J. Robertson, *J. H. Scullin* (Perth, 1974); L. Ross, *John Curtin* (Melb, 1977); F. W. Eggleston, Confidential notes (Menzies Lib, ANU); B. Fitzpatrick papers (NL); family papers (held by Mrs L. Hamilton, Battery Point, Tas).

SUSAN BLACKBURN ABEYASEKERE

BLACKET, JOHN (1856-1935), Methodist minister, was born on 13 February 1856 at Kent Town, Adelaide, son of Ebenezer Edward Blacket, shoemaker and market gardener, and his wife Matilda, née Puddy. When he was 6 the family moved to Goodwood, two miles south of Adelaide. Blacket attended the Methodist Sunday school and two village schools run by Mrs Grace Etheridge and Mrs Capper in Arthur Street, Unley, a near-by village whose 'drowsy contented' qualities he later remembered with nostalgia. He was a member of the local literary and mutual improvement societies and attended both the Anglican and Methodist churches at Unley. He acquired some further education at Richmond Baker's academy at St Luke's Anglican Church, Whitmore Square, Adelaide.

Although at first apprenticed to a printer at the *Register*, in 1878 Blacket became a lay preacher, and three years later a probationary minister, in the Wesleyan Methodist Church. His first circuit was at Minlaton in 1881. The six years of pre-ordination study that he undertook were probably decisive in the germination of his later intellectual interests. On 31 March 1885 he married Martha Jane Fidler at Mount Gambier; they had fourteen children. Blacket went on to serve in thirteen Methodist circuits in South Australia, most of them in the country. As a preacher 'he tried to pass on the results of the latest criticism and research'. In 1893 he visited England, in 1904 he spent a year resting, and in 1922 he became a super-numerary minister.

Despite covering large rural areas with only a horse and buggy to travel many miles on gravel roads, Blacket had a productive life: in the midst of heavy church and family responsibilities, and with only occasional access to Adelaide's libraries, he wrote eight books of philosophy and history, the latter mostly about the first thirty years of South Australian settlement. His research was meticulous but his style hortatory, as in the introduction to his *History of South Australia* (Adelaide, 1911): 'So long as the heart of the British race in the Australian Common-wealth beats true to God we have nothing to fear'.

As a Christian philosopher Blacket pro-pounded a theology of divine immanence that facilitated an accommodation of scientific discovery with the Christian claim to historical revelation. Always respected by his opponents, he opposed socialist and single-tax doctrines but approved of trade unionism: these ideas were outlined in sever-al pamphlets and his book, *Theistic essays for thoughtful men and women* . . . (Adelaide, 1891). He engaged in controversies in the press and in later life was often caricatured, the sketches showing his predilection for the frock coat long after it had gone out of fashion.

Predeceased by his wife, Blacket col-lapsed and died at the gate of his Payneham home on 7 June 1935 and was buried in the local cemetery. A son Arthur also went into the ministry and, after missionary terms in Fiji and India, became principal of Wes-ley Theological College, Wayville, South Australia.

Methodist Church of A'sia (SA), *Conference minutes*, 1936; *Aust Christian Cwlth*, 21 June 1936; *Observer* (Adel), 4 Mar 1922; *Advertiser* (Adel), 8 June 1935; J. Blacket, The history of Unley and Goodwood (NL); A family record (held by Mrs A. H. Blacket, Burnside, SA); file no 1340 (SAA).

ARNOLD D. HUNT

BLACKET, WILFRED (1859-1937), bar-rister and littérateur, was born on 27 Sep-tember 1859 in Sydney, son of Russell Blacket, clerk and later a schoolmaster, and his wife Alicia, née Jackson. For much of his youth he lived at Keira Vale near Wollon-gong where his father conducted a school at which Wilfred was educated. At 15 he became a bank clerk; after nearly ten years service with the English, Scottish and Aus-tralian Chartered Bank he briefly pursued mining ventures. Throughout these early years he contributed paragraphs and verses to journals, notably the *Bulletin* which

published the whole of his 1600-line 'Hymn to humbug'. His literary bent led to ap-pointment as the *Bulletin*'s first formally styled sub-editor, in which he exhibited 'a pungent gift in knocking other people's work into shape'. He was also an occasional leader-writer for several newspapers.

Meanwhile he began to read for the Bar, to which he was admitted on 27 August 1887. His early work was at common law es-pecially on District Court circuits – those at Newcastle, Maitland, Cobar and Bourke being favourites of his. In those days he often conducted successful defences of Aborigin-als brought before the courts. On 24 April 1894 at Marrickville he married Gertrude Louisa, daughter of William Lovegrove, and granddaughter of Prosper de Mestre [q.v.1]. He was by that time well established at the Bar and said to be 'doing three or four men's work' and 'carrying a large and varied practice'.

At the turn of the century Blacket was appointed part-time secretary to the Statute Law Consolidation Commission. The com-missioner Judge C. G. Heydon [q.v.] thought him 'a model of industry and intelligent care' and, being often absent from Sydney, im-posed on him a heavy administrative re-sponsibility. Mr Justice A. B. Piddington [q.v.] rightly said that for this 'colossal labour [Blacket] never received his due meed'. Extraordinarily, the State govern-ment did not appoint him to the bench, for which experience equipped him well. In 1916-17 he conducted the royal commission on the Federal capital administration and inquired into charges of extravagance against W. B. Griffin [q.v.]; at other times he presided or assisted at various inquiries or tribunals.

Blacket took silk in 1912 at which time he commanded an extensive High Court prac-tice. With radical leanings, he sympathized with industrial aspirations and the advanced or experimental side in politics, and was recognized by trade unionists as a 'very sound legal adviser'. Of spontaneous wit, he was said to be 'inexhaustible, whether your need was a good case or a good story'. His entertaining reminiscences, *May it please your Honour*, were published in 1927. In them he also expressed some of his attitudes to the law, including the view that 'the jury system now in force in the British Empire is the most perfect guarantee of liberty that human wisdon has ever devised'.

Survived by his wife, Blacket died child-less and intestate at Lindfield on 6 February 1937. He was privately interred in the Ang-lican section of Northern Suburbs cemetery, with Methodist rites.

Cyclopedia of N.S.W. (Syd, 1907); A. B. Piddington, *Worshipful masters* (Syd, 1929); *V&P* (LA NSW), 1902, 2, 39; *Punch* (Melb), 10 Aug 1916; *SMH,* 8 Feb 1937; *Bulletin,* 10 Feb 1937.

J. M. BENNETT

BLACKETT, WILLIAM ARTHUR MORDEY (1873-1962), architect, was born on 18 September 1873 at Fitzroy, Victoria, eldest son of Cuthbert Robert Blackett [q.v.3], chemist, and his second wife Margaretta, née Palmer. He was educated at Scotch College, Melbourne, was articled to H. J. Proctor, and won several prizes in student competitions sponsored by the *Australasian Builder and Contractor's News.* In 1895-97 he worked as a draftsman in the Department of Railways and Public Works of Western Australia, and designed several post offices.

After his return to Victoria Blackett was in continuous practice from 1899 to the early 1940s. In 1900-03 he was in partnership with T. H. P. Rankin. His cousin William Blackett Forster served articles with the firm and joined him as partner in 1914-32. For a time Blackett was in partnership with Gawler & Churcher, and in 1936-41 he worked in association with (Sir Arthur) Stephenson [q.v.] & Turner on the Royal Melbourne Hospital complex.

At the outset of his career Blackett designed the Presbyterian Church, Heidelberg, and the children's wing and laundry of the Austin Hospital. He was noted for his house remodelling and as a designer of interior decoration and fittings. The partnership of Blackett & Forster designed several city buildings including Victor Horsley Chambers (1926) and Francis House (1927), both in Collins Street; in 1929 the firm received the Royal Victorian Institute of Architects' medal for Francis House. Outside the city, a few designs are known, including the Warburton Chalet (1929) and the Jessie Fraser Wing of Somers House, Black Rock (1935). The known houses of the practice are at Brighton Beach (1914), South Yarra (1917) and Euroa (1932). His short article on 'The smaller two-storey house' appeared in the *Australian Home Builder,* June 1924.

Blackett had a long and distinguished association with both the Royal Victorian and later the Royal Australian institutes of architects. He was an associate of the R.V.I.A. from 1892 and a fellow from 1905, a council-member in 1907-52 and president in 1916-18 and 1928-30. A founder and first president in 1930 of the R.A.I.A., he wrote one of its earliest publications, *The work of an architect* (Sydney, 1935?); in 1952 he was honoured with a life fellowship. In 1932 he

was made a fellow of the Royal British Institute of Architects.

In February 1917 Blackett enlisted in the Australian Imperial Force and was assigned to the Educational Service. After the war he was active in the Melbourne Legacy Club, was vice-president in 1926-27 and designed its badge. He was also a force behind the realization of the Shrine of Remembrance, Melbourne. He was president of the Arts and Crafts Society of Victoria in 1927-49, a trustee of the Allied Societies Trust Ltd in 1924 and a director of Ozapaper Ltd. Blackett was a solid, energetic man committed to the public advancement of the profession through the creation of strong and respectable State and national institutes. His achievements in this field far outstripped the fruits of his architectural practice.

On 14 September 1904 at Brighton Beach, Blackett had married Gertrude Lewis (d. 1924); on 30 December 1930 at Sydney, Anne Lewis, née Hancock (d. 1937); and on 12 April 1960 at Brighton Beach, Isabel Margaret McCallum, née Wills. He had no children. He died on 2 June 1962, survived by his wife, and was buried in Brighton cemetery. His estate was valued for probate at £25 637.

His brother, Charles Edward Blackett (1880-1964) was born on 25 March 1880 at Fitzroy and educated at Queen's College, St Kilda. He was a metallurgist at Kalgoorlie, Western Australia, in 1901-35, then general manager of New Occidental Gold Mines, Cobar, New South Wales, until 1946. Blackett had married Edith Bradley in 1901. He died on 20 July 1964 at East Melbourne, survived by one son and two daughters.

J. Smith (ed), *Cyclopedia of Victoria,* 1 (Melb, 1903); Roy Vic Inst of Architects, *J,* Mar 1916; *A'sian Builder and Contractor's News,* 31 Mar, 7 Apr, 25 Aug 1894; *Age,* 4 June 1962.

GEORGE TIBBITS

BLACKLOCK, WALTER (1862-1935), trainer, was born on 11 December 1862 at Mount Brisbane Station, Brisbane valley, Queensland, son of Thomas Blacklock, a Crimean War veteran and baker, and his wife Elizabeth, née Devlin. Under the patronage of John Finnie of Rose Vale stud, near Drayton, 'Watty' Blacklock and his brother Richard James (1861-1951) became leading light-weight jockeys on a circuit that extended from Brisbane to Charters Towers and Townsville. Although he rode until 1890, increasing weight reduced Walter's opportunities: his last important successes were the Queensland Cup of 1885 on My Love and next year the Queensland Turf

Club Spring Sapling Stakes on Rose; earlier wins included the Queensland Derby of 1882 on Goldfinder, and in 1883 the St Leger on Medusa and the Brisbane Cup on Mozart.

Blacklock married Mary Edith Peak at Drayton with Wesleyan rites on 11 July 1889. He set up as a public racehorse-trainer in stables at Ormond Lodge, bordering Eagle Farm race-course. His early patrons included D. C. Seymour for whom he trained Beggar Boy, a jumper which proved 'a veritable goldmine', and A. C. Sandeman, owner of Babel which won the Stradbroke Handicap in 1895 and 1896. Blacklock's own horse, Yelverton, had won the Brisbane Cup in 1894.

For about twenty years Blacklock was among the leading trainers in Brisbane. Owners liberally commissioned him to buy yearlings; he schooled his two-year-olds early and thoroughly and won the Hopeful Stakes nine times between 1901 and 1914. Among the three-year-old classics he won the 1897 St Leger with Sandeman's Brazenface, the 1898 Queensland Guineas and Derby with D. Beattie's Boreas, the 1900 Queensland Guineas with Beattie's Araxes, the 1902 Queensland Guineas and Derby, the 1903 St Leger with H. Mosman's [q.v.5] Balfour, and came first and second in the 1906 Queensland Derby and the 1907 St Leger with J. Taylor's Togo and 'T. West's' Inglewood. High weights and competition from New South Wales horses proved too much for most of his classic winners in the top handicaps, but he still trained the winners of the 1898 and 1902 Stradbrokes, the 1900 Prince of Wales Cup, and the 1906 King's Cup. He won the Queensland Cup in 1906 and 1908 and the 1912 Moreton Handicap.

Blacklock was always ready to take his good horses to the Sydney and Melbourne carnivals but usually won only minor events. Exceptions were the 1908 Doncaster Handicap with Togo and the 1920 Caulfield Futurity with Gold Tie, his best horse of the period, with which he won the 1918 and 1919 Stradbrokes. He trained many winners of the feature events in annual carnivals at Charters Towers, Townsville and Toowoomba. From about World War I his activities diminished and in September 1924 he retired from training, selling Ormond Lodge to A. H. Whittingham [q.v.]. He died at Hendra on 2 July 1935, survived by his wife, two daughters and a son, and was buried in Nundah cemetery with Methodist rites. His estate was sworn for probate at £1698.

Blacklock's career spanned a transition in Queensland racing from highly decentralized irregular meetings, with jockeys and trainers often the retainers of wealthy owners, to an organized industry based on metropolitan tracks with freelance professionals. Small, sturdy and jovial, with a sweeping white moustache, he remained always the quintessential horseman. He failed to learn to drive a motor car, purchased in 1923, which he would try to stop by pulling on the steering wheel and shouting 'Whoa'.

N. Gould, *The magic of sport* (Lond, 1909); J. L. Collins and G. M. Thompson, *Harking back* (Brisb, 1924); *Qld Turf Guide*, 1874-75; *A'sian Turf Register*, 1880-1925; information from Mr Jack Colley, Clayfield, Qld.

S. J. ROUTH

BLACKLOW, ARCHIBALD CLIFFORD (1879-1965), soldier, pharmacist, grazier and politician, was born on 11 October 1879 at Bagdad, Tasmania, son of Frederick Henry Blacklow, farmer, and his wife Mary Ann, née Hallam. Educated at Bagdad State School and The Hutchins School, Hobart, he went to Sydney in 1895 to be apprenticed as a pharmacist to his uncle J. C. Hallam. Four years later he joined the 1st Infantry Battalion, New South Wales Militia, was made a non-commissioned officer in 1901, but resigned to attend the University of Sydney. After studying pharmaceutical chemistry in 1902-05, he worked with Hallam Ltd and later became managing director. On 17 December 1908, at St Andrew's Anglican Cathedral, he married a widow Blanche Geraldine Woodforde, née Soane. He joined the Australian Rifle Regiment in 1909 and was commissioned lieutenant; in 1913, the year of his promotion to captain, he represented Australia at the international rifle-shooting championships at Bisley, England. He was to lead the Bisley team in 1924.

On the formation of the Australian Imperial Force Blacklow became staff officer for musketry training, 2nd Military District, until 1 April 1916 when he enlisted as captain. Soon promoted major, he was posted to the 36th Battalion and sailed for England. His unit eventually occupied a quiet sector of the Western Front near Armentières. Blacklow was transferred to the 35th Battalion in May 1917 and served as its temporary commander in the Messines offensive. Sent to England in July to attend a senior officers' school, he resumed temporary command for the second battle of Passchendaele on 12 October and was later mentioned in dispatches. The battalion then served at Le Touquet and Armentières a. Blacklow remained in charge until 15 March 1918 when he was promoted lieut-colonel to command the newly formed 3rd Machine-Gun Battalion, which served with the 3rd

Division in all its 1918 operations on the Somme. Blacklow was again mentioned in dispatches in May and awarded the Distinguished Service Order on 3 June.

Demobilized in May 1919, he resumed work as a pharmacist in Sydney. In 1921-24 he commanded the 34th Battalion, Australian Military Forces; this was his last appointment, though he remained on the reserve of officers until 1940. In 1924 Blacklow gave up pharmacy and returned to Tasmania where he acquired pastoral properties at Orielton, Wattle Hill and Sorell. He took an active interest in local affairs and was district coroner and a member of the Sorell Council for many years. After contesting the Federal seat of Franklin in 1929, he won it for the United Australia Party in 1931: a firm advocate of States' rights, he strongly pressed for aid to Tasmanian primary industries, especially fruit export. After being defeated in 1934 he was elected to the Tasmanian Legislative Council in 1936 and held the seat of Pembroke until 1953; his outstanding interest was dairy produce legislation. During World War II he had commanded a Volunteer Defence Group; he was appointed O.B.E. in 1944.

Blacklow sold the last of his properties in 1951 and returned to Rosetta; he later lived at Richmond. Survived by his only son, he died in Hobart on 4 May 1965 and was buried in St Mark's churchyard, Pontville. His estate was sworn for probate at £15 963.

London Gazette, 28 Dec 1917, 28 May, 3 June 1918; *Mercury,* 5 May 1965; Blacklow file (AWM); War diaries, 35th Battalion, *and* 3rd Machine-Gun Battalion (AWM); information from R. McC. Blacklow, Glenorchy, Tas.   H. J. ZWILLENBERG

BLACKMAN, MEREDITH GEORGE (1876-1957), soldier and farm-hand, was born on 8 October 1876 at Ben Bullen, New South Wales, son of Charles Samuel Blackman, drover, and his wife Christina, née Nicholson. Little is known of Blackman's early life; he was working as a linesman in the Toowoomba district, Queensland, when he enlisted as a private in the Australian Imperial Force on 17 August 1915. He understated his age by four years in order to meet the enlistment requirements. Next December he sailed for Egypt with reinforcements for the 26th Battalion.

In May 1916 Blackman was posted to the 12th Battalion and left for the Western Front; he went into the line at Fleurbaix, was wounded in the head on 10 June and rejoined his unit for the final attack on Pozières. He was specially commended for gallantry in this engagement, and was later awarded the

Military Medal. Wounds received at Pozières kept him from active service for two months, after which he served at Amiens and at Switch Trench, Flers. He was promoted lance corporal next December and corporal in April 1917. At Lagnicourt on 15 April, while leading a patrol which had come under shell-fire, Blackman occupied a shell hole and opened fire on the enemy; though nearly all his men had been wounded, he held on until ordered to retire, and for this action, which helped to prevent a German counter-attack from developing, was awarded the Distinguished Conduct Medal. Further work in the Lagnicourt sector won him a Bar to his Military Medal.

In September Blackman took part in the attack on Polygon Wood where he gained a second Bar to his Military Medal; later that year he fought in the decisive battle of Broodseinde Ridge. His battalion was posted to the Ypres-Comines Canal zone during the German offensive of spring 1918 and served at Hazebrouck and Strazeele before taking part in the final advance on the Hindenburg Line. Blackman, who was promoted sergeant in August and temporary company quartermaster sergeant in September 1918, returned to Australia next August with a rarely equalled number of decorations for individual courage.

After demobilization he worked as a linesman at Toowoomba for several years and in 1925-39 he and his brother moved around the Gwabegar-Narrabri district of New South Wales, working as farm-hands and rabbit-trappers. In World War II Blackman joined the Citizen Military Forces and was allotted to Eastern Command Headquarters as a cook; discharged in July 1944 (he was then 67 years old), he returned to Gwabegar where he worked as a farm-hand until his death on 19 October 1957. He was buried in the local Presbyterian cemetery.

L. M. Newton, *The story of the Twelfth* (Hob, 1925); C. E. W. Bean, *The A.I.F. in France,* 1917 (Syd, 1933); *London Gazette,* 14 Nov 1916, 15 June, 6 July, 14 Dec, 1917; The war diary of the 12th Battalion (AWM).   G. R. VAZENRY

BLACKWOOD, ROBERT OFFICER (1861-1940), businessman and pastoralist, was born on 24 June 1861 at Woodlands, near Crowlands in the Wimmera district of Victoria, eldest son of Richard Blackwood (d. 1881), of Woodlands and Hartwood, near Deniliquin, New South Wales, and his wife Isabella, née Officer. He was a nephew of James and John Hutchison Blackwood [qq.v.3].

Blackwood attended Melbourne Church of England Grammar School in 1878-79; he was a keen athlete and was in the football and rifle teams. In 1882 he matriculated and was admitted to Trinity Hall, Cambridge, where he took up boxing; he left the university that year. In 1886 he was runner-up for the amateur light-weight boxing championship of England. When Hartwood was put up for sale by his father's executors in 1889, Blackwood returned to Australia and purchased it with his brothers George and Harry, taking over the management himself. In 1913 they sold the property to J. H. Patterson [q.v.].

Blackwood was active in the Deniliquin district in his support of railway extension and water-conservation. He was a council-member of the Pastoralists' Association of Victoria and Southern Riverina and in 1906 became a trustee and later vice-president of the Pastoralists' Union of Southern Riverina. In 1907 he became first president of the Conargo Shire. A free trader and supporter of (Sir) George Reid [q.v.], Blackwood was elected by five votes to the House of Representatives seat of Riverina in December 1903. However, he was unseated on petition by the former member J. M. Chanter [q.v.] who claimed electoral irregularities, based on statements by one Edward Healy. In the subsequent election of May 1904 Blackwood lost to Chanter. He was later cleared of all allegations (known as the Healy charges) but never stood for parliament again.

In 1905 Blackwood was appointed to the local board of advice of Dalgety [q.v.4] & Co., Melbourne, becoming chairman in 1925-27. He was a director of many companies, including the Broken Hill Proprietary Co. Ltd and several associated companies, the Trustees, Executors & Agency Co. Ltd and Australian Iron and Steel Ltd, and was chairman of directors of Australian Farms Ltd, which went into liquidation in 1925. Blackwood was president of the Victorian Employers' Association for five years and of the Registered Clubs' Association of Victoria in 1916-30, and was a member of the Edward Wilson [q.v.6] Trust in 1921-40. He was a councillor of the Royal Agricultural Society from 1917, vice-president in 1920-38 and a trustee thereafter.

Blackwood was Presbyterian by birth; his marriage at St Paul's Cathedral, Melbourne, on 23 July 1895 to Constance Ferrier Hamilton was a fashionable occasion. A slim, elegant man of great integrity and little humour, Blackwood devoted himself to music and business while Constance dwelt mostly overseas. He enjoyed collecting paintings, cabinet-making, shooting and golf. He was president of the Melbourne Club in 1911, and a member of the Royal

Melbourne Golf and the Victoria clubs. Despite failing health he maintained close contact with his business affairs almost to the day of his death on 22 September 1940 at Landene, St Kilda Road. He was buried in Melbourne general cemetery, survived by his wife; there were no children.

His cousin ARTHUR RANKEN BLACKWOOD (1850-1905) was born on 12 January 1850 at Hobart Town, only son of James Blackwood and his wife Eliza, née Officer. He was educated at Melbourne Grammar School (1858-64), Harrow School (1865), and Balliol College, Oxford (B.A., 1873; M.A., 1888) and was called to the Bar of the Middle Temple in 1875. In Melbourne on 15 October 1885 he married May Cunningham; their only child died young. Admitted a partner in 1879 in the firm of Dalgety, Blackwood & Co., in 1884 he became joint managing director with James Aitken of Dalgety & Co. Ltd. He was first chairman of directors of B.H.P. in 1885, but resigned next April after disagreements with G. McCulloch [q.v.5]. He was also a director of the Silverton Tramway Co. Ltd and of several other companies. In 1889 he was appointed colonial superintendent of Dalgety & Co.; in 1900-05 he was a member of the company's local board of advice.

Blackwood was a partner in Nyang, near Deniliquin, and Talawanta, on the Darling; he was also part-owner of the Morven Hills estate in New Zealand where he used to go deer-shooting. He was a member of the Melbourne Club and chairman of the Victoria Amateur Turf Club in 1884-85; his horse Vengeance won the Caulfield Cup in 1890. He died at Malvern on 2 February 1905 of cerebral haemorrhage and was buried in Melbourne general cemetery. His estate was valued for probate at £4606.

PD (Cwlth), 1904, 1041; *Cwlth Law Reports,* 1 (1903-04), 39, 121; *Pastoral Review,* Feb 1905, Mar 1906; *Dalgety's Review* (A'sia), 1 Mar 1905; *A'sian Insurance and Banking Record,* 21 Oct 1940; *BHP Review,* Dec 1940; *Leader* (Melb), 6 July 1895; *Riverine Grazier,* 14, 18 Dec 1903, 9 Feb, 10, 20 May, 29 July, 18 Oct, 8, 22 Nov 1904; *SMH,* 25 Dec 1903, 12-14 Mar 1904; *Argus,* 8, 10, 11, 19 Mar, 26 July, 23 Sept 1904, 3 Feb 1905; *Pastoral Times,* 15 Oct 1904; *Table Talk,* 7 Oct 1909, 20 Sept 1928; Dalgety & Co. papers (ANU Archives, *and* RHSV); family and private information.

MARGARET CARNEGIE

BLAIR, SIR JAMES WILLIAM (1870-1944), politician, barrister and judge, was born at Coalfalls, Ipswich, Queensland, on 16 May 1870, younger son of Gordon Blair, a Scots customs officer, and his wife Julia, née Droughton. Educated at first by his Irish mother – a strong personality – he later attended Ipswich West State School, then Ipswich Grammar School from 6 March 1882 to the end of 1888 when he passed the University of Sydney senior public examination. In 1889 he was reading in Brisbane for the preliminary Bar examinations with F. ff. Swanwick, a barrister and schoolmaster who had been a member of parliament. He lived with Swanwick, published some newspaper verse and was admitted to the Queensland Bar on 6 March 1894 on the motion of Dr A. H. Boone.

Blair made friends in 1894 with another 'native son', the then attorney-general T. J. Byrnes [q.v.], and the two shared chambers until Byrnes's death in 1898. Over twenty years later Blair said, 'I was a hero-worshipper. Byrnes was my hero'. Already considered a master of both written and spoken English, Blair also possessed other attributes valuable in public speaking: he could be forceful, his voice was particularly pleasant and he had many 'graces of speech'. He was junior counsel for the Crown in prosecuting directors of the Queensland National Bank, and was briefed in the libel actions, *Hoolan* [q.v.] v. *directors of the Eagle* and *Jarvis* v. *Charters Towers Evening Telegraph.* In the criminal jurisdiction he was counsel on appeal in the Kenniff [q.v.] trial. He had laid the reputation for the later widely held belief in his profession that, 'if the need arose, Jimmy Blair could make a jury weep'.

Association with the politicians Swanwick and Byrnes had its effect. On 11 March 1902 Blair contested a general election as an independent candidate for Ipswich which then returned two members to the Legislative Assembly. He was placed second to T. B. Cribb [q.v.], a member since 1896 who had been treasurer from February 1901. Blair achieved some notoriety by papering Ipswich with heart-shaped cards about an inch square: some said 'In the hearts of the people', others bore the humble legend 'Give Jimmy a vote'. There was only one Jimmy on the ballot paper and sufficient electors gave him a vote.

For one who subsequently gained a reputation as something of a bon viveur, Blair's parliamentary policy suggested either that the crusading zeal of a young man had not yet faded or that he could shrewdly assess his strongly Nonconformist constituents. He opposed Sunday opening of public houses and favoured rigorous enforcement of the Licensing Act and the introduction of local option without compensation; bars should be restricted to the hours imposed on shops by the Factories and Shops Act and should be closed on polling days. He also favoured more stringent enforcement of the

Gambling Act, the minimization of Sunday labour, suppression of Sunday trading and prohibition of the sale of tobacco to children. His education policy sought to restrict government scholarships to State grammar schools, and envisaged a take-over by the State of the grammar schools and the grant to them of more scholarships. State-school parent-committees should not have to contribute to the repair of schools and school-residences. In other fields he sought extension of the Factories and Shops Act to the whole State, and the opening of polls under the Act not only to ratepayers but to all electors.

(Sir) Arthur Morgan [q.v.] formed a coalition government with Labor's W. H. Browne [q.v.] on 17 September 1903. Needing a lawyer for attorney-general, he invited Blair, who thus became a minister at 33 and *ex officio* leader of the Queensland Bar. He was given the additional portfolio of mines on 27 April 1904 and retained both offices under Kidston [q.v.]. He was out of office during the brief reign of the Philp [q.v.] government from November 1907 but he regained his former portfolios when Kidston resumed power on 18 February 1908.

Blair's first major bill became the Worker's Compensation Act of 1905 – a useful protective addition to the industrial laws. It was published with annotations in 1906 with Blair, T. W. McCawley [q.v.] and Thomas MacLeod as joint editors. The preface claimed that the Act introduced a principle well known in the United Kingdom but hitherto unknown in Queensland law. In 1905 he and MacLeod had revised and edited R. A. Ranking's [q.v.] *Queensland police code and justices' manual of the criminal law.* Blair had little success with his mining legislation: the 1905 Mining Act amendment bill was rejected, and a 1906 bill to consolidate and amend the laws relating to mining fields, mines and mining lapsed after the second reading. His Children's Court Act of 1907, which took offenders under seventeen into special closed courts, was a success, but his technical instruction bill of the same year was not returned by the Legislative Council.

In the first session of the seventeenth parliament in 1908 Blair produced and steered through parliament two measures that were to play a part nine years later in the T. J. Ryan [q.v.] government's efforts to abolish the Legislative Council. In November 1907 the council had refused to pass a trades disputes bill and an election Act amendment bill. Kidston sought to appoint enough councillors to have these measures passed. Lord Chelmsford [q.v.], the governor, refused this on the ground that Kidston had no mandate to increase the size of the

Upper House. Kidston asked for a dissolution, was refused, and resigned. Philp tried to form a government, was defeated, and thereupon sought and, to Kidston's consternation, was granted a dissolution. On Kidston's return to power with a large following in February 1908, he sought to resolve future conflicts with the Upper House by constitutional means. First, Blair brought down an amendment of the Constitution repealing the clause in section 9 (amendment of the Constitution) which required a two-thirds majority on the second and third readings of bills for amendment. This paved the way for a further amendment – the Parliamentary Bills Referendum Act – under which measures rejected by the council, or which it refused in two consecutive sessions to pass in the form which the assembly desired, could be submitted to the people by way of referendum and, if approved, automatically become law.

During the parliamentary recess in 1908, Blair made a 3500 mile (5600 km) motor trip in his 1905 Panhard with four companions through outback Queensland. It enabled him to educate himself in the needs of remote districts, and attracted world-wide interest as automotive pioneering. Given the condition of the roads – where they existed – it was a remarkable achievement; Blair felt he had demonstrated 'the utility of motor transit in the heart of Queensland'.

Kidston had spent the recess in the United Kingdom. On his return, he decided that the government could survive only by a fusion with the Opposition. Some Opposition members had to be brought into the cabinet and Blair was one of the ministers displaced. It was said that Kidston promised to compensate him with a seat on the southern Supreme Court bench, and that he had accepted, but he was in fact offered a seat on the northern bench so that C. E. Chubb [q.v.3], who had been there for over fifteen years, could be transferred to Brisbane. Blair refused and had to wait fourteen years for another approach. With Peter Airey and George Kerr [qq.v.], who had also lost portfolios, Blair then led what was called 'the Independent Opposition'. He could have been a thorn in Kidston's side, but came to his rescue in October 1910 when Ryan and Edward Macartney [q.v.] were hammering home the auditor-general's criticism of government expenditure on the University of Queensland. He was unable, however, to stomach Kidston's offer to bear the cost of opposition by the Queensland Tramway Employees' Association to an application for registration under the Commonwealth Arbitration Act by the rival Australian Tramway Employees' Union; the latter ceased work on 19 January 1912. As other unions became involved, the dispute escalated into a general strike. Although Blair actively preached moderation throughout, and persuaded the Ipswich railway workers to go back, his mining constituents and the waterside workers remained out some time longer.

D. F. Denham [q.v.], who had succeeded Kidston as premier in February 1911, called a general election for 27 April 1912 as soon as the strike had collapsed. A requisition signed by nearly a thousand voters invited Blair to accept nomination as the government candidate for Ipswich. He accepted and worked with a committee of crusty conservatives and former Labor supporters who had 'thrown off the Trades Hall yoke', and who admired his stand in the strike.

Having been re-elected, Blair returned to the ministry on 3 September as secretary for public instruction, replacing K. McD. Grant [q.v.] who had resigned on a point of principle. He held office until 1 June 1915, usually deputizing on legal matters for Attorney-General T. O'Sullivan [q.v.] who sat in the council. In this last phase of his political career, Blair was responsible for further social legislation. The Criminal Code was amended in 1913 to raise the age of consent from 14 to 17 and to provide elaborately for the protection of girls. The Testator's Family Maintenance Act (1914) gave the court discretion to prevent unjust disinheritance of immediate family. The Friendly Societies Act was also amended that year to permit them to become the only corporate owners of pharmacies in Queensland. State secondary school scholarships, instead of being awarded by competition, went to all those who qualified, and scholarship-extensions were granted to those who passed the junior public examination.

After Labor's sweeping victory in the general election of 22 May 1915, the government majority of 22 became a minority of 18. Blair, who had declined Denham's endorsement, stood again as an independent and lost his seat to D. A. Gledson [q.v.], a Labor candidate, by 400 votes. The mining areas of his electorate abandoned him completely. He claimed to have been sick throughout the campaign and, when it ended, he spent several days in hospital.

Henceforth Blair concentrated on his legal practice. In 1917 he appeared with Ryan for the government in the Legislative Council referendum case, arguing the validity of the constitutional legislation he had had passed in 1908. The State Full Court declared both Acts invalid. The High Court of Australia unanimously reversed this decision and declared that the Legislative Council could be abolished by an Act in accordance with the Parliamentary Bills Referendum Act. Blair was also in great demand as a counsel in criminal cases.

The Judges Retirement Act (1921) removed a number of over-age judges, and Blair accepted the position on the northern bench offered him by Labor Premier E. G. Theodore [q.v.] in 1922. He and his wife moved their home to Townsville. On 24 January 1923 he was transferred to the central bench at Rockhampton. When McCawley died prematurely on 16 April 1925, Blair succeeded him as chief justice on 24 April, spending his first few days of office arranging a memorial fund. From 1930 he acted as deputy governor for brief periods, served as administrator in April 1932 pending the arrival of Sir Leslie Orme Wilson [q.v.], and was formally appointed lieutenant-governor on 23 May 1933. On 1 June 1930 he had been knighted on the instigation of the A. E. Moore [q.v.] government, and on 3 June 1935 was appointed K.C.M.G. — seemingly directly by the King whose jubilee year it was, for his name did not appear on the Commonwealth list and the W. Forgan Smith [q.v.] government made no recommendations.

There were three classic cases in Blair's term as chief justice. In 1929 the Country National Progressive ministry set up a royal commission to investigate the purchase by its Labor predecessors of two mines at Mungana in North Queensland. The report condemned W. McCormack [q.v.] and Theodore, both former premiers, and the government immediately proceeded against them and two others for conspiracy, seeking £30 000 in damages. Although complex and highly technical, the case created intense interest and political passion because it was said to be designed expressly to destroy the career of Theodore, then Federal treasurer. The trial lasted twenty-one days before Blair and a jury of four, and was decided in favour of the defendants. Newspapers of all political colours agreed that his 4½-hour summing-up was extremely fair. The suggestion, under a thin fictional veil, of his venality in Frank Hardy's political novel *Power without glory* rests on no more than malicious contemporary gossip.

In October 1939 Blair presided over an extraordinary criminal trial. On 4 August 1937 members of the League for Social Justice had invaded a Labor caucus meeting in the old Legislative Council chamber at Parliament House, armed with batons, coils of barbed wire and hammers. They were committed for trial on charge of 'assembly in such a manner as to cause fear that they would tumultuously disturb the peace'. With so many accused, the trial had to be held in the Brisbane City Hall. Although Blair made it perfectly clear to the jury that he believed all the accused to be guilty, they were all found not guilty.

Blair's third *cause célèbre* is known as the Ithaca election petition. E. M. Hanlon, a Labor minister and member for Ithaca, was opposed in 1938 by George Webb of the Protestant Labour Party and won by only 456 votes. Webb appealed to Mr Justice E. A. Douglas, sitting as an elections tribunal, that Hanlon in his campaign had distributed illegal leaflets: the appeal was upheld. Hanlon's counter-appeal to the Full Court was sustained and Webb's application for leave to appeal to the High Court was refused. Douglas felt aggrieved by the removal of judicial pension rights in 1922 by the Labor government and was concerned at what he saw as threats to judicial independence. Resentment at the reversal of his decision in the Ithaca petition case and suspicion of Blair's attitude over the pensions issue finally boiled over into a statement published in the Brisbane *Truth* on 22 October 1944. He asserted that Blair had suppressed a pension plan for judges submitted to him for consideration by the government, had received a salary as lieut-governor, and had been given large undisclosed payments by the government without statutory authority. Other judges united in condemning Douglas but Blair, now retired, maintained a dignified silence. Questions asked in parliament and statements in the ensuing controversy made it clear that Douglas was mistaken on the pensions question, that Blair had not received any salary as lieut-governor, and that the alleged undisclosed payments were in fact the salary equivalent of accumulated periods of sabbatical leave.

In the parliamentary debates on the establishment of the University of Queensland, Blair had argued unsuccessfully for the waiving of all fees and in 1915-16 became a member of the senate. He was reappointed in 1926 and was elected chancellor in 1927. He moved immediately to improve the university's primitive accommodation and by 1930 had accepted a gift of 200 acres (81 ha) at St Lucia from Dr J. O. Mayne [q.v.]. The work of creating a new campus occupied much of his time, but World War II prevented its completion before his death.

In 1912-13 Blair was a committee-member of the Ipswich Grammar School Old Boys' Association and became joint patron of its Brisbane branch in 1932. He held office also in both the Queensland Scottish Union and the Queensland Irish Association. A notable athlete in his youth, he was later president of the Queensland Rugby Union. Ipswich district cricket competitions of the early twentieth century included a team called Blair's. In his later years he became more interested in the turf and was president of Tattersall's Club in 1911-22. He was also a member of the Queensland and Johnsonian clubs.

On 16 May 1940 Blair retired from the bench but remained lieut-governor and chancellor of the university. He died of cerebro-vascular disease on 18 November 1944 at the Mater Misericordiae Hospital in South Brisbane, leaving an estate valued for probate at £3718. After a service at St John's Cathedral, the state funeral proceeded to Bulimba cemetery. He was survived by his wife May Christina, née Gibson, nineteen years his junior, whom he had married on 29 February 1912 at St Andrew's Church of England, South Brisbane; they had no children.

Blair was regarded as something of a dandy: he frequently wore a 'white gardenia in his buttonhole and a silk handkerchief peeping from his breast pocket'. Like all public men he had his detractors — he was venal, he was weak, he 'married beneath him' because of that weakness, and he lacked dignity. Others saw outstanding gifts which took him, a native son of the people, to some of the highest offices in the State, and delighted in his colourful personality, his gift of ready and apt speech, his wit and love of humour, his kindness of heart and genuine interest in his fellow men.

C. A. Bernays, *Queensland – our seventh political decade, 1920-30* (Syd, 1931); *PD* (Qld), 1944-45, 961; *Aust Law J,* Mar 1930, 14 June 1940, 15 Dec 1944; *Brisbane Courier,* 12 Mar 1902, 17 Sept 1903, 3 Apr 1907, 29 Jan, 6, 26 Feb 1912, 1, 20 Apr 1922, 22, 24, 25 Apr 1925; *Qld Times,* 1 Feb 1908; *Queenslander,* 28 Apr 1927, 9 Jan 1930; *Telegraph* (Brisb), 24 May 1939; *Courier Mail,* 10 Aug 1939, 13 Feb 1940, 20 Nov 1944; H. Bryan, The University of Queensland 1910-1960 *and* Hayes MS 193 (Fryer Lib, Univ Qld); Ipswich Grammar School Archives; information from Hon. E. J. D. Stanley, Ascot, Qld.   J. C. H. GILL

BLAIR, JOHN (1857-1910), newspaper editor and proprietor, was born on 18 August 1857 at Ayr, Scotland, son of John Blair, watchmaker, and his wife Agnes, née Mitchell. He was educated at Ayr Academy and then apprenticed to his father. In 1886 he migrated to Queensland and established himself as a watchmaker in Mackay.

Blair's occasional press contributions in 1886-88 impressed editors by their simple but forceful literary style. He joined the staff of the Brisbane *Telegraph* about 1888, then went to Rockhampton in May 1889 as chief of staff of the *Morning Bulletin;* in 1896 he became its editor and part-owner with William McIlwraith. His political editorials,

whether on Queensland, Australian or international affairs, created considerable interest in the eastern States. His views, nurtured in the Scottish Liberal Party, were stimulated by the colony's political climate. Rockhampton not only reflected the struggles surrounding the rise of the Labor Party, but was also divided on two local issues, Central Queensland Separation and the deepwater port site.

The *Morning Bulletin*'s leading articles and reports of major election campaigns strongly urged the claims of William Kidston [q.v.]. Under this influence the Rockhampton electorate returned him as an endorsed Labor candidate in 1896-1904 and subsequently as an Independent. Kidston's famous 'gang forward' policy speech in 1907 illustrated his bid for independence from Labor, when Kidstonian candidates signed his personal pledge. Each policy plank had been introduced through Blair's editorials in the preceding weeks, while both Labor and the conservative (Sir) Robert Philp [q.v.] and his supporters were strategically attacked. When another election followed in 1908, he diplomatically prepared the way for Kidston's compromise with Labor: no socialism, but legislative support from Labor for approved bills. During the campaign a Rockhampton conservative candidate A. H. Feez [q.v.] referred to Blair as 'the kingmaker up the street'; another opponent attributed 'the deplorable result of the election' to the *Morning Bulletin* and wrote privately to another local editor: 'I know you can do much good in checkmating the dark and wily schemes of the Blair-Kidston combine'.

Blair's attitude to the Central Queensland Separation Movement and its dedicated apostle G. S. Curtis [q.v.] was possibly influenced by political expediency. He supported the separationists' anti-Federal campaign in 1899, but was careful to emphasize that the opposition of Curtis and Kidston 'arose exclusively from the insuperable obstacle which the constitution places in the path of Central Queensland ever obtaining self government'. After the Federation bill succeeded in Queensland, Blair unemotionally commented that it was a democratic vote and must be accepted. When Curtis opposed Kidston in the 1907 election, Blair scathingly attacked him for trying to revive the Separation issue which had been 'slain and buried by the people of Central Queensland themselves'.

The Rockhampton Harbour Board had been divided for years on the suitability of Broadmount as a deepwater port, so when Blair's skilful articles appeared in 1907 with apparently irrefutable arguments in favour of Port Alma, it was not long before the

Kidston government agreed to build a rail-link with Rockhampton, provided the Harbour Board would guarantee its profitable operation. A board election was fought on the issue and won by the candidates supported by Blair. Significantly, at the turning of the first sod for the Port Alma railway in January 1910, Premier Kidston proposed a toast 'to the ablest and most unselfish public man in the district — John Blair'. When Kidston abandoned public life soon after Blair's death, the allegations of 'kingmaker' and the comparison drawn between the 'Blair-Kidston combine' and the association of David Syme [q.v.6] and Alfred Deakin [q.v.] seemed confirmed.

Blair had married Elizabeth Riggall in Melbourne on 21 March 1893; they had four sons and one daughter. When he collapsed and died of a heart attack in Rockhampton's main street on 19 December 1910, local people were shocked and the *Morning Bulletin* staff was 'plunged into deep grief' by the loss of a brilliant colleague at the height of his career. His tombstone in Rockhampton cemetery carries two lines from Scott's 'Marmion':

> But in close fight a champion grim,
> In camps a leader sage.

D. J. Murphy et al (eds), *Prelude to power* (Brisb, 1970); *Morning Bulletin,* 18, 30 Aug, 2 Sept 1899, 11 Feb, 13 Apr, 27 May 1907, 20 Jan, 6 Feb 1908, 20, 22, 28 Dec 1910, 7 Feb 1911, 9 July 1931, 8 July 1961; K. Allen, The city and district of Rockhampton (1923, Rockhampton District Hist Soc); P. F. MacDonald, Letter-book 1908 (Rockhampton Municipal Lib); family information from Mr A. R. Blair, Syd.   LORNA L. MCDONALD

BLAKELEY, ARTHUR (1886-1972), trade unionist and politician, was born on 3 July 1886 at Gilberton, South Australia, son of Simeon Blakeley, a house-painter from Yorkshire, and his wife Catherine Ann, née Greenwood. The family soon moved to New South Wales and he attended North Broken Hill Convent School, leaving at 13 to work in the mining camps. Next year he became a shearer and apart from a brief return to mining, continued in pastoral occupations. He became an organizer for the Australian Workers' Union in 1912, and secretary of its western (Bourke) branch in 1915-17. From 1912 he was a delegate to A.W.U. conventions and New South Wales Labor Party conferences, and was also a member of the State party executive in 1915-17.

In 1917 Blakeley was elected to the House of Representatives for Darling, defeating W. G. Spence [q.v.6]. He campaigned against conscription in New England in 1916 and in his electorate next year. Although opposed

to the Industrial Workers of the World, at the 1917 A.W.U. convention he sought support for a royal commission into the conviction of 'the twelve' for conspiracy. He was summonsed under the War Precautions Act in December 1917, with other anti-conscriptionists, but the charge was seemingly not pressed. He twice failed in July 1919 to have details of his case tabled in parliament.

Blakeley was general president of the A.W.U. in 1919-23. In 1920 he became secretary to the Federal Parliamentary Labor Party, narrowly defeating J. H. Catts [q.v.]; he remained secretary until 1928 and served on the Parliamentary Standing Committee on Public Works in 1923-25. In April 1928 he, unexpectedly, narrowly won the deputy leadership of the party from E. G. Theodore [q.v.] who, however, next year defeated him, but he was elected to J. H. Scullin's [q.v.] ministry. As minister for home affairs in 1929-32, he was responsible for Canberra, and moved there with his family in 1929; he announced in 1930 the establishment of a university college and next year the abolition of the Federal Capital Territory Commission. He was one of Scullin's more loyal supporters. In 1932-34 he was again caucus secretary.

Blakeley's main interests were industrial affairs, particularly as they affected the A.W.U., and public health. In what Sir Neville Howse [q.v.] described as his 'excellent and lucid speech' on the 1924-25 budget, he showed his mastery of the statistics on tuberculosis, cancer, venereal disease and industrial diseases, and deprecated the small allocation for public health. Capable of sharp witticisms, Blakeley had claimed in 1917 that the country was run by the prime minister and the government printer.

Defeated in the 1934 election by a Lang [q.v.] Labor candidate, Blakeley moved to Melbourne and next year was appointed an inspector of the Commonwealth Court of Conciliation and Arbitration, becoming a senior inspector in 1940. On 13 November 1942 he became a conciliation commissioner, and was attached as industrial officer to the Allied Works Council; he resigned in June 1943 when his advice was rejected and an award made without consulting the unions or the court, but was reappointed in August. He retired in 1952.

Blakeley died at Glen Iris on 27 June 1972; after a state funeral he was cremated. Predeceased by his wife Ruby Pauline McCarroll (d. 1962), whom he had married at Christ Church St Laurence, Sydney, on 21 February 1914, he was survived by two sons and two daughters. His estate was valued for probate at $8175.

His elder brother FREDERICK (1882-1962),

opal miner, was born on 1 October 1882 at Gilberton and moved with his family to Broken Hill. At 12 he joined a gang of navvies and a year later went to the opal-fields at White Cliffs. He spent the rest of his life roaming in the outback prospecting. In 1908 with two friends he cycled 2200 miles (3500 km) from White Cliffs to Darwin; years later he described the journey in *Hard liberty* (London, 1938), one of the most remarkable books on the inland. He led the 1930 expedition to search for L. H. B. Lasseter's [q.v.] lost reef, although he doubted its existence. In his *Dream millions,* published posthumously in Sydney in 1972, he questioned Lasseter's veracity, and suggested that he had faked his own death. Blakeley also wrote occasional articles for the *Sydney Morning Herald* on the Aboriginals and on fossil monsters in the sandhills of Central Australia; in World War II he suggested using wild horses for transport and pack bullocks in the New Guinea jungle. Unmarried, he died of cancer in Sydney on 31 August 1962.

J. Robertson, *J. H. Scullin* (Perth, 1974); P. M. Weller (ed), *Caucus minutes,* 1-3 (Melb, 1975); *PD* (Cwlth), 1917-19, 10660, 1923, 18, 1924, 2937-43; *Aust Worker,* 19 Apr 1917, 23 Jan, 6 Feb, 13 Nov 1919; *SMH,* 13 Oct 1934, 4 Aug 1940, 3 June 1942, 29 May 1943, 30 Jan, 13 Feb 1947, 1 Sept 1962, 28 June, 29 Oct 1972.   NORMA MARSHALL

BLAKEY, OTHMAN FRANK (1897-1952), engineer, was born on 10 November 1897 at Herberton, Queensland, son of Othman Blakey, schoolteacher, and his wife Eleanor, née Shackleton, a sister of the Antarctic explorer. After the accidental death of his father in 1899 left the family badly off, Blakey began schooling at Brisbane Boys' Central School, then won a scholarship in 1911 to Brisbane Grammar School. He matriculated in 1915 and was awarded a Queensland Open Scholarship, studied engineering at the university, won the Sir Thomas McIlwraith [q.v.5] Engineering Scholarship, and graduated with first-class honours in civil engineering (B.E., 1920; M.E., 1924). On 19 April 1922 in Sydney he married Barbara Lucy Gwendoline Fraser; they had two children.

Blakey joined the Melbourne architects Barlow and Higgins in 1921 as a structural engineer. A consultant in private practice from 1924, he worked on many large new buildings in Melbourne and Adelaide, and was a leader in the application of techniques such as welded steel framework and reinforced concrete. His high professional standards, both of conduct and performance, and his punctiliousness about job safety were later impressed on his students.

In 1927 Blakey was appointed lecturer-in-charge of the department of materials and structures in the school of engineering at the University of Western Australia. On becoming full-time vice-chancellor, Hubert Whitfeld [q.v.], who had been professor of mining and engineering, recommended – unwisely perhaps – that the school be divided into departments under lecturers. Blakey was promoted to associate professor and in 1947 to the new chair of civil engineering. The 57 students when he joined the school had grown to 228 by 1945. Although he was reserved in nature, many students valued his open house on most Sunday nights. He always stressed the importance to engineers of human relationships, and in post-war years relinquished the right of private practice that went with his appointment rather than risk competing with former students.

A councillor of the Institution of Engineers, Australia, from 1938 until his death, Blakey was its president in 1945; he took a leading role in the Perth division and was chairman in 1936 and 1942. He was on the State branch committee of the Standards Association of Australia from 1948 and served during World War II on technical manpower committees. Long, lean and lantern-jawed, he had few interests outside his profession: his entry in *Who's who in Australia* listed only two recreations; student activities and Rugby football. He was also a Freemason and an office-bearer of the university rowing club. Like most of his professional contemporaries, he did not often turn his mind to the larger social issues of engineering and technology.

After World War II the engineering school under Blakey was slower to take up research than other schools and faculties. Students who returned to resume interrupted courses noticed a change in him; he seemed more conservative, and impatient with colleagues. He died in Perth of cancer on 27 March 1952, and was cremated with Anglican rites.

F. Alexander, *Campus at Crawley* (Melb, 1963); Inst of Engineers (Aust), *J,* 24 (1952); *Univ of WA Gazette,* 2 (1952), pt 1; *West Australian,* 24 March 1955.   D. E. HUTCHISON

BLANC, GUSTAVE (1876-1959), axeman, was born on 11 August 1876 at Alberton, Victoria, son of Francis (François) Edward Blanc, French-born vigneron and farmer, and his Irish-born wife Hannah, née Dorgan. Francis Blanc had come to Gippsland to manage a vineyard at Alberton but, as the climate was unsuitable, selected land at Alberton West (1880) where he built up a mixed farm, and at Binginwarri (1889).

Gus Blanc was educated at Alberton West State School. He showed early talent as an all-round athlete, but excelled as an axeman, a skill he developed clearing virgin bush on the Binginwarri selection. He won his first woodchopping contest at Foster on Boxing Day 1899, and during 1900 succeeded in several events in the 2 ft. (61 cm) standing and underhand events; in his first year of competitive chopping he was made a back-marker. In 1901 he tried his luck in Tasmania and at Burnie won the 2 ft. underhand contest — his first world championship. In 1903 Blanc reached the peak of his career when, in Davenport, Tasmania, he captured the world championship 2 ft. standing block event in the time of 3 minutes 58 seconds — a record still unbroken when he died. A week later he won the underhand 2 ft. log championship, thus completing the first world championship double. At Launceston in 1904 he again won the double championship in 2 ft. logs. The same year he toured New Zealand and was successful in the national 2 ft. standing block championship. He visited Western Australia in 1910 and carried off the State's standing and underhand championships. In 1905 he cut a 36 in. (914 cm) blackbutt standing block in eleven blows. Next year he won the Australian 6 ft. (1.8 m) girth underhand championship in 1 minute 56 seconds — another record which stood for many years.

During his long career as an axeman Blanc gave away many long starts in handicaps. He once conceded 40 seconds in a 36 in. standing block contest and the first, second and third logs fell before he began; cheered by the crowd, he then cut his log in 16 seconds. In his prime he was such a fine athlete that at one gathering in Gippsland, Victoria, he won every event in the woodchopping programme; he then went on to win the 75 (69.5 m) and 100 (91.4 m) yards foot races, the high jump, the long jump, the hop, step and jump, putting the shot and tossing the caber. Tall and broad-shouldered, he exemplified perfect physical fitness.

On 26 April 1911 at St Mary's Catholic Church, Yarram, Blanc married Eliza Newton, daughter of pioneers of the Port Albert district. After his marriage he did little competitive chopping — partly because handicapping made it almost impossible to win, and partly because of the demands of his dairy farm at Binginwarri. For many years he acted as official handicapper and starter for local axemen's events and helped to organize woodchopping and other sporting events at district meetings. He was president of the football club, played competitive cricket into his fifties and delighted in encouraging young people to join in sporting activities; his bright and breezy personality made him widely popular and he helped many a neighbour in trouble.

Blanc died on 1 October 1959 in the Alfred Hospital, Melbourne, predeceased by his wife and survived by his four daughters. He was buried in Alberton cemetery with Catholic rites.

J. Preston, Racing axemen (held by author); information from Mrs H. E. Hogan, Binginwarri, Vic.
JAMES PRESTON

BLANCH, GEORGE ERNEST (1864-1920), educationist, was born on 30 July 1864 at Great Malvern, Worcestershire, England, son of Joseph Benson Blanch, a Wesleyan minister of yeoman stock, and his wife Mary Spencer, née Hall. Blanch was educated at Kingswood School, Bath, and went up to Christ Church, Oxford, on a natural science scholarship. He graduated B.A. with first-class honours in chemistry in 1886 (M.A., 1890), and had also entered for the examinations of the University of London, where he graduated B.Sc. in pure mathematics, chemistry and physics in 1886.

That year, after beginning to read for the Bar, Blanch became a science demonstrator to the London School Board. He was responsible for the subject's teaching in three districts, giving experimental lectures in chemistry and physics to teachers and to the older boys in selected schools; he also supervised the work of school-board teachers.

In 1890 he was appointed to Sydney Grammar School by A. B. Weigall [q.v.6] and took up his duties as senior mathematical and science master next year. Through the Teachers' Association of New South Wales (formed in 1892), and at his own school, Blanch pressed the claims of science as a means of strengthening pupils' powers of observation and reasoning. He contributed towards an increasingly respectful view of science as a liberal study. In 1894 he was in charge while Weigall was on a years leave in England.

Blanch became headmaster of Melbourne Church of England Grammar School in February 1899. The 1890s had been a trying time but enrolments increased fourfold during Blanch's sixteen years at the school. He caught its fortunes as the tide turned, and his signal contribution was the harnessing of old boys' enthusiasm for the school; he also reinvigorated the prefect system. With the school in excellent heart, Blanch unexpectedly accepted the headship of Christ's College, Christchurch, New Zealand, in September 1914. He was diabetic, and hoped to find a less demanding post.

Christ's College had no academic pretensions, its boys coming from comfortable landed families. Blanch found himself accepting a task of reformation a second time. He saw the school through the war years, encouraging both patriotism and science. Numerous building projects to cope with increasing enrolments were begun under his guidance.

Blanch died of influenza on 18 September 1920 at the school and was buried in Linwood cemetery. At the time of his death, he was a member of the Standing Committee of the Anglican synod and of the Diocesan Education Board in Christchurch. He was of gentle demeanour, with a courtly manner but firm resolve. A copy of his portrait (original destroyed by fire), held by Melbourne Grammar School, shows a man of apparent softness but with steel underneath. On 13 February 1896 at Hove, Sussex, England, he had married Margaret Cochrane Whyte McLean; she survived him, together with a son and two daughters, one of whom married (Vice Admiral Sir) Roy Dowling.

Melb C. of E. Grammar School, *Melburnian*, Dec 1898, Dec 1914, May, Dec 1915, Dec 1920; *Punch* (Melb), 31 Aug 1911; G. E. Blanch, Letter to Edwin Bean, 1 May 1890 (Memorial Lib, Syd Grammar School); Christ's College register, Dec 1920 (Canterbury, NZ).   I. V. HANSEN

BLASHKI, MYER; *see* EVERGOOD

BLEAKLEY, JOHN WILLIAM (1879-1957), protector of Aborigines, was born on 17 December 1879 at Manchester, England, during a visit by his parents, John Close Bleakley, boilermaker, of Ipswich, Queensland, and his wife Caroline, née Mason. His family returned home while he was an infant and he was educated at state primary and technical schools at Ipswich. He took the public service examination in December 1899 and next August became a clerk in the Home Secretary's Department. He was transferred in December 1902 to the government shipping office on Thursday Island.

From August 1905 to 1907 Bleakley was shipping master and inspector of pearl-shell and bêche-de-mer fisheries on the island, and was then appointed clerk to the chief protector of Aborigines in Brisbane. In May 1908 his experience on Thursday Island made him an important witness before a royal commission on the pearl-shell and bêche-de-mer industries. He was promoted to deputy chief protector of Aborigines in April 1911, becoming chief protector in February 1914. He filled this position until age and ill health forced his retirement in 1942; from 1939 he was known as director of native affairs, under an amending Act he had helped to draft.

By the late 1920s Bleakley was a well-known Australia-wide voice upon Aboriginal welfare. His influence was enhanced when the Bruce-Page [qq.v.] government invited him in May 1928 to investigate the 'status and condition of aboriginals, including half-castes' in central and northern Australia. His characteristically clear, competent, conscientious report, presented the following January, trenchantly criticized existing race relations in the territories. Commonwealth conferences in Melbourne in April 1929 and at Darwin during 1930 considered reforms, but the onset of the Depression, a change of government and the powerful pastoral lobby minimized the result. The Bleakley report nevertheless helped to expedite the creation in 1931 of the Arnhem Land Reserve, a decision of lasting significance.

Bleakley's record in Queensland displays a similar combination of limitation and achievement. His professional knowledge was built on common sense, hard work and accumulated experience, not on a liberal education and training in social anthropology or native administration. Although he was affectionately remembered by both black and white for his compassion, his approach was nevertheless rigidly parochial and paternalistic. His fervent advocacy of segregation, his long-standing preoccupation with 'the half-caste problem' – summarized in his pamphlet *The half-caste Aborigines of North and Central Australia: suggestions towards solving the problem* – and his persistent theorizing on 'breed', 'blood' and 'race purity' show his acceptance of current racial ideas, since discredited. Yet by 1922 he had publicly questioned prevailing orthodoxy about the 'inevitability' of Aboriginal 'extinction', and in his 1935 paper, 'The Aborigines: past and present treatment by the state', published in J. S. Needham's *White and black in Australia* (London, 1935), he faced racial injustice with a frankness and sensitivity uncommon at the time.

Bleakley's energetic administration encouraged greater expenditure on Aboriginal affairs in Queensland than elsewhere in Australia: the rigidly controlled wages were higher, and the inadequate housing better, than in other States. Bleakley was perhaps best known to the public for his active involvement in the careers of Aboriginal middle-weight boxers Jerry Jerome and Ron Richards [q.v.], his encouragement of Aboriginal football competitions, and especially for his championing of fast bowler Eddie Gilbert [q.v.] during the highly publicized 'throwing' controversy of 1936.

While still at Thursday Island in 1905, Bleakley had married Catherine, daughter of Thomas Grisewood of Brisbane; by 1920 they had five children. He was a justice of the peace, a member of the Sherwood District Local Association and the Sherwood Boy Scouts' Committee, and treasurer at St David's Church of England, Chelmer. After retirement he condensed his ideas on Aboriginal questions into a major work, *The Aborigines of Australia,* published posthumously in 1961. Late in February 1957 he had suffered a stroke at his home at Virginia and died at Brisbane General Hospital on 4 March. He was buried in Toowong cemetery.

E. Foxcroft, *Australian native policy* (Melb, 1941); G. Nettheim, *Outlawed: Queensland's Aborigines and islanders* (Syd, 1973); R. Evans et al, *Exclusion, exploitation and extermination* (Syd, 1975); M. A. Franklin, *Black and white Australians* (Melb, 1976); *PP* (Qld), 1908, 2, 305, (Cwlth), 1929, 2, 1162.   RAYMOND EVANS

BLOCKSIDGE, WILLIAM; *see* BAYLE-
BRIDGE

BLUEGUM, TROOPER; *see* HOGUE,
OLIVER

BLUNDELL, REGINALD POLE (1871-1945), tobacco-twister, trade unionist and politician, was born on 4 February 1871 at Norwood, South Australia, son of John Pole Blundell, accountant and early Adelaide pioneer, and his wife Ida Rathburg, née Young. A Protestant, he was educated at Norwood Public School and then apprenticed as a tobacco-twister. On 10 January 1894 he married Alice Clara Gates at Norwood.

Blundell was involved with the labour movement as a young and active member of the Tobacco Twisters' Union of which he was secretary for eight years. Among other positions he became president of the Women's Employment Mutual Association (later Working Women's Trades Union), secretary of the Drivers' Union, and a member of the Richmond Democratic Club,

the Eight Hours' Day Committee, the board of management of the *Daily Herald* and the United Trades and Labor Council of South Australia. He was secretary of the T.L.C. for some years and president in 1905. He was also a staunch member of the Australian Labor Party and president of the State branch in 1912

Blundell was first elected to the House of Assembly at a by-election for Adelaide in 1907. He was re-elected in 1910, 1912 and 1915, and was government whip and secretary of the parliamentary party in 1910-12. He continually argued for the reduction of the working week, the rights of women workers and improved factory legislation. He took a special interest in the state of the Destitute Asylum. Optimistic, he saw 'on all sides . . . an expansion of life, new possibilities of enjoyment, physical, intellectual . . . daily opening for the masses'. He was always well prepared with facts, figures and the views of overseas authorities, and was fond of quoting poetry.

On the formation of the Labor ministry of Crawford Vaughan [q.v.] in 1915, Blundell held the portfolios of industry, mines and marine. In 1917, however, he left the A.L.P. over the conscription issue and joined the National Labor Party. He was in A. H. Peake's [q.v.] Liberal-National coalition ministry from 17 August 1917 as minister for repatriation, agriculture and industry, but was defeated in the 1918 election. He had been a member of select committees on northern railways in 1910 and on the metropolitan abattoirs in 1913-15.

In 1918 Blundell was the organizing secretary of the National Party of South Australia and won the Federal seat of Adelaide as a Nationalist in the 1919 elections. In 1922 the A.L.P. candidate defeated him and he returned to his former trade, working for W. D. & H. O. Wills (Aust) Ltd for the next fifteen years as a traveller on the west coast.

Blundell was described by T. H. Smeaton [q.v.] as 'an enthusiast among enthusiasts; he has been ubiquitous in service in every movement that has any relation to the welfare of the workers'. His colleagues praised him as 'energetic and capable' and as 'an active worker for trade unionism'. He died of pernicious anaemia at Helmsdale on 9 August 1945 leaving an estate sworn for probate at £440. Survived by his wife, three daughters and three sons, he was buried in North Brighton cemetery.

T. H. Smeaton, *The people in politics* (Adel, 1914); S. O'Flaherty, *The Australian Labor Party, South Australian Branch* (Adel, 1956); D. J. Murphy (ed), *Labor in politics* (Brisb, 1975); *PD* (SA), 1907-15; *Advertiser* (Adel), 10 Aug 1945.
                               DEAN JAENSCH

BOAN, HENRY (1860-1941), retailer and sportsman, was born on 4 November 1860 at Jones Creek near Dunolly, Victoria, son of Thomas Boan, miner and road contractor, and his wife Rachel, née Isaacs. Sketchily educated at Dunolly, where his English-born parents had settled in the 1850s after some time in California, United States of America, he left his poor but secure Jewish home at 16 to work as a messenger in Flegeltaub's Ballarat warehouse for 10s. a week and keep. Promoted to town-traveller at £2 10s. a week, he soon resigned, failed to find a niche in Melbourne and, after working his way to Sydney, lived a hand-to-mouth existence. Posts in mercantile houses like Anthony Hordern's and David Jones's [qq.v.4,2] were lost from pride and impulsiveness. For four years he drifted from job to job in Sydney, Brisbane, Toowoomba, Charters Towers and elsewhere, and was often penniless.

Harry Boan never lost faith in his ability or prospects, and in 1886 his parents offered him their £200 savings to make a fresh start. With his brother Ernest, he opened a store in booming Broken Hill. His imaginative buying and advertising soon produced a turnover of £1000 a week. Expanding steadily, Boan Bros was soon the leading drapery establishment of the 'Silver City'. In the mid-1890s Broken Hill was crippled by strikes; in 1895 Harry sold out to his brother and migrated with another brother Benjamin to Western Australia, where gold-fever had created an expanding market. The site selected for their store was marginal and swampy, but was directly opposite the central railway station. Despite a chronic shortage of labour and materials and the need to borrow £62 000, a single-storey building was erected within four months. On 17 June 1896 in Sydney, with Hebrew rites, Harry married Sophie, daughter of the merchant Barnett Bebarfald; they had four children.

Boan had a fine physique, a neat beard and a distinguished manner. He dressed smartly, talked fluently and well, and loved an audience. His promotional methods startled parochial Perth. When Boan Bros opened on 7 November 1895 it almost sold out, and had to close for a day to replenish stock and recruit a hundred more assistants. By the 1920s it was called 'the people's store'; free trains and taxis brought customers to and from its birthday-sales. Though much was spent on lifts and other facilities, little went on frills and the floor-boards remained bare. Local enterprise was encouraged by special promotion of Western Australian goods, and a factory was established to service the store.

Benjamin's death in 1901 gave Harry sole control, and he bought land adjoining the store in 1910. Before expanding through to Murray Street next year, he toured Europe and America, seeking ideas. About 1913 his wife and children settled in England; henceforth he lived alone in Perth hotels.

Boan was elected unopposed to the Legislative Council in April 1917, but resigned suddenly in February 1918 after criticism of the opening in his store of a branch of the State Savings Bank. Soon afterwards, he floated the store as a limited company, left for England, living in Park Lane, London, and at Cobham, Surrey. In July 1919 at the Guards' Chapel, his second daughter married the earl of Athlumney, an Irish peer. In 1928 his elder daughter, widowed in World War I, married Lieutenant P. G. Agnew, R.N., who was created a baronet in 1957. Returning to Perth about 1920 Boan was re-elected to the Legislative Council as a Nationalist candidate in November 1922; he did not renominate in 1924.

Politics seemingly bored him, but horses, both on the turf and in the hunting-field, were a consuming passion. He was a fine judge of horseflesh and his racing stud brought him many trophies: Tanami cost him £300 and won over £5000, including the Australian Jockey Club Derby of 1910, while Maltfield won £1750 and Maltblossom £1250. He took a close paternal interest in the Children's Hospital, served as president of its board, and made frequent generous donations.

Following the death of an elder son who had been intended to succeed him, Boan gladly relinquished control of the store to his son Frank who returned from England late in 1929. By about 1932 Harry turned to serious horse-breeding and racing, and settled in Melbourne near a brother and sister. He died at Caulfield of chronic heart and kidney conditions on 18 March 1941, and was buried in Karrakatta cemetery, Perth, with Anglican rites.

J. S. Battye (ed), *Cyclopedia of Western Australia*, 1 (Adel, 1912); V. Courtney, *Perth and all this* (Syd, 1962); *Daily News* (Perth), 2, 5 May 1928, 6 Nov 1930, 16 Oct 1931; *Westralian Worker*, 9 Nov 1928, 8 Nov 1929; *Mirror* (Perth), 24 Aug 1929, 7 Nov 1930, 30 Nov 1935; *West Australian*, 8 Nov 1931, 19 Mar 1941; *New Call*, 14 Apr 1932; *Weekend Mag*, 7 July 1969.   TOBY MANFORD

BOARD, PETER (1858-1945), director of education, was born on 27 March 1858 at Wingham, New South Wales, son of William Board and his first wife Margaret, née Cameron. William had migrated from Scotland in 1842 and farmed on the Manning River but he became a teacher soon after

Peter's birth. Educated at his father's schools, Peter was able and studious. His uncle Rev. Archibald Cameron, a Scots graduate appointed to the Manning at the instigation of Rev. J. D. Lang [q.v.2], influenced him strongly in his youth, helping to determine his intellectual interests and his less than orthodox Presbyterianism.

After two years at Fort Street Model School, Sydney, in 1873 Board passed the university junior examination, and when he turned 15 became a pupil-teacher at Glebe. Following a year on a scholarship at Fort Street Training College he was appointed as a trained teacher in 1877. While in charge of the small school at Gunning, on 26 September 1878 he married Jessie Allen (d. 1932), daughter of Rev. John and Euphemia Bowes [q.v.]; their only child Ruby [q.v.] was born there in 1880. At 26 Board was headmaster of the large metropolitan Macdonaldtown (Erskineville) Public School. On 1 July 1893 he became inspector of schools at Lismore. Meanwhile in 1885 he had been one of the first group of evening students to enrol at the University of Sydney (B.A., 1889; M.A., 1891); he graduated with second-class honours in mathematics and, in that subject, was second in his year which included J. A. Pollock and J. J. C. Bradfield [qq.v.].

After his term at Lismore, Board served as inspector in the Albury and Newcastle districts. He became known as a sound administrator who stimulated and sustained his teachers through his own enthusiasm for teaching and his interest in children. By 1903 educational reform had become a political issue. Professor (Sir) Francis Anderson's [q.v.] scathing attack upon existing practices, in his address to the conference of the Teachers' Association of New South Wales in June 1901, had been seized upon by the press and followed by a public meeting organized by (Sir) Joseph Carruthers [q.v.]. John Perry [q.v.], minister for public instruction, responded by calling a conference of school inspectors and senior officers of his department, and by appointing G. H. Knibbs and J. W. Turner [qq.v.] royal commissioners to examine and report on educational practices overseas.

Board then went abroad on long service leave. His experiences were to have deep and lasting effects upon his thinking, but their more immediate significance lay in the quick printing and wide distribution by the minister of his succinct report on *Primary education* (Sydney, 1903), which he had submitted on his return. Available almost simultaneously with the massive *Interim report of the commissioners on certain parts of primary education* (Sydney, 1903), Board's report became the better known. He was outstanding among those who took part in another and more widely representative conference convened by Perry in 1904. Appointed to a committee to draw up a syllabus for primary schools, he was so influential that it became known as 'Board's syllabus'.

The government adopted the commissioners' strong recommendation to appoint a director of education by making Board both under-secretary of the Department of Public Instruction and director on 8 February 1905. One of his signal contributions was the manner in which he established both the procedures and the traditions of this dual office, maintained by his successors until the reorganization of 1975. He saw his first task as that of ensuring that the spirit and intention of the new primary syllabus were comprehended by teachers: accordingly, he planned a new orientation for inspectors, and he frequently addressed teachers. But, above all, he came to see the necessity of changing the pupil-teacher system as soon as possible, and replacing it by full-time pre-service preparation. In 1905-06 he established the Teachers' College, Sydney, at Blackfriars School as an interim provision until he could find better means of achieving a closer association between teacher preparation and university training. In 1906 Alexander Mackie [q.v.] was appointed principal of the college and a relationship of mutual respect and trust quickly developed between the two men. As soon as he could muster resources, Board facilitated advances in teacher education, leaving Mackie remarkably free to develop its internal programme. In 1910 Mackie was also appointed professor of education at the university. By 1912 the phasing out of the pupil-teacher system was completed. In 1919 the first wing of the Teachers' College building was erected on a site in the university grounds set aside by legislation in 1911.

Board's interest extended to children of pre-school age. Not only did he include them in his statement of principles underlying the primary school syllabus, but he also supported the Kindergarten Union of New South Wales by becoming a member of its executive and by nominating two of his officers as members of the Kindergarten College Council. By 1912 he induced the minister to increase the government grant to the union and that year to send Miss Martha Simpson [q.v.] abroad to study the methods of Dr Maria Montessori; on her return, her class at Blackfriars became a demonstration centre for teachers from New South Wales and other States. Gradually it was assumed that public schools would enrol children a year earlier than required by law.

In his annual report for 1906 Board had set out objectives for secondary education, some of which anticipated developments by more than fifty years. In 1907 he proposed the establishment of a leaving certificate to mark the completion of the high-school course, and of a council to co-ordinate curricula and standards in both government and non-government secondary schools; he was opposed by the latter and by the university, which was already considering a proposal making it responsible for the co-ordination and supervision of secondary school standards. In 1909 Board again went overseas, visiting Canada and the United States of America. The breadth of his interests was indicated by his *Report upon observations of American educational systems* (Sydney, 1909), which contained reports on rural schools, education for industrial purposes, secondary education, and the university as a public institution. Many of his views were to find their way into later legislation and administrative decisions.

Confirmed in his outlook on secondary education and declining to wait for co-operation from his opponents, Board submitted draft regulations to govern the conduct of (public) secondary schools under the Act: they defined the scope of secondary and, thus, primary education for the first time, though in terms of examinations. The 1910 elections intervened while the regulations were under consideration and they came before (Sir) George Beeby [q.v.], minister of public instruction in the first Labor government in New South Wales. Though Labor policy had given priority to evening-continuation rather than to full-time high schools, he tabled the regulations, which were not challenged in the remaining fifteen days of the session. Even before that, Board had completed arrangements to reorganize the secondary classes of Fort Street School into two high schools, and had adopted a new curriculum produced by Mackie and his staff.

Sent overseas in 1911 to report on continuation schools, Board attended the Imperial Education Conference in London. He visited centres in Britain and Europe with S. H. Smith [q.v.], an inspector of schools on leave. On his return he set up the first day-continuation schools, and placed Smith in charge of them. They failed as the government could not demand day-release from employers and because of the outbreak of World War I.

Board made a significant contribution to the Bursary Endowment Act of 1912, if only for the reason that so much was left to regulations. The composition of the Bursary Endowment Board provided the foundations of the bridges he had sought to build between government and the non-government schools, and between the school system and university. Thereafter, the 'regis-tration' of non-government schools at which bursaries would be also tenable involved inspection on behalf of the board, and parliament rightly assumed that bursaries tenable both at schools and at the university would be awarded on the basis of the department's examinations.

A. C. Carmichael [q.v.], Labor minister of public instruction, directed Board to prepare a first draft of a bill to achieve the government's intention of reforming the university, 'and such other matters as may suggest themselves to him'. The University Amendment Act 1912 reconstituted its senate, provided for the establishment of evening tutorial classes open to unmatriculated students, and instituted a scheme of exhibitions. Board prepared these provisions in accordance with government policy and on the basis of his own convictions. He added, as part of his bridge-building strategy, the statutory recognition by the university of the Leaving Certificate, in approved subjects, for purposes of matriculation and the award of exhibitions; and the establishment of a conjoint board of examiners, comprising officers of the department and representatives of the university, to 'recommend the award' of certificates. The Act opened the way for his membership in 1913-24 of the senate, where he increasingly won the respect of the chancellor and fellows.

When David Stewart [q.v.] was attempting, in the face of a reluctant university, to establish the Workers' Educational Association in Sydney, Board provided him with an office, telephone and travel vouchers, and secured a special subvention from the government. He arranged for Albert Mansbridge, on a visit to Sydney in 1913, to address the university senate; the outcome was the establishment of the department of tutorial classes which, with Francis Anderson, he later defended in the senate. To the end of his life he maintained personal links with the W.E.A.

In 1912 Board devoted his annual report to a systematic outline of necessary developments in technical education, which set the pattern for growth in that field for the next decade. On the death of Turner in 1913 Board obtained the appointment as superintendent of technical education of James Nangle [q.v.], who was eager to develop similar ideas. Only on one issue did they differ significantly: Nangle was convinced that technical education should have its own director, with direct access to the minister, but Board insisted on the unity of the educational system.

He had been fortunate in serving under governments whose policies gave him scope, within the limits of available funds, to foster new ideas in primary education, and to promote the establishment of high schools both in the city and in the country. He was able to sustain his professional momentum, despite the stringencies of the war years, and after 1918 quickly turned his attention to the post-war tasks which he could discern. In 1922, however, he found himself serving a minister, Albert Bruntnell [q.v.], who had little interest in other than primary and vocational education, and who thought to save funds by re-imposing fees in high schools. Board's protests were dismissed and he resigned from the end of 1922, three months earlier than he was due to retire. By this time he had realized a considerable part of his intentions in teacher-training and other ideals. From all sides came tributes to the man and to his services to education, mingled with angry regret at the manner of his going.

Board's years of retirement were full, and his activities reflected the range of his interests and the vigour of his mind. In 1920 the Commonwealth government had accepted the report of a committee, which he had chaired, that there should be established under the Repatriation Commission a Soldiers' Children Education Board, to administer funds on behalf of children who had lost their fathers through war-service; the money was made available, in the first instance, under the McCaughey [q.v.5] bequest. It was established in New South Wales in 1921, with Board as its chairman. He was re-elected each year until 1945, taking an active interest in its work, especially after his retirement. In 1921 he had chaired the Western Australian royal commission on public elementary education and, in 1924, an inquiry on state secondary schools in Tasmania. Living now in Leura, he became involved in the project for an Anzac memorial hospital; in 1928 he was elected chairman of the Blue Mountains District Anzac Memorial Hospital and took a characteristically personal interest in its operation over the next decade. He also continued his association with the Kindergarten Union, becoming chairman of its college council; in that capacity he attended the New Education Fellowship Conference in Sydney in 1937. He contributed chapters to P. R. Cole's [q.v.] *The primary school curriculum in Australia* (Melbourne, 1932) and *Education of the adolescent in Australia* (Melbourne, 1935), and wrote *Whither education?* (Sydney, 1939). He had been appointed C.M.G. in 1916.

Survived by his daughter, Board died at Chatswood on 12 February 1945 and was cremated after a service attended by a large and representative gathering at St Stephen's Presbyterian Church, Sydney. His estate was valued for probate at £1474.

No director of education in New South Wales has matched Board's achievements. Winning the respect of a succession of ministers, he gave to the Public Instruction Act of 1880 a reality which it had lacked for a generation. Moreover while it is manifest that at the time of his appointment he was the man for the hour, his unique combination of qualities made him a dynamic force in education for nearly twenty years, and the far-sightedness of some of his ideas left tasks for others to complete.

His portrait by Norman Carter [q.v.] is held by the Art Gallery of New South Wales; another, by George Lambert [q.v.], at the Teachers' College, Sydney, succeeds in reflecting much of the spirit of the man.

A. R. Crane and W. G. Walker, *Peter Board* (Melb, 1957), and for bibliog; P. Board papers (ML).

HAROLD WYNDHAM

BOARD, RUBY WILLMET (1880-1963), voluntary welfare worker, was born on 15 October 1880 at Gunning, New South Wales, only child of Peter Board [q.v.] and his wife Jessie Allen, née Bowes. She was educated in Sydney, Berlin and Paris; her social conscience was moulded by childhood happiness in 'this small and closely linked family' and by the progressive ideals of her father. With no financial need to work, she was free to combine her aptitude for language with an interest in welfare. In 1927 she published pamphlets on *Australian pronunciation* and the *Pupils' practice book for vowel sounds*.

In the early 1920s Ruby Board moved with her parents to Leura and nursed her mother until her death in 1932. She became a leading figure in the Country Women's Association and was president of the Blue Mountains branch in 1930-38. A member of the National Council of Women of New South Wales for fifty years, she had been general honorary secretary in 1914-18 and led the Australian delegates to the sixth quinquennial convention of the International Council of Women in Washington in 1925; as New South Wales president in 1938-48 she refused to be appointed M.B.E. because she believed that her office, reflecting the work of the council, deserved higher recognition; she accepted a C.M.G. In 1931 she had been founding honorary treasurer of the National Council of Women of Australia, and was president from 1942 to 1944. In 1939-58 she was also a vice-president of the Rachel Forster Hospital for Women and Children.

Ruby Board was founding president of the Women's Voluntary National Register in 1940 and was defence director of the

Women's Auxiliary National Service, helping to co-ordinate the work of women's organizations during World War II. She also served on the executive of the Australian Comforts Fund, and in 1943 was a founder and first president of the Housekeepers' Emergency Service.

A diabetic from the 1930s, she demonstrated effectively how little this condition need interfere with a busy and productive life. She was an office-bearer of the Diabetic Association of New South Wales from 1949 and served as president in 1951-60. Anxious to inform the public of the problems associated with the disease, she organized a lecture tour in 1953 by two world authorities and in 1955 and 1958 attended congresses of the International Diabetes Federation at Cambridge, England, and Dusseldorf, Germany. In 1957 she was founding president of the Diabetic Association of Australia and presided at its first conference held in Sydney.

From 1960 Ruby Board lived at the Mowll Memorial Village, Castle Hill, until she had a fall in December 1963; she died on Christmas Day in the Rachel Forster Hospital and was cremated after a Presbyterian service.

Selfless and generous, with boundless energy, she inspired those around her to similar enthusiasm and commitment; she was not interested in power for its own sake, or in office for its prestige, and always sought to provide opportunities for the individual's expansion. Her work was commemorated by the naming of the diabetic wing of the Rachel Forster Hospital after her in 1966.

Diabetic Federation of Aust, *Conquest,* no 5, July 1960, no 21, Apr 1964; *N.C.W. News,* Feb 1964; *SMH,* 23 May 1940, 27 Dec 1963; J. F. Arnot, Ruby Board 1880-1963 (notes held by author).

ANDRÉE WRIGHT

BOAS, ABRAHAM TOBIAS (1842-1923), Jewish minister, was born on 25 November 1842 at Amsterdam, son of Tobias Eliesar Boas, rabbi, and his wife Eva Salomon Levi, née Linse. It was a family of distinguished Jewish scholars and ministers who had fled from Poland to Holland late in the seventeenth century. After training at the Amsterdam Theological Seminary, Boas went to England at 23 to continue studying. In 1867 he became minister at the Southampton Synagogue, where his conduct encouraged Chief Rabbi Dr N. M. Adler to recommend him to the South Australian congregation late in 1869.

Arriving at Semaphore on 13 February 1870 in the *Temesa,* Boas was carried ashore on the shoulders of a sailor and met by several members of his congregation with whom he walked to Port Adelaide. There followed half a century of energetic spiritual, social, and intellectual leadership: for forty years he did not take a holiday. Within a year a new synagogue in Rundle Street was consecrated, accommodating 350 worshippers. Here on 15 May 1873 Boas married Elizabeth Solomon; they had ten children. His pastoral visits later extended as far as Fremantle, Perth and Coolgardie, Western Australia, where new synagogues and schools were opened. He actively created goodwill both within and outside the Jewish community by membership of numerous philanthropic, social, and cultural bodies.

Boas was short and thickly built with dark beard, hair turning grey, and piercing eyes behind steel-rimmed glasses. He was a popular lecturer, whose voice was 'sonorous' although with a pronunciation often 'unfamiliar'. He was esteemed as a student of English literature and drama, particularly of Shakespeare; from 1888 he was vice-president of the University Shakespeare Society. He was a foundation member of the District Trained Nursing Society, chairman of the board of the James Brown Memorial Trust for housing indigent tuberculosis patients, president of the Jewish Literary Society, and first chairman of the Jewish Choristers' Club. Boas was headmaster of the Adelaide Synagogue's Sabbath and Sunday schools — in 1895 the enrolment was over 80 — and chairman of the Chevra Kadisha (burial society) which he helped found in 1907. His efforts to introduce the triennial reading of the law in Australian synagogues failed. He looked upon 'Christianity as the foster-child of Judaism' and his standing in the wider religious community was attested at Easter 1899 by his successful intervention in a bitter controversy between Catholics and Protestants, which gained the thanks of both the Catholic archbishop and the Anglican bishop; a newspaper commented that 'such a genuine Jew would make a splendid Christian'.

By 1914 Boas was the oldest officiating Jewish clergyman in Australasia and the longest-serving Jewish minister in the British Empire. His activityy was much curtailed by a stroke in 1918, but in 1921 during a visit from London by Chief Rabbi Dr J. H. Hertz, he was honoured with the status of rabbi, as he was regarded as 'the most learned of Anglo-Jewish Rabonim'. He died at his home in Gover Street, North Adelaide, on 20 February 1923, and was buried in West Terrace cemetery.

His son Isaac Herbert [q.v.] was a prominent scientist and two others were active in public life in Western Australia.

The eldest, Lionel Tobias (1875-1949), after moving to Perth in 1896, was secretary to the Karrakatta Cemetery Board, 1918-37. Elected to the Subiaco City Council in 1906, he served for thirty-six years and was mayor in 1917-20. He was prominent on behalf of ex-servicemen and in civil defence, as well as in numerous local sporting, cultural and philanthropic organizations. His main achievement was the foundation in 1905 with J. J. Simons [q.v.] of the Young Australia League, of which he was president for over forty years until his death. His brother Harold (b. 1883), an architect, was a prominent town planner.

Aust Jewish Hist Soc, *J*, 7 (1972), no 2; *Register* (Adel), 30 Mar 1899; *Bulletin*, 1 Mar 1923; Boas material (Aust Jewish Hist Soc, Syd); Boas family records (J. S. Battye Lib, Perth, *and* Perth Hebrew Congregation Lib).   LOUISE ROSENBERG

BOAS, ISAAC HERBERT (1878-1955), scientist, was born on 20 October 1878 in Adelaide, son of Abraham Tobias Boas [q.v.], Jewish rabbi, and his wife Elizabeth, née Solomon. He was educated at Prince Alfred College, the South Australian School of Mines and Industries, and the University of Adelaide (B.Sc., 1899). In 1901 he was appointed lecturer in geology and mineralogy at the university and later worked as a demonstrator in physics with (Sir) William Henry Bragg and Professor E. H. Rennie [qq.v.]. At Bragg's urging, Boas accepted in 1903 a lectureship in physics and chemistry at the technical school at Charters Towers, Queensland, in two colourful and exacting years there he learnt 'how to tackle problems of which I had no experience'. In 1906 he became lecturer in chemistry at the Technical School, Perth. He married Adela Isabella Solomon in Adelaide on 1 January 1908. For his survey of Collie coals, made in 1914 at the request of a State royal commission, he was awarded the degree of M.Sc. by the University of Western Australia.

Boas became increasingly interested in the chemistry of wood and associated products. The shortages of World War I convinced him that Australia needed a central organization to deal with the problems of the forest industries. In his makeshift laboratory at the Technical School, he investigated the fundamental and chemical reactions involved in the soda process of paper-making, uninhibited by existing techniques and undismayed by adverse reports of visiting experts. Making pulp from karri and producing a few sheets of paper from it, he showed that the apparent unsuitability of Australian hardwoods was due to misconceived techniques rather than the timber itself.

In 1919 Boas persuaded the Australian States to establish a forest products laboratory, to be set up in Perth under the auspices of the projected Commonwealth Bureau of Science and Industry. Appointed officer-in-charge, in 1919-20 he toured similar laboratories in North America, England, Europe and India. When by 1921 the bill to establish the bureau had not been passed, Boas resigned to become chief chemist in the Melbourne leather firm of Michaelis [q.v.5], Hallenstein & Co. He soon found a common interest with Professor D. O. Masson [q.v.] in the problem of scientific control of the tanning, glue and gelatin industries in Victoria. Meanwhile in Perth, a former student L. R. Benjamin [q.v.] was carrying on where Boas had left off. Despite difficulties, pulping and paper-making continued, extending to almost all Australian eucalypts.

Boas was appointed chief of the forest products division when it was set up in Melbourne in 1928 under the reorganized Council for Scientific and Industrial Research. In 1935 he toured North America and Europe and attended the Fourth British Empire Forestry Conference in South Africa. During World War II he was, among other positions, assistant controller for timber supplies in the Department of Supply and Development, and was on the advisory committee of aeronautical research; he was also a member of the Commonwealth committees on development of secondary industries and flax production. In April 1944 he retired as chief of his division so that he could join the board of New Zealand Forest Products Ltd, but he remained on half time with C.S.I.R. until May 1945, working as a consultant and completing a book (published in Melbourne in 1947) on *Commercial timbers of Australia*. He held a number of offices after retirement, including the chairmanship of an advisory panel on furniture standards. A foundation member of the Royal Australian Chemical Institute, and fellow in 1944, he was elected general president in 1952.

Throughout his life Boas was closely associated with the Jewish community. He was president of the St Kilda Hebrew Congregation in 1930-32 and 1934-36, a member of the Victorian Jewish Advisory Board, and chairman of the Australian Jewish Welfare Society in 1936-46. A member of the Australian Friends of the Hebrew University, Jerusalem, he took a great interest in Israel and helped its forest development; the Wood Technology Institute of Israel was named after him.

Survived by his wife, three sons and a daughter, he died at Hawthorn, Victoria, on

16 October 1955. The University of Melbourne's Boas Memorial Lectures for secondary school students were inaugurated in 1961.

N. Rosenthal, *Look back with pride* (Melb, 1971); H. E. Dadswell, 'To honour a pioneer', *APM News*, Aug 1961; J. G. Campbell, 'Papermaking and Australia's scientific contribution', *Printing and Graphic Arts* (Melb), no. 48, Oct 1963; E. Boas, I'll eat my hat – sketches in the life of I. H. Boas (LaTL); Establishment of newsprint industry in Aust – proposed paper pulp industry, Tas, correspondence 1929-33 (LaTL).

NEWMAN ROSENTHAL

BODY, ELIEL EDMUND IRVING (1881-1965), sheep-breeder, was born on 30 March 1881 at Wambandry, near Warren, New South Wales, second son of Frederick Edmund Body (1842-1906), grazier, and his wife Helen Harriet, née Irving, of Lake Terramungamine station. Frederick Edmund had migrated from Cornwall in 1850 with his parents, and about 1865 took up land on the Macquarie River. In 1881 he bought Bundemar, near Trangie, and later Lake Terramungamine; he began clearing the heavily timbered country and in 1890 laid the foundations of the Bundemar flock. That year he represented Dubbo on the first council of the Pastoralists' Union of New South Wales. In 1901 his eldest son Frederick Irving founded the renowned Bundemar merino stud with 1700 Peppin [q.v.5] ewes, and rams bought from Thomas Millear's Wanganella estate: thereafter the Body family did not introduce any outside blood. F. E. Body died at Bundemar on 28 April 1906, leaving an estate valued for probate at £102 407 deficit. The properties were administered as the estate of the late F. E. Body.

Eliel Edmund Irving, always known as 'Ted', was educated from 1894 at The King's School, Parramatta, and in 1901-02 studied arts at the University of Sydney. He returned home without a degree and enthusiastically helped to manage Bundemar. In 1914 the family bought Ardgour, Quirindi, and in 1924 a section of Buttabone, Warren, which were run as part of the stud. The sheep were classed by Charles Mallinson until he received a merino sheep appointment from the South African government in 1919. That year Body became a co-trustee of his father's estate and for many years thereafter was the guiding hand, first as studmaster, then as manager. The first famous sheep bred by Body was Sir Charles, whose progeny were sold throughout Australia and exported to South Africa and South America. Bundemar won many championships at the Sydney Sheep Show and the group prize (later the Stonehaven [q.v.] Cup) more often than any other stud.

From 1921 Body was a councillor of the New South Wales Sheepbreeders' Association, and president in 1925-30, 1937-40 and in 1947-49, serving almost continuously as one of its eight vice-presidents until he was made a life governor in 1960. He was also a member of its flock register committee and, in 1961, aged 80, was one of the provisional committee which set up the Australian Stud Poll Merino Flock Register. He played a leading part in negotiations with the Federal and State governments on closer settlement and the export embargo on merino rams. In 1932 he had declined Country Party nomination for the State electoral seat of Castlereagh.

Body was a keen footballer, cricketer, tennis-player, golfer and race-goer, and was a member of the Australian Club, the Australian Jockey Club and Royal Sydney Golf Club; he spent his last years in Sydney. In 1960 he was appointed C.B.E. for his services to the sheep industry. On 8 June 1965 he died at his flat at Edgecliff and was cremated with Anglican rites; he was survived by his wife Doris Elaine, née Walsh, whom he had married at St Kilda, Victoria, on 20 August 1913, and by his only son. His estate was valued for probate at £71 705. After his death the close family partnership was impossibly unwieldy, with shareholders spanning three generations: Bundemar and the other stations were ultimately sold in 1973. The phenomenal success of the stud had been due to a close-knit family effort under Ted Body's sagacious control.

NSW Sheepbreeders' Assn, *The Australian merino* (Syd, 1955); *Pastoral Review*, July 1906, Aug 1909, Dec 1910, Aug 1925, July 1965; *SMH*, 30 Apr 1932, 20 July 1934, 18 June 1936, 28 Jan, 22, 26 June 1939, 9 Sept 1947; records (NSW Sheepbreeders' Assn. Paddington). H. ALEXANDER

BOEHM, TRAUGOTT WILHELM (1836-1917), schoolmaster, was born on 18 October 1836 at Muschten, Zuellichau, Brandenburg, sixth son of Johann Georg Boehm, carpenter, and his wife Caroline, née Koenig, who were Old Lutherans. On 2 January 1839 the family arrived at Port Adelaide in the group of Lutheran pilgrims on Captain Hahn's *Zebra*, and helped form the settlement at Hahndorf. Boehm was educated at the church school before going at 12 to G. D. Fritzsche's [q.v. Kavel, 2] tiny Lobethal College to train as a teacher. He later had practical training at the Bethany

Lutheran Church School and studied under Dr C. W. L. Muecke [q.v.5] at Tanunda. 'A gifted, industrious and God-fearing scholar', he was called as a teacher by the Hahndorf congregation in 1854 and took charge of the Lutheran school where he remained three years.

In 1857, aided by an annual government grant of £70, Boehm opened a private, unsectarian advanced school in his home, calling it the Hahndorf Academy. Next year, on 12 August, he married Anna Maria Dolling; they had two children. He offered instruction, based on the German classical gymnasium, to boys and girls, including some boarders, from all religions and national groups. Although a member of the Evangelical Lutheran Synod of South Australia, Boehm disapproved of excessive scriptural teaching. Languages, music and the first-hand study of natural history and science were emphasized, and conversation was 'induced' in German. The school was extended gradually from 1871, when a large two-storey building was begun. Boehm was made a justice of the peace. In 1874 his grant ended and three years later, financially embarrassed, he sold the school at a loss to the Lutheran Church for £700. It was renamed Hahndorf College and Boehm remained as principal.

In 1881 he was involved in disputes with sections of the Lutheran synod, who possibly found his views too liberal; conscious only of striving 'for light and truth', he threatened to resign. Two years later he bought back the college at the original price, and made large extensions. In 1884 he was declared insolvent, partly because he had supported his son farming in the north. Allowed to keep the college, Boehm carried on for two more years, but then had to sell. The purchaser, D. J. Byard (B.A. Oxon., 1882), was an Englishman with a love of German language and culture; he carried on in Boehm's tradition until the college closed in 1912.

Boehm moved to Murtoa, Victoria, where in 1887 he opened a private school; this was taken over by the Lutheran Church about 1894 and named Concordia College. Boehm stayed as music teacher until the college removed to Adelaide in 1904, when he retired to Warracknabeal to live with his daughter. For some years he wrote on meteorology for the local newspaper. He settled briefly on land at Yaapeet before dying at Warracknabeal on 12 May 1917. His estate was sworn for probate at £1331.

Many prominent South Australians had studied at Hahndorf College and consistently did well at the University of Adelaide's matriculation examinations. A small man nicknamed 'Chibby', Boehm wore a wide waxed moustache; some of his

lessons were held in the bush, and he used a harpsichord at the college to help sweeten with music and song 'the bitterness of beginning term'. In evidence in 1882 before a commission on the working of the Education Acts, he attacked the state school system as 'little better than a mere farce', with its 'cramming and word-drenching' of pupils and its payment by results; he advocated a knowledge of psychology for teachers and the study of natural science 'to fascinate and cultivate the youthful mind'. Aware that these views would be thought 'queer', he concluded his submission with a couplet:

I may not pretend, though teaching, to find
A means to improve or convert mankind.

H. T. Burgess (ed), *Cyclopedia of South Australia*, 2 (Adel, 1909); W. Iwan, *Um des Glaubens willen nach Australien* (Breslau, 1931); A. Brauer, *The one hundredth anniversary of the arrival of the Lutheran pilgrim fathers . . .* (Adel, 1938), and *Under the Southern Cross* (Adel, 1956); F. J. H. Blaess, *Hahndorf and its academy* (Hahndorf, 1968), and 'The college in the hills . . .', *Aust Lutheran Almanac,* 1952-62; *Walkabout,* Apr 1964; *Register* (Adel), 21 Sept 1883; *Warracknabeal Herald,* 15 May 1917; J. W. Hayes, Education in the German Lutheran community of South Australia circa 1838-1914 (M.Ed. Hons thesis, Univ Syd, 1971); news-cuttings, Boehm box (Lutheran Archives, Adel).   SUZANNE EDGAR

BOGUE LUFFMAN; *see* LUFFMAN

BOISMENU, ALAIN MARIE GUYNOT DE (1870-1953), Catholic missionary bishop, was born on 27 December 1870 at St Malo, Brittany, France, son of François Guynot de Boismenu and his wife Augustine Marie, née Thomas. Educated at St Malo and in Antwerp, he joined the Congregation of the Sacred Heart in 1886, was ordained on 10 February 1895, and was soon rewarded for zeal as a seminary professor with a posting to British New Guinea. Arriving at Yule Island on 25 January 1898, he was appointed counsellor and became virtual substitute for the ailing vicar apostolic, Archbishop Louis-Andre Navarre (1836-1912), as well as pro-vicar general and deputy superior. The mission suffered from an inappropriate European parochial system, from the government's confining 'spheres of influence' policy and from competition from the heretics of the London Missionary Society. Navarre thought a push to the mountains impossible, but in 1899 Boismenu entered the Fuyuge hinterland. The party was saved from massacre only by sang-froid: they refused to use guns 'in order to show we were not double-minded when we said we were men of peace', and thus retreated. On his return Boismenu found that he had been appointed co-adjutor to Navarre and titular bishop of Gabala; he was consecrated in Paris in 1900. He succeeded Navarre in 1908 in what became the vicariate apostolic of Papua in 1922.

By 1900 Boismenu had won the mountains for the Sacred Heart. The mission was reorganized with a system of head stations under directors. The functions at headquarters were also more carefully defined, while systematic annual reports were elicited from the districts and carefully sifted for future planning. From 1898 to 1945 the mission grew from five districts of 8000 people with 2400 adherents to eleven districts of 65 000 with 23 500 adherents, and had new centres at Onongge (1913), Port Moresby (1915), Toaripi (1927) and Samarai (1932).

Boismenu did not envisage any rapid progress towards political autonomy for Papuans, but his episcopacy was humane and practical. Recruits included the controversial stigmatic and mystic Marie-Thérèse Noblet [q.v.], the World War I air-ace Lucien Bourjade ('Le Papou'), the publicist André Dupeyrat and a community of contemplative Carmelite nuns. More concerned to redeem communities than to convert individuals, Boismenu concentrated on an elite of young Christians. By 1933 his catechists numbered 219, and an order of local nuns – the Handmaids of the Lord (fostered by Noblet) – flourished.

His administration kept religion as its central focus. Financial deficits were overcome more by austerity than by means of plantations, which tended to identify missionaries with European exploiters. Boismenu promoted primary and technical education, and pupils increased from 800 in 1898 to 7000 in 1945. By 1932 forty-eight 'graduates' were employed by the Papuan administration. Education was in English to ensure ability to participate in the wider community.

At the Australasian Catholic Congress in Melbourne in 1904 Boismenu had hoped to win support for 'liberty of conscience' against the 'Erastian' 'spheres of influence' policy. He declared that even compared to Polynesians, the Papuan 'was unquestionably of an inferior nature . . . which has lived too long a prey to original sin'. He told the 1906-07 royal commission that the Papuans were 'children'. This attitude may explain his inability to respond adequately to the papal call for an indigenous clergy: only two candidates were presented for the priesthood during his episcopacy. In 1918 Joseph Taurino, significantly part-Polynesian, was sent to France but died in 1922. In 1928 Louis

Vangeke (created bishop in 1970) was sent to Madagascar for his studies; abandoned in infancy, he had lived only with missionaries. Vangeke was never given a parish of his own nor did he work among his Mekeo group as a pastor, but he continued to revere Boismenu as a saint.

He retired in 1945, was especially commended by Pope Pius XII and made archbishop of Claudiopolis in Honoriade. He lived out his remaining years 'in almost eremetical retirement among the citrus trees in the green valley of Kubuna'. Boismenu died there on 5 November 1953. Jesus-bearded, gaunt and bright-eyed, he seemed a living ikon of Christian benignity. Paul Claudel called him 'that lion-hearted bishop worthy of the most dazzling ages of the Church', and the poet James McAuley saw him as 'the man who most exemplified greatness', with 'a rare sanctity and unerring spiritual discernment'. His grave at Kubuna is a place of pilgrimage.

B. Grimshaw, *Adventures in Papua with the Catholic mission* (Melb, 1913); A. Dupeyrat, *Papouasie: histoire de la mission, 1885-1935* (Paris, 1935), and *Papuan conquest* (Melb, 1948); A. Dupeyrat and F. de la Noe, *Sainteté au naturel* (Paris, 1958); P. Ryan (ed), *Encyclopaedia of Papua and New Guinea*, 1, 2 (Melb, 1972); Roy Com into . . . Papua, Report, *PP* (Cwlth), 1907; J. McAuley, 'My New Guinea', *Quadrant*, 5 (1960-61), no 3; information from Bishop L. Vangeke, A. Aoae and personnel, Sacred Heart Mission, PNG.

JAMES GRIFFIN

BOLD, WILLIAM ERNEST (1873-1953), town clerk, was born on 6 May 1873 at Birkdale near Southport, Lancashire, England, son of Charles Bold, secretary to the Leeds Canal Co., and his wife Elizabeth, née Turner. Educated in Lancashire and later at the Haberdashers' School, London, he was an apprentice electrical engineer on the Forth railway bridge at Queensferry, Scotland, in 1888-90. Returning to London he taught himself shorthand and worked as a clerk-typist with an Australian mercantile firm in the Baltic Exchange. At the suggestion of a relation in Fremantle, he migrated to Western Australia in 1896.

Bold worked briefly with a merchant, and late in 1896 he was clerk-typist to the town clerk of the city of Perth, becoming known as his assistant. He became acting town clerk on 27 November 1900, after the forced resignation of the inefficient H. E. Petherick. The council initially rejected his application for the vacant office and appointed a Melbourne candidate, who resigned ten days later; indeed, Bold's reappointment in an acting capacity in April 1901 was approved only after long debate and a close vote. On 30 September he was appointed town clerk, the youngest in any Australian capital, and when he resigned forty-three years later he was the longest serving.

Bold's first problem was Perth's most flamboyant mayor, W. G. Brookman [q.v.], mining speculator, urban landlord and social visionary, who dreamed of Perth as 'a fairer Athens', but regularly failed to attend ordinary council meetings. In the opinion of councillors Brookman dipped into the entertainment fund too often and too deeply and allowed the lady mayoress too much say in the affairs of the city. As the bearer of unwelcome messages from the council, Bold suffered at the mayor's hands but it was he, not Brookman, who lasted beyond 1901. The mayoralty went to less troublesome men and the council became less faction-ridden.

Bold needed also to boost the morale and efficiency of the staff, for both his predecessors had been poor managers. Using as a model the technically efficient Birmingham of Joseph Chamberlain, he soon expanded the size and improved the quality of the staff and streamlined its operations. Working from an increasingly sound administrative base with a relatively inexperienced council and mayors who were not strong leaders of opinion, Bold became a powerful driving force in policy formation, not only preparing detailed reports for councillors but even intervening often and at length in council debates. By 1905 it could be written of him that 'he comported himself like the boss Panjandrum'; he was 'the real mayor and [mayor] Brown merely his easy going factotum'.

Bold was a strong advocate of municipal socialism and described its advantages in his presidential address to the Western Australian Municipal Officers' Association in 1906. He and the mayor T. G. Molloy [q.v.], a kindred spirit, partly convinced and partly tricked the council in 1908 into buying out the Perth Gas Co., which produced both gas and electricity; a costly and controversial purchase at the time, it eventually proved a valuable asset to the city. In 1912 Molloy and Bold also fought hard to secure the tramways company, but were outmanoeuvred and outbid by the Scaddan [q.v.] Labor government.

After several reports by Bold had failed to induce the ministry to create a 'Greater Perth' authority and pass a town planning act, the council sent Bold in 1914 on a tour of Britain and North America to gather information about municipal experiments and improvements. In London he attended both the Imperial Health and Town Planning and the Garden Cities and Town Planning Association conferences; he also inspected innovative cities, towns and suburbs in both Britain and the United States. On his return he refined his 'Greater Perth' concept to embrace satellite garden and seaside suburbs, a redeveloped civic centre like Chicago's, and an overall plan on 'City Beautiful' lines.

The 'Greater Perth' movement made some headway during World War I when Leederville, North Perth and Victoria Park voluntarily joined the city; the inner suburb of Subiaco resolved to remain independent. In 1917, on Bold's recommendation, the 1300-acre (526 ha) Limekilns Estate was bought, adjacent to western seaside endowment lands already owned by the city. Despite opposition from works minister W. George [q.v.], an old council enemy of Bold's, (Sir) James Mitchell's [q.v.] government passed the City of Perth Endowment Lands Act in 1920 which empowered the council to develop and sell the land in its trust. In the mid-1920s the council, at Bold's suggestion, invited the architects Hope and Klem to design satellite towns on the new lands. Floreat Park, Wembley Park and City Beach owed much to Raymond Unwin's writings and the 'City Beautiful' movement. Early homes there were functional and cheap enough for the thrifty worker, for Bold was a strong advocate of 'national efficiency'.

Another of his dreams was fulfilled in 1928 when the first Australian town planning Act was passed by the State parliament. It owed much to the work of the Town Planning Association of Western Australia, established in 1916. Its principals were Bold, Carl Klem, and the architect and city councillor Harold Boas. In 1930 Bold and Boas persuaded the council to establish a town planning committee.

Bold's ideas prevailed in the 1920s, but in the 1930s he was less successful. The creation of Riverside Drive in 1937 enhanced the city foreshore but public criticism of his administration culminated in 1938 in a royal commission. His chief critic was D. L. Davidson, the first town planning commissioner appointed under the 1928 Act, who alleged that health and building regulations were not being observed and that there were far too many slums. Bold's contention that there had been only minor irregularities was accepted, but the commission recommended immediate revision and updating of the by-laws. Though it described him as 'very efficient and conscientious', the report recognized that in pursuing his 'City Beautiful' ideals he had become a little careless in his administration of the central city area. In his long typescript reminiscences, written in 1944, Bold did not mention the royal commission, though it had dominated his life at the time. At the request of the mayor and council, he deferred his retirement through World War II and, although ill, resigned only after he had trained a successor. An auto-biographical address to the Royal Western Australian Historical Society was published in its journal in 1946.

Bold is generally acknowledged to be the founding father of town planning in Western Australia. Uniquely among Perth's town clerks he developed a vision of his ideal city, much of which he brought into being. Yet he was formally honoured with a C.B.E. only as late as 1948. Most mayors recognized his ability and some spoke of him as a friend. Many other people were openly hostile. His severest critic was Thomas Walker [q.v.6], editor of the *Sunday Times*. E. G. ('Dryblower') Murphy [q.v.], who wrote verse for that paper, characterized him as 'Beau Brummel Bold' and as 'a toffy young spark'. The *Times* spoke for that 'temper, democratic; bias, offensively Australian', which found Bold's appearance and manner intolerable. He always wore a top hat and morning coat with a stiff, high-collared shirt, and in council was bewigged. He was formal, rather unbending and, unlike his predecessor and several of his mayors, he was abstemious. He had been organist and choirmaster at the Hornsey Road Methodist Church, London, in 1892-96; he became assistant organist at St George's Cathedral, Perth, and from 1897 organist at Wesley Church and later at St Aidan's Presbyterian Church, Claremont. He was also a Rotarian and, at one time, a Freemason.

Bold had married Nellie Cooper, daughter of Nicholas Jeffrey of Eaglehawk, Victoria, on 9 October 1907 at Claremont; they had three children. He died at Tresillian Hospital, Nedlands, on 25 November 1953 and was cremated. His estate, valued for probate at £7927, was left to his family.

J. S. Battye (ed), *Cyclopedia of Western Australia*, 1 (Adel, 1912); *V&P* (LA WA), 1938, 2 (20); R. Clark, 'The city beautiful', *and* 'Garden City Movement', *Architect*, 10 (1969), no 2, 4; M. Webb, 'Planning and development in metropolitan Perth to 1953', *Perth city and region*, Aust Planning Inst congress (Perth, 1968); *West Australian*, 28 Nov 1900, 10, 24, 30 Sept 1901; *Western Mail*, 30 Oct 1930; R. E. Robertson, W. E. Bold (M.A. thesis, Univ WA, 1970); H. Boas, Bricks and mortar (1971, Battye Lib, Perth); Minute books and reports, *also* records connected with roy com, 1938 (Perth City Council).   Tom Stannage

BOLTON, WILLIAM KINSEY (1860-1941), soldier and politician, was born on 1 November 1860 at Lostock Gralam, Cheshire, England, son of John Hammersley Bolton, corn-dealer, and his wife Hannah,

née Kinsey. In 1868 he migrated with his parents to Victoria where his father was a storekeeper at Camperdown, Darlington and Mortlake.

After education at Darlington State School and apprenticeship as a carpenter in Mortlake, Bolton went to Melbourne and then in 1879 to Sydney, where he studied architecture for three years while working as a foreman-carpenter. In 1884 he set up as a builder in Warragul, Gippsland. From 1890 he was inspector of works in the Victorian Public Works Department, employed in the Bendigo and Ballarat districts.

In 1878 Bolton had joined the Southern Rifles and was commissioned lieutenant in the 3rd Battalion, Victoria, on 12 December 1891; he was promoted captain in 1897, major in the 7th Australian Infantry Regiment in 1903 and lieut-colonel in 1910. In 1900-01 he had led the officers' team at the inauguration of the Commonwealth and won the officers' shooting-match.

In 1912 Bolton took command of the 70th Regiment. On 19 August 1914 he enlisted in the Australian Imperial Force and was sent to command the Queenscliff Fort, but was soon back in Melbourne mobilizing the 8th Battalion, which sailed for Egypt on 19 October. They landed on Gallipoli on 25 April 1915 and Cape Helles on 9 May. After the gruelling Battle of Krithia (7-8 May) and brief command of the 2nd Infantry Brigade, Bolton's age and collapsing health led to his repatriation in the hospital ship *Ballarat*. C. E. W. Bean [q.v.] described him as 'a soft-hearted commander very solicitous for his men'. A hill and ridge on Gallipoli were named after him.

From August Bolton commanded successively the Ballarat Training Depot and the Defended Ports of Victoria, retiring as honorary brigadier general in 1920. He had been a founder of the Returned Sailors' and Soldiers' Imperial League, and became its first national president on 3 June 1916. Soon he was embroiled in the conscription debate and he attended the inaugural meeting of the National Party in January 1917. At the invitation of W. M. Hughes [q.v.] Bolton ran for the Senate and was elected on 5 May 1917. His early attempt to have aliens and their descendants barred from holding commissions in the Australian Military Forces was unsuccessful. Next year he was appointed C.M.G.

Bolton insisted on orthodox, polite representation of R.S.L. views through recognized channels and he discouraged undisciplined demonstrations by returned men. As dissatisfaction grew with government treatment of ex-servicemen, Bolton's 'law and order' policy met with opposition in the R.S.L. In 1917 the central council had approved his nomination to the Senate but by 1919 he was criticized for his inability to devote enough time to league affairs. A Victorian faction campaigned for his replacement by (Sir) Gilbert Dyett [q.v.] and he was defeated as president on 15 July.

In December 1919 Bolton was re-elected to the Senate after a campaign embittered by accusations that he had been cowardly at Gallipoli. He successfully refuted these charges. After his defeat as R.S.L. president, he was less prominent in politics, and in the December 1922 election he was defeated.

Bolton occupied himself as partner in a building firm and in other business concerns. He contested the Federal seat of Henty unsuccessfully in 1929. For many years he lived at Ballarat and owned a house at Brighton and a small property near Camperdown. He died of cancer at Brighton on 8 September 1941 and was cremated. Bolton was married twice: on 29 December 1881 at Warrnambool to Jane Morpeth Gillies (d. 1893), and on 18 August 1894 at Bendigo to Margaret Ford, both times with Presbyterian rites. He was survived by two sons and a daughter of the first marriage and a son and three daughters of the second. Three sons and a daughter served in World War I.

M. M. McCallum, *Ballarat and district citizens and sports at home and abroad* (Ballarat, 1916); C. E. W. Bean, *The story of Anzac*, 1, 2 (Syd, 1921, 1924); L. Hills and A. Dene, *The RSSILA: its origin, history...*, 1 (Melb, 1927); H. Copeland, *The path of progress* (Warragul, 1934); W. F. Whyte, *William Morris Hughes* (Syd, 1957); G. L. Kristianson, *The politics of patriotism* (Canb, 1966); *Argus*, 27 Mar 1917, 9 Sept, 9 Oct 1941; *Ballarat Star*, 8, 10-13 Dec 1919; *Geelong Advertiser*, 25 Apr 1936; *Age*, and *Sun-News Pictorial*, 9 Sept 1941.

J. N. I. DAWES

BON, ANN FRASER (1838-1936), philanthropist, was born on 9 April 1838 at Dunning, Perthshire, Scotland, daughter of David Dougall, physician, and his wife Jane, née Fraser. On 12 January 1858 at Dunning, Ann married a family friend John Bon, thirty-three years her senior, who had farmed in Perthshire until ruined by economic depression. In 1837 he had been chosen by Watson and Hunter, partners in a Scottish pastoral company with extensive properties in the Port Phillip District, to take stud cattle to Wappan (Wappang) on the Delatite River. In the 1840s the company had to sell its holdings and Bon was able to buy Wappan. Years of good management increased his wealth and in 1857 he had returned to Dunning to pay his creditors in full. He stayed there long enough to marry,

returning to Australia in 1858 with his bride.

On their voyage Ann Bon took a piano, a cargo of bulbs, seeds, shrubs and fruit trees, five servants and enough hand-woven linen to last her a lifetime; John took a champion Clydesdale stallion and a celebrated bull. In spite of the birth of three sons and two daughters between 1860 and 1868, Ann was increasingly active in station management; in this she had the backing of her husband, a humane and greatly respected man. When on 21 November 1868 he died suddenly, she took over the management of Wappan, developed it with determination and foresight, and remained in complete charge until her sons were old enough to share in the work, and then only under her direction.

Devoutly religious, imperious in her manner, a loving but stern mother, an autocrat with her domestic staff and stationhands, Ann Bon held firmly to her course even if it meant defying authority. Lonely and in many ways shy, she made few close friends, but to those in need, especially the Aboriginals, she showed compassion and generosity. Dispossessed members of the Taungerong tribe had found a refuge at Wappan; in the 1860s they were resettled at Coranderrk near Healesville, but on their annual return for shearing they kept Mrs Bon informed of their treatment by the Board for the Protection of the Aboriginals. Her home at Kew was a refuge for the sick and needy and she regularly visited Aboriginal patients in Melbourne hospitals. When her efforts to provide jobs and clothing were rebuked as 'interference' in 1879, she began to support Aboriginals who opposed protection board policy, notably Thomas 'Punch' Bamfield, henchman to William Barak [q.v.3]. Using her influence with leading Presbyterian clergymen and politicians, she persuaded the government to investigate conditions at Coranderrk in 1881; she accepted membership of the inquiry and succeeded in reversing policy. The antagonism of officials prevented her appointment to the protection board but she continued her direct intercessions with government members. In 1904 she became a board-member and attended regularly until 1936. She maintained a voluminous correspondence with Aboriginals all over Victoria, remaining uniquely responsible to them; she earned reprimands for 'disloyalty' in 1921, 1923 and 1936 when she protested to the minister that her colleagues' decisions had caused injustice or hardship.

Ann Bon was a member of the first ladies' committee of the Austin Hospital and a generous benefactor; she was a foundation member of the committee of the Charity Organisation Society and a lifelong supporter of the Salvation Army. She established a school for Chinese children in Melbourne and worked towards a more enlightened approach to mental sickness. She gave generously to the Presbyterian churches at Mansfield and Bonnie Doon and in World War I donated an ambulance to the Belgian Army, for which she was decorated in 1921 by King Leopold. Each Christmas she gave £20 to every blinded soldier in Victoria. As 'Sylvia', she wrote and published books of homely verse and hymns.

When it was clear that the construction of the Sugar Loaf Weir and Lake Eildon would eventually flood much of Wappan land, Mrs Bon retired to the Windsor Hotel, Melbourne, where she lived as a virtual recluse. She died, aged 98, on 5 June 1936 and was buried in Kew cemetery. In her later years she had been visited daily by William, the younger of her two surviving sons, who took up residence in Menzies Hotel when water reached the Wappan homestead; he too lived as a recluse.

A. Sutherland et al, *Victoria and its metropolis,* 2 (Melb, 1888); C. S. Ross, *The Scottish Church in Victoria* (Melb, 1901); J. Gillison, *Colonial doctor and his town* (Melb, 1974); *PD* (Vic), 1881, 37, 703; *PP* (Vic), 1882, 2 (5), 1882-83, 2 (5, 15); I. MacDonald, 'A woman of many parts', *Messenger* (Presbyterian, Vic), Feb 1951; A. Massola, 'Painting by Berak', *Vic Naturalist,* 76 (1959-60); *Australasian,* 19 Nov 1930; *Argus,* 12 June 1936, 10 Jan 1951; D. Barwick, Rebellion at Coranderrk (held by Barwick).   JOAN GILLISON

BOND, GEORGE ALAN (1876-1950), manufacturer, was born on 22 May 1876 at Louisville, Kentucky, United States of America, son of George Henry Bond, a Scottish horticulturist, and his wife Jane, née Redman. While still operating a small trading firm in New Jersey, Bond came to Sydney in 1906, followed by his wife Jeanette, née Hall, whom he had married in New York. He was naturalized in 1922.

Bond began business in Sydney as an importer of hosiery and underwear. With the outbreak of war in 1914 and consequent import shortages, he began manufacturing hosiery on a small scale at Redfern. The enterprise flourished and in June 1920 was converted into a public company, George A. Bond & Co. Ltd, with an issued capital of about £200 000. Bond as managing director supervised the firm's rapid growth in the 1920s; by 1927 it employed some 2600 people and had assets valued at £1 582 000. He and his wife held most of the ordinary shares and the firm was directly under the control of 'the chief'. Aided by substantial tariffs the manufacture of hosiery and knitted goods grew rapidly in the 1920s, and by 1925 he was

apparently producing about one-quarter of the total Australian output.

In 1923 Bond had begun the first significant attempt to spin and weave cotton in Australia by establishing a mill at Wentworthville. With government support, cotton was grown mainly in Queensland where his company owned two cotton farms; from 1926 it received a bounty for manufacturing yarn from local cotton. In 1926 he formed a subsidiary company, George A. Bond Cotton Mills Ltd.

Bond's profitable expansion and diversification of interests came to an abrupt halt in 1927: the value of stocks held by the parent company had risen to the ruinous figure of £650 000 and the Bank of New South Wales, which held a large overdraft, forced the firm into liquidation in December. The companies were carried on by the liquidators until sold in 1930 to an entirely new group, Bond's Industries Ltd, which ultimately flourished. The loss involved in the liquidation was probably the largest by a manufacturing company to that date: all the share capital to the value of £700 000 had to be written off.

Bond's whole fortune and much of his reputation were lost in the crash. He opposed the terms of the liquidation but was defeated in the Equity Court, and was held liable to his company for £90 000 for improperly drawn director's fees, commissions and other payments. Commonwealth, State and New Zealand taxation authorities claimed payment on concealed income. Bond fought bankruptcy proceedings to the High Court, lost and was declared bankrupt in April 1931. The principal unsecured claim was his debt to the company, but no assets were available and he was finally discharged in April 1935. He found employment at Summer Hill as manager of a small hosiery firm, the Jeanette Manufacturing Co., founded by his wife in 1928. Unable to re-establish himself, he was described as a commission agent when he died of atherosclerosis on 1 June 1950 at Ashfield and was cremated with Presbyterian rites. His wife had predeceased him in 1937; they had no children. His estate was valued for probate at £642.

Yarn Spinner (Syd), 1 (1926-27); file NSW 166 of 1930, District of NSW and ACT (Federal Court of Bankruptcy, Syd); George A. Bond & Co. Ltd papers (held by Bonds Coats Patons Ltd); G. A. Bond, CRS-A435, 50/4/4886 (AAO).   COLIN FORSTER

BONYTHON, SIR JOHN LANGDON (1848-1939), editor, newspaper proprietor and philanthropist, was born in London on 15 October 1848, second son of George Langdon Bonython, carpenter and builder, and his wife Ann, née McBain. The family arrived in South Australia in July 1854. Bonython attended Brougham School, North Adelaide, and in 1864 joined the *Advertiser* as a reporter. His abilities were recognized by J. H. Barrow [q.v.3], the editor, who soon put him in charge of the literary staff. On 24 December 1870 Bonython married Mary Louisa Fredericka Balthasar in Adelaide; they had eight children of whom three daughters and three sons survived infancy.

Successful speculation in mining shares helped Bonython to buy into the business in 1879 and when he was only 36 he became editor, a post he held for forty-five years. He became sole proprietor in 1893 and began to amass a personal fortune, which at the time of his death was one of the largest in Australia. The business remained under his direct control until 1929 when it was sold for £1 250 000 and turned into a public company.

Bonython had an unswerving ambition to excel. He possessed good health, abundant self-confidence, an unusual capacity for hard work and an ability to disengage himself in private from business worries. These attributes, together with his journalistic ability, sure business acumen and shrewd appreciation of public taste, were the basis of his remarkable success. Under his direction the *Advertiser* became a prominent Australian daily newspaper, addressing itself less to the conservative pastoral interests than to the small businessman and landholder. It reflected the aspirations of the growing middle class and its pride in the developing State and came to be identified with South Australia's progress. Through this the *Advertiser* prospered, although its financial success can also be attributed to the prominence given to the small advertisement. Above all, Bonython stressed that a newspaper should be full of news and its coverage as complete as possible. He was no friend of the Australian Journalists' Association.

Bonython maintained an independence from the ruling political and social élite and in fact did not join the Adelaide Club until his retirement at 81. However he exerted great influence. He expounded a liberal progressive policy, which in the 1890s had much in common with that of C. C. Kingston [q.v.], the radical premier. He was the confidant of many men in political and economic affairs at home, interstate and abroad and his aid was often enlisted in particular causes. In 1895 he assisted Chief Justice Sir Samuel Way [q.v.] to obtain a seat on the Judicial Committee of the Privy Council. He prevailed on Kingston to back Way's nomination despite a feud between the two,

and got David Syme [q.v.6] of the *Age* to secure the support of (Sir) George Turner [q.v.], the Victorian premier. Finally, he persuaded Kingston to visit Turner to clinch the matter. During these negotiations he abrogated his rule never to visit the office of a politician even though his own door was open to all-comers. Apart from Way, Bonython numbered Sir James Penn Boucaut [q.v.3], Alfred Deakin, Sir John (Earl) Forrest and Sir John Cockburn [qq.v.] among his friends.

Early in his career the cause of universal elementary education interested Bonython and the *Advertiser* commented fully on the developments which followed the Education Act, 1875. He was chairman of the board of advice for the school district of Adelaide in 1883-1901 and became particularly interested in technical education, considering it 'the master-key to that efficiency without which there can be no industrial or commercial success'. In 1886 he was appointed to a board to inquire into technical education and as a result of its report the South Australian School of Mines and Industries was established; from 1888 until his death he was a member, and for fifty years president, of its council. He was chairman of Roseworthy Agricultural College in 1895-1902, and a member of the Council of the University of Adelaide in 1916-39. He was knighted in 1898: that year he and (Sir) J. R. Fairfax [q.v.] of the *Sydney Morning Herald* became the first Australian newspaper proprietors to be so honoured.

Through the *Advertiser* Bonython advocated Federation, but he wanted the rights of the smaller States to be more explicitly safeguarded than was proposed. In 1901 he was elected to the House of Representatives, being second to Kingston in a State-wide poll. He was re-elected unopposed in 1903 for the division of Barker. In the House he favoured protection, retrenchment, and the White Australia policy. He advanced the interests of South Australian local industry and urged the Commonwealth to take over the Northern Territory. He became a follower of Alfred Deakin, who wanted him to give his full time to politics; their friendship survived a sharp disagreement over the composition of Deakin's ministry of July 1905 and his disappointment that Deakin's recommendation of him for a K.C.M.G. in 1908 was not accepted. Bonython did not contest the 1906 election although the Labor Party proposed to grant him, and other Protectionists, immunity from opposition; he suspected that his party would soon be out of power and travelling to Melbourne for parliamentary sittings was becoming irksome.

Bonython was a member of the royal

commission on old-age pensions in 1905-06 and helped to establish the Commonwealth Literary Fund, serving as chairman in 1908-29. He was a trustee and one of seven commissioners appointed under the Australian Soldiers' Repatriation Acts of 1916 and 1917. He was appointed C.M.G. in 1908 and K.C.M.G. in 1919 for his services to the Commonwealth.

To some he seemed parsimonious, but most found him more than generous. Bonython made many important public benefactions, mostly to educational institutions. In 1902-37 he gave £22750 to the School of Mines and Industries, £20 000 to the University of Adelaide in 1926 to endow a chair of law, and £50000 in 1930-34 for the erection of the Bonython Hall. His largest benefaction was made in 1934, when he gave £100000 towards the cost of completing Parliament House. He distributed meal tickets to the needy in bad times, guaranteed the account of a printing firm, Mail Newspapers Ltd, for £2500 during a difficult period, and helped the government pay the salaries of the civil service during a financial crisis in the Depression. Bonython contributed to a variety of causes and institutions during his lifetime and beneficiaries under his will included the Pirie Street Methodist Church, where he always worshipped and of which he was a trustee; St Peter's Cathedral, to which he donated the cost of the canons' and choir stalls in 1925 in memory of his wife who had died the previous year; and the Salvation Army.

Bonython was descended from an old Cornish family and, inspired by his grandmother, took an interest in his heritage. He had a fine library of books on Cornish history and was patron of the South Australian Cornish Association and a member of the English Royal Institution of Cornwall. Although he acquired some family relics, he deeply regretted that he could not buy back Bonython, the family seat in Cornwall. He was proud of the honours bestowed on him though, towards the end of his life, he desired an hereditary title, a baronetcy or a barony, but it was not forthcoming.

Bonython was a short, distinguished-looking man who could be stern and was strict with his children. His family were somewhat awed by his achievements and his expectation that his male descendants at least should strive to follow his example. Personally fastidious, and suspicious of anything that might harbour germs, he enjoyed good health until the end of his life. He died on 22 October 1939, aged 91, and after a service in St Peter's Anglican Cathedral and a state funeral he was buried in West Terrace cemetery. His estate was sworn for probate at over £4 million. Portraits hang in Parliament House, Adelaide, the board room of Advertiser Newspapers Ltd and Bonython Hall; others are held by the family.

A. J. Hannan, *The life of Chief Justice Way* (Syd, 1960); D. Green (ed), *An age of technology 1889-1964* (Adel, 1964); J. A. La Nauze, *Alfred Deakin* (Melb, 1965); E. G. Bonython, *History of the families of Bonython . . .* (Adel, 1966); T. T. Reed, *A history of the Cathedral Church of St Peter* (Adel, 1969); P. M. Weller (ed), *Caucus minutes*, 1-3 (Melb, 1975); 'The great Australasian dailies', *Review of Reviews* (A'sian ed), 1892; *Advertiser* (Adel), 24 Feb 1903, 15 Oct 1928, 26 Sept 1934, 23 Oct 1939; *Mail* (Adel), 12 Oct 1918; *Smith's Weekly* (Syd), 15 Oct 1938; R. L. Butler papers (SAA); Deakin papers (NL); information from the late Sir William Bishop, Sir Fred Drew, Glenelg East, and Mr L. C. Hunkin, Marion, SA.   W. B. PITCHER

BONYTHON, SIR JOHN LAVINGTON (1875-1960), newspaper editor and company director, was born in Adelaide on 10 September 1875, eldest son of (Sir) John Langdon Bonython [q.v.] and his wife Mary Louise Fredericka, née Balthasar. Educated at Prince Alfred College, he entered the *Advertiser* office after a world tour in 1896. He was associated with his father in the management of the *Advertiser,* the *Chronicle* and the *Express,* and edited the *Saturday Express* in 1912-30; he was proud of his accuracy as a journalist.

Much of Bonython's energy was devoted to civic affairs. He was elected to the Adelaide City Council in 1901; this association spanned over fifty years. In 1907 he became an alderman and in 1912-13 was the youngest man to have become mayor of Adelaide; in 1928-30 he was lord mayor. The affairs of the city that he loved, and which he seldom left, absorbed much of his public life and he became concerned with preserving the heritage, particularly the Park Lands, bequeathed to its citizens by Colonel Light [q.v.2]. In 1935 he presented a clock for the town hall tower. He was a member, sometime chairman, of the boards of the abattoirs, Municipal Tramways Trust, Royal Adelaide Hospital, Metropolitan Infectious Diseases Hospital, fire brigade and other public utilities. He also held high office in the Adelaide School Board, the Botanic Garden, the South Australian Institution for the Blind and Deaf and Dumb, the Taxpayers' Association, the Royal Society of St George, and the Royal Commonwealth Society. Bonython served on the board of Minda Home for retarded children from its inception in 1898 for sixty-two years, for twenty-six of which he was president; in 1956 he provided a large sum for a building there which was named for him. He was knighted in 1935.

Temperamentally, Bonython was not suited to succeed his father as sole proprietor of the *Advertiser,* but when it was sold in 1929 and converted into a public company he became a director; for a time he was vice-chairman and retained the association until his death. His business interests extended to other fields: he was chairman of directors of the Executor Trustee & Agency Co. and served on the boards of several other companies. He also had close associations with the South Australian Housing Trust, the Adelaide Chamber of Commerce and the Liberal and Country League of South Australia. He was a member of the Adelaide Club.

Bonython was twice married: first on 16 April 1904 to Blanche Ada Bray, who died in childbirth in 1908 leaving two daughters and a son; second on 11 December 1912 to Constance Jean Warren; they had two sons and a daughter. Lady Bonython (1891-1977) was educated at Dryburgh House School and the Geelong Church of England Girls' Grammar School. Shortly after her marriage, when she was 21, she became mayoress and carried out her duties with great assurance. She was prominent in the Mothers' and Babies' Health Association, the Kindergarten Union of South Australia, the Pre-School Association and other welfare organizations. In 1936 she was one of two women on the Adelaide Centenary Committee. For many years she encouraged contemporary painters and was involved in the affairs of the South Australian Symphony Orchestra from its inception. In 1954 she was appointed O.B.E.

Bonython was a regular churchgoer and a trustee of the Pirie Street Methodist Church for over thirty years. Of slightly more than average height and of slim build, he was a careful man of abstemious and frugal habits: he used public transport to go to his office. He was possibly rather inhibited by close and lengthy association with his forceful father, to whom he was devoted. He died on 6 November 1960 and was buried in the family grave. His estate was sworn for probate at £276412. A large portrait hangs in the council chamber of the Adelaide City Council and a smaller one is held by the family.

Bonython's son by his first marriage, John Langdon (b. 1905) is a prominent businessman; Charles Warren (b. 1916), conservationist and chemical engineer, and Hugh Reskymer (Kim), D.F.C., A.F.C. (b. 1920), art dealer and jazz and speedway entrepreneur, are sons of the second marriage.

H. T. Burgess (ed), *Cyclopedia of South Australia,* 1 (Adel, 1908); E. G. Bonython, *History of the families of Bonython* . . . (Adel, 1966); *SA Methodist,* 11 Nov 1960; *Advertiser* (Adel), 7 Nov 1960, 13 June 1977; information from Mr J. L. Bonython, Medindie, and Mr C. W. Bonython, Magill, SA.

W. B. PITCHER

BOOTE, HENRY ERNEST (1865-1949), Labor propagandist, journalist and writer, was born on 20 May 1865 at Liverpool, England, eldest child of Joseph Henry Boote, mercer, and his wife Elizabeth Hampden, née Jolley. He had left school by 10 and was apprenticed to a printer. He educated himself by reading in local free libraries and developed an interest in painting. An art-dealer engaged him at 20 as a copyist and later commissioned works for sale. Boote saved some money and in 1889 migrated to Australia, finding work as a compositor in Brisbane. He had a strong working-class consciousness, was a keen trade unionist and soon became closely involved in the affairs of the Queensland labour movement, displaying talent as a socialist propagandist and writer. He experienced a sense of being 'born again' and developed a lifelong belief in the moral righteousness of the organized working-class cause and the inevitability of socialism.

In 1894 Boote was sent to Bundaberg by the Australian Labour Federation to edit the *Bundaberg Guardian,* a twice-weekly paper noted for its opposition to the employment of Kanaka labour in the sugar industry. Two years later he moved to Gympie to found and edit the Gympie *Truth* for Andrew Fisher [q.v.] with whom he lodged. In 1902 he became editor in Brisbane of the *Worker,* to which he had long contributed articles. He established a reputation as an essayist and poet among fellow contributors such as Henry Lawson, (Dame) Mary Gilmore, R. J. Quinn [qq.v.] and Norman Lilly. His regular articles under the pseudonym 'Touchstone' led to the publication of his first book of essays, *A fool's talk* (Sydney, 1915).

In 1911 Boote had moved to Sydney as leader and feature writer on the *Australian Worker,* the official organ of the Australian Workers' Union; he was editor in 1914-43. A close confidant and friend of Labor leaders such as E. G. Theodore, J. H. Scullin [qq.v.], Fisher, John Curtin and H. V. Evatt, he came to exercise a profound influence on the shape and direction of party policy as well as on the wider political and industrial scene. His regular editorials, signed 'H.E.B.', were closely followed by serious students of labour affairs. Often he tried to reconcile socialist idealism with the practical day-to-day realities of Australian politics, and to produce a guiding philosophy — radical but gradualist and Fabian in style — to which all members of the labour movement could subscribe.

When Labor split over conscription in 1916 Boote became probably the foremost Australia-wide publicist for the 'No' case in the referenda. The 1917 A.W.U. convention unanimously passed a resolution of thanks to him, with vociferous cheering. Ian Turner has remarked that no man at that time was 'more widely known and respected' in the labour movement. In November he was prosecuted under the War Precautions Act for publishing articles, notably 'The lottery of death', which were prejudicial to recruiting. Despite W. M. Hughes's [q.v.] promise that political matter would not be subject to censorship, he was fined £100 and costs. Late in 1916 Boote had begun to champion the cause of the twelve gaoled Industrial Workers of the World and in March 1917 was convicted of contempt of court. One hundred thousand copies of his pamphlet *Guilty or not guilty?* were distributed. He began his campaign largely from loyalty to one of the prisoners, his friend Donald Grant [q.v.], but became convinced that none of the twelve should have been convicted. His sustained agitation was largely responsible for the N. K. Ewing [q.v.] royal commission of 1920 after which ten of the twelve were freed.

At first a supporter of the radical 'one big union' idea, which swept through the labour movement at the close of World War I, Boote later assisted conservative elements in the A.W.U. to defeat the proposal. Left-wing attacks on his employers' leadership made his support for them inevitable; but, to Boote, his about-face was justified by leftist excesses. Though an ardent internationalist he had been soured by developments in Russia after 1917; he also saw the coloured races excluded, by their numbers and underdevelopment, from real unity with the Australian labour movement, and was repelled by left-wing attempts to develop links with Communist front organizations such as the Pan-Pacific Trade Union Secretariat to which the new Australasian Council of Trade Unions was affiliated in 1927-30. He was also angered by the support given by left-wing unionists to J. T. Lang [q.v.], whom he regarded as a potential dictator.

Nevertheless, with the rise of the Fascist powers in the 1930s and the adoption of a conciliatory united front policy by the Comintern after 1934, Boote moved back towards outspoken endorsement of some leftist causes. In the late 1930s he supported collective security and severely criticized the Australian Labor Party for its isolationism. In 1940 he threatened to resign from the *Australian Worker* when his article supporting the 'Hands Off Russia' resolution by the New South Wales branch of the A.L.P. was suppressed by A.W.U. officials. Despite increasing disenchantment he continued as editor until grave illness forced him to retire in March 1943.

In private life Boote was shy and reticent, known to his friends and acquaintances as a talented artist and lover of music. In 1926-42 he was a trustee of the Public Library of New South Wales and also served as a member of the Mitchell Library committee. On 6 October 1889 in Brisbane, with Roman Catholic rites, he had married Mary Jane Paingdestre; they had two daughters and a son. Boote separated from his wife just before he moved to Sydney in 1911, but they were not divorced. For the rest of his life he lived with the journalist and writer, Mary Ellen Lloyd (d. 1967) at their home, May Day, at Rose Bay; it seemed to friends an 'idyllic existence – a living, warm, fragile, friendly serenity'. He remained in quiet retirement until his death on 14 August 1949; he was buried in South Head cemetery after a service conducted by the rationalist H. Scott Bennett [q.v.].

Boote has been all but ignored by literary historians, yet he was one of the most prolific writers of his era; in old age he was granted a Commonwealth Literary Fund pension. His publications range across numerous straight political and social commentaries, mainly pamphlets, to political novels such as *The human ladder* (1920); a satirical allegory entitled *The land of Wherisit* (1919); essays and sketches in *Tea with the Devil and other diversions* (1928); and several volumes of verse. All these works carry the stamp of Boote's socialist philosophy, but their didacticism is to some extent redeemed by his very competent and lively style.

H. E. Boote, *Sidelights on two referendums, 1916-1917,* M. E. Lloyd ed (Syd, 1952); I. Turner, *Sydney's burning,* 2nd ed (Syd, 1969); D. J. Murphy, 'Henry Boote's papers', *Labour Hist,* Nov 1968, no 15; *Worker* (Syd), 1 Apr 1911, 15, 22 Aug 1949; *Aust Worker,* 29 June, 17, 24, 31 Aug 1949; F. Farrell, International socialism and Australian labour (Ph.D. thesis, ANU, 1975); T. J. O'Sullivan, Saga of events in the trade union movement and political Labor party (1946, ML); H. E. Boote-T. J. O'Sullivan correspondence (ML); Boote papers (NL).
FRANK FARRELL

BOOTH, DORIS REGINA (1895-1970), nursing volunteer and goldminer, was born at South Brisbane on 1 October 1895, daughter of Henry Wilde, clerk, and his wife Minna Christina, née Gerler. After a state school education, she enrolled as a trainee nurse at Brisbane General Hospital but met Captain Charles Booth, a shell-shocked soldier who had prospected in Papua before the war; she discontinued her training when they married on 14 May 1919. After twelve penurious months at Mitchell in western Queensland, Booth became a plantation manager for the New Guinea Expropriation Board at Raniolo near Kokopo. When he was discharged late in 1923, his wife took a share in four trade-stores and broke local convention by becoming a licensed recruiter of labour. Financed by Burns Philp [qq.v.] & Co. Ltd, they went surreptitiously to Salamaua in 1924 following rumour of gold. Booth went ahead to the Bulolo valley while his wife secured her own miner's right, refused earlier in Rabaul; single-handed, she then spent five weeks taking a line of carriers from Salamaua to Bulolo. There, while her husband prospected, she was employed by William ('Sharkeye') Park to 'man' his lease.

Booth pegged a lease in his wife's name, then left her as the only resident white woman at Bulolo to work it while he prospected at Edie Creek. From September 1926 to January 1927 she also organized and managed a racially segregated bush hospital to control a dysentery epidemic, treating over 32 patients at one time and more than 130 all told. For this work she received the O.B.E. in 1928 and became known locally as 'the Angel of Bulolo'.

One of their leases was sold in April 1927 to Morobe Guinea Gold Ltd and Mrs Booth became a director of the firm.

While Mrs Booth went to Australia for her health and for business between 1927 and 1930, the marriage began to collapse. Nevertheless, the couple travelled to the United States of America and England and while in London in 1928, with M. O'Dwyer as ghost-writer, she published *Mountain gold and cannibals*, a popularized version of her experiences. After her return to New Guinea in March 1929 she slowly wrested control over the family business affairs from her husband, whom she left early in 1932.

Booth sued in the Central Court of the Territory of New Guinea in August 1933 for restitution of property. Since no Mandated Territory law explicitly safeguarded married women's property rights, it was a test case. Judge F. B. Phillips [q.v.] held that British and Australian Acts passed before 1921 superseded the common law notion of male control of joint property and gave Mrs Booth the verdict. When Booth appealed this particularly acrimonious case to the High Court of Australia, the judgment was upheld and territorial law was amended by the Status of Married Women Ordinance 1935-36.

There is no evidence that the couple were ever formally divorced; Booth returned to prospecting while his wife became a suc-

cessful mine-manager and company director. Settling in Brisbane in July 1938, she worked for the Mothercraft Association until after 1945 when she was involved in rebuilding her business from war-damage insurance. Appointed as the sole woman member of the first and second Legislative Councils of Papua-New Guinea in 1951-57, she supported mining interests, public health, secondary education for black and white, land and housing loans for Europeans and the sexual protection of native women. Doris Booth was a strong opponent of the liquor (natives) bill of 1955, and of a section in the public service bill (1953) restricting married women to temporary or exempt positions. She represented the women of Papua-New Guinea at the Pan-Pacific Women's Conference of 1955 in Manila. She retired to Brisbane in 1960, did volunteer work with the Methodist Blue Nursing Service, and died of coronary vascular disease at St Andrew's War Memorial Hospital on 4 November 1970.

L. Rhys, *High lights and flights in New Guinea* (Lond, 1942); *Cwlth Law Reports*, 53 (1935), 1-32; *Pacific Islands Mthly,* June 1954, Dec 1970; *Rabaul Times,* 8 Dec 1933; High Court of Aust, Transcript of procs, 1934, annotated by C. Booth, MS 5669 (NL); A518: AJ/824/1, AC836/3, A846/1/66, 81 (AAO, Canb); information from Mrs Eileen Bulmer, Caloundra, Qld.   SUSAN GARDNER

BOOTH, HERBERT HENRY (1862-1926), Salvationist, was born on 26 August 1862 at Penzance, Cornwall, England, fifth child of William Booth and his wife Catherine, née Mumford. William Booth had resigned from the ministry of the Methodist New Connexion Church in 1861 and established in London the East London Revival Society which, after several changes of name, became known in 1878 as the Salvation Army, with William as general.

Herbert received little formal elementary education but became a student at Allesly Park College and the Congregational Institute at Nottingham. Along with others of the family, he threw himself into army work in France (1880-82) and in Britain as principal of the Officers' Training Home. After an overseas tour in 1888 Herbert was given the title of commandant by the general and placed in charge of army operations in Britain. An able musician and splendid showman, in 1890 he organized a grand demonstration at the Crystal Palace for which later that year he published *Songs of peace and war*. On 18 September at Clapton he married Cornelie Schoch, daughter of a Dutch Salvationist.

Herbert was involved in family arguments that developed after his mother's death in 1890. Because of disagreements with his brother Bramwell he successfully requested in 1892 a posting to Canada; in 1895 he reluctantly obeyed orders to take up the Australasian command.

The Booths and their three sons arrived in Melbourne on 25 August 1896. Three months later Herbert launched his 'Move-on Manifesto', an ambitious plan for the Australian army based on the general's scheme of social salvation outlined in his *In darkest England and the way out* (London, 1890). The Booths, talented in public relations and administration, attracted financial support for the army's social work, especially in Victoria where the organization was well established and respected and where state aid was available for welfare work. Institutions established by the Booths in Victoria became models for army work in other countries and for welfare work in Australia.

Many Salvationists were critical of Herbert's leadership. A decline in membership strengthened accusations that he was promoting social at the expense of spiritual work. Most dissatisfaction concerned his dictatorial leadership. He refused to implement new regulations from headquarters which weakened the powers of territorial commanders and insisted on choosing his own staff. Family arguments again came to the fore and in 1901 Herbert asked to be relieved of the Australasian command and to be appointed superintendent of the army's farm for boys and girls at Collie, Western Australia, where he arrived on 1 October. Early next year, after hearing of his sister Catherine's resignation from the army, he decided to follow her. In February he and Cornelie left Collie quietly and in August embarked for San Francisco.

The 'five conquering years' of Herbert Booth's leadership left an indelible imprint on the Australian Salvation Army. Apart from the extension of the social wing, his legacy included the establishment of a national training college for officers in East Melbourne and the growth of the *War Cry* to a sixteen-page national paper printed on the army's own press. He also steered to completion the spectacular *Soldiers of the Cross*, a mixture of slides and moving picture; produced in order to raise money for the army's work, it has an important place in the history of Australian film.

In the United States of America Herbert became an Evangelist, and travelled in North America and South Africa with *Soldiers of the Cross*. In 1915 he established the Christian Confederacy in America, whose pacifist philosophy he expounded in several publications including *The saint and the sword* (New York, 1924).

Cornelie Booth died in 1919. In November 1923, on his return to New York from an evangelistic tour of New Zealand and Australia, Herbert married Australian-born Anna Ethel Lane. She and two sons of his first marriage survived him when he died at Yonkers, New York, on 25 September 1926.

F. C. Ottman, *Herbert Booth: Salvationist* (Lond, 1929); R. Sandall, *The history of the Salvation Army*, 3 (Lond, 1955); R. Howe, '"Five Conquering Years". The leadership of Commandant and Mrs H. Booth . . . 1896 to 1901', *J Religious History*, 6 (1970-71), no 2; *New York Times*, 26 Sept 1926; information from Mr John Blake, South Blackburn, Vic. RENATE HOWE

BOOTH, MARY (1869-1956), physician and welfare worker, was born on 9 July 1869 at Burwood, Sydney, eldest of three daughters of William Booth, schoolmaster, and his wife Ruth, née Sewell. Educated by Mrs Cornell, she matriculated from Airlie School in 1886 and attended the University of Sydney (B.A., 1890). In 1891-93 she was governess to the children of the earl of Jersey [q.v.], governor of New South Wales. A legacy from her maternal grandfather Thomas Sewell in 1893 gave her some financial independence. After briefly studying as a medical student at the University of Melbourne in 1894, she left for Scotland, accompanied by her sister Eliza (Bay), and in July next year enrolled at the College of Medicine for Women, University of Edinburgh (M.B., C.M., 1899). After some experience in infirmaries, she returned to Sydney in 1900.

Dr Booth's medical career was relatively short lived and she never worked in an Australian hospital. Although she kept rooms near Macquarie Street until 1910, much of her practice was contractual with, for example, the Australian Mutual Provident Society. Appointed to the Department of the Government Statistician as anthropometrist in 1900, she lectured on hygiene at girls' secondary schools. Strongly feminist, she was a founder of the Women's Club in 1901, and corresponding secretary in 1905-07 and later a vice-president of the National Council of Women of New South Wales. She was lecturer in hygiene for the Department of Public Instruction in 1904-09, and then in 1910-12 was employed by the Victorian Department of Education to help to establish the first school medical service in that State. She published in the *Transactions* of the Australasian Medical Congress and of the Australasian Association for the Advancement of Science, and in the *Australasian Medical*

Gazette. In 1913 she visited Britain and represented the Commonwealth government at the English-Speaking Conference on Infant Mortality, London.

Back in Sydney by 1914, Mary Booth quickly responded to the domestic problems raised by World War I; her offer to supervise refugee camps in Egypt was refused as she was too well qualified. In November she founded the Babies' Kit Society for the Allies' Babies and in June next year opened the Soldiers' Club in the Royal Hotel, George Street; she was its honorary secretary until it closed in 1923, and she ran it very strictly. From September 1915 she was a member of the executive committee of the Universal Service League and campaigned vigorously for conscription. Other war-work included organizing the Centre for Soldiers' Wives and Mothers and setting up a war widows' fund. In 1918 she was appointed O.B.E. She was defeated in 1920 for the North Shore seat in the Legislative Assembly as an independent feminist candidate and, supported by the Women's Reform League, failed after negotiations to stand for a Senate seat in 1922.

Fiercely patriotic, Dr Booth determined to promote and protect the Anzac tradition; in 1921 she founded the Anzac Fellowship of Women and remained president until 1956. It was the only civilian organization granted the right by W. M. Hughes [q.v.] to use the name 'Anzac'. An equally ardent advocate of increased immigration, she was an office-bearer of the New Settlers' League of Australia, and a member of the Women's Migration Council of New South Wales. When British ex-servicewomen began arriving in Sydney, mostly as assisted migrants, she founded the Ex Service Women's Club. From 1921 she looked after boys migrating under the 'Dreadnought scheme' and in 1923 set up the Empire Service Club. She raised funds, supervised the Empire Service Hostel and in 1925-44 published the monthly *Boy Settler*, all as a contribution to maintaining 'our own British Stock' and counteracting communism. She kept in contact with her boys and worked closely with the Department of Labour.

Incorrigibly active, Dr Booth belonged to the University of Sydney Society for Combating Venereal Diseases after the war, and in the 1920s to the League of Nations Union and the English-Speaking Union. A member of the Town Planning Association of New South Wales, in 1920 she told the royal commission on the basic wage that young families could be happily brought up in a flat if it was designed with proper space for the children; in 1929 she attended the 12th Congress of the International Federation for Housing and Town Planning in Rome, and visited Britain.

In 1931 the Anzac Fellowship of Women set up the Anzac Festival Committee, with Dr Booth as chairman and the governor-general Lord Gowrie and Lady Gowrie [qq.v.] as patrons, to encourage the arts rather than sport in the 'Anzac Season'. In 1939 Mary Booth persuaded Sir Robert Garran [q.v.] to write the script for a historical pageant beginning with Richard Coeur de Lion. Her last major initiative was to found in 1936 the Memorial College of Household Arts and Science, on land adjoining her home at Kirribilli; she firmly believed that 'good wives make good husbands'. In 1961 its funds were used to found the Dr Mary Booth scholarship for women economics students at the University of Sydney.

She died in the Rachel Forster Hospital for Women and Children on 28 November 1956 and was cremated with Anglican rites. Her estate was valued for probate at £14335.

Royal Commission on the basic wage (Syd, 1920), Evidence; National Council of Women (NSW), *Jubilee Report, 1896-1946*; *MJA*, 23 Feb 1957; R. F. H. Row, 'School medical services in Victoria', *Health Bulletin* (Vic), 5 (1959); *SMH*, 21 Feb 1920, 26 July, 9 Nov 1929, 27 Apr 1958, 17 May 1969; I. L. Marden, Dr. Mary Booth ... (1957, ML); R. Mackinnon, Mary Booth, a biography (1969, ML); Anzac Fellowship of Women papers (NL); Mary Booth papers (ML); Miles Franklin correspondence, 1923-53 (ML); R. R. Garran papers (NL).

J. I. ROE

BOOTH, NORMAN PARR (1879?-1950), analytical chemist and businessman, was born at Honley near Huddersfield, Yorkshire, England, son of Clarkson Booth of Cadbury Bros Ltd at Bournville. He was educated at Huddersfield, at King Edward VI Grammar School, Camp Hill, Birmingham, and Mason Science College.

In 1898-1901 Booth was employed in the analytical laboratory of the Worshipful Society of Apothecaries of London, rising to chief assistant. In 1900 he became an associate of the Institute of Chemistry of Great Britain and Ireland and in 1903 a fellow. He joined Cadbury Bros in 1901 as its first analytical chemist. His research was central to the development of both Cadbury milk chocolate, produced commercially in 1905, and the famous Bournville cocoa, marketed in 1906. He was responsible for the technical aspects of the company's first milk-condensing factory at Knighton in 1911 and of the later Frampton plant.

In 1924 Booth, by now chief chemist at Bournville in charge of a large research laboratory, succeeded William Cooper as chairman and managing director of Cadbury-Fry-Pascall Ltd, opened in 1922 at Claremont, Tasmania. Following in the tradition of the Quaker Cadbury family, Booth excelled in industrial relations and was respected for his fairness, firmness and courtesy. He presided over a remarkable expansion at Claremont, despite temporary 'heartbreaking' cut backs in production and employment during the Depression.

In England Booth had been a member of the Bournville works and village councils, a trustee of the men's pension fund, and a substantial contributor to the firm's war effort for men on leave during World War I. He also contributed to the Tasmanian community. He had a lifelong interest in theatre and had been a founder of the Bournville Dramatic Society: he helped to establish the Hobart Repertory Theatre Society, was later its president and took the lead in the acquisition, renovation and extension of its present playhouse. Tall and handsome, Booth himself was an enthusiastic player, his performances being notable for their force and gusto.

Interested also in technical education, Booth was a member of the Engineering Board of Management of the University of Tasmania and the Hobart Technical College; served on the latter's council, where he emphasized the importance of chemistry; and was a promoter in 1938 of the Tasmanian section of the Australian Chemical Institute. He was a member of his State's committee of the Council for Scientific and Industrial Research, the Food Standards Committee, the Hobart Chamber of Commerce, the Tasmanian Chamber of Manufactures and the Tasmanian branch of the Economic Society of Australia and New Zealand. He was active in Rotary, a justice of the peace, a trustee of the Tasmanian Museum and Botanical Gardens and a member of the Tasmanian Club. He visited England after his retirement in December 1938 but returned to lend his expertise to the wartime control of industry as a member of the Administrative Authority for Tasmania.

Booth married Ellen Fellows (d. 1945) on 28 May 1902 at Balsall Heath, Birmingham. She shared his theatrical interests, was a special magistrate under the Infants' Welfare Act (1935) and also a justice of the peace. Booth died of hypertensive heart disease in Hobart on 18 February 1950, aged 71, survived by two sons. In Hobart he was remembered for the part he played in the community and at Cadbury's as the man who made 'Claremont something more than a factory and who was something more than a Chairman of Directors'. His estate was sworn for probate at £33 925 in Tasmania and £3344 gross in England.

I. A. Williams, *The firm of Cadbury 1831-1931* (Lond, 1931); Hobart Repertory Theatre Soc, *Golden jubilee, 1926-1976* (Hob, 1976); *Bournville Works Mag*, Aug 1939; *Tas Mail*, 6 Mar 1924; *Mercury*, 24 Sept 1934, 19 Dec 1938, 20 Feb 1950; notes from Mr J. Reynolds, West Hobart.

G. P. R. CHAPMAN

BOOTHBY, GUY NEWELL (1867-1905), novelist, was born on 13 October 1867 at Glen Osmond, South Australia, son of Thomas Wilde Boothby [q.v.3], stock and station agent and politician, and his wife Mary Agnes, née Hodding; he was a grandson of Judge Benjamin Boothby [q.v.3]. About 1874 Guy went with his mother and brothers to England where he was educated at the Priory School, Salisbury, and Warminster Grammar School. Aged 16 he returned to his father and worked as a clerk in the Adelaide town clerk's office. He became private secretary to the mayor (Sir) Lewis Cohen [q.v.] in 1890.

The *South Australian Register* had been accepting some of Boothby's contributions and he also wrote plays and musical comedies which he showed to leading actresses. Several of his works were performed locally, and included the author as actor, but none was really successful. *The Jonquille* (1891), which the *Observer* said 'fell flat', was an ambitious melodrama with a French Revolution setting; a repeat 'author's benefit' performance was financially unrewarding.

With a friend, Longley Taylor, Boothby sailed steerage for England in December 1891, but they ran out of funds, landed at Colombo and wandered for some months. Sometimes working before the mast, they touched at Singapore, Borneo and Java, stayed on Thursday Island where Boothby dived for pearl-shell, drifted down the Queensland coast, and travelled overland by buggy from Normanton to the Darling River.

Next year Boothby wrote up this experience in the autobiographical *On the wallaby* which he took to England and had published in 1894. That year his first novel, *In strange company*, also appeared and did well. On 8 October 1895, with four more novels written, he married Rose Alice Bristowe in London. Six thousand words a day became his average output and fifty novels appeared over the next ten years. The stories, packed with bizarre events ingeniously linked, were related in a light ironic tone. Boothby claimed that he was encouraged by his 'pal' Rudyard Kipling. The early novels about Australia were among his best; he later used more exotic settings and themes, of which a series about Dr Nikola was extremely popular. Nikola resembled Mephistopheles, possessed hypnotic powers and studied witchcraft and the occult. 'Frank sensationalism carried to its furthest limits', said *The Times* critic, but Boothby unashamedly aimed to entertain his avid audience: 'I give the reading public what they want . . . in return my readers give me what I want'. His income rose to possibly £20000 a year: he lived comfortably, collecting books, breeding horses, cattle and bulldogs, and keeping an exotic aquarium at his mansion, Winsley Lodge, at Boscombe near Bournemouth. With success, his method of working became more eccentric. He retired at nine o'clock, rose in the small hours, dictated into a wax-cylinder phonograph, and required his two secretaries to get up at 5.30 a.m. and transcribe the result into typescript.

Survived by his wife, two daughters and a son, Boothby died suddenly of pneumonia on 26 February 1905, aged 37, and was buried at Bournemouth.

Windsor Mag, Dec 1896; *Athenaeum* (Lond), 4 Mar 1905; *Bulletin,* 7, 14, 21 Nov 1891, 9 Mar 1905, 24 Feb 1960; *Australasian,* 9 Nov 1901; *The Times,* 28 Feb 1905; *Advertiser* (Adel), and *Register* (Adel), 1 Mar 1905; *Bournemouth Guardian,* 4 Mar 1905.

BORCHGREVINK, CARSTEN EGEBERG (1864-1934), Antarctic explorer, was born on 1 December 1864 in Christiania, Norway, son of Henrik Christian Borchgrevink, barrister, and his wife Annie, née Ridley. Educated at Gjertsen College, he later studied natural science at the Royal College in Tharandt, Saxony. After returning to Norway in 1888, he migrated to Australia where he worked on survey teams in Queensland and New South Wales. In 1892-94 he taught languages and natural science at the Cooerwull Academy, Bowenfels, New South Wales.

Borchgrevink claimed to have had a continuing interest in polar exploration, and to have been stimulated by the work of local scientific enthusiasts on the first Australian Antarctic Committee. In 1894 the Norwegian H. J. Bull, a former resident of Victoria, organized an Antarctic whaling expedition in the ship *Antarctic;* it called at Melbourne and Borchgrevink signed on as a deck-hand, with permission to carry out scientific work as well. After many vicissitudes a landing was made at Cape Adare on the Antarctic continental mainland on 24 January 1895 with Borchgrevink claiming to be the first man to set foot thereon. Re-

turning to Australia and later to England, he read numerous papers to learned societies and worked to gain support for an expedition, led by himself, to spend a winter and carry out scientific work at Cape Adare. His scientific writings encouraged the English geographical authorities to increase their efforts to organize a large expedition, but when he gained the financial support of his employer, the publisher Sir George Newnes, their approval turned to resentment. Nevertheless his plans proceeded; the *Pollux* was purchased and renamed *Southern Cross,* barque-rigged, and fitted with steam-engines. A small scientific staff was chosen, including L. C. Bernacchi [q.v.].

The party left Hobart on 19 December 1898; a base was set up at Cape Adare next February. Man's first winter on the continental mainland was spent with only one death to mar the achievement; they landed on the Ross Barrier for the first time, and made a sledge journey thereon to latitude 78°50'S, the highest southern latitude reached in the Antarctic to that date. Valuable scientific work of a pioneering nature was carried out, but did not receive due recognition at the time because of Borchgrevink's low standing in England. None the less, he was made a fellow of the Royal Geographical Society on his return. His own sovereign appointed him a knight of St Olaf and he received similar honours from Denmark (1907) and Austria (1911). In 1904 the Royal Scottish Geographical Society awarded him its silver medal. Finally, in 1930, after the value of his work had been fully recognized, the Royal Geographical Society awarded him its Patron's Medal. The English edition of Borchgrevink's book, *First on the Antarctic continent* (London, 1901), was criticized for its journalistic style; the German and Norwegian versions carried fuller accounts of the party's scientific achievements. His only other field-work of note was during 1902 when he went to the West Indies on a scientific expedition for the National Geographic Society to study the effects of recent volcanic eruptions.

On 7 September 1896 at the parish church of Thorpe-le-Soken, Essex, Borchgrevink had married Constance Prior Standen; they had two sons and two daughters. He died in Oslo on 21 April 1934 and was cremated. Although he had been somewhat obsessed by a desire to be first and was not a properly trained scientist, his pioneering work in the Antarctic was valuable to later, more elaborate, scientific expeditions.

R. A. Swan, *Australia in the Antarctic* (Melb, 1961); *JRAHS,* 46 (1960), pts 1, 3; *PRGSSA,* 68 (1966-67); *Polar Record,* 17 (1975), no 108.

R. A. SWAN

BOREHAM, FRANK WILLIAM (1871-1959), preacher and writer, was born on 3 March 1871 at Tunbridge Wells, Kent, England, eldest child of Francis Boreham, solicitor's clerk, and his wife Fanny, née Usher. He was educated and was later a pupil-teacher at Grosvenor United School, Tunbridge Wells. In December 1884 he became junior clerk with a local brickworks where, in a locomotive accident, he lost his right foot, necessitating the life-long use of a stick. Late in 1887 he went to work as a clerk in London, becoming increasingly involved in church, debating and writing activities. Although his family was Anglican, he was baptized at Stockwell Old Baptist Church in 1890; he preached from pavement and pulpit and published *Won to glory* in 1891. He was admitted to Spurgeon's College, London, in August 1892, serving as a student-minister at Theydon Bois, Essex, where he met Estella Maud Mary Cottee.

In 1894 Boreham was called to the Scottish community at Mosgiel near Dunedin in New Zealand, and was inducted on 17 March 1895. Stella, then 18, followed to marry him at Kaiapoi on 13 April 1896. Boreham became president of the Baptist Union of New Zealand in 1902, and published *The whisper of God and other sermons* (London). He wrote editorials for the *Otago Daily Times,* contributed to theological journals and, as a keen temperance advocate, participated in liquor polls in 1905 and 1907.

In June 1906 Boreham was called to the Baptist Tabernacle, Hobart. He edited the *Southern Baptist* and later the weekly *Australian Baptist* and in 1910 became president of the Tasmanian Baptist Union. His *George Augustus Selwyn* was published in 1911. He wrote a biographical series for the Hobart *Mercury,* which in 40 years covered 2000 persons; in 1912-59 he contributed 2500 editorials to the *Mercury* and the Melbourne *Age.* Boreham's 80 publications, including religious works, homiletic essays and novels, sold over one million copies. Some were written around Mosgiel people, and one character, John Broadbanks, closely resembled the author. The Broadbanks Dispensary in Bengal, India, was established from proceeds of this series. Other writings were woven around everyday problems, with literary references to English writers and Australians such as Marcus Clarke [q.v.3], Henry Lawson and C. J. Dennis [qq.v.]; most originated as sermons to responsive congregations. In 1940 he published his autobiography, *My pilgrimage.*

In May 1916 Boreham had accepted a call to Armadale Baptist Church in Melbourne. He retired from that charge in 1928 to tour North America and Britain, where his writings were well known. On his return he preached at the Methodist Central Mission, Melbourne, and then at Sydney's Pitt Street Congregational Church. For many years he conducted Wednesday lunch-hour services at Scots Church, Melbourne. In 1936 he made another preaching tour abroad. McMaster University, Canada, had conferred on him a doctorate of divinity in 1928, and, for his 'services to religion and literature as a preacher and essayist', he was appointed O.B.E. in 1954.

Boreham never wore clerical garb. His physical activity was restricted by lameness and he broke his leg and hip several times in falls. He was a devotee of cricket. Friendly and unassuming, he had a gentle, sensitive face, a large drooping moustache, and a 'lingering Kentish flavour' to his voice. He died in Melbourne on 18 May 1959 and was buried in Kew cemetery, survived by his wife, son and three of their four daughters. His estate was sworn for probate at £22379. He is commemorated by the F. W. Boreham Baptist Hospital in Canterbury.

T. H. Crago, *The story of F. W. Boreham* (Lond, 1961); *Age,* 19 May 1959. IAN F. MCLAREN

BORELLA, ALBERT CHALMERS (1881-1968), soldier and farmer, was born on 7 August 1881 at Borung, Victoria, son of Louis Borella, farmer, and his wife Annie, née Chalmers, both native-born. His mother died when he was 4 and his father remarried. Educated at Borung and Wychitella state schools, he later farmed in the Borung and Echuca districts; he also served for eighteen months with a volunteer infantry regiment, the Victorian Rangers.

From April 1910 Borella was employed by the Metropolitan Fire Brigades Board, Melbourne. He resigned in January 1913 and took up a pastoral lease, drawn by ballot, on the Daly River, Northern Territory. With the help of Aboriginal boys he built a house and ring-barked and partly fenced his holding before mounting costs forced him to abandon it early in 1915. On 15 March he enlisted in the Australian Imperial Force as a private and was posted to 'B' Company, 26th Battalion, on 24 May. After training in Egypt his unit landed at Gallipoli on 12 September and Borella, who was promoted corporal later that month, served there until November.

The 26th Battalion sailed for the Western Front in March 1916; Borella was wounded in the battle of Pozières Heights on 29 July and was evacuated for four months. He was promoted sergeant in January 1917, and in March was awarded the Military Medal for conspicuous bravery at Malt Trench, Warlencourt. Commissioned second lieutenant on 7 April, he was mentioned in dispatches soon afterwards and in August was sent to England for officer training and promoted lieutenant. In the early months of 1918 the 26th Battalion held the line at Dernancourt, where Borella was mainly engaged in patrolling and raids. He fought at Morlancourt and Hamel and on 17 July, for 'most conspicuous bravery in attack' at Villers-Bretonneux, won the Victoria Cross. While leading his platoon in an assault on an enemy support-trench, he noticed a machine-gun firing through the Australian barrage; he ran out ahead of his men into the barrage, shot the gunners with his revolver and captured the gun. He then led a small party against the strongly held trench, bombed two dug-outs and took thirty prisoners. Only weeks after this incident he was invalided to Australia owing to wounds and illness.

In 1920-39 Borella farmed on a soldier-settlement block near Hamilton, Victoria. He was National Party candidate for Dundas in the 1924 Legislative Assembly election and was only narrowly defeated. He married Elsie Jane Love at Wesley Church, Hamilton, on 16 August 1928; from September 1939, when he changed his name by deed-poll, he and his family used the surname Chalmers-Borella. On the outbreak of World War II Borella was appointed lieutenant in the 12th Australian Garrison Battalion with which he served until 1941 when he was attached to the Prisoner of War Group at Rushworth. Promoted captain on 1 September 1942, he served with the 51st Garrison Company at Myrtleford until discharged in 1945. He then moved to Albury, New South Wales, joined the Commonwealth Department of Supply and Shipping, and was an inspector of dangerous cargoes until his retirement in 1956. Survived by his wife and two of his four sons, he died on 7 February 1968 and was buried with full military honours in the Presbyterian cemetery.

'A big tough-looking bloke, the image we conjure up of the digger', Borella was yet a humane, quietly spoken and unostentatious man, ever ready to assist a worthy cause. Streets in Albury and Canberra are named after him.

K. R. Cramp, *Australian winners of the Victoria Cross . . . 1914-19* (Syd, 1919); C. E. W. Bean, *The A.I.F. in France, 1918* (Syd, 1942); L. Wigmore (ed), *They dared mightily* (Canb, 1963); *London Gazette,* 11 May 1917, 16 Sept 1918; *Mufti* (Melb), 1 July 1937; *Reveille* (Syd), Jan 1967, Mar, Apr 1968; *Courier Mail,* 27 Feb 1919; *Border Morning Mail,* 16, 17 Aug 1954, 6, 8 Dec 1960, 8-10 Feb 1968.

JEAN P. FIELDING

BORTHWICK, THOMAS (1860-1924), medical practitioner, was born on 13 January 1860 at Peebles, Scotland, son of William Borthwick, shepherd, and his wife Janet, née Hudson. He graduated in medicine at the University of Edinburgh in 1881. After brief medical practice in Scotland and a short stay in South Africa, he arrived in Adelaide in 1883 and practised at Kensington. From 1885 he was medical officer of health for Kensington, Norwood, St Peters and Burnside. His monograph, *A contribution to the demography of South Australia,* earned him an M.D. degree in 1891 from Edinburgh University, where that year he began a course in practical sanitary science. He returned to Adelaide with sufficient equipment to fit up a bacteriological laboratory, possibly the first of its kind in Australia, at his home.

In 1894 Borthwick was selected for the new position of honorary bacteriologist at the Adelaide Children's Hospital and his equipment was transferred to its new Thomas Elder [q.v.4] laboratory. In London in 1895 he studied the anti-toxin treatment of diphtheria under Dr. G. Sims Woodhead, and he probably visited the Pasteur Institute in Paris to study the control of diphtheria. On his return home, the new treatment was adopted by the Children's Hospital and by the medical profession in general. In addition to diagnostic work in the hospital, he lectured 'with infinite patience and tact' to nurses on hygiene and bacteriology. His work with diphtheria had shown him that the period of contagion lasted much longer than previously supposed and convalescents were subsequently detained until all fear of infection had passed. In 1899 the University of Adelaide made him examiner in hygiene and lecturer in bacteriology, a post he retained until 1920. In 1902 he was offered the position of honorary bacteriologist at the Adelaide Hospital and he became consultant there in 1911. He resigned from the Children's Hospital as its emphases shifted from extensive to intensive medicine, but continued to advise it on sanitary matters.

Borthwick brought about the Health Act of 1898, which introduced notification of infectious diseases and established a Central Board of Health; but he was also one of the first to recognize the Act's practical weaknesses. In 1900-24 he was the part-time medical officer of health for the city of Adelaide, the corporation having acknowledged the need for a qualified person. He was also health officer for the Metropolitan Dairies Board (later the Metropolitan County Board of Food and Drugs) and was appointed consultant medical officer to the Metropolitan Abattoirs Board in 1913. He introduced inspection of dairies and licensing of milk vendors, instituted a mother and child health service, showed the need for a separate infectious diseases hospital, and regularized the inspection of insanitary dwellings. In 1922 he initiated a three-year campaign to eliminate the city's mosquitoes by compulsorily screening domestic water-tanks and treating breeding-grounds in the River Torrens. He also suggested the creation of a Greater Adelaide area to secure uniform action on such matters as hygienic food supplies. He never hesitated to express his opinion in the most emphatic and un-equivocal manner and wrote several highly respected papers on bacteriology and public health.

Borthwick was amiable, but shy and re-tiring: his work was hence inadequately publicly recognized. Family tradition has it that he had left South Africa after losing a breach of promise case. On 22 April 1885 he married Mary Borthwick at Norwood. She died four years later aged 28, leaving a three-year-old son, who died in 1903. On 24 March 1891 Borthwick married Annie Bucephala Thompson Giffen. He was dis-appointed in his public life: when the presi-dency of the Central Board of Health fell vacant, it was, for political reasons, bes-towed elsewhere. Borthwick suffered from cancer of the throat, but remained at his post until six weeks before his death at Largs Bay on 11 March 1924. Survived by his wife, he was buried in North Road cemetery.

H. T. Burgess (ed), *Cyclopedia of South Aus-tralia,* 1 (Adel, 1908); *MJA,* 5 Apr 1924; *Health,* May 1924; *Advertiser* (Adel), 12 Mar 1924; Medical Officer of Health, Reports 1900-01 to 1923-24 (Adel City Council); Adelaide Children's Hospital, An-nual reports 1894-1924 (SAA); (Royal) Adelaide Hospital, Annual reports 1898-1924 (SAA).

NEVILLE HICKS
ELISABETH LEOPOLD

BOSANQUET, SIR DAY HORT (1843-1923), admiral and governor, was born on 22 March 1843 at Alnwick, Northumberland, England, third son of Rev. Robert William Bosanquet and his second wife Caroline, née MacDowall. He was an elder brother of Bernard Bosanquet, the philosopher. He entered the Royal Navy in 1857, and as a midshipman he was present at the taking of Canton. As commander-in-chief, East In-dies, in 1899-1902, he had some success in suppressing the Arab slave trade and preventing the Boers from importing arms. Meanwhile, much of his career had been spent in command of training ships and colleges. Promoted commander in 1874, captain in 1882, rear admiral in 1897 and vice admiral in 1902, he was commander-in-chief on the North America and West Indies Sta-

tion in 1904-07, and at Portsmouth in 1907-08. He was appointed K.C.B. in 1905 and G.C.V.O. in 1907.

On retirement Bosanquet was appointed governor of South Australia. Soon after his arrival on 29 March 1909, he called on the ailing premier of the Labor-Liberal coali-tion, Tom Price [q.v.], who confided that he intended to resign in June and to recommend that Labor's John Verran [q.v.] be commis-sioned to succeed him. Nevertheless, the governor believed that the acting premier A. H. Peake [q.v.], a Liberal, was 'the proper person to be sent for', because Verran had never held cabinet rank. He acted accord-ingly when Price died six weeks later, and the 1910 election brought Verran to power.

Bosanquet plagued four successive min-istries with memoranda demanding an end to the practice of requiring the governor periodically to sign warrants for excess ex-penditure pending parliament's grant of supply. The practice was regularized by the Governor's Appropriation Act, 1911. He sympathized with Labor's plans to curtail the Legislative Council's power of veto, and when the Imperial government was asked to intervene, in November 1911, he at first suggested ways in which his ministers could strengthen their case. However, he was an-gered when Verran sought to force the matter by tacking two extraordinary items to a supply bill, thus ensuring its rejection by the council. He consented to use the Governor's Appropriation Act to pay civil servants' wages, but refused to entertain a request for a dissolution until Verran un-dertook to use all means of obtaining supply. In telegrams to the Colonial Office he sug-gested that the crisis was of Verran's own making and observed that interference by the Imperial government 'would be strongly resented by the Opposition'. The Asquith ministry declined to intervene, supply was obtained, parliament was dissolved and Downing Street rejoiced. Bosanquet encou-raged both Peake and Verran to fight for South Australia's rights, especially in the boundary dispute with Victoria, the struggle for a fair share of Murray water, and the building of the Oodnadatta-Pine Creek rail link as a quid pro quo for the transfer of the Northern Territory to the Commonwealth.

Bosanquet returned to England in March 1914 and was appointed K.C.M.G. In 1881 he had married Mary Butt, by whom he had a son and two daughters. After his son was killed in action in 1916, he sold Brom-y-Clos, his estate in Herefordshire, and moved to the Old Vicarage, Newbury, Berkshire, where he died on 28 June 1923.

P. A. Howell, 'Varieties of vice-regal life in South Australia', *JHSSA,* no 3, 1977; *Advertiser*

(Adel), 1909-14; *Register* (Adel), 1909-14, 22 Dec 1923; *The Times,* 30 June 1923, 24 May 1930; CO 418/73, 82, 92, 103, 115, 126.   P. A. HOWELL

BOSCH, GEORGE HENRY (1861-1934), merchant and philanthropist, was born on 18 February 1861 at Osborne's Flat near Yackandandah, Victoria, son of George Bosch, a miner from Bavaria, and his wife Emily, née Spann, of Hamburg. Through the Spanns he was connected with an old Hanseatic Lutheran merchant family. Educated at T. and C. McAlpine's private school, Richmond, he was apprenticed to a Melbourne watchmaker. In 1881, in partnership with his father as Bosch & Son, he started importing watch materials and tools, and that year began business in Sydney. By 1885 he was joined by Emil Barthel and the business gradually expanded into dental and optical supplies and diamonds. He made his first business visit to Europe in 1885; he spoke German well, and was probably assisted by the Hamburg connexion. In 1894 he bought out Barthel but kept the name, Bosch, Barthel & Co.; branches were set up in Melbourne and Brisbane.

His business was his life and Bosch sometimes gave fourteen hours a day to it, to the eventual detriment of his health. A sound and efficient manager, he developed a highly profitable enterprise and invested successfully in stocks and Sydney real estate. In 1924 he retired and, prompted partly by his view of the obligations of great wealth, tried in vain to devise schemes to permit his employees to acquire ownership and control.

In 1909 Bosch had given handsomely to the Dreadnought Fund. His interest may have been directed towards medical science by his knowledge of physical disabilities — his mother was a partial cripple and a friend was paralysed. Impressed by John Hunter [q.v.], professor of anatomy, he gave £1000 to the University of Sydney in 1924 for research into spastic paralysis and next year £2000 for cancer research; in 1927 he provided £27 000 to establish chairs of histology and embryology. In 1928 he transferred to the university almost £200 000 in property and securities: the income was to be used for chairs of medicine, surgery and bacteriology. On a visit to the United States of America in 1930, Bosch ably carried out some of the negotiations with the Rockefeller Foundation for a grant to build a new medical school building, opened in 1933. He also gave £10 000 in 1928 to Trinity Grammar School, Summer Hill, contributed largely to the upkeep of the Milleewa Boys' Home, Ashfield, and the Windsor Boys'

Farm, and assisted St John's Church of England, Gordon.

A bachelor for most of his life, Bosch had few recreations, but literary and political allusions in his letters show him to have been widely read and interested in current affairs. He enjoyed walking and was an honorary treasurer of Manly Golf Club for many years. After a breakdown in health in 1928 he visited east Asia; on 11 October 1929 at Beechworth, Victoria, he married 28-year-old Gwendoline Jupp, who had nursed him. Survived by his wife and two sons, Bosch died of coronary occlusion at his home at Gordon on 31 August 1934, and was buried in the Anglican section of Northern Suburbs cemetery. His estate was valued for probate at £257 046 in New South Wales, £5379 in Victoria and $31 000 in Hong Kong. Believing that sons should make their own way, he left them each £15 000; he provided an annuity to his wife during her widowhood and, after several small bequests, the residue to the university's medical school. His will was contested and eventually the Privy Council awarded an additional £10 000 to each son.

Bosch's portrait by George Lambert [q.v.] is held by the University of Sydney and there is a memorial window to him in St John's Church, Gordon.

SMH, 11 Sept, 12 Oct, 13 Dec 1928, 5 Apr, 17 Sept, 12 Oct 1929, 1, 4 Sept 1934; *Sunday Telegraph Pictorial,* 21 Oct 1928; papers held by Mr H. Bosch, Syd; Bosch estate and benefaction papers (Registrar's office, Univ Syd).

BOSWELL, WILLIAM WALTER (1892-1959), soldier, labourer and railway ganger, was born on 20 July 1892 at Broombee, near Mudgee, New South Wales, son of Arthur William Boswell, farm-labourer, and his wife Rebecca, née Winter. Educated at Hargraves Public School, he worked as a farm-hand and fettler in the Mudgee district until World War I.

Appalled by the sinking of the *Lusitania* by a submarine in May 1915, Boswell enlisted as a private in the Australian Imperial Force on 10 June and embarked for Egypt with reinforcements for the 2nd Battalion. On 31 March 1916 he was posted to the 45th Battalion, which sailed for France in June and occupied a quiet sector of the front near Fleurbaix. They took over the newly captured line east of Pozières on 5 August and, in the continuous German bombardment of the next ten days, suffered severe casualties. Boswell, who 'worked unceasingly' as a stretcher-bearer, received the Military Medal. The citation specially referred to his bravery on 7 August in the attack on Munster Alley and Toor Trench; though exposed to heavy fire he had spent three hours treating wounded men and carrying them to the aid-post. In November Boswell was promoted lance corporal. He served at Gueudecourt in the early months of 1917 and at Messines and Passchendaele later that year.

On 5 April 1918 the Germans attacked the 4th Australian Division at Dernancourt and the 45th Battalion took part in a spirited counter-attack which drove them back. The stretcher-bearers worked under artillery fire throughout the engagement and Boswell was awarded a Bar to his Military Medal for 'gallant conduct and untiring energy in collecting and attending the wounded'. A month later he was promoted corporal. From Dernancourt the battalion moved on to Villers-Bretonneux where it fought in the decisive battle of 8 August. Its last engagement was at Le Verguier on 18 September and he gained a second Bar to his Military Medal: in charge of a party of stretcher-bearers, he continued to tend the wounded despite a heavy barrage.

Boswell returned to Australia in June 1919 and in October joined the New South Wales Government Railways as a labourer. Next year, on 20 October, he married Sarah Jane Bunyan at Emu Plains. He was promoted to railway ganger in 1928 and worked in the Blue Mountains, Tamworth and Bathurst areas until 1944 when he retired because of poor health. In 1945-49 he worked as a ganger in the Department of Main Roads.

In retirement Boswell lived at Windsor where, survived by his wife, he died of cardiac disease on 22 June 1959; his ashes were placed in the memorial wall at St Matthew's Anglican Church. Boswell's elder brother James Harold also served in World War I; he was in the 1st Signals Squadron, Australian Mounted Division.

J. E. Lee, *The chronicle of the 45th Battalion, A.I.F.* (Syd, 1924); C. E. W. Bean, *The A.I.F. in France, 1918* (Syd, 1942); J. E. Lee, *A brief history of the 45th Battalion, A.I.F., 1916-1919* (Syd, 1962); *London Gazette*, 9 Dec 1916, 16 July 1918, 17 June 1919; staff records (Dept of Main Roads, Syd, *and* Public Transport of NSW, Syd); information from Mrs I. Griffiths, Queanbeyan, NSW.

R. SUTTON

BOTTRILL, DAVID HUGHES (1866-1941), philanthropist and journalist, was born on 11 February 1866 in North Adelaide, son of William Bottrill, bootmaker, and his wife Mary Ann, née Evans. Bottrill went to England for four years when his mother died in 1872 and attended a private school in Lancashire. In 1882 he entered the South Australian Public Service as a clerk in the postal branch. His position was made permanent in 1890 and on 9 April that year he married Sophie Annie Degenhardt at Norwood.

Bottrill was active in the Norwood and Kent Town literary societies; he wrote poetry and in 1891, when secretary of the University Shakespeare Society, won a prize for a novelette, 'Her Husband'. On 14 July 1894 he published a letter in the *Observer* which originated the Sunbeam Society of South Australia, a children's club to teach 'the blessedness of helping others . . . loving kindness and self-denial'. They were encouraged to form 'Sunbeam circles', each consisting of about six children and taking its name from an eminent public or historical figure, which met monthly for social activities or fund-raising. By 1903 there were 285 circles. The club was run through 'Uncle Harry's' sentimental, doting letters in the children's column of the weekly *Observer* and Saturday's issue of the *Evening Journal*. Bottrill was wont to discourse on his emotions as he read the 'much-treasured missives' from his young correspondents. He often signed himself as their 'friend and playfellow'. The society grew rapidly to a membership of over twelve thousand and, to organize it, in 1896 Bottrill became a full-time journalist with the *Register*. A column by a rival, 'Aunt Dorothy', appeared in the *South Australian Chronicle*. 'Sunbeams' raised large sums to assist the Adelaide Children's Hospital and other local and overseas children's charities. Bottrill's wife and children were incorporated into the society as 'aunt' and 'cousins'. Congratulations arrived from Queen Alexandra and Florence Nightingale.

Bottrill was appointed a justice of the peace in 1905. He became an active member of the committees of several of the charities to which, by 1906, his society had contributed the published total of £4756. In 1898 he had been made a life governor of the Adelaide Children's Hospital, and he was a lay preacher and superintendent of the Knightsbridge Baptist Church Sunday school. He also gave literary lectures to municipal institutes and was a founder of the State branch of the Dickens [q.v.4] Fellowship. In August 1909 Bottrill left the *Observer* and formed a company to publish his own children's paper, the *Sunbeam*. Over the next two years he managed to produce numerous issues but in 1911 announced his financial failure. Next year he found a temporary 'home' for his column with the Saturday *Daily Herald*.

On 24 March his youngest son, Robert Harry Sunbeam Bottrill aged 9, died from shock following severe burns. Two days later the *Herald* dismissed Bottrill, who then attempted unsuccessfully to maintain the flagging society from his home. He returned to the public service as a clerk in the Hydraulic Engineer's Department and in 1920 was again made permanent. Survived by his wife, three daughters and two sons, he died on 22 December 1941 in the Royal Adelaide Hospital after surgery.

H. T. Burgess (ed), *Cyclopedia of South Australia,* 2 (A dl, 1909); *SA Literary Societies' Union Year Book,* 1891; Children's Sunbeam Soc (Adel), *Sunbeam,* 28 Aug 1909, 22 Oct, 15 Dec 1910, Mar, Nov 1911; *Observer* (Adel), 14 July, 18 Aug, 17 Nov 1894, 13 July, 14 Dec 1907, 14 Aug 1909; *Advertiser* (Adel), 25 Mar 1912, 23 Dec 1941; *Daily Herald,* 6 Apr 1912; Board of Management minutes (Adelaide Children's Hospital); family papers and news-cuttings.   MARGARET BARBALET

BOTTRILL, FRANK (1871-1953), blacksmith and inventor, was born on 1 April 1871 at Sturt, Adelaide, son of John Lucas Bottrill, market gardener, and his wife Eliza, née Macklin. Frank was brought up as a Methodist and probably attended Payneham School before serving an apprenticeship as a blacksmith. Later he worked in the mines at Moonta and Wallaroo where he obtained his certificate as an engine driver (steam). About 1889 he went to Broken Hill, New South Wales, but by 1896 was working as a blacksmith at East Payneham; in September he applied for a patent for improvements in windmills.

In the early 1900s Bottrill and his brother Reuben were employed by the Triumph Plough Co. of Adelaide to clear scrub in the Tintinara district, in the south-east of the State. The major problem of using conventional tractors was loss of traction in sandy soil and wet ground through skidding. Bottrill invented an improved road wheel in which a series of flat bearers rotated with the wheel and provided a track for it to run on. This device, analogous to the later caterpillar tread, was patented on 6 September 1907.

In 1908 Bottrill moved to Victoria and in Ballarat he became a Seventh Day Adventist. He met Margaret Young, a Bible-worker for the church, and on 31 March 1909 at North Fitzroy they were married.

Living in South Melbourne, Bottrill worked as a blacksmith and engineer in close association with A. H. MacDonald & Co. of Richmond. In 1911 an engine and wagon to his design was built by MacDonald's and Austral Otis Engineering Co. for delivery to the Mount Gunson coppermine in South Australia. Tractors using his

patent wheels were used on the Cloncurry mines in Queensland and in the construction of the transcontinental railway. However the most famous use of his device, known variously as 'Dreadnought wheel' or 'Pedorail', was on 'Big Lizzie', an enormous traction engine designed by Bottrill and built by MacDonald's in 1915: 34 feet (10.4 m) long, weighing 45 tons (46 tonnes), with two trailers attached it could carry almost twice that weight. Bottrill had hoped to use it in Broken Hill but the huge vehicle only got as far as Mildura. He settled at Red Cliffs and under his direction 'Big Lizzie' was used for extensive land-clearing operations in the Mallee. In 1926-28 the engine was used at Glendinning near Balmoral and was then abandoned until 1971.

In 1926 Bottrill set up as an engineer at Vasey near Glendinning. In 1931 he moved to Lismore near Camperdown, working as a mechanic, and in 1934 became a blacksmith at Dareton, New South Wales, not far from Mildura. Independent, modest, of strong build and unusual endurance, Bottrill was a vegetarian and teetotaller; he had a rich bass singing voice. His favourite book was the Bible. In 1919-24 he had been a founder, an elder and treasurer of the Mildura Seventh Day Adventist Church. He was elder and treasurer of the Dareton church until his death in hospital at Mildura on 7 January 1953. Childless, he was survived by his wife.

Bottrill's 'Big Lizzie' is preserved at Red Cliffs. His invention was important in the mechanical clearing of sandy country but had no long-term impact on the development of the traction engine.

F. Wheelhouse, *Digging stick to rotary hoe* (Melb, 1966); A. S. Kenyon, 'Clearing by traction engine', *J of Agr* (Vic), 8 (1908); *Qld Government Mining J,* 14 June, 15 Aug 1913; *Sunraysia Daily,* 9 Jan 1953; *Canb Times,* 30 June 1964; information from Mr J. R. Gates, Mildura, Vic.

                                          F. J. KENDALL

BOURCHIER, SIR MURRAY WILLIAM JAMES (1881-1937), grazier, soldier and politician, was born on 4 April 1881 at Pootilla, Bungaree, Victoria, eldest son of Edward Bourchier, Geelong-born farmer, and his wife Francis (Fanny), née Cope. In 1878 Edward and his three brothers had taken up four adjoining selections on the Murray River near Tocumwal. Within a few years their properties had expanded considerably: Edward's, near Strathmerton, was called Woodland Park; the other three were known collectively as Boomagong. After a private education in Melbourne, Murray returned to Woodland Park. From 1909 until the outbreak of World War I he commanded a troop of light horse at Numurkah, attending annual camps and courses.

Bourchier's military service was distinguished. He enlisted in the Australian Imperial Force in August 1914 and sailed as a lieutenant in the 4th Light Horse Regiment, serving seven months on Gallipoli. After the Sinai campaign in 1916-17, during which he was promoted lieut-colonel commanding his regiment, he made the crucial final assault on Beersheba. On 31 October 1917 he led his men, many of them from his own district, at full gallop over two miles into Turkish entrenchments and on for a further two miles into Beersheba to capture vital wells before the Turks could destroy them. Lacking sabres, the regiment used bayonets held in their hands as shock weapons. For this exploit he was awarded the Distinguished Service Order and earned the sobriquet 'Bourchier of Beersheba'. Eleven months later, after fighting north through Palestine, he commanded a joint force of the 4th and 12th Light Horse regiments (Bourchier Force) in the final advance on Damascus; on entering the city the 4th captured 12 000 Turks and set about relieving their sufferings.

Bourchier was three times mentioned in dispatches. He was appointed C.M.G. in June 1919 and his A.I.F. appointment ended in October. In 1921 he was promoted colonel, commanding the 5th Cavalry Brigade, and in 1931 brigadier, in charge of the 2nd Cavalry Division. He returned to Strathmerton but later farmed a property at Katandra, which he named Kuneitra. On 16 June 1921 at Holy Trinity Church, Kew, he married Minona Francis, daughter of Sir Frank Madden [q.v.].

In 1920 Bourchier entered the Legislative Assembly as the Victorian Farmers' Union member for Goulburn Valley; he had to contest the 1921 election but between 1924 and 1935 he was unopposed as Country Party member. The plight of returned soldiers had been his active concern; fittingly, his maiden speech was an attack on the (Sir) Harry Lawson [q.v.] government's neglect of ex-servicemen and the subject remained a constant theme. He was fiercely loyal to his electorate and its particular rural interests. He allied himself with the conservative John Allan against (Sir) Albert Dunstan's [qq.v.] breakaway group of 1926, the Country Progressive Party. Bourchier would not tolerate the notion of an alliance with Labor, which Dunstan favoured. He opposed the unemployed workers' insurance bill of 1928 on the conflicting grounds that there would always be the 'unemployable' in the community and that lack of work was a temporary problem: he considered the money would be better spent on national undertakings, such as irrigation schemes. Similarly, in 1931, he opposed the unemployment relief bill, because it discriminated against the unemployed in country areas. He was typical of the aggressive parochialism of his party.

Bourchier was minister of agriculture and of markets in the Allan government in 1924-27 and deputy leader of the party in 1927-30. When the party and the breakaway group amalgamated to form the United Country Party in 1930 he was obliged to stand down for Dunstan. Bourchier was not one of those approved by Sir Stanley Argyle [q.v.] to join his United Australia Party-Country Party coalition from May 1932. Next year, when Allan had to resign after a revolt by three members, Bourchier won the leadership ballot which followed. He was a principled and predictable man who never lacked a solid bloc of supporters, but he was an uninspired leader, and he seemed almost destined to lose in the end to the more resourceful Dunstan. His March 1935 election campaign was unimpressive; he concentrated almost entirely on rural matters in the general context of sound finance, a balanced budget, and no additional taxation. Although the party improved its position, his supporters grew impatient. On 14 March, at a meeting over which Bourchier presided, his leadership was challenged: Dunstan won by 13 votes to 11. In the Country Party government formed with Labor support on 2 April, Bourchier was named chief secretary and minister of labour and deputy premier.

In January 1936 his appointment as agent-general in London was announced. It is likely that Bourchier had in fact been in Dunstan's cabinet under sufferance. Nevertheless, government members insisted that, with his sound knowledge of primary industry and the needs of farmers, he was well qualified for the job. The appointment was extended from the usual three years to five, and Bourchier left for London in August. On 16 December 1937 he died in London of pernicious anaemia and cancer and was cremated; he was survived by his wife, a daughter and two sons, and left an estate valued for probate at £17 520. Bourchier was knighted posthumously in January 1938. His portrait by Longstaff [q.v.] is in the possession of the family. His son Murray Goulburn Madden became ambassador to the Union of Soviet Socialist Republics in 1977.

H. S. Gullett, *The A.I.F. in Sinai and Palestine* (Syd, 1923); M. H. Bourchier, *'Boomagong' and the Bourchier family* (Tocumwal?, 1973, copy LaTL); *PD* (Vic), 1921, 277-79, 1928, 1085-87, 1931, 1086-89; *Argus*, Feb, 15 Mar 1935, Feb-June 1936; *Age*, 18 Dec 1937; *Shepparton Advertiser*, 20 Dec 1937;

J. B. Paul, The premiership of Sir Albert Dunstan (M.A. thesis, Univ Melb, 1961); D. M. Hudson, The role of the Country Party in the formation of governments in Victoria 1924-29 (4th year Hons essay, Univ Melb, 1963).   DON WATSON

BOURKE, JOHN PHILIP (1857-1914), schoolmaster, prospector and poet, was born on 6 August 1857, at Nundle, New South Wales, son of William David Bourke, butcher, and his wife Jane, née Shepherd. After primary schooling, he prospected with his father and at 17 sold his first mining lease for £600. William Bourke became a schoolmaster in 1875 and in September 1882 John also joined the Department of Education as temporary teacher at Wilson's Downfall in northern New South Wales. He was transferred in 1886 to manage two half-time schools at Wandsworth and Tenterden and in January 1887 was suspended for drunkenness. Given charge in May of a full-time school at Tenterden, in September he was found very drunk by an inspector. He claimed in defence that he had lived alone in a bark hut, three miles from the school, and drank mainly from desperate loneliness. He was permitted to retire, never to be again employed by the department.

Bourke arrived in Western Australia about 1894 and prospected over the northern and eastern goldfields, particularly at Broad Arrow and Paddington. According to A. G. Stephens [q.v.] he was consistently lucky in making small rises worth £200 to £1000 (with a record of £1250) 'but never handled a wingless coin'. By 1899 he had settled in Boulder as a working miner and, under the pseudonym 'Bluebush', began submitting poems and paragraphs to the local press; he had previously been an occasional contributor to the Sydney Bulletin. Bourke rapidly became popular and from 1906 was staff poet for the Kalgoorlie Sun; his work was also published in the Perth Sunday Times. When continual heavy drinking took its toll he visited the eastern States briefly in 1913 to seek medical advice on his failing health and to arrange publication of a book of verse. Soon after his return he died, unmarried, of pneumonia on 13 January 1914 at Nurse Egan's private hospital in Kalgoorlie. His burial by a Catholic priest in the Boulder cemetery was attended by the mayor, most of the journalists in the district and representatives from the Boulder Liedertafel. His Off the Bluebush . . ., edited and introduced by Stephens, was published in 1915.

'Bluebush' Bourke is remembered as one of the leading poets of the Western Australian goldfields, along with (E. G.) 'Dryblower' Murphy [q.v.], 'Crosscut' and 'Prospect Good'. They comprise a group whose verse Stephens praised in a series of articles in 1910-11 in the Perth magazine, Leeuwin, for its 'vigour and versatility': 'The East has more refined writers, more cultivated and more artistic writers; but not more manly writers'. He compared the goldfields versifiers to writers of marching songs and referred to their 'striking phraseology' and 'real singing talent'. Bourke's own estimation of his talent, in self-effacing mood, was more modest:

We singers standing on the outer rim
Who touched the fringe of poesy at times
With half-formed thoughts, rough-set in halting rhymes,
Through which no airy flights of fancy skim —
We write "just so", an hour to while away,
And turn the well-thumbed stock still o'er and o'er . . .

The verse and prose of 'Bluebush' is a barometer of changing feelings and attitudes on the Western Australian goldfields. His poems depict local 'characters', scenes of poverty and hardship and the consolation of 'booze'. But a sense of humour is evident and a strong commitment, as part of a radical movement, to mateship and social justice. Many of the poems are addressed specifically to the wide audience of miners and prospectors who read his verse.

B. Smith, 'Bards of the backblocks', Westerly, Mar 1977; Sunday Times (Perth), 8 May 1908; Sun (Kalgoorlie), 18 Jan 1914; Colebatch memoirs (Battye Lib, Perth); Dept of Education, School files — teachers' records (NSWA).   BRUCE BENNETT

BOURNE, ELEANOR ELIZABETH (1878-1957), medical practitioner, was born at South Brisbane on 4 December 1878, eldest child of John Sumner Pears Bourne, clerk in the Land Commission Court, and his wife Jane Elizabeth, née Hockings. She was educated at the Brisbane Central School for Girls, the Leichhardt State School and the Brisbane Grammar School, whose trustees awarded her an extension scholarship; she passed the 1896 senior examination with distinction, winning the Grahame and the John West gold medals. The government exhibition awarded to her late that year to the University of Sydney was the first to a woman; she thus became the first Queensland woman to study medicine. Despite a severe attack of typhoid fever during the course, she won honour passes in four of the annual examinations and graduated as bachelor of medicine and master of surgery on 6 July 1903.

In 1903-07 Dr Bourne was resident medical officer at the Women's Hospital, Sydney, at the Brisbane General Hospital, where she was the first woman resident, and at the Hospital for Sick Children, Brisbane. In 1907 she entered general practice at 69 Wickham Terrace, serving as honorary out-patient physician to the children's hospital and as an anaesthetist. Appointed the first medical officer in the Department of Public Instruction on 1 January 1911, she had to establish principles for the medical examination of children and the conditions under which they studied; she also briefed teachers and laid down the procedure for notifying parents of marked physical defects. She saw medical inspection as 'likely to do its work, more by relieving slight defects in a large number of children than by making a few improvements in marked and startling conditions'. In 1910-11 she visited Charleville, Cunnamulla, Thargomindah, Augathella, Eulo, Blackall, Longreach and Barcaldine, while in 1912 she worked in North Queensland, particularly in the Cairns and Mackay districts. The results of her research on hookworm disease, published in the annual school medical report, were used in the Rockefeller-financed hookworm survey of North Queensland after World War I; she also reported on ophthalmia in the western area. At the request of J. D. Story [q.v.], under-secretary for public instruction, she prepared a brochure on diet which was distributed to parents of all schoolchildren.

Disagreements with the department and her heavy work-load reinforced her desire for war service and, though dedicated to child health, she applied for leave in January 1916. She went to England at her own expense and served as a lieutenant of the Royal Army Medical Corps in the Endell Street military hospital, London, staffed entirely by women. Promoted major in 1917, she became medical officer to Queen Mary's Army Auxiliary Corps.

Awarded a Diploma of Public Health in 1920 by the Royal College of Physicians and of Surgeons, Dr Bourne was appointed assistant medical officer to the city of Carlisle, responsible for organizing child welfare services and for the new maternity hospital and associated maternal welfare services. In 1928 she applied for and was offered a position as Commonwealth director of maternal hygiene and children's welfare in Australia; but after discovering that the conditions were unsatisfactory, she withdrew her application. Forced to resign by ill health in June 1937, she left Carlisle and retired to Manly near Brisbane.

After fifty years membership of the Queensland branch of the British Medical Association, Dr Bourne was made an honorary life member in 1953. She was also interested in the Queensland Medical Society and was the first honorary medical officer to the Crèche and Kindergarten Association. Her family had supported the Women's College within the University of Queensland from its foundation in 1914 and the Bourne wing was named in their honour. She was a life vice-president of the college standing committee and donated £1000 shortly before she died. She was also prominent in other cultural activities.

Dr Bourne was an unusually confident and self-reliant woman within Australian society up to the outbreak of World War II. She was also noted for her excellent relations with hospital staff and patients. She died unmarried in Nundah Private Hospital on 23 May 1957 and was buried in South Brisbane cemetery with Anglican rites; her estate was sworn for probate at £11 040. A sister, Florence Ida Bourne, retired in 1948 after thirty-one years as principal of the Maryborough Girls' High School; a brother, George Herbert [q.v.], had a distinguished record in World War I.

E. S. Morgan, *A short history of medical women in Australia* (Adel, 1970); *Brisb Girls' Grammar School Mag,* Dec 1957; Qld Women's Hist Soc, *News Sheet,* no 46, 1957; Bourne papers (Oxley Lib, Brisb); G. H. Bourne correspondence (RHSQ); Education Dept files, A/15844-45, A/15971, EDU/BC89 (QA).   JACQUELINE BELL

BOURNE, GEORGE HERBERT (1881-1959), soldier and bank manager, was born on 21 November 1881 in Brisbane, son of John Sumner Pears Bourne, civil servant, and his wife Jane Elizabeth, née Hockings. Educated at Queensland state schools and Brisbane Grammar School, he joined the Bank of New South Wales in 1898 and was stationed at Brisbane until 1907, then at Toowoomba until 1913. In 1905 he joined the Commonwealth Military Forces, was commissioned second lieutenant in the 14th Australian Light Horse Regiment in 1908 and by World War I was a major.

Bourne enlisted in the Australian Imperial Force on 21 August 1914 and was appointed to the 2nd L.H.R. as major commanding 'B' Squadron. The unit reached Egypt in December and in May 1915 was sent to Gallipoli to fight as infantry; there it served at Quinn's Post and Pope's Hill. In the general offensive of 7 August he took temporary command of the regiment whose role was to attack Turkish positions near Quinn's Post in four successive waves. The first wave was annihilated and, realizing that similar attempts must meet the same fate, he ordered his men to stay in the trenches. This decision, which saved many men from certain death, was endorsed by higher authority. On 20 September Bourne was evacuated because of illness.

Rejoining the 2nd L.H.R. in Egypt on 12 March 1916, he participated in the advance into Sinai and in the many patrols and reconnaissances that preceded the battle of Romani on 3-5 August. Bourne was made commanding officer of his regiment on 27 June and was patrolling with it when the Turks attacked an outpost line on the night of 3 August. Against great odds, the light horsemen held up their advance until reinforcements arrived at dawn. He was mentioned in dispatches and awarded the Distinguished Service Order for 'conspicuous gallantry' in this engagement and in the subsequent advance to Katia and Bir-el-Abd. In September he was promoted lieut-colonel and two months later his regiment joined Major General Sir Philip Chetwode's Desert Column which defeated Turkish forces at Magdhaba and Rafa. Evacuated sick on 13 January 1917, Bourne returned to duty for the second battle of Gaza, and from October 1917 to February 1918 was brigade commander. He resumed regimental command for the advance into the Jordan valley. In the fierce fighting at Abu Tellul the 2nd L.H.R. 'fought doggedly in the face of irresistible odds'. C. E. W. Bean [q.v.] was later to describe Bourne's leadership as 'cool and admirable' and the work of the regiment as 'never excelled in the career of the light horse'. He contracted malaria late in August and resumed duty only two weeks before the armistice with Turkey.

Bourne's A.I.F. appointment was terminated in June 1919, when he rejoined the Bank of New South Wales. In 1921-24, while stationed at Brisbane, he commanded the 2nd L.H.R., Queensland Mounted Infantry. He married Frances Blanche McConnel at St Faith's Anglican Church, Mondure, on 24 April 1924 and later that year was made manager of the bank's Tamworth (New South Wales) branch. While there he wrote *Nulli secundus, the history of the 2nd Light Horse Regiment, A.I.F.* (1926); he commanded the 33rd Battalion in 1926-27, and retired in 1941 as honorary colonel. His banking career continued until 1946: he was manager at Christchurch, New Zealand, in 1936-38 and at Rockhampton in 1938-46. On retirement he settled at Brisbane where, survived by his wife and three sons, he died after an operation for prostate on 8 March 1959. He was buried in Lutwyche cemetery after a service at St Colomb's Anglican Church, Clayfield; all his life he had been a strong churchman.

Bourne's sister, Eleanor [q.v.], was the first woman in Queensland to study medicine. His brother Harold was also a physician and his sister Ida was a teacher.

H. S. Gullett, *The A.I.F. in Sinai and Palestine* (Syd, 1923); C. E. W. Bean, *The story of Anzac* (Syd, 1924); *Courier Mail*, 9-10 Mar 1959; staff records (Bank of NSW Archives, Syd).

M. W. FARMER

BOURNE, UNA MABEL (1882-1974), pianist and composer, was born on 23 October 1882 at Mudgee, New South Wales, daughter of James George Bourne, storekeeper, and his wife Margaret, née Webber. The family moved to Melbourne when Una was a child. An infant prodigy, she was playing by ear when 4. She was taught first by her elder sister, and later by Benno Scherek; in the 1890s Una made her first public appearances in orchestral concerts under his conductorship. In her mid-teens she gave many solo recitals which established her as an artist of considerable promise. In May 1899 she was enthusiastically praised for her contribution at a benefit concert for the soprano Amy Castles [q.v.].

In 1905 Una Bourne undertook an eighteen-month study tour during which she visited Leipzig, Dresden, Berlin, Prague, Vienna, Paris and London. She had not intended to perform publicly but, before her return home, friends arranged recitals in the Bechstein Hall, London, which were acclaimed by English critics. Nellie Melba [q.v.] selected her as her associate artist for tours of Australia in 1907, 1909 and 1912. She occasionally accompanied Melba and these engagements established her as a solo performer. Their lifetime association and friendship contributed substantially to Una Bourne's international repute as a concert pianist.

In November 1912 Una sailed for England to pursue her career. On her arrival she was engaged by Melba for a provincial tour, during which she performed many of her own compositions with success. In February 1914 she gave concerts in Berlin, Dresden and Leipzig, as well as a command performance before Queen Mary at Buckingham Palace. Throughout World War I she remained in England, giving many concerts for hospitals and the Red Cross. She established herself as a pioneer recording artist when in 1915 she began a thirteen-year association with the English Gramophone Co. (His Master's Voice). She recorded over eighty titles, including many works by Chaminade as well as several duets with the violinist Margaret Hayward, and her own compositions – *Caprice, Petite caprice valse, A little song, Cradle song, Humoreske, Gavotte, Marche grotesque* and *Nocturne*. Unfortunately, most of her forty-four recordings were deleted from the H.M.V. catalogue by 1930 and no long-playing reissues of her discs have been made.

Following a tour of Australia in 1920 with Melba, Una Bourne performed both on the Continent and in North America. In the United States she made player-piano rolls for the Duo-Art Co. and emerged as an important broadcaster. She made several return visits to Australia, including one in 1939 when she gave celebrity concerts under (Sir) Bernard Heinze and Eugene Ormandy. She remained in Melbourne to work throughout World War II giving concerts and broadcasts; in 1942 she established a master school of piano-playing at the Melbourne Conservatorium of Music, Albert Street, and a scholarship bearing her name. After the war she gave private piano tuition and continued to write and broadcast. Her declining years were spent at her South Yarra home with a lifetime friend and companion artist, Mona McCaughey (d. 1964). She died on 15 November 1974 and was cremated. Her estate, much of it inherited from Miss McCaughey, was valued for probate at $169168.

Una Bourne had great musical intellect and integrity, coupled with magnificent technique. It was said she played with her mind, her brain and her heart, as well as her fingers.

I. Moresby, *Australia makes music* (Melb, 1948); *Lone Hand*, 1 June 1914; *Aust Musical News and Musical Digest*, 1 May 1942; P. Burgis, Interview with Mr A. Brahe (tape, NL).   PETER BURGIS

BOUTON, WILBUR KNIBLOE (1855-1936), homoeopath, was born in the United States of America, probably in Buffalo, New York, son of James Daniel Bouton, clergyman, and his wife Harriet Eliza, née Knibloe. First trained in mechanical engineering, Bouton turned to medicine and graduated from Boston University (Ch.B., 1884; M.D., 1885). Aged 30 he was appointed first resident medical officer of the new Melbourne Homoeopathic Hospital.

Bouton was the hospital's only 'pure homoeopath'. This system of cure, assuming a benevolent Nature, asserted that disease could be conquered by gentle administration of drugs which produced 'similar' symptoms in the sufferer. He utterly eschewed allopathic treatment and, as a 'high potency man', believed that drug potency increased with dilution.

Bouton practised surgery at the hospital from 1891, soon becoming senior surgeon. He was both renowned and criticized for his dexterous keyhole appendectomies, which were fashionable but risky, and for his staunch resistance to the germ theory and consequent inattention to asepsis and antisepsis. Tolerance of the hospital's poor pathology facilities may have further reflected his commitment to homoeopathy which regarded causes as irrelevant to cure.

As a member of the hospital's board of management from 1894, its vice-president (1909) and president (1918-34), Bouton strongly influenced policy, especially on treatment of patients and medical staff appointments. Doggedly determined to engage only homoeopaths, he was chiefly responsible for attracting numerous American doctors through personal contacts in Boston; he occasionally visited the United States. He resisted attempts by the orthodox in 1906 to eliminate homoeopathy with restrictive legislation, and gained permission for an annual quota of its practitioners. But growing difficulties in retaining satisfactory staff and a decline in homoeopathy's appeal, as acceptance of the germ theory widened, seriously threatened the hospital's viability. From 1924 the British Medical Association, seeking appointments for members, lifted its black ban on the hospital; this move was welcomed by the staff but it isolated Bouton in his bitter but vain efforts to obstruct it.

With dynamic personality and restless energy, Bouton was single minded, opinionated and somewhat domineering, brusque in manner although not unkind. His chief diversions were punting and motoring: his Pullman saloon, the first in Australia, built by James Flood, was a familiar sight at the hospital. His intimate identification with the institution, to which he contributed funds as well as personal devotion, gained it, for a time, the nickname 'Dr Bouton's Hospital'.

On 11 May 1892 at St Silas's Church of England, South Melbourne, Bouton had married Mrs Mary Jeannett Muffitt, née Spenser, a matron of the hospital in 1886-92. She died aged 84 on 4 February 1936; he died aged 80 on 13 May at 7 Collins Street where he had long resided and conducted a flourishing practice. He was survived by a stepdaughter Gertrude, who had assumed his name; she inherited his estate which was valued for probate at £29851.

J. Templeton, *Prince Henry's: the evolution of a Melbourne hospital 1869-1969* (Melb, 1969); *V&P* (LA Vic), 1892-93, 4 (60); *Age, Argus* and *Herald* (Melb), 15 May 1936; Melbourne Homoeopathic Hospital records (Prince Henry Hospital, Melb).   JACQUELINE TEMPLETON

BOWDEN, ERIC KENDALL (1871-1931), solicitor and politician, was born on 30 September 1871 at Parramatta, New South Wales, second son of John Ebenezer Bowden, solicitor, and his wife Sarah Anne, née Smith. His great-grandfather was Thomas Bowden [q.v.1] and the family had lived at Parramatta for four generations. After education at Newington College and Sydney High School, he entered articles with his father and qualified as a solicitor in 1894. At Ashfield Wesleyan Church on 2 February 1898 he married Reinetta May Murphy. In 1904-07 he was an alderman in Granville. In December 1906 he won the seat of Nepean in the Federal parliament. Defeated in 1910, he returned to practise in partnership with his father until he was re-elected for Nepean, as a Nationalist, in 1919; in 1922 he won Parramatta which had absorbed Nepean.

In 1923-25 Bowden was minister for defence in the first Bruce-Page [qq.v.] government. The appointment caused surprise. He had not been a leading speaker in parliament; he had been described as 'an urbane gentleman with an atrocious memory'; and his main interests had been the Federal capital site and the financial aspects of federalism. On defence matters his concerns had been the governor-general's powers to call out the citizen forces; the rights of parents, on religious grounds, to prevent their children receiving military training; and suitable areas for army manoeuvres. But his appointment came at an important time in the development of Australia's armed forces. In June 1923 he introduced legislation to establish the Royal Australian Air Force. After the Labor Opposition had argued that incorporating the Imperial code of discipline was un-Australian, Bowden withdrew the bill in August and introduced another. There was still doubt about discipline and the Opposition forced an amendment before the bill passed. In June 1924 Bruce introduced the government's five-year defence programme, in the defence equipment bill, which provided for the creation of a cruiser and submarine force. Again Bowden was unimpressive in debate.

He was, however, alive to the threat from Japan and the weakness of British sea power, and in November 1923 he had argued that Australia should spend up to £25 million a year to counter possible Japanese intentions. But there is no evidence of his urging a larger defence vote on the Treasury. He admitted that Australia was not ready to meet an emergency, but funds for the Royal Military and Royal Australian Naval colleges were reduced to a minimum; though he felt that Australia might have to be defended by air power he was content to see the air force receive the lowest share of the three services. When he resigned his portfolio in January 1925 it was said that he had been for long in poor health.

In 1926-27 Bowden was a member (sometime chairman) of the joint select committee on electoral law, and in 1927-29 sat on the royal commission on the constitution. He lost his seat in the 1929 election. His last years were shadowed with financial difficulties. He died suddenly of chronic respiratory disease on 13 February 1931, survived by his wife, three sons and two daughters. He had been a Methodist lay preacher and was buried in the Methodist cemetery, Rookwood.

J. C. Wharton (ed), *The jubilee history of Parramatta* (Parramatta, 1911); *PD* (Cwlth), 1906-10, 1919-29; *Cwlth Parliamentary Handbook*, 5 (1901-26); *Aust National Review*, 19 Feb 1923; *SMH*, 14, 16 Feb 1931, 31 May 1932; *Smith's Weekly*, 19 Dec 1931; Bankruptcy papers 491/31 (NSWA).

JOHN MCCARTHY

BOWEN, ESTHER GWENDOLYN (1893-1947), portrait painter and official war artist, was born on 16 May 1893 at North Adelaide, daughter of Thomas Hopkins Bowen (d. 1896), surveyor, and his wife Esther Eliza, née Perry (d. 1913). She was known in Adelaide as Estelle and in London as Stella. After leaving Miss Caroline Jacob's [q.v.] school, Tormore House, with first place in English in the senior certificate examination, she began her art training with Margaret Preston [q.v.]. Early in 1914, with an allowance from her parents' estate, she sailed for England.

Soon after the outbreak of war Stella Bowen enrolled at the Westminster School of Art under Walter Sickert. Her association with the novelist Ford Madox Ford (1873-1939) began in 1919 and lasted nine years. ('Valentine Wannop' in Ford's Tietjens tetralogy is a fictionalized portrait of Stella — 'a bit too near the knuckle', she remarked to Ford). During that period they lived mainly in Paris and the south of France, where she painted landscapes, still-life, and portraits on commission. She also developed a talent for drawing quick 'likeness' sketches. After a visit to Italy in 1923 she became attracted to Giotto and the Italian Primitives; five years later El Greco tended to influence her work. Despite a successful visit to the United States of America in 1932, the calamitous effects of the Depression forced her to leave her 'beloved' Paris and return to London with her daughter Esther Julia Madox. For a time she wrote art critiques for the *News Chronicle*, taught students, and painted an occasional portrait; but it was a constant struggle to make ends meet despite Ford's erratic help.

During her lifetime Stella Bowen painted portraits of (among many others) Aldous Huxley, T. S. Eliot, Edith Sitwell, Naomi Mitchison, Gertrude Stein, Clifford Bax, Robert Lynd, Dorothy Thompson, D. N. Pritt, Isobel Cripps, Theaden Hancock, and G. D. H. and Margaret Cole. She also painted 'several "conversation pieces", of whole families, with little figures of Hogarthian dimensions sitting about in their own houses'. A landscape, 'Embankment Gardens', was bought in 1943 by the National Gallery of South Australia. Other paintings (including a self-portrait) are in the possession of relations and friends in Adelaide and Canberra.

During World War II Stella Bowen published an excellent autobiography, *Drawn from life* (1940), broadcast talks for the Pacific Service of the British Broadcasting Corporation, and on 7 February 1944 became the second woman war artist to be appointed by the Australian government. This was arduous and often distressing work; some portraits of Royal Australian Air Force bomber crews based in England had to be finished with the aid of photographs. The Australian War Memorial, Canberra, holds forty-six of her wartime oils and pencil drawings. Group portraits are treated as a formal decorative scheme, with emphasis on linear design. She had keenly desired to return to Australia but died of cancer in London on 30 October 1947, after having been denied pension and rehabilitation rights and a passage on a troopship. The National Gallery of South Australia presented a memorial exhibition of her paintings in 1953.

M. I. Cole, *Growing up into revolution* (Lond, 1949); D. D. Harvey, *Ford Madox Ford 1873-1939* (Princeton, 1962); A. McCulloch, *Encyclopedia of Australian art* (Lond, 1968); D. H. Skinner and J. Kroeger (eds), *Renniks Australian artists*, no 1 (Adel, 1968); N. Benko, *Art and artists of South Australia* (Adel, 1969); A. Mizener, *The saddest story* (Lond, 1971); R. Biven, *Some forgotten, some remembered* (Adel, 1976); J. Loewe, 'Epilogue', S. Bowen, *Drawn from life*, rev ed (Maidstone, Kent, 1974); *Age*, 7 Jan 1967; F. D. Davison papers (NL); records (AWM); family information.

C. B. CHRISTESEN

BOWEN, ROWLAND GRIFFITHS (1879-1965), naval commander, was born on 14 January 1879 at Taggerty, Victoria, seventh child of David Bowen, farmer, and his wife Margaret, née Hughes, both of whom were natives of Wales. His father died

when he was 7 and the family moved to Petrie, Queensland, where Rowland attended the local state school; in 1895-1911 he worked in Brisbane as a railways clerk. He served in the Queensland Naval Brigade, became a sub-lieutenant in 1900 in the emerging Commonwealth naval forces and in 1911 joined the Royal Australian Navy as a lieutenant. He was district naval officer at Thursday Island until February 1914 and assistant D.N.O. in Melbourne until the outbreak of war. On 14 August, at All Saints Anglican Church, East St Kilda, he married Agnes Grace Mary Bell.

On 19 August Bowen sailed with the Australian Naval and Military Expeditionary Force which had been hastily raised to destroy German wireless stations in the Pacific. In the force's first operation in German New Guinea he led a party of twenty-five naval reservists in an attack on the radio station at Bitapaka. The party was put ashore at Kabakaul on 11 September and, while pushing forward through dense jungle, was ambushed by a patrol of native soldiers led by three German officers. In the skirmish that followed one of the Germans was wounded, and surrendered. Bowen ordered him, under threat of shooting him, to call on his comrades to surrender, for 800 Australians were advancing. Soon afterwards Bowen was shot in the head by a sniper and evacuated; he was mentioned in dispatches for gallantry and was promoted acting lieut-commander in November. His action in coercing a prisoner to act as a decoy was later described by the official historians as an apparent infringement, through ignorance, of the rules of warfare. Legal or otherwise, the incident had unforeseen consequences: the false report of the strength of the Australian troops reached the acting governor of German New Guinea who ordered his small force to abandon the defence of the coastal belt. The military occupation of the colony followed without opposition.

Bowen resumed duty on the Melbourne naval staff in April 1915. Six months later his wife died, leaving him with an infant daughter. In 1916 he became first State president of the Returned Sailors' and Soldiers' Imperial League of Australia. Next year he was posted to Perth and on 22 November married Corinne Elizabeth Bruce-Nicol in St George's Anglican Cathedral. He was promoted commander in April 1919 and was D.N.O. in Tasmania in 1919-23 and in Western Australia in 1923-35. He retired in 1936 and settled in Sydney. An officer of the Order of St John of Jerusalem from that time, he was secretary of the New South Wales Centre, St John's Ambulance Association, in 1939-44 and first Australian registrar and priory secretary of the order in 1942-57. He retired to Canberra in 1957 and two years later was appointed O.B.E. Survived by a son and a daughter, he died on 21 October 1965 and was cremated with Presbyterian rites.

Tall and distinguished in appearance, brisk in manner and speech, conscientious and inflexibly high-principled, Bowen probably commanded respect more readily than he inspired affection. At ease with his friends, he was a man of considerable charm and had a fund of amusing stories.

S. S. Mackenzie, *The Australians at Rabaul* (Syd, 1927); A. W. Jose, *The Royal Australian Navy* (Syd, 1928); Blue book, *PP* (Qld), 1903, vol 1; *Reveille* (Syd), 1 Sept 1936; *Canb Times,* 20 Aug 1964, 22 Oct 1965; Dept of Defence (Navy), MP124, 6, 580/201/27 (AAO, Melb); information from Mr B. G. Bowen, Forrest, ACT.

MERRILYN LINCOLN

BOWES, EUPHEMIA BRIDGES (1816-1900), wife, mother and social reformer, was born in Edinburgh, daughter of Joseph Allen and his wife Eliza. A houseservant, Euphemia arrived as a bounty migrant in the *Fairlie* on 6 December 1838; she could read and write. On 13 September 1842 at Parramatta, with Wesleyan Methodist rites, she married John Bowes, a baker. He had reached Sydney in October 1841 and soon moved to Parramatta, where he continued his work as a Wesleyan lay preacher. They apparently lived in Sydney before going to Wollongong about 1848, where he was accepted into the ministry.

Euphemia bore eleven children, eight of whom survived childhood. She and her numerous family moved at three-year intervals as John was appointed to country circuits – Camden, Mudgee, the Turon, Singleton, the Macleay, the Manning, and Mittagong in 1878; he retired to Stanmore in 1880 as supernumerary. Euphemia shared her husband's qualities of 'piety and unobtrusiveness'. Her Bible was always at hand; her work as class leader and visitor to the sick was praised; it was said repeatedly that she was greatly loved.

After the move to Stanmore, Euphemia's talent for organization was soon engaged in founding the first Woman's Christian Temperance Union in Sydney in 1882. She was elected president in 1885, and president also of the subsequent New South Wales union. She represented the Sydney union at the Melbourne congress in 1889. Aided by extensive contacts from the years of her husband's active ministry, she carried the work of setting up other unions to country districts, visiting in 1892, despite increasing age and poor health, Young, Yass, Cootamundra and Goulburn, and next year Bathurst, Dubbo, Newcastle, Maitland and Singleton. Forty-two unions had been formed in New South Wales by 1892 when she expressed a desire to retire, granted by her election as honorary life president in 1893 when the active presidency passed to Mrs Sarah Nolan [q.v.].

While her major achievement was the creation of a network of unions throughout the colony, she also had some success in restricting licenses and Sunday trading; she campaigned vigorously, but vainly, for local option and the banning of barmaids. Practical measures appealed to her: a soup kitchen at the Mission Church, Sussex Street, and a home for inebriate women, opened in 1892.

In 1886 Euphemia Bowes was one of five good women who, on an appeal from the New South Wales Social Purity Society, formed a ladies' committee. It aimed to promote morality and to secure legislation for the better protection of women, notably the raising of the age of consent from 14 to 18, improvements in the law regarding affiliation, and measures against soliciting, child prostitution and brothels. An early advocate of votes for women, Euphemia secured from the Woman's Christian Temperance Union's 1889 convention a favourable resolution, the creation of its suffrage department in 1890, and its support in 1892 for the Womanhood Suffrage League of New South Wales. Confident of the reforming influence of women's votes, she appealed to other organizations, such as the New South Wales Local Option League, to support the movement.

In his retirement, John Bowes had opened a 'ladies college' in their home, Auburn, at Marrickville, which Euphemia, and more likely her daughters, continued to conduct after his death on 11 October 1891. She died there on 12 November 1900, aged 85, and was buried in the Wesleyan section of Rookwood cemetery. She was survived by three sons and four daughters. Her eldest son, John Wesley Bowes represented Morpeth in the Legislative Assembly in 1887-89, two other sons joined the Methodist ministry, one daughter married Peter Board [q.v.] and another, Eva (Evangeline Grace), continued her mother's work for temperance as corresponding secretary for the Woman's Christian Temperance Union of New South Wales in 1912-36.

E. J. Ward, *Womanhood suffrage* (Syd, nd); *Golden records: pathfinders of Woman's Christian Temperance Union of New South Wales* (Syd, 1926); W.C.T.U., Annual Convention Reports,

1890, 1892-1901; *Dawn* (Syd), 5 Feb 1890, 1 Nov 1894; *Weekly Advocate* (Syd), 19 Oct 1878, 17, 31 Oct 1891; *SMH*, 15 Nov 1900; *Methodist* (Syd), 17 Nov 1900; R. G. Cooper, The women's suffrage movement in New South Wales (M.A. thesis, Univ Syd, 1970); Womanhood Suffrage League, Minute-book 1892 (ML).   HEATHER RADI

BOWLES, WILLIAM LESLIE (1885-1954), sculptor, was born on 26 February 1885 at Leichhardt, New South Wales, son of William Hixson Bowles, an Irish-born compositor, and his wife Rachel, née Mark. He attended the Kangaroo Point State School, Brisbane, then studied carving and modelling at the Brisbane Technical College under Lewis J. Harvey, a careful and dedicated teacher who stressed drawing and the proper use of materials. Harvey's fine art nouveau furniture and pottery introduced Bowles to the style and to current academic techniques before he went to England on a scholarship from the college in 1910. He worked there with several sculptors, including (Sir) E. Bertram Mackennal [q.v.], and attended night classes at South London School of Sculpture and at the Royal Academy. In Mackennal's studio work was then concentrated mainly on large public monuments, such as the London Memorial and Tomb for King Edward VII, and equestrian statues of the king for Melbourne, London and Calcutta. It is not surprising that Bowles's later independent work reflects that of Mackennal, and almost never stems directly from other contemporaries.

During World War I Bowles enlisted in the 2nd/25th London Regiment, and then joined the Royal Tank Corps at its inception. After the war he exhibited regularly at the Royal Academy and was employed on the Wembley British Empire Exhibition. He married Mary Lees of Kelso, Scotland, on 24 February 1924; late that year he returned to Australia and settled in Prahran, Melbourne. He was employed with other artists in the Melbourne Exhibition Building on the projected Canberra War Memorial, for which he executed several sculptures, the models for figures in the dioramas, and two plans for the Hall of Memories. Though forced to sell hire-purchase radios during the Depression, his War Memorial work provided security which evaded other sculptors.

Bowles's work depends heavily on narrative or moral content with little exploration of materials or their surfaces: it conformed with the almost exclusive use of sculpture in the 1930s and 1940s to expand civic and national pride and myth-making. His most interesting artistic quality is his subjection

of sculptural elements of large monuments to an overall 'architectural design'. The 1939 proposal for the Hall of Memories was a draped female figure on a sarcophagus surmounted by soldiers' arms and equipment; his excellent 1949 version was a pale yellow marble shaft representing the four freedoms, carefully relating its central location to the Hall's other features. Unfortunately, political interference prevented its execution. The King George V Memorial in Melbourne, designed in 1935 and cast after World War II, acknowledges the site's importance by minimizing both sculpture and variations of stone colouring. This attention to site and simplicity seems stronger than in the case of his contemporaries George Lambert, C. D. Richardson, or even Rayner Hoff [qq.v.]. In 1937 he won the competition for a memorial to Sir John Monash [q.v.] and his equestrian statue was erected in Melbourne Domain in 1951.

Bowles had strong, if predictable, views on art criticism, art ethics and the art clique that ruled Melbourne taste in the 1940s. He especially disliked George Bell [q.v.] who criticized Ivor Hele's work for the War Memorial. The only critic Bowles approved of was his friend James S. MacDonald [q.v.], who also maintained that symmetry and beauty were the proper goals of art. In 1926 Bowles had been made a member of the Royal Society of British Sculptors. He sometimes exhibited with the Victorian Artists' Society between 1925 and 1932, and with the Australian Art Association in the mid-1930s and 1940s. He was a foundation member and secretary of the Sculptors' Society of Australia, founded in 1932 at a meeting in Ola Cohn's [q.v.] studio, and held this office until the war when the society ceased to function. He also adjudicated the Jubilee Medal award, and was a foundation member of the Australian Academy of Art.

When poor health stopped his work for the War Memorial, Bowles asked that it be completed by his former assistant Ray Ewers. In 1938 he had established a studio and home at Frankston; he died there of coronary vascular disease on 21 February 1954 and was cremated. His wife survived him.

A. McCulloch, *Encyclopedia of Australian art* (Lond, 1968); J. Johnson and A. Greutzner (eds), *Dictionary of British artists 1880-1940* (Suffolk?, 1976); *SMH*, 25 Nov 1937, 22 Nov 1951; records (AWM).   NANCY D. H. UNDERHILL

BOWLING, PETER (1864-1942), coalminer and union leader, was born at Dunfermline, Fifeshire, Scotland, son of Patrick

Bowling, miner, and his wife Marguerite, née MacGuire. At 12 he began work in the local mines. Arriving in New South Wales at 20, he worked in several coal-mines around Newcastle. On 5 September 1889 at the Roman Catholic church, Branxton, he married Mary Ann Madden. In the early 1890s Bowling worked briefly in the Gippsland mines and helped to found a miners' union. Returning to New South Wales, in 1893 he was elected an official of the Back Creek (Minmi) miners' lodge.

From 1897 Bowling was a member of the Australian Socialist League. He was later influenced by the ideology of the anarcho-syndicalist Industrial Workers of the World and favoured strong union organization and direct action. In 1904 he became treasurer of the northern Colliery Employees' Federation and was president in 1906-10. Largely due to his influence, the unions on northern, southern and western fields were brought together in 1908 as the Coal and Shale Employees' Federation. That year he was vice-president of the Trades Union Congress in Sydney; at the 1909 congress he led a bitter attack on the State Labor politicians.

Unrest was endemic on the coalfields, aggravated by the nature of the work and the intransigence of the owners; a militant socialist, Bowling believed that a full-scale battle would win concessions, strengthen the new federation and establish the truth of the direct action philosophy. Taking advantage of an accumulation of grievances, he agitated for a general strike, which was called on 6 November 1909; he devised an ingenious scheme to finance it 'by keeping two mines independent of the Vend at work and sharing the profits with their owners'. Bowling and W. M. Hughes [q.v.] were the outstanding members of the Strike Congress of representatives of miners, waterside workers and coal-lumpers, formed in Sydney to manage the strike. Throughout, Hughes counselled moderation and urged the miners to accept the State government's proposal of a wages board. Defying the congress, Bowling encouraged the coal-lumpers to refuse to unload a Japanese ship carrying coal and openly differed from Hughes on tactics. On 4 December he returned to Newcastle and was arrested with two other union officials on a charge of conspiracy. Out on bail, he addressed a mass meeting and violently attacked Hughes.

Bowling was tried under (Sir) Charles Gregory Wade's [q.v.] amendments to the Industrial Disputes Act, rushed through parliament on 16 December. Sentenced to two and a half years imprisonment, he was taken to Goulburn gaol in leg-irons. By March 1910 the strike had been completely defeated. However, in April the issue contributed to the rout of Deakin's [q.v.] Federal government and in October, after an electoral campaign which featured posters depicting Bowling in prison-dress and in leg-irons, Labor won office for the first time in New South Wales. Bowling was promptly released.

Invited by the Federation of Labor, he visited New Zealand on a lecture tour and in his absence lost the presidency of the northern miners to a moderate. For a short time, until December 1913, Bowling was secretary of the southern miners, then worked in the Balmain colliery and at the Homebush abattoirs. In 1916 he actively campaigned in Newcastle against conscription, but he had four sons at the front, and next year changed his mind.

From about 1920 until he retired in the 1930s Bowling worked mainly on the Sydney wharves. At the time of the miners' strike he was of medium height, broad-shouldered and florid, with grey hair, a moustache and jutting chin. Aged 78 and survived by six sons and a daughter, he died of cerebral arteriosclerosis in the Sacred Heart Hospice, Darlinghurst, on 22 February 1942 and was buried in the Roman Catholic section of Woronora cemetery.

R. Gollan, *The coalminers of New South Wales* (Melb, 1963); L. F. Fitzhardinge, *William Morris Hughes,* 1 (Syd, 1964); I. Turner, *Industrial labour and politics* (Canb, 1965); E. Ross, *A history of the Miners' Federation of Australia* (Syd, 1970); *V&P* (LA NSW), 1896, 3, 835; *Commonweal* (Melb), 1 Dec 1910; *Punch* (Melb), 28 Nov 1907, 25 Nov 1909; *Australasian,* 9, 11 Dec 1909; *Argus,* 28, 29 Oct, 2, 17, 21 Nov, 23 Dec 1910, 10, 17 Jan 1911, 16 Sept 1913; *Bulletin,* 6 May 1926; *SMH,* 16 July 1937; *Common Cause,* 20, 28 Feb 1960; MS cat under P. Bowling (ML).   ROBIN GOLLAN
                                    MOIRA SCOLLAY

BOWMAN, DAVID (1860-1916), bootmaker, union official and politician, was born on 24 August 1860 at Bendigo, Victoria, son of Archibald Bowman, miner, and his wife Isabella, née Spence, both of whom were Scottish-born. Trained as a bootmaker, he had been working in Melbourne when on 20 May 1885 he married Elizabeth Jane Fisher at Ballarat; they had two daughters and two sons. In 1888 the Bowmans moved to Queensland, hoping that the climate would cure his throat condition. When a Brisbane bootmakers' union organized by him struck unsuccessfully in 1889 he was blacklisted. Following the failure of a strike by printers in Brisbane that year, the Brisbane Trades and Labor Council was replaced by the Brisbane District Council of the Australian Labour Federation, with Bowman as president and Charles Seymour [q.v.] as secretary.

In 1891, as an employee of the A.L.F., Bowman was responsible for organizing shearers and bushworkers during the pastoral strike. He was elected vice-president of the A.L.F. next year and president in 1893, when he made his first attempt to enter parliament for Brisbane South. Appointed as an organizer in western Queensland by the Amalgamated Workers' Union in 1894, he stood unsuccessfully for Warrego in 1898, but won the seat next year in a by-election. Beaten in 1902, he returned to Brisbane and opened a newsagency at New Farm.

Bowman remained closely associated with the new Labor Party. He attended each triennial Labor in Politics Convention after 1898 and was a member of the Central Political Executive from 1892 to 1916, except for a period in 1894-95 when it was not functioning. Elected to the Legislative Assembly in 1904 for Fortitude Valley, he held that seat until his death.

Though accepting his party's decision to join the Morgan-Browne [qq.v.] coalition in September 1903, Bowman believed that Labor should not ally itself with other parties but should aim to govern in its own right. By 1905, after the passage of the Adult Suffrage Act, he had joined Albert Hinchcliffe and Mat Reid [qq.v.], secretary and president of the C.P.E., and Henry Boote [q.v.], editor of the *Worker,* in opposing the continuation of the Liberal-Labor coalition, now dominated by William Kidston [q.v.]. Bowman became vice-president of the C.P.E. in 1904 and at the 1905 and 1907 Labor in Politics conventions led a parliamentary faction opposed to Kidston, which succeeded in committing the party to fighting future elections alone. When George Kerr [q.v.] was forced to stand down as party leader after the 1907 convention, Bowman was elected in his place. He was not an outstanding parliamentarian and was disabled as a leader by poor health. He was, however, liked and respected for his personality and integrity by colleagues and opponents, who in 1911 subscribed £1400 to send him on a health voyage to England. To C. A. Bernays [q.v.3, L. A. Bernays] 'he had no very wide command of language, but he had a powerful voice and a stout heart, and what he lacked in polished diction he made up in earnest vigour'.

Bowman was overshadowed by T. J. Ryan [q.v.] during the 1912 general strike and gave way to him as parliamentary leader after he collapsed in the Legislative Assembly later that year. When the Australian Workers' Union was formed in 1913, Bowman became the Queensland vice-president and a member of the board of trustees of the *Worker* newspaper. He was a delegate to the 1908 and 1912 Commonwealth conferences of the Labor Party, and as vice-president of the 1908 conference opposed electoral alliances with other parties.

Labor won the State election in May 1915 and Bowman became home secretary, but his health was so poor that John Huxham [q.v.] became his assistant minister. Bowman died in Brisbane on 25 February 1916 as the Labor in Politics Convention began. He was buried in Toowong cemetery with Presbyterian rites; his estate was sworn for probate at £960. His memory as an honest, forthright Labor man survived: in 1948 a new Federal electorate in Queensland was named after him.

D. J. Murphy et al (eds), *Prelude to power* (Brisb, 1970); D. J. Murphy (ed), *Labor in politics* (Brisb, 1975); *Worker* (Brisb), 2 Mar 1916; Qld Labor Party, Central Political Executive minutes, 1892-1916 (Labor House, Brisb). D. J. MURPHY

BOWSER, SIR JOHN (1856-1936), politician and journalist, was born on 2 September 1856 at Islington, London, son of John Henry Bowser, Indian Army veteran, and his wife Marian, née Hunter. The family migrated to Victoria when John was 3 and settled at Bacchus Marsh, where he attended the local school. He gained his first experience of printing and journalism at 14, working for the *Bacchus Marsh Express* under Christopher Crisp [q.v.3]. He had moved to printers McCarron [q.v.5], Bird & Co. of Melbourne, heading their poster section, when eye trouble necessitated a sea voyage to Scotland; there he worked for his uncle on the *Dumfries and Galloway Standard.* His sight improved; he studied journalism and English literature, and gained his first political experience as a shorthand writer for the commission into the condition of the Skye crofters.

About 1880 Bowser returned to Victoria and settled at Wangaratta. In 1884 he became editor and part-owner, with George Maxwell, of the *Wangaratta Chronicle.* He travelled extensively in the district and established himself in community life; he later pioneered the local rifle and tennis clubs and the library committee, and acquired a small farm on the Ovens River.

In 1894 a meeting of residents at Milawa convinced him it was his duty to represent them in parliament. On 20 November he won the Wangaratta and Rutherglen seat in the Legislative Assembly by only thirteen votes, and his enthusiastic supporters celebrated by pulling his carriage through the streets; he held the seat more comfortably thereafter. In parliament Bowser associated himself with the Kyabram movement and the rural groups which demanded economical government and balanced budgets. He had represented the Citizens' Reform League in the 1902 election, and supported (Sir) William Irvine's [q.v.] ministry as a 'country liberal' to these ends. In 1908 he was a leader of the 'country' faction of twenty-six members, and held the public instruction portfolio briefly in Sir Thomas Bent's [q.v.3] cabinet from October to January 1909. Late in 1916 he founded a new parliamentary group, the Economy Party, as a response to the Peacock [q.v.] government's accumulating deficits; during 1917 his group forced three supplementary budget statements, all reductions in expenditure. Contemporaries, such as the Nationalist J. Hume Cook [q.v.], defined it as 'essentially a country party'. When Peacock raised railway freights and fares later in 1917, Bowser's party challenged him in parliament, failing to defeat him by only two votes; in the election in November they campaigned as the 'Liberals' and defeated Peacock, who resigned.

Bowser then became premier, chief secretary and minister of labour. He was the rare politician who had never sought office for himself and had hoped his party would choose (Sir) John Mackey [q.v.] as premier; he later made no effort to retain the leadership. His ministry won the support of the Victorian Farmers' Union, and held office from 29 November 1917 to 21 March 1918. It was defeated unexpectedly on the issue of railway estimates by a combination of the Labor Party and the sixteen-strong 'corner' group of Nationalists led by Peacock and (Sir) Harry Lawson [q.v.]. A coalition was then formed between the Economy Party and the Nationalists, under Lawson; Bowser became, until 27 June 1919, chief secretary and minister of public health. He resigned after a dispute with Lawson over the sharing of cabinet posts between the parties.

In June 1920 Bowser joined the V.F.U. with some of his associates, and in that party he was influential at a time when it held the balance of power in parliament. On 30 April 1924 he was elected Speaker, on the combined votes of Labor and the V.F.U. When the Prendergast [q.v.] Labor government held office later that year, he occasionally used his casting vote to save it. His most difficult task came in 1926, in the standing orders debate, when Labor members walked out in protest at his rulings. Within his own party he was working to heal the breach with the breakaway Country Progressives of A. A. Dunstan [q.v.], which was fully achieved only in 1930.

Bowser was knighted in January 1927. He did not seek re-election as Speaker when his term ended in May and retired from politics in 1929. His services to his electorate included his work for the establishment of Wangaratta High and Technical schools. He had become sole owner of the *Wangaratta Chronicle* in 1905, and only relinquished full control, due to ill health, in the eighteen months before his death. He was a founder, and for many years president, of the Country Press Co-operative Co. Ltd.

Noted for 'an absurd shyness' with women, Bowser had married late, on 11 October 1914, Frances Rogers, aged 51, who died in 1934. He died of cancer at his home on 10 June 1936 and was buried in Wangaratta cemetery with Presbyterian rites. His estate was valued for probate at £10 490. Contemporary assessments of him referred to his courtesy, sensitivity, kindliness, sense of fair play, and lack of self-interest, rare in a political figure.

M. Whittaker, *Wangaratta* (Wangaratta, 1963); B. D. Graham, *The formation of the Australian Country Parties* (Canb, 1966); *Age*, 22 Oct-29 Nov 1917, 11-12 June 1936; *Punch* (Melb), 29 Nov 1917, 6 Feb 1919; *Smith's Weekly* (Syd), 2 Oct 1926; *Wangaratta Chronicle*, 13, 17 June 1936; C. P. Kiernan, Political parties in the Victorian Legislative Assembly, 1901-1904 (M.A. thesis, Univ Melb, 1954); Hume Cook papers (NL).

MARGARET VINES

BOXALL, ARTHUR d'AUVERGNE (1895-1944), artist, was born on 19 June 1895 at Port Elliot, South Australia, son of George Albert Boxall, carpenter and builder, and his wife Ellen, née Pratt. He was educated at Victor Harbour High School and studied architecture on a scholarship at the South Australian School of Mines and Industries. After being awarded the diploma of the South Australian Institute of Architects, he was articled for seven years to the firm of Woods, (W. H.) Bagot [q.v.], Jory & Laybourne-Smith [q.v.]. He also studied drawing at the Adelaide School of Art under Will Ashton [q.v.] and at the School of Fine Arts, North Adelaide.

When appointed art master at the Collegiate School of St Peter he gave up architecture, although evidence of this training remained in his drawing. A fellow of the South Australian Society of Arts, he won its Melrose Prize for portraiture in 1923 and 1925 and the landscape award in the latter year. At this time he shared a studio with Horace Trenerry [q.v.], and their work, regularly seen at the society's exhibitions, was often compared; both were influenced by Elioth Gruner [q.v.]. Boxall's first one-man exhibition, from which all the works were reportedly sold, was in Adelaide in 1925. Next year a successful 'Farewell Exhibition' was held at the Dunster Galleries.

Boxall then spent three years in England and, as an honorary commissioner, reported to the South Australian government on art. He studied under Henry Tonks and Wilson Steer at the Slade School of Fine Art, University of London, where he gained an honours diploma in fine art, prizes for composition, figure study and landscape, and a scholarship which enabled him to travel widely in Europe. In 1928-29 he exhibited with the Royal Academy of Arts, London, the Paris Salon, the Royal Institute of Painters in Water Colours, the Royal Institute of Oil Painters and the less conventional New English Art Club. While returning to Australia he studied and sketched temples and tombs in Egypt and visited Fiji. He arrived home in 1930 but, disheartened at the prospects in Adelaide, went to stay with a friend in New Zealand and exhibited with art societies there.

In 1932 Boxall was appointed to the East Sydney Technical College as teacher of life-drawing. He became head teacher of art and remained there until he resigned owing to ill health in 1940. His successor Douglas Dundas described him as 'having a cheerful disposition' and as an 'enthusiastic teacher', with a 'profound knowledge of the history of art', who often discoursed to artists and students at his home on the qualities of his numerous reproductions of master works. Boxall believed that 'a pupil must teach himself and the work which counts most is that which is done away from class'. His own draftsmanship was meticulous, confident and sensitive, mirroring his quiet, studious nature. His many small landscapes in oils, which were painted directly and briskly with an apparent ease of style, were carefully thought out initially, as some of his sketches show.

Boxall died, unmarried, of tuberculosis at his father's home at Rose Park, South Australia, on 7 January 1944 and was buried in North Road cemetery. His estate was sworn for probate at £3454. From a bequest of his sister Ella a trust was established for the National Gallery of South Australia known as the d'Auvergne Boxall Bequest which took effect from 1954. This added many paintings, drawings and prints by Boxall to the collection, and a room was renamed the d'Auvergne Boxall Gallery. That year a memorial exhibition of his works was held at the Royal Society of Arts, Adelaide.

Catalogue of d'Auvergne Boxall exhibition, June 1925 (Soc of Arts, Adel); D. Dundas, 'Foreword', *Catalogue – Memorial exhibition, Arthur d'Auvergne Boxall, December 1954* (Roy SA Soc of Arts, Adel); Albert Smith, 'Introduction', *Catalogue of Horace Trenerry exhibition, March 1964* (SA School of Art, Adel); L. Klepac, *Horace Trenerry* (Adel, 1970); *Art in NZ*, no 12-19 (1931-33); National Gallery of SA, *Bulletin*, 5 (1944), no 3; *Observer* (Adel), 15 May 1926; *Advertiser* (Adel), 10 Jan 1944; Boxall files, with biog notes, *and* correspondence file 1954 (Art Gallery of SA, Adel); research material (Sarjeant Gallery, Wanganui, NZ).
                                                    JUDITH THOMPSON

BOXER, WALTER HENRY (1893-1927), soldier, labourer and clerk, was born on 30 March 1893 at Violet Creek near Hamilton, Victoria, eleventh child of John Boxer, boundary rider, and his wife Maria, née Beaton. He was educated at Wannon State School and the Ballarat School of Mines where he obtained his intermediate certificate.

Until World War I Boxer worked in the Wannon district as a labourer and rabbit-trapper. Concealing the fact that he was an asthmatic, he enlisted in the Australian Imperial Force on 22 February 1916 and embarked for Egypt with reinforcements for the 57th Battalion. Transferred to the 58th Battalion on 1 September, he sailed for France three weeks later as a stretcher-bearer. He joined his unit at Fleurbaix, then moved to the Somme where, in the winter of 1916-17, the 5th Division held the line around Flers and Gueudecourt. His battalion took part in a raid on Barley Trench, near Warlencourt, on 25 February 1917 and Boxer was severely wounded in the left arm. Evacuated to England, he resumed duty next June and in September served in the battle of Polygon Wood. He was wounded again at Passchendaele on 16 October when the Germans bombarded the valleys behind the lines with shells and mustard gas; he remained on duty and on 5 November was promoted lance corporal.

In the early months of 1918 the 58th Battalion served in the Messines-Wytschaete sector, then returned to the Somme where the Germans had launched their spring offensive. Boxer was awarded the Military Medal for devotion to duty at Aubigny in May and gained a Bar to his medal for gallantry at Ville-sur-Ancre two months later. On the night of 20 June he was slightly wounded in a raid on a trench in the Morlancourt sector. His brigade advanced from Villers-Bretonneux for the decisive battle of 8 August and in the next major engagement, the battle of Péronne, he won the Distinguished Conduct Medal for conspicuous gallantry on 2 September. Under a heavy barrage of high explosive and gas he brought two men to the dressing-station, then went back through the barrage four times and carried more men from the outpost line before being severely wounded by shrapnel. He was evacuated to England and on 13 December was invalided to Australia, where he spent a further eight months in hospital.

After discharge Boxer worked in Melbourne as a clerk and began an accountancy course. He married Isobel Willis on 28 April 1923 at the Presbyterian Manse, Armadale. Survived by his wife and his three-year-old son, he died of tuberculosis at the Repatriation Hospital, Caulfield, on 16 June 1927 and was buried in Kew cemetery with full military honours.

A. D. Ellis, *The story of the Fifth Australian Division* (Lond, 1920?); C. E. W. Bean, *The A.I.F. in France, 1916-18* (Syd, 1929, 1933, 1937, 1942); *London Gazette,* 13 Sept, 21 Oct 1918, 18 Feb 1919; *Argus,* 17 June 1927; War diary of the 58th Battalion, A.I.F. (AWM); information from Mr K. W. Boxer, Elsternwick, Vic.   G. R. VAZENRY

BOYCE, FRANCIS BERTIE (1844-1931), Anglican clergyman, was born on 6 April 1844 at Tiverton, Devon, England, son of Francis Boyce, accountant, and his wife Frances, née Dunsford. In 1853 the family sailed for Australia in the *Earl of Charlemont* and, after shipwreck on 18 June at Barwon Heads, Victoria, settled in Sydney. Boyce attended St James's Grammar School and James Kean's Cleveland House School. His father's death in 1858 cut short his education and he joined the Union Bank of Australia, showing considerable promise. Seriousminded, Boyce taught Sunday school at Redfern and at Enfield, and resolved to enter the Anglican ministry. After studying at Moore Theological College, Liverpool, under W. Hodgson and R. L. King [qq.v.4, 5], he was made deacon by Bishop Barker [q.v.3] on 21 December 1868 and ordained priest on 19 December 1869.

Boyce was stationed in western New South Wales, soon to be the diocese of Bathurst: he served at Georges Plains (1868), with Blayney attached (1869), Molong and Wellington (1873), and from 1875 at Orange. On 5 July 1871 at Georges Plains he married Caroline (d. 1918), daughter of William Stewart of Athol, near Blayney. Energetic and innovative, Boyce was a missioner on the Darling (described in his *Our Church on the River Darling,* Sydney, 1910), a builder of churches, a champion of denominational education (on which he later wrote pamphlets), an advocate of inter-church co-operation, and a keen member of the diocesan synod. He declared that his early training as an original member of the Volunteer Artillery Corps helped him in outback life. Failing to obtain a more sedentary post at Bathurst Cathedral he returned to Sydney in 1882. After two years in the industrial parish of St Bartholomew, Pyrmont, where he gained his first insight into slum housing, Boyce was appointed to St Paul's, Redfern. He remained there for forty-six years.

St Paul's parish, first developed by Canon A. H. Stephen [q.v.6], was important in diocesan affairs. As its incumbent, and aided by his own administrative ability and diplomatic skill, Boyce rose in ecclesiastical rank. He became a canon of St Andrew's Cathedral in 1901 and archdeacon of West Sydney in 1910, serving on most diocesan committees and representing Sydney in the provincial and general synods. A convinced Evangelical but no narrow 'party' man, he claimed to have been decisive in securing the election of the moderate J. C. Wright [q.v.] as archbishop in 1910.

The growing working-class character of Boyce's Redfern parish, which included Sydney's railway-yards and workshops, made him a vigorous social reformer. He joined the Christian Social Union in the 1890s and worked for the alleviation of unemployment distress. He campaigned for slum clearance and helped to erect 'model' dwellings for some of his parishioners, and claimed that he had helped materially in bringing about old-age pensions; he also promoted female suffrage. A skilful publicist from the time when he had unsuccessfully championed church schools, Boyce became a notable public figure. Temperance was his chief concern, his motive being humanitarian rather than puritanical. He was president of the New South Wales Alliance for the Suppression of Intemperance in 1891-1915, fighting for local option and, later, for early closing. An astute campaigner, not averse to exercising strong political pressure, Boyce believed that his work was crucial in the legislative restrictions introduced from 1904. He used interdenominational means also, being leader of the New South Wales Council of Churches in 1911-17 and 1926-27.

Boyce had no distinct political creed; he worked with Labor politicians such as J. S. T. McGowen [q.v.], whom he admired, but was happier with the Liberals. An ardent Imperialist, he was first president of the British Empire League in Australia in 1901 and also in 1909-11, and helped to bring about the proclamation of Empire Day in 1905. He viewed the Empire as a great moral force in the world; after 1918 he supported the League of Nations as an extension of this ideal. A good Australian, he was no narrow patriot, and was interested in history, writing on the Church of England and some of its notable figures. He was a fellow of the (Royal) Australian Historical Society, and saw history as recounting the development of a moral sense in mankind; in this way, he could account for, and defend, his own reformist activities.

Boyce resigned his parish in 1930 and died at Blackheath on 27 May 1931. He was survived by two sons of his first marriage, and by his second wife Ethel Elizabeth, née Rossiter, widow of Captain Burton, R.N.R., whom he had married on 8 September 1920. Memorials to Boyce were placed in the Sydney and Bathurst cathedrals and his portrait by Julian Ashton [q.v.] was presented to the National Art Gallery of New South Wales in 1917. His memoirs were published posthumously in 1934 as *Fourscore years and seven*.

Aust Church Record, 11 May 1917, 4 June 1931; *SMH*, 28 May 1931, 28 June 1940; *Bulletin*, 1 July 1931; Synod reports, 1870-82 (Diocesan Registry, Bathurst). K. J. CABLE

BOYCE, FRANCIS STEWART (1872-1940), barrister and politician, was born on 26 June 1872 at Rockley, New South Wales, elder son of Rev. Francis Bertie Boyce [q.v.] and his first wife Caroline, née Stewart. Known as Frank, he was educated at The King's School, Parramatta, Sydney Grammar School, and Rugby School, England, and the University of Sydney (B.A., 1893; LL.B., 1896). He played football for the university and was president of the union in 1894; he was admitted to the Bar on 19 February 1897. Fascinated by politics, he was honorary secretary of (Sir) Edmund Barton's [q.v.] New South Wales Federal Association and in 1904 was defeated as a Liberal for the Legislative Assembly seat of Phillip. On 9 January 1901 at Christ Church, Blayney, he had married Norah Leslie Glasson.

Boyce was attached to the Western Circuit for many years. In 1900 he made his name as counsel for the Aboriginal murderer Jimmy Governor [q.v.]: he argued that as Governor had already been attainted, he could not be tried for the same crime and the case had to go to the Full Court. An outstanding and 'vigorous' advocate, he soon built up a large practice and in 1916 was an acting District Court judge; King's Counsel from 1924, he spent nearly three months at Rabaul, New Guinea, in 1927 appearing for the lessees before the royal commission on the Edie Creek gold-mining leases.

A member of the finance committee of the Universal Service League in 1916, Boyce later became active in the National Association of New South Wales; on 3 August 1923 he was nominated to the Legislative Council. In 1924-25 he was an honorary minister in Sir George Fuller's [q.v.] coalition government. In the matrimonial causes (amendment) bill, he tried unsuccessfully to get incurable insanity included as a ground for divorce, and to tighten the use of restitution of conjugal rights to get a quick decree 'virtually by mutual consent'. He also introduced the controversial marriage amendment (ne temere) bill; he took a lawyer's view that civil law should prevail over ecclesiastical law. He was attorney-general, vice-president of the Executive Council and leader of the government in the Legislative Council in (Sir) Thomas Bavin's [q.v.] 1927-30 ministry. In 1931 he led the Opposition in the council and was an architect of its reform in 1934. There were persistent reports in the press that he would replace Bavin as leader of the National Party.

Boyce was appointed to the Supreme Court bench in June 1932 and became judge in divorce, showing 'conspicuous ability' and 'a deep sense of human sympathy'. He also occasionally sat in equity cases. In England in 1938 he was invited to sit on the Divorce Court bench.

A temperance advocate, Boyce shared his father's reformist activities: he was a member of the executive of the New South Wales Alliance for the Suppression of Intemperance, honorary secretary, then president of the Discharged Prisoners' Aid Society, foundation chairman of Barker College Council until 1940, chancellor of the diocese of Grafton and advocate for the diocese of Sydney. A leading Freemason, he was grand registrar of the United Grand Lodge of New South Wales in 1917-25 and deputy grand master in 1926-27.

Survived by his wife, two sons and three daughters, Boyce died of coronary vascular disease on 27 June 1940 at his home in Pymble. After a memorial service at St Andrew's Cathedral he was buried at Blackheath. His estate was valued for probate at £20 489.

Cyclopedia of N.S.W. (Syd, 1907); T. R. Bavin (ed), *The jubilee book of the law school of the University of Sydney* (Syd, 1940); *NSW Law Reports*, 21 (1900), 40 (1940); *SMH*, 12 Mar 1924, 30 June 1926, 27 June 1927, 15 Oct 1928, 5 Mar 1931, 26 Mar, 17 June 1932, 16 Mar, 15 Nov 1938, 5, 6 Jan, 15, 23 Feb 1939, 28 June 1940; *Daily Telegraph* (Syd), 5 May 1929; *Bulletin*, 1 July 1931.

MARTHA RUTLEDGE

BOYCE, SIR HAROLD LESLIE (1895-1955), politician, businessman and lord mayor of London, was born on 9 July 1895 at Taree, New South Wales, son of Charles Macleay Boyce (d. 1936), solicitor, and his wife Ethel May, née Thorne, and grandson of Charles Boyce [q.v.3]. He was educated at the Sydney Church of England Grammar School, North Sydney, in 1906-11, and at Sydney Grammar School, 1911-13. Describing himself as a medical student, he enlisted in the Australian Imperial Force while on holidays in Adelaide in March 1915 and sailed as a second lieutenant with the 27th Battalion in May. He served in Egypt, at Gallipoli and in France where he was promoted lieutenant in the 10th Battalion and seriously wounded at Pozières in July 1916. Invalided back to Adelaide early next year he helped inventor L. E. De Mole [q.v.] with his 'tank', promoted recruiting and returned to England with reinforcements for the 10th Battalion.

After the war Boyce went to Balliol College, Oxford, on Huth and Rhodes Trust scholarships and read modern history (B.A., 1920; M.A., 1924). On a further Rhodes Trust award he read for the Bar and in 1922 was called to the Inner Temple. The same year he was legal adviser and substitute Australian delegate to the third assembly of the League of Nations; he was also adviser to Sir Joseph Cook [q.v.] at the Mandates Commission at Geneva.

Boyce made his home near Cheltenham, Gloucestershire, and soon became active in industry and public life. He revived the Gloucester Railway Carriage and Wagon Co. Ltd and became chairman and managing director; it gained large contracts for rolling stock from Canada and Queensland. His business activities were extensive and varied: apart from a number of engineering firms in the West Midlands they included shipping, gas and newspaper interests.

Boyce entered the House of Commons as Conservative member for Gloucester in 1929, and in 1930 was a member of the Empire Parliamentary Delegation to Northern Rhodesia. An 'outspoken advocate of a forward Imperial policy', he exerted much influence on matters affecting the British Empire until his defeat in 1945. He was indefatigable in raising money for war charities and his K.B.E. in 1944 was held to be richly deserved. After the war he moved to Badgeworth near Gloucester and in 1946 he led the United Kingdom trade mission to China.

A liveryman of the Worshipful Companies of Loriners and Carpenters, Sir Leslie Boyce became an alderman of the City of London in 1942, high sheriff in 1947-48 and in 1951-52 lord mayor — the first citizen of a dominion to achieve the distinction. In recognition, the lord mayor's procession halted outside Australia House where the high commissioner (Sir) Thomas W. White presented him with an illuminated address from Prime Minister (Sir) Robert Menzies. On 4 June 1952 Boyce presided at a court of common council which admitted Menzies to the freedom of the City. On retirement as lord mayor Boyce was created a baronet.

He was prominent in the Masonic craft and the Primrose League, and served on several hospital boards including the Masonic and Royal hospitals. Boyce was a knight of justice of the Order of St John of Jerusalem, his wife being a dame of grace of the order; high sheriff of Gloucester in 1941-42; a council-member of Bristol University; a commissioner of the Central Criminal Court; and a lieutenant and justice of the peace for the City of London. He was a keen and active outdoor sportsman; horticulture was one of his hobbies.

Though Boyce was very ambitious, hard working and unconquerably tough, he was unostentatious and genial; his courtesy and tact contributed much to the success of everything he undertook. In his public duties he was ably assisted by his wife Maybery Browse (d. 1978), née Bevan, of Melbourne, whom he had married on 16 July 1926. His many friends included Leo Amery, Viscount Bruce [q.v.], (Baron) Casey and the Cilento family. He died in hospital near Cheltenham on 30 May 1955, survived by his wife and three sons, the eldest Richard Leslie (1929-1968) succeeding to the title. A portrait of Sir Leslie by James Gunn is in the possession of the third baronet.

London's roll of fame (Lond, nd); L. S. Amery, *My political life*, 3 (Lond, 1955); *Reveille* (Syd), 1 Nov 1961; *Lone Hand,* 1 Apr 1920; *SMH,* 30 Oct 1919, 29 Oct 1931, 1 June 1955; *The Times,* 10, 31 Dec 1930, 3 Aug, 10 Oct, 20 Dec 1946, 1 Oct, 9, 10 Nov 1951, 9, 10, 25 June 1955; *Manning River Times,* 10 Nov 1951; *Advertiser* (Adel), 22 Mar 1952.

G. P. WALSH

BOYD, ADAM ALEXANDER (1866-1948), mining engineer, was born on 15 April 1866 at Eastwood near Glasgow, Scotland, son of Adam Boyd, commission merchant, and his wife Margaret, née Stewart. Educated at the Alan Glen School and Glasgow Technical College, he was articled to Dixon & Marshall, civil and mining engineers, and on 21 December 1888 was granted his certificate as a coal-mine manager. In 1889 he migrated to Melbourne but soon moved to New South Wales where he was assistant mine-manager at the Bellambi Colliery in 1891 and at the Newcastle Wallsend Colliery in 1893.

Appointed mine-manager at the Broken Hill Proprietary Mine in 1898, Boyd devised the steel water-curtain, applying coal-mine practice to restrict underground fires, and modernized practice by standardizing extraction methods and introducing improved systems of haulage and handling. When he left Broken Hill for the Wallsend Colliery in 1911 he was considered one of the best mining engineers in Australia.

In 1913 Boyd went to Queensland as general superintendent of the Mount Morgan Gold Mining Co. Ltd and became its general manager in 1915, when it had settled down as a big, prosaic, hard-to-manage industrial firm. The mine lost heavily after the war from falling copper prices, increased costs, industrial unrest and technical problems. It closed down in 1921-22 and in 1925, but was reopened with State government assistance. An experimental open-cut scheme and new ore-treatment processes introduced in June 1926 revived methods used when the mine produced only gold, but after an adverse technical report in 1927 the directors announced a voluntary liquidation.

On 7 March 1929 Boyd was appointed to the Queensland Mining Industry Commission, for which he toured America and Australia. He floated a new Mount Morgan company on 1 July 1929; the Australian Loans Council provided £15 000 to begin operations on 28 June 1932 – the loan was soon repaid. By 1935 the mine's treatment of low-grade ore had made it an assured success. Boyd resigned to live in retirement at Emu Park near Rockhampton, but returned as chairman and managing director in 1938-41 and was a director till his death. In 1939 he wrote a history of Mount Morgan, but it was not published. Believing that industrial unrest derived from concentration of union power in a few hands, he urged all workers to be active unionists; he also provided recreation, profit-sharing and family security as positive incentives for industrial peace.

Boyd had joined the Australian Institute of Mining and Metallurgy in 1910, was a council-member in 1917-48 and vice-president in 1925-26. He read a paper on the history of Mount Morgan to the institute in 1939 and won its medal in 1941. That year he became a foundation member of the Central Queensland Advancement League, and was elected first vice-president representing country interests. His scheme 'covering greater production of copper and cotton to meet the Commonwealth's requirements and the industrialization of the Central District by the establishment of a copper refinery and pyrites production works', presented to the Federal Manpower and Resources Survey Committee on 3 August 1941, helped to ensure the reopening of the Mount Chalmers copper-mine in 1942.

On 3 August 1892 Boyd had married Margaret Moses (d. 1917) at Hamilton, New South Wales. He died at Brisbane on 16 December 1948 after an operation and his ashes were buried in his wife's grave in Box Hill cemetery, Melbourne. His estate, valued for probate in Queensland at £23 117 and £9713 in New South Wales, was left to their three children. His son Eric Ewart Gladstone made a notable career in Malaya and at Mount Morgan.

Mount Morgan Ltd, *The story of the Mount Morgan Mine, 1882-1957* (Mt Morgan, 1957); *Chemical Engineering and Mining Review,* 10 Jan 1949; *Government Gazette* (Qld), 27 Aug 1927, 7 Mar 1929; *Qld Government Mining J,* 50 (1949), no 567; A'sian Inst of Mining and Metallurgy, *Procs,* 31 Mar 1942; *Morning Bulletin,* 21 Dec 1948; news-cuttings held by Mr S. R. L. Shepherd, Rockhampton, Qld; A461 C373/1/6 (AAO, Canb).

J. M. B. McINERNEY

BOYD, ARTHUR MERRIC (1862-1940), artist, was the father of WILLIAM MERRIC (1888-1959), potter, and THEODORE PENLEIGH (1890-1923), artist.

Arthur Merric was born on 19 March 1862 at Opoho, New Zealand, son of Captain John Theodore Thomas Boyd, formerly of County Mayo, Ireland, and his wife Lucy Charlotte, daughter of Dr Robert Martin of Heidelberg, Victoria. The Boyds came to Melbourne in the early 1880s and on 14 January 1886 Arthur married Emma Minnie à Beckett, artist; they settled at Brighton. In 1890 they left for England to live at the à Beckett seat, Penleigh House, near Westbury, Wiltshire. They both exhibited at the Royal Academy in 1891 after which they moved briefly to Paris. On their return to Melbourne in 1894 they lived at Sandringham. In 1898 their works were included in the Exhibition of Australian Art in London at the Grafton Galleries. The family travelled overseas from time to time, and spent summers in Tasmania where the scenery inspired some of Boyd's best work; he exhibited regularly with the Victorian Artists' Society.

At some time Boyd had studied to become an engineer but he did not practise. He was an artist of charm and ability, who painted best in water-colour, without reaching the heights of his contemporaries in the Heidelberg School. While he was friendly with Frederick McCubbin and E. Phillips Fox [qq.v.], he did not associate much with other artists. According to his son Martin (1893-1972), the novelist, he was, if a little remote, just and generous, with a tolerant and enlightened way of bringing up children.

His wife EMMA MINNIE (1858-1936) was born on 23 November 1858 at Collingwood, second daughter of William Arthur à Beckett [q.v.3] and his wife Emma, née Mills. Many critics believe her work to be superior to her husband's. She, too, painted landscapes in Tasmania and many seascapes, but she had a particular talent for genre. At their farm at Yarra Glen she painted the four seasons in a frieze around the dining-room. She was lively, handsome, cultivated and compassionate. Restless, she had something of the religious mystic in her make-up. After her death at Sandringham on 13 September 1936, her husband lived at Rosebud where he was joined by his grandson Arthur, to whom he gave painting lessons. Boyd died at Murrumbeena on 30 July 1940, survived by two sons and a daughter.

His son William Merric, known as Merric, was born on 24 June 1888 at St Kilda, and attended Haileybury College and Dookie Agricultural College. Unsuccessful as a farmer at Yarra Glen, at one time he considered entering the Church of England ministry; he was the model for 'a difficult young man' in Martin Boyd's novel under that title. However, in 1908 at Archibald McNair's Burnley Pottery, he successfully threw his first pot. His parents helped to provide a workshop for him at Murrumbeena and pottery kilns were established there in 1911 (destroyed by fire in 1926).

Merric studied at the Melbourne National Gallery School under L. Bernard Hall [q.v.] and McCubbin. He held his first exhibition of stoneware in Melbourne in 1912 and a second exhibition soon afterwards, and was employed by Hans Fyansch of the Australian Porcelain Works, Yarraville. On 12 October 1915 he married Doris Lucy Eleanor Bloomfield Gough, a fellow student and potter. In May 1917 he joined the Australian Flying Corps but was discharged later in England. Before his return to Australia in September 1919 he undertook training in pottery technique at Wedgwood's, Stoke-on-Trent.

Merric produced his best works in the 1920s and 1930s. These were mostly pieces for domestic use, often decorated by Doris, and some pottery sculptures. He believed that 'the first impulse of the maker of hand-pottery is to obtain pleasure in making and decorating an article, and making that pleasure intelligible . . . the use of our own fauna and flora is of the first importance'. In spite of his aversion to creating art that would sell well, he worked hard to provide for his growing family. In the 1930s he was employed at the Australian Porcelain Co. Pty Ltd, Yarraville, in the manufacture of Cruffel art porcelain; he earned £4 a week. Doris worked there also on a half-time basis.

In his later years Merric became something of a recluse. He had adopted his wife's faith in Christian Science and from the 1930s read little beyond its teachings and the Bible. Subject to epileptic fits, he died at Murrumbeena on 9 September 1959. Doris died on 13 June 1960. They were survived by their five children, all noted artists: Lucy, Arthur, Guy, David and Mary. Merric had considerable influence on younger artists. 682 of his drawings were collected and published by Christopher Tadgell as *Merric Boyd drawings* (London, 1975). His portrait by his son-in-law John Perceval is one of several.

Theodore Penleigh was born on 15 August 1890 at Penleigh House, Wiltshire, and was educated at Haileybury College and The Hutchins School, Hobart. He studied at the Melbourne National Gallery School (1905-09) and in his final year exhibited at the Victorian Artists' Society. He arrived in London in 1911 and his 'Springtime' was soon hung at the Royal Academy. He occupied studios at Chelsea, Amersham and St Ives, but for a time made Paris his headquarters. There his studio adjoined that of Phillips Fox who brought him into contact with the French modern school and through whom he met Edith Susan Gerard Anderson; they were married in Paris on 15 October 1912.

After touring France and Italy, the couple returned to Melbourne. In 1913 Boyd held an exhibition and won second prize in the Federal capital site competition; he also won the Wynne Prize for landscape in 1914. In October he exhibited at the Athenaeum Hall paintings of Venice, Paris, Sydney, Tasmania and Victoria, including some of Warrandyte, where he had built The Robins, a charming attic house set in bushland.

In 1915 Boyd joined the Australian Imperial Force, becoming a sergeant in the Electrical and Mechanical Mining Company, but was badly gassed at Ypres and invalided to England. In 1918 in London he published *Salvage,* for which he wrote a racy text illustrated with twenty vigorous black and white ink-sketches of army scenes. Later that year he returned to Melbourne and in November held an exhibition at the Victorian Artists' Society's gallery. Although he suffered from the effects of gas, he held one-man shows in 1920, 1921 and 1922; his work, both water-colours and oils, sold quickly. In September 1922 he visited England to choose a collection of contemporary European art for a government-sponsored exhibition to Australia.

On 28 November 1923 Penleigh Boyd was killed instantly when the car he was driving to Sydney overturned near Warragul; he

372

was buried in Brighton cemetery. Next March, Decoration Co. auctioned most of his remaining work, including some of his finest paintings, without reserve.

In his short career Penleigh Boyd was recognized as one of Australia's finest landscape painters, with a strong sense of colour controlled by smooth and subtle tones. 'Wattle Blossoms', hung at the Royal Academy in 1923, was much admired. He loved colour, having been influenced early by study of Turner and the example of McCubbin.

His wife EDITH SUSAN (1880-1961), was born on 16 February 1880 in Brisbane, daughter of John Gerard Anderson [q.v.3], head of the Department of Public Instruction, and his wife Edith Sarah, née Wood. She studied at the Slade School, London, and in Paris with Phillips Fox. After her marriage she continued to paint and excelled in drawing. In later years she wrote several dramas, staged by repertory companies, and radio plays for the Australian Broadcasting Commission in which she took part. She died at East Burwood on 31 March 1961, survived by her two sons, of whom Robin Gerard Penleigh (1919-1971) was a distinguished architect and writer. She may be recognized as the beautiful red-haired woman in several of Phillips Fox's paintings; three of his portraits of her are held by the family.

T. P. Boyd, *The landscapes of Penleigh Boyd,* with biog by James MacDonald (Melb, 1920); K. Hood, *Pottery* (Melb, 1961); Bernard Smith, *Australian painting 1788-1960* (Melb, 1962); J. Reed, *Australian landscape painting* (Melb, 1965); M. Boyd, *Day of my delight* (Melb, 1965); *Modern Art News,* 1 (1959), no 2; *Pottery in Aust,* 14 (1975), no 2; *Home,* 1 Dec 1921; *Aust Women's Weekly,* 26 Apr 1972; *Herald* (Melb), 30 Oct 1920, 9 Sept 1959; *The Times,* 29 Nov 1923; *Age,* 4 Feb 1933, 10 Sept 1959, 3 Apr 1961, 1 Feb 1975; P. Nase, Martin Boyd's Langton novels: an interpretative essay (M.A. thesis, ANU, 1969); M. Boyd, Boyd-à Beckett family tree and associated papers (LaTL); Doulton Insulators Aust Pty Ltd Archives (Yarraville, Vic); family information.   MARJORIE J. TIPPING

BOYD, JAMES ARTHUR (1867-1941), businessman and politician, was born on 7 July 1867 at Portsea, Hampshire, England, son of John Boyd, draper, and his wife Janet Moffatt, née McTurk. About 1869 the family moved to Ayrshire, Scotland. James was educated at St John's Academy, Glasgow, but left school early to become a farm-labourer. He was then apprenticed as a ship's painter on the Loch line. He arrived in Melbourne in 1885 and became first a painter of buildings and later a storeman. He attended night classes at the Working Men's College, dabbling with Henry George's

[q.v.4] single-tax theories. In 1887-88 he took charge of the Peninsular and Oriental Steam Navigation Co.'s models at the Melbourne Centennial International Exhibition.

In the mid-1890s Boyd prospected for gold in Western Australia. He returned to Melbourne and became proprietor of the Fidelity Free Storage Co., where he had previously been employed. For a time he was in partnership with W. J. Bradshaw, but by 1910 traded as Fidelity Storage Co. From small beginnings he expanded his commercial interests. In the 1920s and 1930s he was a director of Mutual Store Ltd, Rolfe & Co. Ltd, and Jumbunna Wool Co. which also had coal interests in Gippsland. From the early 1900s Boyd had been active in the Melbourne Chamber of Commerce and was president in 1920-22 and 1930-32. He was president in 1922-23 of the Associated Chambers of Commerce of Australia which he represented at a congress in London in 1934. By 1941 he was chairman of directors of Melbourne Hotels Ltd, Southern Union Insurance Co. of Australia Ltd and Union Investment Co. Ltd, and was a director of Australian Provincial Assurance Association Ltd, Australian Gypsum Products Pty Ltd, Victor Electric Plaster Mills Ltd and Windsor Hotel Ltd.

Boyd was a member of the Port Melbourne Town Council in 1898-1904, serving as mayor in 1903. In 1897, as a free trader, he had contested the seat of Port Melbourne in the Legislative Assembly. In 1900 he stood for Melbourne, and in March 1901 for the Federal seat of Corio. In July he won Melbourne in a bitterly fought assembly by-election. He continued to defend free trade; on the political issues of the nature and extent of government expenditure and the proper direction of rural development, he remained conservative, but as forceful and independent as his self-made background presaged. He was one of the first to throw off (Sir) William Irvine's [q.v.] attempts in 1902-03 to impose rigid party discipline and was outspokenly critical of the Bent [q.v.3] government's policy and tactics in 1904-06. In February 1907 Bent appointed him minister without office. However, when Boyd returned in 1908 from London, where he had been Victorian representative at the Franco-British Exhibition, he found the ministry reconstructed in his absence and he resigned in late October in protest against concessions to the country faction. In the ensuing election he stood as a Liberal but lost the seat to his Labor rival. He was a member of the royal commission on the University of Melbourne (1902-04), and of the board of inquiry into cancer remedy claims (1906-11). He was also on the committee of the Queen Victoria Hospital.

In 1913 Boyd won Henty in the House of Representatives as a Liberal. He renewed his long-standing dispute with Labor, especially on mining issues; in 1917, as a strong conscriptionist, he accepted W. M. Hughes's [q.v.] leadership of the National Party. In December 1919 he stood as a Liberal Nationalist but lost on preferences. Without party endorsement, he was defeated once more in 1922, and did not stand again.

'Admiral' Boyd retained his interest in the sea, with yachting as his chief hobby. In 1909-19 he chaired a committee set up to train delinquent boys for maritime life, and was responsible for the purchase of an old Loch line sailing-ship for training purposes. He was a commissioner of the Melbourne Harbor Trust in 1913-41, representing exporting interests. A Presbyterian, Boyd had married Emma Flora McCormack on 5 January 1894 at Flemington. Of their two daughters, Alva became a medical practitioner, and Esna was an Australian tennis champion. Predeceased by his wife, Boyd lived at the Hotel Windsor until his death of coronary vascular disease on 12 April 1941. He left an estate valued for probate at £14755.

Punch (Melb), 13 Feb 1908, 31 July 1913; *Argus*, 12 Apr 1941; K. Rollison, Groups and attitudes in the Victorian Legislative Assembly, 1900-1909 (Ph.D. thesis, La Trobe Univ, 1972).

KAY ROLLISON

BOYD, WILLIAM ALEXANDER JENYNS (1842-1928), agricultural journalist, schoolmaster and soldier, was born in Paris on 27 November 1842, son of Captain Charles Boyd, 95th Regiment, who had been a lieut-colonel in the Anglo-Spanish Legion of 1835, and his wife Mary, née Vachell, an aunt to the writer H. A. Vachell. He was educated in England, in Germany at Mannheim and Bonn, in Switzerland at Cully (near Lausanne) and the Italian School at Zurich, and at the Lycée de Versailles, France. Placed in a Manchester mercantile house while being coached for the army, he preferred to go to sea and, as a teenager, sailed the world in American ships. He migrated to Queensland in 1860 and, immediately selecting a small block at Oxley Creek, grew cotton, arrowroot and rice, and energetically and with characteristic initiative built the district's only cotton-mill. On 2 December 1862 he married Isabella Dawson, who soon began teaching privately; in 1867 Boyd became headmaster of the new West Oxley State School. He was a successful teacher with a progressive concern for in-

dividual needs and an 'intimate conversational style'.

Boyd began to grow sugar at Pimpama in 1871 and built his own mill. When cane-rust and frosts defeated him, he became headmaster of Townsville State School. He was made 'Occasional District Inspector and Promoter of New Schools' in 1874 and for nearly two years travelled alone through goldfields and remote stations observing northern life and manners. As agricultural editor of the *Queenslander* from 1874, he published a series of sketches of colonial characters noticed in those years. He resigned from teaching in 1875 to buy and edit the *Cleveland Bay Express* at Townsville and returned to southern Queensland considerably wealthier in 1878.

Boyd selected 1000 acres (400 ha) near Helidon for citrus-growing, and opened a private school at Milton. Visiting London in 1882, he wrote the immigration handbook, *Queensland*, and republished his earlier sketches as *Old colonials*. He owned Eton School at Nundah in 1883-89, but had to close it because of depressed rural economic conditions; he became headmaster of Toowoomba Grammar School, but reopened Eton in 1891-93.

As first editor of the *Queensland Agricultural Journal* from 1897, Boyd set out to improve the standard of agriculture. His practical and readable periodical emphasized the application of science, experiments with new crops, particularly in the tropics, and the formation of co-operative agricultural and industrial societies whose basic theme of self-help satisfied his own individualist ideal. 'Union is muscle', he urged, but nevertheless exhorted farmers not to defy authority: above all the farmer 'must not only be a strenuous worker but also a reader'.

Boyd argued for agricultural development as an aspect of defence, and also promoted it in education. In the *Education Office Gazette* he advocated the rejuvenation of school gardens with object lessons on the basic principles of agriculture and natural science. His enthusiastic propaganda probably influenced the inclusion of optional agricultural courses in the 1905 primary syllabus. In 1906 he began a schools' section in the journal and wrote an agricultural textbook in 1908.

An enthusiastic amateur soldier in 1885-97, Boyd commanded the Brisbane Garrison Artillery from 1891 and was largely responsible for recruiting the Darling Downs Mounted Infantry; he retired as major. Fluent in French, Italian and German, he served for three months in 1914 as a censor at Bundaberg. He had long been active in the Queensland branch of the Royal Geographical Society of Australasia.

A widower for many years, he was married again on 22 January 1918 in Brisbane to Violet Picton Cora White. Retiring as editor of the *Agricultural Journal* in April 1921, he continued to write for Brisbane and interstate publications. When his second wife died in 1927, he joined an adopted widowed daughter in Sydney where he died on 19 May 1928. He was buried in Toowong cemetery, Brisbane, with Anglican rites.

Sherwood Shire first annual show (Brisb, 1921); *V&P* (LA Qld), 1875, 2, 75, 1876, 2, 894; *Education Office Gazette* (Brisb), July 1900; *Muses' Mag*, Sept 1928; *Brisbane Courier*, 21 Jan 1915, 21 May 1928; *Queenslander*, 24 May 1928; Board of Education, Register of teachers 1860-75 (QA).

G. N. LOGAN

BOYLAND, JOHN (1874-1922), miner, unionist and politician, was born on 11 September 1874 at Sandhurst (Bendigo), Victoria, son of John Boyland, miner, and his wife Jane Fraser, née Duncan. He went to work at an early age and was involved in the Queensland shearers' strike of 1894. He moved to Western Australia in 1895 and worked as an underground miner at Menzies and on the Murchison goldfield. A prominent racing cyclist, he won the classic Coolgardie Austral wheel-race in 1897. He worked in South Africa, went briefly to England and, on 21 May 1906 in Perth, married a South Australian girl Bertha Bridges. He then joined his father and a brother in Kalgoorlie; his wife stayed in Perth until 1914.

An enthusiastic unionist, possibly because he had contracted miner's phthisis, Boyland represented the Federated Mining Employees' Association at the Australian Labor Federation Conference of 1913. He volunteered for the Australian Imperial Force in 1914 but was rejected because of his disease and sought to serve by, from late 1915, fervently advocating conscription on democratic grounds. His frequent press controversies, his belief in standing by the Empire 'in its hour of need' and his executive membership of the Boulder National Referendum League made him unpopular with leftist leaders. Although a marked man, he convincingly won the powerful position of secretary of the mining union in November 1916, and in December he also became its president and delegate to the federal council.

When the labour movement split, Boyland became president of the National Labor Party, formed first on the goldfields. He stood unsuccessfully for the Brownhill-Ivanhoe seat in the Legislative Assembly in September 1917, and in November resigned as secretary of the mining union, complaining of '... the hottest bosses I ever worked for. The capitalistic boss is not to be compared ...' He soon became secretary of the Eastern Goldfields Mining and General Workers' Union, the National Labor Party's industrial wing. The struggle to maintain and extend what was generally seen as a 'scab' union strained his weakening constitution and in 1918 he resigned from party office but retained his union position. In October 1919 he entered the Wooroloo Sanatorium and stayed there probably until the middle of 1920. When he was discharged, his union gave him £100 to start a stall in the Kalgoorlie Municipal Markets. On 12 March 1921, as an independent Nationalist, he defeated the Labor candidate A. E. Green [q.v.] for the Legislative Assembly seat of Kalgoorlie by 205 votes. On 14 December 1922 after a long severe winter, he died of pulmonary fibrosis at his Leederville home. He was buried in the Methodist section of Karrakatta cemetery, survived by his wife, a daughter and two sons.

Aust. Labor Federation (WA), *Official Report ... of General Council*, 1913, 1916; *Western Argus*, 21 Nov, 19 Dec 1916, 7, 14 Jan, 18 Feb 1919, 10 Feb 1920, 22, 29 Mar 1921, 19 Dec 1922; *Kalgoorlie Miner*, 19, 27, 28 Nov, 7 Dec 1917; *West Australian*, 14 Mar 1921, 15 Dec 1922.

H. J. GIBBNEY

BOYLE, IGNATIUS GEORGE (1882-1960), publican and politician, was born on 1 January 1882 at Fremantle, Western Australia, son of Francis William Boyle, warder, and his wife Ellen, née Kelly. Educated at St Joseph's Convent, Fremantle, and a foundation student of Christian Brothers' College, Perth, he left school in 1897 for a clerical job in the West Australian Government Railways. He resigned in 1903, then kept a store at Kelmscott where on 9 September 1908 he married Catherine Mary Murphy; they had four children.

Boyle was briefly licensee of the Serpentine Hotel in 1912, then went to Albany as manager for Barnett Bros. While licensee of the Premier Hotel, he became a member of the Albany Municipal Council in 1915-20. He had the Cleopatra Hotel at Fremantle in 1920-22, and was employed by the United Licensed Victuallers' Association in 1922-23 before moving to the Newcastle Hotel at Toodyay. Standing for the Legislative Assembly in 1924 and 1927, he polled well round Toodyay but lost each time to his fellow Country Party member John Lindsay who controlled the eastern wheat-belt. Boyle became a member of the Toodyay Road Board in 1928 and at once mounted a successful challenge to the retiring chairman. In two years he substantially reduced overdrafts and improved local amenities, but on resigning in April 1930 to contest the Toodyay seat a third time he was again defeated.

The Depression brought him to prominence as an agrarian demagogue. Wheatgrowers who had met the State government's pleas for a record crop were bitterly disappointed when falling export prices increased their debts. Boyle, who had bought a farm at Buntine West, became one of the moving spirits of the Wheatgrowers' Union, formed late in 1930; he was president in 1931-35 and chairman of directors of its propaganda organ, the *Wheatgrower*. Modelling its tactics partly on the trade union movement, the union was more militant than the older Primary Producers' Association, and gained strong support in the newer and poorer wheat-belt areas. Boyle led a well organized agitation for guaranteed minimum prices which culminated at the harvest of 1932 in the 'wheatgrowers' strike'. In many central and eastern districts, farmers voted not to market wheat until they were satisfied. The Commonwealth refused to increase the wheat subsidy and the State parliament voted against a levy on wheat sold for home consumption. By mid-December the strike collapsed.

Yet Boyle's reputation still stood high. He was national president of the Australian Wheatgrowers' Federation in 1933 and in Western Australia strongly supported the secession movement, popular among wheat-farmers. At a by-election in May 1935, however, he accepted nomination from the Country Party and became its member for Avon. It was a disastrous mistake. The Wheatgrowers' Union saw him as a deserter, and the Country Party remained in opposition throughout his time in parliament. His main achievement, with the support of rural Labor members, was establishment of a select committee on the education system in 1938; country schoolchildren benefited from its report. Defeated narrowly by a Labor candidate in 1943, Boyle appealed against the result but was beaten more soundly at the ensuing by-election in 1944. Two years later he stood unsuccessfully for the Senate. The Wheatgrowers' Union amalgamated reluctantly with its old rival, the Primary Producers' Association, in 1947. He died of hypertension and heart failure at his home at Mount Lawley on 15 June 1960, and was buried in Karrakatta cemetery.

Boyle was a lifelong Roman Catholic and a keen and good amateur footballer and cricketer. A heavily built florid man, he was resourceful, resilient and energetic. He showed no great originality in his political ideas, but proved himself almost too shrewd and assiduous as fixer and organizer for a rural protest movement. With a little more luck and a little less literacy, he might have been the Albert Dunstan [q.v.] of Western Australia.

G. C. Bolton, *A fine country to starve in* (Perth, 1972); B. K. Hyams, The political organisation of farmers in Western Australia from 1914 to 1944 (M.A. thesis, Univ WA, 1964).   G. C. Bolton

BRACEGIRDLE, Sir LEIGHTON SEYMOUR (1881-1970), rear admiral and secretary to governors-general, was born on 31 May 1881 at Balmain, New South Wales, son of Frederick Bracegirdle, an English-born master mariner, and his wife Sarah Elizabeth, née Drewe. He was educated at Sydney High School and became a clerk. In August 1898 he joined the New South Wales Naval Brigade (naval militia) as a cadet, was promoted midshipman two years later and in 1900-01, during the Boxer Rebellion, served with the New South Wales contingent to the China Field Force. Next year he saw action in the South African War as a lieutenant in the South Africa Irregular Horse; once he narrowly escaped death when he was shot by a sniper after being thrown from his horse.

After the war Bracegirdle resumed work as a clerk, remained in the naval militia and on 19 December 1910 married Lilian Anne Saunders at St Philip's Anglican Church, Sydney. He joined the Royal Australian Navy as a lieutenant in 1911 and was district officer at Newcastle until World War I. In August 1914 he enlisted in the Australian Naval and Military Expeditionary Force, served as a staff officer in the seizure and occupation of German New Guinea and in November was made acting lieut-commander. The A.N.M.E.F. was disbanded on 18 February 1915 and later that month Bracegirdle was appointed commander of the 1st Royal Australian Naval Bridging Train.

Originally intended for service in Flanders, the train embarked in June, was diverted to the Dardanelles, and attached to the IX British Army Corps under General Bland. Its first operational task, carried out under continual shrapnel fire, was the erection of piers and pontoons for the Suvla Bay landing of 7-9 August. The unit served at Suvla until the evacuation and had charge of pier-building and maintenance, the landing of troops, stores and ammunition and the provision of the beach water-supply. On 28 September Bracegirdle was wounded while salving a wrecked store-lighter but he remained on duty. From early December the bridging train was preparing for the evacuation; Bland praised its work during this period, describing it as a specially valuable and well-commanded unit. Bracegirdle, who was hospitalized with malaria and jaundice on 19 December, was twice mentioned in dispatches for distinguished service at Suvla.

He resumed command on 31 January 1916 and for the next three months the train served with I Anzac Corps, operating on the Suez Canal. Late in April it was reassigned to IX Army Corps in the southern section where, in addition to controlling canal traffic and conveying military stores, it built substantial wharves for unloading heavy engines for the desert military railways. Bracegirdle was awarded the Distinguished Service Order in June and was mentioned in dispatches in September. In mid-December, during the advance into Palestine, his unit landed stores on the open coast of the Sinai Desert off El Arish. Early in 1917 the Naval Bridging Train was disbanded; he relinquished his command on 5 March. In April he was promoted commander and returned to Australia as officer-in-charge of troops on the *Willochra*. He was district naval officer at Adelaide in 1918-21 and at Sydney in 1921-23. He had also been a president of the Commonwealth Coal Board in 1919-20. He was made director of naval reserves in 1923 and next year was promoted captain.

In 1931 Bracegirdle became military and official secretary to the governor-general Sir Isaac Isaacs [q.v.], and moved to a cottage in the grounds of Yarralumla, Canberra. His appointment continued during the terms of office of Lord Gowrie [q.v.] and the duke of Gloucester, and extended into the early part of Sir William McKell's term. He brought to the post an appropriately commanding manner and an imposing presence but also coped well with the economies forced upon Government House administration by the Depression and World War II. He retired from the navy in 1945 in the rank of rear admiral, and from his post as official secretary in 1947; in January he was appointed K.C.V.O.

'Brace', as he was generally known, remained active throughout his retirement, working for many years for his friend Essington Lewis [q.v.] as a part-time liaison officer with the Broken Hill Proprietary Co. Ltd and holding directorships of three other companies. He had always enjoyed fishing, shooting and tennis and he and Lady Bracegirdle liked tending the garden at their French's Forest home. A custom which they observed daily was the hoisting of the flag in the grounds. Survived by his two sons Bracegirdle died on 23 March 1970 and was cremated.

S. S. Mackenzie, *The Australians at Rabaul* ... (Syd, 1927); A. W. Jose, *The Royal Australian Navy* (Syd, 1928); J. J. Atkinson, *Australian contingents to the China Field Force 1900-1901* (Syd, 1976); *London Gazette*, 28 Jan, 2 June, 11 July, 22 Sept 1916; *SMH*, 3 June 1916, 21 June 1921, 19 Jan 1931, 1 Jan 1935, 2, 9 Jan 1947, 26 Mar, 10 June 1970; Bracegirdle file (AWM); Roy Aust Naval Bridging Train, Records (AWM); family papers.

W. S. BRACEGIRDLE

BRACY, HENRY (1841?-1917), tenor and stage-director, was born at Maestag, Glamorganshire, Wales, son of an ironworks manager. He began his theatrical career at the Plymouth Theatre in 1866 where he remained for three seasons. In 1870 he made his London début at the Gaiety Theatre and in 1873 was engaged as a principal tenor with the Opera Comique.

In September Bracy sailed for Australia with his wife Clara Thompson, and on 6 December they made their first appearance at the Theatre Royal, Melbourne, in Offenbach's operetta *Lischen and Fritzchen*. After a series of small parts he and Clara were engaged by W. S. Lyster [q.v.5] for his English opera company. They opened in Offenbach's *Princess of Trebizonde* with Armes Beaumont [q.v.3]; Bracy was also stage-manager and Clara delighted audiences with her 'mercurial vivacity'. The Bracys toured the United States of America then settled in London in 1879. Among other successful performances Henry was principal tenor with Florence St John in the comic opera *Madame Favart*, which ran for 502 consecutive performances. In October 1881 he sang Frittelini in *La mascotte* and his song, *Love is blind*, became the rage. At the Savoy Theatre in January 1884 he created Hillarion in *Princess Ida* under the direction of Gilbert and Sullivan. He then turned to management and lost heavily.

Late in 1888 the Bracys returned to Melbourne. In June next year Henry directed John Solomon's English and Comic Opera Company in Sydney and Melbourne. The *Australasian* critic found Bracy's voice mellower and richer: 'his solos were delivered with a directness and a purity of tone most refreshing'. In October 1890 he produced *The gondoliers* for J. C. Williamson's [q.v.6] Royal Comic Opera Company, and from that time produced almost all Williamson's Gilbert and Sullivan performances. Clara also sang in many of the operas. Bracy's productions were set in the Savoy mould, with replicas of the original costumes and sets, and he took no liberties with the text.

Williamson and George Musgrove [q.v.5]

disbanded the company in 1896. Lacking an engagement, next March in Sydney Bracy formed and toured with his own troupe who cheerfully 'shared his risks', until some nine months later he disbanded it. In September 1898 he voluntarily sequestered his estate and was not released from bankruptcy until 1900.

Re-engaged by Williamson, Bracy managed the concert tours of Madame Albani in 1898 and Ada Crossley [q.v.] in 1903, and was stage-director for the Bel Sorel season of grand opera. He 'developed into a splendid all-round man ... operatic artist, stage-director, producer and business manager in turn. Never was there a cooler and more unperturbable stage-boss'. His last role was as Colonel Fairfax in *The yeomen of the guard* in 1908. Bracy was also Williamson's chief adviser in the selection of vocalists. He retired with a special pension in 1914, then visited his wife who 'had for some time been identified with the moving pictures' at Los Angeles, California. In 1913 Williamson had left him 500 shares in his company.

Survived by his wife and two sons, Bracy died, aged 75, of cerebro-vascular disease at Darlinghurst, Sydney, on 31 January 1917 and was buried in the Anglican section of Waverley cemetery: twelve choristers from J. C. Williamson's sang Sir Arthur Sullivan's *The long day closes* at his graveside. As a singer Bracy was 'mechanical, sweet-voiced, unimpassioned' and he remained wooden as an actor; however he was very successful as a producer and director.

V. de Loitte, *Gilbert and Sullivan opera in Australia*, 1879-1933, 7th edn (Syd, 1933); *Argus*, 8 Dec 1873, 3 Jan, 23 June 1874, 19 Apr, 7 Oct 1875, 23 Sept 1879; *The Times*, 7 Jan 1884; *Bulletin*, 10 Aug, 14 Sept 1889, 8 Feb 1917; *Australasian*, 28 Sept 1889, 3 Feb 1917.   TONY MILLS

BRADDON, SIR EDWARD NICHOLAS COVENTRY (1829-1904), civil servant and politician, was born on 11 June 1829 at St Kew, Cornwall, England, son of Henry Braddon, solicitor, and his wife Fanny, née White. A sister Mary Elizabeth became a popular novelist. Braddon was educated at a preparatory school in the Fulham Road, London, and later at a private school at Greenwich. He may have taken commercial subjects at University College. His parents' marriage was a 'loveless' one which led to an 'amiable' separation. Unlike his two sisters, Braddon was permitted to visit his father, and he did so while he remained in England.

In 1847 he went to India to work in a cousin's merchant firm in Calcutta. He found the life of a clerk, imprisoned behind a counting-desk, hard to bear and in 1850 or 1851 he eagerly left the city for the rural districts, to manage a number of indigo factories near Krishnagar. Braddon worked there for about five years, displaying the usual planter arrogance towards the Indians. A European deputy magistrate once actually found him guilty of 'aggravated and unprovoked assault', a decision that was later reversed. In July 1855 his work was interrupted by skirmishes and cleaning-up operations against the Santal people who had revolted briefly. The opportunity for martial activity pleased him, and he later spoke of it as 'a splendid substitute for tiger-shooting which came not to my hand'. Two years later he was able to enlist under (Sir) George Yule in a volunteer force which saw Indian Mutiny service in Purnea.

The Santal insurrection stimulated a change in the organization of government in the area. A new, non-regulation province, the Santal Parganas, was created, with Yule as its first commissioner. His assistant commissioner of Deoghar division, from October 1857, was Braddon who soon found that the arduous life of a district officer suited him admirably. It required a wide range of administrative skills and occasionally caused him to chafe at the need for routine, but he was relatively free from the interference of superiors and could spend about half of each year travelling about his domain. The early administration of the Santal Parganas seems to have been a great success, and he is referred to as having played his part creditably.

Braddon was promoted to Lucknow where in 1862-76 he was superintendent of excise and stamps for the recently annexed province of Oudh; he also served in other administrative posts. As in Deoghar, much of his time was spent in the saddle, and he claimed to have covered 3000 miles (4800 km) a year on tour. Despite his obvious competence, Braddon was eventually forced into a premature retirement upon the amalgamation of Oudh and the North-West provinces. His post disappeared, and he was offered no other — apparently to his chagrin.

Braddon had married twice in India: on 24 October 1857 to Amy Georgina Palmer (d. 1864), by whom he had two sons and four daughters; and on 16 October 1876 to Alice Harriet Smith, by whom he had one daughter. One son was (Sir) Henry Yule [q.v.]. At an age when many Anglo-Indians retired home, he set sail in March 1878 for Tasmania and a new life. He settled on a small, run-down property at Leith on the north-west coast, and worked extremely hard to make it a worthwhile enterprise. Few people then lived in that part of the colony, and Braddon undoubtedly stood out as a man of experience and proven ability. He was soon asked to join community committees, and accepted nomination for the seat of West Devon, an election he won in July 1879 – as he won all that he contested thereafter.

Braddon soon proved himself a sharp debater and accomplished strategist. The Agnew [q.v.3] goverment, third of the so-called 'continuous ministry', began to show signs of confusion and indecision in mid-1886, and an Opposition caucus began to form about Braddon. The immediate reason given for the group's appearance was the need to publicly denounce 'jobbery', most obvious in the appointments of (Sir) John Dodds [q.v.4] and E. D. Dobbie [q.v.] as puisne judge and solicitor-general. When, in early 1887, a determined campaign blocked the re-election of Agnew's appointee to the attorney-generalship, the duty of the premier was made clear, and he advised that Braddon be called to form an administration, which he did. But, for reasons that remain unclear, P. O. Fysh [q.v.] became premier, with Braddon as minister for lands and works, and A. Inglis Clark [q.v.3] as attorney-general.

Braddon had been in office for eighteen months when he was appointed agent-general in London. There is a suggestion that he saw this post, accepted when he was 59, as the culmination of his career, and entered it with his usual zest. He performed a valuable service in attracting money to Tasmania, especially in the flotation of a number of companies, including the Mt Lyell Mining and Emu Bay railway companies. In 1891 he was appointed K.C.M.G. He retained his post until September 1893, when he returned to the colony to active politics and the leadership of the Opposition.

The unsettled nature of Tasmanian politics soon saw Braddon immersed in intrigues designed to destroy the government of Henry Dobson [q.v.]: in April 1894 Dobson was defeated in the House over his land tax bill, and from 14 April Braddon became premier of an administration which was not expected to last long; it survived the 1897 general election and was not defeated until 12 October 1899.

The Braddon ministry did much to restore Tasmania's finances. There was a determined and successful effort to reduce unnecessary expenditure, while industry was given every encouragement to establish, and expand, by a premier who believed that a prosperous business community meant a prosperous colony. At the same time, the government vigorously constructed roads, railways, harbours and waterworks. He licensed his friend George Adams [q.v.3] to conduct Tattersall's lotteries from which the State profited.

Braddon was the first Tasmanian premier to have been a professional public servant before taking office, and he was noted as a conscientious yet ruthless administrator. As premier he was bound to the policies of retrenchment and efficiency, and he attacked both with vigour. His administrative skills had been hard learned in India, and his performance in Tasmania shocked many: public servants long remembered the savagery of 'Braddon's axe'. The need for a devious diplomacy in the Indian setting also prepared him well for Tasmania, where the fate of governments and individual careers depended so much on ability to understand the parliamentary game.

Braddon's government introduced proportional representation and challenged the obstruction of the Legislative Council by an appeal to the Privy Council to define its powers, which was refused. He survived a crisis late in 1897 over a conflict between the Emu Bay and Great Western railway companies, although Clark resigned on the issue. At the Colonial Conference in London that year, Braddon was appointed a privy councillor. As premier, he drew no salary.

Braddon was a convinced Federalist. He was a member of the Federal Council of Australasia in 1888 and in 1895-99, being president in 1895. He hosted the 1895 premiers' conference at which the Federal cause was revived, and was elected top of the poll for Tasmanian delegates to the convention of 1897-98. His conservative voice had as its main refrain the protection of colonial rights. He was particularly concerned with the likely effect of Federation upon colonial finances, and his successful introduction of what became section 87 (quickly dubbed Braddon's 'Blot'), whereby three-quarters of the revenue from customs and excise was to be returned to the States for ten years, was one of the essential steps which ensured acceptance of the Constitution by the smaller colonies. In the referendum battles he participated fully in the 'Yes' campaign, and Tasmania's overwhelming acceptance was due in part to his personal convictions and effort. Deakin [q.v.] described him as 'the most distinguished-looking delegate of the Convention ... slight, erect, stiff, with the walk of a horseman and the carriage of a soldier, he had the manner of a diplomat ... An iron-grey lock fell artistically forward upon his forehead, bright grey eyes gleamed from under rather bushy eyebrows, a straight nose leading to a heavy moustache and a Vandyke beard ... He was a most amiable cynic, an accomplished strategist and an expert administrator ... he introduced into the Convention an element of manners'.

Braddon headed the Tasmanian election for the first Commonwealth parliament with a resounding 26 per cent of the vote. As (Sir) George Reid's [q.v.] deputy, he sometimes acted as leader of the Opposition. At the 1951 jubilee celebrations, he was the Founding Father honoured by Tasmania.

In private life Braddon was scornful of physical danger, domineering with his children (though probably not his wives), fully prepared to participate in the social events of the neighbourhood, and a sartorial disaster. He shared his sister's skill with the pen, writing a number of journal articles, as well as *Life in India* (London, 1872) and *Thirty years of Shikar* (Edinburgh, 1895).

'Ned' Braddon died at Leith on 2 February 1904 and was buried in the Pioneers' cemetery, Forth; there is a memorial to him at Braddon's Lookout, within view of his small property. His estate was valued for probate at £8720 in Tasmania and £679 in New South Wales.

Cyclopedia of Tasmania (Hob, 1900); F. C. Green (ed), *A century of responsible government 1856-1956* (Melb, 1956); A. Deakin, *The federal story*, J. A. La Nauze ed (Melb, 1963); J. A. La Nauze, *The making of the Australian constitution* (Melb, 1972); *Mercury*, 3 Feb 1904.   SCOTT BENNETT

BRADDON, SIR HENRY YULE (1863-1955), businessman and financier, was born on 27 April 1863 near Calcutta, India, second son of (Sir) Edward Nicholas Coventry Braddon [q.v.], and his first wife Amy Georgina (d. 1864), née Palmer. He was brought up at Lucknow until he went to Germany in 1869, where he was educated at Dusseldorf. He spent 1874-75 at Caen, Normandy, France, and in April 1875 went to Alleyn's College of God's Gift (Dulwich College), London. In April 1878 he left to join his father in Tasmania (and was very disappointed at the lack of active bushrangers); he attended Launceston Church Grammar School and late in 1879 joined the Commercial Bank of Tasmania. In 1882 he transferred to the Bank of Australasia at Invercargill, New Zealand.

A notable all-round sportsman Braddon had represented Northern Tasmania at cricket, and played Rugby for Invercargill Club and Otago Province and seven times for New Zealand as full-back. He was a member of the 1884 team that toured New South Wales, where he remained and joined Dalgety [q.v.4] & Co. Ltd as a clerk at Newcastle. He played six times for the colony, against Great Britain in 1888, Victoria in 1889 and Queensland in 1890-92. In 1892 he captained the New South Wales eight in intercolonial races.

On 2 September 1891 Braddon had married Bertha Mary Mathews Russell of Invercargill at St Anne's Church of England, Strathfield. With Dalgety's for forty-four years, he became secretary in Sydney, sub-manager of the Sydney branch in 1904, manager in 1906 and Australian superintendent in 1914-28. Under his leadership the company prospered and expanded. He soon became prominent in business circles: he was president of the Employers' Federation of New South Wales in 1905-07, of the Sydney Chamber of Commerce in 1912-14 and of the Associated Chambers of Commerce of Australia in 1913-14 and 1920-21. In 1907-24 he was a part-time lecturer in business methods at the University of Sydney, and in 1909 published *Business principles and practice*; throughout his life he promoted commercial education. With (Sir) T. R. Bavin [q.v.] in 1911-13 he sat on the royal commission into food supplies and fish.

On the outbreak of World War I Braddon was a founding vice-president of the New South Wales division of the British Red Cross Society and was a member of its council throughout the war. In 1914-20 he was also president of the Australian Comforts Fund (Citizens' War Chest Committee): its executive met every weekday. In 1916 he was a founder of the Universal Service League and a member of its financial committee, and for two years was a member of the State Recruiting Committee: all his three sons were on active service, and all survived the war. He was also a director of Royal Prince Alfred Hospital in 1915-17 and honorary treasurer of the Benevolent Society in 1916-18.

Braddon was appointed commissioner to represent Australia in the United States of America in September 1918 and, soon after his arrival in October, set up an office in New York. Although the governor-general Sir Ronald Munro Ferguson [q.v.] had limited his original 'very wide and comprehensive' mission to trade matters, he reported secretly to London in 1919 that 'Braddon had been undoubtedly accepted in America as more than a Commercial Agent'. The quantity of American imports had risen sharply during the war and he insisted that every matter concerning Australia be put first to him to decide if it were 'diplomatic' and to be passed on to the British Embassy, or 'commercial', when he would deal with it himself. He left America in June, and in London helped to organize the commercial side of the high commissioner's office. He returned to Sydney by November and published *American impressions* in 1920. Appointed K.B.E. that year, he was awarded the Belgian King Albert Medal in 1921.

After the war Braddon was again prominent in financial circles: he was a director of many companies including Sydney Ferries Ltd, W. R. Carpenter [q.v.] & Co. Ltd, and the Goodyear Tyre & Rubber Co. (Australia) Ltd; in 1921-27 he was a member of the Sydney section of the Board of Trade and in 1922-24 a director of the Commonwealth Note Issue Board. He gave innumerable lectures on business and finance, including unemployment, paper money, income tax and the financial position of Europe and Australia; some he published as pamphlets. After he retired as Australian superintendent of Dalgety's in 1928, he was appointed to the Council for Prevention and Relief of Unemployment in 1930. He was a director of the Mutual Life & Citizens' Assurance Co. Ltd in 1933-55, a local director of the Bank of New Zealand in 1929-54, and chairman of the Sydney boards of Babcock & Wilcox Ltd in 1930-48 and of the Union Trustee Co. of Australia in 1942-54.

Braddon's activities were almost innumerable. He had been appointed to the Legislative Council in 1917, and after it was reconstituted in 1933, was elected for a six-year term in 1934; he bitterly opposed J. T. Lang's [q.v.] financial policies, actively campaigned for the Nationalists in the 1930 elections, and next year defended Bavin from his critics. Braddon was a member of the university senate in 1919-29, sat on its finance committee and the University Extension Board in 1920-29 and encouraged it to found a chair of commerce. He was also president of the Women's Hospital, Crown Street, in 1925-44, of the Rotary Club of Sydney from 1922, and first president of the New South Wales Society for Crippled Children from 1930. Active as an Imperial publicist, he gave many addresses to school children, the Boys' Brigade, and to the Police Boys' clubs, of which he was a founder. He was a member of the Round Table group, vice-president of the Millions Club from 1917, president of the English-Speaking Union in 1922-44, a founder of the Australian-American Association and was involved with the Sane Democracy League.

Braddon remained interested in sport: he was president of the New South Wales Rugby Union in 1916-25; he took up tennis and golf, was a member of the Australian and Royal Sydney golf clubs, and late in life was a regular ringsider at Sydney Stadium fights and White City tennis. In 1930 he published *Essays and addresses, historical, economic, social*, whose subjects included the Olympic Games, Shakespeare and the French 'assignat' issues of 1790-97, and also *Making of a constitution*. He was a member of the Royal Australian Historical Society, and in 1933 contributed his 'Reminiscences' to its *Journal*.

Braddon was handsome, with short, very dark hair as a young man, and a neatly clipped moustache which he kept all his life, and had a keen sense of humour. He was a member of the Australian, Union and Warrigal clubs in Sydney and of the Melbourne Club, and visited England and New Zealand several times. He always chaired the Sydney dinners of the old Alleynians and was president of the English Public Schools Association in Sydney in 1931-42. In 1940 he and his wife gave £1000 to the war effort. She died in 1942, and at the Registry Office, Jersey Road, Paddington, on 31 August 1944 he married a divorcee Violet Mary Inglis, née Wheelihan.

Braddon died on 8 September 1955 at his home Rohini, Edgecliff Road, Woollahra, and was cremated with Anglican rites. He was survived by a son and daughter of his first marriage and by his second wife; his estate was valued for probate at £26 216, and his will was challenged in the Supreme Court. His portrait, painted by W. A. Bowring on his retirement from Dalgety's, is held by the University of Sydney.

Braddon's firm belief that 'we should take pride in doing the simplest work as artists rather than as drudges' was perhaps the secret of his success, although he ascribed it to never despising one's job, courtesy and working with one's 'mind on the task, not on enrichment'. He contributed much as a financial expert, as a teacher and publicist, and not least as a humanist.

Trade and Commerce J, 28 Aug 1918; *Commerce* (Syd), Dec 1929; *SMH*, 16 July, 19 Nov 1919, 16 Oct 1920, 12 Apr 1921, 21 Dec 1922, 3 Jan 1929, 4 July 1930, 24 May 1939, 28 Apr 1943, 8 Sept 1955, 11 May, 11 Dec 1956; Braddon material (held by Mr D. A. Wilkey, Canb); Dalgety & Co. papers (ANU Archives); Reports and minutes (Syd Chamber of Commerce Archives); Board of Trade, Minutes CP 703/3, *and* Trade Commissioners, Personal file for H. Y. Braddon CP 360/11, 19/446 (AAO, Canb); Senate, Faculty, *and* Finance Cttee minutes (Univ Syd Archives); CO 418/176; information from Lady Violet Braddon.   H. McCREDIE

BRADFIELD, JOHN JOB CREW (1867-1943), civil engineer, was born on 26 December 1867 at Sandgate, Queensland, fourth son of John Edward Bradfield, labourer and Crimean War veteran, and his wife Maria, née Crew. His parents, brothers and four sisters had arrived in Brisbane from England in 1857. Educated at the North Ipswich State School and the Ipswich Grammar School on a scholarship, Bradfield passed the Sydney senior public examination in 1885, gaining the medal for chemistry. Dux of his school, he won a

Queensland government university exhibition and in 1886 matriculated at the University of Sydney. From St Andrew's College, he continued his brilliant academic career, graduating B.E. with the University Gold Medal in 1889.

From May, Bradfield worked as a draftsman under the chief engineer, railways, in Brisbane. On 28 May 1891 at St John's Pro-Cathedral he married Edith Jenkins. That year he was retrenched and joined the New South Wales Department of Public Works as a temporary draftsman, becoming permanent in 1895. An associate from 1893 of the Institution of Civil Engineers, London, he graduated M.E. with first-class honours and the University Medal in 1896. He had been a founder of the Sydney University Engineering Society in 1895 and was president in 1902-03 and 1919-20. In his 1903 presidential address he drew attention to the competition, initiated in 1900, for the design of a bridge across Sydney Harbour; there had been agitation for a bridge or tunnel since the 1880s.

Bradfield was associated with a great range of engineering work including the Cataract Dam near Sydney and the Burrinjuck Dam which formed part of the Murrumbidgee Irrigation Area. In January 1909 he was promoted assistant engineer at a salary of £400. He had worked on some important projects, but he was not his own master. In August 1910 he applied for the foundation chair of engineering in the new University of Queensland, but was unsuccessful despite twenty-two testimonials from senior public servants, academics, engineers and architects such as Norman Selfe [q.v.6.], (Sir) George Knibbs, (Sir) Edgeworth David, R. F. Irvine and (Sir) John Sulman [qq.v.].

In February 1912 in evidence to the Parliamentary Standing Committee on Public Works Bradfield proposed a suspension bridge to connect Sydney and North Sydney, but in April also submitted a cantilever design. Next year the committee recommended acceptance of his scheme for the construction of a cantilever bridge from Dawes Point to Milsons Point. In 1913 his title was changed to chief engineer for metropolitan railway construction.

Plans for a city railway were already well developed by his predecessors when, in 1914, Bradfield went overseas to investigate new approaches to metropolitan railway construction. Early next year he reported on the proposed electric lines for the city of Sydney. Aware that a bill was soon to come before parliament, he went to considerable effort to show the practicality of his scheme. He was at his most convincing in this report, as in all his later publications, when he managed to combine both the functional and the 'city beautiful' aspects of his plan. In the debates on the bill, his engineering talents were praised by both sides. However all sections of his scheme were postponed as a general war economy measure.

In October 1913, with J. D. Fitzgerald [q.v.] and Sulman, Bradfield had attended the inaugural meeting of the Town Planning Association of New South Wales; at the first Australian Town Planning Conference and Exhibition held in Adelaide in October 1917, he argued in his paper, 'The transit problems of greater Sydney', that his scheme of suburban electrification would benefit large property owners, new home purchasers and the general public by opening up new land, with quicker transport and cheaper fares. He predicted that Sydney's population would reach at least 2 226 000 by 1950. Bradfield maintained – apparently without reprimand from government – an extraordinary barrage of articles and public addresses advocating his plan.

In March 1922 he was sent overseas to inquire into tenders for a cantilever bridge. Later that year the Harbour Bridge Act was carried; Bradfield had advised R. T. Ball [q.v.] to amend the bill to provide for either a cantilever or an arch bridge, according to his specifications, as developments in light steel made the latter possible. In 1924 he recommended that the government should accept the tender of Dorman Long & Co. of Middlesbrough, England.

The easy passage of the Harbour Bridge Act undoubtedly increased Bradfield's determination to promote other sections of his scheme. By mid-1923 the public could see results of the Bradfield plan in the massive excavations and tunnel-building in Hyde Park for the underground railway. In 1924 he received the first doctorate of science in engineering awarded by the University of Sydney, for a thesis entitled 'The city and suburban electric railways and the Sydney Harbour Bridge'. One of his examiners, Sir John Monash [q.v.], wrote: 'these works are undoubtedly of exceptional magnitude, being in some respects unique in Engineering practice'. The opening of the St James and Museum stations and the new section of the Central Station at Chalmers Street on 20 December 1926 marked his plan's first result. In February 1930 he was curtly retired by the railway commissioners; however cabinet preserved his status in the Department of Public Works and £3000 salary, and he continued to represent the government in dealings with the contractors and to supervise construction of the bridge.

During this extended period of public and parliamentary exposure Bradfield's expertise was never questioned. But in 1929 controversy flared over who really designed the bridge, inspired by a series of articles in the *Sydney Morning Herald* by (Sir) Ralph Freeman (1880-1950), consulting engineer to Dorman Long, who was described by the *Herald* as 'the designer' of the bridge and who conveyed the same impression in his articles. Ball, now minister for lands, said it was difficult to determine what was really meant by the term 'designer'; he would describe the bridge as a Bradfield-Dorman Long design. E. A. Buttenshaw [q.v.] called for a report on the matter from Bradfield, who wrote, 'I originated the cantilever bridge design recommended by the public works committee in 1913 and subsequently the arch bridge design of 1650 feet span'; he went on to say Freeman was not the designer and that tenders were called on his own design. The controversy was never finally resolved, but when Bradfield retired in 1933, the director of public works stated that Bradfield was the designer of the bridge and that 'no other person by any stretch of imagination, can claim that distinction'. However, modifications had been made to the design after Freeman's visit in 1926, and in 1932 Dorman Long threatened to sue the government if it erected a plaque naming Bradfield as the designer. One informed view was that the 'detail design was entrusted to Lawrence Ennis who became first Honorary Member of the Institution [of Engineers, Australia] in 1932'. Professor Crawford Munro also considered that Bradfield 'did not design the Sydney Harbour Bridge which we now behold'.

The highlight of Bradfield's career undoubtedly was the opening of the bridge on 19 March 1932 (despite the antics of Captain de Groot of the New Guard). He was a member of the official party and the governor Sir Philip Game [q.v.] named the bridge highway after him. The Depression was to suspend the Bradfield plan for well over a decade, and the construction of the Eastern Suburbs railway was far in the future. In 1933 he was appointed C.M.G. and he retired from the public service in July.

In 1934 Bradfield was appointed consulting engineer for the design, fabrication and construction of a bridge and approaches across the Brisbane River from Kangaroo Point to Bowen Terrace. The Story [q.v.] Bridge was a symmetrical cantilever of 1463 ft. (446 m) in length, with a clear span of 924 ft. (281.6 m); construction began in 1935 and the bridge was opened in 1940. He was also technical adviser to the constructors of the Hornibrook Highway near Brisbane and helped to plan and design the University of Queensland's new site at St Lucia; the university admitted him to an *ad eund.* doctorate of engineering in 1935.

Although in most respects severely pragmatic, Bradfield had a penchant for the grandiose that was revealed in some of his wilder plans for high-rise office blocks astride the southern approaches of the Harbour Bridge and in his proposals for a massive water-diversion scheme in Queensland. In his early seventies he put considerable time and energy into publicizing a plan to irrigate the western districts of Queensland and part of Central Australia by damming certain coastal rivers and running water-pipes through the Great Dividing Range. Aspects of this scheme, and especially his lack of scientific evidence, were publicly attacked by G. W. Leeper of the school of agricultural science at the University of Melbourne.

Bradfield had wide interests within his chosen profession. Early in 1916 he was appointed by the New South Wales government to a committee to establish and manage a school of aviation at Richmond. In 1919 he was a founder of the Institution of Engineers, Australia, and as a councillor in 1920-24 and 1927 represented it on the Australian Commonwealth Standards Association; he was also a member of the Australian National Research Council. He always maintained close links with the University of Sydney: he was a member of its senate in 1913-43, a trustee of Wesley College in 1917-43, a councillor of the Women's College from 1931, and from 1942 deputy chancellor. He was a member of the University Club and from 1922 of the Royal Society of New South Wales.

Bradfield regularly attended St John's Church of England, Gordon, and was a keen gardener. He died at his home at Gordon on 23 September 1943 and was buried in St John's cemetery; a memorial service was held at St Andrew's Cathedral. He was survived by his wife, five sons and a daughter; his youngest son Keith inherited his father's interest in aviation and was assistant director general, Department of Civil Aviation, in 1957-68. Bradfield's estate was valued for probate at £13 843: his salary had been 'by no means commensurate' with his importance. A portrait by F. W. Leist [q.v.] is at the University of Sydney, and others by Gerard Nathan and Joseph Wolinski are held by descendants.

Bradfield was small in stature, with a quiet and humorous disposition. His life was one of total professional zeal and commitment, and he became an outstanding Australian engineer in his generation. Florence Taylor [q.v.] noted his 'tremendous faith in his ability which is not a conceit when there is an enormous knowledge behind that faith and ability'. He was honoured by the award of the (Sir) Peter Nicol Russell [q.v.6] Medal by the

Institution of Engineers, Australia, in 1932, the (W. C.) Kernot [q.v.5] Memorial Medal by the University of Melbourne in 1933, and the Telford Gold Medal of the Institution of Civil Engineers, London, in 1934. His vision of Sydney captured the imagination of many, including J. T. Lang [q.v.] who later wrote: 'Bradfield wanted to be the Napoleon III of Sydney. He wanted to pull down everything in the way of his grandiose schemes. He was always thinking of the future. He was probably the first man to plan for Sydney as a city of two million people'.

J. T. Lang, *I remember* (Syd, 1956); A. H. Corbett, *The Institution of Engineers, Australia* (Syd, 1973); P. Spearritt, *Selected writings of Sydney planning advocates, 1900-1947* (Canb, 1973); Univ Syd Union, *Union Recorder*, 30 Sept, 14 Oct 1943; G. W. Leeper, 'Restoring Australia's parched lands...', *Aust Q*, June 1942; E. J. Brady, 'Wizard of construction', *Life Digest*, May 1949; *Sydney Mail*, 8 Mar 1922; *SMH*, 6 May 1924, 12 Oct, 17 Nov 1927, 11-14, 23, 25, 28 Mar, 23 Nov 1929, 11, 12, 28 Feb, 12 June 1930, 17 Mar, 29 July 1933, 16 June 1934, 24 Sept 1943; P. Spearritt, The consensus politics of physical planning in Sydney (B.A. Hons thesis, Univ Syd, 1972); Bradfield technical papers (ML, NL, NSWA), *and* Engineering School, Univ Syd); Public Works Dept, Special bundles 4/7582-7588 (NSWA); information from and family papers held by Dr K. N. E. Bradfield.

PETER SPEARRITT

BRADLEY, JOSEPH (1857-1935) musician and music teacher, was born on 28 February 1857 at Newton near Hyde, Cheshire, England, son of Matthew Henry Bradley, later publican, and his wife Mary, née Heywood. Trained by Dr Frederick Bridge of Manchester Cathedral, at 12 he was appointed assistant organist of St Paul's Church, Stalybridge, Lancashire. In 1873 he became a fellow of the Royal College of Organists, matriculated to New College, Oxford, in October 1874 and graduated Bachelor of Music next year. As organist in 1876-80 at St Thomas's Church, Heaton Norris, Stockport, he formed and conducted a fifty-piece orchestra. On 8 August 1877 with Anglican rites he married Catherine Mary Pickering at Manchester; they had two children.

Bradley's first major post was as deputy conductor and organist for the Hallé Orchestra of Manchester in 1881-87. There he once conducted Handel's *Messiah* seven times in a week. As chorus-master and conductor of the Glasgow Choral Union in 1887-1908 he controlled over 400 members; the leader of its orchestra was Henri Verbrugghen [q.v.]. Bradley opened the organ at the International Exhibition of 1888, Glasgow, and in 1890 applied unsuccessfully for appointment as city organist of Sydney.

Appointed conductor of the Royal Philharmonic Society of Sydney in 1908, Bradley arrived with his wife on 23 March in the *Somerset*. With the Philharmonic Choir and the new Sydney Symphony Orchestra, which he also conducted (always without a baton), in 1908-14 he was able to introduce such contemporary works as Elgar's *Caractacus* and César Franck's *Les béatitudes*. In 1915 he presented the difficult *Grande messe des morts* of Berlioz to mark the death of Sir William P. Manning [q.v.], long president of the society.

In Bradley's twenty years in Sydney he conducted 126 performances including 29 of the *Messiah*, 8 of Mendelsohn's *Elijah*, 5 of Haydn's *The creation*, 4 of Berlioz's *La damnation de Faust* and 4 of Elgar's *Caractacus*. Conforming with the style of the society, his performances were safe rather than adventurous.

Verbrugghen was chosen in preference to him as first director of the new State Conservatorium of Music, but Bradley philosophically accepted the professorship of theory and later also taught solfeggio. He published *A solfeggio manual for teachers* (1919) and *A manual of musical ornamentation* (1924). He was one of three conductors for the opening concert of the conservatorium in 1915 but, being bald, rotund and impassive, he seemed stodgy compared to Verbrugghen. Though dreaded by students as something of a martinet, he was recognized by all as peerless in theoretical and practical musicianship.

When Verbrugghen resigned, Bradley was on the committee which governed the conservatorium in the interregnum, then in 1924 went on a short visit to Europe, partly to introduce Gladys Cole, a favourite singing pupil, to the musical world. Soon after his return his eyesight began to fail. Pugnaciously proud and reserved, he told nobody, not even his wife, conducted from memory as long as he could and resigned without explanation only when faced with a new score. The Philharmonic Society was angered and gave him only a lukewarm farewell and a meagre cheque. He returned to England in January 1928 to join his son Julius who had spent years in China. An operation for a cataract left him blind. Aged 78, he died of cerebral vascular disease at Harrow, Middlesex, on 3 March 1935.

W. A. Orchard, *The distant view* (Syd, 1943); R. Craig, *A short history of the Glasgow Choral Union* (Glasgow, 1944); E. Wunderlich, *All my yesterdays* (Syd, 1945); W. A. Orchard, *Music in Australia* (Melb, 1952); *Sydney Mail*, 5, 23 Mar, 1 Apr 1908; *SMH*, 12 Dec 1923, 3 June, 14 Dec 1927, 5, 7, 9 Mar 1935; letter from J. Bradley, 20 Aug 1890 (Syd City Council Archives); Roy Philharmonic Soc, Concert programmes 1909-27, MS 5335 (NL); informa ton from Mr R. Wood, Mittagong, NSW.

P. F. LEIGHTON

BRADLEY, LUTHER (1853-1917), cartoonist, was born on 29 September 1853 at New Haven, Connecticut, United States of America, son of Francis Bradley, estate agent, who later moved to Chicago. After a course at Northwestern University he went to Yale College, graduating in 1875. His education included no art training of any sort, although he drew occasional sketches of fellow-students and staff. After five years in his father's business he left Chicago in 1882 on a world trip for health reasons. He arrived in Melbourne from London, saw a cartoon magazine displayed in a bookseller's window and decided that he could do better himself. Soon he was chief cartoonist and proprietor of the journal, which he restored to new life on 19 June 1884 at 83 Queen Street, as the weekly *Australian Tit-Bits* (incorporated in *Life* in June 1886).

Fortunately, Bradley's individual, lively style coincided with the general introduction of photo-engraving which allowed artists to express their own individuality to the full. He contributed to various papers, among them the Sydney *Bulletin*, and on the retirement of *Melbourne Punch's* F. T. D. (Tom) Carrington [q.v.3], Bradley became the paper's chief cartoonist. His first full-page cartoon appeared on 12 January 1888. By then he had overcome the defects apparent in his earlier drawings: the insensitive wiry line and tentative approach arising out of his early lack of training. He lacked Carrington's satirical venom, but his joyous topicality was attuned to the optimistic outlook of young Australia. The former personifications of the colonies as massive matrons in classical draperies were replaced by Bradley with pretty girl types and fashionable young matrons. Bradley's 'You're a big girl now', on 26 January 1888, showed a smart matron, Britannia, advising her up-to-date teen-age daughter, Australia, to throw away her ugly rag dolls of parliamentary obstruction and clowning, and 'in future behave like one who has reached years of discretion'.

Bradley was important for his record of the significant days of the challenge of the trade unions, the golden colonial afternoon of the 'Boom' and the great strikes and financial collapse that followed. He is wrongly credited with being the creator of the 'King Working Man' image of the unions; in June 1892 *Melbourne Punch* published a special issue of Bradley cartoons under this title but Carrington had originated the character. Bradley's graphic imagination blew up the image into a mythical, menacing ogre, the embodiment of middle-class fears.

In mid-1893 news came of his father's illness and Bradley returned to Chicago where he worked successively for the *Journal* and *Inter Ocean*, until in 1899 he became art director and cartoonist on the *Chicago Daily News*. In 1901 he married Agnes Floyd Smith. On 9 January 1917 he died suddenly at his home in Wilmette, Illinois, survived by his wife and their four children. An album of one hundred of his cartoons was produced in America in March 1917 by Rand, McNally & Co.

M. H. Mahood, *The loaded line* (Melb, 1973); *Review of Reviews for A'sia*, Aug 1892; *Cartoons Mag* (Chicago), Mar, Apr 1917; M. H. Mahood, Australian political caricature, 1788-1901 (Ph.D. thesis, Univ Melb, 1970).

MARGUERITE MAHOOD

BRADY, ALFRED BARTON (1856-1932), civil engineer and architect, was born at Manchester, England, on 1 February 1856, son of William Brady, cotton-spinner, and his wife Eliza, née Barton. Educated locally, he entered the service of C. W. Green, architect, in January 1872; he then became chief assistant to G. W. Stevenson, civil engineer and architect, in London. From March 1881 to October 1882 he was surveyor to the Docking Rural and the Hunstanton Urban authorities in Norfolk, and then engineer and surveyor to the District of Maldon, Essex. On 8 July 1879 he had married Lucy Bywater in the Wesleyan chapel at Prestwich, Lancashire. That year they migrated to Queensland in the *Waroonga*, arriving in Brisbane on 15 December.

On 22 January 1885 Brady began his thirty-seven years of service with the Queensland government, joining the railways as supernumerary assistant engineer, southern division. He became assistant engineer of bridges, southern and central division, on 1 January 1887, but transferred to the Public Works Department as engineer for bridges on 1 July 1889. The professional branches of the department were amalgamated in September 1891 and Brady took full responsibility; he became government architect and engineer for bridges on 7 April 1892. A lengthy royal commission into the administration of the Public Works Department was held in 1900. Brady received some criticism, but the report stressed the need for a professional head of department and he was appointed under-secretary, government architect and engineer for bridges on 1 February 1901. He reached retirement age on 1 February 1922 and later became government gas referee.

Brady was closely associated with many major public works in Queensland. He supervised the temporary reconstruction of the Victoria Bridge in Brisbane after several spans were destroyed in the February 1893 floods, and was responsible for the design and construction of the new bridge completed in June 1897. He also erected the Lamington Bridge at Maryborough (1896), the Burnett Bridge at Bundaberg (1900) and the Border Bridge over the Macintyre at Goondiwindi (1915), as well as smaller bridges elsewhere in Queensland. Major buildings overseen by Brady include, in Brisbane, the Lands and Survey (later Executive) Building (1905), the Central Technical College (1914), and the Queensland Government Savings Bank (later Insurance) Building (1921) and, in 1900-02, customs houses at Rockhampton, Townsville, Maryborough and Mackay. From 1901 to 1919 Brady had responsibility under a Federal-State agreement for the construction and maintenance of Commonwealth buildings in Queensland; he represented his government in negotiations over valuation and subsequent transfer of State property in the post-Federation period. Within his department he encouraged the use of day labour under the direct supervision of his own officers, and agreed to the introduction of quantity-surveying techniques in 1911-12 after approaches by the building industry.

An associate of the Institution of Civil Engineers, London, by 1893 and a member by 1899, Brady conducted its examinations in Queensland after their introduction in 1896. The institution awarded him the Telford Premium in 1900 for his paper on the Lamington Bridge at Maryborough, and the Crampton Prize in 1902-03 for his paper on the construction of the Victoria Bridge. Brady was sent overseas by the government in 1913 on a tour of the United States of America and Europe to investigate developments in construction and design.

During his 'long and meritorious' service, Brady moved gradually from professional engineering to the varied and wide-ranging responsibilities of a departmental head. He was described as having 'simple directness of speech ... sincerity of manner' and 'dignified candour'. An architect termed him 'perfectly fair', though reputed to be 'difficult to get on with', and commented further that, while there was no doubt as to his designing and administrative ability, 'he was more the Engineer than the Architect'.

Brady died of recurring epithelioma on 31 May 1932 in Sydney, predeceased by his wife and survived by five sons and a daughter.

Alcazar Press, *Queensland, 1900* (Brisb, nd); C. M. Norrie, *Bridging the years* (Lond, 1956); *V&P* (LA Qld), 1900, 3, 979, 1921, 2, 924; Commercial Publishing Co. of Sydney, Ltd, *Annual Review of Qld*, 1 (1902), no 1; *Queenslander*, 9 June 1932; J. V. D. Coutts, Early Queensland architecture *and* D. J. Garland, Engineer names for Canberra streets (Oxley Lib, Brisb); Annual reports, 1892-1922 (Dept of Public Works, Brisb); Register of arrivals, IMM/119 (QA).   PAUL D. WILSON

BRADY, EDWIN JAMES (1869-1952), journalist and writer, was born on 7 August 1869 at Carcoar, New South Wales, son of Irish parents, Edward John Brady, mounted police constable, and his wife Hannah, née Kenny. His father had migrated first to the United States of America where he had fought in the civil war. Brady was educated at Oberon Public School, then in Washington D.C. where his family settled in 1881. Homesick, they returned to Sydney next year, and Brady went to two Catholic schools, then in 1884 passed the junior public examination from St Patrick's Boys' School. He worked on the Ben Buckler sewer and matriculated, but only attended a few evening lectures at the University of Sydney.

Brady became interested in sailing-ships while a timekeeper for Dalgety [q.v.4] & Co. Ltd on the Sydney wharves; he refused to be sworn in as a special constable during the maritime strike of 1890 and was dismissed. He became secretary of the Australian Socialist League, a member of the Labor Electoral League, editing its newspaper, the *Australian Workman*, and joined a clerks' union. He was narrowly defeated for Labor pre-selection in West Sydney in 1890. Through these activities he became friendly with many early socialists and Labor supporters. Between attempts at farming Brady worked as a dramatic reporter for *Truth*, wrote features for the *Sunday Times*, the *Freeman's Journal*, and the *Bird O'Freedom*, and edited the *Arrow* from 1896. On 30 October 1890 at Paddington he had married Marion Cecilia Walsh, whom he divorced for adultery on 28 May 1895. At Smithfield on 28 June he married a divorcee Annie Creo Dooley (d. 1940), née Stanley, but they soon separated and she, reputedly, refused him a divorce. From about 1902 he lived with Norma Linda Dalby (d. 1936).

Brady's verse appeared in the *Bulletin* from May 1891. The publication of his first volume, *The ways of many waters*, in 1899, reinforced his many literary friendships with Henry Lawson, A. G. Stephens [qq.v.], J. F. Archibald [q.v.3], and others. After a wagon journey from Sydney to Townsville in 1899-1900, Brady bought a half-share in the Grafton *Grip*, and edited it until 1903. Wearying of country life, he sold out, set up the Commonwealth Press Agency in Sydney and briefly edited the Labor paper, *Australian Worker*, until he moved his press agency to Melbourne in 1906. He edited there a short-lived literary monthly, the *Native Companion*, in which he published Katherine Mansfield's first short stories and contributions from Katharine Susannah Prichard [q.v.]. 1911 was a prolific year for Brady: he published an account of his wagon trip as *The king's caravan* (London); a book, *River rovers* (Melbourne), about a trip in an open boat down the Murray from Albury; another volume of collected verse, *Bells and hobbles* (Melbourne); and *Tom Padgin, pirate* (Sydney), illustrated by Lionel Lindsay [q.v.]. Next year he visited parts of south-east Asia, and soon after set up camp at Mallacoota, Victoria, to write free of distractions. His only very profitable book was *Australia unlimited* (Melbourne, 1918), a comprehensive survey of Australia's primary industries.

Brady spent the rest of his life at Mallacoota, with intervals in Melbourne. His interests were wide-ranging: he attempted to establish a south-coast railway, timber-mills, and gold-mines; to grow medicinal plants; to sell a mechanical voting machine; to set up a commercial publishing venture with Randolph Bedford [q.v.], and a co-operative for some of Melbourne's unemployed; but he continually reverted to publicity work and journalism. He wrote *The land of the sun* (London, 1924) after a visit to Queensland, and contributed weekly to *Labor Call* (Melbourne) in the early 1930s under the pseudonym 'Scrutator'. He ghosted several books on economics, compiled a biography, *Doctor Mannix, archbishop of Melbourne* (1934), and wrote many unpublished short stories and poems. Brady received Commonwealth literary fellowships, in 1941 to write *Two frontiers* (Sydney, 1944), an account of his father's adventures, and, in 1944, for a biography of Archibald which was not published. His most substantial literary achievement is as a balladist of the sea – John Masefield, for one, keenly appreciated his energy and enthusiasm.

Brady died in hospital at Pambula, New South Wales, on 22 July 1952 and was buried with Anglican rites in Mallacoota West cemetery. He was survived by three sons and three daughters, and by his third wife. Florence Jane, née Bourke, an artist, whom he had married on 10 June 1942 at St Augustine's Church of England, Mentone, Victoria, and by their daughter.

Table Talk, 12 Dec 1929; J. B. Webb, A critical biography of Edwin James Brady (Ph.D. thesis, Univ Syd, 1973), and for bibliog; Brady papers (NL and Oxley Lib, Brisb).   JOHN B. WEBB

BRAGG, SIR WILLIAM HENRY (1862-1942), and BRAGG, SIR WILLIAM LAWRENCE (1890-1971), physicists, were father and son. William Henry was born on 2 July 1862 at Westward near Wigton, Cumberland, England, son of Robert John Bragg, merchant navy officer and farmer, and his wife Mary, née Wood. His mother died when he was 7 and, almost isolated from other children, he was raised by his uncle William Bragg at Market Harborough, Leicestershire. He won scholarships to the local grammar school and to King William's College, Isle of Man, where he became head of the school and won an exhibition to Trinity College, Cambridge. There he worked almost entirely at mathematics; later he regretted this early specialization. Lacking both spending money and easy sociability, he was saved from loneliness by his skill at games. In 1884 he graduated as third wrangler and a year later was awarded a first in part III of the tripos.

In 1886 Bragg arrived in Adelaide to take up the university post of '(Sir Thomas) Elder [q.v.4] Professor of Pure and Applied Mathematics, who shall also give instruction in Physics'; it had been recently vacated by (Sir) Horace Lamb [q.v.5]. He was ignorant of physics, in which he was to become one of the most eminent men of his time. Although at first he had only two students, he did not proceed to engage in any research. He apprenticed himself to a firm of instrument-makers to make apparatus for his deficient teaching laboratory.

Meeting with a friendly reception, particularly from the family of (Sir) Charles Todd [q.v.6], Bragg enjoyed a wide popularity, and his personality blossomed. He played tennis and golf and helped to introduce lacrosse to South Australia. On 1 June 1889 he married Todd's daughter Gwendoline, a skilled water-colourist; Bragg took up painting and they exhibited together. They had two sons, one of whom was later killed at Gallipoli, and a daughter. Bragg was active in the affairs of the Public Library, Museum and Art Gallery of South Australia, the School of Mines and Industries and the Teachers' Guild.

At the university he encouraged student activities, particularly the formation of the union. He believed that the greatest work a colonial university could do was to act as 'the centre from which all education radiates' and help to bring all teachers in touch with the best thinking. Country teachers were welcomed to his lectures and not required to pay fees. His academic interest shifted to physics: he developed a flair for expounding the subject both in formal classes and in public lectures often enlivened with experimental demonstrations. Electromagnetism interested him; one day in 1895 he was experimenting with a Hertzian oscillator when he was visited by Ernest Rutherford who was on his way to Cambridge and had worked on radio transmission at Christchurch, New Zealand. It was the beginning of a valuable lifelong friendship.

Early next year Bragg learned of W. K. Röntgen's discovery of X-rays and, with his able assistant A. L. Rogers, set about producing the new radiation. On 13 June they obtained a photograph with their own Röntgen tube. One of the first beneficiaries was Bragg's 6-year-old son William Lawrence, whose broken elbow was photographed with the primitive equipment. But many years passed before Bragg began his serious studies of X-rays and other ionizing radiations.

In 1898 he spent a year's leave in England; he reported on technical education and the central importance of design in industry. On his return Bragg carried out experimental work on radio communication with Todd. Their transmissions from the State Observatory were successful over a distance of 600 yards (550 m) on 10 May 1899, and by 20 July, over five miles (8 km) from the Observatory to Henley Beach.

The turning-point in Bragg's career came in 1904 when he gave the presidential address to section A of the Australasian Association for the Advancement of Science at Dunedin, New Zealand, 'On some recent advances in the theory of the ionization of gases'. He discussed the penetration of matter by α and β particles, concluding that the massive α particles, unlike the β and γ rays, would move undeviated through a gas until all the energy was lost through ionization of the gas molecules, and consequently α particles of a given initial energy should have a definite range in the gas. This idea was followed up in a brilliant series of researches which within three years earned him a fellowship of the Royal Society of London. He was helped by a student R. D. Kleeman, whom Bragg had invited to act as his assistant.

The first experiments showed clearly the well-defined ranges of α particles and distinguished the four groups of α particles emitted by radium, radon, RaA and RaC. They also showed the 'stopping power' of substances was approximately proportional to the square roots of the atomic weights. Bragg wrote long accounts of his work to

Rutherford at McGill University, Canada. The work continued with studies of the ionization of gases by α particles, in which Bragg was helped considerably by J. P. V. Madsen [q.v.]. Bragg concluded that X-rays and γ-rays were streams of neutral-pair particles rather than electromagnetic waves. This made him the centre of a controversy for several years. In January 1909, shortly before leaving to occupy the Cavendish chair of physics at the University of Leeds, Bragg delivered the presidential address to the A.A.A.S. meeting at Brisbane, in which he summarized his work of the past five years and commented on the significance of scientific research for the development of Australia.

In 1912 Max von Laue showed that X-rays could be diffracted by crystals and established their wave nature. During that summer Bragg and his son William Lawrence, who was then at Trinity College, Cambridge, discussed this development. While the father, with his experience of ionization measurements, went on to construct an X-ray spectrometer for the further study of the properties of X-rays, the son found a brilliant simplification of Laue's diffraction problem and formulated Bragg's Law, relating the location of maxima of the diffraction pattern to the wavelength of the radiation and the distance between the appropriate planes of atoms in the crystal. He also realized that analysis of X-ray diffraction patterns provided a means of locating the atoms in crystals. From Laue patterns W. L. Bragg derived the structures of ZnS and the alkali halides, and then, joining forces with his father who now had a superior experimental method, they together initiated the whole subject of X-ray crystallography, for which they received the Nobel prize for physics in 1915. W. L. Bragg was then 25.

The outbreak of war temporarily ended this work. W. H. Bragg became occupied with the problems of submarine detection and his son worked on sound-ranging for the artillery in France; both made notable contributions.

In 1915 W. H. Bragg was appointed to the Quain chair of physics at University College, London. Here, and on becoming Fullerian professor of chemistry and director of the Royal Institution of Great Britain in 1923, he built up vigorous schools of X-ray crystallography concerned principally with the study of organic molecules. At the institution he established a tradition of popularizing science in his Christmas lectures for young people, which were models of clarity and intellectual excitement.

W. H. Bragg maintained an active interest in X-ray crystallography until his death and made a monumental contribution to the subject, as well as serving the scientific world in other capacities. Many honours were bestowed upon him by learned institutions, including election in 1920 as an honorary fellow of Trinity College, Cambridge. He was appointed C.B.E. (1917) and K.B.E. (1920) and admitted to the Order of Merit (1931). He received the Rumford (1916) and Copley (1930) medals of the Royal Society of which he was president in 1935-40. Predeceased by his wife, he died in London on 12 March 1942 after a period in which heart trouble reduced his activity.

Sir William Bragg was a tall, rosy-cheeked man, whose large eyes were dark and kindly. His religious beliefs were strong, but not dogmatic, and are admirably expressed in his Riddell Memorial Lecture of 1941. He was always modest and ready to change his views, and his personal character shines through the records as that of a gentle and humane man.

William Lawrence Bragg was born in Adelaide on 31 March 1890 and educated at the Collegiate School of St Peter and the University of Adelaide (B.A., 1908). He graduated also at Trinity College, Cambridge, where he became a fellow and lecturer in natural science. Following the period of collaboration with his father and the war years, he was in 1919 appointed Langworthy professor of physics at Victoria University, Manchester, where he fostered a school of X-ray crystallography devoted mainly to the study of inorganic structures, notably silicates, metals and alloys. On 10 December 1921 at Cambridge he married Alice Grace Jenny Hopkinson who pursued a successful career in municipal affairs.

In 1937 Bragg became director of the National Physical Laboratory, Teddington, but a year later succeeded Rutherford as Cavendish professor of experimental physics at Cambridge. Here he joined in the attack upon the structures of the proteins, haemoglobin and myoglobin. In 1954 he was appointed to the positions earlier held by his father at the Royal Institution. At his retirement in 1966 he had seen the subject of X-ray crystallography, pioneered by his father and himself, grow from the elucidation of the structures of the simplest crystals to that of enormously complicated molecules containing thousands of atoms. He visited Australia in 1960 and spoke at the University of Adelaide of the latest triumphs of crystallography.

Sir Lawrence Bragg was widely honoured: he had been the youngest-ever Nobel laureate. His war service earned him the O.B.E. and M.C.; he was elected F.R.S. (1921), knighted (1941) and appointed C.H. (1967), and received the Hughes, Royal and Copley medals of the Royal Society. He died on 1 July 1971, survived by his wife, two sons and two daughters.

K. Grant, *The life and work of Sir William Bragg* (Brisb, 1952); C. C. Gillespie (ed), *Dictionary of scientific biography*, 2 (New York, 1970); G. M. Caroe, *William Henry Bragg... man and scientist* (Lond, 1978); G. Caroe, 'Notes on Gwendoline Bragg', R. Biven (ed), *Some forgotten, some remembered* (Adel, 1976); *V&P* (LA Vic), 1901, 3 (36); *Obituary Notices of Fellows of the Roy Soc,* 4 (1943), and for publications; *British J for the Hist of Science*, 5 (1970-71); *Physics Bulletin*, 22 (1971); *Aust Physicist*, May 1976; *The Times*, 2, 8 July 1971.   S. G. TOMLIN

BRAHE, MARY HANNAH (MAY) (1884-1956), composer, was born on 6 November 1884 at East Melbourne, daughter of Richard Dickson, Melbourne-born cordial manufacturer, and his wife Margaret, née Dickson, formerly of Glasgow, Scotland. May, as she was known, was taught piano by her mother, and continued her studies at Stratherne Girls' School, Hawthorn. When May was 12 her mother died, and three years later, when her father's business faltered, she left school to earn a living teaching piano. She took private lessons, first with Mona McBurney [q.v.], who taught her accompanying, and then with the singer Alice Rebotarro, whose training in vocal technique later helped her to compose songs that were easy to sing.

On 12 November 1903, with Congregational rites, May married Frederick Charles Brahe, a clerk. After the birth of her two sons she continued her music, and by 1910 was playing in a trio organized by Marshall Hall [q.v.] and accompanying singers at recitals of her own songs. In 1912, encouraged by her publishers (G. L.) Allan [q.v.3] & Co., she decided to go to London to establish herself as a composer, and left her children in the care of their father and paternal grandmother. After several months of struggle, during which she played piano in a cinema, her first success came with the song, *It's quiet down here*; the publishers, Enoch & Sons, paid her a royalty of 2d. per copy. By early 1914 she had earned enough to visit Australia briefly in order to bring her family back to England. In 1919, soon after returning from war service, Frederick Brahe was killed in a motor accident. On 24 August 1922, at the registry office, Paddington, May married an Australian-born actor George Albert Morgan.

May Brahe's songs were performed at fortnightly concerts organized by her publishers. When the firm was taken over by Boosey & Hawkes in 1925, she became one of their few composers on an annual retainer.

In the next eighteen years she published more than 400 compositions, mainly ballads, which were recorded by Dame Nellie Melba, Peter Dawson [qq.v.] and other singers of the day. These rather sentimental songs with titles such as *I passed by your window, To a miniature* and *The piper from over the way*, were also often chosen as items for school concerts in Britain, Australia and the United States of America. She collaborated with many lyric writers, including her sister Madge Dickson, and made settings of poems by Walter de la Mare, Dorothea Mackellar [q.v.] and others. However, she worked most successfully with Helen Taylor, whose appealing, if somewhat facile, rhymes blended with May Brahe's music to create songs that had 'a direct simplicity which went straight to the hearts of the people'. Helen Taylor wrote the words for Brahe's most famous song, *Bless this house*, which, published in 1927 and made famous by John McCormack in 1935, became even more popular in America during World War II.

Shortly before returning to Australia to settle in Sydney in 1939, May Brahe composed a musical comedy, *Castles in Spain*, with a libretto by Sydney and Muriel Box. From 1940 she lived in semi-retirement, becoming an enthusiastic contract bridge player, adding to her extensive library, and maintaining a constant, if reduced output of songs and piano pieces, many of which were composed for children. She often gave talks to women's clubs and over radio. She died at Bellevue Hill on 14 August 1956 of coronary vascular disease, and·was cremated with Presbyterian rites; she was survived by two sons and a daughter of her first marriage and a son of her second.

Theatrecraft (Lond), May 1939; *Woman's World*, 1 Dec 1939; *A.B.C. Weekly*, 9 July 1949, 5 June 1954; *Woman's Day and Home*, 13 Apr 1953; *Argus*, 27 Mar 1912; letter from L. Boosey (held by Mr H. G. Morgan); information from Mr D. Brahe, Killara, NSW, Mr A. Brahe, Melb, and Mr H. G. Morgan, Armidale, NSW.   MIMI COLLIGAN

BRAND, CHARLES HENRY (1873-1961), soldier and politician, was born on 4 September 1873 at Ipswich, Queensland, fifth child of Charles Hayman Brand, farmer, and his wife Elizabeth, née Elliott. His father was a native of Exeter, England, and his mother of Londonderry, Ireland. Educated at Bundaberg and Maryborough state schools, he joined the Department of Public Instruction as a trainee-teacher in November 1887. In 1898 he was commissioned lieutenant in the Queensland Volunteer Infantry and on the outbreak of war in South Africa enlisted as a sergeant in the 3rd Queensland (Mounted Infantry) Contingent. He served with the Rhodesian Field Force and in operations in the Transvaal and the Orange River and Cape colonies; on 25 June 1900 he was commissioned lieutenant. He returned home with the contingent in June 1901 but next May re-enlisted in the 7th Commonwealth Horse as captain in command of 'C' Squadron. The regiment never saw action as, by the time it reached South Africa, peace had been proclaimed.

In 1903-04 Brand taught at Charters Towers State School and in 1905 joined the permanent military forces as a temporary lieutenant. He was attached to the administrative and instructional staff in Melbourne; his rank was confirmed in 1906, and on 25 June he married a schoolteacher Ella Arline Armstrong at the Methodist parsonage, Bondi, New South Wales. In 1906-09 he was on the instructional staff, was promoted captain in July 1909 and spent the next two years in India on exchange duty. On his return he was appointed to the South Australian staff and was promoted major and acting commandant in 1912. A contemporary described him as 'the most energetic officer and best instructor' he had ever known.

When the 1st Division, Australian Imperial Force, was raised in August 1914 Major General (Sir) William Bridges [q.v.] selected Brand as brigade major of the 3rd Infantry Brigade. He embarked for Egypt on 21 October. At Mena Camp he was a familiar sight, going about his duties on a hired donkey when other transport was scarce, doing the work of a messenger, an instructor or a staff officer exactly as each task came to hand. The 3rd Brigade was first ashore at Gaba Tepe, Gallipoli, on 25 April 1915. Brand was conspicuous that day when he helped to direct troops on Plateau 400, organized stragglers under fire at Gaba Tepe and led an attack which resulted in the disablement of three enemy guns. Often in the following weeks he delivered messages to the forward troops and when the Turks advanced in mass attacks on Lone Pine he manned the only telephone at 3rd Brigade headquarters.

During the Turkish counter-attack of mid-May Brand was temporary commander of the 3rd Battalion and was slightly wounded when a German naval shell landed in his headquarters. He remained on duty and on 14 July was promoted lieut-colonel and given command of the 8th Battalion which relieved the 6th and 7th Battalions at Steele's Post on 18 July. Here, because of constant bombardment, there was a high incidence of shock in the casualty lists. Except for a rest period at Lemnos in November, the 8th remained at Steele's until the evacuation. Brand was awarded the

Distinguished Service Order for devotion to duty and gallantry at Anzac; he was the first Australian to receive this award for Gallipoli service. His battalion reached the Western Front late in March 1916 and went to the Somme. In June Brand took temporary command of the 6th Brigade and on 10 July was promoted colonel and temporary brigadier general and was given command of the 4th. He lived down the effects of an 'extraordinarily inept and egoistic' oration to his troops and held his command for more than two years.

In 1916-17 the brigade served at Pozières, Bullecourt, Messines, Polygon Wood and Passchendaele. Its heaviest losses were at Bullecourt where, after a few hours fighting, there were more than 2000 casualties. Brand, who had strenuously opposed the plan to attack with the assistance of tanks only and without artillery support, wept as he saw the remnants of his troops emerging from the line. At Messines he was wounded when a shell exploded outside brigade headquarters and was out of action for a month. When the German offensive on the Somme began in March 1918, the brigade was drawn into a gap in the Gommecourt-Hébuterne area, where it hung on for three critical weeks. Afterwards Brand led the brigade in the capture of Morcourt and Méricourt in July during the semi-open warfare near Madame Wood, and in its last operation close to the Hindenburg Line. Between 27 September and 4 October he was one of a group of 100 Australian officers and men who helped to lead the 27th American Division through its first big battle. Afterwards the original Anzacs in the force, including Brand, left for Australia, though before his departure he was invested at Buckingham Palace with the C.B., C.M.G. and D.S.O. During the war he was eight times mentioned in dispatches.

Brand's A.I.F. appointment was terminated on 21 February 1919 and he resumed duty with the Australian Military Forces. He was commandant in Victoria in 1919-20, confirmed in the rank of brigadier general on 1 April 1920, and was base commandant in New South Wales in 1921-25. He was made 2nd chief of general staff and a member of the Military Board in 1926 and two years later became quartermaster general, retiring in 1933 in the rank of major general. In the 1934 general election he won a Victorian Senate seat for the United Australia Party and held it until June 1947. In parliament he mainly concerned himself with defence policy and the needs of ex-servicemen; he was chairman of the Federal Parliamentary Ex-Servicemen's Committee in 1942-47.

Survived by his wife and two daughters, Brand died at his Toorak home on 31 July 1961 and was cremated with full military honours. A portrait by W. B. McInnes [q.v.] is in the Australian War Memorial, Canberra. Brand was a soldiers' general and was trusted and well liked by his troops who honoured him with the nickname 'Digger'.

Aust Defence Dept, *Official records of the Australian military contingents to the war in South Africa*, P. L. Murray ed (Melb, 1912); C. E. W. Bean, *The story of Anzac* (Syd, 1921, 1924), and *The A.I.F. in France, 1916-18* (Syd, 1929, 1933, 1937, 1942); *London Gazette*, 3 June 1915, 29 Dec 1916, 1 Jan 1918; *Reveille* (Syd), Mar, July, Oct 1930, Apr, June 1933, Apr 1935; records (AWM).
                                              A. J. SWEETING

BRAND,   HENRY   ROBERT;   *see* HAMPDEN

BRASSEY, THOMAS, first EARL BRASSEY (1836-1918), governor, was born on 11 February 1836 at Stafford, England, eldest son of Thomas Brassey, railway contractor, and his wife Maria Farrington, née Harrison. He was educated at Rugby School and University College, Oxford (B.A., 1859; M.A., 1864; D.C.L., 1888) and was called to the Bar, Lincoln's Inn, in 1866. After several attempts between 1861 and 1866 to enter parliament as a Gladstonian Liberal, he won Hastings in 1868, holding the seat until 1886. He was civil lord of the Admiralty in 1880-84 and its parliamentary secretary in 1884-85.

Brassey's passionate love of the sea dated from boyhood and as often as he could he cruised in his yacht the *Sunbeam*. He was an enthusiastic publicist of naval and maritime affairs and labour conditions: in the House, in public lectures, letters to the press and in pamphlets and books, most notably *Work and wages* (1872), *The British Navy* (1882-83) and the periodical *Brassey's Naval Annual* (from 1886).

For his work in establishing volunteer naval reserves he was appointed K.C.B. (1881) and was raised to the peerage as Baron Brassey of Bulkeley, Cheshire, in August 1886. In 1860 he had married Annie Allnutt, who wrote lively, popular accounts of their travels together; she died aboard the *Sunbeam* on 14 September 1887, seven days out of Port Darwin. On 8 September 1890 he married Sybil de Vere Capell, youngest daughter of Viscount Malden. Brassey was lord-in-waiting to Queen Victoria in 1893-95 and president of the Institute of Naval Architects in 1893-96. He had joined the Imperial Federation League soon after its foundation in 1884, serving as honorary treasurer and vice-president; in July 1892 he chaired the committee which recommended its dissolution.

In 1895 Brassey accepted the position of governor of Victoria, arriving in Melbourne in the *Sunbeam* on 25 October with his wife and little daughter. He travelled within Victoria, visited other Australian colonies including Western Australia where he owned land, and returned to England on leave from March to October 1898. In November 1899 Brassey refused Sir George Turner's [q.v.] request for a dissolution but, accepting his resignation, he adopted his suggestion that Allan McLean [q.v.] be sent for. A year later the McLean government was defeated at a general election and subsequently in the House, and Turner returned to office on McLean's recommendation. No one seriously disputed the governor's discretionary right to refuse the dissolution, although the *Age* considered it unnecessarily postponed the people's political judgment. Brassey had simply followed a well-defined procedure; he explained to the Colonial Office that the change of ministry would not affect either Australian Federation or Victorian support for the British government's action in South Africa.

Brassey's support for Federation was unwavering, and impulsive to a degree which embarrassed Imperial officials involved in negotiating the final form of constitution. He gave unqualified praise to Deakin's [q.v.] part in the movement. Brassey's insistent proposals for careful selection of the first Australian governor-general were dismissed as emanating from an impractical ass whom some officials suspected of hankering for Federation honours himself. His eager reports of premature Victorian volunteering for service in South Africa, and his promotion of Australian naval reserves, met with a cool reception although Chamberlain was readier than his colleagues to appreciate the loyal sentiments behind the dispatches.

Brassey's governorship marked the end of an era. He left Melbourne on the *Sunbeam* on 13 January 1900, before his full term was completed and, after his return to England, pursued his creditable but undistinguished career. He continued to write and speak on Imperial and naval subjects, frequently making warm references to Victoria. Further honours were bestowed on him: G.C.B. in 1906, lord warden of the Cinque Ports in 1908, an earldom in 1911. Characteristically he sailed the *Sunbeam* to Gallipoli in 1915 and then handed her over to the Indian government for use as a hospital ship. He died in England on 23 February 1918, survived by his second wife and their daughter, three daughters of his first marriage, and briefly by his heir.

A. Brassey, *Lady Brassey's three voyages in the Sunbeam* (Lond, 1887); S. Eardley-Wilmot (ed), *Voyages and travels of Lord Brassey, 1862-1894*, 1-2 (Lond, 1895); A. H. Loring and R. J. Beadon (eds), *Papers and addresses by Lord Brassey; Imperial federation and colonisation, 1880-1894* (Lond, 1895); *Australasian*, 9 Mar 1895; *Argus*, 25 Feb 1918; CO 309/141-149.   B. R. PENNY

BRAUND, GEORGE FREDERICK (1866-1915), merchant, politician and soldier, was born on 13 July 1866 at Bideford, Devonshire, England, eldest son of Frederick Braund, draper, and his wife Ellen, née Doidge. He was educated at Bideford Grammar School and, when 15, migrated to New South Wales with his parents and their nine other children. He worked in Sydney at the York Street warehouse of (A.) McArthur [q.v.5] & Co. until 1889 when his father bought out J. Moore & Co., general merchants of Armidale. From then until his father's death in 1899 he was accountant in the family business; he then became manager. As a young man Braund was a talented all-round sportsman, excelling at boxing, fencing and Rugby; he was also an active member of local literary and drama groups. On 30 January 1895 he married Lalla Robina Blythe at St Matthew's Anglican Church, Drayton, Queensland.

In May 1893 Braund had been commissioned second lieutenant in the Armidale company, 4th Australian Infantry Regiment. He was promoted lieutenant in 1898, captain in 1899 and major in 1912, and was company commander in 1899-1912. He took a continuing interest in local affairs and by World War I was 'Armidale's most prominent citizen'. A magistrate, he was also for many years president of the Armidale Chamber of Commerce, a member of the public school board, and a director of the New England Building Society and of various local business concerns. In 1910 the Liberal Party invited him to contest the Federal seat of New England; he declined because of family commitments but in 1913 became Liberal member for Armidale in the Legislative Assembly.

That year Braund was promoted lieut-colonel, and from July 1914 commanded the 13th Infantry Regiment. On the formation of the Australian Imperial Force he was appointed by Colonel H. N. MacLaurin [q.v.] to raise and train the 2nd Battalion and on 17 August became its commanding officer. The unit embarked for Egypt two months later. Braund trained his officers and men with extreme thoroughness and, largely by his own example, exacted a high standard of discipline. He was a convinced theosophist;

self-discipline was part of his creed; he was a teetotaller, a non-smoker and a vegetarian and was almost obsessive about physical fitness. He was short in stature, alert, active and of a lively disposition. He probably commanded respect, rather than affection, from his troops. Once on Gallipoli, however, all appreciated his insistence on fitness, discipline and mental alertness.

On the morning of 25 April 1915 the 2nd Battalion landed at Gallipoli and two of its companies were at once assigned to the 3rd Brigade, already engaged in fierce fighting at The Nek. 'B' and 'C' Companies were held in reserve until 1.30 p.m. when, under a harassing fire, Braund led them up steep goat-tracks to the junction of Walker's Ridge and Russell's Top. There, in a vital but isolated position, they dug in and held on for two days against a sustained Turkish attack. Casualties were high and only Braund's tenacious leadership held his seriously weakened force together. On 27 April, when reinforcements from Lieut-Colonel W. G. Malone's Wellington Battalion reached him, he led the combined force in a steady bayonet charge through the scrub to the crest of Russell's Top. Forced to withdraw before a strong enemy counter-attack, his men resumed their original positions and retained them until the morning of the 28th; by then Braund's exhausted battalion had withstood the main Turkish advance for three days and nights without rest. They withdrew to the beach, leaving Malone's men in control of the sector.

Malone kept a diary in which he was critical of Braund's command. His comments seem unjustified; far from voicing any criticism of Braund, his own men paid tribute to his courage and gallantry. C. E. W. Bean [q.v.] judged that he had shown 'every quality of a really great leader'. On 2 May 1915 Braund was ordered from the beach, where his battalion was held in reserve, to Victoria Gully. After midnight on 3-4 May he was asked to send part of his unit to reinforce the 3rd Battalion in the line. After dispatching 'C' Company he set out for brigade headquarters and instead of using the normal track took a short cut through the scrub. Slightly deaf, Braund failed to hear a challenge from a sentry, who shot him. He was buried in Beach cemetery, Gallipoli, and was survived by his wife, two sons and a daughter. He was mentioned in dispatches posthumously. Braund was the first Australian legislator to enlist for World War I and the second to die in battle.

C. E. W. Bean, *The story of Anzac* (Syd, 1921); C. F. Aspinall-Oglander, *Military operations: Gallipoli* (Lond, 1929); F. W. Taylor and T. A. Cusack, *Nulli secundus, a history of the Second Battalion*

A.I.F., 1914-19 (Syd, 1942); *London Gazette*, 3 Aug 1915; *Reveille* (Syd), Oct 1931, Aug 1932, Oct 1933, Feb, Apr 1935; *SMH*, 13 May 1915; *Armidale Chronicle*, 15 May 1915; War diaries, 2nd Battalion and 1st Division, A.I.F. (AWM).

DARRYL McINTYRE

BRAZENOR, WILLIAM (1888-1945), soldier and administrator, was born on 7 April 1888 at Ballarat, Victoria, son of William Brazenor, architect, and his wife Ellen, née Coogan. Educated at the Pleasant Street State School until 12, he later joined the Ballarat Water Supply as a clerk and began a part-time course with the Victorian Institute of Accountants. He was active in the St Andrew's Young Men's Club where he became a competent debater. In 1909 he was commissioned second lieutenant in the 1st Battalion, 7th Australian Infantry Regiment, and was promoted lieutenant in 1911 and captain in 1912. On 22 November 1911 he married Anne Mabel Cunningham at St Peter's Anglican Church, Ballarat.

Brazenor joined the Australian Imperial Force in March 1915 and in May was allotted to the 23rd Battalion as captain commanding 'C' Company. He sailed for Egypt that month, was promoted major in August and, from September until the evacuation, fought with distinction at Gallipoli, particularly Lone Pine. His unit served in the Sinai Desert in early 1916 then, in March, left for France where it saw action on the Somme. Promoted lieut-colonel in December, Brazenor commanded the battalion in all its 1917-18 operations; in 1917 these included the battles of Bullecourt and Ypres and in 1918 Amiens, the Somme, Hamel and Mont St Quentin. Between October 1917 and December 1918 he also temporarily commanded the 6th Brigade on five occasions. His brigade commander spoke of him as a man of 'very great initiative, coolness and determination' and 'a born fighter in the field'. He was mentioned in dispatches three times for outstanding service and was awarded the Distinguished Service Order in January 1918. For conspicuous gallantry in the battle of Hamel he received a Bar to this award.

In March 1919 Brazenor returned to Australia and his A.I.F. appointment ended in July. Next year he completed his accountancy studies, received rapid promotion in his civilian career, and between the wars was secretary of the Ballarat Water Commission and then of the Sewerage Authority; in both capacities he showed keen interest in conservation and afforestation schemes. He served in the Citizen Military Forces as a lieut-colonel in the

2nd Battalion, 39th Regiment, in 1920-21. Promoted colonel in 1923, he commanded the 6th Brigade for four years, and was placed on the unattached list in 1927 and on the reserve of officers in 1932. In World War II, in spite of chronic bronchitis, he commanded the 3rd Garrison Brigade and the 20th Battalion, Volunteer Defence Corps. Survived by his wife, two daughters and two sons, he died suddenly on 22 September 1945 at Ballarat and was cremated.

Brazenor achieved prominence in both his military and civilian careers through natural ability and hard work. He was involved in many community projects and served terms as president of Ballarat Legacy, the orphanage committee, the Mechanics' Institute and the Old Colonists' Association. A keen sportsman, he was a first-class rifleshot, had a handicap of 5 at golf and was a 100-break man at billiards. He was a foundation member of Wendouree Masonic Lodge.

His step-brother John Alexander Smyth Brazenor, D.S.O. (1877-1953) served as a major in the Australian Army Service Corps in France.

C. E. W. Bean, *The A.I.F. in France*, 1916-18 (Syd, 1929, 1933, 1937, 1942); *London Gazette*, 2 Jan, 28 Dec 1917, 1 Jan, 24 Sept, 31 Dec 1918; *Ballarat Courier*, 24 Sept 1945; Brazenor file (AWM); information from W. G. Brazenor, Palm Beach, NSW.   M. AUSTIN

BREDT, BERTHA; see McNAMARA, BERTHA

BREINL, ANTON (1880-1944), medical scientist and practitioner, was born on 2 July 1880 in Vienna, son of Anton Breinl, lace manufacturer, and his wife Leopoldina, née Stammhammer. The family came from Graslitz near Pilsen in the Sudeten German part of Bohemia. Educated at a gymnasium at Chomutov, Breinl entered Charles University, Prague, in 1899 and took its medical degree in April 1904. He decided to satisfy his interest in both research and travel by taking up tropical medicine, in which dramatic advances were then being made; with funds for only three months, he went to England to the Liverpool School of Tropical Medicine in May. Appointed John Garrett international fellow in bacteriology, he worked under Sir Ronald Ross, discoverer of the malarial life cycle, and Professor Rupert Boyce. In April 1905, he accompanied Dr H. Wolferstan Thomas, with whom he had worked on trypanosomiasis, to Brazil on the school's Yellow Fever Expedition. Six

months later Thomas contracted the disease, then Breinl. Despite a normal mortality rate of 95 per cent both recovered, though Breinl developed a lifelong facial palsy. Wrecked at the mouth of the Amazon on the way home, he lost all his records, apparatus and personal effects.

He continued his research on pathogenic protozoa at the school in the Runcorn Research Laboratory and became its director in May 1907. He investigated tick fever and developed work on the effect of the drug, atoxyl, in trypanosomiasis. Bitten by an experimentally infected rat in 1907, he became the first European to be cured of sleeping sickness by atoxyl. Professor Paul Ehrlich visited Runcorn, saw the work of Thomas and Breinl on trypanosomiasis, tried organic arsenical compounds in syphilis and in 1907 developed salvarsan (606), the first successful treatment for the disease. As a referee for Breinl's Australian appointment, he described him as 'one of the leaders of modern chemotherapeutic work'. While at Liverpool, Breinl wrote or contributed to one book and twenty-one papers.

Appointed as first director of the Australian Institute of Tropical Medicine at Townsville in 1909, Breinl began work on 1 January 1910 in converted wardsmen's quarters at the Townsville Hospital, with one assistant who had accompanied him from Liverpool. He was awarded the Mary Kingsley medal for research in tropical medicine in 1910, his engagement was extended in May 1914 for five years, and a few days later he was naturalized. Meanwhile he had investigated his territory as far north as Thursday Island, examined the Northern Territory in 1911, and in July-August 1912 had surveyed the health of Papuan coastal peoples from Port Moresby to the Mambare River. In June-October 1913 he travelled by canoe and on foot from Port Moresby to Daru. His major research in Australia was pioneering work into the physiology and biochemistry of Europeans living in the tropics. With W. J. Young [q.v.] he published a major paper, 'Tropical Australia and its settlement' in 1919; the institute published twenty-two scientific papers while he was director.

In October 1920 Breinl quietly retired from the institute to a busy private practice in Townsville. There is strong evidence that he was under pressure to resign because of his national origin. Throughout World War I he had suffered some social ostracism through the gossip of ultra-patriots. He unsuccessfully volunteered three times for army service and, while continuing his own work, replaced, without salary, the enlisted superintendent of the Townsville General Hospital. His authoritative treatment of serious malaria cases, sent by the army from New Guinea, saved many. The biochemist Professor H. Priestley [q.v.] believed it a 'great tragedy' that he 'felt compelled to give up active scientific research at the height of his career. Breinl was a splendid man to work with, enthusiastic, very hard working ... His knowledge of protozoology in particular, and of tropical medicine generally was great, and as a laboratory technician, he was superb'.

Besides his native German, Breinl spoke English fluently, French moderately and had some knowledge of Portuguese and Italian. He was an accomplished violinist and met his future wife Nellie Doriel Lambton, a nurse, when she accompanied him on the piano. Married in Townsville on 21 April 1919, they had three sons including twins who became medical practitioners. Having suffered for years from hypertension, he died of renal failure on 28 June 1944 in the Royal Prince Alfred Hospital, Sydney, and was cremated.

Aust J of Science, 7 (1944); *MJA*, 21 Oct 1944; R. A. Douglas, 'Dr Anton Breinl and the Australian Institute of Tropical Medicine', *MJA*, 7 May 1977; Breinl papers (James Cook Univ, Townsville).

                                   R. A. DOUGLAS

BRENAN, JENNIE FRANCES (1877-1964), dancing teacher, was born on 24 April 1877 at Carlton, Victoria, fifth daughter of James Joseph Brenan, Irish-born estate agent, and his wife Annie Bryce Cooper, née Livingston, of Edinburgh. She was educated at the Catholic Ladies' College, East Melbourne. Despite family disapproval, Jennie always wanted to dance and J. C. Williamson [q.v.6], a frequent visitor to the Brenan home, encouraged her to take lessons from Mary Weir. Her early training in 'fancy dancing', from the gavotte to the Irish jig, gave her an artistic eclecticism she never lost. In the 1890s she studied ballet in Melbourne under Rosalie Phillipini and in 1901-02 under Alexandre Genée in London.

Ironically, the qualities which were to impress her thousands of students, early restricted her stage career. One young pupil recalled Miss Jennie as 'a tall, graceful creature with a cloud of dark hair, lovely eyes, long legs like a race horse and elegant ankles'. Too tall for classical ballet, she recoiled from the immodesty of the popular theatre. At her début in J. C. Williamson's production of *Trilby* at Bendigo in July 1896, her high-kick number stopped the show, but shyness overcame her and she refused to dance in Melbourne where she knew too many people. Williamson persuaded her to turn to teaching and her first pupils were his

daughter and the young Dorothy Brunton, who became a star in musical comedy.

Jennie Brenan opened her first studio in 1904 at 163 Collins Street and with her sisters Margaret (1884-1964) and later Eileen (b. 1891), taught ballet, ballroom and fancy dancing. In the 1920s, she added the Embassy Cabaret to her enterprises, and the sisters taught in private schools in Melbourne, Geelong and Frankston, producing pantomimes and *tableaux vivants* on sacred themes, lavishly costumed from the J. C. W. wardrobe. The Brenan school became the major supplier of dancers for J. C. W. productions for more than thirty years and Jennie created ballet and dance sequences for operettas, musicals and pantomimes. Her insistence on decorum and elegance in her pupils helped to make theatrical dancing more respectable. Her outstanding pupils included Ivy Schilling, Joan Cadzow, Pat Keating, Phyllis Kennedy, Lois Green, Roy Currie and Martin Rubinstein.

However, it was as much as an 'entrepeneur of teaching' that Jennie Brenan made her contribution to the dance in Australia. With Eileen she travelled annually to London where they continued to study and could engage teachers of the highest quality for their school. Through her friend (Dame) Adeline Genée, president of the Association for Operatic Dancing of Great Britain (later the Royal Academy of Dancing), she organized the teaching and examination of its syllabus in Australia, and examiners were brought from London for the first tests in 1935. Academy scholarships then gave Australian students entry to the Sadler's Wells school. Jennie was the first president of the R.A.D. in Australia and in 1936 was the first overseas representative to be elected to its grand council. She died, unmarried, on 2 February 1964 and was buried in Melbourne general cemetery. In 1965 the R.A.D. (Victoria) gave a teacher's scholarship bearing her name.

V. Tait, *A family of brothers* (Melb, 1971); J. Cargher, *Opera and ballet in Australia* (Syd, 1977); A. Lubbock, *People in glass houses* (Melb, 1977); H. C. Walker, 'A chat with Jennie Brenan', *Lone Hand*, 1 Aug 1914; information from Miss E. Brenan, Fitzroy, and Mr E. H. Pask, Aust Ballet School, Flemington, Vic.   JANET McCALMAN

BRENNAN, ANNA TERESA (1879-1962), lawyer, was born on 2 September 1879 at Emu Creek, Victoria, thirteenth child of Michael Brennan, farmer, and his wife Mary, née Maher. Anna was born into a household devoutly Catholic and intellectually stimulating, conducive to social conscience and individual achievement. Several of her brothers enjoyed distinguished careers, notably Thomas and Frank in both law and politics, and William [qq.v.] in journalism. She attended the co-educational St Andrew's College, Bendigo, and in 1903 continued to drive daily by buggy to a coaching college some ten miles distant. Her brothers encouraged her to take up a profession, and as each in turn was supported financially by the others throughout his studies, so was she. She entered the University of Melbourne in 1904 to study medicine but 'was ploughed', being 'too nervous to do the dissections'. In 1906 she began a law course and graduated in 1909. In 1904 she had joined the Princess Ida Club for women students, held office in 1907-09 and remained on the committee until 1913; she represented the club on the National Council of Women in 1912.

Anna did her articles with Frank Brennan & Rundle and Thomas moved her admission on 1 August 1911. She was the second woman, and the first native-born woman, admitted to practice in Victoria. She was active in the firm to the end of her life: the partnership had become Frank Brennan & Co., with Anna, the senior partner, calling herself 'the Co.'. The practice was general but, despite early reservations, Anna entered the matrimonial field. She campaigned within the profession and publicly for the revision of laws which obstructed proceedings, invited collusion, or brought inequitable ancillary relief; she favoured the payment of maintenance to husbands in justifiable circumstances. In spite of personal objections to divorce, she stressed in the late 1940s the need for more expeditious dissolution, where sought, of hasty unions between Australian war brides and American servicemen.

In the 1940s the National Council of Women appointed Miss Brennan to appear before a Commonwealth parliamentary commission, whose findings eventually produced revision of the law governing nationality of married women; she later worked to remedy situations created by conflict of matrimonial laws between the States. For some time she was president of the Legal Women's Association, formed in 1931; it awards an annual prize in her name to the woman placed highest in the final-year law class-list at the University of Melbourne.

Anna Brennan supported the assumption by women of responsibility. With her brother Frank she attended the League of Nations Assembly at Geneva in 1930 and observed that 'Women delegates might have much to contribute on legal, economic and international questions . . . valuable aid was perhaps lost because it was taken for granted

that their interests would be solely humanitarian'. When the Lyceum Club for women was founded in 1912, Anna joined as an 'original' member. She immediately became a trustee of club property, was honorary legal adviser until 1918, and president in 1940-42. A short-lived venture of the club was her 'Walking Circle' (1928): the bush tracks defeated all but its founder.

Her Catholicism was deep and rational, and she had that sense of Christian duty which leads to serving others. When admitted to practice she was a committee-member of the Newman Society at the university. She sat on the first central committee of the Catholic Women's Social Guild, established in 1916, which undertook, among other things, hospital visiting, the management of hostels and girls' clubs, and provision of catechists to lay schools. She lectured widely, wrote for *Women's Social Work*, organ of the guild, and for its successor, *Horizon*, and was the guild's second president in 1918-20. Her principles and devotion to Joan of Arc encouraged her association with the international St Joan's Alliance, which originated in England in 1910 as the Catholic Women's Suffrage Society, and championed innumerable humanitarian causes, predominantly those affecting women. Anna attended the inaugural meeting of the Australian foundation of the alliance in 1936, having joined the English chapter while abroad, and was president of the Victorian section in 1938-45 and 1948-62.

Diminutive, ever sprightly and an individualist, Anna Brennan had an incisive mind, and a delightful wit. Her opinion was valued, her criticism was constructive; she condemned only prejudice and culpable ignorance. She appreciated beauty, intellect and people, about whom she could be less than flattering but never cruel. She never married and had little domestic inclination, her sister Mary Catherine (May) (1874-1963) gladly undertaking the household duties. According to Frank, Anna was 'Always looking for experience when she ought to be saying her prayers'; her spirit never dulled. She fell while negotiating steps at the university before a lecture on nuclear fission and succumbed to pneumonia on 11 October 1962; May soon followed, for want, it seemed, of Anna's companionship. They were buried side by side in Coburg cemetery.

J. M. Gillison, *A history of the Lyceum Club* (Melb, 1975); *Austral Light*, Sept 1911; *Catholic Citizen* (Lond), Nov 1962; *Law Inst J*, Feb 1963; *Horizon* (Melb), Oct 1966, jubilee no; *Southern Sphere*, Sept 1911; *Lone Hand*, Sept 1914; *Herald* (Melb), 12 Oct 1962; Princess Ida Club, Minutes and papers (Univ Melb).   RUTH CAMPBELL
                                        MARGARET MORGEN

BRENNAN, CHRISTOPHER JOHN (1870-1932), poet and scholar, was born on 1 November 1870 in Harbour Street, Sydney, eldest of five surviving children of Irish migrants Christopher Brennan (d. 1919), brewer, and his wife Mary Ann (d. 1924), née Carroll. His father had learned his trade at the Guinness brewery, Dublin, and after reaching Sydney about 1864, worked in R. and F. Tooth's [qq.v.6] Kent Brewery; he later became a publican. Young Christopher's childhood sickliness (he had typhoid at 6), coupled with precocious academic ability, helped to make him the object of his mother's special affection and set him apart somewhat from his brothers, sisters and other children. In 1880 he became the solitary acolyte at the Good Samaritan School and Convent, Pitt Street, and was intended for the priesthood. At 11 Brennan went to the Jesuit St Aloysius' College, where he first read Milton, whose poetry later had a deep influence on him. Three years later, with a scholarship from Cardinal Moran [q.v.], he went as a boarder to St Ignatius' College, Riverview. He had already raised himself far above the rest of his family, both intellectually and socially.

Life at Riverview under the founding rector Fr Joseph Dalton [q.v.4] changed Brennan greatly. He grew rapidly into a big, strong youth and experienced a major intellectual awakening: despite stringent physical and academic discipline, the school gave him great intellectual freedom, and whatever he wanted he was given to read. Most importantly, in Fr Patrick Keating, the classics master, he found the only teacher ever to make a deep impression on him. Not an exceptional scholar by Jesuit standards, Keating influenced him not so much intellectually as morally. Brennan was captivated by his discipline, charm and elegance, and above all by his air of perfection, and was never to cease searching for that perfection, completeness and apparent infallibility which he had known in the faith of his youth, and in his favourite teacher. Just before leaving Riverview, Brennan abandoned his vocation, which distressed his parents, but not Moran or the Jesuits.

In March 1888 he went to the University of Sydney where to all appearances he led an adventurous, wayward life. None of his university teachers could stimulate him profoundly; for some, such as Professor Walter Scott [q.v.], he felt little more than contempt. But for the first time he began to form strong and lasting friendships, with men of or near his own age, including J. B. Peden, A. B. Piddington, Dowell O'Reilly and J. Le Gay Brereton [qq.v.]. As a student, Brennan distinguished himself for his scandalous neglect of set texts, and his

ability to get good results without appearing to try. As editor of *Hermes* (1889-90) and as a prankster he seemed to his fellow students 'just a rollicking carefree chap'.

In private however, Brennan worked very hard at classical texts of his own choice, forming in 1888 an independent theory (now substantially accepted) about the descent of the extant manuscripts of Aeschylus. He also apparently suffered from moods of black melancholy and became passionately attached to the poetry of Tennyson and Swinburne. During the long vacation of 1889-90 he lost his faith and spent the rest of his life trying in philosophy, love and poetry to establish some new kind of absolute. He graduated B.A. in 1891 with first-class honours and the University Gold Medal in logic and mental philosophy, but only second-class honours in classics. In 1892 he won an M.A. in philosophy (conferred in 1897).

Systematic logical inquiry did not satisfy Brennan's fundamental religious needs. In 1891, most of which he spent rather adventurously as a teacher at St Patrick's College, Goulburn, he wrote his earliest surviving poems and, after an affair, embarked on a 'virtuous' attachment. Returning to Sydney in October he taught part time at Riverview and had a second virtuous romance. In 1892 he won the James King [q.v.2] of Irrawang Travelling Scholarship and studied at the University of Berlin in 1892-94. He fell in love and became engaged to his landlady's daughter Anna Elisabeth (1870-1943), daughter of Rudolph Werth, of Ragnit, East Prussia. Brennan also discovered the work of Mallarmé, which led him to believe that poetry might offer the means of recovering Eden. Having abandoned his university studies he decided to 'go in' for verse: for the next ten years it became the most important thing in his life.

In July 1894, without his fiancée and without the expected doctorate, Brennan returned to Sydney, then in the depths of an economic depression. Unable to find work of any kind for a year, he was employed from September 1895 in the Public Library of New South Wales to catalogue D. S. Mitchell's [q.v.5] collection, becoming second assistant librarian on 1 January 1907. He was at that time better read in, and a more original critic of, European literature than anyone else in Australia. But the university waited until October 1909 before offering him a permanent position as assistant lecturer in French and German in the department of modern languages and literature. He had been temporary lecturer in modern languages in 1896-97 and 1908-09, and in classics in 1908. Apparently his heavy drinking and the erotic interests shown in his first printed book of verse, *XXI Poems* (1897), told against him when he was being considered for various teaching posts.

Elisabeth Werth came out to Sydney late in 1897, and Brennan married her in St Mary's Cathedral on 18 December; for a time they seemed happy. She had studied music: those who knew her in the 1890s remembered her playing the piano and singing songs of 'haunting sweetness'; they also remembered her beauty – her glorious golden hair and blue eyes. Many factors drove them increasingly apart: he drank heavily; they argued over money; there was a wide gulf between his interests and attitudes, and those of his wife; the birth and rearing of four children created tensions. The arrival in December 1900 of Frau Werth, with a deranged daughter, to live in their household, added to the strains and conflicts. Slowly his marriage drifted towards disaster.

Brennan's spiritual pilgrimage, the quest for Eden as recorded in his verse, ended nowhere: 'The wanderer', mostly written in 1901-02, concludes with the tacit abandonment of that quest. His attempt to fashion a mythic unity out of the individual poems he wrote, to create a 'single concerted poem' after the model of the French Symbolist 'livre composé', made the misery and the spiritual loss which lay at the heart of some of his finest poems inconvenient to his larger design. After 1902 he ceased to write verse regularly, although the poetry he wrote between that year and the publication of his 'livre composé' *Poems* in 1914 tended to revert to the view of himself as the seeker after Eden.

As his poetic output declined, and his domestic situation grew more difficult, Brennan became one of the great talkers and bon vivants of café-life in the city; he dominated successively two dining-and-conversation groups, the Casuals and les Compliqués. He also returned to the study of classical texts, though never again with quite the thoroughness and delight that had marked his studies as a young man.

Brennan did start to produce quantities of poetry again in 1915. The pieces collected as *A chant of doom, and other verses* (1918) expressed vehement support for the Allied cause in World War I; although incomparably the worst poetry he ever wrote, they enjoyed markedly better sales than *Poems*. It seems they were inspired less by the war than by the hostilities in his own household, and his desire to spite his German wife and mother-in-law.

Brennan's marriage finally broke up late in 1922. He went to live with Violet Singer, a cultivated woman seventeen years his junior, who had led a somewhat erratic and unhappy life. She admired him greatly; he felt she had given him life. He naturally conceived and expressed his love for her in absolute terms, but it was none the less more human and personal than any absolute he had previously embraced. In March 1925 she was run down by a tram; in June Brennan, who since 1921 had been (Sir Samuel) McCaughey [q.v.5] associate professor and head of the university's department of German and comparative literature, was removed from his post on the grounds of adultery. His incontinent, erratic behaviour certainly made him a very difficult employee, but the love and admiration that many of his students felt for him testify that he still had much to offer the university when it turned him out.

After the double blow of 1925, Brennan was a broken man. He wrote a few poems about his love for Violet Singer – some of the finest poetry he had ever composed – but his life became lonely, purposeless and insecure, especially after his salary ran out at the end of the year. He spent much of 1926 as house-guest of Hilary Lofting; in 1927 he taught at the Marist Brothers' High School, Darlinghurst. After that he suffered real privation. In July next year some friends and admirers instituted a fund to assist him in paying for necessities of what had become a very modest (though still disordered) style of living. In 1930 he became a part-time teacher of modern languages at St Vincent's College, Potts Point, a position he held, with some happiness, until his last illness. In March 1931 he was given a Commonwealth Literary Fund pension of £1 a week.

From 1925 onwards, Brennan had reverted more and more to a generally Catholic orientation. He returned fully to the beliefs and the practices of Catholicism in mid-1932, while seriously ill in St Vincent's Hospital. He died of cancer on 5 October in Lewisham Hospital and was buried in Northern Suburbs cemetery. He left his estate, valued for probate at £68, to Robert Innes Kay, solicitor. Predeceased by his two daughters, he was survived by two sons.

Brennan's place in Australian literature is as paradoxical as his character. At a concious level, Australia and its writers count for little in his poetry, which makes few overt references to the landscape and society, and hardly draws at all from Australian literature. Yet he read widely in the works of his contemporaries and predecessors, and the poetry of Henry Kendall [q.v.5], which he greatly admired, is subliminally present in his own work, especially 'The wanderer'. A striking indication that Australia counted for a great deal in Brennan's life as a writer may be seen in the fact that, although he abhorred Henry Lawson [q.v.] as a poet and a man, the progress of their lives was hauntingly similar: promise, achievement, degeneration, disgrace, posthumous legend. The comparison with Lawson, and with earlier writers such as Marcus Clarke, D. Deniehy, A. L. Gordon [qq.v.3,4,5] and Kendall, shows that Brennan's life followed a pattern common among Australian writers. Like them he helped to create a national literary tradition which broke down the loneliness felt by so many writers; in his turn, like them, he suffered from and was partly destroyed by that loneliness.

But Brennan's poetry stands largely outside the mainstream of Australian poetic development. In its attempt to follow the example of the French Symbolists, it was the first of its kind ever to be written here. With its clotted diction and extreme Victorian poeticism, it could not be directly emulated by later generations. None the less some of the most important later poets, such as R. D. FitzGerald, A. D. Hope, Judith Wright and James McAuley found in his work a point of reference and departure, because he was the first Australian to write within, and be worthy of, the great European philosophical-poetic tradition. His interest in human sexuality and psychology, especially the unconscious, and his attempt to use the French Symbolists as a basic model, link Brennan to British writers such as Eliot, Yeats and D. H. Lawrence, although his achievement hardly matches theirs.

Despite his essentially European manner and interests, Brennan's audience was and remains almost exclusively Australian. Even if he failed both in his search for Magian enlightment through poetic symbol, and in his related attempt to create a 'livre composé', he wrote many fine individual pieces, such as 'Lilith', most of the poems in the 'Wanderer' sequence, and some love poems composed in the 1920s. In works such as these his poetry remains challenging, and deeply moving.

A. G. Stephens, *Chris Brennan* (Syd, 1933); R. Hughes, *C. J. Brennan: an essay in values* (Syd, 1934); A. R. Chisholm, *Christopher Brennan: the man and his poetry* (Syd, 1946); G. A. Wilkes, *New perspectives on Brennan's poetry* (Syd, 1953); W. W. Stone and H. Anderson, *C. J. Brennan: a comprehensive bibliography* ... (Syd, 1959); A. R. Chisholm and J. J. Quinn (eds), *The verse of Christopher Brennan* (Syd, 1960), and *The prose of Christopher Brennan* (Syd, 1962); R. Pennington, *Christopher Brennan: some recollections* (Syd, 1970); J. McAuley, *Christopher Brennan*, 2nd edn rev (Melb, 1973); G. A. Wilkes, 'The uncollected verse of C. J. Brennan', *Southerly*, 1963, no 3; R. B. Marsden, 'New light on Brennan', *Southerly*, 1971, no 2; Brennan papers (ML), *and* MSS (NL, and Fisher Lib, Syd); Brereton papers (ML); H. F. Chaplin, A Brennan collection (NL).

AXEL CLARK

BRENNAN, EDWARD THOMAS (1887-1953), surgeon and medical administrator, was born on 13 April 1887 at Stawell, Victoria, son of Edward Thomas Brennan, surveyor, and his wife Anne Mary, née Powell. Educated at Beechworth Grammar School and the University of Melbourne (M.B., B.S., 1909), he was resident surgeon at the Ballarat Hospital in 1909-10 and medical superintendent at Fremantle Hospital, Western Australia, in 1911-14. In June 1913 he was commissioned in the Australian Army Medical Corps.

On 31 August 1914 Brennan joined the Australian Imperial Force as a captain and was made regimental medical officer in the 11th Battalion. He sailed for Egypt in November and went ashore with the covering force at Gallipoli on 25 April 1915. His unit fought at Steele's Post where Brennan had to set up his aid-post on top of a steep cliff; he overcame the problem of evacuating wounded by easing them down a sand-slide to the beach. He received special mention for 'various acts of conspicuous gallantry' in the first ten days at Anzac. Later, at Leane's Post, he risked his life by crawling along a shallow communication trench under heavy fire to attend wounded. He remained at Anzac until the evacuation and was awarded the Military Cross. Promoted major in January 1916, he was transferred to the 7th Field Ambulance and reached the Western Front in April and served in the battles of the Somme. In February next year he was made temporary lieut-colonel and commander of the 1st Field Ambulance and took part in all the 1st Division's major operations in 1917-18. He was awarded the Distinguished Service Order in June 1918 and was mentioned in dispatches four times during the war.

Brennan's A.I.F. appointment ended in January 1920. He resigned his commission on 18 July and next day joined the Royal Australian Navy as surgeon lieutenant on H.M.A.S. *Sydney*. Three years later he left to become travelling medical officer for the Territory of New Guinea, a post which 'for its action and adventure suited him well'. On 26 October 1923 at Rabaul he married an American, Ruth Todd; their home for the next two years was the 45-foot (13.7 m) schooner which Brennan sailed around the coast on his medical duties. He was later stationed at Madang. In 1928 he was made director of public health for the territory and in 1933 became a member of the Legislative Council. A friend observed that these added responsibilities 'sat easily upon him, and the assumption of authority altered his genial bearing not a whit'. He held both offices until World War II when he sought an A.I.F. post but was declared medically unfit for active service. In December 1941 he was appointed assistant director of medical services for the 8th Military District (New Guinea), holding the rank of colonel; after a few months ill health forced his evacuation. He was deputy director of medical services of the Allied Works Council, New South Wales, in 1942-45 and chief medical officer for the United Nations Relief and Rehabilitation Administration in the south-west Pacific in 1945-50.

Survived by his wife and three daughters, Brennan died of coronary vascular disease at Cronulla, Sydney, on 18 August 1953 and was buried in Woronora Catholic cemetery. His courage and vivid personality boosted morale in both peace and war. He had a remarkable aptitude for grasping the essentials of any problem and for making rapid, sound decisions. These qualities, together with his genial disposition and professional knowledge, made him a popular and highly respected medical officer and an excellent administrator.

C. E. W. Bean, *The story of Anzac*, 1, 2 (Syd, 1921, 1924); A. G. Butler (ed), *Official history of the Australian Army Medical Services . . . 1914-18*, 1-2 (Melb, 1930, Canb, 1940); *London Gazette*, 24 July 1915, 28 Jan, 2 Feb, 11 July 1916, 28 May, 3 June 1918; *MJA*, 12 June 1954.   M. AUSTIN

BRENNAN, FRANCIS (1873-1950), lawyer and politician, was born at Upper Emu Creek (Sedgwick) near Bendigo, Victoria, eleventh of the thirteen children of Michael Brennan and his wife Mary, née Maher. Michael (1828-1902), born at Mount Charles, Donegal, Ireland, spent some years in Glasgow, Scotland, during and after the famine, and in 1852 migrated to Victoria, keeping a shorthand diary of the voyage. He mined at Bendigo, worked on the roads and as a carrier, and in 1857 bought a property at Upper Emu Creek, which he named Mary Vale, and worked as a mixed farm. Mary (1838-1920) was born at Thurles, Tipperary, and had a convent education to the age of 15. She migrated with her widowed mother in 1853, settled in Melbourne, and married Michael there on 14 April 1856.

Farming at Mary Vale was, at best, moderately successful and, after three terms as president of Strathfieldsaye Shire, Michael became shire secretary and engineer in 1882. All the boys except the eldest, Joseph (1857-1946), were forced to make their careers elsewhere. Michael Austin (1861-1913), blazed the trail for the family in Melbourne; he completed his B.A. in 1891 and LL.M. in 1898 and worked in the Crown Law Department. Thomas, William and Henry (1869-1936) became journalists; Richard (1868-1950) joined his father at Strathfieldsaye Shire and succeeded him as

secretary in 1898. None of the girls married. Ellen (1858-1947) kept house for her brothers in Melbourne; she enjoyed some reputation as a scholar. Mary Catherine (May) (1874-1963) also kept house for the unmarried members of the family, notably Anna [q.v.].

Frank Brennan stayed on the farm, continuing his education part time under the tuition of a remarkable primary teacher Henry Beetson, until his failure in some of his first year law subjects in 1897 forced him to Melbourne to sit for supplementary exams and thereafter to attend the university full time. The security and richness of his early years developed in him an intense loyalty to his family and the Catholic religion. His family's breadth of ideas, opinions and personalities provided a stimulation and a rapport that were not matched elsewhere for him. His Church's certainties supplied a stable framework for his morality and gave purpose to his existence.

Brennan graduated LL.B. in 1901 and quickly established a modestly successful legal practice which specialized in union business, particularly after the foundation of the Commonwealth Court of Conciliation and Arbitration in Melbourne in 1905. He gained prominence as a Catholic layman through his gifted speaking and his activities in the Catholic Young Men's Society, of which he was president in 1906. He developed no serious legal ambitions to counterbalance an almost inevitable move towards a political career. He joined the Australian Labor Party in 1907 and first stood for pre-selection in 1908. After failing to gain pre-selection for the Federal seat of Batman in 1910, he contested Bendigo against the redoubtable Sir John Quick [q.v.]. He lost narrowly, but entered the Federal parliament in 1911 by winning a by-election in Batman.

In many ways Brennan was not a typical Labor politician of his day. He was better educated and better spoken; nor did he make any effort to develop a 'common touch'. As the first Victorian lawyer to enter the ranks of the Federal Parliamentary Labor Party he belonged to a suspect profession to which he remained loyal — and even exceptional in his deep respect for the law's ramifications. From this, and his rural background, stemmed some of the conservative elements in his political conduct and views. He remained an individualist whose modesty and warmth often nestled behind his volatility, his biting wit, and his acid powers of sarcasm.

Brennan's good fortune in securing what became a safe seat, his being on the 'right' side in the 1916 Labor split, his later association with Scullin [q.v.] and the moderates in the party, plus his undoubted ability, all helped to provide an unchallenged place within the Labor Party. He had little reason to become involved in the internal workings of the party, and he showed a remarkable lack of inclination to do so. He was without intense personal ambition: he served the Labor cause as one who loved that cause — not as one who loved the life that had to be led in order to serve it. He regarded himself as a socialist, by which he meant he stood for the democratic reorganization of the Australian economy to serve the needs of the people in an egalitarian manner. His Catholicism shaped his perception of his public role in a broad philosophical way, but not specifically or consciously. He did not join the Catholic Federation, refused to become involved in Catholic education claims, and spoke only once in parliament about Catholics — on a minor matter concerning allegations of preference for them in the public service. Yet he remained prominent as a public figure in his Church's activities, and was a friend of Archbishop Mannix [q.v.]. He always opposed any form of bloc activity within the Labor Party, Catholic or otherwise. He was a Labor politician who was a Catholic, not a Catholic acting as a Labor politician.

At a ceremony performed by Mannix on 30 December 1913, Brennan married Cecilia Mary (Sheila) (1885-1941), daughter of Dr Nicholas O'Donnell [q.v.], leader of Melbourne's Irish community. They had two children: Mary, who suffered from Down's syndrome and whose care came to dominate her father's existence; and Niall, biographer of Mannix and John Wren [q.v.].

Brennan first gained political prominence through his early opposition to Australia's involvement in World War I. In July 1915 he was involved in a much-publicized clash with W. A. Watt [q.v.], who accused him of being 'pigeon-livered'. When he challenged Watt to enlist with him, Watt failed to appear. The coupling of the Irish uprising and the anti-conscription issue in 1916 ignited Brennan's emotions, consumed all his energies, undermined his health, tarred him with an anti-British brush, and increased his natural scepticism of political realists, especially W. M. Hughes [q.v.]. The Labor Party that survived after 1916 savoured a righteous idealism embodied by men like Brennan. He became a major figure, often brilliant and effective in his oratory and criticism, during the long years Labor spent in Opposition to 1929.

When the Scullin government was elected in 1929 Brennan became attorney-general. He was as ill-prepared as most of his colleagues to cope with the complexities of office during the Depression. Under pressure he was ensnared by his conservative legalism, became impatient with the problems at first, and was later resigned to political impotence. He proved incapable of providing any definite lead, was unable to reach accord with the union movement, and saw his one major legislative initiative, the conciliation and arbitration bill (1930), savagely amended by the hostile Senate. He gave his close friend Scullin unqualified support in his determination to ensure that the party survived as viable and democratic. In this he was shackled to support the implementation of economic policies which he abhorred. Partly as a consequence he was dumped by the electors of Batman in December 1931 after having retained the seat by a record majority in 1929.

Brennan resumed his law practice, but won Batman again in 1934 and was untroubled to hold it until his retirement in 1949. He retained a strong voice in the Parliamentary Labor Party, particularly on foreign policy until 1940. Throughout the 1920s he had kept the issues of peace, defence and military training before parliament. He was proud to be involved in the Scullin government's suspension of compulsory military service. In his one opportunity on the world stage he delivered a ringing plea for peace in an address to the League of Nations in 1930. He went on to attend the Imperial Conference in London soon after. During the 1930s he supported the various peace movements and was prepared to be accused of being a dupe or fellow-traveller for his support of Communist-front peace organizations. His brother Harry broadly shared his views. His pacifism was based on an idealistic belief in the 'practicality' of men being able to live in peace through their innate good will. He abhorred physical violence. He believed intensely in a policy of isolationism for Australia to enable it to get its own house in order, to set an example of anti-militarism. The outbreak of World War II led to general disillusionment for him, particularly because of the attitude of John Curtin and his supporters to the war effort. His earlier outspoken pacifism as the war approached led to a firm identification with Labor's left wing. His political influence waned and he was dropped from the party's parliamentary executive in 1940. He was one of the few Labor members to oppose the Curtin government's introduction of limited conscription for overseas service, but he eventually buckled under the pressures of party loyalty and supported the bill in the House.

In 1941 Brennan's wife died and he struggled to maintain an interest in life. Mary, at a stage when she was difficult to manage and help, became the keystone of his life. He was being progressively robbed of his finest possession as a public man – his power of oratory. By 1943 his speech was often infuriatingly halting, seeming stilted and mannered as he struggled to control it: he became an embarrassment to listen to.

Frank Brennan could be regarded as having failed in his political career, to have achieved little for a man of his ability. He failed in what he made his one great cause – pacifism – but he did so on his own terms. He retired in 1949 and died, aged 77, of hypertensive vascular disease on 6 November 1950. He was buried in Melbourne general cemetery after a state funeral.

THOMAS CORNELIUS (1866-1944) was the seventh child in the family. After leaving the local school he was apprenticed as a typesetter with the *Bendigo Independent*. Upon completing his time he went to Melbourne to work as a printer with the *Argus*, transferred to the reading staff, became a junior reporter, and eventually a cable sub-editor. He had continued his education part time, matriculated on his fourth attempt in 1892 and completed a law degree in 1900. Aged 35, he married Florence Margaret Slattery on 15 April 1902 at St Patrick's Cathedral. He resigned from the *Argus* when admitted to the Bar in 1907. In succeeding years he received many briefs through Frank's law firm and established a leading reputation in the Criminal Court through such cases as the trial of Colin Campbell Ross, on which he published *The gun alley tragedy* (Melbourne, 1922). He was largely responsible for a reform in the practice laid down by the High Court for the hearing of criminal appeals. He became a K.C. in 1928 and was awarded a doctorate of laws in 1932 for his thesis, published in 1935 as *Interpreting the constitution*.

A notable Catholic layman, Tom Brennan was particularly prominent in the period 1910-20, being one of the founders of the Catholic Federation and its first president in 1911; editor of the Catholic *Advocate* in 1915-17 until he clashed with Mannix during the conscription controversy; a committee-member of the Australian Catholic Truth Society; and the first president of the Newman Society at the university. He was a strong advocate of state aid to Catholic schools, but was one of the few Victorian Catholics of Irish descent strongly to support conscription in 1916-17.

Politically conservative, Brennan stood unsuccessfully as a Liberal and later as a Nationalist for the Legislative Assembly seats of Melbourne (1911), Warrenheip (1911), Richmond (1914) and Bendigo East (1921). Eventually he was appointed to the Senate by the Victorian parliament in May 1931 to fill a casual vacancy. He was re-elected in December and served as minister without portfolio assisting the ministers for commerce in the United Australia Party governments of 1932-37, being acting attorney-general and acting minister for industry during parts of 1935-36. He was defeated at the 1937 election.

Brennan was quiet, reserved and unassuming in manner, his obvious determination and strong character giving many an impression of flintiness. Privately he was a man of gentlemanly charm, kindness and simplicity, who delighted in referring to himself as the 'last of the Tories' as a contrast to his radical brother Frank. Survived by his wife and two daughters, he died aged 76 on 3 January 1944.

WILLIAM ADRIAN (1871-1956) was born on 29 April 1871. He left Mary Vale in 1887 and worked in the railways and the Victorian Civil Service, before joining Thomas on the *Argus*. He was a member of the Federal parliamentary press gallery continuously in 1901-27. Deeply conservative politically, he nevertheless remained very close to his brother Frank throughout their lives. As 'Ariel' he wrote with an easy grace and liberal lacings of the Brennan irony. Bill Brennan was small in stature and of a quiet disposition, though very witty. He served as one of the early presidents of the Catholic Young Men's Society and in 1906 was the first secretary of the Melbourne Press Bond, the Australian Journalists' Association's most significant predecessor. However in 1917 he presented the Melbourne newspaper proprietors' case against the A.J.A. before the Arbitration Court. From 1927 until his retirement in 1939 Brennan was chief leader-writer on the *Argus*. He was a member of the Savage, Yorick and Wallaby clubs. He remained unmarried, was appointed O.B.E. in 1952 and died on 9 November 1956.

N. Brennan, *A hoax called Jones* (Lond, 1962), and *Dr. Mannix* (Adel, 1964), and *John Wren* (Melb, 1971); K. Ryan, Frank Brennan: a political biography (M.A. thesis, La Trobe Univ, 1978); family papers (held by Misses C. and L. Brennan, Caulfield, *and* Mr N. Brennan, Kingajanik, via Gladysdale, Vic).   KEVIN RYAN

BRENNAN, FRANK TENNISON (1884-1949), politician and judge, was born on 6 December 1884 at Maryborough, Queensland, son of Martin Brennan, grocer, and his wife Annie, née Byrne. Educated at the Maryborough Christian Brothers' College and the Boys' Grammar School, he entered the family business briefly and was then articled to his brother, a Warwick solicitor.

He practised at Toowoomba in 1913-20, entered the Legislative Assembly as Labor member for Warwick in 1918, and became assistant home secretary and minister in charge of health and local authorities from 2 July 1923 until 14 July 1924, when he was appointed secretary for public instruction. A lively, active, aggressive politician with a genuine passion for social justice and great skill in managing his constituency, he was completely at home in Labor politics, but strong Catholic religious principles kept him always on the far right wing.

As one of the few lawyers who joined the Labor Party, Brennan supported the changes to the judicial and court structure introduced by the Labor government in 1921. To enable the poor to obtain quick and cheap relief from the courts, he urged amalgamation of the two branches of the profession; in 1921 he supported an amendment to the Supreme Court Act which allowed solicitors of five-years standing to be admitted as barristers. The amendment became known as 'the Brennan Clause' when, in 1924, he himself took advantage of it.

In 1922 he reported an attempt to bribe him into voting with the Opposition on a no confidence motion. Two men were subsequently convicted in the 'Brennan bribery case'. Appointed to the Supreme Court bench in March 1925, he was forced to fight for the position when the Queensland Bar Association argued that the high standards usually required for judges were being disregarded. Since he had been a barrister for too short a period, he was briefly readmitted as a solicitor to gain the necessary standing, and his elevation was upheld by the Full Court. Critics continued to assert that the appointment repaid his caucus vote which had made W. N. Gillies [q.v.] premier.

Brennan served in 1925-47 at Rockhampton on the central bench of the Supreme Court. He dealt mainly with routine matters arising in the circuit courts and made no great contribution to Australian jurisprudence. He was criticized for his short prison sentences, for dispensing with counsel's arguments to provide quick relief for litigants, and for his extra-judicial and political comments from the bench. His habit of interrupting counsel was no doubt due to his long-held belief that justice should be available to all and should not be hindered by lawyers. In 1934 he wrote a novel about public life called 'Your obedient servant', which was not published because of possible libel proceedings.

Transferred to Brisbane in 1947, Brennan died there on 6 August 1949 and was buried in Nudgee cemetery after a state funeral. On 19 July 1922 he had married Hanna Maria Gertrude Koenig; a son and two daughters survived him.

C. A. Bernays, *Queensland – our seventh political decade 1920-1930* (Syd, 1931); P. S. Cleary, *Australia's debt to Irish nation-builders* (Syd, 1933); *Court privileges abused in Red-baiting attack on F. W. Patterson MLA* (Brisb, 1945?, copy Oxley Lib, Brisb); *PD* (Qld), 1921, 1258-82; *Brisbane Courier*, 29 Aug, 26 Sept 1922, 10, 12-14, 19 Mar 1925; *Daily Standard*, 25 Feb 1925; M. Cope, A study of labour government and the law in Queensland, 1915-1922 (B.A. Hons thesis, Univ Qld, 1972); K. H. Kennedy, Bribery and political crisis 1922 (held by author).   MALCOLM COPE

BRENNAN, MARTIN (1839-1912), police superintendent, and SARAH OCTAVIA (1867-1928), teacher and nun, were father and daughter. Martin was born in September 1839 at Kilkenny, County Kilkenny, Ireland, son of Martin Brennan, farmer, and his wife Sarah, née Tobin. He migrated to New South Wales in 1859 and joined the mounted patrol under Captain Zouch [q.v.6]. Stationed at Braidwood, Brennan ran the gold escort to Goulburn for two years, and distinguished himself at the Lambing Flat (Young) riots, where he was wounded in the arm and had four horses shot under him.

In 1862 Brennan became a senior constable at Moruya, and on 4 July 1865 he married Elizabeth McKeon, from Galway. He was one of the first policemen to use Aboriginal trackers successfully. Promoted sergeant, he was transferred to Araluen and from 1872 was in charge of the Queanbeyan station; while there he became senior sergeant. In 1880 he became a sub-inspector in the Young district, and served at Wagga Wagga, moving to Newcastle in 1886. Promoted inspector next year, he was praised for his handling of disturbances during the coalminers' strike in 1888. He became superintendent of the north-western districts in 1894 with headquarters at Tamworth. Later that year he was recalled to Sydney to take charge of the training depot and the eastern districts. By 1902 he was superintendent of the Mounted Police Barracks at Moore Park. E. C. Day [q.v.], inspector-general, praised the 'incalculable value' of his work 'in the training of recruits, which he brought up to a very high standard'.

Brennan's only child Sarah Octavia was born at Moruya on 14 April 1867. She was educated as a boarder from 1879 at the Sisters of the Good Samaritan St Benedict's Convent at Queanbeyan and passed the junior public examination in 1883. Her father took a keen interest in her education; from 1878 he took a correspondence course in Latin and French from Professor Badham [q.v.3] and both he and Sarah matriculated at the University of Sydney in 1885. Although he followed his daughter's courses there, he could not sit for a degree as he was unable to attend lectures. Sarah graduated B.A. in 1889 and M.A. in 1891 in the schools of classical philology and history. From 1894 she studied science, graduating B.Sc. in 1898. Next year they travelled overseas. Sarah belonged to the Australian Naturalists' Society of New South Wales and late in 1899 read a paper to the local Linnean Society.

Brennan retired on 1 February 1907 and that year published his *Australian reminiscences*, having been encouraged by Sarah to record some of his adventures during the bushranging days. Predeceased by his wife, he died of a strangulated femoral hernia in St Vincent's Hospital on 8 August 1912 and was buried in the Catholic section of Waverley cemetery.

From 1901 Sarah had lived at the Sisters of the Good Samaritan Glebe convent and taught science and Latin at their St Scholastica's High School. On 11 January 1920 she joined the Congregation of the Sisters of the Good Samaritan and took the religious name Sister Mary Elizabeth. She taught at the Randwick novitiate, returned to St Scholastica's, then at the Balmain novitiate helped to train Sisters to teach science. With great zest she worked to improve the teaching of science in Catholic high schools, and was greatly beloved for her gentleness, courtesy, refinement and affectionate concern for others. She died of coronary vascular disease at Lewisham Private Hospital on 8 January 1928 and was buried in Rookwood cemetery.

T&CJ, 13 Oct 1888, 14 Aug 1912; *SMH*, 9 Aug 1912; Sister M. Elizabeth Brennan, File 59D, and note-books (St Scholastica's Archives, Glebe Point, Syd).   M. IMELDA RYAN

BRENT OF BIN BIN; *see* FRANKLIN, STELLA

BRENTNALL, THOMAS (1846-1937), chartered accountant, was born on 30 December 1846 at Escomb, County Durham, England, son of Joseph Edmund Brentnall, grocer, and his wife Mary Ann, née Strutt. The family lived at Eston, Yorkshire, and Brentnall was educated at private schools at Great Ayton and Darlington. He matriculated at the University of Durham but on leaving school joined the Middlesbrough branch of the National Provincial Bank of England. In 1874 at Bedford he married Caroline Crossley, and for the next few years

they lived at Prestonpans, Scotland, where Brentnall worked for a colliery company.

In 1878 Brentnall decided to migrate to Australia and with his wife and small son arrived in Melbourne in November in the *Loch Tay*. He brought rigid standards of business ethics and social behaviour, combined with elegant good manners. After working briefly with the London Bank of Australia he established himself as a public accountant, and acquired two existing practices which brought him an immediate clientele of leading businessmen and pastoralists. Despite an early financial setback, owing to a defaulting partner whose liabilities Brentnall fully repaid, he developed sound and valuable connexions as an auditor. His firm was successively Brentnall & Riley, Brentnall, Norton & Co., and Brentnall, Mewton & Butler. In 1886 he helped to found the Incorporated Institute of Accountants, Victoria, becoming president in 1898. In 1907 he was first president of the Australasian Corporation of Public Accountants and in 1928, when a royal charter was granted, he became first president of the Institute of Chartered Accountants in Australia. For many years he served the Victorian Companies Auditors' Board as examiner, director and chairman.

Brentnall always loved music. As a boy he learned the violin and organ, and sang in choirs. In Melbourne he played his violin, a magnificent Andreas Guarnerius instrument, sang with the Metropolitan Liedertafel and in the Centennial Exhibition choir of 1888, and acted as organist for several local churches. He was president of the Melbourne Music Club and the Victorian division of the British Music Society, and ultimately was a financial guarantor of the Melbourne Symphony Orchestra in the late 1920s. He welcomed visiting musical celebrities, often entertaining them at his home. On his several visits to London he attended a round of concerts and performances which he recorded in his copious critical diary and later described in his autobiography, *My memories* (Melbourne, 1938).

Brentnall was a keen golfer; as early as 1874 he had been a member of the Royal Musselburgh Club in Scotland. His friendship with J. M. Bruce [q.v.3] led to the founding of the (Royal) Melbourne Golf Club. Brentnall was the third captain and at 85 claimed that for the previous thirty-five years he had played golf once a week. He presented a set of his early primitive sticks to the club.

Brentnall was an active trustee and vice-president of the Melbourne Newsboys' Society; he was also a director of the Royal Humane Society for forty years, and president for eleven. From 1880 he lived at

Newnham, Caroline Street, South Yarra. Predeceased by his wife in 1909 and survived by a son and daughter, Brentnall died at his home on 10 July 1937 and was buried in Boroondara cemetery.

A. D. Ellis, *The history of the Royal Melbourne Golf Club* (Melb, 1941); *Chartered Accountant in Aust*, July 1937; *Argus*, 30 Dec 1935; *Sun-News Pictorial*, 12 July 1937.   DOUGLAS KEEP

BRERETON, JOHN LE GAY (1871-1933), scholar and writer, was born on 2 September 1871 in Sydney, fifth son of John Le Gay Brereton [q.v.3], medical practitioner, and his wife Mary, née Tongue. His parents had arrived in Melbourne in the *Dover Castle* on 25 July 1859 and moved to Sydney. His father practised in the city, was a minor poet and a leading member of the Swedenborgian community. In 1882 the family moved to a new home, Osgathorpe, at Gladesville. Brereton was educated at Sydney Grammar School from 1881 and at the University of Sydney (B.A., 1894), where he read English under Professor (Sir) Mungo MacCallum [q.v.] and, as editor of the student magazine *Hermes*, began to write seriously.

Brereton tried a variety of occupations – schoolteacher, tea merchant, clerk in the New South Wales government statistician's office. At the same time he continued to write, and made many literary friends, notably Henry Lawson and C. J. Brennan [qq.v.]. His first book, *The song of brotherhood and other verses*, was published in 1896. *Landlopers*, a prose work based on a walking tour to the Blue Mountains and the South Coast, followed in 1899. Much of his writing in the 1890s conformed to the prevailing attitudes of egalitarianism and nationalism. At its best, it was distinguished by the mystic pantheism which was the basis of his personal religious faith. His poetry was characterized by his love of mountains and streams. Regarding himself as a 'brother of birds and trees' he was a vegetarian; he loved to spend holidays tramping through the bush.

On 21 December 1900 Brereton married Laura Winifred Odd, daughter of a neighbour. In 1902 he was appointed assistant librarian at the University of Sydney under the titular librarian H. E. Barff [q.v.]. He advised the government architect W. L. Vernon on the design of the first permanent library building. Under his direction its holdings were greatly expanded and the catalogue made systematic. He encouraged students, young writers and artists and, a member of the Casuals Club from 1907, moved in literary and artistic circles outside

the university. In 1908 he published another book of poetry, *Sea and sky*.

In the 1900s Brereton started to build his European reputation as a literary scholar and in 1909 published *Elizabethan drama: notes and studies*. He contributed articles on Shakespeare and Marlowe to learned journals and in 1914 sent a critical edition of *Lust's dominion* (of disputed authorship) to the Catholic University of Louvain, Belgium. The manuscript was lost in the German invasion, and was eventually published in 1931. Although strongly anti-militarist, he was more sympathetic to the British cause in 1914 than he had been to Australian participation in the South African War and in 1915 brought out a book of poems relating to the war, *The burning marl*. That year he was promoted to university librarian.

In 1921 Brereton was appointed professor of English literature. He had a pervasive influence on his students and had long promoted the education of women at the university. Tall and loose-limbed, he was invariably hatless. Academic responsibilities occupied most of his time and energies; nevertheless in 1923 he was a foundation member of the English Association, in 1929 first president of the Fellowship of Australian Writers and in 1931 an organizer of the Sydney P.E.N. Club. He published a further volume of verse, *Swags up!* (1928), and a volume of essays, *Knocking round* (1930); with Bertha Lawson edited *Henry Lawson, by his mates* (1931); and contributed innumerable letters and poems on diverse subjects to the *Sydney Morning Herald*, often under the pseudonym 'Basil Garstang'.

Brereton died suddenly on 2 February 1933 near Tamworth, while on a caravan tour. He was survived by his wife, four sons and a daughter. His portrait is held by the University of Sydney.

Brereton was not a major writer, but his verse did make a distinct contribution to the development of Australian poetry, while *Landlopers* is a uniquely charming prose idyll. His academic labours place him among the leading humanist scholars of his day, he was a rare academic on familiar terms with creative writers, while his gentle, whimsical, and sometimes melancholy personality made him widely loved and respected.

His elder brother ERNEST LE GAY (1869-1932), mining engineer and lecturer, was born on 10 April 1869 in Sydney and educated at Sydney Grammar School and at Christ's College, Christchurch, New Zealand, but did not matriculate. Between prospecting on the New South Wales goldfields, he was apprenticed to a naval architect, worked as a mining engineer and occasionally visited Sydney to attend university lectures on engineering and metallurgy. In

1903 Brereton was elected an associate of the Institution of Mining and Metallurgy, London. He was appointed demonstrator in chemistry at the University of Sydney in 1908, and married Lorna Beatrice Russell in Melbourne on 2 June 1910. In 1916 he was awarded a B.Sc. research degree for work on the origins and nature of gold deposits in New South Wales, and was appointed lecturer. He was a member of the Australian Chemical Institute and of the Royal Society of New South Wales.

Survived by his wife, daughter and two sons, Brereton died at Turramurra on 4 August 1932 and was cremated with Anglican rites.

H. P. Heseltine, *J. Le G. Brereton* (Melb, 1965), and for bibliog; *Hermes*, Lent 1933; *Lone Hand*, June 1920; *To-day* (Melb), 26 Dec 1931; *Art in Aust*, 15 Apr 1933; *SMH*, 17 Mar 1927, 3 Feb, 9 Sept 1933, 21 Feb 1948; *Sydney Mail*, 12 Oct 1927; J. Le G. Brereton letters (LaTL); Brereton papers (ML); information from Dr S. G. Foster, Sydney.

H. P. HESELTINE

BREWIS, CHARLES RICHARD WYNN (1874-1953), naval officer, was born on 7 October 1874 at Ibstone, Buckinghamshire, England, son of Samuel Richard Brewis and his wife Frances Caroline Williams, née Wynn. He joined the Royal Navy at 14, training as a cadet on H.M.S. *Britannia*. He was midshipman on H.M.S. *Curacoa*, part of the Imperial squadron on the Australian station, in 1891-94 when, having attained the rank of acting sub-lieutenant, he undertook further studies in England. Back in Australia in 1896-1902, as lieutenant on H.M.S. *Penguin*, he helped survey much of the Western Australian and Tasmanian coastlines and the South Pacific. He then returned to England to assist as navigating officer in the training of men under the Dreadnought programme, receiving appointment as commander on 30 June 1908.

In 1910 Brewis's wife, Corry Jeannette, whom he had married in Sydney on 20 February 1900, holidayed in Hobart where her father William Crosby, M.L.C., was a prominent ship-owner. During her return voyage to England aboard S.S. *Pericles*, the ship struck an uncharted rock and sank off Cape Leeuwin, Western Australia, on 31 March. The resulting deterioration in his wife's health prompted Brewis to resign from the navy and migrate to Hobart the following August.

His immediate approaches to Prime Minister Andrew Fisher [q.v.] and the first naval member, Captain (Sir) W. R. Creswell [q.v.], seeking a position in the Royal Australian Navy, were unsuccessful and he sought farming opportunities in northern Tasmania. Then in 1911 he was appointed a consultant to the Commonwealth government on the requirements for a national lighthouse service. He urged the use of unattended, quick-flashing acetylene lights, countering opposition by stressing that these could be established in places where the erection of manned lighthouses would be difficult and costly. His recommendations led to the formation in 1913 of the Commonwealth Lighthouse Service, which body thereafter was guided by the administrative procedures he had evolved. His reports were published officially in 1912-14. Brewis was expected to apply for the directorship of lighthouses in 1913 and, after some hesitation, he did so. However, despite being the best-qualified candidate, he was by-passed in favour of J. F. Ramsbotham [q.v.] because of his 'unsuitable temperament', which had already led to conflict with public-service colleagues.

With the outbreak of war Brewis was appointed principal naval transport officer in the R.A.N., commanded the second convoy in December 1914 and was made captain in 1916. In 1920-22 he was district naval officer in Victoria and member of the naval board investigating regulations under the Control of Naval Waters Act (1918). The Royal Navy accorded him a captaincy (retired) in November 1918. Appointed C.B.E. in 1920 and honorary aide-de-camp to the governor-general in April 1922, he retired from the R.A.N. during a period of staff retrenchments at the end of that year. He soon left Melbourne for England where he settled at Bosham, Sussex, and indulged in his lifelong hobby of small-boat sailing.

Brewis died on 31 January 1953, survived by one son and four daughters.

M. B. Komesaroff, 'The Commonwealth Lighthouse Service', *VHJ*, 48 (1977), no 2; *The Times*, 4 Feb 1953; Navy series 1923-50, MP763 series 328/2/5, 358/2/15 (AAO, Melb).

MICHAEL KOMESAROFF

BREWSTER-JONES, HOOPER; *see* JONES, HOOPER B.

BRICE, KATIE; *see under* ARDILL, GEORGE

BRIDGES, SIR (GEORGE) TOM MOLESWORTH (1871-1939), lieut-general and governor, was born on 20 August 1871 at Park Farm, Eltham, Kent, England, third son of Major Thomas Walker Bridges and his wife Mary Ann, née Philippi. Educated at Newton Abbot College and the Royal Military Academy, Woolwich, he was commissioned in 1892 and spent his early service in India and Nyasaland. In the South African War for a few months in 1901 he commanded the 5th and 6th Western Australian (Mounted Infantry) Contingents. On 14 November 1907 in London, he married a widow, Janet Florence Marshall, née Menzies; they had one daughter.

In World War I during the retreat from Mons, Bridges found at St Quentin two exhausted British battalions whose commanding officers had assured the mayor that they would surrender to save the town from bombardment. Despite a shattered cheekbone and concussion, Bridges rallied the men with a tin whistle and toy drum and led them off to rejoin General French's army. The incident became famous. Appointed C.M.G. in 1915, Bridges received many foreign decorations and rapid promotion to major general. He lost a leg at Passchendaele and subsequently led two war missions overseas. For exploits in the Balkans, Russia and Asia Minor, he was appointed K.C.M.G. (1919) and K.C.B. (1925). His uncle Robert Bridges, the poet laureate, honoured him with an ode, 'To His Excellency'.

In 1922, at the instigation of his friend and admirer (Sir) Winston Churchill, Bridges accepted appointment as governor of South Australia on specially favoured terms; he arrived in Adelaide in December. A thorough conservative, he was a staunch defender of capital punishment and the Legislative Council, scorned indolent 'unemployables', and was popular with returned servicemen. Two themes dominated his speeches: the horrors of Bolshevism and the desirability of promoting immigration. He played bridge at the Adelaide Club almost daily and the Colonial Office staff found that his reports reflected the opinions of 'the usual government house entourage' and lacked 'independent judgment'. When the prohibition issue loomed, Bridges created a storm by entertaining a Licensed Victuallers' dinner with quotations from G. K. Chesterton's drinking songs and hilarious prohibition stories.

Bridges had private quarrels with the Labor ministries of 1924-27. He was incensed when the premier, John Gunn [q.v.], published a secret memorandum from a former premier to the governor. Gunn refused to apologize or to compel his attorney-general W. J. Denny [q.v.] to correct an allegation that the British government made retired army officers governors to be 'relieved of the payment of [their] military pensions'. When Labor ministers blundered, through ignorance of convention or Imperial decisions,

Bridges received no thanks for helping to right their mistakes. He refused a second term and returned home in 1927.

Bridges had studied at the Slade School of Fine Art, University of London, and was a competent painter. Many of his Australian oils and water-colours were sold for charity at one-man exhibitions in Adelaide and London. In retirement he wrote his memoirs, *Alarms and excursions* (1938). His private papers were destroyed in World War II, but a diary-extract recording a visit to the Northern Territory in 1923 survives in the Public Record Office, London. Predeceased by his wife he died at Brighton on 26 November 1939.

DNB, 1931-40; P. A. Howell, 'Varieties of vice-regal life in South Australia', *JHSSA*, no 3 (1977); *Advertiser* (Adel), 27 Nov 1939; *The Times*, 27 Nov 1939; information from Liddell Hart Centre for Military Archives (Lond), and Mrs J. Lees-Milne, Badminton, Gloucestershire; CO 532/223, 233, 272, 308, DO 35/2, 23 (NL).   P. A. HOWELL

BRIDGES, ROYAL TASMAN (ROY) (1885-1952), journalist and novelist, was born in Hobart on 23 March 1885, son of Samuel Bridges, basketmaker, and his wife Laura Jane, née Wood, descendants of Tasmanian pioneers. He was educated at Queen's College, Hobart, in 1894-1901, and graduated B.A. from the University of Tasmania in 1905. A small man, shy, sensitive and given to nervous depression, he held a great affection for his mother. From tales retold by her he developed an interest in Tasmanian and family history and an intense attachment to Wood's Farm, near Sorell, the Wood home for over a century.

Bridges began his journalistic career in December 1904 as a cadet on the *Tasmanian News*. In May 1907 he became junior reporter on what he later termed that 'rotten sweatrag', the *Mercury*. In 1908-09 he worked in Sydney for the *Australian Star*, leaving after a change of editor for a brief term as freelance novelist. Late in 1909 he joined the Melbourne *Age* where he remained until 1919, advancing from court reporter to chief parliamentary reporter. He was a founding member of the Australian Journalists' Association in 1911. Until January 1922, when he rejoined the *Age*, he made his living as a novelist. He suffered from an habitual dread of noise, which prompted frequent changes of dwelling. In 1925 his mother died; with his elder sister Hilda, she had followed him to Sydney and Melbourne. Next year he abandoned his position on the *Age Literary Supplement* and spent several months in London. Homesick, he returned to Melbourne in February 1927 to work for six months on the *Herald*. Nervous tension wrecked a further engagement with the *Age* in October 1928. In November 1930, after the death of his uncle Valentine Wood, he fulfilled a long-standing promise by moving with Hilda to Wood's Farm and beginning its restoration. Apart from a few months in 1931 and the years 1933-35, which he spent with Hilda researching in Melbourne, he stayed there for the rest of his life, lonely and often ill, but unable to summon the financial or mental resources to forsake his inheritance.

As an undergraduate Bridges had written stories for the *Tasmanian News*. Further stories were published in the *Australian Star* in 1908 and his first novel *The barb of an arrow* (Sydney, 1909) was serialized in that year. In the following 41 years he wrote 36 novels, thus becoming Tasmania's most prolific author. Some of his writings deal with convictism and bushranging in Victoria and Tasmania; others use English episodes to explain and emphasize the Australian sections; another group of lighter works is set almost wholly in England. He elicits compassion for the victims of the transportation system, and occasionally touches on religious intolerance. He revealed, however, that his early 'thrillers' were hurriedly written for £50 'whenever I was hard up'; he described a later one as 'punk'. His more mature works include a group of six known as The Hobart-Richmond-Sorell novels which evidence his deep delight in the beauty of the Orielton valley running between Richmond and Sorell; others are studies in morbid psychology. The style, both in dialogue and narrative, is mannered in an attempt to recapture the atmosphere of the time.

Bridges was a serious writer with a feeling for and a considerable knowledge of the times of which he wrote. This and the volume of his work must make his contribution to Australian and Tasmanian literature substantial, although his novels lack profundity. Apart from many articles, he wrote the non-fictional *From silver to steel: the romance of the Broken Hill Proprietary* (Melbourne, 1920), *One hundred years: the romance of the Victorian people* (Melbourne, 1934) and *That yesterday was home* (Sydney, 1948), a family history and unusually revealing autobiography.

He died, unmarried, of cardio-vascular disease on 14 March 1952 and was buried at Sorell. His final work, *Youth triumphant*, was posthumously serialized in the *Saturday Evening Mercury* in 1954. Next year his sister Hilda presented a collection of his manuscripts to the University of Tasmania.

His sister HILDA MAGGIE (1881-1971), writer, was born in Hobart on 19 October

1881 and educated at Scotch College there. Roy's lifelong companion, housekeeper and amanuensis, she still found time to produce thirteen novels, three children's tales and hundreds of short stories and sketches. Her first novel, *Our neighbours* (London, 1922), was a tale of Melbourne suburban families, while her ensuing works were light narratives of mystery and romance set in Victoria or the east coast of Tasmania, the plots frequently depending upon smuggling, hidden treasure, secret caves and unknown identities. The characters are stereotyped, but her prose smooth, with effective, intimate descriptions of interior ornamentation, fashions and small natural scenes. Her main concern is entertainment but in *Men must live* (London, 1938) she touches upon the denudation of land by firewood carters, a matter of considerable personal concern. She died in Hobart on 11 September 1971 and was buried at Sorell.

D. H. Borchardt and B. Tilley, 'The Roy Bridges collection . . . A catalogue', *Studies in Aust Bibliog*, no 4, 1956; *Age*, 17 Mar 1952, 26 Feb 1955; H. H. Pearce papers (NL).

J. C. HORNER

BRIDGES, SIR WILLIAM THROSBY (1861-1915), soldier, was born on 18 February 1861 at Greenock, Scotland, son of William Wilson Somerset Bridges, naval officer, and his wife Mary Hill, née Throsby, great-niece of Charles Throsby [q.v.2] of Moss Vale, New South Wales. He was educated at Ryde, Isle of Wight, and from 1871 at the Royal Naval School, New Cross, London. When his father retired in 1873 the family migrated to Canada, settling at Shanty Bay, Ontario, and Bridges continued his schooling at Trinity College School, Port Hope. In April 1877 he entered the Royal Military College of Canada at Kingston, intending to train for a commission in the British Army. Next year, however, his parents were ruined by a bank failure and left Canada to settle at Moss Vale, leaving Bridges behind. He contrived to follow them by failing his studies and left the college without completing the course, thereby becoming the first Kingston cadet discharged for academic failure. He arrived in Sydney in August 1879 and that month joined the colony's civil service as assistant inspector of roads and bridges at Braidwood; he held similar appointments at Murrurundi and Narrabri until 1885.

That year Bridges volunteered for service with the Sudan Contingent but was too late. In May he was made a lieutenant in the temporary forces raised to protect the colony in the contingent's absence, and a vacancy in the permanent artillery allowed the confirmation of his commission in August. He married Edith Lilian Francis at St John's Anglican Church, Darlinghurst, on 10 October. In 1886 he attended the first course conducted at the School of Gunnery, Middle Head, and for the next four years served on its staff, gradually acquiring a reputation as a serious student of the military art. He became a founding member of the United Service Institution of New South Wales in 1889. That year he qualified as an instructor of gunnery and on his promotion to captain in September 1890 left for England to attend several gunnery courses which he passed with distinction. He returned in February 1893 to take up dual posts as chief instructor of the School of Gunnery and the colony's artillery firemaster, holding both until March 1902. He was promoted major in September 1895. Bridges came to the notice of Major General (Sir) Edward Hutton [q.v.], in command of the colony's forces, who selected him to act as secretary to three major military conferences and committees in 1893-96. These appointments ensured that, though only a comparatively junior officer, he had a sound background knowledge of defence issues.

With the outbreak of the South African War Bridges was selected for special service with the British Army and from December 1899 was attached to the cavalry division at Colesberg. He took part in the relief of Kimberley and the battles at Paardeberg and Driefontein before being evacuated to England in May 1900 with enteric fever. While convalescing in London he gave evidence before a royal commission on the care and treatment of casualties in the South African campaign. He returned to Sydney in September and resumed duty at the School of Gunnery. In March 1901 he acted as secretary to a conference of State commandants convened by Sir John (Earl) Forrest [q.v.] to draw up a defence bill for the amalgamated colonial defence forces now under Commonwealth control. He was involved in a second conference in June to comment on proposed amendments to the draft bill and was later appointed to a committee of inquiry to gather data for the formulation of a defence policy. In August he was called to give evidence to a Commonwealth committee considering service pay and allowances.

With the appointment of Major General Hutton to command the Australian forces, Bridges's career was again advanced. In March 1902 he became assistant quartermaster general on Hutton's headquarters, one of the prime staff appointments, which gave him responsibility for military intelligence, the formulation of defence schemes and organization of the forces. In May Hutton sent him to collect information on the defences of Noumea, New Caledonia, on behalf of the War Office, a task he successfully performed. He was promoted lieutcolonel in July. Next month Bridges was a member of a committee convened by the minister for defence to consider alternatives to the system of command of the military forces, and on 12 January 1905 he became chief of intelligence on the first military board of administration, which followed Hutton's return to England. He also became entitled to a seat on the five-man Council of Defence intended to settle policy and coordinate the naval and military boards. From the first meeting of the council in March 1905 Bridges came into sharp conflict with the director of the naval forces, Captain (Sir) William Creswell [q.v.], over the proposal to form an Australian navy. Bridges opposed the concept, mainly because he believed a local navy would duplicate a task which could be done more effectively by the Royal Navy, but also because Creswell's scheme could seemingly only be funded by disbanding the major part of the military forces. His differences with Creswell extended into an acrimonious conflict over the question of control of procedures to establish the identity of all vessels entering Australian ports in wartime, a dispute which Bridges lost in June 1908.

On the military board he became a relentless advocate of efficiency within the forces. From early 1905 he urged it to pay at least as much attention to ensuring that Australia had properly trained officers as to acquiring war *matériel*. In 1906 Bridges was prominent in the establishment of a department of military science at the University of Sydney to qualify graduates for commissions in the militia forces – although he held that the 'proposed Courses of Instruction would not form a substitute for a Military College' – and he remained associated with the department until 1909. While working on the defence schemes Bridges realized the necessity of learning from the experience of other countries in mobilizing military forces, and induced the minister for defence to send him to the 1906 Swiss manoeuvres. His impending departure in January was seized upon by Prime Minister Deakin [q.v.] as an opportunity to refer the question of Australian defence to the Committee of Imperial Defence in London. Deakin directed Bridges to assist the committee but expressly restricted him to furnishing information and not opinions. Although Deakin recognized Bridges as 'the ablest of our Imperial officers' he also viewed him as being 'imperfectly in sympathy' with certain nationalist aims.

Bridges was promoted colonel in October 1906 and on returning to Australia next January came into conflict with the new minister for defence (Sir) Thomas Ewing [q.v.], who insisted on the immediate implementation of a scheme for the protection of vital areas of Australia. Bridges argued that such a scheme was worthless unless a general staff was established to plan the work involved. Further differences developed in October when his report on the Swiss military system was used by the government as evidence that Australia needed compulsory military training, a proposal which Bridges privately deplored. In December he was successful in founding an intelligence corps and this body became the forerunner of a general staff.

Bridges had long had a hobby of canoeing, which he pursued frequently in these years on the Yarra River. In January 1908 he fulfilled a long-standing ambition by navigating the rapids of the Snowy River from near Dalgety, New South Wales, to near Buchan, Victoria – an astonishing voyage of nearly 200 miles (322 km), accomplished with three friends in two canoes.

Bridges's attempts to improve the efficiency of the forces also brought him into conflict with the inspector general, Major General (Sir) John Hoad [q.v.]. Long-standing antipathy between the two was compounded by Bridges's appointment as first chief of the Australian general staff in January 1909, during Hoad's absence in London. Bridges remained in the post less than five months, however, having been selected to attend the Imperial Conference that year. On his departure he was promised that he would be reappointed C.G.S. on his return, and the minister for defence agreed to put this in writing. After the conference he became Australian representative on the Imperial General Staff in London and was appointed C.M.G. in July. Queries were soon raised as to why he was at the War Office and whether his duties were those of observer or exchange officer. Bridges insisted that his proper function was to act as official representative, but his efforts to have his view accepted were cut short in January 1910 when he was recalled to found Australia's military college. At first he attempted to decline the post of college commandant but, on Defence Minister (Sir) Joseph Cook's [q.v.] insistence, accepted and arrived back in Australia in May, having visited military schools in England, America and Canada. On taking up his new appointment he was promoted brigadier general.

Following a recommendation to the government by Lord Kitchener, Bridges began establishing the college along the lines of the United States Military Academy, West Point. His personal impact was evident, however, in nearly every aspect of the college, from its location at Duntroon in the Federal Capital Territory to its organization and routine. It opened on 27 June 1911, and Bridges remained commandant until May 1914, by which time its reputation was firmly established. He left the college to assume the Australian Army's senior appointment as inspector general.

After the declaration of war Bridges was instructed by the government to raise an Australian contingent for service in Europe. His determination that the troops would fight as an entity instead of being fragmented among British formations did much to satisfy nationalist sentiment and set a precedent retained throughout the war. Despite his suggestion that command of the Australian Imperial Force (a name he chose himself) be entrusted to Hutton, Bridges was appointed commander, with the rank of major general, in August.

On arrival in Egypt in December, Bridges began a heavy programme of training for his division. Disciplinary problems with high-spirited troops were, in part, a reaction to the detailed training on which Bridges insisted, though the thoroughness of the training was essential preparation for the untried Australians. In the Gallipoli landing in April 1915 his division was first ashore on Anzac Cove. At the end of the first day Bridges and Major General Godley, commanding the New Zealanders, were convinced that disaster would follow next day and proposed taking the force off the beach. The suggestion was overruled and the Allied forces began consolidating the position.

In the following weeks Bridges became well known to his troops for the first time, through his daily inspections of the firing line; during these he showed great disregard for his personal safety. On the morning of 15 May he was shot by a sniper in Monash Valley, and both artery and femoral vein in his right thigh were severed. He was evacuated to the hospital ship *Gascon* but his condition was such that doctors decided against operating to remove his leg. The wound became gangrenous and he died en route to hospital in Egypt on 18 May. He had been appointed K.C.B. the previous day. His remains were interred at Alexandria but in June it was decided to return the body to Australia for burial. After a memorial service in St Paul's Cathedral, Melbourne, on 2 September, and a funeral procession through the city, his body was transferred to Canberra and reburied overlooking the Royal Military College. He was survived by two sons and two daughters; Lady Bridges died in 1926. His portrait, painted in 1919 by

Florence Rodway [q.v.], is in the New South Wales Art Gallery; copies hang in the Australian War Memorial collection and in the Royal Military College, Duntroon. His second son William Francis Noel (1890-1942) served with the A.I.F. at Gallipoli and on the Western Front, reaching the rank of major. He was awarded the Distinguished Service Order in 1918.

Bridges's career was essentially that of an able staff officer who had had few opportunities to command troops before being placed at the head of a division. A shy and sensitive man, he attempted to mask himself behind an aloof, diffident and sometimes rude manner. He was not therefore a popular commander, though his personal courage was respected. Well-read in his profession, motivated by high ideals and possessed of uncompromising standards, he made many enemies, yet all he undertook was stamped with efficiency and success. His death early in the war caused his career and achievements to slip from public view, but he can rightfully be regarded as Australia's first notable general.

C. E. W. Bean, *Two men I knew* (Syd, 1957); C. D. Coulthard-Clark, *A heritage of spirit* (Melb, 1979), and for bibliog.   C. D. COULTHARD-CLARK

BRIENT, LACHLAN JOHN (1856-1940), journalist, was born on 16 October 1856 and baptized a Catholic on 7 December in Hobart Town, son of Michael Joseph O'Brien (alias Bryant), carpenter, and his wife Margaret, née McLean. His father had been transported for ten years for stealing a handkerchief, and arrived in Van Diemen's Land in the *Forfarshire* on 12 October 1843. After two years on Norfolk Island in 1850-52, he received his certificate of freedom in 1853; in 1855 he was granted permission to marry Margaret McLean, who had been sentenced in Glasgow to seven years transportation for theft and had reached Hobart on 21 April 1853 in the *Duchess of Northumberland*.

Lachlan became a reporter in Hobart and on 5 April 1876 married Alice Harriet Alberta Tasker with Congregational forms. About 1878 he moved to Melbourne to work on the *Age* and later joined the *Sydney Morning Herald*. In 1883 he left to become news editor of the *Daily Telegraph*. With its chief editor F. W. Ward [q.v.] he helped to make the paper more pithy and arresting. Next year when the Daily Telegraph Newspaper Co. Ltd was formed he became a shareholder. In May 1890 with Ward and H. Gullett [q.v.], he resigned after a dispute with the directors over future policy and limitations on editorial independence. At the end of the year Brient was recalled as editor.

In 1891 he also became Australian cable-correspondent for *The Times* (London). Under Brient's guidance, the *Telegraph* took advantage of technological developments and its reputation was enhanced by the quality of its maps, portraits and sketches accompanying reports on the South African War. The paper's editorial policy strongly favoured free trade. In the New South Wales general election in 1898 Brient launched an intensive campaign for (Sir) George Reid against (Sir) Edmund Barton [qq.v.]; while the paper supported Federation, by next year when the second referendum was held it had changed to opposition. Reserved and somewhat mysterious to his staff, which included such notable journalists as (Sir) Frank Fox and W. Farmer Whyte [qq.v.], Brient was rarely seen in the office until late in the evening and would severely snub any proof-reader who dared to point out a mistake. He made the *Telegraph* into an 'audacious, unscrupulous, mendacious go-ahead sheet'.

From 1899 Brient had been a trustee of the Public Library of New South Wales, in which he took a keen interest although unable to attend meetings. Troubled by a heart condition he resigned in 1901 from the *Telegraph* and went to London, where he joined the editorial staff of the *Morning Post*, and survived into old age. He was a handsome man, with a neat George V beard, curling moustache and wavy hair, and was a member of the Savage Club. He died of cerebro-vascular disease at Walton-upon-Thames, Surrey, on 24 July 1940, survived by two sons. Although as editor he had written little himself, he was remembered as 'a great pressman with a wonderful nose for news'.

His son Albert Lachlan was born on 20 February 1877 in Hobart and was a reporter on the *Daily Telegraph* under his father. Later he became relieving editor of the Melbourne *Argus* and of the *Australasian*. He attended the opening of the first Federal parliament, was one of the earliest members of the parliamentary press gallery and became an authority on foreign affairs. He was a Freemason and belonged to the Yorick and Royal Melbourne Golf clubs. On 7 May 1946 he married Grace Sloan McMillan; she survived him when he died, childless, on 29 June 1955 at Leura, New South Wales.

Review of Reviews for A'sia, Oct 1892, p73; Daily Telegraph Newspaper Co. Ltd *Annual Report*, 1884-1902; *Cosmos Mag*, 30 Sept 1895, p4; *Punch* (Melb), 22 Aug 1901; *Catholic Press*, 24 Aug 1901; *Bulletin*, 5 May 1904; *SMH*, 15 Nov 1940; *Argus*, 29 June 1955; Brient to E. Barton, Feb 1893, D. Maughan papers (ML); Convict registers 1804-53, *and* parish registers (TA).   JILL WATERHOUSE

BRIER, PERCY (1885-1970), musician, was born on 7 June 1885 at North Pine (Petrie) near Caboolture, Queensland, son of George Blyth Brier, schoolmaster, and his wife Amelia, née Welsby, both of whom were English migrants. He was educated until 1898 at the Yeronga State School, Brisbane, where his father was headmaster, and later attended the Brisbane Technical College at night. Brier began to study the piano under Miss Birkett in 1893; by 1898 he had decided on a career as a musician. As a pupil of Mrs Harry Reeve in 1900, he secured 99 per cent in the senior examination of the Trinity College of Music, London, and topped the lists. He learned harmony and counterpoint from A. A. Burford in 1901, and won a scholarship to study at Trinity College under Bainbridge, Ogbourne, Pearce, Saunders and Warrener. He was awarded the licentiates of Trinity College and the Royal Academy of Music in 1904, and next year became an associate of the Royal College of Organists.

Returning to Brisbane in 1906, Brier began the professional practice of music. As an organist, his main church appointments were at the City Tabernacle Baptist Church in 1912-19, and as acting organist at St James's Church of England, Sydney, in 1926. As director or deputy, he conducted the Queensland State and Municipal Choir, the Apollo Club, the Brisbane Austral Choir, and the Indooroopilly Choral Society which he had also founded. He was popular as an adjudicator in musical competitions throughout Queensland and northern New South Wales, and also in Sydney, Melbourne and Adelaide. From 1922 he was an examiner for the Australian Music Examinations Board and travelled widely in this capacity, especially in his home State.

Brier was a founder of the Musical Association (later the Music Teachers' Association) of Queensland, and was its president twelve times between 1924 and 1951. He established the Queensland branch of the Guild of Australian Composers in 1940 and was later its patron. On his retirement in 1963, Brier estimated that he had taught 912 students, many of whom achieved some prominence. Possibly the most distinguished was James Mursell, musical psychologist at Columbia University, New York.

An old-fashioned composer with Victorian roots, Brier was gentleman enough not to become publicly ruffled by musical innovations. He published only *Intermezzo giocoso* (for piano), but left in manuscript two piano concertos, many songs, choral and chamber music, and some organ solos and church music. He also wrote three small textbooks, printed privately, and a historical compilation, *The pioneers of music in Queensland* (1962), extended to *One hundred years and more of music in Queensland* and published posthumously in 1971. It was followed by his *Autobiography of a musician* in a limited edition in 1973.

Brier was a convinced High Anglican from his youth and subsequently served his local church, St Andrew's, Indooroopilly, as parochial councillor, rector's warden and lay reader. When hurt or offended he could retreat behind a chilling hauteur and a slightly precious old-fashioned manner of speech; normally he was a polite Christian gentleman. With ordinary students, he was always patient — with a dry wit, a ready laugh and an intellectual approach which sometimes seemed pedantic. To the gifted student he was an inspired and inspiring teacher, using his own personality only as a catalyst to prompt the student to think for himself.

On 1 July 1915 Brier had married Eva Baynes (d. 1943) in the City Tabernacle. 'I an Anglican, my bride a Congregationalist, the officiating minister a Methodist and all in a Baptist Church!!!', he wrote in recollection. Survived by one of two sons, he died of coronary vascular disease on 9 May 1970 at Scarborough; he was cremated and the ashes interred at St Andrew's Church. The University of Queensland awards an annual prize for composition in his memory, and a Canberra street is named after him.

W. A. Orchard, *Music in Australia* (Melb, 1952); *Canon*, Feb 1958; *Brisbane Courier*, 29 Apr 1925; *Courier Mail*, 12 May 1970, 23 June 1975; reminiscences (Mr L. Sitsky, Canberra School of Music, ACT); family information from Mr E. B. Brier, Fig Tree Pocket, Qld.   ROBERT K. BOUGHEN

BRIGDEN, JAMES BRISTOCK (1887-1950), economist, administrator and diplomat, was born on 20 July 1887 at Maldon, Victoria, son of James Bristock Brigden, bootmaker and later tram-conductor, and his Welsh wife Mary, née Griffiths. He received his early education in state schools, but left at 16 to ship as a cabin-boy on a brief adventure to England. On his return to Victoria he sought a career in political journalism, but had to eke out his freelance earnings in a variety of pursuits, including poultry-raising and operating an ice-run. He participated extensively in political movements, and was prominent in the early struggles to organize the Shop Assistants' Union.

Jim Brigden enlisted as a private in the Australian Imperial Force in October 1915, qualified as a musketry instructor, and by late 1916 was in France with the 29th Battalion. After being promoted acting corporal, he suffered severe wounds at Beaumetz, and was hospitalized in Oxford, England, for a protracted period from March 1917. There he had the good fortune to attract the care and interest of Mrs Edwin Cannan and, through her, of her husband the distinguished economist. Then followed the award of a Kitchener Memorial Scholarship to Oriel College, Oxford, enabling him to read jurisprudence (B.A., 1920; M.A., 1925) and to follow up his interest in economics under Cannan's unofficial tutoring. He married Dorothy James of London at Ide Hill, Kent, on 26 June 1920; they were childless. After his graduation he took posts as a tutorial class lecturer for the Workers' Educational Association first at Sheffield, England, and in 1921 at Queenstown, Tasmania, His pamphlet, *The economics of Lyell* (Hobart, 1922), contains one of the earliest attempts to estimate the national income of Australia.

In January 1923 Brigden became the first Pitt Cobbett [q.v.] lecturer in employment relations at the University of Tasmania, where he came under the influence of L. F. Giblin [q.v.]. During this period he also served on the Queensland Economic Commission on the Basic Wage, which reported in February 1925, and published *Employment relations and the basic wage* (Hobart, 1925). These works broke new ground by stressing the idea that wage policy should be guided mainly by the principle of 'capacity to pay'. In June 1924 he succeeded (Sir) D. B. Copland as professor of economics in the University of Tasmania. The following year Brigden and Giblin, as members of the committee appointed to inquire into Tasmanian disabilities under Federation, produced a report which was largely responsible for setting Commonwealth-State financial relations on a new course.

Brigden made his most important contribution to theoretical economics in 1927-29 when he served on the prime minister's committee which produced *The Australian Tariff: an economic enquiry* (Melbourne, 1929). 'Brigden and Giblin wrote that report . . . no one else had much of a hand in it', Professor Torleiv Hytten noted later, while Giblin himself recalled: 'I have a strong impression that Jim supplied the ideas which were the basis of the more significant parts'. Brigden's original challenge to the doctrine of free trade under Australian conditions had come to notice earlier in the first issue of the *Economic Record*.

By now he was becoming widely known in business and political circles; and with the threat of depression his advice was eagerly sought. In May 1929 Brigden was economist of the Oversea Shipping Representatives' Association, with the task of rationalizing and co-ordinating shipping movements to hold down freight rates in overseas trade. Next month he became economist and deputy chairman of a newly formed body, the Australian Oversea Transport Association. In early 1930 he was appointed first director of the Queensland Bureau of Economics and Statistics (soon the Bureau of Industry), a position he held for eight very productive years. Initially the bureau was concerned with economic research and public education, but it later also became the authority for large public works throughout the State. During 1932 Brigden was also a commissioner of the Queensland State Industrial Court and a member of the Commonwealth Wool Inquiry Committee. In 1935 he was formally made Queensland government statistician.

In these years Brigden believed it his duty to disseminate economic knowledge, a job to which he brought a sense of humour, 'In order that it may have a chance of competing in the din, this book shouts a bit itself', he wrote of the introductory volume of *Economic News* in 1932. With export prices plummeting, he based his thinking on a reversal of Giblin's famous 'multiplier', and had begun to publicize his findings with a series of radio talks, collected as *Escape to prosperity* (Melbourne, 1930). He followed this with *PP: on purchasing power and the pound Australian* (Brisbane, 1931) and *Credit: what is; what is proposed; what is practicable* (Brisbane, 1932). *Railway economics* (Brisbane, 1931) and *The story of sugar* (Brisbane, 1932) were explanations of the working of industry. The first of his Queensland year-books appeared in 1937. As a Commonwealth consultant on development, he was also active in the conferences of economists which formulated the Premiers' Plan. But by 1932 he had personally abandoned the original recommendation to reduce government spending and was advocating reduction of wages and an increase in government spending, a position which led to long-term disagreement with some members of the Industrial Court.

In July 1938 Brigden welcomed an appointment as chairman of the National Insurance Commission, set up to introduce a national scheme of contributory health and pension insurance, somewhat along the lines of the English system. However, despite his enormous efforts to get satisfactory legislation passed, to build up an adequate organization, to defend the proposals against entrenched vested interests and to explain it to the public, the scheme foundered. After Munich the threat of war gave its critics the opportunity to claim that finance was not available simultaneously for war preparations and social reform. Brigden never quite recovered from the abandoning of this great project into which he had poured his very soul.

With other members of his ill-fated commission, he went in June 1939 to the new Department of Supply and Development, first as economist and a few months later as secretary. In August 1940 Brigden also became secretary of the newly formed Ministry of Munitions, assisting to get the great munitions drive under way at that critical time, and in July 1941 was appointed secretary of the Department of Aircraft Production. By the end of 1941 he was exhausted and was given relief by a posting as financial counsellor to the Australian Legation (later Embassy) to the United States of America, thus entering on what was probably the most rewarding phase of his varied career.

He spent the next five years in unobtrusive and self-effacing economic diplomacy — at the time when relations with the United States were not only sensitive but also critical for the defence of Australia, and the foundations were being laid for post-war political, social and economic reconstruction. Brigden won the confidence and support of the highest authorities in the American administration. In the international field he was able to use to advantage his skill and experience in negotiation, his gentle and urbane demeanour, and his patent integrity and good sense. His advice was widely sought and his views accorded a respect out of all proportion to the position he and his country occupied. Particularly notable was his work with reciprocal lend-lease; with the difficult birth of the United Nations Relief and Rehabilitation Administration (of which he was chairman of the committee of supplies); with the International Monetary Fund, the International Bank for Reconstruction and Development, and with the Food and Agricultural Organization (of which he was chairman of the finance committee). At the same time he provided intellectual leadership to the contributions committee of the United Nations.

Brigden's career was characterized by intense vigour. In early life a 'battler', in young manhood a valiant soldier, he developed into an innovative economist, and served faithfully and well as an administrator. He reached his full flower, after tasting the bitter fruits of frustration and mental despair, as a highly regarded diplomat on the wartime and post-war world stage. A tallish man, whose sandy hair had sometimes earned him the nickname 'Blue' or 'Red', he found time to write occasional poetry and, with his wife, maintain an interest in the theatre. His most cherished personal honour was the honorary fellowship of Oriel College to which he was elected in 1941. He retired, ill, in November 1947 and, survived by his wife, died tranquilly on 12 October 1950 at Mitcham, Victoria, from what he lightly used to call his 'bloody old pressure'.

Economic News (Qld), Dec 1950; R. Wilson, 'James Bristock Brigden: a tribute', *Economic Record,* June 1951; N. Cain, 'Political economy and the tariff: Australia in the 1920s', *Aust Economic Papers,* June 1973; Brigden papers, M3730, series 49 (NL).   ROLAND WILSON

BRIGGS, SIR HENRY (1844-1919), headmaster and politician, was born on 17 March 1844 at Kettering, Northamptonshire, England, son of George Briggs, shoemaker, and his wife Sarah, née Tibbutt. Educated at the Collegiate School, Leicester, under Canon Fry, he won the Queen's scholarship at 18 and entered St Mark's College, an Anglican teacher-training centre at Chelsea, London. He subsequently became headmaster of the College of Model Schools for three years and of Mottram Grammar School for twelve years.

Briggs was appointed foundation headmaster in 1882 of the Anglican Fremantle Grammar School. He introduced his students to a wider curriculum than that common elsewhere in the Australian colonies, which followed English tradition by emphasizing classical studies. Despite financial limitations, Fremantle Grammar was soon the leading school in Western Australia; prominent citizens no longer had to send their sons to England or the eastern colonies. When Briggs decided to resign in 1889 to open his own school, the choice of almost all his pupils to follow him forced the Church of England to close the school to allow him to become its proprietor. With an enrolment increased from 29 to 120, it remained under his control until 1897, when he retired to enter politics.

As a bachelor, Briggs was able to devote much spare time to literary, political and civic interests. A member of the examining board of a weak and inexperienced Education Department, he helped to raise educational standards. He sat on a committee established by the Legislative Council in 1889 to investigate technical education, and demonstrated the need to adapt curricula to colonial conditions. In 1903 he became a trustee of the Public Library, Museum and Art Gallery. More significantly, he was one of the first to urge the establishment of a university and was a member of the royal commission which preceded the University Act of 1911.

Briggs had gained political influence as secretary of the Western Australian Chamber of Commerce in 1883-95 and in June 1896 he won the West Province of the Legislative Council by a large majority. A heavy man of more than 18 stone (114 kg), he spoke well though slowly, ponderously and didactically. Although not particularly outspoken, he could be forceful on major issues; he was always a humanitarian on industrial questions. In June 1900 he became chairman of committees and in 1906 succeeded Sir George Shenton [q.v.6] as president of the Legislative Council, an office which he filled with dignified success until his death.

Briggs was examiner for a scheme of commercial qualification launched by the Fremantle Chamber of Commerce in 1904. While president of the Fremantle branch of the Australian Federation League, he represented the colony at the Federal convention of 1897-98 in Adelaide, Sydney and Melbourne, but was largely 'a spectator and a vote'. He was knighted in 1916.

A prominent Freemason, Briggs took the preliminary steps in creating the Royal Arch Chapter in Western Australia, but when he died on 8 June 1919 his will directed that there should be no Masonic rites at his funeral; he was buried with Anglican rites in Fremantle cemetery. His estate, valued for probate at £19 477, was left equally between the Home of Peace at Subiaco and an English cousin.

W. B. Kimberly, *History of West Australia* (Perth, 1897); J. S. Battye (ed), *Cyclopedia of Western Australia*, 1 (Adel, 1912); F. Alexander, *Campus at Crawley* (Melb, 1963); D. Mossenson, *State education in Western Australia, 1829-1960* (Perth, 1972); *Herald* (Fremantle), 4 Mar 1882; *West Australian*, 9 June 1919; CSO 1667/1888, 3489/1889 (Battye Lib, Perth).

TOBY MANFORD

BRINSMEAD, HORACE CLOWES (1883-1934), soldier and administrator, was born on 2 February 1883 at Hampstead, London, son of Edgar William Brinsmead, piano-manufacturer, and his wife Annie, née Bayley. He was educated at Clifton, Cranleigh and Repton schools and at 20 migrated to Australia and settled on the land in North Queensland. This venture was unsuccessful and he became a planter in Tonga, remaining there until World War I.

On 29 December 1914 Brinsmead enlisted in the Australian Imperial Force as a private and was posted to the 24th Battalion. He was commissioned second lieutenant while training at Seymour, Victoria, and on 26 June 1915 embarked for active service. When his battalion reached Gallipoli in September Brinsmead, by then lieutenant, was appointed adjutant. He was firm, just and courteous towards other ranks who, because of his slight build, gentle nature and quiet disposition, thought at first that he was 'too refined to make a leader in war'. He proved his ability during the heavy Turkish bombardment of Lone Pine on 29 November. Sent in to command 'B' Company when the front line had been blown to pieces, he quickly reorganized the men and had the trenches rebuilt so that a fresh Turkish attack could be met with confidence. He served at Lone Pine until the evacuation and commanded the last party to leave the sector.

The 24th Battalion reached the Western Front in March 1916. Brinsmead, who was still adjutant, was promoted captain in May, and for gallantry at Pozières on 27 July was awarded the Military Cross. On the same day he was severely wounded in a leg and evacuated to England. Nine months later he was still unfit for active service and after attending a senior-officers' course at Clare College, Cambridge, transferred to the administrative staff at Australian Flying Corps headquarters, London. From April 1917 until early 1919 he was a senior staff officer in the A.F.C. training wing. He was promoted major in January 1918 and temporary lieut-colonel a year later. From April to November 1919 he was attached to the Foreign Office for special duty with the military section of the British delegation to the Paris Peace Conference. He was appointed O.B.E. in June and in November was sent to Germany with the Disarmament Control Board.

Brinsmead was demobilized in May 1920 and on 8 December, at the Presbyterian Ladies' College, East Melbourne, married Ivy Ernestine, daughter of Charles McDonald [q.v.]. In the same month the civil aviation branch of the Department of Defence was established, and he was appointed controller. Over the next eleven years he directed the growth of civil aviation in Australia, earning a reputation as an efficient administrator with a diplomatic gift for cutting red tape. He framed the air navigation regulations, flew thousands of miles investigating new aerial mail and passenger routes and reporting on landing grounds and general facilities, and was a constant advocate of the local manufacture of aircraft parts.

In December 1931 Brinsmead left for London to conclude a project which he had long striven for; an aerial passenger and mail-service connexion along the Imperial air route between England and Australia. At

Bangkok his aircraft crashed soon after take-off and he suffered severe head injuries. He was brought home next February but remained an invalid until his death at the Austin Hospital Melbourne, on 11 March 1934; he was cremated with full military honours. His wife, a son and two daughters survived him.

W. J. Harvey, *The red and white diamond* (Melb, 1920); C. E. W. Bean, *The story of Anzac*, 2 (Syd, 1924); *London Gazette*, 29 Dec 1916, supp, 3 June 1919; *Sea, Land and Air*, Jan 1921; *Duckboard*, Mar 1933, Apr 1934; *Reveille* (Syd), Apr, May 1934; *SMH*, 3 Dec 1920, 25 Jan 1933, 12 Mar 1934; *Punch* (Melb), 16 Dec 1920; *Table Talk*, 7 Oct 1926; *Argus*, 12 Mar 1934; War diary of the 24th Battalion, A.I.F. (AWM).   DARRYL MCINTYRE

BRISBANE, WILLIAM PETER (1866-1925), breeder and judge of dairy cattle, was born on 7 June 1866 at Berwick, Victoria, son of James Grimmond Brisbane, cattle-breeder, and his wife Elizabeth, née Brisbane, both from Perthshire, Scotland. From the age of 12 William took cattle to the National Agricultural Society's Melbourne show unaided and returned with trophies to present to his father.

Brisbane's career reflects the progress of the Victorian dairying and butter industries. At 19 he took charge of Richard Gibson's Ayrshire stud at Tullamarine. When Gibson died and the best of the herd was purchased by W. B. Cumming, Brisbane went with them as manager to the grazing property of Mount Fyans, near Camperdown. Depressed wool prices in the early 1890s and the foundation of local butter factories induced many graziers to establish dairy herds on portions of their runs. Through Brisbane's judicious importations from Scotland and skill in selection, Cumming's Ayrshires won six consecutive championships at the Royal Agricultural Society's show in Melbourne.

Aspiring to a property of his own, Brisbane approached Edward Manifold [q.v.] who in 1896 offered him leasehold of a farm of 300 acres (120 ha) at Weerite, east of Camperdown. The association with Cumming was retained — he received the benefit of Brisbane's knowledge of the breeder's art and Brisbane initiated his own herd with blood lines which originated at the duke of Buccleuch's famous Scottish stud. Pressure of land taxation in 1911 provoked Manifold to sell his land to his tenants; Brisbane bought his farm, eventually named Gowrie Park, on generous terms.

In 1906, when dairying was still at a pioneering stage, and when farmers cared little about selection of breeding animals, Brisbane purchased a sire, Lessnessock, imported from the Scottish stud of A. Montgomery of Ochiltree. As well as winning the champion's ribbon four times at the Melbourne show, and once at the Sydney show, Lessnessock stock lifted the quality of dairy cattle throughout Australasia and the Pacific islands. Scottish Queen, a three-year-old Lessnessock descendant, topped the Victorian government herd test in 1913-14, and next year Linda of Gowrie Park won again. In 1913-14 thirty-five Gowrie Park Ayrshires easily doubled the average butter-fat figure for Victorian dairy cows. Brisbane's grasp of dairy husbandry went beyond breeding: he was an early advocate of better feeding through pasture improvement, recognizing, in particular, the advantages of subterranean clover before many farmers could even identify it.

A big, bluff, cheerful and outspoken man, Brisbane was well known at show rings throughout Australia as a cattle judge. He was also a councillor of the Royal Agricultural Society of Victoria, taking an active part in organizing the annual exhibitions. He served the Camperdown community as a justice of the peace and a master of the Masonic lodge. His concern for dairymen of the future is illustrated by the advice and gifts of valuable stock to the Geelong Calf Clubs from which the Young Farmer movement developed. Brisbane died suddenly of heart failure on his property on 26 June 1925 and was buried in Camperdown cemetery. His estate was valued for probate at £26 652. On 23 December 1895 at the Portarlington Presbyterian manse he had married Mary Campbell. She survived him, together with their two sons who for many years maintained the reputation of the Ayrshire cattle of Gowrie Park.

J. Smith (ed), *Cyclopedia of Victoria*, 2 (Melb, 1904); *Camperdown Chronicle*, 12 Oct 1922, 30 June 1925; *Terang Express*, 7 Dec 1923; *Colac Herald*, 29 June 1925; *Australasian*, 4 July 1925; Closer settlement files, Leslie Manor estate (Lands Dept, Vic); scrap-book held by Mrs C. M. Brisbane, Newtown, Vic.   L. LOMAS

BROADBENT, GEORGE ROBERT (1863-1947), cyclist and map publisher, was born on 3 November 1863 at Ashby near Geelong, Victoria, son of George Adam Broadbent, Lancashire-born draper, and his wife Elizabeth, née Ruffhead. When the family moved to North Melbourne Broadbent attended the Errol Street school, followed his father's trade, and became an early cycling and cycle-racing enthusiast.

At various times Broadbent held most

Victorian and Australian road records, and two of his performances on solid tyres – 203 miles (327 km) in 24 hours on a penny farthing, and 100 miles (161 km) in 6 hours 20 minutes on a 'safety' bicycle – were never bettered. He established records for all distances between 130 and 220 miles (209 and 354 km), and for all times between 8 and 12 hours, at the Exhibition Grounds track in May 1894, and road records for 50 and 100 miles (80 and 161 km) in October 1896. The *Australian Cyclist* acknowledged him 'the finest road rider that Australia has ever produced'.

A foundation councillor of the League of Victorian Wheelmen in October 1893, Broadbent contested the first Warrnambool-Melbourne race in 1895, and was active in the Good Roads Movement. Next year he issued a road map of Victoria, 'prepared . . . after some sixteen years riding and touring in all parts of the Colony', which indicated general topography, distances, and roads classified as 'good', 'fair' or 'ridden with difficulty'. It was to become Victoria's standard map, and the basis of a continuous publishing programme by Broadbent's Official Road Guides Co.

He bought a steam-driven motor car in 1898, contributed regularly to the *Argus* and *Australasian* on both cycling and touring and, in December 1903, attended the meeting which established the (Royal) Automobile Club of Victoria. Broadbent became an active vice-president of the Good Roads Association of Victoria in November 1912 and was consulted regularly during the preparation of the country roads bill. That year he took over the *Argus* motoring column, wrote tirelessly on road improvements and maintenance, and became manager of the Automobile Club's new touring department in 1914. He was also an active member of the trust created in 1919 to establish the Great Ocean Road from Barwon Heads to Warrnambool. His name was entered in the R.A.C.V. Golden Book in May 1932 for outstanding services to motoring and road development. He retired in December 1937 and was one of fifteen surviving founders to be elected life-members of the R.A.C.V. in May 1947.

Broadbent had married Louisa Santy with Baptist forms at Richmond on 29 December 1887. When he died at his home at Hawthorn on 28 October 1947, three sons and six of his seven daughters survived him. His second son Robert Arthur, also an amateur and professional cycling champion, represented Australia at the Olympic Games in Paris in 1924, succeeded him as tourist manager of the R.A.C.V. and, in 1963, established R. A. Broadbent-Tourist Publications. The youngest son Edward Albert had taken over

Broadbent's Official Road Guides Co. in 1945.

Roy Automobile Club of Vic, *The golden jubilee 1903-1953* (Melb, 1953); League of Vic Wheelmen, *Official Gazette*, 7 Nov 1905, 7 July 1907; *Aust Motorist*, 1 Sept, 2 Nov 1914; *Aust Cyclist*, 7 Sept, 7 Dec 1893; *Aust Wheel*, Oct 1896, Jan 1897; *Radiator*, 15 Jan 1938, 12 Nov 1947; *Herald* (Melb), 27 Mar 1902; *Argus*, 21 Nov 1912, 20-22 Feb, 29 Apr 1919, 11 Oct 1930, 24 Aug 1946, 29 Oct 1947; *Punch* (Melb), 13 Oct 1921; *Sun-News Pictorial*, 29 Oct 1947; *Geelong Advertiser*, 15 Jan 1958.

G. F. JAMES

BROADBENT, JOSEPH EDWARD (1883-1948), parliamentary draftsman, was born on 14 December 1883 at Kelvin Grove, Brisbane, son of Kendall Broadbent (1837-1911) and his wife Maria, née Boreham, both English-born. His father was a noted ornithologist, who worked for thirty years at the Queensland Museum. Educated at the Kelvin Grove State School, Joseph won a scholarship to Brisbane Grammar School and matriculated at the University of Sydney in 1898. A keen student of the classics, he accumulated texts throughout his life.

Entering the Queensland Public Service in 1900, Broadbent served successively in the Stores Department, Stamp Office and Justice Department, becoming in 1917 parliamentary secretary to the government. In this role, he wrote the pamphlets *Socialism at work* (1917) and *Administrative actions of the Labour government in Queensland . . .* (1924).

Admitted to the Queensland Bar in 1919, he was appointed assistant parliamentary draftsman in 1925 and, on the elevation of J. L. Woolcock [q.v.] to the bench in December 1926, became parliamentary draftsman from 10 February 1927. Besides attending to bills during this period, Broadbent was deeply involved in the production, often outside working hours, of numerous statutory collections and annotations. He was a member of the editorial board for volumes 1-9 of the 1939 consolidation, *The public Acts of Queensland* (reprint); he edited several statute compilations including *Labour laws of Queensland* and *Queensland liquor laws* and the *Queensland digest of case law 1861-1924*. He was also the State's contributor to the *Journal of the Society of Comparative Legislation*. His work of collection and clarification was of special importance to a scattered professional body, often far from libraries, and it was recognized in 1932 by the award of the Imperial Service Order.

Broadbent retained an active interest in Brisbane Grammar School, serving as a trustee in 1920-32 and in 1939-47 as vice-chairman; he was president of the old boys' association in 1929 and donated a prize which still subsists. He also served as trustee of the Brisbane Girls' Grammar School in 1920-32 and 1939-47. In the 1930s he undertook evening studies at the University of Queensland (B.A., 1936); he then worked towards a law degree. An unpublished work on Queensland legislation, held in the university library and marked 'thesis', suggests further unrealized ambitions.

The pressure upon Broadbent as sole draftsman was considerable and the strain of his work-load began to tell, especially through the war years when he suffered recurrent illness. He died of arteriosclerotic heart disease at West End, Brisbane, on 14 December 1948, the day after his official retirement. Cremated after a Baptist service, he was survived by his wife Daisy Stewart, née Nelson, whom he had married on 10 June 1914, and by a daughter. He is unanimously recalled by contemporaries as a kindly, courteous gentleman with a sense of humour and a dry wit whose generosity was legendary and whose friendship was prized.

C. Lack (ed), *Three decades of Queensland political history, 1929-1960* (Brisb, 1962); *Brisb Grammar School Mag*, June 1949; *Courier Mail*, 16 Dec 1948.   R. J. N. BANNENBERG

BROCK, HENRY ERIC (1884-1963), pastoralist, and HAROLD JAMES (1887-1941), pastoralist and businessman, were sons of Henry James Brock and his wife Georgina, née Mercer, and grandsons of James Brock of Kirk Liston, Scotland, who migrated to Van Diemen's Land in 1833. Eric (as Henry Eric was known) and Harold were born at Campania on 4 January 1884 and 17 April 1887. Their father was the developer and principal owner of the New Golden Gate goldmine at Mathinna and owner of the Lawrenny estate at Ouse. He died in 1898, leaving to his family an estate valued at £229 347. Harold was educated at Officer College, Hobart, and both brothers attended Launceston Church Grammar School and Geelong Church of England Grammar School, Victoria.

After completing his education Eric undertook a two-year world tour with his eldest brother James, a strenuous athlete later reputed to have lost most of his inheritance on a single horse-race. Eric and Harold were also keen turf sportsmen, running their own horses with considerable local success. Eric was on the first Tasmanian Amateur Jockey Club committee and Harold was a Tasmanian Racing Club committee-man.

In 1909 Eric, Harold and James, with their younger brother Claude as resident manager, formed the pastoral company Brock Bros Pty Ltd; it was based on Lawrenny, destined to become one of the most extensive Tasmanian pastoral ventures and the dairy nucleus of a substantial part of the Hobart milk-supply. The main, five-mile-long Lawrenny irrigation canal, supplied by turbine pumps, was rapidly completed to water 1500 acres (607 ha). From the 1920s until 1940 when Claude died, Eric concentrated on developing the inland runs north of Ouse, particularly the Lake Echo area. Well-known for his lakeside hospitality, he was a persistent, influential advocate of a regional road system; he stocked the lake with fish and established open bird-sanctuaries both there and at Lawrenny.

Harold, too, spent some years in developing pastoral country in the Bashan lakelands area, but after his marriage to Jeanie Macbeth Tulloch on 4 July 1918 in Scots Church, Melbourne, he moved to Stoke, New Town. He was to return to pastoral activity in 1929 on the Brock Bros' Meadowbank estate, but in this intervening period of general economic recession he made substantial contributions to industrial development in Tasmania. Most important was the formation at Railton of the Goliath Portland Cement Co. which took over the old Tasmanian Cement Co.'s works in August 1928, having contracted to supply the British-based firm Dorman Long & Co. with cement to complete Sydney Harbour Bridge. Both initiator and a director, Harold mortgaged property to back the enterprise. His investment was tinged with idealism: 'We wish it to be an object lesson', he was attributed as saying. 'If we have no faith in our own country it is absurd to think that anybody else will'.

Harold's judgment proved well founded: production grew to 500 000 tons (tonnes) per annum by 1967. Moreover the social benefits accruing to the region would have pleased him. He died of complication of a gastric ulcer at Glenora on 22 June 1941, survived by his wife, a daughter and two sons, leaving an estate valued for probate at £30 104. Described by his obituarist as 'a staunch supporter' of causes 'considered likely to improve the lot of the masses', Brock made substantial contributions to such movements, including the Australian Labor Party, an association which brought him into regular contact with J. A. Lyons [q.v.], who visited him on occasions at the Meadowbank homestead.

The death of Harold's sons on active service in 1944 and 1945 ended the family association with Lawrenny; there had been no issue from Eric Brock's two marriages, the first of which, to a widow Ivy Mabel O'Connor McGregor, née Grubb, on 16 February 1920 in Hobart, according to the forms of the Presbyterian Church, had ended in divorce in 1929. The estate was sold by Eric to the Commonwealth government in 1946 for soldier settlement. He then donated land for the Ouse Golf Links, and established another natural reserve at his new homestead on the 40 acres (16 ha) he had retained close to Ouse, employing for its upkeep a well-known lake-country shepherd, A. Daley. Eric died at Lawrenny on 14 May 1963, survived by his second wife Clare Jessie, née Haywood, whom he had married on 28 May 1929 at Sandy Bay. His estate was valued for probate at £114 075. The lush pastures of the Lawrenny irrigation scheme remain as a summer memorial in the upper Derwent valley.

Cyclopedia of Tasmania, 1 (Hob, 1900); Goliath Portland Cement Co. Ltd, *Fiftieth anniversary, 1923-1973* (Railton, 1973); *Mercury*, 10 Apr 1884, 6, 12 Aug 1898, 3 Jan 1910, 6, 12, 27 July, 1-4 Aug 1928, 23, 24 June 1941, 7 June 1946, 16 May 1963; *Tas Mail*, 13 Aug 1898, 10 June 1905, 11 July 1928.

G. P. R. CHAPMAN

BROCKMAN, FREDERICK SLADE DRAKE-; *see* DRAKE-BROCKMAN

BRODNEY, SPENCER; *see* BRODZKY

BRODZKY, MAURICE (1847-1919), journalist, was born on 25 November 1847 at Marggrabowa, East Prussia (Poland), son of Israel Brodzky and his wife Bella, née Czerwynkowsky. A student in Paris when the Franco-Prussian War broke out, Brodzky served as a volunteer in the French Army from August 1870 to July 1871. After discharge he migrated to Australia in the *Sussex*, was shipwrecked off Barwon Heads, and arrived in Melbourne almost penniless. He found employment teaching European languages at Melbourne Church of England Grammar School. For some years he shared lodgings with Richard Birnie and J. F. Archibald [qq.v.3], who later recalled that he 'wrote brightly, was indefatigable, and had a marvellously useful memory'. Brodzky became a journalist first on the Sydney *Evening News*, then the Melbourne *Age*, then the Melbourne *Herald*, also acting as Australian correspondent for the London

Daily Telegraph. He published two short books in Melbourne, *Genius, lunacy, & knavery* (1876), the story of an unscrupulous colonial surgeon, and *Historical sketch of the two Melbourne synagogues* (1877). A defamation case arising from the latter bankrupted him for eight years.

In 1885 Brodzky resigned from the *Herald* and, apparently using borrowed capital, started his own journal *Table Talk*, a weekly miscellany of politics, finance, literature, arts and social notes, which was highly successful during the boom of the 1880s. In 1890 Brodzky began investigating certain speculative land companies and new banks which had shown large paper profits during the land boom. His articles claimed that suspicious and sometimes fraudulent practices had occurred in the Federal and Mercantile banks, and in many other institutions operated by leading politicians and businessmen. As hundreds of such companies failed and were liquidated, *Table Talk* alone exposed the technique of so-called 'secret compositions' by which many directors and shareholders made private arrangements with creditors in order to avoid public exposure in the courts. Even Brodzky's own relations were attacked in the journal.

Table Talk also continued to print fresh revelations on the matter of the stolen parliamentary mace, allegedly discovered in a Melbourne brothel. Dr William Maloney [q.v.] claimed in the Legislative Assembly that Brodzky had 'levied blackmail' on the subject. He retorted in print that Maloney was 'a malicious liar . . . a silly, abusive and foul-mouthed scoundrel . . . an ignorant political quack . . . cowardly . . . a black-guard'. This was contrary to Maloney's general reputation as a noted humanitarian, but he did not sue.

During the severe depression which followed the bank closures of 1893, *Table Talk*'s profitability suffered, and Brodzky was unable to meet debts. In 1902, an article in it claimed that F. H. Bromley [q.v.], State Labor leader, had been accessory to a criminal act. Bromley sued for libel, winning substantial damages and forcing Brodzky into the Insolvency Court. He lost building, plant and journal. The goodwill of *Table Talk* was sold for £15, and it was finally taken over by the Melbourne *Herald*, which continued its publication as a society journal until 1939. Brodzky drifted into casual newspaper work, then took his family to San Francisco, where he became editor of a weekly, the *Wasp*. He survived the great earthquake of 1906, working thereafter as a journalist in London and New York, where he died in 1919. On 3 August 1882 at Fitzroy registry office, he had married Florence Leon (d. 1958), through whose family connexions he met Theodore Fink [q.v.]. They had five sons and two daughters, all of whom assisted their father in the writing and production of *Table Talk*.

The eldest son, LEON HERBERT SPENCER BRODZKY (1883-1973), better known as SPENCER BRODNEY, was born at South Yarra on 29 August 1883. He was influential as a journalist for many years, particularly when his friend Alfred Deakin [q.v.] was prime minister. He contributed articles on the theatre to *Table Talk* and *Lone Hand*, attempting to encourage indigenous drama. In 1904 he organized the Australian Theatre Society, which was active for some years in Melbourne. He wrote and produced two plays: one of them, *Rebel Smith*, with its theme of 'One Big Union' and its main character a member of the Industrial Workers of the World, was published in New York in 1925. In 1914 Lord Northcliffe appointed him editor of the *Weekly Despatch* in London on condition that he change his name from Brodzky to the less-Jewish-sounding Brodney. Spencer Brodney married Esther Siebel in New York in 1918, returned to Australian journalism for four years, and was then appointed editor of the *New York Times*' monthly, *Current History*. When this ceased, he founded his own journal entitled *Events*. He died in New Jersey on 7 May 1973.

HORACE ASCHER BRODZKY (1885-1969) was born at Kew on 30 January 1885. He studied at the National Gallery School in Melbourne and the City and Guilds South London Technical Art School, but finally rebelled against academic techniques. During World War I Horace Brodzky worked as a poster artist for the American Red Cross, and edited art journals in New York. He later became prominent in modern art movements. Early in the 1930s he began to concentrate on single-line pen-drawings using plain steel nibs, his linear style pre-dating by several years similar techniques used by Picasso and Matisse. He wrote biographies of Jules Pascin (1946) and Henri Gaudier-Brzeska (1933), whose bust of Horace (1913) is in the Tate Gallery, London. He died in London on 11 February 1969.

Julius Brodsky (b. 1888) was for many years an instructor in electrical engineering in the United States of America. Vivian Brodzky (1892-1968) became a journalist in London, and Alfred Tennyson (Bob) Brodney (b. 1896) a lawyer in Melbourne.

O. Comettant, *Au pays des Kangourous et des mines d'or* (Paris, 1890); B. Elliott, *Marcus Clarke* (Oxford, 1958); M. Cannon, *The land boomers* (Melb, 1966); L. Rees, *The making of Australian drama* (Syd, 1973); *Lone Hand*, June 1907, June 1908; *Argus*, 2 Jan 1872; *Table Talk*, 20 Jan 1893, 30 Oct 1902; *Age*, 12 Apr, 15 July 1893; *Truth* (Melb), 20 Dec 1902; *The Times*, 17 Feb 1969; Brodzky MSS (LaTL); Enregistrée no 12746-3 (Ministère de la Guerre Archives, Paris); Insolvency files 3757, 90/4124 (PRO, Vic); file CP 407, S1, B1, Weekly Intelligence Summary no 1, May 1917 (AAO, Canb); family information.   MICHAEL CANNON

BROINOWSKI, LEOPOLD THOMAS (1871-1937), political journalist, was born on 28 June 1871 at Carlton, Victoria, third son of Gracius Joseph Broinowski [q.v.3], artist and ornithologist, and his wife Jane, née Smith. His father had migrated from Poland in 1857 and his Australian-born mother was the daughter of a whaling captain. In 1880 Broinowski moved with the family to Sydney and attended St Ignatius' College, Riverview, where his father was drawing-master and his elder brother Gracius Herbert later taught science. He began an arts degree at the University of Sydney in 1889 but before graduating in 1897 he spent some years on his father's farm at Campbelltown and also began a teaching career, first as a private tutor, with his younger brother Robert Arthur [q.v.] among his pupils, then at Newington College, Sydney, and in Melbourne.

During the 1890s Broinowski became a strong Federationist and in 1898, abandoning studies for a law degree, was engaged by (Sir) Edmund Barton [q.v.] as a secretary. He accompanied Barton on the 1899 campaign in New South Wales and Queensland and his notes indicate its frantic pace and heavy physical and mental demands. He also worked with (Sir) R. R. Garran [q.v.] on the literary committee of the United Federal Executive, the co-ordinating body of the New South Wales Federation Leagues. After a period as journalist on the *Goulburn Evening Penny Post*, he moved to Hobart in 1902 to write editorial and special articles for the *Mercury*, becoming associate editor in 1904. He was also a regular contributor to the *Bulletin*.

In December 1922 Broinowski stood unsuccessfully as a National Party candidate for the Federal seat of Denison. 'States' rights' was a strong issue in Tasmania, and he modified his previous unequivocal Federalist stance by adopting the slogan 'Tasmania First'. In October 1921 he had been a member of a delegation to Melbourne which unsuccessfully tried to secure an amendment to the Navigation Act (1912) and he now maintained that Tasmania had been neglected and humiliated, and needed more substantial guarantees. During his campaign, he attracted some adverse criticism by advocating abolition of the Arbitration Court and reversion to a system of State wages boards.

After the 1922 election, Broinowski involved himself outside his profession largely with the welfare of returned servicemen and as an agitator on civic issues. He had already edited *Tasmania's war record 1914-18* (Hobart, 1921), and was awarded the Certificate of Merit by the Returned Sailors' and Soldiers' Imperial League of Australia. In the late 1920s he was active in preparing the case for special financial help for Tasmania, a prelude to the establishment of the Commonwealth Grants Commission.

Broinowski's reputation rests chiefly on his newspaper writing, described in an obituary as 'clear and logical, concise and explanatory'. Through his journalism he had considerable influence in Tasmanian politics. Though by nature and reputation a conservative, his judgment was widely respected throughout State political circles, and after his death from cerebro-vascular disease in Hobart on 26 September 1937 the Labor premier, A. G. Ogilvie [q.v.], gave him a glowing tribute. He was buried in Cornelian Bay cemetery, survived by his wife Annie Coverdale, née Sorell, whom he had married in Hobart in 1908, and by a son and a daughter.

J. Reynolds, *Edmund Barton* (Syd, 1948); *Mercury*, 22 Nov-16 Dec 1922, 28 Sept 1937; *Bulletin*, 6 Oct 1937; information from Mrs K. E. Broinowski, Canb, and Mr and Mrs R. Broinowski, Hob.

PETER BOYER

BROINOWSKI, ROBERT ARTHUR (1877-1959), public servant and poet, was born on 1 December 1877 at Balwyn, Victoria, one of eight children of Gracius Joseph Broinowski [q.v.3], artist and ornithologist, and his wife Jane, née Smith. Educated at St Aloysius' College, Sydney, Broinowski also acknowledged a considerable debt to his father, 'a man of culture and wide knowledge . . . who encouraged me to pursue the things that really matter'. On 21 February 1906 he married Grace Creed Evans, violinist, at Kew, Victoria.

Entering the Commonwealth Public Service in 1902, Broinowski served an apprenticeship as a clerk before securing appointment in 1907 as private secretary to (Sir) Thomas Ewing [q.v.], minister for defence, a position he retained under Ewing's successors, (Sir) George Pearce and (Sir) Joseph Cook [qq.v.]. In March 1911 Broinowski joined the staff of the Senate on which he served as clerk of the papers in 1915-20, then usher of the Black Rod until 1930, clerk-assistant and secretary of the joint-house department 1930-38, and finally clerk of the Senate in 1939-42.

Throughout his long life Broinowski

maintained an interest in the arts, especially literature. While the Commonwealth government operated from Melbourne, he was able to develop this interest as secretary of the Repertory Theatre Club and as a member of various literary societies, notably the Melbourne Literary Club. With friends such as R. H. Croll [q.v.], Broinowski also developed his interest in the bush through membership of the Melbourne Walking Club. He began to contribute poetry to *Birth* and became editor of the poetry page in *Stead's Review*. In 1924, supported by the financial contributions of a few friends, he launched *The Spinner* which, published in Melbourne by E. A. Vidler [q.v.], provided a regular forum for the work of such poets as Mary Gilmore, John Shaw Neilson and Marie Pitt [qq.v.]. It ceased publication in 1927 following Broinowski's transfer to Canberra which deprived him of close contact with his Melbourne literary friends. In 1926 he was divorced and next year, on 20 April, he married Kathleen Elizabeth Knell in Melbourne.

A convivial man, Broinowski belonged to various community organizations in Canberra, being active in the Alliance Française and a member of Rotary and of the local Society of Arts and Literature. He established the rose-garden behind the Senate chamber, and founded a Canberra Tennis Association award, the Broinowski Cup.

After his retirement from the Senate in 1942, Broinowski settled in Sydney where he maintained his interests in the arts, both as a reviewer in the *Sydney Morning Herald* and as an occasional broadcaster for the Australian Broadcasting Commission. He made recordings of his poems, some of which were also bound in typescript as 'Themes and songs' (Canberra, 1962), with a preface by his close friend L. H. Allen [q.v.]. After a long illness he died at his Lindfield home on 16 August 1959. He was survived by two sons from his first marriage; and by his second wife and their daughter.

Herald (Melb), 19 Jan 1931, 16 Jan 1936; *Advertiser* (Adel), 18 Aug 1959; R. A. Broinowski papers (NL); Kate Baker collection (NL); R. H. Croll papers (LaTL); Mackaness papers (NL); information from Mrs K. E. Broinowski, Canberra.

JOHN R. THOMPSON

BROMHAM, ADA (1880-1965), feminist and temperance worker, was born at Gobur, Victoria, on 20 December 1880, daughter of Frederick Bromham, blacksmith and miner, and his wife Charlotte, née Bradford. Educated at Yarck before arriving with her family in Western Australia in 1893, she became a monitor at a Normal school near

Fremantle, then worked as a doctor's receptionist. When her mother died in 1908, she joined the daughters of Thomas Smith, former mayor of Fremantle, in a drapery shop at Claremont; she lived with the Smith family and was inspired by its temperance principles. Mainly through Miss Bromham's ability, the business prospered and, by the early 1920s, she was able to pursue a growing interest in social issues. She stood unsuccessfully for election to the Legislative Assembly in February 1921, then held office in the Women's Service Guilds, was president of the West Australian Temperance Alliance and secretary of the Australian Women's Equal Citizenship Federation in 1925, and next year became secretary of the Australian Federation of Women's Societies. Frugal habits and a substantial return from the sale of her business interests in 1927 enabled her henceforth to work full time for her causes.

Nominated by the Women's Service Guilds to the June 1926 International Suffrage Alliance Congress in Paris, Ada Bromham led the Australian delegation, and then represented her country at a London conference of the British Empire League on emigration; soon after her return she visited the eastern States for a Woman's Christian Temperance Union convention. She left Perth in January 1934 to become national recording secretary for the union in Melbourne. She conducted a Tasmanian campaign for six o'clock closing, then sailed in May 1935 with Isabel McCorkindale, W.C.T.U. national director of education, for a union convention in Stockholm and another British Commonwealth League conference in London. They returned through Italy, Germany, Russia and probably China. A South Australian temperance campaign in July 1935 included an all-night vigil at Parliament House.

In 1937 Miss Bromham became general secretary of the South Australian branch of the W.C.T.U. and corresponding secretary of the national body, now based in Adelaide. She stood unsuccessfully for Unley in the 1941 State election, then devoted much of her time to the legislative department of the national body. She retired at the beginning of 1946, and settled briefly at Hunters Hill, Sydney, but in 1947 went to Melbourne temporarily as Victorian general secretary. There she concentrated on penal reform and retired again at the end of 1949.

Ada Bromham now became interested in the Chinese-Australian Friendship Society and in May 1952 joined a peace delegation to Peking with Dr John Burton and other radicals. Allegations of germ warfare in Korea made the cause extremely unpopular, and on return all the papers and literature collected by the party were seized by the Customs in Sydney.

Miss Bromham next joined Isabel McCorkindale in Brisbane in 1952-53 as a supernumerary assistant and corresponding secretary for the national W.C.T.U. She travelled the State widely on union work and visited relations, but her long-standing Christian Socialist convictions clashed with the union's predominant conservative bias in Queensland; she rejoined her family in Western Australia about 1959.

Miss Bromham had worked for Aboriginal welfare both in South Australia and Victoria, and the last phase of her life in Perth was devoted almost entirely to this cause. She became Australian representative for the world W.C.T.U. council for the advancement of Aboriginals and Torres Strait Islanders, and later divisional superintendent in Western Australia; and she fought against State parliamentarians and the Commonwealth minister for territories for better conditions for these people.

A keen motorist, excellent mechanic and competitor in hill-climbs, she had acquired an Oakland car in 1916 and crossed the Nullarbor Plain several times. According to family tradition, she drove many miles along the lonely Balladonia track in 1931 on a punctured tyre that she had successfully plugged with a cork. She spent her last years in a small room at Willard House, the North Perth headquarters of the W.C.T.U. She died at the Brentwood Hospital of bronchopneumonia on 15 March 1965, and was cremated after an Anglican service. Contemporaries remember her as a handsome woman and as a forthright outspoken socialist whose bark was worse than her bite, who spoke quietly but did not suffer fools gladly.

I. McCorkindale (ed), *Pioneer pathways* (Melb, 1948), and *Torch-bearers* (Adel, 1949); M. M. Bennett, *Human rights for Australian Aborigines* (Brisb, 1957); W.C.T.U., *Convention Reports*, WA 1920-65, National 1934-40, SA 1941-45, Vic 1946-49; *Dawn Newsletter*, 1921-27; *West Australian*, 26 May, 23 June 1952, 18 Mar 1965.

WENDY BIRMAN

BROMILOW, WILLIAM EDWARD (1857-1929), missionary, was born on 15 January 1857 at Geelong, Victoria, son of Thomas Bromilow, bricklayer, and his wife Jane, née Owen. Leaving Grenville College, Ballarat, after matriculating at 14, he taught at Queenscliff State School in 1876-77. At 21 he became a probationer in the Methodist Church and, while serving at Rupanyup in the Wimmera, he volunteered for the mission field. Having been ordained, on 9 April 1879 he married Harriet Lilly Thomson, and sailed from Sydney in the *John Wesley* to serve in Fiji for ten years.

Bromilow returned to Victoria and, after a year on the Box Hill circuit and a short term as foreign mission secretary, he volunteered to lead the Australian Methodist team launching a new venture in south-eastern British New Guinea. Accompanied by Rev. George Brown [q.v.3] he arrived at Samarai in a chartered vessel, *Lord of the Isles*, on 3 June 1891. The party also included S. B. Fellows, J. T. Field, J. Watson, G. H. Bardsley, and twenty-two South Sea island teachers.

Because of its central position and the prestige of its inhabitants among their neighbours, Dobu Island in the D'Entrecasteaux [q.v.1, Bruny] group was chosen as the headquarters. From this centre Bromilow directed the work as chairman of the district. For seventeen years mission stations were established in strategic centres in the D'Entrecasteaux and Trobriand islands and the Louisiade Archipelago; boarding schools for girls and boys and a training institution for local teachers and pastors were also founded. In 1892 Mrs Bromilow established a group of Australian Methodist Sisters.

Bromilow and his wife retired from Papua for health reasons in 1908. Till 1920 he occupied various suburban circuits in Sydney but was also prominent on the mission board, particularly as clerical treasurer in 1913-20. During this time, on Sir William MacGregor's [q.v.5] recommendation, he received a D.D. degree in 1910 from Aberdeen University for his New Guinea language translation work, and became chairman of the New South Wales Methodist Conference in 1911.

Because of post-war staff shortages Bromilow volunteered again. In July 1920 he arrived at the headquarters of the Papuan mission, where he served as chairman of the district until his final retirement in 1924. Besides preparing a translation of the Bible in the Dobuan language (1927), he supervised further developments in the mission. He served on the executive committee of the mission board, from which he resigned about a year before his death. Survived by his wife and daughter, he died in Sydney on 24 June 1929 and was buried in Gore Hill cemetery.

Bromilow was the founder of the Methodist mission in British New Guinea. He established harmonious relations in the field between his own and other missions as well as with successive heads of government. He developed a strong faith in what he termed the spiritual, intellectual and practical capacity of the Papuan. Because of his own religious and moral training he tended, like so many missionaries of his time, to make a stern assessment of many of the values and customs of Pacific peoples. His anthropological writings were said to contain 'a great deal of misinformation and a little fact', and also reveal him as rather paternalistic. He helped to destroy traditional custom wherever if conflicted with his own moral standards.

Bromilow's outstanding achievement was his translation work. The Dobuan language was selected by him as the *lingua franca* for the Methodist mission in British New Guinea. By 1908 he had published a New Testament, which he revised in 1925. His publications included papers to scientific societies on the life of the people, and his autobiography, *Twenty years among primitive Papuans* (London, 1929), which contains valuable information on his mission work and on contemporary administration and society.

British New Guinea Annual Report, 1889-90, 1905-06; *Papua Annual Report*, 1906-07, 1923-24; M. W. Young, 'Doctor Bromilow and the Bwaidoka wars', *J of Pacific Hist*, 12 (1977), no 3-4; Aust Methodist Church, Overseas mission papers (ML); United Church in Papua New Guinea Archives 1884 (New Guinea collection, Univ PNG Lib).

RODERIC LACEY

BROMLEY, FREDERICK HADKINSON (1854-1908), trade unionist and politician, was born on 30 November 1854, probably in south Staffordshire, England, son of Clara Bromley. Little is known of his early life, but after training in art at the School of Design, South Kensington, he became a japanner. About 1877 he came to Victoria under engagement as foreman of the japanning department of Hughes & Harvey, tinsmiths of Melbourne. He made his home in Carlton and on 24 July 1879 at the Holy Trinity Anglican Church, Balaclava, married Rosina Brown.

In the early 1880s Bromley became active in the trade union movement. With J. G. Barrett [q.v.] and David Wyllie he helped to establish the Melbourne Tinsmiths, Ironworkers and Japanners' Society; he was elected its first secretary on 30 April 1883. Reforms were won for the industry but Hughes & Harvey refused to accept the eight-hours system and Bromley was discharged. He set up as a decorative artist, becoming well known as a painter of trade union banners. In 1883 he also helped to organize the Tailoresses' Union, and was elected president in January 1885.

Bromley became his union's representative on the Trades Hall Council on 17 May 1883; in early 1884 he was elected vice-president and on 27 March 1885 president. He was secretary of a T.H.C. subcommittee which conferred in July 1883 with the royal commission on the operation of the 1874 Factory Act; he also gave evidence. He represented the T.H.C. at the third Inter-colonial Trades Union Congress held in Sydney in October 1885 where he presented a paper on the 1874 Act. Congress appointed him to the Parliamentary Committee for Victoria, of which he was first president. In 1885-86 he served on boards of conciliation for settling industrial disputes among boot-makers, wharflabourers and tinsmiths. During the 1890 maritime strike he was a member of the finance and control committee.

In March 1886 Bromley stood unsuc-cessfully for the Legislative Assembly seat of Collingwood. He was elected vice-pre-sident of the Progressive Political League of Victoria in December 1891 and in April next year was successful as its nominee for Carlton on a one-man one-vote platform. C. H. Pearson [q.v.5] described him at the time as a 'thoughtful and cultivated man'. Bromley was secretary of the Parliamentary Labor Party until 1900 when he was elected leader; he resigned on 7 June 1904 because of ill health. His support of George Sangster in a scandal over using union funds without permission led to a libel case in 1903 in-volving H. Brodzky [q.v.], editor and pro-prietor of *Table Talk*; Bromley won the case but it probably lessened his electoral appeal. He had visited New Zealand in 1902 to ex-amine its working-class and social service legislation. He served on boards of inquiry into the working of the Factories and Shops Act of 1890 (1893-94) and into the effect of the fiscal system of Victoria (1894), chaired the life insurance inquiry board (1896) and was a member of the Fisheries Commission.

Bromley was appointed a trustee of the Public Library, Museums, and Art Gallery in November 1895 and voted for their opening on Sunday afternoons. He opposed religion in education and favoured the extension of the state schools system into secondary education. A supporter of the Working Men's College, he was a councillor until 1907 and chairman in 1888-89. His work for the Carlton Refuge was well known.

Bromley died of pneumonia at his home in Carlton on 29 September 1908, pre-deceased by his wife and only son, and was buried in Melbourne general cemetery. His estate was valued for probate at £182.

V&P (LA Vic), 1884, 2 (18); *PD* (Vic), 1908, 933-36; *Speaker* (Lond), 11 June 1892; *Collingwood Mercury*, Feb-Mar 1886; *Argus*, 7 May 1887, 2 Apr 1892; *Daily Telegraph* (Melb), 26 Feb 1889; *Age*, 2 Mar 1889, 21 Dec 1907, 30 Sept 1908; *West Aus-tralian*, 27 Mar 1903; *Table Talk*, 2 Apr 1903;

Council minutes, 24 Nov 1885 (Trades Hall, Melb); Political Labor Council (Melb), Minutes, 18 Oct 1902, 10 June 1905 (Aust Labor Party, Vic Branch); Trades Hall Council (Melb), Autobiog notes (ML).   N. W. SAFFIN

BROOKER, THOMAS HENRY (1850-1927), salesman, wood-merchant and poli-tician, was born on 30 December 1850 at Kensington, London, son of William Brooker, bricklayer, and his wife Jane, née Gemmell. On 25 April 1855 the family ar-rived in South Australia on the *Caroline*. Brooker was educated at Hindmarsh and worked for fifteen years as a salesman in Thomas Hardy's [q.v.4] Bankside vineyard at Torrens, before opening his own business as a salesman and wood-merchant at Rid-leyton. On 6 March 1870 he married Emma Tume at Hindmarsh.

Brooker helped start the local literary society in the 1870s and for over sixty years served the Robert Street Church of Christ, as Sunday school superintendant, elder and member of the home mission committee. He was a founder and director of the West Torrens Starr-Bowkett Building Society, president of the local football club, and en-joyed cricket, tennis and fishing. In 1885-91 he was a councillor, and in 1891 mayor, of the Hindmarsh corporation.

In 1890-1905 Brooker was a member of the House of Assembly, first for the district of West Torrens and from 1902 for Port Adelaide. He supported protection, free education, extension of the franchise, land settlement and water conservation. In his maiden speech he had announced that he was sent to parliament by the labouring classes and that while he might bring with him some of their 'antipathies and prejudices . . . he had also an honest and true heart'. Brooker maintained a humane interest in the poor: on his motion pauper garb was abolished from the Destitute Asylum and he was on the important 1892 shops and factories commission which un-covered sweated labour and recommended material changes in the Health Act to im-prove working conditions in factories. His colleagues nicknamed him 'Honest Tom'. He was whip for the Kingston and Holder [qq.v.] governments and minister of educa-tion and industry in J. G. Jenkins's [q.v.] cabinet in 1901-02. He had successfully guided through parliament legislation to fix a scale for payment of jurors in 1891 and to facilitate the establishment of free libraries in 1902.

In 1905 Brooker was defeated as a can-didate for the Central District in the Legis-lative Council. Since 1903 he, Joseph Vardon [q.v.] and William Charlick, in collaboration with the Adelaide City Council, had operated the Adelaide Fruit and Produce Exchange Co. Ltd. Brooker was its secretary until his death. It was said of the markets that the city's medical officer could have taken 'the most sensitive lady' through them at any time. Questioned about the exchange by a Victorian royal commission of 1915, Brooker asserted stoutly, 'I do not believe in a monopoly . . . State, municipal or private . . . Fair competition brings out the best results'.

Brooker was an active Freemason. A member of the board of governors of the Botanic Garden, he was chairman from 1897 to 1927. Predeceased by his wife, he died on 11 July 1927 at Norwood, survived by four daughters and two sons. He was buried in Hindmarsh cemetery. He had been admired for his piety, steadfastness and commitment to his fellow man.

H. R. Taylor, *The history of Churches of Christ in South Australia, 1846-1959* (Adel, 1959); *PP* (LA Vic), 1915, 2 (58); *Pictorial Aust*, Jan 1885, Dec 1894; *Observer* (Adel), 27 Dec 1890, 6 May 1899, 16 July, 10 Sept 1927; *Register* (Adel), 12 July 1927.

MARLENE J. CROSS

BROOKES, HERBERT ROBINSON (1867-1963), businessman, pastoralist, public official and philanthropist, was born on 20 December 1867 at Sandhurst (Bendigo), Victoria, second son of William Brookes and his wife Catherine Margaret, née Robinson. His younger brothers were Harold Eric (1875-1953) and (Sir) Norman Everard [q.v.]. William Brookes, born in Northampton, England, came to Victoria in 1852 aged 18, made his way to Sandhurst as a bullock-driver and amassed a fortune through mining ventures, notably the Golden Fleece claim; he settled prosperously in Melbourne in 1871. He took up large pastoral leaseholds in Queensland between Longreach and Muttaburra, founded the Australian Paper Mills in 1882 with Archibald Currie [q.v.3] and later became a director of Austral Otis Engineering Co. Ltd. He died on 4 September 1910 leaving an estate valued for probate at £172 000.

William Brookes had apparently intended that the family should become absorbed into a leisured upper-class society. The son who came nearest accepting this dream was Harold, who took some interest in A.P.M. but concerned himself mainly with the Queensland holdings and his own Woodend property, Flinthill. Herbert diverged from the pattern, notably through his early experiences, professional interests and personal character.

In 1878-80 William Brookes, then in partnership with (Sir) Simon Fraser [q.v.4], had taken his family to South Australia on a railway-building contract north of Port Augusta. In 1879 the eldest boy William, aged 13, was killed by a fall from a tree. Harold and Norman were too young to be affected by their outback experience but Herbert worked as timekeeper and storekeeper, mixed with the men, and acquired knowledge and sympathies which influenced him for life. In 1881-85 he attended Wesley College where he showed considerable sporting ability; he graduated from the University of Melbourne with honours in civil engineering (B.C.E., 1890). After about a year spent mainly on the Queensland properties, he went at his father's instigation into the management of a series of small Victorian mines.

For some years Herbert attended Dr Charles Strong's [q.v.6] Australian Church. On 27 October 1897 he married Strong's daughter Jessie (known as Jennie) Denniston; her tragic death on 6 April 1899 affected him deeply. Alfred Deakin [q.v.] befriended him and persuaded him to accompany the Deakin family on a trip to England. On 3 July 1905 in Melbourne Brookes married Ivy, Deakin's eldest daughter. At this time he left Hollybush near Bendigo, where he had been assistant manager of Glenfine south mine and came to Melbourne to improve the management of Austral Otis. He was highly successful and by 1912 was a director of the firm. He grew interested in the problems of Australian secondary industry; in 1913-17 he became president of the Victorian Chamber of Manufactures. While his brothers were absent on war service he carried on as chairman of A.P.M.; in 1921 he handed over to Norman. As well, he was continuously concerned with the William Brookes & Co. pastoral holdings, both in Queensland and in marginal country near Wiluna, Western Australia (purchased in 1929).

Brookes's life was divided between the business career in which he rapidly became an outstanding spokesman for secondary industry, pastoral affairs, responsible public service posts (mainly part-time), political activities, and an active social and cultural life at his homes, Winwick in South Yarra and Penola at Mount Macedon. His personality made this diversity quite natural. His temperament was serious; he was intellectually independent, with deep, if unorthodox, religious convictions; constitutionally shy, but the reverse of self-centred; his public responsibilities grew from morally based concern, as well as a genuine interest in other people which engendered, on their side, respect and admiration, and then great personal affection. Throughout his life he made lasting friendships with men whom he had first met casually, on committees or organizations; revealingly, one of these wrote of him, years after Brookes had left the committee concerned, as 'the most appreciative listener of all ages'. To this human quality he added intelligence and much hard work. It was predictable that he was three times offered a knighthood, and also that he always declined.

Brookes's chairmanship of the Chamber of Manufactures had led to his involvement after 1914 in a series of wartime committees of which the Munitions Committee was the most important. After the war he was appointed to the newly established Commonwealth Board of Trade (1918-28), and the Tariff Board (1922-28), which entailed Australia-wide travel. In 1929 the prime minister (Viscount) Bruce [q.v.] appointed him commissioner-general to the United States of America, to promote Australian achievements in economic, musical, artistic, literary and intellectual fields. Brookes found this work absorbing, sacrificing his post only to save a Depression-cursed Australia the expense of maintaining it. He was a foundation member and vice-chairman of the Australian Broadcasting Commission (1932-39); among associated activities were the promotion of Victorian orchestral music and the initiation of A.B.C. celebrity and children's concerts. He was active in such organizations as the League of Nations Union and the English-Speaking Union. In 1933-47 he was a valued council-member of the University of Melbourne, especially of its finance committee.

Brookes was an able, creative committee-member, whose character could however limit his effectiveness. He would not accept formal leadership even when it was offered him, and even when his refusal later facilitated the adoption of policies he did not approve. This pattern of behaviour was evident on the Tariff Board, and perhaps more importantly on the A.B.C., whose chairmanship he refused in 1932; he then failed to secure for the commission the independence he desired it to have. In two university defeats his stance was determined partly by personal loyalties which perhaps influenced his judgment, and partly by dislike of factional intrigue: he ultimately accepted the 1938 appointment of J. D. G. Medley as vice-chancellor as an excellent one, but always deplored the way in which his friend Sir James Barrett [q.v.] was replaced as chancellor in 1939.

An intense admirer of Deakin, Brookes was associated with the foundation of the Commonwealth Liberal Party (1908) and the People's Liberal Party (1911). He founded and edited the *Liberal* (1911-14), and was P.L.P. president from 1912 until the party dissolved in 1916. He was later prominent in the National Union. Brookes saw W. M. Hughes, Sir George Pearce [qq.v.], Deakin and Bruce as the outstanding Australian statesmen of 1900-40, and later respected and supported (Sir) Robert Menzies. His own working principles were illustrated by his establishment of adult education facilities at the Hollybush mine, his campaign against miners' phthisis and his 1917 introduction of profit-sharing in A.P.M. Soon after joining the Board of Trade in 1918, he demanded information on European social insurance and profit-sharing practices. A belief in sexual equality made him insist that managers' wives on Brookes-owned stations be paid for the work they did. He distrusted the Labor Party as extremist, but in old age was willing to admit that his fears had not yet been realized. He was also an Empire loyalist, and it was this, focused by the conscription controversy in 1916-17, rather than simple sectarian prejudice, which brought him into collision with Archbishop Mannix [q.v.] and 'Irish' Catholicism. This was the only unremitting feud of his public career; he backed the Protestant newspaper, *Vigilant*, from its inception. The conflict seems also to have led in 1918 to a suggestion, from him, that a kind of counter-propaganda network of people with the proper outlook be set up, to pounce on and expose what he saw as insidious subversive propaganda; his interest in this had faded by about 1923, but he could never have intended to take a prominent role himself, since he stipulated that to avert any suspicion of government influence, the leadership should have no connexion whatever with the government institutions.

Living, and dispensing hospitality, in unostentatious comfort, Brookes was unobtrusively generous to employees, friends and causes. With his wife Ivy he financed a wing of the university conservatorium; he suggested a vice-chancellor's house and, with George Nicholas [q.v.], built it. Money existed to be used, he held, on travel within and without Australia (he made minimal claims on the public purse), on children and their education, on books, on pictures (he was an admirer of E. Phillips Fox and Rupert Bunny [qq.v.]), on other people; never on superfluities.

His second marriage brought him lifelong companionship, emotional fulfilment, and children: in his two sons and a daughter, born between 1906 and 1920, he took unusual pleasure. IVY BROOKES (1883-1970), born on 14 July 1883 at South Yarra, was musically gifted, crowning her conservatorium career with the Ormond [q.v.5]

Scholarship for singing (1904); she played in Marshall Hall's [q.v.] orchestra in 1903-13. The musical interests which she shared with Herbert produced a joint participation, from 1908, in the work of the Lady Northcote Permanent Orchestra Trust Fund. She was a foundation vice-president of the ladies' committee of the Melbourne Symphony Orchestra, and a member of the university faculty of music in 1926-69.

Their long marriage was a partnership of joint and separate interests mutually recognized as significant. Politics they shared, and Ivy held executive office in the League of Nations Union and the Empire Trade Defence League. Musical interests were developed partly through their T. E. Brown Society (1906-21), which added music to its basically literary activities, and also through their hospitality to many musicians, notably (Sir) Bernard Heinze. Sir Walter Murdoch [q.v.], whose work and outlook Brookes enjoyed and admired, was the closest of friends; their correspondence was uninterrupted for fifty years. For two generations the Brookes household was a place where creative ideas were exchanged and developed. Their social life reached into the university through Herbert's friend (Sir) Ernest Scott [q.v.] and Ivy's brother-in-law (Sir) David Rivett [q.v.], and thence to most of the professorial board and the council; the Winwick Saturday tennis-parties were famous. Herbert's position on the council was paralleled by Ivy's foundation membership of the boards of physical education (1938-70) and social studies (1941-67). Her particular concerns were the National and International councils of Women, the Playgrounds' and Housewives' associations of Victoria, and above all the Women's Hospital, on whose board she sat for fifty years. She founded the International Club of Victoria, and presided over it for its lifetime (1933-58). In the United States with her husband, she gained recognition as an individual who spoke well and had her own interests.

Brookes died in Melbourne on 1 December 1963, and his wife on 27 December 1970; both were buried in St Kilda cemetery.

R. Rivett, *Australian citizen: Herbert Brookes* (Melb, 1965); H. Brookes papers (NL); Deakin papers (NL).   ALISON PATRICK

BROOKES, SIR NORMAN EVERARD (1877-1968), tennis-player, was born on 14 November 1877 at St Kilda, Victoria, youngest son of William Brookes, contractor, mining entrepreneur and manufacturer, and his wife Catherine Margaret, née Robinson. His elder brother was Herbert

[q.v.]. Educated at Melbourne Church of England Grammar School, Norman matriculated in 1895 and on leaving school joined the Australian Paper Mills Co. Ltd of which his father was managing director. He began as a junior clerk; by 1904 he was a director of the firm.

Brookes showed a precocious aptitude for all ball games. At school he excelled at cricket, football and lawn tennis. Later he took up golf and won the Victorian foursomes championship once and the Australian twice. His great enthusiasm, however, was tennis and he devoted much of his time to improving his game. The family had its own court where he could play regularly; near by, he could study the strokes and tactics of leading players; and he received valuable coaching from Dr W. H. Eaves. Moreover, he had the means to go to Europe and play in tournaments there.

In 1896 Brookes was selected to represent Victoria against New South Wales. At this stage he was a fierce hitter and a baseliner. By the time he made his first journey to Wimbledon in 1905, he had changed his style of play to the controlled speed in ground shots and the aggressive net-attack that were to take him to the top. At Wimbledon in 1905 he won the all-comers' event but lost his challenge to the title-holder H. L. Doherty. That year he and New Zealander Anthony Wilding challenged for Australasia in the Davis Cup; lacking experience, they were eliminated early.

On his second visit to Wimbledon, in 1907, Brookes won the singles, doubles (with Wilding) and mixed events. He was the first player from overseas and the first left-hander to win the world title. That year Brookes and Wilding captured the Davis Cup from Great Britain; their remarkable partnership enabled Australasia to retain it in 1908, 1909 and 1911 (there was no challenge in 1910) and gave tremendous stimulus to tennis in Australia.

In 1914 Brookes again won the singles championship at Wimbledon and, with Wilding, the doubles. They regained the Davis Cup from the United States of America in New York a few days after the outbreak of World War I. Wilding enlisted and was killed in France in May 1915. Brookes, who suffered from stomach ulcers, was rejected for active service. He became a commissioner for the Australian branch of the British Red Cross in Egypt from August 1915 to late 1916; he resigned in January 1917 and in May became commissioner for the British Red Cross in Mesopotamia. Soon after, he was appointed assistant director of local resources for the British Expeditionary Force there, with the rank of lieut-colonel.

After the war, in 1919 and 1920, Brookes

represented Australasia in Davis Cup matches, and in 1924 played for the last time at Wimbledon. Over the years he had won innumerable championships in Australia, Europe and the United States. Known as 'The Wizard', Brookes was a master strategist and a shrewd tactician. Spare in build, his stamina sometimes failed in long matches, but he played with rare determination and concentration. Always immaculately dressed, he wore long-sleeved shirts and a peaked tweed cap and for many years used a heavy flat-top racquet with slack strings. His ground strokes, produced with a minimum of back-swing, were accurate and powerful; his strongest weapons were his service and his volleying. He had phenomenal delicacy of touch and control of angled shots.

Brookes was president of the Lawn Tennis Association of Victoria from 1925 until 1937; it was largely due to his enterprise that Kooyong, purchased in 1919, was developed as a tennis centre. In 1926 he became first president of the Lawn Tennis Association of Australia, holding the office for twenty-eight years. Though naturally taciturn and reserved he could at times be outspokenly blunt, stubborn and uncompromising. Despite his great prestige he did not escape the charge of being autocratic and he came under criticism as a selector of Davis Cup teams, but Brookes's name and fame were legendary. In recognition of his distinguished services to tennis he was knighted in 1939.

On 19 April 1911 at St Paul's Cathedral, Melbourne, Brookes had married 20-year-old Mabel Balcombe, daughter of Harry Emmerton, a solicitor; they had three daughters. (Dame) Mabel was for many years Melbourne's leading society hostess. In 1921 Brookes had resumed his place at A.P.M., becoming chairman of directors of the firm and later of North British and Mercantile Insurance Co. Ltd. He was a director of several other companies and a partner in the family pastoral firm, William Brookes & Co.

Brookes died at his home, Elm Tree House, South Yarra, on 28 September 1968 and was buried in St Kilda cemetery. His wife and two daughters survived him. His portrait by William Dargie is held in the family.

A. W. Myers, *Fifty years of Wimbledon* (Lond, 1926); W. T. Tilden, *The art of lawn tennis*, 10th edn (Lond, 1935); M. Brookes, *Crowded galleries* (Melb, 1956); P. Metzler, *Tennis styles and stylists* (Syd, 1967); R. S. Whitington, *An illustrated history of Australian tennis* (Melb, 1975); *Age*, 14 Oct 1959, 30 Sept 1968; *Herald* (Melb), 30 Sept 1968.

W. H. FREDERICK*

BROOKFIELD, PERCIVAL STANLEY (1875-1921), militant trade unionist and politician, was born on 7 August 1875 at Wavertree near Liverpool, Lancashire, England, son of Cuthbert Brookfield, grocer, and his wife Jane, née Peers. At 13 he went to sea, spent a short time in South America and about 1890 deserted his ship in Melbourne. He humped his swag and prospected in Victoria, New South Wales and Queensland, before settling about 1910 at Broken Hill, New South Wales, as a miner. Known as 'Jack' or 'Brookie', he became vice-president of the underground section of the Amalgamated Miners' Association and early in 1916 successfully led the fight for a 44-hour week for miners.

In July as 'general' of Labor's Volunteer Army, Brookfield led the anti-conscription campaign in Broken Hill: they were harassed by conscriptionists. In August, after a riotous meeting, he was fined £5 despite evidence, accepted by the magistrate, that he had tried to quell the riot. Fined again in September for cursing the British Empire and calling W. M. Hughes [q.v.] a 'traitor, viper and skunk', he was gaoled for refusing to pay the £50. In two years he reputedly paid £700 in penalties and forfeited bonds.

On his release, Brookfield won Political Labor League pre-selection and a Legislative Assembly by-election for Sturt in February 1917, holding the seat with an increased majority at the general election in March. A militant socialist, eloquent and strong in debate, he soon became the leading left-wing spokesman and aroused the hostility of the right. He advocated peace in Europe and reforms in the mining industry, defended the Russian Revolution and supported direct action rather than arbitration. Although not a member of the Industrial Workers of the World, he believed in some of their ideas: more practically, he campaigned with H. E. Boote [q.v.] for the release of Donald Grant [q.v.] and the other eleven imprisoned I.W.W. members. In 1920, when he held the balance of power in parliament, he persuaded J. Storey's [q.v.] government to appoint a second royal commission into the sentences of 'the Twelve'; Mr Justice N. K. Ewing [q.v.] substantially accepted the claim that they had been convicted on perjured evidence.

Brookfield also organized demonstrations in Sydney against the deportation of Paul Freeman [q.v.]. He found himself at odds with the majority of the Parliamentary Labor Party and in July 1919 had resigned from it. Instructed by the Barrier District Assembly of the party, which considered that he had made his point, he withdrew his resignation, but was not readmitted. In 1920 he won Sturt as a member of the Industrial

Socialist Labor Party, and played a vital role in settling the 1919-20 miners' strike, helping to obtain a 35-hour week and maximum compensation for tubercular and fibrotic miners in the Workers' Compensation (Broken Hill) Act.

On 22 March 1921 Brookfield was shot on Riverton railway station, South Australia, while trying to disarm Koorman Tomayoff, a deranged Russian who had already wounded two people; he died that day in Adelaide Hospital and was buried in Broken Hill cemetery, where a memorial headstone was unveiled in 1922. The courageous manner of his death was sufficient answer to those who had attributed his opposition to conscription to cowardice; Mary Gilmore [q.v.] commemorated it in verse in the *Australian Worker*.

G. Dale, *The industrial history of Broken Hill* (Melb, 1918); I. Turner, *Industrial labour and politics* (Canb, 1965), and *Sydney's burning*, 1st edn (Melb, 1967); E. Ross, *A history of the Miners' Federation of Australia* (Syd, 1970); R. H. B. Kearns, *Broken Hill*, 3 (Broken Hill, 1975); B. Kennedy, *Silver, sin, and sixpenny ale* (Melb, 1978); *PD* (NSW), 1917-18, 67-71; *International Communist*, 2 Apr 1921; *Argus*, 18, 19, 23 Aug, 6 Sept 1919, 23 Mar 1921; *Labour News*, 26 Mar 1921.

ROBIN GOLLAN
MOIRA SCOLLAY

BROOKMAN, SIR GEORGE (1850-1927), businessman and politician, was born on 15 April 1850 in Glasgow, Scotland, eldest son of Benjamin Brookman, letterpress-printer, and his first wife Jane, née Wilson. On medical advice the family migrated in 1852 to Adelaide where Benjamin was engaged by the government printer before establishing his own business. After education at James Bath's school and that of R. C. Mitton, George worked for D. & J. Fowler, wholesale grocers and importers. In the 1880s, with William Finlayson, he conducted a large retail grocery business in King William Street. Then, at a time of economic uncertainty, he became a sharebroker and financial agent and, in 1890-96, a member of the Stock Exchange of Adelaide.

After news of promising gold finds in Western Australia, Brookman formed the Adelaide Prospecting Party (later Coolgardie Gold Mining and Prospecting Co. Ltd) with ten paid shares of £15 each and five free shares issued to his brother William and Samuel W. Pearce [qq.v.]. These two prospectors pegged claims at Hannan's Find, north-east of Coolgardie, in June 1893. Despite the waverings of associates, and conflicting reports from experienced men who visited 'Brookman's sheep-run', as the claims were known, Brookman increased the syndicate's capital, then in Melbourne floated the Ivanhoe property as a subsidiary company, and the Lake View and Boulder East Co. in Adelaide. The Great Boulder claims were sold off in London. Difficult conditions on the fields, problems in delivering the first battery, and the financial stringencies of the promoters were surmounted; at the end of 1894 Brookman witnessed in person the satisfactory results of the initial clean-up at the battery. Next year Associated Gold Mines of Western Australia Ltd was formed in London to absorb further claims. By 1896 the success of the many Brookman companies, with the best leases on the 'Golden Mile', was apparent – an achievement realized largely through Brookman's extraordinarily skilful financial transactions and able administration. When the Coolgardie Gold Mining and Prospecting Co. was voluntarily liquidated in 1898, its capitalization represented £9 275 750.

Brookman never lost his interest in Western Australian and South Australian mining, but after a controversy over the management of Associated Gold Mines in 1900 he resigned his directorships and his later years were marked by other activities. He had been chairman of the Walkerville District Council in 1886, 1894 and 1899, and represented Central District in the South Australian Legislative Council in 1901-10. Politically conservative, he favoured orthodox financial policies and opposed general suffrage for the council. He advocated electrification but not nationalization of the Adelaide tramways, ignored the existence of sweating in factories, and believed the public education system had gone too far, except in imparting rudimentary agricultural and technical knowledge. He was a consistent supporter of harnessing the Murray for irrigation, and sought improvements in shipping facilities, more help for the mining industry, development of the Northern Territory with Asian labour, and closer settlement in selected areas.

In business affairs Brookman was associated with several public companies and built substantial offices in Grenfell Street. He bought and restructured the Electric Lighting and Traction Co. Ltd, which from 1895 had sought to supply electricity to Port Adelaide and Adelaide; from 1905 he was chairman of the local, and later central, board of the Adelaide Electric Supply Co. Ltd. In wartime he was also prominent, contributing liberally to the South Australian Bushmen's Contingent for the South African War and raising funds in World War I. A member of the State War Council, chairman of the State Repatriation Board, and active on behalf of the War Savings

Committee and Red Cross Society, he was appointed K.B.E. in 1920. Brookman was also chairman of the Adelaide Hospital, a governor of the Children's Hospital and of the South Australian Public Library, Museum and Art Gallery, a director of the Bank of Adelaide in 1911-27, and a council-member of the University of Adelaide in 1901-26. His benefactions included £15 000 donated to the building fund for the South Australian School of Mines and Industries, and gifts to the Art Gallery.

Brookman was known to his contemporaries as public-spirited, alert, energetic and courteous, with his opinion always well considered; to some people he seemed reticent and retiring. He was above all a shrewd businessman. Small in stature, from his parliamentary days onward he had varying health. He died at Medindie on 20 June 1927 and was buried in North Road cemetery, survived by his wife Eliza Martha, née Marshall, whom he had married on 13 February 1878 with Presbyterian forms at St Kilda, Victoria, and by a daughter and two sons. His estate was valued for probate at £42 748. Two oil portraits are held by the family.

J. J. Pascoe (ed), *History of Adelaide and vicinity* (Adel, 1901); H. T. Burgess (ed), *Cyclopedia of South Australia*, 1 (Adel, 1907); Garden and Field Pty, *Our pastoral industry* (Adel, 1910); *Register* (Adel), 2 Sept 1899, 17 Apr 1919, 29 Oct 1920, 21 June 1927; *Observer* (Adel), 8 June 1901, 23 Oct 1920, 25 June 1927; *Advertiser* (Adel), 21 June 1927; family papers (held by Mr A. Brookman, Meadows, and Mr J. G. Brookman, Hazelwood Park, SA).   R. M. GIBBS

BROOKMAN, WILLIAM GORDON (1859-1910), mining speculator, was born on 8 August 1859 at Prospect, South Australia, third son of Benjamin Brookman, government stamp-printer, and his wife Jane, née Wilson. Educated at Whinham College, he was a public servant in 1875-80 before joining his elder brother (Sir) George [q.v.] in a general merchant and agency business. By 1889 he was principal of Chance & Co., jam and pickle manufacturers, which failed in 1890 in the financial depression and maritime strikes following the collapse of the Victorian land boom. In June 1892 he was an undischarged bankrupt with liabilities of £31 000, members of his family being the principal creditors.

In 1893 George, inspired by the arrival of gold ore samples from Coolgardie, Western Australia, organized a syndicate to send Will and a prospector acquaintance Sam Pearce to Coolgardie to secure mining leases. The pair shared a one-third interest in the syndicate. They walked 300 miles (480 km) from York to Kalgoorlie, arriving on 28 June 1893, within a week of P. Hannan [q.v.] reporting his find. Avoiding prospectors at work round Hannan's hill, they camped four miles south on the 'Golden Mile' where thereafter they pegged over twenty mine leases. The syndicate took up nineteen, and floated three companies in Australia and others in London later.

In 1894 exemptions from costly development conditions were authorized, giving leaseholders opportunity to obtain overseas capital. Brookman acquired control of some 2000 acres (800 ha) of mining leases. On 7 September 1895 he sailed for London, after going to Adelaide to make settlement in full in discharge of his bankruptcy. He arrived in London with his wife Anne Kinder, née Flynn, a widow with four children, who had joined her mother, a Boulder hotelkeeper, in 1894.

Lionized in financial circles, Brookman adopted lavish standards common to other wealthy Australian mining men already in London. He arrived in Perth on 31 December 1896, by private train from Fremantle. Director of some thirty mining companies and reputedly a millionaire, he was to develop a score of mines into dividend-paying investments for a fee of £10 000, and had decided to live permanently in Perth. He bought much land, acquired a country estate, a seaside cottage, a private yacht, and a motor car, and lived in a town mansion with a suite of liveried servants. His opulence was the delight of gold-rush immigrants and the envy of the old families. However, elaborate ceremonial openings of new mine treatment plants stopped suddenly when he was stripped of many English directorships, allegedly for absence without leave. He lost the resultant legal battle in London.

Brookman returned to Perth to find himself acknowledged as a leader by gold-rush migrants hostile to the Sir John (Earl) Forrest [q.v.] government. Twice petitioned to displace the incumbent mayor of Perth, Alexander Forrest [q.v.], Brookman agreed to nominate when he vacated the office. He knew from Forrest that, although the latter was ineligible to serve a fourth successive term, the government proposed to remove the disqualification in order to leave Forrest in office during a royal visit in 1901, for which Forrest had been nominated to an honours list. Brookman sailed for the Paris Exposition of 1900 leaving nominations for the mayoralty and for a newly created seat in the Legislative Council. His supporters won him the council seat, but the government was defeated over the mayoral office. Advised by cable that his nomination for mayor had been lodged, Brookman returned to contest a bitter four-way mayoral election in which his Adelaide bankruptcy figured and his marriage with Anne Kinder was questioned.

Triumphantly elected, Brookman took a neutral stance between city council factions and was thereby left with insufficient support to enforce order in a series of turbulent and well-publicized wrangles at council meetings. Press hostility turned from the councillors to the mayor, and to the public behaviour of the mayoress. It was noted that Brookman was the only capital city mayor omitted from the honours list on the opening of the Federal parliament; the Perth award was a C.M.G. to Alexander Forrest. A few weeks before the royal visit Brookman resigned and retired to Mandurah to live. He had lost heavily in the London stock exchange collapse and his last major venture – to smelt ores at South Fremantle – had failed. The resulting composition with his creditors made him ineligible for office.

He lived at Mandurah while selling assets to meet his debts until 1904. His wife deserted him. He made his last appearance in the Legislative Council on 29 September 1903, and in December his seat was declared vacant. In failing health he travelled to Victoria, New South Wales, Queensland and New Zealand, accompanied by his widowed sister Mrs Ragless and by a nurse on his last journeys. He died in his father's home in Adelaide of pulmonary tuberculosis on 5 January 1910. His estate in South Australia was valued for probate at £7 10s., and in Western Australia at £127. Brookman had claimed proudly that he had secured the investment of £35 million in Western Australia and had established fifty-two mines.

J. J. Pascoe (ed), *History of Adelaide and vicinity* (Adel, 1901); P. W. H. Thiel & Co., *Twentieth century impressions of Western Australia* (Perth, 1901); J. S. Battye (ed), *Cyclopedia of Western Australia*, 1-2 (Adel, 1912, 1913); E. O. G. Shann, *The boom of 1890 – and now* (Syd, 1927); V. Courtney, *All I may tell* (Syd, 1956); G. C. Bolton, *Alexander Forrest* (Melb, 1958); *V&P (LC WA)*, 1903-04, 1, 217; W. E. Bold, 'Looking backwards', *JRWAHS (Early Days)*, Dec 1946; J. W. McCarty, 'British investment in Western Australian gold mining, 1894-1914', *Univ Studies in History* (WA), 1961-62; *British A'sian*, 31 Oct 1895, 4 Aug 1898; *Advertiser* (Adel), 24 Dec 1892; *Morning Herald* (Perth), 31 Dec 1896, 5 Jan 1897, 14-23 Jan 1900; *West Australian*, 30 Oct, 19 Nov 1900, 27, 28 June 1901; *Western Argus*, 2 July 1901, 11, 18 Jan 1910; W. G. Brookman estate papers (held by family); H. C. De Rose estate papers (held by R. J. Trott, Adel); Supreme Court (SA), no 143 of 1897 (Adel); Bankruptcy file GRG 66/5, no 6002 (SAA).

R. O. GILES

BROOKS, GEORGE VICKERY (1877-1956), teacher and educational administrator, was born on 29 March 1877 at Meadows, South Australia, two weeks after the arrival from Canada of his parents Tom Bowden Brooks, an English shoemaker and storekeeper, and his wife Elizabeth Ann, née Wendlesy. He received his primary education at the one-teacher Meadows school where, in 1891, he was appointed monitor. Next year he became a pupil-teacher at Clarendon, serving there and at Le Fevre Peninsula school for four years before attending the Adelaide Teachers' College in 1896. He was appointed assistant at Kadina in 1897, teaching there, at Hindmarsh and East Adelaide for nine years, as well as studying science at the University of Adelaide, attracting attention as an exceptionally gifted and dedicated teacher.

When W. L. Neale [q.v.] became director of the Tasmanian Education Department in 1905 and endeavoured to upgrade teaching standards by recruiting promising South Australian teachers, his first appointment was Brooks, in January 1906, as first assistant at Battery Point, Hobart. The personal and professional qualities Brooks displayed there gained for him, in 1908, appointment as master of method (headmaster) at the new Elizabeth Street School, the first Tasmanian practising school. For nearly twelve years he exercised a potent influence on every student from the Training College, being highly regarded for his enthusiasm, progressive ideas, organizational competence, consideration and ability to inspire his staff and college trainees. Exuding vitality, frequently saying 'I'll do it now', he would almost run from one activity to the next. His public reputation and popularity were mainly responsible for doubling the school's enrolment. He was president of the Teachers' Union in 1917-18, of the Southern Teachers' Association in 1917-19 and of the education section of the Royal Society of Tasmania in 1918. His reputation stood so high that on the resignation of W. T. McCoy [q.v.] in September 1919 he was appointed director of education although he was not a university graduate, having been one subject short of a science degree when he transferred to Tasmania.

Brooks took office at a particularly difficult time but was well aware of the problems he faced. Major handicaps included serious staffing difficulties, stringent financial restrictions and lack of public support for education, particularly in rural areas. He attacked these problems with characteristic vigour. In 1920 he persuaded the legislature to increase teachers' salaries, although he was unable to prevent a temporary cut in 1923. He directed much effort towards improving conditions for children in rural areas, from 1924 transporting pupils to central consolidated schools where improved staffing and better facilities were available. The gradual acceptance of this policy, as parents became aware of the benefits, culminated in the establishment of area schools. This progressive innovation followed his return from a six-month visit to England and the United States of America in 1935, sponsored by a Carnegie Corporation grant.

Brooks had a genuine belief in the worth of the individual and encouraged experiment and staff involvement in all matters. Meetings, committees, conferences, schools of method, interstate and local visits were characteristic of his energetic administration. Apart from area schools, other significant advances during his directorship included: the establishment of one and two teacher model schools, a sight-saving school and a departmental visual education branch; the appointment of a psychologist, school clerks, teacher group leaders and counsellors; the abolition of external examinations in favour of accreditation at primary and sub-secondary levels; a programme of regular visits by education officers to other States; and the use there of student-training facilities for specialized subjects. He retired in 1945, having been appointed C.B.E. the year before.

Brooks also gave leadership in other community activities. A charter member and director of the Hobart Rotary Club, he was president in 1937 and a prime mover of many of the club's community projects and author of its history. He was president of the Tasmanian Free Library Movement in 1939-44 and chairman of the Tasmanian branch of the Soldiers' Children's Board. He was a local Methodist preacher for almost fifty years, a keen gardener and in his youth a first-grade tennis player, for which sport he later substituted bowls. He died in Hobart on 8 January 1956, survived by his wife Ada Louisa, née Mitchell, whom he had married on 28 March 1902 at Kadina, South Australia, and by a son and a daughter.

A. Rowntree, 'Valediction . . .', *Tas Education*, Apr 1956; *Mercury*, 9 Jan 1956; D. V. Selth, The effect of poverty and politics on the development of Tasmanian State education 1900-1950 (M.A. thesis, Univ Tas, 1969); Education Dept files (Hob).
                                                                    D. H. TRIBOLET

BROOKS, JOSEPH (1847-1918), surveyor and astronomer, was born on 2 August 1847 at Stockport, Cheshire, England, son of James Brooks, surveyor, and his wife Ann,

née Goddard. The family arrived in Adelaide when Brooks was 9, and he was educated there at the Collegiate School of St Peter. He joined the South Australian Department of Survey and Crown Lands in 1864 as a draftsman, and was attached to G. W. Goyder's [q.v.4] 1869 expedition of about 150 men to the Northern Territory that led to the establishment of the town of Palmerston (Darwin); although official photographer, Brooks was much involved with drafting and planning for the settlement. In 1875 he was transferred to the field-staff as trigonometrical surveyor.

Brooks moved to Sydney in 1877, joined the Department of Lands as a licensed surveyor in June, and at St Andrew's Cathedral married Amy Florance Beilby Kendall on 20 December. From 1879 he assisted W. J. Conder in the triangulation of New South Wales which had begun from a base measured at Lake George, but he soon became responsible for the field-work. He displayed physical endurance in coping with adverse weather conditions and in carrying instruments to near-inaccessible places on mountain tops; in 1880 his party suffered severely from scurvy 'owing to impossibility of obtaining proper food and vegetables'. At many of the trigonometrical stations Brooks determined astronomically latitude and azimuth, and at some stations found longitude by comparing telegraphically his local time with that at Sydney Observatory. He maintained a high standard of accuracy and the closing error of the triangles was less than that of the great trigonometrical surveys of many other countries. 'He was a born observer with considerable mechanical ability, which enabled him to use his instruments to the best advantage'. He bore the main burden of the extensive surveying work in New South Wales and was aware of its value to Australia; in his report for 1898 he had claimed that 'the trigonometrical survey becomes more important year by year especially to enable the compilation of maps for the various purposes of government'.

After retirement in September 1906, Brooks developed his lifelong interest in astronomy: he joined expeditions to observe total solar eclipses on 3 January 1908 at Flint Island near Tahiti, on 9 May 1910 at Port Davey, Tasmania, and on 28 April 1911 at Vavau, Tonga. On these expeditions he was responsible for establishing by observation the geographical co-ordinates needed to interpret some of the data, and for observation at the time of the eclipse. In 1908 good photographs of the corona were brought back and he assisted with the work on the spectograph, but in 1910 and 1911 they were frustrated by bad weather.

Brooks wrote critical and sometimes derogatory marginal notes in his handbooks and had a somewhat difficult temperament. He could be impatient of shortcomings in others, and his men sometimes thought it necessary to hide their awareness of his foibles — for example, by taking a rest on the way to camp so as to avoid his annoyance when he did not get there first. He was a fellow of the Royal Astronomical Society and of the Royal Geographical Society of London, and a member of the Astronomical Society of the Pacific and of the Royal Society of New South Wales. In his earlier days Brooks was a noted tenor singer and, in 1882, was a founder of the Sydney Liedertafel; he remained a member for many years. Survived by his wife, a son and two daughters, he died of Bright's disease at his home at Woollahra on 9 May 1918, and was buried in the Anglican section of Rookwood cemetery.

Solar eclipse expedition to Flint Island, 1908 — report by F. K. McClean (Lond, nd); *Solar eclipse expedition to Port Davey, Tasmania, 1910* — report by F. K. McClean et al (Lond, nd); G. H. Knibbs (ed), *Federal handbook of the British Association for the Advancement of Science . . . 1914* (Melb, 1914), 380; W. A. Orchard, *Music in Australia* (Melb, 1952); M. G. Kerr, *The surveyors* (Adel, 1971); *Observatory* (Lond), 1911; *Surveyor* (Syd), 27 (1918); Roy Astonomical Soc, *Monthly Notices*, 210 (1924); records held by NSW Dept of Lands (Syd), *and* SA Dept of Lands (Adel); records (SAA).   HARLEY WOOD

BROOKS, WILLIAM (1858-1937), printer, publisher, politician and patriot, was born on 31 December 1858 at Tiverton, Devonshire, England, son of James Brooks, a lacehand, and his wife Mary Ann, née Williams. Educated at Tiverton Board School and trained as a compositor, he worked in London before going to South Africa. He later claimed that he had established the first trade union in South Africa. From 1884 he was in Sydney, and he married Martha Jessie Taylor (d. 1931), of Cape Town, on 20 July at a North Shore Congregational church. After working briefly for the *Sydney Morning Herald*, he set up as a printer.

Brooks's business expanded rapidly after he won a Department of Public Instruction tender for school readers, which were widely used in Australian schools; he also produced a series of Australian Catholic readers. He extended his activities to manufacturing and retailing; William Brooks & Co. Ltd was incorporated in 1901.

Prominent in the Master Printers' and Connected Trades Association, Brooks represented it on wage boards in 1908-11 and was its president in 1911-24. A council member of the Chamber of Manufactures of New South Wales in 1914-25, he was also on the council of the Employers' Federation of New South Wales in 1913, and its president in 1914-20 and 1921-24. He was a vigorous opponent of the trade unions. Claiming he had worked as many hours as he could get when he was on wages, Brooks condemned union opposition to piecework. He established the industrial department of the Employers' Federation to fight arbitration cases for the federation's members. From seeking to consolidate employer organizations, he became fearful that a single organization would be an added incentive for the unions to form 'One Big Union' which would make industrial conflict more hazardous. He redirected his efforts to getting amendments to arbitration legislation which would restrict the operation of arbitration to the minimum wage and the standard working week.

Brooks was involved in negotiations for the National Party, and channelled funds to it from New South Wales employers until 1919 when (Sir Edward) Owen Cox [q.v.] reorganized the financing of the party in the State. Brooks was appointed to the Legislative Council in 1917. Under amending legislation in 1918 responsibility for the minimum wage in New South Wales was removed from arbitration to a specially created Board of Trade. In the absence of legislative change in the direction desired by Brooks, the advisory service which he had set up became more heavily involved in fighting arbitration cases, especially at the Commonwealth level.

Brooks was a co-founder with Mary Booth [q.v.] of the Soldiers' Club in 1915, and a vice-president of the Citizens' Referendum Six O'clock Association; behind both lay the concern that soldiers on leave would be drawn to hotels and brothels at the risk of venereal disease. Brooks expected Australians to go to the help of the 'Old Country', to the last man, and he believed that the contribution of those who went should be fully and formally recognized. At the Soldiers' Club in 1915 he helped organize the Returned Soldiers' Association, acting temporarily as its first president. He was joint honorary treasurer of the Anzac Day fund in 1916 and later a trustee of the Anzac Memorial fund. Among his suggestions to honour the fallen was the creation of memorial parks. He was pledged to 'follow the King' and not take alcohol during the war, but he was no wowser and crossed the floor in 1931 to defend the working man's right to gamble.

In 1916 Brooks was a founding member of the Property Taxpayers and Ratepayers' Association, formed in protest against rent control and to fight adult suffrage in local government, and in 1924 he became president of a new Taxpayers' Association. In 1919-27 he represented Bourke Ward on Sydney Municipal Council, serving on its finance and health committees and advocating a separate authority to control electricity. Until 1933 he continued to be vice-president of the Employers' Federation and a spokesman for the abolition of compulsory arbitration. His criticism of Australian wage levels hardened over the years. In 1926 his firm failed to pay its customary 7 per cent dividend on its paid-up capital of £65 000.

Brooks was honorary treasurer for the Australian National Defence League in 1933 and president in 1925-35 of the Adult Deaf and Dumb Society of New South Wales, a cause his wife had supported since its foundation. She bore him five daughters; possibly he paid tribute to her when he opposed legislation giving illegitimate children a right to a father's estate: he held that a wife and her children had prior claim as family wealth was as much due to the work of the wife as of the husband.

Survived by his daughters, Brooks died at his Double Bay home on 14 October 1937 and was buried in the Presbyterian section of South Head cemetery. His estate was valued for probate at £9136.

Roy Com on industrial arbitration, Report, *PP* (NSW), 1913, 2nd S, 1, 558-65; Employers' Federation of NSW, *Annual Report*, 1913-34; *Property Owner*, 2 June 1916; *Syd Stock and Station J*, 13 July 1914; *SMH*, 7 Feb 1925, 16 Oct 1928, 15 Oct 1937; D. H. Coward, The impact of war on New South Wales (Ph.D. thesis, ANU, 1974); Anzac Fellowship of Women papers (NL).   HEATHER RADI

BROOME, GEORGE HERBERT (1866-1932), mine-manager, was born on 26 September 1866 at Bermondsey, London, son of John Broome, shipbroker, and his wife Martha, née Pounds. He obtained his diploma of mining at Mason Science College, Birmingham, and in 1883-87 worked under Professor W. E. Benton at Wimblebury Colliery, Staffordshire. In 1888 he won the Queen's medal in the mining examination of the Imperial College of Science and Technology, South Kensington. After serving as a deputy in a Yorkshire colliery he obtained his British colliery-manager's certificate (first class) at Merthyr, Wales.

In 1890 Broome went to New Zealand. He was general manager and engineer for the Westport-Wallsend Coal Co., Ngakawau, in 1890-92, the Westport-Cardiff Coal Co. Ltd, Mokihinui, in 1892-99, and the New Zealand Coal and Oil Co. at Kaitangata and Orepuki in 1899-1903. On 19 April 1894 in St John's Church, Westport, he married Margaret Marshall, Sydney-born daughter of a mine-manager.

Broome visited England in 1903, intending to go on to South Africa. Instead he became general manager of a coal and coke company at Frank, Alberta, Canada, until 1905. He returned to New Zealand to design and superintend works associated with the Westport-Stockton Coal Co. Ltd colliery, then the most modern in the country.

In 1909 Broome successfully applied for the widely advertised position of general manager of the new State Coal Mine at Wonthaggi, Victoria. He arrived to take up duty in March 1910, four months after the first coal had been shipped. He proved an able manager, the only man to achieve long-term commercial viability in a Victorian black coal-mine. His technological contributions included the introduction of a central power-station to operate the pits electrically. He devised most of the mechanical coal-handling plant at the Wonthaggi field, including a semi-automatic coal-tipper, a stone-tipping device, and remote control and four-way haulage engines. In 1932 it was estimated that these inventions had saved £12 000 a year in wages. Described as 'calm, just, considerate and urbane', he could claim in 1909 that he had not had a strike in a colliery under his management. Despite the many disputes at Wonthaggi, he was respected by the miners for his policy of dealing with collective bodies, not individuals.

Broome was chairman of the Victorian board of examiners for coal-mine managers in 1910-32, a member of the Institute of Mining Engineers and a councillor of the Institute of Mining and Metallurgy. He was a certificated water-supply engineer and municipal surveyor.

Broome had been closely involved in the development of Wonthaggi from a tent settlement to a thriving town. He was a member of the Church of England and a Freemason. Ill health forced him to resign on 4 August 1932; he died at his home in Broome Crescent on 9 August and was buried in the Wonthaggi cemetery. His wife had died before he came to Australia; five of his six sons and a daughter survived him. Among his writings is an article on the development of the Wonthaggi mine, published in the *Proceedings* of the Australasian Institute of Mining Engineers, 1914.

A. Quilford, *State mines ... the Powlett coalfields* (Wonthaggi, 1977); *V&P* (LA Vic), 1919, 2 (28); *NZ Mining J*, 1896-97; Canada Geological Survey, *Memoir*, no 8, 9, 53; *Buller Miner*, 9 Oct

1908, 4 Mar 1910; *Powlett Express*, 28 Nov 1930, 12 Aug 1932; *Age*, and *Argus*, 10 Aug 1932; *Bulletin*, 17 Aug 1932; *Wonthaggi Sentinel*, 28 Nov 1932.

E. W. RUSSELL

BROOMFIELD, FREDERICK JOHN (1860-1941), journalist, was born on 2 April 1860 at Minstead in the New Forest, Hampshire, England, son of Charles Broomfield, ship's storekeeper and later sea captain, and his wife Elizabeth Ann, née Thrum. In 1868 he migrated to Victoria with his widowed mother; they lived at Little Hampton near Daylesford, where Broomfield was educated and worked with his uncles, who were sawmillers and squatters. He joined an architect's office at Kyneton, also working on the *Kyneton Guardian* and as a correspondent for the *Age*. Later he was briefly on the staff of Melbourne *Punch*, worked for several touring theatrical companies and prospected for gold in Tasmania.

In the early 1880s Broomfield settled in Sydney, where he was based for the rest of his life. He worked as an accountant, probably for O. C. Beale [q.v.], until his review of E. A. Martin's *Life and speeches of Daniel Henry Deniehy* (1884) brought him to the attention of W. B. Dalley [q.v.4], who secured for him a position at £400 a year as editorial assistant to Andrew Garran [q.v.4] in compiling the *Picturesque atlas of Australasia* (1886-88). Already a contributor to the *Bulletin*, he became a sub-editor under J. F. Archibald [q.v.3] and helped him prepare the famous anthology, *A golden shanty* (1890). Tradition has it that Broomfield accepted Henry Lawson's [q.v.] first *Bulletin* contribution. Among other writers he helped at this time were Francis Adams and John Farrell [qq.v.3,4]. In 1888 Broomfield left the *Bulletin* through ill health but was soon working on *Australasia illustrated*, an expansion of the *Picturesque atlas*. In the 1890s he assisted the government statistician (Sir) Timothy Coghlan [q.v.] in preparing his publications; he also 'ghosted' J. W. Turner's [q.v.] educational reports.

Broomfield had been a founder of the *Centennial Magazine* (1888-89), and edited the *Elector* in the 1890s, the *Golden Fleece* (1901-03) and later the *Theatre*. More important, particularly after 1900, was his freelance work for the 'four or five journals which have had a major lump of my energies': the *Freeman's Journal*, *Bulletin*, *Sydney Mail*, *Brisbane Courier*, *Worker* (Brisbane) and the *Australian Worker*. Both as 'hired pen' and journalist his range was impressive: 'for 35 years', he wrote in 1920 when seeking the literary pension he secured in 1929, 'I have acted as an unpaid patriotic teacher of Australian history, a biographer of the achievements of Australians . . . [and] an annalist of the settlement of the continent'. He was equally at home as a critic of art, architecture, literature and the theatre; his articles in the *Salon* (c. 1912) and elsewhere are recognized as having educated Australian artists about contemporary European movements. His creative work included several published songs and contributions to anthologies of prose and verse, and he compiled a useful 'pronouncing gazetteer' for the Australasian supplement of *Webster's international dictionary of the English language* (U.S.A., 1898).

A flamboyant dresser, Broomfield sported 'a peaked beard and upbrushed moustache, a Cavalier hat with a swirling brim', and a cane with which he made rapier thrusts at friends upon meeting. His conversation, like his correspondence, was ornamented by picturesque phrasing and medieval oaths but he had a 'high falsetto voice, and a wobbling, gobbling utterance, as if he had a plum in his mouth'. He was active in the *Bulletin* circle and a central figure in the Dawn and Dusk Club. But behind the melodramatic Bohemian stood the kindly, practical friend who helped 'Price Warung' [q.v.3, Astley] fight drug-addiction, assisted Victor Daley's [q.v.] widow, and defended Lawson in *Henry Lawson and his critics* (1930).

In 1918 Broomfield broke his ankle which never properly healed; he was invalided for three years but later made his greatest contribution to Australian literature. An omnivorous reader and avid collector of Australiana, he was assisting Sir John Quick [q.v.] with a bibliography of Australian literature when Quick died in 1932. The project was taken over by E. Morris Miller [q.v.] whose monumental *Australian literature from its beginning to 1935* (Melbourne, 1940) benefited enormously from Broomfield's bibliographical skills, wide personal knowledge and meticulous research which were acknowledged on the title page.

Broomfield died at Bellevue Hill on 22 May 1941 and was cremated with Anglican rites. He was survived by his wife, Parisian-born Alice François Marie Florence, née Perdrix, whom he had married in Sydney on 2 June 1891, and by their two sons.

N. Lindsay, *Bohemians of the Bulletin* (Syd, 1965); A. McCulloch, *Encyclopedia of Australian art* (Lond, 1968); W. Stone, 'A note on F. J. Broomfield', *Biblionews*, Apr 1967; *Sydney Mail*, 10 Feb 1894; *Bulletin*, 25 Oct 1902, 28 May, 4 June 1941; *Aust Worker*, 25 Feb 1909; *SMH*, 23 May 1941; Morris Miller *and* Palmer papers (NL); B. Stevens papers (ML); MS cat under Broomfield (LaTL, ML, NL).

B. G. ANDREWS
ANN-MARI JORDENS

BROWN, ALFRED REGINALD RAD-
CLIFFE; *see* RADCLIFFE-BROWN

BROWN, DAVID MICHAEL (1913-1974),
footballer, was born on 4 April 1913 at
Kogarah, Sydney, son of Denis Brown,
stonemason, and his wife Annie Elizabeth,
née Hennebry. He grew up alongside Bronte
beach, where his parents ran the surf-sheds,
attending St Charles's School and later the
Christian Brothers' College, Waverley. Despite the loss of the top of a thumb, and a
permanently damaged elbow, at school he
showed remarkable skill at Rugby football.
Unemployed for a time, he became a clerk in
the Department of Labour and Industry
about 1930 and later worked in the publishing department of the *Daily Telegraph*.

In 1930 Dave Brown won a place in the
Eastern Suburbs first-grade Rugby League
team. Next year he was chosen to represent
New South Wales against Queensland.
During the summer of 1931-32 he suffered an
illness which resulted in the loss of all his
hair, and for the rest of his football career his
leather headpiece was his trademark. In
1932, despite his youth, he became captain of
Easts, and represented his State against the
visiting English team and Queensland.
Selected to tour England with the
'Kangaroos' next year, he proved a phenomenal success as a try-scoring centre-
three-quarter and place-kicker: he played in
32 of 36 games, scoring 19 tries and 114 goals
for a tally of 285 points which remains unequalled. In Sydney he led Easts in 1932-36
when they came to dominate the club competition. In 1935 he scored 385 points, beat-
ing 'Dally' Messenger's [q.v.] 1911 total of
270; it remained the record until 1978 when
Mick Cronin broke it. Brown captained the
State team and, at the end of the season, led
an Australian tour of New Zealand, scoring
74 points in four games, with 10 tries and 22
goals. Against the touring English side in
1936 he became the then youngest Australian captain against England.

In December Brown joined the English
club, Warrington, receiving a record £1000
plus £6 per game and a job at £3 per week.
Returning after three successful seasons, as
captain-coach he led Easts to victory again
in 1940 and retired next year. Labelled 'the
scoring machine' and 'the Bradman of
Rugby League', at his peak Brown combined
fast, long-striding runs with exceptionally
adept ball-handling and anticipation.
Though only 5 ft. 10 ins. (1.79 m), he weighed
a solid 14 stone (89 kg). A clean player and

skilful captain, he was no selfish accumula-
tor of points, his records stemming from flair
and remarkable long-range goal-kicking.

In 1940 Brown ran the Albury Hotel,
Darlinghurst, then worked for the Commonwealth Department of Labour and National Service; later he managed the family
surf-sheds. In 1959 he was appointed
schools-liaison officer for the New South
Wales Rugby League. He spent three
months in South Africa in 1962, attempting
to introduce the code there, but the 1964
Australian tour by a South African team,
which he coached, was not a success. A good
cricketer, golfer and surfer, Brown enjoyed
playing cards, and was a member of the
Australian Jockey and Sydney Turf clubs.
He died in Sydney on 23 February 1974 of
pulmonary fibrosis, survived by his wife
Ellen, née Wilson, whom he had married at
Hurstville on 20 November 1936; they had no
children. He was buried in Waverley cemetery after a requiem Mass attended by many
footballers.

SMH, 14 Apr 1941, 8 Oct 1950; *Catholic Weekly*
(Syd), 4, 11, 18, 25 Aug 1960; *Sunday Telegraph*
(Syd), 24 Feb 1974; *Sun* (Syd), 25-27 Feb 1974;
information from Mrs E. Brown, Earlwood, Mrs
M. Hickman, Randwick, and Mr E. E. Christensen,
Bronte, NSW.   CHRIS CUNNEEN

BROWN, FRANCIS ERNEST (1869-
1939), schoolmaster and clergyman, was
born on 12 March 1869 at Bristol, England,
fifth surviving child of James Brown, master
hatter, and his wife Eliza Adelaide, née Gil-
lis. Generations of Browns had been hatters
at Frampton Cotterell, Gloucestershire, but
new techniques and fashions had eroded the
craft by the time James died in 1886. Despite
economic hardship Francis was sent to a
boarding-school from which, in 1884, he won
a scholarship to Bristol Grammar School. He
was head boy in 1888, won a mathematical
scholarship to Hertford College, Oxford, and
graduated B.A. in 1892.

From September Brown was senior
mathematics master at Hulme Grammar
School, Manchester, and from 1905 at King
Edward VII School, Sheffield, where he
became second master and frequently acting headmaster. He was appointed headmaster of Preston Grammar School, Lancashire, in July 1911, on an understanding
that shortly led to his release when his earlier
application for the headmastership of
Geelong Church of England Grammar
School, Victoria, proved successful.

Brown placed great emphasis on religion,
having been influenced strongly at Bristol
by the cricketing Studds and by the Chris-

tian socialist writings of F. D. Maurice. He took the middle road between High Churchmen and Evangelicals and after being ordained in 1896 by Bishop Moorhouse [q.v.5], held two curacies as well as his teaching post. In 1895 he had married Ada Hancock, after a five-year engagement which had confirmed a shared sense of Christian purpose. Brown felt strongly that schoolmasters should be ordained and he hoped that his influence at Geelong would increase the number of boys entering holy orders.

Despite his lack of relevant experience Brown had been selected to run an Australian version of the English public school. Within three years of his arrival in January 1912, Geelong Grammar had been rebuilt, on that model, on an isolated site of 200 acres (80 ha) seven miles (11 km) from Geelong. It was already predominantly a boarding-school and catered particularly for Western District graziers whose ambition was to send their sons to Oxford or Cambridge. But money was short and the new headmaster had to be planner, building supervisor and accountant as well as teacher, administrator and chaplain. The school absorbed all his energies, and he rarely left it. On top of the frustrations of having no chapel and badly overcrowded boarding-houses for several years, the outbreak of World War I led to an acute shortage of qualified staff and forced him to concentrate on administrative and financial rather than cultural and academic goals. His meticulous reports to council reveal both that strain and his energy and judgment.

Chapel services, scripture lessons and confirmation classes were Brown's major points of contact with boys. He worked hard through parents and old boys for a war memorial cloister at the chapel. This became a kind of conscience for the school, linking the living with those who had fallen. His contribution to Christian education was recognized with an honorary D.D., presented at the Lambeth Conference of 1920. Believing that the school needed a younger man, he retired in 1929 to become, for five years, rector of Preston Bagot, Warwickshire. He died of progressive muscular atrophy at Ampney St Peter, Gloucestershire, on 1 June 1939, survived by his wife, two sons and three daughters. A portrait by W. B. McInnes [q.v.] is at Geelong Grammar School.

T. Judd, *Fifty years will be long enough* (Melb, 1971); Geelong Grammar School, *Corian*, 1912-29, Mar 1976; *Argus*, 22 Feb 1930; *Age*, 7 Oct 1939; J. Carolan, A history of Geelong Grammar School, 1912-29 (M.A. thesis, Univ Melb, 1975); family information from Mr P. L. Brown, Newtown, Vic.

WESTON BATE

BROWN, SIR HARRY PERCY (1878-1967), engineer, public servant and company director, was born on 28 December 1878 at Hylton, County Durham, England, son of George Brown, a former superintendent of the London Telegraph Office, and his wife Sarah Emma, née Dawson. Educated at Bede College, Durham, and Durham College, Newcastle upon Tyne, he entered the Post Office and advanced quickly. On 28 September 1904 he married Emily Aldous in the Anglican Church of St Andrew, Leytonstone. In 1913, as an adviser to the Indian government, he introduced management by telephone of rail traffic and dock-handling in Calcutta. Next year Brown was made responsible for the technical planning and management of all telephone and telegraph plant in Great Britain. In 1916 he was placed in charge of 'emergency communications' for home defence. This work, which entailed a high degree of inventiveness and improvisation, won him an M.B.E. in 1918.

On the invitation of the W. M. Hughes [q.v.] government, Brown arrived in Australia late in 1922 to act as technical adviser on a three-man Postal Advisory Committee that had been commissioned to draw up a 'reconstruction' programme for postal and telegraph services. His early work so impressed W. G. Gibson [q.v.], the postmaster-general, that by December he had manoeuvred the retirement of the secretary of the department, J. Oxenham [q.v.], and secured Brown's accession as secretary and director. The appointment was initially controversial. The installation of an 'import', on a salary (£2500) well above that of any other Federal public servant, drew criticism from within the Post Office, from the press and from the Federal Parliamentary Labor Party. Dissatisfaction subsided within six months, however, and the next five years proved a triumph for Brown as the department underwent a period of rapid and overdue development. Allowing for the underlying economic boom and for the decisions taken before his arrival, Brown clearly gave marked impetus to this expansion.

His first undertaking was to strengthen central administration. Previously the State offices had been the main organs, but in his first four years six major sections were created at central office, Melbourne — telegraphs and wireless (1923), telephones (1924), postal services (1924), correspondence, records and staff (1926), chief inspectors' (1926) and research (1927). He also shaped new patterns of staff promotion: the pre-eminence of the career generalist was diminished by the near-abolition of the senior positions of chief clerk and clerk. It was later said that Brown tended to give undue weight to technical qualifications in administrative appointments.

The first engineer to be permanent departmental head, Brown had a personal impact on postal technology. After initial lethargy from departmental engineers, in 1925-31 he pushed through the linking of all State capitals by 'carrier wave' channels, an apparatus conveying multiple circuits on each trunk line. He similarly spurred on mechanized mail-handling, the system completed in 1930 at the Sydney General Post Office being the most extensive in the world.

Brown attached as much importance to public relations as to administration and technology. To raise morale, and hence efficiency, a personnel branch was set up at central office. The interest taken by him in staff matters was intense and never condescending. The same thought was given to his market, the public. Subscriber surveys, advertising campaigns, and press releases were used on an unprecedented scale. These measures had considerable success in improving the poor image of the department. Brown himself received a prominence in the press extraordinary for a Commonwealth public servant.

As he did with the postal and telegraph services, Brown played a key role in the growth of wireless broadcasting between 1923 and 1928. A very active intermediary in the negotiations between industry interests and the minister, he was later credited with the formulation of the 'dual system' of 'A' and 'B' class stations enacted under the Wireless Agreement Act, 1924, and the wireless telegraphy regulations. While he probably did not instigate the 1928 decision of the government to purchase the assets of the 'A' stations – at the time he was actively representing Australia at conferences in Washington and London – he was, as chairman of the Wireless Broadcasting Advisory Committee, the central figure in the planning of the 'National Broadcasting Service' in 1929-30.

After the establishment of the Australian Broadcasting Commision in July 1932, the Postmaster-General's Department continued to have responsibility for the technical side of the national service, something which Brown prized. The department also retained its wide powers over the commercial ('B') stations and Brown, though he always preferred and was renowned for his methods of conciliation and persuasion, was not afraid to deploy these powers. At least three times – in 1931, 1936 and 1938 – he was a willing party to acts of political censorship, which he believed were necessary in times of 'crisis'. He also viewed with some dismay the growth of newspaper-controlled radio stations; in 1935 he helped to frame regulations to limit the number of stations owned by one licensee, a measure which, later weakened by Cabinet, proved of little consequence.

In the field of posts and telegraphs, Brown throughout the 1930s maintained his exacting managerial standards and his flair for public relations. The impact of the Depression could not be warded off, but the department's net profit for the years 1933-39 was an impressive £18 million. His most auspicious initiative in this period was his plan in 1935 for a daily air mail service to all Australian capitals without surcharge, a scheme which was eventually compromised in Cabinet. In 1938-39 he sat on the Defence Communications Committee, completing arrangements for the wartime control of communications.

On 3 October 1939 Brown's resignation was announced, seemingly precipitated by proposals to transfer to the A.B.C. some of the department's technical powers in broadcasting and to devolve some of the administrative functions of the director-general. In December he took up the appointment of chairman and joint managing director of the British General Electric Co. Pty Ltd, a position he had earlier declined.

In May 1940 Brown returned to the Commonwealth public service in the new wartime position of co-ordinator-general of works, his company 'releasing' his services as a war gesture. His task was to advise the Australian Loan Council on the degree of civil and military urgency of the major capital works planned by the State governments. Based on consultation with State officials, his submissions and arguments before the Loan Council facilitated the necessary reduction in civil works expenditure in 1940-42.

In August 1943 the Loan Council decided to retain Brown's services as executive of the National Works Council, planning post-war works to provide employment during demobilization and reconversion. To this end he submitted three reports, collating £150 million worth of projected works. In this phase perhaps an equally important service was his persuading State bodies to place all resource orders to war production authorities through him. In contributing to resource co-ordination he had been able to draw on his experience in rationalizing supply and distribution in the P.M.G. in 1926-27, and from his long membership of the Commonwealth Stores Supply and Tender Board.

Brown's pre-eminent reputation brought him extra wartime tasks. In 1940 he submitted a report on the standardization of State power-supply systems. From July to November 1941, he acted as part-time director of war organization of industry, under a minister but without a department. He was a member of the Treasury's advisory committee on financial and economic policy, and early in 1943 he investigated charges against the New South Wales director and the deputy director of the Allied Works Council. In 1944-45 he wrote a report which provided the framework for the post-war Snowy Mountains hydro-electric scheme.

Following a serious illness in August 1945, Brown resigned from the public service. He remained, however, a co-opted member of the Council for Scientific and Industrial Research until 1952, this arrangement stemming from his formative membership of the Radio Research Board in 1927-39. He did not retire from his post with British General Electric until 1953, having presided over the establishment of local manufacture of small-horsepower motors and light industrial products.

Physically and intellectually robust, Brown was a great and powerful public servant. Gracious and high-minded by nature, he was capable of shrewdness with ministers and sternness with critics. He cherished the Empire and voted conservatively all his life. He had settled religious beliefs. Radiating his conviction of the personal rewards of public service and of the ultimate good of scientific advance, he aspired to social leadership, but his standards were not as lofty or as stern as those of his contemporary, Lord Reith. For all his polish and discipline, Brown was very much at home in the Australia of the inter-war period. He had been appointed C.M.G. in 1934 and was knighted in 1938. Survived by two sons and a daughter, he died in Sydney on 5 June 1967. His estate was valued for probate at $145 817.

S. F. Kellock, 'Sir Harry Brown in public administration, war work and commerce', *Public Administration* (Syd), Sept 1967; PMG's Dept, *Annual Reports*, 1921-39; Cwlth Co-ordinator General of Works, *Report*, 1944-46 (NL); National Works Council, Report, 1944-51 (NL); *Punch* (Melb), 3 Dec 1925; *SMH*, 1 Jan 1934, 22 Dec 1942, 24 Mar 1943, 23 Aug 1945; H. P. Brown papers (held by, and information from, Mr K. S. Brown, Castle Hill, NSW); information from Mr D. Lawrence, Email Ltd, Waterloo, Syd.

M. G. HOWARD

BROWN, HENRY YORKE LYELL (1844-1928), geologist, was born on 23 August 1844 at Sydney, Nova Scotia (Canada), son of Richard Brown, geologist, and his wife Sibella, née Barrington. He was educated at King's College, Windsor, Nova Scotia, and taught there after matriculating

in 1859. He then studied under T. H. Huxley [q.v.1] and John Tyndall at the Royal School of Mines, London, in 1863-64. In 1865-69 he worked on the Geological Survey of Victoria under A. R. C. Selwyn [q.v.6].

Brown was government geologist in Western Australia in 1870-72. He discovered the Weld Range, drilled the first artesian bore near Perth, and forecast accurately that the colony's mineral resources would eventually become a main source of its advance. In 1872 he worked in private mining in Victoria and New Zealand and two years later rejoined Selwyn in Canada. Finding the climate too severe, he returned to Australia to work for the New South Wales government in 1881-82.

In December 1882 Brown became, at twice his previous salary, government geologist of South Australia. He made the first recorded observations of much of the hot, arid interior, often travelling alone but for an 'Afghan' camel-driver or Aboriginal guide, under harsh conditions. In 1883 he journeyed to the far north-eastern corner of the colony and in 1885 to Silverton and from Port Augusta to Eucla and back. He went to the Musgrave Ranges in 1889, and through the Lake Eyre region in 1892. His longest journey was made through the Northern Territory from north to south in 1894. He explored the MacDonnell Ranges in 1888, 1890 and 1896 and the country to the north of the Nullarbor Plain in 1897, and in 1905 journeyed to Charlotte Waters and to the north-west of the Northern Territory. In 1907 he went from Van Diemen Gulf to the McArthur River. On Brown's last major trip in 1909 he assessed the Tanami goldfield. His written reports of these explorations were minimal; mostly he recorded the results on maps. He had achieved a major objective with the production of a geological map of the whole colony in 1899. At this time Brown was described by the *Critic* as 'noted for his Bohemian habits and dry humour'.

In 1887 and 1890 Brown had published records of the mines of South Australia to draw attention to mineral resources and to the unsystematic way in which they were worked. He criticized the licence laws as unfair to genuine prospectors and called for a school of mines. He always worded his reports on sensational 'discoveries' carefully so that 'rarely was it possible to . . . exaggerate a good impression into a glowing opinion'. In controversy he was restrained and polite.

In 1911 Brown resigned, took six months leave and married a New Zealander, Hannah M. Thompson. He continued to act as an honorary consultant to the Department of Mines in Adelaide until his death. This lithe 'little brown man with a hammer in his hand' had stimulated gold-mining and the copper industry in the State, charted the limits of artesian water in central Australia and discovered natural outlets for the disposal of flood waters in the south-east. At his death in Adelaide on 22 January 1928 it was said that 'he knew every mineral belt from Darwin to Mt. Gambier'. He was survived by his wife and only daughter.

E. W. Skeats, *Some founders of Australian geology* (Syd, 1934); *Public Service Review* (SA), Jan 1912; Roy Soc SA, *Trans*, 52 (1928); E. C. Andrews, 'The heroic period of geological work in Australia', Roy Soc NSW, *Procs*, 76 (1942), no 2; *Advertiser* (Adel), and *Register* (Adel), 24 Jan 1928.

P. R. G. DUNLOP

BROWN, HERBERT BASIL (1893-1938), soldier and labourer, was born on 23 June 1893 at Banstead, Surrey, England, son of George Brown, licensed victualler, and his wife Ellen, née Felce. Nothing is known of his early life. He migrated to New South Wales shortly before World War I and was working as a labourer in an Arncliffe brickyard when he enlisted in the Australian Imperial Force on 26 September 1914. He was posted to the 13th Battalion and sailed for Egypt in December.

Brown first saw action at Gallipoli when his battalion was sent into Monash Valley on 25 April 1915; he later fought at Hill 60. He was wounded in action on 15 May and again on 27 August but remained at Anzac until the evacuation. After patrol work in Egypt his unit left for France, taking over the line at Bois Grenier in June 1916. From mid-July Brown served on the Somme and was wounded at Pozières. Having volunteered to take charge of an observation post at Mouquet Farm, where three occupying parties had already been killed, he held on for thirty hours and several times crawled out under heavy fire to tend wounded men in shell holes. He was promoted lance corporal in August and corporal in October, and in December was awarded the Military Medal.

In the winter of 1916-17 Brown served at Flers and Gueudecourt and distinguished himself in the capture of Stormy Trench on 4 February 1917. He led a bayonet charge against a wave of advancing Germans, then with Captain H. W. Murray [q.v.] pursued and routed them. That same day he was made temporary sergeant. He fought at Bullecourt in April and won the Distinguished Conduct Medal for gallantry in the battle of Messines on 7 June. His officer having been killed, he took charge of the platoon which was under heavy shell-fire and, after his unit had been relieved, led his men to safety through a sudden barrage. He later returned and carried two wounded men to the dressing station. He was commissioned second lieutenant on 21 July and promoted lieutenant in November. Next March, in the advance on Hébuterne, he was in charge of a patrol which recaptured a section of the town; on 5 April he led a bombing attack on a nest of machine-guns, destroying the guns and taking prisoners. For these services he was awarded the Military Cross. He fought at Villers-Bretonneux and Hamel and in the battle of 8 August before taking part in the final advance to the Hindenburg Line.

'Hard Boiled' Brown, as he was affectionately known in his battalion, was one of the very few men in the A.I.F. to receive the D.C.M., M.C. and M.M. His A.I.F. appointment ended in January 1919 and he began work as a storeman in the Sydney suburb of Surry Hills. On 28 May 1921 he married Teresa May Cox at St Peter's Catholic Church; there was one son of the marriage which was dissolved in February 1931. For some years before his death Brown used the name of Richard Long. He died of tuberculosis on 23 September 1938 at Waratah Hospital for Infectious Diseases and was buried in Sandgate cemetery with Anglican rites.

T. A. White, *The fighting Thirteenth* (Syd, 1924); *London Gazette*, 8 Dec 1916, 24 Aug 1917, 16 Sept 1918; *Reveille* (Syd), Nov 1938; *SMH*, 13 Feb 1931.

MALCOLM McGREGOR

BROWN, JAMES DRYSDALE (1850-1922), businessman and politician, was born on 21 April 1850 at York, England, son of John Brown, accountant, and his wife Jessie, née Gilmour, both of Scotland. They later moved to France where he was educated at Le Havre and Paris. In January 1862 the family arrived in Victoria, attracted by gold discoveries at Woods Point. From his years in this isolated settlement he developed a lifelong interest in mining, but also retained an almost exaggerated respect for European ways.

In 1866 Brown moved to Melbourne and worked for the Hobson's Bay Railway Co. as a clerk. At 23 he joined the Bank of Victoria, becoming an accountant at Inglewood and St Arnaud. In 1877 he transferred to the Colonial Bank, establishing and managing several suburban branches until 1888 when he contracted typhoid. Living then on savings and mining investments, he travelled first to New Zealand and the south Pacific and then to London to study law. He was called to the Bar at the Middle Temple in

1893, practising only briefly in London, but making useful financial contacts before returning to Australia; he was admitted to the Victorian Bar in May 1894. But he had arrived in the worst of the depression; neither law nor banking offered many opportunities and so he turned to mining investment, just when British capital was bringing about a small boom in gold-mining. He became actively involved through his large shareholding in the Charlotte Plains gold-mine, acquired in 1889. This deep-lead mine at Moolort near Maryborough was waterlogged, and Brown used capital he had attracted while in England to drain it, eventually with some success. He became an influential promoter of deep-lead mining in the area.

In 1904 Brown contested Nelson Province in the Legislative Council; it covered the central mining district where his interests lay. Avoiding overt party allegiance in his campaign, he appealed to the electorate in terms of State development, stressing his interest in mining; he described himself as 'liberal minded'. He was easily elected above two sitting members and retained the seat until his death.

In January 1909 Brown became attorney-general and solicitor-general in the John Murray [q.v.] ministry. Although politically moderate and limited in his legal experience, he was far more compatible with the members of the new government than most of the other councillors and was sympathetic to its land taxation and land resumption policies. He retained his portfolios in the first W. A. Watt [q.v.] ministry from May 1912 to December 1913. He then became minister of mines, forests and public health and vice-president of the Board of Land and Works in the second Watt ministry from December to June 1914, and again under Sir Alexander Peacock [q.v.] until November 1915. As a minister, he made no striking impact, working within the accepted convention that good government was essentially good administration. He was a shrewd, if dour, administrator, mostly concerned with rural development schemes such as promoting Australian timbers and prohibiting gold-dredging in rivers. He was elected chairman of committees on 10 August 1920.

Brown never married. A brother John Vigor Brown was a successful merchant and politician in New Zealand. Drysdale Brown, as he was known to his friends, lived comfortably in South Yarra, never becoming Australian in speech, manner or dress, retaining the habits of an educated English gentleman. He was, however, a follower of Charles Strong's [q.v.6] Australian Church. For the last ten years of his life he suffered from arteriosclerosis, from which he died on 5 April 1922; he was buried in Boroondara cemetery. He left his estate, valued for probate at £10 337, to his nieces in Melbourne and New Zealand.

PD (LC Vic), 1922, 7; *Age*, 24 May 1904, 8 Jan 1909; *Punch* (Melb), 4 Feb 1909; *Argus*, 8 Apr 1922.

KAY ROLLISON

BROWN, JOHN (1850-1930), 'coal baron', shipowner and racehorse breeder, was born on 21 December 1850 at Four-Mile Creek near East Maitland, New South Wales, eldest son of James Brown [q.v.3] and his wife Elizabeth, née Foyle. He was educated at Newcastle, and at 14 began work in the Newcastle office of his father's and uncle's firm, J. & A. Brown [q.v.3]. After experience underground, then as a colliery clerk, surveyor and pit-manager at the Minmi mine, he was sent overseas – to China on the firm's business and to inspect its London agency. He also studied the latest technology and working methods in mines in Britain and the United States of America. In the 1870s he managed the Minmi mines. On 25 January 1881 at Govan, Lanarkshire, Scotland, he married Agnes Bickers Wylie with the forms of the United Presbyterian Church. However she died in Sydney on 17 August the same year.

In 1877 Brown's uncle Alexander had died leaving his £100 000 estate to his nephews; in 1882 James appointed John general manager and handed over his coal interests to his sons in 1886. John Brown remained in control of policy. He extended the Minmi mine and benefited from membership of the Vend, a cartel which regulated prices and shared the trade between Newcastle coal-proprietors, but he left it in 1890. Free to reduce prices and with no shareholders to satisfy, he embarked on a period of trade expansion which contributed to the dissolution of the Vend and thereby helped to impoverish the district. In 1896, when many collieries were idle, his Minmi mines worked on 256 out of a possible 280 days and next year were active on 264: the firm's annual output exceeded 300 000 tons (tonnes) in 1897-1901. In the early 1900s Brown expanded his South Maitland interests, acquiring the high-producing Pelaw Main and Richmond Main collieries, and by 1904 had connected both to the firm's Minmi-Hexham railway. He also built up the fleet of tugboats which operated in both Sydney and Newcastle.

In order to develop the export trade Brown spent much time abroad and opened offices in San Francisco, Valparaiso and in London, where he mostly lived in 1888-93 and 1899-1904 while the business was managed by his brother William. William then claimed the right to participate in the firm's management and from 1905 pursued his claim in the Equity Court. In November 1909 the partnership was dissolved by order of the court and John was appointed receiver and manager; his appeal to the Privy Council against the dissolution was dismissed.

Early in the century, Brown became famous for his horse-breeding and racing exploits. In 1893 he had begun to race horses as 'J. Baron', and in 1897 won the Australian Jockey Club Doncaster Handicap with Superb. In 1902 he imported the stallion, Sir Foote, for his stud, Wills Gully, near Singleton. Sir Foote's most famous son was Prince Foote: in 1909-10 he equalled Poseidon's record in winning the A.J.C. and Victoria Racing Club Derbys and St Legers and the Melbourne Cup in the same season — as well as the A.J.C. Sires' Produce Stakes and the three-mile Australasian Champion Stakes. That season Brown topped the winning-owners' list with £14 610 in stakes. Duke Foote carried his pale blue colours with yellow sleeves and black cap to victory in several important races, but was the unplaced favourite in the 1912 Melbourne Cup won by William Brown's Piastre. In 1919 John's Richmond Main dead-heated with Artilleryman in the A.J.C. Derby and won the Victoria Derby. He bred other notable horses including Prince Viridis, Prince Charles, winner of the 1922 Sydney Cup, Leslie Wallace and Balloon King. Between 1910 and 1924 he reputedly won £90 094 in stakes. Terse with trainers, he frequently changed them, but he pampered his horses. Although by 1930 he owned 240 brood mares and seven stallions he usually refused to sell any horses even if he did not want to race them. He exhibited and imported prize dogs, poultry and turkeys, and bred stud cattle. He bought Darbalara, near Gundagai, another stud near Scone, and in 1927 Dalkeith, near Gundagai, to grow maize and lucerne.

Confirmed in sole management, Brown expended much capital in his desire to be self-contained. Before World War I the firm had two-thirds of Sydney Harbour's towing and carried out much ocean salvage work, also controlling the Newcastle pilot system until it was taken over by the government. He spent large sums on the latest mining plant, colliers, rolling stock and his Hexham shipping point and engineering works, which serviced steam and locomotive engines for other firms: on one excursion abroad he spent over £1 million on locomotives, mining equipment and a steamship to carry them home. In the 1920s he opened up the Stockrington mine and for many years he had a contract to supply the Australian

Gaslight Co. In 1930 he had a large collier, 5 coastal colliers, a schooner and 10 tugs, including the *Rollicker*, one of the most powerful in the world — but there was little work for her. He abhorred the idea of turning his firm into a public company.

Brown's 'antagonism to unionism was bitterly unequivocal and even ruthless', and 'his passion for riding the whirlwind and defying the storm of popular disapproval' in his relations with his miners was well known; he was also extremely reluctant to accept the State and Commonwealth arbitration systems. At Pelaw Main, from 1903 he installed modern cutting machinery manned by American technicians and free labour. In defiance of the Colliery Employees' Federation, in 1913 he pursuaded the Minmi miners' lodge to sign a local agreement for five years. He acquired a reputation for severity, denying his Minmi miners the opportunity to buy the land on which their homes were built, and refusing to renew long leases, so they could be threatened with eviction during strikes, but he believed it was his responsibility to provide employment so long as the miners accepted the exigencies of the industry. In late 1914 he issued a writ against the Colliery Employees' Federation for £100 000 damages for loss of trade and payment of demurrage. For much of World War I Brown was chairman of the Northern Colliery Proprietors' Association.

In the troubled 1920s when the price of coal was depressed and the export trade dwindling, Brown closed Minmi mines (in 1922) when the men refused to accept lower wages (although allegedly he secretly arranged to pay their bills at the local store). He repeatedly warned the government that the coal trade was in jeopardy and advocated a reduction in wages. On 4 March 1929 he began 'something in the nature of a lockout at the Richmond Main and Pelaw Main Collieries', because he could not sell coal interstate or overseas at its current price. It was announced in the House of Representatives that he would be prosecuted; but in April the charge was dropped, to the indignation of the Labor Party which revived the question in September.

Brown died childless at his unpretentious home in Wolfe Street, Newcastle, on 5 March 1930, and was buried in the family vault in the Presbyterian cemetery, East Maitland; huge crowds watched his funeral procession. He left the residue of his personal estate, valued for probate at £640 380, and shares in J. & A. Brown to his general manager Thomas Armstrong and to Sir Adrian Knox [q.v.], as tenants in common, to carry on the firm under the same name during the lifetime of his brother Stephen.

'Shrewd, analytical, and taciturn', Brown shunned publicity and was an enigmatic and legendary figure, who might have stepped out of the pages of a Galsworthy novel. He was tall, spare and upright, and continued to dress 'in sober broadcloth, glossy black boots and ties' with a high square bowler hat. Although he was the focal point for much industrial ill-will and Labor oratory, the *Australian Worker* admitted that in 'his personal relations with his employees he was by no means wholly unkind; indeed, at infrequent times, he was comparatively generous'. He had a 'strong strain of theatricality' and liked playing the part of the relentless capitalist. Nevertheless he made a practice of getting out among the miners.

His brother William (1862-1927) shared his interest in racing: as well as Piastre, he had other winners in Haulette, Thana and Colbert. For a time he managed the Duckenfield colliery at Minmi and was consul-general for Chile. He died unmarried at his home 153 Macquarie Street, Sydney, on 2 February 1927, leaving his estate to his brother John and sister Mary Stephen Nairn. Their youngest brother Stephen (1869-1958) was educated at Newington College, Sydney. After John's death the firm's interest in tugboats was sold to the Waratah Tug & Salvage Co., and from 1931 Stephen was a partner in and a director of J. & A. Brown & Abermain Seaham Collieries Ltd after its amalgamation. He travelled widely, enjoyed fishing and at Segenhoe grew prize dahlias and chrysanthemums. He died unmarried on 19 November 1958 at 153 Macquarie Street, Sydney, and left his estate, valued for probate at £149 977 to (Sir) Edward Warren.

Brown's first cousin ALEXANDER (1851-1926), merchant and politician, was born on 9 February 1851 at Maitland, New South Wales, son of William Brown, medical practitioner, and his wife Mary, née O'Keefe. He was educated at West Maitland, then articled to his stepfather Joseph Chambers, and admitted as a solicitor in 1873. On 8 August 1872 at West Maitland he married Mary Ellen Ribbands. He entered J. & A. Brown and, after his uncle Alexander's death in 1877, took over the Newcastle office. In 1883, following an overseas trip, he was dismissed by his uncle James after selling the Ferndale colliery without approval. Next year he unsuccessfully claimed in two Supreme Court cases that he was a partner in the firm.

Alexander relinquished his interest in J. & A. Brown in return for his cousins' share in the New Lambton mines, which he thereafter managed and turned into the New Lambton Land & Coal Co. Ltd in 1891. During industrial disputes he pursued an independent line from other proprietors and

occasionally supported the miners. In 1885 he became manager of the Newcastle branch of Dalgety [q.v.4] & Co. Ltd and in 1905 managing director. He also built up extensive pastoral interests.

In 1889-91 Alexander represented Newcastle in the Legislative Assembly as a Protectionist and supporter of (Sir) George Dibbs [q.v.4], who was a director of the New Lambton Land & Coal Co. Defeated in 1891 Alexander was nominated to the Legislative Council on 30 April 1892. In 1892-96 he was first president at a difficult period of the Hunter District Water Supply and Sewerage Board at £300 a year; repeated questions were asked in the assembly about his anomalous position of holding an office under the Crown while a member of parliament. In 1895 a select committee investigated the cost of construction works and in 1897 there was a royal commission into the board's management, but Brown emerged well from these inquiries. Although strongly conservative, he was regarded as 'a fair fighter'.

Alexander was president of the Newcastle Chamber of Commerce in 1888 and 1892. He was Belgian consul in Newcastle in 1882-1926 and was appointed chevalier of the Order of Leopold in 1902; he was also consul for Italy. He died on 28 March 1926 at his home, Cumberland Hall, East Maitland, and was buried in the Presbyterian cemetery. He was survived by five sons and three daughters of his first marriage, and by his second wife Edith Mary, née Adams, a nurse whom he had married on 27 March 1920. His estate was valued for probate at £60 871.

C. Inglis, *Horsesense* (Syd, 1950); J. W. Armstrong, *Pipelines and people* (Newcastle, 1967); *V&P* (LA NSW), 1894-95, 5, 1289, 1897, 5, 195; *NSW Law Reports*, 5 (1889), 393, 25 (1905), 412; *Weekly Notes* (NSW), 1 Mar 1910; *SMH*, 17 Sept, 10, 13 Nov 1909, 12 Aug 1925, 30 Mar 1926, 4 Feb, 13 May 1927, 23 Mar, 10 Apr, 16 Aug, 10, 30 Sept 1929, 6, 8 Mar, 21 Apr 1930, 21 Nov 1958; *Punch* (Melb), 10 Oct 1912, 3 Sept 1925; *Argus*, 6 Mar 1930; *Aust Worker*, 12 Mar 1930; *Bulletin*, 12 Mar, 16 Apr 1930; *Daily Telegraph* (Syd), 21 Nov 1958; *NT News*, 30 June 1971; J. W. Turner, The influence of the firm of J. & A. Brown on the ... New South Wales coal industry (M.A. thesis, Univ Syd, 1967), *and* The development of coal mining and manufacturing in Newcastle 1800-1900 (Ph.D. thesis, Univ Newcastle, 1977).

J. W. TURNER

BROWN, JOSEPH TILLEY (1844-1925), politician, was born on 7 February 1844 at Saint John, Surrey, England, son of Joseph Brown, marine captain, and his wife Amelia, née Tilley. He came to Victoria at 7. In 1856-59 he attended Geelong Church of England Grammar School and then began work as a clerk at Bright & Hitchcock [q.v.4], retailers. In December 1863 he joined the Bank of New South Wales, serving at Geelong, Melbourne, Ballarat and elsewhere until his appointment as first manager at Rochester in January 1873. On 6 January 1874 at Christ Church, Rochester, he married Mary Ann, daughter of Thomas Seward, publican.

In January 1875 Brown resigned because of irregularities on the part of a subordinate, and went into a stock and commission agency with his brother-in-law Stephen Seward. At the same time he was a member of the Marathon Co. which acquired land between Echuca and Rochester. In June 1878, at a hearing of the royal commission on the progress of settlement under the 1869 Land Act, he was charged by the Echuca bailiff Charles Tattam with 'boss-cockie dummying'. With some prevarication, Brown admitted that he managed a small group of family and friends to exploit the Act. However, his 'pushing energetic' ways won him as much admiration as dislike in the district. He was president of the Rochester Farmers' Union in 1879 and the Agricultural and Pastoral Society of Echuca in 1881-82, and was active in the Water for the Northern Plains movement and the Decentralization League. A member of the Echuca Shire Council from 1876 he was president in 1888-89.

In 1881 Brown was reported as a partner in the purchase of 350 000 acres (142 000 ha) of virgin land in New South Wales. At the same time he held 9000 acres (3600 ha) in the Echuca district, growing wheat and wool. His partnership with Seward was dissolved in November 1882 with Brown carrying on the business based in Echuca. In 1893 he set up in Collins Street, Melbourne, with his private residence at Hawksburn. By 1905 J. T. Brown & Co. had reopened branches in several country centres, including Chiltern, Violet Town, Wangaratta, Euroa and Seymour; by 1908 he retained only his Wangaratta and Melbourne agencies.

In 1883 Brown had contested the Legislative Assembly seat of Mandurang as a free trader. He was unsuccessful, but by 1886 had adapted his views to win as a moderate protectionist. He was defeated in 1889, and in 1892 ran for Gunbower and in 1893 and 1894 Mandurang. In October 1897 he won the Shepparton-Euroa seat as a supporter of Sir George Turner [q.v.], retaining it until May 1904 when he failed to win the new seat of Goulburn Valley. Encouraged by his contact with electors in the north-eastern border districts, in 1906 Brown won the Federal seat of Indi, because of his anti-socialist stand and his opposition to the supposed extravagance of the Deakin [q.v.]

ministry. He retained the seat until 1910. He contested Indi once more in 1913 but won only 67 votes.

Brown retired to manage a property at Moyhu, south-east of Wangaratta, for some years. Survived by a daughter, he died in hospital at Brighton on 28 September 1925 and was buried in Brighton cemetery. His estate was valued for probate at £12 106.

J. Smith (ed), *Cyclopedia of Victoria*, 1 (Melb, 1903); *PP* (LA Vic), 1879, 3 (72), 1883, 4 (50); *Investigator*, 4 (1968), no 3; *Riverine Herald*, 21 Apr 1875, May-Dec 1881, Jan-Mar 1886; *Argus*, 3 Feb 1886, 1 Nov, 14 Dec 1906, 30 Sept 1925; *Shepparton Advertiser*, 28 Sept, 1, 8 Oct 1897; *Weekly Times* (Melb), 28 Feb 1903; Bank of NSW Archives (Syd).

SUSAN McCARTHY

BROWN, MARGARET HAMILTON (1858-1952), headmistress, was born on 20 May 1858 at Lutton Place, Edinburgh, eldest daughter of James Brown, musicseller and shopkeeper, and his wife Mary, née Home, a trained teacher. In 1863 Mary followed her husband to South Australia with her two daughters. Margaret was educated at Miss Bridgman's private school in Morphett Street, and also attended Adolph Leschen's Gymnastic Institution. She studied at the teachers' Training College in 1877 and completed her qualifications by pupil-teaching at North Adelaide Model School in 1878-83 where she proved herself 'a teacher of ability', of 'more than ordinary skill'.

Her father being unable to provide fully for his five daughters and three sons, Margaret was encouraged by her mother to start, in 1884, a governess class for small boys and girls in their North Adelaide home. Her youngest sister, MARY HOME BROWN (1878-1968), born on 16 May 1878, known as Mamie, and three others were pupils. Next year the family moved to Medindie and Margaret opened the Medindie School and Kindergarten. Probably the first kindergarten in South Australia, it was established on the progressive free principles of Maria Montessori: special infants' equipment was imported from Germany.

The enterprise developed as a girls' school in size and range of classes and was moved to a larger property on Northcote Terrace, which Miss Brown boldly bought for £2500 in 1893 and later named The Wilderness. Boarders were accepted, her sister 'Wynnie', who developed prowess in interstate tennis, helped with sport and infant teaching, and the whole family co-operated in the venture. The second daughter Kate Cormack also trained as a teacher. The school discouraged snobbery, uniforms were not worn and drama and vigorous sport were provided. Mortgage payments were heavy and class-rooms often makeshift: they included the family dining-room, converted stables and an old tram-car in the luxuriant garden. All the sisters helped with teaching: Margaret took English and history, Annie became housekeeper and matron. The brilliant Mamie won a scholarship to the University of Adelaide (B.Sc., 1902) and returned to teach mathematics and Latin. Her reply to a suitor offering marriage was 'Thank you very much indeed, but . . . I must say that I prefer literature'. She was an adventurous cyclist and became an alert, firm and quick-witted teacher with a sense of humour. Margaret invariably maintained a serene equanimity in the class-room. As she aged she concentrated on keeping the accounts and the educational direction of the school passed to Mamie.

Mamie was influenced in the 1920s by the theories of Charlotte Mason who advocated masterly inactivity for teachers and self-direction, close reading and concentration for students. The importance of teaching from the best literature rather than condensed textbooks was emphasized. In 1928 The Wilderness School adopted Mason's methods and joined the Parents' National Educational Union of Great Britain. In 1923 a library had been established, and in 1936 a small laboratory, but science teaching was never strong. Senior students did well in university matriculation examinations from this school where 'the sacredness of personality' was respected.

The Brown sisters' energy had successfully built a highly regarded girls' school, with 360 pupils by 1946, out of the small beginning commonly adopted by many single women as a means of livelihood in the nineteenth century; it had become the longest-established independent girls' school in the State. In 1948 its ownership was vested in a company to ensure continuation beyond the life of the founders; that year Margaret was appointed O.B.E. She died on 5 December 1952 and from her small estate bequeathed a Mary Home Scholarship for free tuition at the school.

In 1958 Mamie retired but continued to live at the school and serve as a governor. All the sisters dressed in long skirts, mainly black, but Mamie wore grey to camouflage the chalk. In 1964 her portrait was painted by William Dargie and hung in the school hall. When she died on 1 December 1968 it was remarked that all pupils had felt 'the love, the humour, the honesty, the humility and complete lack of hypocrisy' by which the Brown sisters had lived.

E. George, *The Wilderness book* (Adel, 1946); M. Scales, *John Walker's village* (Adel, 1974); *Advertiser* (Adel), 1 Jan 1948, 10 Dec 1952, 2 Dec 1968;

PRG 156/1-5 (SAA); information from Mr G. H. Brown, Kensington Gardens, SA.

DEAN W. BERRY

BROWN, THOMAS (1861-1934), farmer and politician, was born on 6 October 1861 at the parsonage, Walla Walla near Forbes, New South Wales, eldest child of Mitchell Brown, domestic servant to Rev. Marcus Brownrigg [q.v.3], and his wife Isabella, née Abernethy. His father migrated from the Shetland Islands, Scotland, arriving in Sydney on 22 February 1856 on the *David McIver*. In 1866 Mitchell selected land at Bedgerebong which he named Clusta. Thomas studied for the Presbyterian ministry at St Andrew's College, University of Sydney, but health problems caused his withdrawal. He remained a lay preacher and was an elder of Forbes Church and later of Chalmers Church, Redfern, where on 15 December 1897 he married his cousin Louisa Jane Brown; he received part of Clusta which he named Browland.

Brown's skill as a farmers' advocate launched his political career: he represented Forbes at the first Farmers and Settlers' Association conference in June 1893 and was a foundation member of its executive. In 1894 he won the Condoublin seat in the Legislative Assembly as a 'non-solidarity' Labor member; next year he joined the Labor 'solidarities'. A free trader, he supported (Sir) George Reid against (Sir) William Lyne and W. A. Holman [qq.v.], and opposed the 1899 referendum on the draft constitution bill. He was a delegate to the interstate conference on the formation of a Federal Labor Party held in Sydney in January 1900.

In 1901 Brown resigned from the assembly and surprisingly defeated B. R. Wise [q.v.] for the Canobolas seat in the House of Representatives. A 'King among Stonewallers', he emerged as the 'Bannerman' [q.v.3] of the Federal parliament. Unopposed in 1903, he was dissatisfied with the general election and secured a select committee on the administration of the Electoral Act and served on it. In 1906 'Honest Tom' Brown won the new seat of Calare; he strongly supported the 1910 land tax bill. A member of the Australian delegation to London for George V's coronation in 1911, he became first secretary of the Australian branch of the Empire Parliamentary Association.

Some months after being defeated for Calare in 1913 Brown returned to the State parliament at a by-election for Lachlan. In September 1915 he embarrassed Holman by introducing a motion on closing hours for licensed premises. The victory of 6-o'clock closing in the referendum of June 1916 owed little to his traditional temperance arguments. That year he joined the Universal Service League but remained with the Labor Party after the split over conscription. He chaired the 1916-17 royal commission into rural, pastoral, agricultural and dairying interests. Defeated by E. A. Buttenshaw [q.v.] in 1917, he worked for a temperance organization, then became secretary to the prime minister W. M. Hughes [q.v.].

Brown was highly esteemed in the Presbyterian General Assembly and was active in committee. In 1909 he had facilitated a public discussion on social issues which ended in a memorable clash between the prime minister Andrew Fisher and Rev. John Ferguson [qq.v.]. Brown was a councillor of Scots College, Sydney, and a member of the Council for Civil and Moral Advancement (1915). Survived by his wife, a daughter and two sons, he died at his residence at Randwick on 23 March 1934 of cerebral haemorrhage and was cremated.

B. Nairn, *Civilising capitalism* (Canb, 1973); *Punch* (Melb), 20 Mar 1913; *SMH*, 24, 29 Mar 1934; *Aust Worker*, 28 Mar 1934; D. H. Coward, The impact of war on New South Wales (Ph.D. thesis, ANU, 1974); Thomas Brown papers 2185, 2234 (NL); L. J. Weir, Genealogy and biog data of the Brown family, 1650-1973 *and* family papers held by, and information from, Mrs L. J. Weir, Queenscliff, NSW).   JOHN ATCHISON

BROWN, VERA SCANTLEBURY; *see* SCANTLEBURY-BROWN

BROWN, WALTER ERNEST (1885-1942), soldier, grocer, brass-finisher and water-bailiff, was born on 3 July 1885 at New Norfolk, Tasmania, son of Sidney Francis Brown, miller, and his wife Agnes Mary, née Carney. He was brought up at New Norfolk and on leaving school worked as a grocer in Hobart until 1911 and at Petersham, New South Wales, until World War I.

On 26 July 1915 Brown enlisted in the Australian Imperial Force as an infantryman, then hoping to see action more quickly transferred to the light horse. He embarked for Egypt in October and joined the 1st Light Horse Regiment on 14 January 1916; he later transferred to the Imperial Camel Corps. In July, having determined to reach the infantry in France, he contrived (on a plea of having lost his false teeth) to be sent to Cairo where he obtained a transfer to the 20th Battalion reinforcements. He sailed for France in October and after serving for a month with the 55th Battalion and for six months with the 1st and 2nd Australian Field Butcheries, joined the 20th Battalion at St Omer in July 1917. In September and October he fought at Passchendaele and was awarded the Distinguished Conduct Medal for attending wounded under heavy fire, and later, after his sergeant had been disabled, taking charge of the section, giving 'a fine example of courage and leadership'. He was promoted lance corporal on 19 October and was wounded in November.

Early in 1918 the 20th Battalion fought at Morlancourt and then moved into the Villers-Bretonneux sector; Brown was promoted corporal on 7 April. On 6 July he was with an advance party which took over some newly captured trenches near Accroche Wood and, on being told that a sniper's post was causing trouble, he located the spot, picked up two Mills bombs and ran towards it under fire. His first bomb fell short, but on reaching the post he knocked one German down with his fist and threatened the others with his remaining grenade; when they surrendered, Brown ordered them back to the Australian lines. He had captured thirteen men, including one officer. He was awarded the Victoria Cross. He remained on the Somme until the Armistice and was wounded in action in August and promoted sergeant on 13 September.

Brown was discharged from the A.I.F. in February 1920. In 1920-30 he worked in Sydney as a brass-finisher and in 1931-40 at Leeton as a water-bailiff with the New South Wales Water Conservation and Irrigation Commission. He married Maude Dillon, an Irishwoman, in Christ Church, Bexley, on 4 June 1932. In June 1940, by giving his age as 40 instead of 54, Brown enlisted in the 2nd A.I.F. His real age and record were soon discovered, and he was promoted lance sergeant and posted to the 2/15th Field Regiment, but he reverted to gunner at his own request. The regiment, part of the ill-fated 8th Division, reached Malaya in August 1941. Brown was last seen on 14 February 1942, the night before the Allied surrender at Singapore. Picking up some grenades he said to his comrades, 'No surrender for me', and walked towards the enemy lines. He was presumed to have died while trying to escape on 28 February. He was survived by his wife, a son and a daughter.

Brown was regarded by those who served with him as 'a born soldier, quiet, friendly and loyal beyond measure'. His portrait by John Longstaff [q.v.] is in the Australian War Memorial collection.

C. E. W. Bean, *The A.I.F. in France, 1918* (Syd, 1942); L. Wigmore (ed), *They dared mightily* (Canb, 1963); *London Gazette*, 3 June, 17 Aug 1918; *Reveille* (Syd), July 1946, Jan 1968; *Sydney Mail*, 28

Aug 1918; *Bulletin*, 12, 26 June, 3, 24 July 1946; War diary of the 20th Battalion (AWM); records (AWM).   K. R. WHITE

BROWN, WALTER FRANKLYN; *see* BARRETT, WALTER

BROWN, WILLIAM JETHRO (1868-1930), political thinker, academic, and jurist, was born on 29 March 1868 at Mintaro, South Australia, son of James Brown, farmer, and his wife Sophia Jane, née Torr. James had migrated from Devon in 1847; of humble background, he became a substantial property-owner. Young 'Willie' worked hard on the family farm, but did well at Stanley Grammar School, Watervale. He spent 1882-86 as a pupil-teacher at Moonta Mines State School. Thence he transferred with remarkable ease and success to St John's College, Cambridge, graduating B.A. and LL.B. with first-class honours, in 1890. F. W. Maitland was among his teachers, and became a friend. Brown's complete degrees were M.A. and LL.D. (Cambridge), LL.D. and Litt.D. (Dublin). In 1891 he was called to the Bar at the Middle Temple, London.

In January 1893 Brown was one of three foundation lecturers in the University of Tasmania, teaching law and modern history. In 1896 he was promoted professor, and in 1898 temporarily occupied the chair of law at Sydney. In May 1900 he left Hobart to return to England, and on 14 August married Aimée Marie Loth. Brown was professor of constitutional law at University College, London, in 1900-01, living the while at an East End 'settlement'. In 1901-06, he was professor of constitutional and comparative law at the University College of Wales, Aberystwyth, and in 1906-16, professor of law at the University of Adelaide. Then, as a wartime sacrifice, he became president of the Industrial Court of South Australia; new legislation in 1920 added the conjoint presidency of the Board of Industry.

Brown wrote four major books: *The new democracy* (1899), *The Austinian theory of law* (1906), *The underlying principles of modern legislation* (1912), and *The prevention and control of monopolies* (1914). His many articles appeared in major English and American journals, although in the 1920s he wrote too for the nascent Australian academic press. As chairman, he prepared the report of the Federal royal commission on the sugar industry (1912). His judgments in the *South Australian Industrial Reports* were subtle and scholarly. Brown is one of the few Australians to

have proposed a deeply thought political philosophy. Owing much to T. H. Green and other Idealists, he responded also to concepts of pragmatic social engineering. Brown saw the modern state as an organic, indeed psychical, entity whose members ought to join in selfless service and thus find a humanitarian faith to fill the vacuum created by hedonist materialism. Government, guided by society's most enlightened members, should secure welfare and efficiency. 'In the reconstructed doctrine of individual rights', he argued, 'the common good takes the place of consent as the justification for the exercise of authority'.

New democracy and *Prevention and control of monopolies* suggested how Australian experience might help secure these aims. The former book included a paper in which Brown enthused over Tasmania's experiment with proportional representation, presenting it as an antidote to corruption and apathy in the electorate and mediocrity among politicians. Conversely he criticized the referendum, then popular with many radicals, because it would encourage 'popular despotism' in opposition to skilled and strong leadership from above. The chief interest of *New democracy* lies in Brown's advocacy of Australian Federation. Thereby, he argued, the country would find peace, prosperity, and 'an inspiring faith in the splendour of the future . . .'. Hitherto, Brown believed, Australia had suffered the modern malaise of lack of purpose and honour.

Prevention and control of monopolies argued for the outlawing of predatory trade practices and for requiring business to disclose its dealings. In some extreme cases nationalization might be appropriate. Brown's loudest call was for the establishment of expert tribunals to control tariffs, wages, and, most important of all, prices. He cited Australia's experiments with New Protection and repeated much of his sugar commission report. The Interstate Commission, enjoying its brief heyday, appealed to him as a splendid example of the kind of expert tribunal which might secure socio-economic justice.

Brown's major contributions to the philosophy of jurisprudence were published in his *Austinian theory of law*, the bulk of which comprised an edition of the major teachings of the Englishman, John Austin. There was some paradox here, as Austin was the supreme representative of the positivist-utilitarian school which viewed law as essentially and always the will of the ruler, whereas Brown had a much more fluid view of that issue. He interpreted law 'as a process, as an activity, not merely as a body of knowledge or a fixed order of construction'; it must adapt to meet the changing needs and nature of society. Roscoe Pound and Rudolph von Ihering were jurists whom he particularly admired.

For a man of these beliefs the role of industrial arbiter had much appeal, for thereby the law could serve social welfare and harmony. Brown put this case with skill and passion in the Industrial Court, hoping to inspire workers with a sense of social adhesion and purpose. Especially interesting was his espousal (1920) of a scheme of co-operative councils, which might unite employers and employees; the idea had affinities with Britain's Whitley councils and even Mussolini's corporativism.

Brown was a thoughtful and creative educator. From Maitland he had learned that academic history centred on documents, while Harvard and other American schools provided his model for the complementary notion of case-study in law. 'In truth it is relatively unimportant how much a student knows when he leaves his University', said Brown in his inaugural lecture at Aberystwyth. 'It is of incalculable importance that he should have ... learnt to give a reason for the faith that is in him, that he should have won his way to freedom of thought'. All this put him in tune with contemporary 'progressive' thought; he traced his attitudes in both education and law to Giambattista Vico. Brown taught by seminar and continuous assessment. He strove to make law a liberal, autonomous study, free from both traditional 'Arts' teaching (his major antagonist in Wales) and narrow professional demands (which confronted him in Adelaide). Brown encouraged other fledgling disciplines. He himself introduced political science (specifically so called) at both Hobart and Aberystwyth, and also urged that a full place be given to economics and commerce. As with jurisprudence, he stressed that these subjects must recognize social change and assist in human welfare.

Similar attitudes shaped Brown's attitude to religion. His mother, whom he revered, was a Methodist fundamentalist. Abandoning formal belief in favour of an ethical pragmatism, he called upon Christians to recognize that theirs was an historical religion, which should ever be ready to shape itself afresh.

Brown had considerable feeling for beauty, both in art and nature – he owned works by Hans Heysen [q.v.]. While, like many of his peers, he argued for eugenic controls and for the glory of family life, yet he upheld feminist ideas. His major piece of imaginative writing, *Who knows?* (1923), was a post-Ibsenesque drama of woman's revolt. At least in earlier days Brown achieved notable rapport with students, and always retained personal appeal. 'He was a man who hid beneath an armor of whimsical gaiety, adventure, courage and loyalty', wrote W. Harrison Moore [q.v.]. He had slight build, fine features, and clipped tones.

Poor health and a dismal marriage increasingly darkened Brown's life. Having originally welcomed World War I as a stimulus to social union, he came to see that it fomented hatreds and tensions. Australian federalism, still earlier among his ideals, vitiated his work as industrial arbiter. Neither employers, employees, nor society at large responded to his hopes. Overwhelmed by work, Brown retired in 1927 and died on 27 May 1930. He was buried in West Terrace cemetery, Adelaide, and his wife and son survived him.

M. Roe, *William Jethro Brown* (Hob, 1977); *Aust Highway*, 10 Sept 1930; personal papers, and a memoir and bibliog by his son, C. M. A. Brown (SAA).   MICHAEL ROE

BROWNE, ALFRED JOSEPH BESSELL-; *see* BESSELL-BROWNE

BROWNE, REGINALD SPENCER (1856-1943), journalist and soldier, was born at Oaklands, Appin, New South Wales, on 13 July 1856, son of William James Merrick Shawe Browne, pastoralist, and his wife Rachel, née Broad. His father, a native-born scion of an already old Australian family, was superintending officer of Yeomanry and Volunteer Corps in 1854. Educated at Appin, at Corowa and in England, Browne became a journalist and precociously published slim volumes of verse in 1874-75 from the offices of the Deniliquin *Pastoral Times* and the *Albury Banner*. He was a sub-editor on the *Townsville Herald* in 1877 and editor of the *Cooktown Herald* in 1878. When Sir Thomas McIlwraith [q.v.5] arranged a cabinet syndicate to control the *Observer* in 1881, Browne moved to Brisbane as its editor and married Violet Edith Fanny Sutton of Maryborough on 13 October. She died soon afterwards.

Browne joined the *Brisbane Courier* in 1882 and stayed there for nearly all his working life. As associate editor of the *Queenslander*, he discovered and encouraged the poet George Essex Evans [q.v.]. Commissioned in the Queensland Mounted Infantry on 20 December 1887, he was said to have found work briefly on the London press to facilitate military study. He published *Romances of the goldfield and bush*, a volume of slight prose sketches, in London in 1890.

Browne commanded a flying column of

his regiment in western Queensland during the shearers' strike of 1891 but was, nevertheless, always sympathetic to trade-unionism. He was promoted captain in 1891 and major in 1896. In November 1899 he sailed for South Africa as a special-service officer with the first Queensland contingent, carrying the local rank of major. With active service in many fields, he was appointed C.B., received the Queen's Medal with five clasps, was invalided to Australia in November 1900 and mentioned in dispatches in 1901. His return to Brisbane was a triumph.

Browne progressed slowly through the literary hierarchy of the *Courier*, but devoted much time still to soldiering as lieut-colonel commanding the 13th Light Horse Regiment from 1903 and colonel of the 5th Light Horse Brigade from 1906; in 1911 he was transferred to the reserve. He was disappointed in his aspirations in 1906 to become lieut-governor of Papua and in 1908 acting State commandant. He presided at a meeting on 20 January 1911 when one faction among Brisbane journalists forestalled another connected with the Trades Hall, and formed an association. As first president he steered it through complications caused by the general strike of 1912 but was never again active, though he urged young men to support the association and he later contributed to its funds while overseas. As an old friend and political adherent of (Sir) Littleton Groom [q.v.], he transmitted regular political intelligence and worked informally for the Liberal Party.

On 4 March 1915 Browne joined the Australian Imperial Force as colonel commanding the 4th Light Horse Brigade; when it was broken up he took over the 6th Infantry Brigade at Gallipoli, at the age of 59. He served at Lone Pine and Quinn's Post and was evacuated on 10 December but, too old for further active service, was given charge of the Australian Training and General Base Depot at Tel-el-kebir, Egypt, on 20 March 1916 as brigadier general. Publication by him in 1915 of *The heroic Serbians* won him the order of the Serbian Red Cross. In 1916 in England he commanded the Australian Training Depot on Salisbury Plain, then moved to No.2 Command Depot at Weymouth where he probably met the novelist Thomas Hardy. He returned to Australia, unfit, in November 1917, commanded the Molonglo Concentration Camp at Canberra from February to December 1918, was then demobilized, and was formally retired on 20 October 1921 as honorary major general. For two years he was State president of the Returned Soldiers' and Sailors' Imperial League of Australia.

Between 1925 and 1927 Browne contributed a weekly article to the *Courier*, giving his memories of men and events in the Queensland of his time. These were published as *A journalist's memories* (1927); the book is still the source of much of both the history and legend of Queensland.

In his later years Browne was a famous Brisbane identity. He was nominally financial editor of the *Courier Mail*, reporting only the limited operations of the Brisbane Stock Exchange; he also edited the *Queensland Trustees Review*. On 7 August 1889 he had married Catherine Fraser Munro (d. 1942), a noted musician and amateur actress. He had been interested primarily in pastimes like polo, shooting and fishing, but henceforth shared wide cultural interests with his wife. He died, childless, on 9 November 1943, and was cremated with Anglican rites. His estate was sworn for probate at £1912. Tolerant and broadminded, Browne had been widely respected as 'in every sense a gentleman'.

D. B. W. Sladen (ed), *Australian poets, 1788-1888* (Lond, 1888); Aust Defence Dept, *Official records of the Australian military contingents to the war in South Africa*, P. L. Murray ed (Melb, 1912); H. J. Summers, 'Spencer Browne, soldier, journalist, historian', *JRHSQ*, 9 (1969-75), no 5, and for bibliog; Groom papers (NL).   H. J. SUMMERS

BROWNE, WILLIAM HENRY (1846-1904), miner and politician, was born on 13 September 1846 at Pimlico, London, son of William Henry Browne, stone-sawyer, and his wife Eliza, née Barton. He went to sea when 11, served for nine years in the merchant navy, and possibly also in the Royal Navy, and in 1866 became a goldminer at Araluen, New South Wales. He followed this occupation in the eastern colonies for the next twenty years. In Queensland he worked at Gympie, Herberton and Croydon, where he lost an eye in an accident.

Browne helped to form a miners' union at Croydon and was successively its president and secretary. In August 1890 he contested a Legislative Assembly by-election for the two-member electorate of Burke, but John Hoolan [q.v.] defeated him by twenty-four votes. Still secretary of the miners' union, Browne organized financial support for the shearers during the 1891 pastoral strike. In 1892 Burke was divided into two single-member electorates: at the election next year he won the new seat, Croydon. Though not a forceful orator, he spoke often in the House. In September 1894 he and six other Labor members were suspended and removed by the serjeant-at-arms when they refused to obey the chairman's call to order during debate on the peace preservation bill.

After the defeat of Andrew Fisher [q.v.] at the 1896 election, 'Billy' Browne became secretary of the Parliamentary Labor Party but was forced to vacate the position in 1898 because of acute asthma associated with miner's phthisis. When Anderson Dawson [q.v.] formed a Labor ministry in 1899, Browne was included as secretary for mines and for public instruction; the brevity of the government's term allowed him no time to prepare any legislation.

'A speck among politicians because of his spare and feeble frame', Browne had a very big heart and a broad mind. He was elected leader in August 1900 on the resignation of Dawson, and was also president of the party's central political executive. In the formation in September 1903 of the (Sir) Arthur Morgan [q.v.]-Browne Liberal-Labor coalition, which ousted the thirteen-year-old 'continuous government', Browne was overshadowed by William Kidston [q.v.]; but the trust in which he was held by executive and party members was the decisive factor in bringing the Labor Party over. A moderate in his political views, who hoped to harmonize relations between capital and labour, Browne saw advantages to the party in holding office as part of the coalition, but reserved the right to withdraw if it attempted to pass legislation unfavourable to the labour movement.

He became deputy premier and secretary for mines and for public works in the new government on 17 September 1903, but died of pneumonia and angina pectoris on 12 April 1904. The state funeral procession was led from the Church of England cathedral to Toowong cemetery by naval personnel. He was unmarried and his estate, sworn for probate at £411, was administered by a sister in Sydney.

C. A. Bernays, *Queensland politics during sixty years* (Brisb, 1919); D. J. Murphy et al (eds), *Prelude to power* (Brisb, 1970); D. J. Murphy (ed), *Labor in politics* (Brisb, 1975); *Brisbane Courier*, and *T&CJ*, 13 Apr 1904; *Croydon Mining News*, 16 Apr 1904.

D. J. MURPHY

BROWNLEE, JOHN DONALD MAC-KENZIE (1900-1969), musician, was born on 7 January 1900 at Geelong, Victoria, son of James Watson Brownlee, farmer, and his wife Isabella Finlayson, née Mackenzie. Educated at a state school until he was about 14, he then briefly attended Gordon Technical College. In 1915 he was employed as a clerk by the Geelong hardware firm of Hawkes Bros.

A member of a musical family, Brownlee played the cornet in the Geelong Municipal Band. By his late teens it was apparent that he had a potentially fine baritone voice, and he was encouraged by the Hawkes family to take professional training. In 1921, after winning the gold medal as champion vocalist at the South Street competitions in Ballarat, he abandoned accountancy studies and moved to Melbourne to study singing under Ivor Boustead of the Albert Street Conservatorium. In 1922 Melba [q.v.] heard him sing Handel's *Messiah* and was so impressed with the quality of his voice that she urged him to go overseas for further tuition; in 1923 he began intensive studies in Paris with Dinh Gilly, and two years later was singing operatic roles in the Trianon Lyrique. There he was again heard by Melba who insisted that he appear in her Covent Garden farewell in 1926. From then on his rise was rapid. He made a sensational début at the Paris Opera House in Massenet's *Thaïs* in 1927 and was a contract singer there until 1936. Between the Paris seasons he appeared in the leading opera-houses of Europe and South America, in international seasons at Covent Garden, and at the Glyndebourne festivals where he established a reputation as an interpreter of baritone roles in Mozart operas. He visited Australia for the Williamson [q.v.6]-Melba Grand Opera Company in 1928 and for a concert tour in 1932-33. During the latter visit he joined the Williamson-Imperial Company as a guest star from 10-21 September 1932 and performed in five operas on six nights.

In 1937 Brownlee made his début at the Metropolitan Opera in New York as Rigoletto, and until his retirement in 1958 performed there in most of the eighty operas of his repertoire. New York became his home, and he appeared in opera and recitals in many parts of North America as soloist with the leading symphony orchestras and in nation-wide broadcasts. In 1952 he made his final visit to Australia, where he sang two of his most famous roles: Don Giovanni, and Scarpia in Puccini's *La Tosca*.

Brownlee was active in the American Guild of Musical Artists and was president in 1952-66. He was on the Advisory Committee on the Arts and the committee for International Cultural Exchanges during the Eisenhower and Kennedy administrations. Appointed as head of the Voice and Opera Department of the Manhattan School of Music in 1953, he became director of the school in 1956 and after 1958 devoted most of his energies to his work there. While actively engaged in teaching, and in directing and staging many of the school's opera productions, he found time to plan a campaign which raised $9.5 million; this enabled the institution to increase substantially its enrolments and to honour an agreement for the purchase of the buildings of the Juilliard

School. Brownlee died on 10 January 1969 and was buried in Ferncliff cemetery, Hartsdale. He was survived by his wife, the former Countess Donna Carla Oddone di Feletto, whom he had married in Paris on 29 November 1928, and by a daughter and two sons.

Australia saw little of the singer during his great career, but Melbourne honours his memory in a simple but practical way – by the John Brownlee Vocal Scholarship, first awarded in 1969.

A. L. Brownlee, *The Brownlee family* (Melb, priv print); I. Moresby, *Australia makes music* (Melb, 1948); J. Wechsberg, *Red plush and black velvet* (Lond, 1962); J. Hetherington, *Melba* (Melb, 1967); B. & F. Mackenzie, *Singers of Australia* (Melb, 1967); *Geelong Advertiser*, 12 Apr 1952; *New York Times*, 26 Nov 1956, 17 Oct 1957, 25 Oct 1962, 7 May 1963, 12 Jan, 3 Oct 1969; *Herald* (Melb), 29 Nov 1969.   MORRIS S. WILLIAMS

BROWNLOW, FREDERICK HUGH CUST (1859-1931), naval officer and public servant, was born on 8 August 1859 at Westminster, London, son of Edward Brownlow, sergeant in the Coldstream Guards, and his wife Charlotte Esther, née Burroughs. Educated at St Olave's Grammar School, Southwark, he began work in a surveyor's office but left in 1873 to be apprenticed to a Sunderland shipowner. He gained his mate's certificate and served in the merchant navy until 1881 when he decided to settle in Australia. Working his way to Sydney as an able seaman, he went into the coachbuilding trade with T. Moore & Son.

In 1885 Brownlow served as a private with the colony's Sudan Contingent and that year joined the New South Wales Naval Volunteer Artillery; he was commissioned sublieutenant in 1889 and lieutenant in 1892. During the Boxer Rebellion he helped to organize and equip the New South Wales contingent to the China Field Force. In 1888 he had joined the Department of Mines as a clerk, becoming mining registrar in 1908-11. He married Ellen Gillespie (1870-1929) in St Michael's Anglican Church, Surry Hills, on 18 March 1891. From 1902 he also held the part-time appointment of officer commanding the naval forces in New South Wales. Promoted lieut-commander that year, he was made commander in 1905, and in 1906-09 was the first and only consultative member of the first naval board of administration. From its foundation in 1905 he had been a State committee-man of the Australian National Defence League, and warmly supported creation of an Australian navy. On the formation of the Royal Aus-

tralian Navy in 1911 he resigned from the public service to become district naval officer for New South Wales; he was promoted captain and awarded the Volunteer Officers' Decoration in 1913. In his time he was the only R.A.N. captain who had not served in the Royal Navy.

Brownlow was D.N.O. at Sydney until 1921; his main duties related to the recruiting, discipline, drafting, accommodation and control of personnel. In 1913, when the Australian fleet took over the Royal Navy's establishments in Australia, he assisted in organizing the transfer of responsibilities, and in World War I carried heavy administrative burdens. During the war years he lived at the naval depot in Rushcutters Bay, never leaving his post; for his devotion to duty he received the thanks of the Admiralty and the naval board and was appointed O.B.E. in 1919. He retired in October 1921, by which time he was the senior captain in the R.A.N.

A man of 'great organising ability', Brownlow was popular and active in naval circles even after retirement, and in 1922-29 was secretary of the Rawson Institute for Seamen. At the time of his death he was secretary of the New South Wales League of Ancient Mariners. Survived by his three daughters, he died in St Luke's Hospital, Darlinghurst, on 1 June 1931 and was cremated after an Anglican service at his Double Bay home.

T. G. Ellery, *Australian defence: the opinions of experts* (Adel, 1907); *Cyclopedia of N.S.W.* (Syd, 1907); *V&P* (LA NSW), Blue Book, 1889, vol 3, 1895, vol 1, Public Service list, 1900-12; *SMH*, 21 June 1921, 21 Dec 1929, 1-3 June 1931.

ROBERT HYSLOP

BRUCE, JOHN LECK (1850-1921), sanitary engineer and teacher, was born on 16 October 1850 at Glasgow, Scotland, son of Robert Bruce, clerk, and his wife Jane, née Leck. Trained as an architect, he joined the firm of Bruce & Sturrock, and was consulting engineer to the Glasgow Corporation. He was a juror on gas-cooking and gas-heating appliances at the Glasgow Gas and Electric Exhibition in 1880, and a member of the city's institute of architects and the philosophical society. On 1 August 1877 he had married Charlotte Florence Cochran at the Hamilton Presbyterian Church, Birkenhead, England.

Bruce arrived in Sydney in May 1887 and set up practice as a consulting engineer and architect. On 15 April 1889 he became a foreman of works in the government architect's branch of the Department of

Public Works at a salary of £250. In May 1891 he was appointed first lecturer in sanitary engineering at Sydney Technical College, and devoted the rest of his professional life to developing that department. In 1901, with Dr T. M. Kendall, medical adviser to the Metropolitan Board of Water Supply and Sewerage, he published *The Australian sanitary inspector's textbook....* At this time he was the Australian examiner for the London Sanitary Institute, Sydney editor of the *Building and Engineering Journal of Australia and New Zealand*, assistant editor of the *Australian Technical Journal* (in which he had published an article on gas-lighting in March 1897), and president of the sanitary department's examining board. His textbook was reissued as the *Australian sanitary inspector's handbook* (1920).

By 1912 Bruce was a member of the Royal Sanitary Institute; in 1914 he was on the editorial advisory committee of the *Technical Gazette of New South Wales* and in 1912-17 contributed articles about ventilation, moisture and temperature control of air, and the lighting of dwellings and factories. He devised simple instruments for use by factory inspectors in determining whether air and lighting conformed to the requirements of the Factories Act. He also wrote an introductory chapter to *Practical Australian sanitation* (vol.1), by Dr C. Savill Willis. On his retirement in 1920 he was made a fellow of the Technical College.

On 29 November 1921 Bruce died of cerebral thrombosis at Blakehurst, Sydney, and was buried in the Presbyterian section of South Head cemetery. He was survived by his wife, two sons and two married daughters.

Quarter century of technical education in New South Wales (Syd, 1909); *Aust Technical J*, Mar 1897; Sanitary Inspectors' Assn (NSW), *Official Report*, 1 (1912); *Technical Gazette of NSW*, 4 (1914), 6 (1916), 7 (1917), 12 (1922).

J. M. ANTILL

BRUCE, MINNIE (MARY) GRANT (1878-1958), journalist and writer of children's books, was born on 24 May 1878 near Sale, Victoria, daughter of Eyre Lewis Bruce and his wife Mary (Minnie) Atkinson, née Whittakers. Her father, a surveyor, migrated to Melbourne from Cork, Ireland, in 1854, settling in Gippsland ten years later. Her mother was a daughter of a Welsh pioneer of the Monaro district, New South Wales. Minnie was fourth in a family of two boys and three surviving daughters.

Her first recorded literary effort was a precocious epic on an insane Czar, written at 7. Three years later she was editing her school magazine. More substantial literary success came when she won first prize in the Melbourne Shakespeare Society's annual essay competition in April 1895. A pupil at Miss Estelle Beausire's Ladies' High School, Sale, Minnie passed the matriculation examination later that year with honours in English, history and botany.

In 1898, in the Christmas supplement of the Melbourne *Leader*, her story, 'Her little lad' was published under the signature 'M.G.B.'. Following publication of 'Dono's Christmas' in the December 1900 supplement under the pseudonym 'Coolibah', she went to live in Melbourne, boarding at first and later as a 'bachelor girl' in a bed-sitting-room. After doing secretarial work, she joined the staff of the *Age* and the *Leader* and began contributing articles and short stories to *Outpost, Table Talk, Lone Hand, Woman's World, Australasian Traveller, Woman, Southern Sphere* and the Ballarat *Evening Echo*, claiming later that the only subject on which she had not expounded was 'dress'. Articles such as a series on Melbourne hospitals in *Woman* (1909) show a spontaneity and incisiveness rare in later works. The short stories brim with the 'exciting and pathetic incidents' praised by later reviewers of the Billabong books: mixtures of sentimentality and pathos, skittishness and stoicism, challenge and safety, relationships between social classes in which benign patronage and good-humoured servitude were balanced, all united by a philosophy of hard work.

Minnie also wrote patriotic verse but after seeing in print one effusion, performed in 1903 at an Empire Day demonstration of the Australian Women's National League, she 'put the paper in the fire, and have since kept to prose'. About this time she combined with other women to form the Writers' Club which later merged with the Lyceum Club.

Although she wrote many books, her most famous were the Billabong series, begun when she was writing weekly stories for the children's pages of the *Leader*, where *A little bush maid* first appeared in serial form. The story proved so successful that the Linton family was launched. At her editor's suggestion she posted the completed novel to Ward, Lock & Co. in London where it was published in 1910 under the authorship 'Mary', regarded as more marketable than 'Minnie'. Other titles followed quickly. 'I was very firm about one point', she said in *Table Talk* in 1939, 'that there should be no love interest in them. I was more or less forced into marrying off Norah and Wally eventually, but beyond that I drew the line'. Reviewers applauded the clean, healthy, wholesome, pleasant, and purely Australian character of the saga. The public responded with joy. For the author it was 'no longer necessary to choose between a meal and a pot-plant'. During World War I her sister-in-law Lady Evelyn Seton wrote a pungent criticism of the series and its central family, advising their creator to break free; but the Lintons had become part of the national life, 'running our own show' as Jim Linton said in the foreword to *Billabong's luck. Billabong riders*, the fifteenth and last of the series, was published in 1942.

In 1913 Mary Grant Bruce had gone to London where English relations provided her with an introduction to Lord Northcliffe. She began writing articles for the *Daily Mail*. In 1914 she met a distant cousin, Major George Evans Bruce of the Norfolk Regiment, ten years her senior, who had served in the British Army in India and South Africa; he was also a writer of exotic melodramas and expert articles on fish and crustacea. They came back to Australia and were married at Holy Trinity Church, East Melbourne, on 1 July 1914, but their stay at the seaside, described by her in *The peculiar honeymoon*, was cut short by the outbreak of war. Bruce was soon called to duty at the War Office. They sailed in the troop-ship *Nestor* to Cork, where Bruce, proscribed from action by a strained heart, was to be second-in-command of the Dublin Fusiliers, training recruits. In the next three years Mary 'produced two babies and four books'. After the war, the family returned to Australia to settle at Traralgon, Gippsland.

Mary Grant Bruce continued to write for magazines while the Billabong series appeared. In 1926 she returned to full-time journalism for six months as acting editor of *Woman's World*. In 1927 the family moved to Omagh, Ireland, with permanent residence in mind. Soon after their arrival their younger son accidentally shot himself. They left Ireland, and the next twelve years were spent on the Continent and in the south of England. In 1939 they returned to Australia to settle their son on the land. During World War II Mary worked for the Australian Imperial Force Women's Association, sold her autograph at charity auctions for the war effort and broadcast three series of talks for the Department of Information.

She was a prolific letter-writer, and took copious notes of her 'European Wanderings', many of which were the basis for articles. Other notebooks contain detailed descriptions of the Australian landscape, impressive in their observation and immediacy. Her respect for Aboriginal traditions, expressed in her book of legends *The stone axe of Burkamukk* (1922), was unusual for her time. Some of her early articles, with their spirited criticism of feminine roles, show an incipient feminism which most contemporaries would not have shared. Much of her success, however, lies in the completeness with which she expressed the philosophy of her times.

Although much of her work was written in England, Mary Grant Bruce's patriotism is more Australian than British. The Lintons' world, threatened from outside, withstood challenge, unchanged and untarnished. Australians, and not only children, looking at Billabong, could see themselves as they wanted to be — mates in fortune and adversity, sturdy, decent and fearless inheritors of a tough, but rewarding land. After her husband died in 1948, Mary Grant Bruce returned to England, visiting Australia from time to time. Survived by her son, she died in Sussex on 2 July 1958, and was cremated at Hastings.

H. M. Saxby, *A history of Australian children's literature, 1841-1941* (Syd, 1969); Mary Grant Bruce papers and news-cuttings (LaTL).

LYNNE STRAHAN

BRUCE, STANLEY MELBOURNE, VISCOUNT BRUCE OF MELBOURNE (1883-1967), businessman, prime minister and public servant, was born on 15 April 1883 at St Kilda, Victoria, youngest of five children of John Munro Bruce [q.v.3] and his wife Mary Ann, née Henderson. His parents were comfortably circumstanced, his father having become a partner in the softgoods importing firm of Paterson, Laing & Bruce in 1878. The family spent some time in England while Bruce was a child, and he began his formal education at Eastbourne, probably with an English governess. In 1891 he entered a Toorak, Victoria, prep school run by Miss McComas, who remembered a delightful boy, serious, earnest, very good-looking, always 'a little gentleman' and very self-reliant. He went on to Melbourne Church of England Grammar School in 1896, where he captained football, cricket and rowing, was a cadet-lieutenant, and in 1901 school captain.

When his father's firm encountered liquidity problems during the 1890s financial crisis, the family moved temporarily from its comfortable Toorak home. His father retained a right to draw £2500 a year and in 1897 he was able to buy out his senior partner, John Paterson. He then formed a limited liability company to which he transferred assets valued at £400 000 and as part payment became majority shareholder. The English partners, or their estates, took up shares and also provided short-term finance. On J. M. Bruce's death in 1901, the English directors controlled London head office. In a manoeuvre to shift that control without a flight of capital, Bruce was made acting chairman in 1907. It was a delicate situation for the family: they could not take up the debt themselves and they could not be sure they would be able to replace the capital if it was withdrawn as the firm's 4 per cent dividend was below market average.

Bruce had worked in the Melbourne warehouse of Paterson, Laing & Bruce in 1902 before going to Trinity Hall, Cambridge. He rowed in the winning Cambridge crew in 1904 and in later years sometimes coached for Cambridge, following the principles of Steve Fairbairn [q.v.]. Known affectionately as 'Bruggins' on the tow-path, he had a winning crew in 1914. After he graduated B.A. in 1905, Bruce trained with Ashurst, Morris & Crisp, a leading firm in commercial law, and read for the Bar. He was appointed acting chairman of Paterson, Laing & Bruce in October 1907, and next month was called to the Middle Temple. The firm appears to have taken priority though he had leave to travel to Mexico in 1908 and to Colombia in 1912 on legal commissions to collect evidence. The management of the firm was the reason for his living in London. His elder brother Ernest was in charge of the Australian end of the business.

Bruce's task was to retain the confidence of the English debt-holders while the firm's profitability improved. His appointment as chairman was confirmed in 1908 and in his first report to shareholders he included a detailed analysis of the effects on the market of political developments in Australia. Intended to show the firm was a growth enterprise, this exercise, which Bruce repeated in later reports, kept him up to date with Australian politics. His tact and courtesy to the older directors, together with his sound advice on the business, ensured their continued backing. By 1910 the company had accumulated reserves of £100 000 and the dividend was raised to 5 per cent and in the following year to 6 per cent. It then matched the market and when capital was needed in 1913, Bruce had no difficulty in arranging a new debenture issue.

At Sonning, Berkshire, on 12 July 1913, Bruce married Ethel Dunlop, daughter of Andrew George Anderson and granddaughter of Thomas Manifold [q.v.2]. Ethel was to be his closest confidant. Letters to friends reveal that the decisions which touched him personally and closely in later years were made in consultation with her. They took motoring holidays together, shared interests in bridge and golf, went regularly to the theatre, and when possible to the Henley regatta. On his numerous journeys overseas and around Australia, she always went with him and he was especially helped by her quick recollection of people they had met.

Bruce had come into business at the top but he acquired a thorough knowledge of the firm's operations; in 1910 he returned to Australia to act as general manager while Ernest was overseas. They again exchanged positions in 1914 and at the outbreak of war Bruce was in Australia. He returned to London in December, was commissioned in the Worcester Regiment in January 1915 and, seconded to the Royal Fusiliers as temporary captain, fought in the Gallipoli campaign. He went ashore at Hellas and on 3 June was wounded. Bruce rejoined the fighting at Suvla Bay where he won the Military Cross for making contact with an isolated section. In October he was wounded in the knee and invalided to England. Later he received the Croix de Guerre avec Palme in recognition of support his battalion had given the French.

He was able to take some part in the management of Paterson, Laing & Bruce during 1916. Despite shipping difficulties and double taxation, against which he spoke forcefully, the firm was better placed than its small competitors to obtain supplies, and Australians were buying more expensive lines: it continued to pay a 6 per cent dividend. Bruce returned to Australia in January 1917 to take over as general manager, Ernest having left to join the British artillery. The business continued to prosper. By 1919 it had over 1000 on its payroll and a nominal capital of £1 million. In 1920 its dividend was raised to 7½ per cent. On Bruce's initiative a profit-sharing scheme had been extended to junior staff.

Bruce took his military discharge in June 1917. The following April he secured National Party endorsement in the by-election for the Federal seat of Flinders. He observed the benefits of co-operation between National and Country parties when the Victorian Farmers' Union candidate withdrew, following agreement to introduce preferential voting. Bruce had an easy victory. Contrary to the later myth, which he fostered, he was not a political innocent nor did he stumble into politics. Sir Walter Manifold [q.v.], president of the Victorian Legislative Council in 1919-23 was Ethel's uncle; J. C. Manifold [q.v.], her second cousin, was a member of the Federal parliament. Fears about socialistic legislation had recurred in his chairman's reports: Labor's land tax was 'a deliberate attack on capital'. Arguing that rising prosperity would counter these tendencies, Bruce had advised vigorous government action on irrigation and immigration. However, the reports reveal a growing disquiet about 'uneconomic' expenditure. In his campaign

Bruce stressed the need for business methods in government.

In the guise of a businessman who disliked 'party politics', he was able to criticize the government for its administration while accepting most of its legislation, departing from the party line only on its land tax amendment bill. The new tariff he accepted, acknowledging a need for new industries, a view which derived ultimately from a businessman's appreciation of the benefits to trade of increased national income.

Bruce spent eight months of 1919 at head office in London. Ernest died that year, leaving Bruce to handle the two positions they had shared. He again went to London early in 1921 and was about to return when rumours circulated that he was to be Australia's delegate to the September meeting of the League of Nations. When the appointment was announced he was golfing at Le Touquet, a favourite holiday then and later. At Geneva he spoke movingly of the horror of war: 'If the League of Nations goes, the hope of mankind goes also'. Five of his fellow officers had been killed in the first weeks on Gallipoli.

His return to Australia coincided with a political crisis. W. M. Hughes [q.v.] failed to get the Country Party to join the government and on Sir Joseph Cook's [q.v.] retirement took the opportunity to reconstruct his ministry. Family and business connexions ensured Bruce would be considered, but in this instance he did hesitate: he could combine his responsibilities in the family firm with those of a back-bencher, but he could not run a department and manage the firm. Only when offered the treasurership was he prepared to hand over the running of the company. He placed Thomas Alston, the firm's solicitor and Ethel's brother-in-law, on the board and relied heavily thereafter on his advice for the business. Bruce attended board meetings until a month after becoming prime minister, though he resigned his directorships of the National Mutual Life Association of Australasia Ltd and Equity Trustees, Executors & Agency Co. He was fortunate in coming to Treasury at the turning-point of the post-war recession. Relieved of defence expenditure by the Washington treaties, he was able to reduce income tax and show a substantial surplus.

Bruce became prime minister on 9 February 1923. Hughes had failed to get an absolute majority in the 1922 election and the Country Party again refused a coalition. He was forced to recommend Bruce. Protecting his flank from Hughes by getting his approval for (Sir) George Pearce [q.v.] to join the ministry, Bruce conceded to (Sir) Earle Page [q.v.] five of the eleven portfolios, sufficient for the Country Party to value the

coalition tactic. Throughout his six and a half years as prime minister his first priority was to maintain the coalition. Repeatedly he arranged electoral pacts well in advance to forestall demands from his own party to go it alone. He was the architect of the most powerful and durable alliance in Australian politics.

Secure in office through Country Party support, Bruce was safe from challenge from within his own party. Unwisely he fell into the practice of consulting the National Party organizers, but few others in the party. In his own view the coalition lacked talent. A steady worker himself, in the office at 8.30 a.m. and using a dictating machine at home, he mastered quickly the detail of government business. His capacity for systematic analysis complemented Page's voluble and erratic brilliance and they worked together harmoniously enough; but it was Pearce to whom he later paid tribute: 'Much of my "courage" as Prime Minister was due to Pearce's pricking me on'.

Attracted to planning big, Bruce set about solving three national problems: economic development, Federal relations and national security. The solutions were interrelated. Security through membership of the Empire would be enhanced if market and investment opportunities between Australia and Britain were maximized; Australia's attractiveness as an investment area would be greater if the outstanding problems between the Commonwealth and the States were solved. Overseas capital must play an important role in its further industrial development. Bruce anticipated Germany would try to regain lost territory and that she would not be in a position to do so for fifteen years. There was no pressing security problem. His willingness to accept British strategic planning, and to add to the Australian fleet in keeping with that plan, should be recognized as being part of a wider strategy on resources. He wanted to attract British capital to Australia. He also wanted to ensure that the links forged by trade and investment would strengthen the country to which Australia looked for its defence.

Bruce was a close observer of American production methods and he warned that a flood of their products would destroy existing price levels. In much the way he lectured his shareholders, he pushed the British to recognize the importance of the Australian market for their ailing industry and the danger to that market of any undermining of prices for Australian exports: to protect their own market, they should protect Australia's market. He expected them to see the logic of Imperial preference. The Empire had 'Men, Money and Markets'; utilized properly these could ensure the industrial strength of Britain as well as of Australia.

For Australia to be an attractive investment area, the Federal system had to be seen to work satisfactorily. At heart Bruce may have been a centralist; in practice his aim was the elimination of friction between Australia's seven governments, the provision of adequate fiscal sources for the States, and the creation of machinery to set guidelines for public borrowing. Significantly, in 1923 he called the premiers together before putting any legislation to parliament. He failed to get agreement on either of his key proposals: a division of the tax field and a distribution by industries of the arbitration jurisdiction of the Commonwealth and the States. He allowed only a short session of parliament for essential business before leaving for the 1923 Imperial Conference.

Bruce tried to commit the British government to his policies for Empire development but he made little headway, apart from enlarging the existing settlement and migration agreement. As the States had used only a small portion of the money available, this had symbolic rather than real importance. His strategy was to affirm Empire unity, the Chanak incident having strained relations in 1922. He quickly abandoned a proposal for a Pacific League of Nations when warned of Canada's objections. Though he was unhappy about the United Kingdom's habit of deciding foreign policy on its own while expecting the Dominions to provide military forces when needed, he was opposed then, and until 1939, to any breaching of the diplomatic unity of Empire. Nevertheless he wished to be better informed, and on his return he arranged for the appointment of R. G. (Baron) Casey as his liaison officer in London. Casey found rooms in the cabinet secretariat, becoming in effect Bruce's personal diplomat. Bruce also placed F. L. McDougall [q.v.] in Australia House as his economic adviser and came to rely heavily on his opinion, especially in trying out an idea.

As an anti-socialist prime minister, Bruce was prepared to sell the Commonwealth Shipping Line, though his requirements on freight charges delayed the sale until 1928. He was not satisfied, however, with the efficiency of Australian industry and hoped to improve productivity by taking expert advice and creating advisory services. His outstanding success was the Council for Scientific and Industrial Research which was to find scientific answers for producers' problems. Bruce wanted the best British scientists to establish it and took a personal interest in finding them. His inclination to seek British experts may have reflected British prejudice or been intended to reassure Bri

tish capital that matters were well managed in Australia. He got J. Ainsworth from the British Colonial Service to report on the administration of New Guinea, appointed (Sir) Harry Brown [q.v.] as secretary to the Postmaster-General's Department, and looked around for a top-class English banker to be governor of the Commonwealth Bank. The bank's charter had been altered in 1924 to provide for the appointment of a board of businessmen and to facilitate its development as a central bank.

During Sir Littleton Groom's [q.v.] absence in 1924 Bruce was acting attorney-general in a period when the unions were ready to test their strength against employers. The post-war recession had passed. The waterfront was busy and both watersiders and seamen were taking advantage of this to regain privileges lost in 1917 and to improve their appallingly bad working conditions. Bruce intervened with Lord Inchcape to assist watersiders but was not prepared to ignore persistent flouting of awards. Before Groom returned in 1925 application was made to deregister the seamen's union.

Bruce never had a consistent policy on industrial relations. He was impatient of complaints by employers about arbitration and included them in his recurring appeal for a new spirit of co-operation in industry. In his own experience he had found the solution to rising costs was to improve efficiency and increase turnover, and it is clear that he believed that too often the employer who complained had not put his own house in order. Yet he had no sympathy for unions persistently using the strike-weapon: in 1925 he had controversial amendments to the Navigation and Immigration Acts passed to break a strike; but he was unresponsive to complaints from employers that the dual system of arbitration allowed unions to shop around. In 1926 he strengthened the Federal court and sought constitutional amendment to gain full industrial powers for the Commonwealth.

When an attempt was made under the amended Immigration Act to deport T. Walsh [q.v. Pankhurst] and J. Johnson, Labor challenged Bruce to go to the country. He won a resounding victory in November 1925. In a campaign which linked strikes and the 'foreign agitator' with loss of wages and rising prices he appealed for law and order, directing that appeal to women especially. Since becoming prime minister Bruce had visited all States and many outback centres. He had been solicitous of women's support, speaking at their meetings and agreeing to the inclusion of women in official delegations. The following he built up by personal contact may have been more important in winning the election than the appeal to law and order; but it was his denunciation of the 'wreckers who would plunge us into the chaos and misery of class war' that afterwards clung to him.

In the new ministry J. G. Latham [q.v.] replaced Groom as attorney-general. Latham had only recently joined the National Party, having entered parliament with the support of the Single Purpose League, its purpose being the abolition of compulsory arbitration. In cabinet Latham argued against penalty clauses in the arbitration Act. It was a curious appointment if Bruce's intention at that stage was to get tough with the unions. Groom resented his demotion to Speaker; in 1929 his refusal to vote lost the crucial division for the government.

After a short session and the unsuccessful campaign for constitutional amendment, Bruce left for the 1926 Imperial Conference. As in 1923 he was indifferent if not opposed to Dominion moves to define autonomy. Again he tried to persuade the British of the merits of Imperial preference. He secured a broadening of the terms of the settlement and migration agreement, which allowed the money to be used not merely for putting migrants on the land but also for associated development works. One of his objectives was a national transport system: he had already provided Federal money for roads and was also working towards standardization of railway gauges.

While in London Bruce had heard criticism in financial circles of Australia's 'vociferous' borrowing. He feared an adverse effect on future loans and, partly to counter that but also in furtherance of his long-term aims, he arranged for an officially sponsored delegation of businessmen to visit Australia. His insistence on getting leading industrialists delayed its departure, and by the time the British Economic Mission reached Australia in September 1928 the deteriorating economic situation made a favourable report unlikely.

Bruce was moving steadily towards firmer Commonwealth control of the economy and a new tariff policy. His intentions were to give full protection to those manufactures where the Australian market was adequate 'to keep going plants of sufficient magnitude to constitute an economic unit', and to give protection only to those manufactures, opening the rest of the market to British goods. Further, he would fix duties for a number of years so British industry could plan production for the Australian market. Finally, he envisaged a trade treaty with similar guarantees for Australian produce. The Economic Mission's role was to report the prospects for British industry and so create the necessary pressure in Britain to bring the plan to completion. He was collecting information for the mission through the Development and Migration Commission and a secret inquiry into the cost of the tariff.

In 1927 Bruce also moved decisively to settle financial relations between the Commonwealth and the States, having terminated *per capita* payments and provided only temporary relief. He changed the basis of negotiation from a division of the tax field to funding State debts, making the offer sufficiently attractive to obtain in return approval for the Loan Council to become the authorizing body for public borrowing. The agreement was made binding by constitutional amendment in 1928. It was to be a more effective weapon against recalcitrant States than he anticipated. Appropriately, given that shift of power, he also oversaw in 1927 the move of parliament and some government departments to Canberra.

In his overarching plan for Australia's future development the pieces were beginning to fall into place. But Bruce's planning went astray. In a major review of the Commonwealth Conciliation and Arbitration Act in 1928 the government required the court to consider the economic effects of its awards, and included in the amended Act penalty clauses and provision for compulsory court-supervised ballots which were objectionable to unionists. On the eve of the 1928 election when a waterside strike threatened, Bruce rushed through legislation to create a system of licensing waterfront labour designed to break the union. On this he had taken Pearce's advice. It was presented to the electorate as a firm stand against industrial anarchy, and endorsed, but the cumulative effect of the two Acts was industrial conflict accompanied by violence. Both helped to discredit Bruce.

When he called the premiers together in January 1929 to meet the Economic Mission, he was still looking forward to new policies. Throughout his years as prime minister Bruce had stalled on social reform, promising national insurance, child endowment and finance for housing, but postponing action on all but the last. He had calculated costs before acting. Yet in 1929 he could write in confidence to McDougall: 'The world is now so far advanced that we have to recognize we must face great expenditure upon social amelioration, and the only way to solve our problems is to adopt the same course as every modern business has been forced to ... of expanding our turnover rather than imagining we can solve our difficulties by reducing our expenses'. He had been patiently putting together a complex plan for greater national turnover.

It was too late. Unemployment was increasing. Employers wanted more immediate solutions to the problem of costs. In March 1929 on the northern coalfields John Brown [q.v.] locked out his miners. Latham insisted he be prosecuted but Bruce, in a futile attempt to negotiate a settlement, stopped the prosecution. He had called a premiers' conference for May to hammer out future economic and social policies. Instead the Nationalist premiers met ahead and agreed they would insist on the Commonwealth vacating the field of arbitration. That ultimatum destroyed Bruce's intentions for the conference: without the support of premiers of his own party he could not succeed. Within the parliamentary party his position had deteriorated. Throughout, he had resisted advice to bring Hughes into the ministry and more recently had brushed aside a concerted attempt by W. A. Watt, (Sir) W. Massy Greene [qq.v] and Hughes for changes. W. M. Marks [q.v.] had a grievance about the entertainment tax. In April Latham had contemplated resigning.

In the August budget session, Bruce introduced the bill to abolish the Commmonwealth Arbitration Court and Hughes marshalled the dissidents to bring about his defeat. Bruce fought a poor campaign in defence of a measure which it seems doubtful he ever desired. When the Labor Party sought some arrangement which would save the court, Bruce offered to stand aside for Latham. Latham insisted the bill go forward. It was a tough budget and Bruce did not expect to win the election but the loss of his own seat was unexpected. On 22 October 1929 he ceased to be prime minister.

Bruce intended to return. He predicted Labor would be unable to meet its election promises and there would be a swing against it. He would drop out of the news for about a year. He sailed for England in December, travelled in Europe and furthered his contacts with British industrialists. He was working down the familiar lines of a rational division of investment opportunities. Behind the scenes he was negotiating for the Bank of England to provide some relief on the acute problem of Australian government overdrafts. It would not do so, Bruce advised, unless convinced Australia was taking steps to get on a sounder financial and economic basis: the purpose of Sir Otto Niemeyer's visit was 'to convey this without appearing to dictate to Australia, and Scullin's [q.v.] job will be to try and make some arrangement without it appearing to the public in Australia that the government had been dictated to'.

In November 1930 Bruce returned to Australia earlier than he had intended. The government had begun to disintegrate, but the more pressing reason was the difficulties of Paterson, Laing & Bruce. As a result of the Scullin tariff it was losing customers. In 1930 it drew on reserves to pay a reduced dividend and in 1931 reported a substantial trading loss. When a snap election was held in December 1931 Bruce found for a second time his business blocked his political advancement, on this occasion irretrievably. He was back in London explaining the firm's poor performance to the shareholders. Though he was returned for Flinders, he was still at sea when the new ministry was formed. His position in it was assistant treasurer. His own conception of his role was as a steadying influence on the changeable Lyons [q.v.] but he later confided he had no desire to serve Joe again.

Lyons never allowed Bruce the opportunity to threaten his position. He appointed him minister in London and leader of the delegation to the Ottawa Conference. When Bruce sailed in June 1932, having briefly filled in for Latham at External Affairs, his career in politics was over. Well before he could make any moves to return, Lyons offered him the high commissionership in London and when Bruce endeavoured to defer his decision, still contemplating a return to politics and expecting Lyons's health would not hold up, Lyons forced the issue in September 1933.

At Ottawa Bruce consolidated his reputation as a tough negotiator, getting last-moment concessions from the United Kingdom on meat quotas. From there he went to London to renegotiate Australia's debt. Blocked by a government embargo on the raising of new capital, Bruce used his old City contacts to break through. To the chancellor of the exchequer he argued that the Australian people could not be held from default much longer and default would seriously damage British interests. He got access to the money market and carried through the series of conversion loans which by 1935 had substantially reduced interest payments. He had finely judged the mood of the market and the terms it would accept.

As high commissioner in 1933-45 Bruce was closely involved in moves to protect and extend the concessions for Australian produce gained at Ottawa. Discussion of these issues occupied much of his three-month visit home in 1934. He represented Australia at the League of Nations in 1932-39, with a seat on the council in 1933-36. He had not sought the latter, and in private was critical of the 'interminable orations' at the League which dodged 'the issues that count'.

Nevertheless Bruce's reputation as an international statesman was established during the years in which he travelled between London and Geneva while crisis succeeded crisis and the League floundered. When Turkey sought revision of the Straits Convention in 1936 Bruce was accepted unanimously as president of the Montreux conference and his chairing of it was widely acclaimed. He declined another invitation that year to chair a commission on Palestine. The League counted less to Bruce than the contacts he established there. Meeting as an equal with British ministers in Geneva, it became easier in London to get access to senior ministers and to confidential information which enabled him to be accepted as an adviser to the British government in his own right, while also acting as the main adviser to the Australian government. His technique was to send a situation-appraisal to his prime minister with prior warning of the decision he might need to take, so that in most instances the decision when made was as Bruce advised. He had a comparable influence on British policy only on the abdication, where his insistence that Mrs Simpson would not be accepted as queen spurred Baldwin to confront the King.

During the Abyssinian crisis Bruce was a reluctant supporter of sanctions and among the first to advise reconciliation with Italy after partial sanctions had failed to save Abyssinia. The key to peace in Europe he thought was to detach Italy from Germany. He urged the British to recognize this and to formulate clearly their intentions regarding Germany's claims. France, he repeatedly warned, would drag England into a European war: France would neither concede anything to Germany nor take effective action to block her, would not fight for Czechoslovakia, and could not assist Poland. An 'unfulfillable guarantee' to Poland was of utmost danger. In the last days before the war Bruce desperately tried to avert that disaster.

His concern throughout was the repercussions on Australia of Britain's situation in Europe and her lack of policy on China: Bruce recognized the danger to Australia lay in a Pacific war coinciding with a European war. As early as 1933 he was warning Australian ministers that the Royal Navy might not be available when needed: nevertheless he went on seeking assurances that it would. He welcomed (Baron) Hankey's visit in 1934 as a step towards more concrete proposals and was hopeful of getting these from the 1937 Imperial Conference. Again disappointed, he switched tactics in 1938. He began negotiations for large-scale aircraft production in the Dominions, seeking guaranteed orders and technical assistance from England to make the Australian plant viable. He was adjusting earlier ideas on rationalizing Empire production to a war situation. The natural follow-on after World War II began was the Empire air training scheme. He anticipated

bombing would interrupt production in Britain and his plans for Australian production had run into difficulties. It was easier, he argued, to take men to the machines for final training than the machines to the men.

In December 1938 on his way to Australia and in May 1939 on his way back, Bruce had seen the American president. The conversations dealt with the likelihood of American support if Japan moved south, but the president regarded a public commitment as premature. When war started Bruce and (Sir Robert) Menzies were in complete agreement that Australia should not commit its forces to a European war while Japan's intentions were unclear. Bruce requested information from the British and he regarded the Admiralty's reply as misleadingly reassuring. None the less it persuaded Casey, then minister in London, and on his advice the troops were promised.

Bruce was already offside with Churchill and he never regained his former standing. Foreseeing the rapidity with which Poland would be over-run, Bruce had tried to mobilize support for a clear definition of peace aims, hoping thereby to avert the destruction of Europe. Meeting with little success, he had put his hopes on Churchill, only to find he had no aim but to smash Germany. Throughout the 'phoney war' Bruce pursued this issue beyond the tolerance of erstwhile admirers in high circles. He had moved almost to President Wilson's position of a quarter of a century earlier. If the world was to be safe after the war the victors had to show something more than acquisitiveness and vindictiveness. The aims he wanted stated as a basis for peace included equality of opportunity for nations, economic and social policies which would obviate recurring boom and depression, and programmes to improve the world food situation. Since the world economic conference in London in 1933 Bruce was concerned about national policies for restricting production as a means of raising prices; at the League of Nations he had chaired the committee which reported on world nutrition. He was moving towards linking these. If more investment was directed to the underdeveloped countries, rising living standards there would ensure the prosperity of the industrial nations. So long as he was trying to mobilize support for a statement on allied peace aims, London was the place where the decisive issues for the future of the world would be determined. To Menzies' increasingly urgent requests in late 1939 for him to go to Washington as Australia's first ambassador, he made excuses.

Bruce continued as high commissioner, loyally serving every wartime Australian government. He joined the War Cabinet in 1942 but had little influence; to his chagrin he found he was invited only on selected occasions. In August 1945 his retirement was announced. In December he returned home. In 1939 on his visit to Australia Lyons had invited him to rejoin the government, but the next day withdrew the offer. Following Lyons's death on 8 April, Page invited him to come back as leader. When it became apparent that the unanimous support of both parties was not forthcoming, Bruce declined the offer. In 1946 the possibility of returning to politics was again canvassed. He was 63 and Labor was securely in office. After allowing the rumours to circulate for four months he left abruptly for England in early April. In the 1947 New Year honours Bruce received a viscountcy, and chose to be Bruce of Melbourne. To an old friend he admitted to having reversed all his previous decisions, having discovered there was 'no niche for me in Australia'. He accepted the honour so as to have a platform if he ever had something to say, but he used it rarely. When he did speak in the Lords it was on familiar lines of doing more for the underdeveloped world. During the Cold War he was arguing that 'well-fed men are not apt to become revolutionaries'.

In London, Bruce was still respected for his business acumen and he became a director of the Peninsular & Oriental and British India Steam Navigation companies and of the Royal Exchange Assurance. He joined the London boards of the National Bank of Australasia and of National Mutual Life. In 1947-57 he was chairman of the British Finance Corporation for Industry Ltd. His inclination always had been to public service and he welcomed an invitation to be chairman of the preparation commission and then of the World Food Council of the Food and Agriculture Organization of the United Nations, 1946-51. It was a fitting culmination to the work he had done on nutrition for the League but its scope was much more limited than the proposals he had tried so doggedly to have accepted as the Allies' peace aims.

Late in life he said the three things which had pleased him most were his Cambridge blue, his captaincy of the Royal and Ancient Golf Club of St Andrews and his fellowship of the Royal Society (1944). This was a characteristic Bruce statement: he had been the dominating figure in Australian politics in the 1920s and later counsellor to leading statesmen of other nations, yet the achievements which he claimed for himself were personal. The others were shared. Bruce believed in the team, though he preferred to lead rather than to follow. He took advice from those whom he trusted and, having made his decision, he accepted responsibility: those close to him remembered, with affection, that if the decision subsequently appeared wrong, there were no recriminations. When invited to return to politics, he waited for evidence that the party was solidly behind him and, finding it was not, he declined. He concealed his disappointment. Accustomed from an early age to exercise authority, he had no relish for serving under others, but neither did he wish to be a focus for division in his party. He was never nakedly ambitious, yet his advice to a younger man that ambition was necessary to succeed in politics undoubtedly was a reflection on himself. He did not like to appear to have been pressured. He could be tough to his own supporters and to his political opponents. The objections of the former were muted but not the latter's: in the folk memory of the Australian labour movement, Bruce was its arch-enemy.

Bruce went out to meet the people, and on tour and as a host he had a charm few could resist. Yet his reluctance to wheel and deal, his propensity to argue from basic principles, and his toughness once a decision was taken, marked him out as exceptional. In consequence, he was regarded, mistakenly, as an Englishman who happened to have been born in Australia: too aloof and reserved to be an Australian. His spats seemed to confirm this. Having worn borrowed spats to the football to protect an old ankle injury from the chill of a damp Melbourne day, when the press scoffed he persisted in wearing them: he would not accept dictation on what he wore. As he was tall, well-built and, in the conventions of his time, handsome, the spats were the joy of cartoonists.

From the time he had been required to live in London to represent the family, Bruce retained a strong sense of being an Australian. The English never doubted whose interests he had at heart. His vision had extended from his own country to the world but, invited in 1951 to be the first chancellor of the Australian National University, he accepted. Other work kept him in England and his visits were infrequent and for ceremonial occasions. This, his last public office, linked his abiding interest in the beneficial uses of science and his long-standing desire to be of service to Australia; he did not relinquish it until 1961. Bruce continued to live in London where he died on 25 August 1967. His wife, who had shared his confidences, had died in March. His will provided a generous endowment for the university and directed that his ashes be scattered over Canberra.

E. C. G. Page, *Truant surgeon*, A. Mozley ed

(Syd, 1963); C. Edwards, *Bruce of Melbourne* (Lond, 1965); A. Stirling, *Lord Bruce: the London years* (Melb, 1974); R. G. Neale (ed), *Documents on Australian foreign policy, 1937-49*, 1-2 (Canb, 1975-76); Paterson, Laing & Bruce, *Annual Report to Shareholders*, 1907-34; D. Carlton, 'The Dominions and British policy in the Abyssinian crisis', *J of Imperial & Cwlth Hist*, Oct 1972; P. G. Edwards, 'S. M. Bruce ... and Australia's war aims and peace aims, 1939-40', *Hist Studies*, no 66, Apr 1976; G. T. Powell, The role of the Commonwealth government in industrial relations, 1923-1929 (M.A. thesis, ANU, 1974); S. M. Bruce papers, CRS A1420-21, M100-14, A1486-96, Accession CP362/4-5, AA1970/555-9 (AAO, Canb); H. Brookes papers (NL); J. Latham papers (NL); Paterson, Laing & Bruce records (ANU Archives); G. F. Pearce papers (NL).   HEATHER RADI

BRUCE, THEODORE (1847-1911), auctioneer and politician, was born on 5 April 1847 at Leeds West, Yorkshire, England, son of William Bruce, wool and oil merchant and his wife Charlotte, née Baines. His maternal grandfather was Edward Baines, author and politician and founder of the influential daily newspaper, the *Leeds Mercury*. The family arrived in South Australia in 1852 and Theodore was educated at J. L. Young's [q.v.6] Adelaide Educational Institution and the Collegiate School of St Peter. He then spent six or seven years on stations in the far north, experience which convinced him of the potential for development of the Northern Territory. He returned to Adelaide to join the office of Messrs (R. I.) Stow [q.v.6] & Bruce, but soon moved to the National Bank of Australasia for which he worked for several years, again in the far north. On 24 August 1876 in St Luke's Church, Adelaide, he married Mary Ellen McFie; at this time Bruce was a commercial traveller.

About 1880 he joined forces with his brother-in-law G. S. Aldridge, chairman of the Stock Exchange of Adelaide, in Henning, Bruce & Aldridge, an auctioneering concern which also established a brewery at Broken Hill. The partnership was dissolved in 1889 and Bruce continued the auctioneering business alone from his offices in the Old Exchange, Pirie Street. 'He was a master in every way with the hammer, being bright, good natured, witty and quick'. In 1885 he had been commissioned lieutenant in the Rifle Volunteer Force. Next year he helped form the Goodwood Literary Society, and he was the first president of the Goodwood Institute.

Much of the last twenty years of his life Bruce devoted to civic affairs. For two years he represented Goodwood Ward in the Unley City Council, and in 1897-98 was mayor. He was also a member of the Adelaide City Council for the Hindmarsh Ward from 1894;

an alderman in 1900, as mayor of Adelaide in 1904-07 he was closely involved with Premier Tom Price [q.v.] in planning the tramways scheme, a very substantial achievement; he was city council representative on the Municipal Tramways Trust until 1909. The regulation of the meat supply and the creation of abattoirs in the metropolitan area were also part of Bruce's municipal work

His parliamentary aspirations were delayed by six electoral defeats, but in 1909 he stood as a Liberal for the Central District in the Legislative Council and 'routed the Socialistic candidate'. Described as a 'Progressivist' he adopted advanced principles wherever desirable and practicable. Bruce's speeches ranged over a wide group of questions: municipal works, quality control of food, and loans for low cost housing. He was respected for his business expertise and was 'fearless in expressing his views'.

Bruce was a patron of the arts and sport, a racehorse-owner and a member of the Stock Exchange of Adelaide. He was elected first president of the Yorkshire Society the day before he died at his Mount Lofty home on 1 July 1911, after suffering for several years from rheumatism for which he had sought relief at hot springs in New Zealand. He was survived by his wife, two daughters and three sons and his estate was sworn for probate at £15 927.

J. J. Pascoe (ed), *History of Adelaide and vicinity* (Adel, 1901); H. T. Burgess, *Cyclopedia of South Australia* (Adel, 1907-09); Universal Publicity Co., *The official civic record of South Australia* (Adel, 1936); G. B. Payne, *History of Unley, 1871-1971* (Unley, 1972); *Evening Journal*, 29 Feb 1896; *Observer* (Adel), 10 Dec 1904; *Advertiser* (Adel), 2 July 1911; biog index, *and* news-cuttings 1223/37 (SAA).   ERIC RICHARDS

BRUCE, SIR WALLACE (1878-1944), insurance broker and commission merchant, was born on 3 August 1878 at Kapunda, South Australia, son of John Albert Bruce, agent, and his wife Harriett Ellen, née Cowie. He was educated at Prince Alfred College, Adelaide, and worked for the Alliance Assurance Co. Ltd for about ten years. For two years he was the commercial manager of the Victoria Tannery at Hindmarsh, but in 1904 he opened his own insurance business, Wallace Bruce & Co., at 3 Old Exchange, Pirie Street, Adelaide. Next year, on 11 October, he married Winifred Drummond Reid at the Congregational Church, North Adelaide.

Bruce built up a successful enterprise which dealt with prominent city, country and overseas clients. He established a

Western Australian agency and employed correspondents in Melbourne and Sydney. His solid business reputation led him into the directorates of many large South Australian enterprises, including Holden's Motor Body Builders Ltd, the Adelaide Cement Co. Ltd, Clarkson Ltd, the British Automobile Finance Co. of South Australia, the South Australian Gas Co., and Clutterbuck Bros (Adelaide) Ltd (of which he was also chairman). From 1923 he was a trustee of the Savings Bank of South Australia and in 1923-25 he was president of the local Taxpayers' Association. In 1925-27 he was president of the Adelaide Chamber of Commerce and in 1927-28 of the Associated Chambers of Commerce of Australia. In 1916-25 he was on the Adelaide City Council and was lord mayor in 1925-27, being twice unopposed. He represented the council on the Municipal Tramways Trust in 1919-25 and, after a visit to Europe and the United States of America in 1922, he produced a report for the government on tramways. He was knighted in 1927. It was said of Bruce that 'although not a prolific speaker, his remarks are listened to with attention and respect'. He chaired the Industrial Peace Conference of 1928-29 in Melbourne and Sydney which sought solutions to industrial relations problems, and in April 1929 presided over a round-table conference on reopening the New South Wales coal-mines.

Bruce's most important appointment was in 1932 when he chaired a Commonwealth government committee to investigate unemployment; its membership included the economists L. F. Giblin, R. C. Mills, E. O. G. Shann [qq.v.] and L. G. Melville. They advised that little could be done to reduce unemployment in the short run, and that the first priority should be the reduction of production costs in the Australian economy. While advocating that the exchange rate should be managed to restore employment and that the tariff be reviewed, the Wallace Bruce report opposed any public works expenditure which was not self-financing. It recommended the creation of State employment councils to co-ordinate sustenance and relief measures being undertaken by numerous government departments and charities, and to prune unproductive programmes. In 1935 Bruce became chairman of the South Australian Harbour Board.

He had wide interests in sport and was a trustee of the South Australian Cricketing Association from 1928. Survived by one son and four daughters, Bruce died in Adelaide of cardio-vascular disease on 16 November 1944. His estate was sworn for probate at £67 028.

H. T. Burgess, *The cyclopedia of South Australia*,
1 (Adel, 1907); Associated Publishing Service, *The civic record of South Australia 1921-1923* (Adel, 1924); E. O. G. Shann (ed), *The Australian price-structure, 1932* (Syd, 1933); Universal Publicity Co., *The official civic record of South Australia* (Adel, 1936); L. F. Giblin, *The growth of a central bank* (Melb, 1951); C. B. Schedvin, *Australia and the great depression* (Syd, 1970); *Observer* (Adel), 11 Mar 1922; *SMH*, 7 Dec 1928; *Advertiser* (Adel), 17 Nov 1944.

ERIC RICHARDS

BRUCHE, SIR JULIUS HENRY (1873-1961), soldier, was born on 6 March 1873 at North Melbourne, son of William Julius Maximilian Bruche, corn merchant, and his wife Elise Dorothea Henrietta, née Goetz, both German-born. Educated at Scotch College and the University of Melbourne, he was admitted to the Supreme Court of Victoria as a barrister and solicitor in 1898, but abandoned the legal profession that year to become a regular soldier. Seven years earlier he had been commissioned in the 1st Battalion, Victorian Rifles; in July 1898 he joined the Permanent Military Forces as a lieutenant and was promoted captain next February. In 1898-1903 he was adjutant of the 1st and 2nd Battalions.

On the outbreak of the South African War Bruche was selected for special service with the British Army and in December 1899-January 1900 was attached to the 3rd Battalion, Grenadier Guards, at Modder River. He served with the Australian Regiment as quartermaster and then with the Victorian Mounted Rifles as adjutant, and took part in operations in Cape Colony and the Orange Free State. He returned home in December 1900 but in February 1902 went back to South Africa with the 2nd Battalion, Australian Commonwealth Horse.

Bruche served on the Victorian administrative and instructional staff in 1903-05. On 12 April 1904 at St Thomas's Anglican Church, North Sydney, he married Dorothy Annette McFarland; there were twin daughters of the marriage. In 1905 he was made deputy assistant adjutant general and was promoted major in 1906. Next year the office of chief commissioner of police fell vacant and Bruche applied, strongly supported by his friend (Sir) John Monash [q.v.] who described him as 'the one real live and up to date man among our Victorian permanent officers', 'young and energetic' with a 'magnetic personality . . . vigour and force of character . . . a cultured mind . . . and a loyal temperament'. Bruche's application failed. He was to try for the position, again unsuccessfully and with Monash's support, in 1912, 1920 and 1922. In 1910 he went to England on a year's exchange duty and on his return was appointed D.A.A.G. in Tasmania; he was promoted lieut-colonel in July 1912 and next February was posted to Queensland, first as D.A.A.G. and then as assistant adjutant general.

Soon after war was declared in 1914 Bruche, who might reasonably have expected a field command, was made commandant in Western Australia. He weathered several virulent attacks made on him because of his German origins and in June 1916 was appointed to the Australian Imperial Force as colonel. He was attached to A.I.F. headquarters in London for four months before joining the 5th Australian Division on the Western Front as assistant adjutant and quartermaster general. Monash, who considered that he had been given 'a very rough spin' by the authorities, had helped secure the appointment and Bruche served with distinction until after the Armistice. The 5th Division historian was later to praise his 'great professional ability', though it was his 'character and broad humanity' that 'made his influence so profoundly and so beneficially felt throughout the division'. In January 1919 Monash chose Bruche to assist him in the Repatriation and Demobilization Department in London as director of non-military employment. He returned to Australia in December, having been mentioned in dispatches five times and appointed C.M.G. and C.B.

Bruche was promoted colonel in 1920 and major general in 1923, and from 1920 until his retirement held the highest posts the Australian Army could offer. He was commandant in New South Wales in 1920-21 and 1926-27 and in Queensland in 1921-25, and was adjutant general of the Australian forces in 1927-29. For the next two years he was senior military representative at Australia House, London, and Australian representative on the Imperial General Staff at the War Office. He returned home in May 1931 to become commandant of the Royal Military College, Duntroon, but held the position only until October when he became chief of the General Staff. He retired in 1935 and was appointed K.C.B. that year. Survived by Lady Bruche and one of his daughters, he died in Melbourne on 28 April 1961 and was cremated with Anglican rites.

Bruche maintained high standards of conduct in both his service and private lives. He was an able staff officer whose attention to detail did not tend to obscure the wider picture. He was a strict disciplinarian with a reputation, perhaps undeserved, of being a martinet. What is true is that he was almost a terror to those who did not match his own estimate of performance. His rather brusque manner could probably be attributed to innate shyness.

Aust Defence Dept, *Official records of the Australian military contingents to the war in South Africa*, P. L. Murray ed (Melb, 1912); A. D. Ellis, *The story of the Fifth Australian Division* (Lond, 1920?); C. E. W. Bean, *The A.I.F. in France*, 1917, 1918 (Syd, 1933, 1942); *London Gazette*, 3 June 1935; *United Service* (Syd), July 1962; *Australasian*, 11 Nov 1899; *SMH*, 25 March 1927, 29 Dec 1928, 14 May 1931, 2 May 1961; *Age*, 29 Apr 1961; Monash papers.   SYDNEY ROWELL*

BRUNNICH, JOHANNES CHRISTIAN (1861-1933), agricultural chemist, was born on 11 September 1861 at Görz, Austria-Hungary (now Gorizia, Italy), son of Christian Christoph Brünnich, Lutheran pastor and mathematician, and his wife Pauline Therese, née Kühne. Reared in Bohemia, he went with his family to Stäfa (canton Zurich), Switzerland, in October 1874 and won entry to the Federal Polytechnic School (Eidgenössische Technische Hochschule) at Zurich. There he studied chemistry under Viktor Meyer and Georg Lunge and was briefly Meyer's personal assistant. After graduation he worked in sugar-beet factories in Bohemia and Russia, and for a firm of wholesale druggists in Tiflis (Tbilisi), Georgia.

In 1884, while performing Swiss military service as a lieutenant of field artillery, Brünnich met Dr J. J. Müller, a pioneer physician of Gayndah recently returned with his family from Queensland, who inspired him to migrate early in 1885. He became manager of a sugar-refinery and maltings at Bulimba near Brisbane. On 22 April 1886 he married Kate Terry, daughter of a Brisbane watchmaker. After briefly managing a sugar-mill at Darwin, he joined the Colonial Sugar Refining Co. in April 1887 as chemist and manager at the Homebush mill near Mackay.

By 1897 Brünnich was so respected that he was offered and accepted the position of government agricultural chemist in the new Queensland Department of Agriculture. Initially, he was also lecturer in chemistry at the new Agricultural College at Gatton, but from 1900 was free to devote all his time to departmental work. Although his plans for experimental sugar-stations were almost completely adopted, he protested about the inadequacy of his budget for 1901-02 and quarrelled with the under-secretary for agriculture, and was nearly dismissed. After a long discussion of the question during the parliamentary debates on the departmental estimates, Brünnich held his job but was subordinated to Dr W. Maxwell [q.v.]. The two clashed constantly and this unhappy conflict had repercussions throughout his career.

More than sixty papers by Brünnich on applied chemistry, soils, and plant and animal nutrition examined the problems and possibilities of agriculture in Queensland: the quality of his work was attested by (Sir) David Rivett [q.v.], Sir John Russell and other scientists. Before 1899 he recommended a survey and an exhaustive analysis of Queensland soils, a topic to which he frequently returned. He investigated water pollution in 1899 and showed how sugarmills could safely discharge waste into streams. Next year he began work on fodders, grasses, poisonous plants and the separation of useful substances from native plants and trees.

Brünnich moved with his laboratory to Brisbane in 1902 and in 1905 regained sole control of his organization. He was vice-president of the Royal Society of Queensland in 1907, president in 1908 and treasurer in 1909-14. In the years before 1918 he worked on Queensland wheat quality, performing both chemical analysis and milling and baking tests. He advised the government on the sugar industry and helped to establish payment for cane by analysis – probably one of his most important achievements.

Naturalized at Homebush in December 1891, Brünnich subsequently became an enthusiastic captain commanding the Gatton squadron of the Queensland Light Horse. Like most enemy aliens, he suffered embarrassing government interference during World War I and in 1920 was still trying to secure the return of confiscated personal papers. After the war he continued his work on animal nutrition, and prepared legislation relating to fertilizers, stock foods, margarine and pure seeds for which no precedents existed. Despite a busy professional life he found time to examine in chemistry at the Queensland College of Pharmacy and Chemistry. A foundation member and fellow of the (Royal) Australian Chemical Institute, he was also a fellow of the Royal Institute of Chemistry of Great Britain (now Royal Chemical Institute). Brünnich wrote for the farmer as much as for the scientist and had the gift of elucidating difficult concepts. His *Elementary lessons on the chemistry of farm, dairy, and household*, first published serially in 1906 in the *Queensland Agricultural Journal*, had monograph editions in 1912 and 1922 and was a text in rural colleges for many years.

Kindly, fun-loving, and enthusiastic in manner, with an unusually liberal outlook for his times, Brünnich was often blunt with superiors; although his colleagues sometimes mimicked him behind his back, they still revered him. When he retired in September 1931 he left to his successor a laboratory with a high reputation. Survived by his wife, two sons and three daughters, he died of cerebro-vascular disease on 3 July 1933 and was buried in Toowong cemetery with Anglican rites. His estate was sworn for probate at £3743.

Dept of Agr and Stock, Annual reports, *V&P* (LA Qld), 1898-1901, *PP* (Qld), 1902-31; *PD* (Qld), 1906, 2093; *Qld Agr J*, Sept 1931, and for publications; *Queenslander*, 6 July 1933.

T. J. BECKMANN

BRUNSKILL, ANTHONY (1859-1936), farmer, was born on 6 December 1859 at Maulds Meaburn, Westmorland, England, eldest son of George Brunskill, farmer, and his wife Mary Ann, née Norman. The family arrived in Sydney as assisted migrants in December 1877. Anthony worked on construction of the Junee-Bomen railway, then as a station-hand near Wagga Wagga for 25s. a week. Hard work and thrift enabled him to buy a three-horse team and plough after two years. His family settled at Wagga in 1879 and acquired a farm, Flowerdale. With his father and brother George, he contract-harvested wheat and oats with the reaping-hook until his father introduced the scythe and cradle to awed locals, who dubbed him 'Old Yankee'. On 24 July 1884, at near-by Lake Albert, Brunskill married Elizabeth Caroline Baker.

In 1888 he purchased 2300-acre (930 ha) Bon Accord with its own railway siding, and by 1890 had 1070 acres (433 ha) under cultivation. In 1892 Brunskill was also share-farming, growing hay for Sydney auctions. A pioneer in costing-practices and time-and-motion studies, he used 'mass production' techniques, in contrast to contemporary farming practices. In 1891 he won the Department of Agriculture's initial prize for the best-managed farm in the south-west. When conditions in the 1890s worsened, Brunskill sold Bon Accord to solve his financial problems.

He then bought Allonby, a 4800-acre (1940 ha) farm near Forest Hill and, by 1900, was the biggest wheat-grower in the district, with 3000 acres (1215 ha). By his common-sense farming practices and system of stock management, Brunskill made Allonby known all over Australia; the farm became one of the show-places of the Riverina. Brunskill's Border Leicester sheep-stud was among the best in New South Wales. In 1907 he won the *Sydney Mail* prize for the best farm in the southern districts. That year, with Telacon Lloyd, he paid £3632 for 1638 acres (663 ha), once part of Borambola station, and they co-operated in stock-dealing throughout eastern Australia. Brunskill's interests extended to part-ownership of Dunlop station, near Bourke. He was also chairman and managing director of Anthony Brunskill & Sons Ltd of Old Borambola station.

A tireless advocate and pioneer of fodder conservation, Brunskill was mainly responsible for the Royal Agricultural Society establishing its important fodder-conservation competitions, and was also a member of the New South Wales Sheepbreeders' Association in the 1920s. He was a member of the Murray Lands Advisory Committee in 1922 and of the Federal Pastoral Advisory Committee in 1928.

Brunskill was strongly interested in immigration; in 1910 he revisited Westmorland extolling the advantages of rural work in Australia. A big, sunburnt giant of a man, almost two metres tall, with black beard and massive shoulders, he made a remarkable impact. In 1924, the year his wool carried off honours at the Wembley Exhibition, he toured England's rural districts interviewing intending settlers for New South Wales.

Survived by his wife, four sons and two daughters, Brunskill died at Allonby on 11 December 1936 and was buried in the Methodist cemetery, Wagga Wagga. His estate was valued for probate at £46 908. His reputation as 'King of Fodder' described a perfectionist who produced hay of superlative quality.

E. Irvin, *Early inland agriculture* (Wagga Wagga, 1962); K. Swan, *A history of Wagga Wagga* (Wagga Wagga, 1970); Standing cttee on public works – proposed Wagga-Humula railway, *V&P* (LA NSW), 1902, vol 5; *Agr Gazette of NSW*, 12 (1901); *British A'sian*, 4 Aug 1910; *Pastoral Review*, Jan 1937; *Wagga Wagga Advertiser*, 15 Nov 1890, 19 Jan 1892, 12, 14 Dec 1936; *SMH*, 25 Dec 1930, 12 Dec 1936; *Land*, 18 Dec 1936; Goldsbrough Mort & Co. records, 2/145/56 (ANU Archives); information from Hon. H. S. Roberton, Curtin, ACT.   JOHN ATCHISON

BRUNTNELL, ALBERT (1866-1929), Salvation Army officer, auctioneer and politician, was born on 4 May 1866 at Llanigon, Breconshire, Wales, son of Edward Bruntnell, master blacksmith, and his wife Harriet, née Owens. Brought up by his sisters and a stern father, he was educated at the local National school, then worked in a tailor's shop. He joined the Salvation Army about 1885 and made rapid progress through its ranks as a cadet in various parts of England.

Promoted captain in July 1888, Bruntnell was sent to Melbourne, and in August next year to Sydney. In October he made a big jump in rank when promoted staff captain.

He was in Melbourne in 1890-93 and married Nellie Whittaker, a fellow officer, on 13 November 1891 in a ceremony at the Exhibition Building performed by General William Booth. In 1894 Bruntnell was promoted major and went to Christchurch, New Zealand, as the army's colonial secretary. He returned to Melbourne in 1897 as brigadier and colony commanding officer, and was in Queensland in 1900-02 in the same capacity. He became State commanding officer in Sydney in January 1903, but resigned in November when the New South Wales Alliance for the Suppression of Intemperance gave him a testimonial; personal gifts were forbidden by the army.

Bruntnell became a Methodist. An active member of the Australian Protestant Defence Association and the Protestant Federation, he was organizing secretary of the New South Wales Alliance in 1904-09, general superintendent in 1910 and vice-president for some years. He lectured on temperance all over the State. Grand chief templar of the International Order of Good Templars in 1907, he attended a meeting of its International Supreme Lodge in Washington in 1908 and that year campaigned for the United Kingdom Alliance in England. By 1912 he had become a partner in Strongman, Bruntnell & Co., auctioneers and estate agents at Burwood, and in 1914-29 was a partner in Bruntnell & Bannerman Ltd.

In 1904 he was defeated as a Liberal by E. W. O'Sullivan [q.v.] for the Belmore seat in the Legislative Assembly, but in July 1906 won a by-election for Surry Hills against John Norton [q.v.]. Next year he unsuccessfully contested Alexandria; in 1910 he won Annandale but lost it in 1913; in 1916 he won a by-election for Parramatta which he represented until 1929. Bruntnell was not essentially a party politician and that was precisely what made him a political asset, anti-wowserism notwithstanding. In 1911-12 he sat on the royal commission on the question of legalizing the totalisator and signed the majority recommendation that its introduction would add to existing evils.

Bruntnell was briefly minister of public health under W. A. Holman [q.v] in 1920, and was minister of public instruction in Sir George Fuller's [q.v.] government in 1922-25. His fondness for debate and warmth of temperament drew him into the great controversies of World War I and its aftermath, and he portrayed the British Empire as 'standing white and clean on the summit of civilization'. In 1922 to counteract disloyalty, he instituted a pledge centred round 'the flag' for schoolchildren. He reintroduced high-school fees to obtain funds not available from a depleted treasury, presided energetically over the construction and renovation of primary schools, secured large subventions for the University of Sydney in 1922-23, and encouraged vocational training for trades and agriculture; he also believed every girls' school should have a kitchen.

Although Bruntnell retained close links with the Protestant cause throughout his political career, as a minister he saw the dangers of extreme legislation and fell out with the prohibitionist R. B. S. Hammond [q.v.]; he took no part in the debates on the controversial marriage amendment (ne temere) bill. He rejected excessive Protestant demands. By refusing to admit temperance lecturers into schools or to ban a procession carrying the Host at the Eucharistic Congress of 1928, he was responding to pressures of office and applying his rule of fair play: the state should 'keep the ring'.

On the resignation of Fuller in 1925, Bruntnell narrowly lost the leadership of the National Party to (Sir) Thomas Bavin [q.v.], under whom he served as colonial secretary from October 1927. Survived by his wife and six daughters, he died of coronary vascular disease at his home at Pymble on 31 January 1929; he was buried in the Methodist section of Northern Suburbs cemetery, where a handsome memorial to him was erected in 1931. His estate was valued for probate at £2444. A portrait by Joshua Smith is held by the family.

'Briggie' Bruntnell had been popular in the party and in parliament. J. T. Lang [q.v.] recognized in him a man devoted to the people, humane, and of broad sympathies, 'whose name would not be associated with any cloud of dishonour'. Bruntnell succeeded as a politician because he had a way of winning respect, even when his views were unpopular; because he caught up and articulated values that were widely held in Australia at his time; and because he was conspicuously not just a politician.

J. D. Bollen, *Protestantism and social reform in New South Wales 1890-1910* (Melb, 1972); B. A. Mitchell, *Teachers, education, and politics* (Brisb, 1975); *Fighting Line*, 18 Oct 1913; *Aust National Review*, 25 Feb 1929, 26 Feb 1931; *Bulletin*, 6 Feb 1929; *SMH*, 9 Feb 1929; A. Fairley, The failure of prohibition in New South Wales ... 1913-1928 (B.A. Hons thesis, Univ NSW, 1968); R. W. Johnston, The Temperance Alliance and New South Wales State politics, 1904 to 1913 (B.A. Hons thesis, Univ NSW, 1972); news-cuttings held by Miss L. M. Bruntnell, Gordon, NSW.

J. D. BOLLEN

BRUNTON, SIR WILLIAM (1867-1938), businessman and lord mayor, was born on 1 February 1867 at Carlton, Victoria, son of David Brunton, mason, and his wife Margaret, née Lonie, both Scottish-born. He was educated at Princes Hill State School and, after his father died, was apprenticed in 1880 as a carpenter and joiner. Seven years later Brunton was invited to join his uncle's business, Currie & Richards, manufacturers of galvanized spouting and ironware. He became a partner and, in 1918 when a proprietary company was formed, a managing director, retaining a lifelong connexion with the firm. He consolidated his business career by accepting directorships with London Stores Ltd, the Standard Mutual Building Society, and the Metropolitan Gas and Australasian Advertising companies.

Brunton entered the Melbourne City Council for Victoria Ward, which took in North Carlton, in January 1913. He was one of the council's many representatives on the Melbourne and Metropolitan Board of Works in 1919-30. In October 1923 he was elected lord mayor to replace the ailing Sir John Swanson [q.v.], served three successive terms and voluntarily relinquished the office in 1926. As chairman of the National War Memorial of Victoria Committee he worked toward the creation of the Shrine of Remembrance. He developed the Lord Mayor's Fund for Metropolitan Hospitals and Charities and in 1926 helped to raise £200 000 for victims of bushfires in Gippsland. Brunton was knighted in 1926 and elected alderman in 1929. Having been a member of the committee of management of the Royal Melbourne Hospital for fourteen years, he resigned as vice-president in December 1936 after a disagreement over the site for its new building.

Brunton had been thrust into public prominence during the police strike which began on 31 October 1923. On 2 November, at the request of the (Sir) H. S. W. Lawson [q.v.] ministry, Brunton made use of council powers to recruit special constables. By Saturday, 3 November, one hundred had been enrolled. That evening saw serious rioting and looting in the city: he interviewed the attorney-general Sir Arthur Robinson [q.v.], and arranged for Sir John Monash and Brigadier General H. E. Elliott [qq.v.] to take charge of the 'specials' and control the situation from the Town Hall. On 5 November the ministry announced Brunton's appointment as chairman of an executive committee, with the responsibility of co-ordinating services and the power to enrol a force of 5000; the committee met regularly over the next few weeks. The minority Labor councillors were highly critical of his actions: they believed that the Lawson ministry had escalated the situation and, with Brunton's active connivance, had shelved responsibility onto the council.

During Brunton's mayoralty, metropolitan growth and the increasing number of motor vehicles presented new problems; while city planning and public works were gravely hindered by the division of authority into some two dozen municipalities and other bodies with limited powers. In 1925, on the suggestion of the minister for public works, the Melbourne City Council convened a conference on the subject of a Greater Melbourne council, with Brunton as chairman. He also chaired the thirteen-man committee that prepared a draft report, which recommended that a federal scheme, like the London County Council, be adopted, with a new metropolitan body co-ordinating and controlling essential services. The report was adopted with amendments by the conference in June and was referred to constituent councils. The city council considered the report in September and rejected it, Brunton himself voting against the scheme. The proposal lapsed, but the 'Brunton Report', as it became known, remained for many years the basis for Greater Melbourne projections.

On 14 February 1894 Brunton had married Jessie Wray of Carlton, who became noted for her philanthropy; she died in 1927. On 16 November 1932 in Sydney he married a lifelong friend, Christine Martha McFadden. Brunton had no children but took a great interest in child welfare, particularly the playgrounds movement. He was a Presbyterian and a prominent Freemason, a keen supporter of the Carlton cricket and football clubs, and for thirteen years president of the Victorian Bowling Association. He was a Gilbert and Sullivan enthusiast.

Brunton died of cancer on 13 April 1938 at his home, Selkirk, Malvern, predeceased by his second wife. He was buried in Melbourne general cemetery and his estate, valued for probate at £184 367, was largely left to charities. Brunton Avenue, Melbourne, is named after him.

A. F. Davies, *Local government in Victoria* (Melb, 1951); *Aust Hardware and Machinery,* 1 Sept 1903; *Argus,* 8 Nov 1923, 8 Dec 1936, 14 Apr 1938; *Table Talk,* 4 Feb 1926; Melb City Council Archives.　　　　　　　　DAVID DUNSTAN

BRUTON, MARY CATHERINE (1862-1937), Sister of Charity, was born on 13 May 1862 in Sydney, daughter of Irish parents John Bruton, schoolmaster and customs officer, and his wife Johanna, née O'Callaghan. She was brought up in a religious family: two aunts and three sisters also joined the Charity Congregation. Mary and her sisters were educated by a German tutor at Tocumwal, then at the Loreto Ab-

bey, Ballarat, Victoria. When their father returned to Sydney they attended St Vincent's College.

Mary joined the Sisters of Charity on 14 June 1886 and at her clothing ceremony on 9 October took the name Canice. She was professed on 13 October 1888. In 1900-13 she was mother superior of St Mary's Convent, Liverpool, and of Monte Oliveto Convent and School, Woollahra, where she directed the erection of a new building. In 1914 she became mother-rectress of the Catholic Ladies' College, East Melbourne. Under her guidance it made rapid progress: her girls achieved good results in public examinations and she widened the curriculum to include a science department.

As first assistant to the superior-general in 1920-24, Mother Canice took charge of the new foundation, St Vincent's Hospital at Toowoomba, Queensland. She was elected superior-general in 1924. During her term of office she founded convents at New Norfolk, Tasmania, and at Ashgrove and Kingaroy in Queensland. In 1925, at the urgent request of Bishop Barry [q.v.], she permitted a team of Sisters of Charity to manage the Catholic hospital at Cootamundra, New South Wales, which was in danger of closing, and make it a sound establishment. In 1932 she represented some 400 Australian Sisters of Charity at a congress in Dublin and visited Rome. At the end of her term of office in July 1936, she became superior of the Sacred Heart Hospice for the Dying which her aunt Mother Cecilia Bruton had conducted for twenty-nine years. Mother Canice died there on 15 October 1937 and was buried in Rookwood cemetery.

Her sister DOROTHY JOSEPHINE (1866-1938) was born on 28 March 1866 at Moama, completed her education at St Vincent's College and in 1887 studied arts at the University of Sydney for a year. She joined the Sisters of Charity on 26 January 1890 and was professed on 9 July 1892, taking the name Dympna. After training as a teacher at her old school, she eventually became principal of Bethlehem College and Convent, Ashfield. In about 1925-35 Sister Dympna was principal of St Vincent's College. She possessed in full the qualities of 'courage and endurance, cheerfulness and humour and, above all, the spirit of "help your mate"'. When the poet C. J. Brennan [q.v.], joined the staff in 1930, she showed great compassion for his fluctuating health. She died in St Vincent's Hospital on 6 April 1938.

SMH, 23 May 1934; *Freeman's J* (Syd), 24 May 1934, 21 Oct 1937; Sisters of Charity Archives *and* Annals of the Irish Sisters of Charity in Australia, vol 2, 1882-1938 (St Vincent's Convent, Potts Point, NSW).　　　CATHERINE O'CARRIGAN

BRUXNER, SIR MICHAEL FREDERICK (1882-1970), politician, was born on 25 March 1882 at Sandilands, Tabulum, New South Wales, second son of English-born Charles Augustus Bruxner, a pioneering grazier on the Clarence River, and his wife Sarah, daughter of Henry Barnes [q.v.3] of Dyraaba. As a child Bruxner was delicate, and nearly died of pleurisy and pneumonia. His education was a mixture of private tuition and boarding-schools; he was captain of The Armidale School in 1900. A good scholar, he lived in St Paul's College while studying arts and law at the University of Sydney in 1901-03, but was sent down for missing law lectures. After a few years on the family property he moved to Tenterfield to help a family friend in his stock and station agency. Liking the life, he bought out his friend, and opened his own business in 1907 as Bruxner & Cotton.

He prospered and soon became a leading citizen: he was a vice-president of the local agricultural society and of the cricket and Rugby clubs. A dashing horseman and successful amateur jockey, Bruxner owned racehorses and in 1909-11 was president of the Tenterfield Jockey Club. On 17 June 1908 at Christ Church, Kiama, he married Winifred Catherine Hay (Midge) Caird, daughter of a medical practitioner. Commissioned as second lieutenant on 11 September 1911 in the 5th Australian Light Horse (Hunter River Lancers), he transferred next year to the 6th (New England) and took command of the local half-squadron. In 1914 Bruxner volunteered and went with his regiment to Gallipoli and was wounded. Later, in 1916, he commanded the 6th during part of the Romani campaign in Sinai, for which he was mentioned in dispatches and in 1917 awarded the Légion d'honneur. That year he joined the staff and rose to be assistant adjutant and quartermaster general of the Anzac Mounted Division. He was promoted temporary lieut-colonel and was awarded the Distinguished Service Order.

On his return to Tenterfield in July 1919 Bruxner sold his stock and station agency and also Emu Park in Queensland which he had bought before the war; and he consolidated Roseneath, near the border, where he bred Hereford cattle. Instead of settling down as a grazier he soon became involved in the emerging Country Party, partly through conviction and partly through friends and family, and agreed to stand as a Progressive in the State elections of 1920, held under proportional representation. Elected as one of three members for Northern Tableland, he was never afterwards troubled to hold his seat (Tenterfield from 1927). In parliament he was not conspicuous

until the Progressive Party split in December 1921 over whether to join with Sir George Fuller [q.v.] in an anti-Labor coalition. The coalitionists, led by Walter Wearne and (Sir) Thomas Bavin [qq.v.] succeeded, but the ministry lasted only seven hours, and the Progressives were permanently divided. The self-styled 'True Blues' who had opposed the coalition maintained their separate identity, elected Bruxner leader for the 1922 elections, and renamed themselves the Country Party in 1925.

An adroit minor-party leader, Bruxner maximized every opportunity to bring his party's name and claims before the public. He became closely involved with the Northern New State Movement, and succeeded in gaining a royal commission into their proposals in 1925. He also helped to establish the Main Roads Board that year. He resigned the leadership at the end of 1925, mainly for family reasons, and handed to his successor E. A. Buttenshaw [q.v.] a united and confident party.

When J. T. Lang [q.v.] was defeated in 1927 Bruxner was included in the Bavin-Buttenshaw coalition as minister for local government. Against strenuous criticism from the non-Labor back-benchers and extra-parliamentary organizations, he found himself defending Bavin's retention of the adult franchise provisions of the Local Government (Amendment) Act, with which he privately disagreed. His chief preoccupation was transport: he expanded the functions of the Main Roads Board, decentralized its control, and brought about a classification of the roads system which became the basis for the funding of road-building. His view that transport should be a public utility, not a source of private profit, was given force in the Transport Act of 1930, which regulated private bus services in order to prevent the collapse of government-owned tramways and railways. His determined opposition to private enterprise in this matter earned him the sobriquet 'Red Mick', but added to his stature as a politician.

When the ministry fell, Bruxner devoted himself to the reviving New State movements, concerned that they should not destroy or weaken the party that was his great love. He helped to amalgamate them in the United Country Movement, which was then joined to the renamed United Country Party. As the political climate in New South Wales grew more uncertain, he took the lead in arguing that the Country Party should remain quite separate from the United Australia Party, and not succumb to the cry that total unity of the non-Labor forces was an absolute necessity. His view prevailed, and in April 1932 the parliamentary party asked him to seek the leadership again. On 13 May Governor Sir Philip Game [q.v.] dismissed the Lang government and called upon (Sir) Bertram Stevens [q.v.] to form a caretaker government whose sole function would be to hold an election; Bruxner and the Country Party joined the coalition and the partnership with Stevens lasted for seven years; Bruxner was minister for transport and deputy premier in 1932-41.

The Stevens-Bruxner government was aided by the weakness and internal strife of the Labor Party, but embarrassed by a huge parliamentary majority. From the beginning Stevens had trouble with his backbench, and increasingly depended upon Bruxner; this dependence in turn gave rise to the claim that the Country Party dominated the ministry. However, Bruxner greatly respected Stevens's financial ability, and had no ambitions to be premier himself; in any case, his party did not have the numbers. In policy terms the charge of domination was unfounded; as deputy premier Bruxner saw himself as a loyal lieutenant, and the initiatives which flowed from his position were few: another royal commission on the question of new States in 1935, the establishment of New England University College in 1938, and an unsuccessful attempt to aid the Australian film industry through quotas.

Bruxner's choice of portfolio reflected his belief that cheap and efficient transport was the key to many of the problems of country people. An Act in 1932 provided for commissioners of main roads, for railways and for road transport and tramways, a system which long remained. He continued his attempts to regulate metropolitan transport by establishing government bus services, to the horror of many government supporters but with the approval of the Opposition; he was described in the *Labor Daily* as 'a real Socialist'. The explanation for his stand was straightforward: as trustee for the people the government could not afford to allow private interests to treat metropolitan transport as simply a business like any other. In railways and roads his successes were less spectacular, but no less important. The railway finances improved from the largest deficit then known to a profit, and the Department of Main Roads built a reputation for productivity and efficiency that had no equal in the State bureaucracy.

Bruxner was not involved in the plot which resulted in the resignation of Stevens in August 1939, and he was able to form a coalition with the new premier, Alexander Mair [q.v.]. But the public disunity which had been displayed, coupled with the decline of factionalism within the Labor Party and the replacement of Lang by the moderate

(Sir) W. J. McKell, made it certain that the coalition would be defeated in the next elections. Bruxner was preoccupied with the coming war, which he had felt to be unavoidable after a trip to Europe for the coronation in 1937. He equipped the railway workshops with modern machine tools, established National Emergency Services in order to deal with air raids, and built strategic roads which became part of the main roads system.

In 1941, when the government fell, Bruxner was only half way through his parliamentary career, but he was not to enjoy ministerial office again. Labor's dominance in New South Wales lasted until 1965. From 1941 to 1958 Bruxner led the Country Party in five more election campaigns. He sold Roseneath in 1950 and next year bought the homestead section of Old Auburn Vale station; he lived at Bellevue Hill, Sydney. He resigned as leader in May 1958; after a final term he retired from the assembly in 1962 and was appointed K.B.E. He was a member of the Union, the Australian Jockey and Sydney Turf clubs; from the 1950s he was chief steward of the horse section and from 1960 deputy president of the Royal Agricultural Society of New South Wales.

Predeceased by his wife, Bruxner died on 28 March 1970 and was cremated with Anglican rites. He was survived by a daughter and two sons: the elder became a District Court judge and the younger represented Tenterfield in the Legislative Assembly from 1962. His estate was valued for probate at $62 758.

Bruxner was a natural politician and a natural leader, who combined a cheerful smile and an approachable manner with a personal dignity which he never lost: for most of his political life he was referred to as 'the Colonel', a style he greatly enjoyed. His political skill and his integrity gave the Country Party in New South Wales a status it did not enjoy in other States, while as a minister he was innovative and highly competent. His portrait by W. Chandler is in the Country Party offices, Sydney, and a sketch by George Lambert [q.v.] is in the Australian War Memorial, Canberra.

H. S. Gullett, *The A.I.F. in Sinai and Palestine* (Syd, 1923); D. Aitkin, *The colonel* (Canb, 1969); Bruxner papers (Dixson Lib, Univ New England); E. C. G. Page papers (NL).   DON AITKIN

BRYANT, CHARLES DAVID JONES (1883-1937), marine artist, was born on 11 May 1883 at Enmore, Sydney, fifth son of John Ambrose Bryant, storekeeper, and his wife Caroline, née Leedon. Educated at

Sydney Grammar School, he was brought up at Manly in a musical family and played the cello. At 9 he began art lessons with W. Lister Lister [q.v.], a family friend, and first exhibited with the Art Society of New South Wales in 1900. On leaving school he worked in the Bank of New South Wales.

In 1908 Bryant went to London where he was a pupil of John Hassall; later, while studying marine painting with Julius Olsson at St Ives, Cornwall, he became a close friend of (Sir) William Ashton [q.v.]. He exhibited with the Royal Institute of Oil Painters, of which he became a councillor, the Royal Academy of Arts, the Salon des Artists Français (Paris Salon), and the Walker Gallery, Liverpool; he was also a member of the Royal Society of British Artists and an associate of the Royal British Colonial Society of Artists. Involved with Australian expatriates in London, he was an *habitué* of the Chelsea Arts Club, the Savage Club and the London Sketch Club.

In 1917 Bryant was appointed an official war artist and honorary lieutenant with the Australian Imperial Force. He painted war-ravaged towns and villages in northern France, but many of his sixty-nine paintings now in the Australian War Memorial, Canberra, were 'studio' pictures such as 'First Convoy crossing the Indian Ocean, November 1914'.

Bryant returned to Sydney in 1922 and his exhibition of seventy pictures was opened on 16 November by Governor Sir Walter Davidson [q.v.]. The National Art Gallery of New South Wales paid 300 guineas for 'Landing the Catch' and 150 guineas for 'Low Tide at St Ives'. That year he was elected a fellow of the Royal Art Society of New South Wales and was a vice-president in 1929. He was commissioned by the Commonwealth government to paint a series of pictures of the Australian occupation of German New Guinea in 1921, and in 1925 by the New South Wales government to depict the American fleet in Sydney Harbour for the president of the United States. In 1924-30 Bryant ran a colour-store in George Street while living at Manly, where he was a founder and committee-man of the Art Gallery and Historical Collection. His portrait by Lawson Balfour [q.v.] shows him incurably neat with black bow-tie, waistcoat and loose white coat for painting, his short black hair brushed straight back from a somewhat heavy face.

About 1931 Bryant went to England and in 1933-34 was president of the London Sketch Club. On his return in 1936, he held one-man exhibitions in Sydney and Melbourne. Unmarried, he died on 22 January 1937 at Manly and was buried in the Church of England cemetery. His estate was valued

for probate at £4670. Although he painted some charming seascapes, he is mainly remembered for his sympathetic studies of ships. Memorial retrospective exhibitions of his work were held in 1937 and 1938. He is also represented in the State art galleries in Adelaide, Brisbane and Melbourne, in regional galleries, and in the Imperial War Museum, London.

Memorial exhibition of paintings by . . . Charles Bryant, A. Hordern & Sons Ltd fine art galleries (Syd, 1937); *Art in Aust,* 1919, May 1937; *B.P. Mag,* Dec 1929-Feb 1930, Mar 1937; *SMH,* 9 June 1921, 20 Dec 1923, 24 Nov 1925, 7 Jan, 18 Nov 1926.

JOANNA MENDELSSOHN

BRYCE, LUCY MEREDITH (1897-1968), haematologist, was born on 12 June 1897 at Lindfield, New South Wales, eldest child of Robert Bryce, commercial traveller, and his wife Margaret Annie Lucy, née Doak, of Sydney. When Lucy was 11 the family moved to Melbourne, where her father later founded the firm of R. Bryce & Sons, merchants and importers. Lucy was educated at Melbourne Church of England Girls' Grammar School and the University of Melbourne (B.Sc., 1918; M.B., B.S., 1922).

In 1922-28 Dr Bryce held research posts at the Walter and Eliza Hall [qq.v.] Institute of Medical Research, spending 1925-26 in London at the Lister Institute. In 1928 she became bacteriologist and clinical pathologist at the (Royal) Melbourne Hospital, resigning in 1934 to enter private practice as a clinical pathologist. She continued part-time research at the Hall Institute (1934-46) and at the Commonwealth Serum Laboratories (1939-44), and was honorary director of pathology at the Queen Victoria Hospital; in World War II she was visiting specialist with the rank of major at the 115th Australian General Hospital, Heidelberg.

The work for which she is best remembered began in 1929. At the initiative of Dr Eric Cooper, the Victorian division of the Australian Red Cross Society agreed to organize a panel of blood donors who were prepared to attend hospitals when required. A Blood Transfusion Service was set up with Dr Bryce as honorary director; she undertook the blood grouping as well as other aspects of laboratory testing and medical care of the donors. Blood storage techniques developed during the Spanish Civil War were adopted under her supervision. In the subsequent complex developments in blood research and transfusion services during and after World War II, her leadership was invaluable.

In 1954 Dr Bryce retired as honorary director of the service but, despite failing health following a stroke, continued as chairman of the transfusion committee until 1966. She had been appointed C.B.E. in 1951. She died on 30 July 1968 and was cremated. Her estate was valued for probate at $385 932.

Lucy Bryce was author or co-author of forty-three scientific articles and of a history of the transfusion service up to 1959, *An abiding gladness* (1965). At the time of her death she was working on a book about her travels in south-east Europe in the 1920s. Her scientific work, her writing and her approach to administrative problems revealed a mind that was meticulous to a fault, while the soft voice and manner of a cultured gentlewoman concealed a surprising firmness of purpose. She made large demands on those who worked for her but had the capacity to inspire great loyalty from them.

Her portrait by William Dargie hangs in the Lucy Bryce Hall at the Central Blood Bank, Melbourne. A duplicate is held by her family.

Aust Red Cross Soc, *Annual report*, 1968-69; Aust Red Cross (Vic Branch), Minutes of special executive and sub-cttee meetings 16 Oct 1929, *and of* Blood Transfusion Service Cttee meetings 19 Dec 1953, 18 Sept 1968; family information from Mrs S. Rigby, Camberwell, and Mrs F. Rigby, Canterbury, Vic.   M. L. Verso

BUCHANAN, FLORENCE GRIFFITHS (1861-1913), missionary and teacher, was born on 16 September 1861 at Canterbury, Kent, England, daughter of Captain Neil Griffiths Buchanan of the 93rd Highlanders and his wife Elizabeth Jane, née Griffiths. Orphaned when young, Florence became the ward of a relation at Torquay, Devon. Despite her extremely delicate constitution and near-blindness, she devoted herself as a young woman to both practical charity and prayer. After a physical breakdown in 1887, she accompanied her two brothers to Bundaberg, Queensland, where they purchased Oakwood, a substantial cane-farm. Seriously injured in a riding accident in 1888, she was left permanently crippled. After teaching her Melanesian servants English and Bible stories, she later assumed responsibility for the fundamentalist non-denominational South Seas Evangelical Mission (also known as the Queensland Kanaka Mission). In addition she served as Queensland secretary of both the International Scripture Union and the Young Women's Christian Association, and maintained at her own expense a hostel for English migrant girls.

After Oakwood was destroyed in the 1893 floods, Florence Buchanan lived at Townsville and competently helped Bishop C. G. Barlow [q.v.] to administer his diocese. Two years later she worked among the multiracial communities of divers on Thursday Island. Forced to go to London for surgery, on her return she met Kashiwagi Taira [q.v.], an educated storekeeper who introduced her into the usually closed Japanese community. Though only modestly successful in proselytizing them, she was revered and respected by everybody on the island for her generous hospitality, friendliness, humour and compassion.

In 1906 Miss Buchanan was engaged first as a teacher and later as acting headmistress of the famed Singapore Chinese Girls' School; she also taught the orphans at St Mary's Home in Singapore. In 1907 she again underwent major surgery in London and, upon recovery, returned to Thursday Island and was ordained a deaconess in January 1908. In May she went to Moa Island and conducted the Anglican mission, taught school, and tried to inculcate skills necessary for economic self-sufficiency. Her former work among Melanesians stood her in good stead, for the mission included Pacific islanders deported from Queensland.

Florence Buchanan resigned her charge of the mission in 1911 because of deteriorating health, but she stayed on as a teacher. She was disappointed at missing the dedication in August 1913 of St Paul's Church, Moa, by her devoted friend Bishop Gilbert White [q.v.]. In September she performed her last public function when she spoke on 'The mission field as a vocation for women' at the annual congress of the Church of England in Brisbane. She died of tuberculosis in St Helen's Methodist Hospital on 30 December and was buried in Toowong cemetery. Her death was profoundly mourned throughout the Torres Straits. The church on Moa installed a memorial stained-glass window, with her face as the gentle but indomitable St Catherine of Genoa to whom Bishop White likened her.

G. White, *Thirty years in tropical Australia* (Lond, 1918); E. Jones, *Florence Buchanan, the little deaconess of the south seas* (Lond, 1921); J. Baynton, *Cross over Carpentaria* (Brisb, 1965).

KAY SAUNDERS

BUCHANAN, GWYNNETH VAUGHAN (1886-1945), zoologist, was born on 21 November 1886 in Sydney, only child of

Thomas Buchanan, banker, and his second wife Gwynneth, née Vaughan. After her father's death in 1897, Gwynneth settled with her mother in Melbourne. An Anglican, she attended Toorak College, and later the University of Melbourne where she graduated B.Sc. with first-class honours, winning the scholarship in biology at the final honours examination in March 1908. In December she won the MacBain [q.v.5] scholarship for her contribution to research on the blood vessels of Australian earthworms. A government scholarship enabled her to continue this work in 1909, when she was also appointed junior demonstrator in biology. In 1910 Miss Buchanan graduated M.Sc., began tutoring in biology at Queen's College, and received a bursary to enable her to study the blood of Australian birds and marsupials. In August 1913 she took an Orient Free Passage for England where she worked, until late 1914, on the embryology of Australian marsupials under Professor J. P. Hill at University College, London. This research together with earlier published work won her a D.Sc. at the University of Melbourne in April 1916.

In 1915 Gwynneth Buchanan received a government scholarship for inquiry into human embryology, and in the following years tutored in biology at Queen's, Ormond and Trinity colleges. Between 1910 and 1920 she was senior biology mistress at the Presbyterian Ladies' College. She was also a public examiner in anatomy and physiology in 1914-16, and in animal morphology and physiology from 1919 to 1922. In 1921 she published her best-known work, *Elements of animal morphology* (Melbourne), which ran to four editions; it was a recommended reference for schools until 1963 and was used by university practical classes for many years.

Dr Buchanan was appointed lecturer-in-charge of biology at the University of Western Australia for two terms in 1920. Next year she became full-time lecturer in zoology at the University of Melbourne and in 1925, after a years study leave in Britain and the United States of America, senior lecturer; in 1926 she was acting head of department. Preoccupied increasingly with teaching rather than research, she was devoted to the interests of her students, energetically carrying out a heavy programme in the senior zoology years.

Gwynneth Buchanan was a leading member of the University Science Club, a founding member in 1935 and sometime secretary of the McCoy Society for Field Investigation and Research, and a staff representative on the Melbourne University Union Committee in 1921-35. Active in the Victorian Women Graduates' Association,

she was its president in 1934-35 and a delegate to the conferences of the International Federation of University Women in Oslo in 1924 and in Cracow in 1936. Co-honorary secretary in 1920-37 of the committee working to establish the University Women's College, she was one of the college's first governors and a council-member until 1945. She was also president of the Lyceum Club in 1929-31, and held office as president and vice-president both of the University Women's Hockey Club and, for most of 1927-37, of the Victorian Women's Hockey Association.

By 1935 Dr Buchanan was already affected by arteriosclerosis and chronic nephritis; she took leave of absence in 1944 and retired at the end of that year. A woman of great energy, compassion and warm friendships – though not without some personal conflicts in her years of failing health – she maintained her interest in university affairs to the end. She died on 21 June 1945 and was cremated. The greater part of her estate, valued for probate at £8588, was left to the Women's College.

Aust J of Science, 8 (1945); *Univ Melb Gazette*, July 1945; Roy Soc Vic, *Procs*, 58 (1946); *Argus*, 22 June 1945; Univ (Women's) College Archives (Melb); Univ Melb Archives.   CECILY CLOSE

BUCK, ROBERT HENRY (1881-1960), always known as Bob Buck, bushman, was born on 2 July 1881 at Alberton, South Australia, son of Robert Buck, labourer, and his wife Sarah Ann, née Breaden. He was mainly self educated and worked at Wallaroo until in 1905 he joined his uncle Joseph Breaden, who had been on D. W. Carnegie's [q.v.] exploring expedition of 1896-97, and owned Todmorden, and Henbury and Idracowra in the Northern Territory. Another uncle, Allan Breaden, managed Idracowra; both Breadens had pioneered in Central Australia from 1875.

Buck's uncles were excellent teachers of bushmanship. He worked as a stockman, was a good saddler, and in 1907 overlanded 800 head of cattle from Brunette Downs to Henbury, of which he later became manager. He was popular with Aboriginals for his kindness and generous rations of beef and referred to them as 'my tribe'. He lived with his Aranda bush-wife Molly Tjalameinta, by whom he had a daughter Ettie.

In 1927, in partnership with Alf Butler, Buck took a new lease of 240 square miles (620 km²) at Middleton Ponds; Ettie became stockman, camp cook and camel boy. The partnership was dissolved and Buck sold out in 1939, then managed Renner's Rock (99 square miles – 256 km²) which he owned in 1939-53 before retiring to Alice Springs. When a neighbour recalled an unnatural increase in his stock, Bob explained, 'My bullocks had calves too'.

In 1930-37 Buck had been contracted by Donald Mackay [q.v.] for three of his four aerial surveys of regions of the Northern Territory and Western Australia, to clear aerodromes, establish supply-dumps, guide aeroplanes with smoke-signals, manage camps, and stand by with his team of Aboriginals and camels ready to mount a rescue party. Lake Buck was named for his contribution to the success of the surveys. The gold expedition seeking L. H. B. Lasseter's [q.v.] reef used the 1930 Ilbilla base. When Lasseter failed to return, the dependable Bob Buck was commissioned to search for him. He started in February 1931 on camels with Johnson Breaden, Lion and Billy Button, found the prospector's body and buried it, and travelled 1000 miles (1610 km) including a nine-day dry stage. Buck and his party then returned into the Petermann Ranges to guide Walter Gill, who wished to study a tribe Buck had encountered.

Despite evidence of Lasseter's identity which he presented to the police, some believed Buck was hoaxing. The ensuing controversy (probably inflated by Bob's brand of exaggerated humour) projected him nationally as an intrepid bushman. He was brought to Sydney, and interviewed and fêted. His sudden fame made him the obvious, and his heavy drought losses a very willing leader of a new expedition in quest of the fabled reef in August 1931. Buck planned a six months search but the venture was abandoned after six weeks.

When he was on the stations Bob Buck was renowned for his hospitality to black and white travellers; he helped many in distress and saved some from perishing. In his later years the now bulky bushman with handlebar moustaches was an identity at the Stuart Arms Hotel: 'Playing crib and drinking rum are the best things in life and you can do 'em together'. He became notorious as a yarn-spinner: most of his tall stories of the Centre were as true as the one about mustering cattle in boats after a drought broke.

On the morning of 9 August 1960 Bob told a visitor in hospital: 'Wind my watch, I'll tell you when I died'. He died that afternoon and was buried in the Catholic section of Alice Springs cemetery. His lifelong mate Alf Butler said: 'He was an outstanding stockman, good tracker and had a way with black fellows'.

D. W. Carnegie, *Spinifex and sand* (Lond, 1898);
I. Idriess, *Lasseter's last ride* (Syd, 1931); E. Coote, *Hell's airport* (Syd, 1934); F. P. Clune, *Last of the Australian explorers* (Syd, 1942); W. Gill, *Petermann journey* (Adel, 1968); T. G. H. Strehlow, *Journey to Horseshoe Bend* (Syd, 1969); F. Blakeley, *Dream millions*, M. Mansfield ed (Syd, 1972); *Centralian Advocate*, 12 Aug 1960; *Sunday Mail* (Adel), 1 Apr 1967; Lands Branch, Letter L506(5), 15 May 1978 (Dept of NT, Darwin); Grazing licence and pastoral lease registers (AAO, NT Branch, Darwin).   ALEX JELINEK

BUCKLAND, SIR THOMAS (1848-1947), goldmine-manager, pastoralist, businessman and philanthropist, was born on 1 August 1848 at Maidstone, Kent, England, son of John Buckland, carpenter, and his wife Martha, née Smith. Educated there at Rocky Hill House Academy, he migrated to Sydney in 1865 and worked for his uncle Thomas Buckland [q.v.3]. He soon moved to Victoria and became a gold-assayer, then in 1867 went to Queensland and joined the Gympie gold rush. In 1869 he returned to Sydney and entered the Bank of New South Wales, became bullion clerk and gold-assayer at head office and was briefly at its Araluen and Gulgong branches.

Three years later Buckland resigned and moved to Charters Towers, Queensland, where he set up as a gold-buyer and assayer and was head of the butchering business, T. Buckland & Co. Here he greatly prospered despite his propensity for fighting and litigation: he twice, in 1877 and 1883, sued T. O'Kane [q.v.5], editor of the *Northern Miner*, for libel and won negligible damages. At the time he owned the *Towers Herald*.

Investing heavily in mining, Buckland paid out a small fortune in 'backing money' before receiving a dividend. He became manager of several companies, and was managing director of the Victory (Charters Towers) Gold Mining Co. Ltd, in 1892, the 'most productive goldmine in Australasia'; earlier he had installed the 'Excelsior' machine to treat tailings. From 1877 Buckland was a member of the Charters Towers Municipal Council and was mayor in 1882 and 1883; he was also president of the hospital committee and the Chamber of Commerce and a vice-president of the Towers Pastoral, Agricultural, and Mining Association and the North Queensland Rifle Association. In 1879 he acquired Cardigan station in North Kennedy, in 1891 St Anns, and next year Bosworth on the Burdekin River.

At Millchester, Queensland, on 8 August 1875 Buckland had married an eighteen-year-old widow Emma Moore, née Barnett; he divorced her for adultery in 1889. In 1890 he went back to England, intending to settle, and on 15 October married Mary Kirkpatrick of Monks Horton Park near Hythe, Kent. However in 1891 he returned to Queensland to manage his interests during the depression, and soon became managing director in Australia for the English principals of Cobar Gold Mines Ltd, New South Wales. Residing in Sydney from about 1898, he became a director of several prominent companies: chairman of the pastoral company Pitt, Son & Badgery [qq.v.5,3] Ltd in 1906-43 and of the United Insurance Co. Ltd from 1935, president of the Bank of New South Wales in 1922-37, and a director of the Permanent Trustee Co. of New South Wales from 1920. After carrying his stations through the depression and the extended drought of the early 1900s, he sold them on a rising market between 1914 and 1916.

Thereafter Buckland devoted his time and energy to his directorships and to philanthropy. He endowed the Buckland Memorial Church of England Boys' Home at Carlingford in 1927, and in 1934 gave £100000 for the construction and endowment of the Buckland Convalescent Hospital at Springwood, stipulating that the State government should build a water-supply to serve both the hospital and the neighbouring part of the Blue Mountains. He was a member of Barker College Council from 1928 and president of the Sydney branch of the Royal Society of St George in 1939; he had been knighted in June 1935.

Slight in build, unobtrusive, with tight waving hair and a pointed beard, Buckland dressed neatly though not fashionably. A member of the Australian Club, he had earned the nickname 'The Sydney Limited', partly for his rapid progress on foot from one board meeting to another. He continued to drive himself when aged more than 90. With a growing concern about the country's lack of defence preparations, in 1938 he donated £10500 to the Commonwealth government to buy an Avro Anson bomber and was taken for a flight in it; rumour had it that he had made this a condition of his gift. In 1940 he gave £20000 to the British government for war expenditure, and next year gave £15000 for another bomber for the Royal Australian Air Force.

Buckland died on 11 June 1947 at his residence, Lyndhurst, Hunters Hill, and was cremated with Anglican rites. Predeceased by his wife, he was survived by two sons and three daughters. His estate was valued for probate at £589958; after bequests of £40000 to each child, legacies totalling £24000 to other members of his family and some £11000 to sundry schools and hospitals, he left two-thirds of the residue to the Buckland Convalescent Hospital, Springwood, and the income of one-third to Church of England homes for children.

D. Jones, *Trinity phoenix* (Cairns, 1976); *Aust Mining Standard*, 18 Feb 1893; *Pastoral Review*, 16 July 1947; *Northern Miner*, 22 July, 5 Aug, 12, 19, 24 Oct, 29 Dec 1882; *Graziers' Review*, 16 Apr 1922; *SMH*, 15 Oct 1928, 8 June 1929, 11 Mar 1932, 26 May 1934, 3 June 1935, 5 Sept 1938, 13 June 1947; Supreme Court, SCT/CH9, case 108 (QA); Civil and Criminal Courts, A17369, A17371, A17389, A17735, A17736, A18281, A18309, A18496 (QA); Lands, LAN/AF 823, 828, 999, N154 (QA); Bank of NSW Archives (Syd). R. F. HOLDER

BUCKLEY, ALEXANDER HENRY (1891-1918), soldier and farmer, was born on 22 July 1891 at Warren, New South Wales, fourth child of James Buckley, selector, and his wife Julia, née Falkanhagan, both of whom were Victorian-born. He was educated at home by his parents and later farmed with his father on Homebush, a property near Gulargambone.

On 3 February 1916 Buckley enlisted as a private in the Australian Imperial Force and embarked for England in June with reinforcements for the 54th Battalion. He joined the battalion at Flers, France, on 17 November, served on the Somme in the winter of 1916-17 and in 1917 fought in the battles of Bullecourt, Polygon Wood and Broodseinde; he was made temporary corporal in November. Next April his unit moved into the Villers-Bretonneux sector and in August took part in the Battle of Amiens.

On 1 September 1918 Buckley's battalion was involved in an operation aimed at clearing the area between Mont St Quentin and Péronne, a medieval walled town surrounded by a moat. The 54th's task was to take the ground between Péronne and the River Somme, then move in on Péronne 'if not too strongly opposed'. Advancing in drizzling rain and under heavy fire, it took the first line of enemy trenches but was held up by a nest of machine-gunners. Accompanied by Corporal A. C. Hall [q.v.], Buckley stalked these gunners and rushed the post, shooting four men and taking twenty-two prisoners. The Germans retreated to Péronne, entering the city by a large bridge which they destroyed. The only remaining bridge on the battalion's front was a footbridge defended by machine-guns. With three other members of his company, Buckley tried to force his way across under heavy fire but was killed in the attempt. He was awarded a posthumous Victoria Cross, the citation for which praised his 'initiative, resource and courage'. He was buried in the Péronne communal cemetery extension.

C. E. W. Bean, *The A.I.F. in France, 1918* (Syd, 1942); L. Wigmore (ed), *They dared mightily* (Canb, 1963); *London Gazette,* 14 Dec 1918; *Reveille* (Syd), 1 Nov 1939; records (AWM).

LIONEL WIGMORE

BUCKLEY, MAURICE VINCENT (1891-1921), soldier, was born on 13 April 1891 at Hawthorn, Victoria, son of Timothy Buckley, brickmaker, and his wife Honora Mary Agnes, née Sexton. His father was a native of Cork, Ireland; his mother was Victorian-born. Educated at the Christian Brothers' school, Abbotsford, he became a coach-trimmer and was working at Warrnambool when he enlisted in the Australian Imperial Force on 18 December 1914. Next June he embarked for Egypt with reinforcements for the 13th Light Horse Regiment but by late September 1915 he had returned to Australia and was discharged.

Buckley re-enlisted in Sydney on 16 May 1916 under the name of Gerald Sexton; Gerald was the name of a deceased brother. He left for France in October with 13th Battalion reinforcements and joined his unit on the Somme in January 1917. That year he fought at Bullecourt, Polygon Wood, Ypres and Passchendaele and early in 1918 at Hébuterne and Villers-Bretonneux. He was promoted lance corporal in January and by June was a lance sergeant in charge of a Lewis-gun section. After being wounded at Hamel he resumed duty for the battle of 8 August in which he won the Distinguished Conduct Medal. While advancing from Hamel towards Morcourt his company was delayed by sudden machine-gun fire on four separate occasions; he quickly silenced each enemy post by using his Lewis-gun with great promptness and skill. Once, when the battalion was advancing through tall crops, a hidden gun fired into its ranks causing several casualties. Buckley stood up in full view of the enemy, calmly noted the position of the gun from the flashes and, firing from the hip, put it out of action. He was confirmed as sergeant on 28 August.

On 18 September the 13th Battalion took part in the attack on Le Verguier. Setting off behind the creeping barrage it cleared several enemy outposts, two of which fell to Buckley's Lewis-gun. When a field-gun held up one company he rushed towards it, shot the crew and raced under machine-gun fire across open ground to put a trench-mortar out of action. He then fired into an enemy dug-out and captured thirty Germans. By the end of the day he had rushed at least six machine-gun positions, captured a field-gun and taken nearly 100 prisoners: he was awarded the Victoria Cross. The award was gazetted under the name Sexton, and Buckley then decided to reveal his identity; a second gazettal was made in his real name.

Buckley returned to Australia and was discharged in December 1919; next year he began work as a road-contractor in Gippsland. On 15 January 1921 he was injured when he tried to jump his horse over the railway gates at Boolarra. He died twelve days later in hospital at Fitzroy, and after a requiem mass in St Patrick's Cathedral was buried in Brighton cemetery with full military honours. Ten Victoria Cross winners were pallbearers. Buckley was unmarried. A friend described him as a 'modest, unassuming young man, with a great fondness for horses and an open-air life'.

T. A. White, *The fighting Thirteenth* (Syd, 1924); C. E. W. Bean, *The A.I.F. in France, 1918* (Syd, 1942); L. Wigmore (ed), *They dared mightily* (Canb, 1963); *London Gazette,* 5, 14 Dec 1918, 8 Aug 1919; *Mufti* (Melb), 1 Nov 1938; *Reveille* (Syd), June 1968; *Western Mail* (Perth), 17 Dec 1936; *Age,* 17, 18 Dec 1918, 15 Mar 1920, 28, 29 Jan, 11 Feb 1921; *Herald* (Melb), 17 Mar 1920; War diaries, 4th Light Horse Brigade, 13th Light Horse Regiment, *and* 13th Infantry Battalion (AWM).

D. M. HORNER

BUDDICOM, ROBERT ARTHUR, also known as BEDFORD, ROBERT (1874-1951), scientist and local entrepreneur, was born on 7 November 1874 at Ticklerton Eaton, Shropshire, England, son of William Squire Buddicom, landowner, and his wife Elizabeth Haughton, née Hornby. He was educated at Charterhouse and at Uppingham where he excelled in metal-work, composition of Greek and Latin verse and the construction of electrical apparatus. Advised against an engineering career by his great-uncle William Barber Buddicom, inventor of the Buddicom locomotive, he crammed in biology and chemistry, and in 1894 was a science scholar at Keble College, Oxford (B.A., 1897); he produced there the prototype of Buddicom's gas regulator, and made studies of muscle control and nervous excitability. He balanced his scientific gifts with interests in drawing, music and classics.

Oxford biological scholar in 1897-98 at the marine biological station, Naples, Italy, Buddicom consolidated his studies of the arts. In 1898 he gave a paper on the potential for life in all matter: an early Teilhardian view from a rationalist standpoint. In 1900-01 he was curator of the Plymouth Museum and Art Gallery, founded and edited the short-lived journal *Life* in 1902, and was a market-gardener at Shiplake, Oxfordshire. While a demonstrator and lecturer at London Hospital Medical College in 1906-14 he became pessimistic about the future of Britain, an attitude strengthened by his work as foundation secretary of the British Legion for Home Defence. After a court action in February 1915 when, as a director of the Stolz Electrophone Co. (1913) Ltd, he was found to have been involved in misrepresentation in a prospectus, he migrated to Australia under the name of Robert Bedford. He had acquired land at Turramurra, New South Wales, in the settlement on his divorce from Laura Lucie Finlay whom he had married in London on 17 January 1900. However, he took up 2000 acres (810 ha) at isolated Kyancutta, South Australia, and grew wheat. Ethel Hilda Lewis, his second wife, and two children had accompanied him from England.

In 1915-20 Bedford strove to provide for the basic needs of the small pioneering community: he served as physician and veterinary surgeon; harried the government to hasten construction of the water-pipeline from Port Lincoln; and worked as a chainman on the Kyancutta tank. He ran a cash store and in 1922 opened a cottage hospital with his wife as matron. He established the radio station 5RB in 1924, next year opened a railway refreshment-room, and subsequently took over the post office. With helpers he constructed an all-weather aerodrome and in 1929 formed Eyre Peninsula Airways, which closed in 1935. Meanwhile the accurate reports which he had been sending to Adelaide resulted in the recognition of Kyancutta as an official weather-station. During the 1930s Bedford founded the doomed Australian Country Library Association. He operated a flour-mill, a smithy and a mail-run, built a printing-press, and experimented with a phonetic system of English. A strong supporter of the South Australian Centre Party, he entered politics in 1928 as a founder of the Kyancutta branch of the South Australian Wheat-growers' Association; in 1933 he drafted a constitution for the Australian Wheatgrowers' Federation. He represented Kyancutta Ward on the district council of Le Hunte in 1934-35. In the face of general government neglect of the district, however, he advocated secession of the peninsula from South Australia as Eyralia.

Bedford continued always to probe into the nature of life. He compiled a list of Aboriginal words and in 1920 was a founder of the Adelaide Rationalist Society. The first of his notorious field-trips was made in 1927, to Nildottie and Swan Reach for Aboriginal fossils and to Ardrossan for archeocyathinae; next year he went to Lake Callabonna for Diprotodon bones and rock-carvings. He housed his collections, excellently arranged to demonstrate the evolution of man from primitive matter, in the remarkable Kyancutta Museum and Library which was opened in 1929.

In 1931-38 Bedford examined the meteorite craters at Henbury, Central Australia. He excavated large meteorite masses there, discovered the associated black silica glass and iron shale balls, and from an analysis of the surface condition of the irons demonstrated that the fall was more recent than originally supposed. He was responsible, too, for the location of the Lake Labyrinth stone; the preservation of the Kyancutta and Silverton meteorites; and the gathering of irons from Boxhole, Central Australia. He considered the Murnpeowie iron the finest meteorite in existence. His work on archeocyathinae and related fossils from 1933 resulted in the description of thirty-two new species and eight new genera, his researches being published as *Memoirs of the Kyancutta Museum*, 1-6 (Adelaide, 1934-39). The museum mounted a display on evolution in Adelaide in 1936 and another on archeocyathinae in Auckland, New Zealand, next year. In 1938 he published the philosophical conclusions to his researches as 'An outline of biosophy: part 1' (*Memoirs...*, 5).

Bedford's success in classifying fossils and in describing both meteorites and tektites drew some unfair criticism. The South Australian Museum opposed his admission to the Museum Association of Australia and New Zealand. The Adelaide *Advertiser* libelled Kyancutta Museum parties for their work at Henbury, but later publicly apologized.

During World War II Bedford acted as a volunteer air-observer, built models of inventions to aid the Allies, and urged the annexation of near-by Pacific islands. His last years were clouded by an obsessive desire to revive Kyancutta aerodrome. Survived by his wife, two sons and three daughters, he died at Kyancutta on 14 February 1951 and was buried as Robert Bedford in the local cemetery. The museum was subsequently closed and its holdings dispersed.

L. H. Daniel, *Life as I see it* (Adel, 1977); *Mineralogical Mag*, Mar 1932, Mar, Sept 1933, June 1934, Mar 1935, June 1936; *S.A. Institutes J*, 30 Apr 1951; M. Brett-Crowther, 'Robert Buddicom: prophet and utopist', *Shropshire Mag*, Aug 1974; *The Times*, 2-6 Feb, 8 May 1915; *Mail* (Adel), 19 Nov 1932; R. F. I. Smith, 'Organise or be damned': Australian wheatgrowers' organisations and wheat marketing, 1927-1948 (Ph.D. thesis, ANU, 1969).
                                    M. R. BRETT-CROWTHER

BUGDEN, PATRICK JOSEPH (1897-1917), soldier, was born on 17 March 1897 at

South Gundurimba, New South Wales, eldest child of Thomas Bugden, farmer, and his wife Annie, née Connolly, both native-born. His father died when Bugden was 6, leaving four children; and his mother remarried. Educated at Gundurimba Public School and the convent school at Tatham, he later worked for his stepfather as a barman at the Federal Hotel, Alstonville; outgoing and popular, he excelled at football, cricket and shot-putting. Before joining the Australian Imperial Force he completed twelve months military training under the compulsory scheme introduced in 1911.

Bugden enlisted in the A.I.F. as a private on 25 May 1916, trained at Enoggera in Queensland, and in September embarked for the Western Front with 31st Battalion reinforcements. He joined the unit on 19 March 1917 at Bapaume and served there until the end of May. On 26 September the battalion took part in the second phase of the battle of Polygon Wood. As it advanced towards its objective the leading platoons were swept by fierce machine-gun fire from a group of pillboxes. Bugden was in a small party sent forward to attack the first strong point: successfully 'silencing the machine-gun with bombs', he 'captured the garrison at the point of the bayonet'. In the next two days he performed several similar acts of gallantry, each of which contributed to the battalion's advance. Once, single-handed, he rescued a corporal who was being taken to the German lines, and at least five times he dashed out into intense shell and machine-gun fire to bring in wounded. 'Always foremost in volunteering for any dangerous mission', he was killed on 28 September. For his bravery during the preceding two days Bugden was awarded a posthumous Victoria Cross. He was buried in Hooge Crater cemetery, Zillebeke, Belgium. He was unmarried.

C. E. W. Bean, *The A.I.F. in France,* 1917 (Syd, 1933); L. Wigmore (ed), *They dared mightily* (Canb, 1963); *London Gazette,* 26 Nov 1917; *Western Mail* (Perth), 25 Mar 1937; *Courier Mail,* 30 Nov 1917; *Northern Star* (Lismore), 30 Nov 1917, 18 Feb 1967; information from Mr T. Marsh, Tatham, Mr S. Abernethy, Banora Point, and Mr R. Daley, Alstonville, NSW.　　　N. S. FOLDI

BUGGY, EDWARD HUGH (1896-1974), journalist, was born on 9 June 1896 at Seymour, Victoria, only child of John Buggy, carpenter and building contractor, and his wife Margaret Teresa, née Boyle, from County Cavan, Ireland. Hugh Buggy attended the convent school at Seymour; early in World War I, after his father had died and he had gone to Melbourne with his mother, he received his first journalistic experience on the South Melbourne *Record.* He joined the Melbourne *Argus* in 1917 and began a course for the diploma of journalism at the university in 1921.

Buggy was one of the most energetic and colourful journalists of his time. He was a pure reporter; he had one five-year stint as a newspaper desk-man, as deputy-news-editor of the Sydney *Sun,* and did not particularly like it. He preferred to be near the action. Major events he covered included the Melbourne police strike (1923), the fatal shoot-out between 'Squizzy' Taylor [q.v.] and 'Snowy' Cutmore (1927), the arrival in Brisbane of Kingsford-Smith [q.v.] and the *Southern Cross* (1928), the last election campaign of S. M. (Viscount) Bruce [q.v.] (1929) and the murder of the 'Pyjama Girl' (1934). Following the *Greycliffe* ferry disaster of 1927, he had a secret night rendezvous with the diver whose job it was to recover bodies from the Sydney Harbour bed. In 1929 at Rothbury, New South Wales, Buggy used his own singlet to apply a tourniquet to the thigh of a wounded miner. 'After that', he said, 'I could do no wrong on the coalfields'. In 1932, following the opening of the Sydney Harbour Bridge, he was the only pressman to secure an interview with Captain de Groot.

Buggy reported more than 200 murder investigations and 83 murder trials, and attended nine hangings. At the same time he managed to be a highly respected writer on sport, particularly football. He had a phenomenal memory, and even in his last years he was able to recall all Victorian league grand final scores, as well as the results (with innings totals) of all Australia-England Test cricket matches. He had a flair for the picturesque sporting phrase: he was widely believed to have coined the term 'bodyline', but this claim was never settled conclusively.

Buggy worked with the *Argus* until 1922, then joined the new Melbourne *Sun News-Pictorial* under the editorship of Montague Grover [q.v.] in 1923. He served on the Melbourne *Evening Sun* in 1923-25, the Sydney *Sun* in 1925-27, 1928-31 and 1937-42, the *Sun News-Pictorial* in 1927 and the Melbourne *Herald* in 1932-37. He was chief operational censor at General Macarthur's headquarters in 1942-46, and then an editor with Radio Australia. In 1950 he rejoined the *Argus,* and became its chief football-writer in 1951. After the *Argus* ceased publication in 1957, he worked for suburban newspapers in Oakleigh, Footscray and Dandenong, and contributed to the Catholic newspaper, the *Advocate,* as well as working as chief court reporter for *Truth* for three years.

Buggy married Mary Eleanor Carolan on

24 April 1929 and a widow Violet Sloane, née Rose, on 17 September 1945. Both marriages ended in divorce and were childless. 'He had only one love', a relation summed up. 'He was absolutely devoted to newspapers . . . nothing else'. He 'ghosted' for Kingsford-Smith and C. T. P. Ulm [q.v.] the *Story of the Southern Cross trans-Pacific flight* (Sydney, 1928), and in 1946 he wrote *Pacific victory*. In 1977 his book *The real John Wren* was published.

Buggy mastered Morse code and was an accomplished shorthand writer. He had a slight impediment in his speech which caused him to pause often and speak tersely; his conversations were described as 'a combination of verbal Morse and short-hand'. For many years he lived with his mother and aunt in McIlwraith Street, Carlton, and after their deaths remained alone in the house. He died following a heart seizure on 18 June 1974 and was buried in Seymour cemetery after a service at St Bernard's Catholic Church, East Coburg. His 300 books of newspaper clippings were bought by a Melbourne second-hand book dealer.

H. Gordon, *An eyewitness history of Australia* (Adel, 1976); *Sun News-Pictorial,* 14 May 1942, 19, 22 June 1974; *Argus,* 26 Mar 1951; *Herald* (Melb), 18 June 1974; *Age,* 19 June 1974, 27 Feb 1976; *SMH,* 19, 20 June 1974; *Truth,* 22 June 1974; *Sydney Sun,* 29 June 1974.   HARRY GORDON

BULCOCK, EMILY HEMANS (1877-1969), poet and journalist, was born on 28 July 1877 at Tinana near Maryborough, Queensland, daughter of Henry Burnett Palmer, schoolteacher, and his wife Mary Jane, née Carson. She attended bush schools, but was educated chiefly by her father, a scholarly man with a deep interest in European literature and history. A younger brother Vance Palmer [q.v.] became a distinguished writer.

In 1891 government economies left her father without assistance in a school of ninety pupils, so Emily became an unpaid teacher for four years, then at 19 was appointed the pioneer teacher of a new school at Razorback (Montville), where she also conducted evening classes for illiterate farm-workers. On 13 April 1903 at Cleveland she married Robert Bulcock (d. 1924), an orchardist who owing to illness had later to give up farming; they moved to Caloundra in 1914, where Mrs Bulcock began to write regularly for Brisbane and southern newspapers. To mark the celebration of Anzac Day in 1922 the Sydney *Bulletin* devoted a full page to her poem, illustrated by Norman Lindsay [q.v.]. In 1917 the family moved to Brisbane.

During the 1920s Emily Bulcock worked as a freelance journalist, writing regular columns for the *Graziers' Journal* and the *Farmers' Gazette.* She was a foundation member of the Queensland Country Women's Association, and of the Queensland Authors' and Artists' Association, of which she was a committee-member from 1925 and vice-president from 1936; when in 1958 the association became the Fellowship of Australian Writers (Queensland), she continued as a vice-president until 1965, when she was made a life member. In 1964 she was appointed O.B.E. for her services to literature and was presented with a collection of verses composed in her honour by nine Queensland poets.

Mrs Bulcock's first poem had appeared in the *Ipswich Times* in 1889, and her last published verses in the *Courier Mail* in 1966. During more than seventy years of writing, her verse had appeared in the main Brisbane and Sydney newspapers, in the Melbourne *Age* and in many periodicals. In 1923 her first collection, *Jacaranda blooms,* was published in Brisbane. In 1945 she produced her second book of poems, *From quenchless springs,* and in 1961 a small collection of occasional verse, *From Australia to Britain.* On her ninetieth birthday the fellowship held a reception in her honour.

Mrs Bulcock was a kind and generous woman, with a quick sympathy for all in trouble. She gave practical help to many young writers, and a number of refugees from Nazi rule remember her with gratitude. In her eighties she was an active member of the Save the Children Fund. She had an easy mastery of technique, and a gift for occasional popular verse, celebrating events in national life with aptness and appealing sentiment. But her best work was on a different plane, and in her mature years her contemplative and nature poems showed depth of feeling, vivid imagery, a passionate love of beauty and poetic discipline.

Emily Bulcock died in Brisbane on 4 September 1969, and was cremated. She was survived by a son and a daughter, both of whom became authors.

Qld Authors' and Artists' Assn minutes (copy, Oxley Lib, Brisb); family papers (held by author).
                              MARJORIE PUREGGER

BULLER-MURPHY, DEBORAH VERNON; *see* HACKETT, DEBORAH

BUNNING, ROBERT (1859-1936), timber merchant and sawmiller, was born on 13

December 1859 at Hackney, London, son of Joseph Bunning, carpenter, and his wife Jane, née Bain. He was apprenticed as a carpenter, and as a boy would travel across London to work in winter with a hot baked potato in each pocket for warmth. In 1872 Joseph took his family to Boston, United States of America, where he worked on church buildings. When the family returned to London, Robert and his younger brother Arthur (1863-1929) stayed to work near Chicago. Joseph later recalled the boys to London to help him put a spire on a church. On 29 June 1886 the brothers arrived at Fremantle, Western Australia, in the *Elderslie* to join a married sister, and set up as building contractors.

By January next year they had won contracts for additions to the Fremantle Lunatic Asylum and for the Roebourne hospital. In 1889 Robert went to Scotland to marry Georgina Taylor at Strathdon near Aberdeen on 28 August. When Arthur was injured in a riding accident, Robert became the driving force in the partnership which built the Weld Club (1892) and Trinity Congregational Church (1893) in Perth and the Coolgardie warden's quarters (1895); they claimed, too, to have owned most of the buldings in Barrack Street, Perth, at one time.

A boom during 1896-97 in the export of jarrah turned Bunning's attention to timber. Although his income of £156 756 for the year came partly from four brickyards, he was anxious to sell them. He bought his first sawmill at North Dandalup in 1897 and was involved with his friend Frank Wilson [q.v.] in the newly formed Timber Merchants and Mill Owners' Association. He was president in 1904-25 and represented it on the executive of the Employers' Federation in 1917-36; he was on the executive too of the Sawmillers' Association from its formation in 1913 to 1936. He had few other outside interests. As a witness to the royal commission on forestry (1903), Bunning stressed freedom of trade for the small man against the Millars' combine, and in later years attacked the State sawmills as a threat to free enterprise.

Despite a constant shortage of capital Bunning established sawmills throughout the south-west, imported the first band-saw in Western Australia to Lion Mill and was the first to instal a timber-drying kiln. He also imported a unique locomotive known as 'Dirty Mary' for use on steep grades, and was one of the first to use a tractor for log-hauling in the bush. In 1929 he leased Garden Island for a holiday resort but was defeated by the Depression.

Bunning's wife had died in 1897 leaving him with two children. In October 1902 he returned to Scotland and married Helen Marion MacRae in Edinburgh; they had five children. On 12 August 1936 during a dinner to celebrate his fifty years of business in Western Australia, Bunning collapsed and died while replying to a toast. He was buried in the Presbyterian section of Karrakatta cemetery and his estate was valued for probate at £29 220.

K. Murray, *Bunning's story,* 2nd edn (Perth, 1964); *V&P* (LA WA), 1903-04, 2 (24); *JR WAHS,* 1 (1927-31) pt 5; *West Australian,* 13 Aug 1936; J. R. Robertson, A history of the timber industry of Western Australia (B.A. Hons thesis, Univ WA, 1956); Sawmillers' Assn minutes *and* Timber Merchants and Mill Owners Assn, Minutes 1904, *and* WA Timber Merchants Assn, Minutes 1895-1902 (held at Forest Products Assn, West Perth); family papers (held by Mr C. R. Bunning, Miss F. M. Bunning and Mrs O. Vincent, Perth).

JENNY MILLS

BUNNY, RUPERT CHARLES WULSTEN (1864-1947), artist, was born on 29 September 1864 at St Kilda, Melbourne, third son of Brice Frederick Bunny [q.v.3], barrister, and his wife Marie Hedwig Dorothea, née Wulsten. Educated at the Alma Road Grammar School, St Kilda, The Hutchins School, Hobart, and in Germany and Switzerland, in 1881 he enrolled at the University of Melbourne to study civil engineering. Abandoning his studies in the hope of becoming an actor, but frustrated by family opposition, he eventually joined the National Gallery schools under O. R. Campbell and G. F. Folingsby [qq.v.3,4]; his fellow students included Frederick McCubbin, E. Phillips Fox [qq.v.] and Louis Abrahams. In 1884 Bunny went to London and enrolled at P. H. Calderon's art school in St John's Wood. Two years later he left for Paris to study under Jean-Paul Laurens.

Bunny exhibited at the Salon de la Société des Artistes Français (Old Salon) from 1888, becoming the first Australian painter to receive a *mention honorable* for his painting 'The Tritons'. He also began exhibiting with British societies and galleries including the Royal Academy, London, the Royal Society of British Artists, the Institute of Painters in Oil-Colours, the Fine Art Society, and the New Gallery, Grosvenor, and Grafton galleries. His participation in the Carnegie Institute's 'Pittsburgh Internationals' was to continue for almost thirty years; he was awarded a bronze medal at the Paris Exhibition of 1900, and was represented in the Bendigo Victorian Gold Jubilee Exhibition of 1901-02. In 1901 he left the Paris Old Salon for the New (Société Nationale des Beaux-Arts). This coincided with a change in his work from large, idealized subject compositions drawn from the Bible and especially classical mythology, painted in a neo-classical style touched with Pre-Raphaelitism, to paintings of women, landscapes, and portraiture. His interest in music is reflected in his portraits of musicians, especially of fellow Australians Nellie Melba, Percy Grainger and Ada Crossley [qq.v.].

In 1902 in Paris Bunny married Jeanne Heloise Morel, a former fellow student and favourite model whose portrait he painted often. His paintings now became more French, both in subject and style. One-man exhibitions were held at the Galerie Silberberg and the Galerie Graves, Paris. He produced some of his most successful works during this first decade of the new century. 'Après le Bain' was purchased for the Jeu de Paume, the first of many to be bought by the French government, followed by 'Endormies' (National Gallery of Victoria), 'Summer Time', his major compositional achievement, and 'A Summer Morning' (both in the Art Gallery of New South Wales). At the height of his powers and with an enviable reputation he visited Australia in 1911 for successful exhibitions in Melbourne and Sydney. His return to Paris in 1912 marked a period of crisis and uncertainty with World War I shattering an age of elegance. His work in the American Hospital in Paris also affected him deeply.

Bunny again turned to the classics for inspiration, producing a brilliant series of mythological decorations that are among his finest works. These new decorative compositions reached their fullest expression in the 1920s with stylistic influences ranging from classical Greek art, through Puvis de Chavannes, Art Nouveau and Fauvism, to Diaghilev's Ballets Russes. Bunny also returned to painting landscapes, especially lyrical views of the south of France.

In the 1920s he held a number of exhibitions in Melbourne and Sydney as well as in Paris, before hard economic times and the death of his wife in 1933 resulted in him finally returning to Melbourne to live. He exhibited with the Victorian Artists' Society, various contemporary groups, and was artist vice-president and inaugural member of the Contemporary Art Society, established in 1939. The same year he began exhibiting annually at the Macquarie Galleries, Sydney.

Bunny devoted increasing time to music in his last years and composed several ballets. In 1946 a major retrospective exhibition of his work was shown at the National Gallery of Victoria, the first time it paid such an honour to a living Australian painter. He died on 25 May 1947 in a private hospital in Melbourne.

Hailed as one of Australia's finest artists of his time, Bunny was a skilfully eclectic painter whose works ranged from large-scale compositions in the grand manner to decorative scenes of feminine intimacy. His first work to enter an Australian Gallery was 'Sea Idyll', presented to the National Gallery of Victoria in 1892 by Alfred Felton [q.v.4], who, on his death in 1904 also bequeathed Bunny a life annuity. A self-portrait (c.1920) and a portrait of his wife (c.1902) are in the National Gallery of Victoria.

D. Thomas, *Rupert Bunny, 1864-1947* (Melb, 1970), and for bibliog.   DAVID THOMAS

BUNTINE, WALTER MURRAY (1866-1953), schoolmaster, was born on 1 August 1866 at Meadowbank near Rosedale, Victoria, second son of Robert Buntine, grazier, and his wife Jessie, née Murray. He entered Scotch College, Melbourne, in 1884 and the University of Melbourne in 1886 (B.A., 1892; M.A., 1906), supporting himself by private coaching and taking a post in 1889 at Rev. E. J. Barnett's school in East St Kilda. On 11 July 1894 he married according to the Presbyterian form Bertha Florence, daughter of Richard Gibbs, barrister.

Observing the excessive number and precarious existence of private schools in the district, Buntine purchased the goodwill first of St Kilda Grammar School and, in 1896, of Caulfield Grammar School, taking his pupils to Barnett's premises. In 1905 he bought the present site and built new premises, which were opened in 1909. Caulfield Grammar School became a public company in 1931 and Buntine retired the next year.

His prime task had been the defence of private schools in competition with church schools and the state. Their best safeguard, Buntine believed, was the Incorporated Association of Secondary Teachers of Victoria (from 1922 Incorporated Association of Registered Teachers of Victoria) of which he was president in 1914, 1926 and 1931. Fearful of state control, yet uneasy about unregulated private enterprise, he urged a policy of public supervision, arguing for the Registration of Teachers and Schools Act of 1905, and campaigning for the clause in the Education Act of 1910 creating the Council of Public Education.

Unfamiliar with educational ideas, Buntine depended greatly in his own school on his headmaster F. H. J. Archer [q.v.] and the able W. S. Morcom (1890-1966), and turned his attention to the external conditions affecting schooling. Concerned for the child of average ability, he used his membership of the Council of the University of Melbourne in 1933-37, the Schools Board in 1919-22 and 1926-33, and the Standing Committee of Convocation in 1926-33 to ensure appropriate standards in public examinations. He was a member of the University Extension Board in 1912-21, the faculty of education in 1926-34, and the Council of Public Education in 1935-38, and in 1935 represented the State government and the university at the Fifth International Congress on Family Education in Geneva.

Buntine had grown up as a Presbyterian. Whether he was confirmed in the Anglican Church is uncertain, but he was a member of the councils of Melbourne Church of England Girls' Grammar School in 1914-27 and of St Hilda's Deaconess and Missionary Training Home. He was a lay reader of the Melbourne Diocese in 1920-49, and first president of the Victorian branch of the Church Missionary Society, to which he donated £1000 for a scholarship in memory of his eldest son Lieutenant W. H. C. Buntine, M.C. With a group of Evangelicals Buntine helped to found Ridley College in 1909; he was first secretary of its council in 1909-22 and a member until 1953. In 1924-50 he was one of the two London representatives on the Commonwealth Council of the British and Foreign Bible Society in Australia and in 1938 he was elected a life governor. His publications include *Caulfield Grammar School jubilee 1881-1931* (Melbourne, 1931).

Survived by his wife, three sons and a daughter, he died on 26 January 1953 and was buried in Box Hill cemetery after an Anglican service. The Buntine oration, endowed by his family, is delivered biennially at the conference of the Australian College of Education. A portrait by Rollo Thompson is at Caulfield Grammar School. His son Lieut-Colonel Martyn Arnold Buntine (1898-1975) became headmaster of Camberwell Grammar School, Hale School, Perth, and Geelong College.

L. L. Nash, *Forward flows the time* (Melb, 1960); P. H. Karmel, *Some economic aspects of education* (Melb, 1962); K. Cole, *A history of the Church Missionary Society of Australia* (Melb, 1971); *PP* (LA Vic), 1894-95, 2 (3), 55-65; Dioceses of Melbourne and Wangaratta, *Yearbook,* 1914-53; *Argus,* 20 Apr 1893, 27 Jan 1953; Inc Assn of Secondary (Registered) Teachers of Vic, Minutes 1907-29 (Elizabeth St, Melb); W. H. Buntine file (Caulfield Grammar School Archives); Council, and Convocation, and Schools Board minutes (Univ Melb Archives); papers held by Dr R. D. Buntine, Cheltenham, Vic.   E. L. FRENCH

BUNTON, HAYDN WILLIAM (1911-1955), footballer, was born on 5 July 1911 at Albury, New South Wales, son of Ernest Edward Bunton, brickmaker, and his wife Matilda Caroline, née Luhrs, both Victorian-born. An outstanding footballer, cricketer and athlete in his youth at Albury, Bunton attracted the attention of many Melbourne football clubs. Fitzroy finally signed him (for both football and cricket) in 1930, but accusations by disappointed clubs that illegal payments had been made caused the Victorian Football League's permit committee to refuse to allow him to play until 1931. Fresh allegations from a disgruntled secretary of the administratively troubled Fitzroy club revived in 1933 the investigation into payments to Bunton. He and his club were found guilty, but Bunton was merely 'admonished'.

Generally as a rover and wearing the number 7, he played 117 games for Fitzroy and kicked 208 goals. He was 5 ft. 9 ins. (175 cm) in height and weighed about 11½ stone (73 kg). The results of a competition held in Melbourne in 1935 for a suitable nickname suggest his qualities: first 'Beau', second 'Tracker', and third 'Pearler'. Statistics indicate that in 1933 he usually won about 25 kicks a game, took 10 marks, and scored infrequently, although in one match he kicked 8 goals (out of 12) against Collingwood, roved all day, and was presented with the ball; 'so he should have been', said an opponent, 'he had the – thing all afternoon'.

Most observers commented upon his balance, his ball-handling which at times 'bordered on the freakish', and his ability to avoid bumps and tackles. Bunton was a good and accurate but not a long kick, and he eschewed the then fashionable drop-kick. He rarely conceded a free kick, and his handsome brilliance was matched by his scrupulous fairness. Hence he won the Brownlow medal for the fairest and best V.F.L. player in 1931, 1932 and in 1935; in 1934 he was runner-up.

In 1938 Bunton went to Perth to play with Subiaco and there won the Sandover [q.v.] medal in 1938, 1939 and 1941. After service in the army in 1942-44, he played for North Adelaide in 1945 (making his only appearance in a finals game with them), and coached the same club in 1947 and 1948. He died in the Royal Adelaide Hospital on 5 September 1955 from the effects of a car crash, and was buried in North Road cemetery, Nailsworth. His wife, Lylia Frances, née Austin, whom he had married at Scots Church, Melbourne, on 22 February 1936, had died suddenly in Adelaide on Christmas Day 1954.

Bunton's career outside football was undistinguished. At various times he was a shop-assistant, a theatre-manager, a car salesman, and at the end an insurance agent.

A popular and generous man, 'he was always good for a bite'. His elder brother Cleaver became mayor of Albury and briefly senator for New South Wales.

Sporting Globe, 7 June 1930, May, June, 4 Oct 1933, 7 Sept 1955; *Herald* (Melb), 8 Oct 1937, 12 Apr 1952, 6 Sept 1955.   W. F. MANDLE

BURDETT, BASIL (1897-1942), journalist, art dealer and critic, was born on 23 July 1897 at Ipswich, Queensland, son of William Burdett, clerk, and Lillie Jane Gray. He enlisted in the Australian Imperial Force in Brisbane in September 1915 and served as a stretcher-bearer with the 1st Field Ambulance. Before his return to Australia late in 1919 he took a three-month course of commercial training in London. In 1919-21 he was a journalist on the *Brisbane Daily Mail* and first contributed art criticism to that paper. Moving to Sydney, he opened the New Art Salon in Pitt Street; in 1923 he managed a gallery in George Street and then briefly ran another art-dealing business. Early in 1925, with John Young, he established the important Macquarie Galleries in Bligh Street. At this time he was also an associate editor for, and frequent contributor to, *Art in Australia.*

On 22 December 1925 in Melbourne Burdett married Edith Napier Birks of Adelaide; the couple lived at Wahroonga in a house designed by their friend J. D. Moore [q.v.] until the break-up of their marriage in 1929. Burdett then travelled in Europe and returned in mid-1931 for divorce proceedings. His association with Macquarie Galleries also ended that year. He sold a valuable collection of old English glass, china, furniture, books and paintings and returned to Europe where, fluent in both French and Spanish, he roamed widely.

On his return to Australia in 1931, Burdett continued briefly as associate editor of *Art in Australia* and then moved to Melbourne where he joined the *Herald.* After a further 2 years away in 1934-35 he became its art critic in 1936; he also reviewed the ballet performances of the de Basil company during their Melbourne seasons. Commissioned by Sir Keith Murdoch [q.v.] to organize an exhibition of European modernist art, he left Australia late in 1938, returning next year; the comprehensive and seminal *Herald* Exhibition of French and British Contemporary Art opened in Melbourne on 16 October 1939. Ill with jaundice, he could not be active in the Melbourne showing.

Between 1936 and 1941 Burdett brought to art criticism in Australia a unique combination of aesthetic perception, intellectual awareness and open-minded sympathy for the work of the young and the *avant-garde.* His closest cultural ties were with the values of European society and he felt frustrated by parochial attitudes towards the arts in Australia. At times he seemed distant and aloof, but this may have been largely a shield for a natural diffidence and, perhaps too, a disappointment with his own creativity. It is to his great credit that he recognized immediately and promoted the work of artists such as Sidney Nolan, Albert Tucker, Arthur Boyd and Danila Vassilief.

Burdett joined the Australian Red Cross Field Force on 15 January 1941 in Melbourne and embarked for Singapore later that month. He was appointed deputy assistant commissioner on 16 September and assumed responsibility for administering both the Australian and British Red Cross operations in the 'Far East'. He was killed at Sourabaya, Java, when the aircraft on which he was a passenger crashed on landing on 1 February 1942. He was survived by his daughter, born in 1927. In 1943 Burdett was posthumously awarded the (New South Wales) Society of Artists' Medal.

S. Ure Smith (ed), *The Society of Artists book* (Syd, 1943); N. Palmer, *Fourteen years* (Melb, 1948); Joan Lindsay, *Time without clocks* (Melb, 1962); A. McCulloch, *Encyclopedia of Australian art* (Lond, 1968); L. Rees, *The small treasures of a lifetime* (Syd, 1969); A Coates and N. Rosenthal, *The Albert Coates story* (Melb, 1977); *Herald* (Melb), 3 Feb 1942; Burdett *and* Lindsay papers (LaTL); Aust Red Cross Soc, Records (Melb).
                                        RICHARD HAESE

BURFITT, MARY BOYD; *see* WILLIAMS, MARY BOYD

BURFITT, WALTER CHARLES FITZMAURICE (1874-1956), surgeon, was born on 16 February 1874 at Dubbo, New South Wales, son of Charles Trimby Burfitt (d. 1927), native-born storekeeper, and his Irish-born wife Annie, née Fitzmaurice. His father later became a stock and station agent in Sydney; he wrote *History of the founding of the wool industry of Australia* (1907) and was honorary secretary of the Australian Historical Society in 1909-14, president in 1915 and an original fellow. Walter was educated at St Aloysius' College, Sydney, from 1885 and in 1890 went on to St Ignatius' College, Riverview. In 1892 he won a scholarship to St John's College, University of Sydney (B.A., 1894; B.Sc., 1898; M.B., Ch.M., 1900). Helped by an aunt, he financed his studies by winning some eight prizes and scholarships, and in 1900 won the University Medal. That year he became resident medical officer at the Royal Prince Alfred Hospital and in 1901-12 was in general practice at Glebe. On 9 June 1908 at Our Lady of the Sacred Heart, Randwick, he married Esmey Mary Elliott Mann.

In 1912 Burfitt moved to Macquarie Street where he practised as a consultant surgeon until 1940. He was surgeon and later gynaecologist at Lewisham Hospital in 1901-40, medical officer at St Vincent's Hospital from 1901 and at the diphtheria clinic of the Royal Alexandra Hospital for Children, and visiting surgeon at Parramatta District and Western Suburbs hospitals. He became known for his deft and extremely rapid operations.

A life member of the Royal Society of New South Wales from 1898, with a lifelong interest in geology, in 1927 he gave £500 to the society (later raised to £1000 by his wife) for the Walter Burfitt Prize and Medal for published research; he always invited the recipients to his home at Elizabeth Bay to meet the family. In 1925 he had given £1000 for the Walter Burfitt Scholarship in physics or chemistry at the University of Sydney. A founding member of the Royal Australasian College of Surgeons in 1928, he was also a founder and sometime president of the Medical Benevolent Association of New South Wales; with Katharine Ogilvie he set up and was sometime chairman of the Hospital Almoners' Guild. He was a member of the Catholic Medical Guild of St Luke, a fellow of St John's College and chairman of the Council of Sancta Sophia College, University of Sydney, from 1929.

Burfitt was a member of the Australian Jockey and Royal Sydney Golf clubs and of the Sydney Cricket Ground, and also of the Union and University clubs. He joined his family at Mount Wilson whenever possible during the summer, and was a keen gardener. In 1940 he was appointed a knight commander of the Papal Order of St Sylvester.

After suffering a stroke in 1944, Burfitt ceased to practise. He died at Lewisham Hospital on 1 June 1956 and was buried in the Catholic section of Waverley cemetery. He was survived by his wife, two sons and three married daughters – both sons and his daughter Barbara followed him in medicine. He left an estate valued for probate at £80 390. His portrait, painted in 1924 by Dorafield Hardy, R.A., is held by the family.

JRAHS, 13 (1927), p 378; Roy Soc NSW, *Procs*, 91 (1957), no 1; *SMH*, 29 Aug 1927.

WALTER FURNEAUX BURFITT

BURGESS, HENRY THOMAS (1839-1923), Methodist minister, was born on 27 March 1839 at Sandbach, Cheshire, England, son of Thomas Burgess, ironmonger, and his wife Ellen, née Bostock. The family migrated to South Australia in 1848 and settled at Kooringa, where his father became an official at the Burra copper-mine. Burgess attended the local public school, and worked for two years in a store, then for three years as an assistant in stores at Adelaide and Mount Barker. In 1859, at the early age of 20, he was accepted as a probationary minister by the Wesleyan Methodist Church. He was appointed to Yankalilla, a rural circuit south of Adelaide, and began the mandatory six-year course of study which culminated in his ordination in 1865. Burgess was conservative in his theology and his emergence as an outstanding preacher was rapid. From 1870 he ministered to a succession of major circuits in South Australia, and remained in parish work till 1902. On 30 September 1863 in Adelaide he had married Ellen Pickford; they had sixteen children.

Burgess was president of the annual Wesleyan Conference in South Australia in 1880 and 1890, and was president-general of the General (federal) Conference in 1897-1901. In the latter capacity he represented the Church at the inaugural celebrations of the Commonwealth of Australia and the opening of the first Federal parliament. His primary ecclesiastical contribution was his advocacy of union of the four branches of the Methodist movement. The Bible Christian Church was particularly strong in the colony largely due to Cornish immigration. The attitude towards union was lukewarm among some of the better-educated and more prosperous Wesleyans. It was largely due to the leadership of Burgess and the respect that he evoked among all the heirs of Wesley that union was realized in South Australia in 1900. He was elected president of the first South Australian Conference of the Methodist Church that year, and played a leading part in the achievement of federal union four years later, especially in drafting the constitution for the first general conference.

Burgess also edited his Church's paper in South Australia, the *Christian Weekly and Methodist Journal*. He was vice-president and secretary of the Adelaide Children's Hospital in 1901-13, and secretary of the South Australian branch of the Royal Geographical Society in 1916-20.

To help support his 'large and afflicted family' – only eight children survived infancy – Burgess engaged in journalism. He was a leader-writer for the *South Australian Register* for several years, and contributed prize-winning essays to religious papers in the United States of America. He had a 'terse idiomatic style' and wrote several small religious works, the best known being *Methodism and the twentieth century* (Adelaide, 1901). A major literary achievement was his editorship of the two-volume *Cyclopedia of South Australia* (1907-09). This massive miscellany of information on aspects of South Australian life gave much space to biographical sketches of leading citizens and remains a useful research source. In 1908 Burgess had been awarded the honorary degree of LL.D. by Wesleyan University, Middletown, Connecticut, U.S.A.

Predeceased by his wife, he died on 19 November 1923 and was buried in West Terrace cemetery, Adelaide.

H. T. Burgess (ed), *Cyclopedia of South Australia*, 2 (Adel, 1909); J. E. Carruthers, *Lights in the southern sky* (Syd, 1924); *Methodist Church of A'sia* (SA), Conference minutes, 1924; *Christian Weekly and Methodist J*, 1 June 1894; *Advertiser* (Adel), and *Register* (Adel), 20 Nov 1923; *Aust Christian Cwlth*, 20 Nov 1923.   ARNOLD D. HUNT

BURGOYNE, THOMAS (1827-1920), politician, builder and journalist, was born on 10 June 1827 at Gobe Farm near Gladestry, Radnorshire, South Wales, son of William Burgoyne, builder and farmer, and his wife Elizabeth. Educated at private schools at Ludlow, when 14 he was articled to a Hereford architect who trained him in trigonometry, surveying and building. On 28 August 1848 he married Jane Jervis, and next year they migrated to South Australia on the *Royal Sovereign*.

Burgoyne worked as a builder before spending a luckless year on the Victorian goldfields in 1852. In 1856 he went to Port Augusta, where he erected the first permanent building and designed St Augustine's Church; and he built homesteads, tanks and woolsheds all over the pastoral north. A teetotal Unitarian, Burgoyne established a drama club, debating society and cricket club.

The 1864 drought meant Burgoyne was unable to collect £10 000 in debts. He sold his business and worked as an auctioneer and correspondent for the *South Australian Register*. His first wife had died and on 30 September 1871 he married Julia Frances Cotter. He led moves towards Port Augusta's incorporation and was the first town clerk and surveyor in 1875-79; councillor in 1879-81, he was mayor in 1882. In 1877 he had founded the *Port Augusta Dispatch* which he edited for three years.

In 1884-1915 Burgoyne represented the enormous seat of Newcastle (Flinders) in the House of Assembly. He published a pamphlet, *The land question* (1884) in which he advocated the land nationalization theories of Henry George [q.v.4], and next year formed a liberal faction, the Independent (Country) Party, which influenced successive land Acts and at times claimed twenty-two members. Nicknamed 'Old Logic', Burgoyne supported free trade, progressive land tax, property tax, payment of members and retrenchment.

On 27 June 1889, against his faction's policy, he accepted ministerial office under (Sir) J. A. Cockburn [q.v.] as commissioner of crown lands and immigration until May 1890 and as commissioner of public works till the government fell in August. He had initiated a Crown Lands Act but later saw his ministerial interlude as a 'mistake' and resumed as party chairman. In November 1899 the six-year-old Kingston [q.v.] ministry reintroduced a previously rejected household franchise bill: Burgoyne and his group sponsored a motion which led to the government's fall. Asked to form a ministry, Burgoyne declined, but was minister for education in the conservative V. L. Solomon's [q.v.] subsequent one-week government. In 1906 Burgoyne chaired the meeting to establish A. H. Peake's [q.v.] Liberal and Democratic Union and spoke eloquently of the need for Liberals to hold the ring between Labor and conservatives. In 1915, aged 87, he lost his seat.

Dignified and respected, Burgoyne had been a founder and first president of the South Australian Institutes Association, whose early journals he edited, and a governor of the Public Library, Museum and Art Gallery of South Australia. In 1908 he painted a portrait of Premier Tom Price [q.v.]. For the last ten years of his life Burgoyne was lame. Predeceased by his second wife, he died on 23 March 1920 at Fullarton and was buried in Magill cemetery. He had three children by his first wife and five by his second. His estate was sworn for probate at £1195.

The 'Register' guide to the parliament of South Australia (Adel, 1887); H. T. Burgess (ed), *Cyclopedia of South Australia*, 1 (Adel, 1908); *SA Institutes J*, 30 Apr 1931; *Register* (Adel), 27 June 1889, 10 June 1916; *Advertiser* (Adel), 10 June 1919, 24 Mar 1920; *Observer* (Adel), 27 Mar 1920; family information.   DAVID GOLDSWORTHY

BURKE, JOHN (1842-1919) and JOHN EDWARD (1871-1947) were shipmasters and ship-owners. John was born in 1842 at Kinsale, County Cork, Ireland, son of Denis O'Hara Burke, fisherman, and his wife Ellen, née O'Connor. In his youth he made several Atlantic voyages as a seaman and was in the United States of America at the outbreak of the civil war. Returning to Ireland, he signed on the *Erin-Go-Bragh*, chartered by a brother of Bishop James Quinn [q.v.5] to take Irish emigrants to Queensland. After a six-months voyage with much sickness, passengers and crew were released from quarantine to land in Brisbane on 8 August 1862.

Burke jumped ship, worked briefly as a pilot, then joined the Australasian Steam Navigation Co., sailing as a deck-hand in the *Queensland* and the *Telegraph*. On 1 October 1863 he married 20-year-old Elicia Swords who had been a passenger on the *Erin-Go-Bragh*. After working for a time on river and bay ships, Burke secured a master's licence restricted to sheltered waters, and commanded the *Fanny*, trading to the Logan and Albert rivers for Honeyman & Sons. In the Logan flood of 22 January 1887, Burke and his crew worked indefatigably to save over fifty lives and earned a public testimonial.

When his employers closed down that year, he bought the *Louisa* from them and traded first to Ipswich and the Logan and Albert rivers and later into Moreton Bay. The *Louisa* brought the first relief supplies to Ipswich after the 1893 flood. Burke acquired other small vessels and lighters for his fleet and in the early twentieth century added coal-bunkering plant. About 1910 he sold the lighters and bunkering plant and bought the *Porpoise* to establish a coastal service. He later added the *Gundiah* and the paddle-steamer *Adonis* for the Maryborough-Townsville timber trade. He retired in 1915 but served as a director of John Burke Ltd until his death from pneumonic influenza on 3 June 1919. He was buried in Toowong cemetery with Roman Catholic rites; his estate was sworn for probate at £6776.

Of Burke's twelve children, Peter Patrick (1877-1963) sailed as a master for the company, while William Joseph (1882-1966) worked as a stevedore and supervised a fuel business owned by the company. John Edward was born on 8 January 1871 in Brisbane. Educated at state schools, he began work as a plumber's assistant, then served as a deck-hand on the *Fanny* and, probably from 1887, shared ownership of John Burke & Son. He married Bridget O'Keefe at St Stephen's Cathedral, Brisbane, on 17 April 1895; they had three children.

When his father retired, John Edward took over management of the company. Services were extended along the Queensland coast and in 1921 to the Gulf of Carpentaria, which was soon described by residents as 'Burke's flaming ocean'. He saw a big future for the company in promoting Gulf settlement and became a provisional director of a proposed Karumba Co-operative Meat and Canning Co. The plan proved abortive but, when eventually in 1934 Shand's Gulf Meatworks were constructed, Burke's supplied the wharf at Karumba where the meatworks continued to operate until World War II.

Difficulties created by waterfront strikes and cost increases in the 1920s and 1930s were compounded by the loss of two ships. The *Douglas Mawson*, chartered from the Queensland government, disappeared during a Gulf cyclone in March 1923 and twelve crewmen and five passengers perished; the company-owned *Dorrigo* sank off Double Island Point on 2 April 1926 with a loss of twenty-two lives.

Burke was an alderman of South Brisbane in 1908-23 and mayor in 1912; he was prominent in the municipal acquisition and extension of the area's wharves, served on the Victoria Bridge Board, represented employers on the Board for Masters and Engineers of River and Bay Steamboats and Barges, and in 1915 failed as a Liberal candidate for the South Brisbane parliamentary seat. He followed the turf and, as chairman of the Kedron Amateur Racing Club, negotiated the purchase in 1923 of the interests of John Wren [q.v.] and his partner Ben Nathan in unregistered Brisbane race-courses. He was involved again with Wren over the Coorparoo Turf Club in 1929, as chairman of directors of Brisbane Amusements Ltd. A royal commission in 1930 on racing found both transactions highly dubious.

Burke's contemporaries remembered him as a strong character with a lively sense of humour. An unrepentant enthusiast for private enterprise, he defined Australia as 'an island surrounded by Navigation Acts ... and vexatious regulations of all descriptions'. The paintwork of his ships, originally Irish green, was changed to black with green funnels after repeated black bans by striking unions. However, the firm held the respect of its men who argued that 'they fed us well and treated us well'; many employees became shareholders. He would have no truck with women, even in his office, because no lady would stand his language.

Burke died on 8 October 1947 at his home at Kangaroo Point and was buried in Toowong cemetery with Roman Catholic rites. His estate was valued for probate at £48 264. His son John Augustine (1896-1972) managed the company in his turn until it was taken over by the Dillingham Corporation in 1968.

J. F. McGill, *Historical happenings and incredible incidents of the Queensland turf* (np, nd. Copy,

Univ Qld Lib); D. Doyle, *A saga of the sea* (Brisb, 1937); N. L. McKellar, *From Derby round to* *Burketown* (Brisb, 1977); *PP* (Qld), 1930, 2, 1289; 'A legend in Queensland's development: John Burke Pty. Ltd.', *Qld Maritime Bulletin*, 5 (1973), no 3, supp; Burke cutting-book (Oxley Lib, Brisb); Immigration records, 1862 *and* Company file 158/1920 (QA).   G. R. C. McLEOD

BURKE, THOMAS MICHAEL (1870-1949), businessman and philanthropist, was born on 30 June 1870 at Norval near Ararat, Victoria, second son of William Marcus Burke, Dublin-born miner, and his wife Mary Ann, née Florence, of Aberdeen, Scotland. After attending Norval State School and Ararat High School, Burke became a railway clerk at Spencer Street, Melbourne, in 1887. Five years later he was promoted to Ararat. There on 25 July 1898 at St Mary's Catholic Church, he married Margaret Duggan Brady, daughter of a railway inspector.

Burke was an active member of the Australian Natives' Association, becoming president of the Ararat branch in the last years of the Federal movement. He was elected vice-president of the Victorian A.N.A. in 1900-01, and chief president in 1902-03, when he led delegations to Western Australia and Tasmania to found branches there.

In March 1902 Burke became secretary of the Civil Service Co-operative Society of Victoria, and was a leader of railwaymen in their confrontation with the (Sir) William Irvine [q.v.] government over its wages and anti-union policies. Burke quit the railways just before the application of coercive legislation against strikers and their spokesmen, and in May 1903 he established the Civil Service Co-operative Store, Flinders Street, Melbourne, becoming manager. In 1904 he was secretary of the first 'Made-in-Australia' Exhibition and frequently spoke out in favour of protection and co-operatives. In September 1914 he stood as Labor candidate for the Federal seat of Corangamite but narrowly lost.

Following large trading losses in mid-1914 the Co-operative Store was sold in 1915. Burke then turned to the real estate business. He bought land in the depressed market of the war years, subdivided it and sold it on nominal deposit and easy terms in the immediate post-war period. His scale of operations made him one of Australia's best-known real estate agents. His advertising spread the 'new gospel' of '8d. a day' to secure a stake in an 'expanding Australia'. By 1924 Burke had diversified into finance and investment, and had set up offices in

country centres as well as in Sydney, Newcastle, Brisbane and Adelaide. In August 1924 T. M. Burke Pty Ltd was incorporated as a holding company with family shareholding.

The Depression caused the temporary collapse of the land market. By the mid-1930s, however, Burke had reverted to more conventional sales and the company both survived and prospered. Branches were set up in Auckland, Singapore and London. In May 1936 he handed over day to day management to his sons while remaining chairman of directors.

Burke was a member of all major Victorian racing-clubs, an owner from the 1920s of successful racehorses (including Quintus, who won the Newmarket and Standish handicaps), and president of the Breeders, Owners and Trainers' Association of Victoria for several years. His philanthropic activities included financial support to the Melbourne University Conservatorium Symphony Orchestra and a gift of land on the summit of Mount Dandenong for a public park. His membership of the Victorian Hospitals and Charities Board in 1931-49 included terms as chairman in 1936-39 and 1944-45. He was also a member of the Victorian Council of the Australian Red Cross. He was appointed consul for Poland in 1933 and kept this post for the rest of his life.

Burke was an ardent Catholic benefactor and lay leader. In 1920 he bought Studley Hall, Kew, and gave it to the Jesuits as a preparatory school for Xavier College; it became known as Burke Hall. His large donations helped to establish Corpus Christi College, Werribee, and St Anthony's Foundling Home, Sydney; smaller gifts sustained many Catholic institutions and activities. He was first national chairman of the Knights of the Southern Cross and in 1926 presented a chalice to Pope Pius XI on behalf of Australian Catholic businessmen. He was on the committee for the National Eucharistic Congress held in Melbourne in December 1934. A member of the Australian Catholic Federation in its heyday, 1911-22, he lobbied in vain Prime Minister (Viscount) Bruce [q.v.] in 1928 to seek a national solution to state aid, gave the opening address in the 'Education Justice' campaign in Victoria in 1929, and was prominent in organizing the Catholic Education Congress of November 1936 in Adelaide, at which he moved the resolution to establish a Catholic Taxpayers' Association.

In 1942 Burke was appointed C.M.G. His last years were spent quietly at his home at Armadale, where he died of cancer on 16 February 1949, survived by his wife, five sons and two daughters; he was buried in

Melbourne general cemetery. His portrait by Max Meldrum [q.v.] hangs in the library of Burke Hall.

J. E. Menadue, *A centenary history of the Australian Natives' Association 1871-1971* (Melb, 1971); K. S. C., *Advance Australia*, Mar 1969; A. W. Hannan, Victorian Catholics, state aid & religious instruction in state schools, 1901-39 (M.Ed. thesis, Monash Univ, 1973); T. M. Burke Pty Ltd, Records (Corporate Affairs Office, Melb); family records and interviews.   TONY HANNAN

BURLEY, JOHNSTON (1873-1955), soldier, carpenter and engine driver, was born on 26 September 1873 at Aghavea near Lisnaskea, Ireland, son of William Burley, dairyman, and his wife Annie, née Trimble. The family came to Australia in the mid-1880s and settled in Melbourne where Joe, as he was known, helped his father run a dairy at Carlton; he was then apprenticed to a master carpenter and while learning his trade served as a soldier in a volunteer unit. In the early 1890s he went to New Zealand in search of work and later earned his passage home by looking after animals in a circus. Unable to find employment in Melbourne, he bought a steerage passage to Western Australia with £2 he had won in a bicycle race, and worked as a carpenter at Perth and Shark Bay until October 1899, when he enlisted for service in the South African War as a private in the 1st Western Australian (Mounted Infantry) Contingent.

The contingent was absorbed into the Australian Regiment and served with the Kimberley Relief Force. At Slingersfontein on 9 February 1900 Burley was in a party of about twenty-five Western Australians who defended a kopje against several hundred Boers, and for outstanding gallantry in this action was awarded the Distinguished Conduct Medal. He served in operations in the Transvaal, Orange Free State and Cape Colony before returning home in December, and was promoted lance corporal on 1 January 1901, two months before his unit was disbanded. He joined the Western Australian Government Railways, qualifying as a locomotive engine driver in March 1903, and on 24 February 1904 at Perth he married Alice Mahala Palmer. He became a member of the Salvation Army on his marriage but he later reverted to Methodism and brought up his six children in that faith.

In 1916 Burley, now a sergeant in the Australian Military Forces, was given a temporary appointment on the instructional staff as a warrant officer. He enlisted in the Australian Imperial Force on 19 January 1917 as a company sergeant major in the 5th Broad Gauge Railway Operating Company and embarked at Fremantle ten days later. He served in Belgium from June 1917 to April 1918 and in France, with the 6th B.G.R.O.C., until the Armistice. In June 1917 he was in charge of a train when a wagon containing explosives was set on fire by enemy shelling. Burley uncoupled the rest of the train and sent it along the line to a safe distance, then tried to put out the fire. The wagon exploded but his action saved the train. He was awarded a Bar to his D.C.M., and was the only Australian to win that medal in the South African War and awarded a Bar for service with the A.I.F.

After demobilization Burley continued as an engine driver until 1934 when he lost the lower part of his right leg and part of his left foot in a railway accident. Until then he was active in the Federated Engine Drivers' & Firemen's Union. In retirement he divided his time between his farm at Bullsbrook (which he had worked with the help of his sons since 1926) and his home at Bayswater, Perth. Survived by his wife, two sons and three daughters, he died at Mt Lawley on 21 June 1955 and was buried in Karrakatta cemetery with Methodist forms.

Burley was a handsome man with a fresh complexion, fair hair and grey eyes. Although quick-tempered, he was popular with workmates and acquaintances. All his life he was an avid reader, with a particular interest in war history. He studied elocution and often recited at church socials. He was a teetotaller.

Aust Defence Dept, *Official records of the Australian military contingents to the war in South Africa*, P. L. Murray ed (Melb, 1912); J. Burridge (ed), *Western Australian contingents to the South African War* (Perth, 1972); *London Gazette*, 27 Sept 1901, 16 Apr 1902, 26 Nov 1917; *Listening Post*, July 1955; *West Australian*, 24-25 June 1955; 5th Australian Broad Gauge Railway Operating Company — a brief record (AWM); information from Mrs B. West, Karrinyup, and Mrs G. Wareing, Chittering, WA.   REX CLARK*
WENDY BIRMAN

BURLEY GRIFFIN, WALTER; see GRIFFIN

BURN, ALAN (1889-1959), academic engineer, was born on 19 October 1889 in Hobart, son of William Alexander Burn of the long-established firm of Burn & Son, auctioneers, and his wife Marion Louisa, née MacMillan. After education at Officer College, Friends' High School and King's Grammar School, he graduated B.Sc. from the University of Tasmania in 1909 and

M.Sc. in 1911. That year he also obtained his B.E. from the University of Sydney while working there as a demonstrator in electrical engineering. In 1912 he became an assistant mechanical engineer with the State Rivers and Water Supply Commission of Victoria. Two years later he received the first Walter and Eliza Hall [qq.v.] travelling fellowship in engineering awarded by the University of Sydney, enabling him to work at the Escher Wyss & Co. establishment in Zurich, Switzerland, on the design and construction of water-turbines and pumps, a topic which was to prove of lasting interest to him. In England, in 1916, he joined the Aeronautical Inspection Department and, having attained the rank of honorary lieutenant in the Royal Air Force, he accepted, in 1918, a position as locum tenens for the chair of civil engineering in the University of Tasmania; he was appointed professor the following year and emeritus professor after his retirement in 1956.

One of the university's best-known personalities, Burn was a member of its council in 1922-27, 1929-41 and 1945-56, dean of the faculty of engineering for many years and chairman of the Engineering Board of Management of the University of Tasmania and the Hobart Technical College. In 1945-49 he was the last part-time vice-chancellor, and he attended the conferences of British Empire universities in 1931 and 1948, receiving the honorary degree of LL.D. from the University of London in the latter year.

Burn regarded engineering as an art, stressing in lectures and papers the role of the professional engineer as a leader in the community. In the 1920s he taught every engineering subject on the syllabus and is remembered by his students, with whom he established close relations, as a thorough, clear thinker, a man who dealt in elementary principles, and a first-class lecturer who kept his mathematics simple. He was idealistic, believed education should encourage moral as well as mental development, and wished university scholars to experience the stimulus of learning from men at the frontiers of knowledge.

Many of his students went on to eminent positions in engineering practice, and through them Burn maintained contacts with industry, contributing practically to the progress of the State. After widespread destruction of timber bridges in Tasmania during the 1929 floods he stimulated much pioneering development in bridge design, including what are claimed to be the first composite beam bridges (Proctor's Road, 1933, and Ulverstone bridges), very early work on the welding of major structures (Kimberley, 1932), and the floating Derwent bridge at Hobart (1943). He was an associate

commissioner for the Hydro-Electric Commission in 1951-59. In 1950 he was president of the Institution of Engineers, Australia, having been a foundation member and in 1925 president of the Tasmanian division. He won the institution's (W. H.) Warren [q.v.6] Memorial Prize in 1939 and, in recognition of his lifetime of service, the Peter Nicol Russell [q.v.6] Memorial Medal in 1955.

Burn was not physically robust. He enjoyed tennis, motoring — in days when there were few motorists — and the amateur theatre, being president of the Hobart Repertory Theatre Society in 1935-36. On 31 March 1926 he had married a widow Olive Grant Harbottle (d. 1970), née Pinnock, of Hobart. She became a well-known producer in repertory theatre and continued an association with Burn & Son, through periodic displays of antiques at Burn's Mart Auction Sales, which were a feature of Tuesdays in Hobart for over a hundred years. Burn died without issue at Hobart on 18 December 1959. His estate was valued for probate at £41 795. The Alan Burn lectures, given annually to the Institution of Engineers, commemorate his name, work and the traditions which he respected. A prize, awarded in engineering at the University of Tasmania, also honours his distinguished career. A complete list of his publications appears in University of Tasmania *Calendar*, 1955.

Inst of Engineers, Aust, *J*, 27 (1955); *Univ Tas Gazette*, Apr 1960; *Mercury*, 19 Dec 1959, 24 Sept 1970.
                                    M. S. GREGORY

BURNAGE, GRANVILLE JOHN (1858-1945), soldier and merchant, was born on 14 December 1858 at Dungog, New South Wales, son of Thomas Burnage, watchmaker, and his wife Kezia Agatha, née Hodges, both English-born. The family moved to Newcastle where Thomas established himself as a wine and spirits merchant; after schooling, Granville became a salesman and later a partner in the family business. In 1878 he was one of the first recruits to join the Newcastle Infantry Company, New South Wales militia. He was commissioned lieutenant in 1883, promoted captain in 1885 and made honorary major in 1896.

In 1901-02 Burnage saw action in the South African War as major commanding 'B' squadron, 3rd New South Wales Mounted Rifles Regiment; he served in operations in eastern Transvaal and the Orange River Colony. Invalided home in 1902, he resumed work as a wine and spirits merchant and continued to serve in the militia. In September he was confirmed as major and made second-in-command of the 4th Australian Infantry Regiment. He commanded the regiment in 1907-13 and in 1908-13 was also officer in charge of the Newcastle port defences; he was promoted lieut-colonel in 1909.

Burnage joined the Australian Imperial Force on 28 September 1914 but, because of his age, did not expect a field command. He was placed in charge of the Rosehill A.I.F. depot, then on 6 October was appointed to raise and command the 13th Battalion. In choosing his officers and other ranks he set an exceptionally high standard and, during the battalion's training period, made himself unpopular by the strictness of his discipline. The battalion reached Egypt in February 1915 and, because its transport always carried streamers in battalion colours to distinguish it from other units during manoeuvres, it became known as 'Bill Burnage's circus'. It landed at Gallipoli on the night of 25 April and went into Monash Valley. Burnage had orders to reinforce Quinn's Post and Pope's Hill and to help clear the enemy from Russell's Top; in the first week of fighting his troops suffered heavy casualties but earned the name of 'the fighting Thirteenth'. He was 'continually in the front line... moving from post to post across the open'; his fearlessness in action and his concern for his men rapidly won him extraordinary esteem and affection.

On 2 May the battalion took part in an attack on Baby 700, a key enemy position. The men of the 13th reached their objective and held their ground but were cut off without support. Burnage went back alone across an area swept by Turkish fire to report to brigade headquarters; he was ordered to withdraw his men under cover of darkness. 'The Colonel', wrote his second-in-command, 'was the last man out of that deadly fight, in which we lost 300 men... The men were thrilled by such leadership and ever afterwards referred to Colonel Burnage as "The Gamest Old Man" '. On 29 May, during a fierce Turkish attack on Quinn's Post, Burnage's left elbow was shattered in a bomb blast. He was invalided home, mentioned in dispatches in August and appointed C.B. in December. For the rest of the war he was officer commanding on various troopships between Australia and England; he won commendation for his leadership when the *Barunga*, carrying over 800 troops, was torpedoed in July 1918.

Burnage was demobilized in September and resumed business in Newcastle. He commanded the 2nd Battalion, 13th Regiment, Australian Military Forces, until March 1921 when he retired with the honorary rank of colonel. Burnage was a staunch churchman. On 25 November 1915 he had married Helen Haslewood at St Peter's Anglican Church, London. Survived by his wife, he died at Toronto on 12 July 1945 and was cremated. His estate was sworn for probate at £28 490.

Aust Defence Dept, *Official records of the Australian military contingents to the war in South Africa*, P. L. Murray ed (Melb, 1912); C. E. W. Bean, *The story of Anzac*, 1, 2 (Syd, 1921, 1924); T. A. White, *The fighting Thirteenth* (Syd, 1924); A. W. Jose, *The Royal Australian Navy* (Syd, 1928); *London Gazette*, 5 Aug, 15 Dec 1915; *Reveille* (Syd), July, Sept 1939, Aug 1940, Aug 1945; records (AWM).
D. V. GOLDSMITH

BURNS, SIR JAMES (1846-1923), businessman, shipowner and philanthropist, was born on 10 February 1846 at Polmont, Stirlingshire, Scotland, son of David Burns, merchant, and his wife Margaret, née Shiress. Educated at Newington Academy and the Royal High School, Edinburgh, he migrated to Brisbane in 1862 with a brother, worked as a jackeroo on stations, and in 1865 combined with his brother in Burns & Scott, Brisbane storekeepers. He joined the Gympie gold rush in 1867, made large profits from three stores of his own and, after the death of his father in 1868, returned in 1870 to Scotland through the United States of America. From Scotland he briefly visited war-torn France as an observer.

Burns brought his mother, sister and two brothers to Queensland in 1872 and opened a store at Townsville, supplying all the North Queensland goldfields. On 8 February 1875 in Brisbane he married Mary Susan Ledingham, who died in May next year, leaving a daughter. The schooner *Isabelle*, which he had chartered in 1873 to ensure supplies from Sydney, became the nucleus of an eventual fleet. Prominent in promoting coastal shipping services and inland trade, he was a member of an 1876 expedition seeking a route from the Hodgkinson goldfield to Trinity Inlet (Cairns), but at the end of the year he was induced by constant attacks of malaria to settle in Sydney. He financed his Townsville manager (Sir) Robert Philp [q.v.] as a partner in a new firm under Philp's name. On 1 April 1877 Burns opened as a merchant under his own name in Sydney. At Elsternwick, Victoria, on 31 March 1880 he married with Presbyterian forms Mary Heron Morris (d. 1904).

Concentrating initially on a regular shipping service between Sydney and Townsville, Burns moved rapidly from sail to steam, and in 1881 joined the British India Steam Navigation Co. Ltd in promoting the

Queensland Steam Navigation Co. Its aggressive competition soon forced the Australasian Steam Navigation Co. to sell out. He played an important part in the negotiations for sale and subsequent creation of the Australasian United Steam Navigation Co. in 1887, and his company became their agents at Sydney, Townsville and other North Queensland ports.

In 1879 Burns had expanded into a new trading firm in the Gulf of Carpentaria and by 1880 had compelled his main rivals, Clifton & Aplin [q.v.3], to accept his monopoly of the trade of Normanton and thus later of the Croydon goldfield. He established a store at Thursday Island at the same time, giving the firm entry to the pearl-shell industry and enabling it to participate in the exploitation of New Guinea from the beginning of government in 1884. Branches were established during the 1880s in most of the major North Queensland ports. The firm also controlled the Townsville lighter fleet and in 1883-85 flirted with the Pacific island labour trade. Always uneasy about the trade, Burns withdrew when some members of the crew of his *Hopeful* were prosecuted for malpractice.

The firms in Sydney, Townsville, Charters Towers, Cairns, Thursday Island and Normanton were amalgamated in April 1883 into Burns, Philp & Co. Ltd. Burns initially held 43 per cent of the shares and remained chairman and managing director until 1923. Although senior staff became shareholders, he remained in strict and unsentimental control; when Philp left the firm in 1893, it was the enterprise of Burns alone that guided its expansion: during the 1890s branches were established at Geraldton and Fremantle in Western Australia, and at Port Moresby and Samarai in Papua.

In 1889 Burns became a shareholder in the Australasian New Hebrides Co. Ltd; and the A.U.S.N. Co. dominated New Hebrides shipping. Following mismanagement and failure of its settlement scheme, the New Hebrides Co. was reconstructed in 1893 with Burns Philp as managing agents, and was later taken over. With subsidies from the Victorian and New South Wales governments and the Presbyterian mission to the New Hebrides, the firm became the principal instrument for Australian imperialism in the group; it also held extensive mail contracts and received an extra subsidy to run its steamers under Australian industrial conditions. When the French government began actively promoting the settlement of its nationals in 1901, the new Commonwealth government accepted a proposal by Burns to provide land and passages for British settlers in return for a new extended mail-service contract. The venture seemed to be commercially sound since the proposed settlers would be practically tied to the company, but it was never very profitable because of labour problems, Australian tariffs and the uncertainties of international administration. Burns and his Pacific manager W. H. Lucas [q.v.] corresponded regularly and maintained personal relations with Commonwealth leaders for over twenty years, often through Atlee Hunt [q.v.].

The firm's interests slowly extended throughout the Pacific islands as far east as Samoa. Its interests in the South Pacific were linked by its extensive line of steamships — by 1907 operating to the New Hebrides, Solomon, Gilbert and Ellice islands and Papuan ports. In addition Burns took a particular interest in their service from Sydney through Java to Singapore. In 1905 a company ship trading at Jaluit in the Marshall Islands had been charged what seemed outrageous port-dues by the German authorities on the ground that the company was exempted from internal charges borne by resident Germans. The case aroused Burns's Imperial fervour. Asserting that the claim breached international law, he used his government friends to seek compensation of £17 500 through the British Foreign Office. When negotiations concluded in 1910, the Germans paid £4100. Complaints from New Hebrides settlers of rapacity and inefficiency brought an investigation of the firm's activities by a Commonwealth royal commission in 1915. The complaints were rejected.

Diverse in his business interests, Burns was chairman of the (North) Queensland Insurance Co. Ltd in 1886-1923, the New South Wales Mortgage, Land, and Agency Co. and the Solomon Islands Development Co. Ltd; he was also a director of the Australian Mutual Provident Society, the Sydney Exchange Co., the Bank of North Queensland, and various collieries. He was a member of the Union Club, Sydney, from 1896. Much of his spare time was devoted to the volunteer defences: having joined the Parramatta troop of the 1st Light Horse Regiment (New South Wales Lancers) as a trooper in June 1891, he was immediately promoted captain, and major in January 1896. From September 1897 to June 1903 he commanded the regiment as its lieut-colonel and, promoted colonel, the 1st Australian Light Horse Brigade from July 1903 to January 1907, when he retired because of age. Through his efforts and financial aid, detachments of the Lancers attended Queen Victoria's Diamond Jubilee in 1897 and the Aldershot Tattoo in 1899; he also helped the same detachment join the first British armies in the South African War. His deep personal interest in his men and 'quiet gentlemanly manner' made him 'more beloved than any other of the regiment's commanders'.

In 1906 Burns served on a royal commission of inquiry into railway administration and in 1908 was appointed to the Legislative Council; that year he was a commissioner for the Franco-British Exhibition, London. Proud of his Scottish descent, he was president of the Highland Society of New South Wales in 1903-23 and probably helped finance its journal, the *Scottish Australasian*. From the late 1880s he lived at Gowan Brae, near Parramatta; the Lancers had their rifle-range in a gully of its extensive grounds. In 1910 he gave land at North Parramatta to endow the Burnside Presbyterian Homes for Children and was chairman of its board for ten years. A trustee of the Australian Museum, Sydney, he collected Australian minerals, especially opals, Pacific island shells and curios, and some artefacts for his own museum at Gowan Brae.

During World War I Burns helped establish a scheme for insuring enlisted men with dependants. At the same time he was quick to establish a shipping service to Rabaul and to profit from the Australian military occupation of German New Guinea. He became a close friend of the governor-general Sir Ronald Munro Ferguson [q.v.], a fellow Scot, and sometimes lent him Gowan Brae. During World War I Burns supplied him with confidential information on Japanese movements in the Pacific. Greatly concerned about the 'swarm of Japanese coming South', and their danger to Australian and British political and trading interests, he repeatedly urged Munro Ferguson and the Commonwealth government to make it clear to the Japanese that they must hand over their recently acquired gains south of the Equator. He also devised a scheme for a Pacific island federation and a single administration for British possessions in the Pacific. In 1915 he went to London and, with three sons on active service, he was able to visit France — he wrote an account of the trip on his return: his youngest son Robert was killed in France in 1916 and his second son died in 1921 as a result of active service. He was appointed K.C.M.G. in 1917.

Burns died of cancer at Gowan Brae on 22 August 1923 and was buried there in its private cemetery. He was survived by a daughter of his first marriage, and by his eldest son James, managing director of Burns Philp in 1923-67, and by two daughters by his second wife. His estate, valued for probate at £227 604 in New South Wales and £8853 in Queensland, included bequests to the Burnside homes, the Presbyterian Church, various hospitals, Presbyterian colleges and the Salvation Army.

Gowan Brae is now the site of The King's School.

A shrewd and tough businessman, Burns was willing to make his headquarters in Fiji, if necessary, to compete with the Japanese; in 1915 he told Munro Ferguson that 'So far as my own company is concerned we can look after ourselves, though very loath to leave the Commonwealth or to have any truck with Asiatics'. Generous in private, he was a stern and somewhat unapproachable father, and would allow no Sunday amusements. Tolerant of other Protestant denominations he was suspicious of the political motivation of the Roman Catholic Church.

P. V. Vernon (ed), *The Royal New South Wales Lancers, 1885-1960* (Syd, 1961); P. Yeend, *Gowan Brae* (Syd, 1965); N. L. McKellar, *From Derby round to Burketown* (Brisb, 1977); G. C. Bolton, 'The rise of Burns, Philp 1873-93', A. Birch and D. S. Macmillan (eds). *Wealth and progress* (Syd, 1967); *PP* (Cwlth), 1914-17, 5, 665; *SMH*, 9 July 1908, 4 June 1917, 23 Aug 1923; R. C. Thompson, Australian imperialism and the New Hebrides, 1862-1922 (Ph.D. thesis, ANU, 1970); Atlee Hunt *and* Novar papers (NL); Philp papers (Oxley Lib, Brisb); Prime Minister's Dept, Pacific Branch, CRS A1108, vols 1, 2, 6, 58 (AAO, Canb); information from Mr J. D. O. Burns, Burns, Philp & Co. Ltd, Syd.

G. J. ABBOTT
H. J. GIBBNEY

BURNSIDE, ROBERT BRUCE (1862-1929), judge, was born on 22 April 1862 at Nassau, Bahamas, West Indies, son of (Sir) Bruce Lockhart Burnside, barrister, and his wife Mary Elizabeth, née Francis. His father became solicitor-general of the Bahamas and was later chief justice of Ceylon. Burnside was educated at Nassau Grammar School, the Royal Naval School, Newcross, London, and at Nancy, France. Entering Lincoln's Inn in 1881, he was called to the Bar there in 1884; he arrived in Perth in July and began practice; two years later he joined D. G. Gawler in a Fremantle partnership. On 10 December 1887 at Fremantle he married Mary Charity, daughter of Samuel Bruce, a London surgeon. Burnside became usher of the Black Rod in the Legislative Council in 1890. Appointed crown solicitor in 1894, he proved to be a capable law officer and fair-minded prosecutor. In December 1902 he succeeded F. W. Moorhead [q.v.], on the Supreme Court bench. With (Sir) Robert McMillan [q.v.], appointed a few weeks earlier, he 'worked . . . for over 26 years in complete friendship'.

In 1903, Burnside became for the first time president of the Arbitration Court, while remaining a justice of the Supreme Court;

his several terms as president totalled almost ten years. His work there was aided by his own technical skills as an accomplished amateur carpenter and metal-worker, and it was said that he was the one judge to leave the Arbitration Court reluctantly. He held the confidence of both employers and employees, but his gold-mining award of December 1920 was blamed by many residents of the goldfields for the closure of a number of marginal mines. Possibly his most important work was the establishment of the apprenticeship system.

Burnside presided in December 1916 over the trial of nine members of the Industrial Workers of the World accused of seditious conspiracy. Unlike an eastern contemporary, he created no martyrs; all the accused were found guilty, but were given suspended sentences. From the dock Montague Miller [q.v.] described Burnside as 'a tolerant and gentlemanly judge'. He presided over royal commissions in 1917 and 1919 to investigate relations between the Scaddan [q.v.] government and S. V. Nevanas, and an industrial dispute in the goldfields firewood-industry.

Burnside was an extrovert with a rousing and sometimes earthy sense of humour; a contemporary was impressed with his 'power of terse, direct and forcible expression'. He carried out judicial duties competently, though sometimes laboriously, and did not suffer fools gladly. A keen sportsman, in 1884 he helped to found the West Australian Rowing Club (the first in Perth) and became its first secretary; he was later captain and president. He was also an enthusiastic yachtsman and his large *Genista*, built to his own design in Scotland, was a familiar sight on the Swan River and at Careening Bay, Garden Island. For some years he was commodore of the Royal Perth Yacht Club.

Survived by his wife and only son, Burnside died in office of pneumonia on 8 August 1929 at his home, Craig Muir, Claremont, and was buried in the Anglican section of Karrakatta cemetery. His estate was sworn for probate at £10 091.

Truthful Thomas, *Through the spy-glass* (Perth, 1905); J. S. Battye (ed), *Cyclopedia of Western Australia*, 1 (Adel, 1912); *WA Industrial Gazette*, May 1921, Dec 1929; E. J. Edwards, 'Robert Furse McMillan', *Univ WA Law Review*, 1 (1963-64), nos 2, 3; *West Australian*, 12-16 Dec 1916, 9 Aug 1929; *SMH*, 9 Aug 1929.   G. T. STAPLES

BURRELL, HENRY JAMES (1873-1945), naturalist, was born on 19 January 1873 at Rushcutters Bay, Sydney, fourth son of Douglas Burrell, architect, and his wife Sarah Rose, née Stacey. After slight schooling he led a wandering, knock-about life which included some years as a comedian on the vaudeville stage. On 28 March 1901 he married a 42-year-old divorcee Susan Emily Naegueli, only child of William and Susan Rebecca Hill of Caermarthen station, Manilla, New South Wales, where he settled as a grazier.

Burrell established a small zoological garden with native fauna and soon became interested in the platypus, *Ornithorhynchus anatinus*. Told by zoologists that it could not be kept in captivity, he determined to try, and so began his celebrated study of monotremes – the platypus and the echidna, *Tachyglossus spp.* Devoting all his spare time to field work on the Namoi, Manilla and Macdonald rivers, he discovered many new facts about the world's most curious mammals, captured some and succeeded in keeping them alive. He devised an ingenious portable artificial habitat called a 'platypusary' which, at the Moore Park Zoological Gardens, enabled him in 1910 to exhibit them for the first time. In 1922 he assisted Ellis Stanley Joseph to exhibit in the United States of America the first live platypus to be seen outside Australia. He was also the first to keep baby platypuses in captivity, organized a recording of their voices, and had a film made depicting the habits of both monotremes.

In 1926 with A. S. Le Souef [q.v.], Burrell published *The wild animals of Australasia* ... (London, 1926), and contributed articles on the monotremes to the *Australian encyclopaedia*. His most notable work is the authoritative *The platypus; its discovery, zoological position form and characteristics, habits, life history, etc* (Sydney, 1927); the book was all the more remarkable because he could not get official sanction to work as a private collector and, unlike earlier unrestricted observers, was prevented from exploring certain branches of his subject. Professor L. Harrison [q.v.], who prepared the historical and technical material, withdrew as co-author after a dispute with the publishers. Late in 1927 Burrell was stricken with paralysis while working in the cold waters of the Namoi, but the 'platypoditudinarian' (his own term) made a remarkable recovery. He continued his work but went to Sydney where he and his wife were willing hosts to visiting naturalists.

Burrell published many papers and notes on his speciality in scientific journals. He was a corresponding-member of the Zoological Society of London and of the Australian Museum, a life-member of the American Museum of Natural History, New

York, charter-member of the American Society of Mammalogists, fellow of the Royal Zoological Society of New South Wales and was associated with other local scientific societies. Much of his collecting was carried out for the University of Sydney and the Commonwealth government, but he donated his excellent collection of photographic negatives to the Australian Museum, Sydney, and his unique complete sequence of monotreme exhibits to the Australian Institute of Anatomy, Canberra. He was appointed O.B.E. in 1937.

Burrell's wife Susan, an able naturalist in her own right, helped him in his research and lectured to schools and other groups on monotremes. She was a charter-member of the American Society of Zoologists, and a member of the Royal Australasian Ornithologists' Union and of the Linnean and Royal Zoological societies of New South Wales. An active Red Cross worker in World War I, she was later president of the Excelsior branch and was also a councillor of the National Association of New South Wales. She died on 27 March 1941, and on 2 December next year Burrell married a divorcee Daisy Ellen Brown, daughter of W. J. Mitchell of Bowen Park, Trangie.

Burrell died suddenly of heart disease on 29 July 1945 at his home at Randwick, and was cremated with Anglican rites; he was childless. His estate was valued for probate at £11 184.

With a keen analytical mind, Burrell was a delightful, well-loved companion: breezy, hearty, quick-witted, with a great sense of humour, he was content to be known simply as 'the Platypus Man' or 'Duckbill Dave'. Surfing and writing amusing prose and verse for his friends were his chief recreations.

Aust Museum Mag, 1 Dec 1945; *Vic Naturalist,* 62 (1945-46); *SMH,* 30 July 1945.

G. P. WALSH

BURSTON, JAMES (1856-1920), businessman and soldier, was born on 1 May 1856 at Kilmore, Victoria, son of Samuel Burston, formerly of Somerset, England, and his wife Sophia, née Keith, from Cambridgeshire. Samuel, a successful storekeeper and later a pastoralist, moved to Melbourne where by 1871 he had bought the maltings of J. Gough & Sons in Flinders Street, trading as Samuel Burston & Co. Although he had no previous experience as a maltster, he became one of the leading innovators in the trade. After a visit to Europe, in the early 1880s he rebuilt the Flinders Street Malthouse, using the new Saladin or pneumatic process for making malt. The product proved a success and he was soon exporting it to all the colonies.

James joined the business at 14. In the years preceding his father's death in 1886 he ran the business with his younger brother George William (1859-1924). It became a limited liability company in 1890, with James as managing director. After a disastrous fire the factory was rebuilt in 1892. Later the firm took over the maltings of the Victoria Brewery Co. and in 1912 merged with Barrett Bros, its chief competitor, to form Barrett Bros & Burston Co. Pty Ltd with James as one of its four original directors. Samuel Burston & Co. Ltd remained separate.

James Burston's chief interest outside the business was the Victorian Volunteers. He joined as a private in 1873, was commissioned lieutenant in 1879, and promoted captain in the 2nd Infantry Battalion in 1885, major in 1889 and lieut-colonel in 1895. Burston's battalion won the Brassey [q.v.] marching and firing competition four times, and in 1897 he represented Victoria at the Diamond Jubilee celebrations in London. While in England he attended a course at Aldershot at his own expense. In 1908 he was appointed staff officer to the officer commanding the Victorian Field Force.

In 1900 Burston was elected unopposed to the Melbourne City Council, serving as lord mayor in 1908-09 and 1909-10. His concerns were the city finances, the beautification of the Yarra and the public gardens, the problem of dusty streets, and the memorial to King Edward VII. Burston wanted the memorial to take the practical form of a new wing to the children's hospital, while popular opinion favoured a statue. Melbourne *Punch* alleged that the wrangles over the memorial cost him a third term as lord mayor, as well as the customary knighthood. He retired from the council in 1912.

When World War I broke out Burston, who had twice been on the unattached list and was now 58, resumed active duty and was made chairman of the Officers' Selection Committee, September 1914 to April 1915. He was then appointed to the Australian Imperial Force to command the 7th Infantry Brigade, which embarked on 2 June 1915 and arrived at Port Said on 30 June. He reached Gallipoli in September where the brigade was stationed at Chalac Dere and the Apex. Despite his determined efforts the physical conditions proved too much for his health and at the end of October he was appointed officer-in-charge of reinforcements at Mudros, commanding 15 000 men at an inspection by Lord Kitchener. In February 1916 Burston went to London on special leave before returning to Australia where he was promoted honorary brigadier general and placed on the reserve of officers in September. He retired in January 1920 with the honorary rank of major general.

Burston was president of the Melbourne Permanent Building Society and vice-president of the Universal Permanent Building and Investment Society, which were later amalgamated through his efforts. He was for some years chairman of the Bank of Victoria. Conservative in tastes, Burston was upright and respectable, unswerving and hard working. While he may have lacked fire and imagination, he was untarnished by the scandals which disfigured the lives of many more colourful men of the age.

On 12 April 1883 at the Collins Street Independent Church Burston had married Marianne, daughter of James McBean, jeweller. He died of cerebro-vascular disease at his home in Hawthorn on 4 March 1920, and was buried in St Kilda cemetery; he was survived by his wife, three of his four daughters and three sons, one of whom (Major General Sir) Samuel Roy became director general of medical services, Australian Military Forces.

His brother George William remained as a director of Samuel Burston & Co Ltd until his death in 1924. His chief interest had been cycling: he helped to found the Melbourne Bicycle Club in 1878, and in 1893 the League of Victorian Wheelmen, and long remained active in cycling administration. He himself concentrated on touring and road racing, and before the introduction of the pneumatic tyre held the Australian 100-mile (161 km) road record of 8 hours 9 minutes. In November 1888, with H. R. Stokes, he undertook a world tour: they were the first Australians to do so, and among the few world cyclists to accomplish the journey on penny-farthing machines. His account of the trip was published in the *Australasian* and as *Round about the world on bicycles* (Melbourne, 1890). He made at least three more cycling journeys abroad.

J. Smith (ed), *Cyclopedia of Victoria*, 1 (Melb, 1903); Barrett Bros and Burston & Co. Pty Ltd, *A short history of the company . . . 1912-1972* (Melb, nd); *Aust Brewer's J*, Aug 1883, Mar 1886, Apr 1892, Nov 1906; *Punch* (Melb), 10 Sept 1908, 20 May 1915; *Table Talk*, 1 Oct 1908; *Argus*, 5 Mar 1920, 13 Dec 1924; *Australasian*, 20 Dec 1924; J. Burston file (AWM).   P. H. DE SERVILLE

BURT, SEPTIMUS (1847-1919), lawyer, politician and grazier, was born on 25 October 1847 at St Kitts, West Indies, son of (Sir) Archibald Paull Burt [q.v.3], Western Australia's first chief justice, and his wife Louisa Emily, née Bryan. He was educated at a private school at Melksham, Wiltshire, England, and from 1861 at Bishop Hale's [q.v.4] school in Perth, where his fellow students included (Sir) John and Alexander Forrest [qq.v.]. After serving as an articled clerk to G. F. Stone [q.v.2], Burt was admitted to the Western Australian Bar in 1870 and occupied some of his leisure as captain of the Perth Cricketers in 1871. He wrote in 1875 that he was doing reasonably well, although there was not as yet much work for lawyers in the colony, and what he was doing was 'not likely to lead one to any great distinction'. However, in 1876 he was taken into partnership by (Sir) Edward Stone [q.v.], son of his former mentor; Stone & Burt quickly established itself as one of Western Australia's leading legal firms. On 13 July 1872, at St George's Cathedral Church, Burt had married Louisa Fanny, daughter of G. E. C. Hare, government resident at Albany.

In October 1874 he accepted Governor Weld's [q.v.6] invitation, inspired no doubt by official friendships with his father, to become a nominated member of the Legislative Council. As was probably expected, Burt supported Colonial Secretary Barlee's [q.v.3] proposals for self-government, which passed through the council but were blocked by the British government. His first political action, however, was to manage a private bill about the temporal affairs of the Church of England.

In January 1879 Burt relinquished his nominee membership of the council; at the general election in 1880 he was returned unopposed for Murray and Williams. As an elected member he both took a more independent line on major issues, and successfully carried through to the statute book private members' bills on subjects ranging from the licensing of firearms and the sale of liquor to the transfer of land-titles and control of scab in stock. However in March 1886 he was temporarily catapulted into the official circle when a long-simmering feud between Governor Broome [q.v.3], Attorney-General A. P. Hensman [q.v.4] and Surveyor-General John Forrest, culminated in Hensman's resignation. By accepting Broome's invitation to act temporarily as attorney-general, Burt aligned himself with the 'Government House party', a posture which he maintained in the related controversy over Broome's suspension of Chief Justice Onslow [q.v.5]. Burt was impatient of the way quarrels between officials threatened to impede colonial progress, and preferred to get on with the job. His six-month term as attorney-general included the longest and most productive council session to that date. Having resigned his seat to accept office, Burt found himself out of politics when his successor arrived. He was 'rewarded' by appointment as one of Western Australia's two representatives at the Colonial Conference held in London in April 1887 and the subsequent jubilee celebrations. He was also appointed Q.C. In 1881-89 he was a member of the Perth City Council.

In May 1888 Burt sought to re-enter the Legislative Council through a by-election for the seat of Perth, but encountered a demagogic style of politics new to Western Australia. John Horgan [q.v.], a radical Irish lawyer, sought successfully to mobilize the working class and his fellow Catholics against the Anglican Burt, linking him with the 'six hungry families'. Though Horgan won by three votes in the highest poll recorded in the colony, Burt was returned soon after for the North Province in time to take a leading part in the debates on Western Australia's new constitution.

His conservative inclinations were tempered by an intelligent and pragmatic appreciation of political realities. Thus he argued for an elected rather than a nominated Upper House on the grounds that nominated Upper Houses 'represent nobody, they do little or no work, and their chief duty . . . is to get out of the way when the popular chamber is coming along'. Burt also startled his friends by rejecting property qualifications for members or electors of the Lower House because the temper of the times was such that manhood suffrage was bound to come before long. To introduce it at once would be to 'cut away all ground for agitation' and to ensure that 'those gentlemen who lived on politics and hoped to get fat on it, would not have a solitary plank left to stand upon'.

In the final tussle with the British government in 1889-90 over the possible partition of the colony and the threatened withholding of control over crown land after self-government, Burt showed himself to be probably the most resolute member of the council. Others were prepared to compromise to safeguard the constitution bill; he argued, correctly as it turned out, that Westminster would give way if Western Australia stood its ground.

At the first election under the new Constitution in 1890 Burt was returned unopposed for the Legislative Assembly seat of Ashburton, which he retained without contest until his retirement from politics in 1900. Both the principal contenders for office as premier, (Sir) S. H. Parker [q.v.] and John Forrest, sought to enlist Burt as attorney-general. Burt committed himself to Parker but, when he withdrew, joined Forrest. They were old friends and business partners but their relationship had been strained by the Hensman and Onslow episodes. Conscious that Burt's abilities complemented his own, Forrest had anxiously sought to repair their relationship throughout 1890 and for the next seven years they worked together closely and harmoniously.

As attorney-general Burt personally drafted most of the legislation during the early 1890s. Although he was not a forceful speaker and suffered from a slight speech-impediment, his cool and precise contributions to debate were a vital counterweight to Forrest's boisterous enthusiasm. When the government's critics seemed likely to tempt Forrest into an indiscretion, 'often might be seen Mr Burt's detaining hand on his leader's coat-tails as he rose excitedly to the fly'. On other occasions Burt would come in towards the end of a debate to defuse opposition by announcing the ministry's willingness to amend or compromise. Although the government was concentrating on development, significant social and political reforms were enacted; Burt sought always to control and channel the demand for such changes rather than to frustrate it and thereby provoke extremism.

Well aware of his dependence on Burt, Forrest begged him to reconsider when he thought of resigning in February 1896, offering part of his own salary if that would help. When Burt finally decided to resign in October 1897 Forrest acknowledged privately: 'You have indeed been my guide, philosopher and friend and I do not know how I shall get on without your friendly advice'. Although Burt remained in the assembly till April 1900 he took little part in proceedings and his career virtually ended in 1897. His decision was due in part to his growing distaste for politics. Western Australia was on the threshold of party politics and Burt had some years earlier declared: 'The tendency of party government . . . is for the opposing parties to bid below each other for popular favour. It is a form of Government I have always detested'.

The need to provide for his six sons and four daughters through his legal practice and pastoral interests also influenced Burt's decision to leave political life. He was regarded by many as the soundest lawyer at the Western Australian Bar; his opinions were keenly sought, and his courtroom manner, though quiet, was persuasive. In 1899 one grateful client offered him £1000 over and above his fees. Burt's pastoral interests dated from 1877 when he joined John, Alexander and David Forrest in a syndicate taking up a lease of 590 000 acres (239 000 ha) on the Ashburton River. Minderoo station, as this lease was called, became in time an extremely profitable enterprise. Other pastoral properties of which Burt became part-owner included Kadji Kadji, Brick House, Yinniethana, Red Hill and Minne Creek. Well before his death he established members of his family on most of these stations.

Throughout his life Septimus Burt was a staunch adherent of the Church of England, which he served as synodsman, trustee, legal adviser and benefactor. He was a close friend of Archbishop C. O. L. Riley [q.v.] who after Burt's death described him as 'a very generous man who did not like his generosity to be known'; his name has however been preserved in connexion with one of his gifts to the church, the Burt Memorial Hall erected in honour of his two sons killed during World War I. Their deaths saddened his last years, when he was himself often in pain; survived by his wife, four sons and four daughters, he died on 15 May 1919 and was buried in the Anglican section of Karrakatta cemetery, Riley conducting the funeral. His estate, valued for probate at £147 357, was left mainly to his family.

Burt was a very private man who disliked the limelight and regarded public life as a duty rather than as a source of pleasure or profit. He rejected such honours as the knighthood offered in 1901 and declined repeated invitations to join the bench of the Supreme Court. His life was lived in accordance with the code he spelled out in a private letter of 1888: 'I endeavour to make the motives of my actions the Glory of God, the welfare of my fellow-man, the honor of my Sovereign and the good of this country. If I can keep to these lines I do not think I can go far wrong'.

His brother OCTAVIUS (1849-1940), public servant, was born at St Kitts on 14 December 1849. After his family's arrival in Perth, he was educated at Bishop Hale's school. In 1869 he entered the civil service as a clerk but soon moved to the National Bank. In May 1872 he returned to the civil service, at first as a clerk in the Governor's Office, and then in 1874-77 as private secretary to the governor and clerk to the Executive Council. In 1877-80 he was clerk and keeper of records in the Survey Office.

Burt was resident magistrate for the Toodyay District in 1880-87. During his years in the Avon Valley he won widespread respect, but his rigorous suppression of sly-grog selling and illegal gambling irritated many and led to an open feud with the honorary magistrates including S. P. Phillips [q.v.5], the 'Squire of Culham', from which Burt emerged victorious. In his response to a measles epidemic in 1883-84, as later in his career, Burt showed himself unusually sensitive to the plight of the Aboriginals.

In 1887 he became assistant colonial secretary and was promoted in 1890 to the colonial secretaryship with a seat in the Executive and Legislative councils. When

self-government was inaugurated a few months later Burt became Western Australia's principal civil servant as under-secretary for the colony. In April-October 1898 he was secretary in the agent-general's office, London. From 1901 until his retirement in 1912 he held the positions of sheriff and comptroller of prisons and also served as a deputy marshal of the High Court of Australia. As Western Australia's chief electoral officer for fifteen years, he conducted the Federation referendum of 1900 and the first Federal election in 1901. In 1903 he was awarded the I.S.O.

In 1877 Burt had married Esther Hare, sister to the wife of his brother Septimus; they had two daughters. Like his brother, Octavius was an active member of the Church of England which he served for more than thirty years as a synodsman, diocesan councillor and member of the cathedral chapter. He was keenly interested in aquatic sports and was for a time a member of the volunteer movement. Survived by one daughter, he died on 1 April 1940, leaving an estate valued for probate at £2881, and was buried in Karrakatta cemetery.

J. S. Battye (ed), *Cyclopedia of Western Australia*, 1 (Adel, 1912); F. K. Crowley, *Forrest: 1847-1918*, 1 (Brisb, 1971); R. Erickson, *Old Toodyay and Newcastle* (Toodyay, WA, 1974); B. K. de Garis, 'Western Australia', P. Loveday, A. W. Martin & R. S. Parker (eds), *The emergence of the Australian party system* (Syd, 1977); *Possum*, 10 Sept 1887; *West Australian*, 9 Mar 1912, 16, 17 May, 5 June 1919, 24 Sept 1932; W. F. P. Heseltine, The movements for self-government in Western Australia from 1882-1890 (B.A. Hons thesis, Univ WA, 1950); C. T. Stannage, Electoral politics in Western Australia 1884-1897 (M.A. thesis, Univ WA, 1967); Burt papers (held by Sir Francis Burt, Cottesloe, WA); biog cuttings (RWAHS).

B. K. DE GARIS
TOM STANNAGE

BURTON, ALEXANDER STEWART (1893-1915), soldier, was born on 20 January 1893 at Kyneton, Victoria, son of Alfred Edward Burton, grocer, and his wife Isabella, née Briggs, both Victorian-born. The family moved to Euroa and, after attending the state school, Burton followed his father into the firm of A. Miller & Co., working in the ironmongery department. He was a chorister in the Euroa Presbyterian Church, a member of the town band, and was active in sport. In 1911 he began his period of compulsory military service.

On 18 August 1914 Burton enlisted in the 7th Battalion, Australian Imperial Force, and embarked for Egypt in October. On 4 April 1915 his battalion embarked for Lemnos and on the 25th took part in the landing at Anzac. Burton, who was ill with a throat infection, watched the landing from a hospital ship but a week later he was in the trenches. The 7th Battalion was then fighting near 400 Plateau; on 5 May it left Anzac beach to participate in the attack on Krithia, then returned to serve at Monash Valley and Steele's Post. Burton was slightly wounded in action and in July was promoted lance corporal for having volunteered for and taken part in a dangerous operation; he was later promoted corporal.

Burton was posthumously awarded the Victoria Cross for conspicuous bravery in the trenches at Lone Pine on 9 August. Early that morning the Turks launched a strong counter-attack on a newly captured trench held by Burton, a personal friend Lieutenant F. H. Tubb, Corporal W. Dunstan [qq.v.] and a few others. The Turks advanced up a sap and blew in the sandbag barricade but Burton, Tubb and Dunstan repulsed them and rebuilt it. Supported by strong bombing parties, the enemy twice more destroyed the barricade but were driven off and the barricade was rebuilt. Burton was killed by a bomb while building up the parapet. Tubb and Dunstan were also awarded the Victoria Cross. Burton's award was gazetted on 15 October and on 28 January 1916 he was mentioned in dispatches.

His kind and manly nature had won him many friends; even before Lone Pine he was frequently mentioned in soldiers' letters for various daring acts. He has no known grave, but his name is commemorated on the Lone Pine Memorial, Gallipoli, and by an oak tree and bridge at Euroa. In 1967 his family presented his V.C. to the Australian War Memorial. He was unmarried.

C. E. W. Bean, *The story of Anzac*, 2 (Syd, 1924); A. Dean and E. W. Gutteridge, *The Seventh Battalion, A.I.F.* (Melb, 1933); L. Wigmore (ed), *They dared mightily* (Canb, 1963); *London Gazette*, 15 Oct 1915, 28 Jan 1916; *Age*, 15 Oct 1915; *Western Mail* (Perth), 19 Nov 1936.   G. P. WALSH

BURTON, JOHN WEAR (1875-1970), Methodist minister, was born on 8 March 1875 at Lazenby, Yorkshire, England, second son of Robert Burton, joiner, and his wife Maria, née Bell. In 1883, to benefit Maria's health, the family migrated to New Zealand, eventually settling at Masterton. Burton left school at 12 and worked as a fleece-picker and in a retail store before becoming apprenticed to his father's wheelwright trade. At 17, influenced by a family missionary tradition and an active local church life, he became a lay preacher and in 1895 began theological training in Auckland. Appointed as a probationer two years later to Paeroa, where he studied part time for matriculation, and then to Malvern, he enrolled for university work at Canterbury, saving for fees and fares by 'batching' in the local church vestry. In 1897 he attended the inaugural meeting in Melbourne of the Student Christian Movement of Australia and New Zealand. There he joined the Student Volunteer Movement whose members were pledged to be missionaries. After ordination in 1901 he was shifted to Christchurch but was soon asked to take charge of Indian missionary work in Fiji. On the day of departure, 24 April 1902, he married Florence Mildred Hadfield (d. 1953).

In Fiji Burton was appalled by the indentured Indian labourers' living conditions on the sugar estates, and exposed the abuses in his most influential and controversial book, *Fiji of today* (London, 1910). It was regarded as a pioneer work by Rev. C. F. Andrews in India, whose later agitation helped to terminate the indenture system in 1920.

Family illness forced Burton to return to New Zealand in 1910. After three years in New Plymouth he was invited by F. J. Cato [q.v.] to be secretary in Victoria for overseas missions. At the University of Melbourne he continued his interrupted studies (B.A., 1918; M.A., 1920). In 1918-20, as an honorary major with the Young Men's Christian Association, he assisted with the demobilization of Australian troops in London, where he was converted to pacifism. Returning to Victoria, he indicated his growing interest in Christian unity, sponsoring United Mission Study Schools and helping to initiate the National Missionary Council, of which he was chairman for eleven years.

In 1925-45 Burton was general secretary in Sydney of the Methodist Missionary Society of Australasia. Though criticized for his dominance, he was an outstanding leader during the Depression and World War II, with a natural organizing ability and a capacity for single-minded pursuit of aims. His astute recommendations often effected decisive changes in mission policy. He regularly visited stations in India, north Australia and the Pacific and was an early advocate of devolution of authority. Convinced of the need for better-qualified missionaries, he introduced training programmes including language study and a course in anthropology devised by A. P. Elkin. For six years secretary of the Australian Intercommunion Group, Burton helped draft a mutual communion formula for use in Papua; it was subsequentlly adopted by Episcopal and Presbyterian churches in the United States of America and by the United Church of North India. In 1935, reputedly while sitting on a log in the outback, Burton and John Flynn [q.v.] originated the concept of a united church in north Australia, which was achieved in 1946.

A student of Bonhoeffer and Tillich and a member of the local 'Heretics' club, Burton acquired a reputation as a theological radical which was confirmed by his support for Professor Samuel Angus [q.v.] though, like others at the time, he was cautious in his public utterances. In 1931 he had been president of the New South Wales Methodist Conference. He was president-general of the Methodist Church of Australasia in 1945-48, his elevation having been deferred during the war because of his uncompromising pacifism. He toured North America in 1945, receiving an honorary doctorate of divinity from Victoria University, Toronto. Retiring from the ministry in 1948, he was one of Australia's two representatives on the South Pacific Commission until 1950. Survived by five children, he died on 22 May 1970. His son John Wear was secretary of the Department of External Affairs in 1947-50.

Burton was handsome yet austere in appearance. Disdaining popular judgments and adhering to principles of justice and utterance of Christian conscience, he belonged to the social and humanitarian tradition of Dr Charles Strong [q.v.6], one of his heroes. For twenty-three years editor of the *Missionary Review,* Burton clear-sightedly analyzed missionary achievement in its editorials. His published works dealt with the responsibility of colonial nations to their dependent territories, and the role of the missions in assisting their peoples through years of rapid modernization.

C. F. Andrews, *India and the Pacific* (Lond, 1937); M. McKenzie, *Mission to Arnhem Land* (Adel, 1976); Methodist Missionary Soc of A'sia, *Missionary Review,* June-July 1970; *Methodist* (Syd), May-July 1970; J. W. Burton papers (ML); Methodist Overseas Missions, Papers (ML); Strong papers (LaTL); biog notes from Rev. Dr A. H. Wood, Melb, and Mrs R. Newman, Syd.

A. W. THORNLEY

BUSHELL, PHILIP HOWARD (1879-1954), tea merchant, was born on 14 September 1879 at Liverpool, England, youngest child of Alfred Thomas Bushell and his wife Agnes, sister of Arthur Brooke, who founded the tea firm Brooke Bond. On his mother's death he was brought up by the Brooke family and educated at Burnham College, Somerset. His father migrated to Brisbane with his three older sons in 1883 and set up as a grocer and tea merchant. At 11 Philip joined them and attended Brisbane Grammar School in 1891-93.

Philip became a taster but, disagreeing with his father's methods, joined his brother Alfred Walter (d. 1955) who had established a Sydney branch in 1895, extending to Victoria in 1899. Bushell & Co., 'The Tea-men', moved to George Street North in 1904 and suspended operations in Victoria. Concerned that his youth and inexperience might alienate the conservative tea-drinker, Bushell put his bearded father's picture on his packets and business flourished. On 13 February 1912 a public company, Bushell's Ltd, was formed, with Bushell as chairman. In 1920 the firm was reconstructed to finance a new building in Harrington Street and extend operations to Western Australia, South Australia and Tasmania, and to Victoria in 1922. Over-extended, it was soon in severe financial trouble, but Bushell persuaded his employees to lend cash and the firm was saved; in 1924 he promoted its products by distributing a free half-pound of tea to every home in Sydney. He restarted direct operations in Brisbane in 1929 and opened a branch in New Zealand in 1937. World War II brought problems of supply and rationing in the tea trade and from March 1942 to 1953, when controls were lifted, he was a member of the (Commonwealth) Tea Control Board. In 1957 Bushell's Investments Ltd was formed to acquire Bushell's Pty Ltd with a nominal capital of £3 million.

Bushell was a man of striking physical appearance and great personal charm. He had a lively mind, read a lot and loved conversation and acquiring knowledge. Energetic and enthusiastic, he travelled widely including a three-year world tour during which he visited the Soviet Union. On his return in January 1936 he averred there was no communism, only state capitalism, in Russia which he predicted would be a huge success. In 1947 he represented the Institute of Industrial Management, Australia, at the eighth International Management Congress, in Stockholm. He was a member of Royal Sydney Golf Club, Royal Sydney Yacht Squadron and the Australian and University clubs in Sydney. His personal friends included Sir Victor Coppleson [q.v.] and (Sir) William Morrow, both of whom helped administer the Bushell Trust, set up by the family in the 1940s to give immense sums of money anonymously to medical research and education.

Bushell died at his home, Carthona, Darling Point, on 29 March 1954 and was cremated with Anglican rites. He was survived by his wife, Myrtle Dolce, née Stewart, whom he had married in Sydney on 12 February 1916, and by two daughters. His estate was valued for probate at £666 695. His wife, a retiring person, served on various committees supporting the arts; she died on

8 September 1959 leaving an estate of £2 558 921. Bushell Place, a public plaza, commemorates the firm's long association with The Rocks area of Sydney.

Bushells employee report 1977-78 (np, nd); *SMH*, 11 Oct 1924, 22 Apr 1930, 18 Nov 1931, 2 Nov 1932, 30 Jan 1936, 11 Jan, 3 Nov 1939, 12 July 1947, 25 Aug 1948, 10 Apr, 9 Sept 1954, 19 Nov 1957, 5 Feb 1960; *Aust Financial Review*, 25, 26 July, 2 Aug 1978; *Australian* (Syd), 26 July 1978; *Bulletin*, 8 Aug 1978; information from Mrs A. Oxley, Darling Point, NSW.   G. P. WALSH

BUSS, FREDERIC WILLIAM (1845-1926), merchant, sugar-planter and manufacturer, was born on 2 January 1845 at Faversham, Kent, England, son of Thomas Buss, chemist, and his wife Frances Helen, née Thorpe. Educated at the Grove House, Highgate, London, he left school when young, served a draper's apprenticeship, and in 1863 arrived in Queensland with his father, sisters and brothers including Charles and George, later his partners. He worked in Brisbane for R. A. [q.v.5] & J. Kingsford and for William Southerden & Co. in Maryborough, then for ten years ran a drapery shop in Maryborough with Thomas Penny; they also had a Bundaberg branch. After visiting England, Buss established a major department store in Bundaberg in partnership with his brother George and W. H. Williams. The firm became Buss & Turner in 1888 and settled in Bourbon Street.

As the sugar industry gained momentum in the late nineteenth century the store became foster-nurse to half the business houses in the town; one of the most important was Woolley, Bergin & Co., which became significant suppliers of agricultural machinery, occupying shops owned by Frederic Buss on Bundaberg's main street. He may well have been the silent partner who enabled the company to buy out the ironmongery section of Buss & Co. in 1885. Discussing his success in 1888, the *Bundaberg Reporter* said, 'he touches nothing now scarcely but it turns to gold'.

The opening of Millaquin refinery in 1882 by the Cran brothers [q.v.] of Maryborough facilitated Bundaberg's transition to a premier sugar district in which Buss and his associates built an empire of plantations and mills. In 1881-1918 Buss, his family (particularly his brother Charles) and partners acquired interests in eleven properties, many of them in the rich Woongarra canefields where he lived. He later invested in Mackay sugar and left his shares in Farleigh Estate Sugar Co. to his two sons. Only Millaquin and the Yengarie refinery at Maryborough extensively practised the system whereby juice was pumped from near-by crushing mills by pipeline. Of sixteen such mills constructed in 1881-85 to serve Millaquin, Buss had interests in three. He joined the Crans in constructing the Duncraggan mill, the refinery's biggest early supplier (absorbed later by A. P. Barton's Mon Repos, Ashfield, and worked by Charles Buss and J. S. Penny from 1882) and the 1000 acres (400 ha) of Pemberton Grange and Glen Morris owned by Frederic Buss and John Ewen Davidson [q.v.] who were white-sugar producers; heavy expenditure on modern machinery designed by the company's own engineer promoted efficiency. Invicta on the Kolan, a highly regarded mill owned by Frederic alone, was sold in 1918. At Knockroe plantation, Buss with his partners T. Penny and Williams followed the lead set by the Colonial Sugar Refining Co. in subdividing for tenant farmers. Although the experiment was not completely successful at first, other family plantations were subdivided.

Frederic Buss was also one of the initiators and directors of the distillery which tided Bundaberg over the crisis years of the 1880s and 1890s. In 1898 his ventures in the sugar industry employed 700 men and produced an output worth £144 000. A member of the Bundaberg Municipal Council in 1891-93, he was active in the chamber of commerce. He was also on the harbour board and a justice of the peace. He declined the offer of a seat in parliament. His donation of £500 for tree-planting in the main streets was a lasting legacy; Buss Park was named for the family.

On 3 October 1870 Buss had married Maria Howard at Maryborough; she and six children survived him when he died at Bundaberg on 20 June 1926. His estate, valued for probate in Queensland at £45 098 and in New South Wales at £62 409, provided bequests for Dr Barnardo's Homes and six institutions in Bundaberg, Maryborough and Brisbane. He was buried in the Bundaberg general cemetery with Anglican rites.

His nephew Garnet Leslie (1886-1973) was born on 2 October 1886 at Bundaberg, son of George Buss and his wife Edith, née Warland. Educated at Bundaberg and at Maryborough Grammar School, he was managing director of Buss & Turner from 1927 and a director of Bundaberg Foundry Co. for many years. Known as 'Mr Bundaberg', he was a leading Rotarian, president of the Burnett Club, an alderman of the Bundaberg City Council and keenly interested in sporting bodies, particularly the golf and surf life-saving clubs. He married his cousin Mabel Howard, Frederic's daughter, at Bundaberg on 30 July 1919 and died there on

21 December 1973, leaving one daughter.

W. F. Morrison, *The Aldine history of Queensland* (Syd, 1888); J. Y. Walker, *The history of Bundaberg* (Brisb, 1890); Alcazar Press, *Queensland, 1900* (Brisb, nd); *Queensland and Queenslanders* (Brisb, 1936); H. Turner, *Rural life in sunny Queensland* (Bundaberg, 1955); C. T. Wood, *Sugar country* (Brisb, 1965); *V&P* (LA Qld), 1889, 4, 431; *PP* (Qld), 1906, 2, 22, Roy Com on the sugar industry, (Cwlth), 1913, 4, 1169, Evidence, 760, 824, 901; *Bundaberg Daily News and Mail*, 21 June 1926.

                                          J. G. NOLAN

BUSSAU, SIR ALBERT LOUIS (1884-1947), farmer and politician, was born on 9 July 1884 at Clear Lake (Natimuk), Victoria, sixth child of Johann Joachim Heinrich Adolph Bussau, German-born carpenter, contractor and farmer of Huguenot extraction, and his wife Maria Ernestina, née Rokesky. At 12 'Lou' Bussau left Warracknabeal State School to work for his father but, influenced by his mother's love of learning, he continued his education, first at night at a private college, and then by correspondence with the University of Melbourne's law faculty. He made weekly legal rounds from Warracknabeal to Hopetoun and Beulah for J. S. Wright-Smith and spent his spare time reading widely, attending Labor Party meetings and lay-preaching for the Baptist Church. On 22 April 1912 he married Ballarat schoolteacher Mary Scott Baird and about three years later they moved to Hopetoun where Bussau represented the Wright-Smith firm.

He purchased 640 acres (259 ha) north of Hopetoun (Wilhelmina parish) after the disastrous drought of 1914-15 and later bought an adjacent block on which, with the aid of share-farmers, he successfully produced wheat, wool and fat lambs. Farm ownership and the possibility of furthering wartime marketing measures won Bussau over to P. G. Stewart's [q.v.] militant Mallee wing of the Victorian Farmers' Union about 1916. Typical of the new breed of country-town leaders, he became an outspoken critic on farming issues and was adept at manoeuvring meeting procedures.

Hopetoun provided opportunities for rapid advancement. Bussau became a councillor of Karkarooc Shire (1921-32), and was shire president in 1926-27. In 1924 he was chief president of the Australian Natives' Association, Victoria. He was an organizer in 1927 of the Victorian Wheatgrowers' Association (later the Victorian Wheat and Woolgrowers' Association), retiring in 1932. He left the V.F.U. to join the breakaway Country Progressive Party and was president in 1929; that year he stood

unsuccessfully as the party's candidate for Lowan in the Legislative Assembly. When differences with the Victorian Country Party were settled, Bussau joined the new United Country Party, standing successfully for Ouyen in 1932. He became vice-president of the party and president of the Australian Wheatgrowers' Federation.

In parliament, Bussau advocated rural rehabilitation measures reminiscent of Roosevelt's New Deal thinking: comprehensive marketing legislation, fixed produce-quotas, protection against foreclosure, a guaranteed consumer price, and bulk handling measures which would provide construction work for the unemployed who 'did not want doles ... or charity'. He enjoyed bandying with the young (Sir Robert) Menzies and his lifelong friend John Cain who mocked him as 'the Socialist' and 'the radical member for Ouyen'. Bussau replied that he was merely protecting the most important section of the State: 'The City of Melbourne would fall without the country', city parties 'could only see the sun rise in the Dandenong Ranges and set on the Werribee Plains'.

When, after the 1935 election, (Sir Albert) Dunstan [q.v.] and the Country Party took office with Labor support, Bussau was made attorney-general, solicitor-general, minister of transport and vice-president of the Board of Land and Works. He proved an excellent minister and a political threat to other leaders – this partly accounts for his posting to London as agent-general early in 1938.

That year Bussau visited the Ruhr brown coal industrial centres. His travels complemented his vast reading knowledge on European and North American agriculture and afforestation. During the air raids, he was a celebrated 'fire watcher' and his daring as a spotter earned him the nickname 'the Mad Australian'. However, he was horrified by the devastation of English cities and relieved to return in 1942-43 via the North American wheat-belt to Victoria where he became air raid precautions adviser. In 1945 he was appointed first chairman of the Australian Wheat Board, a post which he held until his death.

Bussau's humble origins, German parentage and his recognition of the worth of hard-pressed Mallee 'battlers' generated a radical, forthright approach to public office. He was knighted in 1941 but remained 'Plain Lou' – unpretentious and self-made, a wiry, quick-spoken, impulsive person who always wore a smile and loved a verbal fight. Throughout his life, he was a keen sportsman, with special interest in cricket, football, golf and bowls. Shocked by fierce accusations from Country Party colleagues over Prime Minister Chifley's New Zealand wheat-deal, he suffered three strokes and died at South Yarra on 5 May 1947. He was accorded a state funeral and was cremated. He was survived by his wife (d. 1958) to whom he left £13 772; they had no children. In the words of John Cain, Bussau was a 'true democrat', an ambitious Mallee politician whose efforts advanced the cause of the rural sector.

G. H. Mitchell, *Growers in action* (Melb, 1969); *Woomelang Sun*, 6-13 Feb 1931, 6 May 1932; *Ouyen and North West Express*, 13 May 1932, 7 May 1947; *Countryman* (Melb), 7 Mar 1947; *Argus*, and *Horsham Times*, 6 May 1947; *Hopetoun Courier*, 9 May 1947; J. A. Senyard, A Mallee farming community in the Depression: the Walpeup Shire of Victoria, 1925-1935 (M.A. thesis, Monash Univ, 1974); information to author from Mr F. H. M. Cullen, Mr P. B. Leach and Mr G. G. Marshman.

R. C. DUPLAIN

BUSSELL, WILLIAM JOHN (1854-1936), Anglican clergyman, was born on 23 August 1854 at Reinscourt, Western Australia, eldest child of Joseph Vernon Bussell, pioneer, and his wife Mary Elizabeth, née Phillips. As a youth, Bussell's father, with his brothers John, Alfred [qq.v.1,3] and Charles, had taken up land at Augusta in 1830 and on his premature death in 1860 his wife returned to Adelaide. Here Bussell was educated at the Collegiate School of St Peter in 1866-73, remaining for a further three years as assistant to the headmaster Dr G. H. Farr [q.v.4] while preparing for holy orders. He was ordained deacon in 1877 and priest in 1879 and, after a curacy at Mount Gambier, was successively mission curate in the south-east until 1880; incumbent of Strathalbyn, Meadows and Macclesfield in 1880-95 with responsibility for the mission district from 1888; and priest-in-charge of the River Murray mission in 1894-1912. He was organizing chaplain of the Bishop's Home Mission Society in 1903-23; canon of Adelaide in 1906 until his retirement in 1933; archdeacon of the Broughton from 1903 and chaplain of hospitals from 1925.

Essentially a missionary priest, Bussell did his most notable work in ministering to the River Murray settlers from 1891, when the Home Mission Society purchased the steam launch *Etona*. He travelled on it from Goolwa to the Victorian border, providing pastoral care for stations, farms, and camps of woodcutters and fishermen; from 1893 he also ministered to participants in a group-settlement scheme optimistically established by the government to alleviate unemployment – these settlers, untrained for rural life and almost penniless, suffered great hardship.

Except for the years 1892-93 spent at Strathalbyn, Bussell worked continually for the River Murray mission until it closed in 1913, bringing both spiritual ministration and material help and receiving in return wood for the launch's engines and occasionally vegetables and fish. By 1897 the launch, which two years later was replaced by a paddle-steamer with a chapel and deck-accommodation, was travelling 1000 miles (1600 km) every six weeks, calling at some forty places, including the Aboriginal settlement at Point McLeay. Bussell shared the work with his engineer, John McLellan: he steered and cooked, McLellan stoked and tended the engine; both loaded tons of wood. Outlying places, away from the river, were visited in borrowed buggies, on horseback, by bicycle or on foot, and services were held in widely assorted premises.

Although a staunch churchman, Bussell's sympathies extended to all movements designed to benefit the community. President of the Aborigines Friends' Association, he was an early member of the Advisory Council of Aborigines; he also belonged to the Adelaide City Mission and the Adelaide Benevolent and Strangers' Friend Society.

Of medium height and with a strong physique, Bussell had organizing ability, great resource, and remarkable patience; he was widely read and a fluent preacher. It was, however, his transparent goodness, warm-hearted generosity and quiet unassuming manner, combined with a willingness to share their hardships, that won him the enduring friendship of the settlers. On 13 July 1909 in Adelaide he married Susan, sister of J. R. Harmer [q.v.], third bishop of Adelaide; they had no children. Bussell died on 6 June 1936 at North Adelaide and was buried in North Road cemetery, Adelaide.

H. T. Burgess (ed), *Cyclopedia of South Australia*, 2 (1909); G. H. Jose, *The Church of England in South Australia*, 3 (Adel, 1955); Church of England, *Diocese of Adelaide and Willochra Year Book*, 1935-36; *Adelaide Church Guardian*, 1 July 1936; *Inquirer and Commercial News*, 19 Sept 1860; *Advertiser* (Adel), 8 June 1936.

T. T. REED

BUSTARD, WILLIAM (1894-1973), painter, stained-glass artist and book-illustrator, was born on 18 April 1894 at Terrington, Yorkshire, England, son of William Bustard, police constable, and his wife Mary, née Harrison. From the School of Science and Art, Scarborough, he won a scholarship to the Battersea Polytechnic and Putney School of Art in London; he later attended the Slade School of Art. He learned stained-glass techniques under James Powell of Whitefriars, London, and worked in cathedrals in England, Ireland and the United States of America. After exhibiting at the Royal Academy in 1915, he enlisted in the Royal Army Medical Corps on 23 August, became a corporal on 25 June 1916 and served in Salonika, Greece, to November 1917, then in Italy to June 1918. Posted to an officer cadet battalion in October, he was commissioned a reserve second lieutenant in the East Yorkshire Regiment after demobilization on 13 February 1919. He then took a refresher course in art at Oxford and helped repair mediaeval stained-glass in Belgium and France.

Bustard had married Lily Whitmore at Malton, Yorkshire, on 20 October 1918, and in 1921 they migrated to Queensland. He taught art half time at the Central Technical College, Brisbane, from 1924 to 1933, and became a life member of the Royal Queensland Art Society and its president in 1932. A foundation member of the board of trustees of the Queensland Art Gallery in 1931-37 and chairman of the gallery's art advisory committee, he resented conservatism on the board and resigned in disgust.

Windows by Bustard are in St John's Church of England Cathedral, St Stephen's Catholic Cathedral, St Anne's Presbyterian Church and the City Hall in Brisbane; an important group of forty-nine is in St Augustine's Church of England, Hamilton, and others are at Rockhampton, Southport and Coolangatta. Of his many windows elsewhere in Australia, the most impressive is the memorial in the Catholic Star of the Sea Cathedral, Darwin, to those who died in the Japanese air raid in 1942. Through his personal insistence on strong supports, the window remained undamaged in the 1974 cyclone. In World War II he had served in the Royal Australian Air Force, camouflaging installations.

Editions of *Robinson Crusoe* and *Treasure Island* illustrated by Bustard were published in 1949 and 1956; a copy of the former was presented to Queen Elizabeth on her visit to Brisbane in 1954. Paintings by him are in the Queensland Art Gallery, the Australian War Memorial, Canberra, and in private collections.

Remembered by his contemporaries as a kindly, jovial Bohemian with a touch of the larrikin at times, Bustard was respected as 'a fluent painter', 'Bill the Swift'. He envied a musical brother, though he performed creditably himself on piano, violin and accordion and was a regular attendant at concerts. Survived by a daughter, he died at Labrador, Queensland, on 24 August 1973, and was cremated with Church of England rites.

V. Lahey, *Art in Queensland, 1859-1959* (Brisb,

1959); W. Bustard papers (NL); Qld Art Gallery, Biographical files (Brisb); SP110/2-42/28/2298 (AAO, Canb); information from Miss Lorraine Bustard and Mrs Jessie Hanley, Labrador, Qld, and Mr D. Phillips, Spring Hill, Qld.

RAOUL MELLISH

BUTLER, ARTHUR GRAHAM (1872-1949), physician and medical historian, was born on 25 May 1872 at Kilcoy, Queensland, son of William Butler, station-manager, and his wife June, née Graham, both English-born. After attending Ipswich Grammar School, he studied medicine at St John's College, Cambridge (B.A., 1894; B.C., 1897; M.B., 1899); he rowed for Cambridge, was an outstanding middle-distance runner, and warmly sympathized with the labour movement. On returning to Queensland he went into general practice at Kilcoy, then in 1902-07 at Gladstone. On 2 February 1904 at St Paul's Anglican Church, Burwood, New South Wales, he married Lilian Kate Mills. He left Gladstone in 1907 to do twelve months postgraduate work at the University of Sydney, then went into practice in Wickham Terrace, Brisbane, specializing in gynaecology and obstetrics. In 1912-14 he was honorary secretary of the Queensland branch of the British Medical Association.

In 1912 Graham Butler joined the Australian Army Medical Corps and became medical officer of the Moreton Regiment. He enlisted in the Australian Imperial Force as a captain on 20 August 1914 and was appointed regimental medical officer of the 9th Battalion which sailed for Egypt in September. Officers and men were inclined to regard his wise precautions as over-careful, even finicky, and he was soon affectionately known as 'Gertie'. Butler was in one of the first boats ashore at Gallipoli on 25 April 1915; he climbed the cliffs with the leading wave and set up his aid-post between 400 Plateau and Bolton's Ridge. One of his men later recalled 'from the time that he stepped out on the beach dressed like a veritable Christmas tree . . . until several days afterwards when he was on the point of collapse from sheer exhaustion . . . his energy, bravery and devotion to duty were an inspiration to all'. He was the only medical officer to win the Distinguished Service Order at Anzac, where he remained until October.

In February 1916 Butler, who had been promoted major the previous September, was appointed deputy assistant director of medical services, I Anzac Corps. He reached France in April. A medical colleague later described him as 'a most efficient D.A.D.M.S. . . . enthusiastic in his work, quiet in manner and a very brave gentleman'. In November 1916 he was promoted lieut-colonel and next February was given command of the 3rd Field Ambulance. At Bullecourt his unit was in the forward area as the 1st Division's main dressing station, then after two months at Buire served in Flanders, taking over the advanced dressing station on the Menin Road on 15 September. In characteristic fashion Butler turned his hand to any task that required attention. 'Gertie was everything in the unit, from C.O. to sanitary fatigue', one of his men remarked. He was mentioned in dispatches twice in 1917.

After the 3rd battle of Ypres Butler was sent to London to help collate the medical records of the A.I.F. He left the front reluctantly but was to return often to spend hours with unit commanders, instructing them in the compilation of war diaries and medical records. From July 1918 he became commander of the 3rd Australian General Hospital at Abbeville until it closed in June 1919. Before returning home he spent another six months at the war records section, A.I.F. headquarters, London. Two brothers and a sister had also served in the A.I.F.

Demobilized in February 1920, Butler resumed private practice in Brisbane and that year was State president of the B.M.A. In 1923, 'against his wish, but from a sense of public duty', he agreed to write the official history of the Australian Army Medical Services in the war; the task was to occupy the next twenty years of his life. He gave up his practice and moved to Canberra where he became medical officer of the Royal Military College in 1927-30 and of the Federal Capital Territory in 1928-31. The three volumes were published in 1930, 1940 and 1943; Butler wrote them all, except part of the first. Towards the end of his task he was troubled by partial blindness. His literary work displays the qualities that he showed on the battlefield: courage, compassion and meticulousness. He sought to isolate and analyse important problems as a guide to future policy and management. His arguments are trenchant, his scholarship exact and penetrating. His wide-ranging, critical statistical appendices are especially valuable and shocking in their implications. His three volumes are among the most distinguished war history texts of the English-speaking nations.

Butler was an active member of St John the Baptist's Anglican Church, the Canberra Horticultural Society and local ex-servicemen's associations. Always a keen rose-grower, he had been joint author of *National roses of Canberra* in 1933. His final publication in 1945 was *The digger: a study in democracy*. Survived by his wife and daughter, he died of hypertensive cerebral vascular disease at Canberra on 27 February 1949 and was buried in the churchyard at St John's. A colleague once said of Butler: 'he was everything that gentle upbringing, the highest education, Christian philosophy, unbounded comradeliness, fearless integrity, the zeal of an idealist, and boyish humour and enjoyment of life could make a man'. His portrait by John Longstaff [q.v.], hangs in the Australian War Memorial.

C. E. W. Bean, *The story of Anzac*, 1 (Syd, 1921); *London Gazette*, 1 June, 3 Aug 1915, 2 Feb, 25 Dec 1917; *Reveille* (Syd), Oct, Nov 1930, Mar 1935, Feb 1937, Mar 1940; *MJA*, 27 Apr 1940, 8 Oct 1949; *SMH*, 3 July 1943, 28 Feb 1949; *Canb Times*, 27 Feb 1949, 4 June 1951, 14 June 1959; A. G. Butler diary and papers (AWM); family papers held by Lady Hancock, Dalkeith, WA; information from Mrs P. Cunningham, Buderim, Qld.   C. M. GURNER

BUTLER, CHARLES PHILIP (1880-1953), soldier and agricultural journalist, was born on 16 July 1880 in Adelaide, son of (Sir) Richard Butler [q.v.], and his first wife Helena Kate, née Layton. He was educated at the Collegiate School of St Peter and in 1898 joined the South Australian Machine-Gun Battalion, a militia unit. Next year he volunteered for service in the South African War, enlisting as a corporal in the 2nd South Australian Mounted Rifles Regiment; he saw action in the Transvaal and the Orange River Colony. While in South Africa he married Bertha Smeaton Hawkins on 16 July 1901 and, instead of returning home with his regiment next March, obtained a commission in the Canadian Scouts.

Butler returned to Adelaide late in 1902 and joined Butler, Hogarth & Edwards, his father's stock firm. In 1902-07 he was stationed at Northam, Western Australia, and in 1907-09 at Peterborough, South Australia. In 1909 he became auctioneer for the South Australian Farmers' Co-operative Union and by 1916 was manager of the stock department. In 1903 he had been commissioned second lieutenant in the 18th Light Horse Regiment and later served with the 17th and 22nd Light Horse; by World War I he was a major. He joined the Australian Imperial Force on 25 March 1916 in that rank and in May was made second-in-command of the 43rd Battalion. His unit reached the Western Front in November and on 6 February 1917 Butler was promoted lieut-colonel and appointed commanding officer. He led the battalion throughout that year, serving at Messines, Warneton and Ypres; he was mentioned in dispatches and in June was awarded the Distinguished Service Order.

Butler was invalided home in February 1918 after a serious bout of trench fever. Undaunted, he set about raising 500 volunteers to take back to the front. Despite a vigorous campaign 'Butler's 500' was still incomplete when the war ended; he had over 300 names but only 37 had actually enlisted. He returned to the Farmers' Union and to his chagrin was made auctioneer, his old job having gone to another. He now devoted much time to the Returned Sailors' and Soldiers' Imperial League of Australia and was State president in 1922-24. In 1923 he was a central figure in the Ryan case, which secured continued preference for ex-servicemen in public service appointment. He had been promoted colonel in 1922 and commanded the 6th Cavalry Brigade in 1921-24. He remained on the reserve of officers until he retired in 1940.

In September 1924 'Charlie' Butler took up a soldier-settlement wheat-farm of 750 acres (300 ha) at Appila but, after a run of poor seasons, he accepted the agricultural editorship of the *Advertiser* and the *Chronicle* in 1929. He was an innovative editor. His system of estimating the dressed weights of pens of livestock was later adopted by the leading interstate press. He began on-the-spot reporting of interstate shows and published a valuable stud-stock supplement annually. In 1934 he accompanied the State's deputy director of agriculture on a tour of South America, South Africa and New Zealand, and in 1936, under his pen name of 'Yattalunga', he published *Primary production in the southern hemisphere*. Before retiring in 1950 he organized many farmers' fairs and a pasture-improvement competition.

Butler's wife died in 1949 and he married a divorcee Mary Isobel Barclay Thompson, née Shand, on 16 March 1950 at Toorak Presbyterian Church, Melbourne. He died with emphysema and Parkinsonism in the Repatriation General Hospital, Adelaide, on 25 September 1953 and was buried in the A.I.F. cemetery, West Terrace. It was the biggest funeral even seen there. Butler was survived by his wife, and by three daughters from his first marriage. A burly 6 ft. 1 in. (185 cm), 16½ stone (105 kg) extrovert, he was quick-talking and had an infectious enthusiasm for all he did.

E. J. Colliver and B. H. Richardson, *The Forty-third* (Adel, 1920); C. E. W. Bean, *The A.I.F. in France,* 1917 (Syd, 1933); G. L. Kristianson, *The politics of patriotism* (Canb, 1966); *London Gazette,* 1, 4 June 1917, 9 Feb 1924; *Digger,* Sept 1924; *Pastoral Review,* 16 Oct 1953; *Advertiser* (Adel), 1 Nov 1934, 26 Sept 1953.   CARL BRIDGE

BUTLER, HENRY JOHN (1889-1924), aviator, was born on 9 November 1889 at Yorketown, South Australia, son of John James Butler, wheat-farmer, and his wife Sarah Ann, née Cook. Harry Butler showed his enthusiasm and aptitude for mechanics by building models of primitive aircraft while still at school in Koolywurtie; he later accorded farm-work a lower priority than collaboration with a neighbour and lifelong mentor S. C. Crawford in building and flying one of Australia's early aeroplanes. Among the February 1915 candidates, Butler alone gained entrance as an aeromechanic to the Australian Flying School at Point Cook, Victoria. Commissioned three weeks after joining the Royal Flying Corps in 1916, he became fighting-instructor at Turnberry, Scotland, in 1917, and chief fighting-instructor at No. 2 Yorkshire School of Aerial Fighting in 1918. He alternated teaching with studying German aerial combat tactics over France, and he received the Air Force Cross in 1918.

Demobilized as captain, Butler brought back to Australia in 1919 a £2000 Bristol monoplane, a type which had proved its superiority in speed and manoeuvrability. He also purchased an Avro 504-K and three 110 horsepower Le Rhone rotary engines: he converted the Avro to carry two passengers on joy-rides at £5 for fifteen minutes. The monoplane, popularly termed the 'Red Devil', made the first Australian mail-service flight over water on 6 August 1919 when Butler covered the distance of 67 miles (108 km) from Adelaide to his home town, Minlaton, in twenty-seven minutes, reaching an altitude of 15 000 feet (4570 m). With 'luck, pluck and ability' as a formula for success, he also raised funds for patriotic purposes in several daring aerobatic exhibitions, notably a stunt-flying display before a crowd of 20 000 at Unley oval on 23 August 1919, the provision of a low-flying escort for Prime Minister W. M. Hughes's [q.v.] train from Salisbury to Adelaide that year, and the winning of an aerial Peace Loan Derby on 7 September 1920.

With Crawford's administrative help and the mechanical services of H. A. Kauper [q.v.], Butler operated as the Captain Harry J. Butler & Kauper Aviation Co. Ltd. The firm used the Albert Park field which later became South Australia's government airport; it was voluntarily liquidated in 1921, as a result of the public's waning interest in aerobatics. Butler retained the equipment and operated on his own until his flying career was terminated by a crash south of Minlaton on 10 February 1922. Upon recovery he established an aviation and motor-engineering garage at Minlaton and in 1924 became a director of Butler, Nicholson Ltd, motor distributors and engineers.

He died suddenly on 30 July 1924 from an unsuspected cerebral abscess and was buried in North Road cemetery, North Adelaide. He was survived by his wife Elsa Birch Gibson, a nurse from Bool Lagoon whom he had married on 21 July 1920 at St Paul's Anglican Church, Adelaide. The restored 'Red Devil' is housed in the Captain Harry Butler Memorial Museum at Minlaton; an oil portrait of him is held by the Art Gallery of South Australia.

E. R. Burnett-Reid, 'The Harry Butler story', Aviation Hist Soc of Aust, *J*, 4 (1963), no 4; *Advertiser* (Adel), 5 July, 7, 30 Aug 1919; *Observer* (Adel), 14 Jan 1922, 2 Aug 1924; H. Butler collection, PRG 207, *and* letters to G. Ward (SAA).

LEITH G. MacGILLIVRAY

BUTLER, SIR RICHARD (1850-1925), premier, was born at Stadhampton near Oxford, England, on 3 December 1850, elder son of Richard Butler, farmer, and his wife Mary Eliza, née Sadler. On 8 March 1854 the family arrived in Adelaide. Butler was educated at the Collegiate School of St Peter, then worked for his uncle Philip on his property, Yattalunga, near Gawler. In 1876 he took up land in the near-by agricultural district of Mallala and, in 1882, at Spalding. He had married Helena Kate Layton in 1878; they had eight children before her death in 1892. After two years sheep-farming at Crystal Brook near Port Pirie, in 1887-99 he was again at Mallala. On 7 June 1894 he married Ethel Pauline Finey; they had three children.

Butler's social and economic background led easily to an involvement in community affairs. He was a justice of the peace before he was 30, a member of the Crystal Brook School Board of Advice and in 1887-91 a councillor and sometime chairman of the Grace District Council. In August 1890 he won a House of Assembly by-election for Yatala which he represented until 1902; he then became member for Barossa until 1924. He had moved to Adelaide in 1899.

Butler entered parliament at a time of fluid political alignments. He stood as a Liberal without formal affiliations, and his maiden speech supported Thomas Playford's [q.v.] motion of no confidence in (Sir) J. A. Cockburn's [q.v.] government in a dispute over the Broken Hill rail link. He voted for Playford against (Sir) F. W. Holder's [q.v.] successful challenge in June 1892, and backed Sir John Downer's [q.v.] conservative ministry of 1892-93. He opposed C. C. Kingston's [q.v.] attack on Downer in 1893. But with the Liberals united in the new Kingston ministry Butler veered to support it, becoming government whip. He opposed progressive land tax, intercolonial free trade and the introduction of coloured labour, but favoured female suffrage, free education, payment of members and the establishment of a state bank. In 1898 he took over Cockburn's portfolios of agriculture and education, retaining them until the defeat of the Kingston government next year over Legislative Council reform. Butler had supported the range of liberal constitutional and industrial legislation introduced by Kingston's ministry. He admired Kingston, was ambitious for office and may, despite later affiliations, have been genuinely sympathetic to these causes at that time.

In May 1901 Butler became treasurer in J. G. Jenkins's [q.v.] cabinet, and from April 1902 was also commissioner of crown lands and immigration. This ministry claimed linear descent from Kingston's of 1893-99, but became increasingly conservative. Butler's political outlook changed considerably at this time. 1901-04 were years of political and financial readjustment for South Australia, the problems raised by Federation being magnified by drought and depression in 1901-02. Although his realism as treasurer resulted in the nickname 'Dismal Dick', Butler earned a high reputation for financial ability by pursuing a policy of balancing budgets through retrenchment. At Commonwealth-State conferences in 1903 and 1905 he was very critical of the financial provisions of the Federal compact. His concern for reducing expenditure now led him to resist any extension of state services outside those directly connected with rural development and he opposed further Legislative Council reform. He was hostile to the Labor Party's policy of expanding state intervention. These views alienated him from the more liberal of Kingston's old supporters who formed a separate party under A. H. Peake [q.v.] in 1904. Butler's increasing conservatism was exemplified in July when the government was reshuffled to include two members of the conservative opposition.

However he did not fully align himself with the conservatives. Instead, Butler became the parliamentary leader of an informal group of country members supported by the Farmers and Producers' Political Union, set up in September to defend country interests. Non-Labor politics was further fragmented by the formation of an electoral alliance between Peake's Liberals and the Labor Party. In these difficult circumstances, on 1 March 1905 Butler became premier in addition to his other offices. In the

May elections the ministerialists lost seats, Labor gained, and his government was defeated when he met parliament on 20 July. After another defeat he resigned on 26 July and became leader of the Opposition. In June 1909, after Premier Tom Price's [q.v.] death, Butler supported a new ministry led by Peake and an anti-Labor fusion was negotiated in September. In December a reconstruction of the ministry saw him again treasurer and minister for the Northern Territory. However the fusion was defeated by the Labor Party in the 1910 election and Butler accepted Peake as leader of the Opposition.

In February 1912 Butler again took office under Peake as minister of mines, minister of marine, and commissioner of public works (until November 1914 when he became commissioner of crown lands). The ministry was defeated at the March 1915 election. In 1917 after the Labor Party split, Peake again formed a government with Butler as treasurer; he was also minister of railways until May 1919 and of agriculture for five months. He consolidated his reputation for sound though frugal administration, taking some notable initiatives in the building of the Outer Harbour at Adelaide, once named 'Butler's Folly', and the locking of the River Murray. He had been knighted in 1913.

In May 1919 Butler's political career suffered a severe reverse. Irregularities in the bulk-wheat-handling scheme, which he had administered as minister of agriculture, were investigated by three royal commissions in 1917-21. The 1919 commission examined sixteen allegations against him, and found that strained relations between Butler and the scheme's manager had led to expensive administrative blunders and that he had used his position to gain minor electoral advantages. Peake immediately requested his resignation. Butler refused, claiming that he had done his best to protect his brother farmers and that resignation would be an admission of guilt. He was therefore dismissed by the Executive Council and he returned bitterly to the back-bench. In July 1920 the third royal commission found that an employee of the wheat scheme responsible for some of the allegations against Butler was himself guilty of more serious charges. Though the commission made no reference to the charges against Butler, he interpreted its findings as a vindication. His colleagues seemingly agreed, electing him Speaker in 1921. Not relishing 'political extinction', he retained this position but was badly defeated in the 1924 election when the Liberals lost office.

For a man who had 'early learned to "scorn delights and live laborious days" '

and whose only recreation was a 'change of work', this was a considerable blow, but next year he visited England which he revered as the seat of the Empire. He died at South Croydon on 28 April 1925 survived by nine children. A funeral service was held at his old church, St Andrew's (Anglican), Walkerville, and his remains were buried in North Road cemetery. His estate was sworn for probate at £10 998. In 1928 a memorial portrait by George Webb was hung in the House of Assembly. Butler's second son, (Sir) Richard Layton [q.v.] followed his father into politics and was twice premier.

H. T. Burgess (ed), *Cyclopedia of South Australia*, 1 (Adel, 1907); G. D. Combe, *Responsible government in South Australia* (Adel, 1957); *PP* (SA), 1919, 3 (28), 1920, 2 (27); *Observer* (Adel), 30 Oct 1896, 11 Mar 1905, 2 May, 13 June 1925, 20 Oct 1928; *Sunday Mail* (Adel), 24 July 1922; *Advertiser* (Adel), 29 Apr 1925; R. Daunton-Fear, Sir Richard Butler (B.A. Hons thesis, Flinders Univ, 1970).

KAY ROLLISON

BUTLER, SIR RICHARD LAYTON (1885-1966), premier, was born on 31 March 1885 at Yattalunga near Gawler, South Australia, second son of (Sir) Richard Butler [q.v.], grazier and premier, and his first wife Helena Kate, née Layton. After education at Mallala and the Adelaide Agricultural School, he farmed and managed the stock and station firm, Butler, Shannon & Co., at Hamley Bridge, before taking up grazing at Kapunda and Balaklava. On 4 January 1908 he married Maude Isobel Draper at North Adelaide. He gained debating experience in country literary societies and model parliaments, and as an early member of the Liberal Union.

In 1915 Butler was elected to the House of Assembly for Wooroora, but lost his seat in 1918 through his support for conscription. He then managed the Farmers' Bulk Grain Co-operative Co., but in 1921 won back Wooroora and held it till 1938. He learned to study parliamentary papers and acquaint himself with the State industrially and financially, rather than make frequent speeches in the House.

In 1925 Butler became party whip; two months later his financial ability and 'pugnacity' gained him the leadership of the parliamentary Liberal Federation in place of Sir Henry Barwell [q.v.]. In April 1927 he led the party to electoral victory and became premier, treasurer and minister of railways, despite his lack of ministerial experience. Although a country member he was not aggressively rural. His policy speech had deplored the deficit, excessive taxation and the costs of the 44-hour week; he promised to restore sound finance and abolish illegal off-course betting in hotels.

The main achievements of this first Butler government were the Drought Relief Act, 1927, and the Debt Adjustment Act, 1929 — attempts to assist the depressed rural sector. Industrial policy was severe: Butler felt that people should work harder. A 1929 strike by waterside workers resulted in their suppression by a special police force which could call up 3000 men within one week to handle emergencies. Later that year the government attempted to organize a referendum to ratify Saturday afternoon closing of hotels. This, supported by all Protestant and Anglican churches and temperance groups, incensed the powerful United Licensed Victuallers' Association and many who favoured off-course betting. The U.L.V.A. organized against the government and contributed to its electoral defeat in April 1930. By then the grave economic situation had led Liberal organizers to persuade Butler that it would be no bad thing if Labor had to handle the Depression. L. L. Hill's [q.v.] government administered the harsh Premiers' Plan, but collapsed under internal dissension, and Butler again won the election and became premier, treasurer and minister of immigration on 18 April 1933.

Following the merger of the Liberal and Country parties in 1932 in the Liberal and Country League, Butler was forced to include weak ex-Country Party members in his cabinet. Moreover the L.C.L. philosophy of independence for individual members made it difficult for Butler to dominate the parliamentary party and ensure strong cabinet government. Neither cabinet nor any other group could command the loyalty of all the party, which was further divided by its conflicting interest groups outside parliament.

Butler was tactless and impetuous. Although diligent in mastering reports, and convivial and broadminded, he worked in sudden bursts and sometimes gave offence to interest groups by his choice of words. However, by tough bargaining with the Commonwealth, which resulted in extra grants to the State, he was able to prune the deficit and reduce government spending in 1933-34 to the lowest level since 1925-26. South Australia was the first to balance its budget after all States had agreed on this goal in 1930

Primary industry became the cabinet's main problem: no session passed without legislation or proposals to aid that sector, yet actual benefits to farmers were few. The L.C.L. was divided over how extensively government should assist the depressed wheat and dairy industries; finally the conservative view prevailed and the resentful wheat farmers in the marginal lands continued to languish. The main organ of aid was the Farmers' Assistance Board, but it was administered stringently, in accordance with the ministry's frugal policy; the board's supervisory, inquisitorial role alienated many. Those few farmers whom the board deemed economically sound were assisted by the Primary Producers Debts Act of 1935 to prevent their position deteriorating. Butler was unable to establish a bulk-handling scheme for wheat, and he consistently and trenchantly opposed all the Commonwealth's attempts to set up a compulsory wheat pool. When in 1938 the State government leaders agreed to implement a home-consumption price-plan, Butler claimed it as a personal victory. He also opposed Commonwealth plans for rationalization of butter production. With regard to milk controls and prices, his cabinet was humiliated by being forced by one faction to introduce legislation and frustrated by another group opposing it.

Butler was more successful in attracting secondary industry to the State, a policy he had been advocating since 1929. He became an ardent supporter of J. W. Wainwright [q.v.], under-treasurer and auditor-general from 1934, who argued strongly that only secondary industry could make economic expansion possible. The important firm of Holden's Motor Body Builders Ltd, employers of 4000 men, threatened to move their factory to Melbourne while Butler was overseas in 1935. On his return he quickly granted them the desired aid and concessions to prevent the move. In 1937 the Broken Hill Proprietary Co. was offered sites and other valuable incentives to build a blast furnace at Whyalla. Similarly, Imperial Chemical Industries Ltd established a plant at Port Adelaide, and British Tube Mills Ltd and Stewarts and Lloyds Ltd were likewise attracted. Legislation was passed in 1937 to establish a statutory non-profit-making body, the South Australian Housing Trust, with a grant to build cheap homes for working people. With leading firms, the government supported the foundation of an Industries Assistance Corporation of South Australia Ltd, and underwrote Cellulose (Australia) Ltd to manufacture paper by a new process from the State's *pinus radiata* plantations. The interlocking of public and private interests, with the government responding to pressures from, but never adversely affecting, private interests, characterized Butler's industrialization programme.

In the area of social reform, in which opposing pressure groups also attempted to force his hand, Butler was cautious. He had learned in his first premiership that aiding the churches to suppress bookmaking and drinking was administratively impossible and electorally unpopular. He publicly defended the rights of men whose work was 'hard' and 'dirty' and whose 'outlet is often to have a drink or to pick a winner'. Church and temperance groups interpreted his lack of action, on these issues and on their demand for Bible-reading and religious instruction in state schools, as active encouragement of the forces of evil. They mounted a vociferous moral crusade against the government and against licensed betting shops prior to the 1938 election.

Butler's unpopularity had been mounting since his introduction of a bill to extend the life of the parliament to five years in 1933. The proposal had drawn widespread opposition and had finally been passed only as a trial measure; attempts to ratify it permanently had foundered on his inability to control the dissentient forces within his party. Even early in 1934 there had been press rumours of a 'realignment of the Ministerial members for the purpose of displacing Mr Butler'. In 1937 the *Wheatgrower* had revealed that back-benchers tried to dismiss him from the leadership. At the election in April 1938, in spite of repeated successes in balancing the budget, he and the Liberals faced dislike and disillusion with party politics. They lost their absolute majority: in a House of 39 seats the L.C.L. won 15 and independents won 13. Faced with defeat the Liberals closed ranks and unanimously re-elected him to the leadership. Supported by independents, Butler continued as premier

However his political career was faltering. When the member for the Federal seat of Wakefield, C. A. S. Hawker [q.v.], died in an air crash, Butler was induced to seek election in his stead and resigned on 5 November. In an intense, somewhat spiteful campaign the 'so confident' ex-premier was defeated by Labor candidate Sydney McHugh. Although he tried to re-enter politics, claiming that like Kipling 'he could wait and not get tired by waiting', he never succeeded. The L.C.L. refused him pre-selection again. On the opening of additions to Parliament House in 1939 he wryly quoted the adage, 'Fools build houses for other people to live in'.

As premier Butler had maintained good relations with his civil servants. He depended heavily on Wainwright to carry out the policy of prudent government spending dictated by the Depression. Agriculturists came to distrust him. They resented his affinity with the Chamber of Manufactures and industrialists such as (Sir) Edward Holden, Essington Lewis and Harold Darling [qq.v.]. Butler's concern to do his best for the State, combined with

detailed proposals from civil servants and industrialists, had fired his most effective policies. However his personal efforts had been marked by limited ideas and lack of authority. Although he had been premier for a record term of over eight years, he was handicapped by his party's lack of cohesion and did not develop the office to the extent achieved by his notable successors, Sir Thomas Playford and D. A. Dunstan.

Butler was knighted in 1939. During and after World War II he was a director of Emergency Road Transport for South Australia and chairman of the Liquid Fuel Control Board. Later he was a director of Cellulose (Australia) Ltd, Adelaide Cement Co. Ltd, the Adelaide Electric Supply Co. and the Electricity Trust of South Australia. He never varied his country-bred habit of rising at six to work in his garden before going to the office. He died of cerebro-vascular disease in Calvary Hospital, North Adelaide, on 21 January 1966 and, after a state funeral and service at St Andrew's Anglican Church, Walkerville, was buried in Evergreen Memorial Park cemetery, Enfield. Butler was survived by his wife, a daughter and a son; his estate was sworn for probate at £566.

T. J. Mitchell, 'J. W. Wainwright: the industrialisation of South Australia, 1935-40', *Aust J of Politics and Hist*, May 1962; S. Dyer, 'Farm relief in South Australia during the great depression', *JHSSA*, 2 (1976); *Australasian*, 19 Dec 1925; *Observer* (Adel), 26 Dec 1925, 2 Jan 1926; *SMH*, 19 Aug, 24 May 1929, 21 Feb, 12 May, 28 Sept 1934, 13 Dec 1938; *Advertiser* (Adel), 5, 17 Aug 1937, 8 June 1939, 22 Jan 1966; *Sunday Mail* (Adel), 27 Mar 1965; R. F. I. Smith, The Butler government in South Australia, 1933-1938 (M.A. thesis, Univ Adel, 1964); M. J. Thompson, Government and depression in South Australia, 1927-1934 (M.Ec. thesis, Flinders Univ, 1972); J. Lonie, Conservatism and class in South Australia during the depression years 1929-1934 (M.A. thesis, Univ Adel, 1973); A. D. Blatcher, Consensus and revision: the non-Labor political parties in South Australia, 1932-1944 (B.A. Hons thesis, Flinders Univ, 1974); PRG 129 (SAA).   SUZANNE EDGAR
R. F. I. SMITH

BUTLER, ROBERT JOHN CUTHBERT (1889-1950), politician, lay preacher and reformer, was born probably on 20 April 1889 at Pembury, Kent, England, son of John Albert Butler, farmer, and his wife Emma, née Batchelor. Educated at Canterbury, Butler became a tailor, married Rosa May Beaven at Stoke Newington, Middlesex, in 1910 and next year migrated to New South Wales. Active in Labor politics and the Presbyterian Church, he took part in a strike at the Catherine Hill coal-mine, then moved to Brisbane in 1914 as a temperance worker and lay preacher. He unsuccessfully contested the suburban seat of Toombul for Labor in May 1915 and in September was appointed librarian at the Queensland Museum.

Butler was a confidant of E. G. Theodore [q.v.], and his political dedication soon worried the museum authorities. He was prominent in 1916 as an advocate of radical views on peace, conscription and civil liberties; in September he joined the Queensland Anti-conscription Campaign Committee and organized the women's section. He unsuccessfully contested the Federal seat of Moreton in May 1917. Failing to secure appointment as director of the museum in June, he resigned in November and became a paid organizer for the anti-conscription movement. With T. J. Ryan, Lewis McDonald [qq.v.] and Theodore he was summonsed for conspiracy to incorporate Ryan's speeches and writings against conscription in *Hansard*. In March 1918 Butler won the State seat of Lockyer. He became a thorn in Ryan's side as leader of a group urging public support for peace but attended the House for only 51 days of 77 in 1918 and 26 days of 77 in 1919-20. He was soundly defeated by a Country Party candidate late in 1920.

Disillusioned with politics, Butler moved to Perth in 1925 to work with the local temperance organization. Though not ordained, he became minister of the Augustine Congregational Church at Bunbury late in 1931 and was a most successful preacher. Active in relieving distress caused by the Depression, he was secretary of the Unemployed Workers' Movement and late in 1933 became a vice-president of the Relief and Sustenance Worker's Union.

In November Butler became one of two country vice-presidents of the new Douglas Social Credit Movement and by February 1934 was its paid secretary. His skill as an orator enabled him successfully to defend the complex monetary theories of Douglas in debate against both Labor and Nationalist partisans, but he failed to secure election to the Legislative Council in May 1934. In a subsequent series of lecture tours through depressed country areas, his populist fervour attracted many in economic distress.

Butler disagreed finally with the Western Australian Douglas Credit Movement in 1936, resigned, drove across Australia and settled in Sydney. He revived his association there with the movement and with Protestant churches. During World War II he broadcast occasionally for the Australian Broadcasting Commission, then withdrew into retirement. Survived by his wife and four sons, he died of cancer at Hornsby on 8 November 1950 and was cremated.

Butler's beliefs and career ran a full course from Christian unorthodoxy to Labor radicalism and monetary reform. (Sir) Walter Murdoch [q.v.] spoke of his 'eloquence that came from perfect sincerity and an intense eagerness to serve his fellow men', but Patrick Troy, who encountered him in debate, saw him as no more than an astute and unscrupulous demagogue.

D. J. Murphy, *T. J. Ryan* (Brisb, 1975); *PD* (Qld), 1918, 1140, 1166, 1685, 1919-20, 2218; *New Economics . . . Douglas Credit Proposals*, 1933-34; *Daily Standard*, 10 May 1915, 21 Sept, 21 Oct 1916, 30 Apr 1917; *Worker* (Brisb), 30 May 1915, 21 Sept 1916; B. B. Berzins, The social credit movement in Australia to 1940 (M.A. thesis, Univ NSW, 1967).

D. B. WATERSON

BUTLER, THOMAS JOHN (1857-1937), professor of Latin, was born on 4 June 1857 at Windsor, New South Wales, second son of Patrick Butler, draper, and his wife Honorah, née Ryan. He was educated at the local Roman Catholic school and at Lyndhurst College in 1869-73 under Rev. Norbert Quirk; in 1873 he won a scholarship to the University of Sydney. At St John's College in 1874-75, he won the Lithgow, (Daniel) Cooper and Deas Thomson [qq.v.2,3,2] scholarships and graduated B.A. in 1876 with first-class honours and prizes in classics and natural science. In 1876-77 he taught with his elder brother Edmund at St Patrick's College, Goulburn. Resigning because of ill health, he became a private tutor in Sydney. On 21 May 1881 at Christ Church St Laurence, he married Lilian Eliza Trayte (d. 1893) with Anglican rites.

In 1880 Butler had been appointed assistant lecturer in classics at the university, under Professor Charles Badham [q.v.3]. He gave ten lectures in 1886 on the literature of the reign of Queen Anne, one of the first courses offered by the University Extension Board, and edited Badham's *Speeches and lectures delivered in Australia* (1890). Professor Walter Scott [q.v.] suggested dividing the department of classics in October 1890, and became professor of Greek; in March next year Butler was appointed to the chair of Latin, without the usual overseas consultations. He was the first graduate of the University of Sydney to hold a chair therein. In 1888-1913 he was a fellow of the senate, elected by convocation.

Widely read in ancient and modern European literature, Butler when young had no opportunity to travel overseas, and thereby lacked access to fundamental material, which may account for his entire lack of published contributions to classical scholarship. On the other hand he was an able teacher: his students included his successor F. A. Todd and the poet C. J. Brennan [qq.v.]. He was also active in university life: president of the union and of the dramatic society, and vice-president of the sports union and of the boat club. He was a trustee of the Public Library of New South Wales from 1899.

Butler was a prominent member of the Athenaeum Club, Sydney; A. B. Piddington [q.v.] found his 'conversation excelled' anything he had ever known 'for richness, variety, wit and warm good-nature'. He retired because of ill health on 31 December 1920 and died at his home at Greenwich on 19 February 1937; he was buried in the Catholic section of Northern Suburbs cemetery. He was survived by his second wife Annie, née Bugman, whom he had married at St Patrick's, Sydney, on 6 January 1894, and by two sons and two daughters by his first wife.

A. B. Piddington, *Worshipful masters* (Syd, 1929); A. R. Chisholm, *Men were my milestones* (Melb, 1958); *Hermes* (Syd), 21 Oct 1899; *ISN*, 30 Sept 1893.   A. J. DUNSTON

BUTLER, WALTER RICHMOND (1864-1949), architect, was born on 24 March 1864 at Pensford, Somerset, England, fourth son of Henry Butler, farmer, and his wife Mary Yeoman, née Harding. He showed an early talent for sketching and at 15 was articled to Alexander Lauder of Barnstaple. In 1885 W. R. Lethaby encouraged Butler to move to London and work with J. D. Sedding. He was accepted into the arts and crafts and domestic revival circles centred on William Morris and R. N. Shaw, among whom his closest friend was Ernest Gimson (1864-1919). In June 1888 Butler left Sedding's office and sailed for Australia, perhaps at the prompting of the young Melbourne architect Beverley Ussher then visiting London. Three of Butler's brothers and one of his sisters also settled in Australia. On 25 April 1894 at Holy Trinity Church, Kew, Butler married Emilie Millicent Howard.

From 1889 until 1893 Butler was in partnership with Ussher. In 1896 he was joined by George C. Inskip but they parted in 1905 after a dispute with the Royal Victorian Institute of Architects over the conduct of a competition. In 1907-16 he partnered Ernest R. Bradshaw and after World War I he was in practice with his nephew Richard (b. 1892) as W. & R. Butler, which briefly included Marcus Martin. In the late 1930s Butler was in partnership with Hugh Pettit, but he retired when Pettit enlisted for World War II.

Butler was rightly considered an architect of great talent, and many of his clients were wealthy pastoralists and businessmen. His country-house designs include Blackwood (1891), near Penshurst, for R. B. Ritchie, Wangarella (1894), near Deniliquin, New South Wales, for Thomas Millear, and Newminster Park (1901), near Camperdown, for A. S. Chirnside. Equally distinguished large houses were designed for the Melbourne suburbs: Warrawee (1906), Toorak, for A. Rutter Clark; Thanes (1907), Kooyong, for F. Wallach; Kamillaroi (1907) for (Baron) Clive Baillieu [q.v.], and extensions to Edzell (1917) for George Russell, both in St Georges Road, Toorak. These are all fine examples of picturesque gabled houses in the domestic revival genre. Butler was also involved with domestic designs using a modified classical vocabulary, as in his remodelling of Billilla (1905), Brighton, for W. Weatherley, which incorporates panels of flat-leafed foliage. His ardent admiration for R. N. Shaw is reflected in his eclectic works. Butler also regarded himself as a garden architect.

As architect to the diocese of Melbourne from 1895, he designed the extensions to Bishopscourt (1902), East Melbourne. His other church work includes St Albans (1899), Armadale, the Wangaratta Cathedral (1907), and the colourful porch and tower to Christ Church (c.1910), Benalla. For the Union Bank of Australia he designed many branch banks and was also associated with several tall city buildings such as Collins House (1910) and the exceptionally fine Queensland Insurance Building (1911). For Dame Nellie Melba [q.v.] Butler designed the Italianate lodge and gatehouse at Coombe Cottage (1925) at Coldstream.

Butler was of immaculate appearance and had impeccable manners. He was a superb draughtsman and is reputed to have controlled all the designing and detailing in his office. In World War I he suffered a deep personal setback with the death of his only son, and from the 1920s he started to relinquish all but the elite clients to his younger partners. His gradual departure from practice is a moving conclusion to a brilliant career. On visits to London in 1912 and 1929 and perhaps also in 1924, he renewed his friendships with the close associates of his youth. Butler's works included *Modern architectural design* and *Healthy homes*, both published in Melbourne in 1902. Survived by his wife and two daughters, he died at his home in Toorak on 31 May 1949, and was cremated. His estate was valued for probate at £11 255.

Roy Vic Inst of Architects, *J*, July-Sept 1903, Mar 1905, Mar-May 1922; *Building, Engineering and MiningJ*, 9 Jan 1892; *Argus*, 1 June 1949; D. H. Alsop, Walter Richmond Butler, architect (B. Arch. research report, Univ Melb, 1971); W. R. Butler papers (LaTL).   GEORGE TIBBITS

BUTLER, WILLIAM FREDERICK DENNIS (1878-1941), lawyer, was born on 28 July 1878 at Bagdad, Tasmania, son of Francis Frederick Butler and his wife Emma Tregurtha, née Dennis. He attended the local state school and The Hutchins School, Hobart, before entering the University of Tasmania (B.A., 1899; B.Sc., 1900; LL.B., 1903; M.Sc., 1938). He was admitted to the Bar of the Supreme Court of Tasmania on 25 September 1903. After a world tour he joined the legal firm Butler, McIntyre & Butler, founded by his great-grandfather Gamaliel Butler [q.v.1], where he practised for the rest of his life, as a partner from 1910.

After his father's death Butler also managed Korongee orchard at Glenorchy. Politically independent, in 1907-10 he was an elected member and became treasurer of the Moonah Town Board. He had supported Federation and the introduction of the Hare-Clark [q.v.3] voting system in Tasmanian State elections. As a respected equity lawyer and advocate, Butler was conveyancing counsel to the State Supreme Court and belonged to the editorial board responsible for reprinting *The public general Acts of Tasmania 1826-1936.* His article, 'Some aspects of statute law revision in Australia', was published in the proceedings of the first Australian Legal Convention (*Australian Law Journal,* 1935-36, supplement to volume 9). He was president of the Southern Law Society in 1928-39 and the first Tasmanian to be president of the Law Council of Australia in 1938.

Butler was a prominent Anglican layman for more than thirty years. In 1942 Bishop W. R. Barrett wrote of the 1908 synod: 'Butler's name was soon to become a household word in the affairs of the Church . . . His modest and gentle manner and his wide knowledge smoothed the passage of legal business in this and many later Synods'. For the 'nexus' debate at the 1913 synod on the legal relationship between the 'Church at Home' and the Church in Australia, Butler produced a detailed, scholarly treatise. In 1916 he became Church advocate, and he made outstanding contributions to the debates over alterations to the Book of Common Prayer. He was a trustee of Church property in Tasmania, and a lay reader and church-warden of St John's, New Town. He belonged to several church boards and to that of Christ College, whose affairs he had reconstructed as the progenitor of the Christ College Trust Act, 1926. In 1940 he was elevated to diocesan chancellor: Bishop R. S. Hay [q.v.] commented: 'it was a just if somewhat tardy recognition of the Church's great indebtedness to him for the distinguished service which he had so freely and efficiently given to the diocese'.

Butler's 1917 lecture to the Royal Society of Tasmania on the foundation of public institutions for secondary education in Tasmania has been the corner-stone for subsequent research on this subject. He was elected to the Council of the University of Tasmania in 1912-20, was vice-warden of the senate in 1925-36 and warden from 1936 until his death, and encouraged the establishment of the faculties of engineering and commerce; he was also on the board of The Hutchins School. A Rotarian and a bush-walker, he was also president of the Tasmanian section of the League of Nations Union.

Butler had married Constance I. Morrisby in 1896 and when he died on 6 October 1941 at Hobart he was survived by her, by a son who carried on the family legal tradition, and by two daughters.

B. W. Rait, *The official history of The Hutchins School* (Hob, 1935); W. R. Barrett, *History of the Church of England in Tasmania* (Hob, 1942); *Church News* (Hob), Nov 1941; *Mercury,* 7 Oct 1941.   GEORGE DEAS BROWN

BUTTENSHAW, ERNEST ALBERT (1876-1950), farmer and politician, was born on 23 May 1876 at Marengo, New South Wales, eldest son of Henry Buttenshaw, blacksmith and later farmer, and his wife Mary Jane, née West. He was educated at Young Superior Public School; at 14 he began work in the Post Office, but left two years later to work on a farm near Grogan. From 1898 he managed his father's farm at Lake Cowal and in 1904 selected his own block at Billys Lookout near West Wyalong. On 11 February 1903 he had married Lucy Isabel Dean (d. 1925). During World War I he cultivated 1400 acres (567 ha) of wheat. In 1912-18 he was a member of Bland Shire Council and president in 1914-18.

Buttenshaw had joined the Farmers and Settlers' Association in 1897 and, a member of its executive in 1910-27, became president in 1922-23 and 1925-26. He was chairman of the Voluntary Wheat Pool in 1921-25. As a Nationalist, he won the Legislative Assembly seat of Lachlan in 1917, representing Murrumbidgee in 1918-27 and Lachlan in 1927-38. He soon joined the Progressive Party and was whip and parliamentary secretary in 1920-22. One of the 'True Blues' who refused to join Sir George Fuller's [q.v.] coalition ministry in 1922, he was deputy leader in 1922-25, and then leader of the renamed Country Party. Buttenshaw came to an arrangement with (Sir) T. R. Bavin [q.v.] for the 1927 elections and, prompted by (Sir) M. F. Bruxner [q.v.], held out for four portfolios in the coalition: he was secretary for public works in 1927-30, and minister for railways in 1927-29.

An energetic minister, Buttenshaw secured generous funds for water, sewerage and railways in the wheat districts. As acting premier from April to August 1929, he attended the Premiers' Conference in May which met without the Commonwealth and issued an ultimatum to S. M. (Viscount) Bruce [q.v.], the prime minister, on arbitration. He also had to contend with the New South Wales coal strike, and tried to abolish rural wage-awards. Buttenshaw relied heavily on Bruxner for advice and on 26 April 1932 stood down as leader, becoming deputy. He was secretary for lands in the (Sir) Bertram Stevens [q.v.]-Bruxner ministry in 1932-38. Buttenshaw repeatedly visited country electorates and tried to extend closer settlement, especially in areas where irrigation was possible; he also tried to provide recreational and sporting facilities. He resigned his portfolio on 31 January 1938 and did not stand at the general election in March.

A director of the Farmers & Graziers' Co-operative Grain, Insurance & Agency Co. Ltd from 1931, Buttenshaw was chairman and managing director in 1938-50, and presided over record growth by the company. He was also president of the Circular Quay Association from 1938. Well-known as a cricketer and tennis-player, he was a trustee of the Sydney Cricket Ground from 1935, a vice-president of the New South Wales Lawn Tennis Association and of the Royal Agricultural Society, and sometime president of Strathfield Golf Club. From 1942 he sat on the Central Wool Committee.

Buttenshaw had been a warden of St Andrew's Church of England, Strathfield. He died of cancer on 26 June 1950 at his home at Ashfield and was cremated. He was survived by three sons and four daughters of his first marriage, and by his second wife Clare (Clara), née Sugars, a nurse whom he had married on 8 December 1928. His estate was valued for probate at £10 494.

Who's who in the Progressive Party (Syd, 1925); U. Ellis, *The Country Party* (Melb, 1958); B. D. Graham, *The formation of the Australian Country Parties* (Canb, 1966); D. Aitkin, *The colonel* (Canb, 1969); *SMH*, 27 June 1950; *Land* (Syd), 30 June 1950; information from Mrs J. Tinkler, French's Forest, NSW.   BEVERLEY KINGSTON

BUTTERS, SIR JOHN HENRY (1885-1969), engineer, was born on 23 December 1885 at Alverstoke, Hampshire, England, eldest of six children of Richard John Butters, master mariner, and his wife Fanny, née Dunkinson. He attended Taunton's Trade School at Southampton in 1898-1901, then studied at Hartley University College, Southampton, for three years on a county borough scholarship. In 1904 he received a University of London intermediate bachelor of science (engineering) degree and a first-class certificate for electrical engineering from Hartley College.

Butters then joined John I. Thornycroft & Co. Ltd, shipbuilders and engineers of Southampton, as an apprentice and improver. In 1905 he moved to the technical department of Siemens Brothers Dynamo Works Ltd at Stafford and gained experience designing dynamos and motors. In 1908 he became assistant engineer at the head office in London where he was responsible for designing and costing power-station projects. Next year the firm transferred him, as chief engineer, to their Australasian branch based in Melbourne. Butters advised the Waihi Gold Mining Co. on the design and layout of its hydro-electric station at Horahora on the Waikato River in New Zealand and the Municipal Tramways Trust, Adelaide, which was electrifying its system.

In 1910, still employed by Siemens Brothers, he was consulted by Complex Ores Co. Ltd of Melbourne and its subsidiary, the Hydro-Electric Power and Metallurgical Co. Ltd, about their proposals to produce electricity in Tasmania to facilitate the processing of zinc ore. Thus, almost from its inception, Butters was involved in the Great Lake hydro-electric scheme, the first major attempt to harness the water-power of Tasmania in this way. The hydro-electric company started active operations in August 1911 and Butters resigned from Siemens Brothers to become its engineer-in-chief and manager on 1 September. He was responsible for the design, layout and construction of a masonry dam at the Great Lake, intake works on the Shannon River, a power-station and transmission line, and an electricity distribution and sub-station complex for Hobart. In 1914 the company ran into financial difficulties; the hydro-electric undertaking was acquired by the State and became the responsibility of a newly established Hydro-Electric Department, of which Butters was appointed chief engineer and general manager at a salary of £1000 a year. A man of strong mental and physical qualities, he pushed ahead vigorously with the work so that, despite the rigorous winter conditions at high altitudes, the first two turbines (each of 4900 horsepower) of the

Waddamana power-station were brought into operation in May 1916. During the next seven years, in spite of financial stringencies and shortages of labour and materials, the capacity of the installation was raised to 63 000 horsepower and the reticulation system greatly extended. In 1923, on the completion of the scheme which had cost over £3 million, Butters was appointed C.M.G.; he had already been made M.B.E. in 1920. Although he set and demanded high standards, he was warmly regarded both by the project's large work-force whom he treated justly and sympathetically, and by the Tasmanian government which delegated considerable responsibility and authority to him.

Butters had been appointed second lieutenant in the Australian Engineers on 20 September 1909, and was promoted lieutenant on 7 March 1911 and captain on 1 March 1914. Repeatedly during World War I he sought unsuccessfully for permission to go on active service, but had to be satisfied with the post of staff officer Engineers at headquarters 6th Military District, Hobart, which he held in 1915-21; he was promoted major on 1 January 1919.

The Great Lake scheme and these military duties would have taxed the energy of most men, but Butters still found time for other activities. In 1916, as chairman of the Tasmanian State committee, he became an *ex officio* member of the executive committee of the Commonwealth Advisory Council of Science and Industry. The Commonwealth government in 1917 appointed him a member of a royal commission that reported on the handling, storage and transport of wheat. Next year he became president of the newly formed Tasmanian Institution of Engineers, and in 1920 was elected chairman of the Tasmanian division of the Institution of Engineers, Australia. Butters was also a member of the board, set up by the Tasmanian minister for education in September 1919, to investigate the possible co-ordination of engineering courses at Hobart Technical College and at the University of Tasmania, which recommended that a degree in engineering should be established at the university. At its first meeting in September 1921, the university's faculty of engineering elected him as its chairman and later as its representative on the university board of studies; he was appointed by the State parliament to the university council for two years from January 1922. In 1920 the Tasmanian government had appointed him as chairman of a committee to report on the water-supply of Hobart, and in 1922 as its representative on the main committee of the Australian Commonwealth Engineering Standards Association.

In 1922 Butters visited New Zealand to advise the Auckland Electric-Power Board on the system it should adopt for the supply of electricity in its area; next year he prepared a report on water-power in Tasmania on behalf of the Institution of Engineers, Australia, for presentation to the World Power Conference in London in 1924.

Butters successfully applied for the position of full-time chairman of the Federal Capital Commission, a body created under the Seat of Government (Administration) Act, 1924, to expedite the development of Canberra; he was appointed for five years from 3 November 1924 at a salary of £3000. The commission was a statutory corporation in which were vested the whole of the land and other public assets in the Federal Capital Territory: for the first time a single authority had responsibility for the administration, design and construction of Canberra as well as the development of municipal activities and the control of private enterprise. Initially the commission was charged with the job of completing Parliament House at the earliest possible date — January 1927 was suggested — by which time office and residential accommodation was also to be ready for parliamentary staff and a small secretariat. Although some construction work had been undertaken, the task was formidable. The government then decided in November 1925 that the entire central office of the public service, rather than a small secretariat, should be moved to the capital. Some idea of the flurry of activity can be gained from the fact that the commission spent £4 680 000 during the thirty months before the opening of Parliament House on 9 May 1927 and at its peak employed 4000 tradesmen and labourers. Butters, described as 'big, bronzed and direct of speech', was the driving force; he was determined that Canberra would 'have none of the terrible eyesores which mar so many of our cities'. His achievement was recognized when, during the visit of the duke of York for the opening, he was knighted.

Throughout this period, however, Butters had borne the brunt of criticism from Australians who disagreed with the concept of a 'bush capital' and from people whose homes and jobs had been transferred there. He himself argued that the municipal side 'formed a small part of [the commission's] everyday work, and obviously its general activities could not be made subsidiary to the smaller, but troublesome, points associated with local government'. The fact that the commission exercised almost complete control over the life and work of the populace, who lacked any voice in the decision-making process until 1929, led to considerable resentment. In July 1929 the government, which had been unable to reach any long-term solution to the administration of the Federal Capital Territory, proposed to Butters that the life of the commission – due to terminate on 2 November – be extended by one year. He was reluctant to continue on a full-time basis because he had borne 'a very great deal of opprobium which I have not earned', because an extension for a mere twelve months would lead to more abuse but little security for himself or his family, and because the financial restraints being imposed on Canberra's development might reduce the scope of his job from that of designer and constructor to that of administrator. When in August the government indicated that the plan to transfer the rest of the public service had been abandoned for some years, he resigned from 14 October and left Canberra the following day. The naming of Butters Drive in the suburb of Phillip is the only official commemoration of his association with the city.

Depressed conditions in Australia had ended large-scale public works projects that would have satisfied a man of Butters' experience, proven ability and forceful personality. His departure from Canberra, after a hectic five years during which £7 741 000 was spent, seems to have been a turning-point in his career. Not yet 45, he moved to Wahroonga, Sydney, set up as a consulting engineer and continued in private practice until about 1954. But much of his time was spent in other ways: in 1932 he was vice-president of the board of commissioners of the Government Savings Bank of New South Wales; in 1935-36 he was chairman of the Macquarie Street Replanning Committee and in 1937-38 of the Circular Quay Planning Committee. He was a director of a diverse range of companies, becoming chairman of Associated Newspapers Ltd, Radio 2UE Sydney Ltd, The North Shore Gas Co. Ltd, Hadfields Steel Works Ltd and Hetton Bellbird Collieries Ltd.

Butters had been appointed honorary consulting military engineer at Army Headquarters, Melbourne, with the rank of honorary lieut-colonel in 1927. He served on a part-time basis during World War II and was transferred to the reserve of officers (Engineers) with the same honorary rank on 1 October 1952. Interested in advancing the status of engineers, he became councillor in 1920 and president in 1927-28 of the Institution of Engineers, Australia; because of his efforts, in February 1928 it became the first national body to hold its annual conference in Canberra. He was a member of several other professional organizations, including the American Society of Civil Engineers. Another of his continuing interests was the development of motoring: in 1931, when General Motors absorbed (H. J.) Holden's [q.v.] Motor Body Builders Ltd, Adelaide, he joined the first Australian board of General Motors-Holden's Ltd and continued as a director until his death. A member of the Royal Automobile Club of Australia from 1928, he was president in 1937-49 and then vice-patron until 1969.

A self-disciplined, reserved and modest man, Butters continued an active and many-sided career until about 1967 when ill health led him to retire progressively from public life. He died at Turramurra on 29 July 1969 and was cremated with Anglican rites. He had married Lilian Gordon Keele at Waverley on 10 February 1912; she and their three daughters and a son survived him.

Tasmania Hydro-Electric Dept, . . . *Inauguration of the Tasmanian Hydro-Electric Power Scheme* (Hob, 1916); *Government Gazette* (Cwlth), 21 June 1917, 30 Oct 1924; information from Auckland Electric-Power Board, J.W.W. Butters (Syd), Canberra National Memorials Cttee, Dept of Defence (Canb), General Motors-Holden's Ltd (Melb), The Hydro-Electric Commission (Tas), Radio 2UE Sydney Pty Ltd, Richard Taunton College (Southampton), Roy Automobile Club of Aust (Syd), Univ of Southampton, Univ of Tas, and Aust Archives Office (Canb).

G. J. R. LINGE

BUXTON, SIR THOMAS FOWELL (1837-1915), philanthropist and governor, was born on 26 January 1837 at West Ham, Essex, England, eldest son of Sir Edward North Buxton, second baronet, of Warlies, Essex, and Colne House, Cromer, Norfolk, and his wife Catherine, née Gurney; his paternal grandfather of the same name, the first baronet, had been a notable leader of the anti-slavery movement. Educated at Harrow School and Trinity College, Cambridge (M.A., 1859), in 1858 he succeeded to the baronetcy, landed interests and a partnership in the brewing firm of Truman, Hanbury, Buxton & Co. where he worked until 1889.

An Evangelical Anglican, Buxton devoted much energy and money to religious and charitable causes, serving in the Church Missionary and British and Foreign Bible societies. He became vice-president of the British and Foreign Aborigines Protection Society, joined the committee of the British and Foreign Anti-Slavery Society, and secured the amalgamation of these bodies. He was a zealous student of natural history and a conservationist.

On 12 June 1862 at Exton Buxton married Lady Victoria Noel (1839-1916); ten of their thirteen children survived infancy. His wife was crippled by a spinal condition from 1869. Buxton served as a Liberal in the House of Commons in 1865-68, was a promoter of the Imperial Federation League, and represented Britain at several European conferences on slavery and central African affairs. In 1880 he declined a peerage because he was proud to continue the style and forenames of his grandfather. From 1882 he was increasingly critical of the effects of British imperial practice in Africa and Asia and, in a reformist spirit, became a director of the Imperial British East Africa Co. Nevertheless he broke with the Liberal Party over Irish home rule in 1886.

In 1895 Buxton accepted the governorship of South Australia, after anxious and prayerful reflection. The British were amazed at the choice of this critic of the government's colonial policy. The South Australian government was even more surprised. It had requested a long interregnum to follow Governor Kintore's [q.v.5] retirement. The radical premier C. C. Kingston [q.v.] had hoped for participation of the local executive in the nomination of future governors and to save money. He made the post unattractive by abolishing the vice-regal expense allowance and demanded that subordinate posts be filled locally. The Colonial Office tried 'to bring [Kingston and his colleagues] to their senses by sending them a man strong enough to live within his salary'. Kingston retaliated with a bill to reduce the governor's salary by £1000. Although the Colonial Office advised Buxton that this proposal was derogatory to the dignity of the office, he refused to withdraw his acceptance of the office. Kingston applied other petty economies: when Buxton arrived in Adelaide on 29 October he was charged customs duty on his wife's invalid carriage, and told that the governor's salary (reduction) bill had passed both Houses.

When formally advised to assent to the bill, Buxton felt obliged to reserve it but he urged the secretary of state to secure royal assent speedily, and thus negated the conservatives' efforts to embarrass the government. Tension developed next year when Kingston ignored Buxton's advice and left the office of chief secretary vacant for several weeks following the resignation of J. H. Gordon [q.v.]. But the government soon came to appreciate Buxton's gentle courtesy; his unassuming friendliness disarmed all radical criticism. Kingston declared 'Governor Buxton and his flock to be the most genial, sociable and common-sense family who have ever inhabited the Adelaide vice-regal mansion'. He deplored the coloured immigration restriction bill, 1896, but when he reserved it the Colonial Office instructed him to assent to a similar measure if it exempted British subjects from its operation. With that single exception, the *Advertiser* later claimed, 'no one could have more completely identified himself with the aspirations of the people over whom he ruled'. He attended the Federal Convention debates of 1897-98 as an observer and lobbied discreetly to help resolve disagreements.

Uniquely among Australian governors, Buxton regularly visited and chatted with the inmates of the gaols, the Home for Incurables, the lunatic asylum and the destitutes' refuges. These people were to him 'individuals with lives and interests of their own'. He travelled to meet the Aboriginals, tried to explain their tribal land tenure and other customs to the whites, and frequently exhorted government, churchmen and pastoralists to make amends for past mistakes.

The Buxtons stimulated Adelaide's musical life and worked tirelessly for a host of religious, educational and charitable organizations: Government House became the meeting place of numerous committees and Buxton gave very large sums to drought victims. Lady Victoria became the first president of the Church of England Mothers' Union in Adelaide and founded several working-girls' clubs. They 'brought Government House nearer to the people than ever it was before'. Lady Victoria afterwards remembered, with '*real pleasure*', 'our Garden Parties for State school-teachers, for the police and their wives, the hospital nurses, the market-gardeners and their families . . . [and] the Anglican Sunday-School teachers'. The family's tie with South Australia was cemented in 1896 when their daughter Constance Victoria married Rev. Bertram Robert Hawker.

On leave in England in 1898 the Buxtons' eldest son developed a near-fatal illness and Lady Victoria's condition worsened. Buxton resigned without returning to Australia. He had been appointed K.C.M.G. in 1895 and was promoted G.C.M.G. in 1899. He continued to 'stick up for South Australia' and strove to prevent Joseph Chamberlain tampering with the Constitution of the Commonwealth. He continued his philanthropic work. Since 'he used to say that the real advantage of wealth was not the great house but the "stray sixpence in the pocket"', it was fitting that when he died, on 28 October 1915, it was in a cottage at Cromer because he had made Colne House a hospital for wounded soldiers. The Art Gallery of South Australia holds a portrait of Buxton by John Collier.

G. W. E. Russell, *Lady Victoria Buxton* (Lond, 1919); *PP* (GB), 1895 (Cmd 7910); P. A. Howell, 'Varieties of vice-regal life in South Australia',

JHSSA, no 3 (1977); *Bulletin*, 25 Jan 1896; *Register* (Adel), 29 Sept, 21 Dec 1898; *Advertiser* (Adel), 11 Apr 1899; *The Times*, 4 Nov 1915; Buxton papers (held by Mr R. de Bunsen, Upshire, Essex, *and* British Anti-Slavery Soc Lib, Oxford, Eng); CO 13/150-153 (NL).   P. A. HOWELL

BYATT, JOHN (1862-1930), educationist, was born on 7 October 1862 in London, son of John Byatt, printer, and his wife Sarah, née Ferris. Eldest in a family of two boys and two girls, he was educated in London, had five years as a pupil-teacher, trained at the Congregational Borough Road Training Institution, and taught in London elementary schools for seventeen years. He was a graduate, licentiate and examiner of the Tonic Sol-fa College, organizing, and conducting at, many musical festivals. Byatt's other vital interest was sloyd: after two years study at the Slöyd Seminarium, Nääs, Sweden, he organized teachers' woodwork and manual training classes, was appointed an examiner, and gained advanced manual qualifications in London and Leipzig, Germany.

Seeking a qualified manual training organizer and instructor, the Education Department of Victoria engaged Byatt from 2 April 1900 at a salary of £500. With his wife Alice Elizabeth, née Chambers, a teacher whom he had married in London on 29 July 1893, Byatt sailed on 2 April 1900 in the *Karlsruhe*. From 3 April 1905 he was appointed permanently as inspector of manual training and drawing. Training centres, introduced by him into Victoria in 1900, had so multiplied by 1913 that some 10 000 boys were learning woodwork. He lectured to sloyd teachers in Victoria, New South Wales and Tasmania, and in 1902-05 published in the *Education Gazette and Teachers' Aid* articles on paperwork and cardboard modelling.

Talented and painstaking, Byatt was often required for additional duties. He served three periods as an ordinary school inspector; organized and supervised several summer schools for teachers; was treasurer of the 1906 and 1913 education exhibitions; and secretary of the vast State schools jubilee exhibition of September 1922. Asked in 1915 to reorganize school music, Byatt revitalized singing-teaching, personally training and examining many teachers, and promoting the Tonic Sol-fa system; not until 1925, however, was he officially appointed as an inspector of singing as well as of manual training.

A devout Christian, Byatt studied Greek, Hebrew and theology, often while journeying by buggy from school to school. He attended lectures at Ridley College and had gained his Th.L. by January 1923. As a lay preacher, he occupied both Methodist and Anglican pulpits. Interested in dynamics, archaeology, Esperanto, old brasses, trees and philately, he joined various clubs and societies: astronomical, historical, field naturalist, and microscopical. He retired on 7 October 1927, not once since 1900 having been absent from official duty through illness. On 4 September 1930 Byatt died of coronary vascular disease and was cremated; he was survived by his wife, and by his son (a clergyman) and daughter (a teacher).

C. R. Long (ed), *Souvenir of the Summer School, Quarantine Station, Portsea* (Melb, 1909); *Education Gazette* (Vic), 20 Apr 1922, 25 Oct 1927; R. S. Stevens, Music in State supported education in New South Wales and Victoria, 1848-1920 (Ph.D. thesis, Univ Melb, 1977); register of career of J. Byatt (History section, Education Dept, Melb); Education Dept, Special case 1174 (PRO, Vic).
NEVILLE DRUMMOND

BYRNE, FREDERICK (1834-1915), Catholic priest, was born on 22 February 1834 in Dublin. At 14 he began studies for the Benedictine novitiate at Subiaco near Rome, but returned to Dublin because of ill health. In 1855 he migrated with Dom Joseph Serra [q.v.6] to Western Australia, where he taught at a church boys' school. He went to the Adelaide mission in 1857 and then to Sevenhill, the Jesuit college near Clare, to complete his studies for the priesthood. He was ordained in 1860 and for the next five years was in Adelaide and travelling on southern Yorke Peninsula and along the far west coast. Later he described the life of such a priest: 'suffering the most miserable accommodation, he has to eat badly-prepared food, and to sleep on some sort of a shakedown . . . No matter how fatigued he may be, he is expected to be fresh and cheerful, and to talk for hours on subjects in which he has not the smallest interest'.

In March 1865 Byrne was appointed to Kapunda but resigned after conflict with an assistant, Fr Horan. He was posted to Salisbury in 1869, before becoming joint administrator of the Adelaide diocese on Bishop Sheil's [q.v.6] death in 1872. Byrne was appointed vicar-general by the new bishop, his friend Christopher Reynolds [q.v.6] and later twice administered the diocese. In 1881 Byrne was made doctor of divinity by the Holy See and next year was received by the Pope. In 1883-97 he served again at Kapunda and from 1897 was at Goodwood. In 1902 he became a domestic prelate and in 1912 he retired.

Byrne's career coincided with the increasingly uncompromising attitude of Bishop Geoghegan [q.v.4] and his successors towards secular education and the 1851 Education Act. Byrne fostered Catholic schools wherever he served and personally funded the building of the school of St Thomas at Goodwood. His concern for the spiritual well-being of the laity sometimes induced him to criticize his superiors and engage in public controversy. His outspoken *History of the Catholic Church in South Australia* (1896) was equivocal about Bishops Sheil and Murphy's stand on secular education, and he disagreed with Sheil over the treatment of the Sisters of St Joseph in 1871. But despite Byrne's critical attitudes, contemporary accounts emphasize his kindliness, imperturbability and retiring disposition.

He and other priests had been prominent at the meeting called by Geoghegan on 27 September 1860 to petition parliament against the existing education system. Two years later Byrne was directing Catholics' votes in the Yatala electorate. In reviving the Catholic Club in 1881 he had similar political goals and recognized the role of newspapers in furthering the Church's views. He had hoped for much from the *Record and South Australian Catholic Standard* and its successor, the *Catholic Record*, and became a shareholder and chairman of directors of the successful *Southern Cross*.

After his death at Calvary Hospital on 22 July 1915 Monsignor Byrne's body was placed in St Francis Xavier's Cathedral and requiem Mass was presided over by Archbishop Spence [q.v.]. His funeral was largely attended and he was buried at Cabra convent. A friend and benefactor of the Dominican nuns since their arrival in the colony, Byrne had endowed the community at Cabra with grounds in 1884.

Advertiser (Adel), 29 Sept 1860, 18, 19 Nov 1862, 23 July 1915; *Catholic Record*, 18, 25 Feb 1881; *Southern Cross* (Adel), 22 Apr 1910, 30 July 1915, 16 Oct, 6, 30 Nov 1936; Francis Murphy, Journal, 5 Mar 1857, *and* F. Byrne, Letters, 24 Jan, 21 Feb 1880, 24 May 1897, *and* R. A. Morrison, Index file 1866-99, vol 1, MS notes (Roman Catholic Archdiocesan Archives, Adel); information from Fr Newbold, Roman Catholic Church Offices, Perth.

SUSAN PRUUL

BYRNES, THOMAS JOSEPH (1860-1898), barrister and premier, was born on 11 November 1860 in Brisbane, son of Irish immigrants Patrick Byrnes and his wife Anna, née Tighe. Patrick is described variously as farmer, dairyman and grazier. The family, chronically poor, moved to Humpybong on Moreton Bay in 1861, then in 1866 to Bowen, North Queensland, where Patrick died in December next year. Thomas attended the Bowen Primary School where, as an exceptional pupil, he was encouraged by the schoolmasters and the parish priest. In 1873 he was appointed a pupil-teacher but a government scholarship next year took him to Brisbane Grammar School. There in 1875-77, he annually won the Lilley [q.v.5] gold medal for distinction in Greek, Latin and English. He was awarded the University of Sydney prize in the junior public examination of 1876 and granted an extension scholarship which enabled him to complete his secondary education at the Grammar School. Having won an exhibition tenable at any university in the British Empire, he chose the University of Melbourne and began arts and law there in 1879. He graduated in arts in 1882 and law in 1884, with honours in both; in 1882-83 he taught at Xavier College.

Byrnes was admitted as a barrister in Victoria on 8 July 1884 but returned for a Queensland admission on 5 August. In 1884-85 he read law in the chambers of Patrick Real and by 1890 had built up a large, successful practice in Brisbane. In his spare time he chaired the Reunion Society for alumni of the Grammar School, was a cricket and football spectator, translated from the classics and shared membership of a select literary circle with Sir Samuel Griffith [q.v.]. In the new coalition government Premier Griffith retained the attorney-general's portfolio but, as he was drawing up proposals for a federal constitution, he desired to be relieved of day-to-day work, so created the new post of solicitor-general which he offered to Byrnes who was appointed to the Legislative Council.

The support given by Byrnes to the workmen's lien bill of 1891 convinced many that he was a sincere liberal, but he was also deeply influenced by current nationalist and materialist attitudes and was principally preoccupied with Queensland's development, prestige and security. Believing that a short continuation of Kanaka labour was the only way to save the valuable sugar industry, he supported the Pacific islanders (extension) bill of 1892. Concern for Queensland's well-being also led him temporarily to support the idea of Federation. During the shearers' strike of early 1891, in response to Sir Thomas McIlwraith's [q.v.] request for effective action, he invoked an archaic British conspiracy Act under which strike leaders were convicted and imprisoned. Later that year, he forced Crown Solicitor J. H. Gill [q.v.4] to accept an articled clerk without the customary premium. Gill's view that this was not a legitimate occasion for ministerial patronage had strong support, and Byrnes was later criticized in parliament for making unwarranted reductions in Gill's salary.

Byrnes continued his private practice and was engaged in two major Supreme Court cases. In *Queensland Investment Co.* v. *Grimley*, his successful conduct of the defence was widely praised. In the Robb [q.v.6] arbitration case of 1892, praise for his skill was accompanied by public objection to the high fees paid to Griffith as leading counsel and to Byrnes as one of his assistants. In 1891 he was both a member of and a witness before the royal commission on the establishment of a university, and in 1893 he helped to establish the University Extension Council.

After appointment as attorney-general in March 1893 on the resignation of Griffith, Byrnes won the Legislative Assembly seat of Cairns, described by some as 'a Griffith pocket borough'. He revised the law of friendly societies with his Act of 1894. In the same year he championed Premier (Sir) Hugh Nelson's [q.v.] peace preservation bill which permitted imprisonment solely by order of the governor-in-council, and in 1895 he espoused the suppression of gambling bill; both pieces of legislation aroused strong opposition. In 1895 and 1897, he represented Queensland at meetings of the Federal Council of Australasia.

Byrnes now emerged as an opponent of northern separation, arguing that such a colony would inevitably elect a Labor government which would abolish importation of Polynesians. Under-developed and depopulated, the north would then lie open to Asiatic invasion. He realized that this attitude would cost him the support of many Cairns voters and, when the Legislative Council rejected the Mareeba-Atherton railway he had promised his constituents, he took the opportunity to stand for the normally safe ministerial seat of North Brisbane, which McIlwraith had resigned. In the general election of 1896 opponents concentrated on the Peace Preservation Act and sectarian issues. The *Brisbane Courier* saw Catholic bias in appointments to the Department of Justice and recalled Byrnes's support for grants to denominational schools at a meeting in St Mary's Cathedral, Sydney, in January 1895. Some of his fellow ministers believed that his limited resources forced him to neglect his parliamentary duties for his private practice. He was censured too for taking a seven-week pleasure-trip to Honolulu with Nelson and (Sir) Robert Philp [q.v.]. The sectarian issues dominated the contest and no Catholic was elected for the metropolitan seats, but the system of staggered elections gave him another chance. Nelson wanted him for attorney-

general, so invited both the candidates for Warwick to withdraw from the poll in Byrnes's favour. Although John Archibald, the government candidate, complied, the independent candidate refused. Nevertheless the backing of (Sir) Arthur Morgan's [q.v.] *Warwick Argus*, and the large Irish-Catholic vote combined with Byrnes's own prestige and oratory to give him the largest majority ever polled in the electorate.

In 1897 Byrnes accompanied Nelson to England as Queensland representatives at the Diamond Jubilee, and toured Europe. When Sir Arthur Palmer [q.v.5], president of the Legislative Council, died in April 1898, Nelson took his place and on 13 April Byrnes became premier, chief secretary and attorney-general. He had far more electoral appeal than any of his undistinguished colleagues who, despite their covert dislike for him, had to accept their youngest member as leader.

In his 1896 policy speech at Warwick, Byrnes had declared that Queensland needed further time for development before taking her rightful place as leader of a federated nation; government support for early Australian Federation was now withdrawn. He made a two-month triumphal tour through northern and central districts outlining a programme of progressive enterprise. Byrnes joined southern premiers in denouncing an agreement made by Sir William MacGregor [q.v.5] granting land concessions in New Guinea to a British syndicate. The Pacific Islanders (Extension) Act was due to expire in 1902, British policy discouraged removal of Papuans from the Territory and Byrnes, who saw New Guinea as a rich source of coloured labour for the sugar industry and was concerned about mineral rights, feared that the presence of the syndicate would strengthen and prolong British influence. He had signified his agreement to the concessions by initialling the document in January 1898, but when Nelson's correspondence on the affair was published, the section that would have revealed Byrnes's apparent change of attitude was deleted at Byrnes's request.

Byrnes and his treasurer Philp introduced the subsidization of migrants. He promised referenda on women's suffrage and 'one man, one vote', but was unable to get his workmen's lien bill past the committee stage. He succumbed to a sudden attack of measles followed by pneumonia on 27 September 1898 when he seemed to be constituting a more progressive form of government than Queensland had yet seen, though in concrete terms his five months premiership had accomplished little. Byrnes's popular policies and well-publicized defence of Queensland interests contributed to the enormous public distress. After a state funeral proceeding through extraordinary crowds, he was buried in Toowong cemetery. He had never married and his estate, sworn for probate at £20000, was divided between relatives, friends and a religious order.

Byrnes's career embodied cherished contemporary ideals of patriotism and progress: supporters of state education, ignoring the exceptional nature of his success, cited his life as proof that lowly origins did not debar a Queenslander from eminence; Catholic conservatives believed that his success proved the ease of social mobility for the poor Irish which the Labor Party said was impossible under capitalism. A legend developed around Byrnes's memory, hailing him as a man of outstanding integrity and political acumen. A memorial fund initiated the Byrnes medal for scholarship, and statues by public subscription were erected in Warwick and Brisbane. No other Queensland premier has been so honoured. He inspired posthumously a wealth of eulogistic literature, and was enshrined in print by such prominent men as (Sir) James Blair, J. J. Knight, George Essex Evans [qq.v.] and Anthony St Ledger. The literature of the legend offers no criticism of Byrnes, even presenting him as an acclaimed champion of religious toleration – a startling reversal of the charges of sectarianism levelled at him when in office. Byrnes was not, of course, the legendary paragon, but his youthful brilliance, his charm and patriotism evoked great public support in his lifetime, and it is these qualities which survive in the popular hagiography of the legend.

Alcazar Press, *Queensland, 1900* (Brisb, nd); A. St Ledger et al, *Sketches and impressions of Thomas Joseph Byrnes* . . . (Brisb, 1902); R. Gill, 'Thomas Joseph Byrnes: the man and the legend', D. J. Murphy and R. B. Joyce (eds), *Queensland political portraits 1859-1932* (Brisb, 1978); *Echo* (Brisb), 24 Oct 1896; *Worker* (Brisb), 23 Apr, 1 Oct 1898; *Age* (Brisb), 30 Apr, 21, 28 May, 4, 25 June, 17 Sept, 1, 8 Oct 1898; *Bulletin*, 8 Oct 1898; *Brisbane Courier*, 27 Sept 1919; R. H. Gill. The legend and the career of Thomas Joseph Byrnes . . . (B.A. Hons thesis, Univ Qld, 1975); Palmer-McIlwraith papers (Oxley Lib, Brisb).

ROSEMARY HOWARD GILL

BYRON, JOHN JOSEPH (1863-1935), soldier, was born on 10 March 1863 at Harristown, County Wexford, Ireland, son of John Byron and his wife Elizabeth, née Audley. Nothing is known of his early life. He migrated to Australia in the early 1880s and in September 1885 joined the Queensland Defence Force as a lieutenant in the Brisbane Garrison Battery; he was appointed to the Queensland Permanent Artillery on 1 January 1886.

In November 1888 Byron was promoted captain and early in 1891 went to England for eighteen months training with the Royal Artillery. He passed the course with honours, resumed duty in Queensland, and in February 1895 was promoted major and made artillery staff officer. On 25 April, at All Saints' Anglican Church, Petersham, New South Wales, he married Scottish-born Mary Anderson who was later to become well known as a writer. Byron was acting commander of the Queensland Permanent Artillery from 1896 to July 1899 when he was promoted lieut-colonel and confirmed as commander. That month, at the direction of the Queensland government, he went abroad for military instruction, visiting Canada and the United Kingdom and attending manoeuvres in Switzerland.

When war broke out in South Africa in October 1899 the Queensland government arranged for Byron to serve with the Imperial Army; he was recommended as 'an officer of great ability'. With Imperial and Australian detachments in Cape Colony, Orange River Colony and the Transvaal in 1899-1900, he took part in the advance on Kimberley and at Magersfontein was wounded in the leg. In February 1900 he was appointed aide-de-camp to the commander-in-chief Lord Roberts, and was later in action at Paardeberg, Poplar Grove and Driefontein; he was mentioned in dispatches twice and appointed C.M.G. in February 1901. In August Byron returned to resume command of the Queensland Artillery. Next February he was made assistant adjutant general for artillery at headquarters, Australian Military Forces; he resigned this appointment in September 1903 and left for South Africa to manage the duke of Westminster's estate at Cassigholt, Orange River Colony. He did not return to Australia except for a visit in 1932.

In 1907-10 Byron was in the Orange River Colony Legislative Assembly and from 1910 until his death a member of the Union of South Africa parliament. During World War I he was appointed colonel in the South African forces amd held commands in German South West Africa, German East Africa and Central Africa. He was made a temporary brigadier general in 1916. In 1917 he commanded a British artillery group on the Western Front and was then appointed second-in-command of the Dunsterforce Caucasus Military Mission. His war honours included the Distinguished Service Order and the Légion d'honneur, as well as several mentions in dispatches. Survived by his wife and two adopted children, Byron died of coronary thrombosis at Sea Point, Cape

Colony, on 17 February 1935 and was buried at Plumstead.

As a soldier Byron was recognized as being unusually successful in independent command, both as a tactician and an administrator; as a farmer he was considered an authority, progressive and successful; as a parliamentarian he was noted for his commanding presence and gift of oratory.

Aust Defence Dept, *Official records of the Australian military contingents to the war in South Africa*, P. L. Murray ed (Melb, 1912); R. L. Wallace, *The Australians at the Boer War* (Canb, 1976); *Dictionary of South African Biography*, 3 (Cape Town, 1977); Blue Books, *V&P* (LA Qld), 1886-97; *V&P* (LA NSW), 1892-3 (7) 568; *Brisbane Courier*, 15, 28 Feb, 4, 11 Mar 1902, 5 Mar 1905; *SMH*, 9, 16 Feb 1932, 26 Mar 1935; *Cape Times*, and *Rand Daily Mail*, and *The Times*, 18 Feb 1935; *Argus*, 23 Feb 1935; records (AWM); CO 234/69 pt 2.

R. P. SERLE

C

CABENA, WILLIAM WHYTE (1853-1928), businessman and lord mayor, was born on 12 November 1853 at Londonderry, Ireland, son of Francis Cabena, shipmaster, and his wife Rachel, née Whyte. His mother was of Scottish origin and his grandfather was an Italian. Cabena was educated at Londonderry, and apprenticed to a provision merchant there.

Suffering from tuberculosis, he arrived in Melbourne in 1874. He recovered from the disease and in 1877 became manager of Gavin Gibson & Co., a retail boot-business established at Sandhurst (Bendigo) in the 1850s with headquarters in Melbourne from 1870. In 1887 Cabena was admitted as a partner and, after Gibson's death in 1888, purchased a controlling interest. By 1902 he was chairman of directors and manager of the company, now described as shoe and leather merchants and importers of Melbourne and Sydney, and also chairman of a boot-manufacturing firm and a tannery in Adelaide. He was well acquainted with international trends and aware of the benefits of centralized marketing and specialization.

Cabena was politically ambitious but his free-trade views may have lessened his influence in the boot trade. In September 1902 he entered the Melbourne City Council; by 1910 he had virtually retired from his business. In 1906 he became one of the council's representatives on the Melbourne and Metropolitan Board of Works, on which he was influential for many years, especially as a member of its finance committee. In June 1914 he was elected an alderman and was an important member of various council committees, particularly those of finance and electric-supply. He was a member of the Melbourne and Metropolitan Tramways Board from its inception in 1918. He was elected lord mayor for the year 1918-19 after a bitter contest with the retiring candidate, Frank Stapley [q.v.].

An Orangeman and Presbyterian, Cabena responded to public protest at the flying of a Sinn Fein Flag in the 1918 St Patrick's Day procession, stipulating that no permit for the 1919 march would be granted unless the Union Jack and the Australian flag were displayed and *God save the King* sung. Cabena took the St Patrick's Day Committee's ambiguous reply as a rejection of his demands; his decision to refuse a permit provoked considerable bitterness and laid the basis for subsequent St Patrick's Day disputes in Melbourne.

Described in 1918 as a 'most dignified and smallish man' with a resemblance to King Edward VII, Cabena was a dogmatic, forceful and talented businessman. He used his financial ability to advance his own views in the council and was not above resigning or threatening to do so when he did not get his way. He was particularly active in resisting attempts to create a Greater Melbourne Council. On 1 February 1879 he had married Mrs Ann Raisbeck, née Stubbs, who died in 1906. On 22 January 1915 he married another widow, Katie Sarah Ellison, née Willis, who was a well-known worker for patriotic and charitable causes. A diabetic, Cabena collapsed on 11 September 1928 and died at his home in St Kilda Road on 11 December. Survived by his wife and predeceased by a son of his first marriage, he was buried in Melbourne general cemetery.

J. Smith (ed), *Cyclopedia of Victoria*, 1 (Melb, 1903); *V&P* (LA Vic), 1902-03, 2 (31); *Aust Storekeepers' J*, June 1895; *Aust Leather J*, 15 Apr 1905, 15 Feb 1908; *Punch* (Melb), 17 Oct 1918; *Argus*, 12 Dec 1928; Melb City Council Archives.

DAVID DUNSTAN

CAHILL, PATRICK (1863?-1923), buffalo-shooter, farmer and protector of Aboriginals was born, probably in 1863, at Laidley near Toowoomba, Queensland, son of Thomas Cahill, blacksmith, and his wife Sarah, née Scahill; his birth was not registered. Paddy and his brothers Tom and Matt joined Nat Buchanan [q.v.3] and the Gordons in overlanding 20 000 cattle in 1883 for Wave Hill station, Northern Territory. The Cahill brothers later managed Wave Hill, Delamere and Gordon Downs stations.

Paddy was soon attracted by reports of up to 60 000 buffalo running wild on the plains of the Alligator River. One of the first to shoot from horseback, he and his partner William Johnston employed Aboriginals during the dry season in semi-mobile camps to produce hides and horns. Cahill's largest monthly kill was 1605; hides were initially worth £1 each. Much of his success was due to his fast, intelligent horse St Lawrence. In 1898 he wrote a series of articles on hunting for the *Northern Territory Times*.

Early in 1899 when hunting was becoming unprofitable Cahill bought the pearling lugger, *Ethel*. On 18 October at St Mary's Star of the Sea Catholic Church, Darwin, he married Maria Pickford. Within three weeks of the wedding he covered 200 miles (320 km) in three days to assist Johnston who had been gored. Cahill was probably the most popular man in the Northern Territory at this time. Visiting Darwin in 1898, A. B. Paterson [q.v.] light-heartedly listed the main conversational pieces of Darwin as 'the cycloon' (of 1897), G. R. (the government resident) and Paddy Cahill.

Cahill and Johnston settled in 1906 at idyllic Oenpelli in Arnhem Land. The local Kakadu people helped establish a farm, growing fruit, vegetables, sisal, cotton and other products. Naturally intelligent, Cahill had developed a deep interest in and empathy with Aboriginals, learning languages and being careful to use tribal names. He sought to minimize their contacts with Europeans, particularly missionaries, and in 1912 was appointed a protector and manager of a reserve based on Oenpelli. He was visited there by (Sir) W. Baldwin Spencer [q.v.] in 1912, Elsie Masson in 1915 and Carl Warburton, all of whom recorded their admiration for the house, gardens and dairy. Cahill maintained a long friendly correspondence with Spencer and, next to F. J. Gillen [q.v.], was probably his most important collaborator. As a result, Cahill supplied the National Museum of Victoria with zoological specimens and a very important collection of bark-paintings.

In 1915 J. A. Gilruth [q.v.], administrator of the Northern Territory, chose Oenpelli as a government experimental dairy and provided some cows, but the first shipment of butter was boycotted by Darwin unionists because it was produced by black labour. In 1917 one of Cahill's trusted Aboriginal workers attempted to poison him and his family. During the Darwin disturbances of 1918-19 he served as a special constable defending Government House, antagonized the dissidents, and was described in royal commissioner N. K. Ewing's [q.v.] report as a decent man but sometimes careless. It was implied that he had used his friendship with Gilruth to advance his son.

Paddy Cahill was 'a stocky, broad-shouldered extrovert, with ruddy complexion and ever cheerful manner'. He visited Melbourne for the Cup of 1922 with his wife and son. An earlier influenza attack recurred and he died at the Sydney home of his brother Tom on 4 February 1923 and was buried in Randwick cemetery. Mount Cahill, Cahill's Landing and Cahill's Crossing in Arnhem Land and a Darwin street are named after him.

E. R. Masson, *An untamed territory* (Lond, 1915); W. B. Spencer, *Wanderings in wild Australia* (Lond, 1928); C. Warburton and W. K. Robertson, *Buffaloes* (Syd, 1934); E. Hill, *The Territory* (Syd, 1951); K. Cole, *Oenpelli pioneer* (Melb, 1972), and *A history of Oenpelli* (Darwin, 1975); D. J. Mulvaney and J. H. Calaby, *'So much that is new'* (Melb, 1979); *PP* (Cwlth), 1917-19, 6, 1145, 1920-21, 3, 1663, 1671; *NT Times*, 17 Mar, 20 Oct, 10 Nov 1899, 1 Dec 1911, 6 Feb 1923; *Sydney Mail*, 27 June 1899; *SMH*, 6 Feb 1923; *Daily Telegraph* (Syd), 7 Feb 1923; *Argus*, 10 Feb 1923; *Labor Call*, 8 Mar 1923; A1640 1903/419, CRS A3 item NT 17/427, AR NT 14/403 13 June 1914 (AAO, Canb).

M. A. CLINCH

CAHILL, WILLIAM GEOFFREY (1854-1931), public servant and police commissioner, was born on 7 November 1854 at Strokestown, Roscommon, Ireland, son of John Cahill, of Ennis, and his wife. Educated at the Strokestown National School, he served in the Royal Irish Constabulary, then migrated to Australia with his wife Lavinia, née Bernie. They arrived at Maryborough, Queensland, in the *Highflyer* on 2 December 1878.

Cahill joined the Queensland Public Service on 1 August 1879 as second clerk in the registry of the Supreme Court in Brisbane. He became first clerk during 1880, deputy curator of intestate estates from 1 January 1885, registrar of the Southern District Court on 1 June 1887, and secretary to the crown law officers on 19 March 1889; the position was retitled under-secretary for justice on 14 May 1890. On 1 April 1905 he was appointed commissioner of police, and on 7 September protector of Aborigines. Following the Police Act Amendment Act of 1912, which limited the commissioner's term to five years, he was reappointed on 19 December until 1917.

Cahill served in the militia, being promoted lieutenant from sergeant in the Brisbane Volunteer Rifle Corps (Queensland Volunteer Rifles) in 1885, captain in 1887 and major in 1891. He relieved Lieut-Colonel A. J. Thynne [q.v.] as commander of the volunteer infantry in the southern military district while Thynne was overseas in 1894-95. Transferred to the unattached officers list on 18 June 1896, Cahill resigned his commission on 6 April 1897 (probably in protest at the appointment of a non-volunteer commanding officer), but was reappointed major on 9 December. He resigned in 1905 when appointed commissioner of police.

Cahill was a capable administrator in the justice department, supervising a period of expansion and introducing reforms to the Queensland police force, including free uniforms and better pensions. He made every effort to have police relieved of extraneous government duties in rural areas — without notable success. He pressed for better arms and ammunition, and set up a police horse-breeding establishment at Woodford which was moved later to Rewan, south of Springsure. 'Somewhat inclined to be a martinet', he tightened discipline, following the practice of the Royal Irish Constabulary, and in 1913 issued a *Policeman's manual*, adapted from the Irish version for Queensland conditions. He tried to improve training conditions and to modernize the criminal investigation branch. His responsibilities as commissioner included increasing control of urban traffic, closer supervision of liquor licensing and gambling, and enforcement of infant life protection legislation.

The Brisbane general strike of 1912 was the critical point of Cahill's career. Charged with preservation of law and order by the D. F. Denham [q.v.] government, he had to resist the demands for rigorous suppression made by extreme anti-unionists, maintain control of the irregular force of special constables sworn in to assist the regular force, and deal with a potentially serious civil disturbance. After days of increasing tension and some street incidents, the strike leaders ignored his instruction not to assemble on Friday, 2 February. Confronting the demonstrators in Albert Street, Cahill led a baton charge to disperse the crowd and was thrown from his horse in the mêlée. The police prevailed without serious injury to either side and incidents thereafter gradually decreased. Cahill was threatened that a future Labor administration would give him four minutes to resign, but he was complimented by the government and its supporters.

On the election of the T. J. Ryan [q.v.] Labor ministry in 1915, Cahill retained office, with his erstwhile opponent David Bowman [q.v.], one of the 1912 strike leaders, as his ministerial head. After quarrelling with senior officers of the Home Secretary's Office on police policy and control, he clashed with John Huxham [q.v.], who succeeded Bowman as home secretary on 23 March 1916, over the formation of a police union which, to Cahill, constituted a breach of good order and discipline. In December he applied for and was granted early retirement on medical grounds, with a pension of £450 a year.

Cahill was described as 'outwardly stern' and 'reserved', but 'tall, lithe, well set up and strikingly handsome'. He was awarded the Volunteer Officers' Decoration in 1911 and was appointed C.M.G. in December 1912. He was honorary aide-de-camp to two governors in 1912-16. Predeceased by his wife and childless, Cahill died of cirrhosis of the liver at his home at Newmarket, Brisbane, on 25 April 1931; he was buried in the Catholic section of Nudgee cemetery.

Qld Police Dept, *A centenary history of the Queensland Police Force 1864-1963* (Brisb, 1964); D. J. Murphy et al (eds), *Prelude to power* (Brisb, 1970); *V&P* (LA Qld), 1897, 2, 207, 1903, 2, 319; *Queenslander*, 30 Apr 1931; H. M. Draper, Origin and history of the Queensland Police Force to 1900 (Oxley Lib, Brisb); Executive Council, Minutes Dec 1916, A4495 (QA); Home Sec, In-letters 1916/10424, HOM/J215 (QA); Immigration register, IMM/116 (QA).   PAUL D. WILSON

CAIN, SIR JONATHAN ROBERT (1867-1938), lord mayor and businessman, was born on 23 September 1867 at Leamington, Warwickshire, England, son of John Cain, carpenter, and his wife Winnifred, née Anstey. The family migrated in 1877 and John Cain started a furniture shop in North Adelaide. Cain attended the Model School there and was a chorister at St Peter's Cathedral. On leaving school he worked first with his father, and later in Melbourne as an undertaker. At Collingwood, on 30 July 1890, he married Ada Davey, a milliner. They returned to Adelaide and established a confectionery store and, in 1903, a drapery shop in King William Street. From 1908 Cain concentrated on the drapery and millinery trade, in which he remained for the rest of his life.

Outside business Cain was a debater and, before the war, president of the Pirie Street Literary Society and a front-bencher in the Literary Societies' Union parliament. Business and debating drew him into politics and in 1914 he became secretary of the Liberal Union's Adelaide district committee. In 1916 he was elected councillor for the Hindmarsh Ward in the Adelaide City Council, where he served for twenty-two years, and was lord mayor in 1933-37.

Cain's period as lord mayor was marked by his concern for the unemployed and by his efforts to popularize the council. In 1931 he started the Lord Mayor's Relief Fund, an appeal for voluntary contributions to help the unemployed. In 1933 he formed the United Relief Council to co-ordinate the relief work of all metropolitan councils and defeated moves to restrict use of the fund to the city only. He always shunned inter-council jealousies, and as lord mayor persuaded the United Relief Council to operate on the principle of most aid to the areas of greatest need. The council spent £30000 raised by the relief fund in 1931-37 and over £30000 in State grants in 1933-37. Cain greatly increased the number of mayoral receptions, arguing that in times of crisis they heightened the sense of community. He excelled as host for the duke of Gloucester's Adelaide visit in 1934 and as an organizer for the State centennial celebrations in 1936 when he ensured that money spent benefited the unemployed: work was provided to beautify Torrens Lake. For his services to the city he was knighted in 1937.

Cain was interested in bowling, community singing and the Boy Scouts' movement, and was a council-member of the South Australian Acclimatization and Zoological Society. He was also chairman of the Adelaide directors of the Cornhill Insurance Co. Ltd. He was a short man, plump, florid, talkative and hospitable. Not a controversialist, he believed party politics had no place in council affairs. Predeceased by his wife and survived by his only daughter, he died on 4 November 1938 of pneumonia contracted after a motor accident and was buried in North Road cemetery. His intestate estate was valued for probate at £2703.

Associated Publishing Service, *The civic record of South Australia 1921-1923* (Adel, 1924); Universal Publicity Co., *The official civic record of South Australia* (Adel, 1936); Adelaide City Council, *Annual Report*, 1932-38; *South Australian*, 11 Nov 1926; *Advertiser* (Adel), 1, 4 Dec 1933, 30 June 1937, 5 Nov 1938; Notice papers etc (Adel City Council Archives).   CARL BRIDGE

CAIRNS, SIR HUGH WILLIAM BELL (1896-1952), neuro-surgeon, was born on 26 June 1896 at Port Pirie, South Australia, son of William Cairns, timber contractor from Scotland, and his Australian-born wife Amy Florence, née Bell. He was educated at Riverton High School and at Adelaide High School, where he was dux and editor of the journal in 1911, and proceeded to the university with an exhibition. On 11 May 1915 he joined the Australian Imperial Force as a private in the Australian Army Medical Corps, and from 30 July served in the 3rd Australian General Hospital on Lemnos. Next February he returned to complete his medical course at the University of Adelaide which he represented at rowing and lacrosse. He graduated M.B., B.S. in 1917 after being Davies Thomas and Everard Scholar, was commissioned as captain on 7 August, and elected to the South Australian Rhodes scholarship. From 29 March 1918 he served in France with the 2nd A.G.H., the 3rd A.G.H., the 47th British Division and the 15th Australian Field Ambulance.

Cairns entered Balliol College, Oxford, in January 1919, rowed as bow in the University Boat Race and was president of the Balliol Boat Club. After six months in the Radcliffe Infirmary as house surgeon, he utilized his Rhodes scholarship to begin his long connexion with the London Hospital, first in the pathology institute, then in the surgical unit, becoming F.R.C.S. in 1921, the year of his marriage to Barbara Forster, youngest of the remarkable daughters of A. L. Smith, master of his Oxford college.

At this stage Cairns's special interest was genito-urinary work. As Hunterian Professor of the Royal College in 1926, he lectured on testicle tumours and the congenital cystic kidney. His work was marked by thoroughness rather than brilliance. He was already utterly dependable. The time was ripe, in his view, for the development of neurosurgery at the London Hospital, and in 1925-26 he took leave with a Rockefeller fellowship to study the new speciality under Harvey Cushing at the Peter Brigham Young Institute, Boston, Massachusetts. Under Cushing's abiding inspiration, he learned the surgical technique, the organization of a clinic and the system of record collection with which he was to endow generations of his pupils. Returning to England in 1927 he had an assured appointment at the London Hospital but life was not at first financially easy. The young man took some time to make his mark since he insisted on specializing in neurological surgery in a manner which seemed unorthodox. His beds were scattered, theatres not easily made available, and nurses and especially radiologists were untrained in the new kind of surgery which was, moreover, unpopular with anaesthetists. (Sir) Geoffrey Jefferson and Professor N. M. Dott were facing similar obstacles and the three men soon created a new school of British neurological surgery of international stature.

Cairns soon became inordinately busy, his consulting work being carried out in the London Hospital, his operating in West End nursing homes. Another visit to Cushing strengthened his resolve to be an integral part of a medical school freed from the consuming distractions and wealth of a busy metropolitan practice. 'Hugo' Cairns was the vital force in persuading Lord Nuffield, who was stunned by his enthusiastically unyielding energy, to make his farsighted benefaction to Oxford medicine. Cairns had by now an international reputation: when T. E. Lawrence was fatally injured on his motorcycle in May 1935, it was 'Mr Cairns, the brain surgeon' who was immediately called to treat him.

Cairns was the inevitable first tenant of the new Nuffield chair of surgery at Oxford in 1937 and he was elected a professorial fellow of Balliol. He left the London clinic in good hands, characteristically taking copies of his case records, clinical photographs and pathological material with him. He was a pioneer in employing a medical artist in his theatres. Doubts about the adequacy of clinical material were soon dispelled, but eighteen creative months with new wards coming to life were interrupted by war, when Cairns at once became adviser on head injuries to the Ministry of Health and neuro-surgeon to the army, eventually rising to brigadier. A new base hospital for head injuries was established at St Hugh's College where 'The Nutcrackers Suite' became a neurological unit of first importance. Just as Cairns was swift to stress the advantage of air evacuation of battle casualties, so too was he busy in organizing the mobile surgical teams which revolutionized the treatment of wounded in the North African campaigns. Earlier still in the war he had persuaded the army to make crash helmets for dispatch riders compulsory.

Cairns was inevitably active in developing the use and technique of penicillin treatment developed at Oxford by (Lord) Florey, his successor as Rhodes scholar from Adelaide. Having studied the technique of penicillin treatment of pneumococcal meningitis, and tuberculous meningitis with streptomycin, in his last years he became interested in the operation of leucotomy.

He was appointed K.B.E. in 1946. Next year he was elected the first Sims Commonwealth professor appointed by the Royal College and given the honorary M.D. of Adelaide. He was an enthusiastic supporter of the medical research soon to begin in the Australian National University. He travelled widely and in his later years administrative and ambassadorial duties stole time from his clinical work, but he remained to the end first and foremost the 'good doctor'. Every patient became Cairns's personal friend for life. He was always an exacting exemplar, mellowing as he grew older but still fiercely demanding of his pupils as of himself. He played tennis as if his life depended on it; felled or sawed timber at Wytham Woods until his companions were exhausted; snatched holidays at Bamburgh; and listened to music with his own especial raptness. He was the ideal professorial fellow of Balliol, the college he loved; his counsels were all-important.

He faced death stoically when an operation diagnosed cancer. To the end he remained at work, being flown to the pillow of some dying eastern potentate, just as in 1946 – a measure of his international repute – he had been flown immediately to attend to the American general, George S. Patton. He was an eagerly scholarly man who produced more than a hundred papers. His own collection of important early French neurological papers was lost by arson in the Cairns library established in his honour at the Radcliffe. He believed himself to be 'very normal', a claim denied by his own very excellence. 'I don't think I'm very clever: I'm quite ordinary really'. What was unique was his personal bravery, his superb stamina, his integrity, and his capacity to brush aside obstacles. He was always looking ahead and was simple in the directness of his plans; people saw through them but found themselves co-operating because of his unique resolution, his charm and his utter dependability. He could not understand the petty, nor could he neglect any detail in 'working up a case', in Cushing's manner. He died in the Radcliffe Infirmary on 18 July 1952 after a singularly happy marriage, leaving a widow, two sons, and two daughters.

R. Massey, *When I was young* (Toronto, 1976); *DNB*, 1951-60; *British J of Surgery*, 40 (1952-53); *British Medical J*, and *Lancet*, 26 July 1952; *J of Neurology . . .* (Lond), Aug 1959.

E. T. WILLIAMS

CALDER, GEORGE (1839-1903), mariner, was born on 15 October 1839 in Stirlingshire, Scotland, son of John Calder, sea captain, and his wife Janet, née Smith. In his teens he became a seaman on vessels sailing in the Firth of Forth, near Edinburgh.

Calder left Scotland in June 1859 in the crew of a sailing vessel bound for Victoria. When he arrived in Melbourne he signed off, and soon afterwards became chief officer on a Melbourne-owned barque, carrying cargoes and passengers along the east coast of Australia, and to Adelaide, Tasmania and across to New Zealand. In April 1861, during a voyage to Tasmanian and New Zealand ports, Calder was promoted to replace the captain who was dismissed by the ship-owners at Launceston for drunkenness and inefficiency. On 3 December 1863 at St James's Church, Melbourne, while briefly captain of the *Sea Breeze*, he married 19-year-old Sarah Dodd, daughter of a ship-wright. Soon after, he joined the shipping agents McMeckan, Blackwood [qq.v.5,3] & Co.

In 1870 Calder made the first of his voyages in connexion with the laying of the overland telegraph line from Port Darwin to Adelaide. As captain of the steamship *Omeo* he was commissioned to carry cargo to Port Darwin and to investigate how the project might be assisted from the north. Early in 1872 he returned with telegraph equipment and with directions to navigate the uncharted Roper River as far inland as possible. He succeeded in taking the ship to within 40 miles (64 km) of the construction party, naming Calder Range on the way. In Adelaide on 15 November he was accorded a public ovation and presented with a gold watch for his 'able services' to the expedition.

In the mid-1870s Calder was in charge of the *Omeo* on the New Zealand run. He was master of the steamship *Otago* when it ran aground in thick fog off the west coast of New Zealand on 3 December 1876. All the passengers and the cargo, which included five boxes containing 5000 ounces of gold, were saved and the ship later refloated. In 1880-84 he was captain of the *Claud Hamilton* on the New Zealand and Adelaide run. From then until his retirement in March 1887 he was in charge of the Adelaide Steamship Co.'s *South Australian* which ran between Melbourne and Adelaide, and Adelaide and Fremantle, Western Australia. With a gratuity, Calder purchased the leasehold of the Malvern Hotel, Melbourne, but he lost money in the bank crashes of the early 1890s and in 1893 had to relinquish the business.

Making his home in South Yarra with five unmarried children, Calder wrote his memoirs, *Stirring events, ashore and afloat*, published in Melbourne in 1897. The book included a lengthy section on sea ports around the world, with advice to young mariners. In poor health in his last years, he died in hospital in Melbourne on 24 February 1903, and was buried in St Kilda cemetery survived by two sons and five daughters; his wife, a son and a daughter had predeceased him.

Register (Adel), 16 Nov 1872.

R. J. MACDOUGALL

CALDER, WILLIAM (1860-1928), engineer, was born on 31 July 1860 at his father's sheep-farm at Lovell's Flat, Milton near Dunedin, New Zealand, only son of Arther Calder and his wife Margaret Milne, née Strachan. Calder was educated at the local school at Milton and the Otago Boys' High School in Dunedin in 1876-77. From 1881 he attended engineering lectures at Otago University before entering the New Zealand Government Survey Department as a cadet in October 1883; after five years practical training he passed the authorized surveyors' examination with credit in July 1888.

Later that year Calder came to Victoria and worked in private engineering and surveying firms. In October 1889 he became assistant town surveyor for the City of Footscray, and in July 1890 town engineer. At night he studied to gain certificates as municipal engineer (1890) and engineer of water-supply (1892). From December 1897 to March 1913, Calder was city engineer and building surveyor to the City of Prahran. Among his achievements were construction of, allegedly, the first asphalted carpet-road

surface and the first refuse destructor in Australia, and the completion of a major drainage project.

By 1912 the appalling condition of Victoria's rural roads was a major concern to both farmers and motorists. That year a Country Roads Board was set up and Calder was appointed chairman, with W. T. B. McCormack [q.v.] and F. W. Fricke as the other members. In its first two years, the board travelled ceaselessly, inspecting a road system neglected by indigent municipalities since the building of the railways. A meticulous note-taker and enthusiastic photographer, Calder recorded the board's progress; his notes were transcribed and used as a basic reference for many years. Maps were published in 1914 and 1915 showing the roads selected for improvement. The board was endlessly tactful in receiving interest groups pressing for various improvements, while insisting on high standards of construction and financial control.

After 1918 there were shortages of money and manpower for road-building. Calder campaigned publicly and privately for more funds, especially for arterial roads, and invariably attained rapport with a succession of ministers. In 1924 he toured Europe and North America; his report, published that year, is widely regarded as a classic of road-construction practice and road-administration. In it he evaluated the contemporary controversy over the use of cement concrete (the American model) and bituminous pavement (the British); he favoured the latter for Australian conditions. Other recommendations included experiments with new materials and a fuel tax to replace the vehicle tax. Maintenance was to be given high priority, and he also stressed the importance of regulation of motor transport to preserve road surfaces and to raise revenue.

Many of Calder's recommendations were included in the important Highways and Vehicles Act of 1924, which provided for the declaration of State highways, two-thirds financed by the State government through the C.R.B. This network of highways is perhaps Calder's main achievement: the road to Bendigo and Mildura was named after him. The board's organization was copied in other States, New Zealand and Fiji. He long advocated Federal assistance in highway construction, and attended the first meeting of the Federal Aid Roads Board set up under the Act of 1926.

Calder had married Elizabeth Bagley Palmer of Dunedin on 4 November 1889 at Brunswick. He was a devout Presbyterian and member of his church boards of management of Footscray and Armadale. He retained a pleasant but definite Scots burr all his life. Small, with a pointed beard and a 'puckish sense of humour', he was a conscientious and methodical worker, of conservative disposition and unchallenged integrity. He encouraged young engineers with initiative and had close links with Professor Henry Payne [q.v.] of the University of Melbourne. A 'champion shot', he assisted with military training in the Moorooduc area during World War I. Calder had hoped to retire to his small property at Red Hill, but died of cancer at East Malvern on 18 February 1928. Survived by his wife, a son and a daughter, he was buried in the Cheltenham cemetery after a ceremony at Gardiner Presbyterian Church. Calder's wife was saved from financial difficulty by a special State pension.

Memorials to him include an avenue of trees on the road to Geelong beginning one mile past Werribee, cairns at Warragul and elsewhere in Gippsland, and a bridge at Moe. A Tom Roberts [q.v.] portrait hangs in the C.R.B. board room, Kew.

R. Southern, 'William Calder – public servant and engineer . . .', *VHJ*, 48 (1977), no 3, and for bibliog.   ROGER J. SOUTHERN

CALLAGHAN, JAMES JOSEPH (1850-1908), schoolteacher, was born on 25 March 1850 at Mulgoa, New South Wales, son of John Joseph Callaghan, farm labourer, and his wife Mary Ann, née Grymes. James attended the Roman Catholic school at Hartley in 1854-62, then at Bathurst, where he became a pupil-teacher until 1867. He was a student for a year, then taught at St Stanislaus' College, Bathurst, until March 1870.

Callaghan gave all his savings to his father and went to Sydney. He worked as a private tutor but soon joined the staff of the *Freeman's Journal*. At St Patrick's Church, Sydney, he married Mary Teresa Graves on 6 May 1871. He gave up a well-paid position in 1873 to fulfil his ambition to teach; bringing warm testimonials from Bishop Matthew Quinn [q.v.5] and others, he was judged to have a gentlemanly appearance and a becoming demeanour, and was admitted to the Council of Education's Training School.

Callaghan went to the Armidale Catholic school in January 1874; next year he was transferred to Nundle and was briefly correspondent for the *Maitland Mercury*. In 1880 he moved to West Maitland and also taught in the Evening Public School. When state aid ended in 1883, he transferred to the Department of Public Instruction and taught at Hamilton, Newcastle; as the school

grew to become a superior public school, he nursed grievances at the slowness of his promotions and other departmental conflicts and in 1894 attempted to use a member of parliament to advance his interests.

An able public speaker, Callaghan had a strong political conscience and strongly supported Irish Home Rule. He won repute among his opponents as a firebrand and was warned by the department to avoid public political discussions. He also reserved the right as an established headmaster to interpret freely some regulations which did not suit his pupils' needs and was occasionally in trouble for this.

Callaghan quickly became prominent in the New South Wales Public School Teachers' Association formed in 1899; he was vice-president in 1902-03, then president until December 1904, frequently visiting Sydney as the association emerged as an important trade union and pressure group. Callaghan was long remembered for his teaching abilities: his formative influence was acknowledged by educators such as K. R. Cramp and C. B. Newling [qq.v.]. He was also remembered for his hatred of smoking. He put much of his energy into evening teaching, debating clubs, and the Hamilton Mechanics' Institute.

Callaghan retired on 31 December 1906 on account of poor health and, survived by his wife and by thirteen of their sixteen children, died of cerebral haemorrhage associated with renal disease on 13 September 1908 at his home at Newtown, Sydney. He was buried in the Roman Catholic section of Rookwood cemetery.

B. A. Mitchell, *Teachers, education and politics* (Brisb, 1975); *Aust J of Education*, 1903-04; teachers records (NSW Dept of Education, Syd); school files (NSWA).   BRUCE MITCHELL

CALLISTER, CYRIL PERCY (1893-1949), food technologist, was born on 16 February 1893 at Chute near Beaufort, Victoria, son of William Hugh Callister, schoolmaster, and his wife Rosetta Anne, née Dixon. After education at state schools, Grenville College, Ballarat, and the Ballarat School of Mines, he attended the University of Melbourne on a major residential scholarship to Queen's College (B.Sc., 1914; M.Sc., 1917; D.Sc., 1931).

In January 1915 Callister joined Lewis & Whitty, manufacturers of food and household products. In June he enlisted in the Australian Imperial Force. Within three months the Department of Defence withdrew him to join the Munitions Branch. Shortly afterwards he was sent to Britain and spent the war working on explosives manufacture in Wales, and in Scotland where he met and married Katherine Hope Mundell at Annau, on 8 March 1919; they had two sons and a daughter.

On his return to Australia in 1919 Callister rejoined Lewis & Whitty where he remained until that company was taken over. In February 1923 he was appointed to Fred Walker's small food company to develop yeast-extract for retail sale. Although this product was known overseas, no information was available about the process, and Callister developed it *de novo* from brewers' yeast. Under the trademark Vegemite it was placed on the market early in 1924 and slowly became an established item, solely through Callister's technological skill and perseverance. Walker was also interested in methods for preserving cheese, and involved Callister in this as well. Thus the chemist rapidly became well informed in microbiology and began to experiment with cheese-processing. With the help of patents held by the American James L. Kraft, he made a satisfactory product and Walker used this in 1925 to persuade Kraft to grant a license for the manufacture of Kraft cheese in Australia. So the Kraft Walker Cheese Co. was established in 1926 with Callister as chief chemist and production superintendent.

He was the key to the increasing technical emphasis of the company. In 1925 he had sent samples of Vegemite to London to be tested for Vitamin B activity — a far-sighted move in the very early days of vitamin knowledge. The result confirmed Callister's confidence in the product as a valuable nutrient. In 1926-31 he carried out detailed original studies on the scientific background of cheese-making to establish the parameters of good cheese quality. Convinced that background science was essential in any industry, in 1927 he appointed a bacteriologist to his staff, possibly the first such appointment in Australia.

Callister became a director of the company in 1935 shortly before Walker died suddenly. He continued to build up laboratory staff and supervise production and quality as the company emerged from the Depression and shouldered unexpected demands for the production of familiar and unfamiliar products during World War II. Under his personal direction high tonnages of service rations for the Australian and United States armies were produced; the unfamiliar technology of dehydration was undertaken for government; and scientific staff greatly improved Vegemite, developed new knowledge of cheese manufacture and processing and of the behaviour of thiamine (vitamin B_1) in foods, and introduced into Australia methods of assay of the B complex

vitamins. Immediately after the war he stimulated successful attempts to diversify the source of raw-material yeasts for Vegemite.

Prominent in the leadership of the (Royal) Australian Chemical Institute, for which he and (Sir David) Rivett [q.v.] secured the royal charter in 1931, Callister was also closely associated with the Society of Chemical Industry of Victoria. His two greatest attributes were his professional excellence and his high personal integrity, a product of his staunch Baptist upbringing. Callister left few published scientific papers, though his output of company reports was extensive. His contributions to Australian food science and technology include the establishment of two new products, Vegemite and processed cheese; his emphasis on quality control; his demonstration of the value of research in the food industry when little was being done anywhere; and the men he trained and inspired.

Callister suffered his first heart attack late in 1939. Others followed, the fatal one occurring on 5 October 1949. Survived by his wife and two children (a son was killed in World War II), he was buried in Box Hill cemetery. His estate was valued for probate at £45 917.

K. T. H. Farrer, 'C. P. Callister – a pioneer of Australian food technology', *Food Technology in Aust*, Feb 1973, and for bibliog; Kraft Foods Ltd, Records (Port Melbourne); information from Mr W. H. Callister, Hawthorn, Vic.

K. T. H. FARRER

CALVERT, ALBERT FREDERICK (1872-1946), author, traveller and mining engineer, was born on 20 July 1872 at Kentish Town, Middlesex, England, son of John Calvert, mining engineer, and his wife Grace, née Easley. He was brought up principally by his grandfather John Calvert (1814-1897), a widely travelled mineralogist who claimed extensive gold discoveries in Australia in the 1840s. *Leaves from the Calvert papers* (1893) by Albert's secretary G. Hill is a misleading account of his family history.

Calvert first visited Western Australia early in 1890 and in April undertook an expedition from Lake Gairdner in South Australia to the upper Murchison River. In April 1891 and December 1892, he practically repeated the trip on behalf of the General Exploration Co. of London and the British Australian Exploration Co. His most important discovery was the rare spinifex parakeet. Before the third journey, Calvert circumnavigated Australia collecting material for his book, *The discovery of Australia* (London, 1893). Returning to London, he married Florence Holcombe at Kentish Town on 28 March 1894.

In November 1895 Calvert landed at Albany with his fourteen-year-old brother Leonard and two menservants. He was joined by a journalist, an artist, his private secretary and a mining engineer. They visited Perth and the eastern goldfields, were fêted socially, sailed for Roebourne and, leaving the ailing Leonard at the port, visited the inland diggings. Calvert returned to Roebourne on 4 January 1896 with sunstroke; Leonard died of typhoid on the 11th. Calvert visited Adelaide, Melbourne and Sydney before returning to London where he published *My fourth tour in Western Australia* (1897).

In January 1896 the Royal Geogaphical Society (South Australia) accepted his offer to finance an expedition to search for Leichhardt [q.v.2] and open a stock route from the Northern Territory to the western goldfields; L. A. Wells [q.v.] was appointed leader. Although new country including the Calvert Range was examined, Charles Wells and George Jones were lost in the desert and died. When Calvert was unable to meet the expedition's expenses, he was publicly derided.

As a mining investment consultant and as a prolific writer, for a decade he was obsessed with Western Australia. Described in London as 'Westralia's golden prophet', Calvert was courted, wined and dined, and indulged in yachting, motoring and racing. His *West Australian Review*, published in London in 1893-94, dealt mainly in mining information, commentaries and forecasts. His fourteen other Australian books covering forests, Aboriginals, pearls, history, minerals and his own travels were cheap, readable and topical, but often careless.

Calvert was managing director of Big Blow Gold Mines and Consolidated Gold Mines of Western Australia on the Pilbarra goldfields, and consulting engineer for the Mallina gold-mines. Management difficulties, his distaste for Federation and a bankruptcy caused by racing losses in 1898 killed his interest in Australia and he turned to a new area. Thirty-six books on Spain and Spanish art published by 1924 won him appointment as a knight of the Orders of Alfonso XII and of Isabella the Catholic.

After a visit to Nigeria in 1910, Calvert published two books on that country followed by five on German Africa published during World War I. In 1923 a sister of the late Czar of Russia accused him of conspiracy to swindle her out of her jewels, and won substantial damages; a criminal pro-

secution threatened by the trial judge did not eventuate. Initiated as a Freemason in 1893, he became something of an authority on Masonic history in later life, though his work is not now highly regarded. Depending on Masonic help in his last years, Calvert died of cerebro-vascular disease in the Archway Hospital, Islington, London, on 27 June 1946, survived by his wife and four sons.

V&P (LA WA), 1895, 1 (7), 1901-02, 3 (46); *Masonic Secretaries' J* (Lond), no 4, May 1918; *Mining J* (Lond), 4 Sept 1894; *British A'sian*, 5 Jan 1899; *Morning Herald* (Perth), 10 Jan 1896, 12 Jan 1897; *Sheffield Daily Telegraph*, 28 Aug 1898; *Australasian*, 1 Oct 1898, 7 Jan 1899; *Argus*, 10 Apr 1923; *The Times*, 18 Apr 1923; information from Australian Embassy, Madrid, *and* United Grand Lodge of England (Library, Lond).

WENDY BIRMAN

CAMBAGE, RICHARD HIND (1859-1928), surveyor and botanist, was born on 7 November 1859 at Applegarth near Milton, New South Wales, second son of Yorkshire-born John (Fisher) Cambage, blacksmith and later farmer, and his second wife Emma Ann, née Jones. His father had reached Sydney on 5 July 1835 in the *Marquis of Huntley*, sentenced to seven years for housebreaking. Richard was educated at the Ulladulla Public School, was a pupil-teacher there and at 18 began training as a surveyor; in 1880 he helped to survey National Park. On 11 July 1881 at the Elizabeth Street registry office, Sydney, he married Fanny Skillman (d. 1897), daughter of the head-teacher at Ulladulla.

Licensed as a surveyor in June 1882, Cambage became a draftsman in the Department of Lands and on 16 February 1885 transferred to the Department of Mines as a mining surveyor. He covered much of the colony on his field trips and became expert in bushcraft, with 'an intuitive sense of direction', but his professional duties became increasingly concentrated on coal-mining. In 1900 he carried out a difficult and dangerous survey of abandoned Newcastle workings running under the harbour and sea-bed. While investigating the old Balmain tunnels in Sydney he managed the remarkable feat of transferring his azimuth from the surface to a point 2920 ft (890 m) below sea-level in a single operation. Promoted chief mining surveyor in 1902, he investigated the site of an explosion in the Mount Kembla mine which had killed 95 men: his evidence to the royal commission on the disaster led to the reversal of the coroner's verdict that the miners had died of carbon-monoxide poisoning.

Cambage was a member of the board of

examiners for licensed surveyors in 1903-18, and a foundation fellow of the Institution of Surveyors, New South Wales, of which he was president in 1907-09; he also lectured on surveying at Sydney Technical College in 1909-15. On 1 January 1916 he became under-secretary and warden of the Department of Mines and from next March was superintendent of explosives. He also chaired several boards in the public service.

A keen childhood interest in plants, birds and animals of his native district, where there were pockets of sub-tropical rainforest, blossomed during his years in the field. He made plant collections in 1880-90 for Dr William Woolls [q.v.6] who gave him botanical lessons, and his observations formed the basis of two significant contributions to Australian botanical study. Cambage studied systematically the relationship of various Australian genera to their environment, and particularly the importance of the chemical composition of the parent rocks in the distribution of *Eucalyptus* species. If neither completely original nor definitive, his work in this area was remarkably perceptive. He also made a sophisticated analysis of the physiology and morphology of the widely varied Australian species of the genus *Acacia*, which involved years of experiment with seedlings in his garden and greenhouse. He published extensively in the journals of the local Royal and Linnean societies, often with his friend J. H. Maiden [q.v.]. *Acacia cambagei*, the 'gidgea' of the Darling River, and *Eucalyptus cambageana*, the 'Coowarra Box', were named after him.

A fellow of the Linnean Society of London from 1904, Cambage was very active in many local learned societies and was 'a renowned peacemaker'. He was a councilmember of the local Linnean Society from 1906 (president in 1924), honorary secretary of the Royal Society of New South Wales in 1914-22 and 1925-28 (president in 1912 and 1923), president of the Wild Life Preservation Society of Australia in 1913 and of the State branch of the Australian Forest League in 1928, a council-member of the Australian Wattle League from 1909, and an elective trustee of the Australian Museum, Sydney, from 1925. As founding honorary secretary of the Australian National Research Council in 1919-26, he organized the Second Pan Pacific Science Congress held in Melbourne and Sydney in 1923, and as president in 1926-28 he represented the Commonwealth at the third congress held in Japan in 1926. He attended the conference on reorganization of the Commonwealth Institute of Science and Industry in 1925. In 1928 he presided over the Hobart meeting of the Australasian Association for the Advance-

ment of Science. Cambage was also a foundation member in 1901 of the (Royal) Australian Historical Society and president in 1924. He enjoyed tracing the actual paths followed by some of the early explorers, including Barrallier's [q.v.1] attempt to cross the Blue Mountains, which he described in papers for the society.

Cambage retired from the public service at the end of 1924 and next year was appointed C.B.E. He was an active Freemason, holding high office in the local lodges, and a keen follower of Test and Sheffield Shield cricket. On 28 November 1928 he died suddenly with angina pectoris at his Burwood home, and was buried in the Anglican section of Rookwood cemetery. He was survived by two daughters and two sons who had both served in World War I.

Public Service J (NSW), 15 Nov 1924; Roy Soc NSW, *Procs*, 63 (1926); Linnean Soc NSW, *Procs*, 54 (1929), 59 (1934), and for publications; *Aust Museum Mag*, 3 (1929); *Aust Mining Standard*, 6 Dec 1916, 6 Dec 1928; *SMH*, 3 May 1923, 29 Nov 1928; *Bulletin*, 5 Dec 1928; Hunt Inst biogs (Basser Lib, Canb); information from Mrs R. S. Kerr, St Lucia, Qld.

W. G. McMINN

CAMERON, ALEXANDER (1864-1940), solicitor and public servant, was born on 5 August 1864 at Morgiana station, near Hamilton, Victoria, twin son of John Cameron, sheep-farmer, and his wife Barbara Winifred, née Taylor. He was educated at Hamilton College and on matriculating in 1881 attended lectures at the University of Melbourne. In March he was articled to Charles James Cresswell, a Hamilton solicitor; in June 1885 the articles were assigned to David Houston Herald of Melbourne, and he was admitted as a barrister and solicitor to the Supreme Court of Victoria on 1 September 1886.

After a trip abroad Cameron began practice in Melbourne. About 1889 he set up in partnership with Samuel Crisp; the firm later became Crisp, Cameron & Rennick, and finally Crisp, Cameron & Hanby. On 29 June 1892 he married Mary Wright in Toorak Presbyterian Church, and settled in Malvern.

In 1902 Cameron was elected to Malvern Town Council and soon after was appointed a council delegate to the Melbourne and Metropolitan Board of Works. His main concerns were tramway services and building regulations in the suburbs. His outstanding work for Malvern was to bring to a successful conclusion the council's long fight for a municipal tramway. He used his legal knowledge and business ability to pave the way for the formation in 1907 of the Prahran and Malvern Tramways Trust in order to construct an electric tramway linking the two suburbs. On 16 March 1908 both councils elected him chairman of the trust, whose activities later extended to seven suburbs. In his years as chairman, Cameron became a recognized authority on the subject of passenger transport, and a tireless advocate of electric trams as the best means of providing quick transport for developing suburbs.

In July 1919 Cameron was appointed full-time chairman of the newly constituted Melbourne and Metropolitan Tramways Board. Tramway lines, for both cable and electric traction, had been constructed by different bodies without any uniform system; under Cameron's guidance the Tramways Board was to bring these under a single control, extend the electric lines, and convert the existing cable-system to electric traction.

In March 1923 Cameron went abroad to investigate traffic problems; he returned next year confirmed in his long-held opinions that electric trams were superior to buses and that overhead wires were preferable to the underground conduit system. Controversy over the use of buses or trams in Melbourne continued, however, despite protests by Cameron that full investigations had been made in 1922 and 1927. That year, despite opposition from town planning bodies and the Melbourne City Council, the construction of electric tramways in St Kilda Road and Collins Street went ahead. He continued to fight off criticisms that electric trams were noisy, that overhead wires disfigured the streets, and that trams caused congestion.

Cameron's term of office was originally five years. The structure of the board was then to be reviewed, but this was continually postponed and Cameron's term extended. Finally, on 18 December 1935, reconstruction was announced and at the same time Cameron's retirement. He first read of this decision in the press and the members of the board protested at the grave discourtesy shown to him; they paid tribute to him when he chaired his last meeting on 19 December.

Cameron was a member of the Institute of Transport, London, and kept himself well informed of modern trends by reading technical journals and corresponding with traffic experts overseas. He was well read in the works of Virgil, Horace, Washington Irving, Emerson and others. 'Short and burly, affable and homely', Cameron was known for his friendliness, and his enthusiastic dedication to his work. 'He talks and thinks trams', wrote an interviewer in 1928. He was president of the Club Cameron of

Victoria and a member of the Melbourne Scots and the Rotary and Yorick clubs. Among his club associates he was well known as a golfer, fisherman, 'bridge-maestro', raconteur and philosopher. He died of cancer at his home in South Yarra on 23 February 1940, survived by his wife; their only son had died in infancy.

Melbourne and Metropolitan Tramways Board, . . . its progress and development 1919-1929 (Melb, 1929), and Centenary souvenir, 1934-5 (Melb, 1935); J. B. Cooper, A history of Malvern (Melb, 1935); A. Henderson (ed), Early pioneer familes of Victoria and Riverina (Melb, 1936); J. D. Keating, Mind the curve! (Melb, 1970); Inst of Engineers, Aust, J, 6 (1934); Punch (Melb), 3 July 1919; Argus, 5 Feb 1924, 28 Jan 1929, 5 Apr 1930, 1 Jan 1936; Table Talk, 8 Mar 1928; Age, 24 Feb 1940; M.M.T.B., Annual report, 1919-36 (Melb).

KATHLEEN THOMSON

CAMERON, DONALD (1877-1950), soldier and grazier, was born on 21 August 1877 at Rouchel near Scone, New South Wales, son of Kenneth Cameron, grazier, and his wife Mary Ann, née McMullin both native-born. After attending Rouchel Public School he worked on near-by grazing properties and became skilled in bushcraft, horsemanship and rifle-shooting.

In 1899 Cameron enlisted for service in the South African War as a trooper in the 1st Australian Horse and sailed for Cape Town in January 1900. His squadron was attached to the Royal Scots Greys at Modder River and served in operations through the Orange Free State and Transvaal. At Zand River in May Cameron was involved in a Boer ambush; his horse was shot and he was captured, but escaped a few weeks later. He returned home with his unit in May 1901 but re-enlisted and was commissioned as a lieutenant in the 3rd New South Wales Imperial Bushmen's Regiment. He served for fifteen months in the Transvaal where his unit was engaged in dispersing concentrations of Boer troops; because of his bushcraft and tactical skill Cameron excelled at this work which involved long night-marches over unknown and sometimes rugged country. Although still a subaltern, he commanded the squadron for ten months in 1901-02.

On returning home Cameron purchased grazing land at Rouchel and worked this property until World War I; he was active in the local Presbyterian church and in political and sporting organizations. He enlisted in the Australian Imperial Force as a captain on 4 May 1915, was promoted major on 1 June and appointed to 'C' Squadron, 12th Light Horse Regiment. The unit fought as infantry at Gallipoli from 29 August until the evacuation; Cameron was attached to the 6th L.H.R. at Holly Spur, Wilson's Lookout and Ryrie's Post. He rejoined his own regiment in Egypt and served in all its engagements in Sinai, Palestine and Syria; from April 1917, when he was promoted lieut-colonel, he was commanding officer. His transparent honesty of purpose and sense of fairness quickly won him the loyalty of his men and his unit was noted for its excellent discipline.

Cameron was a tall, wiry man with a direct eye and a quiet manner. In action he was imperturbable, a trusted leader and sound tactician. He frequently urged the use of mounted action and was prominent in the famous charge which captured Beersheba in October 1917. The 4th and 12th L.H.Rs. surprised and over-ran Turkish defences; Cameron's men galloped on to seize the town, capturing guns and taking prisoners on the way. He was awarded the Distinguished Service Order for directing the attack in 'an extraordinarily able and determined manner'. He gained a Bar to this award in operations leading to the capture of Damascus in 1918; on 30 September he led a spirited mounted charge on Kaukab, 'seized his objective with great dash, and drove the enemy in disorder towards Damascus'. After the Armistice he commanded the 4th Light Horse Brigade for a month before returning to Australia in July 1919.

After demobilization Cameron returned to his property at Rouchel and on 11 December at Singleton married Ivy Eliza Dawes. From 1920 until he retired in 1933 he was a lieut-colonel in the Australian Military Forces. He was active in local affairs and in World War II helped organize the Volunteer Defence Corps in the Hunter Valley. Survived by his wife, a daughter and one of his two sons, he died of diabetes at Muswellbrook on 7 October 1950 and was buried in Rouchel Presbyterian cemetery.

Aust Defence Dept, *Official records of the Australian military contingents to the war in South Africa*, P. L. Murray ed (Melb, 1912); H. S. Gullett, *The A.I.F. in Sinai and Palestine* (Syd, 1923); *London Gazette*, 18 Jan, 17 Aug 1918; *Reveille* (Syd), Oct 1937; War diary of the 12th Light Horse Regiment, AIF (AWM); records (AWM); information from Mr R. Cameron, Singleton, NSW.

RONALD HOPKINS

CAMERON, SIR DONALD CHARLES (1879-1960), soldier, pastoralist and politician, was born on 19 November 1879 in Brisbane, son of John Cameron [q.v.] and his wife Sarah Annie, née Lodge. His father was born in British Guiana, his mother in New South Wales. He was educated at Toowoomba and Brisbane Grammar schools and at 18 became a clerk in the Queensland Meat Export and Agency Co., of which his father was chairman of directors.

In 1899 Cameron went on a tour of Europe and Asia. He was in China during the Boxer Rebellion and after attaching himself to an American infantry regiment which had been dispatched from Manila, accompanied it to Peking. He returned to Australia in 1901, volunteered for service in the South African War, and on 19 March was commissioned lieutenant in the 6th (Queensland Imperial Bushmen) Contingent. He reached Cape Town in May and for the next year participated in patrolling and mopping-up operations in the Transvaal and the Orange River Colony. On 16 June he risked his life to rescue a wounded trooper and was mentioned in dispatches. His unit was disbanded in June 1902.

In 1902-14 Cameron, with his brothers, managed the family property, Kensington Downs, near Longreach, and was involved in their associated pastoral and other business activities. He visited Europe and the United States of America in 1903. On 18 February 1914 he married Evelyn Stella Jardine, granddaughter of John Jardine [q.v.4], at St John's Anglican Cathedral, Brisbane, and soon afterwards toured China and Japan; he had just returned home when World War I broke out. He enlisted in the Australian Imperial Force on 30 September and was appointed captain in the 7th Light Horse Regiment; on 17 November he transferred to the 5th L.H.R. and embarked for Egypt in December as second-in-command of 'C' Squadron. From 20 May 1915 until the evacuation his regiment fought as infantry at Gallipoli. Cameron was wounded on 9 June and again, quite severely, on 28 June in the heroic but fruitless attack on Turkish trenches known as the Balkan Gun Pits. This wound was to trouble him for the rest of his life as removal of the bullet which had entered just below his ribs was considered too hazardous.

Cameron was promoted major on 9 September and rejoined his unit in Egypt on 3 January 1916. After serving in the Suez Canal zone he crossed into Sinai in April and for the next ten months commanded his squadron in numerous patrols and skirmishes; he fought in the battle of Romani on 4-5 August. In February 1917 the light horse advanced into Palestine and took part in the battles of Gaza and in operations and patrols in the Wady Ghuzze. Cameron was promoted lieut-colonel on 30 October and took command of the regiment which he led in the attack on Beersheba and the advance on Jerusalem.

In the early months of 1918 he went to

England on leave, returning in April to resume command for the offensives against the retreating Turks which ended in their capitulation at Ziza on 30 October. Here Cameron was faced with the task of protecting the enemy force from Allied Bedouin troops while he arranged the surrender. For service in the Palestine campaign he was mentioned in dispatches three times, awarded the Distinguished Service Order and the Order of the Nile, and appointed C.M.G. He was an able commanding officer with a gift for obtaining 'machine-like discipline' from his men without having to demand it; morale in his regiment was always high. The writer Ion Idriess, who served under him, remembered him as 'a nuggety chap, not very tall, with a rugged face that [broke] easily into a smile'; in action he was 'never flustered' and was a 'cool but a quick thinker'.

After demobilization Cameron returned to Kensington Downs and in 1919-31 represented Brisbane for the National Party in the House of Representatives. Ill health forced his retirement but he was Nationalist member for Lilley in 1934-37; he contested the Senate election in 1937 but was defeated. As a parliamentarian he represented Australia at the League of Nations Assembly in 1923 and sat on the joint select committee on Commonwealth electoral law and procedure in 1926-27. A tireless worker, he always had the interests of ex-servicemen at heart; and in parliament was a leading spokesman for the Returned Sailors' and Soldiers' Imperial League of Australia; when a history of the 5th L.H.R. was printed in 1926, he paid the publishing costs and presented a copy to every member of the regiment. He commanded the 14th L.H.R. in 1921-24, was president or patron of many social organizations and hospitaller and almoner of the Order of St John in Australia. He was appointed K.C.M.G. in 1932. In World War II he served as chairman of the New South Wales recruiting drive committee for the Royal Australian Air Force.

After the war Cameron lived in retirement in Sydney and Brisbane and towards the end of his life he and his wife were hospitalized in Brisbane; she predeceased him, as did their only daughter. He died on 19 November 1960 and was cremated with Presbyterian forms. In accordance with his wishes his ashes were buried near the grave of his grandfather in the family cemetery on Home Creek station near Barcaldine. His estate was sworn for probate at £2382.

Aust Defence Dept, *Official records of the Australian military contingents to the war in South Africa*, P. L. Murray ed (Melb, 1912); H. S. Gullett, *The A.I.F. in Sinai and Palestine* (Syd, 1923); L. C.

Wilson and H. Wetherell, *Fifth Light Horse Regiment, 1914-1919* (Syd, 1926); *London Gazette*, 1 Dec 1916, 16 Aug, 1 Dec 1917, 14 Jan 1918, 12 Dec 1919, 16 Jan 1920, 5 April 1923; *Reveille* (Syd), June 1932; *Pastoral Review*, Feb 1961; *Courier Mail*, 21 Nov 1960.
                                                    S. W. WIGZELL

CAMERON, DONALD JAMES (1878-1962), trade unionist, labour journalist and politician, was born on 19 January 1878 at North Melbourne, son of Alexander Cameron, a Scottish slater, and his wife Mary Ann, née Nairn. He was educated at the City Road primary school, South Melbourne, and South Melbourne College. His earliest work was with various slaters and plumbers. He went to Western Australia about 1895 in search of gold but, apart from weekend fossicking, he worked mainly with the *Coolgardie Miner* as a junior machinist, later as a compositor, and experienced his first strike. He completed a printer's apprenticeship.

After a brief sojourn in Perth Cameron returned to Melbourne in 1899, and married Georgina Eliza Werrin according to Free Christian Church forms on 26 April. In 1901 he volunteered for the South African War, serving with the 5th (Victorian) Mounted Rifles, was wounded and carried a bullet in his leg for the rest of his life. More importantly, however, the war awakened his consciousness of social injustice. He was discharged in 1902, returned to Perth next year, and worked as a plumber, wharf labourer and miner. He was a member of the Fremantle Lumpers' Union in 1910-12 but was not active in its organization. After leaving the wharves he worked as a plumber with the railways, becoming secretary of the Plumbers' Union in 1912-19. At various times he was also part-time secretary of the Undertakers', Saddlers' and Musicians' unions.

His earliest active political involvement was with a small 'socialist propaganda group', though he did not believe in purely direct action. Cameron became an active member of the Australian Labor Federation (the Western Australian branch of the Labor Party), was a member of its metropolitan district council and was a delegate to the party's interstate conferences of 1915 and 1918. A leading figure in the anti-conscription movement, he was president of the Western Australian Anti-Conscription League during the split in the party. He was Labor candidate for the State seat of Canning in the 1917 elections, but in polling only 43 per cent failed to unseat Attorney-General R. T. Robinson [q.v.], partly because he campaigned from Victoria where he was detained on union matters.

Cameron was also a member of the Western Australian Socialist Party, a small offshoot of the influential Victorian Socialist Party, regularly contributing a Western Australian column to the *Socialist*. Impressed with Cameron during his 1917 visit to Victoria, R. S. Ross [q.v.] and other V.S.P. leaders decided to offer him the job of party organizer. Cameron accepted, taking up the position in March 1919, later editing the *Socialist* (1920-23) and holding the V.S.P. secretaryship (1920-32). During this time, however, he retained his membership of the Australian Labor Party.

In the trade union movement Cameron was an active member of the Marine Stewards' Union; for many years he was its delegate to the Melbourne Trades Hall Council and to national trade union congresses. He also represented the Kalgoorlie branch of the Australian Tramway Employees' Association at its national conferences. He was president of the Melbourne T.H.C. in 1930-31 and was elected assistant secretary in August 1934. He was a foundation member of the interstate executive of the Australian Council of Trade Unions (from 1927) and was a regular member of its emergency committee between 1927 and 1937. As such he played a major part in the A.C.T.U.'s development. In the 1920s and 1930s he was a prolific contributor to labour journals including the *Tramway Record* and the *Marine Stewards' Journal*, both of which he at one time edited, and the *Union Voice* and *Labor Call*, his articles ranging from bread and butter issues to ideological polemics.

Within the A.L.P. Cameron was a regular member of the Victorian state executive in 1928-49, president of the Victorian branch in 1932 and a delegate to federal conference in 1934-48, attending fourteen conferences in all. He was also frequently a delegate to the federal executive. He was the unsuccessful Labor candidate for the Federal seats of Balaclava in 1929, and Fawkner in a 1935 by-election against a future prime minister, Harold Holt. Cameron headed the Victorian Labor Senate ticket for the 1931 elections, but no Labor candidates were elected. In 1937, placed only second on the ticket, he was elected to the Senate, taking his place on 1 July 1938; he was re-elected in 1943, 1949, 1951 and 1955.

Cameron was a member of the standing committee on regulations and ordinances (1938-41); minister for aircraft production from 7 October 1941 to 2 February 1945; minister assisting the minister for munitions from 7 October 1941 to 27 February 1942 and member of the production executive of Cabinet (1941-45). Throughout the war he maintained his opposition to conscription for overseas service. After a reshuffle in February 1945 Cameron became postmaster-general, holding the portfolio until 19 December 1949. From 18 June 1946 to 19 December 1949 he was deputy leader of the government in the Senate and he served on the select committee on the Commonwealth Bank bill (1950) in 1951. He was president of the Melbourne Technical College in 1934-38 and a member of the Melbourne University Extension Board. Having become very deaf, he retired from the Senate on 30 June 1962, at the end of his fifth term, aged 84.

Cameron, if not leaving a clear personal imprint on the labour movement, was one of its great activists this century. Although an avid reader of most works influencing the labour movement and a polemical writer, at times bordering on the iconoclastic, he never fully shared the scepticism about labour in politics which pervaded the V.S.P. ideology, or supported the direct actionist, anti-parliamentary stance of the industrial unionists at a time when these attitudes were dominant in the movement. He was diffident about the One Big Union concept which, around the early 1920s, had widely been seen as a panacea for the political and industrial weakness of the working class, suggesting that it could lead to a 'trades hall dictatorship'. Instead, he preferred a strong national superstructure for the trade union movement to be erected on the existing, though rationalized, base, and hence he threw his weight behind the formation of the A.C.T.U. which he saw as embodying this principle.

Cameron's opposition to the Soviet communist model, which he once described as 'ultra-capitalism', was firmly rooted in his belief in democracy and working-class struggle within the arena of parliament. The objective of socialization of industry was, he believed, consistent with this model of political action. Although he considered that revolution was possible, and during the Depression hailed its approach, he always insisted that capitalist rulers must not merely be replaced by socialist rulers as in the Soviet Union, but that the new order must be based on an educated and politically conscious public and an open system of government. His political career exemplified the development of these views, though he was often accused of opportunism by V.S.P. contemporaries during his early enunciation of them.

Square-jawed and bushy-browed, with a mop of silver-grey hair, Don Cameron was a quiet person, reticent about himself and his past, even to his immediate family, but was liked in parliament for his shrewd and pithy humour. He disclaimed any religion. Less than two months after retiring from parliament Cameron died at East Malvern on 20 August 1962 and was cremated. His estate was valued for probate at £23 174. He was survived by his wife and three sons; his third son Roy was active in Victorian Labor politics and the union movement from the 1930s and particularly from the 1950s.

Socialist (Melb), 17 Feb, 8 Nov, 1922; G. Dunkley, The ACTU 1927-1950: politics, organization and economic policy (Ph.D. thesis, Monash Univ, 1974); D. Cameron papers (NL); I. Turner, Interview with Senator Don Cameron, 1960 (LaTL); documents held by and information from Mr R. Cameron, Glen Iris, Vic.   GRAHAM DUNKLEY

CAMERON, DONALD NORMAN (1851-1931), landowner and politician, and CYRIL ST CLAIR (1857-1941), soldier, landowner and politician, were brothers. Donald Norman was born at Fordon, Nile, Tasmania, eldest son of Donald Cameron [q.v.3; d. 1890] and his Scottish wife Mary Isabella, née Morrison, and grandson of Donald Cameron [q.v.3; d. 1857] who migrated from Scotland in 1820. At 8 Cameron attended Glenalmond College, Perthshire, Scotland, returning to Tasmania in 1870 to take up sheep-breeding on his property, Bentley, at Chudleigh: he became one of the colony's foremost farming authorities. On 8 June 1880 at St John's Church of England, New Town, he married Anne Lillias Scott.

Cameron was elected to the House of Assembly for Deloraine in 1893 but resigned after six months to unsuccessfully contest Tamar for the Legislative Council. He represented Deloraine again in the assembly from 1897 to 1899. He became a free-trade member for Denison in the first Federal House of Representatives; defeated in 1903, he regained the seat next year in a by-election following the death of Sir Edward Braddon [q.v.] and held it until 1906. A member of the select committee on the Electoral Act administration in 1904, he was regarded as an energetic member who, although he spoke seldom, had a forceful personality. He represented Wilmot in the House of Assembly in 1912-13 and 1925-28.

Lean and lanky, conspicuous for wearing a panama hat in all weathers, Cameron was known for his pugnacity. It was said that 'if he had no foes . . . he would fight his friends'. He challenged the taxation commissioner in the High Court of Australia in 1923 and 1924 over the valuation of his livestock; an obituarist remembered him for a famous 'dripping' case arising from a servant using butter instead of dripping, and for another lawsuit concerning threepence exchange

owing on a cheque. He died on 17 February 1931 at Chudleigh, survived by his wife, a daughter and two of his three sons.

Cyril St Clair was born on 5 December 1857 at Fordon and educated at Launceston Church Grammar School and in Edinburgh, where he received a commission in the Royal Southdown Militia. After joining the 1st (King's) Dragoon Guards in 1879, he posted to the 9th (Queen's Royal) Lancers; he fought in the Afghan War in 1879-80 and marched with (Lord) Roberts from Kabul to Kandahar. In 1894 he returned as captain to Fordon with his wife Margaret Honeywood, née Hughes, whom he had married on 30 August 1887 in the Anglican church at Bovey Tracey, Devonshire, England.

Cameron embarked for the South African War in October 1899 as a captain in the Tasmanian Mounted Infantry; in December he was promoted major and in November 1900 was appointed C.B. Although his eccentric 'sudden personal predilections' annoyed him, his bravery was admired by all: when captured and disarmed by the enemy he reputedly fought with his bare fists. He returned to Tasmania in 1901 a hero, and was elected to the Senate as a Liberal on the single question of universal military training; the subsequent Australian training scheme owed much to his advocacy. A reticent parliamentarian, he was defeated in 1903 but was re-elected in 1906 and sat until 1913.

In 1901-03 and in 1909-14 Cameron was lieut-colonel of the 26th Light Horse, Tasmanian Mounted Infantry. He commanded the Australian Commonwealth Corps at the coronation of Edward VII in 1902 and next year was given command of the 12th Australian Light Horse and made aide-de-camp to the governor-general Lord Northcote [q.v.]. On the outbreak of war in 1914 he travelled to England where he was appointed to Headquarters Imperial Staff as assistant-adjutant-general and was adviser to General (Baron) Birdwood [q.v.]. Cameron took part in the landing at Gaba Tepe on 25 April 1915. Later that year he was invalided back to Australia and honoured by the Senate which admitted him to a seat on the floor of the House and presented him with a copy of the proceedings. In 1916 he was gazetted honorary colonel of the 26th Light Horse, Tasmanian Mounted Infantry, and in 1921 honorary colonel of the 22nd.

Tall and slightly stooped, with a typical weather-beaten military face, Cameron had 'a gentle disposition under the armour'; his ideal was 'determinedly and quietly to do our duty'. He died on 22 December 1941 at Fordon, survived by two sons and one daughter.

Cyclopedia of Tasmania (Hob, 1900); *British*

A'sian, 19 Nov 1914; *Punch* (Melb), 16 Sept 1915; *Examiner* (Launc), and *Mercury*, 18 Feb 1931, 23 Dec 1941; *Bulletin*, 25 Feb 1931; MS cat under Cameron (TA); family papers (held by Colonel D. Cameron, Fordon, Nile, Tas).

CAROLINE L. CAMERON

CAMERON, JAMES (1846-1922), farmer, entrepreneur and politician, was born probably early in 1846 at Logie-Almond, Perthshire, Scotland, eldest child of Alexander Cameron and his wife Anne, née Pullar. Heeding the advice of a brother already in Victoria, Alexander and his wife and children left Liverpool in the *Oliver Lang* as unassisted migrants, arriving at Geelong in 1854. During nine years of tenant farming at Batesford, the children received a rudimentary education at home from an itinerant parson. Eventually the family was able to select six small blocks totalling 250 acres (101 ha) at Beremboke, but this failed to provide sufficient livelihood for a large family of eleven; hence James and two other brothers sought work as contractors, surveyors and leasehold farmers in the Western District. Angered at restrictions on small farmers, the brothers turned to the remote wilds of East Gippsland. In 1877 they each selected 340-acre (138 ha) blocks, with leasing rights to higher ground, on the Snowy River estuary at Orbost. On 30 April 1879 at Colac, James married 19-year-old Sarah Scouller, of Birregurra.

With a Highlander's perseverance, Cameron set to work draining and clearing the rich Orbost flats. Pioneering difficulties were compounded by labour shortages, distance to markets and flooding. He experimented with flax, beans and tobacco while relying on maize, pig-rearing and scientific dairying. Several times he resorted to hiring 'Hindoo' harvesters, a measure which was later to cause political embarrassment. He diversified into grazing and marble extraction at South Buchan and mining investment at Nowa Nowa; he became a director of the Orbost Butter and Produce Co., a distributor of farm-machinery and a manager of the schooner service to Melbourne.

In 1882 Cameron was the first Orbost councillor of the newly constituted Tambo Shire. In the next twenty years he served as justice of the peace, shire councillor, guardian of St James's Anglican Church, Sunday school superintendent, and president of the local agricultural society and railway league. His home was a large barn-like structure, built to serve as guest-house, hospital, post office, church and community hall. Cameron called it Lochiel after his traditional clan residence. Its grounds were the centre for community gatherings, agricultural fairs and sports such as tossing the caber. During floods he had '300 pigs in the loft . . . a family on top of that, and 10 to 12 feet of water under them'. By 1895 Cameron paid rates of £192 on thirteen properties; had a family of eight children; employed house-servants and farm-hands, and had time to lecture on Dickens [q.v.4] and Sir Walter Scott to the local debating society. He was never too busy to conduct Melbourne officials over the bad roads with his skilfully driven four-in-hand team.

In 1902 Cameron won a by-election for Gippsland East and took his seat in the Legislative Assembly amid the cry for retrenchment created by the Kyabram reform movement. He was typical of the 'parish pump', 'roads and bridges' member who gave support to country-oriented Liberal and National ministries for concessions to his vast riding. During his eighteen years in parliament, Cameron proved to be a pragmatic, argumentative man, devoid of humour, who defended the small entrepreneurial designs of rural Victoria. He was unsympathetic to the urban unemployed, the aged poor and village settlers who, he considered, had not shown themselves to be thrifty. His proudest accomplishments were securing £1 million for East Gippsland development, bringing the railway to Orbost in 1916 and fathering the Country Roads Board.

Cameron was remembered for his startling no confidence motion against Sir Thomas Bent [q.v.3] in December 1908, which took all the adversaries by surprise and ushered in the John Murray-W. A. Watt [qq.v.] ministries. He had petitioned Bent in vain 'to buy an estate, put such families as you would find in Brighton . . . market gardening types' on the land and to develop a broader railway programme. As minister without portfolio in 1909-13 he tackled levee building on Victorian rivers, sewerage and harbour works and agricultural inspection. Although he initially felt that 'there was really too much talk in Parliament' and was 'opposed to Royal Commissions', he proved a vigorous debater and served on five inquiries relating to the Lands Department, the Melbourne police (as chairman), vaccination efficiency, smallholdings and the drift of rural population. After winning six elections, he lost to a Victorian Farmers' Union candidate in 1920.

Cameron spent his last days at his beloved Lochiel suffering from a prolonged illness which was aggravated by a botched operation. Three of his sons served with distinction on the Western Front. He died on 13 July 1922, heart-broken at the loss of his youngest son from a riding accident. Cameron was buried in the Orbost cemetery, leaving an estate valued at £30 436 to his wife and seven surviving children who had managed his many enterprises.

A. Sutherland et al, *Victoria and its metropolis*, 2 (Melb, 1888); J. Smith (ed), *Cyclopedia of Victoria*, 1-3 (Melb, 1903-05); E. H. Sugden and F. W. Eggleston, *George Swinburne* (Syd, 1931); *Snowy River Mail*, 18 Jan 1898, 14 June 1902, 9 Mar, 13 Apr 1895, 16 Jan 1916, 4 Nov 1920; *Gippsland Times*, 3 Dec 1908; *Argus*, 15 July 1922; M. Gilbert (ed), Personalities and stories of the early Orbost district (Orbost); information from Mary Gilbert, Orbost, Vic.   R. C. DUPLAIN

CAMERON, JOHN (1847-1914), pastoralist, company director and politician, was born on 13 March 1847 at New Amsterdam, British Guiana, son of Donald Charles Cameron, plantation manager, and his wife Margaret Anne, née Moore. John's grandfather had been an officer of the 79th Highlanders at Waterloo. His father, after managing a sugar-plantation at Berbice, British Guiana, migrated to Victoria in 1852, and next year his wife and family followed on the *Great Britain*. The Camerons took up Native Creek and later Berremboke stations, north-west of Geelong.

John was educated at Scotch College, Melbourne, and at Geelong Church of England Grammar School, where 'I never did any good beyond being a good fighter'. He began work as a jackeroo in 1859; in 1861-63, with the Crombie brothers [q.v.], the Camerons and their flocks pushed north-west from Inverell, New South Wales, to Barcaldine, Queensland. After eighteen months at Barcaldine Downs, John became overseer of Alice Downs and subsequently manager of Wilby. When the Camerons, Crombies, T. S. Mort [q.v.5], J. T. Allan and Herbert Garrett formed a partnership embracing an empire of seven huge runs, John entered the firm. The partnership was dissolved in 1877 but he retained, with his brother-in-law James Crombie, Kensington Downs and Greenhills. The agreement with Crombie disintegrated in 1881 and Cameron and his mother kept Kensington Downs of 625 square miles (1619 km²), 62 miles (100 km) north-east of Longreach. He lived there until 1891 when he retired to Brisbane.

Cameron was more a representative of the second phase of Queensland pastoral pioneering, when capital and managerial skill generally superseded physical endurance, luck and personal persistence as prerequisites for survival. Yet he experienced many early vicissitudes and hardships which shortened his life: he once spent several days in the branches of a gum (a marooned pastoral mariner) during a terrible Dawson River flood. He took pains to avoid the homicidal problems of squatter-Aboriginal confrontation.

Cameron's 'peculiar' attitudes towards Chinese labour – 'He has always contended that the Chinese gardener or cook is unnecessary and Kensington Downs has been always for a White Australia' – blunted Labor opposition to both his person and his business interests. Cameron, whose hospitality, courtesy and essential fairness demonstrated both his generous tolerance and strong personality, survived long enough to receive the respect of western Labor politicians who had sprung from the same genre. George Kerr [q.v.] remarked in 1904: 'The member poses, and has a right to pose, as a good and kind employer'. In 1891, however, Cameron had fulminated that 'in the fight for a principle [free contract] he was prepared to lose every sheep that he possessed'.

On 15 April 1889 Cameron convened a meeting of employers at Barcaldine 'to consider the advisableness of forming a Union for the prevention of strikes and the amicable settlement of disputes which may arise'. This body subsequently became the Central Queensland Pastoral Employers' Association: Cameron was its president in 1893-1908. On an intercolonial level he helped organize, co-ordinate and direct the pastoralists' campaign against the labour thrust of the 1890s, an activity which quietly paralleled, and historically may well have been as effective as, the 'new unions' and the colonial Labor parties. In 1897-1908 he was president of the United Pastoralists' Association of Queensland during a critical period of labour, economic and climatic problems.

Helping the conservative coalition pick up the pieces following the Queensland National Bank disasters (he served as pastoral valuer and consultant to the 1896-97 committee, which revealed unpalatable truths), Cameron became part of that brief revival and consolidation of Queensland quasi-capitalism which followed the depression of the 1890s, when he was hard hit. He was wise enough to avoid purchasing pastoral freeholds: 'I would sell land to anybody who would be fool enough to buy it', he declared in 1904, 'I do not own an acre in Western Queensland; and I do not wish to own any'. But he was forced to rely heavily on bank and agency credit: in 1896 he mortgaged Kensington Downs's 113 117 sheep to Dalgety's [q.v.4], the Mercantile Bank and the Commercial Bank of Australia.

Cameron survived the depression, only to suffer a serious set-back during the great drought and wool-price slump of 1900-02. Yet his probity, political influence and individual solvency enabled him to replace the old, discredited entrepreneurs as chairman of Morehead [q.v.5] Ltd, and as a director of the Queensland National Bank, the Darling Downs and Western Lands Co., the Queensland Meat Export and Agency Co. Ltd, the Union Trustee Co. and the Alliance Insurance Co.

Elected to the Legislative Assembly for Mitchell in 1893 as a central separationist, free trader and stern retrencher, Cameron used his qualities of honesty, shrewdness and even temper to influence coalition ministers. Declining office, he worked for the pastoral interest behind the scenes. He spoke infrequently but always to the point, preferring to argue the pastoralists' case for effective wage-reduction and voluntary arbitration in public, while privately urging the government to smash the shearing strikes of 1891 and 1894. These tactics were successful and Cameron never attracted the opprobrium heaped on Tozer and Sir Samuel Griffith [qq.v.].

His defeat by Labor candidates in 1896 (Mitchell) and 1899 (Barcoo) signified that the squatters' position was now electorally hopeless in western Queensland. Having declared publicly in 1895 that 'I have never believed in the principle of one man one vote, and nothing will ever convince me that men should have equal voting rights', he was clearly an anachronism. But he remained undaunted. Deeply disturbed by the pastoral industry's plight, Cameron re-entered parliament for Brisbane North in 1901 and, with his co-member E. B. Forrest [q.v.], was never seriously challenged. Ill health compelled his retirement in February 1908.

A staunch Philp [q.v.] adherent, he was prepared to be flexible if it would help the pastoralists. By 1905 he was even conceding the right of women as well as pastoral workers to vote, although the idea of an income tax remained particularly obnoxious. Cameron never denied that he entered parliament as a squatters' delegate to retrieve a disastrous situation. Parliament, he said, 'must revive the great primary industries of the State so that all else would flourish'. 'The city', he declared in 1904, 'was only the great emporium, the great mart where primary products were distributed, where buyer and seller most easily met. Without a prosperous back-country, the city would languish'.

Most Queenslanders agreed with him. Although he failed to extend pastoral leases and revise pastoral classifications in the Pastoral Holdings New Leases Act of 1901,

Cameron worked for thirty amendments in a bill of sixteen clauses. His tactics succeeded in extracting from the government more generous provisions than they were initially prepared to concede. In 1902 he effectively used the Queensland financial lobby in London and skilfully conducted a model campaign that generated light for the squatters rather than heat amongst the politicians. This was his apogee. The (Sir Arthur) Morgan [q.v.] ministry was less sympathetic. In March 1904, replying to Cameron's presentation of a memorial by 400 leading squatters pleading for further relief, Morgan was unsympathetic and allowed only some minor concessions.

Cameron visited Japan for his health in 1906 and never again spoke in the assembly. His political career concluded on a bizarre note which indicated that the shape of Queensland politics had decisively altered. In 1905 he had published the text of a land tax bill in the *Daily Mail*, alleging that he had found it on the floor of a room in Parliament House. It is probable that the text had been leaked to Cameron, whose desire to injure a Liberal government and defeat a land tax momentarily got the better of him. The tactic backfired and the conservative rump of a dozen or so members was tactically outmanoeuvred by the government. Cameron's declining health had undoubtedly affected his judgment.

On 18 April 1877 at Mudgee, New South Wales, he had married Sarah Annie (1850-1893), daughter of Oliver Lodge. Three sons survived him, the eldest of whom, (Sir) Donald Charles [q.v.], had an illustrious military and political career. Cameron married in 1899 Louise Christine (1861-1917), daughter of J. C. Heussler [q.v.]; their only son predeceased him.

After a long illness, Cameron died of intestinal neoplasm at his home Avoca, Albion, Brisbane, on 29 June 1914. He was buried in the Toowong cemetery with ceremonies befitting an elder of the Presbyterian Church and the chief of the Caledonian and Burns clubs. Cameron had published 'A review of the pastoral industry of the State of Queensland since 1865' in *Royal Queensland Geographical Journal* (1905-06). He left an estate valued for probate at £73 978.

A. MacKenzie, *History of the Camerons* (Inverness, 1884); Alcazar Press, *Queensland, 1900* (Brisb, nd); *PD* (Qld), 1895, 73, 700, 1901, 86, 484, 1904, 92, 168-72; *Pastoral Review*, Aug 1893, July 1914; *Western Champion* (Barcaldine), 9 May 1893, 4 July 1914; *Brisbane Courier*, 16 Aug 1904, 10 Apr 1907; *Morning Bulletin*, 30 June 1914; *Queenslander*, 4 July 1914, 3 Aug 1918; Central Qld Pastoral Employers' Assn, Minutes 1891-1908 (Barcaldine); family information from Mr S. Archer, Brisb.   D. B. WATERSON

CAMERON, SAMUEL SHERWEN (1866-1933), veterinary surgeon and public servant, was born on 29 June 1866 at Haile, Cumberland, England, son of John Cameron, farmer, and his wife Sarah, née Sherwen. After attending a commercial school at Barrow in Furness, Lancashire, he was articled to a solicitor but two years later enrolled at the Royal (Dick) Veterinary College in Edinburgh. Following a distinguished student career he graduated as a qualified veterinary surgeon in 1888. Next year he migrated to Victoria to join the staff of the recently established Veterinary College, Fitzroy, as lecturer and hospital surgeon, a post which he held for five years. In 1893 he was elected to the Veterinary Board of Victoria.

In 1895 Cameron took up an appointment as veterinary officer to the municipality of Dunedin, New Zealand. Here he was closely associated with the establishment of the country's first public abattoirs. He returned to Melbourne in mid-1896 to become veterinary inspector for the Board of Public Health. He continued to direct his efforts in the field of meat hygiene, and together with Dr D. A. Gresswell [q.v.] was responsible for the Meat Supervision Act of Victoria, 1901, which regulated for the first time the slaughtering of cattle. Concerned also with conditions in the milk industry, Cameron set about designing legislation and, largely owing to his initiative and determination, the Milk and Dairy Supervision Act was passed in 1905. This Act was administered by the Department of Agriculture to which Cameron was transferred as chief veterinary inspector. In this post he was also responsible for the first organized efforts to control and eradicate diseases of livestock in Victoria.

In 1910 the government decided that a thorough reorganization of the Department of Agriculture was imperative: Cameron became director in January 1911 with the onerous task of restoring efficiency to a badly run-down instrumentality. Ignoring possible hostility to his appointment among senior officers of the department, Cameron went ahead with the reorganization with some ruthlessness, and much of the ultimate success of his work was undoubtedly due to his initiative and sense of purpose. He was eminently successful in bridging the gulf between the scientific agriculturist and the practical farmer; he supported the university's faculty of agriculture set up in 1906, and by 1931, when he retired, he was employing thirty-five of its graduates. Another of Cameron's progressive moves was the issue of government certificates for soundness in stallions; similar legislation came into being in the other States. The success of the State Research Farm at Werribee owed much to his enthusiasm and foresight.

Cameron was also associated with the formation of Young Farmers' clubs in Victoria. Among his other interests were the Better Farming Exhibition train, the Red Poll and Friesian Cattle Breeding societies and standard and grade herd-testing. In 1927 he represented Australia at the Imperial Conference on Agriculture held in London. He was a council-member of the Royal Agricultural Society of Victoria, and a committee-man of the Pastures Improvement League and the Clydesdale Horse Society. From 1916 Cameron was a member of the Advisory Council of Science and Industry and, in 1925, of the conference to reorganize the Commonwealth Institute of Science and Industry.

In 1909 a faculty of veterinary science had been set up at the university and Cameron was appointed lecturer in veterinary hygiene and dietetics; that year he graduated doctor of veterinary science. He became senior lecturer in 1924 and also taught fourth-year state sanitary science. In 1928 the teaching of veterinary science ceased at the university; ironically the decline in student numbers was in part a result of Cameron's encouragement of trained laymen, such as dairy supervisors, to carry out functions previously taken on by veterinarians. He also lectured in animal husbandry and veterinary hygiene in the faculty of agriculture in 1927-33.

Dr Cameron had a gruff manner, and to a young graduate had a rather austere and forbidding presence. On 18 May 1897 he had married Williamina Milne in Dunedin. She survived him, together with one of their two sons and a daughter when he died of cancer at his Hawthorn home on 31 December 1933; he was cremated. His estate was valued for probate at £11 979.

G. Currie and J. Graham, *The origins of CSIRO* (Melb, 1966); *Science and Industry*, Dec 1919; *Aust Veterinary J*, Feb 1934; *J of Agr* (Vic), Feb 1934; Aust Veterinary Assn, *Vic Veterinary Procs*, 1958; *Punch* (Melb), 22 Mar 1911.

HAROLD E. ALBISTON

CAMFIELD, JULIUS HENRY (1852-1916), gardener and horticulturist, was born on 30 March 1852 at Islington, London, son of Henry Camfield, bricklayer, and his wife Ellen, née Baker. Apprenticed at 13, he later worked on several estates near London as head gardener, in his last position having charge of fourteen men. On 30 November 1875 at Marylebone he married, with Wesleyan forms, Louisa Dinah Millichap, daughter of a gamekeeper; in October 1881, with a young family, they embarked for Australia.

Arriving in Sydney on New Year's Day 1882 Camfield presented his credentials to Charles Moore [q.v.5], director of the Botanic Gardens, who on 23 January appointed him overseer of the Garden Palace Grounds, which had been established for the 1879 Sydney Intercolonial Exhibition. Situated at the main entrance, the Garden Palace Grounds were not part of the Botanic Gardens, but set apart solely for public pleasure and devoted chiefly to lawns and popular flowers. Some of the public's pleasures were less than respectable, and led Camfield in 1903 to call for police to patrol the grounds, in place of the less-respected bailiffs. In 1912 he was appointed overseer of the inner Domain, formed by incorporating the Garden Palace Grounds with part of Government House gardens, and made responsible for their consolidation.

Camfield was fascinated by the flora of the Sydney region, especially to the south of his Kogarah home. He assisted J. H. Maiden [q.v.], who succeeded Moore as director in 1896, to collect material for his new National Herbarium of New South Wales and compiled his own small herbarium which he presented to the Botanic Gardens in 1912. Considered a sound botanist by Maiden, he could only rarely be persuaded to publish: in 1898 with Maiden he published notes on plants native to the Port Jackson area, and in 1904 a modest but sensible paper on the cultivation of native flowering plants, in the *Agricultural Gazette of New South Wales*. Camfield's annual reports were careful and meticulous, reflecting his personality. A member of the Linnean Society of New South Wales, he read widely and haunted Sydney's book shops, alerting Maiden to many rare volumes which were then purchased for the Botanic Gardens library. He had a lively interest in sociology, anthropology, history and philosophy, and an extensive library in these fields, but, being shy and withdrawn, rarely shared his interests with others.

Camfield retired in July 1916. Survived by his wife and three sons, he died of cancer on 26 November and was buried in the Methodist section of Woronora cemetery. Maiden claimed that no director 'ever had a more competent or more loyal colleague' and in 1920 named an uncommon species of Eucalyptus after him, *E. camfieldii*, known popularly as 'Camfield's Stringybark'.

Report ... Botanic Gardens, government domains ... 1916, *PP* (NSW), 1917-18, 4, 12; J. H. Maiden, 'History of the Sydney Botanic Gardens',

JRAHS, 14 (1928) pt 1, 17 (1931), pt 2; W. W. Frogatt, 'The curators and botanists of the Botanic Gardens, Sydney', *JRAHS*, 18 (1932), pt 3.

MARK LYONS
C. J. PETTIGREW

CAMIDGE, CHARLES EDWARD (1837-1911), Anglican bishop, was born on 2 October 1837 at Nether Poppleton, Yorkshire, England, eldest son of the vicar (Canon) Charles Joseph Camidge and his wife Charlotte, née Hustwick. Educated at St Peter's School, York, and Wadham College, Oxford (B.A., 1860; M.A., 1863; D.D., 1887), he was made deacon on 31 December 1860 and priested on 22 December 1861 by Archbishop Longley of York. On 3 July 1862 at Sheffield he married Laura Carow Sanderson, daughter of a wealthy merchant; they had no children. After a brief curacy in Sheffield, in 1861 he became curate to his father, now vicar of Wakefield; Charles organized the Wakefield Industrial and Fine Art Exhibition of 1865 and wrote an account of it.

Camidge became successively vicar of Hedon in 1868, rector of Wheldrake in 1873 and vicar of Thirsk in 1876. The archbishop presented him to the canonry and prebend of Wetwang in York Minster in 1882; he became rural dean of Thirsk next year. A moderate churchman with leanings toward Tractarianism, he was recommended for the bishopric of Bathurst in New South Wales by the Evangelical Bishop Hill of Sodor and Man, who described him as 'a good man all round, [who] has a nice wife, good means, and [is] ready to accept the post'. He was consecrated on 18 October 1887 in Westminster Abbey and was tendered a choral farewell in York Minster: all the music had been composed by his great-grandfather, grandfather and uncle, organists of the minster since 1756.

Enthroned at Bathurst on 3 January 1888, Camidge searchingly reorganized his huge diocese of 73 000 square miles (189 000 km^2) and encouraged bush clergy to conduct services in numerous small centres, thereby dramatically increasing the official attendance figures for the diocese. He elevated the standards of church music, resuscitated the offices and expounded the duties of rural dean and archdeacon, stiffened the examination for ordinands, and in 1891 amended the patronage ordinance to permit episcopal presentation to all vacant cures.

In the *Sydney Morning Herald* in March 1890, Camidge ably defended the Church of England against Cardinal Moran [q.v.]; his half of the controversy was later published privately in Bathurst. Although reputed to have declined nomination to the sees of Sydney in 1889 and Goulburn in 1892, he accepted a crozier presented that year by the Bathurst diocese. He was a business-like president of synod, whose addresses were well prepared and comprehensive, and on social issues analytical and thoughtful.

In 1900-07 a dispute engineered by Dr J. T. Marriott, incumbent of All Saints Cathedral, Bathurst, which involved the conflicting cathedral and parochial functions of that church, undermined Camidge's failing health. In July 1902 he took a cruise to Vancouver, Canada, and in 1904-05 another to Western Australia. In January 1906 he visited England after his episcopal concession had facilitated a settlement at All Saints. On the advice of Revs F. H. Campion [q.v.] and E. H. Lea he established the Brotherhood of the Good Shepherd in January 1902, to minister in the isolated parts of the diocese. He himself purchased the site of Brotherhood House, Dubbo, which he opened and dedicated in September 1905. A Freemason, Camidge was grand chaplain of the United Grand Lodge of New South Wales in 1888-89. He preached and spoke frequently in Sydney, and as senior bishop in Australia acted as primate in 1909-10.

A fine musician, knowledgeable about art and a keen gardener, he died suddenly on 5 May 1911 at Bishopscourt, Bathurst, and was buried in the churchyard of Holy Trinity Church, Kelso. His estate was valued for probate at £13578. Survived by their adopted daughter, his wife died on 13 May 1914.

Bathurst Times, and *Daily Telegraph* (Syd), and *Evening News* (Syd), 6 May 1911; *SMH*, 6, 8 May 1911; R. M. Teale, The Anglican diocese of Bathurst, 1870-1911 (M.A. thesis, Univ Syd, 1968); S. E. Marsden papers, uncat MS (ML).

RUTH TEALE

CAMPBELL, ALFRED WALTER (1868-1937), neurologist, pathologist and research worker, was born on 18 January 1868 at Cunningham Plains, near Murrumburrah, New South Wales, son of David Henry Campbell, pastoralist, and his wife Amelia Margaret, daughter of T. C. Breillat [q.v.3]. He was educated at Oaklands, Mittagong, and in 1885 entered the medical school of the University of Edinburgh (M.B., Ch.M., 1889; M.D., 1892); he captained the university cricket and football teams. Interested in the developing mental science, he sought experience in various British institutions, then visited the main clinics and laboratories in Europe. In Vienna he was assistant to Krafft-Ebing. He published his first scientific paper – in German – while he was in Prague.

Returning to Britain in 1892, Campbell gained his doctorate with a thesis on 'Alcoholic neuritis: its clinical features and pathology'. That year he was appointed medical officer and director of pathology at Rainhill County Mental Hospital, near Liverpool. His investigations placed him in the forefront of British neuropathologists, and caused the asylum to become a school of the University College, Liverpool, and a Mecca for overseas visitors. His research combined clinical observations with microscopic studies of rare completeness, and he advanced the knowledge of a wide range of ailments. In 1900-03 he completed as intensive study of the histological structure of the human cerebral cortex which defined the functional areas of the brain. His monograph, *Histological studies on the localisation of cerebral function* (Cambridge, 1905), was hailed as a landmark; it was partly illustrated with his own clear drawings.

Campbell returned to Australia in 1905 and next year set up in private practice in Sydney as a specialist in neurology and mental diseases; he became an honorary consultant to the Royal Alexandra Hospital for Children and the Coast (Prince Henry) Hospital. On 30 May 1906 in St Stephen's Presbyterian Church, he married his childhood friend Walterina Jane (Jean) Mackay, daughter of a neighbouring pastoralist.

An honorary captain in the Australian Army Medical Corps Reserve from 1909, Campbell enlisted in the Australian Imperial Force in November 1914 and embarked for Egypt. As a major he served at the 2nd Australian General Hospital in Cairo and organized the treatment of nerve injuries and of the results of mental stress. He returned to Australia in December 1915 and was appointed to the Military Hospital, Randwick. In 1916 he published in the *Medical Journal of Australia* 'Remarks on some neuroses and psychoses in war'. Despite his outstanding ability his advice to segregate mental cases was 'very imperfectly implemented'. After the war he became a consultant to the Department of Repatriation.

Though his busy practice restricted research, Campbell continued to publish numerous papers, notably on further work on the brain, poliomyelitis and 'Australian disease', later known as Murray Valley encephalitis. An able linguist, he also published in French, German and Italian. A member of the Royal Society of New South Wales from 1907, he helped to convene the section of neurology and psychiatry of the New South Wales branch of the British Medical Association in 1924 and was chairman of the section in 1925 and in 1932. Campbell enjoyed golf and knew all names and habits of the birds that found sanctuary in his garden at Rose Bay. Widely read and with a keen sense of humour, he was 'an excellent companion'.

Survived by his wife and two daughters, Campbell died of cancer on 4 November 1937 in his home at Rose Bay and was cremated with Anglican rites. He was 'one of the most scientific, broadminded and able neurological specialists that the country has produced'.

F. Tilney and H. A. Riley, *The form and functions of the central nervous system* (Lond, 1921); F. W. Jones and S. D. Porteus, *The matrix of the mind* (Lond, 1929); J. F. Fulton, *Physiology of the nervous system* (Lond, 1938); A. G. Butler (ed), *Official history of the Australian Army Medical Services... 1914-18*, 3 (Canb, 1943); *MJA*, 22 Jan 1938, and for publications; *Lancet*, 3 Sept 1938.

EDWARD FORD

CAMPBELL, ALLAN (1836-1898), medical practitioner and administrator, was born on 30 April 1836 in Glasgow, Scotland, fifth child of Allan Campbell, print-cutter, and his wife Agnes, née Dawson. Poor health cut short his study of architecture, but he qualified as a homoeopathic physician (L.R.C.P., Edinburgh, L.F.P. & S., Glasgow, 1864) and worked in London. He arrived in Adelaide on 24 January 1867 and practised with Dr H. Wheeler. Next year on 30 April, Campbell married Florence Ann, sister of (Sir) Samuel Way [q.v.].

In 1876 Campbell's practical suggestions formed the basis of the report of the government's commission on sanitation, of which he was a member. It suggested increased power for the Central Board of Health, to which he was later nominated, and the appointment of district health officers. Soon Adelaide became the first Australian capital to undertake a deep-drainage sewage system. When an epidemic struck the city, Campbell and his brother Dr William Macdonald Campbell rented a Currie Street shop which they called the Children's Outpatients' Dispensary, and treated the sick, often free of charge.

He then formed a committee to raise funds to build a hospital for poor children. Two years later the Adelaide Children's Hospital and Training School for Nurses opened; Campbell's architectural knowledge had influenced its design. He lectured there on physiology and hygiene and tended the poor at the Adelaide Homoeopathic Medical Charity. In 1879-91 he was on the board of management of the Adelaide Hospital.

In 1878 Campbell had been elected to the Legislative Council; he remained a member until his death. A liberal free trader, he was no orator, but was exact, 'honest and industrious', studying political economy, Whitaker's *Almanack* and the *Statesman's Yearbook* incessantly. He sat on many parliamentary commissions, one of which recommended progressive reforms for the Adelaide and Parkside lunatic asylums.

In 1889 Campbell was made minister without portfolio to strengthen (Sir) J. A. Cockburn's [q.v.] cabinet, but arguments over its constitutional propriety caused Campbell to resign the appointment after two weeks. In December he spoke at a public meeting to discuss sweated labour among female shirtmakers, showing thorough knowledge of their frequently dehumanizing conditions. A similar sensitivity to the difficulties of the unemployed in the winter of 1893 led him to collaborate with Edith Noble and Rev. B. C. Stephenson to devise a home-nursing scheme for Bowden, one of Adelaide's poorest suburbs. Next year he used his 'social influence and prestige' to extend this project to found the District Trained Nursing Society.

In 1895 the Children's Hospital, whose board Campbell headed, became reputedly the first in the southern hemisphere to set up a specifically bacteriological laboratory for the treatment of typhoid, diphtheria and tuberculosis. Two years later new isolation wards, the Allan Campbell buildings, were added. Campbell saw the projects as 'part and parcel of a great system of public hygiene'. He worked unsparingly on improvements to South Australia's health laws: the innovative Health Act, 1898, carried his stamp, particularly in the clauses relating to infectious diseases. His inaugural address to the Institute of Hygiene and Bacteriology, on tuberculosis and public health, urged government inspection of food supplies. Shortly afterwards another Campbell scheme, the Queen Victoria Home for Convalescent Children at Mount Lofty, was completed.

Survived by his wife, two daughters and six sons, two of whom were doctors, Campbell died of cardio-vascular disease in Adelaide on 30 October 1898 and was buried in North Road cemetery. He had been a prolific anonymous contributor to the *South Australian Register* in an effort to increase public understanding of sanitation, and had belonged to many religious, political, artistic, philanthropic, academic and professional societies. Active in all of them, he was 'no mere figure-head'.

The 'Register' guide to the parliament of South Australia (Adel, 1887); W. F. Morrison, *The Aldine history of South Australia* (Adel, 1890); J. J. Pascoe (ed), *History of Adelaide and vicinity* (Adel, 1901); *PP* (SA), 1876, 2 (18), 1884, 3 (136); *Critic* (Adel), 11 Nov 1899; *Advertiser* (Adel), 28 Jan 1867, 31 Oct, 2 Nov 1898; *Observer* (Adel), 1 Oct, 12 Nov 1887, 14 Dec 1889, 5 Nov 1898; *Register* (Adel), 9, 10 July 1889, 2 July 1897, 10 Sept, 31 Oct 1898; notes and information from Ms M. Barbalet, Wayville, SA; A. Campbell, Notes, *and* Jean Stewart, Letter, Jan 1960 (records, Adel Children's Hospital).

SUZANNE EDGAR

CAMPBELL, ARCHIBALD JAMES (1853-1929), ornithologist, was born on 18 February 1853 at Fitzroy, Victoria, eldest son of Archibald Campbell, who came to Australia in 1840, and his wife Catherine, née Pinkerton, both of Glasgow, Scotland. After education at a private school in Melbourne, Campbell entered the Victorian civil service in 1869, and by 1872 was a weigher in the Department of Trade and Customs; he retired from the Federal Customs Department in July 1914. His interest in nature was aroused in childhood at Werribee where he lived with his grandparents until the age of 10. His first love was egg-collecting, and his general interest in birds was further inspired by study of John Gould's [q.v.1] works at the Public Library.

'A.J.', as he was familiarly known, was described as 'tall, somewhat lean, but suggesting energy and tireless activity, small shrewd eyes . . . with a decidedly humorous twinkle . . . a thick crop of stiff hair, face well covered with a moustache and beard, dressed always in rough surfaced tweed such as Scotchmen love'. He was for many years active in the Field Naturalists' Club of Victoria. The most popular of his accounts, such as *Scraps about bird-nesting*, provide interesting descriptions of rural Melbourne environs. By 1896 his collection of eggs represented 500 species. Campbell initiated the first of several dinners which led to the formation in 1901 of the (Royal) Australasian Ornithologists' Union; he was president in 1909 and 1928 and co-editor of its journal, the *Emu*, for thirteen years.

In the 1890s he had contributed a series of articles on Australian birds to the *Australasian* and in 1905 was a founder of the Bird Observers' Club. In quest of eggs and bird-lore he travelled throughout Australia, often under rough conditions. He scientifically described and named over thirty Australian birds although only a few of these names have resisted synonymy. He published papers on eggs in the *Southern Science Record*, the *Victorian Naturalist* and the *Proceedings* of the Royal Society of Victoria; one was read at the International Ornithological Congress at Budapest in 1891. These papers formed the basis for his major and still useful *Nests and eggs of Australian birds* (1900), in an edition of 600 copies published in both one and two volumes. His pioneer collection, made when custom divided sets of eggs for exchange rather than preserved them as full clutches, is now held in the National Museum of Victoria.

Campbell was elected a colonial member of the British and an honorary fellow of the American ornithologists' unions. He was a keen conservationist, showing concern for disappearing species, and a pioneer bird-photographer (having photographed Lesser Noddies as early as 1889). A lover of acacias, he was founder in 1899 of the Victorian Wattle Club (later League). His descriptive nature-writing was hampered sometimes by studied literary striving, but in less self-conscious moments he showed a youthful sense of fun and an innocent colonial vigour that evokes a freshness of bush scene and experience. He was a member of the board of management of Toorak Presbyterian Church, a tenor in its choir, and an elder of Box Hill Presbyterian Church.

Campbell had married a teacher, Elizabeth Melrose Anderson (d. 1915), at South Yarra on 11 March 1879; they had five children. By his second marriage to Blanche Ida Rose Duncan, a trained nurse, at Toorak on 27 March 1916, he had one son. He died at Box Hill on 11 September 1929 and was buried in St Kilda cemetery.

His eldest son ARCHIBALD GEORGE (1880-1954) was born at South Brighton on 2 May 1880. Educated at Armadale State School and the Working Men's College, he was a student at the School of Horticulture, Burnley, in 1895-98. After three years of orchard-work at Rutherglen he returned to Burnley to lecture. Later he became an orchardist at Pomonal and then from 1913 at Kilsyth.

Archie Campbell had absorbed an interest in birds from his father and he early began field trips in and beyond Victoria. His extensive list of ornithological publications, some important in their time, show attention particularly to distribution, migration and ecology. He was a fellow of the R.A.O.U., an honorary associate in ornithology at the National Museum, and lectured in nature study to the Workers' Educational Association. Deeply interested also in geology, botany and nature appreciation, he filled many notebooks, now preserved at the National Museum. A pocket full of raisins or oatmeal, a water-flask and an overcoat sufficed him for a day or two walking in the Mallee. He was ahead of his time in conservation. In later life a tall, austere, white-haired man, taciturn and ostensibly dourly studious, Campbell was at heart a deeply religious and somewhat mystic romantic, as his manuscript verses and philosophical writing on nature show.

He had married Amy Dethridge on 29 June 1907 in the Australian Church, Melbourne; the eldest of their four sons was killed in World War II. On 19 July 1954 Campbell was accidentally drowned in Dandenong Creek, near Bayswater. He was buried in the Methodist section of Lilydale cemetery.

W. J. Sowden, *Outline history of the wattle blossom celebration in Australia* (Adel, 1913); H. M. Whittell, *The literature of Australian birds* (Perth, 1954); D. L. Serventy and H. M. Whittell, *Birds of Western Australia*, 4th edn (Perth, 1967); *SA Ornithologist*, Oct 1929; *Aust Zoologist*, 5 (1930); *Emu* (Melb), Jan 1930, Oct 1954; *Age*, and *Argus*, and *Sun-News Pictorial*, 12 Sept 1929; Roy A'sian Ornithologists' Union, Records (LATL); Ornithology archival and MS collection (National Museum of Vic); family papers (held by Mr D. Campbell, Beecroft, NSW).   ALLAN McEVEY

CAMPBELL, DONALD (1886-1945), engineer, newspaper proprietor and politician, was born on 16 September 1866 at Robe, South Australia, son of Alexander Campbell, farmer and storekeeper, and his wife Jane, née Draper, immigrants from Glasgow, Scotland, in 1851. Campbell was educated at public schools and at the Collegiate School of St Peter, Adelaide, where he was sent by a neighbouring family as schoolmate for their son. After apprenticeship as an engineer, he 'drifted round the Riverina with a swag, rabbiting, tank-sinking, scrub-cutting'. He worked on Murray River steamers and in the Broken Hill mines, where he was in the 1892 strike. His satirical caricatures of the Broken Hill Proprietary Co. bosses published in Sydney newspapers allegedly led to his dismissal.

His brother Roland had begun the weekly *Millicent Times* in July 1891 and, after his return to South Australia, Donald took it over in 1894. He contributed to the Sydney *Bulletin*, helped run the Millicent flour-mill, built a substantial house, and married on 23 December 1901 Florence May Carne, a schoolteacher. In his editorship of the *Millicent Times* he proved an able journalist, concerned with local issues though not afraid to write strongly on wider questions. His pro-Boer sympathies and attacks on local landed proprietors brought him disfavour. Faced with competition, he sold his printing business in December 1905 to a group which set up the *South Eastern Times*.

Campbell had also been clerk to the shire district council of Kennion and secretary of the Millicent Caledonian Society. In 1906 he stood as a Labor candidate for Victoria and Albert in the House of Assembly. Though platform-shy, he was elected after a campaign in which reform of the Legislative Council franchise was a dominant issue. In parliament he refused to join commissions and committees, concentrating on local affairs but retaining his concern for the powers of the Lower House against the Upper.

Campbell also matriculated and studied law (LL.B., 1912) while a member of parliament. On losing his seat in 1912, he became Australian representative on the Dominions royal commission on Empire trade, an appointment which took him overseas. His private travels in Africa and Egypt were recorded in his book *Wayfarings among the Pharaohs* (Adelaide, 1923).

Returning to Adelaide in 1915, Campbell practised law. Hampered by deafness and recovering from a stroke, he moved to Bordertown in 1919, editing the *Border Chronicle* and continuing legal practice. His editorials and political opinions had a force and authority rare among provincial newspapers. He retired from the paper in December 1931, doing some legal work in his last years in Bordertown, Gawler and Adelaide. He died at North Walkerville on 21 October 1945, survived by his wife, three sons and three daughters.

There was nothing superficial about Campbell. He was a man of industry, scholarship and humour, who thought deeply, read widely and expressed himself fluently. A kindly man, fond of gardening and devoted to his family, he made his mark in several spheres, but above all as a forthright and gifted journalist.

Freelance, *The birth of a country newspaper* (Mt Gambier, nd); G. C. Newman, *From student's lamp to lawyer's gown* (Adel, 1912); J. Melano, *Walking tall* (Adel, 1973); *Worker* (Syd), 6 May 1905; *Border Chronicle*, 25 Dec 1931; *Advertiser* (Adel), 23 Oct 1945; *South Eastern Times*, 26 Oct 1945; information from Miss B. Campbell, Payneham South, SA.   R. M. GIBBS

CAMPBELL, EDWARD (1883-1944), businessman and lord mayor, was born on 26 May 1883 at Footscray, Victoria, second son of Edward Campbell (d. 1931), Scottish-born engineer, and his wife Annie Smith, sister of James Cuming junior [q.v.]. Young Edward was educated at Yarraville State School, University High School and Wesley College. In the mid-1880s his father had managed the Victorian Sugar Co.'s refinery at Yarraville, but about 1889 he established a blacksmithing and engineering business in Carlton. Edward was apprenticed to his father in

1900, but received no special privileges as the owner's son.

After completing his apprenticeship, Campbell was sent to Edinburgh in 1907 to study structural engineering. He returned to Australia in 1909 and was soon appointed a governing director of his father's firm. On 4 May 1910 at St Columb's Church, Hawthorn, he married Beatrice Caffin; they made their home in East St Kilda. In 1913 the firm of Edward Campbell & Son Pty Ltd was formed, and a year later it was joined by Edward's elder brother James, an accountant.

Campbell enlisted in the Australian Imperial Force in March 1917, embarking in the *Nestor* for England in June. He spent some months at the engineers' and signallers' depot at Parkhouse camp, Wiltshire, before serving in the battles of Mont St Quentin and the Hindenburg Line as a sapper in the 14th Field Company. After his return home in May 1919 he resumed activities in the family business, later becoming chairman and managing director. In the 1920s and 1930s the company supplied structural steel for many major buildings in Melbourne, including St Andrew's Hospital, East Melbourne.

In 1921 Campbell gained a seat in the Melbourne City Council as a member for Smith Ward. He was a representative of the council on the Melbourne and Metropolitan Board of Works and served on three of its committees. Elected lord mayor in 1937, he strongly opposed government proposals to reform the city council's constitution. Next year he failed by four votes to win a second term of office.

Campbell regularly attended the meetings of the Old Wesley Collegians' Association. A Freemason, he was a foundation member of the Wesley Collegians' Lodge and of the Victorian Engineers' Lodge No. 411. He and his wife worked untiringly for various charities, especially the Children's and Prince Henry hospitals, and Campbell was made a life governor of the Royal Victorian Institute for the Blind in 1938. During World War II he travelled extensively to raise money for the Australian Comforts Fund, of which he was an executive member. In 1942 he was appointed C.B.E. He was a great gardener. A charming and unassuming man, he had a keen sense of public responsibility and was generous with his time to those who sought his assistance.

Campbell died of coronary vascular disease in hospital at Richmond on 6 August 1944 and was cremated. He was survived by his wife, three sons and three daughters, and left an estate valued for probate at £64 742.

Argus, 11, 30 Oct 1937, 6, 16, 29 Apr, 11 Oct 1938, 8 Aug 1944; *Age*, 7 Aug 1944; information from Mr K. Campbell, Sunbury, Vic.

C. G. T. WEICKHARDT

CAMPBELL, ELIZABETH (BESSIE) (1870-1964), banjoist, was born on 21 July 1870 in Melbourne, daughter of Irish parents John Christopher Campbell (d. 1912), wigmaker and hotelkeeper, and his second wife Eliza, née McMullen. Her father was born in Dublin and worked for Madame Tussaud, before migrating to Victoria about 1849. He continued his trades and exhibited waxworks; in the early 1870s the family moved to Sydney.

In 1884 Bessie went to London with her parents; she recorded that she 'took a great fancy to the five-stringed banjo' and was taught by Joe Daniels. After returning to Sydney next year, she learned for three months from the American Hosea Easton. In the early 1890s she studied under Walter Stent who taught her different American 'systems of finger-picking' (playing different arpeggio arrangements with the thumb and fingers); she deplored people who used a plectrum.

Bessie Campbell began to appear in concerts for charity about 1891. In September 1893 she played a solo at the American Banjo Club's concert at the Centenary Hall, York Street, in aid of the Seamen's Mission. By 1897 she had been acclaimed as 'Australia's greatest lady banjoist', had become the first female member of the American Banjo Club (founded by Stent in 1892), and was receiving 'six to eight letters a week for concerts great and small'. In April 1904 she was paid five guineas for appearing at the Bathurst agricultural show. Billed as 'The Banjo Queen', in 1907 she toured the northern rivers with the National Concert Company: one critic found her 'a wonder for she plays the banjo with so much ability as to render it almost a classical instrument'. Nevertheless she had had to contend with a good deal of prejudice against it.

At this time Bessie had 'a petite, pretty figure . . . soulful eyes, and the peach bloom complexion of an Andalusian . . . quick nervous ways that betray an inexhaustible amount of activity, and much talent'. She liked to include Christy-minstrel songs and Negro spirituals in her repertoire and was often accompanied on the piano by her sister Fanny. She made friends with many theatre people, such as Nellie Stewart [q.v.]. During World War I, at the peak of her professional career, she gave frequent performances for servicemen and the Australian Red Cross Society.

After the war Bessie held benefit concerts

for the Western Suburbs Leagues Club and the Returned Sailors' and Soldiers' Imperial League. She was also involved in charitable work for Burwood Municipal Council and in the 1920s was the honorary secretary of the Wanderers' Club. By the early 1930s arthritis was making it difficult for her to play and she never made commercial recordings. During her latter years she shared a house at Burwood with her brother Jack, who had also been involved in show business for J. C. Williamson's [q.v.6]. She was a great follower of cricket.

Bessie Campbell did not marry but she had never lacked suitors. She died on 28 April 1964 at Burwood, and was buried in the Anglican section of Rookwood cemetery.

G. Shearston, 'Bessie Campbell: Australia's queen of the banjo', *Aust Tradition*, Oct 1966; *Daily Telegraph* (Syd), 14 Sept 1893; *Clarion* (Grafton), 2 Jan 1907; diaries and news-cuttings held by and information from Mr & Mrs T. J. Ball, Rhodes, NSW.   PAUL COMRIE-THOMSON

CAMPBELL, ERIC (1893-1970), solicitor and leader of the New Guard, was born on 11 April 1893 at Young, New South Wales, fourth son of native-born parents Allan Campbell, solicitor, and his wife Florence Mary, née Russell. He was educated privately and was a cadet-member of the Coronation Contingent which visited England in 1911. While an articled clerk in his father's office, he was commissioned in 1914 in the volunteer Australian Field Artillery. In April 1916 he joined the Australian Imperial Force as a lieutenant and was promoted captain in May and major next year. He served first in France with the 27th battery of the 7th A.F.A. From August 1917 until the Armistice he was with the 12th Australian (Army) Field Artillery Brigade, attached to General Headquarters, in Flanders, on the Somme, and in the final advance to the Hindenburg Line. He was gassed in November 1917, twice mentioned in dispatches in 1918, and was awarded the Distinguished Service Order in January 1919.

Campbell returned to Australia in February, resumed his legal studies and was admitted as a solicitor on 29 August 1919. In 1920-26 he was in partnership with S. G. Rowe, then established with his brothers Campbell, Campbell & Campbell, a successful practice with a clientele of pastoralists, merchants, professional men and financial institutions. On 22 October 1924 at Memagong station, near Young, he married Nancy Emma Browne, daughter of a grazier. In 1931 he was a reputable businessman

living at Turramurra: a director of Australian Soaps Ltd, Discount and Finance Ltd and other companies, he belonged to the Imperial Service Club, the Union and New South Wales clubs and Royal Sydney and Killara Golf clubs; he was also a Freemason and a member of the Rotary Club of Sydney. He was fond of tennis, gardening, surfing and motoring.

Actively interested in the militia, Campbell commanded the 9th Field Artillery Brigade in 1924 and was promoted lieut-colonel next year; he was transferred to the reserve in 1932. He first turned to paramilitary activity in 1925: with Major John Scott [q.v.] he recruited a secret force of 500 ex-officers to try to put down a seamen's strike. In 1930 he became recruitment officer for the committee run by (Sir) Robert Gillespie and (Sir) Philip Goldfinch [qq.v.], a secret vigilante group of businessmen, ex-officers and graziers alarmed by the Depression and the election of J. T. Lang's [q.v.] Labor government; they were later known as the Old Guard. At a meeting at the Imperial Service Club on 18 February 1931 Campbell, disappointed with the Old Guard, was the principal founder of the New Guard, which stressed loyalty to the throne and British Empire, and wanted 'sane and honourable' government and the 'abolition of machine politics'; Campbell saw patriotism as its key virtue. The guard aimed at uniting 'all loyal citizens irrespective of creed, party, social or financial position'. As general officer commanding, Campbell organized it on military lines. He claimed that in an 'emergency' it could maintain essential services including Bunnerong power house; the police attested to the guard's efficiency. With a peak membership of over 50 000, the guard rallied in public, broke up 'Communist' meetings, drilled, vilified the Labor Party and demanded the deportation of Communists.

In January 1932 Campbell asserted that Lang would never open the Harbour Bridge, referred to him as a 'tyrant and scoundrel', and claimed to prefer Ebenezer (Lang's bull) as premier. Fined £2 at Central Police Court for using insulting language, Campbell successfully appealed. In the tense atmosphere of early 1932, rumours were rife that the New Guard was plotting a coup or the kidnapping of Lang; but Captain F. de Groot's Harbour Bridge ribbon-cutting antics were an anti-climax and the guard's popularity began to wane after eight of its members were charged with assaulting J. S. (Jock) Garden [q.v.]. After raiding its headquarters, the police, according to the *Labor Daily* (7 June), were about to lay charges of conspiracy against Campbell when Lang was dismissed by the governor.

With the easing of tension, members of the New Guard melted away, and there was dissension among those remaining as Campbell grew more authoritarian and militant. In 1933 he visited Europe and met Fascist leaders; next year he published *The new road*, a case for Fascism and Mussolini's 'corporate state'. He tried to take the remnant of the guard into party politics and formed the Centre Movement, but was defeated for Lane Cove at the 1935 State election.

In 1938 Campbell was charged with conspiracy to prevent the course of justice and to cheat and defraud Du Menier Laboratories Ltd, a subsidiary of Australian Soaps Ltd, of which he was chairman. He was acquitted. Next year, arising out of an Equity suit brought by him, Judge (R. H.) Long Innes [q.v.] submitted a report alleging that Campbell had committed perjury; however, the Full Court ruled that the charges were not sustained and that his name should not be struck from the roll of solicitors; but it directed him to pay costs. In 1941 he returned to Billaboola, part of Memagong station. He practised in Young, was president of Burrangong Shire Council in 1949-50, and bought a property near Yass where he settled in 1957. In 1961 he threatened a libel suit against *Nation* for an article on 11 March on the New Guard: no further articles appeared. He published his own account, *The rallying point* (Melbourne), in 1965. Next year he moved to Canberra where he practised, but his health was increasingly impaired by serious injuries received in an accident in 1959.

Survived by his wife, two sons and two daughters, Campbell died of cancer on 2 September 1970 in Canberra and was cremated after a Presbyterian service. Good-looking, with a neat military moustache, he had a certain panache: in retrospect he had 'thoroughly enjoyed' the experience of the New Guard and 'the association with so many grand loyal Australians'.

K. Amos, *The New Guard movement 1931-1935* (Melb, 1976); P. Mitchell, 'Australian patriots: a study of the New Guard', *Aust Economic Hist Review*, Mar 1969; *SMH*, 12, 16 Jan, 3 Feb, 9 Mar 1932, 28 Feb 1934, 9 June 1938, 13, 15, 17, 21-22, 28-29 Sept, 1, 8 Oct 1938, 28 Feb, 1-3, 8 Mar, 6 Apr 1939, 4 Sept 1970; Col Sec file B568 (NSWA).

KEITH AMOS

CAMPBELL, FREDERICK ALEXANDER (1849-1930), engineer and educationist, was born on 27 November 1849 at Melrose, Scotland, son of Rev. Alexander James Campbell, Free Church minister, and his wife Mary Turner Wedderburn, née Heriot-Maitland, granddaughter of the earl of Lauderdale. In 1859 Alexander accepted a call to Brighton, Victoria. On arrival, however, he was appointed to St George's, Geelong, and was active in establishing Geelong College and the Presbyterian Theological Hall.

Frederick was a foundation student at Geelong College. Matriculating in 1871, he reflected his father's missionary interests by travelling in the Pacific. On his return he published *A year in the New Hebrides, Loyalty Islands, and New Caledonia* (Melbourne, 1872). Among a collection of plants that he brought back was a new species of *Pittosporum*, which (Sir) Ferdinand Mueller [q.v.5] named after him.

Campbell enrolled at the University of Melbourne in 1875, and graduated with the Certificate of Engineer in 1879 (M.C.E., 1898). On 1 July 1879 he was appointed assistant engineer to the railways branch of the New South Wales Department of Public Works, and was based at Tamworth, Glen Innes, Bolivia and Deepwater before his services were dispensed with in May 1886. In Brisbane on 16 April 1884 he married Mary Pitts. During these years he published in the *Transactions and Proceedings* of the Royal Society of Victoria — of which he became a council-member in 1893-1900 — several papers on the properties of Australian timbers and on the effects of wind pressures on the stability of structures.

In March 1887 Campbell was appointed secretary and director of the Working Men's College in Melbourne (Royal Melbourne Institute of Technology). His father's long association with Francis Ormond [q.v.5] may have assisted his claims. Always a pragmatist where technical education was concerned, Campbell canvassed widely for support for the new institution. He was no doubt aware that his appointment had aroused the ire of the Trades Hall, whose candidate D. Bennet [q.v.3] was not selected. In an initiative rare in Australian education, Campbell offered to teach students what they wanted to be taught. The college initially succeeded beyond expectations: there were 2000 students within two years. Its trade classes were an interesting innovation, for they broke with the received wisdom that technical education should not concern itself with workshop training.

In the 1890s Campbell faced two major problems. Government subsidies were abolished and replaced by capitation grants, with a disastrous effect for some years on enrolments, subjects taught and morale. His second problem, the unpreparedness of many of the students for any form of technical college work, was partially solved in 1898 by the inauguration of full-time preparatory classes. Another important innovation was the establishment of full-time, three-year diploma courses in 1899.

The royal commission into technical education in 1899-1901 did little either to reform the technical schools of Victoria or to improve their position. Campbell continued to write and agitate for the development of training in the skilled trades, and for technical colleges to take over apprentice-training functions previously carried out by the master. His closing years at the college were clouded by bitter internal disputes. A government board of inquiry in 1910-11 exonerated him and praised his services, but Campbell's position *vis-a-vis* his council was of extreme difficulty. He retired in ill health in 1913.

Campbell lived in active retirement for many years. In 1921 he was decorated by the Belgian government for his war-work, and he advised on the vocational training of returned soldiers. He was an active churchman, following his wife's Anglican persuasion, a keen and successful golfer, and an amateur artist of merit. He read in history and the arts, was a knowledgeable gardener and numbered among his friends Frederick McCubbin and Sir John MacFarland [qq.v.]. He had published *Some facts, opinions, and conclusions about technical education* (1898), *Education and industry in Victoria* (1907), and *The Working Men's College in the making 1897-1913* (1925).

Predeceased by his wife, Campbell died on 13 February 1930. He was buried in Boroondara cemetery and was survived by a son.

PP (LA Vic), 1911, 1st S, 2 (14); *Argus*, 7 Mar 1887, 14 Feb 1930; *Age*, 14 Feb 1930; S. Murray-Smith, A history of technical education in Australia (Ph.D. thesis, Univ Melb, 1966).

S. MURRAY-SMITH

CAMPBELL, GERALD ROSS (1858-1942), barrister, soldier and publicist, was born on 21 July 1858 at Paddington, Sydney, son of Scottish parents Alexander Campbell [q.v.3] and his second wife Sarah Robertson, née Murray. Educated in Scotland at the Royal Academy, Tain, County Ross and Cromarty, and at Craigmount House School, Edinburgh, he returned to attend the University of Sydney and graduated B.A. in 1880 with first-class honours in classics (M.A., 1884). Admitted to the Bar on 31 October 1882, he practised at Denman Chambers and joined the Australian Club. On 25 August 1897 at St Cuthbert's parish church, Bedfordshire, England, he married Mary Fraser; she bore him two sons and died in 1902. On 26 April 1905 in Sydney he married Marion Veitch Mein; they were childless.

More interested in soldiering than the law, Campbell had helped to raise the 1st Regiment, New South Wales Scottish Rifles, in 1885 and next year was commissioned captain. Promoted major in 1894 and lieut-colonel in 1898, he commanded the regiment until 1907. As colonel he commanded the Sydney Fortress (Garrison Troops) in 1907-09.

Campbell fiercely believed in universal, adult military training on the Swiss system and in 1905 took the initiative in forming the New South Wales division of the Australian National Defence League; he was joint honorary secretary with W. M. Hughes [q.v.]. Although Hughes sometimes stumped the country for the league, Campbell was its real head and heart. Single-minded and tireless in his advocacy, he badgered every prime minister and minister for defence: he repudiated the Victorian division for trying voluntarism first and feuded with (Sir) George Reid [q.v.] for equivocating on the issue. When thwarted, he was caustic. 'There is going to be a good deal of trouble', (Sir) Thomas Ewing [q.v.], minister for defence in 1908, warned him, 'but stick to it, and in public give your advice in the friendliest way you can. You are rather inclined to write in Doric'. Campbell edited the league's quarterly journal, the *Call*, and listed Federal election candidates who were 'sound' on defence. At its zenith in 1909 the league had nineteen branches and some 1500 members, but suddenly diminished in membership after the Defence Act that year provided for compulsory training of youths.

In 1914 Campbell was appointed to the State committee for the selection of officers for the Australian Imperial Force. In 1915 and 1916-17 he served with the Sea Transport Service as officer commanding troops for two voyages to Egypt and England, and retired from the army as honorary brigadier general in 1920. Meanwhile the league advocated conscription and in 1919 raised its voice against any reduction in compulsory training but it was feeble and out of harmony with the times. Campbell remained honorary secretary until its demise in 1938.

After the war he lived at The Dell, Moss Vale, where he was largely content to garden and to administer his father's estate. After suffering from paralysis agitans for fourteen years, Campbell died at his home on 30 November 1942 and was buried in the Presbyterian section of Bong Bong cemetery. He was survived by his second wife, and by his sons: the younger, Major General Ian Ross Campbell, C.B.E., D.S.O., served with distinction in Crete in World War II and in Korea, and became commandant of the Royal Military College, Duntroon, Australian Capital Territory.

Aust National Defence League (NSW Division), Minute-books and correspondence, 1905-38 (AWM); records (AWM); family information.

JOHN BARRETT

CAMPBELL, JAMES (1830-1904), businessman and manufacturer, was born on 6 March 1830 at Auchterarder, Perthshire, Scotland, son of John Campbell, farmer, and his wife Helen, née Morison. Trained as a plasterer, he took an assisted passage to Moreton Bay, arriving in Brisbane by the *John Fielding* on 12 June 1853. Finding little work at his trade, Campbell took other building jobs and opened a store for building materials in George Street in 1854; he soon moved to Creek Street. Demand increased substantially in the 1860s and Campbell found an expanding market for the lime, cement and plaster he won from the corals of Moreton Bay. In the 1870s he began milling and selling timber procured initially near Brisbane and Ipswich. He also purchased several ships and built up a thriving shipping trade. The firm James Campbell & Sons was founded in 1882.

The exhaustion of local timber forced Campbell to cover much of the coast from Gympie to Kyogle, New South Wales, with numerous mills. The sawn timber was shipped to the firm's wharf near Creek Street in its own ships. In the 1880s and 1890s the firm diversified its activities, prefabricating houses and buying Petrie's quarry at Albion, the Buderim sugar-mill and the Redbank brickworks. In 1896 it became a limited liability company.

Campbell was described as quick tempered, easily provoked and easily appeased. A born fighter and political radical, he was involved in the Queensland Liberal Association of the 1850s, spent two years as an alderman of the Brisbane Municipal Council and was also a member of the Ithaca Shire Council. A frequent press correspondent on what he saw as injustices, he was an unofficial spokesman for migrants, particularly Scots, and befriended many. He was an ardent advocate of improved working conditions and gave his men the eight-hour day willingly. He refused, however, to accept trade unions, but was respected by his men for his strong personality and genuine charity.

Throughout his life Campbell remained a strong Scots patriot, and was a committee-member of the Caledonian Society from its inception in 1861 and of the Queensland Scottish Association. He visited Scotland after his retirement in 1896. Brought up as a rigid Calvinist destined for the Presbyterian ministry, he rebelled and became aggressively anti-clerical. He died of chronic hepatitis on 11 April 1904 at his home at Kelvin Grove, Brisbane, and was buried in Toowong cemetery. At his own request there were no religious rites but his old friend S. W. Brooks [q.v.3] delivered a eulogy at the graveside. In memory of his foundation membership of the Brisbane Gymnasium, a son equipped a gymnasium at Fortitude Valley.

Campbell had married Mary Isabella Mitchell at Callender, Perthshire, in February 1853; seven children survived him. His daughters married William Aplin [q.v.3], (Sir) Robert Philp and James Forsyth [qq.v.]. Of his sons, JOHN DUNMORE (1854-1909) was born in Brisbane on 19 April 1854 and was baptized by Rev. John Dunmore Lang [q.v.2]. Educated at the Brisbane Normal School, he left early to join his father's business. He received a partnership in James Campbell & Sons and when the firm became a limited company in 1896 was appointed chairman and managing director. Particularly interested in the timber trade, he spent many years in the north coast district mainly at the firm's Coochin Creek sawmill, Campbellville. A strong advocate of reafforestation, he was elected to the Caboolture Divisional Board in 1883 and urged the government to open up the district with a railway. He spent nine years in local government and in 1889-90 was president of the Brisbane Chamber of Commerce. Concerned, too, with the improvement of harbour facilities, he was a member of the Queensland Marine Board in 1890-99.

Campbell won West Moreton in the Legislative Assembly in 1899 and held it until just before his death. He opposed Federation, believing that it was premature and could damage Queensland, and he had a brief undistinguished term as minister for railways in the 1907-08 ministry of his brother-in-law Philp. Outside politics Campbell was associated with many organizations. He was a councillor of the Industrial Association of Queensland in 1890-93, a vice-president of the Queensland Employers' Association in 1893-96, and a member of the Brisbane Hospital Committee of Management in 1893-1907. From 1894 to 1905 he was a vice-president of the Queensland Rugby Union. A visit to England and the United States of America in 1906 stimulated his interest in migration and in 1907 he was president of the Queensland

Immigration League. He died of cerebro-vascular disease on 19 June 1909 and was buried in Toowong cemetery with Presbyterian forms. His estate, valued for probate at £13067, was left for the benefit of his wife Mary, née Cameron, whom he had married at Brisbane on 11 May 1876, and their nine surviving children.

His brother CHARLES WILLIAM (1871-1949) was born in Brisbane on 28 May 1871 and educated at Brisbane Grammar School. Managing the firm's Albion sawmill, he pioneered the export of Queensland timber to Melbourne by rail. He was an alderman of the Hamilton Municipal Council in 1912-19 and mayor in 1916-17; when Hamilton was absorbed by 'Greater Brisbane', he represented the suburb on the Brisbane City Council in 1926-31. Chairman of the Clayfield Nationalist Political Association, he was president of the Queensland Employers' Federation for fourteen years and was connected also with the Brisbane Timber Merchants' and Timber Export associations, and the Queensland Society for the Prevention of Cruelty to Animals. In his youth he was a well-known boxer and crack rifle-shot. In April 1897 he had married Minnie Hill; they had six children. He died at Clayfield on 3 July 1949 and was cremated. His estate was valued for probate at £33 584 in Queensland and £3181 in New South Wales.

Queensland and Queenslanders (Brisb, 1936); 'Pioneering Queensland families', *Steering Wheel*, Dec 1936, Jan 1937; *Telegraph* (Brisb), 11 Apr 1904; *Brisbane Courier*, 13 Apr 1904, 21 June 1909; *Sunday Mail* (Brisb), 6 June 1954, supp; J. Whiteley, Two families of early Brisbane (B.A. Hons thesis, Univ Qld, 1962).   A. L. LOUGHEED

CAMPBELL, JAMES LANG (1858-1936), judge, was born on 28 November 1858, son of George Murray Campbell of Lochgilphead, Argyleshire, Scotland, and his wife Christina. He was brought to Australia about 1865. Educated privately, for some eight years he pursued pastoral and mining interests in Queensland, then was employed in New South Wales by the Australian Joint Stock Bank. While a bank officer he read in the chambers of R. E. O'Connor [q.v.]. He was admitted to the Bar on 17 August 1886.

On 9 September 1885 Campbell had married Laura Augusta Georgina (Lily), eldest daughter of Roger Gadsden, a London barrister; they were childless. He was acting secretary to the attorney-general in 1887-88, then commenced private practice. Although successful, his forensic weapon was the

bludgeon, not the rapier; his convoluted sentences were notorious, but so was his remarkable diligence. He became a standing counsel for the State taxation commissioners and for the Crown in closer settlement resumptions, taking silk in 1910. During World War I he was a committee-member of the Universal Service League and in 1919 was royal commissioner on the coal-trade inquiry.

Campbell's appointment as a Supreme Court judge in August 1922 was criticized because of his age. R. C. Teece [q.v.] recalled that 'despite his success at the Bar, he was a very poor lawyer'. His judicial term was distinguished most by problems arising out of his failure to stand down on reaching the statutory retiring age of seventy. He had publicly given the date of his birth as 1860 but, in *Celebrity Pictures Pty. Ltd.* v. *Turnbull* (1929), it was alleged that he had already attained his seventieth birthday and that his hearing the case rendered it void. A summons was brought before another judge to set aside the verdict. A Scottish birth certificate was tendered and Campbell was called as a witness. The summons was dismissed, but parliament was persuaded to legislate in 1929 'to validate certain judicial acts of the Honourable James Lang Campbell'. Sir Owen Dixon, describing this as 'a curious if not remarkable, incident in the history of our courts', pointed out that remedial legislation was unnecessary: the judge, having acted with colourable authority, was invested with jurisdiction by the common law unless challenged in the very exercise of that authority.

Campbell, while a judge, inquired in 1924 as a royal commissioner into the costs of production and distribution of gas by the Manly Gas Co. Ltd, and in 1927 presided over the court of inquiry into the Sydney Harbour collision between the *Tahiti* and the ferry *Greycliffe*. After retiring in May 1929 he acted as royal commissioner in 1930 on a controversial inquiry into mining leases at Mungana and Chillagoe in Queensland, involving E. G. Theodore and W. McCormack [qq.v.] whom he found 'guilty of fraud and dishonesty'; Theodore denounced Campbell as 'merely a pensioner in retirement'.

Survived by his wife, Campbell died at his home, Caradon, Woollahra, on 7 December 1936. His estate, including The Bowery, near Coolah, was valued for probate at £3430.

Owen Dixon, *Jesting pilate* (Syd, 1965); K. H. Kennedy, *The Mungana affair* (Brisb, 1978); *V&P* (LA NSW), 1887-88, 1, 558; *Weekly Notes* (NSW), 46 (1929); *SMH*, 31 Aug 1922, 10 Nov 1927, 23 May, 21 June 1929, 9 Dec 1936; R. C. Teece, Reminiscences (held by NSW Bar Assn, Syd); Halse-Rogers, J., Note-book, 1929 (NSWA).   J. M. BENNETT

CAMPBELL, JOHN ARCHIBALD (1854-1916), pastoralist, was born on 28 June 1854 at Bullock Creek, Victoria, second son of Donald Campbell (1813-1868) and his wife Margaret, née Sinclair. Donald, a bounty immigrant who had arrived in Sydney on 8 November 1841 in the *Trinidad* from Elleric, Argyllshire, Scotland, was one of the many hard-working, ambitious Highlanders who fled from the great distress in Scotland after the Napoleonic wars. He overlanded to Gippsland in 1842 with sheep, discovering the first practical land route from Port Albert to Western Port, and squatted at Bullock Creek (near the site of Bendigo) in 1846, opening Campbell's (or Bullock Creek) Camping Ground and Inn. He married Margaret Sinclair on 6 February 1851 at the Free Presbyterian Church, Melbourne; their elder son Donald (b. 1852) was drowned in 1860 at Glengower, near Clunes where Campbell had moved as manager for or partner of Hugh Glass [q.v.4] sometime after 1854. Campbell built the Glengower Hotel to cater for the goldfields population; near-by Campbelltown was named after him in 1861. He died suddenly at Glengower on 26 January 1868, leaving an estate valued for probate at £18 000.

John Archibald was tutored privately before attending Ballarat College and then Scotch College, Melbourne, but he had to leave school after his father's death. He worked at the London Chartered Bank until he came of age, and then spent some four years inspecting country before buying, on 18 September 1879, Murrill Creek, near Narrandera, New South Wales. At St Kilda, on 18 November 1879 he married Jane (d. 1939) only child of John Gordon of Borambola, Wagga Wagga, New South Wales. Selling out of Murrill Creek profitably he entered into partnership with his father-in-law in a large grazing property, Dungalear, at Walgett, shearing 100 000 sheep, which he purchased in 1885 when Gordon returned to England. In 1887 Campbell formed a partnership with W. P. McGregor of Broken Hill to buy Tubbo, Narrandera, from the estate of his wife's uncle, John Peter [q.v.5]; as managing director he built it into one of the finest wool-producing properties in the colony. Noted for his fine merino wool, stud sheep and cattle, Campbell was also a keen judge of thoroughbred horses and bred the Grand National Hurdle winner, Wingarra.

Campbell was one of the originators in 1890 of the Pastoralists' Association of Victoria and Southern Riverina (president in 1902-06) and was a New South Wales representative on the Pastoralists' Federal Council of Australia. He was heavily involved in the negotiations with the Amalgamated Shearers' Union of Australasia (later the Australian Workers' Union) at the time of the 1890 shearers' strike, and was one of the ten signatories to the famous freedom of contract agreement on 7 August 1891. Although firm and determined, Campbell was also a liberal man, always in favour of doing 'a fair thing' by the shearers, leaving them no reasonable cause for complaint. President of the Pastoralists' Union of Southern Riverina from 1906, his forceful and masterful addresses were appreciated for their practical knowledge, and he took a leading part in the lengthy arbitration proceedings with the A.W.U. A vice-president of the Australian Sheepbreeders' Association, he was appointed in December 1915 to the local board of advice of Dalgety [q.v.4] & Co. Ltd, and at the time of his death he was a growers' representative on the Central Wool Committee formed to arrange the sale of the Australian woolclip to the British government.

Campbell suffered from a duodenal ulcer. Saddened by the deaths on active service in France of two of his sons on 3 September and 7 October 1916, he died suddenly on 9 December at his home Ottawa, Irving Road, Toorak. Mourned throughout the pastoral industry, he was buried in Kew cemetery. He was survived by his wife, two sons and four daughters. His estate in Victoria was valued for probate at £21 115 and in New South Wales at £120 030.

Campbell's youngest son John Alan (1899-1939) who was educated at Melbourne Church of England Grammar School and Jesus College, Cambridge, was an outstanding oarsman. Before enlisting in the Royal Air Force he rowed in the Melbourne Grammar first crew from 1915 to 1918 when he was captain of boats. At Cambridge he rowed in the winning crews of 1920 and 1921 when he was president of boats. He represented England in the winning inter-allied peace regatta crew in Paris in 1919 and rowed in the winning Leander crew at the 1920 Olympic Games. He bought Dungalear from his father's estate in 1924 for £185 000, and later Soho, Drysdale, Victoria. At Melbourne Grammar on 6 February 1923 he married Beatrice Helen Chambers, who survived him together with their three children when he died on 5 February 1939 of pneumonia; he was buried in Boroondara cemetery, Kew. He left an estate in Victoria valued for probate at £42 836 and in New South Wales at £98 325.

E. J. Brady, *Australia unlimited* (Melb, 1918); G. C. Drinkwater and T. R. B. Sanders (eds), *The University boat race* (Lond, 1929); Clanalder Archives, *Historical papers, no. 1 – Campbelltown*, J. Alderson ed (Maryborough, Vic, 1967); *Pastoral Review*, Dec 1893, May 1905, Aug 1906, Nov 1910, Dec 1916, Jan 1917; *Scottish A'sian*, Jan 1917;

Argus, 11 Dec 1916; *Australasian*, 24 Oct 1936; information from Dr J. G. Campbell, Toorak, Vic.

MARGARET CARNEGIE

CAMPBELL, JOHN FAUNA (1853-1938), surveyor, was born on 21 August 1853 at Loch Leven, Kinross-shire, Scotland, second son of Donald Campbell and his wife Jane (Jean), née Robertson. After schooling at Redgorton and Monzie, Perthshire, he was apprenticed to an architect, then he migrated to Dunedin, New Zealand, in 1879. After employment with the New Zealand Public Works Department and the Southland Agricultural Co., Campbell reached Sydney on 3 January 1881. Here he adopted the name 'Fauna' for identification purposes. He joined the Department of Lands as a cadet draftsman and was soon promoted. Completing examinations, he was registered as a licensed surveyor on 10 January 1884, and that year attended W. H. Warren's [q.v.6] lectures in engineering at the University of Sydney; he was registered as valuer in August 1894.

Late in 1888 Campbell was sent to the Walcha district of the Armidale Land Board. On 7 February 1889 in Sydney he married Althea Louisa Gissing, an Englishwoman. Well-known locally, he served on the Walcha Municipal Council for eight years. Until 1903 he pioneered cadastral survey of southern New England, recording his intimate knowledge of rural development before intensive settlement. A member of the Linnean Society of New South Wales, he studied and collected new botanical specimens, working with Ernst Betche [q.v.3], and with J. H. Maiden [q.v.] who named a papilionaceae *Pultenaea campbellii* after him. His geological notes were incorporated in Sir Edgeworth David's [q.v.] *Geological map of the Commonwealth of Australia* (1931). In 1903 Campbell moved to Sydney for the education of his children. He returned to New England as crown representative and chairman of the Armidale Forest Board in 1906-07 and was surveyor to the Closer Settlement Advisory Board from 1909, advising on land valuation, improvements and subdivision in the Monaro and Riverina.

An active member of the Institution of Surveyors, New South Wales, from 1893, Campbell was a council-member in 1909-12, and published sixteen papers in the *Surveyor*. Retirement from December 1913 at his Burwood home was creative and fruitful. He regularly contributed scientific articles to newspapers, chiefly for the *Sydney Morning Herald*'s column 'On the land'. He was president of the metropolitan branch of the Farmers and Settlers' Association in 1915-17. In 1916 he seconded a proposal for a national soil and feature survey to aid post-war settlement and increase production; to further this campaign he published *Story of the soil* (1917).

Campbell's varied interests crystallized around history as he delved into land settlement. He was a council-member of the Royal Australian Historical Society in the 1920s: 'The discovery and early settlement of New England' was the first of twenty-eight papers that he published in its *Journal and Proceedings*. A reticent man who combined the practical and scientific, Campbell shunned publicity but had 'unflagging zeal and patience' in detailed research. His publications remain a valuable source on early settlement.

Survived by his wife, two sons and a daughter, Campbell died in the Masonic Hospital, Ashfield, on 25 January 1938 and was cremated with Anglican rites.

J. F. Campbell, *'Squatting' on crown lands in New South Wales*, B. T. Dowd ed (Syd, 1968); N. C. W. Beadle, *Students flora of north eastern New South Wales*, pt 3 (Armidale, 1976); *Scottish A'sian*, Mar 1916; *Aust Surveyor*, June 1938; *JRAHS*, 24 (1938), and for publications; *SMH*, 26, 27 Jan 1938; *Walcha News*, 28 Jan 1938; information from Mr E. F. Campbell, Faulconbridge, and Mr L. N. Fletcher, Gordon, NSW.   JOHN ATCHISON

CAMPBELL, THOMAS IRVING (1861-1942), rural lobbyist, was born on 24 July 1861 at Richmond, Victoria, third son of Scottish-born parents James Campbell, carpenter, and his wife Isabella, née Irving. In January 1876 he left Melbourne to work for his uncle on Tuppal station, near Deniliquin, New South Wales. In the early 1880s he selected a farm, Waverly, near Carrathool, but soon moved to Ilkadoon, near Tabbita. In 1895 he let his farm and opened a stock and station agency at Whitton. On 11 October 1899 at Gunbar homestead, near Hay, he married with Wesleyan forms Mary Lugsdin.

The rabbit plague and his knowledge of land tenures precipitated Campbell into prominence at the Cootamundra meeting of the nascent Farmers and Settlers' Association in June 1893. There and at the Sydney conference he successfully stressed the need for government assistance against the rabbit. His emphasis on branch combination and vigorous representation became part of the association's platform.

A founding member of the F.A.S.A., Campbell was general secretary in 1897-1925, and from 1900 also manager of its co-operative, formed to market produce and export wheat. He moved to Sydney and set up an office at the Queen Victoria Markets, meanwhile putting the association on a business-like basis and instituting annual reports. As nominal editor with Charles White [q.v.6], he organized the publication of the *Farmer and Settler* in 1906; after being unsuccessfully sued for damages and breach of contract over the publication of annual reports in 1909, he helped to establish the *Land* newspaper in 1911.

Campbell was secretary to the council of the Commonwealth Farmers' Organisation at its first interstate conference in Sydney in 1906, founding secretary of the Shires Association of New South Wales in 1908-14, secretary to the Australian Farmers' Federal Organisation in 1916, assessor to Mr Justice R. D. Pring [q.v.], the royal commissioner inquiring into the administration of the State Wheat Office in 1919-20, and a member of the New South Wales Board of Trade. He stressed the need for political organization by farmers and defended the F.A.S.A.'s link with the Liberal Party before 1914. With (Sir) Arthur Trethowan [q.v.] he organized the 'Loyal Camp' during the 'Great Strike' of 1917, and allied the association with the National Party. When the F.A.S.A. resolved on a separate political organization, Campbell provided secretarial services for the central council; he subsequently strongly opposed any amalgamation with the National Party. In 1921 he voted against the Progressives joining the Nationalists in a coalition ministry, thus fostering the development of the Country Party.

Construction of the Hay-Hillston railway and his eldest son's departure for Ilkadoon rekindled Campbell's yearning for the land: he resigned as general secretary of the F.A.S.A. in 1925, but returned as president in 1927 and remained a vice-president until 1931. The Campbells developed large-scale wheat and sheep-farming, and 'T.I.' was primarily responsible for several water-leagues and trusts using drainage water from the Murrumbidgee Irrigation Area.

Survived by his wife, four sons and two daughters, Campbell died at Griffith on 24 July 1942 and was buried in the Presbyterian section of Griffith cemetery. His estate was valued for probate at £2648. With his energy, ability and pertinacity and the confidence of the farmers, Campbell had helped to make the association into a powerful political force.

W. A. Bayley, *History of the Farmers and Settlers' Association of N.S.W.* (Syd, 1957); Goolgowi Jubilee Cttee, *Corridors of gold* (Griffith, 1977); F.A.S.A., *Annual Report*, 1898-1932; *Land* (Syd),

24 Apr, 21 Aug 1925, 28 Aug 1931, 31 July 1942; *Narrandera Argus*, 28 July 1942; *Area News*, 7 Aug 1942; information from Mr F. P. Campbell, Ilkadoon, Goolgowi, Mr E. A. Eldridge, Berangerine, Hay, and Mr A. Sides, Glen Innes, NSW.

JOHN ATCHISON

CAMPBELL, WALTER SCOTT (1844-1935), public servant, was born on 11 June 1844 at Maitland, New South Wales, son of Irish-born Francis Rawdon Hastings Campbell [q.v.3], medical practitioner, and his wife Selina, née Porter. He was educated at Rev. William Woolls's [q.v.6] school at Parramatta, Fort Street Model School, and Sydney Grammar School where he was an original pupil in 1857-61. In 1862 he joined the surveyor-general's branch of the Department of Lands as a draftsman. On 5 October 1867 at Holy Trinity Church, Sydney, he married Mary Ann Holt.

Campbell became chief draftsman in the new Department of Mines on 19 October 1874. In 1886 he studied suitable locations for 'experimental or demonstrating farms' for the government; in his *Extracts from reports on certain agricultural districts of New South Wales* (1888), he concluded that the 'greater part of the farming is carried out in an extremely rough, primitive and slovenly manner without method or the remotest attention to economy'. Next year with R. L. Pudney, principal of Longerenong Agricultural College in Victoria, he reported on a suitable site for the Hawkesbury Agricultural College (founded 1893).

When H. C. L. Anderson [q.v.] became public librarian in 1893, Campbell became chief clerk in the drastically reduced agricultural branch of the Department of Mines and Agriculture, and found himself doing in addition the work of the ex-director and secretary of forests and the ex-director of agriculture at a salary reduced from £600 to £400. Despite depressed economic conditions, the long drought in 1895-1903 and the rabbit plague, in Campbell's time the colony became self-sufficient in wheat production in 1897. He established horse studs at Arrawatta and Bangaroo, a vineyard at Morpeth, and experimental farms at Wollongbar (1894), Bathurst (1896), Grafton (1902), Glen Innes and Cowra (1903) and Yanco (1908). By 1896 he had reputedly spent £100000 on Hawkesbury Agricultural College. In 1898 he persuaded William Farrer [q.v.] to join the department; after 1902 the distribution by the department of the Federation wheat-variety developed by Farrer made possible a vast increase in the State's wheat acreage.

Campbell became chief inspector of agriculture and travelling instructor in

1900. He proved level-headed, 'practical and resourceful' in administering the jungle of land laws, and establishing new settlers on the land under the Closer Settlement Act of 1904. He retired in 1908 and in 1911 investigated agricultural prospects in the Northern Territory for the Commonwealth government. He wrote many articles for the *Agricultural Gazette of New South Wales*, and in 1893 had published an exhaustive and scholarly report on sericulture.

Deeply interested in botany, Campbell collected for Sir Ferdinand Mueller [q.v.5] and Dr Woolls and was a friend of R. D. FitzGerald [q.v.4]. In 1901 he was elected a fellow of the Linnean Society of London. He was also a keen historian and a council-member of the (Royal) Australian Historical Society (president 1916), contributing many articles to its *Journal and Proceedings*.

Proud of his 'remarkable physique and retentive memory', he visited England for the first time at the age of 90, and next year wrote a paper on 'The flour milling industry' for the Commonwealth royal commission on the wheat, flour and bread industries. Survived by a son and a daughter, he died on 25 July 1935 at his home at Vaucluse and was buried in the Anglican section of South Head cemetery.

V&P (LA NSW), 1896, 2, 113, Evidence 38-42, 1903, 4, 589, Evidence 166-173; 'Annual report', *JRAHS*, 21 (1935); *T&CJ*, 15 Apr 1903; Hunt Inst biogs (Basser Lib, Canb).   C. J. KING

CAMPBELL PRAED; *see* PRAED

CAMPION, FREDERICK HENRY (1872-1957), Anglican priest, was born on 8 September 1872 at Danny Park, Hurstpierpoint, Sussex, England, second son of William Henry Campion, gentleman, and his wife Gertrude, née Brand. He was educated at Eton and New College, Oxford (B.A., 1895; M.A., 1908). A nephew of Lady Hampden, he arrived in Sydney in 1895 as tutor in the household of the governor Viscount Hampden [q.v.]. While shooting near Warren with (Sir) Norman Kater [q.v.], he was appalled by the spiritual destitution of bush-dwellers and discussed ways to overcome it with Bishop Camidge [q.v.] and Rev. E. H. Lea. He soon returned to England, in 1896 entered Wells Theological College where he met C. H. S. Matthews [q.v.], and was made deacon on 25 September 1898 and priested on 21 December 1899. While curate of St Mary Handsworth, Birmingham, he was invited to

bring out another clergyman to test his plans for a bush brotherhood in Lea's parish of Dubbo. Campion and Matthews reached Sydney on 2 January 1902 in the *Runic* and on 9 January Campion was licensed as curate to the rector of Dubbo. Next year he began regular campaigns and formed an active committee in Sydney.

At Dubbo in May 1904 Campion formally established and became principal of the Brotherhood of the Good Shepherd. Through his able management it became the most stable and successful of Anglican brotherhoods in Australia. In September he founded the society's journal, the *Bush Brother*, in which he published sermons and accounts of pastoral work.

In May 1906 Campion began a mission to Aboriginals and canvassed the idea of a theological college to train Australian-born Brothers. Above all, he established by example the pattern of a Bush Brother's life: trips into his district, interspersed with frequent short visits to the central house and by quarterly reunions there with all members of the Brotherhood. Despite disappointments, especially in recruitment, by 1907 the Brotherhood of the Good Shepherd was financially viable; it owned its central house at Dubbo, opened in September 1905, and was welcomed by the clergy and laity.

On 19 November 1907 at Dubbo Campion married Noël Blaxland, great-granddaughter of Gregory Blaxland [q.v.1], and soon returned to his Sussex home. He became vicar of West Grimstead, Sussex, in 1909, an army chaplain in 1914, vicar of Leigh, Lancashire, in 1916 and rector of Tillington, Sussex, in 1930. He was rural dean of Petworth in 1932-45 and a prebendary of Chichester in 1938-57. In 1908 he had established the home association of the Brotherhood of the Good Shepherd in London, becoming its treasurer in 1909. He was long a commissary in England for the bishops of Bathurst and in 1924 visited Australia. In 1952 he and Matthews appealed to the Brothers to extend their mission to the diocese of Carpentaria, a challenge taken up in 1957.

Campion died at Petworth on 27 January 1957, survived by a son. In 1907 he had donated the window of the Good Shepherd in Holy Trinity Church, Dubbo, but his Australian memorial remains the Brotherhood itself.

C. H. S. Matthews, *A parson in the Australian bush*, 1st edn (Lond, 1908); J. W. S. Tomlin, *The story of the Bush Brotherhoods* (Lond, 1949); *Bush Brother*, Sept 1904, Oct 1905, Nov 1906, Jan 1908, Mar 1957; *The Times*, 6 Feb 1957; *Anglican*, 15, 22 Feb 1957; R. M. Teale, The Anglican diocese of Bathurst, 1870-1911 (M.A. thesis, Univ Syd, 1968).
                                        RUTH TEALE

CAMPION, SIR WILLIAM ROBERT (1870-1951), governor, was born on 3 July 1870 in London, son of Colonel William Henry Campion and his wife Gertrude, née Brand, daughter of Viscount Hampden [q.v.]. Educated at Eton and New College, Oxford, where he took fourth-class honours in history, he became a member of the London Stock Exchange at the time of the Western Australian mining boom of the 1890s. A Liberal Unionist in politics, he twice unsuccessfully stood for the House of Commons before being returned at a by-election in June 1910; he held his seat till 1924 as a strong advocate of economic and defence co-operation within the British Empire. On 5 July 1894 he had married Katherine Mary Byron.

During World War I, Campion was colonel commanding the 4th Battalion of the Royal Sussex Regiment at Gallipoli. Invalided late in 1915, he went to France in 1916 commanding the 15th Battalion, Royal Fusiliers, and transferred to the 6th Bedford Regiment. Awarded the Distinguished Service Order and mentioned three times in dispatches, he returned to the Royal Sussex Regiment for service with the army of occupation in Germany.

In June 1924 Campion was appointed governor of Western Australia. Back-bench supporters of the prime minister, Ramsay MacDonald, complained of an appointment from the Conservative Party, but from October 1924 to June 1931 Campion worked with Labor and Nationalist premiers alike in harmony during a period without major political crises. Bald with prominent blue eyes, Campion was regarded as the pattern of an English gentleman; he and his wife were highly popular. They travelled widely in Australia and he was particularly active in the Toc H Society. He presided with dignity over the State's centennial celebrations in 1929.

On his return to England in 1931 Campion retired to his country house in Sussex, but spoke frequently in favour of organized migration to Australia, in support particularly of the Fairbridge Farm and other schemes involving young people. He was a member of the Empire Settlement Committee in 1935. He also accepted appointment as chairman of a number of gold-mining companies promoted by Claude de Bernales [q.v.], such as the Anglo-Australian Gold Development Co. and the Commonwealth Mining and Finance Co. He visited Australia with de Bernales in 1935-36 to inspect properties and in 1939, on the board of the Great Boulder Pty Ltd, faced with him an attack by a dissident group of shareholders. When de Bernales tried to transfer the company to Australia in 1940, the com-

pensation proposed for Campion and other directors was criticized as excessive. An investigator from the Board of Trade was not satisfied that the directors had done their duty, but no action was taken. Campion died at Hassocks, Sussex, on 2 January 1951, survived by his wife and three children.

Chemical Engineering and Mining Review, 10 July 1940; *SMH*, 17, 18, 23 May 1929, 5, 12 May 1930, 26 June 1939, 23 Sept 1940; *The Times*, 18 June 1924, 26 June 1934, 20 May 1935, 24 June 1939, 1 July, 23 Sept 1940, 27 Mar 1947, 4 Jan 1951; *West Australian*, 9 May 1934, 5 Jan 1951; *Kalgoorlie Miner*, 30 Oct, 17 Dec 1935.

G. C. BOLTON

CANN, JOHN HENRY (1860-1940), politician and railway administrator, and GEORGE (1871-1948), politician, were born on 19 April 1860 at Horrabridge, Sampford Spiney, Devonshire, and on 30 May 1871 at Shankhouse, Cramlington, Northumberland, England, sons of Richard Cann, signalman, and his wife Rebecca, née Sowden. John Henry moved with his family to Northumberland in 1866; at 9 he was a trapper in a coal-mine, continuing as a miner until he went to London in 1882 and worked as a porter and signalman on the Metropolitan District Railway. On 20 August 1885 at St Mary's Anglican Church, Lambeth, he married a widow Elizabeth Ann Callard, née Wright; they migrated to Sydney in February 1887. He hoped to get a job in the railways but became a miner at Port Kembla; next year he went to Broken Hill and in 1889 was employed by the Broken Hill Proprietary Co. Ltd. He became a Primitive Methodist lay preacher and president of the local branch of the Amalgamated Miners' Association; his leadership during the 1890 maritime strike ensured his pre-selection as parliamentary candidate when the A.M.A. formed the district's first Labor Electoral League in 1891.

In June the Labor Party won thirty-five seats in its first electoral campaign; Cann won Sturt and held it until 1916 (Broken Hill in 1894-1912). He gradually emerged as a skilful and eloquent parliamentarian, remaining 'solid' in the party disputes of 1891-94. He was the director of Labor's campaign at the 1897 election for delegates to the Australasian Federal Convention. At the 1899 party conference at Woonona he supported J. C. Watson [q.v.] in a vital division that ensured that Labor would not oppose the submission of the Constitution bill to a second referendum.

By 1900 Cann was one of only three original Labor members left in parliament and his ability and seniority helped him to become chairman of committees, until 1904, in an agreement with the Protectionist government. When Labor gained office with a majority of one in 1910 he became Speaker, but stood down in July next year when W. A. Holman [q.v.] arranged for H. Willis [q.v.], a Liberal, to take over following the unexpected resignation of two Labor men. In the cabinet reshuffle after J. R. Dacey's [q.v.] death, Cann succeeded A. C. Carmichael [q.v.] as treasurer on 6 May 1912. When Holman formed his first ministry in June next year, Cann became deputy leader and remained at the Treasury until 29 January 1914, when he exchanged posts with Holman to become colonial secretary and secretary for mines. Carmichael's resignation in March 1915 led to Cann's last portfolio, public works.

By then he was a classic self-made Labor man who, through the party, had overcome his lack of formal education and developed his innate intelligence and ability. He exhibited another facet of his background when his Empire sentiments made him a conscriptionist in 1916; he was expelled from the Labor Party. His omission from Holman's National ministry was followed in December by his appointment as assistant railways commissioner. He retired at the end of 1924 and died, childless, at his home at Petersham on 21 July 1940. He was buried in the Congregational section of Rookwood cemetery. His estate was valued for probate at £19 993.

George Cann was educated at Cramlington National School. At 11 he worked at Hartford colliery and later became a member of the Northumberland Miners'. Association. On 8 March 1890 at the Primitive Methodist Chapel, Cowpen Quay, Blyth, he married Catherine Roberts; they had one daughter and one son, and migrated to New South Wales in 1900. He found work in the western coalfields around Lithgow and in 1905-07 he was president of the Western Miners' Association. He joined the Labor Party and in 1910-13 held the Federal seat of Nepean and was also an alderman on Lithgow council.

Cann contested the State seat of Upper Hunter in 1913, but lost; next year he won Canterbury at a by-election, and in 1915-16 was a member of the Labor Party central executive. He enlisted in the Australian Imperial Force on 14 March 1916, became an acting sergeant, and served in various training groups in England, reverting to private on 13 September 1917. He returned to Australia and was discharged on 22 January next year. He had missed the party split – he was probably opposed to conscription – and resumed his political career, retaining his seat in 1917 and in 1920 (St

George). He was elected chairman of caucus in 1919.

In the Storey-Dooley [qq.v.] cabinets, 1920-22, at various times Cann was secretary for mines, minister for labour and industry and minister for local government. In factional wrangles early in 1923, the State executive, dominated by J. Bailey [q.v.], expelled him; but, after the intervention of the Federal executive, a State conference in June restored the *status quo*, and in J. T. Lang's [q.v.] cabinet, 1925-27, he was variously minister for local government, health and labour and industry.

Cann had opposed Lang's leadership; as a result he lost Labor pre-selection in 1927, ran unsuccessfully as an independent and was expelled. He became critical of Lang's 'red dictatorship' and in 1930 contested Lakemba as a Nationalist, but lost. He was a trustee of the National Park (president in 1932) and a Freemason. He died on 18 October 1948 and was buried in the Methodist section of Rookwood cemetery, survived by his wife. His estate was sworn for probate at £577.

H. V. Evatt, *Australian Labour leader . . . W. A. Holman*, 2nd edn (Syd, 1942); B. Nairn, *Civilising capitalism* (Canb, 1973); H. Radi and P. Spearritt (eds), *Jack Lang* (Syd, 1977); B. Kennedy, *Silver, sin, and sixpenny ale* (Melb, 1978); *Bulletin*, 14 July 1900, 9 May 1915; *SMH*, 21 Dec 1916, 4 Apr 1923, 17 Oct 1924, 22 July 1940, 19 Oct 1948; *Punch* (Melb), 4 Jan 1917.   BEDE NAIRN

CANN, WILLIAM HENRY (1857-1942), Methodist minister, was born on 4 May 1857 at Huckworthy, Sampford Spiney near Horrabridge, Devonshire, England, second of ten children of John Cann, farm labourer and miner, and his wife Sophia, née Down. When he was 7, the family moved to Cramlington, Northumberland, where William and his father belonged to the Bible Christian congregation. At 10 he began work in the coal mines at Shankhouse colliery, but following his conversion at 16 he became a local preacher and class leader with 'scores of conversions'; he attended the Bible Christians' Shebbear College, North Devon, in 1878. He began his ministry at Southampton in 1879 and was subsequently appointed to Lee in London, Portsmouth and Yarmouth. In 1878 his family had migrated to America, where Cann's mother was anxious for him to join them. He handed in his resignation as minister at Portsmouth but was persuaded to withdraw it. On 7 August 1884 at York Town, Surrey, he married Mary Plowright Booth de Peare, an organist, and, having been influenced by Rev. James Rowe, migrated to South Australia, arriving in November.

Cann's first ministry was at Port Adelaide. In 1887 his request for transfer to New Zealand, because of his wife's distress in the Adelaide summer, was refused; however he was given a choice of circuit and in 1888 moved to Mount Torrens. He also ministered at Franklin Street, Adelaide (1890-94), Mount Lofty (1894-98), Goodwood (1898-1901) and, after Methodist union, at Quorn, Hindmarsh and Mount Gambier. He was president of the State Bible Christian Conference in 1897 and of the State Methodist Conference in 1912. In 1903 Cann was full-time organizing secretary of his Church's Twentieth Century Fund. His ability as a fund-raiser had become apparent in each of the churches where he had been minister: he had paid off existing debts or raised money for new buildings. His compelling personality was hard to resist and by 1904 he had raised almost £4000 for the fund.

Cann's appointment to the Adelaide Central Methodist Mission was probably in the hope that he would raise money for its development. When he arrived it was hamstrung by inadequate facilities and lack of finance; he remedied both these deficiencies. He was also interested in the work of other missions. When a breakdown in health forced him to take leave in 1915 he visited relatives in the United States of America and observed city church programmes there. Cann recognized that Adelaide's population was changing and the mission's activities were broadened and expanded to attract suburban dwellers. He also raised funds for a young men's hostel and for the Methodist Children's Home at Magill.

Cann was an evangelist and his ministry was characterized by its intensity of purpose. This no doubt accounted for the financial support which he attracted from the well-to-do, but that very support precluded him from attacking the economic conditions which produced human need and suffering in the inner city. Further, he was not free to follow the principles of charity organization which were emerging in relief work elsewhere. In 1929 he retired and lived for a while at the Magill children's home. He died on 9 December 1942 at Henley Beach and was buried in Dudley Park cemetery. Predeceased by his wife, he was survived by a son and a daughter.

W. Hunt (ed), *Methodist ministerial index for Australasia* (Melb, 1914); Sister Dora (F. S. George), *Rev. W. H. Cann* (Adel, 1943); *Aust Christian Cwlth*, 1 Nov 1929; *SA Methodist*, 8 Jan 1943; N. Hicks, The establishment of a Central Methodist Mission in Adelaide (B.A. Hons thesis, Univ Adel, 1966); PRG 192 (SAA).

NEVILLE HICKS
ELISABETH LEOPOLD

CANNING, ALFRED WERNAM (1860-1936), surveyor, was born on 21 February 1860 at Campbellfield, Victoria, son of William Canning, farmer, and his wife Lucy, née Mason. Educated at Carlton College, Melbourne, Canning entered the survey branch of the New South Wales Lands Department as a cadet, and in January 1882 was appointed a licensed surveyor under the Real Property Act. He served at Bega in 1883-86, Cooma in 1887-89 and as a mining surveyor at Bathurst in 1890-92. On 17 April 1884 he had married Edith Maude Butcher in Mary Immaculate Roman Catholic Church at Waverley, Sydney; they had one son who died in 1923.

Canning joined the Western Australian Lands Department in 1893 and, in routine surveying in the south, soon proved himself a first-class bushman and reliable surveyor. About the turn of the century rabbits from the east were beginning to invade Western Australia and Canning was instructed to survey a route for a rabbit-proof fence. The line took him from Starvation Harbour on the south coast to Cape Keraudren, east of Port Hedland, through 1175 miles (1890 km). Said at the time to be the longest single survey in the world, it took him three years. On one bad stretch when a camel died, he had to walk 210 miles (338 km).

In 1906 the State government planned a stockroute to bring live cattle from the Kimberley district to feed the goldfields. David Carnegie [q.v.], who had explored further east in 1897, had concluded that it was 'absolutely impracticable', but Canning proved it to be practicable. With 8 men, 23 camels and 2 horses, he left Daydawn in May 1906, aiming to find water sufficient for stock every 15 miles (24 km) of the 925-mile (1490 km) route, and reached Halls Creek in January 1907 with the task successfully accomplished. On return to Perth he had to face the publication of charges by Blake, the expedition cook, that Aboriginals had been ill treated. A royal commission exonerated him in January 1908, although he had admitted chaining Aboriginals at night.

Canning's optimistic report to the government was accepted, and he organized a second, larger expedition, of 20 men, 62 camels, 2 horses, and 400 goats for milk and meat, to construct the necessary wells along the route. In temperatures varying from below freezing at night to blazing heat, Canning led his party with mild courtesy and resolute example. Calculating distances principally by his own unvarying pace, he would walk for hours, regardless of the weather. Much of the course included desert sand-ridges 50-60 feet (15-18 m) high, which had to be crossed every half-mile or so. He finished this herculean task in March 1910, then went to England, where he addressed the Royal Geographical Society.

In July 1912 Canning became district surveyor for Perth. He worked on the Land Repricing Board in 1915 and in 1917-22 was surveyor for the northern district. He resigned from the public service in 1923 and went into partnership with H. S. King as a contract surveyor.

In 1929, at the invitation of the government, Canning led a new expedition designed to reopen his old stock route, which had been virtually abandoned. Subordinates remembered how he walked the whole distance twice, leading the men to a well, then while the men were cleaning it, walking on fifteen miles (24 km) ahead to locate the next one. After this tremendous feat, he lived in retirement until he died of progressive muscular atrophy at his home in Perth on 22 May 1936. He was buried in Karrakatta cemetery with Church of England rites. His estate was valued for probate at £1012.

D. W. Carnegie, *Spinifex and sand* (Lond, 1898); P. Hasluck, *Black Australians* (Melb, 1942); E. P. Smith, *The beckoning west* (Syd, 1966); H. W. Talbot, 'Geological observations ... ', *WA Geological Survey Bulletin*, 1910; *Aust Surveyor*, 1 Sept 1936, Mar 1970; Thomas Burke diary *and* proposed memorial leaflet, PR 288 (Battye Lib, Perth); interviews with survivors of the 1929 expedition.   JOHN SLEE

CARD, MARY (1861-1940), crochet pattern designer, was born on 24 September 1861 at Castlemaine, Victoria, daughter of David Card, Irish-born watchmaker and jeweller, and his wife Harriet Wooldridge, née Watson, Welsh-born daughter of an actress. Mary was the eldest of a family of ten. About 1873 the family moved to Melbourne where David commenced business in Bourke Street.

In 1880 Mary was a student at the National Gallery School of Design. In the late 1880s she wrote a novel, probably never published. By 1890 she had established a small school in Auburn Road, Hawthorn, and had developed a particular interest in speech training; however by 1903 she had to relinquish it because of increasing deafness. Faced with the need to find an occupation in which her disability was not a handicap, she decided to combine her writing, drawing and needlework abilities to become a 'professional designer and teacher of needlework through the press'. Choosing Irish crochet as her medium, she joined a Ladies' Work Association which undertook repairs of valuable crochet pieces and taught herself to mend old lace. From these heirlooms she learned the principles of Irish crochet, discovering that she could make new and effective designs to be worked from a chart method of her own invention rather than the usual printed directions.

Her first designs were published in the *Ladies' Home Journal* in the United States of America. These were very successful but returns from overseas were slow and in 1909 she decided to offer her designs and a monthly article to the *New Idea* (later *Everylady's Journal*), Melbourne. Her patterns became so popular that the editor reprinted many: her first book (later *Mary Card's crochet book No. 1*) was published in 1914 and others followed, No. 3 being devoted to Irish crochet. She then developed 'giant charts' for more ambitious designs and to cater for workers with failing eyesight, drawn on the scale of ten squares to the inch with a guiding line at every inch. As her popularity grew she no longer had to test all her own patterns but sent them out to be worked by correspondents 'on stations in Queensland, in Western Australia ... in lighthouses, at lonely railway gates on the great trunk lines... wherever a good worker in need of an interest is to be found'.

With five books published, Mary went to the U.S.A. late in 1917 to launch some of her newer designs. In New York, The Mary Card Co. was set up to reprint her crochet books. Later she settled in England in a studio-cottage at Barkham, Berkshire. She continued to produce designs for more than twenty years, some of which she reputedly sold to publishers for several hundred pounds each. She became steeped in English history and was an authority on ecclesiastical architecture, although she once wrote, 'I have had to nail up a placard on my study wall with Advance Australia in big letters just to remind myself that I belong to a pioneer land'.

Mary Card revisited Australia occasionally. Early in 1940, in poor health, she returned to Victoria to live at Olinda, where she shared a cottage with her sister Harriet. She died there on 13 October 1940 and was cremated.

Everylady's J, 6 July 1917; *Aust Home Beautiful*, Nov 1940; *Aust Women's Weekly*, 18 June, 23 July 1975; *Argus* and *Herald* (Melb), 14 Oct 1940.
                                          SALLY O'NEILL

'CARDIGAN'; *see* WOLFE, HERBERT AUSTIN

CAREW-SMYTH, PONSONBY MAY (1860-1939), educationist, was born on 7 August 1860 at Cork, Ireland, son of Emmanuel Uniacke Smyth, gentleman, and his wife Catherine Giles, née Carew. Carew-Smyth's initial art training and teaching was at the Belfast Government School of Art and Design. In 1885 he entered the National Art Training School at South Kensington, London, where he remained as student and teacher for five years. He also taught at Rugby School, studied at the Royal School of Wood Carving and the Guild School of Handicrafts, London, and was sent by the Department of Science and Art to study art, art education and museum procedures in Paris. Testimonials to his career in England affirm his ability and dedication as an educationist and his integrity as a man.

On 23 December 1890 Carew-Smyth married Marie Reynolds of Brixton; they migrated to Australia next January. In September Carew-Smyth applied from Melbourne for the position of master of the school of art and design, established under the auspices of the Ballarat Fine Art Gallery. Opening in November, the school offered day classes and a broad curriculum, and under Carew-Smyth's guidance, established a sound reputation.

In November 1899 he was appointed inspector of drawing in the Department of Education. Carew-Smyth saw drawing as a crucial link between primary and technical education, insisting on it as a 'mental process quite as much as a manual'; he believed strongly in the utilitarian value of drawing to the artisan class and of art as 'craftmanship'. By his emphasis on teacher-training, by his role in the Teachers' Training College, and by his constant travels, writing and lecturing, he upgraded both the standard and importance of drawing early in the century. His meticulous mind formulated the *Austral drawing books* which provided the basis of instruction in the subject in Victoria until 1927.

Although he gave his occupation as 'artist', Carew-Smyth was primarily an educationist. He was actively involved in the early years of Prahran and Swinburne Technical colleges, and especially the Working Men's College which held his interest even after his retirement. In 1906 he was appointed chairman of the Victorian State Schools' Equipment and Decoration Society, and he was important in the organization of the state schools' exhibition that year. He designed the commemorative wall plaques installed in state schools after World War I, and the art teachers' certificate. He was prominent in bringing about the 1922 Jubilee Exhibition, and the 1926 showing of work of overseas schools, and especially the 1934 Melbourne centenary 'Early Victorian Art' exhibition. In the 1930s he wrote wide-ranging, informative

and sometimes humorous articles for the *Argus* on various aspects of the decorative arts. In mid-1936 he was acting director of the National Gallery of Victoria.

To students his single-mindedness sometimes suggested sternness, but Carew-Smyth was always held in the highest regard both professionally and personally. His colleagues recalled a man of kindness, unstinting devotion to work, and humour; he was considered quite a raconteur. Survived by his wife, a son and a daughter, he died in his home at South Yarra on 9 October 1939, and was cremated.

C. R. Long (ed) *Record and review of the State Schools Exhibition . . . 1906* (Melb, 1908); F. A. Campbell, *The Working Men's College in the making 1887-1913* (Melb, 1925); D. Clark, *Some notes on the development of education in Victoria* (Melb, 1929); L. J. Blake (ed), *Vision and realisation*, 1 (Melb, 1973); A. G. Austin and R. J. W. Selleck, *The Australian government school, 1830-1914* (Melb, 1975); N. Carew-Smyth papers, and Annual reports, 1907, 1908, *and* School Committee minute-books (Ballarat Fine Art Public Gallery).

MARGÔT LETHLEAN

CAREY, JOHN RANDAL (1834-1923), businessman and newspaper proprietor, was born on 14 April 1834 at Cork, Ireland, son of John Westropp Carey, of the Connaught Rangers, and his wife Margaret, née McCarthy. Educated at Hamblin's College, Cork, he worked for a merchant before leaving for the Australian goldfields. He reached Victoria in the *Countess of Yarborough* in December 1853 and tried his luck on the diggings before setting up as a general agent and auctioneer as partner in Richards & Carey at Castlemaine. An excellent horseman, he rode his own steeplechasers and later owned Mazeppa, a champion trotter. About 1862 he followed the gold-seekers to New Zealand and joined Arthur William Gilles as general agents, auctioneers and importers of stock from the Australian colonies; they soon established branches at Invercargill, Hokitika and Auckland. From April 1869 Carey was captain of the Auckland Troop of the Royal Cavalry Volunteers; he probably fought in the Maori wars.

On 14 June 1873 at St John's College, Auckland, he married Mary Taylor; that year he and Gilles moved their business to Sydney. With experience of auctioneering and shipping, Carey recognized that transport and land development were inextricably linked. In 1875 he acquired the Manly run which had five boats operating a freight, passenger and towing service across the harbour; he continued as managing director and a major shareholder in the Port Jackson Steamboat Co. in 1877, remaining a director of the reconstituted Port Jackson Steamship Co. Ltd and, on its absorption of a competitor, of the Port Jackson Co-operative Steamship Co. Ltd in 1896-1904. In 1877 he visited England to oversee construction of ferries. He also helped to form the Balmain Steam Ferry Co. Ltd in 1882 and, as a partner in Mann, Carey & Co., extended his activities to railway construction, tendering successfully for the Nyngan to Bourke line. With less success he set up the Sydney Tramway & Omnibus Co. Ltd which was in liquidation in 1899.

In 1879 he was one of a syndicate which started the *Daily Telegraph*, a four-page penny newspaper. With Watkin Wynne [q.v.] as manager, and Carey as chairman of the company from 1884, it succeeded: other newspapers were forced to drop their prices. In 1890 its editorial staff Frederick Ward, L. J. Brient and Henry Gullett [qq.v.] resigned when a direction on editorial policy restricted them from commenting on Carey's other business enterprises. The paper featured sensational news and in 1894 introduced linotype machines against opposition from printers. He remained chairman and the controlling influence of the paper until February 1921.

In 1899 the *Daily Telegraph* campaigned to send troops to help Britain in the South African War and sponsored an insurance fund for Australian volunteers. Carey believed the Australian outback produced the right type of man for South Africa: in 1900, as chairman of a Citizens' Bushmen's Committee, he organized the recruitment of the Bushmen's Contingent and the purchase of horses. A major in the reserve of officers from January 1900 to December 1904, he rode at the head of the contingent when it paraded through Sydney.

Carey was also a trustee of the Savings Bank of New South Wales, a member of the Rocks Resumption Advisory Board, and a director from 1899 and chairman in 1906-23 of Royal North Shore Hospital. His business enterprises and membership of the Athenaeum Club had brought him into close association with leading politicians and he used his connexions to obtain additional land for the hospital. His wife presided over its fund-raising committee and his daughter Beatrice was for some years its masseuse.

Survived by his wife, two sons and two daughters, Carey died at his residence at Milson's Point on 9 June 1923. After the funeral his body was taken by special ferry to be buried in the Anglican section of South Head cemetery. His estate was valued for probate at £79 052.

Cyclopedia of N.S.W. (Syd, 1907); H. Mayer, *The press in Australia* (Melb, 1964); R. B. Walker, *The newspaper press in New South Wales, 1803-1920* (Syd, 1976); Sel cttee on . . . the Military Dept, *V&P* (LA NSW), 1900, 4, 900–Evidence, 225; Roy North Shore Hospital, *Annual Report*, 1923; *Daily Telegraph* (Syd), 14 Oct 1899, 5 Jan, 1 Mar 1900, 11 June 1923; *SMH*, 14 Apr, 12 June 1923; military records (National Archives, Well, NZ). HEATHER RADI

CARINGTON, RUPERT CLEMENT GEORGE, fourth BARON CARRINGTON (1852-1929), soldier, grazier and politician, was born on 18 December 1852 at Whitehall, London, third son of Robert John, second Baron Carrington, and his second wife Charlotte Augusta Annabella, daughter of Peter Robert, Lord Willoughby D'Eresby. His grandfather, the first baron, was the banker Robert Smith, friend of William Pitt. From 1839 the family used the surname Carrington. Educated at Eton, Rupert was commissioned as a lieutenant in the Grenadier Guards in October 1871.

Coming from such a well-known Liberal family it was not surprising that he turned his attention to politics, and when the elevation of Disraeli to the peerage left a vacant seat in Buckinghamshire, he unsuccessfully contested it in 1876. He served in the Zulu War in 1879 as acting adjutant of the 1st Battalion, 24th Regiment of Foot, and later commanded a troop of mounted infantry. In August 1880 he and his brothers were authorized, by royal licence, to continue the use of the family name Carington, in lieu of Carrington which was the title of the barony. That year he became Liberal member for Buckinghamshire; he supported land reform and lowering the county franchise. He was defeated for High Wycombe in the general election of 1885.

In 1884 Carington had retired from the Grenadier Guards with a gratuity and in 1887 came to New South Wales where his brother Charles [q.v.3] was governor. He was appointed a captain on the headquarters staff, New South Wales Military Forces, and next year on 23 March was made aide-de-camp to his brother; he held this post until 1890. On 23 March 1891 at St Matthew's Anglican Church, New Norfolk, Tasmania, he married Edith, daughter of John Sutcliffe Horsfall [q.v.4] and became a grazier and part-owner, with his father-in-law, of Momalong station in the Riverina. His share in the property was financed by a £10 000 loan which Horsfall had negotiated with Goldsbrough, Mort [qq.v.4,5] & Co.

Carington was placed on the reserve of officers in 1900 but in February 1901 went to the South African War as a major in the 2nd Regiment, New South Wales Mounted

Rifles; he was promoted lieut-colonel in May 1902 and that month at Klerksdorp, Transvaal, formed and commanded the 3rd New South Wales Imperial Bushmen's Regiment. This unit was made up of time-expired men from other Australian regiments and was later augmented by a draft of 200 Riverina bushmen raised by his father-in-law. Letters to his brother Charles give a vivid account of the actions and skirmishes of this stage of the war and he and his men received high commendation from Major General R. S. Fetherstonhaugh for their services in western and eastern Transvaal; Carington was awarded the Distinguished Service Order and mentioned in dispatches.

He returned to Momalong in July 1902 and was appointed C.V.O. in 1905. Carington commanded the 6th Australian Light Horse Brigade in 1904-10 and the 2nd A.L.H.B. in 1910-15, and was an honorary aide-de-camp to the governors-general in 1912-17; he had been promoted colonel in 1911 and retired from the Australian Military Forces in 1918. In May 1915 his brother's only son had been killed in action and Carington became heir to the barony. He returned to England after World War I and in 1928 succeeded as fourth baron. He died of heart disease on 11 November 1929 at his residence in Eaton Place, Westminster, and was buried at Moulsoe, Buckinghamshire. His wife had died in 1908 and his only son succeeded to the title.

Aust Defence Dept, *Official records of the Australian military contingents to the war in South Africa,* P. L. Murray ed (Melb, 1912); *London Gazette,* 29 July, 31 Oct 1902, 9 Nov 1905; *The Times,* 12-13 Nov 1929; Marquess of Lincolnshire letters (held by 6th Baron Carrington, Lond).

G. P. WALSH

CARLILE, SIR EDWARD (1845-1917), parliamentary draftsman, was born on 26 April 1845 in London, son of John Carlile, merchant of Houston, Scotland, and his wife Anne, née Williams. The family arrived in Victoria in 1854, and Edward was educated at Dr T. P. Fenner's collegiate school, Prahran. In May 1861 he became a clerk in the Census Office. He was appointed to the staff of the Registrar-General's Office in 1862, and after passing the civil service law examination was transferred to the Crown Law Office in 1865. He was the law gold medallist at the University of Melbourne in 1869-70, and was admitted to the Bar in 1871, becoming parliamentary and professional assistant to the law officers of the Crown in 1873.

On 27 April 1878 at the Catholic Apostolic Church, Carlton, Carlile married Isabella Sophia, daughter of Robert Hunter Young of Edinburgh. He was appointed parliamentary draftsman upon the creation of that position in July 1879, but at the request of the Speaker, Peter Lalor [q.v.5], he became clerk assistant of the Legislative Assembly in April 1882. His historical and legal survey of the constitution and form of government of the various Australasian colonies was published as an appendix to the *Victorian yearbook for 1883-4.* In April 1889 he returned to his position as parliamentary draftsman with much improved status and salary. His *Comparative analysis of the Australian Commonwealth bill 1891 and four federal constitutions* was published in Melbourne in 1897. His standing in the legal profession was recognized in 1900 when he was appointed Q.C. Carlile retired in 1910 and visited England and Europe, but on his return was asked to supervise parliamentary bills for the session of 1912. Next year he was knighted.

Diligent and energetic in his professional duties, Carlile personally supervised the drafting of most Victorian legislation during his term of office. He fought strenuously to uphold and improve the status and responsibilities of the new office of parliamentary draftsman, in particular mounting an impressive personal campaign to obtain the support of the Victorian Bar in resisting a proposal to downgrade the position in 1899. He served as a trustee of the Public Library, Museums, and National Gallery from July 1902 (honorary treasurer in 1911-17); he was a committee-member of the Melbourne Hospital and the Athenaeum Club (president in 1916); and a councillor of the Working Men's College and the Old Colonists' Association. He founded the Civil Service Rowing Club in 1866, was its president for many years, and was also prominent in the Victorian Rowing Association.

Carlile died of cerebro-vascular disease at his home, Yarraby, South Yarra, on 15 November 1917 and was buried in Brighton cemetery after a service conducted by a minister of the Catholic Apostolic faith. He was survived by his wife, three daughters and a son. His elder son had been killed in February 1917 while serving with the Australian Imperial Force in France.

J. Smith (ed), *Cyclopedia of Victoria,* 1 (Melb, 1903); W. Perry, *The Science Museum of Victoria* (Melb, 1972); *PD* (Vic), 1879-80, 1499-1502; *Age,* and *Argus,* 16 Nov 1917; Carlile papers (LaTL).

ROSS GIBBS

CARLTON, JAMES ANDREW (1909-1951), athlete, was born on 10 February 1909 at South Lismore, New South Wales, eldest son of native-born parents Vincent Leslie Carlton, butcher, and his wife Catherine Mary, née Brennan. He was educated by the Marist Brothers at Lismore and at their high school, Darlinghurst, then at St Joseph's College, Hunters Hill. He matriculated in 1927, winning an exhibition in law at the University of Sydney. In 1929 he lived at St John's College and studied first-year arts as an evening student, then took a post in life assurance.

In 1924 at St Joseph's 'Jimmy' Carlton won the junior 100, 220, and 440 yards events, and in 1925-27 the senior treble at the Great Public Schools' championships, establishing records in all three events. He became the first schoolboy in New South Wales to run 100 yards in 10 seconds in 1927, and on the same day ran 220 yards in 21.8 seconds: both records lasted twenty-nine years. That year Carlton was the youngest athlete to that time to win the two sprints at the New South Wales and Australian championships. He repeated the double in 1928 and 1929. With the Botany Harriers, he improved in physique, stamina and style: of medium height, he was strongly built with broad shoulders, powerful arms and well-developed torso and legs. A relatively slow starter, he overcame the problem of body roll and had a powerful driving finish.

At the 1928 Amsterdam Olympic Games, Carlton failed to reach top form because of illness and was defeated in the 100 and 200 metres semi-finals. In 1930 at Newcastle, New South Wales, he equalled Eddie Tolan's world record of 9.2 seconds for 100 yards, but the run was not recognized as there were only two timekeepers. However, in December 1930 at the Sydney Cricket Ground he set an Australian record, which lasted twenty-three years, of 9.6 seconds. In January 1932 at the Australian Championships he ran 220 yards in 20.6 seconds on a curved grass track, but the time was not recognized because of wind assistance. He was also a successful Rugby Union wing three-quarter, playing for St Joseph's College, and for New South Wales in 1930.

Although certain of selection for the 1932 Los Angeles Olympic Games, Carlton decided to train for the priesthood. He was ordained as a missionary priest at Croydon, Victoria, in 1939, and entered the Sacred Heart Monastery, Kensington, New South Wales. He left the priesthood in 1945 and on 10 April at St Paul's Church of England, Chatswood, Sydney, married Enid Alison Symington, a stenographer. After living in Melbourne, Carlton returned to Sydney in 1947 and taught mathematics at Barker College. Next year he was appointed a selector and coach for the New South Wales

Amateur Athletic Association. He devoted most of his spare time to helping young athletes and also wrote for the *Sydney Morning Herald*.

Survived by his wife and two infant sons, Carlton died of asthma at his home at Waitara, Sydney, on 4 April 1951 and was buried in the Roman Catholic section of Northern Suburbs cemetery.

St Joseph's College Mag, 1925-27; *SMH*, 18 Nov 1927, 27, 28 Jan 1930, 27 Jan, 16 Nov 1931, 19, 21 Jan 1932, 17 Aug 1945, 6 Apr 1951; news-cuttings (St Joseph's College Archives, Hunters Hill, NSW).
                                            JAMES BROCK ROWE

CARMICHAEL, AMBROSE CAMPBELL (1866-1953), politician, soldier and accountant, was born on 19 September 1866 in Hobart Town, son of William Carmichael, commission agent, and his wife Emma, née Willson, both Scottish-born. Educated at the High School of Hobart Town (Christ College) he trained as an accountant and studied law for a time. In 1888 he went to Brisbane and worked as a teacher and legal coach; on 18 May 1891 at Wickham Terrace Presbyterian Church he married Mabel Pillinger (d.1931); they had no children. He then went on the land in the Lachlan River district in New South Wales near Lake Cargelligo. He cleared and fenced his holding for stock-breeding and helped to found the local branch of the Farmers and Settlers' Association. By 1900 the venture had failed and that year, in debt, he moved to Sydney and worked as a teacher, a journalist and as a book-keeper for O. C. Beale [q.v.] & Co. He became a member of the Sydney School of Arts debating club.

Campbell Carmichael joined the Leichhardt branch of the Labor Party and helped (Sir) George Beeby [q.v.] at the 1904 State general election. After Beeby's transfer to Blayney, Carmichael won Leichhardt in 1907 and was soon a leading parliamentarian; a forceful and, at times, a brilliant speaker, with an effective flow of sarcasm, he contributed much to the growing status of the party. When J. S. T. McGowen [q.v.], as treasurer, formed the first Labor ministry in 1910 he became an honorary minister and prepared the first budget; he acted as treasurer in March-September next year. N. R. W. Nielsen's [q.v.] resignation in August 1911 resulted in his promotion to the ministries of public instruction and labour and industry, but he resigned in November. Next year Beeby's defection brought cabinet reshuffling and Carmichael returned to public instruction on 1 March; he was also treasurer in April-May and minister for labour and industry from December to June 1913. W. A. Holman [q.v.] became premier on 30 June and Carmichael remained in public instruction until he resigned on 5 March 1915. He was party treasurer from 1910 and on Labor's central executive committee in 1910-11, but was rebuked by it in 1912 when he spoke up for Beeby.

Carmichael's brief work in the labour and industry portfolio did not please Labor's industrial wing, and did nothing to dispel the belief that New South Wales was 'the storm-centre of industrial unrest in Australia'. But he introduced administrative reforms at the Treasury and, with the help of P. Board [q.v.], he proved an energetic, innovative and successful minister of education, reinforcing the growing repute of the parliamentary Labor Party as an efficient manager of affairs of state: his University Amendment Act, 1912, liberalized senate representation, brought in free places and linked the school system with the university; his radical Bursary Endowment Act of the same year helped children in both church and state schools and reduced the disabilities of bush students. He reorganized the medical check-up of pupils, appointing school doctors and nurses; and he set up day-time training for apprentices at technical colleges. He reserved part of the Art Gallery's annual grant for the purchase of Australian work, and in 1914 he established the State Conservatorium of Music.

Carmichael's achievements were accompanied by some personal strain. His resignation in 1911 arose out of irritation with Holman over questions of precedence in cabinet, and belief that he was compromised by a murder charge laid against his nephew. Early in 1914 he suffered a nervous breakdown. To recuperate he took a holiday and business trip to the Continent and Britain, also seeking a director for the conservatorium. In London in June he complained that 'almost the only news cabled from Australia seems to be of frozen meat, Tasmanian apples, and strikes'; he did his best to redress the balance. But he was disturbed by war preparations and when he returned to Sydney in September he organized voluntary rifle-drilling companies. The outbreak of hostilities had unsettled the stability of the cabinet, and Carmichael's rivalry with Holman sharpened as the war exerted strong emotional pressures on him. His resignation from the ministry in March 1915 reflected his state of mind. In June he was appointed a royal commissioner to inquire into the administration of the Murrumbidgee Irrigation Area; after his report in October he declined the position of irrigation commissioner and decided to enlist. Holman extolled his 'high spirit of devotion to public duty'.

Carmichael announced in November that he had the support of the military and recruiting authorities to carry out his own programme 'to raise a thousand rifle reserve recruits', who would join the Australian Imperial Force with him. 'Car's' successful campaign became the talk of Sydney. He gave his age as 43 when he enlisted on 23 November. Allotted to the 36th Battalion, he was promoted from sergeant to second lieutenant on 16 March 1916 and to lieutenant on 1 August; he embarked for England on 13 May and proceeded to France on 12 November. He was wounded at Houplines on 21 January 1917 in an action for which he was awarded the Military Cross. On 2 May he became a captain and was wounded again on 4 October. He returned to Sydney in February 1918.

By then conscription had been rejected at two referendums and the Labor Party had split over it, with many expulsions, including Holman, who had formed a Nationalist ministry. Carmichael had not been involved in the disputes and in March he attended the Labor executive, explained that he favoured conscription but it was now a dead issue, and appealed for 'a great sustained recruiting campaign'. He was not expelled but gradually drifted from the party. He got the support of the new Labor leader, J. Storey [q.v.], and other prominent people, became chairman of the State Recruiting Committee, and again threw himself into his self-imposed task. He raised another 'Carmichael's thousand', and rode at their head when they left Sydney on 19 June. By late September when he arrived in France the war was ending, and he came back to Sydney on 20 February 1919.

Carmichael, still a parliamentarian, was now something of a national figure: an over-age and mercurial war hero, but with panache, courage and resource, tapping great reserves of admiration and goodwill. In March he disclosed his antipathy to 'machine politics' to his constituents, and announced the formation of the People's Party of Soldiers and Citizens, stressing the needs of returned soldiers and seeking profit-sharing. The Soldiers and Citizens' Federation backed him, but the Labor and National parties were critical. He soon found that his ideals of war service, modified by his radicalism, did not correspond with the new, complex politics of peace. After a report that his party had joined with Beeby's Progressives, he announced in January 1920 that it was independent. With two colleagues he ran for Balmain in February; they polled 8.8 per cent of the votes, against Labor's 59.6 per cent.

Carmichael set up as a public accountant and by 1922 had joined the National Party.

Carmichael

He contemplated contesting the Federal seat of North Sydney that year, but stood aside for W. M. Hughes [q.v.]. In 1929 he praised the flexibility of the British system of government and agreed with P. F. Loughlin [q.v.] that cabinets should be selected from all parties. He died at Darlinghurst on 15 January 1953, and was cremated after a Christian Science service. His second wife, Clive Thorngate, née Weston, died five days later; they had married at St Stephen's Presbyterian Church on 4 May 1934, and were childless.

H. V. Evatt, *Australian Labour leader... W. A. Holman*, 2nd edn (Syd, 1942); *British A'sian*, 2 July 1914, 17 Aug 1916; *Scottish A'sian*, 6 May 1919; *T&CJ*, 23 Oct 1907; *Punch* (Melb), 3 Apr 1913; *Daily Telegraph* (Syd), 6 Mar 1915; *SMH*, 16 Mar, 13 Apr 1918, 31 Oct 1929, 17 Jan 1953.

BEDE NAIRN

CARMICHAEL, GRACE ELIZABETH JENNINGS (1867-1904), poet and nurse, was born on 24 February 1867 at Ballarat, Victoria, daughter of Archibald Carmichael, a miner from Perthshire, Scotland, and his wife Margaret Jennings, née Clark, from Cornwall, England. Her father died in 1870 and in 1875 her mother married Charles Naylor Henderson of Melbourne. About 1880 the family moved to Gippsland where Henderson managed a station near Orbost. Grace learned to love the Gippsland forest. She began to express in verse her understanding of the sights, scents and sounds of the bush, often writing in some remote clearing, her manuscripts stored for privacy in a hollow trunk. Henderson and his wife disapproved of her 'scribbling', but a kindly tutor persuaded them that her verse had merit, and she was allowed to continue. The *Bairnsdale Advertiser* published her first story, and the *Weekly Times* an early poem; then on 28 November 1885 her poem 'The old maid' was published in the *Australasian* under her pen name Jennings Carmichael. Encouraged by its editor, David Watterston [q.v.], Grace sent nearly all her subsequent verse to that newspaper.

At 20 she left home to earn her own living, first as a lady's companion and then as a trainee nurse at the Hospital for Sick Children in Melbourne. Her book, *Hospital children*, a distilled, sympathetic account of her experiences there, was published in 1891. Several poems and an essay, 'My old station home', had appeared in the *Centennial Magazine* between September 1889 and March 1890. After qualifying in 1890 Grace worked as a private nurse near Geelong, and found more time for writing; the fruits of her labours were published as *Poems* in Mel-

bourne and London in 1895. In the early 1890s she was a member of the Austral Salon, and in September 1895 gave a well-publicized lecture on 'The spirit of the bush', with Alfred Deakin [q.v.] in the chair.

On 1 April 1895 at the United Methodist Free Church, Fitzroy, Grace had married Henry Francis Mullis, a 35-year-old architect from Northampton, England. They moved to South Australia and then to England. She continued to send verse to the *Australasian* but it seems that her family disapproved of her marriage and lost touch with her. In England she and her husband lived in poverty. One son and their only daughter predeceased Grace, who died of pneumonia in Leyton workhouse near London on 9 February 1904. Her three surviving sons lived in the Northampton workhouse until a group of her admirers in Victoria discovered their whereabouts; an appeal was launched, and in 1910 they were brought to Victoria, and reared in private homes, taking the name Carmichael. That year a small selection of her poems was published in Melbourne. In 1927 at Wood Grange Park cemetery, London, a white marble book was placed on Grace's grave, inscribed with a few brief lines of hers on wattle blossom; plaques were later unveiled to her memory at Orbost (1937) and Ballarat (1938).

In the 1890s Jennings Carmichael had been regarded as a 'graceful and genuine poetess'; later generations found her verse cloying rather than sweet, and its philosophy homespun. Its best feature is the accurate and loving descriptions of the Australian bush, as in 'A bush gloaming'. Her prose work, *Hospital children*, displaying qualities of shrewd observation, sound judgment and quiet humour, is perhaps a worthier memorial.

Table Talk, 5 June 1891; *Argus*, 16 Mar 1904, 11 May 1917; *Australasian*, 19 Mar 1904, 14 May 1910; *SMH*, 26, 27 Oct 1927; family information.

LYNDSAY GARDINER

CARMICHAEL, SIR THOMAS DAVID GIBSON, 1st BARON CARMICHAEL OF SKIRLING (1859-1926), governor, was born on 18 March 1859 at Edinburgh, eldest son of Rev. Sir William Henry Gibson Carmichael (d. 1891), tenth baronet, and his wife Eleanora Anne, née Anderson. He was baptized in the Church of England, but had strict Presbyterian training. At school in Hampshire, England, his devotion to entomology and scientific discovery received every encouragement. He entered St John's College, Cambridge, in 1877 (B.A., 1881; M.A., 1884); his second-class in history reflected parental direction, not natural bent.

A Liberal, he became in 1886 private secretary to two successive secretaries for Scotland in Gladstone's third administration. His reserved manner concealed what his friend Sir Edward Grey described as 'the acutest brain in Europe'. Intelligent, curious, self-deprecatory, compassionate, with a gift for friendship, he was not eloquent and no politician, though he succeeded Gladstone as member of parliament for Midlothian (1895-1900).

In 1908 Sir Thomas Carmichael was appointed governor of Victoria: to this post, which he took up on 27 July, he brought both his farming skills (he was a breeder of polled Angus cattle) and his artistic taste as a collector and connoisseur. He was happiest visiting country areas, where he demonstrated his dry wit: forced to speak on one occasion, he referred to a Scottish tombstone of an infant inscribed 'I expected to be called, but not so soon'. He cut down on overlapping ceremonial between himself and the Melbourne-based governor-general but he enjoyed purposeful ceremonial, as in the rituals of the Church and Freemasonry.

In 1886 Carmichael had married Mary Nugent, niece of the second Baron Nugent; they had no children. In Victoria Lady Carmichael took an interest in kindergartens, arts and crafts training, the Bush Nursing Association and the Victoria League. Both she and her husband promoted art education. He exhibited from his excellent collection, which included water-colours by Turner and Constable.

Carmichael made two important constitutional decisions. He granted a dissolution of parliament to the premier Sir Thomas Bent [q.v.3], who had been defeated on 3 December 1908 in a no confidence vote. Bent, confident of popular support, lied to Carmichael about cabinet unanimity for dissolution and about financial resources for payments till the next parliament met. Carmichael, conscious of his duty to take advice from the premier, was misled. He did not ask the opportunist John Murray [q.v.] to form a government and did not exhaust other alternatives, a point that was clearly made by *The Times* (8 December 1908). Carmichael was supported, however, by the colonial secretary Lord Crewe. Bent failed to win enough support at the election and Murray became premier.

Carmichael's second important constitutional decision related to the 1909 royal commission on Bent's alleged misuse of ministerial influence to make a personal profit. On 5 July the governor refused a request to allow ministers to disclose to the commission cabinet discussions about land issues, emphasizing the necessity for pre-

serving cabinet secrecy.

Carmichael left Melbourne on 29 May 1911 to become governor of Madras. In April 1912, as first Baron Carmichael of Skirling, he was appointed governor of Bengal. He left India in 1917. Survived by his wife, he died in London on 16 January 1926.

M. H. E. Carmichael, *Lord Carmichael of Skirling* (Lond, 1929); *Australasian*, 16 May 1908; *Argus*, 4, 5, 7, 8, 10, 15, 21, 26, 30 Dec 1908, 8 Jan, 24 Feb 1909; *Age*, 7, 8 Dec 1908, 24 Feb 1909; *The Times*, 20 Jan 1926; CO 418/64, 418, 423-32, 439, 462-66, 74/35-45, 51-54, 163-68.   L. R. GARDINER

CARNE, JOSEPH EDMUND (1855-1922), geologist, was born on 12 February 1855 probably at Nowranie station near Urana, New South Wales, second son of Joseph William Carne (1822-1894), pastoralist, and his wife Emma, née Woodhouse. His Cornish grandfather Lieutenant Thomas Carne (1787-1829) had come to Sydney in 1814 with the 46th Regiment. The noted geologist Joseph Carne, F.R.S., was a relation.

Brought up mainly at Appin, Carne attended a private school at Campbelltown. Soon after his mother died in 1871 the family returned to the Riverina. Unsuccessful at the Gulgong diggings, Carne worked as a station-hand in outback New South Wales and Queensland, gaining a mastery of bushcraft. While droving for his uncle T. B. Carne he was practically blinded by sandy-blight. After bush care for some weeks, spent mainly away from sunlight in a dry well, Carne travelled back to Sydney for medical treatment. There he met C. S. Wilkinson [q.v.6], who urged him to study geology. As his sight improved Carne in due course attended classes at the Sydney Technical College.

Early in 1879 he joined the Geological Survey of New South Wales as temporary assistant to Wilkinson. On 9 September 1882 at Burwood he married Louisa McArthur (d. 1892), but the destruction by fire on 22 September of the Garden Palace which housed the Mining and Geological Museum brought him from his honeymoon to begin salvage. He became curator in 1883 and thanks largely to his efforts the museum, in new premises and with new collections, was again open by 1886. Meanwhile, he had organized material for the Colonial and Indian Exhibition, London (1886), and for the exhibitions in Adelaide (1887-88), Melbourne (1888-89) and Dunedin, New Zealand (1889). In May 1890 he accompanied Wilkinson to London to arrange the colony's display for the International Exhibition of Mining and Metallurgy at the Crystal Palace and to report on various museums, mines and metallurgical works in the United Kingdom. He did some preparatory work for the World's Columbian Exposition, Chicago (1893), but in March 1892 transferred to the field staff as a geological surveyor and in 1894 became a member of the Prospecting Board.

Thereafter Carne was increasingly concerned with field geology and compiling reports on the mineral resources of New South Wales. His major works, *The kerosene shale deposits of New South Wales* (1903), *Geology and mineral resources of the western coal field* (1908) and, with L. J. Jones, the classic *Limestone deposits of New South Wales* (1919), like all Carne's writings, combined clarity with meticulous scholarship.

Carne became assistant government geologist in 1902 and in January 1916 succeeded E. F. Pittman [q.v.] as government geologist. He retired from active duty in December 1919. For some time his health had been affected by malaria, contracted while seconded to the Commonwealth government to report on coal deposits in the Purari River district of Papua in 1911-12. The coal proved disappointing but he found promising signs of petroleum; drilling was delayed by the outbreak of World War I. The Carne River in Papua was named in his honour.

A fellow of the Geological Society, London, from 1889, Carne was a councillor of the Linnean and Royal societies of New South Wales; he was awarded the (W. B.) Clarke [q.v.3] Medal in 1920. He died of disseminated sclerosis at his Strathfield home on 23 July 1922 and was buried in the Anglican section of Rookwood cemetery. Carne was survived by three sons and a daughter of his first marriage and by his second wife Clara Grace Hudson, whom he had married at St Andrew's Cathedral on 1 July 1895, and by their daughter and two sons.

His second son WALTER MERVYN (1885-1952), agricultural botanist, was born on 16 September 1885 at Croydon, Sydney, and was educated at Fort Street Public School, Sydney Boys' High School and Sydney Technical College. In 1906-11 he was a laboratory assistant at Hawkesbury Agricultural College. As a scientific cadet with the Department of Agriculture he studied at the University of Sydney in 1912 and next year at the University of California. On his return he became an assistant agrostologist with the department.

In August 1915 Walter enlisted as a private in the Australian Imperial Force, and on 27 November married Blanche Nellie Gertrude Hudson, his stepmother's sister. He served with the 2nd Light Horse Field Ambulance in the Middle East, was mentioned in dispatches in 1916, and awarded the Serbian Silver Medal. Commissioned in 1919, he was appointed to the Education Service; he managed to collect scientific specimens in Palestine and Jordan.

Carne was science master at Hawkesbury Agricultural College for two years, before joining the Western Australian Department of Agriculture in 1923 as economic botanist and plant pathologist. From 1929 he was stationed in Perth as senior plant pathologist for the Commonwealth Council for Scientific and Industrial Research and worked on non-parasitic disorders in apples. Invited by the Empire Marketing Board, he visited England in 1931 to examine Australian apples and pears on arrival.

In 1932-35 Carne was in Tasmania, and in London as fruit officer at Australia House in 1936-37. Now a principal research officer at C.S.I.R., he was seconded in 1938-41 to the Department of Commerce and Agriculture in Melbourne as supervisor of fresh fruit and vegetable exports. Carne joined the staff of the department in 1941, remaining there until his retirement nine years later. During World War II he was attached to food control as technical supervisor of vegetable dehydration. He was a pioneer of plant pathology and fruit storage in Australia.

Carne published many articles and was a fellow of the Linnean Society of London. He was president of the Royal Society of Western Australia in 1927-29 and in 1933 was awarded its gold medal. Survived by his wife and son, he died of coronary occlusion on 20 November 1952 at Chatswood, Sydney, and was cremated.

Linnean Soc NSW, *Procs*, 48 (1923), 78 (1953); Roy Soc NSW, *J*, 57 (1923); Roy Soc WA, *J*, 19 (1932-33); *Aust J of Science*, Feb 1953; *SMH*, 24, 25 July 1922; J. E. Carne diary (ML), *and* letters MS1652 (NL); Hunt Inst biogs (Basser Lib, Canb); family papers held by Miss L. Carne, Cremorne, NSW, and Dr P. B. Carne, Canb.

T. G. VALLANCE

CARNEGIE, DAVID WYNFORD (1871-1900), explorer, was born on 23 March 1871 at Carlton House Terrace, London, fourth son of James, sixth earl of Southesk, and his second wife Susan Catherine Mary, daughter of the earl of Dunsmore. Educated at Charterhouse School and the Royal Indian Engineering College, Staines, he spent a short unhappy term in Ceylon on a tea plantation and, in September 1892 with his friend Lord Percy Douglas, joined the rush to Coolgardie, Western Australia. For eighteen months Carnegie cheerfully worked as a partner and employee in various mines. Between March 1894 and March 1895 he made two commissioned prospecting expeditions for the Hampton Plains Pastoral Co. He found little gold but learned much bushcraft, principally from Gus Luck, an Alsatian who shared the first trip and laughed at his conservative and royalist fervour.

Carnegie now had both the experience and the funds to seek fame by an inland crossing of Western Australia from south to north. Planning to establish the nature of the country between the 1874 route of (Earl) John Forrest [q.v.] and the 1872-73 route of Warburton [q.v.6], he was concerned particularly with gold and the possibility of a direct stockroute between the Kimberley district and Coolgardie. His four companions were Joseph Breaden of Central Australia and his Aboriginal servant Warri, Godfrey Massie of Sydney and Charles Stansmore of Perth. Eight pack-camels carried five months provisions and the necessary equipment; there was only one riding camel.

They started from Coolgardie on 9 July 1896 and intersected Forrest's route at Mount Worsnop 280 miles (450 km) away. At one point, after nearly a fortnight without finding water, Carnegie began to capture Aboriginals, and deprive them of water if necessary or even feed them salt beef as an inducement to reveal secret water-supplies; he was subsequently criticized severely. From Mount Worsnop, Carnegie struck north into the Gibson Desert; they crossed 370 miles (595 km) of this country and on 16 September entered the Great Sandy Desert. For nearly a month the course led across a succession of regular spinifex-clad sand ridges fifty to sixty feet (15-18 m) high. Sandstone tablelands on 16 November led to better country but three camels died of poison plant and on 30 November Stansmore accidentally shot himself dead. The expedition reached Halls Creek on 4 December.

The return trip began on 22 March 1897 and took them east of the outward course; they reached Coolgardie early in August after travelling 3000 miles (4800 km) in thirteen months. Though his results were disappointing, Carnegie was a thoroughly professional explorer. An experienced bushman said of him that 'no explorer since 1862 has covered so much difficult and unknown territory in the time, or accomplished his task with so little loss or with such efficiency'.

Returning to England late in 1897, Carnegie was awarded the Gill medal of the Royal Geographical Society and published his *Spinifex and sand* in 1898. In December 1899 he went to Northern Nigeria as an assistant resident under Sir Frederick Lugard. He served at Illorin and while based at Lokoja was killed by a poisoned arrow in a minor skirmish at Kerifi on 21 November 1900. He was buried at Lokoja; a memorial was erected in Brechin Cathedral, Scotland, and a replica placed in St George's Cathedral, Perth, in 1925. His sister privately published his *Letters from Nigeria* in 1902.

G. Buchanan, *Packhorse and waterhole* (Syd, 1933); D. O'Callaghan, . . . *reminiscences and adventures throughout the world* (Perth, 1941); *Vic Geog J*, 21 (1903); *JR WAHS (Early Days)*, Dec 1948; *British A'sian*, 16 Dec 1897, 29 Sept 1898, 13 Dec 1900; *Australasian*, 25 Sept, 30 Oct 1897, 15 Dec 1900; *Western Argus*, 15 Jan 1901.

PATRICIA MORISON

CARPENTER, SIR WALTER RANDOLPH (1877-1954), merchant, was born on 31 October 1877 at Singapore, Straits Settlements, son of John Bolton Carpenter and his English wife Emma Frances, née Griffin. John, a merchant, whaler and sea captain, came from New Haven, Connecticut, United States of America. Restricted by the American Civil War he had made the Straits Settlements his base and been naturalized a British subject. In 1885 he moved his family to Sydney and became a skipper for Burns, Philp [qq.v.] & Co. In 1891, while commanding the company's *Costa Rica Packet*, he was arrested at Ternate in the Dutch East Indies and then involved in the long struggle for compensation.

To help the family, Walter left Forest Lodge Public School at 14 and joined the Sydney office of Burns Philp. After a year at Esperance, Western Australia, about 1896 he moved to the Thursday Island branch. There on 18 December 1899 he married Edith Anderson, daughter of a sugar-planter. That year he left Burns Philp, bought three luggers and set up a family pearl-shelling business, registered as J. B. Carpenter & Sons Ltd in 1901; Walter was managing director at a salary of £300. In 1905 he was chairman of the Torres Shire Council. Leaving his brother William in charge, Carpenter left Thursday Island late in 1908 and rejoined Burns Philp. After a year in Sydney, he went to Fiji and managed Robbie, Kaad Co. Ltd, recently bought by Burns Philp.

In 1914 Carpenter returned to Sydney and in September registered W. R. Carpenter & Co. Ltd: its first shareholders apart from himself, were P. A. Morris and (Sir J.) Maynard Hedstrom, who later founded Morris Hedstrom Ltd, Fiji. When World War I began Carpenter realized the importance of copra in making munitions and for food, and bought it wherever he could find it and raise credit, chartering 'almost anything that would float', including an old sailing ship, to get it to England. He took enormous risks but made huge profits, and was ideally placed to expand into New Guinea after the Australian government had expropriated German property. Under his able management, the company helped to finance, and later took over, the plantations of some Australian ex-servicemen who became heavily indebted when copra prices fell; it became large storekeepers, traders and property owners in New Guinea and the Solomon Islands – in 1922 he had set up W. R. Carpenter & Co. (Solomon Islands) Ltd. Although much abused by some planters and small traders – W.R.C. was said to stand for 'Would Rob Christ' – Carpenters' also earned the gratitude of those who survived on long-term credit and who looked to it to transact all their business.

Carpenter took advantage of the development of the rich Morobe goldfields in New Guinea; he acquired hotels in Wau and Bulolo, set up electrical power plants and cold stores in various centres, operated a small fleet of inter-island steamers, built and equipped a slip in Rabaul, and operated a desiccated coconut factory. In 1933 he established the first air service between Salamaua and Wau with two De Haviland Fox Moths and next year a direct shipping-line between Australia, the Western Pacific and European ports: most of his ships were built in Australia. Between 1924 and 1934 the company never failed to pay an 8 per cent dividend and extended its trading operations into the Gilbert and Ellice Islands. In 1935 Carpenter set up the Southern Pacific Insurance Co. Ltd, next year acquired a controlling interest in Jobson Brown & Joske Ltd of Suva, Fiji, and soon expanded his airline when he successfully tendered for the government-subsidized route between Rabaul and Australia.

Carpenter had strongly advocated devaluation as a solution to trading difficulties. He had long deplored the effects of 'socialist' trends on the Australian economy and as the 1930s progressed he criticized the Commonwealth government's negative attitude to Australian defence, shipping and ship-builders and urgently stressed the need to develop a strong navy: 'We should concentrate on cruisers, with the Singapore Base as the bulwark of our defence'; in 1938 he also advocated compulsory military training. Fearing the worst he gradually transferred most of his capital out of Australia.

A considerable philanthropist, Carpenter subsidized pound for pound the Home for Destitute Children, and in 1935 gave a house at Wollstonecraft worth £15000 and £5000 in cash to the Commonwealth government for a jubilee maternity hospital. He was knighted in 1936.

On the outbreak of World War II Carpenter's ships and aeroplanes were commandeered by the British and Australian governments. However in 1940 he visited the U.S.A. and managed to purchase two freighters 'under conditions which allow him to operate in the Pacific free of European control'. He then formed a new company in Canada, built a copra-crushing mill near Vancouver and found a healthy North American market. Although his buildings and plantations in New Guinea and the Solomon, Gilbert and Ellice islands were destroyed when Japan entered the war, he did well from the wartime prosperity of Fiji, and later received compensation for war damage. Soon after the war he bought two British ships for the Australian-Canadian run. In November 1941 he had settled permanently in Vancouver and in May 1948 he and his wife took out Canadian citizenship.

In Sydney Sir Walter belonged to the National, Millions and Tattersall's clubs and the Royal Automobile Club of Australia – he enjoyed playing tennis, billiards and 'bad golf', but 'revelled in work'. Bald and bespectacled, he was tall and powerfully built, of 'a merry habit and breezy personality' with 'an admirable habit of laughing at himself'. He was a brilliant manager, far-sighted and enterprising, kind to his employees but tough with competitors. Having survived high risks in early trading, he later built up huge internal reserves to cope with fluctuations in marketing conditions.

After several heart attacks, Carpenter died on 1 February 1954 at Killara, while on a visit to Sydney, and was cremated with Anglican rites. He was survived by his wife, two sons and three daughters; his sons succeeded him as managing directors of W. R. Carpenter & Co. Ltd, and in 1956 bought a controlling interest in Morris Hedstrom Ltd. His estate was valued for probate at £50387 in New South Wales and $923481 in Canada.

With Burns Philp and the Colonial Sugar Refining Co., W. R. Carpenter & Co. had been the most tangible signs of Australia's involvement in the south-west Pacific. The extent to which they did good while doing well, or insensitively exploited islands and islanders has largely determined Australia's reputation in the region.

J (LC NSW), 1894-95, 53, pt 2, 345-437; *Pacific Islands Mthly*, Jan 1936, May 1941, Feb 1954, Dec 1955; *Rydge's*, June 1936; J. B. Carpenter papers (NL).   H. N. NELSON

CARR, THOMAS JOSEPH (1839-1917), Catholic archbishop, was baptized on 10 May 1839 at Moylough, County Galway, Ireland. His father, a farmer of some substance, sent him to St Jarlath's College, Tuam, for his early education. At 15 he was admitted to St Patrick's College, Maynooth, where he was ordained priest in 1866. After two years as a curate in his native diocese, he taught at St Jarlath's and then returned to Maynooth in 1874 where he became professor of dogmatic theology, prefect of the Dunboyne establishment, and in 1880 vice-president of Maynooth. In 1879 he published an extensive work on recent developments in canon law entitled *A contribution on Church and censures*; next year he was appointed editor of the *Irish Ecclesiastical Record* which had lapsed under the editorship of (Cardinal) P. F. Moran [q.v.] in 1876.

The formative years of the young cleric were spent in an ecclesiastical climate in which Cardinal Cullen [q.v.3], as archbishop of Dublin (1852-78), devoted his talents and influence to strengthening the bonds between the Roman see and the Irish Church. The new direction was not lost on Carr and from the time of his appointment to the bishopric of Galway in 1883 he proved unswerving in his loyalty to Rome, became a firm defender of the prerogatives of that see and lectured regularly on its historical claims. While remembered at Maynooth as an uninspiring but painstaking teacher, and a scholar of considerable ability, Carr was more inclined to an active life of leadership and administration. In Galway he took a keen interest in the welfare of his people, especially the poorer classes, and promoted the foundation of technical and industrial schools to equip the young with the skills necessary to gain a useful livelihood.

By the early 1880s Archbishop Goold [q.v.4] of Melbourne had become enfeebled in body and difficult in temperament. At the plenary council, held in Sydney in 1885, Carr's name was put forward as Goold's coadjutor. But as Goold died on 11 June 1886 Carr was appointed directly to the archbishopric on 29 September and received the pallium from Leo XIII in Rome on his way to Melbourne. He was there accorded a friendly and enthusiastic reception in June 1887. Moran had experienced some difficulty in establishing a working relationship with the old pioneer missionary Goold, and when he heard that Carr had been appointed to Melbourne, he exclaimed: 'All the Australian Bishops will now be thoroughly united!'. It was a hope that was fulfilled, at least in so far as the sees of Sydney and Melbourne were concerned, for until his death in 1911 Moran constantly consulted Carr on matters affecting both his own diocese and the general state of the Catholic Church in Australia.

At the time of Carr's arrival the colony of Victoria had settled to a period of peaceful prosperity after the rapid growth and tumult of the gold period. This stability reflected itself in the Catholic Church which had begun to assume the shape of a normal ecclesiastical organism with bishops in Ballarat and Bendigo since 1874; Carr himself consecrated the first bishop of Sale, James Corbett [q.v.], in 1887. Before the financial collapse of the early 1890s Carr was able to administer with ease the structural changes consequent upon population growth and he caused new churches, convents and schools to be built. New religious Orders were introduced while the number of priests on the diocesan mission doubled in ten years to over 100.

The archbishop took a keen interest in the foundation of St Patrick's College at Manly, New South Wales, which opened in 1889 and, being convinced of the necessity of a sound educational standard in his clergy, Carr would not accept students for the priesthood unless they had matriculated. His zeal in that regard was modified by inordinate parsimony, induced by the financial depression, which he rationalized with the stated conviction that parents of ecclesiastical students ought to make sacrifices for the upkeep of their sons. As a result of this policy he lost eight students for his archdiocese in 1908 because he refused to pay their fees at Manly. Independent means, rare in an Irish Australian family in the period, became a yardstick upon which a vocation to the priesthood partially rested.

Carr shared with his episcopal contemporaries the attitude to the necessity of a Catholic education enunciated by Roger Vaughan [q.v.6] who, as archbishop of Sydney (1877-83), regarded a secular education as anathema. Carr summed up his own convictions with the statement: 'Banish faith from the schools in one generation, and you have banished God from the country in the next'. Not content with slogans, the archbishop devoted a great deal of energy to promoting the Catholic school system, with the result that the number of children receiving a Catholic education in Victoria rose from 10 000 at the time of his arrival to almost 50 000 when he died. When training colleges for teachers were required, Carr immediately set up one at Albert Park in 1906 and then turned his mind to tertiary education by founding the Newman Society in 1911 with himself as its first president. On 11 June 1916 he blessed the foundation stone of Newman College, University of Melbourne, and although the major inspirational force in its development was his coadjutor Daniel Mannix [q.v.], Carr was remembered as its founder by the erection of a chapel in his honour.

As a political figure Carr, while determined to uphold his personal convictions on such matters as the Roman primacy and related dogmatic beliefs, about which he engaged in vigorous debate with Professor J. L. Rentoul, Bishop Goe [qq.v.] and others, none the less remained on cordial personal terms with his adversaries; and when birth control met with his public condemnation in 1908 he received letters of congratulation and support from many non-Catholics, including one from the Council of Churches. He was regular in attendance at government levees, formed a firm friendship with the earl of Hopetoun [q.v.] and his wife and, while standing aloof from the political arena, evinced his belief in Federation and attended the opening of Federal parliament in 1901. His interest in the social question was neither doctrinaire nor sectarian and in his public addresses he supported child endowment, housing policies for the masses, the development of educational facilities for women and assistance for Aboriginals. Theoretical notions on the need to help the underprivileged were quickly translated by Carr into practical action, and he helped in the foundation of St Vincent's Hospital and a home for foundlings at Broadmeadows.

In 1913 Mannix was appointed as Carr's coadjutor. The archbishop quickly handed over to him much of his administrative affairs and stood prudently aside while the younger man threw himself into public life with alacrity. To the Australian hierarchy, Carr had become a figure of quiet, balanced, moderate common sense who acted among them as a conciliatory agent and who never permitted his Irish background to override his concern for the consolidation of the Catholic Church in Australia. When the Irish delegates had visited Australia in 1889 Carr expressed considerable unease, but agreed to receive them while making it clear that he took no political stand and, on the continuing problem of Ireland, he maintained a detached attitude despite his love for his native land on whose art and culture he frequently lectured. Thus, when the conscription issue arose, he was able to retain his conciliatory tone while rejecting an overture from the State Recruiting Committee of Victoria which asked that a pronouncement be read in the churches calling on recruitment as a 'Christian duty'. Carr replied courteously: 'Catholics know perfectly well what their interests and duties are . . . they resent the invasion of the State into Church management'.

Carr himself, together with his contem-poraries, regarded his completion of St Patrick's Cathedral in 1897 as the finest visible token of his archiepiscopate. He was aware, however, that stone speaks in a muted voice and his foundation of the *Austral Light* (1892), the *Tribune* (1900) and the enduring Australian Catholic Truth Society (1904), together with the publication of his own *Lectures and replies* (1907), bore testimony to his concern with the problem of educating and informing his laity. Recognizing the deleterious effects of the over-consumption of liquor amongst his people, he did all in his power to inculcate the virtue of temperance without inclining to the extreme of wowserism. He founded the League of the Cross and he obliged children to take a pledge at confirmation binding them not to drink alcoholic beverages until the age of 21.

An excellent shot, card-player and club-man, Carr was at ease in any company, whether that of children or vice-royalty, and at his table all felt the conviviality of his urbane character. With the passing years his geniality seemed to transmit itself into a physical characteristic so that his obesity became the outward sign of a spirit at peace with all its surroundings: Tom Roberts [q.v.] said, 'He's a man you could tell anything to – except something trumpery'. By 1916 he was suffering from cancer and a trip to New Zealand was to no avail. He died in Melbourne on 6 May 1917 and was buried in his cathedral. His episcopate had been one marked by stability, tranquillity and growth, guided by his reliance upon the Roman Church and its central authority; he had visited Rome in 1898 and 1908. In the words of Sir Ronald Munro Ferguson [q.v.], by his 'wisdom, tact and Christian goodness [Carr had] endeared himself to the Australian people'; while the prime minister W. M. Hughes [q.v.], doubtless mindful of Mannix's succession, mourned this 'great and good man' who 'strove always to promote peace and goodwill amongst all sections of the community'.

P. F. Moran, *History of the Catholic Church in Australasia* (Syd, 1895); *Australasian*, 6 Nov 1897, 9 Apr 1898, 27 Sept 1902; *Argus*, 7 May 1917; *Advocate* (Melb), 12 May 1917; Carr papers (MDHC Archives, Fitzroy, Vic).

JOHN N. MOLONY

CARR, WILLIAM JAMES (1883-1966), naval medical officer, was born on 30 January 1883 at Thornton-in-Craven, Yorkshire, England, son of James Carr, solicitor, and his wife Mary Ellen, née Spencer. He was educated at Marlborough College and Trinity College, Cambridge (B.A., 1904; B.C., 1908), and did the clinical training for his medical degree at the London Hospital (L.R.C.P., London; M.R.C.S., England, 1908). He remained at the hospital as a resident medical officer in 1909-10, was medical officer on a tramp-steamer in 1911, and a locum tenens in London and Kent in 1912.

Carr joined the Royal Australian Navy in London on 9 December and was posted to the cruiser H.M.A.S. *Melbourne* in the rank of surgeon lieutenant. He remained in the *Melbourne* until late 1917, seeing war service in the Pacific, North Atlantic, West Indies and the North Sea. His experiences in the West Indies led to a paper on tropical bubo, delivered to the Australasian Medical Congress in 1923. In October 1917 he was transferred to the battle-cruiser H.M.A.S. *Australia*, then in March 1918 to the cruiser H.M.A.S. *Sydney*. He was promoted surgeon lieut-commander in December and next year, on 5 August, married Leonora Constance Eddington at St John's Anglican Church, Toorak, Melbourne. He was medical officer at the Royal Australian Naval College, Jervis Bay, Australian Capital Territory, from August 1920 to March 1923 and was then appointed to the naval wing of the Prince of Wales Hospital, Randwick, Sydney; he was promoted surgeon commander in June 1924. Next year he went on an exchange posting to the Royal Naval Hospital at Haslar near Portsmouth, England, and on his return in June 1927 joined the hospital staff at Flinders Naval Depot, Victoria.

In December 1932 Carr was appointed director of naval medical services and held this post until his retirement in 1946; he was promoted surgeon captain in December 1934. In World War II his considerable administrative ability was directed to the medical problems of the much enlarged R.A.N. which expanded from 5300 personnel in 1939 to almost 40 000 in 1945. The medical supply system which he developed stood the test of war and his pre-war emphasis on reserve training bore fruit in the numbers of competent doctors who chose to serve in the navy: by 1945 the service had 110 medical officers, most of whom were reservists. Carr oversaw the formation of the Women's Royal Australian Naval Nursing Service in 1942 and coped well with the additional strains imposed on the medical supply organization by the requirements of the British Pacific Fleet from 1944.

Carr retired on 8 March 1946 as surgeon rear admiral, the first R.A.N. officer to attain this rank. However, it appears that the promotion was more the result of agitation by the *Medical Journal of Australia* than recognition by the naval board of his pioneering work. He was appointed C.B.E. in 1937 and became a fellow of the Royal Australasian College of Physicians in 1943. In retirement at Frankston, Victoria, he took an active interest in Liberal Party politics and was a keen follower of many sports. Survived by his wife, a son and two daughters, he died on 16 May 1966 and was cremated after an Anglican service.

A. G. Butler (ed), *Official history of the Australian Army Medical Services... 1914-18*, 3 (Canb, 1943); A. S. Walker, *Medical services of the R.A.N. and R.A.A.F.* (Canb, 1961); *MJA*, 26 Jan 1946, 28 Jan 1967; War cruises of the H.M.A.S. *Melbourne* and *Sydney* (held by Mr J. Carr, Melb); MP124 551/202/237, MP150 437/201/301,408,921, MT574 21/8918, MT1214 448/201/874,2237 (AAO, Melb).   DENIS FAIRFAX

CARRICK, ETHEL; *see* FOX, E. PHILLIPS

CARROLL, EDWARD JOHN (1868-1931) and DANIEL JOSEPH (1886-1959), theatrical and film entrepreneurs, were born on 28 June 1868 at Gatton, Queensland, and on 28 June 1886 at Redbank Plains, second and seventh sons of John Carroll, schoolteacher, and his wife Mary, née Dwyer, both from County Cork, Ireland. The boys began their education at Redbank Plains State School where their father was head teacher in 1874-1909; Dan went on to St Edmund's Christian Brothers' College, Ipswich.

'E.J.' joined the Queensland Department of Railways as a clerk in 1883. By the mid-1890s with James Bell he had set up as a fruit-merchant at Gympie and later in Brisbane. In 1901-07, with Bell and C. J. Stewart, he held the catering contracts for railway refreshment rooms at Ipswich, Landsborough and Gympie. On 14 February 1906 at St Stephen's Cathedral, Brisbane, he married Jessie Dee. In Brisbane in 1905-22 he and Stewart leased the Albion Hotel and by 1914 owned the Criterion.

Meanwhile in 1906 Carroll acquired the Queensland rights for the first Australian feature film, *The story of the Kelly gang*, and screened it so successfully that he established an open-air picture circuit round Brisbane suburbs. He also owned touring side-shows and vaudeville acts and later built skating-rinks in several rural centres which were used in summer for picture shows. He gradually built up a chain of theatres.

In 1908 E.J. was joined by Dan, who had worked for E. Rich & Co. Ltd in Brisbane since 1903. When E.J. moved his interests to Sydney about 1913 Dan remained in charge of his Queensland enterprises. They began to bring British and American plays to Australia and had a major success in 1914 with a tour by the Scottish entertainer (Sir) Harry Lauder, who became a close friend.

In 1918 the Carrolls invested in their first film production, *The lure of the bush*, starring R. L. 'Snowy' Baker [q.v.], and it proved highly popular. They also undertook distribution in Australia and overseas of Raymond Longford's [q.v.] film, *The sentimental bloke* (1919), and following its enormous commercial success, decided to enter production themselves. In partnership with Baker and with the South Australian firm, the Southern Cross Feature Film Co. Ltd, they formed Carroll-Baker Australian Productions in 1919 with capital of £25 000. To attract overseas distribution of their films, the company arranged for a team of Americans from Hollywood to form the nucleus of the production staff. Three 'Westerns' starring Baker were made, including *The man from Kangaroo*, and released in 1920 with commercial success. The Carrolls also formed a production association with Longford and Lottie Lyell [q.v.] and made three films including *On our selection* (1920).

During 1920 E.J. travelled widely overseas to market the films and to manage a world tour by Lauder. Late in 1921 the Carrolls withdrew from film production because of disagreement with the Americans over their expensive production methods, and because of difficulties in ensuring adequate exhibition of their films in Australia and abroad.

In 1920 the brothers had formed Carroll Musgrove Theatres Ltd to build the Prince Edward Theatre in Sydney which, from its opening in 1924, became one of Australia's leading cinemas. In 1923 they set up Birch, Carroll and Coyle Ltd to control and modernize their extensive theatre circuit in northern and coastal Queensland. Their other cinema interests, often in association with the Tait brothers and Stuart Doyle [qq.v.], included the Wintergarden Theatre, Brisbane. The Carrolls remained active in live-theatre management and arranged Australian tours by major performers such as the Sistine Choir in 1922 and the violinist Fritz Kreisler in 1925.

Handsome, with a military moustache, E.J. was always impeccably dressed. In 1926 he took his sons to England to be educated and established himself in London. He returned to Sydney in March 1931 and died of cancer at Lewisham Hospital on 28 July, survived by his wife and two sons. He was buried in the Catholic section of South Head cemetery. His estate was valued for probate at £19 236 in Queensland and £17 461 in New South Wales.

Dan was managing director of the family companies until 1959 and chairman of the Motion Picture Industry Benevolent Society in 1932-59. A 'real Beau Brummell', he had an Irish wit and was a devout Catholic. Survived by his wife Muriel Ruby, née Treble, whom he had married at St Mary's Cathedral, Sydney, on 28 April 1928, he died in Sydney of cardiac disease on 11 August 1959, and was buried in South Head cemetery.

The brothers were famous in the entertainment world for their boldness as entrepreneurs and for their integrity as businessmen: their name carried a certain guarantee of professionalism.

Cwlth of Aust, *Roy Com on the moving picture industry in Australia: minutes of evidence* (Canb, 1928); H. Lauder, *Roamin' in the gloamin'* (Lond, 1928?); Redbank Plains State School (Qld), *Centenary, 1874-1974* (Redbank Plains, 1974); E. Reade, *The Australian screen* (Melb, 1975); *Picture Show*, 6 Sept 1919, 1 Apr, 1 Nov, 1 Dec 1920; *Theatre Mag*, 1 Oct 1919, 1 Feb 1920, 1 Dec 1921; *Everyone's* 2 Nov 1921; *Film Weekly*, 30 July 1931, 13 Aug 1959; *Showman*, Oct, Dec 1950, Mar 1953; *A'sian Exhibitor*, 20 Aug 1959; *SMH*, 3 Sept 1919, 26 May, 19 July 1921, 29, 31 July 1931, 4 Dec 1934, 14 Dec 1944; *Table Talk*, 16 Aug 1928.

A. F. PIKE
MARTHA RUTLEDGE

CARROLL, JACK; *see* HARDWICK, ARTHUR

CARROLL, JOHN (1891-1971), soldier, labourer and railway employee, was born on 16 August 1891 in Brisbane, son of John Carroll, labourer, and his wife Catherine, née Wallace, both Irish-born. When he was 2 the family moved to Donnybrook, Western Australia, and then to Yarloop. About 1905 they settled at Kurrawang where John and his father joined the Goldfields Firewood Supply Co. as labourers. Tall and well built, John was a good athlete and a prominent member of the local football club; he was working as a railway guard on the Kurrawang line when he enlisted in the Australian Imperial Force as a private on 27 April 1916.

Carroll embarked for England in August with reinforcements for the 44th Battalion, then on 14 November was transferred to the 33rd Battalion. He went into the line at Armentières, France, and served there until April 1917 when his unit moved into position for the Messines offensive. On 7 June, in the battle of Messines Ridge, he rushed an enemy trench and bayoneted four men, then rescued a comrade who was in difficulties. Later in the advance he attacked a machine-gun crew, killing three men and capturing the gun, and, in spite of heavy shelling and machine-gun fire, dug out two of his mates who had been buried by a shell explosion. During the battle his battalion was in the line for ninety-six hours and Carroll 'displayed most wonderful courage and fearlessness' throughout. He was awarded the Victoria Cross and in September was promoted lance corporal. On 12 October, in the second battle of Passchendaele, he was severely wounded and did not rejoin his unit until June 1918; next month he was transferred to A.I.F. headquarters, London, and in August returned to Australia.

After demobilization Carroll resumed work as a guard on the Kurrawang line. He married Mary Brown in the Catholic Cathedral, Perth, on 23 April 1923; they had no children. In the mid-1920s he moved to the Yarloop district and in November 1927, when he was working as a railway truck examiner at Hoffman's Mill, he slipped while boarding a train during shunting operations and crushed his right foot; it was amputated but he continued working for many years as a labourer and railway employee. In 1956 he went to London for the Victoria Cross centenary celebrations, then retired to the Perth suburb of Bedford. He died in the Repatriation General Hospital, Hollywood, on 4 October 1971 and was buried in Karrakatta cemetery with full military honours. His wife had predeceased him.

Carroll, who was known among his A.I.F. comrades as 'the wild Irishman', was casual and happy-go-lucky by nature. He missed three dates for his investiture with the V.C. and had to be sent for on the fourth occasion; after the ceremony he amused himself by exercising the Victoria Cross winners' right to turn out the Buckingham Palace Guard. He was also known as 'Referendum Carroll' because he rarely said anything but yes or no. Two of his brothers served as privates in the A.I.F.

C. E. W. Bean, *The A.I.F. in France*, 1916-17 (Syd, 1929, 1933); L. Wigmore (ed), *They dared mightily* (Canb, 1963); *London Gazette*, 2 Aug 1917; *Western Argus*, 21 Aug 1917; *Daily News* (Perth), 1-2 Nov 1927.   REX CLARK*

CARROLL, ROBERT JOSEPH (1877-1940), trade union and Labor Party official, was born on 16 June 1877 in Dublin. Migrating in 1882 with his mother and sister, he was educated at St Joseph's College, Brisbane, worked as a shop-assistant, and was apprenticed to the Australian United Steam Navigation Co. in 1892. Qualifying as an engineer in 1897, he served in ships trading with China and Japan. He joined the Amalgamated Society of Engineers in 1897, and was president of the Brisbane branch when he left Australia early in 1902 for the South African goldfields.

Carroll held office in the A.S.E. in South Africa, became the first secretary of the Kimberley Trades and Labour Council, and was dismissed by the De Beers Co. for inducing the Cape Colony parliament to reject 'contracting out' provisions in a workers' compensation bill. On 28 March 1904 at Cape Town, he married Edith Maude Robinson, who had come from Brisbane for the wedding; they had three children.

A foundation member of the South African Labour Party, Carroll campaigned successfully for a Labour candidate against his own mine-owning employer in the Transvaal provincial election of 1907. Labour fared badly in the election: Carroll lost his job and returned to Australia where, unable to find work at his trade, he went pineapple-farming at Cribb Island near Brisbane. Employed at the South Brisbane dry dock in 1911, he became secretary of the Brisbane district committee of the A.S.E. and was spokesman for engineering workers during the 1912 general strike. In February 1913 Carroll toured Queensland organizing for the union and in July became its first full-time official; in two years membership almost trebled. He represented it on the Trades Hall board of management, on the Brisbane Industrial Council and on the Trades and Labor Council when it was reconstituted in 1922. Elected to the central political executive of the Australian Labor Party in 1917, he remained a member till his death; from 1920 he was on its executive committee and was its returning officer in 1919-34. In 1920 he was appointed to the Legislative Council and next year his vote helped to abolish it. He stood unsuccessfully for the Senate in 1934.

Usually a militant, Carroll opposed conscription strongly in 1916-17 and was one of several unionists imprisoned in June 1919 for flying the red flag. He was released from Boggo Road Gaol on 1 August under a peace amnesty after an unsuccessful Supreme Court appeal by T. J. Ryan [q.v.] against the sentence. Despite his militancy and vocal contempt for arbitration, he abided by his party's policy and became a competent and respected advocate in the Industrial Court; he shared with Tim Moroney [q.v.] the presentation of cases for the combined railways' unions. He was also appointed secretary of the Trade Union Research Committee set up in 1925 to assist the investigation into the basic wage commissioned by T. W. McCawley [q.v.]. Carroll's children saw little of him at night and remember him as always either attending a meeting or working at home on a case for the Industrial Court.

He became a director of the *Daily Stan-*

dard in 1918 and as chairman in the 1930s was able to persuade the Australian Workers' Union to continue financing the paper until it closed in 1936. Carroll was a senator of the University of Queensland from 1920, and was active in the Ambulance Transport Brigade, the Authors and Artists' Association and the Royal Geographical Society of Australasia. He was also a trustee of the National Art Gallery.

By the early 1930s, Carroll was one of the most powerful Labor leaders in Queensland, the confidant of W. Forgan Smith [q.v.] and of the central executive president Clarrie Fallon. He resigned his union office in 1935 to become a full-time organizer for the party and in 1937 succeeded Lewis McDonald [q.v.] as secretary. He codified and modernized the confused party rules while rebutting charges of Catholic domination.

Though born a Catholic, Carroll had abandoned all religion when young. When he died of intestinal neoplasm on 7 February 1940, it was found that he had willed his body to the university medical school. His estate was valued for probate at £1508. In December his remains were cremated and the ashes scattered in the bush. He did not believe in stone memorials.

K. D. Buckley, *The Amalgamated Engineers in Australia, 1852-1920* (Canb, 1970); T. Sheridan, *Mindful militants* (Cambridge, 1975); D. J. Murphy, R. B. Joyce and C. A. Hughes (eds), *Labor in power . . . Queensland 1915-1957* (Brisb, 1979); Particulars relating to the working life of Robert J. Carroll (held by Mr C. Carroll, Fryer Lib, Univ Qld). D. J. MURPHY

CARRUTHERS, GEORGE SIMPSON (1879-1949), clergyman, fruit-grower and Douglas Credit politician, was born on 1 February 1879 at Lancaster, England, son of George Brockbank Carruthers, merchant, and his wife Emma, née Roberts. Educated at Lancaster School, Selwyn College, Cambridge (B.A., 1901), and Ripon Theological College, he was ordained deacon in 1903 and priest in 1905, and in 1903-09 held curacies at Clapham, Yorkshire, All Hallows, Leeds, and Wetheral, Cumberland. Illness forced his retirement and he migrated to Tasmania where he tried fruit-farming near New Norfolk. In 1911-13 he lived at Pelham, but by 1914 had transferred to Magra. Though one of the original directors of the Derwent Valley Fruitgrowers' Co-operative Co. Ltd, Carruthers did not prosper. From 1929 to 1931 he farmed at Kingston, ten miles south of Hobart, again without success.

Moving to Hobart, Carruthers campaigned for the Depression unemployed, condemning the large fruit companies for ensuring the eviction of small farmers like himself. He joined the local Labor Party, forming an alliance with Edmund Dwyer-Gray [q.v.], State politician and editor of the Labor *Voice*. In his contributions to the *Voice* after 1931, Carruthers moved steadily towards Douglas Credit ideas, a progress shared by Dwyer-Gray. In 1934 Carruthers incurred automatic expulsion from the party by contesting the State election solely as an endorsed Douglas Credit candidate. In a dramatically close contest he won the sixth Denison seat and the balance of power in the House of Assembly. His benevolent neutrality enabled the Tasmanian Labor Party to begin a period in office, unbroken till 1969.

Carruthers' single parliamentary term, though he chaired a select committee on monetary reform whose report vaguely favoured Douglas Credit, was unhappy. While generally supporting Albert Ogilvie's [q.v.] government, Carruthers incurred the hostility of the fiery premier by voting against the extension of gambling facilities and liquor licences, five-year parliaments and the suspiciously high payments to private companies constructing the Derwent Bridge. Defeated in the 1937 election, he at once applied for readmission to the Labor Party and, after several rebuffs from conference, was restored by the party's State executive in 1940, thanks mainly to Dwyer-Gray. Carruthers advocated his monetary views in the *Voice*, at State Labor conferences, and even on the council of the University of Tasmania, on which he served in 1935, 1939-40 and 1942-47. In the 1943 Commonwealth election he stood unsuccessfully for the Senate as an endorsed Labor candidate.

Carruthers died at Hobart of cancer on 29 June 1949 and was cremated. He endured bachelor loneliness and poverty in his final years, relying heavily on the Anglican Church for which he occasionally ministered, having obtained admission into the diocese of Hobart in 1938. Never an outstanding intellect or magnetic personality, Carruthers had the quiet dignity of a man of principle.

PP (HA Tas), 1935 (25); R. Davis, 'G. S. Carruthers and the Tasmanian A.L.P.', *PTHRA*, 23 (1976), no 4; *Mercury*, 30 June 1949; Aust Labor Party (Tas), Executive minute-book, Dec 1930-Nov 1942, *and* State Conference minutes, 1930-36, 1937-42 (Univ Tas Archives). R. P. DAVIS

CARRUTHERS, SIR JOSEPH HECTOR McNEIL (1856-1932), politician, solicitor and investor, was born on 21 December 1856

at Kiama, New South Wales, sixth son of nine children born to Scottish immigrant, John Carruthers (Cruthers), and his English wife Charlotte, née Prince. He was educated at William Street and Fort Street schools, as a boarder at George Metcalf's Goulburn High School, and at the University of Sydney (B.A., 1876; M.A., 1878). Articled to A. H. McCulloch, he was admitted as a solicitor on 28 June 1879 and soon made investment in land a sideline. On 10 December at St James's Anglican Church, he married Louise Marion, daughter of William Roberts, solicitor.

The same year Carruthers supported (Sir) Arthur Renwick [q.v.6] against (Sir) Edmund Barton [q.v.] for the university seat. In 1887 he topped the poll for the four-member electorate of Canterbury on a platform of local interests, free trade 'pure and simple', social reform, land reform, industrial conciliation and arbitration, an elective legislative council, local government and local option. His maiden speech pleaded for a tramway from Kogarah to Sans Souci, where he lived, but he soon earned respect as a free trader, businessman and reformer. On 17 April 1888 he introduced a private member's bill for a non-compulsory conciliation board and blamed employers as well as employees for industrial unrest; a select committee was appointed but it never reported.

In 1889 Carruthers, who had helped to draw up the ephemeral Liberal Party platform of 6 March, became minister of public instruction in Sir Henry Parkes's [q.v.5] last ministry. He wanted a centralized system, to include the independent schools and technical education, with the university as the apex. He introduced a bill to endow a women's college within the university. Abolishing the Board of Technical Education, he brought technical colleges under the Department of Public Instruction. In 1890 he announced that a teachers' college would be set up within the grounds of the university. He disapproved of payment of members of parliament on democratic grounds.

At the National Australasian Convention in Sydney in March 1891 Carruthers argued for Federation for the sake of 'White Australia'. When Parkes sought approval of the draft Federation bill, (Sir) George Reid [q.v.] and (Sir) George Dibbs [q.v.4] began the manoeuvres that led to the dissolution of parliament. The elections left Parkes premier with Labor support; Carruthers emerged as the leading tactician of the cabinet. Labor's demand for an eight-hour day in mining legislation caused the ministry's resignation on 22 October. Reid became leader of the free traders.

Carruthers, in ill health, found opposition hard to bear, objecting to the 'Socialistic roughs' among Labor, to the selfish liberals, who failed to resist them, and to Barton's failure to promote Federation. He blamed the Dibbs ministry for much of the trouble during the 1892 strike at Broken Hill. Many of his opinions were refined in 1891-94. He did not dislike the principle of income tax, but opposed its introduction lest it delay the return of prosperity. Partly following Henry George [q.v.4], he rejected taxation of the improved capital value of land. He castigated the government's economy proposals to keep children under six away from school and to raise high-school fees.

Depressed by family problems and influenza, Carruthers saw the Free Trade Party in 1894 as split into factions led by Parkes, Reid and B. R. Wise [q.v.]. In June, however, he rallied to Reid's shrewd linking of free trade with direct taxation and retrenchment, and reforms of local government, the Legislative Council and the civil service. The elections next month were conducted on the new single-member seats, contested on the same day. Carruthers won St George and held it until 1908. He joined Reid's ministry as secretary for lands, a portfolio appropriate to his reforming interests, investment experience and legal practice. With many pastoral leases falling in, he proposed crown lands reform, chiefly by a system of homestead selections, which were virtually perpetual leaseholds, giving access to land to people with little capital; new improvement and settlement leases were made available; lands were classified and speculative selections hampered. The proposals gratified land reformers by encouraging genuine closer settlement, while relieving pastoralists' fears of reckless reforms by city-based free traders. Proclaimed in 1895, the Act was Carruthers' first political master-stroke. Public commendation helped him endure private affliction. Late that year he divorced his wife in an undefended suit and was granted custody of the children.

In June the Legislative Council rejected the government's land and income tax bill. Carruthers called for reform of the 'irresponsible' council and wanted an election to 'purify' the Free Trade Party. The government won the elections of 24 July and the council compromised on the taxation proposals. He continued to make his mark as an efficient and sympathetic secretary for lands, although a persistent drought was creating hardship from 1895. In 1897 in Adelaide he was inconspicuous among ten elected representatives of New South Wales at the Australasian Federal Convention, but he took charge of the resulting draft constitution bill while Reid was in London.

Carruthers supported Federation without commending all the detailed proposals; he opposed equal representation of States in the Senate and foresaw conflicts between the Houses. At the referendum of 3 June 1898 a majority favoured the draft constitution but the minimum number of votes was not reached. Reid with Carruthers and other ministers formed a short-lived Liberal and Federal Party for the July general election, but the voters left them dependent on Labor, which was losing faith in Reid. Carruthers continued as secretary for lands until July 1899, when he became treasurer.

The new parliament met in the same month as Carruthers' son Jack died. To private grief, he added frustrations from the Federation movement, having to defend himself and Reid against charges of tergiversation. He was not prominent in the second referendum campaign, which culminated on 20 July 1899 in the acceptance of the constitution. Labor withdrew its support for Reid in September and (Sir) William Lyne [q.v.] became premier. Carruthers did not enter Federal politics in 1901 because on 15 January 1898 he had married Alice Burnett, aged 21, and enjoyed his new family life, and also because his solicitor's practice kept him in Sydney.

In 1901, after Lyne had gone into the Commonwealth parliament, (Sir) John See [q.v.], leader of the Progressives, became premier and wanted party fusion in a non-Labor ministry, including Carruthers; he was tempted, but declined in April. C. A. Lee [q.v.] became party leader and Carruthers was prominent in the new Liberal Party of New South Wales, which absorbed the free traders before they lost the July elections. In August he opposed the vote for women, although praising those 'few women who have earnestly advocated' it. When he replaced Lee on 18 September 1902, he had been already seeking less public expenditure and denouncing 'over-government', on the lines of the Kyabram movement in Victoria. He did not join the People's Reform League, Kyabram's counterpart in New South Wales, preferring the Liberal and Reform Association which he had helped to found in 1902. As its president he encouraged working-class and lower middle-class members. He castigated the government for its financial mismanagement and the declining population growth.

Carruthers expected new political alignments, based on social and industrial matters, with non-Labor comprising Liberals and Progressives; but he misjudged the distorting effects of sectarian and temperance groups, which were linking up with the Liberals. His brother James Edward (1848-1932) was a Wesleyan minister. The P.R.L.

accused Joseph of being too near Labor but he told the assembly on 12 November 1903 that, 'I would sooner sit till eternity on this side of the House than accept the domination by the labour party under which this government exists'. The L.R.A. was then strong, the government disintegrating and the electoral appeal of unity against Labor apparent. See resigned in 1904, and was succeeded as premier by Thomas Waddell [q.v.]. Labor was unprepared for such changes, and was still not strong in suburban electorates; victory at the elections of 6 July 1904 was Carruthers' second master-stroke, helped by 'an alliance of Liberalism, temperance and Protestantism'.

Carruthers, now both premier and treasurer, wanted a fusion ministry, but feared to split his own party, and the strong, reforming cabinet announced on 29 August was wholly Liberal. In the new parliament he required strict party discipline and kept ministers in touch with party members through regular meetings. In a third master-stroke he took advantage of better seasons to implement measures of economic recovery. He aided business by reducing public expenditure, reforming the civil service and cutting rail freights; he also stimulated regional initiative with local government reform, culminating in the Local Government Act, 1906, which set up the modern system of shires and municipalities and encouraged local participation through voting procedures.

Carruthers improved the State's financial standing overseas and tried to improve the quality of English immigration. In 1906 he merged the old Savings Bank, the Post Office Savings Bank and the Advances to Settlers Board into the new Government Savings Bank under independent commissioners, a decision which the *Sydney Morning Herald* doubted, and which the P.R.L. opposed. When J. S. T. McGowen [q.v.] supported Carruthers on it against the obstructive Upper House the *Herald* wrongly blamed the premier for allying himself with Labor. As the Progressives' difficulties increased, some sought coalition with the Liberals in 1907, but Carruthers wanted only fusion; Waddell agreed and in May joined the ministry as colonial secretary. Carruthers' success in marshalling anti-Labor forces in New South Wales was not matched federally. In 1905 he wrote to Alfred Deakin [q.v.] regretting that he and Reid had not 'come together' in a non-Labor government.

In June 1905 Albert Gardiner [q.v.], Labor member for Orange, moved unsuccessfully that the royal commissioner inquiring into land scandals be empowered to investigate alleged abuses under Carruthers and other secretaries for lands. The charges recalled scabrous attacks made on him by John Norton [q.v.] in *Truth* in 1897, claiming irregularities in his divorce, immorality in his private life and land abuses under his administration. Carruthers had instigated a criminal libel action which ended with a divided jury. The 1905-06 innuendos again lacked foundation but, while leader of the Opposition, Carruthers had appeared in the Lands Appeal Court for R. Sims, whose agent W. N. Willis [q.v.] was a principal suspect in the scandals. In 1902 Carruthers had commended the work of W. P. Crick [q.v.], secretary for lands, but the commissioner's report in 1906 claimed that Crick had taken bribes. Carruthers' law firm, without his knowledge and without impropriety, had acted for Willis in what proved to be dubious acts. He gave evidence eight times at the commission and produced his accounts and papers. The commissioner reported that he felt bound 'to add that nothing in the evidence . . . implicated Mr. Carruthers', who decided to give up his law practice temporarily to avoid future embarrassment.

In 1907, election year, some of Carruthers' opponents revived the scandals. He fought back hard, introducing or promising reforms that he had long advocated, and carried the Liquor (Amendment) and antigambling Acts. He induced banks to lower their interest rates to encourage investment, decided to erect the (D. S.) Mitchell [q.v.5] wing of the Public Library of New South Wales and promised financial support to initiate teaching in agriculture and veterinary science at the University of Sydney. The Liberals were still supported by elements which regarded Labor as proliquor, socialist, and dominated by Roman Catholics, but which Carruthers now found tending to conflict with his outlook and his investments in race-courses.

Before polling day, 10 September, Carruthers launched a free-trade, States-right attack on the Federal government. When the Deakin ministry announced new protective duties, including a charge of 30 per cent on wire netting, his indignation overflowed. Up and down the State he attacked the duty as inimical to closer settlement and protective to manufacture of that product in Victorian gaols. Claiming that wire netting on Sydney wharves was State property, he had it seized despite protests from customs officers. Talking of secession, he said that unification would have been better than Federation for it would have prevented the aggressive provincialism of Victoria. His strong words on wire netting and the Federal capital were much criticized, but they directed attention from the land scandals to Carruthers as a

vigorous leader, and helped him to win the elections.

The Liberals were less united than they had seemed at the elections. The land allegations had embarrassed them; Carruthers' vehemence against Labor offended some colleagues; his reform measures alarmed others; the wire-netting affair increasingly seemed a misjudgment that McGowen would exploit. Exhausted by campaigning and vilification, he suddenly resigned the premiership at the end of September, pleading ill health, and advised Governor Sir Harry Rawson [q.v.] to send for (Sir) Gregory Wade [q.v.]. After brief rest at his Manildra property, Carruthers remained in the assembly until October 1908 when he was appointed to the Legislative Council. He declined to be agent-general in London, but represented the State at the Franco-British Exhibition in London of 1908 and reported on immigration, fisheries, banking and overseas representation. In Britain he received the honorary degree of doctor of laws from the University of St Andrews and was appointed K.C.M.G.

Carruthers became active in the council. He approved the choice of Canberra as national capital, and supported an amendment of the Industrial Disputes Act to increase penalties on strikes. In 1910 he opposed amendments of the Australian Constitution sought by the Federal Labor government, fearing financial domination of the States. Next year he combated proposals to tax rents and incomes from farming and grazing on freehold land. Taxation on unimproved land values he would support; taxation of personal exertion he thought unsound in principle although sometimes expedient. In the 1912 debates on industrial arbitration, he defended trade unions but attacked compulsory unionism, partly because the unions were influential in the Labor Party. In 1913 he again opposed an eight-hours bill.

The outbreak of war did not surprise him. An ardent patriot, Carruthers had been active in instituting Empire Day in 1905 so that school children might commemorate Queen Victoria's birthday, 24 May, and Empire virtues. In 1915 he rebuked the government for going on with a land valuation bill when thousands of Australians were dying overseas; he assisted in recruiting and was strongly anti-German and anti-Turk. A conscriptionist, he now accepted a greater role for the Commonwealth, because the States had not done enough for the war. He criticized a 1916 bill to allow unions to help political parties or newspapers, supported the testator's family maintenance legislation, demanded funds for the Parliamentary Library and complained of miners and railwaymen who went on strike. In 1920 he opposed re-recognition of unions that had impeded the war effort. He had moved towards conservatism, but his basic liberalism remained strong: although he favoured W. A. Holman's [q.v.] National government, he opposed the sedition bill of 1918 as a threat to civil liberties. He was a constructive force in the council.

In 1919-20 Carruthers chaired a select committee on improvement of agriculture, and his work led to moves to make him premier again, uniting Nationalists and Liberals against Labor; but he was willing for only a subordinate post. His 'Million Farms' campaign, to settle a million farms with a million families, reflected his nineteenth-century formation and epitomized his attempts to emphasize enterprise and production. On 20 December 1921 he became vice-president of the Executive Council in Sir George Fuller's [q.v.] 'Seven Hours' Ministry'. He was active behind the scenes in the 1922 elections and was again vice-president of the council and leader of the government in the Upper House in 1922-25. He was acclaimed in the *Sydney Morning Herald* as a bulwark against Labor extravagance. When Labor regained power in 1925 under J. T. Lang [q.v.] on a platform including abolition of the council, and obtained 25 additions to it to ensure an abolitionist majority, he led 50 out of 98 members of the Upper House in publishing a strong protest. His own preference was then for a council elected on a restricted franchise. By 1929, however, in reaction to Lang and despairing of attempts to obtain agreement on an electoral system, he favoured nomineeism.

Carruthers had wide interests, despite ill health and a slight frame. At various times he was fellow of the Senate of the University of Sydney, president of the New South Wales Chamber of Agriculture, a member of the Royal Agricultural Society of New South Wales, a trustee of the National Park and of the National Art Gallery; he was an active supporter of cricket and in 1907 became president of the New South Wales Cricket Association; he played bowls well and enjoyed fishing and shooting. He was a trustee of the Mutual Life and Citizens' Assurance Co. Ltd from 1911 to 1932 and at various times a director of Kembla Grange Racecourse Ltd, Moorefield Racecourse Ltd, the Timor Oil Co., the Monaro Community Settlement Co-operative Society, the National Insurance Co. and the Australian Widows' Fund. His pastoral and other landholdings were enterprising, extensive and complicated.

Fascinated by Captain Cook [q.v.1], Carruthers was for many years chairman of the trustees of Cook's landing place at Kurnell;

in 1928 he represented Australia at Hawaiian celebrations of his landing, and in 1930 produced *Captain James Cook R.N.: one hundred and fifty years after*. He died on 10 December 1932 at Waverley, survived by his wife, three sons and four daughters. He was buried in South Head cemetery after a funeral service at All Saints Anglican Church, Woollahra. His estate was valued for probate at £19 490.

H. V. Evatt, *Australian Labour leader . . . W. A. Holman* . . . (Syd,1940); J. Rydon and R. N. Spann, *New South Wales politics, 1901-1910* (Melb, 1962); B. Dickey (ed), *Politics in New South Wales, 1856-1900* (Melb, 1969); D. I. Wright, *Shadow of dispute* (Canb, 1970); B. Nairn, *Civilising capitalism* (Canb, 1973); J. D. Bollen, 'The temperance movement and the Liberal Party in New South Wales politics, 1900-1904', *J of Religious History*, 1 (1960-61), no 3; Carruthers papers (ML); Deakin papers (NL); Parkes correspondence (ML).

JOHN M. WARD

CARSLAW, HORATIO SCOTT (1870-1954), mathematician, was born on 12 February 1870 at Helensburgh, Dumbartonshire, Scotland, fifth son of Dr William Henderson Carslaw, Free Church minister, and his wife Elizabeth, née Lockhead. He was educated at Glasgow Academy and the University of Glasgow (M.A., 1891). That year as a scholar he entered Emmanuel College, Cambridge (B.A., fourth wrangler, 1894; M.A., 1898; Sc.D., 1908). In 1896 he became assistant to Professor William Jack at Glasgow and next year studied at the universities of Rome, Palermo, and Göttingen. A fellow of Emmanuel College in 1899-1905, he continued to teach at Glasgow until he was appointed to the chair of pure and applied mathematics at the University of Sydney in 1903 in succession to T. T. Gurney [q.v.4]. On 12 February 1907 at Bowral he married a widow Ethel Maude Cruickshank, daughter of Sir William Clarke [q.v.3], but she died on 3 June the same year.

Admirably fitted by inclination to cope with his neglected and run-down department, he described himself as 'a teacher who enjoyed teaching'. He faced a complete lack of suitable mathematics textbooks in English, and a further limitation was the importance attached to Euclidean geometry with its difficulties in the theory of parallels. Partly to interest schoolteachers, he wrote *The elements of non-Euclidean plane geometry and trigonometry* (London, 1916).

In Glasgow Carslaw had been inspector of mathematics in secondary schools. In Sydney there was no inspection of schools offering secondary courses or co-ordination of standards and syllabuses, and the final examination was entirely in the hands of the university. He was also concerned both with the general nature of the schools' curriculum and with their relation to the university. While seeking quality in the curriculum, he deplored specialization at the school level. He became involved in the exchanges between the university and Peter Board [q.v.] between 1907 and 1912 and came to accept Board's suggested leaving certificate, and to welcome the principal features of A. C. Carmichael's [q.v.] University (Amendment) Act, 1912. Indeed, in a situation of recurrent tension, Carslaw's ultimate appreciation of the merits of the government's intentions, and his moderating influence in university circles helped to prevent a serious confrontation. He was a member of the first board of examiners established under the Act, and was chief examiner in mathematics for the next thirty years.

Carslaw's most important and enduring work in mathematics was on the theory of conduction of heat. He extended Fourier's great work of 1822 and made the discussion of trigonometric series more rigorous in his book *Introduction to the theory of Fourier's series and integrals and the mathematical theory of the conduction of heat* (London, 1906). As a first step he had to supply a satisfactory treatment in English of real variable theory and the integral calculus. In 1921 the book was enlarged into two, one on Fourier series and one on conduction of heat. The latter was expanded with J. C. Jaeger into *Conduction of heat in solids* (Oxford, 1947; 2nd edition 1959); during work on it they produced *Operational methods in applied mathematics* (Oxford, 1941; 2nd edition 1948), which was a successful attempt to replace the controversial Heaviside operational methods, of which he much disapproved as lacking in rigour, by an integral transform approach. In all he wrote ten books and some seventy papers.

In 1921 Carslaw attended the Second Congress of the Universities of the Empire at Oxford. He contributed many articles to the *Sydney Morning Herald* on such subjects as the need for a closer association with English universities, the development of progressive income tax schedules, and on Lewis Carroll. A fellow of the Royal Society of Edinburgh, he joined the Royal Society of New South Wales in 1903. He was awarded honorary doctorates – of science by the University of Adelaide in 1926 and of laws by the University of Glasgow in 1928.

Although rather shy Carslaw enjoyed company, was a member of the Australian Club and had a large circle of friends, both at home and overseas, with whom he had a prodigious correspondence. This, coupled with sabbatical leaves spent at Emmanuel, kept him in touch with developments overseas and assisted in placing students in whose welfare he took a keen interest. In his earlier days he enjoyed sailing with his close friend (Sir) Alexander MacCormick [q.v.] and, later, gardening and country life.

In 1935 Carslaw retired to his house at Burradoo where he produced much of his most important work until stopped by failing eyesight. He died there on 11 November 1954 and was buried in the Anglican section of Bowral cemetery. His estate was valued for probate at £55579.

J. C. Jaeger, 'Horatio Scott Carslaw', Lond Mathematical Soc, *J*, 31 (1956), and for publications; *SMH*, 12 Jan 1911, 28 Sept 1912; information from Sir Harold Wyndham, Roseville, NSW.

J. C. JAEGER

CARSON, ALFRED (1859-1944), journalist and social worker, was born on 7 November 1859 at Upper Swan, Western Australia, son of George Carson, wheelwright, and his wife Charlotte, née Hadley. Educated at the Guildford government school, he became an assistant master at Perth Boys' School at 18 and about a year later headmaster of the Geraldton Boys' School. The school building also housed the weekly *Victorian Express* and, in his leisure, Carson sometimes set type and read proofs. Having joined the *Express* staff in the mid-1880s, he soon became its editor. He married Eva Massingham of Dongara on 5 August 1884.

When the *Geraldton and Murchison Telegraph* was founded in July 1892, Carson was appointed editor. On his return to Perth, after a short period as leader-writer on the *Daily News*, he joined the *West Australian* in January 1896 as cable-editor and leader-writer, and was later associate editor. He succeeded Robert Robertson as editor of the *Western Mail* in 1912. He represented the *West Australian* at newspaper conferences in Sydney and Melbourne and in 1917 conducted the company's case before the Commonwealth Court of Conciliation and Arbitration when Mr Justice (Sir Isaac) Isaacs [q.v.] made the first journalists' award. Among other overseas assignments, Carson represented Western Australia on a press delegation visiting the Western Front and the United Kingdom in 1918. In 1922 he resigned to contest Perth in the House of Representatives as a Nationalist but was unsuccessful and resumed journalism. He retired in 1938 but was recalled in 1941 because of wartime staff shortages.

Carson was involved in social work for most of his career and in 1908 was appointed by the (Sir) Newton Moore [q.v.] government as a special commissioner to investigate liquor-licensing legislation in the eastern States. He was a founder of the Infant Health Association, president of the Silver Chain District Nursing Association for thirty years, and chairman of the Bush Nursing Society in 1923-44 and the McNess Housing Trust; he was also on the executives of the Flying Doctor Service and of the Australian Red Cross, a justice of the peace, an honorary magistrate of the Children's Court and a keen Freemason. He was appointed O.B.E. in 1941. When Carson died on 24 August 1944, warm tributes were paid for a lifetime of devoted service to young and old in need. Survived by his wife, two sons and three daughters, he was cremated at Karrakatta after a Methodist service, leaving an estate sworn for probate at £688.

N. Stewart, *Little but great* (Perth, 1965); *West Australian*, 5 Jan 1933, 2 Jan 1941, 25 Aug 1944; *Daily News* (Perth), 1 Jan 1941; staff records (W.A. Newspapers Ltd, Perth).   O. K. BATTYE

CARSON, DUNCAN (1860-1931), woolbroker and pastoralist, was born on 8 November 1860 at Clutha, Kew, Victoria, youngest son of John Carson (d. 1902) of Glasgow, and his wife Elizabeth, née Duncan, who had both arrived in Melbourne in the *Robert Benn* in 1842. Educated at Scotch College, Melbourne, he went in 1876 with his family to Britain via the United States of America and the Philadelphia International Exhibition. His father, a prominent Melbourne horticulturist, set him to study horticulture and botany under Sir Joseph Hooker [q.v.4] until November 1878 when the family returned to Melbourne. In 1879 he went as a botanist on the brief Pacific cruise of H.M.S. *Wolverine*. After a short period in the office of William Sloane & Co. in Sydney, Carson turned his attention to wool. With an introduction from A. van Rompacy, he went to Europe in March 1881 to study the trade, mostly at Verviers, Belgium, but also at Bradford, England, and in France.

On his return to Australia, Carson acted as buyer and valuer for his brother William during the wool season and spent the rest of the year acquiring station experience, sometimes on his father's property, Goangra, Walgett, acquired in 1883. His practical experience in the industry was wide: long droving-trips in New South Wales and Queensland, sheep-classing in the Riverina and Victoria, and sheep-judging at many country shows. In 1888 he started a com-

mission agency in Brisbane in partnership with J. H. Geddes, but soon sold out. After acting as wool expert for J. H. Geddes & Co. in Sydney, he joined a partnership with F. E. Winchcombe [q.v.], C. L. Wallis and E. J. Turton in March 1889 to found the woolbrokers, Winchcombe & Co. [Ltd]. In 1899 the firm (styled Winchcombe Carson Ltd from 1910) was incorporated in New South Wales. Carson's wide and expert knowledge of the trade soon made it one of the largest of its kind in the southern hemisphere. In 1917 he became its chairman and succeeded Winchcombe on the State Wool Committee, helping to direct the British-Australian wartime wool purchase scheme.

Carson was a director of the Australian Bank of Commerce and the New South Wales Land and Agency Co. Ltd. At first in partnership with Alfred Brown, he owned Bomera station on the Liverpool Plains and was chairman of the Rockwood Pastoral Co. in Queensland. Associated with almost every movement to benefit the pastoral industry, he was a council-member of the Sydney Chamber of Commerce, the Graziers' Association and the Royal Agricultural Society, acting president of the New South Wales Sheepbreeders' Association and an active worker for the Sydney Sheep Show. He took a keen interest in pasture improvement and maintained his early interest in botany and horticulture. A member of the local Linnean Society from 1890, he accompanied a German botanist on an expedition to North Queensland in 1900, hybridized the early flowering peach known originally as 'Carson's Peach', and had one of the finest collections of orchids in Australia. He also travelled widely to Japan, China, the East Indies and South America, as well as Africa where he shot big game.

Rather short and stocky, friendly and generous, Carson devoted the same energy and enthusiasm to all his interests whether business, family, or the activities of the Highland Society of New South Wales of which he was president from 1923. On 10 June 1891 at Randwick he had married Constance Haidee (d. 1932), daughter of Robert Richards of Sydney; they formally separated in 1925. He was extremely fond of children. Three sons served in World War I, and the loss at Gallipoli of Ronald, who had also learned the trade in Belgium, was a great blow.

Survived by his wife, four sons and three daughters, Carson died of cerebro-vascular disease on 6 January 1931 at his residence Weeroona, Wahroonga, and was cremated after a Presbyterian service. Two sons settled on the land, another joined the firm, and a daughter Haidee Margaret married the eminent physician and surgeon (Sir) Norman Gregg. Probate of his estate was sworn at £67979.

Pastoral Review, 16 Jan 1931; *Scottish A'sian*, 21 Jan, 21 Feb 1931; *SMH*, and *Sydney Mail*, 7 Jan 1931; family information held by author.

G. P. WALSH

CARTER, ARTHUR JOHN (1847-1917), businessman, was born on 27 September 1847 at St Ives, Huntingdonshire, England, son of Charles Carter, Wesleyan minister, and his wife Margaret, née Jarvis. Educated at Woodhouse Grove School, Yorkshire, Bedford Modern School and King's College, London, he lived briefly in France before entering the underwriters' room of Lloyd's of London in 1863. He married Jane Nodes in London in February 1867 and in January 1871 reached Brisbane by the *Light Brigade*. His wife died in May, leaving him with three young sons; on 9 November 1872 he married a widow Frances Eliza Elgin Koch, née Johnson.

Carter soon joined the merchants J. & G, Harris [qq.v.4] and worked for them till 1876. He subsequently became Brisbane manager of the Adelaide Milling & Mercantile Co., and held directorships in Millaquin Sugar Co., John Hicks & Co., Dath Henderson & Co. and J. Leutenegger Ltd, and was chairman of directors of E. Rich & Co. Ltd and of Queensland Trustees Ltd. He was also agent for several overseas insurance companies.

Emulating George Harris, Carter became vice-consul for Sweden and Norway, consular agent for France in 1902 and consul for Norway in 1906. He was made an officer of the French Academy in 1911 and next year received the Norwegian Order of St Olav. He was president of the Brisbane Chamber of Commerce for five terms between 1898 and 1906, and was active in the Immigration League of Queensland, the Committee of Fire Underwriters, the Marine Board, the Brisbane and South Brisbane fire brigades, the General Hospital, the Technical College, and the State committee for the selection of Rhodes Scholars. A foundation member of the Johnsonian Club and a member of the Queensland Club, he was also an active Freemason. He wrote frequently to the press on defence, port facilities and bimetallism and was an energetic and effective lobbyist. Portly, urbane and genial, a kindly employer, popular and respected, he was an acknowledged leader of Brisbane's commercial community.

Carter was a liberal, a free trader and one of the few ardent Federationists in Brisbane commerce. As a leader of the Federation League he visited Sydney for the June 1899 referendum and represented Queensland there at the free-trade conference of February 1900. Appointed to the Legislative Council in July 1901, he spoke rarely but attended regularly.

When the T. J. Ryan [q.v.] government in 1915 proposed amendment of the Workers' Compensation Act to give the State Government Insurance Office a monopoly, Carter was a leading opponent on behalf of private insurance interests. The council amended the bill to remove the monopoly but Carter's failure to secure a consequential amendment negated the victory. The government refused to resubmit the bill on the ground that it was ready for royal assent, thus achieving a major triumph and damaging the council's reputation as a house of review.

Carter only spoke once more in the council, on an insurance bill in December 1916. Survived by his wife and their five children, and by one son of his first marriage, he died of cirrhosis of the liver on 4 November 1917 at his home at Kangaroo Point and was buried in the South Brisbane cemetery. He is commemorated by a plaque in St Mary's Anglican Church, Kangaroo Point, where he was a churchwarden. His estate was sworn for probate at £12392.

His son HUBERT REGINALD (1875-1934) was born in Brisbane on 31 January 1875. Educated at Brisbane Grammar School, he qualified as a solicitor but in 1893 entered his father's business. A volunteer soldier in the Moreton Regiment, he served in South Africa as a captain in the 5th (Queensland Imperial Bushmen's) Contingent and was severely wounded on 4 January 1902. As a major in the 15th Battalion, Australian Imperial Force, he served on Gallipoli until he was wounded again on 10 August 1915, then became a transport officer. He was second State president of the Returned Sailors' & Soldiers' Imperial League of Australia in 1918-19, and was promoted honorary lieut-colonel. He died at Kangaroo Point on 14 July 1934.

Newspaper Cartoonists' Assn of Qld, *Queenslanders as we see 'em* (Brisb, 1916); D. J. Murphy, *T. J. Ryan* (Brisb, 1975); Commercial Publishing Co. of Sydney, Ltd, *Annual Review of Qld*, 1 (1902), no 1; Qld Trustees Ltd, Trustees' Quarterly Review, Jan 1918; *Brisbane Courier*, 6, 7 Nov 1917; *Queenslander*, 10 Nov 1917, 19 July 1934; GOV/69, 20 Jan 1916, 17 Dec 1917 (QA); family papers (held by Judge R. F. Carter, St Lucia, Qld).

BETTY CROUCHLEY

CARTER, FRANCIS MOWAT (1879-1956) and BRYCE MORROW (1882-1939), musicians, were born on 17 June 1879 and 15

February 1882 in Melbourne, fourth and fifth sons of English parents Harold Richard Carter, merchant, and his wife Janet, née Morrow. Norman Carter [q.v.] was an elder brother. They were educated at Haileybury College. Frank took up the violin and Bryce at 14 began to learn the cello under George Howard in Melbourne. About 1899 the family moved to Sydney: Frank rapidly became prominent and his brother continued studies under the eminent Dutch cellist Gerard Vollmar and reputedly inherited his master's valuable instrument. In the early 1900s Bryce played with G. R. Allpress's string quartet and by 1907 he was considered one of the rising stars of Sydney musical circles: he was chosen as an associate artist in the Sydney concerts for Melba's [q.v.] tour that year; the programmes included cello sonatas with Una Bourne [q.v.].

Frank Carter taught from 1904 and shared chambers with his brother from 1908. Bryce taught the daughter of the governor Lord Chelmsford [q.v.] and arranged musical evenings at Government House. In May 1908 the brothers attended the meeting of professional musicians which established a symphony orchestra and played with it throughout its existence. Frank was deputy leader and Bryce principal cellist; Bryce refused a solo role in one concert. They were members of Henri Staell's string quartet and appeared regularly as supporting artists in concerts by other local musicians but rarely, if ever, undertook solo recitals. In 1913 Frank was an associate artist for the tour of Dame Clara Butt and her husband Kennerley Rumford. On 9 September 1908 at Strathfield Frank had married Edith Anne Bunting, a musician twelve years his senior.

Bryce married Emily Christiana Josephson at Redfern on 25 January 1911. He was principal cellist with the Royal Philharmonic Society of Sydney's orchestra and in 1916 was appointed one of the first two teachers of the cello at the New South Wales State Conservatorium of Music, but resigned in 1918. Both played with the State orchestra under Henri Verbrugghen [q.v.] but their lack of overseas experience now began to tell against them. Bryce, however, made solo and orchestral appearances and joined the Sydney Symphony Orchestra under the Australian Broadcasting Commission. He was originally principal but was soon reduced to second then third desk. In 1938 he retired with cancer and died at his Longueville home on 5 January 1939. Survived by his wife, son and daughter, he was buried in the Northern Suburbs cemetery with the rites of the Catholic Apostolic Church. Frank Carter slipped into obscurity in the late 1920s; he probably played in the Prince Edward Theatre orchestra, and lived for many years in retirement while his wife taught the piano. Survived by her and a daughter, he died at Strathfield on 24 March 1956 and was buried in Rookwood cemetery with Anglican rites.

The Carter brothers were typical of the many musicians who provided the basis of the concert life of Australia in the period. Bryce was quite unusual in the standing that he achieved without overseas experience.

V. Herbert (ed), *World's best music*, rev edn (New York, 1907); W. A. Orchard, *The distant view* (Syd, 1943), and *Music in Australia* (Melb, 1952); NSW State Conservatorium of Music, *Prospectus*, 1916-18; *British Australasian*, 23 Mar 1911; *Splashes Weekly*, 26 June 1913, 2 Apr 1914; *SMH*, 6, 7 Jan 1939; Syd Symphony Orchestra, Minutebook 1908-10, T7/7 (ANU Archives); programme files (NL).   TONY MILLS

CARTER, HERBERT GORDON (1885-1963), engineer, was born on 24 March 1885 at St Leonards, Sydney, eldest son of Herbert James Carter [q.v.], entomologist, and his wife Antoinette Charlotte, née Moore. Educated at Sydney Grammar School and The King's School, Parramatta, he lived at St Andrew's College while at the University of Sydney; he graduated B.E. with first-class honours in 1908. In April he started work for the railway commissioners, in June next year transferring to the Department of Public Works as an assistant electrical engineer.

Commissioned as a 2nd lieutenant in the Sydney University Scouts in 1907, Carter was promoted lieutenant in July 1913, appointed to the 1st Battalion, Australian Imperial Force, in September 1914, and sailed in October. He served throughout the Gallipoli campaign and in 1915 was promoted captain, then major. In March 1916 he joined the 5th Pioneer Battalion when it was organized as a unit in Egypt, and from August, as lieut-colonel, he commanded it in France and Flanders 'with conspicuous ability and success' until the end of the war; the battalion built tramways in trenches at Fromelles, improved communication trenches, drained and 'corduroyed' roads, helped to establish the Anzac light-railway system on the Somme, built bridges and was involved in forward defence and road construction in the advance on the Hindenburg Line. Three times mentioned in dispatches, Carter was awarded the Distinguished Service Order in January 1918. On 31 January 1917 in London, he had married Lydia Kate King from Orange, New South Wales, who was then working in the Australian Hospital, Southall.

Carter returned to Sydney in mid-1919 to

the Department of Public Works. In his absence he had been appointed a supervising engineer and in 1924 became chief electrical engineer. In 1929 he resigned to enter private practice. He was responsible for the design and construction of many large electrical works in Australia and Papua-New Guinea, most notably at Burrinjuck, several projects in New Guinea in 1931 and a hydro-electric power-station and transmission lines for the Bega Valley County Council. A council-member of the Institution of Engineers, Australia, in 1924-48, he was president in 1943 and published in its *Journal*. He was also a member of the Institution of Civil Engineers, London, and a fellow of the American Institute of Electrical Engineers.

From the late 1930s Carter built up large business interests: he was chairman of Australia Silknit Ltd, Carrier Air Conditioning Ltd, Non-Metallics Ltd, the Hawkesbury Development Co. Ltd and of W. G. Watson Holdings Ltd, and was a director of Rabaul Electricity Ltd and Concrete Industries (Australia) Ltd. Active in civic and community affairs, he was a director of Royal North Shore Hospital and a trustee of Lane Cove National Park. He was an alderman on the Ku-ring-gai Municipal Council in 1935-41 and mayor in 1938-39. An alderman for Macquarie Ward on the Sydney Municipal Council in 1944-50, he was vice-chairman of its electricity committee in 1942 and city planning and improvements committee in 1945-48, and a delegate to the Cumberland County Council in 1946-49.

Carter was a member of the Australian and University clubs, Sydney, and lived at Golfers Parade, Pymble. An accomplished pianist he regularly played the organ at near-by St Swithun's Church of England. He died suddenly at Killara Golf Club on 11 July 1963 and was cremated with Anglican rites. He was survived by his wife, two sons and a daughter: his second son John was killed while serving with the Royal Australian Air Force in World War II. Carter's estate was valued for probate at £88 123.

A. D. Ellis, *The story of the Fifth Australian Division* (Lond, 1920?); A. H. Corbett, *The Institution of Engineers, Australia* (Syd, 1973); Inst of Engineers, Aust, *J*, 35 (1963).   D. G. GALLON

CARTER, HERBERT JAMES (1858-1940), schoolmaster and entomologist, was born on 23 April 1858 at Marlborough, Wiltshire, England, son of James Carter, farmer, and his wife Mary Ann, née Freeman. Educated at Aldenham Grammar School, Hertfordshire, and Jesus College, Cambridge (B.A., 1881), he was a keen

cricketer and, like his father who bred hunters, loved horses, the open air and music. In 1882 he migrated to Australia, arriving in Sydney in the *Potosi* on 19 February, and was appointed assistant mathematics master at Sydney Grammar School. On 21 December 1882 at St Andrew's Cathedral he married Antoinette Charlotte Moore, of Haskerton Manor, Woodbridge, Suffolk.

Helped by his wife, Carter had charge of various houses used as hostels for some of the boys and became senior mathematics master. In 1902 he fulfilled a Utopian dream of running an enlightened girls' school when he bought Ascham, Darling Point, from its founder Miss Marie Wallis, and became its principal. That year he leased the mansion, Mount Adelaide, with its lovely grounds, for the school, and in 1908 bought Glenrock. In the curriculum he emphasized mathematics, singing and natural history, and established a matriculation class. He was a council-member of the Teachers' Association of New South Wales and of Barker College, and worked on the Teachers' Central Registry. In 1914 Carter retired as principal and sold Ascham to Margaret Bailey [q.v.].

During World War I Carter was a founding member of the executive committee of the Australian branch of the British Red Cross Society and in 1916 joined the general committee of the Universal Service League. His three sons enlisted in the Australian Imperial Force and one daughter Ursula served overseas with the Australian Army Nursing Service: his second son Edward died of wounds in 1915. Carter was active later in the Big Brother Movement.

His friend Dr Charles Dagnall Clark had aroused his interest in entomology, especially in the Coleoptera (beetles and weevils), and he began collecting with his schoolboy sons from his cottage at Medlow Bath in the Blue Mountains. His early friendship with Commander J. J. Walker, R.N., later president of the Entomological Society, London, gave him contacts with English scientists and the British Museum. An energetic collector, Carter made numerous field-trips throughout New South Wales and other States; of particular interest were his visits to areas of comparative isolation: Mount Kosciusko in 1898, 1900 and 1905 and Barrington Tops, New South Wales, in 1916 and 1925-27. He recorded many of his field experiences in his book *Gulliver in the bush* (Sydney, 1933); companions included (Sir) Edgeworth David, L. Harrison, J. H. Maiden and G. A. Waterhouse [qq.v.]; in bad weather he gave them detective stories to read.

Carter became particularly interested in the families Tenebrionidae, Buprestidae,

Cistelidae and Dryopidae as well as certain groups of the Cerambycidae and Colydiidae. His work has formed the basis of all future studies on these sections of the Australian fauna. He described some 44 new genera and 1167 new species in his papers, as well as another 11 genera and 67 species with E. H. Zeck. He published 65 papers, 7 with Zeck, in learned journals, and was a meticulous worker whose descriptions of new species were usually accompanied by revisionary work on the various families and genera, often by keys to assist other workers in determinations.

Carter was a council-member of the Australian Naturalists' Society of New South Wales in 1905-07 (vice-president 1907-09) and the local Linnean Society in 1920-39 (president 1925-26); he was also a fellow of the Royal Zoological Society of New South Wales from 1931 and of the Entomological Society, London, and honorary entomologist to the Australian Museum, Sydney. With A. W. Jose [q.v.] he was joint editor of *The Australian encyclopaedia* (Sydney, 1925-26). He used his entomological knowledge to control pests in his garden.

Predeceased by his wife, Carter died on 16 April 1940 at his home at Wahroonga and was cremated with Anglican rites. He was survived by two daughters and two sons, one of whom was Herbert Gordon [q.v.]. He had donated a collection of Coleoptera to the National Museum, Melbourne; after his death another collection was given to the Council for Scientific and Industrial Research, Canberra. Portraits by his sister Rosa Carter are held by the family.

A. Musgrave, *Bibliography of Australian entomology, 1775-1930*, and *1931-1958* (Syd, 1932, 196?); M. Flower (ed), *The story of Ascham School* (Syd, 1952); Linnean Soc NSW, *Procs*, 68 (1943); *SMH*, 24 Apr 1940; information from Mr E. G. Carter, Tamworth, NSW.   G. T. FRANKI

CARTER, NORMAN ST CLAIR (1875-1963), portrait-painter and stained-glass artist, was born on 30 June 1875 at Kew, Melbourne, third son of English-born parents Harold Richard Carter, grain merchant, and his wife Janet, née Morrow. His brothers Bryce and Frank [qq.v.] became musicians. Norman completed his education at Melbourne Church of England Grammar School in 1888-90, leaving when his father's business was hit by the depression. He had a succession of jobs which included training with 'Kalizoic' decorators, and in 1890-94 was apprenticed to a stained-glass maker. While selling artists' supplies by day, he attended Frederick McCubbin's and L. Bernard Hall's [qq.v.] evening classes at the National Gallery School, and later, helped by a small allowance from his father, studied under E. Phillips Fox [q.v.].

With his close friend Hugh McCrae [q.v.], Carter moved to Sydney in 1903, set up a city studio and joined the Royal Art Society of New South Wales where he was an instructor until 1916. He also worked as a freelance commercial artist and contributed to the *Bulletin* and *Sydney Mail*. Later he moved his studio to Hunter Street, then Vickery's [q.v.6.] Chambers, although he lived at Wollstonecraft. Invited to join the Society of Artists by S. Ure Smith [q.v.], he became a vice-president in 1926. He lectured at the Sydney Technical College in 1915-40 and on freehand drawing in the department of architecture, University of Sydney, in 1922-47. He 'always liked teaching' and found it 'useful as a form of ballast to one's income'. He came to regard 'contemporary art' as a 'fungoid growth' and in 1937 was a founder of the short-lived Australian Academy of Art.

Although Carter never travelled overseas, he was encouraged by Fox and Rupert Bunny [q.v.] to exhibit in Europe and was awarded a bronze at the 1913 Salon des Artistes Française (Paris Salon) for his portrait of Florence Rodway [q.v.], entitled 'Portrait of Mlle X'; it was hung next year at the Royal Academy of Arts, London. An extremely competent and fashionable portraitist, he painted fellow-artists, governors, judges, professors, and other notables such as (Sir) P. Gordon Taylor, and Peter Board [qq.v.]. His portraits of prime ministers Sir Edmund Barton and W. M. Hughes [qq.v.] are in Parliament House, Canberra. Carter always tried to make his subject talk so he could 'see him in different expressions'. His early tonalist works reveal the influences of Hall and Max Meldrum [q.v.].

Carter also found making stained-glass windows 'remunerative' and after World War I received commissions for memorial windows such as those in St Stephen's Church, Sydney, the 'Warriors' Chapel' in All Saints Cathedral, Bathurst, and the Teachers' College, Armidale; other major works include the north clerestory windows in St Andrew's Cathedral, Sydney. He also enjoyed painting such murals as those in the philosophy lecture room, University of Sydney (1921), the Rural Bank of New South Wales, Martin Place, Sydney (1938), and the Maritime Services Board (1952). A lover of nature, at weekends he painted landscapes for a change, and occasionally exhibited them. A retrospective exhibition was held at the Blaxland Gallery in 1959. His later works were more high-keyed in colour and reveal the influence of mural design.

Carter died on 18 September 1963 at

Gordon and was buried in the Anglican section of Northern Suburbs cemetery. Predeceased by his wife Ruby Eva, née Burnell, whom he had married at Toowoomba, Queensland, on 3 November 1908, he was survived by two sons and three daughters. His estate was sworn for probate at £2337. A self-portrait is in the Art Gallery of New South Wales.

Bernard Smith, *Australian painting 1788-1960* (Melb, 1962); *Salon*, 1912, no 1, 1913, no 2, 1914, no 2; *Art in Aust*, 1916, no 1; *Daily Telegraph* (Syd), 9 May 1914; *Bulletin*, 9 Oct 1919; *SMH*, 18 June 1921, 9 Jan, 9 July 1925, 30 June 1931, 10 Mar 1937, 19 Sept 1963; *Sun* (Syd), 23 May 1922, 25 Mar 1959; *Sunday Times* (Syd), 28 May 1922; *Australasian*, 3 June 1922; H. Carter, letter to M. Carter 28 Feb 1977 (Art Gallery of NSW); N. St C. Carter letters (ML); S. A. Howard letters (ML); S. Ure Smith papers (ML); uncat MSS set 471 (ML).

FRANCES LINDSAY

CARTER, THOMAS (1863-1931), ornithologist and pastoralist, was born on 6 April 1863 at Masham, Yorkshire, England, son of James Carter, merchant, and his wife Amelia Mary, née Rhodes. He was educated at Sedbergh and his interest in ornithology was encouraged by his father, a keen naturalist. Before migrating to Western Australia Carter had published a number of papers in British wildlife journals and had been to Iceland to study birdlife. Landing at Carnarvon in 1887, he was employed as jackeroo on Boolathanna station and wrote his first notes for the British wildlife magazine the *Zoologist*, launching the modern period in intensive studies of Western Australian birds.

In 1889 Carter acquired a 135 000-acre (55 000 ha) pastoral lease centred on Point Cloates; he was the first to hold a lease in the area. His characteristic energy and tenacity were needed to cope with sheep losses incurred by poison plants, dingoes and recurring drought in a largely waterless area. His real reward was the magnificent birds which he sought, often dangerously, in the yawning canyons and towering cliffs of Cape Range. An unsuccessful operation on his left eye had rendered it practically useless but he was an excellent shot. Living off the land on his expeditions he was forced sometimes to eat valuable specimens through sheer hunger. His Crusoe-like existence was emphasized by his house built from wreckage of two ships lost near by. Carter's charts of entrances through the dangerous reefs are still in use. An assistant was speared but Carter remained on good terms with the Talaindji tribe, recording their bird names in 'Birds occurring in the region of the North-West Cape', published in the *Emu* on 1 July 1903. He identified 180 birds and secured specimens of 170, two entirely new — Rufous-crowned Emu-wren and the Spinifex-bird which bears his name, *Eremiornis carteri*.

Carter sold out and returned to England in 1903. On 8 September at Twickenham, Middlesex, he married Annie Ward whom he had known all his life and whose rejection of his proposal when she was 17 had prompted his departure to Australia. Returning to Western Australia the following year they settled on a southern sheep-property at Broomehill. 'Birds of the Broome Hill district' appeared in the *Emu* in 1923-24.

While in England in 1909, Carter was warned by doctors to relax his strenuous life-style. After a near-tragic fire at Broomehill, heart trouble was apparent by 1913. Urged by his wife, Carter disposed of his property. With their three children they returned to England in 1914, settling at Sutton, Surrey. Two years later he was back in Western Australia visiting Dirk Hartog Island where mouse plagues invaded his blankets while he slept. He rediscovered there the Black-and-white Wren and the Western Grass-wren, collected only by the French naturalists J. R. C. Quoy and J. P. Gaimard nearly a century earlier on the Freycinet [q.v.1] expedition. He paid three more visits to Western Australia, the last in 1928.

Carter died on 29 January 1931 and was buried at his birthplace. Remarkable in quality and quantity, his Australian contributions occupy two pages in H. M. Whittell's *Literature of Australian birds*. Four species and fourteen sub-species bear his name. Birds collected by him are in the American Museum of Natural History, being part of the famous 'Tring' collection and that of his friend Gregory M. Mathews [q.v.], to which he gave many specimens. Others are in the Western Australian Museum and a collection of eggs is in the British Museum (Natural History). He was a member of the British Ornithologists' Union and a foundation member of the Royal Australasian Ornithologists' Union.

G. M. Mathews (ed), *Austral avian record*, 3 (Lond, 1919); D. L. Serventy and H. M. Whittell, *Birds of Western Australia*, 5th edn (Perth, 1976); *Emu*, 30 (1930-31); *JRWAHS*, 6 (1968) pt 7; *Yorkshire Post*, 2 July 1968; family information.

FREDA VINES CARMODY

CASE, JAMES THOMAS (1884-1921), cartoonist, was born on 21 March 1884 at Boggy Creek near Caboolture, Queensland, son of Thomas Joseph Case, gardener, and his wife Margaret Elizabeth, née Feenan. Leaving school at 14, he worked in the machine-room of the Brisbane *Worker* where it was part of his duty to take the drawings of Monty Scott [q.v.6] to the engraver. While still in his teens, Case became a painter and decorator. He maintained his contacts with the *Worker* and occasional cartoons by him, published therein through 1906 and 1907, showed an aptitude for drawing and a keen sensitive feeling for political humour.

In February 1908 the *Worker* was expanded. The editor, H. E. Boote [q.v.], conducted a competition to produce a cartoon from a blank outline of a human face, which Case won. He was employed as its artist and produced the front-page cartoon of May Day in Brisbane. For the rest of that year he shared the work with Scott but, from February 1909, became the official cartoonist. When the *Daily Standard* was established by the labour movement in December 1912, Case also produced cartoons for that paler.

His cartoons and drawings showed both artistry and wit. Honest upright workmen battled 'Fat' and 'Boodle', whose demise was imminent, as well as unscrupulous Liberal politicians like Digby Denham and Sir Robert Philp [qq.v.] and Labor renegades like William Kidston [q.v.]. Case's depiction of a shocked maiden 'Australia' drawing back the Queensland curtain to reveal the police brutally clubbing Brisbane workers on 'Black Friday' during the 1912 general strike became a classic among Australian political cartoons. 'Australia' was rather scantily clad about the bosom in the original cartoon, but was more fully covered in the reproductions for postcards and for the posters which were hung in union offices and in the homes of Labor stalwarts. His national reputation was made as an anti-conscription cartoonist in 1916 and 1917. During the two referenda his work appeared in Labor and union papers throughout Australia.

In October 1920 Case accepted a position on Sydney *Truth*. Only a few months after arriving in Sydney, he was found to have cancer; he died at Bondi on 24 October 1921. He was survived by his wife Elizabeth Victoria, née Hancock, whom he had married at Brisbane on 1 January 1914, and by a son and a daughter. At his own request his body was returned to Brisbane to be buried in Bulimba cemetery with Anglican rites.

Case's cartoons represented political and industrial Labor in Queensland in its most radical phase. In the 1940s and 1950s the Queensland *Worker*, lacking a comparable cartoonist, reprinted his work, which was also used in *Labor in politics* (Brisbane, 1972) and *The emergence of the Australian party system* (Sydney, 1977).

Worker (Brisb), 4 Mar 1911, 28 Oct 1921; *Daily Standard*, 25 Oct 1921.   D. J. MURPHY

CASEY, GILBERT STEPHEN (1856-1946), labour organizer and agitator, was born in County Clare, Ireland, son of Patrick Casey, storeman, and his wife Susan, née O'Dea. With little formal education, he went to sea and soon absorbed trade union ideas. He probably arrived in Queensland as a seaman in the emigrant barque *Southesk* in October 1883 and was subsequently employed as a seaman, bushworker, coalminer and wharflabourer. On 14 October at the General Registry Office, Brisbane, he married Alice Tighe, née Shile, who had already been twice married.

From February 1886 Casey was associated with the Queensland Maritime Council through the Brisbane Wharf Labourers' Union which he had helped to form in the previous year. In 1888 the council sent him on an organizing mission to Maryborough, Bundaberg, Rockhampton, Mackay and Townsville; there he helped to found the Townsville Trades and Labor Council.

As a member of the Brisbane T.L.C., Casey became a trustee for the Trades Hall reserve, worked for the June 1889 reconstitution of the council into the Australian Labour Federation, and became a member of its central district council. In December he joined Thomas Glassey and Albert Hinchcliffe [qq.v.] in a successful mission to bring the bush unions into the A.L.F. Casey was appointed full time in April 1890 and in his first frenetic three months organized new unions and established district councils at Maryborough, Rockhampton, Charters Towers and Townsville, a considerable feat. At a meeting in February he was appointed chairman of the board of trustees of the *Worker*.

Embroiled in the maritime and pastoral strikes of 1890-91, Casey obstinately pursued the romantic chimera of a general strike even when more pragmatic leaders were anxious to arrange a return to work before defeat turned to rout. His extremism attracted attack from anti-labour forces. The newspaper *Judge* accused him of incest and, in a subsequent libel action, he was awarded contemptuous damages which did not cover costs. Arrested at Barcaldine in 1891 on a charge of inciting to arson, he was remanded in custody for two weeks before being released without the charge being heard.

Casey was a self-proclaimed evangelist for the 'new unionism', believing it would radically transform existing society, which he saw as dominated by 'those who rob legally, those who rob illegally and those who it pays to maintain the law'. After the 1891 strike he found it hard to accept the federation's support for a gradualist political Labor Party which he believed would be easy prey for 'wirepullers'. He became a fervent member of William Lane's [q.v.] New Australia Co-operative Settlement Association and donated his Brisbane home as a prize in a fund-raising raffle for its projected Utopia in South America. On 31 December 1893 Casey and his wife left with the second expedition to New Australia.

Friction rather than fraternity proved to be the keynote of his Paraguayan career. He stayed when the colony split, returning briefly to Australia in 1894 as agent for the New Australians in the struggle for the assets of the association. He was elected president of the Sociedad Co-operativa Colonizadora Nueva Australia in 1896, but the colony's income improved rapidly after his defeat in 1900. His wife had left him in 1895 and married another disenchanted New Australian in South Africa; Casey married a Paraguayan, Maria Antonia Sosa. With their two sons he raised cattle at La Novia, dabbled in sidelines at Asuncion, and contributed occasional letters and articles to the Labor press in Australia. After long service as chief of police at New Australia, he died there on 2 October 1946.

G. Souter, *A peculiar people* (Syd, 1968); D. J. Murphy (ed), *Labor in politics* (Brisb, 1975); *PD* (Qld), 1891, 156; J. Stoodley, 'The development of gold-mining unionism in Queensland in the late nineteenth century', *Labour History*, Nov 1966, no 11; *Worker* (Brisb), 7 July 1890, 21 Feb, 4 Apr, 11 July 1891, 17 Sept 1892, 17 June 1893; *Brisbane Courier*, 24-26 Mar 1891; R. J. Sullivan, The A.L.F. in Queensland 1889-1914 (M.A. thesis, Univ Qld, 1973).   RODNEY SULLIVAN

CASS, WALTER EDMUND HUTCHIN-SON (1876-1931), soldier and teacher, was born on 28 August 1876 at Albury, New South Wales, son of Charles Edmund Cass, publican, and his wife Catherine Lee, née Hutchinson. His father was born in England, his mother in New South Wales. Educated at Albury Superior Public School, he later moved to Melbourne with his family and on 7 October 1890 joined the Victorian Department of Public Instruction as a trainee teacher. Among his early postings were Toora, Derrinallum and Whitehead's Creek.

In February 1901 Cass enlisted for service in the South African War as a corporal in the 5th Victorian Mounted Rifles Contingent. He saw action in the Transvaal, Orange River Colony and Cape Colony, and was promoted sergeant. Returning home in April 1902, he resumed teaching and from 1904 served in the militia as a lieutenant in the 6th Australian Infantry Regiment. He joined the permanent staff of the Australian Military Forces in June 1906 and was a lieutenant on the administrative and instructional staff in South Australia in 1906-08 and in Western Australia in 1908-10. Promoted captain in July 1910, next year he went to India on twelve months exchange duty; he then held staff appointments in Sydney and Hobart until World War I and was promoted major in December 1913.

On 18 August 1914 Cass was appointed brigade major of the 2nd Brigade, Australian Imperial Force. He took part in the landing at Anzac Cove but the unit was transferred to Cape Helles to advance against the Turks at Krithia on 8 May – the first time that an Australian brigade had attacked in open country. Cass dauntlessly led the 7th Battalion across the moorland, was wounded in the chest when he reached the Krithia road, and wounded again as he lay by the roadside. He rejoined his brigade at Anzac on 28 July, was promoted lieut-colonel on 7 August, and until the evacuation commanded the 2nd Battalion.

On 21 February 1916 Cass was appointed commander of the 54th Battalion which reached the Western Front in July, taking over a section of the line at Fleurbaix. He was prominent in the defence of the 5th Division's sector in the battle of Fromelles on 19 July: after his brigade had captured several lines of enemy trenches he crossed No Man's Land and established his headquarters in one of them; there, throughout a night in which his battalion lost over 500 men, he maintained command in the forward area and made the final arrangements for withdrawal. After Fromelles he broke down in health and was evacuated to England where he later held an A.I.F. administrative command. On 18 October, at St James's Anglican Church, Westminster, he married Helena Holmes of Truro, Nova Scotia.

Cass was mentioned in dispatches twice during the war and appointed C.M.G. in 1916. He was demobilized in April 1917 and became director of military training at A.M.F. headquarters, Melbourne, in 1917-21, general staff officer in Queensland in 1922-23 and base commandant in Hobart in 1924. For the next two years he was director of organization and personnel services at Melbourne, then base commandant there in 1926-29 and in Adelaide in 1929-31; he was made temporary brigadier in December 1929. In September 1931 he returned to Melbourne as base commandant; he was operated on for appendicitis and died several days later on 6 November in Caulfield military hospital. He was buried in Melbourne general cemetery with full military honours; his wife and five-year-old daughter survived him.

Cass was a leading Freemason. He also took a keen interest in rifle-shooting and at the time of his death was president of the Victorian Militia Forces Rifle Union and of the Victorian Rifle Association. C. E. W. Bean [q.v.] wrote of him: 'The leaders of the A.I.F. were mostly generous men, and marked for their sense of duty; but there were perhaps few in whom the recognition of duty was quite so strong, or sympathy with the rank and file so keen, as in Walter Cass'.

Aust Defence Dept, *Official records of the Australian military contingents to the war in South Africa*, P. L. Murray ed (Melb, 1912); A. D. Ellis, *The story of the Fifth Australian Division* (Lond, 1920?); C. E. W. Bean, *The story of Anzac* (Syd, 1921, 1924), and *The A.I.F. in France*, 1916 (Syd, 1929); F. W. Taylor and T. A. Cusack, *Nulli secundus, a history of the Second Battalion A.I.F., 1914-19* (Syd, 1942); C. E. W. Bean, *Gallipoli mission* (Lond, 1948); *London Gazette*, 14, 28 Jan 1916, 1 June 1917; *Reveille* (Syd), Nov 1931; *Advertiser* (Adel), and *Argus*, 7 Nov 1931.

L. D. MATTHEWS

CASTLES, AMY ELIZA (1880-1951), dramatic soprano, was born on 25 July 1880 at Melbourne, eldest child of Joseph Castles, printer, and his wife Mary Ellen, née Fallon, both Victorian-born. In the early 1880s the family moved to Bendigo where Amy was educated at St Kilian's primary school and then at St Mary's College.

The Castles family was highly musical. Amy's sister Ethel (Dolly) became well known in Gilbert and Sullivan opera both in Australia and abroad; Eileen sang in grand opera, making her début in Australia with the Melba [q.v.] Grand Opera Company in 1911; and George, a tenor, sang professionally at home and overseas. The other three sons were locally known as singers.

Amy's talent was discovered by E. Allan Bindley while she was still at school. He became her teacher and directed one of her earliest public performances in a local production of Gilbert and Sullivan's *Patience*, in October 1898. Next year, on 16 March, she made her début in Melbourne at the annual meeting of the Austral Salon. The 'magnificent quality' of her voice astonished her audience and public concerts were immediately arranged: the 'slip of a girl in a simple white frock' with her hair down to her shoulders created a sensation, although her promotion was not without its critics. To help raise money for overseas tuition she toured Australia and, backed by an unprecedented sum of £4000, left in September to study with Madame Marchesi in Paris. Alarmed when Marchesi attempted to produce her as a contralto, Amy left her to study with Jacques Bouhy.

In November 1901 she made her first London appearance at a St James's Hall concert with Ada Crossley [q.v.] and Clara Butt, and was enthusiastically received. In 1902 she returned to Australia to tour for J. C. Williamson [q.v.6]; 20 000 attended her farewell concert at the Exhibition Building, Melbourne. After further study in Europe, she reappeared in London in 1905 at Queen's Hall concerts and in 1906 gave a command performance before King Edward VII. She sang in the larger German centres, making her European début in grand opera in 1907 at Cologne in Ambroise Thomas's *Hamlet*. She appeared in seasons of Gounod's *Romeo and Juliet* and *Faust* and became a favourite of the Queen of the Netherlands. She also took part in the Harrison tours of Great Britain and at various times sang under the batons of Hans Richter, (Sir) Henry Wood and Landon Ronald, achieving success in concert, opera and oratorio.

In September 1909 Amy Castles returned to Australia for a four-and-a-half month tour of seventy-two towns for J. & N. Tait [qq.v.]. Her voice at this time was described as astonishingly even and full. At the end of this tour she appeared in the Australian première of Puccini's *Madame Butterfly* for J. C. Williamson. She returned to London in 1911 for a special series of Chapell concerts. In 1912 she accepted an offer of a four-year contract from the Imperial Opera in Vienna and was appointed chamber singer to the Imperial Court. With the outbreak of war she was obliged to leave Austria, returning to Australia in 1915 to tour the capital cities. In 1917 she made her American début in New York at Carnegie Hall. With American involvement in the war Amy gave concerts for the sick and wounded and opened her Manhattan home to visiting Australians. At this time Dolly and Eileen were also working in the United States.

In 1919 Amy toured Australia with the Williamson Grand Opera Company, opening in Sydney. She returned to Sydney again in 1925, at the end of a concert tour of Australasia managed by her brother George and including Eileen. In 1930-31 she visited Hollywood to take part in a 'talkie' but although she still gave occasional concerts she was 'happiest in retirement' and never fulfilled the promise of her pre-war years. 'From time to time' a newspaper article commented, 'Miss Castles has picked up the loose threads of her career, but never with the same enthusiasm'.

A diabetic for many years, Amy Castles died in hospital at Fitzroy, Victoria, on 19 November 1951 and was buried in Box Hill cemetery. She had been living with her sister Dolly in Camberwell. She did not marry.

I. Moresby, *Australia makes music* (Melb, 1948); B. and F. Mackenzie, *Singers of Australia* (Melb, 1967); *Lone Hand*, 2 Aug 1909; *Southern Sphere*, 1 Aug 1910; *Argus*, 17 Mar 1899; *Punch* (Melb), 3, 24 Apr 1902; *Weekly Times* (Melb), 7, 14 Aug 1909; *SMH*, 14 Feb, 2 Mar 1925; *Herald* (Melb), 24 Feb 1932; *Age*, 20 Nov 1951; A. E. Castles papers and news-cuttings (LaTL).

MAUREEN THÉRÈSE RADIC

CASTLETON, CLAUD CHARLES (1893-1916), soldier, was born on 12 April 1893 at Kirkley, Suffolk, England, son of Thomas Charles Castleton, bricklayer, and his wife Edith Lucy, née Payne. He was educated at Lowestoft municipal secondary school and worked as a pupil-teacher in the local council school before migrating to Australia at the age of 19. He reached Melbourne in the autumn of 1912, then travelled through the eastern States and on to New Guinea. According to his father, his interest in nature and geography led to his migration and his journeys after arrival.

When World War I broke out Castleton was in Port Moresby and, on offering his services to the Papuan administration, worked with native troops preparing for coastal defence; he also helped to man the Moresby wireless station. On 11 March 1915 he enlisted in the Australian Imperial Force at Sydney, stating his occupation as prospector. He was posted to the 18th Battalion and sailed for Egypt in June. His unit, which was to serve with the 2nd Brigade until the evacuation, reached Gallipoli on 6 August and on the 22nd took part in the attack on Hill 60. Castleton was promoted corporal on 7 December and temporary sergeant in February 1916. On 8 March, soon after his arrival in France, he was transferred to the 5th Australian Machine-Gun Company and was confirmed in his rank. He served on the Somme with this unit and on the night of 28 July took part in an attack on enemy trenches at Pozières Heights. The Australian advance was stopped by machine-gun fire and shelling, and for three hours troops lay out in No Man's Land under withering fire. Castleton twice brought back wounded men but, while bringing in a third, was hit in the back and killed instantly. He was awarded the Victoria Cross posthumously, and was buried in the Pozières British cemetery at Ovillers-la-Boiselle, France. He was unmarried.

C. E. W. Bean, *The A.I.F. in France*, 1916 (Syd, 1929); L. Wigmore (ed), *They dared mightily* (Canb, 1963); *London Gazette*, 26 Sept 1916; Castleton file (AWM).   J. K. HAKEN

CATANI, CARLO GIORGIO DOMENICO ENRICO (1852-1918), civil engineer, was born on 22 April 1852 at Florence, Italy, son of Enrico Catani, merchant, and his wife Augusta, née Geri. He was educated at the Technical Institute of Florence, where he received his civil engineering diploma. As a young man he was employed in railway construction in Italy.

Early in 1876 Catani and two of his colleagues, P. Baracchi and E. Checchi [qq.v.] resolved to migrate from Italy; it is likely that they were recruited by the New Zealand immigration agency in Germany. They sailed as 'labourers' from Hamburg in the *Fritz Reuter*, reaching Wellington on 7 August. There was no professional work for the new arrivals, so Catani and his friends decided to go to Australia. Describing themselves now as miners, they took steerage passages in the *Alhambra*, arriving in Melbourne on 27 September.

Within a few weeks all three had joined the Department of Lands and Survey as draftsmen. In 1880 Catani was registered as a surveyor under the Land Act. Two years later he and Checchi were transferred to the Public Works Department, where they were employed as engineering draughtsmen preparing plans for harbours, jetties and coast works, and by early 1886 they were both assistant engineers. On 18 May that year at Fitzroy Catani married, according to the rites of the Free Church of England, 26-year-old Cathrine Hanley, daughter of a Belfast (Port Fairy) farmer. On 15 March 1892 he was naturalized.

In November Catani was promoted head of his section. One of the projects under the direction of his department was the draining of the Koo-Wee-Rup swamp, West Gippsland. Finding the work of the contractors unsatisfactory, he devised a system of using the labour of unemployed married men who were offered small farms on the newly drained land. Despite the mixed success of his scheme, most of the works were finished by the end of 1897. He had taken a close personal interest in the project, visiting all parts of the work and getting to know many of the men. A new township in the area was named after him.

Catani was next concerned with the widening and improvement of the River Yarra upstream from Princes Bridge, Melbourne. Through his urging, the scope of the flood mitigation programme was greatly enlarged. Work began in August 1896; next winter he began to plant elms, oaks and poplars along the left bank and the newly formed Alexandra Avenue. His river works extended upstream as far as Cremorne railway bridge, and included the road bridge at Anderson Street. The laying out and planting of the Alexandra Gardens was executed by the Public Works Department under Catani's direction.

Other works associated with him are the roads to Arthur's Seat and to Mount Donna Buang, the draining of Kow Swamp, the Elster Canal, the River Murray levees in the Strathmerton district, and drainage at Framlingham. He was also closely involved in the opening-up of the Mount Buffalo Plateau and the damming there of Eurobin Creek to form the lake which bears his name.

Catani's last major project was the reclamation of the foreshore of St Kilda. He was an original member of the St Kilda Foreshore Trust, set up in 1906, and after his retirement in 1917 he continued as government representative. He designed the landscaping of the gardens at the beach end of Fitzroy Street, later named the Catani Gardens, and was responsible for the foreshore works all the way to Point Ormond.

In 1914 the Catani family had moved from Armadale to St Kilda where they became regular attenders at Holy Trinity Church. Carlo Catani never returned to Italy. He died, intestate, at St Kilda on 20 July 1918, and was buried in Brighton cemetery. He was survived by his wife (d. 1925), one of his three sons and two of his three daughters: his second son had been killed in action in 1916.

Sir Kingsley Norris recalled Catani as a 'remarkable little bald-headed, bearded man'. One officer of his department remembered that he was always clad in Fox's serge and wore his spectacles on the end of his nose. A close associate wrote that 'he saw possibilities to which others were blind'. Other contemporaries recorded his 'unfailing courtesy and kindly nature', qualities which are not always found in persons of energy and imagination. There is a bronze bust of Catani at the foot of Schefferle's memorial clock tower on the St Kilda Esplanade.

J. Smith (ed), *Cyclopedia of Victoria*, 1 (Melb, 1903); J. B. Cooper, *The history of St Kilda* (Melb, 1931); N. Gunson, *The good country* (Melb, 1968); F. K. Norris, *No memory for pain* (Melb, 1970); *Argus*, 22 July 1918; Public Works Dept files (PRO, Melb).   RONALD MCNICOLL

CATO, FREDERICK JOHN (1858-1935), grocer and philanthropist, was born on 15 May 1858 in a tent at Pleasant Creek (Stawell), Victoria, third son of Edward Cato, goldminer and formerly builder, of Surrey, England, and his wife Catherine, née Nimmo, of Glasgow, Scotland. Cato was educated at Stawell State School to the age of 13 and worked in a grocery shop while studying to become a pupil-teacher. He taught at his old school until 1878 before moving to New Zealand where he was eventually in charge of a school at Invercargill. Worried about his health and tired of teaching, in May 1881 he wrote to his cousin Thomas Edwin Moran, who had established two grocery shops in Fitzroy and Carlton, asking him if there were any chance of joining in the business. On 24 July they entered partnership with £411 capital: Moran was to have two-thirds of the shares. In 1884 Cato returned to Invercargill to marry on 12 December Fanny Bethune, daughter of a minister.

The partners prospered. When Moran died in 1890, aged 30, his widow became partner in the business which by then had thirty-five branches. Cato was among the first, in 1893, to introduce six o'clock closing. The business expanded into Tasmania and into New South Wales, where Moran & Cato Ltd was formed in Sydney in 1909. In 1912 it was converted to a proprietary company with the Moran family and Cato as shareholders; Cato became governing director. In 1924 he set up wholesale companies in Melbourne and Sydney. By 1935 there were about 120 branches of Moran & Cato in Victoria and Tasmania and about 40 in New South Wales, with nearly one thousand employees.

Cato had been a founder in 1895 of the Rosella Preserving Co. and became its chairman of directors. He was also a founder in 1911 and chairman of Austral Grain & Produce Pty Ltd, and chairman of Hagita Pty Ltd, coconut-planters of Papua.

An ardent Methodist, Cato fought staunchly for union within the denomination. He was founder in 1913 and long president of the Laymen's Missionary Movement, a pillar of the Auburn Church, president of Queen's College, University of Melbourne, and a member of the Wesley College Council. He donated many scholarships to Church schools and gave extensive properties to the Methodist Ladies' College of which he was a trustee from 1927. He supported the Methodist Boys' Home and Training Farm, Cheltenham, was active in home-mission affairs, and was a generous donor to Methodist missions in Arnhem Land, New Britain and India, which he visited in 1926. He also made generous donations to metropolitan churches of several denominations and to Stawell hospital;

parks are named after him there and in Hawthorn. His Methodist endowments probably amounted to some £150 000 and his total gifts to twice that sum, but he 'never gave or helped anyone blindly . . . He liked to know all about the circumstances and position of those people and causes whom he helped'. A. Wesley Amos commented that 'with the gift came the charm and personality of the giver'.

Cato had long suffered from chronic bronchitis. He died at Hawthorn on 4 June 1935 and was buried in Melbourne general cemetery. His estate was valued for probate in Victoria at £591 176 and in New South Wales at £20 795. He was survived by two of his four sons of whom Edward went into the business and Edwin became a doctor, and by three of his four daughters. The eldest, Frances Gertrude, married Dr Karl Kumm, founder of the Soudan United Mission. Dr Una Beatrice (Porter), his youngest daughter, started the psychiatric clinic at the Queen Victoria hospital and became world-president of the Young Women's Christian Association. The Y.W.C.A. building in Canberra is named after her.

C. I. Benson (ed), *A century of Victorian Methodism* (Melb, 1935); C. E. Sayers, *Shepherd's gold* (Melb, 1966); L. R. East, *The Kiel family and related Scottish pioneers* (Nunawading, 1974); *Argus*, and *Age*, 5 June 1935; Moran & Cato papers (LaTL); information from Ms A. G. Zainu'ddin, Monash Univ, Vic.

CATTANACH, WILLIAM (1863-1932), administrator, was born on 17 May 1863 at Hotham (North Melbourne), son of Thomas Cattanach, builder, and his second wife Mary, née Masterton, both Scottish-born. He was educated at denominational and state schools and matriculated from Scotch College in 1880. After six years as an accountant with the Bank of Victoria, he became town clerk of Flemington and Kensington and then Essendon.

In May 1906 (Sir) Thomas Bent's [q.v.3] government appointed Cattanach one of the three members of the newly constituted State Rivers and Water Supply Commission. He succeeded Dr Elwood Mead [q.v.] as chairman in 1915. The commission was set up to direct the investigation, development and control of country water-supplies throughout Victoria. It became responsible for the administration of closer settlement in irrigation districts in 1912, and after 1918 for the settlement of discharged soldiers from World War I; by 1923 some two thousand soldier settlers were located in irrigated areas, notably Red Cliffs, Woorinen, Merbein, Nyah, Stanhope, Tongala, Shepparton and Rodney. With the assistance of quite a small settlement branch he had to deal with practically every problem of allocation, many of which were very difficult.

Cattanach played a leading part in obtaining government support for co-operative canneries at Kyabram and Mooroopna on the lines of the successful Shepparton cannery set up in 1916. He also aided establishment of co-operative packing sheds for dried vine-fruits at Red Cliffs, Merbein and Woorinen and was active in the negotiations for marketing canned fruits overseas. Under his administration, new and enlarged reservoirs added greatly to the capacity of the country water-storages of the State, and the irrigated areas increased by 50 per cent.

Cattanach was tall and well built, with crisp curly hair, but he was acutely cross-eyed and this certainly disturbed any who might argue with him. Except for the very few who worked closely with him, most of his officers feared rather than liked him. He was very hard-working, and he took no recreation leave in his years as chairman. In 1912 he had visited the United States of America, and in 1927 he toured Canada to seek markets for Victorian canned and dried fruits.

Away from the office Cattanach was friendly and even charming. He was several times president of the Old Scotch Collegians' Association, was a popular member of the Wallaby (walking) Club, and an interesting travelling companion on visits to country districts. In 1925 he was appointed C.M.G.

Cattanach married Kate Lachlan Robertson at the age of 39; they had no children. For many years they lived at the George Hotel, St Kilda. He died on 20 July 1932 while still in office, and was buried in Melbourne general cemetery. His estate was valued for probate at £14 591.

Cattanach had made a substantial contribution to the development of Victorian water-resources, the expansion of irrigation, the subdivision of large holdings for closer settlement and the development of the fruit industry.

PP (LA Vic), 1910, 2 (46); J. N. Churchyard, 'Pioneers of irrigation in Victoria . . . William Cattanach', *Aqua*, July 1957; *Argus*, 1 Jan 1925, 21 July 1932; F. W. Eggleston, Confidential notes (Menzies Lib, ANU).   RONALD EAST

CATTS, JAMES HOWARD (1877-1951), union secretary, politician and businessman, was born on 12 August 1877 at Wagga Wagga, New South Wales, son of James Catts, joiner and grocer, and his wife Amy, née Hedger. As a child he lived with his stern

Methodist paternal grandfather at Stanmore and attended Macdonaldtown Public School, leaving at 13 when the family business at Orange failed.

From 1894 Catts helped his parents run a bakery at Forbes, earning extra money in a brick-pit and as a shearers' cook. At 17 he became secretary of the Forbes branches of the Farmers and Settlers' and the Progress associations; in 1900-03 he was general secretary of the United Progress Association of New South Wales. A teetotaller and firm advocate of temperance, he was organizing secretary in Sydney in 1901-02 of the New South Wales Temperance Alliance. In 1903 he became general secretary of the 350-man New South Wales Amalgamated Railway and Tramway Service Association and editor of the *Railway and Tramway Review* (later the *Co-operator*), and in 1905 federal secretary of the Railway and Tramway Employees' Association. In 1913, when he resigned, the State union had 15000 members. He was the workers' representative on the Railway Superannuation Board in 1910-15, general secretary of the Australian Union Federation and president of the Australasian Labour Federation in 1913-14, and founder of the United Secretaries' Association in 1915.

An unsuccessful Labor contender for Granville in the 1904 State elections, Catts won Cook in the House of Representatives in 1906, being the youngest member to that stage. He quickly became friendly with King O'Malley [q.v.], supporting his Commonwealth Bank scheme, at the same time laying the foundations of a much-tried but firm friendship with W. M. Hughes [q.v.]. Despite a halting delivery he spoke frequently in parliament on many subjects, seeking to make up with persistence what he lacked in size and personality. He strongly supported protection and as a fervent Australian nationalist wanted legislation to ensure that only the Australian-born could become prime minister. He married Eva Alice Weber on 12 August 1907 at St James's Anglican Church, Sydney; they had one son and were divorced in 1920.

Catts's painstaking industry and ability were soon recognized: he became caucus secretary and directed the Federal and State Labor campaigns in New South Wales from 1914 until January 1922. A member of the Federal Parliamentary War Committee, he was New South Wales director of voluntary recruiting in 1915-16, producing the weekly *Call to Arms* and organizing the highly successful route-marches of country volunteers. In March 1916 he was appointed chairman of the Commonwealth Prices Adjustment Board, but soon resigned to lead the New South Wales no-conscription campaign. Loyal to the majority group when the party split over conscription, he was prosecuted seven times under the War Precautions Act (1914) for asserting that a pro-German Japan had designs on Australia.

After the war Catts denounced communism and the 'criminality, graft and corruption' of the Australian Workers' Union faction which controlled the State Labor executive under J. Bailey [q.v.]. Accusing him of sectarianism, the executive expelled him from the party in April 1922; he ran unsuccessfully at the December elections for the breakaway Majority Australian Labor Party. With his second wife Dorothy Marguerite, née Purcell, whom he had married on 8 September 1920 at St Stephen's Presbyterian Church, Sydney, Catts now established a successful printing and publishing agency, Associated Business Services, editing and publishing the *Australian Home Budget* and several suburban papers. As a (Federal) Labor candidate he failed to win the seat of Martin in 1931; he became a member of the party's State executive, opposed to the (State) Lang [q.v.] Labor Party. As a United Australia Party candidate he lost in East Sydney in 1940; he also failed to be elected to the Sydney Municipal Council in 1944, the year he retired.

Catts subsequently pursued his hobby of astronomy, becoming secretary and treasurer of the New South Wales branch of the British Astronomical Association. Survived by his second wife and their son and three daughters, he died on 26 November 1951 at Huntley's Point, and was cremated after a Methodist service.

DOROTHY MARGUERITE CATTS (1896-1961), businesswoman and writer, was born on 1 March 1896 at Beecroft, New South Wales, daughter of Peter Purcell, builder, and his wife Frances Eliza, née Lepherd. Through the *Australian Home Budget* she established the first large paper-pattern service in Australia and ran a medical and home guidance department by post. Well-known for her journalism and public speaking, she co-edited with Ruth Beatrice Fairfax [q.v.] the *Countrywoman in New South Wales*, and wrote eight historical novels with Australian themes, and biographies of O'Malley and her husband. A friend of (Dame) Mary Gilmore [q.v.] from childhood, she was a president of the Society of Women Writers of New South Wales, and foundation president of the Huntley's Point branch of the Australian Red Cross Society. She died on 10 March 1961 at Young.

British A'sian, 6, 13 Apr 1911; *Punch* (Melb), 1 July 1909, 17 Apr 1913, 23 Mar 1916; *Australasian*, 11 Apr 1914, 26 July 1919, 17 Apr 1920; *Aust Worker*, 11 Dec 1919, 10 May 1922; *SMH*, 7, 12, 25

Jan, 8, 10 Apr, 7 July, 22 Oct 1922, 26 Aug 1940; D. and J. H. Catts papers (NL); O'Malley papers (NL).

ARTHUR HOYLE

CAVILL, FREDERICK (1839-1927), 'professor of swimming', was born on 10 July 1839 at Kensington, London, son of John Cavill, coachmaker, and his wife Isabella, née Strachan. He joined the navy as an apprentice in the royal yachts *Victoria and Albert* and *Fairy*, fought in the Baltic war and later took up professional swimming. While teaching at Brighton, he won the English 500 yards swimming championship in 1862. On 13 January at St Dunstan's, Fleet Street, London, he married Maria Theophila Rhodes, a cousin of Cecil Rhodes.

In July 1876 Cavill swam over twenty miles from London Bridge to Greenhithe, the longest distance to that time on the Thames. Next month he swam from Southampton to Southsea Pier and from Dover to Ramsgate, before attempting to swim the English Channel. He was taken from the water three miles from his destination, but achieved considerable fame. Having a 'robust constitution, broad chest, and great muscular power', he tried again next year but was dragged from the water within 220 yards of the English coast. Although the 'success' of the swim was heatedly challenged, it was recognized by the Serpentine Club.

Cavill migrated to Australia, reaching Melbourne with his family in the *Somersetshire* in February 1879. He soon moved to Sydney and set up as a 'professor of swimming'. In 1884 he published a pamphlet *How to learn to swim* which outlined his theories on 'natations'. His floating baths or 'natatoriums' at Lavender Bay, Farm Cove, and after 1902 at Woolloomooloo, were popular haunts, despite some opposition to them. All his children gave demonstrations of aquatics and life-saving. Cavill's greatest Australian feats included swimming from Parramatta to Sydney, and eighteen miles from Glenelg (South Australia) to the Semaphore. Crippled by rheumatism for thirty years, Cavill died on 9 February 1927 at Marrickville and was buried in the Anglican section of Waverley cemetery. He was survived by four of his six sons and three daughters.

All his sons were excellent swimmers. The eldest Ernest (1868-1935) was 1000 yards champion of New South Wales at 15 and was placed in championship races in London. Charles (1870-1897) was the first man to swim the Golden Gate, San Francisco, United States of America, in 1896, but was drowned next year at Stockton Baths,

California. Percy (1875-1940) was the first Australian to win a race abroad when in 1897 he won both the 440 yards and the long distance (5 miles) events in the English Amateur Swimming Association Championships. He also won four State and four Australian championships in 1895-98, but left for the United States in 1900 and coached swimmers for fifteen years, before disappearing, and living as a beachcomber in the Bahamas. Arthur (1877-1914), known as 'Tums', won the New South Wales 500 and 1000 yards amateur championships. At 21 he was 220 yards professional champion of Australia; W. F. Corbett [q.v.] credited him with originating the crawl stroke. In 1901 he went to the United States: he successfully swam the Golden Gate but was frozen to death in 1914 trying to swim Seattle Harbour. Sydney (1881-1945) was 220 yards amateur champion of Australia at 16 and was the originator of the butterfly stroke. He followed his brothers to America where he coached notable swimmers, mainly at San Francisco's Olympic Club. Cavill's three daughters were also outstanding swimmers and Fredda's son Richard (Dick) Eve won a gold medal for diving at the 1924 Olympic Games in Paris.

The youngest son RICHMOND THEOPHILUS (1884-1938) was born on 16 January 1884 in Sydney. He was the first to use the crawl stroke in a competition when in 1899 he won the 100 yards State championship. In 1900-04 he won 18 Australian and 22 New South Wales championships. In England in 1902 he was the first officially to swim 100 yards in under a minute, clocking 58.6 seconds. After living in New Zealand and the United States, Dick returned to Australia in 1913 and for a time played 'Father Neptune' in Wirth's [q.v.] circus. He died of a heart attack at the pool he leased at Balmoral, Sydney, on 2 May 1938, and was survived by his wife Mabel Clara, née West, whom he had married in Sydney on 3 November 1903 and by four children.

Frederick Cavill received three awards, for saving life, from the Royal Humane Society, London, between 1860 and 1870, and two from the Royal Humane Society of Australasia, which also made an award to Percy. Charles, Arthur and Sydney received medals from the National Shipwreck Relief Society of New South Wales – a total of nine awards for bravery before 1900. In 1970 the Cavill family was honoured in the International Swimming Hall of Fame at Fort Lauderdale, Florida, United States of America.

I. and C. Pearl (eds), *Our yesterdays* (Syd, 1954); P. Besford, *Encyclopaedia of swimming* (Lond, 1971); *V&P* (LA NSW), 1892-93, 8, 1227-31; *Tatler*

(Lond), 12 Feb 1898; *Sydney Mail*, 31 July 1897; *Sun* (Syd), 7 Jan 1913; *SMH* 10 Feb 1927; *Sunday Mirror* (Syd), 26 Mar 1961; E. S. Marks sporting collection (ML).

J. G. WILLIAMS

CAWOOD, DOROTHY GWENDOLEN (1884-1962), nurse, was born on 9 December 1884 at Parramatta, New South Wales, seventh child of John Cawood, carpenter, and his English-born wife Sarah Travis, née Garnett. No details of her education are known but in 1909 she began four years nursing training at Coast Hospital, Little Bay, Sydney, and was registered with the Australasian Trained Nurses' Association on 14 May 1913.

Dorothy Cawood enlisted in the Australian Imperial Force on 14 November 1914 as a staff nurse in the Army Nursing Service; she was posted to the 2nd Australian General Hospital and embarked for Egypt on the *Kyarra* with the first A.I.F. contingent. The hospital was based at Mena in 1915 and Sister Cawood served there throughout the Gallipoli campaign as well as doing duty on hospital ships and transports. She was promoted to nursing sister in December, then in March 1916 went with the 2nd A.G.H. to France. After serving at Marseilles and at Wimereux, near Boulogne, she was briefly attached to the 8th Stationary Hospital and the Australian Voluntary Hospital; she returned to the 2nd A.G.H. in July, then from December 1916 to August 1917 was attached to the 2nd Australian Casualty Clearing Station at Armentières. On the night of 22 July 1917 the station was bombed and Sister Cawood, with Sisters Claire Deacon and Alice Ross-King [qq.v.], risked her life to rescue patients trapped in the burning buildings. The three were awarded Military Medals – the first won by members of the A.A.N.S. – for their 'coolness and devotion to duty'. Advising her parents of the award Sister Cawood wrote: 'Do not blame me for this. It is Fritz's fault. He will do these dastardly tricks'.

On 1 August she was transferred to the 38th Stationary Hospital at Calais and in November to the 6th A.G.H.; while there she was mentioned in dispatches for 'distinguished and gallant service in the field'. She was soon posted to Genoa, Italy, with the 38th Stationary Hospital and, except for several months in 1918 when she was hospitalized, served there until January 1919. She was then transferred to England and was attached to the 3rd Australian Auxiliary Hospital at Dartford and the 2nd A.A.H. at Southall before returning to Sydney in May.

After demobilization Sister Cawood nursed in the State hospital at Liverpool, then from 1928 until her retirement in 1943 was matron of the David Berry Hospital, Berry. In 1944 she moved back to her old home in Parramatta and, unmarried, died there on 16 February 1962; she was buried in Rookwood cemetery with Anglican rites.

A. G. Butler (ed), *Official history of the Australian Army Medical Services... 1914-18*, 3 (Canb, 1943); J. Gurner, *The origins of the Royal Australian Army Medical Corps* (Melb, 1970); *London Gazette*, 28 Sept, 24 Dec 1917; *A'sian Nurses' J*, Jan, June 1913, Oct 1917, May 1918; *Sydney Mail*, 2 Jan 1918; S. G. Kenny, The Australian Army Nursing Service during the Great War (B.A. Hons thesis, Univ Melb, 1975).

JACQUELINE ABBOTT

CAWTHORNE, CHARLES WITTO-WITTO (1854-1925), music-seller and concert-manager, was born on 30 June 1854 in Adelaide, eldest son of William Anderson Cawthorne and his wife Maryann Georgina, née Mower, a pianist. His father had come to South Australia in 1841 and established the Victoria Square Academy in that year; he taught until 1862 when he became founder and secretary of the National Building Society. He had a serious interest in and knowledge of Aboriginals and published *The islanders* (1854), an enlightened account of white-Aboriginal relations in South Australia before colonization, and *The legend of Kuperree, or the red kangaroo ...* (1858), concerning the traditions, customs and dialect of the Port Lincoln tribe. He had held an exhibition of his water-colours in 1855 and died in 1897.

At 14 Charles began studying piano with Louis Eselbach and violin with F. Draeger. He also became proficient on the bassoon. In 1870 he began work with his father in a newsagent's business in Morphett Street. The firm became Cawthorne & Co. with father and son as partners in 1884, and they soon occupied part of a new building in Grenfell Street and Gawler Place; they now advertised for the first time as 'music-sellers and artists' colormen'. By 1887 Charles ran the business alone. In 1911 a prime site in Rundle Street was leased and named Cawthorne's Building.

By 1896 Cawthorne's were carrying sheet music from sixty publishers from England, France and Germany. Cawthorne would sit at the piano and try the new songs, throwing those he considered 'rubbish' on the floor. The 'music warehouse' also stocked instruments, books, opals and fine art. The firm acted as a box-office for most musical events in Adelaide, and by 1900 was also printing and publishing original compositions.

On most nights of the week Cawthorne was busy conducting, performing in and organizing musical entertainments. At 18 he was conducting the Adelaide Amateur Orchestra of forty players and had composed a prize-winning waltz. Another successful piece, the *Olivia waltz*, sold well in London as the *Southern Cross waltz*. On 9 September 1885 he married Amanda Dorothea Lellmann who shared his musical interests.

In the early 1890s Cawthorne formed a group of fifteen players known as the Adelaide Orchestra, which from 1893 formed the nucleus of Herman Heinicke's [q.v.] Grand Orchestra; Cawthorne continued to play bassoon and was secretary and treasurer. They became very popular: by 1896 they were staging thirteen concerts a year and the town hall was too small to hold all their patrons. In 1898 he began managing the short-lived students' Conservatorium Grand Orchestra. By now he was seen as a peerless manager. The two orchestras amalgamated to form the Conservatorium Grand Orchestra, soon renamed the Adelaide Grand Orchestra with Cawthorne as bassoonist and business manager. On Christmas night 1899 they combined with the Adelaide Choral Society and the Orpheus Society in a splendid production of *The Messiah*. This became an annual highlight. Cawthorne continued composing: his orchestral piece *Romance* won the prize at a concert judged by public ballot in 1902. In 1910 he became founder and conductor of the Adelaide Orchestral Society.

In World War I he leased the German Club which became Queen's Hall, a venue for patriotic concerts. Cawthorne's 'breezy personality attracted talented musicians from all over Australia'. He also managed concerts for and helped to promote Clara Serena (Kleinschmidt), the Adelaide Choral Society, the Bach Choir, the Adelaide Liedertafel Society, the Metropolitan Male Voice Choir and the Adelaide Glee Club. He encouraged young musicians of talent and helped raise money for them to study abroad.

The portly Cawthorne, though usually jovial, could become somewhat peppery and outspoken. In 1924 a limited company was formed and his eldest son 'Gus', who had joined the firm in 1903, became managing director. Two other sons were directors and Cawthorne himself was chairman. Predeceased by his wife and survived by his four sons, he died of cerebro-vascular disease on 26 June 1925 at his home at King's Park, and was buried in North Road cemetery. His estate was sworn for probate at £7927.

W. A. Cawthorne, *Menge, the mineralogist* (Adel, 1859); Cawthorne's Ltd, *Music in the nine-*

ties (Adel, 1925); Universal Publicity Co., *The official civic record of South Australia* (Adel, 1936); H. Brewster-Jones, 'Music', *Progress in Aust*, 5-6 (1934-36), and 'Pioneers and problems', *Aust Musical News*, Oct 1936; J. Horner, 'A short history of music in South Australia', *Aust Letters*, Mar 1960; J. J. Healy, 'The treatment of the Aborigine ...', *Aust Literary Studies*, May 1972; 'Trade notes', *Music* (Adel), Nov, Dec 1896, Apr 1897, June, July, Dec 1898, Dec 1899, June, Aug, Oct 1900; *Critic* (Adel), 21 June 1902; *Observer* (Adel), 2 Oct 1897; *Advertiser* (Adel), 25, 27 Dec 1899, 27 June 1925; Adel Orchestral Soc, Minutes 1879-80 (SAA); Cawthorne notes 1047/64 (SAA); information from Mr F. Cawthorne, Kurralta Park, SA.

SUZANNE EDGAR
JOYCE GIBBERD

CAYLEY, HENRY PRIAULX (1877-1942), naval officer, was born on 29 December 1877 at Clifton, Bristol, England, son of Henry Cayley, surgeon major in the Indian Medical Service, and his wife Letitia Mary, née Walters. Educated at Eastman's Naval Academy, he joined the Royal Navy's training ship *Britannia* in 1891 as a cadet and was promoted midshipman in 1893 and sub-lieutenant in 1897. His early sea-going appointments were to the Mediterranean Station and the Channel Fleet; then in 1899, after being commissioned lieutenant, he served on H.M.S. *Undaunted* during the Boxer Rebellion. On 14 July 1906 he married Ethel Mary Hewitt at Kensington, London.

In 1909 Cayley, now a lieutenant, was posted to the Australian Station as the Royal Navy's inspector of warlike stores. To take advantage of better career opportunities, he resigned in mid-1912 and joined the newly established Royal Australian Navy, retaining the position of inspector of warlike stores; in due course he was appointed lieut-commander. When war broke out next year he was made an acting commander and sailed with the first Australian convoy as transport officer on the troopship *Euripides*; he was transferred to H.M.S. *Isis* in January 1915 and promoted commander in April. In March 1917 he was appointed second-in-command to Captain John S. Dumaresq [q.v.] in H.M.A.S. *Sydney*, then carrying out patrol and convoy duties in the North Sea. *Sydney* engaged no enemy ships, though Cayley, in typically humorous fashion, reported 'differences of opinion' between his ship and a Zeppelin which 'amused herself by sitting up overhead, well out of range, and thoroughly bombing us'.

He was promoted captain on 1 April 1919 and took command of the *Sydney*. He was a popular but firm commander, who took a humane interest in his men. In June, when the *Sydney* was returning home, Cayley was asked to help quell civil riots in the Straits

Settlements. He promptly supplied landing parties at Singapore and Penang, and as a means of quietening unrest, is said to have ridden by rickshaw, in full uniform, through the streets of Penang. In November the *Sydney* grounded (without damage) at Townsville, Queensland, and Cayley and his navigating officer were court-martialled and reprimanded for negligence; the findings against the navigator were quashed on appeal, but those against Cayley were confirmed. He was held solely responsible for the incident; however, he retained the confidence of Dumaresq, who was then commodore commanding the Australian Fleet, and the mishap does not appear to have prejudiced his chances of preferment.

In 1922-23 Cayley was captain-in-charge at Flinders Naval Depot, Victoria, and then went to England for twelve months training. On his return he was appointed second naval member, one of the few R.A.N. men to serve before 1939 on the Australian Naval Board; appropriately, he concerned himself mainly with personnel matters. In May 1927 he became commander of H.M.A.S. *Melbourne*, then in October was made captain superintendent in Sydney. He was posted back to London in 1929 as naval representative on the Australian high commissioner's staff but, when his position was retrenched during Depression cuts in defence spending, he retired on 7 August 1931 in the rank of rear admiral. He spent the rest of his life in England and in retirement devoted himself to Christian Science, the study of which had led him to abandon the Catholic faith and to become a teetotaller. Survived by his son, he died of pulmonary embolism on 31 December 1942 at his home in Chelsea.

A. W. Jose, *The Royal Australian Navy 1914-1918* (Syd, 1928); *SMH*, 19 July 1919, 30 Apr, 30 May 1924, 8 Oct 1927, 18 July 1929, 12, 14 Feb 1931, 4 Jan 1943; Naval Board, Minutes, 1922-31 (AAO, Melb); MP150/1 437/201/252, MP472 5/15/2871, 5/20/7714, 5/20/10863, MP1049/2 303/1/14 (AAO, Melb); family papers held by Mr F. Cayley, Wollstonecraft, NSW; information from Rear Admiral H. Showers, Watson's Bay, NSW.

MARGOT Z. SIMINGTON

CAYLEY, NEVILLE WILLIAM (1886-1950), ornithologist and artist, was born on 7 January 1886 at Yamba, Clarence River, New South Wales, son of Neville Henry Penniston Cayley, bird-artist from Kent, England, and his native-born wife Lois Emmeline, née Gregory. Educated at local public schools, he moved with his family to Sydney about 1894. He later attended an art school and soon followed his father's example – painting mostly birds. He was a founder of the Cronulla Surf Life Saving Club and a member of the executive of the Surf Life Saving Association of Australia and the Royal Life Saving Society.

On 15 December 1917 at Marrickville Cayley married Beatrice Lucy Doust. Next year he published his first booklet, *Our birds*, and displayed the 'somewhat romantic' originals in the Hunter Street gallery of the art dealer William Aldenhaven. Increasingly interested in ornithology, he became associated with George Robertson [q.v.] and illustrated birds' eggs for *The Australian encyclopaedia* (1925-26) using partly mechanical methods. His popular book *What bird is that?* was published in 1931 and reprinted many times. He followed it with *Australian finches in bush and aviary* ... (1932), *Budgerigars in bush and aviary* (1933), *Australian parrots* ... (1938) and *The fairy wrens of Australia* (1949). Cayley 'was irresistibly attracted by the brilliant colours' and 'elfin forms' of the wrens: the illustrations first appeared in the *National Geographic Magazine* (October 1945). He also did the colour drawings for G. A. Waterhouse's [q.v.] *What butterfly is that?* (1932) and Ellis Troughton's *Furred animals of Australia* (1941). His projected work covering all Australia's birds, their habits, nests and eggs was never completed, although he amassed over 500 colour illustrations.

Cayley's love of birds was an integral part of his life: he was a council-member of the Royal Zoological Society of New South Wales (president 1932-33), the Royal Australasian Ornithologists' Union (president 1936-37), the Gould League of Bird Lovers and the Wild Life Preservation Society of Australia, and was a trustee of the National Park in 1937-48. He also held several exhibitions of his paintings: in 1932 one was presented to King George V. His main medium was water-colours; his pictures were vibrant and steeped in sunlight and shadow.

Cayley died at his Avalon home on 17 March 1950 and was cremated with Anglican rites. He was survived by two sons of his first marriage, and by his second wife Phyllis Mary Linton, née Goodson, a divorcee whom he had married at Chatswood on 2 November 1944.

Emu (Melb), 5 (1950); Roy Zoological Soc, NSW, *Procs*, May 1950; *Wild Life* (Melb), 12 (1950); *SMH* 11, 12 June 1924, 20 July 1932, 16 Mar 1940, 18 Mar 1950.

A. H. CHISHOLM*

CAZALY, ROY (1893-1963), footballer, was born on 13 January 1893 at South Melbourne, tenth child of English-born James Cazaly and his wife Elizabeth Jemima, née

McNee, midwife and herbalist from Scotland. James had been a champion oarsman and a physical instructor but had lost his money in the collapse of the land boom and was a labourer when Roy was born. Educated at the Albert Park and Middle Park State schools, Roy was trained athletically by his father and elder brothers in their backyard gymnasium, and starred early at cricket and football. While still in his teens he rowed for South Melbourne in Victorian championships; he also played as a medium left-hand bowler for Port Melbourne Cricket Club. In his youth he worked in a butcher's shop and as a motor mechanic. On 18 October 1913 at Brunswick he married Agnes Murtha.

In 1909-20 Cazaly played for St Kilda Football Club, without pay, winning the club's 'best and fairest' award in the last two seasons. In 1921 he transferred to South Melbourne, where he formed 'The Terrible Trio' ruck combination with 'Skeeter' Fleiter and rover Mark Tandy. Though only 5 ft. 11 ins. (181 cm) and 12½ stone (79 kg), Cazaly was a brilliant high-mark; he daily practised leaping for a ball suspended from the roof of a shed at his home. He could mark and turn in mid-air, land and in a few strides send forward a long accurate drop-kick or stab-pass. Fleiter's constant cry 'Up there Cazaly' was taken up by the crowds. It entered the Australian idiom, was used by infantrymen in North Africa in World War II, and became part of folk-lore.

Cazaly was paid £6 a week by South Melbourne and regularly played for Victoria. A critic eventually described him as the 'greatest Australian Rules footballer between the two World Wars'. After a year at Minyip as playing coach at £12 a week, he returned to South in 1926-27, then began an extraordinary career as a playing coach with reputedly as many retirements as Nellie Melba [q.v.]. Laurie Nash regarded him as the greatest coach of his experience, the complete player, strategist and tactician, able to impart his knowledge persuasively, without histrionics. He coached City (Launceston, Tasmania) in 1928-30, North Hobart in 1932-33, South Melbourne in 1937-38, Hawthorn in 1942-43, New Town, Hobart, in 1934-36 and 1948-51,and Preston and Camberwell in the Victorian Football Association. His last professional game was with Camberwell when he was 48, but in 1951 when 58 he played in a short veterans' match, then a full game for New Town in which he kicked a goal.

Cazaly was obsessed with sport, the body and physical movement. While with South he had studied, under the club doctor and masseur, muscular anatomy and the treatment of muscular injury, mastering Swedish massage theory and practice. During the Depression, he worked on the waterfront, played with waterside workers in the mid-week competition, and treated muscular injuries at night. In the 1930s he practised Sister Kenny's [q.v.] controversial treatment of poliomyelitis, without charging fees. He developed theories of diet and the 'art of breathing', filling his lungs before going for the ball in the belief that oxygen gave him added levitation and energy. A non-smoker and non-drinker, he 'dried out' late in the week, sipping only a little water and eating sparingly.

During World War II Cazaly worked at Johns [q.v.4] & Waygood and represented fellow employees in negotiations. On moving to Hobart he opened a health clinic, which prospered. On 35 acres (14 ha) at Lenah Valley he bred horses and, with Master Barry, won the first Tasmanian Trotting Championship in 1956. In May 1950 he had stood unsuccessfully as a Liberal Party candidate for Denison for the House of Assembly. His family life was close; he played the piano and they often had sing-songs at night. After a long illness following heart attacks, Cazaly died on 10 October 1963 at Lenah Valley, survived by his wife, a son and four daughters.

Football Life, July 1969; *People* (Syd), 11 Mar 1953; *SMH*, 7, 13 Jan, 11 Oct 1963; *Age*, 11 Oct 1963; information from Mr R. Cazaly, Lenah Valley, Hobart, and Mr L. J. Nash, South Yarra, Vic.

NOEL COUNIHAN

CAZNEAUX, HAROLD PIERCE (1878-1953), photographer, was born on 30 March 1878 in Wellington, New Zealand, son of Pierce Mott Cazneaux, an English-born photographer, and his wife Emily Florence, née Bentley, a colourist and miniature painter from Sydney. In the 1890s the family moved to Adelaide and Mott became manager of Hammer & Co.'s Rundle Street studio. Harold went to a local state school; he started to work in his father's studio and attended H. P. Gill's [q.v.] evening classes at the School of Design, Painting and Technical Arts. In 1898 his passion for photography as an art was aroused by an exhibition of new 'pictorial movement' photographs from England.

Cazneaux moved to Sydney and from about 1904 worked in Freeman [q.v.4] & Co. Ltd's studio, becoming manager and chief operator. On 1 September 1905 at Lewisham he married Mabel Winifred Hodge. In his leisure time he began to document old Sydney. In 1907 he showed photographs at the members' exhibition of the Photographic

Society of New South Wales and two years later held the first one-man exhibition in Australia: the critics praised the diversity of his work. He sent some of his pictures overseas and was recognized as a pioneer of the pictorial movement. In 1916 with five friends, he founded the amateur Sydney Camera Circle. Opposed to slavish imitation of overseas trends, he argued for a break with the typical low-toned British print in favour of 'truly Australian sunshine effects'.

In 1914 Cazneaux won Kodak's 'Happy Moments' contest and used the £100 as a deposit for a house in Roseville where he lived and from 1920 worked for the rest of his life. Frustrated and in poor health, he had left Freeman's in 1918 and was rescued from penury by S. Ure Smith [q.v.], who gave him regular work for his new publications the *Home* and *Art in Australia*. His cover photograph for the first issue of the *Home* in 1920 used sunshine effects so successfully that it sparked a new trend in local photography. 'Caz' benefited greatly from the publicity. A member of the London Salon of Photography, he exhibited there in 1923 and next year, with other members of the camera circle, opened the short-lived Australian Salon with a hanging of 170 pictures.

Cazneaux's stature is based on the extraordinary diversity of his work — landscapes and portraits. He produced a series of portraits of well-known artists, musicians, and actors and many books including *Canberra, Australia's Federal capital* (1928), *Sydney surfing* (1929), *The Bridge book* (1930), *The Sydney book* (1931), *Frensham book* (1934), and the jubilee number of the *B.H.P. Review* (1935). As a critic he wrote for the *Australasian Photographic Review* and the *Gallery Gazette*, London, and columns for the *Lone Hand* and *Sydney Mail*. Sometime president of the Photographic Society of New South Wales, he was elected an honorary fellow of the Royal Photographic Society of Great Britain in 1938.

Survived by his wife and five daughters, who all helped in his studio, Cazneaux died at his Roseville home on 19 June 1953 and was cremated with Anglican rites. His only son was killed at the siege of Tobruk, North Africa, in 1941.

F. J. Mortimer (ed), *Photograms of the year 1919* (Lond, 1920); M. Dupain (ed), *Cazneaux* (Canb, 1978); *A 'sian Photographic Review*, Mar 1909, May 1924, Dec 1952; *Aust Photographic J*, Mar 1909; *Contemporary Photography*, May-June 1948; *Etruscan*, Dec 1970; Keast Burke, Correspondence with H. Cazneaux (ML).   LESLEY G. LYNCH

CHAFFEY, FRANK AUGUSTUS (1888-1940), farmer and politician, was born on 31 March 1888 at Rock View near Moonbi, New South Wales, sixth son of William Adolphus Chaffey, farmer from Somerset, England, and his native-born wife Amelia, née Chad. Educated at Nemingha and Tamworth public schools, he went to Hawkesbury Agricultural College in 1904, gaining its diploma and prizes in 1906. Next year he received a certificate in woolclassing from Sydney Technical College, then joined his brothers in a mixed-farming partnership at Nemingha.

Chaffey represented Tamworth at football and later was an almost fanatical fisherman. An active Freemason, he became grand master of the Peel Lodge. From 1911 he was the first secretary of the Tamworth district council of the Farmers and Settlers' Association. On 1 May 1912 at St John's Church of England he married a nurse Amy Stella McIlveen, daughter of a grazier. Next year, as the Liberal and F.A.S.A. candidate, he defeated R. H. Levien [q.v.] for the Tamworth seat in the Legislative Assembly.

Joining the 5th (New England) Light Horse Regiment as a trooper, Chaffey was promoted second lieutenant in 1913. In September 1915 he was commissioned in the Australian Imperial Force in the 1st Light Horse Regiment. In 1916-18 he served as quartermaster and adjutant at the 2nd Division Base Depot in France and the Anzac Corps Reinforcement Camp at Etaples. Promoted captain in 1917, he was later mentioned in dispatches.

In 1919 Chaffey returned to Australia and his parliamentary duties (his seat had been successfully defended on his behalf in 1916) and resisted pressure to join the Progressives, though he supported the New England New State Movement. Representing the Namoi as a Nationalist until 1927, then Tamworth until 1940, he was a member of Sir George Fuller's [q.v.] seven-hour cabinet on 20 December 1921. In Fuller's coalition ministry he was assistant minister for lands and agriculture from April to June 1922, then minister of agriculture until June 1925. His recommendations on the rationalization of wheat-pools were adopted, he helped to improve dairy-produce standards and founded the Agricultural Bureau of New South Wales. He was secretary for mines and minister for forests under (Sir) Thomas Bavin [q.v.] in 1927-29, then colonial secretary until November 1930. Although he had moved his formal place of residence to Sydney in 1922, Chaffey proved an able and forceful representative for Tamworth and district, procuring water and sewerage supplies, flood-mitigation works, many public buildings and schools, extension of rural electricity, and roads. He continued to enjoy the pleasures of country life, and from

1928 was a councillor of the Royal Agricultural Society of New South Wales, and later became chief steward.

Chaffey returned to office in 1932 as colonial secretary under (Sir) Bertram Stevens [q.v.]. In this position he wielded considerable power, pushing, for example, the Vagrancy (Amendment) Act, 1929, the Charitable Collections Act, 1934, and legislation favourable to rural interests through parliament. As minister in charge of police during the difficult Depression years, he was under constant attack and occasional death-threat for alleged police misconduct. He was very active in the foundation of Police boys' clubs as a means of diverting youthful offenders. In April 1938 Stevens removed him from office in a general reshuffle, despite Chaffey's vigorous denials of ill health.

His health had in fact been poor for some time. Survived by his wife, two sons and four daughters, Chaffey died of coronary occlusion at his Rose Bay home on 9 July 1940 and was cremated. His son William Adolphus Chaffey represented Tamworth in 1940-73.

Generous and friendly if somewhat reserved, Chaffey was deeply, sometimes quite emotionally, concerned with rural pursuits. He was an unrelenting foe of the Left. The honesty of his private and public dealings was never doubted, and his estate, valued for probate at £4872, indicates that he put the public good before his own pecuniary interests. He was a staunch Anglican.

Fighting Line, 19 Nov 1913; *Northern Daily Leader*, 10, 11 July 1940; *SMH*, 10 July 1940; W. A. Chaffey, Memoirs (held by him, Tamworth); Hawkesbury Agr College Archives (Richmond, NSW).   TERRY HOGAN

CHAFFEY, GEORGE (1848-1932), irrigation pioneer, engineer, inventor and entrepreneur, and WILLIAM BENJAMIN (1856-1926), agriculturist and irrigation planner, were born on 28 January 1848 and 21 October 1856 at Brockville, Ontario, Canada, sons of George Chaffey, a Canadian born at Zanesville, Ohio, United States of America, and his wife Anne, née Legoe, of Quebec. In 1859 the family moved to Kingston on Lake Ontario. George attended Kingston Grammar School. He seems to have been in poor health, and was certainly uninterested in classroom instruction. But even at that early age he keenly sought out engineering books at the local library. He left school at 13, and soon became fascinated by the machinery in his father's shipbuilding yard and in the Lakes steamers. In May 1862 he was apprenticed as a marine engineer on

Lake Ontario. Although entirely self-instructed, he obtained a United States certificate at 18, but in 1867 went to work in his uncle Benjamin's bank in Toronto. On 21 May 1869 he married Annette, only child of Thomas McCord, city chamberlain. In 1870-80 George was a partner in his father's shipyard, achieving a deserved reputation as designer and builder of shallow-draught steamers for the Great Lakes and the Ohio and Frazer rivers in British Columbia. During this period his three sons, Andrew, Benjamin and John, were born.

In 1878 George Chaffey senior moved to Riverside, near Los Angeles, California, to join other Canadian families in the Santa Ana River irrigation settlement. William Benjamin, who had been in his employment at Kingston, accompanied him. Their reports induced George junior to join them, since he had grown into a restless entrepreneur. The large profits that flowed from the Riverside venture encouraged George and William to become partners in the new irrigation colonies, named by them Etiwanda and Ontario, on the Cucamonga Plain. These settlements were based upon the purchase of land and water-rights by the Chaffeys at a low price, and resale to settlers in 10-acre (4 ha) blocks, with a mutual irrigation company to distribute water on a non-profit basis. Much of the success of irrigation at Etiwanda and Ontario was due to the use of cement pipes in the main water channels. Planned towns, social institutes and prohibition were features of both colonies, which were regarded as model settlements throughout western America. In addition to his vigorous and innovatory irrigation schemes, George became interested in electric lighting. He was president and joint engineer of the Los Angeles Electric Co., which gave to that city the most extensive lighting by electricity in the United States at the time. He also set up the first trunk line telephones in California.

In 1877-84 northern Victoria suffered from drought, and Alfred Deakin [q.v.], a minister in the Service-Berry [qq.v.6,3] government and chairman of a royal commission on water supply, visited the irrigation areas of California in 1885. He met George and William Chaffey, admired their skill and energy and discussed the possibilities of irrigation in Victoria. Deakin's progress report, the dispatches of two journalists, (Sir) Edward Cunningham [q.v.] and J. L. Dow [q.v.4], who travelled with him, and the exaggerated tales of Stephen Cureton, a new-comer in Los Angeles, who had travelled in Australia, combined to tempt George to Melbourne, where he arrived in February 1886. Despite the later allegations of his political enemies, Deakin certainly never invited him to Victoria. At this juncture George's strong entrepreneurial instincts gravely affected his business judgment. He was plainly warned by Deakin and officials of the Water Supply Department that he would have little chance of obtaining a land grant on terms similar to those in California, but failed to understand the extent to which the Australian national outlook had diverged from the Anglo-American pattern of economic individualism. He was persuaded to look at the Murray Valley and returned to Melbourne excited about its potential for irrigation. Without fully realizing the import of his offer, Deakin assured George that the government would make available 250 000 acres (100 000 ha) of crown land on favourable terms. In April George somewhat rashly cabled his brother William to sell their Californian interests, which he did at a fraction of their real worth and then hurried to Victoria.

George returned to the Murray and selected a derelict sheep station at Mildura as the site for his first irrigation settlement. It was in the Mallee, described in a famous phrase as 'hissing desert', and 163 miles (262 km) from the nearest railhead at Swan Hill. But the Chaffey brothers signed an agreement with the Victorian government on 21 October, committing themselves to spend at least £300 000 on permanent improvements at Mildura in the next twenty years. A bill to validate this agreement, introduced into the Legislative Assembly by Deakin on 30 November, was violently opposed, the Chaffeys being termed 'cute Yankee land grabbers'. The disposal of crown lands was a sensitive issue, and some of the Chaffeys' associates and salesmen were indeed deficient in truth and honesty. An amendment inviting tenders for the 250 000 acres at Mildura was passed. Meanwhile (Sir) John Downer [q.v.], premier of South Australia, journeyed to Melbourne and offered a suitable block of 250 000 acres in his colony. The two brothers acted with their usual alacrity and selected river frontages in the Renmark area.

Since no tenders were received, the Chaffeys decided to go ahead at Mildura also. On 31 May 1887 they signed an indenture with the colony of Victoria, but in September transferred all their rights under it to the firm of Chaffey Brothers Ltd; twelve months later J. F. Levien [q.v.5] replaced Cureton as a director, taking responsibility for the company's finances. With 500 000 acres (200 000 ha) of desert to develop, George showed astonishing energy and initiative in the next four years. William remained at Mildura, and a younger brother Charles came from California to manage the Renmark area. An expensive sales promotion campaign was initiated in Australia and Britain and, despite extreme difficulties of transport, 3300 people were at Mildura by December 1890 as well as 1100 at Renmark – about half of them new British migrants. The towns were well laid out and street trees planted lavishly in the style of Chaffey's American settlements. Difficulties and disputes abounded, but while revenue from land sales flowed in the Chaffeys remained confident. However, dissatisfaction among the settlers because of the loss of water from seepage was accentuated when B. C. Harriman [q.v.4], who had served in the Crown Law Department, told them that the operations of the Mildura Irrigation Co. were illegal and that the subdivisions were entitled to free water. Attacks on the Chaffeys' practices were carried to the Victorian parliament. A storm broke over their heads, intensified by the collapse of the land boom in Melbourne and a drift away from Mildura. City newspapers magnified the troubles at Mildura into a public scandal. Ministerial reports and a select committee failed to offer a solution. The radical elements among the settlers were determined to get rid of the Chaffeys and substitute government control.

In August 1893 Stuart Murray [q.v.5] was instructed to report on the complaints against Chaffey Brothers Ltd. He found that some were justified, and, largely on his recommendation, the Mildura Irrigation Trust was set up in September 1895 to take over the functions of the Mildura Irrigation Co. George had visited London in 1894 in a desperate effort to save his firm by selling the ailing Renmark concession, but failed to raise any money. On 10 December Chaffey Brothers Ltd went into liquidation, owing £22 000 in wages to its employees and with assets of some 438 000 acres (177 000 ha) of unsold land at Mildura and Renmark. The Bank of Victoria foreclosed on the mortgages of hundreds of settlers, but eventually the irrigation colonies at Mildura and Renmark grew to prosperity with assistance from the relevant governments.

In 1896 (Sir) George Turner's [q.v.] administration appointed a royal commission to inquire into the Mildura settlement and make recommendations for its future. The Chaffey brothers and Deakin were subjected to long questioning, and the commission's report, tabled on 2 August 1897, largely blamed the Chaffeys for the troubles at Mildura, claiming that they had operated on insufficient capital and committed serious errors in planning.

In August 1897 George sailed to the United States where he plunged into subdivision ventures before returning to irrigation projects. He tapped underground water to revive the Ontario settlement, diverted the waters of the Colorado River to irrigate the desert which he renamed Imperial Valley, and developed new colonies near Los Angeles. Finally he formed a banking partnership with his son Andrew, involving much travel in the United States and Canada. He died at Ontario, California on 1 March 1932. Extremely vigorous in both body and mind, George was a figure of Pacific importance, described by a friend as 'limited only by his excesses'. No responsible person doubted his complete integrity, despite his astonishing variety of enterprises and the fact that some of the men closely associated with him later acquired reputations for very doubtful financial practices. In particular Deakin spoke of him frequently as a great pioneer in Australian agriculture and a valued personal friend. Chaffey's son Ben (1876-1937) had stayed in Australia, building up business interests in Mildura before becoming a prominent Riverina pastoralist and well-known racehorse owner.

William Benjamin Chaffey also remained in Mildura to 'see it through'. He worked long hours to bring his orchard of some 200 acres (80 ha) into production and established the Mildura (later Mildara) Winery Pty Ltd which in 1914 moved its headquarters to Merbein. Active from 1895 in the development of marketing procedures for local fruit, he became a leading member of both the Mildura and the Australian Dried Fruits associations and was president of the latter for many years. In 1903 he was elected president of the Mildura Shire Council and in 1920 first mayor of Mildura Borough. Known affectionately as 'The Boss' or W.B., he was president of the Old Pioneers' Association and of the local horticultural and agricultural society, and was an active Freemason. In December 1911 the residents of Mildura presented him with a Ford motor car, in appreciation of the 'ability and determination' shown by him in 'aiding the development of the area and in proving conclusively the value of irrigated horticulture'. He was appointed C.M.G. in 1924.

Chaffey's first wife Hattie, née Schell, whom he had married in Canada aged 23, died in Mildura in 1889 leaving a young family. On a return visit to the States in 1891 he married Heather Sexton Schell at Hamilton, Ohio. Chaffey died at Mildura on 4 June 1926 survived by his second wife, two sons and a daughter of the first marriage and two daughters and a son of the second; a son had been killed in World War I. His estate was valued for probate at £11 199; his home Rio Vista became a cultural centre. A statue of him by Paul Montford [q.v.] was unveiled in Mildura in 1929; he was commemorated by another in Renmark in 1930.

J. E. M. Vincent, *The Australian irrigation colonies on the River Murray in Victoria and South Australia* (Lond, 1887); J. Smith (ed), *Cyclopedia of Victoria*, 3 (Melb, 1905); J. A. Alexander, *The life of George Chaffey* (Melb, 1928); M. Cannon, *Land boom and bust* (Melb, 1972); *PP* (LA Vic), 1896, 3 (19); F. D. Kershner, 'George Chaffey and the irrigation frontier', *Agr Hist* (Baltimore), Oct 1953; *ISN*, 27 June, 11, 25 July, 8, 22 Aug 1889; *Australasian*, 16 May 1896; *Argus*, 22 Dec 1911, 4 Mar 1932, 4 Mar 1937; *Sunraysia Daily*, 5 June 1926; *SMH*, 18 Apr 1932; *Herald* (Melb), 8 Oct 1936; Chaffey Bros records (SAA), *and* papers (Univ Melb Archives); Elder Smith & Co. Ltd records (ANU Archives).   PETER WESTCOTT

CHALLINOR, RICHARD WESTMAN (1874-1951), chemist, was born on 26 April 1874 in Darlington, Sydney, second son of native-born parents Thomas Challinor, bootmaker, and his wife Ellen, née Westman. He was educated at Glebe Superior Public School and Sydney Technical College, where he became a laboratory assistant in August 1900 and joined the teaching staff in 1903. In 1904-05 he also attended second and third year science lectures at the University of Sydney as an unmatriculated student. On 19 September 1900 at St Barnabas's Church of England he had married Eliza Quidington Poole; she died at their Leichhardt home in 1911. At Grafton on 7 June 1915 he married Beatrice Eleanor Syer who died next year in childbirth.

By 1909 Challinor was assistant teacher and demonstrator in the department of chemistry and metallurgy at the Sydney Technical College. Next year his professional standing was enhanced when he became, by examination, a fellow of the (Royal) Institute of Chemistry of Great Britain and Ireland. From 1912 he was head teacher of organic chemistry; he expected high standards from his students and 'took a keen personal interest' in them. He was a founder and councillor of the Sydney Technical College Chemistry Society in 1913 and presided over it in 1915-16 and 1938-39.

Challinor carried out research into the chemistry of several Australian plants, in collaboration with E. Cheel [q.v.] and A. R. Penfold, and published in the *Technical Gazette of New South Wales* and the *Journal* of the local Royal Society. Active in scientific societies, in 1917 he was a founder and the first applicant for membership of the (Royal) Australian Chemical Institute; in 1928-29 he was president of its New South Wales branch. He was also president of the Sydney section of the Society of Chemical Industry in 1920-22 and of the Royal Society of New South Wales in 1933-34.

Closely associated with the growth of technical education in the State, Challinor played a vital role in the planning and development of the chemistry and allied diploma courses of the Sydney Technical College, following the reorganization of technical education in 1912-14 under A. C. Carmichael, Peter Board and James Nangle [qq.v.]. By the 1930s chemistry diplomates held many senior positions in industry, and the qualification, Associate of the S.T.C. in chemical courses, was the equal of any in relevant fields in New South Wales. When he retired in 1938 he was made a fellow of the college. He practised as a consulting chemist and in 1940 became a director of the Nightingale Supply Co. Ltd. During World War II he was on the staff of the director-general of manpower in the scientific section. After the war he continued as part-time liaison officer, chemical profession, in the Commonwealth Employment Service.

Challinor died on 3 February 1951 in hospital at Waverley and was cremated after a Presbyterian service. He was survived by a son and two daughters of his first marriage and by his third wife Ethel Annie Atkinson, whom he had married at Narrabeen on 24 May 1924, and their daughter.

Inst for Research in Biog, *Biographical encyclopedia of the world* (New York, 1946); Aust Chemical Inst, *Procs*, 18 (1951); Roy Soc NSW, *Procs*, 85 (1951); *SMH*, 5 May 1938; ML printed cat under R. W. Challinor.   D. P. MELLOR

CHALMERS, FREDERICK ROYDEN (1881-1943), farmer, soldier and administrator, was born on 4 January 1881 at Brighton, Tasmania, son of Robert Hamilton Chalmers, farmer, and his wife Emily Louisa, née Walter. After attending school at Brighton, Chalmers farmed with his father at Bagdad. At 18 he went to South Africa as a trooper in the 1st (Tasmanian) Contingent (later Tasmanian Mounted Infantry). Returning in December 1900, he re-embarked in April 1901 with the 4th (Second Imperial Bushmen) Contingent as second lieutenant, and in August was promoted lieutenant. After the war Chalmers remained in Tasmania until 1907 when he joined the Victorian Railways and later worked at Moe as a salesman.

On 4 January 1910 at the Traralgon Catholic Church he married Mary Cecilia Bennett. She died in November 1914 and the following April Chalmers enlisted as a private in the Australian Imperial Force, and was commissioned lieutenant at Broadmeadows next month. He saw service with the 27th Battalion in Egypt, Gallipoli, France and Belgium. Promoted captain in August 1915, he attended a senior-officers' school at Aldershot, England, late in 1916 and was promoted major; he commanded the battalion from October 1917, as lieut-colonel from January 1918. He received the Distinguished Service Order in November, temporarily commanded the 7th Infantry Brigade in December, and was mentioned in dispatches and appointed C.M.G. in 1919.

Chalmers returned to Tasmania in charge of troops on the *Ormonde*, accompanied by his second wife Lenna Annette, née French, whom he had married in London on 26 May 1917. He farmed for several years at Bagdad, then mined on the west coast, in 1931 joining the Siamese Tin Syndicate at St Helens. He was president of the local branch of the Returned Soldiers' and Sailors' Imperial League of Australia and involved in the Boy Scouts movement.

In October 1938 Chalmers was appointed from seventy applicants to succeed R. C. Garsia [q.v.] as administrator of the Australian mandated territory of Nauru. An imposing figure, tall, white-haired and mustachioed, Chalmers looked the typical administrator of the period; his easy manner ensured his popularity. He introduced Berkshire boars to Nauru to improve the native razorback stock, and *Gambusia* fish to eradicate mosquitoes. In December 1940 when the German raiders *Komet* and *Orion* shelled the phosphate installations, Chalmers stormed along the sea-front shouting at the enemy. On the evacuation of the non-native population in February 1942 he elected to stay.

The Japanese landed on 26 August and Australian contact with Nauru ceased: Chalmers did not know of his wife's death on 14 September. He and four other Europeans were interned until the Allied bombing raid of 25 March 1943. During a lull before midnight the Japanese second-in-command took, without orders, the Europeans from their quarters. They were executed, and apparently buried, on the beach, their manner of death remaining unknown until the restoration of Australian administration in 1945. The executioners were tried in 1946 by war crimes tribunals in Rabaul; one was sentenced to death and one to 20 years imprisonment. Chalmers was survived by a son and two daughters from his first marriage and by four daughters from his second. A monument to him and the other victims was erected at Nauru in 1951.

Reveille (Syd), 1 Oct 1938; *Qld Digger*, Jan 1952; *Examiner* (Launc), 5, 15 Sept 1938; *Sunday Sun*, 6 June 1943; *SMH*, 20 Sept 1945; External Territories, A518 BU118/12 (AAO Canb); records, A2663 item 1010/9/118 (AWM).   KERRY F. KENEALLY

CHAMBERS, CHARLES HADDON SPURGEON (1860-1921), dramatist, was born on 22 April 1860 at Petersham, Sydney, son of Irish parents John Ritchie Chambers, public servant, and his wife Frances, née Kellett. Educated at Marrickville and Fort Street public schools, Chambers left at 13 after his father's pension was halved: he worked as a clerk for a Sydney merchant and in 1875-76 for the Department of Mines. Finding the routine irksome, Chambers became a boundary rider for two years near Camden until invited by visiting cousins to return with them to Ulster. From there he went to London, returned briefly to Sydney where he was an agent for the Montague-Turner opera company and for the Australian Mutual Provident Society, and settled in England in 1882.

As a youth in Sydney, Chambers had 'loitered in the outer courts of journalism', meeting poets such as 'Harold Grey', G. H. Gibson and Victor Daley [q.v.]. In London he wrote to support himself, drawing partly on his Australian experiences for the stories and sketches he contributed to *Society*, *Truth*, the *Sunday Times* and other journals from 1884; several were reprinted in the miscellanies of A. Patchett Martin [q.v.5] and Philip Mennell [q.v.]. Chambers also wrote London letters for the *Bulletin*, and helped W. H. Traill [q.v.6] to secure the services of the cartoonist Phil May [q.v.5].

In 1886 Haddon Chambers had his first play performed, but wider recognition did not come until 1888 when *Captain Swift* was successfully staged in London, with Herbert Tree in the title role of the Queensland bushranger whose past catches up with him in England. The only Chambers play with significant Australian colour, it is chiefly remembered for the phrase 'The long arm of coincidence has reached after me'. During three decades as a playwright Chambers wrote or collaborated on some twenty plays which were staged in the West End; several had long runs and were performed also in New York. The best were the comedies *The tyranny of tears* (1899) and *The saving grace* (1917), in which Chambers displayed a lightness of verbal touch and a characteristic economy in the management of plot and characters. Among his other successes were *The fatal card* (1894), one of the best melodramas of the 1890s, and *Passers-by* (1911).

Chambers carefully planned his plays but seldom revised them, and had a reputation for indolence despite his sporting passions.

He was a man of great personal charm: well-read, widely travelled, witty, strikingly handsome with his youthful looks and chiselled features, and a superb conversationalist. He was prominent in London club life and much in demand with society hostesses. In 1891 he published *Thumb-nail sketches of Australian life* (New York) and later coached Melba [q.v.] in acting, but after *Captain Swift* he retained few Australian connexions. The first Australian dramatist to win recognition overseas, he was also, ironically, a striking example of the 'cultural cringe'. As a result he won repute as a 'citizen of the world' during his lifetime and was forgotten after his death.

On 29 October 1920 Chambers married 28-year-old Nelly Louise Burton, an actress known professionally as 'Pepita Bobadilla'. Survived by his wife and a daughter by his first wife Mary, née Dewer, he died of cerebro-vascular disease at the Bath Club, London, on 28 March 1921 and was buried at Marlow-on-Thames. He died intestate leaving property worth £9195.

H. Russell, *The passing show* (Lond, 1926); A. Nicoll, *A history of English drama, 1660-1900*, 2nd edn, 5 (Cambridge, 1959); A. A. Phillips, *The Australian tradition*, 2nd edn rev (Melb, 1966); J. Hetherington, *Melba* (Melb, 1967); M. Booth, *English plays of the nineteenth century*, 3 (Oxford, 1973); A. Nicoll, *English drama, 1900-1930* (Lond, 1973); 'The genesis of "The Bulletin"', *Lone Hand*, Nov 1907; G. Hill, 'Charles Haddon Chambers', *Lone Hand*, Sept 1915; J. D. Williams, 'A play-boy of two worlds', *Century Mag*, Dec 1921; *Bulletin*, 25 Aug 1888, 15 Feb 1912; *The Times*, 29 Mar, 2 Apr, 6 May 1921; *SMH*, 30 Mar 1921.

         B. G. ANDREWS

CHAMPION, HENRY HYDE (1859-1928), socialist propagandist and journalist, was born on 22 January 1859 at Poona, India, son of Major (Major General) James Hyde Champion and his wife Henrietta Susan, née Urquhart, who was of aristocratic Scottish descent. He saw little of his parents in his childhood: at 4 he was sent to England to attend a day school and at 13 to Marlborough, where his career was undistinguished. However Champion graduated from the Royal Military Academy, Woolwich, was commissioned in the artillery and served in the Afghan War. He caught typhoid and was invalided home. A radical friend showed him the East End slums and accompanied him to the United States of America where he was impressed by the writings of Henry George [q.v.4]. He read Adam Smith, Mill, Ricardo, Marx and others, resigned from the army on 17 September 1882, and next night 'was preaching

Socialism on Clerkenwell Green', London. On 9 August 1883 he married Juliet Bennett (d. 1886).

Champion bought a half-share in a printing-plant and started *To-day*, a monthly magazine in which he published work by Ibsen and Bernard Shaw. In 1883 he joined the Land Reform Union, then the Social Democratic Federation of which he became secretary; he was very soon a dynamic and notorious public speaker. By 1886 he was close to advocating violent revolution and, after a Trafalgar Square meeting which he chaired and which developed riotously, was charged with seditious conspiracy; he was acquitted after conducting his own defence. Champion had been forced to resign as secretary of the S.D.F., largely because of his tendency to act independently, financial lapses and maintenance of Tory associations; he founded the *Labour Elector*. His close associate Tom Mann [q.v.] admired his organizing and literary capacity. During the London dock strike of 1889 Champion was prominent in arranging strike-pay and picketing and in the successful negotiations with the employers.

Seeking relief from recurrent illness, Champion arrived in Melbourne on 12 August 1890. Introduced by a letter from John Burns, he was warmly welcomed by the Trades Hall Council. He announced himself a neutral observer in the developing maritime strike and spoke temperately at the mass meeting on the Yarra Bank on 31 August. A week later, however, he wrote to the *Age* suggesting terms of settlement including acceptance by unionists of freedom of contract. He believed the unions were heading for disastrous defeat and perhaps cast himself in the part of Cardinal Manning in the dock strike. The unions were outraged and refused him admission when he sought to address the Sydney strike conference. His gentlemanly manners, fashionable dress, silk hat, eyeglass and cigar contributed to the Australian workman's bitter resentment and his subsequent scapegoat-role. He continued to deride the union leadership in the *Age*, in October cabled Burns advising against financial support from English unions, and eventually described Australian unionists as 'an army of lions led by asses'. When the strike ended on 13 November he was denounced again as a 'traitor and capitalist stooge'. Champion returned to England and became acting editor of the *Nineteenth Century*. He resigned to stand unsuccessfully for Aberdeen and revived the *Labour Elector*; but by late 1893 he had been repudiated by the Independent Labour Party which he had helped to found and by most socialists.

Hyde Champion returned to Melbourne on 5 April 1894, determined to take the lead in the socialist movement. He nominated for Albert Park in the Legislative Assembly and conducted a campaign which attracted wide interest, but withdrew in favour of another radical candidate. He helped to found Fabian and co-operative societies and joined the committee of the Women's Suffrage League; 'the oppressed sex must needs make common cause with the oppressed class', he remarked. He published *The root of the matter; being a series of dialogues on social questions* (Melbourne, 1895). He became secretary of the May Day committee for 1895 and, as a consequence, the T.H.C. refused to take part. Next year there was a similar conflict and the Trades Hall withdrew again and ran a rival demonstration. From the May Day committee of 1895 Champion had formed the Social Democratic Federation of Victoria, of which he was secretary from 2 June. On 18 October he futilely appealed for a fusion of the S.D.F., the Liberal Party and the Trades Hall. He was a founder of the National Anti-Sweating League and became a vice-president; with Samuel Mauger [q.v.] he helped to draft the 1896 Factories and Shops Act and was one of the league's representatives conferring with hostile legislative councillors.

In 1896 Champion stood for Melbourne South in the assembly, but polled poorly; again his campaign attracted wide audiences but his polished wit, sarcasm and name-dropping of 'men I have met' were marginal assets against unionist interjections. He was leading organizer of the appeal for funds, in support of female doctors, which led to the opening of the Queen Victoria Hospital in 1899. From 22 June 1895 to 29 May 1897 he conducted the *Champion*, a lively weekly full of exposés and propaganda for societies in which he was involved. Early in 1896 he was committed for trial for criminal libel arising out of his racing column, 'The quick and the dead', but the charge was withdrawn. From August 1897 to January 1899 he conducted a weekly society paper, the *Sun*, and in this period wrote many leading articles for the *Age*. All his attempts to find a base for a viable socialist movement and to convert Labor parliamentarians had failed, but in July 1898 he joined the Victorian Socialist League. He made a last parliamentary attempt at Albert Park in 1900, supported now by many at the Trades Hall; the campaign revolved round his personal reputation and he had the satisfaction of prosecuting Max Hirsch [q.v.] and extracting an apology and costs.

On 8 December 1898 Champion was married by his friend Rev. Charles Strong [q.v.6] to Elsie Belle (d. 1953), sister of Vida Goldstein [q.v.]. From 1896 Elsie had conducted the Book Lovers' Library, which she and Hyde were to run for over thirty years. In May 1899, in association with the library, he founded the monthly *Book Lover*. Champion suffered a stroke in 1901 which left him semi-paralysed, with his speech affected and a limp, and unable ever again to use his right hand for typing. The Goldsteins were Christian Scientists: Champion attended meetings of the sect and was converted at least to the extent that he rejected the advice of conventional physicians. Somehow, he kept the *Book Lover* going, largely writing it himself.

He recovered sufficiently to be prominent in the Victorian Socialist Party in 1906-09. Tom Mann's respect for him raised his standing, and he remained loyal to Mann. He was appointed to the executive, became treasurer and then president for a year. He was interested in party administration rather than policy, but spent much of his effort on the Socialist Co-operative Trading Society, the Socialist Savings Bank and a co-operative farming venture. He wrote much for the *Socialist*, usually under such pseudonyms as 'Tenax', and in Mann's absence in 1908 edited the journal. He became involved in bitter factional brawls and in January 1909, after further illness, ended his work for the party.

Champion continued to write occasionally for the *Socialist* and the *Bulletin*, but appeared only rarely in public. He had formed the Australasian Authors' Agency in 1906 and published two or three dozen books, including early works of Dorothea Mackellar [q.v.], Martin Boyd and Marjorie Barnard. In 1911 he printed the sex-reformer W. J. Chidley's [q.v.] *The answer* and engaged Maurice Blackburn [q.v.] to defend him against the charge of obscenity. In 1916 Champion published in the *Book Lover* Frank Wilmot's [q.v.] 'To God from the weary nations'. The *Book Lover* appeared for the last time in August 1921; it had been a rare beacon of appreciation of international and Australian literature. He was declared bankrupt in 1922.

Survived by his wife, Champion died at South Yarra on 30 April 1928 and was cremated after a Christian Science service. Although over-confident in his judgment and lacking in tact and balance, he had great journalistic talent and a pleasant personality, despite his capacity for making enemies: he had retained the affectionate esteem of Mann and many other pioneers of the labour socialist movement in England and Australia in which he played a leading part over twenty-five years.

L. M. Henderson, *The Goldstein story* (Melb, 1973); H. M. Pelling, 'H. H. Champion: pioneer of Labour representation', *Cambridge J*, 6 (1953); *Recorder* (Labour Hist, Melb), Jan 1965; P. Kellock, H. H. Champion: the failure of Victorian socialism (B.A. Hons thesis, Monash Univ, 1971), and for bibliog; C. G. W. Osborne, Tom Mann: his Australasian experience, 1902-1910 (Ph.D. thesis, ANU, 1972).   GEOFFREY SERLE

CHAMPION, HERBERT WILLIAM (1880-1972), public servant, was born on 8 August 1880 at Kaiapoi, South Island, New Zealand, son of Charles James Champion, accountant, and his wife Frances Mary, née Stringer. Educated in Christchurch, possibly at Canterbury College, he left home for Sydney about 1897 following a family crisis. He found employment with Burns, Philp [qq.v.] & Co. who sent him in 1898 to their store in Port Moresby, British New Guinea. The lieut-governor, George Le Hunte [q.v.], brought him into the public service as assistant government storeman.

When the royal commission on the government of Papua arrived in 1906 Champion was chief clerk in the Treasury. Partly because of a feud with (Sir) Hubert Murray [q.v.], David Ballantine was dismissed from the service and Champion was made treasurer in his place. His resentment at what he saw as the ruthless disposal of Ballantine did not affect his official loyalty to Murray when he became lieut-governor. Murray trusted him absolutely and in 1913 recommended his appointment as government secretary.

Partially deaf from about 1904, Champion was at a serious disadvantage between the erudite Murray and the ebullient M. Staniforth Smith [q.v.], but he became known for his quiet efficiency. As the chief executive officer he had to devise many of the improvisations demanded by a meagre budget. During World War I, in addition to his normal duties, he acted at times as commissioner of lands, registrar of titles and public curator. He also undertook, partly for recreation, the management of parks and gardens and personally planted and tended many trees which remain an important scenic feature of the city. He was appointed C.B.E. in 1934.

Champion was respected and trusted by the residents of Port Moresby, and he was often embarrassed when individuals sought his help and advice in matters where a conflict of interest could arise between his official position and personal concern. Despite the traditional antipathy between public and private sectors, his friends included both fellow government officers and members of the commercial community. He belonged to and was twice elected president of the Papua Club, the meeting-place of leading businessmen and planters. As chief of the public service he was noted for impartiality in his dealings with subordinates. He found a position in the service for his step-son on the grounds that he was a returned serviceman and thus eligible for preferential treatment but, conscious of possible charges of nepotism, rejected his own sons' applications for government appointments. They were not employed until the lieut-governor himself had intervened on their behalf. Champion then scrupulously avoided showing any special treatment towards them.

For nine months after Murray's death in February 1940, Champion acted as lieut-governor and was bitterly disappointed when the permanent office went to Leonard Murray. He wished to resign but was prevailed upon to stay. However, both men were virtually deported when a military government was proclaimed on 14 February 1942. Champion said later that he had arrived in Port Moresby with one suitcase and had left with one suitcase forty-four years later. He had collected a fine library in this time and carried out private research on the history of Papuan nomenclature, but all his books and notes were lost during the war. The humiliating end to a career, which he sometimes called 'a long nightmare', encouraged him to forget Papua during his retirement at Chatswood, New South Wales.

In 1902 at Port Moresby, Champion had married Florence (d. 1924), née Foran, widow of H. N. Chester. All three sons of the marriage joined the Papuan service and two of them won distinction as explorers. In 1926 Champion married Haidee Wallace. She survived him with their two daughters when he died on 12 May 1972; he was cremated.

G. Souter, *New Guinea* (Syd, 1968); F. West, *Hubert Murray* (Melb, 1968); J. H. P. Murray, *Selected letters of Hubert Murray*, F. West ed (Melb, 1970); I. Stuart, *Port Moresby, yesterday and today* (Syd, 1970); N. D. Oram, *Colonial town to Melanesian city* (Canb, 1976); Roy Com into . . . Papua, Report, *PP* (Cwlth), 1907). IAN STUART

CHAMPION DE CRESPIGNY, SIR CONSTANTINE TRENT (1882-1952), medical practitioner, was born on 5 March 1882 at Queenscliffe, Victoria, second son of Philip Champion de Crespigny, bank-manager, and his first wife Annie Francis, née Chauncey (d. 1883). PHILIP (1850-1927) was born on 4 January 1850 at St Malo, Brittany, France, son of Philip Robert Champion de Crespigny, police magistrate and goldfields warden, and his wife Charlotte Frances, née Dana. Family tradition claims descent from hereditary champions to the dukes of Nor-

mandy in the eleventh century. Huguenots, they had moved to England after the revocation of the edict of Nantes in 1685.

Philip was a careful, conservative bank official who from 1866 aided the steady expansion of the Bank of Victoria. From 1916, as general manager, he played a diplomatic role in negotiations which led, at the time of his death, to the amalgamation of his bank with the Commercial Banking Co. of Sydney. He had been a chairman of the Associated Banks of Victoria, president of the Bankers' Institute of Australasia, and a council-member of the Commonwealth Bureau of Commerce and Industry. Philip died at Brighton on 11 March 1927. He was survived by the two sons of his first marriage, by his second wife Sophia Montgomery Grattan, née Beggs, whom he had married on 2 November 1891, and by their four children.

Constantine Trent was educated at Brighton Grammar School and Trinity College, University of Melbourne (M.B., 1903; B.S., 1904; M.D., 1906). In 1904-07 he was a resident in Melbourne hospitals, in 1907 he practised in the country at Glenthompson. Specializing in pathology, in 1909 he was appointed to the Adelaide Hospital. He continued his interest in laboratory medicine, being honorary director of the hospital's pathology services and lecturer in pathology in the medical school of the University of Adelaide in 1912-19, but began private practice as a specialist physician in 1912.

Trent Champion de Crespigny was commissioned in the Australian Army Medical Corps in 1907. In May 1915 he joined the Australian Imperial Force as a lieut-colonel and was posted to the 3rd Australian General Hospital during the Gallipoli campaign. From February 1916 he commanded the 1st A.G.H. at Rouen, France, returning to Australia in November 1917. He had been mentioned in dispatches and awarded the Distinguished Service Order in June. He then went back to England and in 1918 became consulting physician at A.I.F. headquarters in London. Next year he became a member of the Royal College of Physicians and returned to Adelaide.

His standing steadily grew as one of Adelaide's most reliable doctors. He was an honorary physician at the Adelaide and the Adelaide Children's hospitals. He became F.R.C.P. in 1929 and was one of the senior Australian medical men involved in founding the Royal Australasian College of Physicians, of which he was president in 1942-44. He published a number of medical papers, mainly in the *Medical Journal of Australia*, between 1914 and 1944.

Trent de Crespigny had a tall, spare figure, was well dressed and wore pince-nez.

Proud of his ancestry, he spoke slowly, with a superior manner which isolated him from his associates and patients, especially women. Nevertheless his intellectual gifts as a diagnostician and his knowledge of scientific medicine were outstanding in South Australia in his time. A daughter-in-law said that he looked upon medicine as a detective looks upon crime – never ceasing to hunt for clues.

For nineteen years from 1929 he was dean and chief examiner in medicine at the medical school of the University of Adelaide. In 1908 he had started a research laboratory in pathology in a tin shed at the back of the Adelaide Hospital. He then solicited funds from private persons, charitable bequests and the State government so that an Institute of Medical and Veterinary Science could be built. In 1937 it was established by Act of parliament and he became the first chairman of its council. His portrait by Ivor Hele hangs there today.

Trent de Crespigny was president of the South Australian branch of the British Medical Association in 1925-26. In 1929 he presided over the medical section of the Australasian Medical Congress in Sydney. In 1941 he was knighted and became known as Sir Trent. Four years later he visited the United States of America where he inquired for the university into medical postgraduate education, especially as it affected medical officers returned from World War II.

His few intimates found 'Crep' a rationalist and a man of dry humour. Adelaide generally saw him as somewhat eccentric. He figured in apocryphal medical anecdotes: some of these concerned his deliberate manner and others his acerbic wit, or his inability to drive a motor car safely. In the 1930s he had been one of the first doctors to hire an aeroplane and pilot to visit distant cases. His advice to one of his children was: 'When in doubt, my dear, do the *difficult* thing'. He had a serious sense of private and national duty.

Sir Trent had married, on 11 September 1906 at Beaufort, Victoria, Beatrix Hughes (d. 1943). On 13 December 1945 he married in St Peter's Cathedral Mary Birks Jolley, a teacher thirty years his junior. He died in Adelaide of hypertensive cardio-vascular disease on 27 October 1952, survived by two sons and two daughters of his first marriage and by his second wife and their daughter. His estate was sworn for probate at £8015. A colleague described his death as 'probably the greatest loss to the South Australian medical profession for the past thirty years'.

His eldest son Colonel Richard Geoffrey, O.B.E. (1907-1966) was a noted physician. His half-brothers, Air Vice Marshal Hugh Vivian, C.B., D.F.C., M.C., Croix de Guerre (1897-1969) and Group Captain Claude Montgomery, C.B.E. (b. 1908) had distinguished careers in the Royal Air Force.

A. Henderson (ed), *Early pioneer families of Victoria and Riverina* (Melb, 1936); R. F. Holder, *Bank of New South Wales: a history*, 2 (Syd, 1970); Inst of Medical and Veterinary Science, *Annual Report*, no 14 (1951-52); *Lancet*, 1 Nov 1952; *British Medical J*, 8 Nov 1952; *MJA*, 21 Mar 1953; Brighton Hist Soc, *Newsletter*, June 1965, supp pt 1; *Industrial and Mining Standard*, 17 Mar 1927; *A'sian Insurance and Banking Record*, 21 Mar, 21 Apr 1927; *Herald* (Melb), 11 Mar 1927; *Argus*, 12 Mar 1927; *Advertiser* (Adel), 1 Jan 1941, 28 Oct 1952; Personalities remembered, ABC radio script 28 Nov 1971 (SAA).   EARLE HACKETT

CHANDLER, ALFRED ELLIOTT (1873-1935), nurseryman, property entrepreneur and politician, was born on 1 July 1873 at Gardiner (Malvern), Victoria, son of William Chandler and his wife Kate, née Timewell. William had left his father's market-garden complex at Gardiner in November 1872 to clear 40 acres (16 ha) at The Basin, Bayswater, at the foot of the Dandenongs; he prospered with vegetables, flowers and fruit on small acreages. Alfred, his seven brothers and three sisters, were all brought up in the market-garden tradition and given a cursory education at The Basin's first primary school. The children worked arduous hours without pay but in the expectation of acquiring property and economic support when they left home.

From 1895 'A.E.' Chandler, with financial backing from his father, developed 47 acres (19 ha) which became known as the Everson Nursery. Originally Chandler specialized in daffodils and boronia, but rust which began in 1928 forced him to abandon the delicate West Australian boronia in favour of the hardier daffodil, which he grew on a huge scale. Chandler also proved to be an enterprising judge of suburban property – buying and selling land as the city expanded over dairy-farms, garden blocks and bushland.

On 24 May 1897 Chandler had married Elizabeth Ann Intermann, daughter of a Carlton cartage-contractor who had fled to the hills during the 1890s depression. Elizabeth died on 3 January 1899 following childbirth. Chandler married her younger sister Marie on 27 August 1901.

Like his father, Chandler became a Ferntree Gully shire councillor, and served in 1901-35. He urged the government to improve roads and to extend the suburban railway to the area he had recently named Boronia. He was elected shire president four times and from 1922 held various positions in the Municipal Association of Victoria.

Chandler succeeded D. E. McBryde [q.v.] on 5 June 1919 as member of the Legislative Council for the South-Eastern Province. His interests were fruit supervision, land settlement problems, plant pests and rural emergency measures. He served on many committees dealing with the railways, government road-transport, the employment council, flood control relief and local government. He was minister of public works and mines and vice-president of the Board of Land and Works in Sir William McPherson's [q.v.] government in 1928-29 and an honorary minister with Sir Stanley Argyle [q.v.] in 1932-35. His tactful negotiations over the contentious railway bridge at Kew were rewarded when the Chandler highway was named after him.

Chandler was a committed community man. He donated land for the Boronia Progress Hall and the Methodist Church. He was a justice of the peace and a member of the Bayswater Brass Band. His nursery was opened to the public to raise funds for local charities which he and his wife sponsored. He kept wickets for a local cricket-team and encouraged his sons at football. Chandler died suddenly at Boronia on 12 February 1935 and was buried in Box Hill cemetery after a state funeral. He was survived by his second wife, their four sons and one daughter, and a daughter of the first marriage. His estate was valued for probate at £29222. His son Gilbert succeeded him as shire councillor and was Victorian minister for agriculture in 1955-73.

A. Sutherland et al, *Victoria and its metropolis,* 2 (Melb, 1888); J. B. Cooper, *A history of Malvern* (Melb, 1935); H. Coulson, *Story of the Dandenongs, 1838-1958* (Melb, 1959); *PD* (Vic), 1919, 838, 1935, 6; *Argus,* 12 Feb 1935; *Age,* 13 Feb 1935; H. Coulson, History of the Chandler family (held by and information from Mr D. Chandler, Boronia, Vic).   R. C. DUPLAIN

CHANDLER, THOMAS CHARLES (1873-1936), headmaster, was born on 24 April 1873 in Sydney, son of Thomas Chandler, mining engineer, and his wife Selina Sarah, née Brown. Educated at Emmaville Public School, New England, in February 1889 he was appointed a pupil-teacher there and won a scholarship to the Fort Street Training School in Sydney, graduating in December 1894. He was selected to teach at the Fort Street Public School, went to Hillgrove in 1898 under Henry Tonkin, an energetic and innovative head who emphasized the role of the school

in community life, and returned in 1902 to Fort Street where he took charge of the matriculation class. On 4 September at the Australian Church he was married by George Walters [q.v.] to Grace McNaught.

Western Australia was still attracting immigrants: a number of teachers from Fort Street School quickly won important posts in its Education Department. At the end of 1902 Chandler applied for a position and was appointed to the Beaconsfield School. His promotion within the department was rapid. Later that year he was transferred to Perth Boys' School where he taught before being promoted to headmaster at South Boulder (1907), Boulder Central (1909), and Fremantle Boys' Central (1912). In January 1913 he returned as headmaster to Perth Boys' School, the largest three-year secondary school in the State; he held the position until his death.

Chandler was a born teacher and the school flourished under his leadership; during his time enrolment increased from 300 to 750 and about 10000 boys passed through. He won the confidence of his pupils because he took a keen personal interest in their welfare, and maintained contact with many of them after they left school. Unlike most of his contemporaries, he regarded corporal punishment as a sign of weakness on the teacher's part and preferred to control the boys by appealing for their co-operation. He specialized in teaching English and his enthusiasm for physical training sometimes disrupted school routines.

Throughout his career Chandler publicly questioned authority when he considered it unfair or discriminatory. He was bitterly disappointed in 1919 to be categorized as too old to be appointed a departmental inspector although he had the requisite qualities. In the early 1920s he again clashed with authority over the fact that his school was not classified as a first-class high school taking students to matriculation level. He threatened to sue the government for the appropriate allowance and eventually a settlement was reached, but not without leaving him embittered.

To some extent frustrated in his profession, Chandler took up a new activity in the 1930s which won him a considerable reputation. Dismayed to see so many of his former pupils unemployed with no prospects, he conceived and promoted the Chandler Boys' Settlement Scheme, launched in 1932. With public support, 1500 acres (600 ha) were leased at Roelands, between Collie and Bunbury, and named Seven Hills. The scheme aimed at giving unemployed boys a chance to learn the fundamentals of farming with a view to establishing them on farms of their own. It won temporary acclaim but collapsed when he died.

Chandler was an ardent lover of sports, playing cricket for West Perth, tennis, golf and bowls. In 1897-98 he had been one of two honorary secretaries of the New South Wales Public Schools Athletic Association. In later life he developed an interest in angling. While on the goldfields, he was major in charge of the goldfields association of senior cadets. In 1916 he was briefly in command of a training battalion at Blackboy Hill Camp but was discharged at the end of the year. Survived by his wife and a son, he died of cardiac disease on 27 October 1936 and was buried in Karrakatta cemetery with Anglican rites.

J. K. Ewers, *Perth Boys' School, 1847-1947* (Perth, 1947); *West Australian*, 28, 29 Oct 1936; Education Dept (WA), Personal files 795/02, 752/13, 2545/26 (Battye Lib, Perth); information from Dept of Education (NSW), *and* Mr E. Huck, Nedlands, WA, *and* Dr B. Mitchell, Univ New England.

DAVID MOSSENSON

CHANTER, JOHN MOORE (1845-1931), farmer, auctioneer, commission agent and politician, was born on 11 February 1845 in Adelaide, son of John Chanter, shoemaker, who migrated from Devonshire, England, in 1840, and his second wife Elizabeth, née Moore. His father became a publican in Adelaide and from 1856 in Melbourne before farming at Trentham and Arcadia in Victoria.

Chanter was educated at the Albert House Academy and the Collegiate School of St Peter in Adelaide and the Model Training Institution in Melbourne. He worked on his father's farm and rented land at Tylden where he became a general storekeeper. In 1874 he selected 320 acres (130 ha) at Rochester, and became first secretary of the Victorian Farmers' Union in 1878. In 1881 he moved to Moama, New South Wales, as an auctioneer and commission agent and was elected first mayor in 1891. He formed an agricultural and pastoral association, a race-course and a jockey club there, and became a director of the Murray River Stock Co. Prominent in establishing the Australian Natives' Association in New South Wales, he was its first president in September 1900-01. He was also a member of the New South Wales Chamber of Mines and a founder of the Masonic Club in Sydney.

Chanter represented Murray in the Legislative Assembly in 1885-94 with the support of the Selectors' Association, and then was returned for Deniliquin. He was secretary for mines and agriculture in (Sir)

George Dibbs's [q.v.4] ministry early in 1889 and in 1893 headed the 'Country Party', a radical protectionist group within the assembly advocating land law reform. He was chairman of committees and in 1894 a member of the public works committee. Noted for his 'democratic views', Chanter argued for an elective Upper House and against plural voting; he supported protection as essential for the development of industries and employment of 'our children' in areas such as Deniliquin. As a representative of a border area plagued by the tariff question, he strongly favoured Federation and in 1901, as a supporter of (Sir) Edmund Barton [q.v.], won Riverina in the House of Representatives.

In the first Commonwealth parliament and again in 1914-22 Chanter was chairman of committees. He was a member of royal commissions on ocean shipping service (1906) and on stripper harvesters and drills (1908-09). In 1903 he narrowly lost Riverina to R. O. Blackwood [q.v.], but after a petition to the High Court regained it in the 1904 by-election. He supported the Barton and Deakin [q.v.] ministries, but with his close friend Sir William Lyne [q.v.] opposed the fusion of 1909; when it was achieved he alone of the Deakinite protectionist members joined the Labor Party whose platform, he declared, embraced policies he had consistently followed. He held Riverina for Labor in 1910, was defeated by the Liberal F. B. S. Falkiner [q.v.] in 1913, but was re-elected after the double dissolution of 1914.

When Labor split over conscription, Chanter joined the Nationalists, having been a strong supporter of Britain in the Boer War. He retained Riverina in 1917 and as a Nationalist and Farmers' candidate in 1919, but was defeated in 1922 by W. W. Killen of the new Country Party.

In some respects typical of many rural politicians in New South Wales — both Labor and Protectionist — Chanter was praised as a hard-working local member who was well acquainted with the vast areas he represented and considered every request from his constituents. Tall and rugged, he was a quiet man who spoke infrequently in debates, but when he did, explored all details of his subject and held tenaciously to his viewpoint.

On 16 November 1863 at Campbell's Creek Primitive Methodist Church, Victoria, Chanter had married Mary Ann Clark (d. 1920); they had six sons and four daughters. Chanter lived in retirement at Caulfield, Victoria, where he died on 9 March 1931. He was buried in the Anglican section of Brighton cemetery. His estate was valued for probate at £1044 in Victoria and £60 in New South Wales.

Chanter's fifth son John Courtenay (1881-1962) fought with the Bushmen's Contingent in the South African War and in the Australian Imperial Force in World War I in the Middle East. He was commissioned lieutenant in 1915 and promoted major in 1917, serving with the 9th and 4th Light Horse Regiments; he was awarded the Distinguished Service Order in 1919. Chanter was president of the Australian Wheatgrowers' Federation in 1934, sometime president of Deakin Shire, Victoria, and Lachlan Shire, New South Wales, and Labor member for Lachlan in the New South Wales Legislative Assembly in 1943-47.

G. L. Buxton, *The Riverina 1861-1891* (Melb, 1967); A. W. Martin, 'Free trade and protectionist parties in New South Wales', *Hist Studies*, no 23, Nov 1954; *Aust Mag* (Syd), 1 Mar, 1 June 1909; *A.N.A.*, July 1926; *Punch* (Melb), 13 Mar 1913; *Argus*, 10, 11 Mar 1931; R. F. I. Smith, 'Organize or be damned': Australian wheatgrowers' organizations and wheat marketing, 1927-1948 (Ph.D. thesis, ANU, 1969); family papers (held by and information from Mr A. A. L. Chanter, Goulburn, NSW).   JOAN RYDON

CHAPMAN, ALFRED GODWIN; *see* ALANSON

CHAPMAN, SIR AUSTIN (1864-1926), businessman and politician, was born on 10 July 1864 at Bong Bong near Bowral, New South Wales, son of Richard Chapman, wheelwright and publican, and his Irish wife Monica, née Cain (or Kean or Kein). Registered as Austen, his Christian name was officially corrected in 1897. He attended the Marulan Public School and after being apprenticed at 14 to a local saddler worked in Goulburn and Mudgee. In 1885 while operating Chapman's Hotel at Bungendore he championed the cause of E. W. O'Sullivan [q.v.], Protectionist candidate for Queanbeyan in the Legislative Assembly, and in 1887 moved to Sydney as managing partner of the auctioneering firm E. W. O'Sullivan, Chapman & Co. At the same time he kept the Emu Inn in Bathurst Street.

When the partnership with O'Sullivan was dissolved in October 1889 Chapman opened the Royal Hotel at Braidwood, and in 1891-1901 held the Braidwood seat in the assembly as a Protectionist. He married Catherine O'Brien of Belle Vue station on 23 October 1894 with Roman Catholic rites. He set up business as an auctioneer and commission agent, raced his own horses and invested heavily in and directed local dredging companies, including the Araluen Central Gold Dredging, Redbank Gold

Dredging and Victorian Araluen Dredging companies. He was a member of the local literary institute and secretary of the Braidwood Hospital and the Railway League. As a parliamentarian he worked assiduously for his electorate, and in the 1890s was a keen supporter of moves to introduce the old-age pension bill.

An enthusiastic advocate of Federation, Chapman won Eden-Monaro in the first Federal election and held it until 1926 as a leading New South Wales Protectionist and later Liberal and Nationalist: he was unopposed in the 1903 general election and also in 1910 when, after the fusion of 1909, he stood as an independent. Although he moved his auctioneering and commission agency to Sydney and established households there and in Melbourne, he toured his electorate frequently and took a tireless personal interest in local affairs. He was an 'infectiously genial man' and his prominence was aided by continuing family connexions within the district: his father was a well-known Braidwood resident who had kept the Commercial and Queanbeyan Club hotels; the new publican of the Braidwood Royal was Chapman's brother-in-law T. Pooley; another brother-in-law, M. Byrne, owned the Royal Hotel in Queanbeyan. Chapman's younger brother Albert Edward, a former teacher who had entered Austin's auctioneering business, represented Braidwood in the Legislative Assembly in 1901-04.

In the Federal parliament Chapman was government whip during the (Sir Edmund) Barton [q.v.] ministry, minister for defence in the first Deakin [q.v.] government of 1903-04, postmaster-general in 1905-07 and minister for trade and customs in 1907-08. He chaired the royal commission of 1906 which successfully recommended old-age and invalid pensions and was responsible for the introduction into the wheat industry of a standard light-weight wheat-bag, familiarly known as the 'Chapman sack'. Common sense was his greatest attribute as a minister. He claimed with pride to have introduced penny postage into Australia, and made his second overseas trip as Australian, New Zealand and Fijian representative at the International Postal Union Congress at Rome in 1906; in 1902 he had been Barton's personal companion at the coronation of King Edward VII. After a stroke in 1909 paralysed one arm and sapped his vitality, he sat on the back-benches until February 1923 when his work towards the formation of the Bruce-Page [qq.v.] coalition and his seniority brought him the portfolios of trade and customs, and health. His term as minister for trade and customs was fraught with tension: his appointment was not generally popular among the Nationalists and the Country

Party was strongly critical of the Tariff Board. In May 1924 he resigned from the ministry on the grounds of ill health and in June was appointed K.C.M.G.

Chapman was one of the most expert constituency-managers in Australian political history. His greatest coup was the selection of the site for the Federal capital, which he was determined to have within the Eden-Monaro district. Initially he supported Dalgety and Bombala but eventually backed the Canberra proposal. His running battles for over ten years against Victorian interests opposed to the site lent some credence to his claim to be 'father of Canberra'. He also advocated a railway link between the south coast of New South Wales and Gippsland in Victoria, and supported proposals to harness the Snowy River for hydro-electricity. He died of cerebro-vascular disease on 12 January 1926 in Sydney, survived by his wife, two daughters and two sons, both of whom became distinguished professional soldiers. His funeral service was held in St Mary's Cathedral, Sydney, and he was buried in the Catholic section of Randwick cemetery. His estate was valued for probate at £34 811.

E. C. G. Page, *Truant surgeon*, A. Mozley ed (Syd, 1963); B. D. Graham, *The formation of the Australian Country Parties* (Canb, 1966); E. J. Lea-Scarlett, *Queanbeyan* (Queanbeyan, 1968); *V&P* (LA NSW), 1891 (1) 471; *Aust Mag* (Syd), 1 June 1909; *Daily Telegraph* (Syd), 29 June 1891, 21 July 1894; *Punch* (Melb), 22 Dec 1904; *SMH*, 15 Dec 1922; *Argus*, 16 Apr, 27 May 1924; *Braidwood Dispatch,* 15 Jan 1926; *Aust National Review*, 20 Jan 1926; *Australasian*, 23 Jan 1926; Crouch memoirs (LaTL).   H. J. GIBBNEY

CHAPMAN, EDWARD SHIRLEY (1859-1925), insurance-manager, was born on 9 September 1859 at Lower Fort Street, Sydney, son of Edward Chapman, insurance-manager and merchant from Cornwall, and his wife Elizabeth Steele, née Perkins, born in Devon, England. Educated at Sydney Grammar School, and later at Alleyn's College of God's Gift (Dulwich College), London, in 1878 he went to St John's College, Cambridge (B.A., 1882; M.A., 1885), where he won his blue for Rugby football. On returning to Australia he played for New South Wales between 1883 and 1887 against Queensland and New Zealand.

His father had established the insurance firm of Edward Chapman & Co. in Sydney in 1854 and extended operations to Melbourne in 1875; in 1884 he retired and Edward became a senior partner of the firm with his brother Percy Steele. The main office remained at Bond Street, Sydney; by 1908 he had opened branches in Brisbane and Perth, with chief agencies in Adelaide, Hobart, in Newcastle and Tamworth, New South Wales, and Bendigo and Geelong in Victoria. The firm had the unusual feature of conducting only insurance business at a time when most of it was largely carried on as a side-line by estate agents, chartered accountants and importers. While Chapman & Co. were the Australian managers and underwriters for the Aachen & Munich Fire Insurance Co., Reliance Marine Insurance Co. Ltd, Merchants' Marine Insurance Co. Ltd and World Marine and General Insurance Co. Ltd, the greatest volume of business came from representing the Employers' Liability Assurance Corporation Ltd of London. Chapman was an ardent worker in the interests of his profession, and was a foundation member and later chairman of the Fire Underwriters' Association of New South Wales, and vice-president of the Council of Underwriters. He was also a director of the Port Jackson and Manly Steamship Co. Ltd, the Port Jackson Investment and Insurance Co. Ltd and D. Mitchell & Co. Ltd, wholesale grocers and general merchants.

Chapman was closely associated with the Australian Jockey Club and was a member of the Australian clubs in Sydney and Melbourne, the Royal Sydney Golf Club, and the National Liberal Club, London. On 11 January 1905 at Glebe, he married a widow Mina Rowland, née Aird. They were enthusiastic supporters of the (Royal) Society for the Prevention of Cruelty to Animals, becoming life governors in 1922. A stall and a kennel were named the 'Shirley Chapman' after he made donations to the Convalescent Home for Horses at Little Bay and to the King Edward Dogs' Home at Waterloo. Mina's gifts, totalling £450, in 1922-23 helped to establish a dispensary and motor ambulance for dogs. In June 1924 the Chapmans represented the Australian branches of the society at its centenary congress in London.

Survived by his wife, Chapman died of cancer at his Longueville home on 31 December 1925 and was buried in the Church of England section of the Northern Suburbs cemetery. His estate was valued for probate at £11 395.

Sydney Chamber of Commerce, *Commerce in congress* (Syd, 1909); D. Mitchell & Co. Ltd, *50 years of progress, 1866-1916* (Syd, 1916); S.P.C.A. (Lond), *Report of the International Humane Congress* (Lond, 1924); R.S.P.C.A., *Annual Report*, 1922-26; *R.S.P.C.A. Journal*, Nov, Dec 1924, Nov 1926; *A'sian Insurance and Banking Record*, 21 Jan 1926; *SMH*, 1 Jan 1926; G. G. Pursell, The development of non-life insurance in Australia (Ph.D. thesis, ANU, 1963).   RAYMOND NOBBS

CHAPMAN, FREDERICK (1864-1943), palaeontologist, was born on 13 February 1864 at Camden Town, London, son of Robert Chapman, surgical instrument maker, and his wife Eleanor, née Dinsey. His father was an assistant to Michael Faraday and John Tyndall and his brother Robert was a physicist with an interest in microscopy and botany. Chapman went to school in Chelsea and also studied privately. When disappointed in his hopes to secure a cadetship at the British Museum, in 1881 he became assistant to Professor J. W. Judd in the geology department, Royal College of Science, London. He later qualified at the college as a teacher of geology and physiography. Encouraged by Judd's study of material from borings around London and guided by his mentor Professor T. R. Jones, he became interested in the Foraminifera. He was later a world authority on these small organisms.

In 1902, on Judd's recommendation, Chapman was appointed by the Victorian government to the newly created position of palaeontologist to the National Museum, Melbourne. His first duty was to transfer to the museum large collections of fossils housed at the Geological Survey of Victoria and at the University of Melbourne. As most specimens in these large collections were undescribed, he published papers on land plants, sponges, corals, mollusca, fishes and other forms. In 1920-32 he was part-time lecturer in palaeontology at the university and was honorary palaeontologist to the Geological Survey of Victoria from 1920. Interested in Australian flora, he was honorary curator of the Maranoa wildflower gardens near his home at Balwyn. In 1927 Chapman retired from the museum to become first Commonwealth palaeontologist, his work involving examination of both micro and macro-fossils from bore and surface material submitted in the search for oil. He retired in 1935. In 1936 he returned to the National Museum as honorary palaeontologist.

Chapman was honoured by many learned societies. In 1896 he was elected associate of the Linnean Society of London and was a fellow of the Geological Society, London, which in 1899 awarded him the Lyell Prize for research and in 1930 the Lyell Medal. He was elected a fellow of the Royal Microscopical Society, London, in 1892 and an honorary fellow in 1929. In 1920 he received the David Syme [q.v.6] prize and medal for research. From 1920 he was a member of the International Commission on Zoological Nomenclature. In 1919-20 he was president of the Microscopical Society and Field Naturalists' Club of Victoria and was a member of the Australian National Research Council

from 1922. In 1926 and 1932 the royal societies of South Australia and New Zealand made him an honorary fellow. He was president of the Royal Society of Victoria in 1929-30, and in 1932 received the (W. B.) Clarke [q.v.3] Medal from the Royal Society of New South Wales. In 1933 he became corresponding member of the Paleontological Society (United States of America) and in 1941 the Field Naturalists' Club of Victoria awarded him the Australian Natural History Medallion.

Outstanding among Chapman's qualities were his quiet gentlemanly manner, his patience and his willingness to pass on his experience and guidance to all-comers. He was an expert photographer and artist. Fossiliferous and Recent material was sent to him for micro-examination from all parts of the world, including material collected by Sir Ernest Shackleton and Sir Douglas Mawson [q.v.] during British expeditions to Antarctica.

Chapman was a prolific writer, publishing five books and some 500 scientific papers, some in collaboration, on geology, palaeontology and zoology. Between 1886 and 1902 he wrote much on Foraminifera, both fossil and living, and on some geological subjects. His last important paper appeared in 1941. Chapman published work in organisms other than the Foraminifera in scientific journals in many different countries. The most important of his books was *The Foraminifera. An introduction to the study of the Protozoa* (London, 1902) which remained the only work of its kind until 1928. *Australian fossils* was published in Melbourne in 1914. His *Book of fossils* (London and Sydney, 1934) was his last major effort.

Chapman had married Helen Mary Dancer of Northampton, England, on 12 August 1890. She had predeceased him by three years when he died at Kew on 10 December 1943; he was survived by his son Wilfred, a distinguished engineer and soldier, and one daughter. His magnificent collection of slides was presented by his son in 1949 to the Bureau of Mineral Resources, Canberra, which purchased his library. A fire in 1953 destroyed many of his microfossils and rare books.

Linnean Soc (Lond), *Procs*, 1943-44, pt 3; Roy Soc (NZ), *Procs*, 75 (1944), no 3; *Herald* (Melb), 13 Dec 1943.   IRENE CRESPIN

CHAPMAN, HENRY GEORGE (1879-1934), professor of physiology, was born on 13 January 1879 at Ealing, Middlesex, England, son of Henry Chapman, solicitor's clerk, and his wife Mary Ann, née Ryden.

About 1886 he accompanied his family to Melbourne and was educated at Hawthorn College. While at Ormond College, University of Melbourne (M.B., 1899; B.S., 1900; M.D., 1902) he won the Beaney [q.v.3] (1899) and MacBain [q.v.5] (1901) scholarships. He then attended the University of Adelaide (M.B., 1901), where he was acting professor of physiology before returning to the University of Melbourne in 1902 as demonstrator in pathology.

In 1903-13 Chapman was lecturer and demonstrator in physiology at the University of Sydney; he was awarded the David Syme [q.v.6] research prize by the University of Melbourne in 1910. In 1913-18 he was assistant professor of physiology under Sir Thomas Anderson Stuart [q.v.], becoming professor of pharmacology in 1918 and succeeding to Stuart's chair in 1921. In 1907 he had been appointed honorary pathological chemist at Royal Prince Alfred Hospital. Always interested in public and industrial health issues, he gave evidence next year before a Western Australian royal commission into meat supply. In 1908 he began lecturing on the technology of breadmaking at the Sydney Technical College where, under his direction, a school of bakery was established in 1916; he gave detailed evidence on diet to the Commonwealth royal commission on the basic wage in 1920.

Active in local scientific societies, Chapman was honorary treasurer of the Royal Society in 1912-34 and president of the Linnean Society in 1918; he was honorary treasurer of the national council and New South Wales branch of the Australian Chemical Institute from 1919 and State president in 1931-33, and president of the Australasian Institute of Mining and Metallurgy in 1920. He published on his research into biochemistry and plant products in learned journals and the *Medical Journal of Australia*, often with D. A. Welsh [q.v.] and J. M. Petrie.

Probably Chapman's most useful work was as chairman in 1919-20 of the complex technical commission of inquiry into the prevalence of miners' phthisis and pneumoconiosis in the Broken Hill mines. Tall and craggy, with a dominating personality, he managed to win the confidence of the unionists and the assistance of the mine-managers and companies despite a bitter strike. After reporting that the Broken Hill mines did cause the industrial disease as the result of inhaling dust, he made strong recommendations for immediate measures including compensation for all persons affected and, implicitly, the 35-hour week. He then 'played an honourable and courageous part in settling the strike', doggedly refusing to divulge the names of the 251 men found suffering from lung disease until compensation was certain.

In 1924 Chapman visited England on behalf of the Australian Meat Council and next year attended the conference on the reorganization of the Commonwealth Institute of Science and Industry. In 1928 he presided over the physiology section of the Hobart meeting of the Australasian Association for the Advancement of Science.

An appeal in 1926 had raised over £120 000 for the university's Cancer Research Fund. After the successful British applicant had declined the appointment, in 1928 Chapman was made director of cancer research despite opposition from members of the science faculty, who doubted both his integrity and his scientific status and distrusted his public image. He made little contribution to research, and in 1930 a series of newspaper articles exposed bitter dissension within the cancer committee and some dubious aspects of Chapman's career.

On 30 December 1903 at Walkerville, South Australia, he had married Julie Adelaide Elizabeth Ramsay Cox, by whom he had a son and two daughters. About 1916 Chapman separated from his wife, and thereafter resided at the University Club, Sydney, also maintaining flats in the city and at Bondi—by 1928 he was living prodigally. On 24 May 1934 in his university rooms he took poisons, never isolated, and died next day. He was buried in the Anglican section of Northern Suburbs cemetery after a service at St Mark's Church, Darling Point. Ten days later his estate was sequestrated on the petition of the Royal Society, which claimed he owed its funds £3360. The other principal claimant, for £15 280, was the Australian National Research Council, of which Chapman had been honorary treasurer. Officers of both bodies had been pressing for an audit and Chapman had just been asked to resign his university post. His assets realized £2380. The circumstances of his troubled last years and death prevented any balanced assessment of his achievements in the field of social and preventive medicine.

H. M. Moran, *Viewless winds* (Lond, 1939); B. Kennedy, *Silver, sin, and sixpenny ale* (Melb, 1978); Linnean Soc NSW, *Procs*, 43 (1918); *Hermes* (Syd), 34 (1928); Roy Soc NSW, *J*, 69 (1935); *Smith's Weekly*, 12 July 1930; *SMH*, 26, 29 May, 2, 6, 7, 20 June, 18 July 1934; Bankruptcy file 138/34 (NSW Supreme Court).   RUTH TEALE

CHAPMAN, SIR ROBERT WILLIAM (1866-1942), engineer, was born on 27 December 1866 at Stony Stratford, Buckinghamshire, England, son of Charles Chapman, a currier from Melbourne, and his wife Matilda, née Harrison. In 1876 the family returned to Melbourne where Chapman attended Wesley College and the university (B.A., 1886; M.A., B.E., 1888). He then worked for a few months for a contractor on railway construction work.

In 1889 Chapman became an assistant lecturer in mathematics and physics at the University of Adelaide, and next year also began teaching mathematics at the South Australian School of Mines and Industries. In 1901 he became lecturer in engineering and in 1907 first professor of engineering at the university. In 1910-19 he replaced (Sir) William Bragg [q.v.] as professor of mathematics and mechanics but in 1920 was reappointed to the chair of engineering, which he occupied until his retirement in 1937. In Melbourne, on 14 February 1889, he had married Eva Maud Hall.

Chapman's 'faculty, amounting almost to genius, of being able to recognize the fundamental essentials in almost any problem', made him an excellent teacher. He was beloved by his students especially for his kindliness and for his 'great gift of lucidity'. He was also more than competent as an experimental investigator and as a practical engineer. His first association with the university had occurred at a time when the training of professionally qualified engineers was still based on the system of pupilage. Physical teaching conditions were depressing. He urged the establishment of joint courses between the university and the school of mines; from 1903 they were instituted, leading to diplomas being awarded by the school. Courses leading to degrees awarded by the university in various branches of engineering were later established on a similar basis, and continued until after his retirement when additional chairs were created within the faculty. He had foreseen the changes that would follow the adoption of these joint courses, embracing theoretical and practical study, and perceived that engineer graduates would need to develop a corporate outlook in order to serve the community effectively.

Chapman made it his personal concern to promote professional status and was a foundation member and president of the South Australian Institute of Engineers, established in 1913, and a foundation councillor and later president of the Institution of Engineers, Australia. His pupils were employed at 'almost every power plant throughout Australia' and in senior positions all over the world. They included G. C. Klug, Essington Lewis, W. E. Wainwright [qq.v.], H. Angwin, chief engineer of the South Australian Harbors Board, and

Chapman's son Robert Hall, chief engineer for railways in South Australia from 1924; other students headed the forestry departments of Great Britain and New South Wales. In 1927 Chapman was appointed C.M.G.

Despite his heavy burden of teaching, Chapman was active in many fields of applied science. His involvement extended well beyond his professorial ambit. Long interested in tidal phenomena and astronomy, he was a member of the Adelaide Observatory Committee. He carried out original research, having extramural applications, into properties of timber, the micro-structure of metals and phenomena related to concrete. Active in setting up a standards laboratory in the State, he was a member of the Australian Commonwealth Engineering Standards Association. His services were often sought as consultant to governments in the field of public works: his chairmanship of an inquiry, which reported to the Victorian government in 1929, into a major subsidence of an embankment at Eildon Weir, was of a pioneering character.

Chapman was a council-member of the University of Adelaide from 1919 and occasionally acted as vice-chancellor. Upon retirement in 1937 he was made emeritus professor and knighted. From 1939 until his death he was president of the council of the School of Mines and Industries. Chapman was a member of many learned societies, and had been president of the South Australian Institute of Surveyors in 1917-29. A fellow of the Royal Astronomical Society from 1909, he consistently nourished the struggling Astronomical Society of South Australia. He was awarded the Peter Nicol Russell [q.v.6] memorial medal, the premier distinction conferred by the Institution of Engineers, in 1928 and the (W. C.) Kernot [q.v.5] memorial medal of the University of Melbourne in 1931. In addition to his learned and scientific papers Chapman published *The elements of astronomy for surveyors* (London, 1919) and *Reinforced concrete* (Adelaide). Survived by his wife, five sons and two daughters, he died in Adelaide on 27 February 1942 and was buried in North Road cemetery. His name is perpetuated by the Institution of Engineers' R. W. Chapman medal and by a prize at the University of Adelaide. A portrait by Ivor Hele hangs in the Chapman theatre in the engineering school of the university.

SA Inst of Technology, *An age of technology, 1889-1964* (Adel, 1964); *PP* (Vic), 1929, 1st S, 1 (11); *Aust J of Science*, 5 (1942-43); Inst of Engineers, Aust, *J*, 14 (1942), and for publications; *SMH*, 9 Aug 1937; *Advertiser* (Adel), 28 Feb 1942; R. B. Potts, Mathematics at the University of Adelaide 1874-1944 (held by Professor Potts); Astronomical Soc of SA, Records (Adel); Inst of Surveyors, Aust,

SA Division, Records (Adel); correspondence 101/1929, 97/49, *and* Council minutes 31 May 1949 (Univ Adel).   R. J. BRIDGLAND

CHAPPLE, FREDERIC (1845-1924), headmaster, was born on 12 October 1845 at St Pancras, London, son of John Chapple, mason, and his wife Louisa, née Brewin. He studied at King's College, University of London (B.A., 1870; B.Sc., 1873) and at Westminster College, a Wesleyan teacher-training institution where he later taught for five years. He was a founding member of the National Union of Elementary Teachers, which he represented in 1870 at a congress on the desirability of religious teaching in government schools. It was a cause he was to espouse again in South Australia. During this period he declined appointment as principal of a Wesleyan university in Illinois, United States of America.

In 1876 Chapple agreed to succeed J. A. Hartley [q.v.4] as headmaster of Prince Alfred College and arrived in Adelaide on 8 April. An early achievement was to secure in 1878 the incorporation of the school. This removed its financial control from 'the hands of four or five gentlemen who might do as they liked' and vested it in a board of management. He continued to shift the school's emphasis away from classical subjects and towards mathematics and natural science, aiming to broaden the boys' minds. Chapple considered that colleges such as Prince Alfred were 'freer' than state schools to devote themselves to 'education' as distinct from 'instruction'. As president of the Collegiate Masters' Association, he told the 1881-83 commission on the working of the education Acts, that provision by the state of advanced or secondary education for 'the people' would be 'a very perilous experiment' and should not be 'one of the functions of government'.

Chapple played an active community role outside the school: he was warden of the Senate of the University of Adelaide in 1883-1922, vice-president of the Royal Society of South Australia in 1880-81, president of the Literary Societies' Union and vice-president of the South Australian branch of the Teachers' Guild of Great Britain and Ireland. In 1900 he published *The boy's own grammar*... and he supported Our Boys' Institute, the State athletic association, and the Young Men's Christian Association of Adelaide of which he was president for seven years. He impressed his contemporaries as being a man of energy and whimsicality and pre-eminently of a 'simple, earnest religious faith'. A Methodist, he was a president of the Council of Churches and, on leave in England in 1901, was a delegate to the Methodist Ecumenical Conference.

On 16 April 1870 at Bethnal Green, London, Chapple had married Elizabeth Sarah Hunter, a schoolmistress. They took great pride in the excellent academic achievements of their four daughters and four sons. Phoebe [q.v.] was an intrepid medical doctor. On Chapple's retirement at the end of 1914 he was appointed C.M.G. It was said by a successor, J. F. Ward [q.v.], that Chapple had been 'the man who really founded Prince Alfred College as a great school'. He died on 29 February 1924 at his home in Norwood and was buried in West Terrace cemetery. A bronze bust by G. A. Barnes [q.v.] is in the school's Old Assembly Hall.

J. J. Pascoe (ed), *History of Adelaide and vicinity* (Adel, 1901); H. T. Burgess (ed), *Cyclopedia of South Australia*, 2 (Adel, 1909); J. F. Ward, *Prince Alfred College* (Adel, 1951); *PP* (SA). 1878, 4 (157), 1883-84, 3 (27a); *Prince Alfred College Chronicle*, Jan 1915, May 1924; *Observer* (Adel), 24 Mar 1894, 1 Nov 1902, 8 Mar 1924; *Advertiser* (Adel), 3 Mar 1924.   ALAN H. DENNIS

CHAPPLE, PHOEBE (1879-1967), medical practitioner, was born on 31 March 1879 in Adelaide, youngest daughter of Frederic Chapple [q.v.] and his wife Elizabeth Sarah, née Hunter. Educated at the Advanced School for Girls, she entered the University of Adelaide at 16 (B.Sc., 1898; M.B., B.S., 1904). In 1905 she was a house-surgeon at the Adelaide Hospital and later worked for a time at the Sydney Medical Mission. Until 1914 she practised from her father's school, Prince Alfred College, attending the boarders and travelling in a phaeton driven by a liveried coachman when visiting patients.

Dr Chapple, a feminist, was one of a handful of Australian medical women who served in World War I. The army refused to appoint female doctors, so she left Adelaide in February 1917 for England and became attached first to the Royal Army Medical Corps and later to Queen Mary's Army Auxiliary Corps, although women were not accorded formal military status. Her first appointment was as surgeon at Cambridge Hospital, Aldershot. In November she went to France where she worked with the Women's Auxiliary Army Corps at Abbeville till August 1918 and also at Rouen and Le Havre. On the night of 29 May 1918 she was inspecting the women's camps when, because of intense bombing, she and forty women sheltered in trenches. A direct hit killed nine and injured several others. For 'gallantry and devotion to duty' on this occasion, Dr Chapple received the rare award for a woman of the Military Medal. Like most of her contemporaries, she tolerated military conservatism but was aware that women were '[squeezed] dry like an orange'.

She returned to Australia in 1919 and resumed practice, on North Terrace, until 1937. Supported by the Women's Non-Party Association, Dr Chapple was narrowly defeated in the 1919 Adelaide municipal elections. In 1921-22 she was honorary medical officer, night clinic (venereal diseases), for women patients at the Adelaide Hospital. For about thirty years from 1910 she was honorary doctor at the Salvation Army maternity hospital for unmarried mothers, first at Carrington Street, Adelaide, then at McBride Hospital, Medindie. 'She was a courageous and clever obstetrician . . . but was jealous of her authority'; although untiring in her work, she never involved herself in the adoption of patients' babies or their non-medical problems.

On the last of her six overseas trips, in 1937 she was the Australian delegate to the Medical Women's International Association conference in Edinburgh. She continued her practice from her home in Norwood until she was 85. She was known as 'Auntie Doc' by her large family whom she kept together and in touch. She was blunt, confident, dominating. A tall strong woman, for years she headed the nursing units marching each Anzac day. She died unmarried on 24 March 1967 and was cremated with full military honours. Her estate was sworn for probate at $93 910; St Ann's College, University of Adelaide, received a bursary from it which is administered in her name.

H. T. Burgess (ed), *Cyclopedia of South Australia*, 2 (1909); *Observer* (Adel), 6 Sept 1919; *Advertiser* (Adel), 17 Oct 1937, 7 Jan 1955, 25 Mar, 6 Apr 1967; Adelaide Hospital, Annual Report, 1891-1922 (SAA); Women's Non-Party Assn minutes (SAA); information from Brigadier Isobel Ferguson, Sunset Lodge, Kingswood, SA.

JOYCE GIBBERD

CHARLESTON, DAVID MORLEY (1848-1934), engineer, unionist and politician, was born at St Erth, Cornwall, England, on 27 May 1848, son of John Charleston, blacksmith, and his wife Elizabeth, née Williams. Following primary education he was apprenticed at the ironworks of Harvey & Co. at near-by Hayle, and in 1870 joined the Amalgamated Society of Engineers. In 1874 he moved to San Francisco, United States of America, to work as a marine engineer on ships of the Pacific Mail Steamship

Co. He migrated to South Australia in 1884 and worked for his brother, a lime-merchant, and for the government as supervising engineer on the Hackney Bridge. He was again a marine engineer in 1886, but resigned next year from the Adelaide Steamship Co. after labour troubles and worked as an engineer with the English & Australian Copper Co. at Moonta until 1891. He married in 1895 but his wife Mary died two years later and there were no children.

Charleston had been associated with the labour movement in London, joined the Democratic Club in Adelaide, and was a delegate to the United Trades and Labor Council. In 1888 he was one of the first U.T.L.C. members to be made a justice of the peace. He was a conciliator in labour disputes in the late 1880s, chaired the Eight Hours Protection Society and was president of the U.T.L.C. in 1889-90.

At the general election in 1891 Charleston stood for the newly formed United Labor Party and headed the poll for the Central District of the Legislative Council. In 1894 he was a delegate to the intercolonial conference of Labor parliamentarians in Sydney. He travelled in the South Australian countryside, lecturing on politics; one such talk, 'Universal depression: its cause and cure', was printed in 1895. The first major dissident in the party, in 1897 he was called a traitor by his leader Tom Price [q.v.]. On 18 August Charleston resigned from the U.L.P. and the council. At the by-election, as an independent Liberal he defeated the Labor nominee, a result which horrified the party but which was described by the conservative *Observer* as 'a triumph for political honour and personal reputation'.

Charleston had been a strong supporter of Federation and in 1901 he was elected to the Senate as a free trader; by this time he had become a relatively large rural property-owner. He was defeated by Labor in the 1903 election and next year was a foundation member and organizing secretary of the Farmers and Producers Political Union; in 1908 he became its general secretary. He stood again for the Senate unsuccessfully in 1906 as a candidate for the F.P.P.U. and in 1910, after amalgamation, for the Liberal Union.

In the 1890s Charleston had been closely connected with the Homestead Blockers League, especially over village settlements on the River Murray. He was a prominent member of the South Australian Cornish Association and a long-term council-member of the South Australian School of Mines and Industries; in 1914 he spent six months in London with a government commission to inquire into technical education. A largely self-educated man, Charleston was praised for the 'clearness, earnestness and comprehension' shown in his speeches. He died at his home at Mile End on 30 June 1934, leaving an estate sworn for probate at £254.

J. J. Pascoe (ed), *History of Adelaide and vicinity* (Adel, 1901); *Pictorial Aust*, May 1891; *British A'sian*, 9 Apr 1914; *Observer* (Adel), 23 May 1891, 28 Aug, 18 Sept 1897, 2 June 1928; *T&CJ*, 3 Feb 1894; *Mail* (Adel), 31 Jan 1914; *Advertiser* (Adel), 2 July 1934; J. Scarfe, The Labour wedge: the first six Labour members of the South Australian Legislative Council (B.A. Hons thesis, Univ Adel, 1968).   DEAN JAENSCH

CHARLTON, ANDREW MURRAY (1907-1975), swimmer, was born on 12 August 1907 at North Sydney, only son of Oswald Murray Charlton, bank manager, and his wife Ada Maud, née Moore. Known as 'Boy', he was brought up at Manly where he revelled in the surf. Educated at Manly Public School, and at Sydney Grammar School in 1921-22, he entered Hawkesbury Agricultural College in January 1923.

On 13 January at the State championships Charlton swam 880 yards freestyle in 11 minutes 5.2 seconds, taking 19 seconds off the world record. In January next year at the State titles held at the Domain baths in Sydney he defeated the great Swedish swimmer Arne Borg over 440 yards freestyle, equalling Borg's world record of 5 minutes 11.8 seconds – the cheering was heard in Martin Place. Next Saturday before a wildly enthusiastic crowd he beat Borg in the 880 yards freestyle event by 15 yards, setting a world mark of 10 minutes 51.8 seconds. These feats helped to revive public interest in competitive swimming and, dubbed the 'Manly Flying Fish', he became a popular sporting idol. His trainer was Tom Adrian.

At the 1924 Olympic Games in Paris Charlton won the 1500 metres title in 20 minutes 6.6 seconds, setting new Olympic and world records; he was only the third Australian to be awarded a gold medal in swimming. In the same race, 13 minutes 19.6 seconds was a world mark for 1000 metres. He was third in the 400 behind Johnny Weissmuller and Borg, and one of the 4 × 200 relay team which came second. Despite illness, he won other races in Europe, including every event he entered in the Tailteann Games in Ireland, before returning to a tumultuous welcome in Sydney. In December he left Hawkesbury Agricultural College without graduating in the diploma course, and worked on Malcolm McKellar's station, Kurrumbede, at Gunnedah. On 8 January 1927 Charlton, now trained by Harry Hay, set a new world record of 10 minutes 32 seconds for 880 yards. He re-

turned to Gunnedah and next year was seriously ill with rheumatic fever. In 1932 he set new Australian records for 440 and 880 yards, but was unplaced in the 400 and 1500 metre events at the Los Angeles Olympic Games.

In 1934 Charlton moved to Canberra and entered a pharmacy business with a friend and former Manly swimmer John L. Davies; he became captain of Manuka Swimming Club. Representing Canberra at the New South Wales championships in Sydney in January 1935, he beat the French and Australian champions Jean Taris and Noel Ryan in the 880 yards in one of his greatest swims and last race. Next year he took up sheepraising with J. Hyles on part of Woolowolar, near Tarago. On 20 March 1937 at St Mark's Church, Darling Point, Sydney, he married Jessie Muriel Hyles. He then settled on a 12 000-acre (4850 ha) property, Kilrea, at Boro near Goulburn, and became a successful grazier. Extremely shy and modest, 'Boy' shunned publicity. He refused offers to turn professional saying: 'I would never be forgiven by the Australian public . . . I am not in the sport for what I can get out of it'. He never won an Australian title, but to Australians in the 1920s he was a popular idol and national hero.

Survived by his wife, son and daughter, Charlton died suddenly of a heart attack at his Avalon home on 10 December 1975, and was cremated. His estate was valued for probate at $131 850.

Charlton's stroke was a four-beat, trudgen crawl, called by some at the time the single trudgen crawl. There was very little leg movement: the wide scissor kick was made horizontally at the end of the left arm drive with the body turned well sideways, then followed two or three vertical kicks. His powerful arms and withering final sprint made him a champion, despite the fact that he rarely trained, preferring to surf instead. In 1968 the new Sydney Domain baths were named after him and in 1972 he was honoured by the International Swimming Hall of Fame at Fort Lauderdale, Florida, United States of America.

Forbes Carlile on swimming (Lond, 1963); P. Besford, *Encylopaedia of swimming*, 2nd edn (Lond, 1976); *Lone Hand*, 14 Feb 1920; *SMH*, 15 Jan 1923, 14, 17, 21 Jan, 14-19, 22, 28, 31 July, 14-19 Aug 1924, 10, 27 Jan 1927, 8, 17, 27, 28 Aug 1928, 18, 25 Jan, 10 Feb 1932, 27 Feb, 29 Oct 1935, 9 Aug, 12 Dec 1975; *Daily Mirror* (Syd), 12 Nov 1971; *Canb Times*, and *Sun* (Syd), 17 Dec 1975.   G. P. WALSH

CHARLTON, MATTHEW (1866-1948), Labor politician, was born on 15 March 1866

at Linton near Ballarat, Victoria, son of Matthew Charlton, a miner from Durham, England, and his wife Mabel, née Foard. In 1871 the family moved to Lambton, a mining village outside Newcastle, New South Wales, where the Scottish-Australian Co. had established coal-mining operations. Educated at Lambton Public School, young Charlton worked in the mines as a trapper, then at the coal-face. On 26 June 1889 at New Lambton he married Martha Rollings according to the forms of the Particular Baptist Church.

Becoming active in union politics, Charlton supported strike action in 1896 to resist wage reductions. When this failed, he followed many fellow miners to the goldfields near Kalgoorlie, Western Australia, and spent over two years there before returning to Lambton and employment in the Waratah pit. He rejoined the northern district Colliery Employees' Federation as a lodge official: in 1901-06 as treasurer he negotiated members' grievances with employers and prepared arbitration cases for the union in addition to normal duties. In November 1902 he represented the New South Wales miners at the first national trades union congress since 1891. There he moved for nationalization of the coal-mining industry, not because of ideological principle but with the practical aim of eliminating the cut-throat competition between owners that depressed miners' wages and conditions. After other delegates opposed this as too radical a demand, Charlton agreed to an amendment urging State governments to fill their needs from their own mines and affirming the ultimate desirability of full nationalization. A moderate in other matters, he supported extension of compulsory industrial arbitration, although warning of defects in current New South Wales legislation.

On 5 December 1903, after colleagues urged him to stand, Charlton won the Waratah by-election for the Legislative Assembly. Next year he transferred to Northumberland. In parliament he spoke principally on mining matters. During the coalminers' strike of 1909-10, marked by a clash between labour leaders over tactics, Charlton accepted the invitation of the Colliery Employees' Federation to represent it before a wages board strongly repudiated by the rank and file. With the strike collapsing, he performed the thankless task of negotiating a return to work under the old conditions in order to preserve the union, and personally urged coalfield meetings to accept the board's decision. Charlton's role, although unsuccessful in securing industrial improvements, failed to impair his stature. Immediately after the strike he won the Federal seat of Hunter from the sitting Liberal member at the general election in April 1910 and held it until retirement.

In 1913 Charlton was elected to the Federal Parliamentary Labor Party executive and became a temporary chairman of committees in the House. In Andrew Fisher's [q.v.] second government he was appointed chairman of the joint parliamentary committee of public accounts and attempted to secure increased powers for it. On 3 May 1915 he offered to resign as chairman in protest against government delay in meeting caucus support for him on this matter. However Fisher conciliated him and Charlton went on until 1922 to develop a useful role for the committee. On the outbreak of war he had supported Australian involvement and in 1916 voted for W. M. Hughes's [q.v.] conscription referendum bill. While conceding the sincerity of its adherents, Charlton personally believed conscription unnecessary and he campaigned against it in his constituency. However, he appeared willing to accept an affirmative result in the referendum and maintained loyalty to Hughes as leader. On 14 November when Hughes faced a motion of censure in caucus, Charlton attempted to avert a party split by moving an amendment to refer the controversy to a party federal conference. Hughes cut debate short by walking out and Charlton stayed to support F. G. Tudor [q.v.]. For the remainder of the war he encouraged voluntary recruiting. He publicly opposed a federal conference recommendation in 1918 to make further support of the war effort subject to certain conditions being met by the Australian and Allied governments.

During the immediate post-war years Labor faced a leadership crisis. The party respected Charlton, but preferred T. J. Ryan [q.v.] as successor-designate to the ailing Tudor. After Ryan's untimely death on 1 August 1921, Charlton succeeded him as deputy party leader in the House. When Tudor died in January 1922 Charlton became acting leader by common consent and was confirmed in the position at a party meeting on 16 May. Always a moderate, he regarded the Labor socialization objective as electorally embarrassing. As leader of the Opposition he offered at the 1922 elections policies of national development under a unified government with regional devolution of powers, tariff protection and limited immigration. Midway through the campaign he was hospitalized for a serious illness. Labor emerged as the strongest single party in parliament though unable to divide the government coalition.

Following its wartime experience, the Australian Labor Party opposed compulsory military training, and insisted that no commitments of Australian forces be made abroad without the clear consent of parliament and people. Charlton strenuously protested against Australian involvement in Britain's minor Imperial crises and urged maintenance of an independent foreign policy. He criticized Australian participation in the Singapore defence strategy and supported the creation of armed forces best suited technically for continental defence. In the belief that the League of Nations offered the only prospect for peace and disarmament he accepted a government invitation in 1924 to attend the assembly of the league at Geneva. At the opening session on 4 September Charlton urged positive action. Subsequent deliberations produced the Geneva Protocol, intended to make international disputes between members justiciable and to establish collective security with a view to eventual disarmament. Charlton and the leader of the Australian delegation, Sir Littleton Groom [q.v.], joined at closed meetings of the British and Dominion delegates to oppose Japanese demands that certain domestic policies, such as immigration, be exempt from compulsory arbitration: they were eventually obliged to compromise.

After returning to Australia Charlton urged adoption of the Protocol; however the government agreed with British misgivings and the scheme lapsed. On the most vexatious political issue of the 1920s, industrial relations, Labor supported extension of Federal conciliation and arbitration but was embarrassed by militant union action. Charlton blamed the seamen's strike for his loss of the election in November 1925. He courageously backed part of the government's referendum proposals on increased industrial powers in 1926, despite deep disagreements within the labour movement on the matter.

Charlton was conscientious in his duties and 'grasped a good many nettles firmly'. Several times he lent assistance to attempts to resolve internal conflicts in the New South Wales branch of the party. This strengthened the party's federal structure but did not produce the desired unity. While universally admired and respected for his integrity and humanity, he failed to gain office in a period of eclipse for Federal Labor. His resignation as leader on 29 March 1928 and retirement from parliament was sudden but not unexpected. For some time J. H. Scullin and E. G. Theodore [qq.v] had been shaping up for the inevitable succession. Charlton left with the full confidence and affection of his colleagues. Tall and distinguished-looking even in old age, in his later years he supported the party with advice and encouragement, adhering to the Federal (official)

Labor Party against the State (Lang [q.v.]) party in the 1930s. He declined to stand for Federal parliament in 1931 and 1934, but was an alderman on Lambton Council in 1934-38. He died on 8 December 1948 at Lambton, survived by his wife, son and daughter. His estate was valued for probate at £7671.

N. Makin, *Federal Labour leaders* (Syd, 1961); R. L. Wettenhall, 'Federal Labor and the Public Corporation under Matthew Charlton', *Labour Hist*, May 1964, no 6; *Punch* (Melb), 5 Nov 1925; *Newcastle Morning Herald*, 27 Sept 1930; *Daily Telegraph* (Syd), 1 Aug 1947; *Canb Times*, 1 Feb 1966.   MURRAY PERKS

CHARTERIS, ARCHIBALD HAMILTON (1874-1940), international lawyer, was born on 22 April 1874 at Glasgow, Scotland, elder son of Matthew Charteris (1840-1897) and his wife Elizabeth, née Greer. He belonged to a distinguished academic family: his father was senior professor of materia medica at the University of Glasgow, his uncle Archibald Hamilton Charteris was professor of biblical criticism at the University of Edinburgh in 1868-98, and his younger brother Francis James became the professor of materia medica at the University of St Andrews.

Charteris was educated at Edinburgh Collegiate School, the Moravian Brothers' school at Neuwied near Koblenz, Germany, and the University of Glasgow (M.A., 1894; LL.B., 1898). After working in law offices in Glasgow, in 1904 he became a member of the Faculty of Procurators, Glasgow, and in 1904-19 was lecturer in public international law and international private law at the university. An active council-member of the International Law Association, he met the leading international lawyers, and published in its *Transactions*. In a notable paper read to the association in 1910, he compared the Scots procedure as to criminal indictments with the corresponding English and French practices. He was also a member of the Royal Institute of International Affairs. During World War I he worked in the trade division of the Admiralty, then for the War Trade Intelligence Department, gaining first-hand experience of the operation of the naval blockade of Germany in 1916-18 and the associated legal problems. In 1919 in Berlin he became legal assistant to the resident agent of the clearing house for enemy debts.

In 1920 Charteris was appointed to the new Challis [q.v.3] chair of international law and jurisprudence at the University of Sydney law school. At St Mary of the Angels Catholic Church, Paddington, London, on 10

January 1921 he married Marguerite (Margaret) Rossiter, from Devonshire; they arrived in Sydney in the *Osterley* on 27 February. Fluent in French and German, a good linguist and broadly cultured, Charteris inspired his students and embellished his lectures with his wit and wartime experiences, and was always approachable.

Outside the university, Charteris fostered in Australia an interest in international law, already to some extent generated by the establishment of the League of Nations in Geneva and the Permanent Court of International Justice in The Hague. He acted as Australian correspondent of the *British year book of international law*, to which he had contributed a classic study of merchant vessels in foreign ports and national waters in its first volume (1920-21).

Charteris also contributed many authoritative articles to law journals including several on Australian immigration laws, and to the press, notably the *Sydney Morning Herald*. In his radio broadcasts he reached a nation-wide public, and was described by (Mr Justice) W. S. Sheldon as 'far and away the best broadcaster in this country'. He became president of the New South Wales branch of the League of Nations Union in 1923 and of the short-lived Australian and New Zealand Society of International Law in 1933. He represented Australia at the third conference of the Institute of Pacific Relations at Kyoto, Japan, in 1929 and at the British Commonwealth Relations Conference at Toronto, Canada, in 1933. The law school published in 1940 a selection of his lectures, entitled *Chapters on international law*, which has been of lasting value. That year he launched his monthly notes for the *Australian Law Journal*.

Careless in his dress, Charteris had an 'incorrigible elfishness', and was one of the most colourful legal and academic figures in Sydney: 'a great scholar and a very lovable man', he published a notable book on Scottish wit and humour, *When the Scot smiles, in literature and life* (London, 1932). Survived by his wife and son, he died of emphysema at his home at Turramurra on 9 October 1940 and was buried in the Presbyterian section of Northern Suburbs cemetery.

T. R. Bavin (ed), *The jubilee book of the law school of the University of Sydney* (Syd, 1940); *Aust Law J*, Oct 1940, 216; *Blackacre*, Michaelmas, 1941; Charteris papers (Fisher Lib, Univ Syd).

J. G. STARKE

CHASE, MURIEL JEAN ELIOT (1880-1936), journalist and philanthropist, was born on 2 July 1880 at Geraldton, Western Australia, eldest of the four children of John Henry Cooper and his wife Priscilla Richenda, née Eliot. On her mother's side she was descended from the Marshall Waller Cliftons [q.v.3], pioneers of Australind, and through Mrs Clifton was related to the great English social worker, Elizabeth Fry. Her maternal grandfather, George Eliot, arrived in Western Australia in 1829, accompanying his cousin (Sir) James Stirling [q.v.2], first governor of the colony.

Muriel's father, a senior officer of the Union Bank of Australia Ltd, died in 1888 and his widow and four children then lived for some years with the Eliot family. Muriel was educated at Amy Best's [q.v.3] school and she married, at the age of 20, Ernest Edward Chase, some fifteen years her senior. They left immediately for England where, on the recommendation of Sir Alexander Onslow [q.v.5], chief justice and acting governor, Ernest became secretary to Sir Charles Rose, a Conservative member of the House of Commons; however, Ernest's ill health obliged them to return to Australia a year later. On the homeward voyage Muriel formed a close friendship with Sister Kate Clutterbuck [q.v.] which greatly influenced her life. Always an essentially religious woman, she early became deeply interested in theosophy, though maintaining a close association with St George's Cathedral, where she had been married.

In 1903, at the invitation of (Sir) J. Winthrop Hackett [q.v.], she became social editress of the *West Australian*, and 'Aunt Mary' of the *Western Mail*'s Children's Corner. Her journalistic career continued until her premature death. Writing under the name 'Adrienne' in the *West Australian*, and also as 'Aunt Mary', Muriel Chase continually stressed the need for more social welfare services in the rapidly expanding Western Australian community. Meanwhile her husband had been seconded to Government House where he served as private secretary and aide-de-camp until his death in 1927.

The State-wide organization known today as the Silver Chain District Nursing Association had its genesis in Aunt Mary's Children's Corner, through which Mrs Chase enrolled her young readers as silver links in a chain of service. By 1904 she had raised sufficient money to appoint a district nurse (Sister S. L. Copley); she was succeeded after one year by Sister Frances Cherry, who served the organization and helped supervise its initial expansion until her death in 1941. These two pioneer nurses visited their patients first by bicycle and then by horse and buggy, their work being financed by the Silver Chain.

From the many visits of the Silver Chain

nurses, the need for a maternity hospital, infant health clinics, cottage homes for the aged and bush nursing services was soon recognized, and all these gradually came into being. Behind them was the gentle, unobtrusive influence of Muriel Chase. She lent practical support to many worthwhile women's organizations, more particularly those caring for children and the aged, and was a foundation member of the Karrakatta Club and the Women Writers' Club. Her devotion to the city's sick and aged extended at times to her relieving the district nurse on night duty.

Survived by two daughters, Muriel Chase died suddenly of cardiac disease on 13 February 1936. Next day the *West Australian* wrote: 'Of all the women of the State, none, it may safely be said, was so well-known and certainly none more widely beloved for her rare qualities of mind and heart'. At her memorial service, St George's Cathedral was filled to overflowing with citizens who wished to pay tribute to a great West Australian woman. One of the Silver Chain Cottage Homes in North Perth bears her name.

N. Stewart, *Little but great* (Perth, 1965); M. L. Skinner, *The fifth sparrow* (Syd, 1972); *Western Mail*, 3 June 1905, 27 Sept 1907, 16 Feb 1936; *West Australian*, 14 Feb 1936; Women Writers' Club, News-cuttings 1937 (Battye Lib, Perth).

NOËL STEWART

CHATAWAY, JAMES VINCENT (1852-1901), and THOMAS DRINKWATER (1864-1925), newspaper proprietors and politicians, were sons of Rev. James Chataway and his wife Elizabeth Ann, née Drinkwater. Born on 6 September 1852 at Aston, Warwickshire, England, and educated at Winchester College, James abandoned plans to enter the Indian Civil Service when his health failed, and migrated instead to Victoria in 1873. After ten years pastoral experience throughout the eastern colonies, he settled at Mackay, Queensland, as partner in an auctioneering and livery-stable business. Turning to journalism in late 1883, he became editor of the *Mackay Mercury* and, with W. G. Hodges, purchased the paper in 1886.

James acquired an interest in the Eton plantation and was soon identified with Mackay's sugar lobby, which supported North Queensland separation until 1892 when Sir Samuel Griffith [q.v.] reintroduced Pacific islands labour, which James believed was fundamental to the industry's prosperity. He toured Egypt in 1889 to study sugar-cane cultivation, and in 1892 established the *Sugar Journal and Tropical Cultivator*; his brother was editor and manager.

Elected to represent Mackay in the Legislative Assembly in April 1893, he emerged as a leading spokesman for the Farmers' Union. He was appointed to the ministry in February 1898, as minister without portfolio, by H. M. Nelson [q.v.], possibly to circumvent the formation of a separate country party. On 2 March 1898 he became secretary for agriculture and held the portfolio, except for the seven days of the A. Dawson [q.v.] ministry, until his death three years later. Temporary responsibility for the ministry of public lands for nearly six months from October 1898 was no doubt connected with his membership of the 1897 royal commission on land settlement. A competent minister, Chataway sponsored several significant progressive measures. The Slaughtering Act of 1898 licensed slaughter-houses and required regular inspections to prevent the marketing of tubercular meat; the Agricultural Bank Act of 1898 provided for improvement loans up to £800 to individual farmers; and the Sugar Experiment Stations Act created research laboratories at Mackay, Bundaberg and Ayr.

James was a member of many local organizations and held a commission in the Mackay Mounted Infantry. When he died of heart disease at South Brisbane on 12 April 1901, he was survived by his wife Jessie Carlyle, née Little, whom he had married in Brisbane on 8 December 1882, and by two sons and two daughters. He was buried in Cleveland cemetery after a state funeral.

Thomas Chataway followed his brother into both journalism and politics. Born on 6 April 1864 at Wartling, Sussex, and educated at Charterhouse, Thomas arrived in Sydney in 1881, worked on the Liverpool Plains for a year, and moved to Habana near Mackay where he was engaged as a sugar-boiler until offered a post on the *Mackay Mercury* in 1886. By 1896 he was editor and manager of the *Mercury* and the *Sugar Journal and Tropical Cultivator*, and in 1905 concluded an amalgamation of the *Mercury* and the *Mackay Chronicle* to form the *Daily Mercury*, which he eventually sold in 1911.

Active in municipal affairs, he was mayor of the town in 1904-06 before successfully standing for the Senate on the anti-socialist ticket in December 1906. Politically conservative and ardently protectionist, he had agitated in the late 1880s for the reintroduction of Pacific islands labour, and nearly two decades later unsuccessfully petitioned the Commonwealth government to contract European migrants for the cane fields. Understandably, he clashed regularly with Thomas Givens [q.v.] in parliament over white labour in the sugar industry. He consistently argued for agricultural bounties to counterbalance tariff protection for southern manufactures. As a member of the parliamentary printing committee and of the 1909 select committee on press cable services, he was the Senate's acknowledged authority on the press, posts and telegraphs. Serving only one term, he was defeated in 1913.

Chataway was employed in Sydney in 1916 as secretary to the Federal leader of the Opposition. In 1917 Senator E. D. Millen [q.v.] asked for his services as a personal assistant when taking responsibility for repatriation. After the war Chataway returned to journalism in Melbourne. He died of arteriosclerosis at Toorak on 5 March 1925, survived by his wife Anna Maria, née Altereith, whom he had married at Rockhampton on 8 November 1890, and by two sons and a daughter. He was buried in Brighton cemetery.

PD (Cwlth), 1907-08, 38, p2635; *Government Gazette* (Qld), 1 Aug 1896; *Sugar J and Tropical Cultivator*, 15 Aug 1901; *Brisbane Courier*, 13 Apr 1901, 6 Mar 1925; *Mackay Mercury*, 14 Apr 1901; *Daily Mercury*, 7 Mar 1925; J. A. Nilsson, History of Mackay, the sugar town 1862-1915 (B.A. Hons thesis, Univ Qld, 1963); Corporate Affairs, Registers 78 book 10 (Brisb); CP601/1, 1917-19 (AAO, Canb).   K. H. KENNEDY

CHATFIELD, FLORENCE (1867-1949), and BARRON, ELLEN (1875-1951), were nurses. Florence Chatfield was born on 1 February 1867 at Worthing, Sussex, England, daughter of William Chatfield, confectioner, and his wife Jane, née Porter. Educated in Worthing and London, she and her sister Emily migrated to Queensland as domestic servants, arriving on 3 June 1885 by the *Chyebassa*. Her widowed father brought out the rest of the family two years later.

With her sisters Florence trained in nursing at Brisbane General Hospital in 1889-92; for a short time she was personal nurse to Dr E. Sandford Jackson [q.v.], and in 1892-96 she was a charge nurse there, then became deputy matron. From 1900 to 1934 she was matron and then superintendent of the Diamantina Hospital for Chronic Diseases; her work showed a 'very broad outlook and great human sympathy'. She was also supervisor and organizer of the Queensland Government Baby Clinics from their inception in 1918, and in 1920 investigated infant welfare in the southern States. She relinquished the position in 1923 to Ellen Barron, as the Diamantina Hospital had expanded from 32 to 216 beds. She was ap-

pointed O.B.E. in 1932.

Miss Barron was born in 1875 at Abingdon, Berkshire, England, daughter of John Joseph Barron, railway stationmaster, and his wife Annie, née Cox. Migrating to Queensland with her parents in or before 1884, she trained as a nurse at the Brisbane General Hospital in 1896-99 and was a staff nurse there until 1901. Head nurse at the Maryborough General Hospital in 1902-04, she trained in obstetrics at the Women's Hospital, Rockhampton, in 1904-05, and was matron of the Lady Musgrave Hospital, Maryborough, in 1906-08 and of the Chillagoe Hospital in 1909. She returned to England in 1912-13, won the certificate of the Incorporated Society of Trained Masseuses, and became a life member of the Chartered Society of Massage and Medical Gymnastics.

Late in 1914 Miss Barron returned to Australia and on 1 May 1915 enlisted in the Australian Army Nursing Service. As a staff nurse in the 3rd Australian General Hospital, she nursed Anzac casualties on Lemnos and served in England and France. Discharged on 18 April 1917, she began work in Brisbane in 1918 under Miss Chatfield in the baby clinics. Four years later she was sent to the Karitane training school in Dunedin, New Zealand, to work under (Sir Frederic) Truby King. On her return in 1923, she became superintendent of the baby clinics and started a training course for clinic nursing staffs. She retired as superintendent in 1939.

Florence Chatfield and Ellen Barron worked tirelessly for their profession of nursing throughout their lives. Miss Chatfield presided over the founding meeting in 1904 of the Queensland Branch of the Australasian Trained Nurses' Association (now Royal Australian Nursing Federation), and worked for it in many ways for over forty years. Both women were members of its council for many years, and were joint honorary secretaries in 1922-33; Miss Chatfield then became vice-president. Both served on the federal council of the association, the Australasian Nurses' Federation. They were foundation members and trustees of the Nurses' Rest Home and Benevolent Fund, Miss Chatfield becoming president, Miss Barron secretary. They were also members of the Queensland Nurses and Masseurs Registration Board. Miss Chatfield served in 1912-21 and was an examiner for many years; from 1930 she also chaired a board providing lectures for student nurses.

Tall and distinguished-looking, the two nurses lived together for part of their retirement and were seen frequently at Brisbane theatres. Florence Chatfield died on 5

November 1949 in Nundah Private Hospital. Ellen Barron died in the War Veterans' Home at Caboolture on 8 July 1951. Both were cremated with Anglican rites.

A biographical register of Queensland women (Brisb, 1939); *PP* (Qld), 1930, 1, 645; *A 'sian Nurses' J*, Feb 1932, Oct 1951; *Brisbane Courier*, 1 Jan 1932, 28 June 1934; *Courier Mail*, 7 Nov 1949; History of the Maternal and Child Welfare Service, Queensland (Maternal and Child Welfare Division, Brisb); Aust Trained Nurses' Assn, Council minutes, 1904, 1922-45, *and* Annual reports 1922-35 (Roy Aust Nurses' Federation, Qld Branch Brisb); Health and Home Affairs correspondence (QA); Immigrant lists, IMM 120, 122 (QA).

GLENDA LAW

CHAUVEL, CHARLES EDWARD (1897-1959), film director, was born on 7 October 1897 at Warwick, Queensland, second son of native-born parents James Allan Chauvel, grazier, and his wife Susan Isabella, daughter of Henry Barnes [q.v.3]. His father, aged 53, joined the Australian Remount Unit in 1916 as a lieutenant and served with the Australian Imperial Force in Sinai and Palestine; he ended the war as a temporary major and was appointed O.B.E. in 1919. Educated at Ipswich Grammar School, Charles worked on several southern Queensland stations then studied commercial art in Sydney. He also attended drama classes and from 1920 worked as a production assistant, primarily responsible for the horses, with R. L. ('Snowy') Baker [q.v.] and other film-makers.

In April 1922 Chauvel followed Baker to the United States of America; he survived in Los Angeles by writing articles about Australia and taking small jobs in Hollywood studios. He returned late in 1923, fired with enthusiasm to produce his own films. Financed by Queensland businessmen and friends, he embarked on *The moth of Moonbi* (released January 1926) and *Greenhide* (released November). The heroine of *Greenhide* was played by Elsie May Wilcox, an actress known professionally as Elsie Sylvaney (Silveni). On 5 June 1927 Elsa (as she became known) and Charles were married in Sydney at St James's Church; thereafter she worked closely with him as a production associate.

Chauvel was self-reliant – serving as his own business manager, director, writer, publicist and distributor. His publicity was flamboyant and both of his silent films were modest commercial successes. In 1928 he went to Hollywood to seek American releases but found the market in the throes of transition to sound. He returned to Australia and worked as a cinema-manager in Melbourne before settling at Stanthorpe, Queensland.

Chauvel's first feature with sound was *In the wake of the Bounty* (released March 1933), which merged a dramatic reconstruction of the *Bounty* mutiny in 1789 with documentary footage of life on Pitcairn Island nearly 150 years later. He had a strong urge to find spectacular backgrounds for his films, even at considerable personal discomfort and risk, and in 1932, with Elsa and a cameraman, he spent three months on Pitcairn shooting material for the film.

In 1935 Chauvel won the Commonwealth government's film competition with *Heritage*, a panoramic view of Australian history. Next year he made a jungle adventure, *Uncivilised*, then visited Hollywood. In July 1937, inspired by the distinguished war records in Palestine of his father, his uncle General Sir Harry Chauvel and his first cousin (Sir) Michael Bruxner [qq.v.], he began preparations for *Forty thousand horsemen*, a tribute to the Australian Light Horse in the campaigns of World War I. Shot in and around Sydney, with sand-dunes at Cronulla representing the Palestinian desert, the film was released in Sydney on 26 December 1940 and was an immediate success with both public and critics. It served as an important boost to Australian morale throughout World War II, and was screened widely overseas, helping to form popular American and British attitudes to the Australian 'digger'.

After another war feature, *The rats of Tobruk* (1944), and several short propaganda films for the Department of Information, Chauvel directed *Sons of Matthew* (1949), a saga of pioneering life in the rugged mountain forests of south-eastern Queensland, filmed on remote locations under difficult physical conditions. The result was considered by many to be his finest work. His final feature, *Jedda* (1955), was Australia's first in colour. It was shot largely in central and northern Australia and told the story of a young Aboriginal torn between her own people and her white foster-parents. He then made a series of thirteen half-hour films entitled *Walkabout* for British Broadcasting Corporation television. The series taxed Chauvel's energy, and he died of coronary vascular disease at his home at Castlecrag, Sydney, on 11 November 1959 and was buried in the Anglican section of Northern Suburbs cemetery. He was survived by his wife and daughter.

Chauvel was the only major director to persevere with production after World War II in the face of increased foreign domination of the Australian film trade. Intense and tireless, he often made severe demands on his employees and took extravagant physical and financial measures to perfect his work. Like many of his contemporaries, he was obsessed by the romance of the movies as exemplified by Hollywood; yet he expressed in most of his films, with varying clarity and strength, a heroic vision of Australia as a grand and exotic land, peopled by spirited sons of the soil.

M. Dunn, *How they made Sons of Matthew* (Syd, 1949); E. Chauvel, *My life with Charles Chauvel* (Syd, 1973); *Picture Show*, 1 Apr 1922; *Everyone's*, 21 July, 15 Sept 1926, 23 Mar 1927; *Film Weekly*, 18 Aug, 12 Dec 1935, 1 Oct 1936, 26 Dec 1940, 2 Jan 1941, 21 Dec 1944, 4 Aug, 15, 22 Dec 1949, 13 Jan, 14 Apr, 12 May 1955; *Sydney Mail*, 24 Mar 1926, 12 Feb 1936; *SMH*, 21 Mar 1927, 20 Mar 1933, 14 Apr 1935, 20, 25, 30 Dec 1940, 17 June, 11 Dec 1944; *Canb Times*, 12 Dec 1970; C. E. Chauvel papers (ML); Chauvel scrap-books and material, *and* films (National Film Archives, NL); Dept of Information, SP109/1 item 78/7/14 (AAO, Canb).   A. F. PIKE

CHAUVEL, SIR HENRY GEORGE (1865-1945), soldier, was born on 16 April 1865 at Tabulam, New South Wales, second son of Charles Henry Edward Chauvel, grazier and cattle-breeder, and his wife Fanny Ada Mary, née James. Chauvel was educated at Sydney Grammar School but had a final year at Toowoomba Grammar before taking his place on his father's cattle-station on the Clarence River. He learned to manage a property, and became a most accomplished horseman.

His ambition was to follow family tradition and join the British Army, there being little scope in the diminutive colonial forces, but his father's losses from drought made Sandhurst and the cavalry impossible. In 1885, when the volunteer movement was reviving, C. H. E. Chauvel raised the Upper Clarence Light Horse in which his son was commissioned next year. In 1888 the family moved to the Darling Downs in Queensland. Harry Chauvel was compelled to resign from the New South Wales forces, but he was commissioned in the Queensland Mounted Infantry in 1890. He had been managing Canning Downs South for three years when in 1896 he obtained an appointment in the Queensland Permanent Military Forces as a captain and adjutant of the Moreton Regiment. He went to England with the Queensland Jubilee Contingent in 1897, staying on for a year for courses and attachments to regular infantry.

Chauvel served with distinction in the South African War as a major in the 1st Queensland Mounted Infantry, taking part in the relief of Kimberley, the advance to Pretoria and the battle of Diamond Hill. At the crossing of the Vet River he personally captured a troublesome machine-gun. For a time he led a mixed force, known as Chauvel's Mounted Infantry, in operations in eastern Transvaal. Returning to Australia in 1901 he took command of the 7th Australian Commonwealth Horse as lieutenant-colonel, but the war ended before he reached Durban. For his services in South Africa, Chauvel was appointed C.M.G. and mentioned in dispatches; he was also given the brevet of lieut-colonel.

In the next decade Chauvel established a reputation as a trainer, especially of officers; many who attended his staff rides were to distinguish themselves in World War I. Apart from a short period in South Australia reorganizing the mounted troops, he remained in Queensland in staff appointments until 1911. He was one of the group, including (Sir) William Bridges and (Sir) Brudenell White [qq.v.], which was close to Major General Sir Edward Hutton [q.v.], commander and organizer of the Australian Army in 1901-04. Chauvel was a strong supporter of the existing militia, and the organization from 1910 of the compulsory system around its officers and non-commissioned officers owed much to his advocacy. On 16 June 1906, at All Saints Anglican Church, Brisbane, he had married Sibyl Campbell Keith Jopp; they had two sons and two daughters.

In 1911 Chauvel became adjutant general and second member of the Military Board. He was at the centre of affairs during the critical period when the compulsory system was being set up and the Royal Military College was being developed at Duntroon. This work was only partly completed when, in 1914, he was sent to London to be Australian representative on the Imperial General Staff. By the time he and his family reached England, Europe was at war and Australia was preparing an expeditionary force. Bridges chose Chauvel to command the 1st Light Horse Brigade; he was the only Australian regular, other than Bridges himself, to obtain a senior command in the original Australian Imperial Force. He served usefully at the War Office until he went to Egypt in December. His visits to Salisbury Plain had convinced him that the camps would not be ready for the A.I.F.; his urgent representations to Sir George Reid [q.v.], high commissioner in London, influenced the historic decision to disembark the force in Egypt.

When the Australian and New Zealand Army Corps assaulted the Gallipoli Peninsula north of Gaba Tepe on 25 April 1915, the three light horse brigades remained in Egypt. They were quickly called for as reinforcements for the infantry, but Chauvel and the other brigadiers stubbornly insisted that their brigades go as complete units, although dismounted. Chauvel landed on 12 May, taking command of the vital sector around Pope's, Quinn's and Courtney's posts. He held these positions against all Turkish attacks until he was sent to a quiet sector in September. During that time, he became known for his coolness and courage especially in the critical fight of 29 May. Like Lieut-General (Baron) Birdwood [q.v.], the corps commander, he spent much of his time walking his trenches and closely observing the state of his troops and their positions.

After two short periods in command of the New Zealand and Australian Division, Chauvel took command of the 1st Division on 6 November. He led it through the evacuation in December and the subsequent expansion of the A.I.F. in Egypt. In December he was promoted major general and in January 1916 was gazetted C.B. Although Birdwood offered him command of one of the infantry divisions soon to go to France, Chauvel elected to remain with the light horse as commander of the new Australian and New Zealand Mounted Division. He also took command of all Australian forces in Egypt including the 1st Squadron, Australian Flying Corps; however, for virtually all matters other than operations, he was responsible to Birdwood in France during the rest of the war.

The new division was still settling down when, on 23 April, the Turks raided the British outposts covering the northern approach to the Suez Canal. Chauvel immediately moved across the canal to restore the situation, beginning an advance which was to continue for two and a half years until the enemy was driven from Aleppo on the northern borders of Syria. His division was the only desert-worthy force in Sinai, so that when the second Turkish thrust for the canal was defeated at Romani on 4-5 August 1916, Anzac Mounted became the spearhead of Eastern Force in the advance across the desert into Palestine. At Romani, with only two of his four brigades under command, Chauvel outfought the Turks in blazing heat. He pursued them, but his division was too light a force to complete their destruction. Under Lieut-General Sir Philip Chetwode, commanding the newly created Desert Column, he destroyed Turkish garrisons at Rafa (December 1916) and Magdhaba (January 1917), thus clearing the way for an assault on the main Turkish positions around Gaza and Beersheba. After Magdhaba he was appointed K.C.M.G.

In the first battle of Gaza on 26-27 March 1917, Sir Harry Chauvel took advantage of the fog to place his division across the Turkish communications. He had forced his way into Gaza when he and the victorious British infantry were ordered to withdraw owing to the approach of fresh Turkish forces. In these operations, the newly formed Imperial Mounted Division was placed under his command. Immediately after the unsuccessful second battle of Gaza, 17-19 April 1917, Chetwode was given command of Eastern Force and Chauvel succeeded to the command of the Desert Column, thus becoming the first Australian to lead a corps. When General Sir Edmund Allenby became commander-in-chief in June 1917, he reorganized the army into three corps, giving Chauvel the Desert Mounted Corps of three divisions. In August he became the first Australian to attain the rank of lieutgeneral.

In Allenby's offensive from 31 October, Chauvel attacked Beersheba from the east, seizing the wells intact by a surprise charge at sunset. The myth that he launched the 4th Light Horse Brigade as a last desperate throw after a brusque order from Allenby does not sustain examination; Allenby's signal, which arose from misunderstanding an earlier message from Chauvel, was sent after the light horse had entered the town. However, when Gaza was taken and the Turkish centre rolled up, Chauvel was in no position to administer the *coup de grâce* as four of his nine brigades had been detached and the remainder were almost exhausted. Nevertheless the Desert Mounted Corps, supported by the 60th Division, drove the Turks up the Plain of Philistia beyond Jaffa and the Nahr el Auja, and Jerusalem was entered by the infantry early in December. For his part in these successes, Chauvel was appointed K.C.B.

In the reorganization in the spring of 1918, a fourth division was added to Chauvel's corps, which now consisted of the Anzac and Australian Mounted Divisions and the 4th and 5th Cavalry Divisions. Allenby attacked twice across the Jordan during this period; the first operation was a powerful raid but the second, under Chauvel, was designed to seize ground with a view to advancing on the vital Turkish rail junction of Deraa. Doubting the feasibility of this plan with the limited forces and logistic support available, he made objections and obtained most of the 60th Division for the assault. Despite the rapid capture of Es Salt on 30 April, the battle swung against him. The Turks repeatedly repulsed the attacks of the 60th Division and drove in his left flank, threatening to cut off his brigades around Es Salt. Moreover, the promised aid from the Arabs did not materialize. As the Turks were being strongly reinforced, on 3 May he decided to withdraw, with Allenby's gruff approval.

This operation was in no sense a raid and deserves the title of second battle of the

Jordan given it by the enemy commander-in-chief, General Liman von Sanders. If Chauvel failed to seize and hold all his objectives, the blow had important psychological results in that it convinced the enemy that the next British offensive would be launched in the same area and by the same troops. When it came on 19 September, the offensive began on the Mediterranean flank, with his corps poised to dash forward as soon as the infantry had cut a path through the Turkish defences. The secret movement of three cavalry divisions and their impedimenta from the Jordan Valley to the orchards near modern Tel Aviv was a triumph for Chauvel and his staff. Within twenty-four hours, by hard riding, his corps was positioned thirty to forty miles behind the disorganized Turkish armies, astride their communications and moving to seize the few crossings of the Jordan. The battle of Megiddo was one of the most completely successful operations of the war; only the Turkish army beyond the Jordan escaped the catastrophe and it was harried across the desert by the Anzac Mounted Division and the Arabs. Giving the Turks no time to recover, Chauvel destroyed their forces around Haifa and Lake Tiberias and made plans for the pursuit to Damascus; then having forced the passage of the Jordan north of Lake Tiberias on 28 September, he drove the enemy across the Golan Heights and rode for Damascus with two divisions while his third entered Deraa and drove the Turks northwards with Arab help. He entered Damascus on 1 October; after a short pause he was ordered to march on Aleppo, 200 miles (320 km) to the north.

Aleppo fell to an Arab force on 25 October. There had been little fighting during the advance; this was fortunate, for Chauvel's tired divisions were melting away, ravaged by malaria and typhus. Six days later the war in the Near East came to an end. In the five weeks since the opening of the offensive, the divisions of the Desert Mounted Corps had advanced from 300 to 500 miles (480 to 800 km), taking over 78 000 prisoners and great quantities of booty. Their battle casualties were only about 650. Many reasons may be adduced for this overwhelming success but not the least was Chauvel's planning of his successive thrusts, his co-ordination of his widely spread forces, and the special care that he gave to the logistical basis of all his operations. Although the headquarters of his polyglot corps was British, he had appointed to key administrative positions Australian officers of outstanding capacity, such as Colonel R. M. Downes and Lieut-Colonel W. Stansfield [qq.v.]. In 1919 he was appointed G.C.M.G.; he was also awarded the French Croix de Guerre, the Order of the Nile (twice) and was mentioned in dispatches ten times.

Returning to Australia in September 1919, Chauvel was appointed inspector general and made a member of the Council of Defence. He was chairman of the senior officers' committee which, in February 1920, advised the government on the strength, organization and equipment of the post-war army. But disarmament and economy were in the air and the government, although at first willing to approve the sizeable force recommended, opted for a token force of 38 000 with six days of camp training a year. Further economies followed.

In these straitened circumstances Chauvel succeeded White as chief of the general staff in June 1923. At the government's request he continued to act as inspector general. Chauvel's reports of 1921-30 are not only a prime source of Australian military history but also his own testament. In plain, unambiguous terms he warned in report after report of the deterioration in Australia's strategic position owing to the relative decline of British sea power; he cast doubt on the efficacy of Singapore as the first line of defence and he argued that the army must be strong enough to hold out until help arrived. He also made it clear that the existing skeleton force of partly trained men was unfit to fight.

In 1924 Chauvel persuaded the government to increase the duration of annual camps from six to eight days and to extend the period of service for trainees from two to three years, but he was unable to obtain funds to rearm the coast defences or even to maintain the army's vehicles and equipment. Nevertheless, he pressed for better pay and conditions for the exiguous permanent force on which the army depended. In particular, Chauvel sought to keep a close relationship with the British Army, by sending officers to the staff colleges and to the Imperial Defence College and on exchange duty in various British headquarters. Insistence on this policy prepared the more senior officers of the Australian Staff Corps for their outstanding part in World War II.

It was not until 1925-29 that the army's first few motor vehicles and tanks began to arrive from England. Chauvel was well aware that this was only a gesture; the army remained what it was, a force of 1918 vintage in which the officer corps struggled to keep up with British developments. Nevertheless, the foundations were laid, as in army-air force co-operation exercises beginning in 1925, Chauvel's own exercise for senior officers the same year, and the establishment in 1926 of the Defence Committee of which he was chairman until 1930.

In his role as inspector general, Chauvel frequently travelled to every State to inspect brigades in camp and watch their training. He preferred this to the paperwork and committees which beset him as chief of the general staff. Like all true commanders, he drew strength and refreshment from contact with troops, and his long term as inspector general gave him an unrivalled knowledge of the service. When J. H. Scullin [q.v.] became prime minister in October 1929, one of his first acts was to suspend compulsory training. Chauvel had not been consulted but was required to provide a plan for a smaller, voluntary force. He at once put his authority and influence behind the organization of the new militia which, in spite of the economic crisis, enlisted 25 000 volunteers and 5000 senior cadets in less than six months.

In November 1929 Chauvel was promoted general, the first Australian to attain this rank. His retirement next April was almost a national occasion; large public dinners were held in his honour in Melbourne and Sydney. But the only official recognition of his service was a ministerial direction for the provision of an army horse for his daily ride in the Melbourne Domain, a privilege he valued immensely.

Retirement was for Chauvel a fruitful experience; directorships in three important companies gave him new interests and he now had time for ex-servicemen's causes. He was for many years chairman of the trustees of the Australian and Victorian war memorials, a senior patron of Melbourne Legacy, and active in the work of the Australian Red Cross and the Young Men's Christian Association. On the eve of Anzac Day 1935, one newspaper wrote that Chauvel 'has come by his quiet work in the interests of returned men to be regarded as their peace time leader'. Such work was but one manifestation of the religious faith on which his life had been built and which was recognized by his Church when he was made a lay canon of St Paul's Cathedral, Melbourne, in 1930.

In 1937 Chauvel led the Australian Services Contingent at the coronation of King George VI. He represented the Returned Sailors' and Soldiers' Imperial League of Australia on the committee which drew up plans for reserve and garrison forces early in 1939. When the Volunteer Defence Corps was set up in June 1940, Chauvel became its inspector-in-chief. At 75 he was in uniform again and on the move around the country. When White, who had been recalled to be chief of the general staff, was killed in 1940, it was to Chauvel that the prime minister, (Sir) Robert Menzies, turned for advice on a successor. In 1944 his health began to fail and he died in Melbourne on 4 March 1945,

survived by his wife and children. He was cremated after a state funeral.

As a soldier, Chauvel's courage and calmness were matched by his humanity which was extended to the enemy as well as his own men. He was always well forward in battle; in the field he lived simply, sleeping in his greatcoat on the sand when his force was on the move. Loyalty was one of his chief characteristics: he stood by Birdwood when Allenby tried to interfere with the A.I.F. command, and by the New Zealanders when there was an attempt to make Anzac Mounted wholly Australian. He has been criticized for lack of resolution at Rafa and Magdhaba but this was probably an unwillingness to accept more casualties for a prize he did not value; there was no question of his resolution at Quinn's Post, or Romani or Beersheba. Besides, he knew that if Anzac Mounted were to suffer a disaster, the Desert Column would be crippled.

Chauvel seemed shy and reserved, in Birdwood's phrase 'very retiring', so that some found him aloof. In reality he was a warm, uncomplicated man, with a keen sense of humour. He rarely sent written orders of the day but he made a point of visiting and addressing troops who had done well or had suffered heavy casualties. Because he understood the British and knew how dependent the small Australian and New Zealand forces were, his policy was to co-operate rather than confront. Because Chauvel was relatively junior and responsible to Birdwood in France, tact and diplomacy were required. His successes in the field and his obvious integrity strengthened his position, but some senior officers seem to have resented a mere 'colonial' having the best command in the Egyptian Expeditionary Force.

His long period of office at the head of the army showed Chauvel at his best. In an adverse political and economic environment he knew that, as he could neither train nor equip the army for war, he must ensure the survival and efficiency of the officer corps. Nor could governments pretend they had not been warned. Lieut-General Sir Sydney Rowell summed up: 'Chauvel was the sheet anchor of the Army in this period ... It says a great deal for the esteem in which he was held and for his wisdom and integrity that he held the Army together at a time when it was always on the rundown and was, in 1929-31, approaching the critical point where it would have collapsed completely, had it not been for Chauvel's work and influence'.

Portraits are in the Australian War Memorial, the Naval and Military Club, Melbourne, and the Imperial War Museum, London. A fine portrait by G. W. Lambert [q.v.] is in the possession of the family. There is a bronze tablet to Chauvel's memory in St Paul's Cathedral, Melbourne, his sword is in Christ Church, South Yarra, and there is a memorial window in the chapel of R.M.C., Duntroon. His two sons were graduates of R.M.C. and served with the Indian Army; his daughter Elyne Mitchell became a well-known writer.

A. J. Hill, *Chauvel of the Light Horse* (Melb, 1978), and for bibliog.   A. J. HILL

CHECCHI, ETTORE (1853-1946), engineer, was born on 11 July 1853 at Pisa, Italy, twelfth child of Leopoldo Checchi, police officer and later teacher, and his wife Carlotta, née Botti. Ettore was 5 when his father died. After obtaining a degree in civil engineering in Florence he decided to migrate with his friends C. Catani and P. Baracchi [qq.v.]; after going to Wellington, New Zealand, they arrived in Melbourne on 27 September 1876 in the *Alhambra*.

On 31 October Checchi was appointed a draftsman in the Department of Lands and Survey. On 14 January 1882 he became engineering draughtsman in the Public Works Department, working on harbours, jetties and coast works; by 1887 he was assistant engineer at a salary of £265. Next year he was transferred to the Department of Water Supply to supervise water-trusts and minor works. By 1889 he was in charge of river-gaugings and measurements of water, and also supervised water-boring operations.

Checchi's early hydrographic work attracted world-wide attention for his organization of systematic river-gaugings throughout Victoria under the direction of Stuart Murray [q.v.5], and it laid the foundation of a scientific water-conservation policy in Victoria. During an arduous six years from 1894 as engineer-in-charge of river-gaugings, irrigation-trusts and the extensive Coliban and Geelong water-supply systems, he took only one day's leave a year. In 1906 he was transferred to the newly constituted State Rivers and Water Supply Commission.

Checchi's greatest contribution to Australian water resources development was the supply of most of the technical data required in connexion with harnessing the River Murray. This data formed the basis for the recommendations in the report of the Interstate Conference of Engineers in July 1913, which were embodied in the River Murray agreement of 1915 between the three neighbouring States and the Commonwealth. Checchi was highly qualified to advise on the contentious matter of the construction of reservoirs and weirs on the Murray and the distribution of its waters between Victoria, New South Wales and South Australia. As chief engineering officer, he was responsible for hydrographic examinations and investigations for storage sites along the Upper Murray, including the site of the future Hume Reservoir. He was also closely associated with investigations for many other major water-conservation projects, including the first Eildon Dam.

At his own request, Checchi retired in 1926, to enjoy his hobby of making guitars. On 13 November 1889 he had married Rebecca Rodgers of Attunga, New South Wales; they had a daughter and three sons, two of whom became doctors. Checchi was a large and powerful man whose great physical strength allowed him, with very few assistants, to establish gauging-stations on most Victorian rivers and to carry out flow measurements under difficult conditions. For a pastime he built and successfully raced model yachts on the Albert Park Lake. He was highly respected as a sound designing engineer, a fine mathematician, and as 'a gentleman in the continental sense of the word at all times'. Survived by his children, he died on 19 July 1946 at his home in Hampton, and was cremated.

J. N. Churchyard, 'Pioneers of Victorian irrigation . . . Ettore Checchi', *Aqua*, Mar 1957; information from Dr C. Checchi, Willaura, Vic, and Mr L. Checchi, Rome.   RONALD EAST

CHEEL, EDWIN (1872-1951), botanist, was born on 14 January 1872 at Chartham Hatch near Canterbury, Kent, England, son of Reuben Cheel and his wife Elizabeth, née Manual. Educated at Newcastle upon Tyne and in Kent, he migrated as a farm-labourer to Mackay, Queensland, on the *Jelunga* in May 1892 and worked in the cane-fields, before moving to Sydney.

Cheel found work as a carpenter and on 14 April 1897 married Ada Spencer. In December he was employed as a gardener at Centennial Park. Encouraged by J. H. Maiden [q.v.], Cheel showed an unusual aptitude for botanical studies and developed a particular interest in cryptogams. In 1901 he was given 'honorary charge' of lichens in the National Herbarium, Sydney, and next year transferred to the outdoor staff of the Botanic Gardens. He took unpaid leave to study lichen herbaria in England in 1905. Returning to Sydney, he had the fungi section added to his care and was appointed botanical assistant in 1908, becoming principal botanical assistant, in charge of the herbarium, on the death of Ernst Betche [q.v.3] in 1913. His appointment in 1924 as curator inaugurated a period of administrative separation between herbarium and Botanic Gardens. He was botanist and curator from 1933 until 1936 when he retired.

Cheel's botanical interests extended beyond cryptogams to most groups of plants. He made a special study of the Myrtaceae, many species of which he cultivated and observed at his home at Ashfield and at Hill Top, south of Picton. He published numerous papers, frequently exhibited botanical specimens and was an enthusiastic leader of field excursions. Recognized as an authoritative, self-trained naturalist, he was praised for his 'unfailing courtesy', 'generous help and unstinted devotion' over many years.

Cheel was president of the local Naturalists' (1911-12 and 1923-24) and Linnean (1930) societies, also of the Horticultural Association (1929-31) and of the Royal Society of New South Wales (1931) whose bronze medal he received in 1943 for 'his contributions in the field of botanical research, and to the advancement of science in general'. President of the botanical section of the Australian and New Zealand Association for the Advancement of Science in 1937, he was also a trustee of the National Park from 1933 and that year represented the Australian National Research Council at the fifth Pacific Science Congress in Canada. A warm supporter of the friendly society movement from the age of 12, he was grand master of the Manchester Unity Independent Order of Oddfellows in New South Wales in 1926.

Survived by his wife and daughter, Cheel died at Ashfield on 19 September 1951 and was cremated with Anglican rites. His extensive collection of New South Wales botanical specimens is housed in the National Herbarium, Sydney.

Botanic Gardens . . . report of the director, *V&P* (LA NSW), 1898-1924; *Aust Naturalist*, 3 (1915), pt 8; *A'sian Herbarium News*, June 1947; Linnean Soc NSW, *Procs*, 86 (1952); Roy Soc NSW, *Procs*, 77 (1952); *Daily Telegraph* (Syd), 22 Oct 1925; *SMH*, 21 Dec 1929; Hunt Inst biogs (Basser Lib, Canb).

ANN G. SMITH

CHEESEMAN, WILLIAM JOSEPH ROBERT (1894-1938), soldier and businessman, was born on 12 January 1894 at Wickham, New South Wales, son of Joseph Ernest Cheeseman, cab driver, and his wife Annie Amelia, née Wells, both native-born. Educated at Islington Public School and Wickham Superior Public School, he became a salesman with David Cohen & Co.,

merchants, of Newcastle. At 18 he joined the militia, was commissioned in the 16th Infantry Battalion in February 1913 and on the outbreak of World War I became signals officer at Newcastle Defended Port. He married Marguerite Ruperta Tracy Scott on 30 January 1915 at St Clement's Anglican Church, Marrickville.

On 18 October 1915 Cheeseman joined the Australian Imperial Force as a lieutenant, embarked for Egypt in November with the 30th Battalion, and was promoted captain in February 1916. He reached France in June and commanded his company at Fromelles and on the Somme where he took part in the battalion's raid at Fleurbaix. He was mentioned in dispatches in January 1917. In the advance on Bapaume on 17 March he organized a bombing and Stokes-mortar attack which captured a section of German trench and then, when his company was held up by machine-gun fire, dislodged the enemy by a flanking movement; six days later at Beaumetz, he launched a successful counter-attack when the outpost line he was commanding was surprised and outflanked by a strong enemy force: his gallantry earned him the Military Cross, and the Légion d'honneur, and he was promoted major in April.

Cheeseman took part in the battle of Polygon Wood in September and, when the commanding officer of the 53rd Battalion was killed, was promoted lieut-colonel; aged only 23, he was one of the youngest battalion commanders in the A.I.F. He was gassed at Villers-Bretonneux in April 1918 but returned to his unit and saw further action at Morlancourt, Amiens, Péronne and Bellicourt. At Bellicourt, on 1 October, his unit was ordered to move up for a dawn attack; but the men lost their way and as dawn broke they came under heavy machine-gun fire. Cheeseman rallied them into columns and led them, under fire, to the start-line; later in the attack he made a dangerous reconnaissance under heavy shelling. These actions won him the Distinguished Service Order, and he was mentioned in dispatches twice in 1918-19.

Cheeseman returned to Australia in June 1919 and in July next year was promoted lieut-colonel in the Australian Military Forces; he commanded the 2nd Battalion, 2nd Infantry Regiment, until July 1921 when he went into business as a storekeeper. He owned stores at Comboyne and Taree, then in the early 1930s became manager of a Woolworths branch in Sydney; in 1936 he moved to Adelaide as general manager for Woolworths Ltd in South Australia. Survived by his wife and two daughters, Cheeseman died on 23 April 1938 after an operation for appendicitis. He was cremated in Adelaide and his ashes were buried in Sandgate cemetery, Newcastle.

Noted for his giant physique and genial disposition, Cheeseman was a popular A.I.F. leader who had the confidence of his superiors despite his youth. After the war he was president of the 53rd Battalion Association for many years.

J. J. Kennedy, *The Whale Oil Guards: 53rd Battalion* (Dublin, 1919); H. Sloan (ed), *The purple and gold ... 30th Battalion, AIF* (Syd, 1938); *London Gazette*, 2 Jan, 18 June, 14 July 1917, 28 May 1918, 8 Mar, 11 July 1919; *Reveille* (Syd), July 1938; *SMH*, 19 June, 17 July, 22 Nov 1917, 11 Mar, 21 July 1919.   C. D. COULTHARD-CLARK

CHELMSFORD, 3RD BARON (1868-1933), governor, was born on 12 August 1868 at Belgrave, London, and baptized Frederick John Napier, eldest son of Frederic Augustus Thesiger, army officer and later Baron Chelmsford, and his wife Adria Fanny, née Heath. After education at Winchester and at Magdalen College, Oxford, he graduated B.A. (first-class honours in law) in 1891 (M.A., 1894), was a fellow of All Souls College in 1892-99 and was called to the Bar of the Inner Temple in 1893. A keen cricketer, he had captained the Oxford XI and played occasionally for Middlesex. On 27 July 1894 he married Frances Charlotte Guest, daughter of Lord Wimborne. He sat on the London School Board in 1904-05, resigning upon succeeding to the barony. In July 1905 he accepted the surprise appointment as governor of Queensland.

Chelmsford arrived in Brisbane and was sworn in on 20 November. His term was dominated by conflict between the Upper and Lower Houses and the emergence of three evenly divided parties in the Legislative Assembly. In November 1907 he refused the premier William Kidston's [q.v.] request to appoint sufficient legislative councillors to ensure the passage of the wages boards bill. Kidston resigned and (Sir) Robert Philp [q.v.] formed a ministry which was promptly defeated in the assembly. Chelmsford then blundered by granting Philp a dissolution, though the parliament was only six months old. Supply was denied, and the governor was sharply criticized in the assembly. Kidston was returned to office in the February 1908 election. Though the Colonial Office considered Chelmsford had erred, his acceptance of the financial burden of an Australian governorship, his intellectual ability and attention to the social duties of the office ensured that he retained the British government's confidence.

In May 1909 Chelmsford left Brisbane to become governor of New South Wales. His term in Sydney was distinguished by cordial relations with the State's first Labor government under J. S. T. McGowen [q.v.]; D. R. Hall [q.v.] later commented that 'without attempting to usurp the functions of his advisers, the Governor was their guide philosopher, and friend'. In October 1912, when his intention to resign for the sake of his sons' education was announced, McGowen praised him as 'more than a Governor to me. He has been a friend with his advice'. Ada Holman [q.v.] described him as 'pale, slim, handsome, cultivated'. He played the cello capably and had encouraged chamber music at Government House in Brisbane and Sydney. From 21 December 1909 to 27 January 1910 he had acted as governor-general when Lord Dudley [q.v.] was on leave. He returned to England in March 1913.

Chelmsford was a captain in the 4th Dorset Territorials. Upon the outbreak of war in 1914 he joined his regiment and went with it to India. In January 1916 he was unexpectedly appointed viceroy of India. Though 'more nearly an agent, and less of a policy maker than any viceroy in the last period of British rule', he helped introduce the Montagu-Chelmsford reforms which set India on the path to responsible government. He was criticized for equivocating over an inquiry into General Dyer's actions at Amritsar in April 1919 and was also faced with Gandhi's first non-co-operation campaign. Chelmsford resigned in 1921, returned to England and was raised to the rank of viscount.

Chelmsford was chairman of the Miners' Welfare Committee under the Mining Industry Act of 1920 and of the royal commission on mining subsidence in 1923-24. From January to November 1924 he was first lord of the Admiralty in Ramsay MacDonald's government, explaining that, detached from politics, he was prepared 'to help carry on the King's Government on a disclosed programme'. The last of Chelmsford's series of surprising appointments was the post of agent general in London for New South Wales, which he accepted in June 1926. Labor premier J. T. Lang [q.v.] explained to his caucus that 'it was absolutely necessary that the State should be represented by a gentleman who would be in close touch with the London financial market'. The appointment was not renewed when (Sir) Thomas Bavin [q.v.] came to office in October 1927.

Again elected a fellow of All Souls in 1929, Chelmsford became warden in 1932. He died of coronary vascular disease on 1 April 1933, survived by his younger son and four daughters. His eldest son had been killed in action in 1917.

A. A. Holman, *Memoirs of a premier's wife* (Syd, 1948); V. A. Smith, *The Oxford history of India* 3rd edn, P. Spear ed (Oxford, 1967); R. J. Moore, *The crisis of Indian unity 1917-1940* (Oxford, 1974); D. J. Murphy and R. B. Joyce (eds), *Queensland political portraits 1859-1952* (Brisb, 1978); *Qld Government Mining J*, 15 Feb 1927; *DNB*, 1931-40; *Brisbane Courier*, 26 July 1905; *SMH*, 29 Mar 1909, 28 Oct 1912, 24 Jan 1924, 15, 16 June 1926, 11 Nov 1927, 3 Apr, 29 May 1933; *The Times*, 3 Apr 1933; CO 418/90/p102-03; GOV/68 (QA).

CHRIS CUNNEEN

CHENEY, SYDNEY ALBERT (1883-1968), car-salesman, was born on 22 March 1883 at Smithfield, South Australia, fifth son of Samuel Cheney, labourer, and his wife Mary Ann, née Goodger. He left the local state school at 12, became a farm-hand and then worked in a fruit-shop in Adelaide. He joined a Baptist young men's Bible class, of which he was secretary for eight years, studied fitting, turning and drawing at the South Australian School of Mines and Industries and took lessons in accountancy and commercial law. When 20 he put an advertisement in a newspaper, offering his services free to an employer for three months. The coachbuilders, Duncan & Fraser, engaged him to sell Oldsmobile cars at £2 a week and commission; he became the State's first car-salesman. He switched to selling Argyll cars and, for publicity, sensationally drove to the top of the Mount Gambier crater; in 1905 he took part in a Melbourne-Sydney reliability trial. Aided by his skill in conjuring, card tricks and recounting yarns, he sold many cars to farmers on Yorke Peninsula. On 4 May 1907 at the Baptist church, Mount Barker, he married Marjorie Olive Fidler.

After selling Fords by the hundred, Cheney resigned from Duncan & Fraser in 1914 and went to the United States of America to seek a Dodge agency. He won it by pertinacity, floated the Cheney Motor Co. Ltd in 1915, had 130 employees next year, and made three more trips to the U.S.A. in the next three years. In 1917 the Federal government imposed a wartime ban on imported completed cars but allowed unrestricted entry of chassis. Alert to the opportunity of developing a new Australian industry, Cheney approached Holden & Frost, saddlers, and enthused H. J. and (Sir) E. W. Holden [qq.v.] who agreed to build Dodge bodies and formed a new company. The results, in the long term, were to be momentous. Early profits were so great that Cheney voluntarily abandoned the part of the original agreement whereby his share was 1 per cent of turnover.

In 1920 Cheney decided to take up a Chevrolet agency, left his Adelaide company and founded S. A. Cheney Pty Ltd in Melbourne; he soon climbed Mount Buffalo in thirty-seven minutes in top gear to demonstrate what a Chevrolet could do. In 1922 in South Melbourne he set up the first assembly line in the Australian motor industry. However, when General Motors themselves opened assembly works in 1926, Cheney switched to selling Austin and Morris cars, launched an advertising campaign to 'Buy British and be proud of it!', and persuaded William Morris (Lord Nuffield) to visit Australia to see why his cars were unsuited to local conditions.

Early in the Depression, after successful efforts to place his employees elsewhere, Cheney closed down his business in good order, and had a years holiday. He then began selling used cars and in 1932 took an agency for Vauxhall cars and Bedford trucks, which he continued until the late 1950s when he finally took a Holden agency. He had also operated Sanderson & Cheney Pty Ltd as a large service-station enterprise. During World War II he was active, with governmental support, in promoting gas-producers and charcoal production. In Adelaide in 1965 he published his autobiography *From horse to horsepower*.

Predeceased by his wife, Cheney died on 22 April 1968 at Toorak and was cremated. He was survived by two sons, and a daughter who for many years was Australian golf champion. His estate was sworn for probate at $135 477.

C. Forster, *Industrial development in Australia 1920-1930* (Canb, 1964); L. J. Hartnett, *Big wheels and little wheels* (Melb, 1964); *Age*, 23 Apr 1968.

L. J. HARTNETT

CHERMSIDE, SIR HERBERT CHARLES (1850-1929), soldier and governor, was born on 31 July 1850 at Wilton, Wiltshire, England, son of Rev. Richard Seymour Conway Chermside and his wife Emily, née Dawson. Educated at Eton and the Royal Military Academy, Woolwich, Chermside graduated top of his year and was commissioned in the Royal Engineers in 1870.

After service on an Arctic expedition of 1873, Chermside was appointed military attaché in Turkey, then military vice-consul in Anatolia in 1876-83. He served with the Egyptian army in the Sudan and as governor of the Red Sea Littoral (1884-86), was consul in Kurdistan, then returned as military attaché to Constantinople in 1889-96, and was British military commissioner and commander in Crete in 1897-99. He served in the South African war as a brigade and later a divisional commander. After briefly commanding The Curragh, Ireland, he was appointed governor of Queensland in 1901. He had been promoted captain and major in 1882, colonel in 1887 and major general in 1898, and appointed C.M.G. in 1880, C.B. in 1886, K.C.M.G. in 1897 and G.C.M.G. in 1899.

Arriving in Brisbane on 24 March 1902, in the midst of a prolonged drought and an economic depression, Chermside promptly offered to forego 15 per cent of his salary during retrenchment. Lady Tennyson described him as 'a very short plain little general with a biggish moustache'. But his readiness to share sacrifice, his approachable personality, wide range of interests, clear and forthright public speeches and his willingness to learn by travel soon made him popular. In his dispatches he was critical of the lack of water conservation, the high cost of land, absentee landholders, excessive overseas borrowing and the poor map coverage of Queensland. He noticed particularly the inefficiencies of the railway network which involved an enormous public debt for a large mileage of lines, 'many being in the wrong places'.

Despite the popularity of his salary remission in 1902, Chermside became increasingly disturbed at what he felt was public derogation of the office of State governor. When in June 1904 the Legislative Assembly debated a private member's bill to reduce the salary of the next governor, he decided to resign, but delayed during a political crisis in June and July. He refused (Sir Arthur) Morgan's [q.v.] request for a dissolution in late June, and after (Sir Robert) Philp [q.v.] declined his commission and Arthur Rutledge [q.v.] failed to form a government, Chermside had no option but to grant Morgan a dissolution on 8 July. He withheld announcement of his resignation until he had opened the new parliament and then left Brisbane on 8 October on pre-retirement leave. There were many expressions of regret at his early resignation for, despite his short period of service, he had made every effort to fulfil the office to the very best of his ability and had won much respect.

Chermside retired from the British Army in 1907 as a lieut-general. In 1899 he had married Geraldine Katherine Webb (d. 1910) and in 1920 Clementine Maria, second daughter of Paul Julius, first Baron de Reuter, and widow of Count Otto Stenbock; both marriages were childless. Chermside died in London on 24 September 1929. A

suburb of Brisbane was named after him following his departure in 1904.

D. J. Murphy et al (eds), *Prelude to power* (Brisb, 1970); *PD* (Qld), 1902, p194, 1904, 92, p110-22, 93, p121; Commercial Publishing Co. of Sydney, Ltd, *Annual Review of Qld*, 1 (1902); *Queenslander*, 24 Mar 1902; *Daily Mail* (Brisb), and *Telegraph* (Brisb), 8 Oct 1904; *Brisbane Courier*, 10 Oct 1904; GOV/34, 36, 39, 40, 48 (QA).   PAUL D. WILSON

CHERRY, PERCY HERBERT (1895-1917), soldier, was born on 4 June 1895 at Drysdale, Victoria, son of John Gawley Cherry and his wife Elizabeth, née Russel, both Victorian-born. When he was 7 the family moved to Tasmania and took up an apple orchard near Cradoc. Percy attended the local state school until he was 13 and was then privately tutored. He played the cornet in the Franklin brass band, sang in the Anglican church choir and belonged to the local cadet corps. He worked with his father and became an expert apple-packer, winning a championship title in case-making at Launceston Fruit Show. In 1913 he was commissioned in the 93rd Infantry Regiment.

On 5 March 1915 Cherry enlisted in the Australian Imperial Force and was posted to the 26th Battalion; he was considered too young for an A.I.F. commission and he sailed for Egypt in June as a quartermaster sergeant. In August he was made a company sergeant major and next month reached Gallipoli where he served at Taylor's Hollow and Russell's Top. He was wounded on 1 December and evacuated; a week later he was promoted second lieutenant. Cherry remained in Egypt until March 1916 when, after attending a machine-gun school, he was transferred to the 7th Machine-Gun Company and sent to France. He commanded the company's 1st Battery at Fleurbaix, Messines and on the Somme until 5 August when he was wounded in a duel with a German officer at Pozières. After sniping at each other from their shell-holes both officers fired together and both were wounded, the German mortally. When Cherry went to him he was given a package of letters which he promised to post; his opponent's dying words were 'And so it ends'. Cherry was promoted lieutenant on 25 August and resumed duty on the Somme in November; next month he was made a temporary captain and transferred back to the 26th Battalion as a company commander. Unpopular at first, for he was 'a little martinet on parade', he was soon to gain the respect of his men for his leadership in action.

Cherry's rank was confirmed in February 1917 and at Warlencourt on 1-2 March he took part in an attack on Malt Trench. When he and his men found a small gap in the enemy wire, he rushed two machine-gun posts, capturing one single-handed and turning the gun on the fleeing Germans before being wounded himself. He was to receive the Military Cross for this gallant episode, though the award was not announced until the day of his death and he never knew of it. On 26 March 1917 his battalion was ordered to storm the village of Lagnicourt. Cherry's company encountered fierce opposition and after all the other officers had been killed or wounded, he 'carried on with care and determination . . . and cleared the village of the enemy'. The Germans counter-attacked and the battle raged all day long. Though wounded in the leg, Cherry remained at his post and in the late afternoon was killed by a shell; he was buried in Quéant Road cemetery, Buissy. He was awarded a posthumous Victoria Cross, an honour for which his battalion commander had recommended him for 'bravery beyond description'. He was unmarried.

C. E. W. Bean, *The A.I.F. in France*, 1916-17 (Syd, 1929, 1933); L. Wigmore (ed), *They dared mightily* (Canb, 1963); *London Gazette*, 24 Apr, 11 May 1917; *Reveille* (Syd), May 1968; *SMH*, 23 May 1917; War diaries, 7th Machine-Gun Company, *and* 26th Battalion AIF (AWM).   REX CLARK*

CHERRY, THOMAS (1861-1945), bacteriologist and agricultural scientist, was born on 27 October 1861 at Gisborne, Victoria, son of Edward Cherry (1830-1910) from Hertfordshire, England, and his wife Ann Appleby, née Davis. His father had established a joinery workshop at Gisborne soon after his arrival in Australia in 1855; various models of his 'Cherry Churn' were used for over eighty years throughout rural Victoria. Thomas was educated at the Gisborne Board School and later at St Paul's School, Geelong. He matriculated at 16, and worked in the family business for seven years, though his connexion with the firm remained lifelong. He later said that his interest in farming and its problems developed in this early period, as well as a love for working with his hands, especially with stone.

In 1885 Cherry began a medical course at the University of Melbourne, with a scholarship to Ormond College. He topped each of his five undergraduate years and graduated M.B. (1889), M.D. (1892) and M.S. (1894). He was senior house surgeon at the Melbourne Hospital in 1890 before continuing his studies in pathology and bacteriology, encouraged by Professor (Sir) Harry Allen [q.v.], at King's College, London, and the University of Aberdeen. He returned to Melbourne in 1892 to become assistant lecturer and demonstrator in pathology; he also took charge of the department's first postgraduate classes.

Revisiting Europe in 1894, Cherry worked with leading bacteriologists in London, Cambridge, Paris and Berlin, and on his return inaugurated a service to hospitals and doctors for the bacteriological diagnosis of diphtheria, tuberculosis, typhoid and related diseases. He undertook regular examinations of Melbourne's water-supply and also worked for the Department of Agriculture, discovering in 1895 the link between the freshwater snail and liver fluke in sheep. In 1900 he was appointed first lecturer in bacteriology, and for a few months in 1901-02 was acting registrar of the university. In 1902 additional work for the government involved training butter-factory managers in bacteriological procedures.

Harassed by Allen's efforts to retain control over bacteriology, in 1905 Cherry accepted appointment as director of agriculture at a salary of £850. He travelled and lectured extensively, and published thirty-four papers on such diverse subjects as silo-construction, bee-keeping and pasture improvement as well as further works on scientific dairy production and water purification. His appointment expired in March 1910 amid controversy over the role of the director and disorganization within the department: Cherry had no statutory authority over his staff, and senior officers often dealt directly with the minister without reference to him. His term was extended until the end of the year, when he was succeeded by Dr S. S. Cameron [q.v.]. Backed by the strong recommendations of cabinet, Cherry was then appointed by the university to the newly created chair of agriculture in 1911. He was active at this time in the movement to establish a national laboratory, in anticipation of the Council for Scientific and Industrial Research.

In 1916 his tenure expired when the government withdrew financial support for the chair, and Cherry enlisted as a major with the Australian Army Medical Corps. He worked as a pathologist in Egypt with the 14th Australian General Hospital and later with the 2nd Light Horse Field Ambulance in the attempt to prevent the introduction into Australia of Mediterranean bilharziosis. Interested in archaeology and historical evolution, he gave many lectures for the army's education programme.

In 1921-34 Cherry was John Grice [q.v.]

Cancer Research Fellow, working first at the Walter and Eliza Hall [qq.v.] Institute of Medical Research in Melbourne, and from 1930 at the university's Veterinary Research Institute. His study was directed to discovering a link between cancer and tuberculosis: he published nineteen papers on his experiments with mice and the statistical analysis of causes of human death. From 1934 his work was sponsored by the Cancer Causation Research Committee.

On 6 February 1894 at East St Kilda, Cherry had married Edith Sarah (b. 1870), daughter of F. J. Gladman [q.v.4]; she had graduated M.A. in 1891. Cherry had an extremely lively mind and encyclopaedic general knowledge and was a skilled sculptor and draughtsman. An active member and churchwarden of St James' Church of England, Glen Iris, and councillor of Ormond College from 1893, he remained robust and energetic until his death on 27 May 1945. He was survived by his wife, three sons, one of whom became Sir Thomas Cherry, F.R.S., and a daughter; his eldest son had been killed in action in France in 1918. Cherry was buried in Box Hill cemetery. His portrait by Aileen Dent was presented to the university in 1944.

G. Currie and J. Graham, *The origins of CSIRO* (Melb, 1966); K. F. Russell, *The Melbourne Medical School 1862-1962* (Melb, 1977); *Aust J of Science*, 8 (1945-46); *MJA*, 28 July 1945; E. S. J. King, 'The story of the Melbourne School of Pathology', *MJA*, 28 July 1951; *Argus*, 29 July 1910; Cherry family papers (held by author).   JILL STOWELL

CHEWINGS, CHARLES (1859-1937), geologist and anthropologist, was born on 16 April 1859 at Woorkongoree station, near Burra, South Australia, third son of John Chewings, pastoralist, and his wife Sarah, née Wall. Educated by tutor and at Prince Alfred College, Chewings also received a thorough practical training from his father, who died in 1879 leaving his family well-to-do.

In 1881 Chewings set out alone from Beltana with two camels to explore the possibility of establishing a cattle-run in the western MacDonnell Ranges. Next year he toured England, Europe and America. In 1883 he travelled from Murat Bay to the Warburton Range to assess the area's pastoral possibilities. Impressed with the efficiency of camels in the interior, in 1884 Chewings sailed to India and shipped nearly 300 of them to Port Augusta. Next year he opened a camel transport service based on Hergott Springs (Marree), explored the MacDonnell Ranges more thoroughly, and stocked his cattle-run, Tempe Downs. He

mapped and named Chapple Range and Mount Chapple, Northern Territory, after his old headmaster, F. Chapple [q.v.].

Accounts of his three inland journeys appeared in the Adelaide *Observer*; that of the third was also published as *The sources of the Finke River* (1886), with a large map. Convinced of the interior's excellent pastoral prospects, Chewings became a strong advocate for a railway to facilitate settlement. On 8 February 1887 he married Frances Mary Braddock at Port Augusta and they went abroad for a year. On returning he was a stock and station agent, sharebroker and commission agent in Adelaide as well as maintaining the camel transport service, managed at Hergott Springs by Fushar Ackbar.

Chewings was excited by marine fossils discovered on Tempe Downs by his manager F. Thornton, and in 1891 published 'Geological notes on the Upper Finke basin' in the *Transactions* of the Royal Society of South Australia. He listed the fossils and tentatively began an interpretation of the region's succession of rock strata. That year he left with his family to study geology at the University College, London, and the University of Heidelberg, Germany (Ph.D., 1894). He was elected to fellowships of the Royal Geographical and Geological societies, London. In his paper 'Central Australia' (1891) in the former society's *Proceedings*, he reviewed the region's history and praised its pastoral possibilities, mineral wealth, and suitability for date-growing and ostrich-farming.

In 1894 Chewings became a mining consultant at Coolgardie, Western Australia, where he was esteemed for his honest, factual reports during the goldfields' boom years. In 1902 he returned to South Australia and spent almost two decades in Central Australia as a mining consultant and camel-carrier of supplies from the railhead, Oodnadatta, to Northern Territory stations and mines. In 1909 he surveyed a stock route from Barrow Creek to Victoria River, and by means of light boring-equipment transported on camels, proved the availability of water throughout at shallow depth. He described in detail this country, long notorious for its lack of surface waters, in the *Geographical Journal*, October 1930. During World War I he mined wolfram in the Northern Territory and transported it by camel to Oodnadatta. After retirement Chewings published frequently on Central Australian geology in the Royal Society of South Australia's *Transactions*.

All his life Chewings had much contact with Aboriginals and he published a popular account of them, *Back in the stone age* (1936). In retirement he compiled an Aranda vocabulary including all the words previously recorded by other students and himself. This and the manuscript of his translation of C. F. T. Strehlow's [q.v.] 'Die Aranda-und Loritja-Stämme in Zentral-Australien' (1915) are in the University of Adelaide's library.

Chewings was an earnest, energetic man with the practicality to work successfully in adverse conditions: he accomplished notable pioneer work in geology and the study of Aboriginal culture. Survived by his wife, two daughters and two sons, he died on 9 June 1937 at Glen Osmond and was buried in West Terrace cemetery. His estate was sworn for probate at £1079. His name is perpetuated in the Chewings Range, Mount Chewings and a street in Alice Springs, Northern Territory.

W. F. Morrison, *The Aldine history of South Australia* (Adel, 1890); W. B. Kimberly (ed), *History of West Australia* (Melb, 1897); R. Cockburn, *Pastoral pioneers of South Australia*, 1 (Adel, 1925); *Observer* (Adel), 22, 29 July, 5 Aug 1882, 29 Sept 1883, 22 May-7 Aug 1886.   HANS MINCHAM

CHIDLEY, WILLIAM JAMES (1860?-1916), sex reformer and eccentric, was a foundling, probably born in Victoria, and adopted as an infant by John James Chidley (d. 1891), toyshop-owner, and his first wife Maria, née Lancelott. The Chidleys also adopted three girls and another boy and returned to England for several years in the early 1860s. On their return to Melbourne his adopted father became an impecunious itinerant photographer with a horse-drawn studio; William attended at least four schools in Melbourne before leaving aged 13; he continued his education by reading voraciously in public libraries. Unsuccessfully apprenticed to a solicitor and then to an architect, he failed to matriculate after months of evening study. While working for his father, he learned photography and developed some talent for sketching likenesses.

About 1880 Chidley moved to Adelaide where he did water-colour and crayon portraits. In 1882 he and a friend were acquitted of manslaughter after a street brawl. About 1885 he met a 'promising young actress' Ada Grantleigh, née Harris, who was married to W. Thoms. Chidley lived with her intermittently until her death – in Adelaide until 1890, then in Sydney, New Zealand and Melbourne; an alcoholic, she died in 1908. He, too, lived through abject periods of alcoholism. They never married but adopted a son (reputedly hers).

Blaming himself for Ada's death, Chidley was attacked by obsessive remorse and also suffered from extreme sexual guilt. For years he had been formulating a theory to deal with the inordinate amount of misery among people he knew. While reasonably recommending vegetarianism, fresh air, sunlight and unrestrictive clothing, and criticizing money-making and class distinction, he also postulated a 'correct' method of intercourse that would 'take place only in the Spring . . . and between true lovers only'. He believed that his sexual theory was the answer to all the ills of mankind and reluctantly resolved to 'go on the active warpath' and propagate it, but began to run foul of the authorities when trying to explain its technicalities to audiences. 'I shall become a scandal and a voice crying in the wilderness' he wrote to H. Havelock Ellis [q.v.4], with whom he had been corresponding since 1899.

In Melbourne in 1911 Chidley published *The answer* and sold copies to curious passers-by on the footpath. Soon in trouble with the police, he moved on to Sydney. Tall and suntanned, with 'black curly hair going grey', beard and moustache, he wore only a short white tunic, with bare head, arms, legs and feet – he made an immediate sensation. Twice charged with offensive behaviour, he was deemed insane by the Lunacy Court on 3 August 1912 and sent to the Callan Park Mental Hospital. His case was debated in the Legislative Assembly and his defenders raised fundamental questions about the misuse of power to certify. Released conditionally on 1 October, he quickly broke undertakings to dress in men's ordinary costume, and to refrain from addressing meetings in public places and from selling his book in the streets. He was again deemed insane on 26 December 1913 but was released five days later. Chidley was charged with such minor offences as breaking the Domain by-laws, offensive behaviour and begging alms seven times in 1914 and eight in 1915. His numerous fines were usually paid by his friends.

On 16 February 1916 Chidley was again found insane and committed to Kenmore Mental Hospital at Goulburn. Backed by the Chidley Defence Committee, chaired by Meredith Atkinson [q.v.], in June he appealed in vain to the Supreme Court. There was considerable popular agitation by the press and in parliament for his release, and efforts were made by his friends to have him deported to Canada or the United States of America. However he was granted leave of absence from Kenmore on bond by the colonial secretary, George Black [q.v.], on the usual conditions, but as he was unable to refrain from 'inculpating' himself Black had him recommitted in September. He recovered from a suicide attempt on 12 October but died suddenly of arteriosclerosis at Callan Park on 21 December 1916.

Chidley's lasting reputation must rest on his autobiography, the 'Confessions'. Although he intended no-one to read them until after his death, in 1899 he sent the manuscript to Ellis who used extracts in his *Studies in the psychology of sex* (London, 1897-1910). Chidley made a duplicate copy as his papers were often confiscated and destroyed by the police. In 1935 Ellis sent this manuscript to the Mitchell Library, Sydney, remarking 'Not only is it a document of much psychological interest, but as a picture of the intimate aspects of Australian life in the nineteenth century it is of the highest interest, and that value will go on increasing as time passes'.

Chidley was a victim of morbid elements in his own nature and in his life: coinciding, they led to his destruction. His theory, although ludicrous at first sight, is no more than a doctrine of gentleness and love. To a certain extent, he was a primitive, unschooled forerunner of Freud and Reich, with his message that 'Our false coition makes villains of us all'. *The confessions of William James Chidley* was published in Brisbane in 1977.

PD (NSW), 1912, 4th S, p 534-58; *Advertiser* (Adel), 24 Oct, 8 Dec 1882; *Observer* (Adel), 9 Dec 1882; W. J. Chidley papers (ML); Col Sec papers, special bundles 5/5298, 5/5299 (NSWA).

SALLY McINERNEY

CHILDE, VERE GORDON (1892-1957), archaeologist and political theorist, was born on 14 April 1892 at North Sydney, son of London-born parents Rev. Stephen Henry Childe, rector of St Thomas's Church of England, and his second wife Harriet Eliza, née Gordon. He was reared in an atmosphere of conventional late-Victorian views and strict paternal authority, against which his inquiring spirit chafed. Known as Gordon, he was educated at Sydney Church of England Grammar School (Shore) and the University of Sydney. He graduated B.A. in 1914 with first-class honours in Latin, Greek and philosophy and won the University Medal, Professor Francis Anderson's [q.v.] prize for philosophy and the (Sir) Daniel Cooper [q.v.3] graduate scholarship. At The Queen's College, Oxford, he was awarded a B.Litt. in 1916 for research on Indo-European archaeology and next year obtained first-class honours in *literae humaniores*.

By 1915 Childe was 'reluctantly convinced ... that orthodoxy was impossible intellectually': his socialist and pacifist views were greatly strengthened by wartime conditions in Britain. In 1917 — in some trepidation lest he be forced to enlist — he returned to Sydney and in November became senior resident tutor at St Andrew's College, University of Sydney. He joined the Australian Union of Democratic Control and opposed what he saw as attacks on civil liberties by W. M. Hughes's [q.v.] government. In particular he involved himself in the bitter struggle against the introduction of conscription. Like other pacifists he was under surveillance by the Department of Defence and had his mail censored.

Over Easter 1918 Childe addressed a peace conference and in May resigned his college position at the request of the principal. In July the Sydney University senate refused to confirm his appointment as tutor in ancient history. The university had apparently been advised by the Department of Defence that his appointment in wartime was undesirable. In the State parliament questions were asked if he had been illegally penalized for his political views.

Childe wrote to the chancellor to complain of his treatment, then went to Brisbane. Towards the end of 1918 he taught briefly at Maryborough Boys' Grammar School, then returned to Brisbane. Back in Sydney, from August 1919 he was private secretary to John Storey [q.v.], leader of the Opposition and premier from March 1920 until October 1921. Childe left the same month for England, where he worked for six months in the New South Wales Agent-General's Office, being dismissed with the change of government in New South Wales.

Thirty-five years later in a posthumous article in *Antiquity* (1958), entitled 'Retrospect', Childe dismissed these turbulent years as a 'sentimental excursion' into Australian politics, but in 1923 in London he published *How Labour governs*, an account of the trade union movement in Australia and the emergence of a working-class party which had won power in a parliamentary system. The book firmly established his reputation as a historian of political theory. His first-hand observations of in-fighting and power struggles during one of the most hectic periods of the labour movement led him to conclude that the parliamentary system was a creation of upper classes, embodying their traditions and privileges, and that once within it working-class representatives would of necessity lose their allegiance to their own party, 'rat' on their principles and fail to implement the programmes on which they had been elected. Childe's interpretation has provided a framework for later histories of the Australian labour movement. A second edition was published in 1964.

Sceptical and angry, Childe rejected the vulgar, reactionary quality of much of Australian social and political life. As well, he accepted uncritically the hypothesis that the current organization of society involved some exploitation and enslavement of the workers, and that the object of a labour movement must be to alter the social structure. On the other hand the lack of unity and apathy of the workers discouraged Childe, who saw that to continue to engage in political activities on their behalf was indeed sentimental. If human dignity no longer existed, he believed it had existed in the past and that the evidence for it could be collected: it was to this problem that he now turned.

Childe appears to have been unemployed for several years, during which time he travelled in Europe. In 1925 he became librarian at the Royal Anthropological Institute, London, and that year published *The dawn of European civilization*; by 1930 he had written four more major works. The books not only brought together for the first time a huge array of data from all over Europe, but also synthesized and distilled them in a theoretical fashion which 'pioneered a new way of looking at technology' and revolutionized archaeology.

Childe saw European civilization as 'a peculiar and individual manifestation of the human spirit', and to explain its origins and development became his task. Over the next three decades he published some 20 books and 200 papers where the technical aspects of his search were assembled and argued. From the beginning he was dissatisfied with archaeology being little more than the mere listing of stone tools and pottery types. Instead it should become the preliterate substitute for conventional history 'with cultures instead of statesmen, as actors, and migrations in places of battles'. In the 1930s he became increasingly committed to an economic interpretation of archaeological evidence, and almost inevitably adopted and developed a Marxist framework for explaining the past. He considered the shift from hunting and gathering to food production, and the emergence of professional groups who did not produce their own food so significant that he called them the Neolithic Revolution and the Urban Revolution.

Childe was concerned with archaeology's relevance (and therefore his own) in contemporary society. One method he used to demonstrate his own utility was to write a series of books designed to present the results of his research in a non-academic form for the general public. The most popular were *Man makes himself* (1936), and *What happened in history* (1942), which by 1957

had sold over 300 000 copies. His works were also widely translated.

In 1927 Childe had been appointed first Abercromby professor of prehistoric archaeology at the University of Edinburgh. Although that year he began excavating a Neolithic village, Skara Brae, in the Orkney Islands, most of his 'vital discoveries were made in the library and museum, not in the field'. In 1936 he was awarded an honorary doctorate of literature by Harvard and next year a doctorate of science by Pennsylvania State University. He was appointed a fellow of the Royal Anthropological Institute, the Society of Antiquaries of Scotland, and of the British Academy, and was professor of prehistoric European archaeology and director of the Institute of Archaeology in the University of London in 1946-57. Childe was shy and retiring in society, even to the point of rudeness. As one of his colleagues has put it, learning was 'the austere content of his life'.

After he retired, Childe returned to Australia in April 1957. He gave a number of lectures and completed *The prehistory of European society* (published posthumously in 1958). Seemingly he found Australia still unattractive and unpleasant. When the University of Sydney awarded him an honorary D. Litt. he attended the ceremony in a bright green shirt – typically 'Childeish' (a word he often used). On 19 October Childe fell to his death over Govetts Leap in the Blue Mountains, New South Wales. From his actions after his retirement, both in Britain and Australia, it seems possible that he took his own life, despite the coroner's verdict of accidental death. Childe did not marry.

V. G. Childe, *How Labour governs*, 2nd edn, F. B. Smith ed (Melb, 1964); B. Cunliffe, 'Introduction', V. G. Childe, *The dawn of European civilization*, 6th rev edn (St Albans, 1973); *M.S.N.*, no 3, 1947; British Academy, *Procs*, 44 (1958); *Hist Studies*, no 29, Nov 1957; J. Allen, 'Aspects of Vere Gordon Childe', *Labour Hist*, May 1967, no 12; Dept of Defence – Directorate of Military Intelligence, Censorship reports MP95/1 (AAO, Melb); Univ Syd Archives; information from Mr G. Munster, Lane Cove, NSW.   JIM ALLEN

CHIN KAW (1865-1922), popularly known as Ah Kaw, merchant and community leader, was born on 17 July 1865 at Shui-hu village, K'ai-p'ing district, T'ai-shan county, Kwangtung province, China, son of Chin Lang Lan, merchant, and his wife Yu Chin Lang Lan, née Yugim. Many details of his career cannot be established with certainty. About 1879 he arrived at the Chinese tin-mining community of Thomas's Plains, near Weldborough in north-eastern Tasmania, where his uncle Chin Ah Heang owned a general grocery and herb store. Besides helping in this retail business and later taking up mineral leases in the area, the young Ah Kaw found his basic literacy a great help to his uneducated fellows. He returned to China in the mid-1880s and married Luey Fong, daughter of a well-respected Sunning-shan family, in 1887. He was back in Tasmania by 1890 and the subsequent arrival of his wife as a 'princess' from China stirred local imagination.

In 1899 Ah Kaw moved from Weldborough to Launceston where he established Sun Hung Ack & Co. in St John Street. He took over the general store and wholesale tobacconist business of James (formerly Chin) Ah Catt, another Cantonese who had already had business dealings with Ah Kaw and Ah Heang in the establishment in 1890 of the store Ah Catt & Co. at Thomas's Plains. Ah Catt was a well-known and popular 'Christianized' Chinese whose funeral on 18 November 1907 was the largest in Launceston for some time and at which the hymn 'Rock of Ages' was sung first by the European mourners and then by the Chinese in their own language.

In subsequent years Ah Kaw took an extensive interest in mining and banking enterprises as well as local welfare, including the well-being of his own countrymen. He early identified his interests with those of his adopted land and was naturalized as a British subject. His shop became an important meeting-point for the Chinese migrants who used it for news of their native land, for remitting money home and as a place of rest and recreation.

Before Federation Chin Kaw was one of those who sought to circumvent the impending immigration restrictions by speeding up migration to Tasmania, where, although a poll-tax was exacted from each Chinese migrant, the limitation on numbers was less severe than in the other colonies. He was probably one of the four Launceston merchants who petitioned against the immigration restriction bill in August 1898. His efforts continued to be gratefully remembered by many Chinese families in various parts of Australia. In 1916, as the mining industry in north-eastern Tasmania was tapering off and the Chinese population dwindling, Ah Kaw moved to Melbourne as a herbalist. He died on 11 April 1922 at Hawthorn after a short illness, survived by his wife, four daughters and six sons, two of whom were to graduate in medicine and law respectively from the University of Melbourne. Following traditional custom, his remains were sent back to China to occupy a place of honour in his ancestral temple.

Cyclopedia of Tasmania (Hob, 1931); *Examiner* (Launc), 16, 18 Nov 1907; *Weekly Courier* (Launc), 27 Apr 1922; family information.   K. S. LIEW

CHINN, HENRY (1858-1940), surveyor and engineer, was born on 15 January 1858 at Collingwood, Melbourne, son of Cornish parents John Mitchell Chinn, engineer, and his wife Jane, née Ivey. Educated probably at a state school, he learned some surveying and drawing while a clerk in the water-supply branch of the Department of Public Works from July 1873 until 1877. On 5 February 1878 at St Paul's Church of England, Melbourne, he married Fanny Margaret Hood; they had two sons and two daughters.

In May he became a draughtsman in the New South Wales Department of Public Works and was licensed as a surveyor on 22 January 1882. He resigned in July, joined the railways in November but was dismissed in March 1883 at Armidale. Returning to Victoria, he worked as an engineer at Lakes Entrance, on Melbourne sewerage works and on railway jobs in New South Wales and Tasmania; he was frequently in trouble. In 1885 he set up as a consulting engineer in Melbourne and secured an extensive practice as an expert witness. When his wife died in 1887 their children were reared by her brother (Sir) Joseph Hood [q.v.].

Chinn speculated in land and in 1890 was bankrupt. In 1894 he was accused of fraudulent dealings over moneylending. He returned to engineering and in 1901 was briefly employed by the Metropolitan Water and Sewage Board, Brisbane, but was discharged for absence without leave. He settled in Western Australia as a consulting engineer in 1903 and in 1907 made some political friends with articles in the *West Australian* criticizing the State railway administration. On 14 December 1907 in Perth he married a divorcee Helen, née Crossley, with Congregational forms. While working on an Adelaide tramway job for Henry Teasdale Smith [q.v.], in May 1908, he was accused of trying to profit from a welding invention of State analyst W. A. Hargreaves [q.v.].

Against technical advice, King O'Malley [q.v.] was persuaded to appoint Chinn supervising engineer for the transcontinental railway in Western Australia on 8 February 1912. Directed to build the track eastwards from Kalgoorlie, Chinn complained of lack of authority to engage staff and was frequently in controversy with H. Deane [q.v.], chief engineer of Commonwealth railways. When O'Malley visited the works Chinn made the elementary error of going direct to the minister to obtain his consent for a deviation in the approved route. J. M. Fowler [q.v.] secured a royal commission into charges that Chinn had illicitly trafficked in gold and had committed frauds in 1894; the commissioner (Sir) Henry Hodges [q.v.] dismissed six charges but was equivocal on charges that Chinn had forged references. O'Malley supported Chinn but when the government fell in June 1913 the new minister discharged him at once. The Labor-dominated Senate appointed a select committee which recommended that he should be paid compensation for dismissal without reasonable cause, but no action was taken.

Bitter and frustrated, Chinn returned to Victoria and struggled vainly for compensation. In January 1916 he met Fowler in Collins Street and, after insulting him, blows were exchanged; both were fined. He lived in Sydney in 1916-25 probably working as a consulting engineer, and retired in 1931. Survived by two daughters of his first marriage, Chinn died as an old-age-pensioner at The Basin in the Dandenongs, Victoria, on 29 October 1940; he was buried in St Kilda cemetery with Anglican rites.

J. S. Battye (ed), *Cyclopedia of Western Australia*, 1 (Adel, 1912); *PP* (SA), 1910, 3 (83), (Cwlth), 1913, 3, 1245, *and* Senate, 1, 179, 1914-17, 5, 1341; *PD* (Cwlth), 1912, vol 64, 1425, vol 69, 7281; *Argus*, 27 Mar 1890; *West Australian*, 22 Jan-6 Feb 1913; *Australasian*, 8, 15 Jan 1916; J. M. Fowler papers (NL); O'Malley papers (NL); A3832, RC14 (1), A456, W16/3/31 (AAO, Canb).   ARTHUR CORBETT

CHINNERY,   ERNEST   WILLIAM PEARSON (1887-1972), public servant and anthropologist, was born on 5 November 1887 at Waterloo, Victoria, son of John William Chinnery, miner, and his wife Grace Newton, née Pearson, both of whom were Victorian-born. His father joined the Victorian Railways and the boy was educated in the state schools of towns in which he served. Articled briefly to a Melbourne law firm, Chinnery joined the public service of Papua in April 1909 as a clerk in Port Moresby. Seeking the prestige of field service, he won appointment as a patrol officer in July 1910 and was posted as relieving officer to Ioma in the Mambare division. In the Kumusi division for the next three years his work on routine patrols was said to have 'gained the respect and the confidence of the local tribes'; he reputedly underwent a tribal initiation ceremony. He was not on good terms either with local Europeans or with Lieut-Governor (Sir) Hubert Murray [q.v.] whom he disliked as something of a humbug. In November 1913 Chinnery was charged with

infringing the field-staff regulations and was reduced in rank. In the Rigo district in 1914, a patrol led by him clashed with tribesmen and shot seven; Murray saw the incident as probably unavoidable. By 1917 Chinnery was patrolling into new country in the central division behind Kairuku and into the Kunimaipa valley. There he discovered the source of the Waria River.

In 1915 he sought leave to enlist; it was granted in 1917 and in September he joined the Australian Flying Corps. Chinnery was demobilized in England late in 1919 as a lieutenant (observer). He had already published anthropological papers and now became a research student under A. C. Haddon at Christ's College, Cambridge. He joined the research committee of the British Association for the Advancement of Science, lectured to the Royal Geographical Society and in 1920 won its Cuthbert Peek award. Refused appointment as Papuan government anthropologist in 1921 because Murray distrusted him, he served New Guinea Copper Mines Ltd as labour adviser until in 1924 he was appointed government anthropologist of the Mandated Territory. In that capacity he published in British anthropological journals six official reports, and a series of papers and notes – all of them, because of his official duties, of the survey rather than the intensive investigation type.

Chinnery became the territory's first director of district services and native affairs in 1932 and thus directed the early extension of control in the newly discovered central highland valleys. He encouraged anthropological reporting by his staff and strongly supported the training of field-officer cadets in anthropology at the University of Sydney. In 1930 and 1934 he represented Australia before the Permanent Mandates Commission in Geneva.

Following a major review of Aboriginal policy in 1937-38, Chinnery was seconded from New Guinea in 1939 to head a new department of native affairs designed to introduce New Guinea methods to the Northern Territory. Living alone in his office, he found much to learn; he also had to cope with the massive problems created by military occupation. When his secondment expired in 1946 he planned to return to anthropology in New Guinea but found no support. He was an Australian adviser at the Trusteeship Council, United Nations, in 1947, and retired to Melbourne.

Chinnery served twice on United Nations missions to Africa but never published the book he had planned. His wife Sara Johnston, née Neill, whom he had married in England in 1919, predeceased him. He died at Prahran on 17 December 1972, survived by four daughters, and was cremated. He belonged to the generation before Malinowski and Radcliffe-Brown [q.v.] who so deeply influenced anthropology. He supplied useful contemporary raw material in native society, but his type of work was overtaken by the new professional standards of the 1920s and 1930s.

E. J. B. Foxcroft, *Australian native policy* (Melb, 1941); C. D. Rowley, *The destruction of Aboriginal society* (Canb, 1970); Northern Territory, *Annual Report*, 1938-39; New Guinea, *Report on the administration of the Territory*, 1938-39; *Government Gazette* (Cwlth), 14 Sept 1939; D. J. F. Griffiths, The career of F. E. Williams, government anthropologist of Papua, 1922-1943 (M.A. thesis, ANU, 1977); Gilbert Murray papers (NL); A56, A73, A452 59/6066, 6067, A518 C828/2 (AAO, Canb).

FRANCIS WEST

CHIPPER, ALICIA MARY; see KELLY, ALICIA

CHIPPER, DONALD JOHN (1868-1917), undertaker, was born on 2 February 1868 in Perth, son of Stephen James Chipper, landowner and publican, and his wife Maria Sophia, née Campbell. His grandfather John was one of the Swan River settlement's first colonists, arriving in the *Caroline* on 12 October 1829 as an indentured worker to James Henty [q.v.1] with whom he stayed for approximately two years. Just after Henty left for Van Diemen's Land in January 1832, John was employed on a private contracting job at Greenmount in the hills outside Perth when he and a boy companion named Beecham were attacked by Aboriginals. Beecham was speared and died but Chipper escaped by leaping off boulders on top of a steep hill and running seven miles to safety. Not only was his escape miraculous, but the site of the attack became known as Chipper's Leap and for many years was a reminder to settlers of the days when Aboriginal-European relations were at their worst in the colony.

Donald's father, Stephen, was licensee in 1867-72 of the United Services Tavern in Perth from which horse-drawn coaches left for King George's Sound. It was an important service. Begun in 1856 by D. J. Chipper's uncle Thomas, shortly after Albany became the main port of call for overseas ships when Fremantle was deemed unsafe by the Peninsular and Oriental Steam Navigation Co., the mail service linked the colony's two main settlements. Horses were changed at eight stops on a route which Thomas himself pioneered. At first he used a spring-cart which also carried mail to farmers along the

way. The journey took up to two weeks and Thomas, at his own expense, had to maintain and improve the route including changing the road to avoid seasonal hazards. By 1879 travelling time for passengers and freight had been reduced to two days.

Educated at the Government Boys' School, Perth, Donald was apprenticed as a coach-builder, wheelwright and undertaker in 1884 and in 1889 established his own business in Murray Street in these three trades; by 1892 it was restricted to funerals. New premises were built in 1897 in Hay Street. Branches were opened at Fremantle and Kalgoorlie.

Chipper was a personable man, had a keen sense of humour, never drove a car but owned many, and travelled frequently to the eastern States by ship. He was a foundation member of the Grand Lodge of Western Australia and its first master (1900-01), and also senior trustee of the Grand Lodge of the United Ancient Order of Druids. Anglican by religion, he married at St George's Cathedral on 25 September 1889 Florence Edith Lima Maude, daughter of William Dale, immigration and charities officer with the Western Australian government. They had four children, including a son Donald John who carried on the family business. Chipper died on 13 March 1917 aboard the *Katoomba* off Albany, and was buried in Karrakatta cemetery.

J. S. Battye (ed), *Cyclopedia of Western Australia*, 1 (Adel, 1912); CS093, 5/2/1832 (Battye Lib, Perth); family papers held by Mr K. J. Chipper, Applecross, WA.

R. T. APPLEYARD

CHIRNSIDE, JOHN PERCY (1865-1944), soldier, politician and pastoralist, was born on 2 October 1865 at Carranballac, Skipton, Victoria, youngest son of Andrew Chirnside [q.v.3], pastoralist, and his wife Mary, née Begbie. The family soon went for five years to Scotland where they owned Skibo Castle, Sutherlandshire. On returning to Australia, Percy was educated at Geelong Church of England Grammar School. He then travelled with a tutor for two years, visiting nearly every country in the world. For the next few years he lived at Werribee Park, the mansion built by his father and uncle Thomas [q.v.3] in the mid-1870s; here he shared his enthusiasm for hunting, coursing, polo and shooting with his brothers Robert, Andrew and George.

Bent on a military career, Chirnside was commissioned lieutenant in the Victorian Field Artillery Brigade in June 1887. Two years later his father agreed to contribute to the cost of raising and maintaining a half-battery of horse artillery at Werribee, of which Percy took command. Horses, uniforms, drill hall and stables were provided by Andrew Chirnside, also half the sergeant major instructor's salary. When Andrew died in 1890, Percy and his brother George, who had jointly inherited the Werribee estate, continued to maintain the half-battery. Percy went to England in November for further training at Woolwich and Aldershot and returned next July. He was promoted captain in January 1893, but in February the goverment disbanded the Werribee half-battery rather than meet the cost of replacing obsolete guns. Chirnside was placed on the reserve of officers in March, retiring in October 1897.

In September 1894, standing as an independent tariff reformer, Percy won the seat of Grant in the Victorian Legislative Assembly. He regarded himself as a 'liberal conservative'. While rarely vocal in the House, he maintained a particular interest in defence matters and was popular among his constituents. He did not stand for re-election in May 1904, when the seat disappeared in a redistribution.

At All Saints Church, St Kilda, on 22 February 1893 Chirnside had married Ethel Mary Fenner. After a honeymoon in Japan, America and England, they returned to live at Werribee, where they built The Manor. Percy ran mainly merino sheep, but also had a stud of milking Shorthorn cattle, importing many top quality animals. By 1910 almost the whole property was let in tenant farms, or had been sold in farm-blocks, and in 1921 he moved to Brandon Park, near Oakleigh, where he founded a stud herd of Jersey cattle.

In June 1905 Chirnside was appointed C.M.G., and after World War I received the O.B.E. During the war he had served in England with the Remount Section of the British Army and was twice mentioned in dispatches. Survived by his wife and three sons, he died in Melbourne on 6 January 1944; a daughter predeceased him. In 1946, when his family was reunited in Australia, a memorial service was held at St Thomas's Church of England, Werribee, and his ashes were scattered from the banks of the river.

H. B. Ronald, *Wool past the winning post* (Melb, 1978); W. Perry, 'The Victorian Horse Artillery', *VHM*, 43 (1972), no 1; *Home*, 1 June 1921; *Punch* (Melb), 19 Nov 1903; *Argus*, 7 Jan 1944; letters and papers held by Mr A. F. Chirnside, Toorak, Vic.

HEATHER B. RONALD

CHISHOLM, ALEXANDER (1878-1945), soldier and draper, was born on 8 December 1878 in Brisbane, son of William Chisholm, draper, and his wife Margaret, née Gibson, both Scottish-born. He was educated at Leichhardt Street State School and Brisbane Grammar School, then went into business with his father. In 1897-1900 he worked in Melbourne and Sydney, rejoining his father in 1901; two years later he became manager of the drapery department of Cullinane's Ltd, general merchants of Gympie. He married Alice Ruth Curtis at Bundaberg on 13 October 1909 with Anglican rites.

In July 1911 Chisholm was commissioned in the 13th Light Horse Regiment, Queensland Mounted Infantry, and served with this unit (renamed in 1912 the 1st L.H.R., Australian Military Forces) until World War I. He joined the Australian Imperial Force as a lieutenant on 20 August 1914 and was appointed to the 2nd L.H.R. The regiment reached Egypt in December and in May 1915 was sent to Gallipoli to fight as infantry; he served at Quinn's Post and Pope's Hill until the evacuation and from November was temporary staff captain of the 1st Light Horse Brigade.

Early in 1916 Chisholm took part in operations in Upper Egypt and then, before the advance into Sinai, was made brigade major; he was confirmed as captain in April. He fought in the decisive battle of Romani and at Katia and Bir-el-Abd, and was promoted major in September; his unit was then attached to Major General Sir Philip Chetwode's Desert Column which defeated the Turks at Magdhaba and Rafa. Chisholm fought throughout the 1917 Palestine campaign, participating in the second battle of Gaza and the capture of Beersheba, and on 1 January 1918 was awarded the Distinguished Service Order. At Musallabeh next April he was severely wounded in the neck, and on resuming duty was made general staff officer for the Australian Mounted Division, holding this post until his demobilization in September 1919. During the Sinai and Palestine campaigns he was mentioned in dispatches three times.

After the war Chisholm resumed business at Gympie. He continued to serve in the A.M.F. and in 1921-24 was lieut-colonel commanding the 5th L.H.R. From 1923 he lived at Rockhampton where he established a very successful drapery business; he later opened a branch at Biloela. Always active in local affairs, he held executive positions with the Rockhampton Agricultural Society, the Queensland Bush Children's Health Scheme, the Central Queensland Employers' Association and other organizations. He was a branch official of the Returned Sailors' and Soldiers' Imperial League of Australia and after his death the league's Rockhampton headquarters was named after him. He was appointed O.B.E. in 1939.

Chisholm died on 17 August 1945 when his car went over an embankment at Slater's Creek, near Dululu; he was buried in North Rockhampton cemetery with Anglican rites. His wife and two daughters survived him. While never a significant national figure, he was well known in Central Queensland because of his military career and his involvement in public affairs. He was a sociable man, generous-natured and with a keen sense of humour.

H. S. Gullett, *The A.I.F. in Sinai and Palestine* (Syd, 1923); G. H. Bourne, *Nulli secundus, the history of the 2nd Light Horse Regiment, A.I.F.* (Tamworth, 1926); *London Gazette*, 1 Jan 1916, 1, 12 Jan 1918, 22 Jan 1919; *Morning Bulletin*, 2 Jan 1939, 18 Aug 1945; War diaries, 2nd Light Horse Regiment, *and* 1st Light Horse Brigade, *and* Aust Mounted Division, AIF (AWM); information from Mrs J. Bradley, Curtis Island, Qld, and Mrs R. Soanes, Stafford Heights, Qld.

DAVID CARMENT

CHISHOLM, DAME ALICE ISABEL (1856-1954), organizer and superintendent of soldiers' canteens, was born on 3 July 1856, probably near Goulburn, New South Wales, second daughter of Major Richard John Morphy, pastoralist of Grena Mummell, Goulburn, and his wife Mary Emma, née Styles. Largely brought up by her Styles grandparents at Reevesdale near Bungonia, she was educated at home. On 18 July 1877 at her father's house she married a widower William Alexander Chisholm (d. 1902), a pastoralist of near-by Kippilaw; they had three sons and two daughters.

When her son Bertram was wounded on Gallipoli, Alice Chisholm went to Egypt in July 1915 to be near him. Impressed by the inadequacy of the amenities in Cairo, she decided to open a canteen for soldiers and established it, largely at her own expense, in the outer suburb of Heliopolis. The glad response from the Australian Imperial Force encouraged her to open another at Port Said.

Troops moving into Sinai and Palestine crossed the Suez Canal at Kantara and it was on the west bank that a canteen was set up early in 1916 by Alice Chisholm, Miss Verania McPhillamy of Forbes, New South Wales, and Miss Rout of New Zealand. Beginning with a lone tent near the bridge, and at their own expense, they built up a soldiers' club capable of catering for thousands without distinction of rank or army. Dormitories and dining-rooms were built, flowers obtained, butter on ice was served with freshly baked bread. Perhaps the greatest luxury, especially for men returning from the front, was the showers.

Large as her soldiers' club became, Alice Chisholm saw to it that her service continued to be personal, moving among the troops to greet them and wish them luck. She was highly competent herself and inspired efficiency in her staff; only thus could 4000 soldiers have been fed or 60 000 eggs be cooked in one day. 'Mother Chisholm's' became a cherished institution of the A.I.F. and many soldiers preferred to spend their leave there rather than in Cairo.

In 1918 Rania McPhillamy opened branch canteens, at Jerusalem and, after the Armistice, at Rafa in Palestine. Appreciating the need for amenities on the troopships which would take the Light Horse and the Flying Corps home, the two women insisted that the profits from their canteens be used to provide 'comforts' for the voyage. They made additional gifts to British and New Zealand troops and military charities. Money remaining was given by Mrs Chisholm to help found the Returned Soldiers' Club at Goulburn which she herself had proposed. In recognition of her work in Egypt she was appointed O.B.E. early in 1918 and D.B.E. in 1920.

On her return to Sydney Dame Alice was president of the Cumberland branch of the Country Women's Association in 1923-27; she was also a keen supporter of the Royal Society for the Prevention of Cruelty to Animals. The later years of her long life were passed in quiet retirement broken by occasional visits to England until, during the miners' strike of 1949, aged 93, she sent a dignified letter of expostulation to the *Sydney Morning Herald*. 'My heart aches', she wrote, 'for the thousands of our people now thrown out of work and the hardships the women especially will have to endure'. Four years later, replying to the toast on her ninety-seventh birthday, Dame Alice remarked: 'I have had a pretty good innings but I suppose Don Bradman would not think so'. Survived by two sons and a daughter, she died at her home at West Pennant Hills on 31 May 1954 and was buried in the Church of England cemetery at Kippilaw.

H. S. Gullett, *The A.I.F. in Sinai and Palestine* (Syd, 1923); *R.S.L. News* (Goulburn), June 1954; *Reveille* (Syd), July 1954; *SMH*, 14 July 1917, 8 Aug 1923, 27 May 1926, 8 Mar 1927, 13 July 1949, 7 July 1953, 11 June 1954; family papers (held by Mrs P. G. Thompson, Wollstonecraft, NSW).

A. J. HILL

CHOMLEY, CHARLES HENRY (1868-1942), writer and newspaper editor, was born on 28 April 1868 at Sale, Victoria, son of Henry Baker Chomley, bank manager, and his wife Eliza, daughter of T. T. à Beckett [q.v.3]. Charles was a nephew of A. W. and H. M. Chomley [qq.v.3]. He was related to that circle of pre-gold Melbourne families which his nephew Martin Boyd later commemorated in his novels.

Chomley graduated B.A. (1888), LL.B. (1889) from Trinity College, University of Melbourne, and was admitted to the Victorian Bar in 1891. In that year, on 16 June he married his cousin Ethel Beatrice Ysobel, daughter of W. A. C. à Beckett [q.v.3]. His mother-in-law took him with her family to England for a year. About 1893 Chomley left the Bar to farm in partnership with a cousin Frank Chomley, and with a group of friends settled in the King River valley in north-east Victoria. His mother, who joined him, recalled it as 'quite an exceptional little community there of a few families of our own class, mostly related to each other, their pretty homes, fine orchards and dairy farms within easy distance'; she found the life both beautiful and difficult. Chomley was an Oxley shire councillor in 1896-99 and president in 1898. After straining his heart he was forced to retire to Melbourne about 1900.

Chomley then took to writing and journalism, and edited the *Arena*, a gossipy, illustrated weekly, devoted to the arts, politics and fashionable society. Lionel and Norman Lindsay [qq.v.] provided cartoons, usually on political subjects. Despite its flippant tone, the *Arena* supported the suffragette movement and championed free trade. In February 1903 it took over the *Sun* but ceased publication in 1904. Chomley's first novel, about the vicissitudes of a selector, *The wisdom of Esau*, written with a friend and former fellow-farmer Robert Leonard Outhwaite, had already appeared. He also wrote on incidents in Victorian history, and in 1905 published his second novel, *Mark Meredith*, a fantasy about life in a totalitarian socialist Australia, where political unregenerates were sent to work in the canefields of Queensland.

In 1907 Chomley sailed for England and in April next year became editor (and later proprietor) of the *British-Australasian*, an established weekly which underwent several changes of name. Catering mainly for Australian expatriates and visitors, it dealt with political, economic and commercial matters affecting Britain, Australia and New Zealand. Every quarter Chomley published a supplement on art and literature, with contributions from his numerous relations, his circle of friends and prominent Australian writers and artists. In 1909 he and Outhwaite produced a tract advocating taxation based on the value of land. Regarded by his relations as an independent thinker and somewhat of a radical, he en-

tered into the monetary debate after World War I, with a pamphlet urging that the system should be based on goods and commodities.

Chomley edited the *British-Australasian* until his death in London on 21 October 1942. His wife, a woman endowed (according to Martin Boyd) with the à Beckett wit, had predeceased him in 1940, leaving a son and three daughters.

M. Boyd, *Day of my delight* (Melb, 1965); *The Times*, 23 Oct 1942; Mrs H. B. Chomley, My memoirs (LaTL).   P. H. DE SERVILLE

CHRISTIAN, SYDNEY ERNEST (1868-1931), soldier, was born on 17 April 1868 in Sydney, son of William Bassett Christian, pastoralist of Tenterfield station, and his wife Emma, née Rendall. Educated at The King's School, Parramatta, and the Church of England Grammar School, Geelong, Victoria, he decided on a military career and qualified for entry to the Royal Military College, Sandhurst, England; instead of enrolling, however, he returned to the family property. In 1891 he was commissioned second lieutenant in a volunteer unit, the 4th New South Wales Infantry (Maitland) Regiment.

On 18 February 1895 Christian joined the New South Wales Permanent Military Forces as a lieutenant in 'A' Field Battery; he was also made an aide-de-camp to Major General (Sir) Edward Hutton [q.v.], officer commanding the colony's forces. He saw active service during the South African War, serving in 1900-01 with 'A' Field Battery, Royal Australian Artillery, in Cape Colony, Transvaal and Orange River Colony. He was wounded in action at Paardeberg and Springfontein and in July 1901 was mentioned in Lord Kitchener's dispatches as 'a very good gunner and horsemaster'. After returning home he was made temporary staff captain for artillery, first in New South Wales and then in Victoria. He married his cousin Edith Ina Christian on 11 February 1902 at St John's Anglican Church, Darlinghurst, Sydney; they were an exceptionally devoted couple, but had no children.

Christian was confirmed as captain in 1905 and two years later went to England on twelve months exchange duty with the Royal Artillery. In January 1909 he became chief instructor for militia artillery in New South Wales and Queensland, and though he was 'a severe task-master, intolerant of inefficiency', the soundness of his training was later borne out by the success of citizen artillerymen at Gallipoli and on the Western

Front. Promoted major in November 1910, he commanded the 1st Battery, Royal Australian Field Artillery, until World War I.

On the formation of the Australian Imperial Force Christian was appointed to command the 1st Field Artillery Brigade; he was promoted lieut-colonel in October and sailed for Egypt with the first contingent. Early in May 1915 his brigade was sent to Cape Helles, Gallipoli, where it served with the British Army's 29th Division until October. For distinguished service in the campaign he was appointed C.M.G., awarded the Légion d'honneur and mentioned in dispatches. In February 1916 he was promoted colonel and temporary brigadier general and was appointed to raise and command the artillery of the newly formed 5th Australian Division. Apart from a nucleus of officers and seasoned gunners the artillery had to be drawn from volunteers from the light horse and the infantry. Time for training was short and equipment lacking; however, the formation was ready to leave Egypt for France by the end of May, an achievement which the official war historian described as remarkable. Christian commanded the artillery in the Armentières sector and in July, at the battle of Fromelles, the 4th Divisional Artillery as well. His men served with the New Zealand Division in Flanders in October and November and then spent the winter on the Somme. In January 1917 he was evacuated because of illness and in April was invalided to Australia and demobilized.

Christian retired from the Australian Military Forces in January 1918 with the honorary rank of brigadier general. His wife had died in London just before his evacuation from France and for the rest of his life he lived at the Australian Club in Sydney; his chief interests were golf and fishing. He died of pneumonia on 17 May 1931 and was cremated with Anglican rites.

Aust Defence Dept, *Official records of the Australian military contingents to the war in South Africa*, P. L. Murray ed (Melb, 1912); A. D. Ellis, *The story of the Fifth Australian Division* (Lond, 1920?); C. E. W. Bean, *The story of Anzac* (Syd, 1921, 1924), and *The A.I.F. in France*, 1916 (Syd, 1929); E. T. Dean (ed), *War service record of First Australian Field Artillery Brigade, 1914-19* (Adel, nd); R. L. Wallace, *The Australians at the Boer War* (Canb, 1976); *London Gazette*, 5, 8 Nov 1915, 24 Feb 1916; *Reveille* (Syd), May 1931; *Gunfire* (Syd), Sept 1963, Mar 1973; *SMH*, 18, 19 May 1931.

J. WHITELAW

CHRISTIE, JOHN MITCHELL (1845-1927), detective and sportsman, was born on 30 December 1845 at Clackmannan, Scotland, son of Captain James Christie and his wife Martha, née Reoch. He attended a school at St Andrews, entering Taylor's College, Woolwich, in 1862 with the intention of following a military career. His grandfather was an army officer in Canada, while his father had served in India. A brother, also Captain James Christie, took part in the siege of Lucknow and was later governor of Edinburgh Gaol, and another brother, Alexander, was a manager of the Bank of Australasia in Melbourne.

Christie, described as a clerk, was 17 when he left Liverpool in the *Commodore Perry* in August 1863 to work for his uncle, Hugh Reoch, a partner in Kilmany Park station, Gippsland, Victoria. Reoch was drowned in the Tarra River in August 1864 and Christie lived and worked with A. C. and W. Pearson [q.v.5] at Kilmany Park and at Lemuel Bolden's [q.v.1] Strathfieldsaye station on the banks of Lake Wellington.

In June 1866 Christie joined the Melbourne detective force which was then said to consist of well-educated men of standing. Later described as a 'well-groomed, refined-looking, walking embodiment of good taste', he was also seen in a less favourable light as one who grew rich on his share of fines.

A good athlete, Christie became well known in boxing and rowing circles throughout Australia. After a sparring and 'scientific boxing' exhibition with Abe Hicken in August 1871 he was awarded a silver cup, and in the same month won the Victorian amateur championship from Jack Thompson (brother of Joseph [q.v.6]). In November 1875 he resigned from the detective force to devote more time to sport and in December won a sculling match from James Cazaly. He won the Australasian Cup for sculling next April but gave up rowing after a defeat by the much younger C. A. Messenger in July 1878. He ran an athletic hall in Little Collins Street and later Swanston Street where he taught boxing. He trained W. Miller [q.v.5] for his fight with Larry Foley [q.v.4] and boxed with Jem Mace.

Christie was also deeply involved in charitable works for various disaster funds, including the Police Fund, and is credited with raising over £30000. He spent some years as a hotelkeeper until November 1884, when he joined the Customs Department. His promotion to revenue detective dated from 1 July 1887 and he was thereafter known as 'Inspector' Christie.

During his years as a detective, Christie's famous cases included forgery and counterfeiting, several money swindles, and the theft of William Lyster's [q.v.5] jewels. In the Customs Department his activities ranged from tracking down smugglers of opium and tobacco, breaking up illicit stills in Richmond and on the western coast, holding border smugglers at Wodonga, and catching George Robertson [q.v.6] importing prohibited books, to confiscating bubonic bacilli at Macarthur. Adept at disguises, Christie was variously a travelling tinker, a street-sweeper, a clergyman, but most often a 'gentleman'. The highlights of his career, however, were when he 'shadowed' visiting royalty; in 1867 he travelled throughout Australia and New Zealand with the duke of Edinburgh [q.v.4]; in 1881 he accompanied Princes Albert and George, and in 1901 acted as bodyguard to the duke of York.

At the time of his retirement in December 1910, due mainly to impaired hearing after being assaulted, Christie was described as 'the idol of the Victorian public' because of his 'astounding feats' of athletics, his many hair-breadth escapes, extraordinary ruses and tricks, and his ingenuity and resourcefulness. His successes were well publicized, but unlike the fictional detectives with whom he was compared, Christie was real and his achievements were genuine.

On 5 December 1877 he had married Emilie Ada Taylor Baker, daughter of a bookseller, at the Presbyterian Manse, West Melbourne; she predeceased him. He died at his home Kilmany, Armadale, on 11 January 1927, survived by his only son. His estate was valued for probate at £10069.

J. B. Castieau, *The reminiscences of Detective Inspector Christie* (Melb, nd); *Notes and Queries for Readers* (Lond), 5 (1863); *Morwell Hist Soc News*, 10 Feb 1966; *Australasian*, 12 Aug 1871, 20-27 Nov, 25 Dec 1875, 15 Apr, 21 Oct 1876, 15 Dec 1877, 13 July 1878; *Punch* (Melb), 29 Dec 1910; *Argus*, 12 Jan 1927; shipping lists (PRO, Vic).

HUGH ANDERSON

CHRISTIE, ROBERT (1883-1957), soldier and air force officer, was born on 5 August 1883 at Maryborough, Queensland, son of Archibald Christie, labourer, and his wife Emma, née Spencer. His father was born in Scotland, his mother in England. He was educated at the Maryborough State School, then moved with his parents to Bundaberg where he worked as a labourer and mail contractor. On 29 July 1907 he married Dorothy Ward with Presbyterian forms.

From about 1907 Christie served in the militia and by 1910 was a sergeant in the Wide Bay Infantry Regiment, Australian Military Forces; he was appointed to the Queensland instructional staff in January 1911 and served as a staff sergeant major until World War I. On 24 November 1914 he enlisted in the Australian Imperial Force

and was posted to the 5th Light Horse Regiment; his unit embarked for Egypt in December and, from 20 May 1915 until the evacuation, fought at Gallipoli as infantry. He was a quartermaster sergeant and honorary lieutenant from July.

On the formation of the A.I.F.'s 4th Division in February 1916 Christie transferred as a sergeant to the 51st Battalion, raised in Western Australia. Commissioned as a second lieutenant in March 1916, he was promoted captain at once and major in September. After reaching France he fought at Mouquet Farm, Lagnicourt and Messines. He commanded the 51st in the battle of Polygon Wood in September 1917 and won the Distinguished Service Order especially for his 'tactical handling of the battalion'. He was promoted lieut-colonel on 23 October and confirmed in his command. Next April at Villers-Bretonneux he gained a Bar to his D.S.O.; here he was involved in a difficult night operation and, having already marched six miles, was ordered to counterattack and recover a village. Although there was no time for reconnaissance the approach march and the attack itself were 'a brilliant success'. Christie retained command until the end of the war and was awarded the Belgian Croix de Guerre and twice mentioned in dispatches. His personal courage and coolness in action, his warm nature and his concern for his men made him a popular and respected leader.

Christie was demobilized in October 1919, and became a peace-time soldier with the 16th Battalion, Citizen Military Forces. In January 1924 he joined the newly formed Royal Australian Air Force as a flight lieutenant in the stores and equipment branch. His experience as a quartermaster proved valuable in setting up No. 1 Aircraft Depot at Point Cook, Victoria, and after a posting to Laverton in 1926-35, he was appointed wing commander and commanding officer of No. 2 Aircraft Depot at Richmond, New South Wales. In World War II he was promoted group captain in July 1940 and placed in charge of the Waterloo stores depot. From September 1942 to April 1944 he was senior equipment staff officer at Melbourne headquarters and ended the war as commanding officer of No. 5 Maintenance Group, Sydney. He was promoted air commodore in July 1944 and next year retired and returned to Bundaberg. Christie had been foundation president of the Wide Bay-Burnett branch of the Returned Sailors' and Soldiers' Imperial League of Australia. In 1950 his old 51st Battalion comrades pressed him to lead them in the Anzac Day march and although not well he joined them in Perth.

Survived by a son and a daughter, Christie died at Bundaberg on 6 February 1957 from injuries received in a fall, and was cremated in Brisbane with full military honours.

L. C. Wilson and H. Wetherell, *Fifth Light Horse Regiment, 1914-1919* (Syd, 1926); C. E. W. Bean, *The story of Anzac* (Syd, 1921, 1924), and *The A.I.F. in France*, 1916-18 (Syd, 1929, 1933, 1937, 1942); *London Gazette*, 17 Dec 1917, 23 Apr, 16 Sept 1918; *Canb Times*, and *Courier Mail*, 8 Feb 1957; information from Miss D. Christie, Bundaberg, Qld.

JOHN MCCARTHY

CHRISTMAS, HAROLD PERCIVAL (1884-1947), retailer, was born on 5 May 1884 at Kiama, New South Wales, eldest son of Robert Christmas, bank clerk and later manager, and his wife Mary Caroline, née King. He was educated at Neutral Bay Public School and in 1898-99 at Sydney Church of England Grammar School (Shore). Percy, as he was known, left school at 16 and became a junior and later a commercial traveller with Isherwood & Bartlett, softgoods wholesalers of Sydney. He was warehouse manager when he married Constance Veta Southouse (d. 1914) on 28 March 1912 at St Philip's Church of England, Church Hill. In 1913 he became manager of the Adelaide branch, but returned to Sydney in 1916 to become a salesman for a Melbourne millinery manufacturer. On 16 January 1917 at St James's Church, Sydney, he married Thirza Millard Phillips.

By chance Christmas bought a book, *The clock without hands*, thinking it would be a detective story: instead it was about the commercial benefits of advertising. A correspondence course convinced him that advertising was the key to successful retailing. In partnership with S. E. Chatterton, who had been a department manager in David Jones [q.v.2], Ltd he sold women's clothes by mail order. Less successful than they had hoped, about 1919 they opened a blouse and hosiery shop in the Queen Victoria Building, and used the slogan 'No Shop Rent', to convince customers that they could buy at lower prices. By 1924 the business had grown and more space was needed. They were offered basement space in the Imperial Arcade, which Christmas leased at a very low rent, although it was unsuitable for a dress shop. G. Creed from Melbourne suggested it could be used for retailing low cost, portable merchandise, patterned on the operation at Cash & Carry Ltd in Adelaide. Woolworths Ltd was registered in 1924, after the American company had indicated it would not object to the name. Christmas became managing director. On 5 December, following an advance advertising campaign, 'Woolworth's Stupendous Bargain Basement' opened. After overcoming a minor financial crisis, the company prospered.

Christmas was able to design and introduce new sales methods which attracted customers because of 'his wonderful understanding of how ordinary people thought and behaved'. He took great trouble about hiring staff and had applicants examined by a phrenologist. In 1928 he opened a second branch, in Pitt Street, and introduced the distinctive red and white uniform for shop assistants who knew him as 'Father'. In the 1930s Christmas presided over the expansion of Woolworths into a chain store with companies registered in Victoria, Western Australia and New Zealand. In 1936 criticism of trade practices led to an inquiry by the Industrial Commission of New South Wales into the control and operations of chain stores. Two and a half years later Mr Justice Browne found that Woolworths' operations were in the best interests of the community.

During World War II Christmas was controller of the New South Wales division of the Australian Defence Canteens Service. Until he retired as managing director of Woolworths in 1945, he kept fit by swimming daily and filled his leisure by reading, sailing and farming at Cattai on the Hawkesbury River. He went overseas in April 1947 but died suddenly at Bordeaux, France, on 19 June, survived by a daughter of his first marriage and by his second wife and their son and daughter. His estate was sworn for probate at £405 091.

Draper of A'sia, 21 Dec 1908; G. Newton, 'When Father Christmas ruled the store', *Aust Women's Weekly*, 4 Dec 1974; *SMH*, 20 June 1947; records and public relations material (Woolworths Ltd, Syd); information from Mr C. Hart, Wahroonga, NSW.

G. J. ABBOTT

CHUMLEIGH, HAROLD VERE (1880?-1970), soldier, is believed to have been born on 2 October 1880 at Carstairs, Lanarkshire, Scotland; however, no record of his birth is available and he often gave conflicting information about his origins. His early life remains a mystery. In 1897 he became a trooper in the 12th Royal Lancers, saw action in the South African War, then served in India until 1907, when he was discharged from the British Army for reasons unknown. Soon afterwards he migrated to Western Australia with a regimental comrade Henry Alfred David Ransom, whom he had persuaded to pose as his brother under the name of Harry Chumleigh. Though they later fell out, Ransom was to use this alias until his death.

In 1909 both men enlisted in the Royal

Australian Artillery in Perth and next year, following the introduction of universal training, attended the first Army School for Instructors at Albury, New South Wales. On graduating, Harold Chumleigh was posted in January 1911 to the newly established Royal Military College, Duntroon, as instructor in infantry drill, musketry and signalling. Three years later, as a warrant officer, he was appointed regimental sergeant major to the Corps of Staff Cadets and held this post until 1928 when he was transferred to Townsville, Queensland. That year he was awarded the Long Service and Good Conduct Medal. He retired in 1930 with the honorary rank of lieutenant.

As regimental sergeant major to the Royal Military College in its first seventeen years, Chumleigh was responsible to the director of drill for the drill, deportment and discipline of the staff cadets. He was soldierly and completely efficient in all he did and unequivocal in his practice of discipline, treating his superiors with unfailing respect and his subordinates with dignity and consideration. His attitude towards the cadets, shortly to be his superior officers, was impeccable. Chumleigh is best remembered 'in summer dress, helmet, rounded nose, and red, flushed face — immaculate summer drill, although close inspection revealed a darn or two — swan-necked spurs — leather-thonged riding whip constantly under the left arm — a high-pitched, penetrating command and a most correct salute'. He did not abuse or bully but was patient and encouraging. In cavalry exercises he led the cadets over the plains of Canberra and into the wooded slopes of Ainslie and Majura, revelling in displaying his knowledge of bush lore and horse-mastership.

Over the years Chumleigh became a Duntroon identity. Affectionately known as 'Old Chum' or 'The Marquis', he delighted in telling tales — most of them exaggerated and romanticized — of his experiences in India and South Africa; it was common knowledge that his claimed military service added up to over 100 years. His private life was predictably colourful. There is evidence to suggest that he was married before he came to Australia. In 1909 he named N. C. Chumleigh of Brisbane as his wife but no record of a marriage exists. He apparently went through some form of marriage about two years later at Queanbeyan, New South Wales, giving his name as Harold Vere Vere-Chumleigh, and there was a daughter of this union. On 31 May 1931, stating his condition as bachelor and his name as Harold Vere Douglas Cholmondeley de Chumleigh, he married Alice Christina Mayo; she divorced him for desertion and adultery in 1935. Chumleigh lived with a Gertrude Lawrence Chumleigh in Townsville in the early 1930s, but in 1937 named Elsie Louise Chumleigh of Crows Nest, New South Wales, as his wife. On 20 October 1955, at Sydney Registry Office, he married a widow, Janet Mabel Owen, describing himself as Harold Vere-Chumleigh, widower, of London. He varied his parents' names as frequently as his own.

On retiring from the army Chumleigh lived at Townsville for several years, then moved to Sydney, where in World War II he served briefly with the 2nd Garrison Battalion, Volunteer Defence Corps. After 1941 he claimed to have been employed in naval security, but by 1955 was a caretaker at the Vesta battery factory, Sydney. He and his last wife lived at Katoomba where he died on 3 November 1970.

Chumleigh's contribution as the first regimental sergeant major at Duntroon was considerable. He trained, in their formative years, many graduates who served in World War I and held senior ranks in World War II. He was in no small way responsible for the mutual understanding and respect established between the Australian Staff Corps and the Australian Instructional Corps during the inter-war years of compulsory training. In 1920 he was mentioned for specially meritorious service rendered in Australia in World War I.

J. E. Lee, *Duntroon* (Canb, 1952); S. F. Rowell, *Full circle* (Melb, 1974); Roy Military College of Aust, *J*, Dec 1966; A. J. C. Newton, 'The Australian Instructional Corps', *Army J*, Aug 1971; *Canb Times*, 28 June 1934, 13 Apr 1935; 'Guest of honour' (radio), 31 Oct 1954 (ABC Archives, Syd); reminiscences and family information.

JEAN P. FIELDING
J. H. THYER*

CORRIGENDA

Australian Dictionary of Biography

†Volume 6: 1851-1890 R-Z (1979)

4a RAMSAY, E. P.
line 42 *for* lithology *read* icthyology

48b ROBINSON
line 4 *for* gaity *read* gaiety

66a ROWAN
lines 27-28 *for* District . . . Downs. *read* District.

75a RUSSELL, H. C.
line 39 *for* Three *read* Four

96b SCOTT, H. J. H.
lines 9-10 *for* churchyard . . . Church. *read* Church of England cemetery with Presbyterian forms.

101b SELLHEIM
line 22 *for* Rachael *read* Rachel

126a SIMPSON, A.
line 4 *for* Wesleyan . . . clergyman *read* gentleman,

174a STANTON
line 16 *for* St Giles . . . Fields. *read* Lincoln's Inn Fields.

184b STEPHEN
line 20 *for* Thakombau *read* Cakobau

185a line 1 *for* mischievious *read* mischievous

223a SUTHERLAND, G.
line 33 *for* 1879 *read* 1877

265a THOMPSON, J. L.
line 7 *for* McCoombie *read* McCombie

266b THOMPSON, J. M.
lines 3-5 *for* London . . . for *read* London, son of Samuel Solomon, tobacco manufacturer, and his wife Jessie, née Levi. He used the surname

267b lines 20-25 *for* a widow . . . infant. *read* his wife Rose Maria, née Barnett, whom he had married at Fitzroy on 12 February 1868, three daughters and a son John.

270a THOMSON, R.
lines 56-57 *after* was *add* secretary and *and for* Sydney branch *read* association.

270b line 14 *for* admission *read* re-admission

276a TIGHE
lines 3 *after* born *add* on 3 March 1827
line 5 *for* 17th *read* 28th *and after* Regiment *add* , and his wife Sarah, née McNamara.
lines 5-8 *for* probably . . . 28th Regiment; *read* , with his family and some of his regiment, reached Sydney on 4 February 1836 in the *Susan* and was stationed at Parramatta;

284a TOOHEY
line 58 *for* colony. *read* colony'.

298a TRAILL
line 7 *delete* and London
line 11 *delete* (Westeve)
line 13 *for* 1790 *read* 1793

298b line 15 *for* New Year's *read* Boxing
line 52 *for* 6d. *read* 6d.,

311b TURNER, C. T.
line 6, bibliography for *Wisden's* read *Wisden*

320a TYSON
line 23 *for* £1000 *read* £2000 for two years

332b VERJUS
line 21 *for* Issoudoun, France, *read* Oleggio, Piedmont,

389a WHITE, J. C.
line 12 *for* and *read* but
line 13 *for* stock *read* works

389b line 2 *for* about 1850 *read* in June 1854

409b WILLOUGHBY
line 2, bibliography *for* Mercer *read* Nurser

412a WILSHIRE
line 7, bibliography *for* 1950 *read* 1850

418b WILSON, S.
line 46 *for* Murrumbidgee River *read* Yanko Creek

428b WISE, E.
line 49 *for* Jefferies *read* Jeffreys

433b WOOD, J. D.
line 39 *for* 1903-08 *read* 1903-09

454a YOUNG, J. H.
line 7 *for* 1890 *read* 1880

†all of these corrections are printed for the first time

line 42 *for* March *read* April *and for*
District *read* Province
line 43 *for* January 1867 *read* 1866

263a †MOCATTA
line 32 *delete* on the Darling Downs
263b lines 10-11 *for* in 1857 *read* on 4
March 1858 *and for* Harriet *read*
Harries Hankin, née

270a MONTEFIORE, J. L.
line 5 *after* Hannah *add* , née
Montefiore

279a MOORE, M.
†lines 3-4 *for* of Irish parents *read*
daughter of James Edward Sullivan and his wife Bridget Mary,
née Whelan,
279b line 13 *delete* [q.v.]

285a MORESBY
line 4 *for* Captain *read* Admiral

302a MORTLOCK
signature *after* bibliography *add*
H. KEMPE

309b MULLEN
line 9 *for* Jun. & *read* jun. and

318a †MURPHY, F.
lines 1-2 *delete* Herbert . . . 1912,

349a †OAKDEN
line 4, bibliography *for* Soc *read*
Inst

349b OAKES
line 3 *delete* Rev. *and for* , Wesleyan
read [q.v.]
line 4 *delete* missionary,

353a O'CONNOR, M.
line 25 for *liminem* read *limina*

355a ODDIE
line 2, bibliography *for* 1885 *read*
1855

361b †O'HEA
lines 21-22 *delete* and . . . to

362a line 30 *for* commander *read* colonel

366b O'MAHONY
line 44 *after* Quinn *add* [q.v.]

372b ORMOND
line 6 *for* Essen *read* Esson

373a †lines 28-30 *for* the . . . 1861 *read*
sections of Bangal station across
the river from Borriyaloak
†line 37 *for* Ann *read* Mary

393a †PALMER, J. F.
line 10 *for* Sydney *read* Melbourne
line 12 *for* 1842 . . . Melbourne *read*
1842,

394b PALMER, T. M.
line 25 *for* Kalakua *read* Kalakaua

397b PARKER, H.
line 20 *for* built *read* bought and
improved

412b PATERSON, J. F.
line 9, bibliography *for* 17 Apr *read*
16 Apr

415b †PATTERSON
lines 10-11 *for* outspoken . . . unremarkable, his *read* his administra-
tration was unremarkable, his
outspoken and uncompromising
support for

446b PITT
line 6 *for* Eliza *read* Elizabeth *and*
after Laycock *add* [q.v.]

†new items (since 1976)

CORRIGENDA

Australian Dictionary of Biography

Volume 5: 1851-1890 K-Q (1979)

xiiia AUTHORS
after KEITH *insert* KEMPE, H.: *Mortlock*
xiiib †line 16 for *Loder* read *Loader*
xva line 25 *for* RODGERS *read* ROGERS

25a KIMPTON
line 28 *after* Charles *add* Leslie

29b †KING, P. G.
line 8 *for* Adventurer *read* Adventure

34b KINTORE
line 1 *for* SIR *read* EARL OF,
line 11 *for* earl *read* duke

60a LANGHAM
line 33 *for* Cakubau's *read* Cakobau's

68b †LATHAM
line 60 *after* cemetery. *add* He was survived by his daughter Bertha Martha and a son, Lambert, of his second marriage.

70a †LAWES
lines 50-51 *for* seven sons *read* six children

76a LEE, D.
signature *for* THERESA *read* THERESE

83a LEVIEN
line 8 *for* a . . . Geelong *read* Geelong Grammar School

94b LIVERSIDGE
line 4, bibliography *for* 1961 *read* 1968

99b LOFTUS
line 14 *for* a peer *read* 'a peer'
100a line 1, bibliography *for* governors *read* governor

LONG
line 17 *for* built *read* later bought

117b LYSTER
signature *for* THERESA *read* THERESE

121a MACANSH
line 24 *delete* and Albilah, *and after* 1875 *add* and Albilbah in 1880

124b MACARTHUR, W.
line 14 *for* wool *read* sheep

142b MCCULLOCK, J.
line 28 *for* Wright *read* [F.A.] Wright [q.v.]

143a MCCULLOCH, W.
line 38 *for* Wright *read* [F.A.] Wright [q.v.]

147a MACDONALD, C.
line 1, bibliography *for* McAlister *read* MacAlister

153b †MACFARLANE
line 40 *after* sons *add* and a daughter

161a MCILRAITH, T.
line 46 *for* in *read* at Maxwelltown, Dumfriesshire,

171a †MACKENZIE, E.
lines 5-6 *delete* sold . . . and lines 23-24 *delete* but . . . made

181b †MACLANACHAN
line 10 *for* 1868-83 *read* 1868-84

189a MACMAHON
lines 14-15 *for* in October *read* on 18 November

192a MCNAB
line 10 *for* admitted *read* ordained

212a MARSDEN
line 3 *for* at O'Connell Plains *read* and baptized at St John's Church, Parramatta, on 9 March

216a †MARTIN, A. P.
line 28 for *Literature* read *The beginnings of an Australian literature* (London, 1898)
line 48 *for* Harriete *read* Harriette

236b †MELVILLE, F.
line 29 *for* 1852 *read* 1853

240a †MEREDITH
line 10 *for* September 1860 when *read* June 1861 although *and after* leave *add* from September 1860
line 13 *for* 1866-70 *read* 1866-71
line 14 *for* 1871-75 *read* 1871-76
lines 21-23 *for* Innes . . . [q.v.]. *read* Innes [q.v.], and under Reiby [q.v.] was colonial treasurer from 20 July 1876 to 9 August 1877, and minister for lands and works from 21 July to 21 August 1876.
line 40 *for* 1832 *read* 1835

248b MIKLUHO-MAKLAI
line 1 *after* MIKLUHO-MAKLAI *add* NICHOLAI
250a line 29 *for* favourably *read* unfavourably

252b MILLER
line 41 *for* District *read* Province

†new items (since 1976)

406b HODGSON, C. P.
lines 11-12 *for* died . . . Hakodate
read died at Pau *and after* 1865 *read*
leaving a wife and daughter

408b HOFFNUNG
line 29 *for* 1857 *read* 1858

416a HOLYMAN
line 37 *for* 1883 *read* 1882

423b HORDERN
line 38 *for* Milton *read* Wilton
line 39 *for* and *read* , Picton, and in
1887 to build

424b HORNE, T.
line 10 *delete* attorney-general,

427a †HORSFALL
line 18 *for* Carrington *read*
Carington
line 43 *for* 300 *read* 200

428a HOSE
line 2 *after* born *add* on 24 September 1826

line 3 *delete* Rev.
line 16 *for* 1854 *read* 1855

429b HOSKINS
line 9, bibliography *for* 1893 *read*
1883

449a HUNTER, H.
lines 13-14 *for* but . . . raise *read* and
raised

458b INNES, F. M.
†line 52 *for* Campbell Town *read*
South Esk

459a line 16 *for* 1878 *read* 1880

471a †JARDINE
lines 18-19 *for* government resident *read* police magistrate
line 20 *for* resident *read* magistrate
lines 45-48 *for* acted . . . available
read was appointed police magistrate in 1868.

486a JOHNSTON, J. S.
line 24 *for* Busten *read* Austen

†new items (since 1976)

216b FRASER, Sir Simon
line 46 *for* Anne *read* Anna
line 51 *for* 1897 *read* 1885

229b GARDINER
line 18 *for* after ... leave *read*
skipped bail

232a GARLICK
line 19 *for* 1874 *read* 1832?

237b GARVAN
line 58 *for* 1898 *read* 1908

240b GEOGHEGAN
line 10 *for* Easter ... 1835 *read* 21
February 1830

241b GEORGE
line 44 *for* May *read* March

245a GILBERT, John
line 20 *for* Mann *read* Manns
245b line 14 *for* Wowingragang *read*
Wowingragong
line 16 *delete* who ... them

246b GILES
line 39 *for* Egerton *read* Warburton.

248b †GILL, J. H.
line 27 *delete* John *and after* Appel
add [q.v.]

253b GLADMAN
line 35 *for* 1882 *read* 1886

260a GOLDIE
line 4 *delete* Sir

264a GOODLET
line 28 *for* 1903 *read* 1913
line 36 *for* Boys' School *read*
Academy

267a GOOLD, S. S.
line 38 *for* editior *read* editor

267b GORDON, A. L.
lines 23-24 *after* November *read*
1853

269a GORDON, Alexander
line 2 *after* born *add* on 14 October
1815

272a †GORE, J.
line 6 *for* 1879 *read* 1878

278b †GOYDER
line 1 *for* WOODROOFE *read*
WOODROFFE

282b GRAHAM, James
lines 42-43 *for* a founding *read* an
early

286b †GRAY, J.
lines 5-6 *for* by ... migrated *read* in
1843 was transported *and after*
Town *add* for subornation
line 57 *for* his wife died *read* the
death of his wife Mary, née Newton, whom he had married in April
1848,

294a GREGORY, A. C.
line 13 *for* Charles *read* Henry
294b lines 2-3 *for* 1863 ... 1879. *read*
1863, on 12 March 1875 was replaced as surveyor-general by W.
A. Tully [q.v.], and became
geological surveyor.

295a line 39 *for* Cantini *read* Catani
line 55 *for* Gascoigne *read*
Gascoyne
295b line 17 *for* four *read* five
lines 23-24 *for* 21 August *read* 23
October

303a GRIMWADE
line 16 *for* 1888 *read* 1889

305b †GRUBB
line 3 *after* London *add* , son of
William Grubb and his wife Hannah, née Rockliff

306b GUERARD
line 39 *for* Wetterboro *read*
Wetterbord
307a line 11, bibliography *for* ML *read*
Dixson Lib

308b GUNTHER
line 3 *for* 28 *read* 25
line 21 *for* 1867 *read* 1868

311a GUTHRIE
line 6 *for* bought *read* leased

313a HACK
lines 7-8 *delete* by ... overland

347a HARGRAVES
line 8, bibliography *for* 10 *read* 38

355b HART, John
lines 46-47 *delete* where ... acres

356b †HART, W.
line 6 *after* November *add* 1902
line 15 *for* twelve *read* eleven
line 17 *after* married *add* a widow
and after Noble *add* , née Keam

358b HASSELL
line 6 *delete* [q.v.]

359b line 25 *for* Ethyl *read* Ethel

360b †HAWKER
line 20 *for* 1811 *read* 1821

†new items (since 1976)

2a D'ALBERTIS
line 22 *for* April *read* November
line 30 *after* November *read* 1875
and after Somerset *read* , Queensland,

9b DALLEY
line 14, bibliography *for* Angus
read Augustus

27b †DAVIES, J.
line 55 *delete* George
line 56 *after* Auber *add* George

29b DAVIES, John M.
line 3 *for* Tetfield *read* Tetbury
lines 25-27 *for* most . . . second.
read 4 of 6 sons and 2 of 6 daughters
of his first marriage, and 1 of 4 sons
and the one daughter of his second
marriage.
line 39 *for* five *read* eight
lines 59-64 *for* London . . . Jessie
read Bank of Australasia. He
moved to Melbourne, joined the
London Chartered Bank of Australia and later the Australian
Deposit and Mortgage Bank Ltd,
becoming manager in 1883. He had
married Sarah Ann Staples in 1877
but she died in 1879, survived by
their infant son; in 1887 he married
Jessie

30a line 1 *for* MacMurtrie *read*
McMurtrie
lines 2-3 *delete* became . . . He

30b line 50 *for* second . . . Boyle *read*
wife
line 51 *for* two *read* three
line 62 *for* two *read* three *and for*
seven *read* six

31a line 8 *for* his . . . Malvern *read*
Windaree, Williams Road, Toorak,
line 49 *for* three *read* four
line 50 *for* thirteen *read* fourteen

38b DE BOOS
line 21 *for* 73 *read* 71

44b DENIEHY
line 32 *for* 1844 *read* 1845

45a line 19 *for* world *read* word

46a line 3 *for* Jamieson *read* Jameson

46b lines 11-12, bibliography delete
Bathurst . . . 1865;

57a DERHAM
line 23 *for* 1856 *read* 1854

64b †DEXTER
line 18 *for* 1857 *read* 1858

80a †DODDS
line 22 *for* 1878-87 *read* 1878-86 *and
after* Hobart *add* , and in 1886-87
South Hobart,

81b †DODERY
line 48 *after* for *read* Longford
(Westmorland)

83a DONAGHY
line 3 *for* After *read* Before
lines 4-5 *delete* John . . . John
line 6 *for* were *read* had been
line 15 *for* 1868 *read* 1886

88a †DOUGLAS, A.
line 17 *for* 1862-70 *read* 1862-71
line 18 *for* 1870-71 *read* 1871-72

93a DOUGLASS
line 17 *for* March *read* April

113a DUFFY, Charles G.
line 49 *for* Of *read* Duffy's eldest
son was John Gavan [q.v.]; of

123a DYMOCK
lines 9-10 *delete* a councillor . . .
University

132b EGGLESTON
line 14 *for* three *read* two *and for*
one daughter *read* two daughters

136b ELLERY
line 7 *for* 1873 *read* 1870 as a
captain
line 8 *for* Corps *read* and Signal
Corps;
lines 8-9 *delete* (Submarine . . . until
line 10 *for* 1889 *read* December
1888

137a ELLIOTT
line 12 *for* Westrip *read* Neestrip

155a FARNELL
line 13, bibliography *for* 1893 *read*
1883

155b FARR
line 40 *for* 95 *read* 96

176a †FITZGERALD, G. P.
line 12 *for* Lane *read* Love

182a FITZHARDINGE
line 11 *delete* erroneously

186b FLEMING, Joseph
line 18 *delete* [q.v.]

187b †FLEMING, V.
line 58 *for* 1872 *read* 1870

207b FOSTER, W. J.
line 14, bibliography *for* 1893 *read*
1883

†new items (since 1976)

his wife Susanna, née Strudwicke

404a CLARK, C. G. H. C.
line 44 *for* 3 *read* 30
for 1876 *read* 1877
line 49 *for* 15 *read* 16

409a †CLARKE, A.
line 15 *after* Royal *add* Military

411b †CLARKE, G.
lines 5-6 *read* Martha, née
Blomfield

412b line 19 *after* Martha *add* Clarke

415b CLARKE, Lady
lines 13-18 *for* In 1900 . . . president
read In 1898-99 she was a member
of the Women's Hospital Committee and in 1900 president of the
Alliance Française,
line 19 *add* and *after* Children

417b CLARKE, M.
lines 48-50 *for* none . . . traced *read*
at least two married in Victoria and
survived him.

419b CLARKE, W.
line 1 *for* b. 1843 *read* 1843-1903

420a line 60 *add* He died at Cape Town
on 9 March 1903 and in the same
week his only son William Mortimer was killed in a riot.

420b CLARKE, W. B.
line 35 *read* Exequiale

423a CLARKE, W. J.
line 50 *for* Cobram *read* Cobran

426b CLIBBORN
line 46 *for* cousin *read* witness at
the marriage

436b COHEN, Edward
line 7 *for* five *read* four *and for* three
read four

439a COLE, E. W.
lines 53-54 *for* Jordan . . . Hobart
read Jorden, of Lauderdale, New
Town, Tasmania

443a COLLINS, R.
line 42 *read* Gwendoline
443b line 17 *read* Robert and William
were
lines 18-19 *for* He was *read* They
were
line 21 *read* They were
line 22 *for* his *read* the
line 2, bibliography *read* 1923

465a †CORRIGAN, J.
lines 22-23 *for* smoothly . . . divi-

sion. *read* smoothly.

468b COTTEE
line 60 *read* civic
469a line 1, bibliography for *One* read *A*

473b COWIE
line 26 *read* in August

478b COWPER, Sir Charles
lines 13-14 *for* and . . . quarrel *read*
. He had already quarrelled
line 19 *for* 1859 *read* 1858

489b CRACKNELL
line 3 *read* Salomons

493b CREWS
line 9, bibliography *read* 1859-69

495b CRISP
line 48 *delete* 8
lines 4-5, bibliography *for* 4 June
. . . 1916 *read* 7 Dec 1889, 8 May
1897, 4 June, 23 July 1898, 5 Nov
1963, 7 July 1966

498b †CROSBY
line 33 *for* In 1859 *read* On 14
February 1857

503a †CROWTHER
line 33 *for* opthalmology *read*
ophthalmology
line 48 *for* Rosa *read* Elizabeth
Rosaline
503b line 22 *for* 1878-84 *read* 1878-86 and
1897-1909
line 23 *for* 1886-1909 *read* 1886-97
line 42 *for* 1881 *read* 1882

506b CUNINGHAM
line 7 *for* daughter *read* sister

509a CURRAN
line 1 *for* Julian *read* J. E. Tenison-
509b line 23 *for* Julian *read* Tenison-

†CURRIE, A.
lines 14-19 *for* he . . . Melbourne
read, with W. A. Boyd and Thomas
Elder Boyd, junior, he bought the
Elizabeth and from January 1855,
with T. E. Boyd only, traded in
coastal, New Zealand and Chinese
waters. The partners established a
shipping company in Melbourne
and in the 1860s bought at least
nine vessels.

511b CURRIE, J.
line 18 *for* built *read* leased

512b CUSTANCE
line 57 *for* Lawrie *read* Lowrie

†new items (since 1976)

310b †BUSSELL
line 4 *for* fifth *read* sixth

311a lines 33-34 *for* St Mary's ... 1834.
read Wonnerup on 22 August 1850.
line 37 *for* soon *read* later
line 52 *delete* at Bunker Bay

311b line 40 *for* 2 December 1875 *read* 1
December 1876
lines 42 and 48 *for* Isaac *read* Isaacs
line 54 *for* On ... he *read* He
line 55 *for* 1882. *read* 1882, at
Brookhampton   farm,   near
Bridgetown.

315b BUTLER, H.
line 3 *delete* surgeon
†line 7 *for* four *read* five

316a †line 42 *for* 1884 *read* 1885

320b BUZACOTT
line 3 *for* July *read* August

323a BYRNES
line 27 *after* Taylor *add* [q.v.]

338b CAMERON, E.H.
line 13 *for* 1863 *read* 1860

341a CAMPBELL, Alexander
lines 28-29 *for* by 1850 *read* in 1843
line 48 *after* the *read* Sydney
branch of the

347a CAMPBELL, W.
line 3 *for* in *read* on 17 July 1810 at

347b lines 9-10 *for* Macarthur's ...
Mountains   *read*   Macarthurs'
Richlands station near Goulburn

348b line 11 *after* died *add* in London

CANI
line 8 *read* Ferretti

351a CANTERBURY
line 11 *for* 23 *read* 24
line 12 *for* Thomson *read* Tomson

352a *before* CARBONI *add* CARAN-
DINI, ROSINA *see* PALMER,
ROSINA

CARBONI
line 1 *for* 1820 *read* 1817
line 3 *for* 24 June 1820 *read* 15
December 1817

357a CARR-BOYD
line 4 *delete* Dr
line 7 *for* There *read* At Campbell
Town

363a CARTER, G.
line 1 *read* 1830

363b line 36 *delete* aged 71

364a CARY
line 39 *for* 1839 *read* 1838

365a CASEY, J.
line 21 *read* Sandhurst
line 23 *delete* He ... and
line 24 *for* in *read* In *and after* 80 *add*
he

366a CASEY, R.
line 39 *for* Terrick *read* Terrick
Terrick
line 47 *for* 1892 *read* 1893

366b lines 15-16 *delete* remained ... he
line 17 *for* sons *read* children

367b CASSELL
line 23 *read* Bruford

373b CHALLINOR
line 1 *delete* ?
line 2 *add* on 22 June 1814

375b CHALMERS, J.
line 59 *for* 1886 *read* 1885

376b CHALMERS, William
lines   2-3   *for*   February   *read*
September

380b CHAPMAN, H.
line 3 *add* on 21 July 1803

382a line 8 *for* 1867 *read* 1868

384a †CHARLES
line 33 *for* about 1853 *read* on 30
May 1855

391b CHIRNSIDE
line 3 *for* Berwickshire *read* Cock-
burnspath, East Lothian
line 5 *for* Fairs *read* Fair
line 37 *add* later *before* building
lines 38-39 *delete* in the 1850s
line 42 *for* and *read* ; his son later
acquired

392b line 8 *for* Bigbie *read* Begbie

393a CHOMLEY
line 20 *for* infancy. *read* infancy,
and five daughters

395b †CHRISTISON
line 25 *for* Tovey *read* Lovey
line 28 *for* 1884 *read* 1880 in London
and after Mary *add* Godsall

399a CLARK, A. T.
line 21 *read* Alexandrina

399b †CLARK, A. I.
line 30 *after* and *add* South Hobart
in

400b line 7 *for* Edmond *read* Edmund

403a CLARK, C.
line 1 *add* son of Daniel Clark and

116a BASSETT
line 35 *read* in 1854
116b lines 60-61 *for* London ... 1890)
read Edinburgh (M.R.C.S.; M.D., 1880)

122a BAYLY
line 16 *for* objected to *read* disliked *and for* shows. *read* shows;
lines 17-18 *for* His ... reflect *read* but he won several prizes, reflecting

123b BEAN
lines 24-25 *delete* the ... [q.v.],
124b line 2 *for* He was the *read* With J. L. Cuthbertson [q.v.] he was a

137b BELMORE
line 8 *for* Scone *read* Muswellbrook

139b BENJAMIN
lines 12-15 *for* officially ... [q.v.] *read* was present at the formal opening of Princes Bridge

147b BEOR
line 59 *for* July *read* June

150b BERRY, D.
line 8 *delete* [q.v.]

152b BERRY, G.
line 10 *for* 12 *read* 2

157a BEST, J.
line 7 read *Vibilia*
157b line 51 *read* Aidan's

177b BLACKMORE
line 1, bibliography *before* Early *add* M.E.P. Sharp et al,

190b BONWICK
line 4 *for* child *read* son

195a BOOTHBY, B.
line 49 *for* 121 *read* 84

197a BOOTHBY, W.
†line 20 *for* Boothy *read* Boothby
197b line 32 *for* 1864 *read* 1861
line 47 *for* 1866 *read* 1864

206b BOWEN
lines 31-32 *for* four ... daughter *read* one son and four daughters
207a line 3, bibliography *read* Carnarvon

208b BOWMAN
line 15 *for* Carey's *read* Cary's [q.v.]

218b BRAIM
line 47 *for* 1867 *read* 1866
line 49 *for* Islington *read* Ilsington
line 53 *for* September *read* November

221b BRAZIER
line 3 *delete* McMillan
line 5 *for* Eliza, née Warren *read* Mary, née McMillan

239a BRODRIBB
line 8 *for* 96 *read* 95 *and for* rector *read* vicar

240b BROMBY
line 61 *for* 1863 *read* 1864

244a BROOKE, G. V.
lines 44-45 *for* E. *read* C. *and for* (later Vezin [q.v.]) *read* [q.v. Charles Young]

245a BROOKE, J. H.
line 4 *for* and ... Brooke. *read* Brooke and his wife May Ann, née Wright.
line 16 *for* In ... Victoria *read* Brooke arrived in Melbourne in April 1853
245b line 39 *add* In 1849 he had married Harriet Williamson; they had three sons and three daughters.

253a BROUGH
line 25 *for* (b. 1848) *read* [q.v.]

263b †BROWN, N.
line 40 *for* the ... November *read* a poll on 19 December

277a BRUCE, J. M.
lines 19-20 *for* Presbyterian *read* Baptist

280a BRUNTON
line 44 *read* 1868

282a BUCHANAN, D.
line 26 *for* Schools *read* School

283b BUCHANAN, J.
line 24 *read* Southern

284a BUCHANAN, N.
line 28 *for* Thompson *read* Thomson

288a BUCKLAND, J.
line 16 *read* Frederic
line 18 *for* 13 *read* 3

296a †BUNCLE
line 2, bibliography *for* 2 *read* 27

297b BUNNY
line 29 *read* linguist

299b BURGESS
line 6 *read* civic

308b BURT
line 1, bibliography *read* McClemans

†new items (since 1976)

10a à BECKETT, T. T.
line 11 *add* He left his estate to his surviving children and his second wife Laura Jane, née Stuckey.
line 8, bibliography *for* 1860-80 *read* 1859-69

15a ADAMS, F.
line 5, bibliography *read* Gavah

18a ADAMSON
line 1 *for* 1828 *read* 1827
line 3 *after* born *add* on 6 August 1827
line 49 *after* Stevenson. *add* She died in 1864 and on 26 August 1873 at Geelong he married Catherine Synnot.

18b AGNEW
line 1 *for* WILSON *read* WILLSON

20b ALDERSON
line 37 *for* Milford *read* Mitford

22a ALLAN, G.
line 40 *for* His son George *read* He

24a ALLAN, W.
line 3, bibliography *for* 1897 *read* 1891

31b ANDERSON, W.
lines 53-54 *for* by a radical candidate *read* and 1894
line 59 *for* Michael *read* Matthew

32a ANDERSON, W. A.
line 4 *after* only *read* surviving

37a ANGAS
line 38 *for* 1871 *read* 1876

39b APLIN
line 3 *for* Cowl, *read* Combe
line 7 *for* Burton *read* Bourton

43b ARCHIBALD
line 38 *for* 'ease' *read* 'case'
46b line 30 *for* Australia's *read* New South Wales's

49a ARMITAGE
line 14 *delete* at Madras

50a †ARMSTRONG, R.
line 3 *for* on Jersey *read* at St Peter, Jersey,
line 4 *after* Islands *add* , sixth son of Francis Wheeler Armstrong and his wife Esther Françoise, née Quett(e)ville. *and for* 1848 *read* 1847
line 11 *after* Turkey. *add* On 20 August 1857 at St Helier, Jersey, he

married Eliza Susannah Mallet.
and for 1870 *read* 1871

50b line 29 *for* 25 *read* 26 *and after* 1910.
add He was survived by two sons and a daughter.

51a ARMSTRONG, bros
line 40 *for* Rupert *read* Robert
line 53 *add* -72 *after* 1871
line 58 *for* née Elliott, *read* Elliot, née Armstrong,

52a ARMYTAGE
line 47 *for* Geelong *read* the Diocesan
line 48 *after* was *add* part of

56a ASTLEY
line 6 *for* 1855 *read* 1859

58b ATKIN
line 9 *read* Shropshire
line 39 *for* March *read* January
line 41 *for* On 26 April *read* In

70b BADHAM
line 28 read *Mnemosyne*

71a lines 17-18 *for* the . . . Union *read* are the Badham Building, the Badham room in the union.

72a BAGOT, R.
line 3 *read* Edwards
lines 3-4 *read* Sydney in 1849
72b lines 29-30 *read* Gregory.
line 32 *for* nineties *read* eighties

74a BAILEY
line 3, bibliography *for* 27 *read* 28

75a BAKER, E.
line 25 *read* Salomons

78b BALCOMBE
line 24 *for* Juanna *read* Juana
line 30 *for* He *read* In 1846 he
lines 31-34 *for* which . . . variants, *read* Chen Chen Gurruck, or Tichingorourke, changing the name

81a BALFOUR
line 39 *for* south *read* north

95a BARKLY
line 42 *for* 'Left' . . . Conservatives *read* radicals and ministerialists
lines 48-49 *for* was . . . in *read* died on 17

109b BARRY
lines 33-34 *delete* and . . . off

111b BARRY, Z.
line 2 *after* born *add* on 1 February 1827
line 25 *for* 1862 *read* 1861

†new items (since 1976)

their interests in the Brighton Estate were acquired eventually by Were's eldest brother Nicholas who lived in England.

597a WICKHAM
line 3 *for* December *read* November
line 4 *for* Captain *read* Lieutenant
line 18 *for* a *read* on 1 June 1843 Elizabeth, eldest
lines 36-37 *delete* in 1857

606a WILLS
line 5 *for* 2 *read* 4

613a WILTON
line 3 *after* born *add* on 24 October 1795

line 48 *for* B *read* K

613b WINDER
line 18 *read* Leverton

616a WINDEYER
line 26 *reinstate* In July 1846

618a WITTENOOM
line 1 *for* 1789 *read* 1788
line 2 *after* born *add* on 24 October 1788

631a WYNYARD
line 29 *for* Cowe *read* Lowe

633b YOUNG
line 51 *for* [q.v.] *read* junior

line 4 *for* housebreaking *read* stealing

444b SIDDINS
line 30 *read* Siddins

445b SIMMONS
line 1 *for* 1880? *read* 1893

446b line 15 *add* He died in Sydney on 9 August 1893.

448a SIMPSON
line 1 *for* 1792? *read* 1793
line 2 *for* born *read* baptized on 29 July 1793
line 23 *for* a woman *read* in 1838 Sophia Ann Simpson, a relation
lines 59-61 *for* substantial . . . standing, *read* cottage in Goodna, which

453a SMITH, T. W.
line 28 *for* the *read* an

467b SQUIRE
line 3 *add* for highway robbery

471a STANLEY, O.
line 49 *for* Harvey's *read* Hervey

480b STEPHENS, E.
line 1, bibliography *for* F *read* J

482a STEVENSON
line 14 *delete* , neé Hutton,
line 17 *for* widow *read* daughter

495a STRZELECKI
line 12, bibliography *read* Havard
STURT
line 5 *for* Napier Lennox *read* Lenox Napier

498b line 4, bibiography *for* 6 *read* 5

501b SWANSTON
line 21 *for* largely . . . for *read* an early subscriber to

505b TEGG
line 15 *for* W. *read* Gideon
line 16 *delete* Wilson

506b TENCH
line 11 *for* 1792 *read* 1791

528a THOMSON, J.
line 61 *add* and *after* tions),
lines 62-64 *delete* and . . . spire),

531a THROSBY
lines 57-59 *for* and . . . and *read* arrived in the *Mangles* in August 1820 and at Liverpool in 1824 married Betsey, daughter of William Broughton [q.v.];

535a TORRENS
line 24 *read* Association

547a †UNDERWOOD, James
lines 2-9 *for* is . . . 1791. *read* was sentenced to death at New Sarum Assizes on 11 March 1786, for killing five sheep. The sentence was commuted to transportation for fourteen years and he arrived in New South Wales on the *Charlotte* in the First Fleet.

547b lines 33-34 *for* but . . . marriage. *read* who bore him a son William.

548b UNDERWOOD, Joseph
line 14 *for* Surgeon *read* the emancipist
†lines 25-26 *for* three . . . Frederick, *read* four daughters and two sons. The elder, Frederick, was
line 27 *for* who *read* and

550a VALE
line 8 *for* 1811 *read* 1812
line 11 *for* London *read* Ely

550b line 12 *for* 39 *read* 31

557a †VON STIEGLITZ
line 29 *for* 1851 *read* 1856
line 31 *for* council *read* assembly

557b line 19 *for* 1884 *read* 1889
line 28 *for* died in *read* died on 14 April
line 34 *add* Bay District *after* Portland

569a WALSH, W. H.
line 3 *for* 12 *read* 10

569b line 6 *after* Ireland *add* Treherne

570a line 32 *for* March *read* February

575a WATLING
line 8, bibliography *for* N *read* M

576a WEDGE
lines 30-31 *for* by . . . government *read* as a Tasmanian parliamentary paper
†line 51 *after* 1857 *add*, as member for North Esk.

585b WENTWORTH, W. C.
lines 42-45 *for* the . . . Wales *read* civilian juries were allowed in civil cases on the application of both parties and the approval of the Supreme Court.

590a †WERE
lines 13-19 *for* Despite . . . Nicholas. *read* In February 1841 Were had become an agent for Henry Dendy. Were's subsequent business failure and bankruptcy in 1843 forced Dendy into insolvency; both

298b O'FLAHERTY
lines 60-63 *for* played . . . York *read*
appeared at theatres in New York,
Philadelphia and other cities.
299a bibliography add *Bow Bells*, 21 Dec
1864
311a PALMER, P.
line 18 for *William Bryan* read
Warrior
321b PEEL
line 3 *for* many *read* four
lines 4-5 *delete*, and . . . longer
325b PETRIE
line 3 *add* son of Walter Petrie and
Margaret, née Hutchinson.
326a line 47 *after* fied. *add* At Edinburgh
in 1821 he had married Mary
Cuthbertson; they had nine sons
and a daughter.
line 49 *delete* lord
337b PLUNKETT
line 4 *for* Ireland. *read* Ireland, son
of George Plunkett and his wife
Eileen, née O'Kelly.
338a lines 2-6 *for* comma *read* stop *and*
delete beginning . . . lash.
339a line 64 *for* reformed *read* Executive
349a POWLETT
line 4 *for* a *read* Rev. Charles
Powlett, sometime
line 11 *for* two *read* three
line 12 *for* first recorded *read*
foundation
line 49 *for* In 1850 *read* On 23 April
1851
355b PUGH
line 10 *add* by a medical practitioner *after* first
360b †RAINE, T.
line 46 *for* 30 March *read* 6 April
364b RAVEN
line 54 *read* Squire [q.v.]
375b REID, A.
line 34 *for* 1836 *read* 1834
376a REID, D.
line 2 *for* 1856 *read* 1826
382b RITCHIE
line 24 *add* at Launceston *after* her
392b ROGERS
line 4 *for* After admission *read* He
went
lines 5-8 *delete*, he . . . 1844
399a Ross, Robert (minister)

line 7, bibliography *add* -Smith
after Lamb
404a RUMKER
lines 27-28 *delete* , through . . .
Brisbane,
407a RUSSELL, H. S.
line 22 *for* was *read* continued to be
408b RUSSELL, P.
line 1 *for* 1796? *read* 1796
line 12 *after* Russell *add* , born on 30
June 1796,
411a RUTLEDGE
line 5 *read* Longford
412a line 17 *read* 1852
417b SAMSON
line 37 *add* He was a nominee in the
Western Australian Legislative
Council in 1849-56 and 1859-68.
419a SAVAGE, John
line 34 *for* John *read* Thomas
431b SCOTT, T. H.
†line 3 *for* baptized on 24 *read* born
on 17
line 17 *for* was . . . been *read* went
bankrupt as
†line 21 *delete* his brother-in-law
†lines 30-31 *for* advanced . . .
priesthood *read* became a priest
the same year, and
†line 31 *for* and *read* was
line 39 *for* accepted appointment as
read was appointed
432b line 10 *delete* a Tory and
†line 11 *for* progressives of *read*
friends of Governor Brisbane and
†line 63 *for* However, he did *read*
His resignation was accepted on 14
November
433a †line 1 *for* not . . . until *read* and on
and delete , when
436a SHARLAND
line 3 *delete* surgeon, *and* Mary
line 4 *delete* , née Culley
line 14 *for* Frederick *read* Frederic
lines 18-19 *delete* 1829 . . . and in
line 19 *add* he *after* 1835
lines 21-22 *delete* from practice,
436b †line 26 *for* 1849 *read* September
1848
lines 28-30 *delete* was . . . then
line 32 *for* Sara *read* Sarah
line 35 *for* Nodd *read* Nod, Surrey
line 40 *for* Frederick *read* Frederic
444a SIDAWAY
line 1 *for* 1757? *read* 1759

†new items (since 1976)

lines 9-10 *for* in Hereford *read* at Hackney, London,

151b line 57 *for* in *read* from
line 58 *for* licences *read* an annual licence

153b MACARTHUR, John
line 8 *for* Katharine *read* Catherine

163b MACDOUGALL
line 60 *for* John *read* James

172a McKENZIE, A. K.
line 6 *for* sister *read* cousin
172b lines 5-6 *delete* and . . . Australia

190b MACQUARIE, L.
line 15 *for* along *read* among
194a line 26 *read* elegiac

196a MACQUEEN
line 34 *for* debtors *read* creditors

198a MAKINSON
line 12 *for* Bird *read* Sumner

207a MARRIOTT
line 10 *for* 1829 *read* 1833
line 11 *for* 1835 *read* 1836
207b line 14 *for* In December 1859 *read* On 28 January 1860

MARSDEN
lines 1 & 3 *for* 1764 *read* 1765

213a MARTENS
line 43 *for* Church *read* cemetery

218a MEAGHER
†lines 8-9 for *News*, read *News. and delete* which . . . cause.
line 11 *for* Confederate *read* Union

220a MEEHAN
line 24 *for* laid out *read* surveyed

226a MIDDLETON
lines 7-8 *for* his wife's death *read* the death of his wife Mary Ann, née Hull,
226b line 62 *for* Richard *read* Robert

231b MILLS, J. B.
line 25 *for* H *read* N

233b MINCHIN
line 54 *for* George *read* John

234b MITCHEL
†line 51 *for* O'Dogherty *read* Izod O'Doherty [q.v.]
235a †line 15 *for* O'Dogherty *read* O'Doherty
line 58 *for* two *read* three

243b MOLLISON
lines 3-4 *for* overlanders . . . parliament *read* overlanders and

pastoralists
244a line 28 *for* 1856 *read* 1858

251a MONTEFIORE
lines 27-30 *for* Early . . . London. *read* After the depression the Montefiore firm in Sydney went bankrupt. The London firm had suspended payment in 1841 and Montefiore had returned to England.

254a MOORE, J. J.
line 1 *for* d. *read* 1790–

269a MURDOCH, P.
line 1 *delete* ? *after* 1795
lines 2-6 *for* descended . . . Wallaces *read* born on 15 January 1795, son of James Murdoch and his wife Frances, daughter of John Wallace,
269b lines 21-24 *delete* in December . . . He
line 32 *delete* whose Christian names were
line 33 *add* whom he had married on 5 February 1830 at Capelrig; she *after* Brown,
line 34 *add* , survived by four children. *after* later

274b MURRAY, T.A.
line 41 *for* 1840, *read* 1834

278a NAIRN
lines 47-48 *delete* where . . . 1829

280a NATHAN
line 25 *for* 1890 *read* 1898

NEALES
lines 4-5 *for* a sister of Jeremy *read* née

285a NICHOLSON
line 57 *for* He . . . two *read* Of his three

285b NIXON
line 30 *for* 1848 *read* 1847

288b NOBBS
lines 47-48 *delete* as a priest

290b OAKDEN
lines 3-4 *delete* (where . . . discoverer)
line 31 *for* Georgiana *read* Georgina

297a †OFFICER
line 12 *for* Jamima *read* Jemima
298a line 19 *delete* from parliament

†new items (since 1976)

CORRIGENDA

Australian Dictionary of Biography

Volume 2: 1788-1850 I-Z (1979)

2a IMLAY
line 2 *for* 1847 *read* 1846
3a line 4 *for* In . . . 1847 *read* On 26 December 1846

5a IRWIN
line 17 *for* 13th *read* 63rd
line 31 *read* five sons and four
5b line 49 *read* Stirling

17a JOHNSON, Richard
line 1 *for* 1753 *read* 1753?
line 11 *for* London *read* Oxford *and for* 1786 *read* 1784
19a lines 38-40 *delete* Seven . . . Norfolk

19b JOHNSTONE, E.
line 1 *for* 1771? *read* 1767
line 2 *for* about 15 *read* 20

32b KANE
line 57 *add* on 1 May 1883
line 58 *for* Lily *read* Alicia

35b Kay, W.
line 45 *for* 33 *read* 34

36b KELLY
lines 2-3 *read* 24 December
37b line 8, bibliography *for* Mar *read* May

41b KEMP
line 39 *for* 1856 *read* 1854

46b KENT, W.
line 28 *for* principle *read* chief

51a KERR
line 24 *for* Charles *read* William
line 25 *delete* [q.v.]

52a KINCHELA
line 9 *for* 1831 *read* 1832

55a †KING, J. C.
line 4 *after* King *add* (d. 1840)
line 5 *for* farmer. *read* farmer, and his wife Martha Jane, née Henry.

56a KING, P. G.
line 32 *add* 1788 *after* February

61b KING, P. P.
line 43 *for* 83 *read* 84
63a line 42 *for* 1834 *read* 1839
63b line 59 *add* stock *after* became
line 60 *for* 1854 *read* 1851

81a LANG, J. D.
line 27 *delete* In January 1859

85a LANGLANDS
line 10 *for* 1849 *read* 1848
line 5, bibliography *read* Nonconformists

89a LA TROBE
line 3 *for* 30 *read* 20
91a line 16 *for* 1846 *read* 1846-47

96b LAWSON
line 22 *delete* [q.v.]
lines 33-34 *delete* In 1828 . . . horses.

97a LAYCOCK, T. (1756?-1809)
line 4 *delete* and . . . 1790
line 6 *for* 1791. *read* 1791 and arrived in Sydney in H.M.S. *Gorgon* in September.

97b LAYCOCK, T. (1786?-1823)
line 6 *delete* was . . . he

101b LEE
line 16 *delete* [q.v.]

108a †LESLIE
line 50 *for* George *read* John Clements

108b LEVEY
line 1 *after* BARNETT *read* (BERNARD)

119a LILLIE
lines 6-7, bibliography for *Evening* . . . 3 read *Lyttelton Times*, 4

123a LOCKYER
line 3 *for* at Wembury *read* in St Andrew's Parish, Plymouth,
lines 4-5 *for* Edmund . . . Joan *read* Thomas Lockyer, sailmaker, and his wife Ann, née Grose

124a LOGAN
line 44 *read* Allan
†line 46 *for* 5700 *read* 4449

124b LONSDALE
line 1 *for* 1800? *read* 1799
line 2 *after* administrator, *add* was born on 2 October 1799,

143b LYTTLETON
line 22 *read* Lyttleton

144b MACARTHUR, A.
line 19 *for* , and . . . Jones *read* Jones and his wife Fanny Edith

MACARTHUR, E.
line 1 *for* 1767? *read* 1766
lines 2-3 *for* née . . . farmers *read* was born on 14 August 1766 in Devon, England, daughter of Richard Veale, farmer, and his wife Grace, who were

149b MACARTHUR, James
line 2 *after* born *add* on 15 December 1798
line 3 *delete* the . . . and

†new items (since 1976)

on 16 March 1812 his
line 52 *for* 1815 *read* 1811

574a HUTCHINS
line 49 *delete* [q.v.]

575a HUTCHINSON
line 62 *add* Forest *after* Sutton

577b HUXLEY
line 10 *delete* (M.B. London, 1845)

Aberdeen *read* Christ's Hospital. He entered the navy in 1781 but was gaoled in 1783 for stabbing and killing a fellow midshipman. Acquitted in 1784, he married Mary Boutcher (d. 1792) and ran a school at Exeter until 1788 and then an academy at Alphington until he became insolvent in 1796. He was also charged with immorality. A professed Roman Catholic, he recanted in 1792 but never won the Anglican ordination he wanted. In 1797-98 he was in the navy posing as a chaplain. In 1800 he married Anna Hall and was awarded a doctorate in divinity at King's College, Aberdeen.

507a line 18 *after* son. *add* The Colonial Office advised Governor Darling of Halloran's shady career and rejected his appeal for a land grant for his establishment.
line 59 *for* first *read* second

507b bibliography *add* K. Grose, 'Dr. Halloran', *Aust J of Education*, Oct 1970.

520a HARRISON
line 2 *for* in *read* at Bonhill near
line 3 *for* near Ben Lomond *read* , Dunbartonshire,
line 7 *after* Anderson *add* (Anderson's University)
line 8 *for* Mechanics' Institute *read* Glasgow Mechanics' Institution
†line 10 *for* about 1832 *read* in 1835

520b line 20 *after* represented *add* Geelong and
line 21 *for* 61 *read* 60
line 35 *read* Rocky

523b HASSALL, T.
line 45 *read* Queensland

524a HAWDON
line 58 *for* After . . . he *read* She died in 1854. In 1872 his son Arthur Joseph
line 61 *for* at Christchurch. *read* in Canterbury, New Zealand.

524b HAWKINS
line 36 *for* owned *read* leased

525a lines 18-19 *for* and . . . [qq.v.] *read* [q.v.]

526b HAYES, Sir Henry
lines 13-15 *for* defiant . . . and *read* defiance of Governor King earned Grant exile on Norfolk Island,

Margarot and Hayes in

529b HELY
line 3 *for* at . . . Ulster *read* in County Tyrone

534b HEYDON
line 40 *for* 1838 *read* 1839

543a †HOBLER
line 1 *for* 1801 *read* 1800
line 2 *for* probably . . . Devonshire *read* born on 6 September 1800 at Islington, London, son of Francis Helvetius Hobler and his wife Mary, née Furby.
line 5 *after* Hertfordshire *add* On 21 October 1822 at Cadbury, Devon, he married Ann Turner.
line 12 *delete* Ann, née Turner,
line 13 *for* six *read* nine

544a line 5 *for* in 1881 *read* on 13 December 1882 and was buried at San Leander.

544b HOBSON, E. C.
lines 17-20 *delete* The . . . it.

549b HOLDEN
line 5 *for* 7 *read* 8

555a HOSKING
lines 25-27 *for* For a . . . with *read* His father was the London agent of Eagar. [q.v.] & Forbes and John became the partner of

558b HOWE, G.
lines 20-21 *for* as . . . Horatio, *read* a son, Horatio Spencer Wills [q.v.],

562b HULL
line 18 *add* and *after* England

563b HUME, A. H.
line 15 *for* Barker *read* Barber

564a HUME, H.
†lines 19-20 *delete* site . . . village of *and after* Bungonia *add* district
line 60 *after* John *read* and

566a HUMPHREY
†line 11 *for* dolorite *read* dolerite

566b line 40 *delete* [q.v.]

572b HUNTER, J. *et al*
lines 10-22 *for* Phillip with . . . Meanwhile *read* Phillip. An elder cousin John Hunter traded with James Watson in 1839-43.

573 HUON
read KERILLEAU *throughout*

573b line 48 *for* His *read* At Parramatta

lines 6-10 *delete* and . . . corps.

356a †ELLISTON
line 12 *for* an alderman *read* a commissioner
line 13 *for* 1854 *read* 1855

357b ENDERBY
line 39 *for* Gladwyn *read* Goodwyn

361a EWING
line 9 *for* the bishop of Tasmania *read* Bishop Broughton [q.v.]
line 17 *add* He was priested by Bishop Nixon [q.v.] on 21 September 1843.

367a FAITHFUL
line 24 *delete* née Pitt,
line 25 *for* Matcham *read* Pitt, née Matcham,

370a FAWKNER
line 51 *for* Dalhousie *read* Talbot

371a FENTON
line 35 *for* newly *read* new

378b FINNISS
lines 40-42 *for* became . . . 1881. *read* acted as auditor-general in 1876 and served on the Forest Board in 1875-81.

389b FLINDERS
lines 3-4 *for* parish . . . School *read* Grammar School and by the vicar of Horbling

407b FOSTER
line 32 *for* Gippsland *read* Hobart

413a FRANKLIN
line 40 *for* February *read* January

419a FROST
line 3 *for* Wales *read* England
419b line 54 *for* Port *read* Point

422b FYANS
line 8 *for* 1810 *read* 1811
lines 11-12 *for* did . . . July *read* had returned to England by May
line 14 *for* The next month *read* On 3 February 1818
lines 21-22 *delete* after . . . war,
423a line 1 *for* some three *read* four
†line 12 *add* [q.v.] *after* Knatchbull
line 17 *for* sixty *read* fourteen

425b GARDINER
line 23 *read* business

434b †GAWLER
line 24 *for* 15 *read* 10

437a GELLIBRAND
line 9 *for* Risby *read* Kerby

437b lines 44-47 *for* He was . . . Hesse. *read* He and his companion, G. B. L. Hesse, probably lost their horses and perished in the summer heat. The mystery was not solved.

453a GIPPS
line 10, bibliography *for* moments *read* comments

†GISBORNE
line 1 *add* (FYSCHE) *after* FYSHE

454a †GLEADOW
line 13 *for* Kearton *read* Keaston

456a GLOVER
line 24 *for* Mill's *read* Mills

457b GOODWIN
line 34 *read* damages of £400

464b GOULBURN, F.
line 36 *for* in May *read* on 10 February

469b GRANT, John
lines 21-23 *for* and . . . voyage *read* . With Hayes, who joined him briefly in exile on the island that year,

492a GUNN, R.
line 4 *for* youngest *read* fourth
line 21 *for* two children *read* child *delete* and
line 22 *for* Francis were *read* was
493a line 24 *for* Five years later *read* On 18 December 1839
line 27 *for* five *read* nine
†line 37 *for* 23 *read* 21

498a HACKING
line 11 *after* European. *add* In 1794 he was granted thirty acres at Hunter's Hill.
lines 13-14 *delete* and . . . Hill

501b HALL, E. Smith
line 13 *for* George *read* William

502a HALL, E. Swarbreck
line 45 *for* 1831 *read* 1851

505b HALLER
line 1 *for* b. 1808 *read* 1808-1886
†lines 14-15 *for* Presbyterian *read* Congregationalist
506a lines 24-25 *delete* is assumed to have
line 26 *for* daughter *read* two daughters; he died at East Melbourne on 29 March 1886

506a HALLORAN
lines 7-17 *for* Westminster . . .

251b COVER
line 29 *read* Hassall

254b COWPER
line 53 *for* -29 *read* and 1829

255a line 30 *read* Frederic

257b COX, J. E.
lines 3-5 *for* England . . . Suffolk *read* Suffolk, England. On 19 January 1821 he married Mary Ann Halls at St James's, Bristol,

258a line 38 *read* Elliott

261a †CROOKES
line 3 *for* Antrim *read* Tyrone

264a CROWDER
lines 23-24 *for* May 1793 *read* January 1794

266a CUNNINGHAM
line 28 *for* 1829 *read* 1820

275a DACRE
line 19 *read* Bennet

277a DAMPIER
line 1 *for* 1652 *read* 1651
lines 2-3 *for* 8 June 1652 *read* 5 September 1651

278a line 26 *add* He died in London in 1715.
line 5, bibliography *add* L. R. Marchant, 'William Dampier', *JR WAHS*, 6 (1963).

279b DANA, J. D.
line 6 *for* efforts *read* effects

280a DANGAR
line 46 *read* Dartbrook

286a DARLING
line 58 *add* his wife, *after* by

288a DASHWOOD
line 6 *for* six *read* four
lines 8-9 *delete* until . . . granted

289a DAVEY
line 44 *for* 1814 *read* 1815

291a †DAVIES, A.
line 12 *for* George *read* Charles

291b DAVIES, R.
line 11 *for* IV *read* III

295a DAVY
line 5 *add* was a house surgeon at *before* Guy's

300a DAWSON
line 3 *delete* Belford,

†DAY
line 2 *after* of *add* John Day,
line 4 *after* Ireland *add* , and his

wife Charlotte, née Denny

300b lines 19-21 *for* After . . . Maitland. *read* As police magistrate again at Maitland, he was also commissioner, Court of Requests, from 1841 and of insolvent estates from 1842.
lines 47-50 *for* he returned . . . 1850. *read* his estate was sequestrated in 1848. Next year he was appointed to Sydney and from 1 January 1851 was provincial inspector of police for the northern district.
line 55 *for* in *read* on 6
line 56 *for* at Campbelltown. *read* in the Anglican cemetery, East Maitland.

301a DEANE
line 64 *for* violoncello *read* violin

301b line 1 *for* Morris . . . violin, *read* Charles Muzio the violoncello.
line 3 *for* Paine *read* Smith

306b DICKSON
lines 25-26 *for* and . . . England *read* He lost the case *Brown* v. *Dickson* and had to pay £333 in damages. He was also prosecuted for forgery and absconded to England while on bail.

316b †DOWLING, H.
line 39 *for* six *read* seven

327a DRUMMOND, John
line 20 read *Marquis*

329b DRY, Sir Richard
line 26 *delete* the transportationist *and after* Douglas *add* [q.v.]

332a DULHUNTY
line 41 *delete* [q.v.]

338a DUNLOP, E.
line 2, bibliography *read* Threlkeld

338b DUNLOP, J.
line 21 *for* life *read* list

343a EAGAR
line 15 *for* Richard *read* Robert

349b EASTY
line 9 *delete* [q.v.]

351a EDGE
line 1 *add* enlisted in the New South Wales Corps on 6 March 1790 and embarked in April. He
line 3 *for* some . . . March *read* in February
line 5 *for* comma *read* stop

†new items (since 1976)

appears to have died in 1810.

109b BLACKBURN
line 44 *for* where ... 1846 *read*
, which from 1843 became increasingly the main centre of his activities. From 1844 he
line 45 *for* as *read* was
add later *after* and
line 49 *for* 20 *read* 16

110a line 5 *add* Fitzroy *before* Church
line 22 *for* 43 *read* 41
line 23 *for* 1839 *read* 1840
line 44 *delete* and court-house
line 62 *for* − *read*)
line 63 *delete* 40)

111b BLAIR
line 1 *for* 1889 *read* 1880

112a lines 51-54 *for* In 1883 ... 1889. *read*
On 11 June 1880 he died at his
home, Greenmount, Toorak.

118b BLIGH, W.
line 4 *for* customs officer *read*
boatman and land waiter in the
customs service.

127b BOUCHER
line 1 *after* Frederick *add* (1801-
1873)

128b lines 5-6 *delete* may ... who

132a BOURKE
line 18 *for* 2 *read* 4
line 26 *for* 4 *read* 7

132b line 63 *for* 1838 *read* 1837

138a BOWMAN, James
line 32 *for* Elizabeth *read* Mary

145a BRADLEY
line 7 *for* Mitchell *read* Witchell

153a BRISBANE
line 55 *for* Church *read* London

153b lines 10-13 *for* lifted ... ending *read*
did not apply any censorship when
W. C. Wentworth's [q.v.] *Australian* began publication, and
ended

157a BROOKS
line 9 *for* had to row *read* sailed

157b line 5 *delete* Richard

158b BROUGHTON, W.
line 11 *for* three *read* four

169b BROWNING
line 42 *for* Arthur *read* Franklin

172b BRUNY
line 1, bibliography *for* M. *read* E.

177a BUNCE
line 7, bibliography *read* Leichhardt.

178a BUNKER
line 1 *for* 1762 *read* 1761
lines 2-5 *for* married ... 1786. *read*
was born on 7 March 1761 at
Plymouth, Massachusetts, United
States of America, son of James
Bunker and his wife Hannah, née
Shurtleff. On 16 November 1786 at
St George-in-the-East, Middlesex,
England, he married Margrett,
daughter of Captain Henry
Thompson, R.N., and his wife
Isabella, née Collingwood, who
was first cousin to Admiral Cuth-
bert Collingwood.

181b BURN
line 22 *read* Jemima

182a line 5 *read* Castle Town
line 43 *read* Jemima

189a BUSBY, John
line 63 *for* 1886 *read* 1887

195b CALLAGHAN
line 2 *for* 1851 *read* 1815

201b CAMPBELL, P. L.
line 1 *delete* (fl.
line 2 *for* 1826-1841) *read* (1809-
1848)

202b line 46 *add* He died in London on 4
October 1848.

207b CAMPBELL, Robert junior
line 8 *read* Ramsay

215b CATCHPOLE
line 40 *add* on 13 May 1819.

223a CIMITIERE
line 18 *delete* [q.v.]

228b CLARKE, W. J. T.
line 2 *for* 1801? *read* 1805
line 3 *for* in London, *read* on 20
April 1805 in Somerset, England,

229a line 12 *for* Glenorchy *read* Campbell Town

229b line 29 *for* 15 *read* 13

238a COLLINS, D.
line 2 *delete* [q.v.]

247a CORDEAUX
line 19 *for* Cars *read* Caro
lines 62-64 *delete* Thomas Moore
... England,

247b line 1 *delete* and

248a COTTER
line 3 *read* Bantry

vii ACKNOWLEDGMENTS
line 9 *for* H. *read* W.
line 36 *read* O'Keeffe

5b ALLAN, D.
line 24 *for* About *read* In

6a ALLEN, G.
line 15 *delete* Moore's successor

6b line 30 *for* 1860 *read* 1866

7b ALLISON
line 44 *delete* [q.v.]

8a †line 23 *for* September 1846 *read* August 1848

9b ALLPORT
line 28 *for* brother *read* son

11b ALT
line 13 *for* 1758 *read* 1757

14a ANDERSON, Joseph
line 12 *for* 1848 *read* 1841
line 13 *for* returned to England *read* had moved to India

32a †ARTHUR, Charles
line 2 *after* was *add* born on 5 February 1808,
line 4 *for* 18 *read* 16
line 28 *for* next year *read* in 1836
line 29 *for* In *read* On 28 *and for* 1826 *read* 1836

32b ARTHUR, Sir George
lines 9-10 *delete* where . . . port
lines 19-20 *for* thanked . . . on *read* praised his gallantry in action.

33a lines 1-2 *for* his . . . and *read* On his return Arthur was given the freedom of the city of
line 46 *delete* improperly

33b line 8 *for* at the end of *read* in April

38b ARTHUR, Henry
line 35 *after* Charles *add* [q.v.]

ATKINS, R.
line 2 *after* was *add* born on 22 March 1745,
line 4 *delete* Lady

39a line 11 *for* 1791 *read* 1792

42b ATKINSON, J.
lines 17-18 *for* died in infancy. *read* lived to a ripe old age at Orange.

47a †BAGOT
line 1 *for* HARVEY *read* HERVEY

48a BAILEY
line 1 *for* 1873 *read* 1879
line 6 *for* LL.B. *read* LL.D.

50b BALL
lines 37-40 *for* been . . . duty *read* sufficiently recovered to return to duty in December 1792 and in 1795 was promoted captain.

51a BALLOW
line 1 *for* 1809 *read* 1804
line 9 *for* 1837 . . . government *read* 1838 after serving as assistant surgeon at the Sydney general
line 43 *for* Thomson *read* Thompson

56a BANNISTER
line 64 *delete* re-em-

56b line 1 *for* ployment by *read* compensation from

57b BARKER, T.
line 9 *read* October

59b BARNES
line 16 *read* Paterson

64a BARTLEY
line 25 *read* nine

65a BASS
line 1 *for* filled *read* fitted

66b BATE
line 7 *for* His *read* A

71a BAUDIN
line 1 *for* THOMAS NICHOLAS *read* NICOLAS THOMAS
line 3 *for* DESAULES *read* DESAULSES

73a line 3, bibliography *for* Nicholas *read* Nicolas

74a BAUGHAN
line 5 *for* a pair of *read* five

83a BELLASIS
line 35 *for* [qq.v.] *read* [q.v.]

84a BENJAMIN, S.
lines 12-16 *for* The partnership . . . marriages. *read* On 15 April 1840 he married Julia, daughter of Abraham Moses.

92a BERRY
line 3 *for* seven *read* nine

92b †line 37 *for* 21 *read* 22

99a BIGGE
line 4 *for* second *read* third
line 14 *for* 1814 *read* 1813
line 47 *read* weakening

103a BIRABAN
line 2 *for* Known . . . tribe *read* He returned to Lake Macquarie and
line 13 *for* 'Maggill' *read* 'Magill'

108a BISHOP, C.
line 33 *for* Nothing . . . him. *read* He

CORRIGENDA

to accompany volume 7

Australian Dictionary of Biography

Volume 1 : 1788-1850 A-H

Volume 2 : 1788-1850 I-Z

Volume 3 : 1851-1890 A-C

Volume 4 : 1851-1890 D-J

Volume 5 : 1851-1890 K-Q

Volume 6 : 1851-1890 R-Z

This list reprints corrigenda already published for all volumes up to the publication of Volume 6 in 1976 and, in addition, includes corrections to errors discovered since then. These latter corrections are preceded by the sign †.

Note that only corrections are shown; additional information is not included; nor is any re-interpretation attempted. The only exception to this procedure is when new details become available about parents or births, deaths and marriages.

Documented corrections are welcomed from readers. Additional information, with sources, is also invited and will be placed in the appropriate files for future use.

N.B. *For readers who have made previous corrections.* The sign † shown in front of a name indicates in most cases that all the changes listed for that name are new, and the sign is not repeated for each one; however, previous corrections (if any) are also included.